UNIX®
USER'S HANDBOOK

ISBN 0-13-027019-9

90000

9 780130 270191

Hewlett-Packard® Professional Books

OPERATING SYSTEMS

Fernandez	Configuring CDE: The Common Desktop Environment
Lund	Integrating UNIX® and PC Network Operating Systems
Madell	Disk and File Management Tasks on HP-UX
Poniatowski	HP-UX 11.x System Administration Handbook and Toolkit
Poniatowski	HP-UX 11.x System Administration "How To" Book, Second Edition
Poniatowski	HP NetServer Guide for Windows NT®
Poniatowski	HP-UX System Administration Handbook and Toolkit
Poniatowski	HP-UX 10.x System Administration "How To" Book
Poniatowski	Learning the HP-UX Operating System
Poniatowski	UNIX® User's Handbook
Poniatowski	Windows NT® and HP-UX System Administrator's "How To" Book
Sauers, Weygant	HP-UX Tuning and Performance
Stone, Symons	UNIX® Fault Management
Weygant	Clusters for High Availability: A Primer of HP-UX Solutions

ONLINE/INTERNET

Amor	The E-business (R)evolution
Greenberg, Lakeland	A Methodology for Developing and Deploying Internet and Intranet Solutions
Greenberg, Lakeland	Building Professional Web Sites with the Right Tools
Ketkar	Working with Netscape Server on HP-UX
Lee	The ISDN Consultant

NETWORKING/COMMUNICATIONS

Blommers	Practical Planning for Network Growth
Lucke	Designing and Implementing Computer Workgroups
Pipkin	Halting the Hacker: A Practical Guide to Computer Security
Thornburgh	Fibre Channel for Mass Storage

ENTERPRISE

Blommers	Architecting Enterprise Solutions with UNIX® Networking
Cook	Building Enterprise Information Architectures
Sperley	Enterprise Data Warehouse, Volume 1: Planning, Building, and Implementation

PROGRAMMING

Blinn	Portable Shell Programming
Caruso	Power Programming in HP OpenView
Chaudri, Loomis	Object Databases in Practice
Chew	The Java™/C++ Cross-Reference Handbook
Grady	Practical Software Metrics for Project Management and Process Improvement
Grady	Successful Software Process Improvement
Kane	PA-RISC 2.0 Architecture
Lewis	The Art & Science of Smalltalk
Lichtenbelt, Crane, Naqvi	Introduction to Volume Rendering
Mellquist	SNMP++
Mikkelsen, Pherigo	Practical Software Configuration Management
Norton, DiPasquale	Thread Time: The Multithreaded Programming Guide
Ryan	Distributed Object Technology: Concepts and Applications
Simmons	Software Measurement: A Visualization Toolkit

IMAGE PROCESSING

Crane	A Simplified Approach to Image Processing
Day	The Color Scanning Handbook
Gann	Desktop Scanners: Image Quality

Hewlett-Packard Professional Books

MORE BOOKS FROM MARTY PONIATOWSKI

HP-UX 11.x System Administration Handbook and Toolkit

◆

*HP-UX 11.x System Administration "How To" Book,
Second Edition*

◆

HP NetServer Guide for Windows NT®

◆

HP-UX System Administration Handbook and Toolkit

◆

*Windows NT® and HP-UX System Administrator's
"How To" Book*

◆

HP-UX 10.x System Administration "How To" Book

◆

Learning the HP-UX Operating System

UNIX®
USER'S HANDBOOK

Marty Poniatowski

www.hp.com/go/retailbooks

Prentice Hall PTR
Upper Saddle River, NJ 07458
www.phptr.com

Library of Congress Cataloging-in-Publication Data

Poniatowski, Marty
    UNIX user's handbook / Marty Poniatowski.
      p. cm.
    ISBN 0-13-027019-9
      1. UNIX (Computer file).   2. Operating systems (Computers) I. Title.
    QA76.76.063P654 2000
    005.4'469--dc21   00-26325

Editorial/production supervision: *Patti Guerrieri*
Acquisitions editor: *Jill Pisoni*
Marketing manager: *Bryan Gambrel*
Manufacturing manager: *Maura Goldstaub*
Editorial assistant: *Justin Somma*
Cover design director: *Jerry Votta*
Cover designer: *Talar Agasyan*
Manager, HP's Retail Book Publishing Program: *Pat Pekary*
Acquisitions Editor, Hewlett-Packard Professional Books: *Susan Wright*

Published by Prentice Hall PTR
Prentice-Hall, Inc.
Upper Saddle River, NJ 07458

Prentice Hall books are widely used by corporations and government agencies
for training, marketing, and resale.

The publisher offers discounts on this book when ordered in bulk quantities.
For more information, contact: Corporate Sales Department, Phone: 800-382-3419;
Fax: 201-236-7141; E-mail: corpsales@prenhall.com; or write: Prentice Hall PTR,
Corp. Sales Dept., One Lake Street, Upper Saddle River, NJ 07458.

Hummingbird Communications, Exceed, NFS Maestro, and TCP/IP Maestro are registered trademarks of Hummingbird Communications Ltd. UNIX is a registered trademark licensed through
X/Open Company, Ltd. X Window System is a trademark and product of the Massachusetts Institute
of Technology. HP-UX, HP OpenView, GlancePlus, PerfView, and Measureware are registered
trademarks of Hewlett-Packard Company. Microsoft, Windows NT, and MS/DOS are registered
trademarks of Microsoft Corporation. OS/2 is a registered trademark of International Business
Machines Corporation. All other products or services mentioned in this book are the trademarks or
service marks of their respective companies or organizations.

Printed in the United States of America
10 9 8 7 6 5 4 3 2 1

ISBN   0-13-027019-9

Prentice-Hall International (UK) Limited, *London*
Prentice-Hall of Australia Pty. Limited, *Sydney*
Prentice-Hall Canada Inc., *Toronto*
Prentice-Hall Hispanoamericana, S.A., *Mexico*
Prentice-Hall of India Private Limited, *New Delhi*
Prentice-Hall of Japan, Inc., *Tokyo*
Pearson Education Asia Pte. Ltd.
Editora Prentice-Hall do Brasil, Ltda., *Rio de Janeiro*

CHAPTER 12   Introduction to System Administration   735

UNIX and Windows NT Interoperability Section

FOREWORD

UNIX has evolved from its rather inconspicuous beginnings in a research and development environment to immense popularity in the Internet community. It is always amazing to step back and realize how much something has changed. Fortunately, in computing, this doesn't take long. The Unix operating system progressed from R&D through uses within select major industries to the Internet. Today's UNIX options for a computer system include a wide range of products, from utilizing a UNIX command set on non-UNIX systems, through various Linux distributions, to the different variants of UNIX, including HP-UX, Solaris, and AIX. Understanding the processes and procedures of the UNIX operating system has never been more important or necessary. Whether you are an administrator or user, beginning or experienced, the concepts and implementations of UNIX and Linux systems have become essential knowledge in today's computer-oriented world.

Many books, software, and advertisements refer to a "basic knowledge" of UNIX without defining it. Because it is always easier to relate to a known quantity (also called "the bird in the hand is worth two in the bush" theory), here is my definition of basic UNIX knowledge. A user with a fundamental understanding of UNIX should know: the structure of UNIX, how to log in and log off, the commands required to move from one directory to another (and back again), an editor, some shell commands, Internet basics, an electronic mail program, the principles of shell scripting, and a little C. However, because a little knowledge is like eating one potato chip, most readers and users find that reading and learning more about UNIX is not only an accomplishment, but also an enjoyable experience.

Coupled with the necessity for knowledge is the demand for documentation. Some documentation unfortunately resembles the User Guide to your VCR. It tells you something, but you aren't quite sure what. A good computer book can be easily identified. It not only illustrates the concepts you are trying to learn, but also furnishes the ideas and information you'll want in six months. An excellent book can also be used as a reference guide as you learn. The UNIX User's Handbook demonstrates the requisite structure of the UNIX operating system and its accompanying commands. It also details three shell environments, the vi editor, data manipulation tools, a thorough chapter on Common Desktop Environment (CDE), and an elaborate Software Development chapter. It surveys issues related to administration, development, and performance through examples employing several UNIX variants, including Linux. For easy reference, many chapters conclude with the manual pages for commands introduced within that chapter. A vi reference card is also provided as an additional quickly accessed resource. This is a book that can be an aid to both the beginning and the experienced user and administrator.

The UNIX User's Handbook provides the reader with the opportunity to learn UNIX from an experienced UNIX professional and an excellent author. I have read (and reviewed) most of Marty Poniatowski's books. He has a flair for making complex procedures completely understandable, especially for the beginner. When I review a book, I look for logical organization, content, readability, examples, and enthusiasm. There is no substitute for enthusiasm; it is thankfully contagious. An author's enthusiasm can inspire readers to unexpected achievements. All authos try to write the book they wish had existed when they were beginning. Mr. Poniatowski succeeds.

Elizabeth Zinkann

Contributing Editor and Review Columnist for *Sys Admin* Magazine

PREFACE

Since its inception, UNIX® has been viewed as requiring a certain amount of "magic" to understand. Nothing could be further from the truth. Like all operating systems most UNIX commands are simple and easy to use. There are also powerful UNIX commands, to which every user has access, that you will find indispensable once you master them.

That proficiency is, in fact, what I wish to accomplish in this book. Cover all UNIX commands and tools that a new UNIX user needs to know in order to become quickly proficient with UNIX, going from the beginner level of UNIX proficiency to the intermediate level.

I could never tell you everything you need to know about UNIX in just one book. I do, however, cover every essential command and tool to get you started quickly with UNIX. If you take a few seconds to look at the upcoming table of contents, I think that you'll see that I've included every essential UNIX topic to help you gain an understanding of UNIX.

You may very well find that you'll need additional resources as your UNIX knowledge grows. All top UNIX suppliers offer training courses in a variety of forms. In addition, the manuals of the top UNIX suppliers are extensive and cover many topics in great depth. And, of course, there are many reference books available as well. This book should be your first reference for learning UNIX but by no means your only reference.

You won't find any fluff in this book. Most of the UNIX topics covered in this book are essential information for every UNIX user. This book is full of background and examples. The book is heavy on examples because I believe that the easiest way to learn any computer-science-related topic is through examples.

UNIX User's Handbook is comprised of the following chapters:

UNIX Section

- Chapter 1: Getting Started

- Chapter 2: UNIX File System Introduction

- Chapter 3: Working with Files and Directories - Permissions, Commands, File Name Expansion, and Wild Cards

- Chapter 4: Common Desktop Environment (CDE)

- Chapter 5: Introduction to the Bash Shell

- Chapter 6: Introduction to the KornShell

- Chapter 7: Introduction to the C Shell

- Chapter 8: The vi Editor

- Chapter 9: Networking

- Chapter 10: UNIX Tools - grep, awk, sed, and Others

- Chapter 11: Introduction to Shell Programming

- Chapter 12: Introduction to System Administration

- Chapter 13: Introduction to Performance Analysis

- Chapter 14: Introduction to Software Development

UNIX and Windows® Interoperability Section

- Chapter 15: The X Window System

- Chapter 16: Network File System

- Chapter 17: Advanced Server for UNIX®

- Chapter 18: POSIX Commands

- Chapter 19: Services for UNIX (SFU)

- Chapter 20: Samba

Covered in these chapters is everything you need to get started and work through advanced topics in UNIX system administration.

A Word about the UNIX Variants Used throughout This Book

I do not advocate the use of one UNIX variant over another. Don't think, for instance, that because there are many Linux examples in this book I am advocating the use of Linux over other UNIX variants. Linux and a handful of other UNIX variants are used throughout the examples in this book because they are among the most popular UNIX variants and I had easy access to such systems. In fact, there are two different Linux implementations used in the book - Red Hat and Caldera. Not only am I not advocating one UNIX variant over another, but I am also not advocating any Linux implementation over another. I have no intention of swaying you one way or another when it comes to which UNIX variant to use. My only objective is to help you get started with whatever UNIX variant you are using as quickly as possible.

I use a wide variety of UNIX variants in the examples throughout the book. I don't get hungup highlighting the differences in UNIX variants. Rather, I focus on the common denominator of UNIX functionality that you can use. Most UNIX variants are very similar indeed, so what you'll find is that the vast majority of commands used throughout this book are very similar, going from one UNIX variant to another.

Only occasionally throughout the book do I provide an example using many different UNIX variants. Most examples use only one operating system. The use's of many commands, however, are sufficiently different such that the outputs, options, locations of commands, or some other feature would be different among UNIX variants. This statement is especially true of system administration-related commands, which is the area where UNIX variants differ the most. The concepts are the same but the location of files, their options, and the format may differ. As long as you know this fact going from one UNIX variant to another, you'll be ready to change your thinking just enough to get you through the possible variations in commands.

I don't cover any UNIX background or try to position UNIX variants. UNIX has now become mainstream and to try to position one UNIX variant relative to another and to try keeping up with the many advanced UNIX features being introduced on a regular basis would be futile.

Manual Pages Included in This Book

I am most grateful to Hewlett Packard Company for having allowed me to include select HP-UX manual pages in this book. Although specific options for a given command often differ among the UNIX variants, to have a manual page to turn to when reviewing a command is useful. I included the manual pages for select commands where I thought they would be especially helpful. My special thanks to Ram Appalaraju, Michael Nixon, John Verrochi, and Susan Wright of Hewlett Packard for having taken a lead role in helping me receive permission for using the manual pages.

Although the manual pages are for HP-UX, you may find that having a manual page in the same chapter where a command is covered is a great reference. Most UNIX commands are similar going from variant to another in that they provide the same output information or use the same options so the HP-UX manual pages provide a good starting point for researching a given command.

When a command used for an online manual page is in the book, the following information appears in the margin:

This is a "man page" block, which includes the man page icon and the command name, in this case **ps**, and the chapter number in which the online manual page appears, in this case Chapter 12.

The Table of Contents contains a complete list of the man pages appearing at the end of each chapter. The man pages for a command appear in the chapter to which the command is most applicable, even if it is not the first chapter in which the command is used. Commands pertaining to performance, for instance, have their man pages in the performance chapter, even if those commands were used in an earlier chapter.

Conventions Used in the Book

I don't use a lot of complex notations in the book. Here are a few simple conventions I've used to make the examples clear and the text easy to follow:

$ and #   The UNIX command prompt. Every command issued in the book is preceded by one of these prompts.

italics   Italics is used primarily when referencing selections that have been made in one of the examples or specifying options to commands.

bold and " "   Bold text is the information you would type, such as the command you issue after a prompt or the information you type when running a script. Sometimes information you would type is also referred to in the text explaining it, and the typed information may then appear in quotes.

<----   When selections have to be made, this indicates the one chosen for the purposes of the example.

One additional convention is that used for command formats. I don't use command formats more than I have to because I could never do as thorough a job describing commands as the UNIX manual pages. The manual pages go into detail on all UNIX commands. Here is the format I use when I cover commands:

```
form 1     command [option(s)] [arg(s)]
form 2     command [option(s)] [arg(s)]
form n     command [option(s)] [arg(s)]
```

I try not to get carried away with detail when covering a command but, sometimes many components must be covered in order for you to understand a command. Here is a brief description of the components listed above:

`form` # - Sometimes many forms of a command exist. If there is more than one form of a command that requires explanation, then I will show more than one form.

`command` - The name of the executable.

`option(s)` - Several options may appear across a command line.

`cmd_arg(s)` - Command arguments such as path name.

Acknowledgments

Too many people were involved in helping me with this book to list them all. I have decided to formally thank those who wrote sections of the book and those who took time to review it. I'm still not sure whether it takes more time to write something or review something that has been written to ensure that it is correct.

William Russell

Bill is Vice President of Software and Solutions Organization for Hewlett Packard. Bill acted as executive champion and sponsor of this book. His support was invaluable in helping to get the resources necessary to complete this book.

Elizabeth Zinkann

Elizabeth wrote the Foreword for this book. She is a Contributing Editor and Review Columnist for *Sys Admin Magazine*, The Journal for UNIX System Administrators. Her articles have also appeared in Performance Computing, Linux Magazine, and Network Administrator. As an independent computer consultant, she has built Linux servers, maintained computers utilizing Linux, Solaris, Macintosh, and Windows environments, and taught UNIX, shell programming, and Internet essentials. In a former life, she also programmed communications features for both domestic and International databases at AT&T Network Systems.

Donna Kelly

Donna wrote the "Common Desktop Environment (CDE)" chapter of this book. Donna and I have collaborated on a number of projects together. Donna has painstakingly reviewed many of my books for both technical accuracy and readability. Donna is both a technical expert in many operating systems and an excellent evaluator of the usefulness of a topic and the way it is covered. She not only ensures that the material is technically accurate, but she also makes certain that each topic is covered in a useful manner and that it is easy to read and comprehend.

Donna has been responsible for a number of computing environments of Hewlett Packard in Roseville, CA. She has experience with several operating systems, including HP-UX, MPE, and AS/400. Donna also is a Microsoft Certified Systems Engineer (MCSE).

Carollyn M. Carson

Carollyn wrote the "Introduction to Software Development" chapter. Carollyn is a Technical Consultant at Hewlett-Packard, specializing in E-Services, Internet Solutions, and Software Languages. Carollyn was previously employed at AT&T/AT&T Bell Labs for 10 years as a software developer and analyst, working on a network optimization system and telecommunication pricing applications.

Thom Fitzpatrick

Thom generously supplied access to many of the UNIX systems used to write this book. He also performed special setup on many systems so that effective examples could be produced. Thom also reviewed many sections of the book. His experience with many UNIX variants and desire to help were an invaluable resource to me when writing this book.

Thom is a technical consultant retained by HP in Roseville, CA. He provides technical and educational services on a variety of UNIX platforms including AIX, Solaris, SunOS, HP-UX, and NCR. He also provides internet and intranet solution help, such as extensive shell scripting, perl programming, cgi, web server implementation, and various security solutions including SSL and firewalls. Thom can be reached at thom@vintage-bus.com

Marty Poniatowski - Author

Marty has been a Senior Technical Specialist with Hewlett Packard for 13 years in the New York area. He has worked with hundreds of Hewlett Packard customers in many industries including, on-line services, financial, and manufacturing.

Marty has been widely published in computer industry trade publications. He has published over 50 articles on various computer-related topics. In addition to this book, he is the author of eight other Prentice Hall books: *HP-UX 11.x System Administration Handbook and Toolkit* (1999); *HP-UX 11.x System Administrator's "How To" Book* (1998); *HP NetServer Guide for Windows NT* (1998); *HP-UX System Administration Handbook and Toolkit* (1997); *Windows NT and HP-UX System Administrator's "How To" Book* (1997); *Learning the HP-UX Operating System* (1996); *HP-UX 10.x System Administrator's "How To" Book* (1995); and *The HP-UX System Administrator's "How To" Book* (1993).

Marty holds an M.S. in Information Systems from Polytechnic University (Brooklyn, NY), an M.S. in Management Engineering from the University of Bridgeport (Bridgeport, CT), and a B.S. in Electrical Engineering from Roger Williams University (Bristol, RI).

Reviewers

I'm not sure what makes someone agree to review a book. You don't get the glory of a contributing author, but the amount of work is just the same. I would like to thank the many people who devoted a substantial amount of time to reviewing this book to ensure that I included the topics important to new UNIX users and covered those topics accurately.

This book covers many different UNIX variants and topics. I developed a sense of the power and importance of the UNIX industry when working with so many UNIX variants. Virtually every company seems to use UNIX, which turns out to be a good thing when asking experts to review various sections. Roughly a total of 25 UNIX experts reviewed various sections of the book. I would like to thank all reviewers and give special thanks to some of them in this section.

Those who devoted time to reviewing many chapters of the book are: Richard Martino, Manager of UNIX Systems, Estee Lauder Companies; Paul J. Semmer, UNIX Administrator, Estee Lauder Companies; George Fiederlein, Manager of Systems Administration, Barnes and Noble Inc.; Ayelet Senator, Senior Systems Administrator, Barnes and Noble Inc.; Tom Broccoletti, Director of Systems Technology, GabRobins North America, Inc., and Jack Kern, Instructor, The Allied Group Inc.

I hope that you enjoy reading the book and learning the material as much as I did writing it.

Marty Poniatowski

marty_poniatowski@hp.com

CHAPTER 1

Getting Started

Introduction

I'll cover a wide variety of topics in this chapter that help you get started quickly on your UNIX system. The topics I cover include the following:

- Multi-user UNIX
- Uppercase and lowercase
- Login process (text and CDE)
- Login name and password
- Entering commands
- Logoff
- Electronic mail
- Internet access
- UNIX components

The topics in this chapter are covered in overview fashion with many examples. You can read a topic in this chapter while you try out the commands on your UNIX system. As I point out in every chapter in this book, differences occur among UNIX variants in almost every area. For instance, the command options on one UNIX variant may be somewhat different on another UNIX variant. Don't get overly concerned about the differences; just be aware of the fact that they exist and work through them as a matter of course. In an upcoming chapter, for instance, I spend some time on Common Desktop Environment (CDE). This is a graphical user interface found on many UNIX variants. It may not be available on your system, or your system administrator may have chosen a different graphical user interface. The same is true for most topics covered in this book. In general, though, most of what takes place at the command prompt is similar among UNIX variants, so you'll be able to take most of the examples in this chapter and use them on your system.

I put "UNIX Components" at the end of this chapter because you'll appreciate this topic much more after you have logged in and performed some basic commands.

Multi-User UNIX

Most UNIX systems are multi-user, meaning that several users may be using a single computer at the same time. You can connect to a UNIX system in a variety of different ways. You may have a character-terminal, on which you can enter commands at the command line that does not support any graphical interface. You may have a computer with a graphics display connected directly to the computer. You may have an X-terminal that runs a graphical user interface over a Local Area Network (LAN). It is difficult to discern a directly connected graphics display from an X-terminal because both run the same graphical user interface - usually Common Desktop Environment (CDE). Although there are many options available for interfaces among UNIX variants you always have access to the command line in

UNIX. There are wide variety of graphical user interfaces and graphical devices available, all of which support terminal windows that give you access to the command line.

Even systems that have only one character-based or graphics-based terminal connected to them are usually multi-user. With only one terminal connected to a system, why would you need to support multiple simultaneous users? To begin, you may have a user working on the directly connected terminal and additional users connected over the local area network. You may also want to have multiple windows open on your graphics terminal performing different tasks as different users.

Single-user systems are usually those dedicated to an individual user for his or her work. These systems provide a full UNIX environment but provide access for only a single user.

Most of the topics covered throughout this book apply to both single-user and multi-user systems.

All UNIX systems are multitasking, meaning that more than one process and application can be running on a system at a time. Later in the book, we look at the many processes running on a UNIX system all at the same time.

Uppercase and Lowercase

UNIX systems distinguish between uppercase and lowercase for both commands and file names. The meaning of a command or the name of a file takes on a different meaning, depending on the way in which uppercase and lowercase letters are used. The following are examples of *different* file names on a UNIX system:

```
program
Program
prograM
PROGRAM
```

If you wish to compile a file called **program** with the **cc** command on a UNIX system, you must issue the following command:

```
cc program
```

If you were to issue one of the following commands, you would not compile the desired program:

```
CC program
cc Program
```

The first example would not run the desired program called **cc,** because **CC**, with uppercase characters, is different from **cc** with lowercase characters. In the second example, the desired compiler called **cc** would indeed be invoked; however, the file called **Program** that we have specified is different from the desired file called **program**.

In addition to using care with uppercase and lowercase on UNIX systems, you also need to be aware of the fact that there are different file types on UNIX systems. Some different types of files found on UNIX systems, as well as how to determine the type of file you are dealing with, are covered in Chapter 2.

Login Process

All users on a UNIX system have a login name set up for them by the system administrator. The system administrator may consult you on the login name you wish to use. You gain access to the system by supplying both your login name and password. I cover this process shortly.

The rules for the login name you choose are determined by your system administrator. Typically, a login name will be two to eight characters in length. There are usually no special characters used in a login name.

There is not typically any security associated with a login name so pick a name easy for you to remember. Your name may also be used by other system users to send you messages and electronic mail, so a name by which other users know you will also be helpful.

Your password must meet the requirements set forth by the system administrator. The first time you log in you may have no password or only a temporary password that must be changed after you initially login to the system. Passwords normally have such requirements as a minimum of six characters and a minimum of one special character. Your system administrator may also require passwords to be changed on a regular basis. Your password should be complete nonsense so that no one could even begin to guess it.

Let's now look at an example login process. I begin with a character-based login session.

On your terminal you will receive a login prompt as shown in the following example. You respond to the login prompt with the name and temporary password supplied you by your system administrator:

```
*********************************************************************
* This is a private system operated for Your Company                *
* business.  Authorization from management is required to use       *
* this system.  Use by unauthorized persons is prohibited.          *
*********************************************************************
```

```
login: martyp
Password:
Last login: Fri Sep 17 07:12:57 from atlm0547.atl.hp.

TERM set to vt100

martyp $
```

The login was successful. We entered the correct login name and password and were granted access to the system.

You may occasionally enter an invalid user name or password. In the following example we first enter a valid user name and an invalid password. On the next attempt we enter an invalid user name. On the third attempt we enter all the correct information and are granted access to the system.

```
********************************************************************
* This is a private system operated for Your Company              *
* business.  Authorization from management is required to use     *
* this system.  Use by unauthorized persons is prohibited.        *
********************************************************************

login: martyp
Password:                          <-- first attempt, invalid password
Login incorrect


********************************************************************
* This is a private system operated for Your Company              *
* business.  Authorization from management is required to use     *
* this system.  Use by unauthorized persons is prohibited.        *
********************************************************************

login: m                           <-- second attempt, invalid user name
Password:
Login incorrect


********************************************************************
* This is a private system operated for Your Company              *
* business.  Authorization from management is required to use     *
* this system.  Use by unauthorized persons is prohibited.        *
********************************************************************

login: martyp                      <-- third attempt, valid user name
Password:                                      and password

Last login: Fri Sep 17 07:12:57 from atlm0547.atl.hp.
DISPLAY set to atlm0547:0.0

TERM set to vt100

martyp $
```

Note that after both the first and second failed attempts to login to the system we "start over." The system recognizes the invalid user name on the first attempt and the invalid password on the second attempt and in both cases supplies a "Login incorrect" message and starts over. The "Login incorrect" message is intentionally ambiguous, so you don't know whether your user name, password, or both are incorrect; therefore as little information as possible is give to someone attempting unauthorized access to the system.

After the successful login, you are given information about the system, your terminal, and any other information the system administrator thinks would be useful to you. This information surely differs on your system.

After login we want to proceed to issue commands. In this example, first command we'll issue is to change the temporary password supplied to us by the system administrator. You may find that after your first login you are *required* to change your password. The **passwd** command is used to change the password. Let's issue the **passwd** command and try to change our password to the current password, that is, no change. Then let's try to change the password to *passwd*. Finally, we'll change the password to a valid password:

man page

passwd-12

```
martyp $ passwd
passwd:  Changing password for martyp
Enter login password:
New password:                        <-- change to current password
passwd(SYSTEM): Password cannot be circular shift of logonid.
New password:                        <-- change to passwd
passwd(SYSTEM): The first 6 characters of the password
must contain at least two alphabetic characters and at least
one numeric or special character.
New password:                        <-- change to valid password
Re-enter new password:
passwd (SYSTEM): passwd successfully changed for martyp
martyp $
```

When we try to change the password to the current password, which is the same as our user name, we are told that the password can't be a "circular shift of loginid." This means that the login name and the password on this system must differ substantially. When we try to change our password to *passwd*, we are told that the first six characters must contain at least one numeric or special character to make the new password more difficult to guess. Finally, we conform to the rules for a new password and receive an indication that the change was made. Note again that the system supplies no visible characters when we type the new passwords.

Some features of a good password are:

- A minimum of six characters that should include special characters such as a slash (/), a dot (.), or an asterisk (*).

- No words should be used for a password.

- Don't make the password personal, such as name, address, favorite sports team, etc.

- Don't use something easy to type, such as *123456*, or *qwerty*.

- Some people say that misspelled words are acceptable, but I don't recommend using them. Spell check programs that match misspelled words to correctly spelled words can be used to guess at words that might be misspelled for a password.

- A password generator that produces unintelligible passwords works the best.

man page

passwd-12

We'll cover many commands throughout the chapters in this book. The **passwd** command is important to know for your initial login, because you my be required to change your password immediately.

If you gain access to your system through a graphical user interface login screen, you enter your user name and password just as you would at the command line. You can retype your user name and password if you make errors, just as you would at the command line. After successful login, you have a graphical environment in which to work. Figure 1-1 shows a Common Desktop Environment with many windows open.

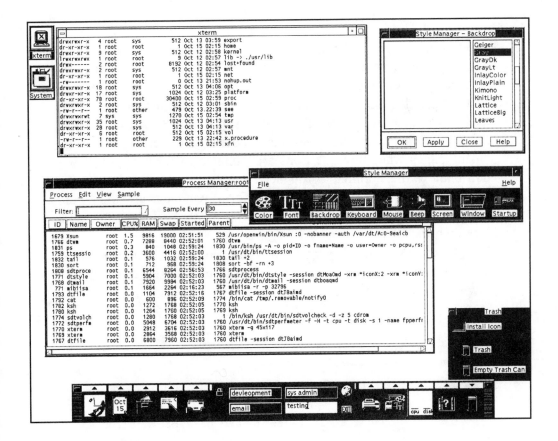

Figure 1-1 Common Desktop Environment after Successful Login

You can see in Figure 1-1 that there are many activities taking place in the graphical environment. Chapter 4, devoted to the Common Desktop Environment, covers many of the components in Figure 1-1 in detail.

Online Manual Pages

A set of on-line manual pages is supplied with most every UNIX variant. The "man" pages, as they are known, are usually complete, current, and an excellent all-around reference. Most other operating systems provide online help that is a small subset of the complete help that is available in the operating system manuals. The "man" pages, on the other hand, are very useful and most UNIX users first go to the "man" pages when any questions arise related to a command. If you don't know the command you need but know a command that is related to the function you wish to perform, you can view the "man" page for the command you know and see the other related commands it references.

To view the "man" page for a command, you simply issue **man** and the name of the command you wish to use, as shown in the following example from a Solaris system:

```
martyp $ man passwd
Reformatting page.  Wait... done

User Commands                                         passwd(1)

NAME
     passwd - change login password and password attributes

SYNOPSIS
     passwd  [-r  | files  | -r nis  | -r nisplus ]  [ name ]

     passwd  [ -r files  ]  [ -egh ]  [ name ]

     passwd  [ -r files  ] -s  [ -a ]

     passwd  [ -r files  ] -s  [ name ]

     passwd  [ -r files  ]  [-d  | -l ]  [ -f ]  [  -n min  ]  [
     -w warn ]  [ -x max ] name

     passwd -r nis  [ -egh ]  [ name ]

     passwd -r nisplus  [ -egh ]  [ -D domainname ]  [ name ]

     passwd -r nisplus -s  [ -a ]

     passwd -r nisplus  [ -D domainname ] -s  [ name ]
```

```
            passwd -r nisplus  [ -l ]  [ -f ]  [ -n min ]  [ -w warn ]
            [ -x max ]   [ -D domainname ] name
```

DESCRIPTION
     The passwd command changes the password or lists password
     attributes associated with the user's login name. Addition-
     ally, privileged users may use passwd to install or change
     passwords and attributes associated with any login name.

     When used to change a password, passwd prompts everyone for
     their old password, if any. It then prompts for the new
     password twice. When the old password is entered, passwd
     checks to see if it has "aged" sufficiently. If "aging" is
     insufficient, passwd terminates; see pwconv(1M), nist-
     bladm(1), and shadow(4) for additional information.

     When NIS or NIS+ is in effect on a system, passwd changes
     the NIS or NIS+ database. The NIS or NIS+ password may be
     different from the password on the local machine. If NIS or
     NIS+ is running, use passwd -r to change password informa-
     tion on the local machine.

     The pwconv command creates and updates /etc/shadow with
     information from /etc/passwd. pwconv relies on a special
     value of 'x' in the password field of /etc/passwd. This
     value of 'x' indicates that the password for the user is
     already in /etc/shadow and should not be modified.

User Commands   passwd(1)

     If aging is sufficient, a check is made to ensure that the
     new password meets construction requirements. When the new
     password is entered a second time, the two copies of the new
     password are compared. If the two copies are not identical,
     the cycle of prompting for the new password is repeated for,
     at most, two more times.

     Passwords must be constructed to meet the following require-
--More--(17%)
```

man page

passwd-12

   This partial listing, as indicated by the "17%" at the end of the
example, shows the "man" page for the **passwd** command we used
earlier in this chapter. You can issue the **man** command for topics
other than commands. You can also get information on system calls,
library routines, and other information. You can even get information
on the **man** command itself, as shown in the following example from
the same system:
```

```
martyp $ man man
Reformatting page.  Wait... done

User Commands                                                              man(1)

NAME
     man - find and display reference manual pages

SYNOPSIS
     man  [ - ]  [ -adFlrt ]  [ -M path ]  [ -T macro-package ]
     [ -s section ] name ...

     man  [ -M path ] -k keyword ...

     man  [ -M path ] -f file ...

DESCRIPTION
     The man  command displays  information  from  the  reference
     manuals.  It displays complete manual pages that you select
     by name, or one-line summaries selected either  by  keyword
     (-k),  or  by  the  name  of  an associated file (-f). If no
     manual page is located, man  prints an error message.

     Source Format
     Reference Manual pages are marked up with  either   nroff(1)
     or   sgml(5)  (Standard  Generalized  Markup  Language) tags.
     The man  command recognizes the type of markup and processes
     the  file accordingly.  The various source files are kept in
     separate directories depending on the type of markup.

     Location of Manual Pages
     The online Reference Manual page directories are convention-
     ally  located  in  /usr/share/man.  The  nroff  sources  are
     located in the /usr/share/man/man* directories.  The
     SGML sources are located in the /usr/share/man/sman* direc-
     tories.  Each  directory  corresponds  to  a  section of the
     manual. Since these directories  are  optionally  installed,
     they  may  not  reside  on  your host; you may have to mount
     /usr/share/man from a host on which they do reside.

     If  there  are  preformatted,  up-to-date  versions  in  the
     corresponding  cat  *  or  fmt  *  directories,  man  simply
     displays or prints those versions.  If the preformatted ver-
     sion  of  interest is out of date or missing, man  reformats
     it prior to display and will store the preformatted version
     if   cat  *  or  fmt  *  is writable.   The   windex database is
--More--(13%)
```

This example shows only 13% of the "man" page for the **man** command. Notice under "SYNOPSIS" that you can specify the section number of the "man" page you wish to view. The "man" pages are grouped into a number of categories. Usually, around eight groupings, or sections, exist for most UNIX variants. Some topics appear in more than one of the sections. You can specify the section number for a command if you know it. In the following example, we search for information on the **passwd** command and see that it appears in more than one section. We can view the "man" page for the command in section 1 and then the "man" page in section 4, as shown in the following example:

```
martyp $ pwd
/usr/man
martyp $ find . -name passwd*
./sman1/passwd.1
./sman4/passwd.4
martyp $ man -s 1 passwd
Reformatting page.  Wait... done

User Commands                                          passwd(1)

NAME
     passwd - change login password and password attributes

SYNOPSIS
     passwd  [-r  | files  | -r nis  | -r nisplus ]  [ name ]

     passwd  [ -r files  ]  [ -egh ]  [ name ]

     passwd  [ -r files  ] -s  [ -a ]

     passwd  [ -r files  ] -s  [ name ]

     passwd  [ -r files  ]  [-d  | -l ]  [ -f ]  [  -n min  ]  [
     -w warn ]  [ -x max ] name

     passwd -r nis  [ -egh ]  [ name ]

     passwd -r nisplus  [ -egh ]  [ -D domainname ]  [ name ]

--More--(3%)

martyp $ man -s 4 passwd
Reformatting page.  Wait... done

File Formats                                           passwd(4)

NAME
     passwd - password file

SYNOPSIS
     /etc/passwd

DESCRIPTION
     /etc/passwd is a local source of  information  about  users'
     accounts.  The password file can be used in conjunction with
```

```
    other  password  sources,  including  the  NIS  maps
    passwd.byname and  passwd.bygid and the NIS+ table  passwd .
    Programs use the getpwnam(3C) routines to access this infor-
    mation.

    Each  passwd  entry is a single line of the form:

    username:password:uid:gid:gcos-field:home-dir:login-shell

    where
--More--(13%)
```

We haven't yet covered some of the commands used in this example, however, all you need to know is that a **passwd.1** and a **passwd.4** were found under the "man" pages.

The "man" page for **passwd** from section 1 is the same as the one used in an earlier example. The "man" page for **passwd** from section 4 is for the **/etc/passwd** file. These are two different "man" pages, one for the **passwd** command and one for the **/etc/passwd** file. It is not uncommon to have multiple "man" pages for the same keyword. By default, the first section in which an occurrence of a "man" page appears is used if no section number is specified.

Some UNIX variants, such as Linux, use a capital "S" for specifying the section number. In our example we used a lowercase "s." As I will point out throughout the book there are many differences among UNIX variants for the ways in which commands are used, the outputs of commands, and in some cases the commands themselves. Please keep in mind that you may encounter such differences in your work, so don't hesitate to use the "man" pages on your system as a reference.

Rather than issuing the **find** command to see what "man" pages cover the **passwd** command, we could have used the **man** command with the "-k" option. This "-k" option combined with a *keyword*, such as *password* in our example, searches all the "man" page descriptions for *passwd*. One-line summaries are produced whereever *passwd* is found. The following example shows what is produced for such a *keyword* search:

```
# man -k passwd

d_passwd            d_passwd (4)- dial-up password file
getpw               getpw (3c)- get passwd entry from UID
```

```
nispasswd        nispasswd (1)- change NIS+ password information
nispasswdd       rpc.nispasswdd (1m) - NIS+ password update daemon
passwd           passwd (1)- change login password and password attributes
passwd           passwd (4)- password file
pwconv           pwconv (1m)- installs and updates /etc/shadow
                 with information from /etc/passwd
rpc.nispasswdd   rpc.nispasswdd (1m) - NIS+ password update daemon
rpc.yppasswdd    rpc.yppasswdd (1m)  - server for modifying NIS password file
yppasswd         yppasswd (1)- change your network password in the NIS database
yppasswdd        rpc.yppasswdd (1m)  - server for modifying NIS password file
```

This command produces a long list of "man" pages from a database, including sections 1 and 4 for **passwd** that our **find** command produced. In order to use the "-k" option, a "man" page database must have been produced by your system administrator by issuing the **catman** command.

man page

passwd-12

I am obviously a big advocate of using "man" pages, because I included many "man" pages at the end of chapters throughout the book. Anytime you see the "man" page icon, there is a "man" page for the command in the chapter number referenced in the icon. Although the "man" page for your UNIX variant may be different from the one appearing in the book, the commands on most UNIX variants are similar, and the "man" pages act as an excellent reference.

man page

find - 10

Electronic Mail

All UNIX variants come with electronic mail programs. You can use one of the electronic mail programs on your system to send and receive electronic mail from other users on the system. You can also communicate with users on other systems and across the internet if your system administrator has set up this capability. In this chapter, we'll cover the basics of sending and receiving electronic mail. I cover this very early in the book because you may receive a message after your first login indicating that you have received mail messages and you'll want to read them. You may receive a welcome message or a request to change your password immediately after your first login.

The most basic electronic mail program, and one that exists on every UNIX variant on which I have worked, is **mail**. This is a very easy program to use that requires very little explanation. In the following example, I invoke the **mail** program, issue "?" to print a list of

mail commands, read a message from *Tom*, reply to his message, and save the original message:

```
* Welcome to sys1

Last unsuccessful login: Mon Mar  8 09:32:13
Last login: Mon Sep 27 07:21:01


   ***********************************************************************
   * This is a private system operated for use by our company only.    *
   ***********************************************************************

* Welcome to sys1

You have mail.

TERM set to vt100

sys1:/home/martyp
martyp $ mail
Mail [5.2 UCB]  Type ? for help.
"/var/spool/mail/martyp": 1 message 1 new
>N  1 tomf            Mon Sep 27 07:23  11/392  "12:00 Phone Call"
? ?
Control Commands:
   q                          Quit - apply mailbox commands entered this session.
   x                          Quit - restore mailbox to original state.
   ! <cmd>                    Start a shell, run <cmd>, and return to mailbox.
   cd [<dir>]                 Change directory to <dir> or $HOME.
Display Commands:
   t [<msg_list>]             Display messages in <msg_list> or current message.
   n                          Display next message.
   f [<msg_list>]             Display headings of messages.
   h [<num>]                  Display headings of group containing message <num>.
Message Handling:
   e [<num>]                  Edit message <num> (default editor is ex).
   d [<msg_list>]             Delete messages in <msg_list> or current message.
   u [<msg_list>]             Recall deleted messages.
   s [<msg_list>] <file>      Append messages (with headings) to <file>.
   w [<msg_list>] <file>      Append messages (text only) to <file>.
   pre [<msg_list>]           Keep messages in system mailbox.
Creating New Mail:
   m <addrlist>               Create/send new message to addresses in <addrlist>.
   r [<msg_list>]             Send reply to senders and recipients of messages.
   R [<msg_list>]             Send reply only to senders of messages.
   a                          Display list of aliases and their addresses.
============================== Mailbox Commands ===============================
? t
Message  1:
From tomf Mon Sep 27 07:23:30
Date: Mon, 27 Sep 1999 07:23:30 -0700
From: <tomf>
To: martyp
Subject: 12:00 Phone Call

Please call me at 12:00 CA time to discuss trip.
Tom

? R
To: tomf
Subject: Re:  12:00 Phone Call

I'll call you then.
Marty
Cc:
? s
"/home/martyp/mbox" [Appended] 11/392
? q
sys1:/home/martyp
martyp $
```

This **mail** session is typical. We first used **mail** to invoke the electronic mail program. We are informed that there is one message from *tomf* with the subject *12:00 Phone Call.* We then use *?* to get a list of **mail** commands. I selected this particular system for the **mail** examples because of the clear help messages that are produced with *?*. We then use *t* to display the message we received, *R* to reply to *tomf* the sender of the message, *s* to save and delete the message, and finally quit with *q*. A file called **mbox** has been produced that contains all of the saved messages.

You can see from this example how easily you can handle the messages in your mailbox. It may be, however, that you wish to view summary information of the messages you have saved and deleted. The file **mbox** in my home directory was created to store messages that were saved and then deleted. We can view summary information of these messages using the option "-f" and **mbox** as an input file as shown in the following example:

```
martyp $ mail -f mbox
Mail [5.2 UCB]  Type ? for help.
"mbox": 4 messages
  1 tomf          Sun Sep 26 18:14  11/343   "Training"
 >2 donnak        Mon Sep 27 07:23  12/402   "Performance"
  3 carollync     Mon Sep 27 07:27  12/380   "Software Update"
  4 tomf          Mon Sep 27 07:38  11/357   "12:00 Phone Call"
```

You can see in this example that there were four messages saved in **mbox** that we can work with simply by specifying the number of the file (1-4). The current message is indicated by the right arrow >. Information is available on the date and time of delivery of the message, the size of the message in lines and characters, and the subject of the message. Saving and deleting files with *s* ensures that a copy of the file is maintained so that you can later access it.

A slightly more advanced electronic mail program is on some systems, called **mailx**. When run, **mailx** produces a list of messages for you rather than displaying them one at a time as **mail** does. The **mailx** list of messages is similar to the list we just saw with deleted

and saved messages using **mail -f mbox**. With **mailx,** you get the status of whether or not you have read the messages. You get a single
character preceding each message indicating that the message is *N* for
new, *O* for old messages that have been read, and *U* for unread messages. On some systems, such as the Red Hat Linux system used for
many of the examples in this book, you get the list of messages when
you run **mail** just as you would when you run **mailx** on other systems.
The following example shows what you would see when you run
mailx:

```
martyp $ mailx
Mail [5.2 UCB]  Type ? for help.
"/var/spool/mail/martyp": 2 messages 1 new 2 unread
 U  1 tomf           Mon Sep 29 08:40  13/394  "Networking"
>N  2 donnak         Mon Sep 29 08:49  10/342  "Interoperability"
?
```

The first message is *U* for unread. The second message is *N* for
new. The right arrow is next to the new message.
    You are not restricted to saving messages to the default file
mbox. You can organize your messages by saving them to different
files. The following example shows saving a message to the file **trip**:

```
martyp $ mailx
Mail [5.2 UCB] [AIX 4.1]  Type ? for help.
"/var/spool/mail/martyp": 2 messages 2 unread
>U  1 tomf           Mon Sep 27 08:49  11/352  "NY trip"
 U  2 donnak         Wed Sep 29 04:44  11/354  "login change"
?
Message  1:
From tomf Mon Sep 27 08:49:09
Date: Mon, 27 Sep 08:49:08 -0700
From: <tomf>
To: martyp
Subject: NY trip

I am going to change the date of the NY trip.

? s trip
"trip" [New file] 11/352
? q
Held 1 message in /var/spool/mail/martyp
martyp $
```

After we invoked **mailx,** a "Return" caused the first message to be read.

The file **trip** was created when this message was saved with **s trip,** and now we can store all related messages in the file **trip.**

Messages saved to a file can be printed with the **lp** command. We'll talk about **lp** later in the book in the system administration chapter; however, at this time it is sufficient to know that files can be printed to the default printer by issuing the command **lp** *filename.* To print the file **trip,** we would issue the command **lp trip.**

Sending electronic mail is just as easy as reading it. The simplest way to send a message is to type **mailx** or **mail** and the *username* of the person to whom you wish to send the message. We'll do just this in the message below to *tomf:*

```
martyp $ mail tomf
Subject: Pickup
I'll be at the airport in NY to give you a ride.
Marty
Cc:
martyp $
```

A *^D* (control D) was used to end the mail message. This message will be in the mailbox of *tomf.* You can send messages using Internet naming if your system has enabled this functionality. The following example shows sending the same message to *tomf* to his Internet electronic mail address:

```
martyp $ mail tomf@tomcompany.com
Subject: Pickup
I'll be at the airport in NY to give you a ride.
Marty
Cc:
martyp $
```

The ability to send messages to other systems and to Internet addresses requires that your system administrator set up this functionality.

If you have a graphical user interface on your system, you probably have a tool that helps you manage mail. Although the tool runs in
your graphical environment, it is probably using one of the mail programs we covered earlier. Figure 1-2 shows accessing mail in the
Common Desktop Environment.

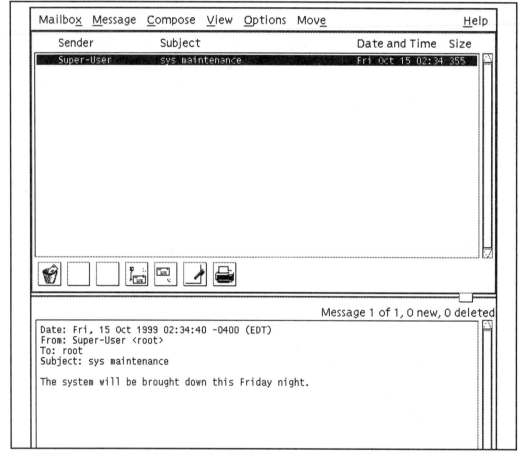

Figure 1-2 Accessing Mail in Common Desktop Environment

The pull-down menus across the top of Figure 1-2 give you
selections that perform the same function as the commands covered
earlier for saving, forwarding, deleting, and so on.

Accessing the Internet

The Internet has been used extensively on UNIX systems since its inception. The first web browser to be widely used was an X Window System application called Mosaic developed at the University of Illinois. Many web browsers are available today that run on UNIX systems including Mosaic, Netscape Communicator, and several others. We'll focus on Netscape Communicator in this section because it is the most widely used on UNIX systems. Many Netscape Communicator packages are available, some with different options from others, and Netscape Navigator, which is a basic web browser. So keep in mind that you may have not have a Netscape browser or you may have a different Netscape browser, from what I cover in this section, but the same principles apply to most browsers.

Your system administrator has probably already set up a browser on your UNIX system. Many UNIX distributions, such as the Linux Red Hat used in many of the examples throughout the book, provide a browser as part of the operating system distribution. The browser and the Internet are invaluable tools when using UNIX systems. You can find the latest information about your UNIX operating system at the web site of the company providing it. Figure 1-3 shows the Netscape Communicator window displaying the home page of Red Hat.

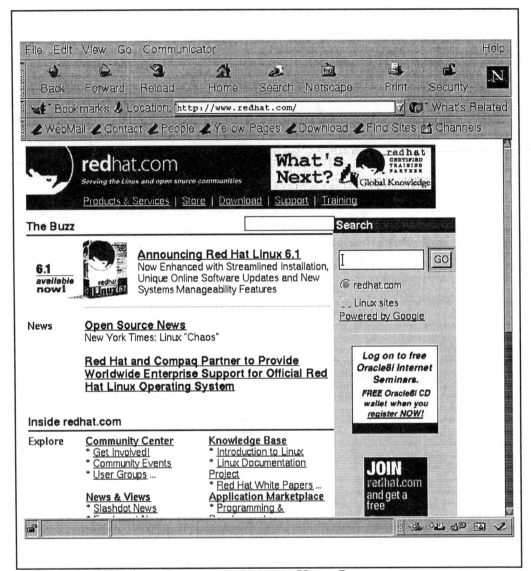

Figure 1-3   Using a Browser to Access a Home Page

From this home page, you can search for any topic related to the Red Hat Linux operating system. We connect to a home page by specifying a Uniform Resource Locator (URL) in the *Location* box of the browser. In this case we have specified *www.redhat.com,* which is the Red Hat URL. The URLs of the companies supplying the four most often cited UNIX variants used in this book are shown in Table 1-1 in alphabetical order.

Table 1-1 UNIX Variant Company URLs Used in This Book

URL	Result
www.hp.com	Hewlett-Packard Company
www.ibm.com	International Business Machines Corp.
www.redhat.com	Red Hat, Inc.
www.sun.com	Sun Microsystems, Inc.

From these home pages, you can work your way through the web site to find the information you need. "Work" is the operative word here. You may be fortunate and use the *Search* mechanism on the home page you are viewing to find just what you need quickly on a web site. On the other hand, you may spend a lot of time hunting around a web site for just what you're after and end up on many related web sites to get your desired information.

Notice in Figure 1-3 that *www.redhat.com* is preceded by *http://.* This is the protocol portion of the URL. *http://* is a protocol used to specify a web page. Many such protocols exist. Table 1-2 lists some of the more commonly used protocols.

Table 1-2 Commonly Used Protocol Specifiers

URL	Result
file:<*pathname*>	Load a local file into browser as specified by <*pathname*>.
ftp://	File Transfer Protocol (ftp) will be used.
gopher://	A host offering Gopher services will be used.
http://	A desired web page to access will be used.
https://	A desired secure web page to access will be used.
news://	A network news server will be used.

These are the most commonly used protocols used in conjunction with a browser.

The next several figures show some of the basic customization you can perform to the browser. These are intended to give you a feel for the type of customization you can perform with most browsers.

Although you may already have your browser loaded for you, there may still be some configuration necessary to get it fully operational or some customization you wish to perform. Figure 1-4, on the left-hand side, shows several areas of customization we can perform in Netscape Communicator with *Fonts* selected in this example:

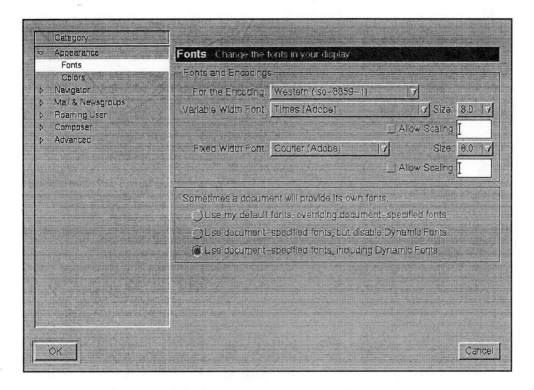

Figure 1-4 Specifying Browser Fonts

In this example, we have selected *Fonts* under *Appearance* to get
the information shown in Figure 1-4. Among the options we have for
customization is to specify the size of the fonts we wish to use in this
application. There is also a *Colors* selection under *Appearance* in
which we would have a similar set of options to adjust the colors in
this application.

The next category of options we can modify is under *Navigator,*
as shown in Figure 1-5.

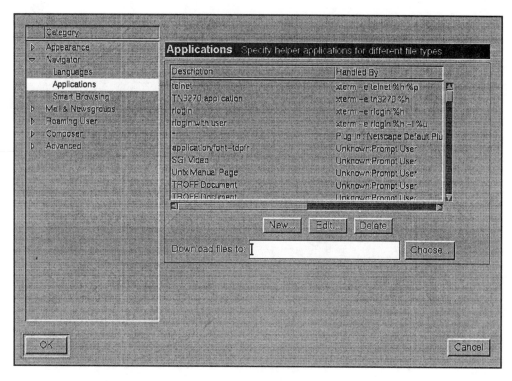

Figure 1-5 Browser Applications

Under *Navigator,* we have three potential areas of customization. We are viewing the *Applications* window. This window lists the applications and the "helper" that will be associated with the application.

The next category is *Mail and Newsgroups,* shown in Figure 1-6.

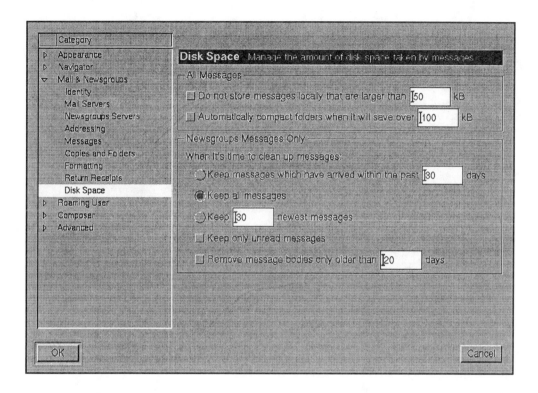

Figure 1-6 Browser Disk Space

In Figure 1-6, we are specifying the amount of disk space that can be consumed by messages. Because mail and newsgroups can both result in a lot of large messages being sent to your system, you want to have control over the size of messages you will receive and what messages will be purged based on their age.

The next category is *Roaming User,* which is related to your setup when Netscape is used on a roaming basis. You are given options for what aspect(s) of your profile will be transferred, as shown in Figure 1-7.

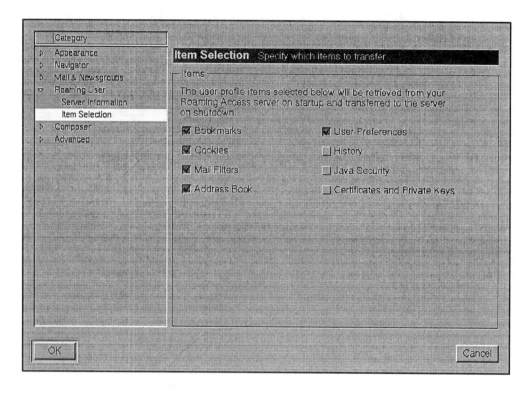

Figure 1-7 Roaming User Items

Figure 1-7 shows some of the items that will be transferred if you are using a roaming access server. No matter where you are using Netscape, you would like to have such a setup as your *User Preferences* be consistent, and this category gives you options for your roaming setup.

The next category is *Composing,* which gives you options related to web documents you publish, as shown in Figure 1-8.

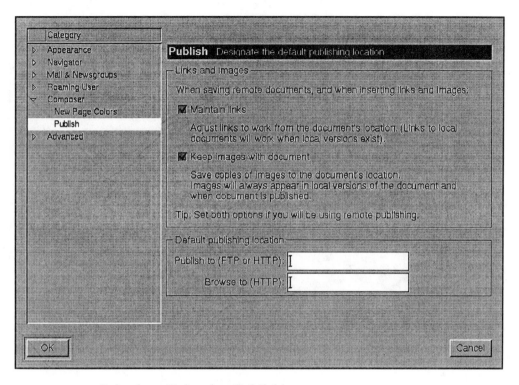

Figure 1-8 Selections Related to Publishing

We are viewing *Publish* under *Composing* in Figure 1-8, which provides options about web-related publishing you may perform, such as the location of documents.

The final category is *Advanced,* which contains information about *Cache* and *Proxies,* as shown in Figure 1-9.

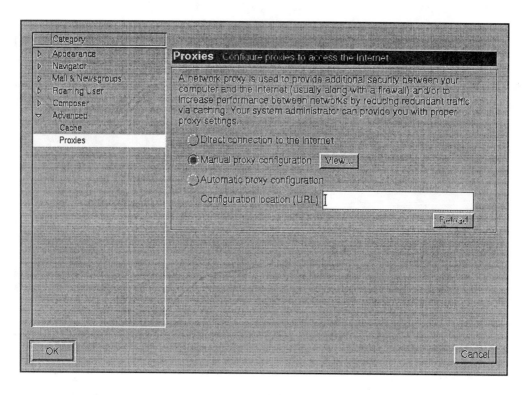

Figure 1-9 Selecting *Proxies*

In the interest of protecting computer systems from intrusion, most companies have set up a firewall for the purpose of restricting access to systems. This restriction means that to getting both in and out of many company networks is difficult. The proxy server is a means by which you can get access to the Internet. We have selected *Proxies* in Figure 1-9 which produces the dialog box shown in Figure 1-10.

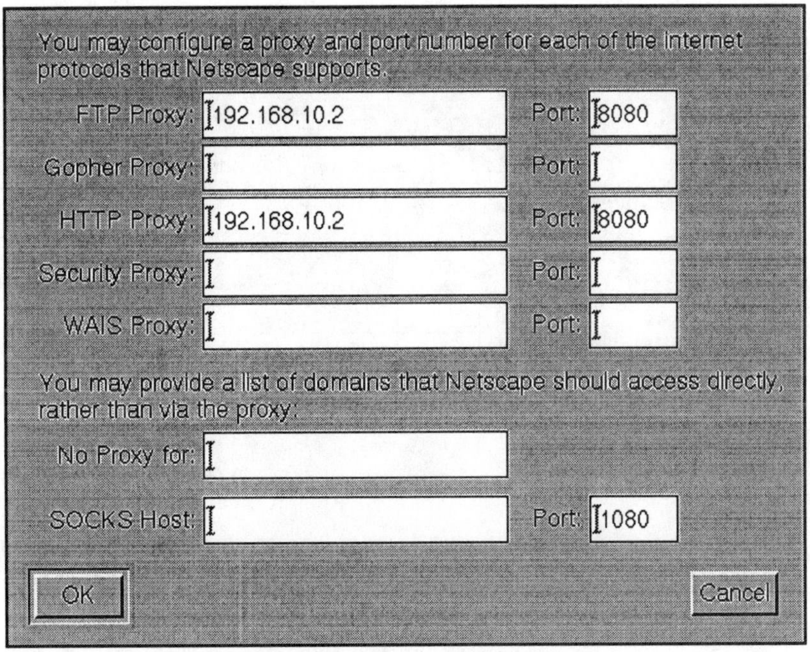

You may configure a proxy and port number for each of the Internet protocols that Netscape supports.

FTP Proxy:	192.168.10.2	Port: 8080
Gopher Proxy:		Port:
HTTP Proxy:	192.168.10.2	Port: 8080
Security Proxy:		Port:
WAIS Proxy:		Port:

You may provide a list of domains that Netscape should access directly, rather than via the proxy.

No Proxy for:		
SOCKS Host:		Port: 1080

OK   Cancel

Figure 1-10 Specifying Proxy-Related Information

In Figure 1-10, we have set up the addresses and port numbers of the proxy servers for two types of internet access. This setup may have already been performed for you by your system administrator. If not, you will want to confer with them prior to making such configuration changes if you don't know this information.

The other category under *Advanced* is *Cache,* as shown in Figure 1-11.

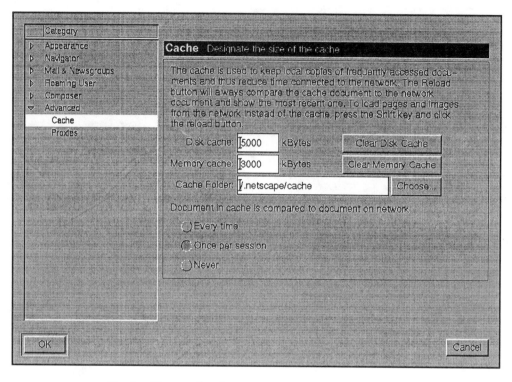

The cache is used to keep local copies of frequently accessed documents and thus reduce time connected to the network. The Reload button will always compare the cache document to the network document and show the most recent one. To load pages and images from the network instead of the cache, press the Shift key and click the reload button.

Figure 1-11   Cache Customization

The browser-related cache is used to increase the speed of your internet work by saving copies of frequently used information locally so that you don't have to continually go out over the network to reload the information. You can specify the size of cache and location for the cached data to be saved in this window.

You will determine the type of customization you want to perform soon after using your browser. Most browsers give you the option to perform the type of customization we have covered in this section.

UNIX Components

I have waited until the end of this chapter to cover the components of a UNIX system, because after login, issuing some commands, and possibly accessing the internet, you have a feel for the way in which you interact with a UNIX system. Now is an appropriate time to cover the high-level components of which a UNIX system is comprised.

Figure 1-12 is a high-level depiction of a UNIX system:

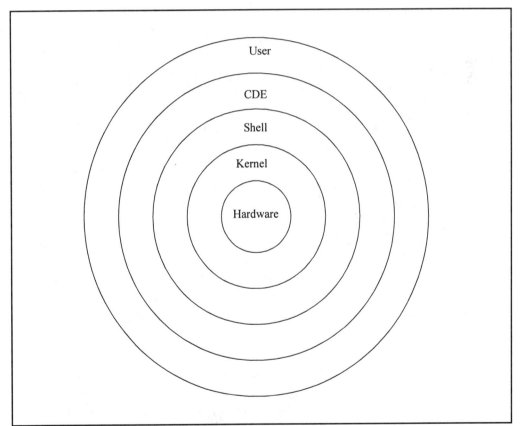

Figure 1-12 High-Level UNIX System Structure

Before describing this figure, I'll first mention that everyone has a somewhat different way of viewing the components of UNIX. This figure contains the most important components from a user perspective.

At the heart of this diagram is the hardware. UNIX, in its many forms, now runs on many different types of hardware. I won't cover much in the way of hardware in this book, because so many options are related to the hardware on which UNIX runs.

The next circle from the center of this diagram is the kernel. The kernel performs many functions including: management of devices, memory, and processes; scheduling and execution of all commands; and containment of drivers that control system hardware. The kernel is an aspect of the system that system administrators spend a lot of time maintaining. When a new device is configured, a device driver may have to be added to the kernel in order to support the new device. There is also substantial tuning that can be performed to the kernel in order to optimize system performance for the application(s) running on the UNIX system. Users have only indirect interaction with the kernel through the commands you issue that work their way to the kernel.

The next circle is the shell. The shell takes commands from you and starts the process of executing the commands. This is about as far into the UNIX diagram as a typical user goes. In addition to passing commands to more inner layers of the system the shell also allows you to run commands in the background and run shell programs. We'll cover three of the most commonly used shells in later chapters and also cover the basics of shell programming. Most of the material in the book is based on work performed by you at the command line, which is part of the shell.

The next circle is the Common Desktop Environment (CDE) or other graphical user interface. Chapter 4 is devoted to CDE in this book, and many examples use CDE and another graphical interface called Gnome that runs on the Linux system. You usually don't see the graphical user interface as a separate circle in such UNIX diagrams, because most of the work done in a graphical user interface works its way down to a shell command. Since most UNIX users use a graphical user interface I think this warrants its own circle.

The final circle is the user. Through all of the layers shown in this figure you accomplish your work on a UNIX system.

Because most of the examples in the book take place at the command line, and the remainder in a graphical user interface, you don't really need to concern yourself with inner UNIX circles as a user. Because your system administrator, database administrator, and others maintaining the system spend a substantial amount of their time dealing with these innermost components, Figure 1-13 is helpful in that it gives you an appreciation for the areas with which your associates are focused. Your shell, mail system, user interface, browser interface, and other components are customized and maintained by you, so these topics will be covered in upcoming chapters, as well as interacting with the UNIX file system and the UNIX commands you'll be issuing.

CHAPTER 2

UNIX File System Introduction

The Basis of UNIX

Most everything in UNIX comes down to files and directories. If you understand the hierarchical UNIX file system layout and how to manipulate files and directories, then you're a long way toward UNIX understanding.

A lot goes into working with UNIX files and directories. This chapter covers the basics and background of files and directories in UNIX. The next chapter covers commands related to files and directories. The only command covered in this chapter is the **file** command, used to determine the type of file.

man page

file - 2

File Types

A file is a means by which information is stored on a UNIX system. The commands you issue, the applications you use, the data you store, and the devices you access such as printers and keyboard are all contained in files. One aspect of UNIX that makes it both simple and complex; simple because you know everything out there is a file, complex because the contents of a file could be anything ranging from simple data you can read to a device file that is created by your system administrator with a unique set of commands.

Every file on the system has a file name. The operating system takes care of all file-system-related tasks; you just need to know the name of the file and how to use it. Many types of files are on UNIX systems. Some file types are peculiar to the UNIX variant you are using. Device files, for instance, contain information about the specific hardware platform on which you are running your UNIX variant. In general, however, most file types are similar going from system to system. The file types we will look at are:

- Text Files

- Data Files

- Source Code Files

- Executable Files

- Shell Programs

- Links

- Device Files

Many times when dealing with various types of files there are extensions are associated with those files. Many applications, for instance, associate a specific extension with that application. Text files, for instance, sometimes have a **.txt** extension. Most C source code programs have a **.c** extension, and most C++ programs have a **.cc** extension. Although the extension can be useful for determining the type of file no written requirements state that a particular type of file must contain an assigned extension.

The following table shows some commonly used extensions for various types of files:

Extension	File Type
.1 to .n	On-line manual source.
.a	An archive or library.
.c	C program source.
.cc	C++ program source.
.csh	C shell script.
.f	FORTRAN program source.
.ksh	Korn shell script.
.o	Object file of compiled source.
.ps	Postscript source.
.shar	Shell archive.
.sh	Bourne shell script.
.tar	**tar** archive.
.txt	ASCII text file.
.Z	Compressed file.

man page

file - 2

A useful technique for determining the file type is to use the **file** command. Most UNIX variants support the **file** command, although the outputs differ somewhat, so I suggest that you use the **file** command to determine file type. The best way to learn about file types and the **file** command is through example, which we'll do later in this chapter after discussing some common file types in more detail.

Text Files

What could be simpler than a file that contains characters, just like the ones you're now reading in this chapter? These ASCII characters are letters and numerals that represent the work you perform. If, for instance, you use an UNIX editor to create an electronic mail message or a letter, you are creating a text file in most cases. Here is an example of part of an ASCII text file from a Linux system:

```
Thu Nov  5 07:29:53 1999 debug: FTS: appending '/dev/hda1'
Thu Nov  5 07:29:53 1999 debug: FTS: appending '/tmp/LST/swap.sel'
Thu Nov  5 07:29:53 1999 debug: Building partition-list with argument <Linux>
Thu Nov  5 07:29:53 1999 debug: Respecting exclude file /tmp/LST/targets.sel:
/dev/hdd
/dev/hda1
/dev/hda2
Thu Nov  5 07:29:53 1999 debug: No ADDITIONAL partitions available
Thu Nov  5 07:29:59 1999 debug: added '8390' to '/root/tmp/modules.handled'
Thu Nov  5 07:29:59 1999 debug: added '8390' to '/root/etc/modules/2.0.29/#1 Tue
Feb 11 20:36:48 MET 1997.default'
Thu Nov  5 07:29:59 1999 debug: added 'scsi_mod' to '/root/tmp/modules.handled'
Thu Nov  5 07:29:59 1999 debug: added 'scsi_mod' to '/root/etc/modules/2.0.29/#1
Tue Feb 11 20:36:48 MET 1997.default'
Thu Nov  5 07:29:59 1999 debug: added 'sd_mod' to '/root/tmp/modules.handled'
Thu Nov  5 07:29:59 1999 debug: added 'sd_mod' to '/root/etc/modules/2.0.29/#1 Tue
Feb 11 20:36:48 MET 1997.default'
Thu Nov  5 07:29:59 1999 debug: added 'sr_mod' to '/root/tmp/modules.handled'
Thu Nov  5 07:29:59 1999 debug: added 'sr_mod' to '/root/etc/modules/2.0.29/#1 Tue
Feb 11 20:36:48 MET 1997.default'
Thu Nov  5 07:29:59 1999 debug: added 'st' to '/root/tmp/modules.handled'
Thu Nov  5 07:29:59 1999 debug: added 'st' to '/root/etc/modules/2.0.29/#1 Tue Feb
11 20:36:48 MET 1997.default'
Thu Nov  5 07:29:59 1999 debug: added 'sg' to '/root/tmp/modules.handled'
Thu Nov  5 07:29:59 1999 debug: added 'sg' to '/root/etc/modules/2.0.29/#1 Tue Feb
11 20:36:48 MET 1997.default'
Thu Nov  5 07:29:59 1999 debug: added 'nfs' to '/root/tmp/modules.handled'
Thu Nov  5 07:29:59 1999 debug: added 'nfs' to '/root/etc/modules/2.0.29/#1 Tue
Feb 11 20:36:48 MET 1997.default'
Thu Nov  5 07:29:59 1999 debug: added 'isofs' to '/root/tmp/modules.handled'
Thu Nov  5 07:29:59 1999 debug: added 'isofs' to '/root/etc/modules/2.0.29/#1 Tue
```

```
Feb 11 20:36:48 MET 1997.default'
Thu Nov  5 07:29:59 1999 debug: 'isofs' is already handled
Thu Nov  5 07:29:59 1999 debug: 'nfs' is already handled
Thu Nov  5 07:29:59 1999 debug: 'sg' is already handled
Thu Nov  5 07:29:59 1999 debug: 'st' is already handled
```

Data Files

A file that contains data used by one of your applications is a data file. If you use a sophisticated desktop publishing tool such as FrameMaker® to write a book, you create data files that FrameMaker uses. These data files contain data, which you can usually read, and formatting information, which you can sometimes read but is usually hidden from you. If your UNIX installation uses a database program, then you may have data files that you can partially read.

Source Code File

A source code file is a text file that contains information related to a programming language such as C, C++, Pascal, FORTRAN, and so on. When a programmer develops a source code file, they create a file that conforms to the naming convention of the program language being used, such as adding a ".c" to the end of the file if creating a C program.

The following is an example of a C source code file:

```
/* this is K & R sort program */

# include <stdio.h>
# include <stdlib.h>

    int N;
    int v[1000000];        /* v is array to be sorted */
    int left = 0;          /* left pointer */
    int right;
    int swapcount, comparecount = 0;
                           /* count swaps and compares*/

     int i, j, t;
    char print;
    char pr_incr_sorts;
```

```
main()


{
    printf("Enter number of numbers to sort : ");
    scanf("%10d", &N);                          /* 10d used for a BIG input */
    printf ("\n");                                /* select type of input to sort */

    printf("Enter rand(1), in-order(2), or reverse order (3)    sort : ");
    scanf ("%2d", &type);
    printf ("\n");                              /* select type of input to sort */

    if (type == 3)
                for (i=0; i<N; ++i)         /* random        */
                     v[i] = (N - i);

    else if (type == 2)
                for (i=0; i<N; ++i)
                      v[i]= (i + 1);             /* in order       */

    else if (type == 1)
                 for (i=0; i<N; ++i)
                      v[i]=rand();              /* reverse order */
    fflush(stdin);
    printf("Do you want to see the numbers before sorting (y or n)? : ");
    scanf("%c", &print);
    printf ("\n");                              /* View unsorted numbers?  */
    if (print == 'y')
      {
            printf ("\n");
         for (i=0; i<N; ++i)
            printf("a[%2d]= %2d\n", i, v[i]);
            printf ("\n");
      }


     fflush(stdin);
    printf("Do you want to see the array at each step as it sorts? (y or n)? : ");
     scanf("%c", &pr_incr_sorts);
     printf ("\n");                             /* View incremental sorts?  */


       right = N-1;                              /* right pointer         */

                qsort(v, left, right);




       {
         fflush(stdin);
         printf ("Here is the sorted list of %2d items\n", N);
            printf ("\n");
         for (i=0; i<N; ++i)
            printf ("%2d\n ", v[i]);
            printf ("\n");
            printf ("\n");                       /* print sorted list       */
                  }
                  printf ("number of swaps = %2d\n ", swapcount);
                  printf ("number of compares = %2d\n ", comparecount);
       }

   /* qsort function */

            void qsort( v, left, right)
                    int v[], left, right;
      {
                int i, last;
                if (left > right)
                 return;
```

```
        swap(v, left, (left + right)/2);
        last = left;
        for (i=left+1; i <= right; i++)
        {
            comparecount = ++comparecount;
              if (v[i] < v[left])
        swap(v, ++last, i);
        }
        swap(v, left, last);
        qsort(v, left, last-1);
        qsort(v, last+1, right);
        }

        /* swap function  */


        swap(v, i, j)
            int v[], i, j;

            {int temp;
                swapcount = swapcount++;
                temp = v[i];
                v[i] = v[j];
                v[j] = temp;


    if (pr_incr_sorts == 'y')
        {
                printf("Incremental sort of array = ");
        printf ("\n");
        for (i=0; i<N; ++i)
            printf("a[%2d]= %2d\n", i, v[i]);
            printf ("\n");
        }
    }
```

Executable Files

Executable files are compiled programs that can be run. You can't
read executable files and you'll typically get a bunch of errors,
unreadable characters, and beeps from your UNIX system when you
try to look at one of these. You may also lose your screen settings and
cause other problems.

You don't have to go far in UNIX to find executable files, they
are everywhere. Many of the UNIX commands you issue are executable files that you can't read. In addition, if you are developing programs on your system, you are creating your own executables.

Here is an example of what you see if you attempt to send an
executable to the screen:

```
unknown/etc/ttytyperunknown<@=>|<@=>|:unknown<@=>
callocLINESCOLUMNSunknownPackaged for
argbad aftger%3
parmnumber missing <@=>|<@=>|:
@ @ 3### @@@A:2TTO|>@#<|2X0OR
EraseKillOOPS<@=>|<@=>|:
<@=>|<@=>|:
<@=>|<@=>|:<@=>|ATOO<@=>|:<@=>|<@=>|:<@=>|<@=>|:<@=>|<@=
>|:
```

Shell Programs

A shell program is both a file you can run to perform a task and a file that you can read. So yes, even though you can run this file because it is executable, you can also read it. I'm going to describe shell programming in more detail in an upcoming chapter.

I consider shell programming to be an important skill for every user to have. I'll spend some time going over the basics of shell programming. Some of the background I'm about to cover relating to file types and permissions is important when it comes to shell programming, so this is important information for you to understand.

Here is an example of part of a shell program that performs an audit of a system:

```
#!/bin/sh
{

echo "PROG>>>>> determining if Ignite-UX loaded on sys-
tem."


igtest=`swlist  | grep Ignite`
echo $igtest
if [ -n "$igtest" ]; then
echo "Ignite-UX installed"
else
echo "Ignite-UX is not installed"
fi
```

```
echo "PROG>>>>> determining if make_recovery has been run
by
                checking for /var/opt/ignite/arch.include."

if [ -f /var/opt/ignite/recovery/arch.include ]; then
echo "make_recovery has been run."
else
echo "make_recovery has not been run."
fi

echo "PROG>>>>> determining if make_recovery was run with
the
                -C (for check_recovery) option."

if [ -f /var/opt/ignite/recovery/makrec.last ]; then
echo "make_recovery with -C has been run. We'll now
                run check_recovery."
/opt/ignite/bin/check_recovery 2>&1
else
echo "make_recovery with -C has not been run. We can't
                run check_recovery."
fi

}   | tee -a /tmp/IMPORTANT/igtest.out
```

The shell program is text you can read and modify if indeed you have permissions to do so. In addition to programming information, shell programs contain comments indicated by lines beginning with a #.

Links

A link is a pointer to a file stored elsewhere on the system. Instead of having two or more copies of a file on your system, you can link to a file that already exists on your system.

One particularly useful way links have been used in UNIX is related to new releases of the operating system. The locations of files sometimes change going from one release to another, and rather than learn all the new locations, links are produced from the old location to the new one. When you run a command using the old location, the link points to the new location.

Links are also useful for centralizing files. If a set of identical files has to be updated often, it is easier to link to a central file and update it, rather than having to update several copies of the file in several different locations.

Device Files

Device files, sometimes called device special files, contain information about the hardware connected to your system. Because device special files are associated with system administration functions they are usually not covered much in user, as opposed to system administration, material. I think the situation should be otherwise. It is very frustrating for a user to want to write a file to a floppy disk or a tape and not have any idea how to access a device file. I'll cover some use of device files so you are not completely in the dark in this area.

Devices on your system can often be accessed with different device files. A disk, for instance, can be accessed with either a block device file or a character device file. Most of this access is the responsibility of your system administrator; however, when you attempt to determine the file type, you may encounter special files of different types such as character and block.

man page

file - 2

Other types of files are on your system as well, but for the purposes of getting started with UNIX, the file types I will describe supply sufficient background to get you started.

The file Command

The **file** command is used to determine the file type. This command is useful because the name of a file does not always indicate its file type. The following examples perform a long listing of a file to provide some background information on the file, and then the **file** command is run to show the file type. I don't cover the command used to list files until the next chapter, but I include it in these examples. The **ls** command provides a listing of files. **ls** is covered in detail in the next chapter. We need to use it in this chapter in only its basic form. I have included the man page for **ls** at the end of this chapter, if you need to view it. Combined with the "-l" option, you can produce a long listing that provides a lot of information about files. Using **ls -l** in the following examples, you will see the name of each file, file type, permissions, number of hard links, owner name, group name, size in bytes, and time stamp. You may not know what much of this information is for now; however, some of this information may be useful when viewing the output of the **file** command. Examples in this chapter for the **file** command show that different UNIX variants may produce somewhat different outputs of the **file** command. The following examples show an HP-UX output for the "UNIX example" and then a Linux output where available.

man page

ls - 2

man page

file - 2

Text File (UNIX example)

(Described by the **file** command as *ascii text*.)

```
# ls -l .mosaic-global-history
-rw-r--r--   1 201       users        587 Dec 22  1999 .mosaic-
global-history
# file  .mosaic-global-history
.mosaic-global-history: ascii text
#
```

Text File (Linux example)

(Described by the **file** command as *ASCII text*.)

```
# ls -l *
-rw-r--r--   1 root      root      251367 Nov  5 07:11 debug
-rw-r--r--   1 root      root        2020 Nov  5 07:11 history
```

```
# file *
debug:      ASCII text
history:    ASCII text
```

Data File (UNIX example)

(Described by the **file** command as *data*.)

```
# ls -l Static.dat
-rw-r--r--  1 201      users     235874 Aug 26  1999 Static.dat
# file Static.dat
Static.dat:    data
#
```

Source Code File (UNIX example)

(Described by the **file** command as *c program text*.)

```
# ls -l krsort.c
-rwxrwxrwx  1 201      users       3234 Nov 16  1999 krsort.c
# file krsort.c
krsort.c:      c program text
#
```

Source Code File (Linux example)

(Described by the **file** command as *C program text*.)

```
# ls -l *.c
-rw-r--r--  1 root     root      4521 Jul 12  1999 intl-bindtextdom.c
-rw-r--r--  1 root     root      6234 Jul 12  1999 intl-cat-compat.c
-rw-r--r--  1 root     root     14128 Jul 12  1999 intl-dcgettext.c
-rw-r--r--  1 root     root      1750 Jul 12  1999 intl-dgettext.c
-rw-r--r--  1 root     root     12759 Jul 12  1999 intl-finddomain.c
-rw-r--r--  1 root     root      1907 Jul 12  1999 intl-gettext.c
-rw-r--r--  1 root     root      1646 Jul 12  1999 intl-intl-compat.c
-rw-r--r--  1 root     root      5361 Jul 12  1999 intl-loadmsgcat.c
-rw-r--r--  1 root     root      7271 Jul 12  1999 intl-localealias.c
-rw-r--r--  1 root     root      2914 Jul 12  1999 intl-textdomain.c
# file *.c
intl-bindtextdom.c: C program text
intl-cat-compat.c:  C program text
intl-dcgettext.c:   C program text
intl-dgettext.c:    C program text
intl-finddomain.c:  C program text
intl-gettext.c:     C program text
intl-intl-compat.c: C program text
intl-loadmsgcat.c:  C program text
intl-localealias.c: C program text
intl-textdomain.c:  C program text
#
```

Executable File (UNIX example)

(Described by the **file** command as *shared executable.*)

man page

file - 2

```
# ls -l krsort
-rwxr-xr-x   1 201      users       34592 Nov 16  1999 krsort
# file krsort
krsort:       PA-RISC1.1 shared executable dynamically linked
-not stripped
#
```

man page

ls - 2

Executable File (LInux example)

(Described by the **file** command as *executable.*)

```
# ls -l a*
-rwxr-xr-x   1 root     root        3888 Jul 24  1999 activate
-rwxr-xr-x   1 root     root        4452 Feb 25  1999 adjtimex
# file a*
activate: ELF 32-bit LSB executable, Intel 80386, version 1,
stripped
adjtimex: ELF 32-bit LSB executable, Intel 80386, version 1,
stripped
#
```

Shell Program (UNIX example)

(Described by the **file** command as *commands text.*)

```
# ls -l llsum
-rwxrwxrwx   1 root     sys         1267 Feb 23  1999 llsum
# file llsum
llsum:        commands text
#
```

man page

file - 2

Shell Program (Linux example)

(Described by the **file** command as *Bourne shell script text*.)

```
# ls -l request-route
-rwx------   1 root     root          1046 Sep 19  1999 request-route
# file request-route
request-route: Bourne shell script text
#
```

man page

ls - 2

Link (UNIX example)

(The link is not referenced by the **file** command; this is shown as a *shared executable dynamically linked*. The reference to *dynamically linked* does not mean that this is a link.)

```
# ls -l /usr/bin/ar
lr-xr-xr-t   1 root     sys            15 Mar 23  1999 ar -> /
usr/ccs/bin/ar
# file /usr/bin/ar
/usr/bin/ar:         s800 shared executable dynamically linked
#
```

Link (Linux example)

(The link is shown is a *symbolic link*.)

```
# ls -l reboot
lrwxrwxrwx  1 root     root            4 Nov  5 01:31 reboot -> halt
# file * | grep link
depmod:          symbolic link to modprobe
ksyms:           symbolic link to insmod
pidof:           symbolic link to killall5
reboot:          symbolic link to halt
rmmod:           symbolic link to insmod
swapoff:         symbolic link to swapon
telinit:         symbolic link to init
udosctl:         symbolic link to /sbin/umssync
umssetup:        symbolic link to /sbin/umssync
#
```

Block Device File (UNIX example)

(Described by the **file** command as *block special*.)

```
# ls -l /dev/dsk/c0t1d0
brw-r--r--   1 bin      sys         31 0x001000 Apr 17  1999 /dev/
dsk/c0t1d0
# file /dev/dsk/c0t1d0
/dev/dsk/c0t1d0:        block special (31/4096)
#
```

Block Device File (Linux example)

(Described by the **file** command as *block special*.)

```
# ls -l loop*
brw-rw----   1 root     disk       7,   0 Sep 23  1999 loop0
brw-rw----   1 root     disk       7,   1 Sep 23  1999 loop1
brw-rw----   1 root     disk       7,   2 Sep 23  1999 loop2
brw-rw----   1 root     disk       7,   3 Sep 23  1999 loop3
brw-rw----   1 root     disk       7,   4 Sep 23  1999 loop4
brw-rw----   1 root     disk       7,   5 Sep 23  1999 loop5
brw-rw----   1 root     disk       7,   6 Sep 23  1999 loop6
brw-rw----   1 root     disk       7,   7 Sep 23  1999 loop7
# file loop*
loop0: block special (7/0)
loop1: block special (7/1)
loop2: block special (7/2)
loop3: block special (7/3)
loop4: block special (7/4)
loop5: block special (7/5)
loop6: block special (7/6)
loop7: block special (7/7)
#
```

Character Device File (UNIX example)

(Described by the **file** command as *character special*.)

```
# ls -l /dev/rdsk/c0t1d0
crw-r-----  1 root     sys        188 0x001000 Mar 23  1999 /dev/
rdsk/c0t1d0
# file /dev/rdsk/c0t1d0
/dev/rdsk/c0t1d0:       character special (188/4096)
#
```

Character Device File (Linux example)

(Described by the **file** command as *character special*.)

```
# ls -l mi*
crw-rw-rw-  1 root     sys       14,   2 Sep 23  1999 midi00
crw-rw-rw-  1 root     sys       14,  18 Sep 23  1999 midi01
crw-rw-rw-  1 root     sys       14,  34 Sep 23  1999 midi02
crw-rw-rw-  1 root     sys       14,  50 Sep 23  1999 midi03
crw-rw-rw-  1 root     sys       14,   0 Sep 23  1999 mixer
crw-rw-rw-  1 root     sys       14,  16 Sep 23  1999 mixer1
# file mi*
midi00: character special (14/2)
midi01: character special (14/18)
midi02: character special (14/34)
midi03: character special (14/50)
mixer:  character special (14/0)
mixer1: character special (14/16)
#
```

File System Layout

Before I begin talking about the file system layout, you need to know that you do not necessarily have a single file system. Your system administrator may have set up a variety of file system types on your system. As a beginning user, you don't care too much about the different types of file systems; however, before proceeding to the file system layout, let me briefly cover some of the different file system types. Your system administrator cares a lot about the different file system types because the commands he or she issues allow them to specify an option such as "-F" followed by the file system type. One good place to start when looking for the different file system types supported by your UNIX variant is the manual page for the **mount** command. The "-F" option, or another option such as "-t" for type in Linux, is usually following by a list of file system types supported. The different file system types and command options to file system types depend on the UNIX variant that you are using. Some commands that commonly support a file system type option are **dcopy**, **fsck**, **mksf**, **mount**, **newfs**, and others, some of which you may need to know as an advanced user if you are going to perform system administration in the future. The following is a description of some of commonly supported file systems on UNIX variants.

man page

mount - 12

• Personal Computer File System (PCFS) is a file system type that allows direct access to PC formatted disks.

• UNIX File System (UFS) is the standard or basic default UNIX file system on some UNIX variants.

• CD-ROM File System (CDFS) is used when you mount a CD-ROM. A CD-ROM is read-only, so you can't write to it. This is called High Sierra File System (HSFS) on some UNIX variants.

• Network File System (NFS) is a way of accessing files on other systems on the network from your local system. An NFS mounted file system looks as though it is local to your system even though it is located on another system.

• Loopback File System (LOFS) allows you to have the same file system in multiple places using alternate path names.

• VxFS is an extent-based Journal File System that supports fast file system recovery and on-line features such as backup on HP-UX.

• High Performance File System (HFS) is HP's version of the UNIX File System. This is used in most of the examples.

• TMPFS is a memory-based file system.

• CacheFS is a file system present in cache.

File system types is an area of high customization on UNIX variants. You will find some of the file systems listed on some UNIX variants and others on other UNIX variants. Although UNIX and its associated commands are very similar, going from one UNIX variant to another, file system types are generally peculiar to a specific UNIX variant. A good place to start when determining what file system types are included with your UNIX variant is to view the file system types listed in the manual page for **mount**.

man page

mount - 12

The manual page for **mount** on the Caldera Linux system we are using lists many file system types. With the Linux **mount** command, you would use the **-t** *vfstype* option to specify one of the file system types to mount:

• minix

• ext

• ext2

• xiafs

• hpfs

- fat

- msdos

- umsdos

- vfat

- proc

- nfs

- iso9660

- smb

- ncp

- affs

- ufs

- sysv

- xenix

- coherent

One common file system I often mount on Linux systems is a DOS floppy disk. For exampl, we would go through the following sequence of events to mount a DOS floppy, copy a file to it, and unmount it:

```
# mount -t msdos /dev/fd0 /mnt/floppy
# cp * /mnt/floppy
# ls /mnt/floppy
file1      file2      file3      file4
# umount /dev/fd0
```

This sequence of commands first mounts **/dev/fd0**, which is the floppy disk device file, under the mount point **/mnt/floppy**. **/dev/fd0** is mounted as type *msdos* as specified by the **-t msdos**. I next copy all files in the current directory to the floppy. All the files on the floppy are then listed with **ls,** producing the list of four files shown. I then umount the floppy disk with the **umount** command, so that I can take the floppy to a DOS system and read the files. Because the floppy was mounted as type *msdos,* the files were written to the floppy in DOS format.

man page

ls - 2

Similarly, to mount a CD-ROM on a Linux system you would issue the following mount command:

```
# mount /dev/hdd /cdrom
mount: block device /dev/hdd is write-protected, mounting read-
only
#
```

man page

mount - 12

You would substitute your CD-ROM device file for **/dev/hdd**. The CD-ROM is, of course, a read-only device, as the message from **mount** indicates.

The file system layout of most UNIX variants is based on the AT&T SVR4 layout. This means that going from one UNIX variant to the next, you see pretty much the same names used in the file system layouts.

Figure 2-1 is a high-level depiction of the file system.

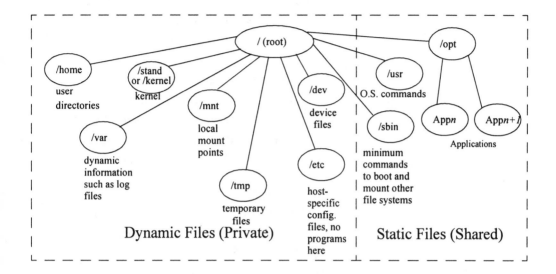

Figure 2-1   General UNIX File System Layout (differs somewhat among UNIX variants)

Here are some of the more important features of the UNIX file system layout:

> • Files and directories are organized by category. The two most obvious categories that appear in Figure 2-1 are static vs. dynamic files. Also, other categories are executable, configuration, data files, and so on. The static files are also labeled "shared," because other hosts on the network may share these. The directories **/usr**, **/sbin**, and **/opt** are shared directories.
>
> • The operating system and applications are kept separate from one another. Application vendors don't care where their applications are loaded; that is up to you. But to a system

administrator it is highly desirable to keep applications separate from the operating system, so you don't inadvertently have application files overwriting operating system files. In addition, if applications are loaded in a separate area, they are "modular," meaning that a system administrator can add, remove, and modify them without affecting the operating system or other applications. Applications are kept in the **/opt** directory.

• Intrasystem files are kept in a separate area from intersystem, or network-accessible files. **/usr** and **/sbin** are shared operating system directories. No host specific information is in these two directories. **/etc** is used to hold the host-specific configuration files.

• Executable files are kept separate from system configuration files so that the executables may be shared among hosts. Having the configuration files separate from the programs that use them also means that updates to the operating system won't affect the configuration files.

I provide descriptions of some of the most important directories of the file system layout.

/   This is the root directory, which is the base of the file system's hierarchical tree structure. A directory is logically viewed as being part of /. Regardless of the disk on which a directory or logical volume is stored, it is logically viewed as a part of the root hierarchy.

/dev   Contains host-specific devices files.

/etc   Contains host-specific system and application configuration files. The information in this directory is important to the operation of the system and is of a permanent nature. There are also additional configuration directories below **/etc**. There are two **/etc** subdirectories of particular interest:

/export Servers export root directories for networked clients. For instance, a server might export user directories such as **/export/home/***username*.

/home Users' home directories are located here. Because the data stored in users' home directories will be modified often, you can expect this directory to grow in size.

/kernel Contains kernel configuration and binary files that are required to bring up a system such as genunix.

/lost+found This is the lost files directory. Here you find files that are in use but are not associated with a directory. These files typically become "lost" as a result of a system crash that caused the link between the physical information on the disk and the logical directory to be severed. The program **fsck**, which is run at the time of boot, finds these files and places them in the **lost+found** directory.

/mnt   This directory is reserved as a mount point for local file systems. You can either mount directly to **/mnt** or have **/mnt** subdirectories as mount points such as **/mnt1**, **/mnt2**, **/mnt3**, etc.

/net   Name reserved as mount points for remote file systems.

/opt   The directory under which applications are installed. As a rule, application vendors never specify a particular location for their applications to be installed. Now, with **/opt**, we have a standard directory under which applications should be installed. This is an organizational improvement for system administrators, because we can now expect applications to be loaded under **/opt** and the application name.

/sbin   Contains commands and scripts used to boot, shut down, and fix file system mounting problems. **/sbin** is available when a system boots, because it contains commands required to bring up a system.

/stand Contains kernel configuration and binary files that are required to bring up a system. Two significant files contained in this directory are the **system** and **vmunix** (kernel) files.

/tmp This is a free-for-all directory where any user can *temporarily store* files. Because of the loose nature of this directory, it should not be used to store anything important, and users should know that whatever they have stored in **/tmp** can be deleted without notice. Application working files should go in **/var/ tmp** or **/var/opt/appname**, not in **/tmp**.

/usr Most of the UNIX operating system is contained in **/usr**. Included in this directory are commands, libraries, and documentation. A limited number of subdirectories that can appear in **/usr**.

/var Holds files that are primarily temporary. Files such as log files, which are frequently deleted and modified, are stored here. Think of this as a directory of "variable" size. Files that an application or command create at runtime should be placed in this directory, including log and spool files. However, some applications may store state information in **/var**.

Linux File System Layout

The Linux file system layout is very similar to the other UNIX variants described earlier, both in concept and in implementation. Files are contained in directories, and directories can have any number of subdirectories. Most operating systems are arranged this way, including UNIX.

The following is a long listing at the root level of a Caldera Linux system:

man page

ls - 2

```
# ls -l /
total 439
-rw-rw-rw-    1 root       root          23 Nov  5 07:10 .lgdb
dr-xr-xr-x    3 root       root        1024 Nov  5 07:10 amd
dr-xr-xr-x    2 root       root         512 Nov  5 07:10 auto
drwxr-xr-x    2 root       root        2048 Nov  5 07:12 bin
drwxr-xr-x    2 root       root        1024 Nov  5 01:44 boot
drwxr-xr-x    2 root       root       10240 Nov  6 22:27 dev
drwxr-xr-x   15 root       root        2048 Nov  7 00:15 etc
drwxr-xr-x    5 root       root        1024 Nov  5 01:43 home
drwxr-xr-x    2 root       root        1024 Nov  5 01:29 initrd
lrwxrwxrwx    1 root       root          11 Nov  5 01:29 install ->
                                                          /var/lib/LST
drwxr-xr-x    4 root       root        1024 Nov  5 01:44 lib
drwxr-xr-x    2 root       root       12288 Nov  5 01:29 lost+found
drwxr-xr-x    4 root       root        1024 Nov  5 01:44 mnt
drwxr-xr-x    4 root       root        1024 Sep 10  1996 opt
dr-xr-xr-x    5 root       root           0 Nov  5 01:59 proc
drwxr-xr-x    5 root       root        1024 Nov  6 20:56 root
drwxr-xr-x    2 root       root        2048 Nov  7 00:03 sbin
drwxrwxrwt    6 root       root        1024 Nov  7 00:10 tmp
drwxr-xr-x   21 root       root        1024 Nov  5 01:40 usr
drwxr-xr-x   14 root       root        1024 Nov  5 01:32 var
-rw-r--r--    1 root       root      404158 Nov  5 01:29 vmlinuz
```

Most of the directories are the same as those described earlier. A couple of directory names did not appear earlier that are significant. The Linux kernel, **vmlinuz**, appears at the root level. The directory /**root** is the home directory of the user *root*.

The /**proc** directory contains information about the Linux system. The /**proc** directory is really a set of data structure information that looks like a directory. The following is a long listing of the **/proc** directory:

```
# ls -l /proc
total 0
dr-xr-xr-x  3 root     root            0 Nov  7 00:13 1
dr-xr-xr-x  3 root     root            0 Nov  7 00:16 1011
dr-xr-xr-x  3 root     root            0 Nov  7 00:13 104
dr-xr-xr-x  3 bin      root            0 Nov  7 00:13 106
dr-xr-xr-x  3 root     root            0 Nov  7 00:13 116
dr-xr-xr-x  3 root     root            0 Nov  7 00:13 118
dr-xr-xr-x  3 root     root            0 Nov  7 00:13 146
dr-xr-xr-x  3 root     root            0 Nov  7 00:13 155
dr-xr-xr-x  3 root     root            0 Nov  7 00:13 156
dr-xr-xr-x  3 daemon   root            0 Nov  7 00:13 162
dr-xr-xr-x  3 root     root            0 Nov  7 00:13 167
dr-xr-xr-x  3 root     root            0 Nov  7 00:13 170
dr-xr-xr-x  3 root     65535           0 Nov  7 00:13 178
dr-xr-xr-x  3 root     root            0 Nov  7 00:13 18
dr-xr-xr-x  3 root     root            0 Nov  7 00:13 19
dr-xr-xr-x  3 nobody   65535           0 Nov  7 00:13 193
dr-xr-xr-x  3 root     root            0 Nov  7 00:13 199
dr-xr-xr-x  3 root     root            0 Nov  7 00:13 2
dr-xr-xr-x  3 root     root            0 Nov  7 00:13 20
dr-xr-xr-x  3 root     root            0 Nov  7 00:13 200
dr-xr-xr-x  3 root     root            0 Nov  7 00:13 201
dr-xr-xr-x  3 root     root            0 Nov  7 00:13 202
dr-xr-xr-x  3 root     root            0 Nov  7 00:13 203
dr-xr-xr-x  3 root     root            0 Nov  7 00:13 204
dr-xr-xr-x  3 root     root            0 Nov  7 00:13 205
dr-xr-xr-x  3 root     root            0 Nov  7 00:13 21
dr-xr-xr-x  3 root     root            0 Nov  7 00:13 273
dr-xr-xr-x  3 root     root            0 Nov  7 00:13 274
dr-xr-xr-x  3 root     root            0 Nov  7 00:13 276
dr-xr-xr-x  3 root     root            0 Nov  7 00:13 3
dr-xr-xr-x  3 root     root            0 Nov  7 00:13 307
dr-xr-xr-x  3 root     root            0 Nov  7 00:13 327
dr-xr-xr-x  3 root     root            0 Nov  7 00:13 358
dr-xr-xr-x  3 root     root            0 Nov  7 00:13 375
dr-xr-xr-x  3 root     root            0 Nov  7 00:13 443
dr-xr-xr-x  3 root     root            0 Nov  7 00:13 444
dr-xr-xr-x  3 root     root            0 Nov  7 00:13 445
dr-xr-xr-x  3 root     root            0 Nov  7 00:13 45
dr-xr-xr-x  3 root     root            0 Nov  7 00:13 482
dr-xr-xr-x  3 root     root            0 Nov  7 00:13 483
dr-xr-xr-x  3 root     root            0 Nov  7 00:16 996
dr-xr-xr-x  3 root     root            0 Nov  7 00:16 997
dr-xr-xr-x  3 root     root            0 Nov  7 00:16 998
-r--r--r--  1 root     root            0 Nov  7 00:13 cmdline
-r--r--r--  1 root     root            0 Nov  7 00:13 cpuinfo
-r--r--r--  1 root     root            0 Nov  7 00:13 devices
-r--r--r--  1 root     root            0 Nov  7 00:13 dma
-r--r--r--  1 root     root            0 Nov  7 00:13 filesys
-r--r--r--  1 root     root            0 Nov  7 00:13 interrupt
-r--r--r--  1 root     root            0 Nov  7 00:13 ioports
-r--------  1 root     root     33558528 Nov  7 00:13 kcore
```

```
-r--------  1 root     root          0 Nov  5 07:00 kmsg
-r--r--r--  1 root     root          0 Nov  7 00:13 ksyms
-r--r--r--  1 root     root          0 Nov  7 00:05 loadavg
-r--r--r--  1 root     root          0 Nov  7 00:13 locks
-r--r--r--  1 root     root          0 Nov  7 00:13 mdstat
-r--r--r--  1 root     root          0 Nov  7 00:13 meminfo
-r--r--r--  1 root     root          0 Nov  7 00:13 modules
-r--r--r--  1 root     root          0 Nov  7 00:13 mounts
dr-xr-xr-x  2 root     root          0 Nov  7 00:13 net
-r--r--r--  1 root     root          0 Nov  7 00:13 pci
dr-xr-xr-x  2 root     root          0 Nov  7 00:13 scsi
lrwxrwxrwx  1 root     root         64 Nov  7 00:13 self->110
-r--r--r--  1 root     root          0 Nov  7 00:13 stat
dr-xr-xr-x  5 root     root          0 Nov  7 00:13 sys
-r--r--r--  1 root     root          0 Nov  7 00:13 uptime
-r--r--r--  1 root     root          0 Nov  7 00:13 version
```

The directories in the long listing, which have a *d* at the beginning of the line, are processes. The file **/proc/kcore** represents the physical memory of your Linux system. Files in **/proc** contain some interesting information about your system. One file you'll want to take a look at is the **/proc/cpuinfo** file. An example of this file is shown in the following listing:

man page

more - 3

```
# more /proc/cpuinfo
processor       : 0
cpu             : 686
model           : 3
vendor_id       : GenuineIntel
stepping        : 4
fdiv_bug        : no
hlt_bug         : no
fpu             : yes
fpu_exception   : yes
cpuid           : yes
wp              : yes
flags           : fpu vme de pse tsc msr pae mce cx8 11 mtrr pge
mca cmov mmx
bogomips        : 266.24
```

more is covered in the next chapter. For now, you need to know just that **more** is used for viewing files.

The **/boot** directory contains the Linux kernel and other files used by the LILO boot manager. The following is a listing of **/boot**:

man page

ls - 2

```
# ls -l /boot
total 452
-rw-r--r--   1 root     root       15954 Feb 11  1997 WHATSIN
-rw-r--r--   1 root     root       15954 Feb 11  1997
                                          WHATSIN-2.0.29-modular
-rw-r--r--   1 root     root         204 Jul 24  1996 any_b.b
-rw-r--r--   1 root     root         204 Jul 24  1996 any_d.b
-rw-r--r--   1 root     root         512 Nov  5 01:44 boot.0300
-rw-r--r--   1 root     root        4416 Jul 24  1996 boot.b
-rw-r--r--   1 root     root          88 Jul 24  1996 chain.b
-rw-------   1 root     root        7680 Nov  5 01:44 map
-r--r--r--   1 root     root        1565 Mar  7  1997 message
-rw-r--r--   1 root     root         192 Jul 24  1996 os2_d.b
-rw-r--r--   1 root     root      404158 Feb 11  1997 vmlinuz-
                                          2.0.29-modular
```

As a user, you are probably most concerned with your home directory, assigned to you by your system administrator, which is most likely in the **/home** directory. I think, however, that as a UNIX user you need to understand the overall UNIX file system layout. Keep in mind that you may find minor differences in the file system layout going from one UNIX variant to another, but in general the layout is similar.

If you're running a graphical user interface on your Linux system, you can view the file system graphically. Figure 2-2 shows the Red Hat Linux *File Manager* that is part of the Gnome user interface.

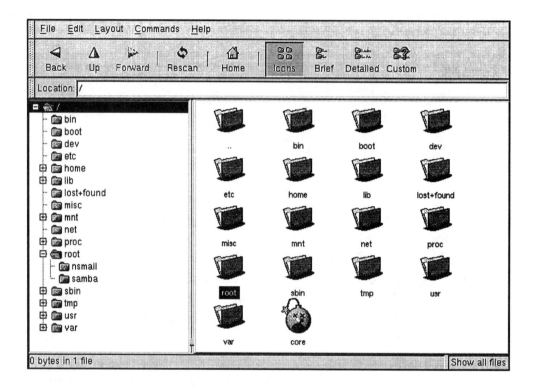

Figure 2-2 *File Manager* in *Gnome* Showing the Red Hat Linux File System

You can see that many of the directories shown on the left-hand side of Figure 2-2 are the same as those described earlier for UNIX systems in general. Although you may be working with any number of different UNIX variants, you'll find most of the system directories to be similar.

Manual Pages of Some Commands Used in Chapter 2

The following are the HP-UX manual pages for many of the commands used in the chapter. Commands often differ among UNIX variants, so you may find differences in the options or other areas for some commands; however, the following manual pages serve as an excellent reference.

file

file - Run test to classify file.

---

file(1)   file(1)

NAME
        file - determine file type

SYNOPSIS

        file [-m mfile] [-c] [-f ffile] file ...

DESCRIPTION
        file performs a series of tests on each file in an attempt to classify
        it. If file appears to be an ASCII file, file examines the first 512
        bytes and tries to guess its language. If file is an executable a.out
        file, file prints the version stamp, provided it is greater than 0
        (see the description of the -V option in ld(1)).

        file uses the file /etc/magic to identify files that have some sort of
        magic number, that is, any file containing a numeric or string
        constant that indicates its type. Commentary at the beginning of
        /etc/magic explains the format.

    Options
        file recognizes the following command-line options:

            -m mfile   use alternate magic file mfile.

            -c   Check the magic file for format errors. This
                            validation is not normally carried out for reasons
                            of efficiency. No file classification is done
                            when this option is specified.

            -f ffile   Obtain the list of files to be examined from file
                            ffile. file classifies each file whose name
                            appears in ffile.

EXTERNAL INFLUENCES
    Environment Variables
        LC_MESSAGES determines the language in which messages are displayed.

        If LC_MESSAGES is not specified in the environment or is set to the
        empty string, the value of LANG is used as a default for each
        unspecified or empty variable. If LANG is not specified or is set to
        the empty string, a default of "C" (see lang(5)) is used instead of
        LANG.

        If any internationalization variable contains an invalid setting, file
        behaves as if all internationalization variables are set to "C". See
        environ(5).

    International Code Set Support
        Single- and multi-byte character code sets are supported. However,
        all non-ASCII text files are identified as "data".

SEE ALSO
     ld(1).

STANDARDS CONFORMANCE
     file: SVID2, SVID3, XPG2, XPG4

ls

man page

ls - 2

ls - List contents of directories.

---

ls(1)   ls(1)

NAME
        ls, l, ll, lsf, lsr, lsx - list contents of directories

SYNOPSIS

        ls [-abcdefgilmnopqrstuxACFLR1] [names]

        l [ls_options] [names]
        ll [ls_options] [names]
        lsf [ls_options] [names]
        lsr [ls_options] [names]
        lsx [ls_options] [names]

DESCRIPTION
        For each directory argument, the ls command lists the contents of the
        directory. For each file argument, ls repeats its name and any other
        information requested. The output is sorted in ascending collation
        order by default (see Environment Variables below). When no argument
        is given, the current directory is listed. When several arguments are
        given, the arguments are first sorted appropriately, but file
        arguments appear before directories and their contents.

        If you are a user with appropriate privileges, all files except . and
        .. are listed by default.

        There are three major listing formats. The format chosen depends on
        whether the output is going to a login device (determined by whether
        output device file is a tty device), and can also be controlled by
        option flags. The default format for a login device is to list the
        contents of directories in multicolumn format, with entries sorted
        vertically by column. (When individual file names (as opposed to
        directory names) appear in the argument list, those file names are
        always sorted across the page rather than down the page in columns
        because individual file names can be arbitrarily long.) If the
        standard output is not a login device, the default format is to list
        one entry per line. The -C and -x options enable multicolumn formats,
        and the -m option enables stream output format in which files are
        listed across the page, separated by commas. In order to determine
        output formats for the -C, -x, and -m options, ls uses an environment
        variable, COLUMNS, to determine the number of character positions
        available on each output line. If this variable is not set, the
        terminfo database is used to determine the number of columns, based on
        the environment variable TERM. If this information cannot be
        obtained, 80 columns is assumed.

    Options
        ls recognizes the following options:

                -a   List all entries; usually entries whose names begin with a
                      period (.) are not listed.

-b   Force printing of nongraphic characters to be in the octal
      \ddd notation.

-c   Use time of last modification of the inode (file created,
      mode changed, etc.) for sorting (-t) or printing (-l
      (ell)).

-d   If an argument is a directory, list only its name (not its
      contents); often used with -l (ell) to get the status of a
      directory.

-e   Print the extent attributes of the file. If any of the
      files has a extent attribute, this option prints the extent
      size, space reserved and allocation flags. This option
      must be used with the -l (ell) option.

-f   Force each argument to be interpreted as a directory and
      list the name found in each slot. This option disables -l
      (ell), -t, -s, and -r, and enables -a; the order is the
      order in which entries appear in the directory.

-g   Same as -l, (ell) except that only the group is printed
      (owner is omitted). If both -l (ell) and -g are specified,
      the owner is not printed.

-i   For each file, print the inode number in the first column
      of the report. When used in multicolumn output, the number
      precedes the file name in each column.

-l   (ell) List in long format, giving mode, number of links,
      owner, group, size in bytes, and time of last modification
      for each file (see further DESCRIPTION and Access Control
      Lists below). If the time of last modification is greater
      than six months ago, or any time in the future, the year is
      substituted for the hour and minute of the modification
      time. If the file is a special file, the size field
      contains the major and minor device numbers rather than a
      size.

-m   Stream output format.

-n   The same as -l, (ell) except that the owner's UID and
      group's GID numbers are printed, rather than the associated
      character strings.

-o   The same as -l, (ell) except that only the owner is printed
      (group is omitted). (If both -l (ell) and -o are
      specified, the group is not printed).

-p   Put a slash (/) after each file name if that file is a
      directory.

-q   Force printing of nongraphic characters in file names as
      the character (?).

-r   Reverse the order of sort to get reverse (descending)
      collation or oldest first, as appropriate.

-s   Give size in blocks, including indirect blocks, for each
      entry. The first entry printed is the total number of
      blocks in the directory. When used in multicolumn output,
      the number of blocks precedes the file name in each column.

-t   Sort by time modified (latest first) before sorting
      alphabetically.

-u   Use time of last access instead of last modification for
        sorting (-t option) or printing (-l (ell) option).

-x   Multicolumn output with entries sorted across rather than
        down the page.

-A   The same as -a, except that the current directory "." and
        parent directory ".." are not listed. For a user with
        appropriate privileges, this flag defaults to ON, and is
        turned off by -A.

-C   Multicolumn output with entries sorted down the columns.

-F   Put a slash (/) after each file name if that file is a
        directory or a symbolic link to a directory; put an
        asterisk (*) after each file name if that file is
        executable; put an at sign (@) after each file name if that
        file is a symbolic link to a file; put a vertical bar (|)
        after each file name if that file is a FIFO.

-L   If the argument is a symbolic link, list the file or
        directory to which the link refers rather than the link
        itself.

-R   Recursively list subdirectories encountered.

-1   (one) The file names will be listed in single column format
        regardless of the output device. This forces single column
        format to the user's terminal.

Specifying more than one of the options in the following mutually
exclusive pairs is not considered an error: -C and -1 (ell), -m and -1
(ell), -x and -1 (ell), -C and -1 (one), -c and -u.

ls is normally known by several shorthand-version names for the
various formats:

    l   equivalent to ls -m.
    ll   equivalent to ls -1 (ell).
    lsf   equivalent to ls -F.
    lsr   equivalent to ls -R.
    lsx   equivalent to ls -x.

The shorthand notations are implemented as links to ls. Option
arguments to the shorthand versions behave exactly as if the long form
above had been used with the additional arguments.

Mode Bits Interpretation (-l option)
The mode printed in listings produced by the -l (ell) option consists
of 10 characters. The first character indicates the entry type:

    d   Directory
    b   Block special file
    c   Character special file
    l   Symbolic link
    p   Fifo (also called a "named pipe") special file
    n   Network special file
    s   socket
    -      Ordinary file.

The next 9 characters are interpreted as three sets of three bits each
which identify access permissions for owner, group, and others as
follows:

        +------------------ 0400   read by owner (r or -)

```
|  +---------------- 0200  write by owner (w or -)
|  |  +-------------- 0100  execute (search directory) by owner
|  |  |                     (x, s, S, or -)
|  |  |  +------------ 0040  read by group (r or -)
|  |  |  |  +---------- 0020  write by group (w or -)
|  |  |  |  |  +-------- 0010  execute/search by group
|  |  |  |  |  |                (x, s, S, or -)
|  |  |  |  |  |  +------ 0004  read by others (r or -)
|  |  |  |  |  |  |  +---- 0002  write by others (w or -)
|  |  |  |  |  |  |  |  +-- 0001  execute/search by others
|  |  |  |  |  |  |  |  |        (x, t, T, or -)
|  |  |  |  |  |  |  |  |
r  w  x  r  w  x  r  w  x
```

Mode letters are interpreted as follows:

-       Permission not granted in corresponding position.

r   Read permission granted to corresponding user class.

w   Write permission granted to corresponding user class.

x   Execute (or search in directory) permission granted to
        corresponding user class.

s   Execute (search) permission granted to corresponding user
        class. In addition, SUID (Set User ID) permission granted
        for owner, or SGID (Set Group ID) permission granted for
        group, as indicated by position.

S   Same as s except that execute (search) permission is
        denied to corresponding user class.

t   (last position only) Execute (search) permission granted
        to others and "sticky bit" is set (see chmod(2) S_ISVTX
        description).

T   Same as t except execute (search directory) permission
        denied to others.

When an option is specified that results in a listing of directory
and/or file sizes in bytes or blocks (such as the -s or -l (ell)
option), a total count of blocks, including indirect blocks, is also
printed at the beginning of the listing.

Access Control Lists (ACLs)
    If a file has optional ACL entries, the -l (ell) option displays a
    plus sign (+) after the file's permissions. The permissions shown are
    a summary representation of the file's access control list, as
    returned by stat() in the st_mode field (see stat(2)). To list the
    contents of an access control list, use the lsacl command (see
    lsacl(1) and acl(5)).

EXTERNAL INFLUENCES
    Environment Variables
        If the COLUMNS variable is set, ls uses the width provided in
        determining positioning of columnar output.

        LANG determines the locale to use for the locale categories when both
        LC_ALL and the corresponding environment variable (beginning with LC_)
        do not specify a locale. If LANG is not set or is set to the empty
        string, a default of "C" (see lang(5)) is used.

        LC_COLLATE determines the order in which the output is sorted.

        LC_CTYPE determines which characters are classified as nongraphic for the -b and -q options, and the interpretation of single- and/or multibyte characters within file names.

LC_TIME determines the date and time strings output by the -g, -l (ell), -n, and -o options.

LC_MESSAGES determines the language in which messages (other than the date and time strings) are displayed.

If any internationalization variable contains an invalid setting, ls behaves as if all internationalization variables are set to "C" (see environ(5)).

International Code Set Support
Single- and multibyte character code sets are supported.

RETURN VALUE
    ls exits with one of the following values:

    0   All input files were listed successfully.

    >0   ls was aborted because errors occurred when accessing files.
         The following conditions cause an error:

         -   Specified file not found.

         -   User has no permission to read the directory.

         -   Process could not get enough memory.

         -   Invalid option specified.

EXAMPLES
    Print a long listing of all the files in the current working directory
    (including the file sizes). List the most recently modified
    (youngest) file first, followed by the next older file, and so forth,
    to the oldest. Files whose names begin with a . are also printed.

        ls -alst

WARNINGS
    Setting options based on whether the output is a login (tty) device is
    undesirable because ls -s is very different from ls -s | lp. On the
    other hand, not using this setting makes old shell scripts that used
    ls almost inevitably fail.

    Unprintable characters in file names may confuse the columnar output
    options.

DEPENDENCIES
    NFS The -l (ell) option does not display a plus sign (+) after the
         access permission bits of networked files to represent existence
         of optional access control list entries.

AUTHOR
    ls was developed by AT&T, the University of California, Berkeley and
    HP.

FILES
    /etc/passwd   to get user IDs for ls -l (ell) and ls -o.
    /etc/group   to get group IDs for ls -l (ell) and ls -g.

    /usr/share/lib/terminfo/?/*
                                   to get terminal information.

SEE ALSO

chmod(1), find(1), lsacl(1), stat(2), acl(5).

STANDARDS CONFORMANCE
     ls: SVID2, SVID3, XPG2, XPG3, XPG4, POSIX.2

CHAPTER 3

Working with Files and Directories - Permissions, Commands, File Name Expansion, and Wild Cards

Permissions

man page

ls - 2

The best place to begin discussing permissions is by issuing the **ls** command, which lists the contents of directories. Permissions are the means by which files and directories are made secure on your UNIX system. Because UNIX is multi-user, potentially thousands of users could be accessing the files on a system. Permissions controls who has access to what files.

Here is an example **ls -l** command and output:

```
$ ls -l sort
-rwxr-x--x   1 marty      users      120 Jul 26 10:20 sort
```

Issuing this command has produced a lot of information relating to a file called **sort**. Let's begin to understand what this listing has produced by analyzing the first set of characters (-rwxr-x--x). This set of characters is made up of four distinct fields, as shown in Figure 3-1.

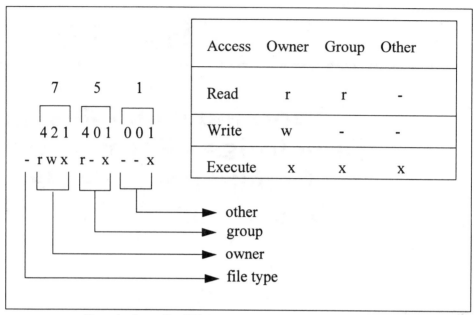

Figure 3-1 Permissions for File **sort**

The first character in this group is related to the file type. I covered some file types earlier, but the **ls -l** command does not analyze files to the same level of detail. Among the types of files **ls -l** will list are shown in Figure 3-2.

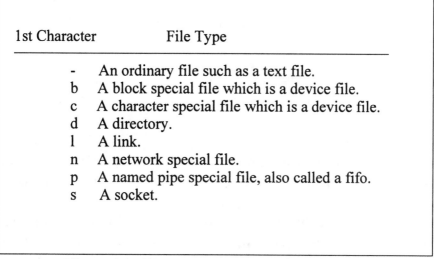

1st Character	File Type
-	An ordinary file such as a text file.
b	A block special file which is a device file.
c	A character special file which is a device file.
d	A directory.
l	A link.
n	A network special file.
p	A named pipe special file, also called a fifo.
s	A socket.

Figure 3-2 File Types of the ls Command

Keep in mind the file types can vary slightly from one UNIX variant to another. The file types listed in Figure 3-2 are common to most UNIX variants. For every file on the system, UNIX supports three classes of access:

- User access (u). Access granted to the owner of the file.

- Group access (g). Access granted to members of the same group as the owner of the file.

- Other access (o). Access granted to everyone else.

These access rights are defined by the position of read (r), write (w), and execute (x) when the long listing command is issued. For the long listing (**ls -l**) issued earlier, you see the permissions in Table 3-1.

man page

ls - 2

Table 3-1   Long Listing Permissions for the File **sort**

Access	User Access	Group Access	Other
Read	r	r	-
Write	w	-	-
Execute	x	x	x

Permissions are not granted where a "-" appears. In addition, there are other permissions such as s, S, t, and T, which I don't cover at this time.

You can see that access rights are arranged in groups of three: three groups of permissions with three access levels each. The owner, in this case *marty*, has read, write, and execute permissions on the file. Anyone in the group *users* is permitted read and execute access to the file. *other* is permitted only execute access of the file.

The definitions of read, write, and execute differ somewhat for files and directories. Here is what you can do if you have read, write, and execute permissions for files:

> **read**   You have permission to read the file.
>
> **write**   You have permission to change and to write to the file.
>
> **execute**   You can run, or execute, the program.

Here is what you can do if you have read, write, and execute permissions for directories:

> **read**   You can list the contents of the directory.
>
> **write**   You can create files in the directory, delete files in the directory, and create subdirectories in the directory.

execute You can change to this directory using the **cd** command, which we'll cover shortly.

man page

cd - 3

We will cover permissions again when the **chmod** command is described.

Absolute and Relative Path Names

We have already covered two topics that can serve as the basis for a discussion of absolute and relative path names: some important directories on the system and user login. If you take a look at the user **denise** and the way some of her files may be organized, we can get to the bottom of relative and absolute path names quickly.

The UNIX file system covered in Chapter 2 showed a hierarchy. In this hierarchy there was the root (/) directory at the top, and files and directories were below root. The two means by which you can traverse this hierarchy to get to a "lower" point are with absolute path names and relative path names. Let's take a closer look at the files and directories that **denise** may have in her user area.

First of all we'll assume that **denise** has many files. This activity is one of the things users do - create files. In addition, your system administrator has provided several default files for purposes such as defining your user environment after login (we'll get into this in a lot more detail in upcoming chapters). **denise** probably has many files under her user area, and subdirectories as well. Her user area may look something like that shown in Figure 3-3.

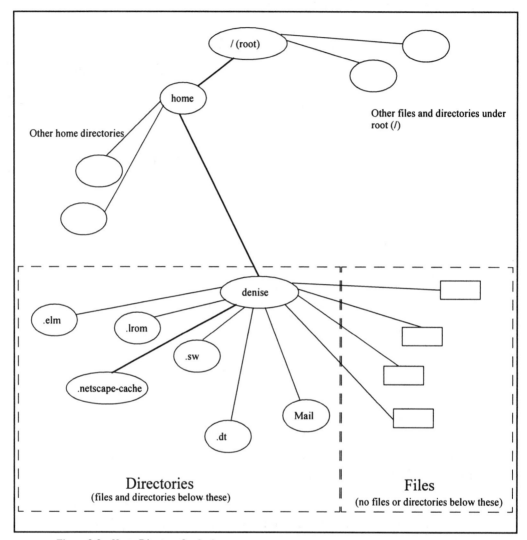

Figure 3-3   Home Directory for **denise**

Most users will have their home directory under **/home** (and who said UNIX doesn't make any sense?). If you want to get to a sub-directory of **denise** using an absolute path name, you traverse the hierarchy using the complete path. To get to the directory **.netscape-cache** under **denise**, you could view the absolute path as shown in Figure 3-4.

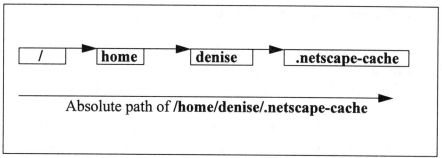

Figure 3-4   Absolute Path

You are progressing from root (/), to **home**, to **denise**, and finally to the directory **.netscape-cache**. The change directory (**cd**) command you issue looks like the following:

```
$ cd /home/denise/.netscape-cache
```

This is an absolute path because it starts at root and progresses through the hierarchy. No matter what directory you are currently working in, even if it is **.netscape-cache**, you could use the absolute path name. In many cases, however, you may not need to issue an absolute path name. You may be so close to the file or directory you wish to access that the absolute path would be a waste of time for you. If, for instance, you are already in **/home/denise**, then you could change to **.netscape-cache** using a relative path name easily:

```
$ cd .netscape-cache
```

The relative path name is shorter because you don't begin with a slash (/) that brings you back up to the top of the hierarchy to work your way down. Instead, you are starting at some point in the file system hierarchy, such as **/home/denise**, and entering a path relative to that directory, such as **.netscape-cache**.

The ls Command

man page

ls - 2

The **ls** command brings about a lot to discuss. I haven't yet described the options to **ls**, yet we have already used the **-l** option as part of the permissions discussion in this chapter, as well as in the **file** command discussion in Chapter 2. The best way to cover the most important options to **ls** is to show examples. I do just that in the upcoming description of the **ls** command.

ls

The following is an example of **ls** without any options other than the directory to list:

```
# ls /home/densie

27247b.exe
410pt1.exe
410pt2.exe
41ndir.exe
41nds1.exe
41nds4.exe
41nwad.exe
41rtr2.exe
HPDA1.EXE
Mail
N3212B6.EXE
SCSI4S.EXE
clean
clean2
clean3
content.exe
dsenh.exe
eg1
```

```
eg2
en0316bz.exe
en0316tb.exe
explore.exe
flexi_cd.exe
fred.h
hal.c
hpdl0117.exe
hpdlinst.txt
hpux.patches
j2577a.exe
ja95up.exe
msie10.exe
n32e12n.exe
nfs197.exe
pass.sb
plusdemo.exe
ps4x03.exe
psg
quik_res.exe
rclock.exe
rkhelp.exe
roni.mak
sb.txt
smsup2.exe
softinit.remotesoftcm
srvpr.exe
steve.h
target.exe
tcp41a.exe
tnds2.exe
upgrade.exe
whoon
win95app.exe
total 46718
```

Which of these are files? Which are directories? Have all of the entries been listed? There are many options to **ls** that will answer these questions.

man page

ls - 2

There is not a lot of information reported as a result of having issued this command. **ls** lists the contents of the directory specified, or the current working directory if no directory is specified.

ls -a

man page

ls - 2

To list all the entries of a directory, you would use the **-a** option. Files that begin with a "." are called hidden files and are not usually listed with **ls**. The following example shows the output of **ls -a**:

```
$ ls -a /home/denise
.Xauthority
.cshrc
.dt
.dtprofile
.elm
.exrc
.fmrc.orig
.glancerc
.gpmhp
.history
.login
.lrom
.mailrc
.netscape-bookmarks.html
.netscape-cache
.netscape-cookies
.netscape-history
.netscape-newsgroups-news.spry.com
.netscape-newsgroups-newsserv.hp.com
.netscape-preferences
.newsrc-news.spry.com
.newsrc-newsserv.hp.com
.profile
.rhosts
.sh_history
.softbuildrc
.softinit.orig
.sw
.xinitrc
.xsession
27247b.exe
410pt1.exe
410pt2.exe
41ndir.exe
41nds1.exe
41nds4.exe
41nwad.exe
41rtr2.exe
HPDA1.EXE
Mail
N3212B6.EXE
SCSI4S.EXE
clean
clean2
clean3
```

```
content.exe
dsenh.exe
eg1
eg2
en0316bz.exe
en0316tb.exe
explore.exe
flexi_cd.exe
fred.h̄
hal.c
hpdl0117.exe
hpdlinst.txt
hpux.patches
j2577a.exe
ja95up.exe
msie10.exe
n32e12n.exe
nfs197.exe
pass.sb
plusdemo.exe
ps4x03.exe
psg
quik_res.exe
rclock.exe
rkhelp.exe
roni.mak
sb.txt
smsup2.exe
softinit.remotesoftcm
srvpr.exe
steve.h
target.exe
tcp41a.exe
tnds2.exe
upgrade.exe
whoon
win95app.exe
total 46718
```

Notice that this output includes hidden files, those that begin with a ".", as well as all other files listed with just **ls**. These did not appear when **ls** was issued without the **-a** option. All subsequent examples include the **-a** option.

man page

ls - 2

ls -l

To list all information about the contents of directory, you use the **-l** option to **ls**, as shown in the following example (some of these file names were shortened to fit on the page):

```
$ ls -al /home/denise
-rw-------    1 denise    users         98 Oct  6 09:19 .Xauthority
-r--r--r--    1 denise    users        814 May 19 10:10 .cshrc
drwxr-xr-x    7 denise    users       1024 Sep 26 11:14 .dt
-rwxr-xr-x    1 denise    users       8705 Jul  7 12:04 .dtprofile
drwx------    2 denise    users       1024 Jul 31 18:48 .elm
-r--r--r--    1 denise    users        347 May 19 10:10 .exrc
-rwxrwxrwx    1 denise    users        170 Jun  6 14:20 .fmrc.orig
-rw-------    1 denise    users         97 Jun 12 18:59 .glancerc
-rw-------    1 denise    users      17620 Sep 21 16:11 .gpmhp
-rwxr-xr-x    1 denise    users        391 Sep 19 09:55 .history
-r--r--r--    1 denise    users        341 May 19 10:10 .login
drwx--x--x    2 denise    users       1024 Jul 31 18:48 .lrom
-rw-r--r--    1 denise    users        768 Jul 28 12:54 .mailrc
-rw-------    1 denise    users       1450 Oct  6 13:58 .netscape-bookmarks.html
drwx------    2 denise    users      10240 Oct 10 15:24 .netscape-cache
-rw-------    1 denise    users         91 Sep 18 14:16 .netscape-cookies
-rw-------    1 denise    users      43906 Oct 10 15:32 .netscape-history
-rw-r--r--    1 denise    users        566 Aug 25 14:36 .netscape-news.spry.com
-rw-------    1 denise    users      46514 Jun 28 12:35 .netscape-.hp.com
-rw-------    1 denise    users       1556 Sep 28 15:02 .netscape-preferences
-rw-------    1 denise    users        104 Jul 11 11:01 .newsrc-news.spry.com
-rw-r--r--    1 denise    users        223 Sep 26 13:26 .newsrc-newv.hp.com
-r--r--r--    1 denise    users        446 May 19 10:10 .profile
-rw-------    1 denise    users         21 Jul  6 13:21 .rhosts
-rw-------    1 denise    users       2328 Oct 10 15:22 .sh_history
-rw-r--r--    1 denise    users       1052 Sep 22 15:00 .softbuildrc
-rwxrwxrwx    1 denise    users        161 Jul 11 12:19 .softinit.orig
drwxr-xr-x    3 denise    users       1024 Aug 31 15:44 .sw
-rw-------    1 denise    users         23 Jun  2 15:01 .xinitrc
-rwxr-xr-x    1 denise    users      11251 May 19 10:41 .xsession
-rw-r--r--    1 denise    users     611488 Oct  3 12:00 27247b.exe
-rw-r--r--    1 denise    users     114119 Sep 29 12:49 410pt1.exe
-rw-r--r--    1 denise    users     136979 Sep 29 12:53 410pt2.exe
-rw-r--r--    1 denise    users     173978 Sep 29 12:40 41ndir.exe
-rw-r--r--    1 denise    users     363315 Sep 29 12:52 41nds1.exe
-rw-r--r--    1 denise    users     527524 Sep 29 12:57 41nds4.exe
-rw-r--r--    1 denise    users    1552513 Sep 29 12:50 41nwad.exe
-rw-r--r--    1 denise    users     853424 Sep 29 12:24 41rtr2.exe
-rw-r--r--    1 denise    users    1363011 Sep 20 12:20 HPDA1.EXE
drwx------    2 denise    users         24 Jul 31 18:48 Mail
-rw-r--r--    1 denise    users    1787840 Aug 31 09:35 N3212B6.EXE
-rw-r--r--    1 denise    users      13543 Sep 23 09:46 SCSI4S.EXE
-rw-r--r--    1 denise    users      28395 Aug 30 15:07 cabview.exe
-rwx--x--x    1 denise    users         66 Jun  8 17:40 clean
-rwx--x--x    1 denise    users         99 Jun 20 17:44 clean2
-rwx--x--x    1 denise    users         66 Jun 20 17:51 clean3
-rw-r--r--    1 denise    users      15365 Aug 30 15:07 content.exe
-rw-r--r--    1 denise    users     713313 Sep 29 12:56 dsenh.exe
-rwx------    1 denise    users        144 Aug 14 17:10 eg1
-rwx------    1 denise    users        192 Aug 15 12:13 eg2
-rw-r--r--    1 denise    users     667890 Sep 20 12:41 en0316bz.exe
-rw-r--r--    1 denise    users     641923 Sep 20 12:42 en0316tb.exe
-rw-r--r--    1 denise    users       6251 Aug 30 15:07 explore.exe
-rw-r--r--    1 denise    users      23542 Aug 30 15:08 flexi_cd.exe
-rw-r--r--    1 denise    users         30 Aug 14 17:02 fred.h̄
-rw-r--r--    1 denise    users          0 Aug 14 17:24 hal.c
-rw-r--r--    1 denise    users     895399 Sep 20 12:32 hpdl0117.exe
-rw-r--r--    1 denise    users      14135 Sep 20 12:39 hpdlinst.txt
-rw-------    1 denise    users       2943 Jun 19 14:42 hpux.patches
-rw-r--r--    1 denise    users     680729 Sep 20 12:26 j2577a.exe
-rw-r--r--    1 denise    users     930728 Sep 20 15:16 ja95up.exe
-rw-r--r--    1 denise    users      53575 Oct 10 10:37 mbox
-rw-r--r--    1 denise    users    1097728 Aug 30 15:03 msie10.exe
-rw-r--r--    1 denise    users    1790376 Sep 18 14:32 n32e12n.exe
-rw-r--r--    1 denise    users    1393835 Sep 29 12:59 nfs197.exe
-rw-------    1 denise    users        977 Jul  3 14:25 pass.sb
-rw-r--r--    1 denise    users    1004544 Aug 30 15:00 plusdemo.exe
-rw-r--r--    1 denise    users     229547 Sep 29 12:27 ps4x03.exe
-rwxr-xr-x    1 denise    users        171 Aug  9 13:43 psg
-rw-r--r--    1 denise    users      16645 Aug 30 15:08 quik_res.exe
-rw-r--r--    1 denise    users      14544 Aug 30 15:08 rclock.exe
-rw-r--r--    1 denise    users    2287498 Aug 30 15:12 rkhelp.exe
-rw-r--r--    1 denise    users          0 Aug 15 12:10 roni.mak
```

```
-rw-r--r--   1 denise    users        1139 Sep 28 10:35 sb.txt
-rw-r--r--   1 denise    users      569855 Sep 29 12:55 smsup2.exe
-rw-------   1 root      sys           161 Jul 11 12:18 softinit.remotesoftcm
-rw-r--r--   1 denise    users          39 Sep 29 12:48 srvpr.exe
-rw-r--r--   1 denise    users          38 Aug 15 12:14 steve.h
-rw-r--r--   1 denise    users       14675 Aug 30 15:08 target.exe
-rw-r--r--   1 denise    users      229630 Sep 29 12:54 tcp41a.exe
-rw-r--r--   1 denise    users     1954453 Sep 29 12:26 tnds2.exe
-rw-r--r--   1 denise    users      364270 Sep 23 09:50 upgrade.exe
-rwx-----x   1 denise    users          88 Aug  9 13:43 whoon
-rw-r--r--   1 denise    users      191495 Aug 30 15:00 win95app.exe
total 46718
```

man page

ls - 2

Because I find this to be the most commonly used option with the **ls** command, I describe each of the fields produced by **ls -l**. I'll use the earlier example of the **ls -l** command, which showed only one file when describing the fields:

```
$ ls -l sort
-rwxr-x--x   1 marty     users         120 Jul 26 10:20 sort
```

The first field is the access rights of the file, which I covered in "Permissions" earlier in this chapter. The *owner* has read, write, and execute permissions on the file. The *group* has read and execute permissions on the file. *other* has execute permissions.

The second field is the link count. This lists how many files are symbolically linked to the file. We will get into the details of the **ln** command used to link files later. In this case, the link count is 1, which means that this file is linked only to itself. For directories, such as **.dt** shown below, the number of subdirectories is shown rather than the link count. This number includes one for the directory itself as well as one for the parent directory. This means that a total of five directories are below **.dt** .

```
drwxr-x--x   7 denise        users     1024 Jul 26 10:20 .dt
```

The subdirectories below **/home/denise/.dt** are:

> **/home/denise/.dt/Desktop**
> **/home/denise/.dt/appmanager**
> **/home/denise/.dt/palettes**
> **/home/denise/.dt/sessions**

/home/denise/.dt/types

These five subdirectories plus the directory itself and the parent directory make a total of seven.

The third field lists the owner of the file. Your login name, such as **denise**, is listed here. When you create a file, your login name is listed by default as the owner of the file.

The fourth field lists the group to which the file belongs. Groups were covered earlier in "Permissions."

The fifth field shows the size of the file. The file **sort** is 120 bytes in size.

The sixth field (which includes a date and time such as Jul 26 10:20) lists the date and time the file was created or last changed.

The seventh field lists the files and directories in alphabetical order. You first see the files that begin with a ".", then the files that begin with numbers, then the files that begin with uppercase letters, and finally the files that begin with lower case letters. There are a lot of characters a file can begin with in UNIX, so if you perform an **ls -l** and don't see the file you are looking for, it may appear at a different spot in the listing from what you expected.

man page

ls - 2

ls -i

To get information about the inode of a file, you use the **-i** option to **ls**. The following example includes both the **-i** and **-l** options to **ls**:

```
$ls -ail /home/denise

137717 -rw-------   1 denise    users           98 Oct  6 09:19 .Xauthority
137623 -r--r--r--   1 denise    users          814 May 19 10:10 .cshrc
140820 drwxr-xr-x   7 denise    users         1024 Sep 26 11:14 .dt
137629 -rwxr-xr-x   1 denise    users         8705 Jul  7 12:04 .dtprofile
180815 drwx------   2 denise    users         1024 Jul 31 18:48 .elm
137624 -r--r--r--   1 denise    users          347 May 19 10:10 .exrc
137652 -rwxrwxrwx   1 denise    users          170 Jun  6 14:20 .fmrc.orig
137650 -rw-------   1 denise    users           97 Jun 12 18:59 .glancerc
137699 -rw-------   1 denise    users        17620 Sep 21 16:11 .gpmhp
137640 -rwxr-xr-x   1 denise    users          391 Sep 19 09:55 .history
137625 -r--r--r--   1 denise    users          341 May 19 10:10 .login
185607 drwx--x--x   2 denise    users         1024 Jul 31 18:48 .lrom
137642 -rw-r--r--   1 denise    users          768 Jul 28 12:54 .mailrc
137641 -rw-------   1 denise    users         1450 Oct  6 13:58 .netscaperks.html
179207 drwx------   2 denise    users        10240 Oct 10 15:24 .netscape-cache
137656 -rw-------   1 denise    users           91 Sep 18 14:16 .netscape-cookies
137635 -rw-------   1 denise    users        43906 Oct 10 15:32 .netscape-history
137645 -rw-r--r--   1 denise    users          566 Aug 25 14:36 .netscapes.spry.com
137646 -rw-------   1 denise    users        46514 Jun 28 12:35 .netsca
137634 -rw-------   1 denise    users         1556 Sep 28 15:02 .netscaperences
137637 -rw-------   1 denise    users          104 Jul 11 11:01 .newsrcws.spry.com
137633 -rw-r--r--   1 denise    users          223 Sep 26 13:26 .newsrc-hp.com
137626 -r--r--r--   1 denise    users          446 May 19 10:10 .profile
137649 -rw-------   1 denise    users           21 Jul  6 13:21 .rhosts
137694 -rw-------   1 denise    users         2328 Oct 10 15:22 .sh_history
137698 -rw-r--r--   1 denise    users         1052 Sep 22 15:00 .softbuildrc
137636 -rwxrwxrwx   1 denise    users          161 Jul 11 12:19 .softinit.orig
 33600 drwxr-xr-x   3 denise    users         1024 Aug 31 15:44 .sw
137648 -rw-------   1 denise    users           23 Jun  2 15:01 .xinitrc
137628 -rwxr-xr-x   1 denise    users        11251 May 19 10:41 .xsession
137715 -rw-r--r--   1 denise    users       611488 Oct  3 12:00 27247b.exe
137707 -rw-r--r--   1 denise    users       114119 Sep 29 12:49 410pt1.exe
137710 -rw-r--r--   1 denise    users       136979 Sep 29 12:53 410pt2.exe
137705 -rw-r--r--   1 denise    users       173978 Sep 29 12:40 41ndir.exe
137709 -rw-r--r--   1 denise    users       363315 Sep 29 12:52 41nds1.exe
137714 -rw-r--r--   1 denise    users       527524 Sep 29 12:57 41nds4.exe
137708 -rw-r--r--   1 denise    users      1552513 Sep 29 12:50 41nwad.exe
137696 -rw-r--r--   1 denise    users       853424 Sep 29 12:24 41rtr2.exe
137654 -rw-r--r--   1 denise    users      1363011 Sep 20 12:20 HPDA1.EXE
182429 drwx------   2 denise    users           24 Jul 31 18:48 Mail
137683 -rw-r--r--   1 denise    users      1787840 Aug 31 09:35 N3212B6.EXE
137702 -rw-r--r--   1 denise    users        13543 Sep 23 09:46 SCSI4S.EXE
137638 -rwx--x--x   1 denise    users           66 Jun  8 17:40 clean
137651 -rwx--x--x   1 denise    users           99 Jun 20 17:44 clean2
137632 -rwx--x--x   1 denise    users           66 Jun 20 17:51 clean3
137688 -rw-r--r--   1 denise    users        15365 Aug 30 15:07 content.exe
137713 -rw-r--r--   1 denise    users       713313 Sep 29 12:56 dsenh.exe
137667 -rwx------   1 denise    users          144 Aug 14 17:10 eg1
137671 -rwx------   1 denise    users          192 Aug 15 12:13 eg2
137662 -rw-r--r--   1 denise    users       667890 Sep 20 12:41 en0316bz.exe
137665 -rw-r--r--   1 denise    users       641923 Sep 20 12:42 en0316tb.exe
137689 -rw-r--r--   1 denise    users         6251 Aug 30 15:07 explore.exe
137690 -rw-r--r--   1 denise    users        23542 Aug 30 15:08 flexi_cd.exe
137670 -rw-r--r--   1 denise    users           30 Aug 14 17:02 fred.h
137673 -rw-r--r--   1 denise    users            0 Aug 14 17:24 hal.c
137660 -rw-r--r--   1 denise    users       895399 Sep 20 12:32 hpd10117.exe
137661 -rw-r--r--   1 denise    users        14135 Sep 20 12:39 hpdlinst.txt
137647 -rw-------   1 denise    users         2943 Jun 19 14:42 hpux.patches
137659 -rw-r--r--   1 denise    users       680279 Sep 20 12:26 j2577a.exe
137697 -rw-r--r--   1 denise    users       930728 Sep 20 15:16 ja95up.exe
137684 -rw-r--r--   1 denise    users      1097728 Aug 30 15:03 msie10.exe
137658 -rw-r--r--   1 denise    users      1790376 Sep 18 14:32 n32e12n.exe
137643 -rw-r--r--   1 denise    users      1393835 Sep 29 12:59 nfs197.exe
137639 -rw-------   1 denise    users          977 Jul  3 14:25 pass.sb
137664 -rw-r--r--   1 denise    users      1004544 Aug 30 15:00 plusdemo.exe
137704 -rw-r--r--   1 denise    users       229547 Sep 29 12:27 ps4x03.exe
137666 -rwxr--r--   1 denise    users          171 Aug  9 13:43 psg
137691 -rw-r--r--   1 denise    users        16645 Aug 30 15:08 quik_res.exe
137692 -rw-r--r--   1 denise    users        14544 Aug 30 15:08 rclock.exe
137693 -rw-r--r--   1 denise    users      2287498 Aug 30 15:12 rkhelp.exe
137669 -rw-r--r--   1 denise    users            0 Aug 15 12:10 roni.mak
137657 -rw-r--r--   1 denise    users         1139 Sep 28 10:35 sb.txt
137712 -rw-r--r--   1 denise    users       569855 Sep 29 12:55 smsup2.exe
```

```
137644 -rw-------    1 root    sys        161 Jul 11 12:18 softinittesoftcm
137706 -rw-r--r--    1 denise  users       39 Sep 29 12:48 srvpr.exe
137682 -rw-r--r--    1 denise  users       38 Aug 15 12:14 steve.h
137685 -rw-r--r--    1 denise  users    14675 Aug 30 15:08 target.exe
137711 -rw-r--r--    1 denise  users   229630 Sep 29 12:54 tcp41a.exe
137700 -rw-r--r--    1 denise  users  1954453 Sep 29 12:26 tnds2.exe
137703 -rw-r--r--    1 denise  users   364270 Sep 23 09:50 upgrade.exe
137663 -rwx-----x    1 denise  users       88 Aug  9 13:43 whoon
137678 -rw-r--r--    1 denise  users   191495 Aug 30 15:00 win95app.exe
```

The inode number contains: the location of files and directories
on the disk; access permissions; owner and group IDs; file link count;
time of last modification; time of last access; device identification
number for special files; and a variety of other information. inode
numbers are used extensively by the system as you change directories
and perform various work.

man page

ls - 2

ls -p

Because you may have subdirectories within the directory you are listing, you may want to use the **-p** option to **ls,** which puts a "/" in after
directory names, as shown in the following example:

```
$ ls -ap /home/denise

.Xauthority
.cshrc
.dt/
.dtprofile
.elm/
.exrc
.fmrc.orig
.glancerc
.gpmhp
.history
.login
.lrom/
.mailrc
.netscape-bookmarks.html
.netscape-cache/
.netscape-cookies
.netscape-history
.netscape-newsgroups-news.spry.com
.netscape-newsgroups-newsserv.hp.com
.netscape-preferences
.newsrc-news.spry.com
.newsrc-newsserv.hp.com
.profile
.rhosts
.sh_history
.softbuildrc
.softinit.orig
.sw/
.xinitrc
.xsession
27247b.exe
```

```
410pt1.exe
410pt2.exe
41ndir.exe
41nds1.exe
41nds4.exe
41nwad.exe
41rtr2.exe
HPDA1.EXE
Mail/
N3212B6.EXE
SCSI4S.EXE
clean
clean2
clean3
content.exe
dsenh.exe
eg1
eg2
en0316bz.exe
en0316tb.exe
explore.exe
flexi_cd.exe
fred.h
hal.c
hpdl0117.exe
hpdlinst.txt
hpux.patches
j2577a.exe
ja95up.exe
msie10.exe
n32e12n.exe
nfs197.exe
pass.sb
plusdemo.exe
ps4x03.exe
psg
quik_res.exe
rclock.exe
rkhelp.exe
roni.mak
sb.txt
smsup2.exe
softinit.remotesoftcm
srvpr.exe
steve.h
target.exe
tcp41a.exe
tnds2.exe
upgrade.exe
whoon
win95app.exe
```

ls -R

Because the subdirectories you are listing probably have files and sub-directories beneath them, you may want to recursively list these. The -R option to **ls** shown in the following example performs this recursive listing. This listing is truncated because it would be too long if it included all the subdirectories directories under **/home/denise**:

man page

ls - 2

```
$ ls -aR /home/denise

.Xauthority
.cshrc
.dt
.dtprofile
.elm
.exrc
.fmrc.orig
.glancerc
.gpmhp
.history
.login
.lrom
.mailrc
.netscape-bookmarks.html
.netscape-cache
.netscape-cookies
.netscape-history
.netscape-newsgroups-news.spry.com
.netscape-newsgroups-newsserv.hp.com
.netscape-preferences
.newsrc-news.spry.com
.newsrc-newsserv.hp.com
.profile
.rhosts
.sh_history
.softbuildrc
.softinit.orig
.sw
.xinitrc
.xsession
27247b.exe
410pt1.exe
410pt2.exe
41ndir.exe
41nds1.exe
41nds4.exe
41nwad.exe
41rtr2.exe
HPDA1.EXE
Mail
N3212B6.EXE
SCSI4S.EXE
clean
clean2
clean3
content.exe
dsenh.exe
eg1
eg2
en0316bz.exe
en0316tb.exe
explore.exe
flexi_cd.exe
fred.h
```

                 .   **(skip some of the listing)**
                 .
                 .

```
/home/denise/.lrom:
LRAAAa27637.CC
LRBAAa27637.CC
LROM.AB
LROM.AB.OLD
LROM.AB.1k1
LROM.SET

/home/denise/.netscape-cache:
```

```
cache306C05510015292.gif
cache306C05560025292.gif
cache306C05560035292.gif
```

```
/home/denise/.sw:
sessions
```

.
.
.   **(skip remainder of the listing)**

ls Summary

I have shown you what I believe to be the most important, and most
often used, **ls** options. Because you may have future needs to list files
and directories based on other criteria, I provide you with a list of
most **ls** options. There is no substitute, however, for issuing the **man
ls** command. Whatever I provide is only a summary. Viewing the man
pages for **ls** gives you much more information. The following is a
summary of the more commonly used **ls** options:

ls - List the contents of a directory

Options

-a	List all entries.	
-b	Print nongraphic characters.	
-c	Use the time the file was last modified for producing order in which files are listed.	
-d	List only the directory name, not its contents.	
-f	Assume that each argument is a directory.	
-g	Only the group is printed and not the owner.	
-i	Print the inode number in the first column of the report.	
-m	List the contents across the screen separated by commas.	
-n	Numbers for UID and GID are printed instead of names.	
-o	List the information in long form (-l), except that group is omitted.	

-p	Put a slash (/) at the end of directory names.
-q	Nonprinting characters are represented by a "?".
-r	Reverse the order in which files are printed.
-s	Show the size in blocks instead of bytes.
-t	List in order of time saved, with most recent first.
-u	Use the time of last access instead of last modification for determining order in which files are printed.
-x	List files in multicolumn format as shown in examples.
-A	Same as -a, except that current and parent directories aren't listed.
-C	Multicolumn output produced.
-F	Directory followed by a "/", executable by an "*", symbolic link by an "@", and FIFO by a "|".
-L	List file or directory to which link points.
-R	Recursively list subdirectories.
-1	Output will be listed in single-column format.

man page

ls - 2

Also, some shorthand command names are available for issuing **ls** with options. For instance, **ll** is equivalent to **ls -l**, and **lsr** is equivalent to **ls -R** in some UNIX variants. We will also cover creating an "alias," whereby you can define your own shorthand for any command in an upcoming chapter.

You can selectively list and perform other file-related commands with wild cards. The following section covers file name expansion and wild cards.

File Name Expansion and Wild Cards

Before we cover additional file system related commands, it is worth taking a look at file name expansion. An overview of file name expansion is useful to ensure that you're comfortable with this topic before we cover additional commands.

Table 3-2 lists some common file name expansion and pattern matching.

Table 3-2   File Name Expansion and Pattern Matching

Character(s)	Example	Description
*	1) ls *.c	Match zero or more characters
?	2) ls conf.?	Match any single character
[list]	3) ls conf.[co]	Match any character in list
[lower-upper]	4) ls libdd.9873[5-6].sl	Match any character in range
str{str1,str2,str3,...}	5) ls ux*.{700,300}	Expand str with contents of {}
~	6) ls -a ~	Home directory
~username	7) ls -a ~gene	Home directory of username

The following descriptions of the examples shown in Table 3-2 are more detailed.

1) To list all files in a directory that end in ".c", you could do the following:

```
$  ls *.c
          conf. SAM.c  conf.c
```

man page

ls - 2

2) To find all the files in a directory named "conf" with an extension of one character, you could do the following:

```
$  ls conf.?
          conf.c  conf.o  conf.1
```

3) To list all the files in a directory named "conf" with only the extension "c" or "o," you could do the following:

```
$  ls conf.{co}
          conf.c  conf.o
```

4) To list files with similar names but a field that covers a range, you could do the following:

man page

ls - 2

```
$   ls libdd9873[5-6].sl
            libdd98735.sl   libdd98736.sl
```

5) To list files that start with "ux" and have the extension "300" or "700," you could do the following:

```
$   ls ux*.{700,300}
            uxbootlf.700   uxinstfs.300
```

6) To list the files in your home directory, you could use ~:

```
$   ls -a ~
            .                .cshrc.org  .login       .shrc.org
            ..               .exrc       .login.org   .cshrc
                             .history    .profile
```

7) To list the files in the home directory of a user, you could do the following:

```
$   ls -a ~gene
            .                .history      splinedat   under.des
            ..               .login        trail.txt   xtra.part
            .chsrc           .login.org    ESP-File
            .cshrc.org       .profile      Mail
            .exrc            .shrc.org     opt
```

pwd and cd

When we covered absolute and relative path names, we used the **cd** command to change **directory**. You can be at any point in the file sys-

tem hierarchy and use **cd** to change to the desired directory, provided
that you have the necessary permissions to change to that directory.

We can change directory using an absolute path name, as shown
in the following example:

man page

cd - 3

```
$ cd /home/denise/.netscape-cache
```

Regardless of your current location in the file system hierarchy,
this changes you to the directory **/home/denise/.netscape-cache**. If,
however, your current location in the file system hierarchy is **/home/
denise**, then you could use a relative place-name to change to
.netscape-cache, as shown in the following example:

```
$ cd .netscape-cache
```

In order to change directory to a place in the file system relative
to your current location, you need a way to determine your current
location. The **pwd** command, for **p**resent **w**orking **d**irectory, can do
this for you. Going back to the previous example in which we changed
directories using the relative path, we could have first issued the **pwd**
command to see that our location was **/home/denise**, as shown in the
following example:

man page

pwd - 3

```
$ pwd
/home/denise
$ cd .netscape-cache
$ pwd
$ /home/denise/.netscape-cache
$
```

pwd takes some of the mystery out of determining your current
directory.

Let's now take a look at moving up a level in the directory tree
using two dots:

```
$ pwd
/home/denise/.netscape-cache
```

man page

cd - 3

man page

pwd - 3

```
$ cd ..
$ pwd
/home/denise
$
```

The two-dot notation moves you to the parent directory of your current directory.

To return to your home directory, you could issue the **cd** command with no arguments, as shown in the following example:

```
$ pwd
/tmp
$ cd
$ pwd
/home/denise
$
```

This shows that no matter what your current location in the file system hierarchy, you can always get back quickly to your home directory. I don't get into shell parameters for some time, but there is a shell parameter which defines your *home* location, as shown in the following example:

```
$ pwd
/tmp
$ cd $HOME
$ pwd
/home/denise
$
```

Using the **pwd** and **cd** commands, you can always obtain your current directory and change to any directory.

cd - Change to a new current directory.

man page

cd - 3

Arguments

none	Change to home directory. This is defined by the HOME environment variable
..	The two dot notation moves you to the parent directory of your current directory.
path	You can specify either an absolute or relative path to change to.

pwd - Present Working Directory, so you know your current location.

man page

pwd - 3

Examples

```
$ pwd
/home/denise/.netscape-cache
$ cd ..
$ pwd
/home/denise
$
```

chmod

man page

chmod - 3

The chmod command is used to change the permissions on a file. Let's start our discussion of **chmod** with the listing of the file **sort** shown earlier:

man page

ls - 2

```
$ ls -l sort
-rwxr-x--x   1 marty      users      120 Jul 26 10:20 sort
```

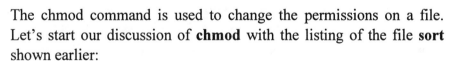

Figure 3-5 shows a breakdown of the permissions on **sort**.

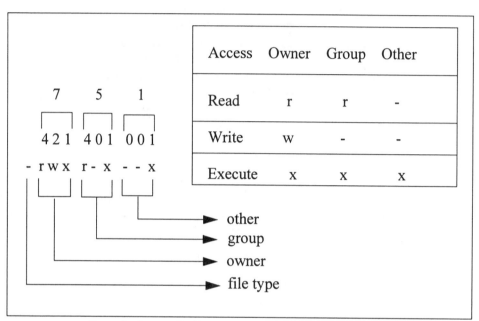

Access	Owner	Group	Other
Read	r	r	-
Write	w	-	-
Execute	x	x	x

Figure 3-5   Permissions of File **sort**

You have very little control over the type of file defined. You do, however, have a great deal of control over the permissions of this file if it belongs to you. The **chmod** command is used to change the permissions on a file or directory. If you are the owner of the file, you can have a field day changing the permissions on the file.

There are two means by which you can change the permissions: symbolic or numeric. I focus first on the numeric mode, because the numbers involved are easy to manage and I sometimes find that new UNIX users get hung up on the meaning of some of the symbols. I'll then cover the symbols and include the symbol meanings in the **chmod** summary. I decided to use the symbols in the summary, because the numeric mode, which I much prefer, is becoming obsolete. In some UNIX variants, the **chmod** manual page is strewn with references to "obsolescent form" whenever the numeric mode is covered.

man page

chmod - 3

First of all, what do I mean by numbers? Looking at the numbers for **sort**, we see permissions of 751: 7 for *owner* (hundreds position), 5 for *group* (tens position), and 1 for *other* (ones position). Figure 3-6 helps with the meanings of the positions.

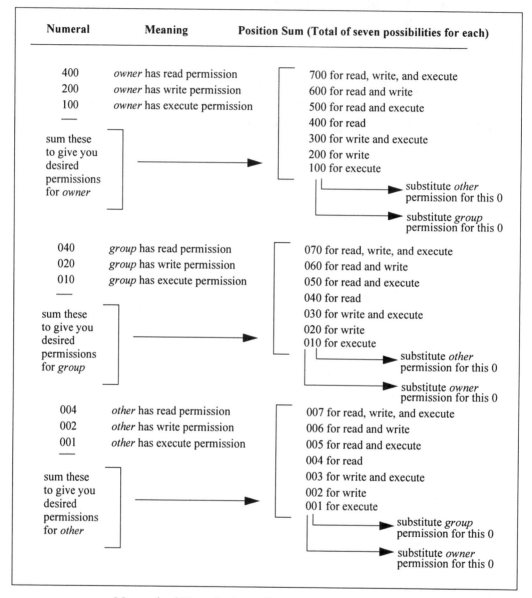

Numeral	Meaning	Position Sum (Total of seven possibilities for each)
400	*owner* has read permission	700 for read, write, and execute
200	*owner* has write permission	600 for read and write
100	*owner* has execute permission	500 for read and execute
		400 for read
		300 for write and execute
sum these to give you desired permissions for *owner*		200 for write
		100 for execute
		substitute *other* permission for this 0
		substitute *group* permission for this 0
040	*group* has read permission	070 for read, write, and execute
020	*group* has write permission	060 for read and write
010	*group* has execute permission	050 for read and execute
		040 for read
		030 for write and execute
sum these to give you desired permissions for *group*		020 for write
		010 for execute
		substitute *other* permission for this 0
		substitute *owner* permission for this 0
004	*other* has read permission	007 for read, write, and execute
002	*other* has write permission	006 for read and write
001	*other* has execute permission	005 for read and execute
		004 for read
		003 for write and execute
sum these to give you desired permissions for *other*		002 for write
		001 for execute
		substitute *group* permission for this 0
		substitute *owner* permission for this 0

Figure 3-6   Numerical Permissions Summary

man page

chmod - 3

     Selecting the desired permissions for *owner*, *group*, and *other*, you use the **chmod** command to assign those permissions to a file or

directory. Some of these permission possibilities are infrequently used, such as execute only, because you usually need to have read access to a file in order to execute it; however, I included all possibilities in Figure 3-6 for completeness. In addition to the permission mode bits shown in figure 3-6, some miscellaneous mode bits also exist that you don't need to be concerned with at this time.

If you decided that you would like to add write permission of the file **sort** for *group* and remove all permissions for *other*, you would simply execute the **chmod** command with the appropriate numeric value. The following set of commands first lists the existing permissions for **sort**, next changes the permissions on **sort**, and finally lists the new permissions on **sort**:

man page

chmod - 3

```
$ ls -l sort
-rwxr-x--x    1 marty       users      120 Jul 26 10:20 sort

$ chmod 770 sort

$ ls -l sort
-rwxrwx---    1 marty       users      120 Jul 26 10:20 sort
```

man page

ls - 2

The same set of commands to change the permissions using the symbolic mode would be:

```
$ ls -l sort
-rwxr-x--x    1 marty       users      120 Jul 26 10:20 sort

$ chmod g+w,o-x sort

$ ls -l sort
-rwxrwx---    1 marty       users      120 Jul 26 10:20 sort
```

In symbolic mode, you issue the **chmod** command and specify who will be affected by the change [user (u), group (g), other (o), or all (a)], the operation you wish to perform [add (+), delete (-), or replace (=)] on permissions, and the permission you wish to specify [read (r), write (w), or execute (x)]. In the previous example using symbolic mode, write (w) permission is being added (+) for *group* (g), and execute (x) permission is being removed (-) for *other* (o).

man page

chmod - 3

The following is a summary of some of the more commonly used symbols of **chmod**:

chmod - Change permissions of specified files using the following symbolic mode list.

Symbol of who is affected:

u	User is affected.
g	Group is affected.
o	Other is affected.
a	All users are affected.

Operation to perform:

+	Add permission.
-	Remove permission.
=	Replace permission.

Permission specified:

r	Read permission.
w	Write permission.
x	Execute permission.
u	Copy user permissions.
g	Copy group permissions.
o	Copy other permissions.

cp

The **cp** command is used to copy a file from one location to another location. You do not alter the original file when you perform a copy. Provided that you have access to the destination directory to which you wish to copy a file, you can place as many copies of a file in that destination as you wish.

man page

cp - 3

The upcoming bullet list describes some of the types of copies you can perform with **cp**. Because there are many file types in UNIX (as covered in Chapter 2) and you have many ways to specify path names for the source and destination files being copied, this list might help you understand the many ways **cp** can be used:

- Copy a source file to a new file name.

- Copy several source files to a different directory.

- Copy several source files to the same directory.

- Copy an entire directory to a different directory.

- Copy several directories to different directories.

The following is an example of copying a file to a new file name within the same directory:

```
$ cp krsort krsort.sav
```

What if the file **krsort.sav** already exists? The answer is that it is replaced by the new **krsort.sav** being copied. To prevent such mishaps (officially called an overwrite) from occurring, you use the **-i** option to **cp**. **-i** asks you whether you wish to overwrite the file before the copy takes place. If your response is affirmative, then the old file is overwritten with the new file.

man page

cp - 3

man page

ls - 2

The following example first shows a listing of the contents of a directory. Using the **cp** with the **-i** option, we copy the file **krsort.c** to **krsortorig.c**, a file that already exists. By responding *n* when asked whether we want to over write **krsortorig.c,** the file is not overwritten and no copy takes place:

```
$ ls -l
total 168
-rwxr-xr-x   1 denise    users       34592 Oct 31 11:27 krsort
-rwxr-xr-x   1 denise    users        3234 Oct 31 11:27 krsort.c
-rwxr-xr-x   1 denise    users       32756 Oct 31 11:27 krsort.dos
-rw-r--r--   1 denise    users        9922 Oct 31 11:27 krsort.q
-rwxr-xr-x   1 denise    users        3085 Oct 31 11:27 krsortorig.c
$ cp -i krsort.c krsortorig.c
overwrite krsortorig.c? (y/n) n
$
```

cp - Copy files and directories.

Options

-i	Interactive copy whereby you are prompted to confirm that you wish to overwrite an existing file.
-f	Force existing files to be overwritten by files being copied if there is a conflict in file names occurs.
-p	Preserve permissions when copying.
-r	Copy recursively.
-R	Copy recursively, except that permissions are different.

mv

man page

mv - 3

The **mv** command is used to move a file or directory from one location to another location. You can also move multiple files.

The following example shows a listing of a directory, the move of a file **krsort.c** to **krsort.test.c** within this directory, and a listing of the directory showing the file has been moved:

```
$ ls -l
total 168
-rwxr-xr-x   1 denise    users      34592 Oct 31 15:17 krsort
-rwxr-xr-x   1 denise    users       3234 Oct 31 15:17 krsort.c
-rwxr-xr-x   1 denise    users       2756 Oct 31 15:17 krsort.dos
-rw-r--r--   1 denise    users       9922 Oct 31 15:17 krsort.q
-rwxr-xr-x   1 denise    users       3085 Oct 31 15:17 krsortorig.c
$ mv krsort.c krsort.test.c
$ ls -l
total 168
-rwxr-xr-x   1 denise    users      34592 Oct 31 15:17 krsort
-rwxr-xr-x   1 denise    users      32756 Oct 31 15:17 krsort.dos
-rw-r--r--   1 denise    users       9922 Oct 31 15:17 krsort.q
-rwxr-xr-x   1 denise    users       3234 Oct 31 15:17 krsort.test.c
-rwxr-xr-x   1 denise    users       3085 Oct 31 15:17 krsortorig.c
$
```

man page

ls - 2

man page

mv - 3

What if the destination file already exists? You guessed it, UNIX is more than happy to write over the destination file. Using the **-i** option, **mv** asks you to confirm overwriting a file before it does so. The following example shows an attempt to move **krsort.test.c** to **krsortorig.c.** The user is alerted to the fact that **krsortorig.c** already exists and chooses not to let the move take place:

```
$ ls -l
total 168
-rwxr-xr-x   1 denise    users      34592 Oct 31 15:17 krsort
-rwxr-xr-x   1 denise    users      32756 Oct 31 15:17 krsort.dos
-rw-r--r--   1 denise    users       9922 Oct 31 15:17 krsort.q
-rwxr-xr-x   1 denise    users       3234 Oct 31 15:17
krsort.test.c
-rwxr-xr-x   1 denise    users       3085 Oct 31 15:17 krsortorig.c
$ mv -i krsort.test.c krsortorig.c
remove krsortorig.c? (y/n) n
$ ls -l
total 168
-rwxr-xr-x   1 denise    users      34592 Oct 31 15:17 krsort
-rwxr-xr-x   1 denise    users      32756 Oct 31 15:17 krsort.dos
-rw-r--r--   1 denise    users       9922 Oct 31 15:17 krsort.q
-rwxr-xr-x   1 denise    users       3234 Oct 31 15:17
krsort.test.c
-rwxr-xr-x   1 denise    users       3085 Oct 31 15:17 krsortorig.c
$
```

Because the response was not in the affirmative, the move does not take place, and the original **krsortorig.c** remains intact.

mv - Copy files and directories.

Options

    -i   Interactive copy whereby you are prompted to confirm that you wish to overwrite an existing file.

    -f   Force existing files to be overwritten by files being copied if a conflict in file names occurs.

    -p   Preserve permissions when copying.

mkdir

How nice it would be to have a command to make a directory any time you wish. You could then use this command to create directories and thereby organize your files in multiple directories in a way similar to organizing files in a filing cabinet. The **mkdir** command allows you to do just that - make a directory.

This is an incredibly simple command. You specify the name of the directory to create. In the following example, we'll look at the contents of a directory with the **ls** command, use **mkdir** to make the directory named **default.permissions**, and then perform another **ls** to see the new directory:

```
$ ls -l
total 2
drwxr-xr-x    2 denise    users        1024 Oct 31 11:27 krsort.dir.old
$ mkdir default.permissions
$ ls -l
total 4
drwxr-xr-x    2 denise    users        1024 Oct 31 11:27 krsort.dir.old
drwxr-xr-x    2 denise    users          24 Oct 31 11:32 default.permissions
$
```

The new directory has been produced with default permissions for the user *denise. group* and *other* have both read and execute permissions for this directory.

What if you wanted to create a directory with specific permissions on it instead of default permissions? You could use the **-m** option to **mkdir** and specify the mode or permissions you want. To give all users read permission on the **krsort.dir.new** directory, you issue the following:

man page

mkdir - 3

```
$ mkdir -m "a=r" read.permissions
$ ls -l
total 6
drwxr-xr-x   2 denise   users        1024 Oct 31 11:27 krsort.dir.old
drwxr-xr-x   2 denise   users          24 Oct 31 11:32 default.permissions
dr--r--r--   2 denise   users          24 Oct 31 11:33 read.permissions
$
```

Remember the symbolic versus numeric mode of permissions? This **mkdir** command shows the symbolic mode, which although I do not like as much as the numeric mode, should be used because the numeric mode is becoming obsolete.

You don't have to stop at creating a directory with only one level of depth. With the **-p** option you can create a new directory with any number of subdirectories in it. Intermediate directories are created with the **-p** option. Let's now create a directory named **level1**, with the directory **level2** beneath it, and the directory **level3** below **level2** in the following example. The **ls** command with the **-R** option recursively lists the directories below **level1**:

man page

ls - 2

```
$ mkdir -p level1/level2/level3
$ ls -R level1
level2

level1/level2:
level3

level1/level2/level3:
$
```

man page

ls - 2

After creating the directory **level1** and issuing the **ls** command, we can see that **level2** is indeed beneath **level1**, and **level3** is beneath **level2**.

man page

mkdir - 3

mkdir - Create specified directories.

Options

        -m   Specify the mode (permissions) of the directory.

        -p   Create intermediate directories to achieve the full path. If you want to create several layers of directory down, you use **-p**.

rm

man page

rm - 3

The **rm** command removes one or more files from a directory and can also be used to remove the directory itself. Going back to our earlier discussion on permissions, you must have both *write* and *execute* permissions on a directory in order to remove a file from it. If you own the directory from which you are going to remove files, then you can probably remove files from it. If, however, you don't have the appropriate permissions on a directory, then the **rm** of files fails.

As with some of the other commands we have covered, you can use the **-i** option, which asks you to confirm each file as it is removed. This means that if you are asked whether you really wish to remove a file and you respond *n*, then the file is not removed. If you respond *y*, the file is removed.

You can also use the **-r** (or **-R**) option to recursively delete the contents of directories and then delete the directories. This means you can recursively delete the files and directories specified. If there is any question is in your mind about whether or not you wish to recursively delete files and directories, then use the **-i** option along with **-r**.

You can use the -*f* option to remove files and directories, which performs removes *without* asking you to confirm them.

The following example performs a long listing of the directory **krsort.dir.new**, interactively prompts the user to see whether he or she wants to delete the files in this directory, and then lists the contents of this directory again, showing that all files have *not* been deleted, because the user responded *n*:

man page

ls - 2

man page

rm - 3

```
$ ls -l krsort.dir.new
total 168
-rwxr-xr-x   1 denise    users     34592 Oct 27 18:44 krsort
-rwxr-xr-x   1 denise    users      3234 Oct 27 18:46 krsort.c
-rwxr-xr-x   1 denise    users     32756 Oct 27 18:46 krsort.dos
-rw-r--r--   1 denise    users      9922 Oct 27 18:46 krsort.q
-rwxr-xr-x   1 denise    users      3085 Oct 27 18:46 krsortorig.c
$ rm -i krsort.dir.new/*
../krsort.dir.new/krsort: ? (y/n) n
../krsort.dir.new/krsort.c: ? (y/n) n
../krsort.dir.new/krsort.dos: ? (y/n) n
../krsort.dir.new/krsort.q: ? (y/n) n
../krsort.dir.new/krsortorig.c: ? (y/n) n
$ ls -l krsort.dir.new
total 168
-rwxr-xr-x   1 denise    users     34592 Oct 27 18:44 krsort
-rwxr-xr-x   1 denise    users      3234 Oct 27 18:46 krsort.c
-rwxr-xr-x   1 denise    users     32756 Oct 27 18:46 krsort.dos
-rw-r--r--   1 denise    users      9922 Oct 27 18:46 krsort.q
-rwxr-xr-x   1 denise    users      3085 Oct 27 18:46 krsortorig.c
$
```

Note that the response to being asked whether the file should be deleted was *n* in all cases. This means that none of the files have been removed. A *y* response to any question results in that file being removed from the directory. To interactively delete a directory, you combine the options **-i** and **-r** of the **rm** command. If, however, you do not delete every file in a directory, then the directory is not removed if the **-i** option is used. The first part of the following example shows all but the file **krsort** being removed from the directory **krsort.dir.new**. The directory is not deleted, because this file still exists. When the file is removed in the second part of this example, the directory itself is then deleted:

man page

rm - 3

```
$ rm -ir krsort.dir.new
directory krsort.dir.new: ? (y/n) y
krsort.dir.new/krsort: ? (y/n) n
krsort.dir.new/krsort.c: ? (y/n) y
krsort.dir.new/krsort.dos: ? (y/n) y
krsort.dir.new/krsort.q: ? (y/n) y
krsort.dir.new/krsortorig.c: ? (y/n) y
krsort.dir.new: ? (y/n) y
rm: directory krsort.dir.new not removed.  Directory not
empty

$ rm -ir krsort.dir.new
directory krsort.dir.new: ? (y/n) y
krsort.dir.new/krsort: ? (y/n) y
krsort.dir.new: ? (y/n) y
$
```

rm - Remove files and directories.

Options

-i	Interactive remove whereby you are prompted to confirm that you wish to remove an existing file.
-f	Force files to be removed.
-r (-R)	Recursively remove the contents of the directory and then the directory itself.

rmdir

man page

rmdir - 3

The **rmdir** command removes one or more directories. The directory must be empty in order to be removed. You can also specify more than one directory to be removed. Going back to our earlier discussion on permissions, you must have both *write* and *execute* permissions on the parent of a directory to be removed in order to remove it.

As with some of the other commands we have covered, you can use the **-i** option, which asks you to confirm each directory as it is removed. This means that if you are asked whether you really wish to remove a directory and you respond *n,* then it is not removed. If you respond *y,* it is removed.

The order in which you specify directories are to be removed is significant. If you want to remove both a directory and its subdirectory, you must specify the subdirectory to be removed first. If you specify the parent directory rather than its subdirectory to be removed first, the remove of the parent directory fails because it is not empty.

You can use the **-f** option to force removal of directories, an action that performs removes *without* asking you to confirm them.

The following example performs a long listing of the directory **krsort.dir.new**, showing that this directory has in it a file called **.dotfile**. When we attempt to remove this directory with **rmdir,** a message is displayed informing us that this directory is not empty. The file **.dotfile** in this directory prevents the **rmdir** command from removing **krsort.dir.new**. After removing **.dotfile,** we are able to remove the directory with **rmdir**:

man page

rmdir - 3

man page

ls - 2

```
$ ls -al ../krsort.dir.new
total 4
drwxr-xr-x   2 denise    users          1024 Oct 27 18:57 .
drwxrwxr-x   4 denise    users          1024 Oct 27 18:40 ..
-rw-r--r--   1 denise    users             0 Oct 27 18:56 .dotfile
$ rmdir -i ../krsort.dir.new
../krsort.dir.new: ? (y/n) y
rmdir: ../krsort.dir.new: Directory not empty
$ rm ../krsort.dir.new/.dotfile
$ rmdir -i ../krsort.dir.new
../krsort.dir.new: ? (y/n) y
$
```

rmdir has now successfully removed **krsort.dir.new** with **.dotfile** gone:

man page

rmdir - 3

rmdir - Remove directories.

Options

	-i	Interactive remove whereby you are prompted to confirm that you wish to remove a directory
	-f	Force directories to be removed.
	-p	If, after removing a directory, the parent directory is empty, then remove it also. This goes on until a parent directory is encountered that is not empty.

Using Commands

Using the cd, pwd, ls, mkdir, and cp Commands

Now that we have covered some of these commands in an "isolated" fashion, let's put some of the commands together.

man page

cd - 3

Let's start by viewing the hierarchy of a directory under *denise's* home directory called **krsort.dir.old,** as shown in Figure 3-7:

man page

pwd - 3

man page

ls - 2

```
$ cd /home/denise/krsort.dir.old
$ pwd
/home/denise/krsort.dir.old
$ ls -l
total 168
-rwxr-xr-x    1 denise    users       34592 Oct 27 18:20 krsort
-rwxr-xr-x    1 denise    users        3234 Oct 27 17:30 krsort.c
-rwxr-xr-x    1 denise    users       32756 Oct 27 17:30 krsort.dos
-rw-r--r--    1 denise    users        9922 Oct 27 17:30 krsort.q
-rwxr-xr-x    1 denise    users        3085 Oct 27 17:30 krsortorig.c
$
```

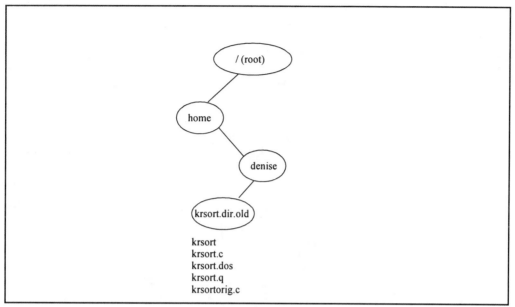

Figure 3-7 **/home/denise/krsort.dir.old**

We can then make a new directory called **krsort.dir.new** and copy a file to it, as shown in Figure 3-8:

```
$ mkdir ../krsort.dir.new
$ cp krsort ../krsort.dir.new
$ ls -l ../krsort.dir.new
total 68
-rwxr-xr-x   1 denise   users       34592 Oct 27 18:27 krsort
$
```

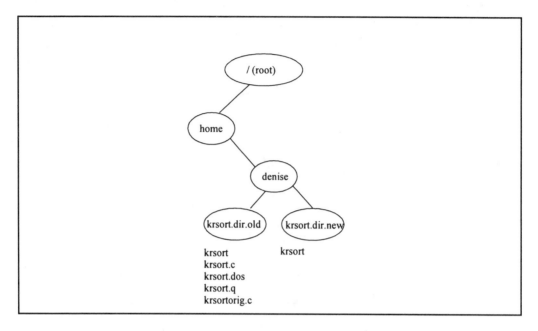

Figure 3-8   **/home/denise/krsort.dir.new**

Now let's try the **-i** option to **cp**. If we attempt to copy a file to an existing file name we'll be asked if we wish to overwrite the destination file. We are alerted to the fact that the destination file already exists and we can then select a new name for the file we wish to copy, as shown in Figure 3-9:

```
$ pwd
/users/denise/krsort.dir.old
$ cp -i krsort ../krsort.dir.new
overwrite ../krsort.dir.new/krsort? (y/n) n
$ cp krsort ../krsort.dir.new/krsort.new.name
$ ls -l ../krsort.dir.new
total 136
-rwxr-xr-x   1 denise   users    34592 Oct 27 18:27 krsort
-rwxr-xr-x   1 denise   users    34592 Oct 27 18:29
krsort.new.name
$
```

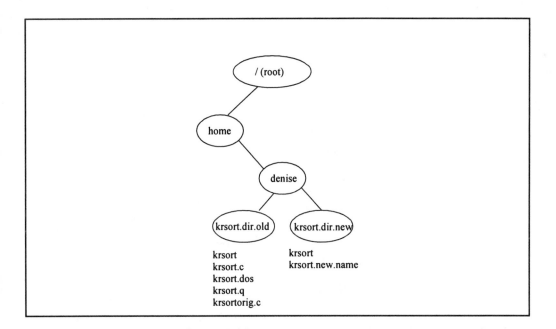

Figure 3-9 **/home/denise/krsort.dir.new/krsort.new.name** Added

We can also use a wild card with **cp** to copy all files in **krsort.dir.old** to **krsort.dir.new,** as shown in Figure 3-10:

man page

cp - 3

```
$ cp * ../krsort.dir.new
$ ls -l ../krsort.dir.new
total 236
-rwxr-xr-x   1 denise   users    34592 Oct 27 18:30 krsort
-rwxr-xr-x   1 denise   users     3234 Oct 27 18:30 krsort.c
-rwxr-xr-x   1 denise   users    32756 Oct 27 18:30 krsort.dos
-rwxr-xr-x   1 denise   users    34592 Oct 27 18:29
krsort.new.name
-rw-r--r--   1 denise   users     9922 Oct 27 18:30 krsort.q
-rwxr-xr-x   1 denise   users     3085 Oct 27 18:30 krsortorig.c
$
```

man page

ls - 2

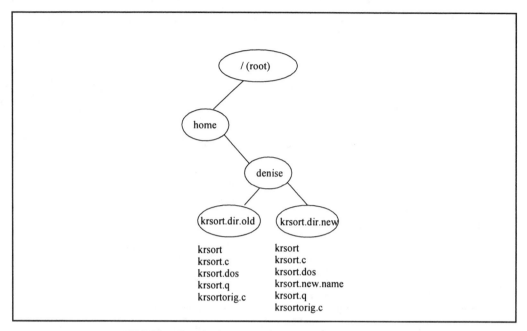

Figure 3-10   All Files Copied to **/home/denise/krsort.dir.new**

Using the mv Command

Let's start over at the point where the **krsort.dir.new** directory is empty, as shown in Figure 3-11:

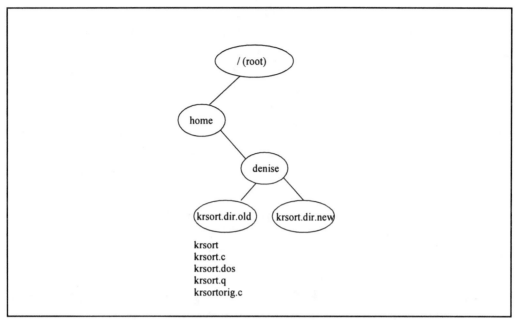

Figure 3-11   Empty **/home/denise/krsort.dir.new** Directory

We can now move the file **krsort** to the **krsort.dir.new** directory, as shown in Figure 3-12:

```
$ mv krsort ../krsort.dir.new
$ ls -l ../krsort.dir.new
total 68
-rwxr-xr-x   1 denise   users        34592 Oct 27 18:20 krsort
$
```

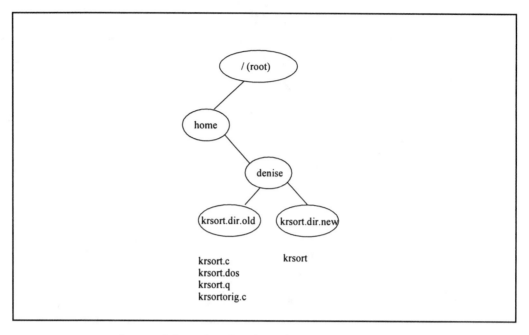

Figure 3-12   **krsort** Moved to **/krsort.dir.new**

If we now attempt to move **krsort** to the **krsort.dir.new** directory with the **-i** option and write over the file **krsort** we get the following:

```
$ mv -i krsort ../krsort.dir.new/krsort
remove ../krsort.dir.new/krsort? (y/n) n
$
```

Because we used the **-i** option to **mv** we are asked whether we wish to allow a file to be overwritten with the move. Because we responded *n* to the question, the file is not overwritten.

We can also use a wild card with the **mv** command to copy all files from the **krsort.dir.old** directory to the **krsort.dir.new** directory. Without the **-i** option, any files in the **krsort.dir.new** directory are overwritten by files that have the same name, as shown in Figure 3-13:

```
$ mv * ../krsort.dir.new
$ ls -l ../krsort.dir.new
total 168
-rwxr-xr-x  1 denise   users   34592 Oct 27 18:44 krsort
-rwxr-xr-x  1 denise   users    3234 Oct 27 18:46 krsort.c
-rwxr-xr-x  1 denise   users   32756 Oct 27 18:46 krsort.dos
-rw-r--r--  1 denise   users    9922 Oct 27 18:46 krsort.q
-rwxr-xr-x  1 denise   users    3085 Oct 27 18:46 krsortorig.c
$
```

man page

mv - 3

man page

ls - 2

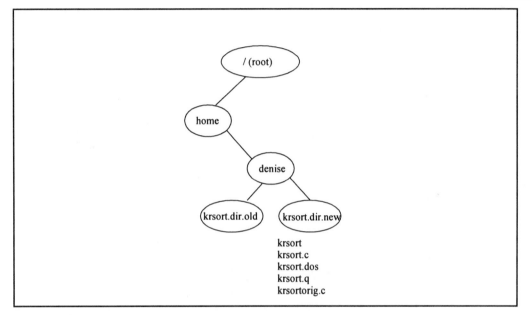

Figure 3-13   All Files Moved to **/home/denise/krsort.dir.new**

Down and Dirty with the rm and rmdir Commands

The most feared command in the UNIX world, with good reason I
might add, is the **rm** command. **rm** removes whatever you want
whenever you want with no questions asked unless you use the **-i**
option.

man page

rm - 3

    Want to blow away your system instantly? **rm** would be more
than happy to help you. As an average user, and not the system admin-

istrator, you probably do not have the permissions to do so. It is, how-ever, unnerving to know that this is a possibility. In addition, it is likely that you have permissions remove all of your own files and directories. All of this can be easily avoided by simply using the **-i** option to **rm**.

man page

rm - 3

Let's assume that **krsort.dir.new** and **krsort.dir.old** are identi-cal directories, as shown in Figure 3-14:

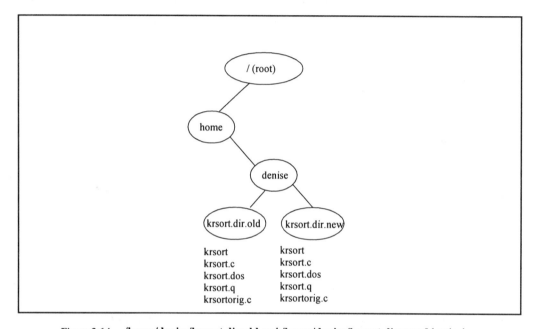

Figure 3-14   **/home/denise/krsort.dir.old** and **/home/denise/krsort.dir.new** Identical

To interactively remove files from **krsort.dir.new**, you do the following:

```
$ rm -i ../krsort.dir.new/*
../krsort.dir.new/krsort: ? (y/n) n
../krsort.dir.new/krsort.c: ? (y/n) n
../krsort.dir.new/krsort.dos: ? (y/n) n
../krsort.dir.new/krsort.q: ? (y/n) n
../krsort.dir.new/krsortorig.c: ? (y/n) n
$ ls -l ../krsort.dir.new
total 168
-rwxr-xr-x   1 denise    users      34592 Oct 27 18:44 krsort
-rwxr-xr-x   1 denise    users       3234 Oct 27 18:46 krsort.c
-rwxr-xr-x   1 denise    users      32756 Oct 27 18:46 krsort.dos
-rw-r--r--   1 denise    users       9922 Oct 27 18:46 krsort.q
```

man page

ls - 2

```
-rwxr-xr-x   1 denise    users     3085 Oct 27 18:46 krsortorig.c
$
```

This obviously resulted in nothing being removed from **krsort.dir.new**, because we responded *n* when asked whether we wanted to delete files.

Let's now go ahead and add a file beginning with a "." to **krsort.dir.new**. The **touch** command does just that, touches a file to create it with no contents, as shown in Figure 3-15:

```
$ touch ../krsort.dir.new/.dotfile
$ ls -al ../krsort.dir.new
total 172
drwxr-xr-x   2 denise    users     1024 Oct 27 18:54 .
drwxrwxr-x   4 denise    users     1024 Oct 27 18:40 ..
-rw-r--r--   1 denise    users        0 Oct 27 18:56 .dotfile
-rwxr-xr-x   1 denise    users    34592 Oct 27 18:44 krsort
-rwxr-xr-x   1 denise    users     3234 Oct 27 18:46 krsort.c
-rwxr-xr-x   1 denise    users    32756 Oct 27 18:46 krsort.dos
-rw-r--r--   1 denise    users     9922 Oct 27 18:46 krsort.q
-rwxr-xr-x   1 denise    users     3085 Oct 27 18:46 krsortorig.c
$
```

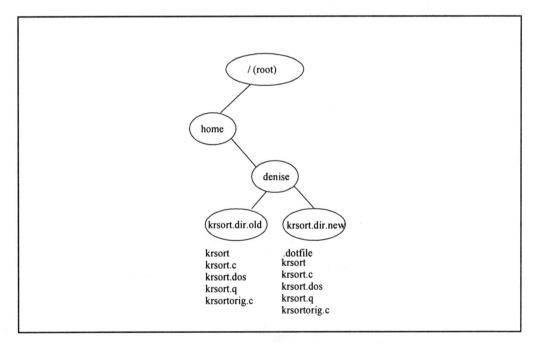

Figure 3-15 **/home/denise/krsort.dir.new** with **.dotfile**

If we now attempt to remove files using the same **rm** command earlier issued we'll see the following, as shown in Figure 3-16:

man page

rm - 3

man page

ls - 2

```
$ rm -i ../krsort.dir.new/*
../krsort.dir.new/krsort: ? (y/n) y
../krsort.dir.new/krsort.c: ? (y/n) y
../krsort.dir.new/krsort.dos: ? (y/n) y
../krsort.dir.new/krsort.q: ? (y/n) y
../krsort.dir.new/krsortorig.c: ? (y/n) y
$ ls -al ../krsort.dir.new
total 4
drwxr-xr-x    2 denise    users         1024 Oct 27 18:57 .
drwxrwxr-x    4 denise    users         1024 Oct 27 18:40 ..
-rw-r--r--    1 denise    users            0 Oct 27 18:56 .dotfile
```

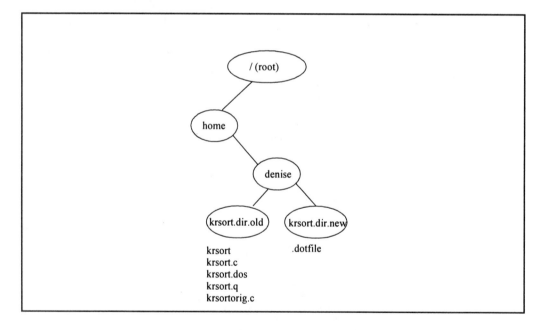

Figure 3-16   Only **.dotfile** Left in **/home/denise/krsort.dir.new**

man page

mkdir - 3

The "*" used as a wild card with the **rm** command does not remove the file **.dotfile**. The file .dotfile in this directory prevents the **rmdir** command from removing **krsort.dir.new**. This file must first

be removed before the **rmdir** command can successfully delete
krsort.dir.new.

```
$ rmdir -i ../krsort.dir.new
../krsort.dir.new: ? (y/n) y
rmdir: ../krsort.dir.new: Directory not empty
$ rm ../krsort.dir.new/.dotfile
$ rmdir -i ../krsort.dir.new
../krsort.dir.new: ? (y/n) y
$
```

rmdir has now successfully removed **krsort.dir.new** with **.dotfile**
gone, as shown in Figure 3-17:

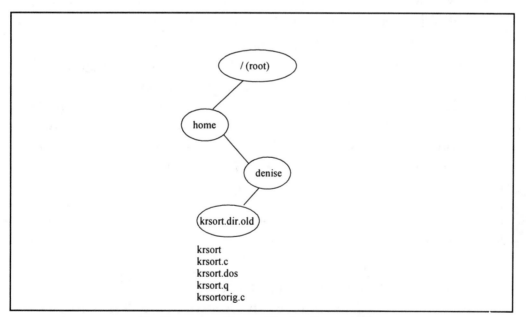

Figure 3-17   **rmdir** Removes **/home/denise/krsort.dir.new**

Redirection

Before we cover viewing files, let's talk about redirection for a minute because I use some redirection in the upcoming section. I'll cover redirection under shell programming, but for now I want to give you just a quick introduction to redirection so that we can more effectively cover some of the commands in this chapter.

UNIX is set up such that commands usually take their input from the keyboard, often called *standard input,* and usually send output to the screen, often called *standard output.* Commands also send error information to the screen. You do not always want input to come from standard input and output and errors to go to standard output. You are given a lot of control to override these defaults. This is called redirection. Table 3-4 shows many common forms of redirection.

As shown in the table, to redirect the output of a command from standard output to a file, you use ">". This works almost all of the time. If you have an environment variable called **noclobber** set, then redirecting to an existing file does not work (we'll cover environment variables shortly). The **noclobber** does not permit redirection to write over an existing file. If you try to write over an existing file, such as / **tmp/processes** below, you receive a message that the file exists:

man page

ps - 12

```
# ps  -ef  > /tmp/processes
/tmp/processes:  File exists
```

You can, however, use a "!" with redirection to force a file to be overwritten. Using ">!" forces a file to be overwritten and ">>!" forces the output to be appended to the end of an existing file. Examples of these are shown in Table 3-4.

Table 3-4   Commonly Used Redirection Forms

Command or Assignment	Example	Description
<	**wc -l < .login**	Standard input redirection: execute **wc** (word count) and list number of lines (**-l**) in **.login**
>	**ps -ef > /tmp/processes**	Standard output redirection: execute **ps** and send output to file **/tmp/processes**
>>	**ps -ef >> /tmp/processes**	Append standard output: execute **ps** and append output to the end of file **/tmp/processes**
>!	**ps -ef >! /tmp/processes**	Append output redirection and override **noclobber**: write over **/tmp/processes** even if it exists
>>!	**ps -ef >>! /tmp/processes**	Append standard output and override **noclobber**: append to the end of **/tmp/processes**
| (pipe)	**ps | wc -l**	Run **ps** and use the result as input to **wc**.
0 - standard input **1** - standard output **2** - standard error	**cat program 2> errors**	**cat** the file **program** to standard output and redirect errors to the file **errors**.
	cat program 2>> errors	**cat** the file **program** to standard output and append errors to the file **errors**.
	find / -name '*.c' -print > cprograms 2>errors	**find** all files on the system ending in **.c** and place the list of files in **cprograms** in the current working directory and send all errors (file descriptor 2) to the file **errors** in current working directory.
	find / -name '*.c' -print > cprograms 2>&1	**find** all files on the system ending in **.c**, place the list of files in **cprograms** in the current working directory, and send all errors (file descriptor 2) to the same place as file descriptor 1 (**cprograms**).

Using the symbols shown in Table 3-4, you can redirect from *standard input* and *standard output*. For instance, rather than display the output on the screen, you can send the output to file. We will use some of these redirection forms in upcoming examples.

Viewing Files with cat, more, pg, head, and tail

To begin, let's look at a long file. In fact, let's look at a file so long that it would not fit on your screen if you were to print out the contents of the file to your screen.

The **cat** command (short for concatenate) does just this, prints out the file to your screen. If, however, the file is long, then you see only the end of the file on your screen. Remember the user **denise** from earlier in the book? She had a lot of files in her directory. Let's list the files in her directory and redirect the output to a file called **listing** with the following command:

```
$ ls -a /home/denise > listing
```

When we **cat listing** to the screen we see only the end of it, as shown in Figure 3-18. We know that this is the end of the file because I have issued **cat** with the **-n** option that includes line numbers. The line numbers indicate that this is not the beginning of the file.

```
┌─────────────────────────────────────────────────────────────────────┐
│ ⊟ │                        cat −n example                    │ ◦ │☐││
├─────────────────────────────────────────────────────────────────────┤
│    106   rclock.exe                                                   │
│    107   rkhelp.exe                                                   │
│    108   sb.txt                                                       │
│    109   shellupd.exe                                                 │
│    110   smsup2.exe                                                   │
│    111   softinit.remotesoftcm                                        │
│    112   srvpr.exe                                                    │
│    113   tabnd1.exe                                                   │
│    114   target.exe                                                   │
│    115   tcp41a.exe                                                   │
│    116   tnds2.exe                                                    │
│    117   trace.TRC1                                                   │
│    118   trace.TRC1.Z.uue                                             │
│    119   upgrade.exe                                                  │
│    120   uue.syntax                                                   │
│    121   v103.txt                                                     │
│    122   whoon                                                        │
│    123   win95app.exe                                                 │
│    124   wsdrv1.exe                                                   │
│    125   wsos21.exe                                                   │
│    126   wsos22.exe                                                   │
│    127   wsos23.exe                                                   │
│    128   xferp110.zip                                                 │
│$ ▊                                                                    │
└─────────────────────────────────────────────────────────────────────┘
```

Figure 3-18   **cat -n** Command

Seeing only the end of this file is not what we had in mind. Using the **pg** (for page), we will see one screen at time, as shown in Figure 3-19:

man page

pg - 3

```
┌─────────────────────────────────────── pg example ───────────────────────────┬──┬─┐
│ □                                                                              │ ○│□│
├────────────────────────────────────────────────────────────────────────────────────┤
│ .                                                                              │
│ ..                                                                             │
│ .CbtOptSet                                                                     │
│ .Xauthority                                                                    │
│ .cshrc                                                                         │
│ .cshrc.orig                                                                    │
│ .elm                                                                           │
│ .exrc                                                                          │
│ .fmrc                                                                          │
│ .fmrc.orig                                                                     │
│ .glancerc                                                                      │
│ .gpmhp                                                                         │
│ .history                                                                       │
│ .login                                                                         │
│ .lrom                                                                          │
│ .mailrc                                                                        │
│ .netscape-bookmarks.html                                                       │
│ .netscape-cache                                                                │
│ .netscape-history                                                              │
│ .netscape-newsgroups-news.spry.com                                             │
│ .netscape-newsgroups-newsserv.hp.com                                           │
│ .netscape-preferences                                                          │
│ .newsrc-news.spry.com                                                          │
│ :█                                                                             │
└──────────────────────────────────────────────────────────────────────────────┘
```

Figure 3-19   **pg** Command

man page

more - 3

The **more** command produces the same output as **pg,** as shown in Figure 3-20.

man page

pg - 3

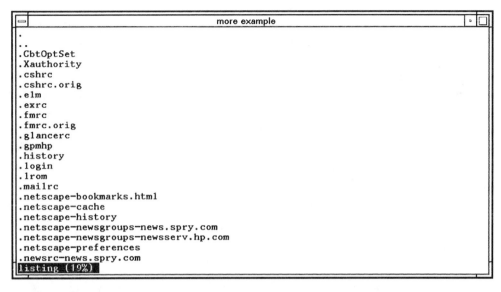

```
⌐──────────────────────── more example ───────────────────────── ◦ ▢
.
..
.CbtOptSet
.Xauthority
.cshrc
.cshrc.orig
.elm
.exrc
.fmrc
.fmrc.orig
.glancerc
.gpmhp
.history
.login
.lrom
.mailrc
.netscape-bookmarks.html
.netscape-cache
.netscape-history
.netscape-newsgroups-news.spry.com
.netscape-newsgroups-newsserv.hp.com
.netscape-preferences
.newsrc-news.spry.com
listing (19%)
```

Figure 3-20   **more** Command

This is more like it; now we can scroll on a screen-by-screen basis with both **pg** and **more**. However, sometimes you want to view only the beginning or end of a file. You can use the **head** command to view the beginning of a file and the **tail** command to view the bottom of a file. The following two examples of **head** and **tail** (see Figures 3-21 and 3-22) show viewing the first 20 lines of **listing** and the last 20 lines of **listing**, respectively.

man page

pg - 3

man page

more - 3

man page

head - 3

man page

tail - 3

```
                                  head example                                    □ □
$ head -20 listing
.
..
.CbtOptSet
.Xauthority
.cshrc
.cshrc.orig
.elm
.exrc
.fmrc
.fmrc.orig
.glancerc
.gpmhp
.history
.login
.lrom
.mailrc
.netscape-bookmarks.html
.netscape-cache
.netscape-history
.netscape-newsgroups-news.spry.com
$ ▮
```

Figure 3-21   **head** Command

```
                                  tail example                                    □ □
$ tail -20 listing
shellupd.exe
smsup2.exe
softinit.remotesoftcm
srvpr.exe
tabnd1.exe
target.exe
tcp41a.exe
tnds2.exe
trace.TRC1
trace.TRC1.Z.uue
upgrade.exe
uue.syntax
v103.txt
whoon
win95app.exe
wsdrv1.exe
wsos21.exe
wsos22.exe...
wsos23.exe
xferp110.zip
$ ▮
```

Figure 3-22   **tail** Command

The command you use depends on the information you wish to display. My personal preference, whether viewing the contents of a large file or a long listing of files, is to use **more**. I don't have a good reason for this, and all I can say is that we are creatures of habit and I have always used **more**. The following are command summaries for **cat**, **pg**, **more**, **head**, and **tail**. I included some of the most frequently used options associated with these commands. Because none of the commands are difficult to use, I suggest that you try each command and see whether one suits your needs better than the others.

man page
more - 3

man page
cat - 3

Here are summaries of the **cat, pg, more, head,** and **tail** commands.

man page
pg - 3

man page
head - 3

cat - Display, combine, append, copy, or create files.

Options

-	Used as a substitute for specifying a file name when you want to use the keyboard for standard input.
-n	Line numbers are displayed along with output lines.
-p	Replace multiple consecutive empty lines with only one empty line.
-s	This is silent mode, which suppresses information about nonexistent files.
-u	Output is unbuffered which means that it is handled character-by-character.
-v	Print most nonprinting characters visibly.

pg - Display all or parts of a file.

Options

-number	The number of lines you wish to display.
-p string	Use string to specify a prompt.
-c	Clear the screen before displaying the next page of the file.

-f	Don't split lines being displayed.
-n	A command is issued as soon as a command letter is typed, rather than having to issue a new line character.

man page

more - 3

more - Display all or parts of a file one screen at a time.

Options

-c	Clear the screen before displaying the next page of the file.
-d	Display a prompt at the bottom of the screen with brief instructions.
-f	Wrap text to fit screen and judge page length accordingly.
-n	The number of lines in the display window is set to n.
-s	Squeeze multiple consecutive empty lines into one empty line.

man page

head - 3

head - Provide only the first few lines of a file.

Options

-c	The output is produced with a specified number of bytes.
-l	The output is produced with a specified number of lines. This is the default.
-n count	The number of bytes or lines is specified by count. You can also use -count to specify the number of bytes or lines, which is shown in the example. The default count is 10.

tail - Provide the last few lines of a file.

man page

tail - 3

Options

-bnumber   Specify number of blocks from the end of the file you
            wish to begin displaying.

-cnumber   Specify number of characters from the end of the file
            you wish to begin displaying.

-nnumber   Specify number of lines from the end of the file you
            wish to begin displaying. You can also specify a num-
            ber or minus sign and number, as shown in the exam-
            ple, to specify the number of lines from the end of file
            to begin displaying.

split

Some files are just too long. The file **listing** we earlier looked at may
be more easily managed if split into multiple files. We can use the
split command to make **listing** into files 25 lines long as shown in
Figure 3-23.

man page

split - 3

```
┌─                                    split example                           ▫ □
│ $ 11 listing
│ -rw--------    1 denise    users         1430 Dec 19 16:30 listing
│ $
│ $ split -1 25 listing
│ $
│ $ 11 x*
│ -rw--------    1 denise    users          330 Dec 19 16:40 xaa
│ -rw--------    1 denise    users          267 Dec 19 16:40 xab
│ -rw--------    1 denise    users          268 Dec 19 16:40 xac
│ -rw--------    1 denise    users          256 Dec 19 16:40 xad
│ -rw--------    1 denise    users          274 Dec 19 16:40 xae
│ -rw--------    1 denise    users           35 Dec 19 16:40 xaf
│ $ ▮
```

Figure 3-23 **split** Command

man page

split - 3

Note that the **split** command produced several files from **listing** called **xaa, xab**, and so on. The **-l** option is used to specify the number of lines in files produced by **split**.

Here is a summary of the **split** command.

split - Split a file into multiple files.

Options

        -l line_count   Split the file into files with line_count lines per file.

        -b n   Split the file into files with n bytes per file.

Manual Pages of Some Commands Used in Chapter 3

The following are the HP-UX manual pages for many of the commands used in the chapter. Commands often differ among UNIX variants, so you may find differences in the options or other areas for some commands, however; the following manual pages serve as an excellent reference.

cat

cat - Concatenate files.

```
cat(1)                                                                    cat(1)

NAME
      cat - concatenate, copy, and print files

SYNOPSIS

      cat [-benrstuv] file ...

DESCRIPTION
      cat reads each file in sequence and writes it on the standard output.
      Thus:

            cat file

      prints file on the default standard output device;

            cat file1 file2 > file3

      concatenates file1 and file2, and places the result in file3.

      If - is appears as a file argument, cat uses standard input.  To
      combine standard input and other files, use a combination of - and
      file arguments.

   Options
      cat recognizes the following options:

            -b    Omit line numbers from blank lines when -n option is
                  specified. If this option is specified, the -n option is
                  automatically selected.

            -e    Print a $ character at the end of each line (prior to the
                  new-line).  If this option is specified, the -v option is
                  automatically selected.

            -n    Display output lines preceded by line numbers, numbered
                  sequentially from 1.

            -r    Replace multiple consecutive empty lines with one empty
                  line, so that there is never more than one empty line
                  between lines containing characters.

            -s    Silent option.  cat suppresses error messages about non-
                  existent files, identical input and output, and write
                  errors.  Normally, input and output files cannot have
                  identical names unless the file is a special file.

            -t    Print each tab character as ^I.  If this option is
                  specified, the -v option is automatically selected.

            -u    Do not buffer output (handle character-by-character).
                  Normally, output is buffered.
```

-v   Cause non-printing characters (with the exception of tabs, new-lines and form-feeds) to be printed visibly. Control characters are printed using the form ^X (Ctrl-X), and the DEL character (octal 0177) is printed as ^? (see ascii(5)). Single-byte control characters whose most significant bit is set, are printed using the form M-^x, where x is the character specified by the seven low order bits. All other non-printing characters are printed as M-x, where x is the character specified by the seven low order bits. This option is influenced by the LC_CTYPE environment variable and its corresponding code set.

EXTERNAL INFLUENCES
   Environment Variables
      LANG provides a default value for the internationalization variables that are unset or null. If LANG is unset or null, the default value of "C" (see lang(5)) is used. If any of the internationalization variables contains an invalid setting, cat will behave as if all internationalization variables are set to "C". See environ(5).

      LC_ALL If set to a non-empty string value, overrides the values of all the other internationalization variables.

      LC_CTYPE determines the interpretation of text as single and/or multi-byte characters, the classification of characters as printable, and the characters matched by character class expressions in regular expressions.

      LC_MESSAGES determines the locale that should be used to affect the format and contents of diagnostic messages written to standard error and informative messages written to standard output.

      NLSPATH determines the location of message catalogues for the processing of LC_MESSAGES.

   International Code Set Support
      Single- and multi-byte character code sets are supported.

RETURN VALUE
   Exit values are:

      0   Successful completion.
      >0   Error condition occurred.

EXAMPLES
   To create a zero-length file, use any of the following:

         cat /dev/null > file
         cp /dev/null file
         touch file

   The following prints ^I for all the occurrences of tab character in file1

         cat -t file1

   To suppress error messages about files that do not exist, use:

         cat -s file1 file2 file3 > file

   If file2 does not exist, the above command concatenates file1 and file3 without reporting the error on file2. The result is the same if -s option is not used, except that cat displays the error message.

   To view non-printable characters in file2, use:

```
cat -v file2
```

WARNINGS
    Command formats such as

```
cat file1 file2 > file1
```

    overwrites the data in file1 before the concatenation begins, thus
destroying the file. Therefore, be careful when using shell special
characters.

SEE ALSO
    cp(1), more(1), pg(1), pr(1), rmnl(1), ssp(1).

STANDARDS CONFORMANCE
    cat: SVID2, SVID3, XPG2, XPG3, XPG4, POSIX.2

cd

cd - Change working directory.

cd(1)   cd(1)

NAME
     cd - change working directory

SYNOPSIS

     cd [directory]

DESCRIPTION
     If directory is not specified, the value of shell parameter HOME is
     used as the new working directory. If directory specifies a complete
     path starting with /, ., .., directory becomes the new working
     directory. If neither case applies, cd tries to find the designated
     directory relative to one of the paths specified by the CDPATH shell
     variable. CDPATH has the same syntax as, and similar semantics to,
     the PATH shell variable. cd must have execute (search) permission in
     directory.

     cd exists only as a shell built-in command because a new process is
     created whenever a command is executed, making cd useless if written
     and processed as a normal system command. Moreover, different shells
     provide different implementations of cd as a built-in utility.
     Features of cd as described here may not be supported by all the
     shells. Refer to individual shell manual entries for differences.

     If cd is called in a subshell or a separate utility execution
     environment such as:

          find . -type d -exec cd {}; -exec foo {};

          (which invokes foo on accessible directories)

     cd does not affect the current directory of the caller's environment.
     Another usage of cd as a stand-alone command is to obtain the exit
     status of the command.

EXTERNAL INFLUENCES
   International Code Set Support
     Single- and multi-byte character code sets are supported.

EXAMPLES
     Change the current working directory to the HOME directory from any
     location in the file system:

          cd

     Change to new current working directory foo residing in the current
     directory:

          cd foo

or

```
cd ./foo
```

Change to directory foobar residing in the current directory's parent
directory:

```
cd ../foobar
```

Change to the directory whose absolute pathname is
/usr/local/lib/work.files:

```
cd /usr/local/lib/work.files
```

Change to the directory proj1/schedule/staffing/proposals relative to
home directory:

```
cd $HOME/proj1/schedule/staffing/proposals
```

VARIABLES

The following environment variables affect the execution of cd:

HOME   The name of the home directory, used when no
                        directory operand is specified.

CDPATH   A colon-separated list of pathnames that refer to
                        directories. If the directory operand does not
                        begin with a slash (/) character, and the first
                        component is not dot or dot-dot, cd searches for
                        directory relative to each directory named in the
                        CDPATH variable, in the order listed. The new
                        working directory is set to the first matching
                        directory found. An empty string in place of a
                        directory pathname represents the current
                        directory. If CDPATH is not set, it is treated as
                        if it was an empty string.

RETURN VALUE

Upon completion, cd exits with one of the following values:

0   The directory was successfully changed.
>0   An error occurred. The working directory remains
                        unchanged.

SEE ALSO

csh(1), pwd(1), ksh(1), sh-posix(1), sh(1), chdir(2).

STANDARDS CONFORMANCE

cd: SVID2, SVID3, XPG2, XPG3, XPG4, POSIX.2

chmod

chmod - Change permissions.

man page

chmod - 3

chmod(1)   chmod(1)

NAME
     chmod - change file mode access permissions

SYNOPSIS

     /usr/bin/chmod [-A] [-R] symbolic_mode_list file ...

   Obsolescent form:
     /usr/bin/chmod [-A] [-R] numeric_mode file ...

DESCRIPTION
     The chmod command changes the permissions of one or more files
     according to the value of symbolic_mode_list or numeric_mode. You can
     display the current permissions for a file with the ls -l command (see
     ls(1)).

   Symbolic Mode List
     A symbolic_mode_list is a comma-separated list of operations in the
     following form. Whitespace is not permitted.

          [who]op[permission][,...]

     The variable fields can have the following values:

          who   One or more of the following letters:

                           u   Modify permissions for user (owner).
                           g   Modify permissions for group.
                           o   Modify permissions for others.
                           a   Modify permissions for all users (a is
                                equivalent to ugo).

          op   Required; one of the following symbols:

                           +   Add permission to the existing file mode
                                bits of who.
                           -    Delete permission from the existing file
                                mode bits of who.
                           =   Replace the existing mode bits of who with
                                permission.

          permission One or more of the following letters:

                           r   Add or delete the read permission for who.

                           w   Add or delete the write permission for who.

x   Add or delete the execute file (search directory) permission for who.

s   Add or delete the set-owner-id or set-group-id on file execution permission for who. Useful only if u or g is expressed or implied in who.

t   Add or delete the save-text-image on file execution (sticky bit) permission. Useful only if u is expressed or implied in who. See chmod(2).

X   Conditionally add or delete the execute/search permission as follows:
- If file is a directory, add or delete the search permission to the existing file mode for who. (Same as x.)
- If file is not a directory, and the current file permissions include the execute permission (ls -l displays an x or an s) for at least one of user, group, or other, then add or delete the execute file permission for who.
- If file is not a directory, and no execute permissions are set in the current file mode, then do not change any execute permission.

Or one only of the following letters:

u   Copy the current user permissions to who.

g   Copy the current group permissions to who.

o   Copy the current other permissions to who.

The operations are performed in the order specified, and can override preceding operations specified in the same command line.

If who is omitted, the r, w, x, and X permissions are changed for all users if the changes are permitted by the current file mode creation mask (see umask(1)). The s and t permissions are changed as if a was specified in who.

Omitting permission is useful only when used with = to delete all permissions.

Numeric Mode (Obsolescent)
Absolute permissions can be set by specifying a numeric_mode, an octal number constructed from the logical OR (sum) of the following mode bits:

Miscellaneous mode bits:

```
4000  (= u=s)   Set-user-id on file execution (file only)
2000  (= g=s)   Set-group-id on file execution
1000  (= u=t)   Set sticky bit; see chmod(2)
```

Permission mode bits:

```
0400  (= u=r)   Read by owner
0200  (= u=w)   Write by owner
0100  (= u=x)   Execute (search in directory) by owner
0040  (= g=r)   Read by group
0020  (= g=w)   Write by group
0010  (= g=x)   Execute/search by group
0004  (= o=r)   Read by others
```

```
0002  (= o=w)  Write by others
0001  (= o=x)  Execute/search by others
```

Options

-A   Preserve any optional access control list (ACL) entries
      associated with the file. By default, in conformance with
      the IEEE Standard POSIX 1003.1-1988, optional ACL entries
      are deleted. For information about access control lists,
      see acl(5).

-R   Recursively change the file mode bits. For each file
      operand that names a directory, chmod alters the file mode
      bits of the named directory and all files and subdirectories
      in the file hierarchy below it.

Only the owner of a file, or a user with appropriate privileges, can
change its mode.

Only a user having appropriate privileges can set (or retain, if
previously set) the sticky bit of a regular file.

In order to set the set-group-id on execution bit, the group of the
file must correspond to your current group ID.

If chmod is used on a symbolic link, the mode of the file referred to
by the link is changed.

EXTERNAL INFLUENCES
    Environment Variables
        LC_MESSAGES determines the language in which messages are displayed.

        If LC_MESSAGES is not specified in the environment or is set to the
        empty string, the value of LANG is used as a default for each
        unspecified or empty variable. If LANG is not specified or is set to
        the empty string, a default of "C" (see lang(5)) is used instead of
        LANG.

        If any internationalization variable contains an invalid setting,
        chmod behaves as if all internationalization variables are set to "C".
        See environ(5).

    International Code Set Support
        Single- and multi-byte character code sets are supported.

RETURN VALUE
    Upon completion, chmod returns one of the following values:

        0   Successful completion.
        >0   An error condition occurred.

EXAMPLES
    Deny write permission to others:

        chmod o-w file

    Make a file executable by everybody:

        chmod a+x file

    Assign read and execute permission to everybody, and set the set-
    user-id bit:

        chmod a=rx,u+s file

Assign read and write permission to the file owner, and read
permission to everybody else:

        chmod u=rw,go=r file
or
        chmod 644 file   (obsolescent form)

Traverse a directory subtree making all regular files readable by user
and group only, and all executables and directories executable
(searchable) by everyone:

        chmod -R ug+r,o-r,a+X pathname

If the current value of umask is 020 (umask -S displays
u=rwx,g=rx,o=rwx; do not change write permission for group) and the
current permissions for file mytest are 444 (a=r), displayed by ls -l
as -r--r--r--, then the command

        chmod +w mytest

sets the permissions to 646 (uo=rw,g=r), displayed by ls -l as -rw-r-
-rw-.

If the current value of umask is 020 (umask -S displays
u=rwx,g=rx,o=rwx; do not change write permission for group) and the
current permissions for file mytest are 666 (a=rw), displayed by ls -l
as -rw-rw-rw-, then the command

        chmod -w mytest

sets the permissions to 464 (uo=r,g=rw), displayed by ls -l as -r--
rw-r--.

DEPENDENCIES
    The -A option causes chmod to fail on file systems that do not support
    ACLs.

AUTHOR
    chmod was developed by AT&T and HP.

SEE ALSO
    chacl(1), ls(1), umask(1), chmod(2), acl(5).

STANDARDS CONFORMANCE
    chmod: SVID2, SVID3, XPG2, XPG3, XPG4, POSIX.2

cp

cp - Copy files and directories.

```
cp(1)                                                                cp(1)

NAME
      cp - copy files and directory subtrees

SYNOPSIS
      cp [-f|-i] [-p] [-e extarg ] file1 new_file
      cp [-f|-i] [-p] [-e extarg ] file1 [file2 ...] dest_directory
      cp [-f|-i] [-p] [-R|-r] [-e extarg ] directory1 [directory2 ...]
      dest_directory

DESCRIPTION
      cp copies:

            -  file1 to new or existing new_file,
            -  file1 to existing dest_directory,
            -  file1, file2, ...  to existing dest_directory,
            -  directory subtree directory1, to new or existing
               dest_directory.  or
            -  multiple directory subtrees directory1, directory2, ...  to
               new or existing dest_directory.

      cp fails if file1 and new_file are the same (be cautious when using
      shell metacharacters).  When destination is a directory, one or more
      files are copied into that directory.  If two or more files are
      copied, the destination must be a directory.  When copying a single
      file to a new file, if new_file exists, its contents are destroyed.

      If the access permissions of the destination dest_directory or
      existing destination file new_file forbid writing, cp aborts and
      produces an error message ``cannot create file''.

      To copy one or more directory subtrees to another directory, the -r
      option is required.  The -r option is ignored if used when copying a
      file to another file or files to a directory.

      If new_file is a link to an existing file with other links, cp
      overwrites the existing file and retains all links.  If copying a file
      to an existing file, cp does not change existing file access
      permission bits, owner, or group.

      When copying files to a directory or to a new file that does not
      already exist, cp creates a new file with the same file permission
      bits as file1, modified by the file creation mask of the user if the
      -p option was not specified, and then bitwise inclusively ORed with
      S_IRWXU.  The owner and group of the new file or files are those of
      the user.  The last modification time of new_file (and last access
      time, if new_file did not exist) and the last access time of the
      source file1 are set to the time the copy was made.

      Options
```

-i   (interactive copy) Cause cp to write a prompt to standard
            error and wait for a response before copying a file that would
            overwrite an existing file. If the response from the standard
            input is affirmative, the file is copied if permissions allow
            the copy. If the -i (interactive) and -f (forced-copy)
            options are both specified, the -i option is ignored.

-f   Force existing destination pathnames to be removed before
            copying, without prompting for confirmation. This option has
            the effect of destroying and replacing any existing file whose
            name and directory location conflicts with the name and
            location of the new file created by the copy operation.

-p   (preserve permissions) Causes cp to preserve in the copy as
            many of the modification time, access time, file mode, user
            ID, and group ID as allowed by permissions.

-r   (recursive subtree copy) Cause cp to copy the subtree rooted
            at each source directory to dest_directory. If dest_directory
            exists, it must be a directory, in which case cp creates a
            directory within dest_directory with the same name as file1
            and copies the subtree rooted at file1 to
            dest_directory/file1. An error occurs if dest_directory/file1
            already exists. If dest_directory does not exist, cp creates
            it and copies the subtree rooted at file1 to dest_directory.
            Note that cp -r cannot merge subtrees.

            Usually normal files and directories are copied. Character
            special devices, block special devices, network special files,
            named pipes, symbolic links, and sockets are copied, if the
            user has access to the file; otherwise, a warning is printed
            stating that the file cannot be created, and the file is
            skipped.

            dest_directory should not reside within directory1, nor should
            directory1 have a cyclic directory structure, since in both
            cases cp attempts to copy an infinite amount of data.

-R   (recursive subtree copy) The -R option is identical to the -r
            option with the exception that directories copied by the -R
            option are created with read, write, and search permission for
            the owner. User and group permissions remain unchanged.

            With the -R and -r options, in addition to regular files and
            directories, cp also copies FIFOs, character and block device
            files and symbolic links. Only superusers can copy device
            files. All other users get an error. Symbolic links are
            copied so the target points to the same location that the
            source did.

            Warning: While copying a directory tree that has device
            special files, use the -r option; otherwise, an infinite
            amount of data is read from the device special file and is
            duplicated as a special file in the destination directory
            occupying large file system space.

-e extarg
            Specifies the handling of any extent attributes of the file[s]
            to be copied. extarg takes one of the following values.

                    warn   Issues a warning message if extent attributes
                                cannot be copied, but copies the file anyway.

                    ignore   Does not copy the extent attributes.
                    force   Fails to copy the file if the extent attribute
                                can not be copied.

Extent attributes can not be copied if the files are being
copied to a file system which does not support extent
attributes or if that file system has a different block size
than the original. If -e is not specified, the default value
for extarg is warn.

Access Control Lists (ACLs)
       If new_file is a new file, or if a new file is created in
       dest_directory, it inherits the access control list of the original
       file1, file2, etc., altered to reflect any difference in ownership
       between the two files (see acl(5)).

EXTERNAL INFLUENCES
    Environment Variables
       LC_CTYPE determines the interpretation of text as single and/or
       multi-byte characters.

       LANG and LC_CTYPE determine the local language equivalent of y (for
       yes/no queries).

       LANG determines the language in which messages are displayed.

       If LC_CTYPE is not specified in the environment or is set to the empty
       string, the value of LANG is used as a default for each unspecified or
       empty variable. If LANG is not specified or is set to the empty
       string, a default of "C" (see lang(5)) is used instead of LANG. If
       any internationalization variable contains an invalid setting, cp
       behaves as if all internationalization variables are set to "C". See
       environ(5).

    International Code Set Support
       Single- and multi-byte character code sets are supported.

EXAMPLES
       The following command moves the directory sourcedir and its contents
       to a new location (targetdir) in the file system. Since cp creates
       the new directory, the destination directory targetdir should not
       already exist.

             cp -r sourcedir targetdir && rm -rf sourcedir

       The -r option copies the subtree (files and subdirectories) in
       directory sourcedir to directory targetdir. The double ampersand (&&)
       causes a conditional action. If the operation on the left side of the
       && is successful, the right side is executed (and removes the old
       directory). If the operation on the left of the && is not successful,
       the old directory is not removed.

       This example is equivalent to:

             mv sourcedir targetdir

       To copy all files and directory subtrees in the current directory to
       an existing targetdir, use:

             cp -r * targetdir

       To copy all files and directory subtrees in sourcedir to targetdir,
       use:

             cp -r sourcedir/* targetdir

       Note that directory pathnames can precede both sourcedir and
       targetdir.

To create a zero-length file, use any of the following:

```
cat /dev/null >file
cp /dev/null file
touch file
```

DEPENDENCIES
 NFS
   Access control lists of networked files are summarized (as returned in
   st_mode by stat()), but not copied to the new file. When using mv or
   ln on such files, a + is not printed after the mode value when asking
   for permission to overwrite a file.

AUTHOR
   cp was developed by AT&T, the University of California, Berkeley, and
   HP.

SEE ALSO
   cpio(1), ln(1), mv(1), rm(1), link(1M), lstat(2), readlink(2),
   stat(2), symlink(2), symlink(4), acl(5).

STANDARDS CONFORMANCE
   cp: SVID2, SVID3, XPG2, XPG3, XPG4, POSIX.2

head

head - Show first few lines of a file.

man page

head - 3

NAME
     head - give first few lines

SYNOPSIS

     head [-c|-l] [-n count] [file ...]

     Obsolescent:
     head [-count] [file ...]

DESCRIPTION
     head prints on standard output the first count lines of each of the
     specified files, or of the standard input. If count is omitted it
     defaults to 10.

     If multiple files are specified, head outputs before each file a line
     of this form:

          ==> file <==

     Options
     -c   The quantity of output is measured in bytes.

     -count   The number of units of output. This option is provided
                     for backward compatibility (see -n below) and is
                     mutually exclusive of all other options.

     -l   The quantity of output is measured in lines; this is
                     the default.

     -n count   The number of lines (default) or bytes output. count
                     is an unsigned decimal integer. If -n (or -count) is
                     not given, the default quantity is 10. This option
                     provides the same functionality as the -count option,
                     but in a more standard way. Use of the -n option is
                     recommended where portability between systems is
                     important.

EXTERNAL INFLUENCES
     Environment Variables
     LC_CTYPE determines the interpretation of text within file as single
     and/or multi-byte characters.

     LC_MESSAGES determines the language in which messages are displayed.

     If LC_CTYPE or LC_MESSAGES is not specified in the environment or is
     set to the empty string, the value of LANG is used as a default for
     each unspecified or empty variable. If LANG is not specified or is
     set to the empty string, a default of "C" (see lang(5)) is used
     instead of LANG.

If any internationalization variable contains an invalid setting, head
behaves as if all internationalization variables are set to "C". See
environ(5).

International Code Set Support
Single- and multi-byte character code sets are supported.

SEE ALSO
tail(1).

STANDARDS CONFORMANCE
head: SVID3, XPG4, POSIX.2

mkdir

mkdir - Make a directory.

mkdir(1)   mkdir(1)

NAME
     mkdir - make a directory

SYNOPSIS

     mkdir [-p] [-m mode] dirname ...

DESCRIPTION
     mkdir creates specified directories in mode 0777 (possibly altered by
     umask unless specified otherwise by a -m mode option (see umask(1)).
     Standard entries, . (for the directory itself) and .. (for its parent)
     are created automatically. If dirname already exists, mkdir exits
     with a diagnostic message, and the directory is not changed.

   Options
     mkdir recognizes the following command-line options:

          -m mode   After creating the directory as specified, the
                         file permissions are set to mode, which is a
                         symbolic mode string as defined for chmod (see
                         chmod(1)). The umask(1) has precedence over -m.

          -p   Intermediate directories are created as necessary.
                         Otherwise, the full path prefix of dirname must
                         already exist. mkdir requires write permission in
                         the parent directory.

                         For each directory name in the pathname prefix of
                         the dirname argument that is not the name of an
                         existing directory, the specified directory is
                         created using the current umask setting, except
                         that the equivalent of chmod u+wx is done on each
                         component to ensure that mkdir can create lower
                         directories regardless of the setting of umask.
                         Each directory name in the pathname prefix of the
                         dirname argument that matches an existing
                         directory is ignored without error. If an
                         intermediate path component exists, but has
                         permissions set to prevent writing or searching,
                         mkdir fails with an error message. If the dirname
                         argument (including pathname prefix) names an
                         existing directory, mkdir fails with an error
                         message.

                         If the -m option is used, the directory specified
                         by dirname (excluding directories in the pathname
                         prefix) is created with the permissions specified
                         by mode.

Only LINK_MAX subdirectories can be created (see limits(5)).

EXTERNAL INFLUENCES
   Environment Variables
      LANG provides a default value for the internationalization variables
      that are unset or null. If LANG is unset or null, the default value of
      "C" (see lang(5)) is used. If any of the internationalization
      variables contains an invalid setting, mkdir will behave as if all
      internationalization variables are set to "C". See environ(5).

      LC_ALL If set to a non-empty string value, overrides the values of all
      the other internationalization variables.

      LC_CTYPE determines the interpretation of text as single and/or
      multi-byte characters, the classification of characters as printable,
      and the characters matched by character class expressions in regular
      expressions.

      LC_MESSAGES determines the locale that should be used to affect the
      format and contents of diagnostic messages written to standard error
      and informative messages written to standard output.

      NLSPATH determines the location of message catalogues for the
      processing of LC_MESSAGES.

   International Code Set Support
      Single- and multi-byte character code sets are supported.

DIAGNOSTICS
      mkdir returns exit code 0 if all directories were successfully made.
      Otherwise, it prints a diagnostic and returns non-zero.

EXAMPLES
      Create directory gem beneath existing directory raw in the current
      directory:

            mkdir raw/gem

      Create directory path raw/gem/diamond underneath the current directory
      and set permissions on directory diamond to read-only for all users
      (a=r):

            mkdir -p -m "a=r" raw/gem/diamond

      which is equivalent to (see chmod(1)):

            mkdir -p -m 444 raw/gem/diamond

      If directories raw or raw and gem already exist, only the missing
      directories in the specified path are created.

SEE ALSO
      rm(1), sh(1), umask(1).

STANDARDS CONFORMANCE
      mkdir: SVID2, SVID3, XPG2, XPG3, XPG4, POSIX.2

more

more - File viewing filter.

man page

more - 3

---

more(1)   more(1)

NAME
     more, page - file perusal filter for crt viewing

SYNOPSIS
     more [-n] [-cdefisuvz] [-n number] [-p command] [-t tagstring] [-x
     tabs] [-W option] [+linenumber] [+/pattern] [name ...]

     page [-n] [-cdefisuvz] [-n number] [-p command] [-t tagstring] [-x
     tabs] [-W option] [+linenumber] [+/pattern] [name ...]

REMARKS:
     pg is preferred in some standards and has some added functionality,
     but does not support character highlighting (see pg(1)).

DESCRIPTION
     more is a filter for examining continuous text, one screenful at a
     time, on a soft-copy terminal. It is quite similar to pg, and is
     retained primarily for backward compatibility. more normally pauses
     after each screenful, printing the filename at the bottom of the
     screen. To display one more line, press <Return>. To display another
     screenful press <Space>. Other possibilities are described later.

     more and page differ only slightly. more scrolls the screen upward as
     it prints the next page. page clears the screen and prints a new
     screenful of text when it prints a new page. Both provide one line of
     overlap between screenfuls.

     name can be a filename or -, specifying standard input. more
     processes file arguments in the order given.

     more supports the Basic Regular Expression syntax (see regexp(5)).

     more recognizes the following command line options:

             -n number   Set the number of lines in the display window to
                          number, a positive decimal integer. The default
                          is one line less than the the number of lines
                          displayed by the terminal; on a screen that
                          displays 24 lines, the default is 23. The -n flag
                          overrides any values obtained from the
                          environment.

             -n   Same as -n number except that the number of lines
                          is set to n.

             -c   Draw each page by beginning at the top of the
                          screen, and erase each line just before drawing on
                          it. This avoids scrolling the screen, making it
                          easier to read while more is writing. This option

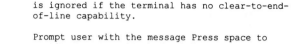

	is ignored if the terminal has no clear-to-end-of-line capability.
-d	Prompt user with the message Press space to continue, q to quit, h for help at the end of each screenful. This is useful if more is being used as a filter in some setting, such as a training class, where many users might be unsophisticated.
-e	Exit immediately after writing the last line of the last file in the argument list
-f	Count logical lines, rather than screen lines. That is, long lines are not folded. This option is recommended if nroff output is being piped through ul, since the latter can generate escape sequences. These escape sequences contain characters that would ordinarily occupy screen positions, but which do not print when sent to the terminal as part of an escape sequence. Thus more might assume lines are longer than they really are, and fold lines erroneously.
-i	Perform pattern matching in searches without regard to case.
-s	Squeeze multiple blank lines from the output, producing only one blank line. Especially helpful when viewing nroff output, this option maximizes the useful information present on the screen.
-u	Normally, more handles underlining and bold such as produced by nroff in a manner appropriate to the particular terminal: if the terminal supports underlining or has a highlighting (usually inverse-video) mode, more outputs appropriate escape sequences to enable underlining, else highlighting mode, for underlined information in the source file. If the terminal supports highlighting, more uses that mode information that should be printed in boldface type. The -u option suppresses this processing, as do the "ul" and "os" terminfo flags.
-v	Do not display nonprinting characters graphically; by default, all non-ASCII and control characters (except <Tab>, <Backspace>, and <Return>) are displayed visibly in the form ^X for <Ctrl-x>, or M-x for non-ASCII character x.
-z	Same as not specifying -v, with the exception of displaying <Backspace> as ^H, <Return> as ^M, and <Tab> as ^I.
-p command	Execute the more command initially in the command argument for each file examined. If the command is a positioning command, such as a line number or a regular expression search, sets the current position to represent the final results of the command, without writing any intermediate lines of the file. If the positioning command is unsuccessful, the first line in the file is the current position.
-t tagstring	Write the screenful of the file containing the tag

named by the tagstring argument. The specified
tag appears in the current position. If both -p
and -t options are specified, more processes -t
first; that is, the file containing the tagstring
is selected by -t and then the command is
executed.

-x tabs   Set the tabstops every tabs position. The default
                 value for the tabs argument is 8.

-W option   Provides optional extensions to the more command.
                 Currently, the following two options are
                 supported:

        notite
                 Prevents more from sending the terminal
                 initialization string before displaying the
                 file. This argument also prevents more from
                 sending the terminal de-initialization string
                 before exiting.

        tite
                 Causes more to send the initialization and
                 de-initialization strings. This is the
                 default.

+linenumber   Start listing such that the current position
                 is set to linenumber.

+/pattern   Start listing such that the current position
                 is set to the line matching the regular
                 expression pattern.

The number of lines available per screen is determined by the -n
option, if present or by examining values in the environment. The
actual number of lines written is one less than this number, as the
last line of the screen is used to write a user prompt and user input.

The number of columns available per line is determined by examining
values in the environment. more writes lines containing more
characters than would fit into this number of columns by breaking the
line into one more logical lines where each of these lines but the
last contains the number of characters needed to fill the columns.
The logical lines are written independently of each other; that is,
commands affecting a single line affect them separately.

While determining the number of lines and the number of columns, if
the methods described above do not yield any number then more uses
terminfo descriptor files (see term(4)). If this also fails then the
number of lines is set to 24 and the number of columns to 80.

When standard output is a terminal and -u is not specified, more
treats backspace characters and carriage-return characters specially.

  - A character, followed first by a backspace character, then by
     an underscore (_), causes that character to be written as
     underlined text, if the terminal supports that. An underscore,
     followed first by a backspace character, then any character,
     also causes that character to be written as underlined text,
     if the terminal supports that.

  - A backspace character that appears between two identical
     printable characters causes the first of those two characters
     to be written as emboldened text, if the terminal type
     supports that, and the second to be discarded. Immediately
     subsequent occurrences of backspaces/character pairs for that

same character is also discarded.

- Other backspace character sequences is written directly to the
  terminal, which generally causes the character preceding the
  backspace character to be suppressed in the display.

- A carriage-return character at the end of a line is ignored,
  rather than being written as a control character.

If the standard output is not a terminal device, more always exits
when it reaches end-of-file on the last file in its argument list.
Otherwise, for all files but the last, more prompts, with an
indication that it has reached the end of file, along with the name of
the next file. For the last file specified, or for the standard input
if no file is specified, more prompts, indicating end-fo-file, and
accept additional commands. If the next command specifies forward
scrolling, more will exit. If the -e option is specified, more will
exit immediately after writing the last line of the last file.

more uses the environment variable MORE to preset any flags desired.
The MORE variable thus sets a string containing flags and arguments,
preceded with hyphens and blank-character-separated as on the command
line. Any command-line flags or arguments are processed after those in
the MORE variable, as if the command line were as follows:

    more $MORE flags arguments

For example, to view files using the -c mode of operation, the shell
command sequence

    MORE='-c' ; export MORE or the csh command

    setenv MORE -c

causes all invocations of more, including invocations by programs such
as man and msgs, to use this mode. The command sequence that sets up
the MORE environment variable is usually placed in the .profile or
.cshrc file.

In the following descriptions, the current position refers to two
things:

- the position of the current line on the screen

- the line number (in the file) of the current line on the
  screen

The line on the screen corresponding to the current position is the
third line on the screen. If this is not possible (there are fewer
than three lines to display or this is the first page of the file, or
it is the last page of the file), then the current position is either
the first or last line on the screen.

Other sequences that can be typed when more pauses, and their effects,
are as follows (i is an optional integer argument, defaulting to 1):

    i<Return>
    ij
    i<Ctrl-e>
    i<Space>   Scroll forward i lines. The default i for <Space>
                    is one screenful; for j and <Return> it is one
                    line. The entire i lines are written, even if i is
                    more than the screen size. At end-of-file,
                    <Return> causes more to continue with the next
                    file in the list, or exits if the current file is
                    the last file in the list.

id i\<Ctrl-d\>	Scroll forward i lines, with a default of one half of the screen size. If i is specified, it becomes the new default for subsequent d and u commands.
iu i\<Ctrl-u\>	Scrolls backward i lines, with a default of one half of the screen size. If i is specified, it becomes the new default for subsequent d and u commands.
ik i\<Ctrl-y\>	Scrolls backward i lines, with a default of one line. The entire i lines are written, even if i is more than the screen size.
iz	Display i more lines and sets the new window (screenful) size to i .
ig	Go to line i in the file, with a default of 1 (beginning of file). Scroll or rewrite the screen so that the line is at the current position. If i is not specified, then more displays the first screenful in the file.
iG	Go to line i in the file, with a default of the end of the file. If i is not specified, scrolls or rewrites screen so that the last line in the file is at the bottom of the screen. If i is specified, scrolls or rewrites the screen so that the line is at the current position.
is	Skip forward i lines, with a default of 1, and write the next screenful beginning at that screenful point. If i would cause the current position to be such that less than one screenful would be written, the last screenful in the file is written.
if i\<Ctrl-f\>	Move forward i lines, with a default of one screenful. At end-of-file, more will continue with the next file in the list, or exit if the current file is the last file in the list.
ib i\<Ctrl-b\>	Move backward i lines, with a default of one screenful. If i is more than the screen size, only the final screenful will be written.
q, Q, :q, :Q, ZZ	Exit from more.
= :f \<Ctrl-g\>	Write the name of the file currently being examined, the number relative to the total number of files there are to examine, the current line number, the current byte number, and the total bytes to write and what percentage of the file precedes the current position. All of these items reference the first byte of the line after the last line written.
v	Invoke an editor to edit the current file being examined. The name of the editor is taken from the

environment variable EDITOR, or default to vi. If
EDITOR represents either vi or ex, the editor is
invoked with options such that the current editor
line is the physical line corresponding to the
current position in more at the time of the
invocation.

When the editor exits, more resumes on the current
file by rewriting the screen with the current line
as the current position.

h   Display a description of all the more commands.

i/[!]expression
                Search forward in the file for the i-th line
                containing the regular expression expression. The
                default value for i is 1. The search starts at the
                line following the current position. If the
                search is successful, the screen is modified so
                that the searched-for line is in the current
                position. The null regular expression (/<Return>)
                repeats the search using the previous regular
                expression. If the character ! is included, the
                lines for searching are those that do not contain
                expression.

                If there are less than i occurrences of
                expression, and the input is a file rather than a
                pipe, then the position in the file remains
                unchanged.

                The user's erase and kill characters can be used
                to edit the regular expression. Erasing back past
                the first column cancels the search command.

i?[!]expression
                Same as /, but searches backward in the file for
                the i th line containing the regular expression
                expression.

in   Repeat the previous search for the i-th line
                (default 1) containing the last expression (or not
                containing the last expression, if the previous
                search was /! or ?!).

iN   Repeat the search for the opposite direction of
                the previous search for the i-th line (default 1)
                containing the last expression

''   (single quotes) Return to the position from which
                the last large movement command was executed (
                "large movement" is defined as any movement of
                more than a screenful of lines). If no such
                movements have been made, return to the beginning
                of the file.

!command   Invoke a shell with command. The characters % and
                ! in command are replaced with the current file
                name and the previous shell command, respectively.
                If there is no current file name, % is not
                expanded. The sequences \% and \! are replaced by
                % and ! respectively.

:e [file]
E [file]   Examine a new file. If the file argument is not
                specified, the "current" file (see the :n and :p

commands) from the list of files in the command
line is re-examined. The filename is subjected to
the process of shell word expansions. If file is
a # (number sign) character, the previously
examined file is re-examined.

i:n   Examine the next file. If i is specified, examines
                the i-th next file specified in the command line.

i:p   Examine the previous file. If a number i is
                specified, examines the i-th previous file
                specified in the command line.

:t tagstring   Go to the supplied tagstring and scroll or rewrite
                the screen with that line in the current position.

m letter   Mark the current position with the specified
                letter, where letter represents the name of one of
                the lower-case letters of the portable character
                set.

' letter   Return to the position that was previously marked
                with the specified letter, making that line the
                current position.

r
<Ctrl-l>   Refresh the screen.

R   Refresh the screen, discarding any buffered input.

The commands take effect immediately; i.e., it is not necessary to
press <Return>. Up to the time when the command character itself is
given, the line-kill character can be used to cancel the numerical
argument being formed.

If the standard output is not a teletype, more is equivalent to
cat(1).

more supports the SIGWINCH signal, and redraws the screen in response
to window size changes.

EXTERNAL INFLUENCES
  Environment Variables
    COLUMNS   Overrides the system-selected horizontal screen size.

    EDITOR   Used by the v command to select an editor.

    LANG   Provides a default value for the internationalization
                    variables that are unset or null. If LANG is unset or
                    null, the default value of "C" (see lang(5)) is used.
                    If any of the internationalization variables contains
                    an invalid setting, more will behave as if all
                    internationalization variables are set to "C". See
                    environ(5).

    LC_ALL   If set to a non-empty string value, overrides the
                    values of all the other internationalization variables.

    LC_CTYPE   Determines the interpretation of text as single and/or
                    multi-byte characters, the classification of characters
                    as printable, and the characters matched by character
                    class expressions in regular expressions.

LC_MESSAGES   Determines the locale that should be used to affect the
                     format and contents of diagnostic messages written to
                     standard error and informative messages written to
                     standard output.

NLSPATH   Determines the location of message catalogues for the
                     processing of LC_MESSAGES.

LINES   Overrides the system-selected vertical screen size,
                     used as the number of lines in a screenful. The -n
                     option takes precedence over the LINES variable for
                     determining the number of lines in a screenful.

MORE   Determines a string containing options, preceded with
                     hyphens and blank-character-separated as on the command
                     line. Any command-line options are processed after
                     those in the MORE variable. The MORE variable takes
                     precedence over the TERM and LINES variables for
                     determining the number of lines in a screenful.

TERM   Determines the name of the terminal type.

International Code Set Support
Single- and multi-byte character code sets are supported.

EXAMPLES
To view a simple file, use:

    more filename

To preview nroff output, use a command resembling:

    nroff -mm +2 doc.n | more -s

If the file contains tables, use:

    tbl file | nroff -mm | col | more -s

To display file stuff in a fifteen line-window and convert multiple
adjacent blank lines into a single blank line:

    more -s -n 15 stuff

To examine each file with its last screenful:

    more -p G file1 file2

To examine each file starting with line 100 in the current position
(third line, so line 98 is the first line written):

    more -p 100g file1 file2

To examine the file that contains the tagstring tag with line 30 in
the current position:

    more -t tag -p 30g

WARNINGS
Standard error, file descriptor 2, is normally used for input during
interactive use and should not be redirected (see Input/Output section
in the manpage of the shell in use).

FILES
/usr/share/lib/terminfo/?/*   compiled terminal capability data base

AUTHOR
    more was developed by Mark Nudleman, University of California,
    Berkeley, OSF, and HP.

SEE ALSO
    csh(1), man(1), pg(1), sh(1), term(4), terminfo(4), environ(5),
    lang(5), regexp(5).

STANDARDS CONFORMANCE
    more: XPG4

mv

man page

mv - 3

mv - Move or rename files and directories.

```
mv(1)                                                                      mv(1)

NAME
     mv - move or rename files and directories

SYNOPSIS
     mv [-f|-i] [-e extarg] file1 new-file

     mv [-f|-i] [-e extarg] file1 [file2 ...] dest-directory

     mv [-f|-i] [-e extarg] directory1 [directory2 ...] dest-directory

DESCRIPTION
     The mv command moves:

          -  One file (file1) to a new or existing file (new-file).

          -  One or more files (file1, [file2, ...]) to an existing
             directory (dest-directory).

          -  One or more directory subtrees (directory1, [directory2, ...])
             to a new or existing directory (dest-directory).

     Moving file1 to new-file is used to rename a file within a directory
     or to relocate a file within a file system or across different file
     systems.  When the destination is a directory, one or more files are
     moved into that directory.  If two or more files are moved, the
     destination must be a directory.  When moving a single file to a new
     file, if new-file exists, its contents are destroyed.

     If the access permissions of the destination dest-directory or
     existing destination file new-file forbid writing, mv asks permission
     to overwrite the file.  This is done by printing the mode (see
     chmod(2) and Access Control Lists below), followed by the first
     letters of the words yes and no in the language of the current locale,
     prompting for a response, and reading one line from the standard
     input.  If the response is affirmative and the action is permissible,
     the operation occurs; if not, the command proceeds to the next source
     file, if any.

     If file1 is a file and new-file is a link to another file with other
     links, the other links remain and new-file becomes a new file.  If
     file1 is a file with links or a link to a file, the existing file or
     link remains intact, but the name is changed to new-file which may or
     may not be in the directory where file1 resided, depending on
     directory path names used in the mv command.  The last access and
     modification times of the file or files being moved remain unchanged.

     Options
     mv recognizes the following options:

          -f              Perform mv commands without prompting for
```

permission. This option is assumed when the
standard input is not a terminal.

-i   Causes mv to write a prompt to standard output
before moving a file that would overwrite an
existing file. If the response from the standard
input is affirmative, the file is moved if
permissions allow the move.

-e extarg   Specifies the handling of any extent attributes of
the files(s) to be moved. extarg can be one of
the following values:

warn   Issue a warning message if extent
attributes cannot be preserved,
but move the file anyway.

ignore   Do not preserve extent
attributes.

force   Do not move the file if the
extent attributes cannot be
preserved.

If multiple source files are
specified with a single target
directory, mv will move the files
that either do not have extent
attributes or that have extent
attributes that can be preserved.
mv will not move the files if it
cannot preserve their extent
attributes.

Extent attributes cannot be preserved if the
files are being moved to a file system that
does not support extent attributes or if that
file system has a different block size than
the original. If -e is not specified, the
default value for extarg is warn.

Access Control Lists (ACLs)
If optional ACL entries are associated with new-file, mv displays a
plus sign (+) after the access mode when asking permission to
overwrite the file.

If new-file is a new file, it inherits the access control list of
file1, altered to reflect any difference in ownership between the two
files (see acl(5)).

EXTERNAL INFLUENCES
Environment Variables
LC_CTYPE determines the interpretation of text as single byte and/or
multibyte characters.

LANG and LC_CTYPE determine the local language equivalent of y (for
yes/no queries).

LANG determines the language in which messages are displayed.

If LC_CTYPE is not specified in the environment or is set to the empty
string, the value of LANG is used as a default for each unspecified or
empty variable. If LANG is not specified or is set to the empty
string, a default of C (see lang(5)) is used instead of LANG. If any
internationalization variable contains an invalid setting, mv behaves
as if all internationalization variables are set to C. See

environ(5).

International Code Set Support
Single character and multibyte character code sets are supported.

EXAMPLES
Rename a file in the current directory:

        mv old-filename new-filename

Rename a directory in the current directory:

        mv old-dirname new-dirname

Rename a file in the current directory whose name starts with a
nonprinting control character or a character that is special to the
shell, such as - and * (extra care may be required depending on the
situation):

        mv ./bad-filename new-filename
        mv ./?bad-filename new-filename
        mv ./*bad-filename new-filename

Move directory sourcedir and its contents to a new location
(targetdir) in the file system (upon completion, a subdirectory named
sourcedir resides in directory targetdir):

        mv sourcedir targetdir

Move all files and directories (including links) in the current
directory to a new location underneath targetdir:

        mv * targetdir

Move all files and directories (including links) in sourcedir to a new
location underneath targetdir (sourcedir and targetdir are in separate
directory paths):

        mv sourcedir/* targetdir

WARNINGS
If file1 and new-file exist on different file systems, mv copies the
file and deletes the original. In this case the mover becomes the
owner and any linking relationship with other files is lost. mv
cannot carry hard links across file systems. If file1 is a directory,
mv copies the entire directory structure onto the destination file
system and deletes the original.

mv cannot be used to perform the following operations:

        - Rename either the current working directory or its parent
           directory using the . or .. notation.

        - Rename a directory to a new name identical to the name of a
           file contained in the same parent directory.

DEPENDENCIES
NFS
Access control lists of networked files are summarized (as returned in
st_mode by stat(2)), but not copied to the new file. When using mv on
such files, a + is not printed after the mode value when asking for
permission to overwrite a file.

AUTHOR
mv was developed by AT&T, the University of California, Berkeley and
HP.

SEE ALSO
cp(1), cpio(1), ln(1), rm(1), link(1M), lstat(2), readlink(2),
stat(2), symlink(2), symlink(4), acl(5).

STANDARDS CONFORMANCE
mv: SVID2, SVID3, XPG2, XPG3, XPG4, POSIX.2

pg

man page

pg - 3

pg - File viewing filter.

---

pg(1)   pg(1)

NAME
     pg - file perusal filter for soft-copy terminals

SYNOPSIS

     pg [-number] [-pstring] [-cefns] [+linenumber] [+/pattern] [file ...]

   Remarks
     pg and more are both used in similar situations (see more(1)). Text
     highlighting features supported by more are not available from pg.
     However, pg has some useful features not provided by more.

DESCRIPTION
     pg is a text file filter that allows the examination of files one
     screenful at a time on a soft-copy terminal. If - is used as a file
     argument, or pg detects NULL arguments in the comand line, the
     standard input is used. Each screenful is followed by a prompt. To
     display a new page, press Return. Other possibilities are enumerated
     below.

     This command is different from other paginators such as more in that
     it can back up for reviewing something that has already passed. The
     method for doing this is explained below.

     In order to determine terminal attributes, pg scans the terminfo data
     base for the terminal type specified by the environment variable TERM
     (see terminfo(4)). If TERM is not defined, terminal type dumb is
     assumed.

   Options
     pg recognizes the following command line options:

          -number   number is an integer specifying the size (in
                           lines) of the window that pg is to use instead of
                           the default (on a terminal containing 24 lines,
                           the default window size is 23).

          -p string   Causes pg to use string as the prompt. If the
                           prompt string contains a %d, the first occurrence
                           of %d in the prompt is replaced by the current
                           page number when the prompt is issued. The
                           default prompt string is a colon (:).

          -c   Home the cursor and clear the screen before
                           displaying each page. This option is ignored if
                           clear_screen is not defined in the terminfo data
                           base for this terminal type.

          -e   Causes pg to not pause at the end of each file.

          -f   Normally, pg splits lines longer than the screen width, but some sequences of characters in the text being displayed (such as escape sequences for underlining) generate undesirable results. The -f option inhibits pg from splitting lines.

-n   Normally, commands must be terminated by a new-line character. This option causes an automatic end-of-command as soon as a command letter is entered.

-s   Causes pg to print all messages and prompts in standout mode (usually inverse video).

+linenumber   Start display at linenumber.

+/pattern/   Start up at the first line containing text that matches the regular expression pattern.

pg looks in the environment variable PG to preset any flags desired. For example, if you prefer to view files using the -c mode of operation, the Bourne-shell command sequence PG='-c' ; export PG or the C-shell command setenv PG -c causes all invocations of pg, including invocations by programs such as man and msgs, to use this mode. The command sequence to set up the PG environment variable is normally placed in the user .profile or .cshrc file.

The responses that can be typed when pg pauses can be divided into three categories: those causing further perusal, those that search, and those that modify the perusal environment.

Commands that cause further perusal normally take a preceding address, an optionally signed number indicating the point from which further text should be displayed. This address is interpreted either in pages or lines, depending on the command. A signed address specifies a point relative to the current page or line; an unsigned address specifies an address relative to the beginning of the file. Each command has a default address that is used if none is provided.

Perusal commands and their defaults are as follows:

(+1)<newline> or <blank>
                Displays one page. The address is specified in pages.

(+1) l   With a relative address, pg simulates scrolling the screen, forward or backward, the number of lines specified. With an absolute address pg prints a screenful beginning at the specified line.

(+1) d or ^D   Simulates scrolling a half-screen forward or backward.

The following perusal commands take no address:

. or ^L   Typing a single period causes the current page of text to be redisplayed.

$ Displays the last windowful in the file. Use with caution when the input is a pipe.

The following commands are available for searching for text patterns in the text. The Basic Regular Expression syntax (see regexp(5)) is supported. Regular expressions must always be terminated by a new-line character, even if the -n option is specified.

i/pattern/   Search forward for the ith (default i=1) occurrence of pattern. Searching begins immediately after the current page and continues to the end of the current file, without wrap-around.

i^pattern^
i?pattern?   Search backwards for the ith (default i=1) occurrence of pattern. Searching begins immediately before the current page and continues to the beginning of the current file, without wrap-around. The ^ notation is useful for Adds 100 terminals which cannot properly handle the ?.

After searching, pg normally displays the line found at the top of the screen. This can be modified by appending m or b to the search command to leave the line found in the middle or at the bottom of the window from now on. The suffix t can be used to restore the original situation.

pg users can modify the perusal environment with the following commands:

in   Begin perusing the ith next file in the command line. The i is an unsigned number, default value is 1.

ip   Begin perusing the ith previous file in the command line. i is an unsigned number, default is 1.

iw   Display another window of text. If i is present, set the window size to i.

s filename   Save the input in the named file. Only the current file being perused is saved. The white space between the s and filename is optional. This command must always be terminated by a new-line character, even if the -n option is specified.

h   Help by displaying an abbreviated summary of available commands.

q or Q   Quit pg.

!command   command is passed to the shell, whose name is taken from the SHELL environment variable. If this is not available, the default shell is used. This command must always be terminated by a new-line character, even if the -n option is specified.

To cause pg to stop sending output and display the prompt at any time when output is being sent to the terminal, press the quit key (normally Ctrl-\) or the interrupt (break) key. Any one of the above commands can then be entered in the normal manner. Unfortunately, some output is lost when this is done, due to the fact that any characters waiting in the terminal's output queue are flushed when the quit signal occurs.

If the standard output is not a terminal, pg is functionally equivalent to cat (see cat(1)), except that a header is printed before each file if more than one file is specified.

EXTERNAL INFLUENCES

Environment Variables
LC_COLLATE determines the collating sequence used in evaluating
regular expressions.

LC_CTYPE determines the interpretation of text as single and/or
multi-byte characters, and the characters matched by character class
expressions in regular expressions.

LANG determines the language in which messages are displayed.

If LC_COLLATE or LC_CTYPE is not specified in the environment or is
set to the empty string, the value of LANG is used as a default for
each unspecified or empty variable. If LANG is not specified or is
set to the empty string, a default of "C" (see lang(5)) is used
instead of LANG. If any internationalization variable contains an
invalid setting, pg behaves as if all internationalization variables
are set to "C". See environ(5).

International Code Set Support
Single- and multi-byte character code sets are supported.

EXAMPLEs
To use pg when reading system news:

    news | pg -p "(Page %d):"

WARNINGS
If terminal tabs are not set every eight positions, undesirable
results may occur.

When using pg as a filter with another command that changes the
terminal I/O options (such as crypt(1)), terminal settings may not be
restored correctly.

While waiting for terminal input, pg responds to BREAK, DEL, and ^ by
terminating execution. Between prompts, however, these signals
interrupt pg's current task and place the user in prompt mode. These
should be used with caution when input is being read from a pipe,
because an interrupt is likely to terminate the other commands in the
pipeline.

Users of more will find that the z and f commands are available, and
that the terminal /, ^, or ? can be omitted from the pattern search
commands.

FILES
/usr/share/lib/terminfo/?/*   terminal information data base

/tmp/pg*   temporary file when input is
                                         from a pipe

SEE ALSO
crypt(1), grep(1), more(1), terminfo(4), environ(5), lang(5),
regexp(5).

STANDARDS CONFORMANCE
pg: SVID2, SVID3, XPG2, XPG3

pwd

pwd - Present working directory name.

---

pwd(1)   pwd(1)

NAME
        pwd - working directory name

SYNOPSIS

        pwd

DESCRIPTION
        pwd prints the path name of the working (current) directory.

EXTERNAL INFLUENCES
    Environment Variables
        LC_MESSAGES determines the language in which messages are displayed.

        If LC_MESSAGES is not specified in the environment or is set to the
        empty string, the value of LANG is used as a default for each
        unspecified or empty variable. If LANG is not specified or is set to
        the empty string, a default of "C" (see lang(5)) is used instead of
        LANG.

        If any internationalization variable contains an invalid setting, pwd
        behaves as if all internationalization variables are set to "C". See
        environ(5).

    International Code Set Support
        Single- and multi-byte character code sets are supported.

DIAGNOSTICS
        Cannot open ..

        Read error in ..
                Possible file system trouble; contact system administrator.

        pwd: cannot access parent directories
                Current directory has been removed (usually by a different
                process). Use cd command to move to a valid directory (see
                cd(1)).

EXAMPLES
        This command lists the path of the current working directory. If your
        home directory were /mnt/staff and the command cd camp/nevada were
        executed from the home directory, typing pwd would produce the
        following:

                /mnt/staff/camp/nevada

AUTHOR
        pwd was developed by AT&T and HP.

SEE ALSO
        cd(1).

STANDARDS CONFORMANCE
    pwd: SVID2, SVID3, XPG2, XPG3, XPG4, POSIX.2

rm

man page

rm - 3

rm - Remove files or directories.

rm(1)   rm(1)

NAME
      rm - remove files or directories

SYNOPSIS

      rm [-f|-i] [-Rr] file ...

DESCRIPTION
      The rm command removes the entries for one or more files from a
      directory. If an entry was the last link to the file, the file is
      destroyed. Removal of a file requires write and search (execute)
      permission in its directory, but no permissions on the file itself.
      However, if the sticky bit is set on the directory containing the
      file, only the owner of the file, the owner of the directory, or a
      user having appropriate privileges can remove the file.

      If a user does not have write permission for a file to be removed and
      standard input is a terminal, a prompt containing the file name and
      its permissions is printed requesting that the removal of the file be
      confirmed (see Access Control Lists below). A line is then read from
      standard input. If that line begins with y the file is deleted;
      otherwise, the file remains. No questions are asked when the -f
      option is given or if standard input is not a terminal.

      If file is of type directory, and the -f option is not specified, and
      either the permissions of file do not permit writing and standard
      input is a terminal or the -i option is specified, rm writes a prompt
      to standard error and reads a line from standard input. If the
      response does not begin with y, it does nothing more with the current
      file and goes on to any remaining files.

   Options
      rm recognizes the following options:

            -f   Force each file or directory to be removed without prompting
                  for confirmation, regardless of the permissions of the
                  entry. This option also suppresses diagnostic messages
                  regarding nonexistent operands.

                  This option does not suppress any diagnostic messages other
                  than those regarding nonexistent operands. To suppress all
                  error message and interactive prompts, the -f option should
                  be used while redirecting standard error output to
                  /dev/null.

                  This option ignores any previous occurrence of the -i
                  option.

            -i   Write a prompt to standard error requesting confirmation
                  before removing each entry.

This option ignores any previous occurrence of the -f
option.

-R   For each argument that is a directory, this option causes rm
      to recursively delete the entire contents of that directory
      before removing the directory itself. When used in
      conjunction with the -i option, rm asks whether to examine
      each directory before interactively removing files in that
      directory and again afterward to confirm removing the
      directory itself.

      The -R option will descend to arbitrary depths in a file
      hierarchy and will not fail due to path length limitations
      unless the length of file name, file specified by the user
      exceeds system limitations.

-r   Equivalent to -R.

Access Control Lists
    If a file has optional ACL entries, rm displays a plus sign (+) after
    the file's permissions. The permissions shown summarize the file's
    st_mode value returned by stat() (see stat(2)). See also acl(5).

EXTERNAL INFLUENCES
    Environment Variables
    LANG provides a default value for the internationalization variables
    that are unset or null. If LANG is unset or null, the default value of
    "C" (see lang(5)) is used. If any of the internationalization
    variables contains an invalid setting, rm will behave as if all
    internationalization variables are set to "C". See environ(5).

    LC_ALL If set to a non-empty string value, overrides the values of all
    the other internationalization variables.

    LC_CTYPE determines the interpretation of file names as single and/or
    multi-byte characters, the classification of characters as printable,
    and the characters matched by character class expressions in regular
    expressions.

    LC_MESSAGES determines the locale that should be used to affect the
    format and contents of diagnostic messages written to standard error
    and informative messages written to standard output.

    NLSPATH determines the location of message catalogues for the
    processing of LC_MESSAGES.

    International Code Set Support
    Single- and multibyte character code sets are supported.

DIAGNOSTICS
    Generally self-explanatory. Note that the -f option does not suppress
    all diagnostic messages.

    It is forbidden to remove the file .., in order to avoid the
    consequences of using a command such as:

        rm -r .*

    If a designated file is a directory, an error comment is printed
    unless the -R or -r option is used.

EXAMPLES
    Remove files with a prompt for verification:

        rm -i file1 file2

Remove all the files in a directory:

```
rm -i mydirectory/*
```

Note that the previous command removes files only, and does not remove any directories in mydirectory.

Remove a file in the current directory whose name starts with - or * or some other character that is special to the shell:

```
rm ./-filename
rm \*filename
etc.
```

Remove a file in the current directory whose name starts with some strange (usually nonprinting, invisible) character or perhaps has spaces at the beginning or end of the filename, prompting for confirmation:

```
rm -i *filename*
```

If *filename* is not unique in the directory, enter n when each of the other files is prompted.

A powerful and dangerous command to remove a directory is:

```
rm -fR directoryname
```

or

```
rm -Rf directoryname
```

which removes all files and directories from directoryname without any prompting for verification to remove the files or the directories. This command should only be used when you are absolutely certain that all the files and directories in directoryname as well as directoryname itself are to be removed.

DEPENDENCIES
  NFS
    rm does not display a plus sign (+) to indicate the existence of optional access control list entries when asking for confirmation before removing a networked file.

SEE ALSO
    rmdir(1), unlink(2), acl(5).

STANDARDS CONFORMANCE
    rm: SVID2, SVID3, XPG2, XPG3, XPG4, POSIX.2

rmdir

rmdir - Remove directories.

man page

rmdir - 3

```
rmdir(1)                                                          rmdir(1)

NAME
     rmdir - remove directories

SYNOPSIS

     rmdir [-f|-i] [-p] dir ...

DESCRIPTION
     rmdir removes the directory entry for each dir operand that refers to
     an empty directory.

     Directories are removed in the order specified.  Consequently, if a
     directory and a subdirectory of that directory are both specified as
     arguments, the subdirectory must be specified before the parent
     directory so that the parent directory will be empty when rmdir tries
     to remove it.  Removal of a directory requires write and search
     (execute) permission in its parent directory, but no permissions on
     the directory itself; but if the sticky bit is set on the parent
     directory, only the owner of the directory, the owner of the parent
     directory, or a user having appropriate privileges can remove the
     directory.

   Options
     rmdir recognizes the following options:

           -f   Force each directory to be removed without prompting for
                confirmation, regardless of the presence of the -i option.
                This option also suppresses diagnostic messages regarding
                non-existent operands.

                This option does not suppress any diagnostic messages other
                than those regarding non-existent operands.  To suppress all
                error message and interactive prompts, the -f option should
                be used while redirecting the standard error output to
                /dev/null.

                This option ignores any previous occurrence of the -i
                option.

           -i   Write a prompt to the standard error output requesting
                confirmation before removing each directory.

                This option ignores any previous occurrence of the -f
                option.

           -p   Path removal.  If, after removing a directory with more than
                one pathname component, the parent directory of that
                directory is now empty, rmdir removes the empty parent
                directory.  This continues until rmdir encounters a non-
                empty parent directory, or until all components of the
```

original pathname have been removed.

When used in conjunction with the -i option, rmdir asks whether to remove each directory component of a path.

EXTERNAL INFLUENCES

Environment Variables

LANG provides a default value for the internationalization variables that are unset or null. If LANG is unset or null, the default value of "C" (see lang(5)) is used. If any of the internationalization variables contains an invalid setting, rmdir will behave as if all internationalization variables are set to "C". See environ(5).

LC_ALL If set to a non-empty string value, overrides the values of all the other internationalization variables.

LC_CTYPE determines the interpretation of dir names as single and/or multi-byte characters, the classification of characters as printable, and the characters matched by character class expressions in regular expressions.

LC_MESSAGES determines the locale that should be used to affect the format and contents of diagnostic messages written to standard error and informative messages written to standard output.

NLSPATH determines the location of message catalogues for the processing of LC_MESSAGES.

International Code Set Support

Single- and multi-byte character code sets are supported.

DIAGNOSTICS

Generally self-explanatory. Note that the -f option does not suppress all diagnostic messages.

EXAMPLES

To remove directories with a prompt for verification:

        rmdir -i directories

To remove as much as possible of a path, type:

        rmdir -p component1/component2/dir

SEE ALSO

rm(1), rmdir(2), stat(2).

STANDARDS CONFORMANCE

rmdir: SVID2, XPG2, XPG3, XPG4

split

split - Split a file into multiple files.

man page

split - 3

    split(1)   split(1)

    NAME
         split - split a file into pieces

    SYNOPSIS
         split [-l line_count] [-a suffix_length] [file [name]]

         split [-b n[k|m]] [-a suffix_length] [file [name]]

         Obsolescent:
         split [-n] [file [name]]

    DESCRIPTION
         split reads file and writes it in pieces (default 1000 lines) onto a
         set of output files. The name of the first output file is name with
         aa appended, and so on lexicographically, up to zz (only ASCII letters
         are used, a maximum of 676 files). If no output name is given, x is
         the default.

         If no input file is given, or if - is given instead, the standard
         input file is used.

    OPTIONS
         split recognizes the following command-line options and arguments:

              -l line_count The input file is split into pieces line_count
                             lines in size.

              -a suffix_length
                             suffix_length letters are used to form the suffix
                             of the output filenames. This option allows
                             creation of more than 676 output files. The
                             output file names created cannot exceed the
                             maximum file name length allowed in the directory
                             containing the files.

              -b n   The input file is split into pieces n bytes in
                             size.

              -b nk   The input file is split into pieces n * 1024 bytes
                             in size. No space separates the n from the k.

              -b nm   The input file is split into pieces n * 1048576
                             bytes in size. No space separates the n from the
                             m.

              -n   The input file is split into pieces n lines in
                             size. This option is obsolescent and is
                             equivalent to using the -l line_count option.

    EXTERNAL INFLUENCES

Environment Variables
    LC_CTYPE determines the locale for the interpretation of text as
    single- and/or multi-byte characters.

    LC_MESSAGES determines the language in which messages are displayed.

    If LC_CTYPE or LC_MESSAGES is not specified in the environment or is
    set to the empty string, the value of LANG is used as a default for
    each unspecified or empty variable. If LANG is not specified or is
    set to the empty string, a default of "C" (see lang(5)) is used
    instead of LANG.

    If any internationalization variable contains an invalid setting,
    split behaves as if all internationalization variables are set to "C".
    See environ(5).

International Code Set Support
    Single- and multi-byte character code sets are supported.

SEE ALSO
    bfs(1), csplit(1).

STANDARDS CONFORMANCE
    split: SVID2, SVID3, XPG2, XPG3, XPG4, POSIX.2

tail

tail - Produce the last part of a file.

man page

tail - 3

```
tail(1)                                                             tail(1)

NAME
     tail - deliver the last part of a file

SYNOPSIS

     tail [-f] [-b number] [file]
     tail [-f] [-c number] [file]
     tail [-f] [-n number] [file]

  Obsolescent:
     tail [+-[number][l|b|c] [-f] [file]

DESCRIPTION
     tail copies the named file to the standard output beginning at a
     designated place.  If no file is named, standard input is used.

  Command Forms
     tail can be used in three forms as indicated above:

          tail -b number...    Copy file starting at number blocks from
                               end or beginning of file.

          tail -c number...    Copy file starting at number bytes from end
                               or beginning of file.

          tail -n number...
             or
          tail number...       Copy file starting at number lines from end
                               or beginning of file.

     tail with no options specified is equivalent to tail -n 10....

  Options and Command-Line Arguments
     tail recognizes the following options and command-line arguments:

          -f                   Follow option.  If the input file is a regular
                               file or if file specifies a FIFO, do not terminate
                               after the last line of the input file has been
                               copied, but read and copy further bytes from the
                               input file when they become available (tail enters
                               an endless loop wherein it sleeps for one second
                               then attempts to read and copy further records
                               from the input file).  This is useful when
                               monitoring text being written to a file by another
                               process.  If no file argument is specified and the
                               input is a pipe (FIFO), the -f option is ignored.


          number               Decimal integer indicating quantity of output to
                               be copied, measured in units specified by
                               accompanying option.  If number is preceded by a +
```

character, copy operation starts number units from beginning of file. If number is preceded by a - character or the option name, copy operation starts number units from end of file. If number is not preceded by a b, c, or n option, -n is assumed. If both the option and number are not specified, -n 10 is assumed.

-b number   Copy file beginning number 512-byte blocks from end or beginning of file. If number is not specified, -b 10 is assumed. See number description above.

-c number   Copy file beginning number bytes from end or beginning of file. If number is not specified, -c 10 is assumed. See number description above.

-n number   Copy file beginning number lines from end or beginning of file. If number is not specified, -n 10 is assumed. See number description above.

file   Name of file to be copied. If not specified, the standard input is used.

If the -c option is specified, the input file can contain arbitrary data. Otherwise, the input file should be a text file.

Obsolescent Form
In the obsolescent form, option letters can be concatenated after the number argument to select blocks, bytes, or lines. If this syntax is used, +-number must be the first argument given. If number is not specified, -10 is assumed. This version is provided for backward compatibility only. The forms discussed previously are recommended for portability.

EXTERNAL INFLUENCES
Environment Variables
LC_CTYPE determines the locale for the interpretation of sequences of bytes of text data as characters (e.g., single- versus multibyte characters in arguments and input files).

LC_MESSAGES determines the language in which messages are displayed.

If LC_CTYPE or LC_MESSAGES is not specified in the environment or is set to the empty string, the value of LANG is used as a default for each unspecified or empty variable. If LANG is not specified or is set to the empty string, a default of "C" (see lang(5)) is used instead of LANG.

If any internationalization variable contains an invalid setting, tail behaves as if all internationalization variables are set to "C". See environ(5).

International Code Set Support
Single- and multi-byte character code sets are supported. However, the b and c options can break multi-byte characters and should be used with caution in a multi-byte locale environment.

EXAMPLES
Print the last three lines in file file1 to the standard output, and leave tail in ``follow'' mode:

```
tail -fn 3 file1
    or
tail -3 -f file1
```

Print the last 15 bytes of file logfile followed by any lines that are appended to logfile after tail is initiated until it is killed:

```
tail -fc15 logfile
   or
tail -f -c 15 logfile
```

Three ways to print an entire file:

```
tail -b +1 file
tail -c +1 file
tail -n +1 file
```

WARNINGS
Tails relative to end-of-file are stored in a 20-Kbyte buffer, and thus are limited in length. Therefore, be wary of the results when piping output from other commands into tail.

Various kinds of anomalous behavior may occur with character special files.

SEE ALSO
dd(1), head(1).

STANDARDS CONFORMANCE
tail: SVID2, SVID3, XPG2, XPG3, XPG4, POSIX.2

CHAPTER 4

Common Desktop Environment

The Common Desktop Environment (CDE) represents the effort of major UNIX vendors to unify UNIX at the desktop level. CDE is widely used by X terminal and workstation users on many UNIX systems, including IBM's AIX systems, Hewlett Packard's HP-UX systems, and Sun Microsystems' Solaris systems. This chapter provides an introduction to CDE: basics of CDE's look and feel, making changes to the CDE environment, and a bit of background about the X, Motif, and CDE relationships. CDE versions used to write this chapter are: AIX CDE 1.0, HP-UX CDE 2.1.0, and Solaris CDE 1.3. Newer releases will have enhanced features, but in general, they should still work the same.

Several features make it easy to customize CDE. The style manager, which every user has access to, makes it easy to customize CDE on an individual user basis. Sooner or later, however, you may want to provide some common denominator of CDE functionality for your users. If, for instance, you have an application that most users will run, you can set up environment variables, prepare pull-down menus, provide suitable fonts, etc., that will make your users more productive. Users can then perform additional customizations such as defining file manager characteristics and selecting backgrounds.

To help you thoroughly understand CDE, I'll cover the following topics:

1. Why a Graphical User Interface (GUI)?

2. CDE Basics

3. Customizing CDE

4. CDE - Advanced Topics

   •The Relationship among X, Motif, and CDE

   •X, Motif, and CDE Configuration Files

   •The Sequence of Events When CDE Starts

   •CDE and Performance

First I'll provide you with the reasoning behind providing a graphical interface rather than the more common, but also more cumbersome, line by line terminal interface. An overview of the CDE desktop workspaces follows. This is divided into two sections: AIX and HP-UX (because they are so similar) and Solaris. Each will give an overview of the front panel features. Next I'll guide you through making some CDE customizations. These customizations will give you a working basis for making more advanced changes on your own. I'll show you how to make some basic, simple changes, and then more complex changes, ending with modifying the login screen with a new logo and new welcome messages. Last, I'll delve into the more advanced topics of X, Motif, and CDE relationships, configuration file usage and location, what happens internally when CDE starts up, and some CDE performance tips.

Why a Graphical User Interface (GUI)?

For computers to be used on every desktop, they had to be made easier to use. A new method of accessing computer power was required, one that avoided the command-line prompt, didn't require users to memorize complex commands, and didn't require a working knowledge of technological infrastructures such as networking. Not that this information was unimportant; far from it. The information was both too important and too specialized to be of use to the average worker-bee computer user. A knowledge of their applications was all that was important for these users. After all, so the reasoning goes, to drive a car, one doesn't have to be a mechanic, so why should a computer user have to understand computer technology? The graphical user interface (GUI) makes computers accessible to the application end-user.

Figure 4-1 illustrates the relationship among the computer hardware, the operating system, and the graphical user interface. The computer is the hardware platform on the bottom. The operating system, the next layer up, represents a character-based user interface. To control the computer at this level, users must type commands at the keyboard. The next several layers, beginning with the X Window System, represent the graphical user interface. To control the computer at these levels, users manipulate graphical controls with a mouse.

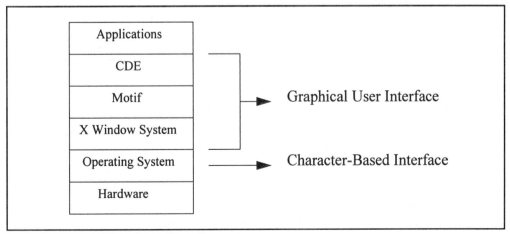

Figure 4-1 User Interface Components

GUIs replaced memorization with exploration. A user could now use pull-down menus, push buttons, sliding scroll bars, and other direct manipulation to use a computer. Typing operating system commands to perform a function is greatly reduced. With a GUI, to use a computer is both easier to learn and easier to use.

While fairly inexpensive in terms of dollars (CDE is bundled "free" with the operating system), GUIs are not without cost in terms of RAM usage and performance. Despite this performance expense, GUIs have become a permanent part of the computing environment. The benefits of their utility are worth the cost.

Beyond the graphical controls that reduce training, make mundane tasks simpler to do, and generally ease the stress of using a computer, two other benefits of GUIs are worth mentioning: multiple windows per display and client-server topology.

The benefit of multiple windows that GUIs provide is that each window (literally a rectangular area surrounded by a window frame) contains a separate application. The user can work with multiple windows open. CDE goes one step further: its multiple workspaces allow users to separate application windows by task into specific workspaces. For instance, in a workspace named "Mail," users may have application windows showing the list of incoming electronic mail, a mail message they are currently reading, and a message they are composing for later transmission. In another workspace called "Financials," they could be working on several spreadsheets, each in its own window.

Client-server topology enables the computing resources spread around a network to be accessed efficiently to meet computing needs. In a client-server topology, powerful computers on the network are dedicated to a specific purpose (file management on a file server and running applications on an application server). Users working on less powerful client computers elsewhere on the network access the files or applications remotely. A file server reduces system administration by centralizing file backup, enabling the system administrator to back up only the file server, not each individual client computer. This setup also ensures that files will be backed up at regular intervals. An application server reduces operating costs by reducing the number and size of storage disks required and the size of RAM required on each client computer. A single version of an application resides and runs on the application server and is accessed by multiple users throughout the network.

Although this topology sounds complicated, the CDE GUI makes it easy. To access a file, users "drag and drop" a file icon from the file manager window. To start an application, users double-click the application icon. To print a file, users drag the file to the icon of the appropriate printer in the front panel and drop it there. Users don't have to know where these files and applications are, what directories they are in, what computers they are on, or how they are accessed. The underlying infrastructure and control you have put in place, along with the power of the GUI, allow users to concentrate on their work and not on the mechanics of their computer.

CDE Basics

Because most systems come with a set of CDE user guides, I'm only going to give an overview of what CDE looks like and the main areas we will be working with when we do some customizations. Along the way, I'll point out similarities and differences among the different flavors of CDE.

The CDE login screen presents you with several choices before you even log in. Under the area where you enter your user name are four buttons: **OK**, **Start Over**, **Options**, and **Help**. **OK** is just the same as pressing *Enter* when you enter your login and then password. The **Start Over** button clears your user login and allow you to start over. **Options** provides you with some initial session configuration that would need to be made before you log in. **Language** allows you to change your default language. Suppose that you need to test your company's software in another language. Assuming that the proper language is preloaded on your system, you can swap between the languages for testing by simply choosing CDE to come up in a different language. **Session** allows you to choose to come up in the CDE desktop session or into a **Failsafe** session, which is an X session but without the CDE desktop. Solaris also has options to log in to their

OpenWindow Desktop or into the **User's Last Desktop**. **Command Line Login** allows you to log in without CDE being invoked. This would be just a regular terminal mode session. **Reset Login Screen** does just what its name suggests. And **Help** lists all these features with a brief description of each.

The login screen itself displays a CDE logo, an operating system logo such as AIX, or possibly your company's logo. A welcome message appears along with a place to enter your user login. After entering your user name, you are prompted for your password. Once entered and verified as correct, CDE is started and the desktop is displayed. On Solaris systems, the first time you log in, you are presented with a choice as to whether you want to log into CDE or OpenWindows Desktop.

The CDE desktop is comprised of four desktop workspaces and a front panel shared by each. The front panel is an easy-to-use interface to various applications, commands, and tools. The various components are easily accessed by the simple point-and-click method. Front panel components are a collection of objects, subpanels, and access to desktop workspaces. Some objects are used only to display items such as the clock, whereas others when clicked either bring up an application, such as the calendar or dtmail, or perform an action, such as the lock or the exit action icons. Subpanels pop up a menu of objects that can be accessed. These objects can also simply display items or bring up applications. By default, on AIX and HP-UX, you see Personal Printer subpanels, Personal Applications subpanels, and Help subpanels. On Solaris, all panels contain subpanels. Subpanels can be added to the other panels on AIX and HP-UX as you see in the next section "Customizing CDE." You can tell that these have subpanels, because they each have a little arrow above the panel where you click to pop it up. In the center of the front panel are four workspaces. These provide areas to perform related tasks, enabling the user to separate work and not clutter up the desktop.

CDE on AIX and HP-UX is very similar and, in general, what is displayed on the front panel on one is the same as on the other. Solaris, however, while retaining the basic CDE look and feel, has greatly expanded on what is included on the default front panel and the subpanels behind it. I'm going to give an overview of CDE as found on HP-UX and AIX first. Then I'll point out the Solaris enhancements to CDE.

CDE as Found on AIX and HP-UX

The front panel is divided into 11 main areas: 5 panels, 1 work-spaces area, and 5 more panels. I'll give an overview of each area from left to right, beginning with the Clock and ending with the Trash Can, as shown in Figure 4-2.

Figure 4-2 Front Panel

Clock - As you would expect, this displays the current time.

Calendar - The Calendar icon displays the current date and when clicked brings up an appointment calendar. The calendar allows you to set appointments and reminders and to create a task list. Appointments can be set as a one-time-only event or as recurring. You can be notified of an appointment by a beep, a pop-up message, or an e-mail. The calendar and associated appointments can be displayed by the day, the week, or the month. A yearly calendar can also be displayed, but without appointments.

File Manager - The File Manager opens a window that displays your home directory and associated files. From here, you can do any number of basic file manipulations, such as copy a file, move a file, delete a file, or execute a program or script. More infrequently used operations, such as creating a symbolic link or changing file permissions or ownership, can also be done here. Removing a file from within File Manager moves it to the Trash Can rather than permanently deleting the file. This way, if you decide that you need it back, you can simply retrieve it from the Trash Can rather than having it restored from a backup - a more time-consuming operating. However, note that the Trash Can is automatically 'emptied' at the end of every session. So when you log off, the files are permanently removed.

Personal Application - The Personal Application subpanel contains the CDE's text editor, **dtpad,** and terminal emulator, **dtterm**. It also contains the Icon Editor. The **dtpad** is an easy-to-use full-screen text editor. As in a PC-based word processor, **dtpad** allows you to move the cursor anywhere to add, change, and delete text, unlike the popular **vi**, which is a line-by-line text editor. CDE's dtterm is a good basic terminal emulator. The Icon Editor opens bitmap (.bm) or pixmap (.pm) files and allows you to edit them.

The Personal Application subpanel is the first place we find the Install Icon application. This is where new icons are added to the subpanel. This allows the application associated with the icon to be executed when the icon is double clicked. We'll be using this when we modify the desktop in "Customizing CDE."

Mail - The CDE mailer, **dtmail**, is invoked when this icon is clicked. From here, mail messages can be composed, messages replied to, and messages forwarded. Most advanced mail features that you've come to think of as basic features are included: items such as adding attachments to messages, replying to just the sender or all recipients, and setting automatic messages saying that you're on vacation. Another feature is when a new message arrives, the *dtmail* icon changes to show a letter popping into the mailbox.

Workspace Area - The next four items comprise the workspace area.

Lock Button - The Lock button allows you to lock your session while you're away from your desk. This security feature keeps others from viewing or accessing your work when you're not there. And it saves you from logging off and on every time you need to step away.

Your login password, or root's password, must be entered to unlock it again.

Workspace Switch - Four in number, these are the separate workspaces created by default. These allow you to organize your work so that your workspace doesn't get cluttered up. By using the workspaces, you can keep work on different tasks, applications, or systems separated from each other. You change from one workspace to another simply by clicking on the workspace number: One, Two, Three, or Four. You'll notice that no matter what workspace you are in, the Front Panel follows you. In "Customizing CDE," you'll see how easy you can increase the number of workspaces and to change the names.

Activity Light - The Activity light, quite simply, blinks when the system is busy doing work.

Exit button - The Exit button is where you log out of CDE, terminating your CDE session. Upon exiting, depending on how you have CDE configured, you are prompted to resume your current session or return to your home session. If you choose to resume your current session, the next time you login, the desktop looks exactly the same is it does when you log out - as closely as possible. Some things, such as remote logins, are not possible, but others are, such as having an application automatically executed. If you choose to return to your home session, the next time you log in, you are returned to a known, preset configuration. This configuration is set in the Style Manager panel, discussed shortly.

Personal Printers - This subpanel contains printers that you have configured on your system, including the default printer designated as such and the Print Manager. The front panel icon is that of the default printer. To print one of your documents, simply drag it from the File Manager and drop it on the printer icon. The Print Manager allows you to view queued print files and remove them before they print. However, this works only with printers directly managed by your system. In today's networked offices, printers are usually shared and the print manager function is on a server probably in the next building.

Style Manager - The Style Manager is one of those places where you can either get really creative getting your desktop to look just like you want or waste a lot of time - depending on your point of view. Here is where you personalize your login to the system to your own preferences. You can change your font size, your background, your mouse speed, and whether or not your session automatically locks after a certain amount of non-activity, or idle time. This is where you can set your home session, as referred to earlier, to come back to every time you log in or set your system to return to the current session or choose the option of being asked every time you log out. One other configuration you can make here is whether your window focus follows your mouse or whether you have to click on a window before it is the active window. On AIX systems, you can toggle on or off whether the workspaces are displayed on the front panel.

Application Manager - When opened, the Application Manager displays folders with useful applications and actions. Although they differ among manufacturers and even operating systems for that matter, AIX, HP-UX, and Solaris all have some basic features: Desktop Applications, Desktop Tools, Information, and System Administration. Desktop Applications contains such applications and tools as Calculator, Man Page Viewer, Icon Editor, and Create Action. Desktop Tools includes tools like xterm, xwd capture, compress files, and reload resources. System Administration contains operating-system-specific applications such as SAM in HP-UX, SMIT in AIX, and Admintool in Solaris, besides more generic actions such as change password. Take the time to look around here. You'll find many items you may want to incorporate on your customized CDE front panel. I, for one, have found the Man Page Viewer to be an invaluable friend and moved it to my front panel, where it can be readily accessed.

Help - The Help subpanel is a compilation of the Help Manager, a Desktop Introduction, Front Panel help, and an On-Item Front Panel help mechanism. The Help Manager is the main online help facility for CDE. This is a comprehensive help system with topic trees and the ability to search the index using keywords or pattern matching, backtrack where you've been in the help manager, and view the history of items for which you requested help. The Desktop Introduction is an overview of CDE and how it works. The Front Panel help facility gives information about how to use the front panel icons, subpanels, and workspaces. The On-Item Front Panel help mechanism allows you to click on the front panel item about which you wish assistance. Along with the Help Subpanel, Help can also be requested by pressing the F1 function key. If installed on your system, AIX may also include Basic Desktop Customization help and Base Library.

Trash Can - The Trash Can, used with the File Manager, holds files and folders that you have deleted during the current session. Using the facility allows you to quickly retrieve files that you should not have removed. The Trash Can can be 'emptied' at any time to permanently remove items. Also, the Trash Can is 'emptied' when you log out of your session.

CDE as Found on Solaris

As mentioned earlier, Solaris has embellished CDE, adding many more subpanels and items to the subpanels, as shown in Figure 4-3. Where Solaris has greatly changed the panel and subpanels, I'll give an overview of what you'll find, as I did in the previous section on AIX and HP-UX. Where they are the same, I'll simply note that they are the same.

Figure 4-3 Front Panel

Like AIX and HP-UX, Solaris' front panel is divided into 11 main areas: 5 panels, 1 workspaces area, and 5 more panels. I'll give an overview of each area from left to right, beginning with the World and ending with the Trash Can.

Links - As you might guess by the World icon, this is where you access the world. Solaris' web browser, HotJava, lives here. There are also actions included to access Personal Bookmarks for the web browser, and a Find Web Page search engine. As indicated on the front panel icon, the world has a clock on it, too.

Cards - The calendar is the same as on AIX and HP-UX. However, included in the subpanel is Find Card, which is a rolodex-type address manager.

Files - Although the title is slightly different, this is where file manager resides. In the subpanel are special icons to perform file actions associated with: Properties, Encryption, Compress File, Archive, and Find File. Solaris has also included actions to manage your floppy disk drive and CD-ROM.

Applications - Renamed simply Applications, here is where you'll not only find the Text Editor, but also Text Note and Voice Note. For the audio enabled, Voice Note allows you to play, record, or save audio files with WAV, AU, and AIFF formats. On this subpanel, you'll also find the Applications subpanel found under Application Manager on the AIX and HP-UX systems. As on the others, this includes Desktop Applications, Desktop Tools, Information, and System Administration. These are basically the same on all systems.

Mail - This subpanel, in addition to *dtmail*, has been enhanced to include a Suggestion Box. A very clever idea, this automatically opens up a message, pre-addressed to Sun Microsystems, Inc., so that you can send them your suggestions.

Workspace Area - The next five items comprise the workspace area.

Lock button - Same as on AIX and HP-UX.

Workspace switch - Same as on AIX and HP-UX.

Progress Indicator - This is the same as the Busy Indicator on AIX and HP-UX.

Exit button - Same as on AIX and HP-UX.

Personal Printers - Same as on AIX and HP-UX.

Tools - The Style Manager is located here and is displayed on the front panel. You'll also find easy access to the CDE errorlog, and Find Process allows you to view all processes running on your system and kill selected ones. The Customized Workspace Menu and Add Item to Menu actions allow you to easily modify the Workspace Menu. The Workspace Menu is accessed by placing the mouse over a blank area of the desktop and pressing the right mouse key. Whereas AIX and HP-UX come with a generic menu, Solaris has incorporated the front panel and subpanel actions into the Workspace Menu as another way to access these actions.

Hosts - Here Solaris differs greatly from AIX and HP-UX. The Hosts subpanel contains system-related actions. On the front panel you'll find the Performance Monitor icons indicating how busy your CPU and disk drives are. From the subpanel, this Host opens up the *dtterm* terminal emulator, and Console opens up a *dtterm* specifically for displaying console messages. System Information provides system information including system name, hardware model, network IP address and domain, physical and virtual memory, operating system version, and date and time last rebooted. Find Host is the same as Find Card in the Cards subpanel.

Help - Same as on AIX and HP-UX.

Trash - The Trash Can is the same, with the addition of a sub-panel icon to 'empty' the Trash Can.

This concludes the overview of the look and feel of CDE. Armed with this knowledge, you can easily navigate around your desktop environment with confidence and ease. Next, you'll learn how to change that look and feel to conform to your work environment.

Customizing CDE

Before you modify any CDE configuration files, first develop a strategy. I know that I've mentioned this before, but it's important enough to mention again.

The following questions should get you started:

1. What are your users' needs?

2. Which of those needs can be met by reconfiguring CDE?

3. At what level should these changes be made (system-wide, groups of users, individual users only)?

4. Which CDE files do you need to modify (names and locations)?

5. What are the changes and what is their order within the file?

It's also a good idea to have handy a binder containing man pages for each of the CDE components (for looking up resources and their values) and a copy of each of the CDE configuration files.

Now that you have a good understanding as to how CDE works, I'll lead you through making changes and customizing the system for either the entire user community or each individual user.

I'll precede each change with a discussion of what is involved with making the change. I'll be making some basic, simple changes and some more advanced changes to show you how versatile CDE can be.

One thing I need to mention is that all these changes can be made on any system. And knowing how to do these tasks "the hard way" increases your understanding of what these tools are doing for you in the background. So be sure to give each one a try.

Changes Using Style Manager

Font Size

When we first log in to CDE and the workspace comes up, as shown in Figure 4-4, one of the first things many users change is the size of the font. Initially set to 4, most users want a bigger font. This change is easy.

Figure 4-4 Style Manager

1. **Click on the Style Manager icon** on the front panel. This action brings up the Style Manager.

2. **Click on Font.**

3. **Highlight 5**.

4. **Click on OK**.

Backdrop and Colors

The Style Manager is also where we can change the backdrop and colors:

1. **Click on Backdrop** and we are presented with a variety of backdrop choices.

2. After we see one we like, such as Pebbles, we can **click on apply** and then **click on close** to change our backdrop. Notice, however, that this action changes the backdrop only for the workspace that we are in.

To change the other workspaces, we can either go to them and bring up the Style Manager in that workspace or, because we already have Style Manager up, we can click in the top right corner on the little "-" on the window itself above "File" and access the pull-down menu. From here, we can choose Occupy All Workspaces. Then we can simply go to the other workspaces, and Style Manager is already up and ready for us there. The Backdrop area is the only place we have to worry about moving to other workspaces.

3. To change colors, **click on the Color icon**. We are given a list of different color schemes from which to choose. And if one isn't quite to our liking, we can easily modify the color, hue, brightness, and contrast. We can even grab a color from somewhere else, such as an image off the Internet, to include in the color scheme. Once we have the colors we like, we can save the scheme with its own name.

Adding Objects to or Removing Objects from the Front Panel

The front panel can make life just a little easier for us by putting frequently used items on it. One of the most frequent actions is opening up a terminal window. And although CDE comes with dtterm as the default terminal window, we sometimes might want to use an xterm window. We'll add it to the Personal Applications subpanel, where dtterm lives on AIX and HP-UX systems. Solaris users can do the same by putting the xterm on the Hosts subpanel, where the This Host terminal emulator lives.

You have two ways to add objects to the CDE front panel:

- Drag and drop them into a slideup subpanel and then make them the default for that subpanel.

- Modify the **/etc/dt/appconfig/types/C/dtwm.fp** configuration file. This approach will be used later when we create actions and file types.

The basic actions to add a control button through drag and drop are as follows:

•Drag the application icon you want as a front panel button from an application manager view and drop the icon onto the installation section (the top section) of the appropriate subpanel.

•Place the mouse pointer over the icon and press mouse button 3 to display the subpanel menu.

• Select Copy to Main Panel.

1. **Click on the up arrow** of the Personal Applications subpanel on AIX or HP-UX or on the Hosts subpanel on Solaris so that it pops up.

2. **Click on the Application Manage**r icon, where Desktop Applications and Desktop Tools live.

3. **Double click on Desktop_Tools**. Here you find **Xterm**.

4. **Drag and drop the Xterm** icon from Desktop_Tools to the Install Icon box at the top of the Personal Applications subpanel on HP-UX and AIX, or Hosts on Solaris.

Now if we want **xterm** to be on the front panel:

1. **Right click on the Xterm** icon in the Personal Applications or Hosts subpanel.

2. **Select Copy to Main Panel** or **Promote to Front Panel** depending on which CDE you are using.

Adding Another Workspace

Another easy change to the front panel is to add another workspace. CDE comes with a default of four workspaces, but this is easy to change. We'll add one more and call it "Web View." This can be the window where we'll access the Internet.

1. **Place the mouse in the Workspace area of the front panel** and **press the right mouse button**.

2. **Select Add Workspace** from the pull-down menu. The work-space "New" has been added.

3. **Right click on the new workspace labeled "New"** and select **Rename**. **Type Web View** and **press Return**.

If we want to delete a Workspace, simply right click on the Workspace to be removed and then select delete.

Making these kinds of changes is easy, and they help personalize the workspace for the individual user.

Changing the Front Panel in Other Ways

In addition to adding or removing buttons, you can shape the front panel in other ways. These other ways use workspace manager resources to modify default values. The following resources relate to the front panel:

- **clientTimeoutInterval** - Length of time the busy light blinks and the pointer remains an hourglass when a client is started from the front panel.

- **geometry** - x and y coordinate location of the front panel.

- **highResFontList** - Font to use on a high-resolution display.

- **lowResFontList** - Font to use on a low-resolution display.

- **mediumResFontList** - Font to use on a medium-resolution display.

- **name** - Name of the front panel to use when multiple front panels are in **dtwm.fp**.

- **pushButtonClickTime** - Time interval distinguishing two single mouse clicks from a double click (to avoid double launching an application accidently).

- **waitingBlinkRate** - Blink rate of the front-panel busy light.

- **workspaceList** - List of workspace names.

- **title** - Title to appear on a workspace button.

Like all other workspace manager resources, these front-panel resources have the following syntax:

```
Dtwm*screen*resource: value
```

For example, suppose instead of the default four workspaces, all that your users need a front panel with six workspaces named Mail, Reports, Travel, Financials, Projects, and Studio. Further, they prefer a large font and have decided upon New Century Schoolbook 10-point bold. As system administrator, you'd make everyone happy with the following resource specifications:

```
Dtwm*0*workspaceList: One Two Three Four Five Six
Dtwm*0*One*title: Mail
Dtwm*0*Two*title: Reports
Dtwm*0*Three*title: Travel
Dtwm*0*Four*title: Financials
Dtwm*0*Five*title: Projects
Dtwm*0*Six*title: Studio
Dtwm*0*highResFontList:
          -adobe-new century schoolbook-bold-r-normal\
          --10-100-75-75-p-66-iso8859-1
```

The screen designation is usually 0, except for displays capable of both image and overlay planes. The order of screens in the **X*screens** file is what determines the screen number; the first screen, typically the image plane, is designated as 0. Note also the inclusion of workspace names (One, Two, Three, Four, Five, and Six) in the six title resource specifications.

These changes can be added to the **sys.resources** file, which is discussed in detail in "Advanced Topics" later in this chapter. These changes can also be made by use of the **EditResources** action to insert the new resource lines into each user's **RESOURCE_MANAGER** property and then restart the workspace manager.

The obvious disadvantage is that you have to physically go to each user's work area and take over the machine for a few minutes. However, on the plus side, the changes are immediate and are automatically saved in the correct **dt.resources** for users who restore their current session. You also avoid having your changes overwritten, which could happen if you modify the right **dt.resources** file at the wrong time, while the user is still logged in.

Modifying Things in Slideup Subpanels

Subpanels are defined in **dtwm.fp** after the front panel and front-panel control definitions. To associate a subpanel with a front panel control button, the front-panel control name is listed as the container name in the subpanel definition.

Note: **/etc/dt** is where global changes are made. **$HOME/.dt** is where local or individual user changes are made.

To add a slideup subpanel to the front panel follow these steps:

1. Copy the file **/usr/dt/appconfig/types/C/dtwm.fp** to **/etc/dt/ appconfig/types/C/dtwm.fp**   or   to   **$HOME/.dt/types/ dtwm.fp**.

2. Decide which control button with which the slideup is to be associated.

3. Create the subpanel definition file in **dtwm.fp**. This will take the following form:

```
SUBPANEL    SubPanelName
{
CONTAINER_NAME   AssociatedFrontPanelControlButton
TITLE   SubPanelTitle
}
```

4. Create subpanel control definitions for the subpanel. These will take the following form:

```
CONTROL   ControlName
{
TYPE   icon
CONTAINER_NAME    SubPanelName
CONTAINER_TYPE    SUBPANEL
ICON   BitmapName
PUSH_ACTION    ActionName
}
```

As with front panel control buttons, it's easier to copy and modify an existing subpanel file than to start from scratch.

Changing the Default Printer Name Display

We'll can make an easy change to one of the slideup subpanels. If we pop up the Personal Printers subpanel, it shows that we have a default printer configured, but not the name of it. Let's go back into the front panel file, **dtwm.fp**, and change that.

man page

vi - 8

1. Bring up your favorite editor, such as **dtpad** or **vi**, and **edit /$HOME/.dt/types/dtwm.fp**.

2. Scroll down to CONTROL Printer. You'll see that the LABEL is Default. **Change** or add to that the name of your default printer. My printer is called a464.

LABEL   Default - a464

3. **Save the file** and **restart Workspace Manager**. Position the mouse over a blank area on your workspace and press the right mouse button. Select Restart Workspace Manager. On Solaris, press the right mouse button to bring up the Custom-

ized Workspace Menu. From here, select Windows, where you'll find the Restart Workspace Manager key.

Pop up the Personal Printers subpanel and now we can see what our default printer really is. Of course, if we change the default, we'll have to change the front panel again. But we know how to do that now, don't we! Figure 4-5 shows the Front Panel.

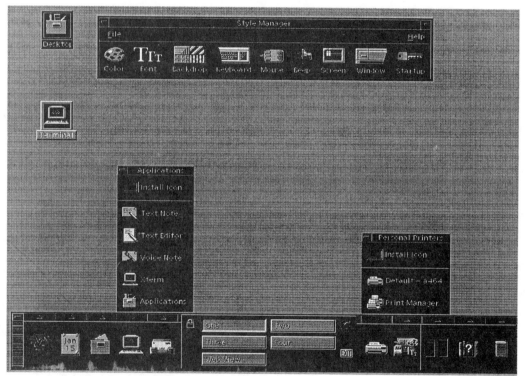

Figure 4-5 Front Panel with Changes

Front Panel Animation

Animation for front-panel or slideup-subpanel drop zones is created by displaying a progressive series of bitmaps. By convention, the bitmaps are in **/usr/dt/appconfig/icons**. The list of bitmaps to display is contained in animation definitions at the end of **dtwm.fp**.

To create an animation sequence for a drop zone:

1. Create a progressive series of bitmaps.

2. Add a list of these bitmap files to the appropriate configuration file using the following syntax:

```
ANIMATION AnimationName
{
 bitmap0
 bitmap1
 bitmap2
 bitmap3
 bitmap4
 bitmap5
}
```

3. Add a line to the appropriate control definition using the syntax:

```
DROP_ANIMATION AnimationName
```

Adding Things to the Workspace Menu

The workspace menu is defined in the **sys.dtwmrc** file. As mentioned in the overview of the front panel for Solaris, the Workspace Menu is accessed by placing the mouse over a blank area of the desktop and pressing the right mouse key. Where AIX and HP-UX come with a generic menu, Solaris has incorporated the front-panel and subpanel actions into the Workspace Menu as another way to access these actions. However, we can create customized Workspace Menu for all three systems using the left mouse key to access it. We'll be doing this task next.

A workspace menu can contain frequently used commands and applications. The customized menu is usually accessed by pressing the left mouse button, which pops up the menu for viewing and selection. A workspace menu comes in handy for those who have a set number of things they do regularly. For instance, a programmer who

uses **C++**, **vi**, and **isql** may have a menu with those items, or a system administrator may have a menu with **df**, **ps -ef**, and **netstat** on it. Or those on an expansive network may want a menu of system logins.

For one or two changes, you can modify the existing workspace menu. For major changes, it's probably easier to insert an entirely new menu definition in **sys.dtwmrc**.

A menu definition has the following syntax:

```
Menu MenuName
{
  "Menu Name"         f.title
  "Frame"             f.exec /nfs/system1/usr/frame/bin/maker
  "Second Item"       action
  "Third Item"        action
}
```

The first line specifies the menu name, following the keyword **Menu**. The lines between the curly braces list the items that appear in the menu in their order of appearance; thus the first line is the title as designated by the function **f.title**. The second line is an example of a definition that would start **FrameMaker** from a remote application server in a distributed environment. Numerous other functions exist, approximately 45 in all. For a complete list, see the **dtwmrc** (4) man page.

For users to display the menu, you need to bind the menu definition to a mouse button and a screen location using the action **f.menu MenuName**. For example, if your users want to post the menu by pressing mouse button 3 when the pointer is on the workspace background, you would insert the following line in the Mouse Button Bindings Description section at the end of **sys.dtwmrc**:

```
<Btn3Down> root f.menu MenuName
```

(Actually, it would be easier to modify the line that's already there by exchanging **MenuName** for **DtRootMenu** on the second line.)

Now, we'll create a simple menu. Our menu is going to include running FrameMaker, running the **vi** editor, and logging into a remote system.

1. First we need a copy of the **/usr/dt/config/C/sys.dtwmrc** file to **/etc/dt/config/C**:

cp /usr/dt/config/C/sys.dtwmrc /etc/dt/config/C/sys.dtwmrc

If we were going to make this a local change for one user only, it would be copied to **/$HOME/.dt** and renamed **dtwmrc**. For the admin1 user, that would be **/home/admin1/.dt/dtwmrc** or on Solaris in **/home/admin1/.dt/C/dtwmrc**.

2. Go into our favorite editor and **modify the file**. We're going to add our new menu just after the DtRootMenu entry, which we see on our system as the left mouse button's "Workspace Menu." Add the following:

```
Menu AdminMenu
{
  "Admin1's Menu"        f.title
  "Frame Maker"          f.exec  "/nfs/system1/usr/frame/bin/maker"
  "VI Editor"            f.exec  "xterm -e /usr/bin/vi"
  "Login systemA"        f.exec  "xterm -geometry 80x50+830+0 -sl 200 -bg
DarkOrchid4 -fg white -n SYSTEMA -T SYSTEMA -e remsh systemA &"
}
```

The **f.title** function shows that this is the menu title. **f.exec** means to execute the following string. Notice that FrameMaker does not need a terminal window, because it uses its own, whereas **vi** and the login both need a terminal window in which to run. Also, I embellished on the **xterm** for the login, making the terminal window very large, with lots of terminal memory, and using specific colors.

Now, let's restart the Workspace Manager and try out our new menu.

3. Position the mouse over a blank area on the workspace and press the left mouse button. Select **Restart Workspace Manager**.

Creating pull-down menus is easy and can easily be expanded on by adding sub-menus to the menu. Just make the function **f.menu** followed by the menu name. We would add the following just after "Admin1's Menu":

```
"Work Menu"        f.menu   WorkMenu''

And then after the } from the Menu AdminMenu section, add:
Menu WorkMenu
{
.
}
```

Performing these advanced functions really isn't so hard. The hardest part is remembering which directories to put the files in: **/etc/dt** for global changes or **$HOME/.dt** for individual changes.

Creating Control Buttons, Actions, and File Types

An action starts a process such as a shell script or an application. An action can be connected to a front-panel button to start when the button is pushed. An action can be connected to a front-panel drop zone to be performed when a data file is dropped on the drop zone. An action can be associated with an icon in a file manager window so tht the action can be started by double clicking the icon. An action can be associated with a particular data type so that double clicking the data file icon starts the action and opens the data file.

In addition to setting up a front panel and default session to meet your users needs, the single most important thing you can do to make computing life easier for the people who depend on you is to create actions and data types.

CDE actions and data types are defined in files that end in **.dt**. Similar to most other CDE configuration files, ***.dt** files have a system-wide version that can be copied into a user's personal directory and customized for personal use. Most system-wide ***.dt** files are found in **/usr/dt/appconfig/types/C**; personal ***.dt** files are created by copying **user-prefs.dt** from **/usr/dt/appconfig/types/C** to **$HOME/ .dt/types**.

The default search path that CDE uses to look for actions and file types includes the following main directories in the order listed:

- $HOME/.dt/types

- /etc/dt/appconfig/types

- /usr/dt/appconfig/types

You can add further directories to the search path using the **DTDATABASESEARCHPATH** environment variable. Insert this environment variable and the new search path into **/etc/dt/config/ Xsession** for a system-wide influence. Insert the environment variable and search path into **$HOME/.dtprofile** for individual users.

Control Buttons - The basic control definition has six parts:

- **CONTROL name** - The definition name. This is the only part of the definition outside the curly braces.

- **TYPE** - The type of control. Several types exist. The most useful for customizing the front panel are probably blank and icon. A blank is useful as a space holder. An icon can start an action or application or be a drop zone.

- **ICON** - The bitmap to display on the front panel. Front-panel bitmaps are located in the **/usr/dt/appconfig/icons** directory.

- **CONTAINER_NAME** - The name of the container that holds the control. This must correspond to the name of an actual container listed in **dtwm.fp**.

- **CONTAINER_TYPE** - The type of container that holds the control. This can be **BOX**, **SWITCH**, or **SUBPANEL**, but it must agree with the type of the container name.

- **PUSH_ACTION** - This is what happens when the control button is pushed. **PUSH_ACTION** is just one of several possible actions. For more information, see the **dtwm** man page.

To remove a control button from the front panel, type a pound sign (#) in the leftmost column of the **CONTROL** definition line. The (#) turns the control specification into a comment line.

Add a control button by editing the **dtwm.fp** file:

1. Copy **dtwm.fp** from **/usr/dt/appconfig/types/C** to **/etc/dt/ appconfig/types/C**.

2. Add the new control definition using the following format:

```
CONTROL NewControl
{
TYPE            icon
CONTAINER_NAME  Top
CONTAINER_TYPE  BOX
ICON            NewControlBitmap
PUSH_ACTION     NewControlExecutable
}
```

Action and File Types have their own peculiarities in that each has a couple of parts, and each must live in its own directory location. This peculiarity will be come clear as we create an action on the sub-panel. The following are the recommended locations in which to create an action or file type definition:

- Create a completely new file in the **/etc/dt/appconfig/types** directory. This file has a system-wide influence. Remember, the file must end with the **.dt** extension.

- Copy **user-prefs.dt** from **/usr/dt/appconfig/types** to the **/etc/ dt/appconfig/types** directory and insert the definition there for system-wide use.

- Copy **user-prefs.vf** to **$HOME/.dt/types** and insert the definition there for individual users.

A typical action has the following syntax:

```
ACTION      ActionName
{
  TYPE      type
```

```
  keyword    value
  keyword    value
}
```

For example, here's a FrameMaker action:

```
ACTION     FRAME
{
  TYPE       COMMAND
  WINDOW-TYPE NO-STDIO
  EXEC-STRING /nfs/hpcvxmk6/usr/frame/bin/maker
}
```

A typical data type has the following syntax:

```
DATA_ATTRIBUTES          AttributesName
{
  keyword        value
  keyword        value
  ACTIONS        action, action
}
DATA_CRITERIA
{
 DATA_ATTRIBUTES AttributesName
 keyword         value
 keyword         value
}
```

Note that all definitions have the following general syntax:

```
KEYWORD value
```

Notice that a data type definition is actually in two parts, an attribute part and a criteria part. The attribute portion of the data type definition specifies the look of the datatype; the criteria portion specifies the behavior of the data type.

For example, here's a file type for FrameMaker files that uses the FRAME action:

```
DATA_ATTRIBUTES      FRAME_Docs
{
  DESCRIPTION        This file type is for FrameMaker documents.
  ICON               makerIcon
  ACTIONS            FRAME
}
DATA_CRITERIA
{
DATA_ATTRIBUTES_NAME   FRAME_Docs
NAME_PATTERN   *.fm
MODE    f
}
```

You can create actions and file types from scratch using these formats. However, the easiest way to create an action is to use the **CreateAction** tool. **CreateAction** is located in the Desktop Applications folder of the Applications Manager and presents you with a fill-in-the-blank dialog box that guides you through creating an **action.dt** file containing the action definition. You can then move this file to the appropriate directory for the range of influence you want the action to have: **/etc/dt/appconfig/types** for a system-wide influence; **$HOME/ .dt/types** for individual users.

Creating a New Icon and Action

Creating an icon is a challenging thing. We could use the Icon Editor found in Desktop_Apps to create a new icon, or we could find a picture we like and use it. One thing to be careful of when pulling in a picture, in order for it to be seen correctly on the front panel, is that it has to be no larger than 32x32 pixels or only a portion of the icon will be displayed. Viewing the picture in the Icon Editor shows you the size of the picture. You may want to search through the application directories for useful icons or pull one down from the Internet.

For this entire example, I'm going to use the Instant Information software that comes with HP-UX. This is the manual set on CD. Other application software will work just as well; just make sure that your paths correspond with the software you are using instead. Also, I'm going to use a fictitious user's home directory: **/home/admin1**.

1. **Bring up the Icon Editor** from the Desktop_Apps (HP-UX), Desktoptools (AIX), or from the Desktop_Tools, on Solaris all in the Application Manager.

2. Choose **File -> Open**.

3. Enter a path or folder name: **/opt/dynatext/data/bitmaps**.

4. Enter the file name: **logoicon.bm**

5. Choose **Open**.

We'll see the icon and that it is indeed 32x32. Now we need to save the icon to our own **.dt** directory.

6. Choose **File -> Save As**.

7. Enter path or folder name: **/$HOME/.dt/icons**. For the admin1 user, that would be in **/home/admin1/.dt/icons**.

If we were going to do this task globally, we'd put this in **/etc/ dt/appconfig/types/C**.

8. Leave the file name as is.

9. **Save**.

Now that we have the icon, we need to create an action file and a description file to go with it.

1. **Using your favorite Text Editor**, enter the following:

```
ACTION instinfo
{
LABEL           instinfo
TYPE            COMMAND
```

```
WINDOW_TYPE    NO_STDIO
EXEC_STRING    /opt/dynatext/bin/dynatext
DESCRIPTION    This action starts Instant Information
}
```

The LABEL is the name of the action, the TYPE is a command, the WINDOW_TYPE is none (no standard I/O or NO_STDIO) because the application has its own window, EXEC_STRING is the command to be executed, and the DESCRIPTION is just a description of what this action does. Make sure that the NO_STDIO has an under-score and not a dash, and don't forget the last }. I've done both of these and then had fun trying to figure out why the action either didn't appear to exist or, if it did appear, why it wouldn't work.

2. **Save this file as /$HOME/.dt/types/instinfo.dt**. For the admin1 user, that would be **/home/admin1/.dt/types/ instinfo.dt**. If this were a global configuration, we'd save the file as **/etc/dt/appconfig/types/C/instinfo.dt**.

Now that we have an action, we need to create a description file. Note that this is a new file with just these 2 lines in it. The contents of this file are irrelevant, but the permissions *must* include executable.

3. Again, **using your favorite editor**, enter:

```
ACTION instinfo
DESCRIPTION  This action starts Instant Information
```

4. **Save this file as /$HOME/.dt/appmanager/instinfo**. For the admin1 user, that would be **/home/admin1/.dt/appmanager/ instinfo**. If this were a global configuration, we'd save the file as   **/etc/dt/appconfig/appmanager/instinfo**.

5. Change the permissions to include execute as follows:

chmod 555 /$HOME/.dt/appmanager/instinfo

Now it's time to modify the front panel to include the icon and action we just created. The front panel file, **dtwm.fp**, is located in the **/usr/dt/appconfig/types/C** directory. Because don't want to overwrite the system file, we need to copy it locally and then modify it for our use.

1. Copy this to **/$HOME/.dt/types/dtwm.fp** for AIX and HP-UX and to **/$HOME/.dt/types/fp-dynamic/dtwm.fp** for Solaris. For the admin1 user, that would be:

man page

cp - 3

cp /usr/dt/appconfig/types/C/dtwm.fp   /home/admin1/.dt/types/dtwm.fp

or on Solaris:

cp /usr/dt/appconfig/types/C/dtwm.fp   /home/admin1/.dt/types/fp-dynamic/dtwm.fp

2. **Using your favorite edito**r, modify the local **dtwm.fp** file.

As we look at the file, we notice that it is in the same order as the front panel is displayed. The clock is the first CONTROL in the file and the first item on the front panel. Also notice that the POSITION_HINTS is 1. Date is next and so is POSITION_HINTS 2. What we want to do is put our new icon and action after POSITION_HINTS 4, the TextEditor CONTROL.

3. Go down just past the } ending CONTROL TextEditor and before CONTROL Mail. At this point, **insert the following exactly as shown below**. Make sure that the uppercase letters are capitalized and the lowercase letters aren't.

```
CONTROL  Info
{
  TYPE                icon
  CONTAINER_NAME      Top
  CONTAINER_TYPE       BOX
  POSITION_HINTS      5
  ICON                logoicon.bm
  LABEL               Instant Info
  PUSH_ACTION         instinfo
}
```

4. Now be careful; this part is tricky. The next items have to have their POSITION_HINTS renumbered. But we are going to **renumber only the next eight items, beginning with Mail and ending with Trash**. Instead of 5 through 12, these are going to become 6 through 13.

5. **Save** the file.

Now, let's restart the Workspace Manager. If we did everything right, we'll have a new icon, which, when clicked, will bring up Instant Information shown in Figure 4-6.

6. Position the mouse over a blank area on the workspace and press the right mouse button. Select **Restart Workspace Manager**.

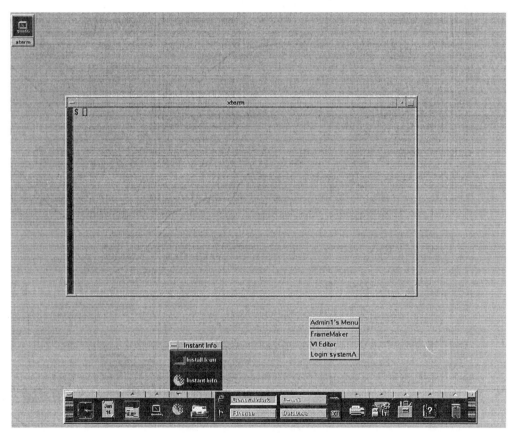

Figure 4-6 Workspace Menu and New Subpanel and Action

A couple of things to remember when creating actions: first and foremost, make sure the PUSH_ACTION and the file names are the same. That similarity is how they find each other. Make sure the that action file ends with **.dt** and make sure that the description file is executable. If any of these are wrong, the action either won't work or won't show up.

To avoid a lot of typing, sometimes the easiest approach is just to copy an existing definition and insert it where you want your new control to be and then modify it. As you move down the list of control definitions, you're moving from left to right across the front panel (notice that the POSITION_HINTS value increases in each definition). So if you want your new control to be to the right of the date on the front panel, you insert the control on the line below "date" and add a POSITION_HINTS 3 line to your definition; if you wanted your new control to be to the left of "date," insert the control on the line above "date" with a POSITION_HINTS of 1.

The new control definition can be located anywhere in the list of control definitions. The POSITION_HINTS line keeps it from getting inadvertently bumped to a new position. It's still a good idea to copy an existing definition and avoid extra typing; it reduces the chance of typing mistakes. And don't forget to include the curly braces.

Using Different Fonts

Although CDE fonts have been carefully selected for readability, you may have valid reasons to prefer other fonts. To make your fonts available system-wide throughout the CDE environment, put them in **/etc/dt/app-defaults/Dtstyle** so that they will appear in the style manager's font dialog box. To make fonts available only for a particular X client application, specify the font in the **app-defaults** file for the application. Just remember, this overrides the fonts in the style manager.

The font dialog box can contain a maximum of seven font sizes. You can adjust this number downward by resetting the value of **Dtstyle*NumFonts** in **/etc/dt/app-defaults/Dtstyle**; however, you can't increase the number higher than seven.

The Font Dialog section of the **Dtstyle** configuration file has seven **SystemFont** resources and seven **UserFont** resources. Again, you can have fewer than seven system and seven user fonts, but you can't have more.

To specify fonts for a particular application, use the ***FontList** resource in the **app-defaults** file for the application.

To modify font resources on an individual-user basis, you can use the **EditResources** action as described in the earalier section "Changing the Front Panel in Other Ways."

Changing the Login Messages

One of the nice things about CDE is the ability to modify so many parts. You can customize individual login accounts or the entire system. By customizing the login screen, you can show those about to log in the name of the system they are accessing, the company logo, and a personalized greeting. These modifications take place in the **Xresources** file:

1. As we've done already with the **dtwm.fp** and **dtwmrc** files, we will need to copy the system file from **/usr/dt/config/C** to **/etc/dt/config/C**.

man page

cp - 3

cp /usr/dt/config/C/Xresources   /etc/dt/config/C/Xresources

2. **Go into your favorite editor** and bring up the **Xresources** file so that it can be edited.

3. **Go to the GREETING area**. Here we'll find the following lines:

!!Dtlogin*greeting.labelString: Welcome to %LocalHost%
!!Dtlogin*greetingpersLabelString: Welcome %s

The first line is the message on the initial login screen. Let's change that so that it welcomes us to our company, ABC, Inc.:

1. **Remove the comment notations**. Unlike shell scripts that most of us are used to, the Xresources file uses two exclamation points as comment notation. Remove the !!.

2. Next, **modify "Welcome to %LocalHost%"**. The %Local-Host% variable is replaced with our system name in the login screen. The line should look like this:

Dtlogin*greeting.labelString: ABC, Inc, Welcomes You to %LocalHost%

3. Next let's **change the second line** to include the department that this system is dedicated to: finance. This second line shows what is displayed when we are prompted for our password. The %s variable is our user name. The line should now look like this:

Dtlogin*greetingpersLabelString: The Finance Department Welcomes %s

4. **Save the file**.

5. **Now log out and back in**. We should see the changes in the login screen. We didn't need to "reload" the file, because the act of logging out and back in does that action.

Changing the Login Picture

Adding a new picture to the login screen is easy if you know one thing. The file has to be a bitmap (.bm) or pixmap (.pm) file. A bitmap file is black and white, and the pixmap file is color. I've tried using other kinds of pictures (.gif and .jpg formats), but they just don't display. The good news is that these can be imported from other systems or the Internet for our use. To make things simple, we're going to use one already on the system. A bitmap showing a birthday cake was found in **/usr/lib/X11/bitmaps** on an HP-UX workstation. However, I have also successfully pulled down pictures of flowers, the Grand

Canyon, and country music singers from the Internet and put them on my system login screen.

1. Once more, let's go into our favorite editor and modify **/etc/dt/config/C/Xresources**.

2. **Go to the MISC area**. Here we'll find the following lines:

!!Dtlogin*logo*bitmapFile: < bitmap or pixmap file >

3. **Delete the leading !!**, which are the comment designators.

4. **Replace < bitmap or pixmap file >** with the name of the bitmap file using the entire path location. The line should look as follows:

Dtlogin*logo*bitmapFile: /usr/lib/X11/bitmap/cake.bm

5. **Save the file.**

6. **Now log out and back in**. We should see the birthday cake in the login screen. Again, we didn't need to "reload" the file, because the act of logging out and back in does that task.

Now that we've seen how easily we can make some simple customizations in CDE for our end users, we should be able to take this knowledge and really make their CDE environments a productive and friendly place to work.

CDE - Advanced Topics

The Relationship among X, Motif, and CDE

X, OSF/Motif, and CDE are enabling framework technologies. Taken together, X, Motif, and CDE make up the three graphical layers on top of the operating system and the hardware platform.

The GUI layers provide increasingly richer ease-of-use functions in a progressive series of layers that buffer the end user from the "user-hostile," character-based interface of the operating system layer.

The X Window System

The X Window System consists of the following:

- Xlib - Low-level library for programming window manipulation; graphics capabilities such as line drawing and text placement; controlling display output, mouse, and keyboard input; and application network transparency.

- Xt Intrinsics - Higher-level library for programming widgets and gadgets (graphical controls components like menus, scrollbars, and push buttons).

- Display servers - Hardware-specific programs, one per display, that manage the graphical input and output.

- Interclient communication conventions (ICCC) - A manual specifying standards for how X client programs should communicate with each other.

- Configuration files - One configuration file that specifies the default session to start (**sys.x11start**) and another specifying values for resources used to shape the X environment (**sys.Xdefaults**).

Through these mechanisms, X provides the standard upon which the graphical part of the network-oriented, client/server, distributed computing paradigm is based. A knowledge of **Xlib** and the **Xt** Intrinsics is important for programming in X and for programming at the Motif level. For system administrators, however, as long as the display servers work and X client applications are ICCC-compliant, you shouldn't need to delve into the X layer. CDE enables you to view X pretty much as part of "all that underlying technological infrastructure stuff" and focus on developing appropriate configurations of CDE to meet your users' work context.

Motif

Motif consists of the following:

- mwm window manager - Executable program that provides Motif-based window frames, window management, and a workspace menu in the X environment.

- Motif widget toolkit - Higher-level library of widgets and gadgets, the graphical components used to control the user environment.

- Motif style guide - A manual defining the Motif appearance and behavior for programmers.

- Configuration files - The **system.mwmrc** file containing configuration information for the workspace menu and key and button bindings. Resources for the window manager are in **mwm** in the **/usr/lib/X11/app-defaults** directory.

Motif provides the window manager for the end user, the widget toolkit for application developers, and the style guide to help developers design and build proper Motif-conformant applications. As with X, system administrators can view Motif mostly as "programmer's stuff," part of the underlying infrastructure, and focus on developing appropriate CDE configuration files.

CDE

As we have already seen, CDE consists of the following:

- Workspace manager - Executable program that provides Motif-based window frames, window management, a workspace menu, and the front panel.

- File manager - Program that iconically manages files and directories through direct manipulation.

- Style manager - Container of dialog boxes that control elements of the CDE environment, like workspace color and fonts.

- Help manager - This program provides context-sensitive help text on CDE components.

- Login manager - Daemon-like application that handles login and password verification.

- Session manager - Manager that handles saving and restoring user sessions.

- Application manager - Manager that registers and keeps track of applications in the CDE environment.

- Configuration files - A big bunch, most of which you can avoid dealing with (see the next section).

CDE also provides a number of basic, end-user productivity-enhancing applications. In general, CDE provides a graphical environment into which users, or you, their system administrator, can incorporate the software tools needed to do their work.

X, Motif, and CDE Configuration Files

X, Motif, and CDE all use configuration files to shape their appearance's and behavior's. Elements of appearance and behavior such as foreground color, keyboard focus policy, and client decoration are resources that can be controlled by values in the appropriate configuration file. In X, Motif, and CDE, the word "resource" has a special meaning. It doesn't refer to vague natural resources or generic system resources, but to rather specific elements of appearance and behavior. Some examples are the **foreground** resource, the **keyboardFocus-Policy** resource, and the **clientDecoration** resource. For example, foreground color could be black, keyboard focus policy could be explicit, and client decoration could be plus-title (title bar only). These would appear in some appropriate configuration file as the following:

    *foreground: black

    *keyboardFocusPolicy:explicit

    *clientDecoration: +title

Which configuration file these resources appear in depends on the scope of the effect desired (system-wide or individual user) and the graphical interface level being used (X, Motif, or CDE).

X Configuration Files

The X Window System has the following configuration files:

    sys.x11start
    sys.Xdefaults
    system.mwmrc
    X*screens
    X*devices
    X*pointerkey

By convention, these files are located in the **/usr/lib/X11** directory; however, I have noticed that many systems have eliminated this directory and moved many of the X-relelated files elsewhere in the system. In addition, each X client application has its own app-defaults configuration file located, also by convention, in the **/usr/lib/X11/ app-defaults** directory. Although six files are listed above, unless you're configuring a workstation for multiple-display screens (X*screens), multiple-input devices (X*devices), or keyboard-only pointer navigation (X*pointerkey), you'll typically need to work with only **sys.x11start**, **sys.Xdefaults**, and **system.mwmrc**.

The **sys.x11start** file was a script used to start X and X clients before the advent of CDE. System administrators or knowledgeable users modified **sys.x11start** so that the appropriate mix of X clients started "automatically." The **sys.Xdefaults** file was read as X started to obtain values for various appearance and behavior resources. Modifications to **sys.Xdefaults** ensured that the X environment and clients had the proper appearance and behavior. **system.mwmrc** contained the configuration of the workspace menu and button and key bindings.

system.mwmrc has been replaced by the Motif version also, **system.mwmrc**.

Motif Configuration Files

Motif added only one new configuration file to the X list: **system.mwmrc**.

By convention, this file is kept with the X configuration files in **/usr/lib/X11**. Actually, this file isn't new; it is the Motif version of **system.mwmrc,** which simply replaced **system.mwmrc** in Motif environments.

Whereas X brought network and interclient communication standards to the graphical user interface, Motif brought a standard for appearance and behavior, the standard originally defined in IBM's System Application Architecture Common User Access (SAACUA), which forms the basis of most PC-based GUIs. Thus, push buttons and scroll bars have a defined look and a defined behavior, and double-clicking always causes the default action to happen.

From a programmer's point of view, the Motif widget toolkit represents quite an advance over programming in "raw" X. From a user's or system administrator's point of view, the Motif user environment is about the same as the X environment, except that the **mwm** window manager is replaced with the Motif window manager.

CDE Configuration Files

It is possible to point to over 80 files that, in one way or another, contribute to configuring some aspect of CDE. By convention, these files reside in the **/usr/dt** directory. However, if you remove from this list such files as those that:

- configure CDE applications as opposed to the environment itself

- establish default actions and datatype definitions that, although you create your own definitions in separate files, you never modify

- are CDE working files and should not be customized

- are more appropriately associated with configuring the UNIX, X, and Motif environments underlying CDE, including the various shell environments, then CDE has approximately 19 configuration files, as shown in Table 4-1

Table 4-1   CDE CONFIGUATION FILES

* .Xauthority	* sys.font	* Xresources
* .Xdefaults	* sys.resources	* Xservers
* .dtprofile	* sys.sessions	* Xsession
* dtwm.fp	* Xaccess	* Xsetup
* dt.wmrc	* Xconfig	* Xstartup
* sys.dtprofile	* Xfailsafe	
* sys.dtwmrc	* Xreset	

Although 19 configuration files are still a lot, don't be alarmed by the number. You won't need to modify many of them, and can ignore a couple you modify once and then forget. You need to understand in depth for periodic modification only one or two, perhaps a system-wide ***.dt** file for custom actions and datatypes or maybe **dtwm.fp**, if you are required to modify the front panel on a regular basis for some reason.

Still, configuring CDE is not something you want to start hacking with without a little preparation and a good idea of what you want to accomplish. All CDE configuration files are pretty well commented, so a good first step is to print the ones you want to modify.

Table 4-2 organizes CDE configuration files according to content and the breadth of their influence.

Table 4-2   CDE Configuration File Influence

Nature of Configuration File	System-Wide Influence	User Personal Influence
Environment Variables	sys.dtprofile Xconfig Xsession	.dtprofile
Appearance & Behavior Resources	sys.resources Xconfig Xresources sys.fonts	.Xdefaults
File Types & Action Definitions	misc *.dt files	user-prefs.dt
Client Startup at Login	sys.sessions Xstartup Xsession Xreset Xfailsafe	.xsession sessionetc
Workspace Manager & Front Panel	sys.dtwmrc dtwm.fp	dtwmrc user-prefs.fp
Clients/Servers & Access	Xaccess Xservers	.Xauthority

The file **sys.dtwmrc** controls the configuration of the workspace manager at the system level. This includes all of the following:

Workspace Menu A menu that displays when mouse button 3 is pressed while the mouse pointer is over the workspace backdrop.

Button Bindings Definitions of what action happens when a particular mouse button is pressed or released while the mouse pointer is over a particular area (frame, icon, window, or root).

Key Bindings   Definitions of what action happens when a particular key or key sequence is pressed

> while the mouse pointer is over a particular area (frame, icon, window, or root).

Unlike configuration files for X or Motif, **sys.dtwmrc** does not control the following configuration elements:

Front Panel   The box, usually at the bottom of the workspace, that contains commonly referenced indicators and frequently used graphical controls, including a six-button workspace switch.

Slideup Subpanels Menus that slide up from the front panel at various locations to provide more functionality without consuming more screen space.

Instead, to avoid a massively large and overly complex configuration file, these elements were separated into their own configuration file in CDE, **dtwm.fp**.

Some front panel configuration elements, like the number of workspaces and their arrangement in the workspace switch, are controlled through resources in a **sys.resources**, **dt.resources**, or **.Xdefaults** file. Like other workspace manager configuration files, **sys.dtwmrc** can be copied to a user's home directory, actually to **$HOME/.dt/** as **dtwmrc**, and modified to personalize the user's environment beyond the system-wide configuration of **sys.dtwmrc**.

The **sys.resources** file is one of those files you might modify once, and then never again. The **dt.resources** file is one of those files you won't ever need to modify and so can ignore. The **.Xdefaults** file is one you or your users may modify on occasion.

The **sys.resources** file is where you put any non-default resources that you want in effect when a brand-new user logs into CDE for the very first time. For example, as system administrator, you may want your users to have a CDE front panel with prenamed workspaces, special colors, particular fonts, or application windows in certain locations. After the first-time login, **sys.resources** is ignored in favor of **dt.resources**. This file, **dt.resources**, resides in **$HOME/.dt/ sessions/current** (or **$HOME/.dt/sessions/home** when the home session is restored) and is created automatically by CDE. You can consider it a CDE working file and forget about it. The **.Xdefaults** file is where you or an end user would list X resources specific to the user's personal CDE environment. **sys.resources**, **dt.resources**, and **.Xdefaults** contain a list of resources and their values.

The **sys.sessions** file controls which clients start the very first time a new user logs into CDE. The **dt.sessions** file is to **sys.sessions** as **dt.resources** is to **sys.resources**.

It may be efficient to configure CDE to start particular applications for your users. You would specify these applications in **sys.sessions**. When a new user logs in for the first time, the CDE environment includes the specified clients. At the end of this first session by logging out, the remaining clients would be recorded in **$HOME/.dt/sessions/current** for CDE (**$HOME/.dt/sessions/home** when the home session is restored).

The **sys.dtprofile** file is a template that is automatically copied at first login into each new user's home directory as **.dtprofile**. **sys.dtprofile** replaces **.profile** or **.login** in the CDE environment (although either **.profile** or **.login** can be sourced in **.dtprofile** by removing the # comment symbol in front of **DTSOURCEPRO-FILE=true**). The **.dtprofile** file holds the personal environment variables that would, in a character-based environment, be found in **.profile** or **.login**. Use **.dtprofile** to avoid the interference tht terminal I/O commands cause to CDE's graphical environment.

The CDE login manager, **dtlogin**, presets the following environment variables to default values:

DISPLAY	The name of the local display
EDITOR	The default text editor
HOME	The user's home directory as specified in **/etc/passwd**
KBD_LANG	The current language of the keyboard
LANG	The current NLS language
LC_ALL	The value of LANG
LC_MESSAGES	The value of LANG
LOGNAME	The user's login name as specified in **/etc/passwd**
MAIL	The default file for mail (usually **/var/mail/$USER**)

PATH	The default directories to search for files and applications
USER	The user name
SHELL	The default shell as specified in **/etc/passwd**
TERM	The default terminal emulation
TZ	The time zone in effect

Variations to these default values belong in each user's **.dtprofile**. Additional environment variables can be added as needed to shape the user's environment to the needs of the work context. Just beware of using commands that cause any terminal I/O.

Like **.dtprofile**, **Xsession** is a shell script that sets user environment variables. The environment variables in **Xsession** apply system-wide. The environment variables in **.dtprofile** apply only to a user's personal environment. Furthermore, Because the login manager runs **Xsession** after the X server has started, the variables in **Xsession** are not available to the X server. Variables typically set in **Xsession** include the following:

EDITOR	The default text editor.
KBD_LANG	The language of the keyboard (usually set to the value of $LANG).
TERM	The default terminal emulation.
MAIL	The default file for mail, which is usually **/var/mail/$USER**.
DTHELPSEARCHPATH	The locations to search for CDE help files.
DTAPPSEARCHPATH	The locations to search for applications registered with the CDE application manager.
DTDATABASESEARCHPATH	The locations to search for additional action and datatype definitions.
XMICONSEARCHPATH	The locations to search for additional icons.
XMICONBMSEARCHPATH	Same as above.

As an example, suppose that you are the system administrator for several mixed workstation and X terminal clusters located at a single site. As usually happens, most users have grown accustomed to certain text editors. Some like **vi**, others prefer **emacs**, and a couple wouldn't be caught dead without **dmx**. An easy way to provide each user with his or her favored text editor would be to reset their EDITOR variable to the appropriate value in the individual **.dtprofile** files.

man page

vi - 8

Xconfig contains resources that control the behavior of **dtlogin** and it also provides a place to specify the locations for any other **dtlogin** configuration files you create. The **Xconfig** file works on a system-wide basis, so it's one of those files that you modify only once and then forget about. When, during login, **Xconfig** is run, several CDE configuration files get referenced: **Xaccess**, **Xservers**, **Xresources**, **Xstartup**, **Xsession**, **Xreset**, and **Xfailsafe**. Like **Xconfig** itself, most of these files are the type that you modify once when installing CDE and then, unless the network topology changes, you never deal with again.

Xaccess, as the name implies, is a remote display access control file. **Xaccess** contains a list of the host names allowed or denied XDMCP connection access to the local computer. For example, when an X terminal requests login service, **dtlogin** consults the **Xaccess** file to determine whether service should be granted.

The primary use of the **Xservers** file is to list the display screens on the local system that **dtlogin** is responsible for managing. **dtlogin** reads the **Xservers** file and starts an X server for each display listed there. It then starts a child **dtlogin** process to manage the server and display the login screen. Note that **dtlogin** works only locally; **dtlogin** can't start an X server on a remote system or X terminal. For remote display servers, some other mechanism must be used to start the server, which then uses the X Display Management Control Protocol (XDMCP) to request a login screen from **dtlogin**.

The **Xservers** file is another of those files that you may spend some time with initially and then, unless the topography of your network changes, never deal with again. When do you use **Xservers**? When a display doesn't match the default configuration. The default configuration assumes that each system has a single bitmap display and is the system console. X terminals, multiple displays (heads), multiple screens, and Starbase applications all require configuration lines in the **Xservers** file.

The **Xresources** file contains the list of resources that control the appearance and behavior of the login screen. After you substitute your company's logo for the CDE logo and change the fonts and colors, you'll probably never have to deal with **Xresources** again (unless your company changes its logo).

Xstartup is a system-wide configuration file executed by the login manager, from which it receives several environment variables:

DISPLAY	The name of the local display.
USER	The login name of the user.
HOME	The user's home directory.
PATH	The value of the **systemPath** resource in **Xconfig**.
SHELL	The value of the **systemShell** resource in **Xconfig**.
XAUTHORITY	The file to access for authority permissions.
TZ	The local time zone.

Because it can execute scripts and start clients on a system-wide basis, **Xstartup** is similar to **sys.sessions**. The difference is that **Xstartup** runs as root. Thus, modifications to **Xstartup** should be reserved for actions like mounting file systems.

Xreset is a system-wide companion script to **Xstartup**. It runs as root and essentially undoes what **Xstartup** put in motion.

The **Xfailsafe** file contains customizations to the standard failsafe session. The failsafe session provides a way to correct improper CDE sessions caused by errors in the login and session configuration files. As such, **Xfailsafe** is something that your users are not ever going to use, but you can make your life a little easier with a few judicious customizations.

The **sessionetc** file resides in a user's **.dt/sessions** directory and personalizes that user's CDE session. **sessionetc** handles the starting of additional X clients like **sys.session**, but on a per-user basis, as opposed to system-wide. Although **dt.session** also starts clients on a per-user basis, the clients are those of the default or current session. **dt.session** resides in **.dt/session/current**. **sessionetc**, which resides in **.dt/session**, and should contain only those clients that are not automatically restored. Typically, these are clients that do not set the **WM_COMMAND** properly, so the session manager can't save or restore them; thus they need to be restarted in **sessionetc**.

The **sys.font** file contains the system-wide, default session font configuration. These default fonts were based on usability studies, so **sys.font** is a file you may never change. However, should you encounter a situation that requires a different mix of fonts on a system-wide basis, this is where you'd change them. Note that the font resources and values mentioned in **sys.font** must match exactly the default font resources specified in the **/usr/dt/app-defaults/C/Dtstyle** file.

CDE has a bunch of files that specify CDE action and data type definitions. All these files end with the file extension ***.dt**. A ***.dt** ("dt" for "desk top") contains both data type and action definitions. The default ***.dt** files are in **/usr/dt/appconfig/types/C** and act on a system-wide basis. Similarly, **user-prefs.dt**, the master copy of which is also located in **/usr/dt/appconfig/types/C**, is used at the personal user level.

The **.Xauthority** file is a user-specific configuration file containing authorization information needed by clients that require an authorization mechanism to connect to the server.

CDE Configuration File Locations

Where CDE looks for particular configuration files depends on the nature of the configuration files, principally what the files configure and how wide their influence is. Table 4-3 shows the location of system and user configuration files based on the nature of the file content.

For each of the default system-wide file locations listed in Table 4-3, a corresponding location exists for custom system-wide configuration files. These custom files should be located in the appropriate subdirectory under **/etc/dt**. The basic procedure is to copy the file you need to customize from **/usr/dt/something** to **/etc/dt/something** and then do your modifications there. For example, to change the default logo in **Xresources**, copy **/usr/dt/config/C/Xresources** to **/etc/dt/**

config/C/Xresources, open **/etc/dt/config/C/Xresources**, and make
your changes.

Table 4-3   CDE System And User Configuration Files

Nature of Configuration File	System-Wide Influence	User Personal Influence
Environment Variables	/usr/dt/config/	$HOME/
Appearance & Behavior Resources	/usr/dt/config/C /usr/dt/app-defaults/C	$HOME/.dt/ $HOME/.dt/sessions/current/ $HOME/.dt/sessions/home/
File Types & Action Definitions	/usr/dt/appconfig/ types/C	$HOME/.dt/types
Client Startup at Login	/usr/dt/config/ /usr/dt/config/C	$HOME/.dt/session/ $HOME/.dt/session/current/ $HOME/.dt/session/home/
Workspace Manager	/usr/dt/config	$HOME/.dt/

This is an important point. Files located under **/usr/dt** are considered CDE system files and will be overwritten during updates. Thus,
any customizations you do there will be lost. Make all modifications
to system-wide configuration files in **/etc/dt** and its subdirectories.

How Configuration Files Play Together

From the material covered so far, you've probably concluded correctly that CDE configuration files aren't something to go hacking
with without a plan - a well thought-out plan. You've probably fig-
ured out that the element you want to configure and the breadth of
influence you want it to have determine which configuration file you
modify.

For instance, if you wanted to set an environment variable, you
have a choice of four configuration files: **sys.dtprofile**, **Xconfig**,
Xsession, and **.dtprofile**. But if you want to set environment variables
that affect only a particular user, your choice immediately narrows to
a single file, **.dtprofile**.

Now the only remaining piece of the puzzle is to understand the order in which CDE reads its configuration files. When a configuration element (an environment variable, resource, action, or data type) is specified twice but with different values, you obviously want the correct value used and the incorrect value ignored.

The following rules apply:

- For environment variables, the last specified value is used.

- For resources, the last specified value is used. However, this is influenced by specificity. Thus **emacs*foreground** takes precedence over just ***foreground** for emacs clients, regardless of the order in which the resources were encountered.

- For actions, the first specified is used.

- For data types, the first specified is used.

Table 4-4 illustrates which specification is used when CDE reads multiple specifications of configuration elements in its configuration files:

Table 4-4   What CDE Uses for Configuration

Configuration Element	Element Used
resource	last encountered or most specific
environment	last encountered
action	first encountered
file type	first encountered

Put in terms of scope, a user configuration file overrides a system-wide configuration file. Looking at the order of precedence of just system-wide configuration files, the files in **/etc/dt** have precedence over those in **/usr/dt**, so global custom configurations have precedence over the CDE default configuration. And **$HOME/.dt** files take precedence over those in **/etc/dt.**

For resources, the elements used to specify a GUI's appearance and behavior, CDE sets values according to the following priorities:

1. **Command line** -   When you start a client from the command line, options listed on the command line have top priority.

2. **Xresources, .Xdefaults, dt.resources, sys.resources,** - When CDE starts, it reads these resource configuration files to determine the value of X resources to use for the session.

3. **RESOURCE MANAGER** - Resources already in the property **RESOURCE_MANAGER** may affect an application that is just starting.

4. **app-defaults** - Specifies "default" resource values that differ from built-in resource values.

5. **built-in defaults** - Default resources that are "hard coded" have the lowest priority.

Specific resource specifications take precedence over general resource specifications. For example, suppose that you want a certain font in your text entry areas. You could correctly specify a ***FontList** resource in your personal **.Xdefaults** file, only to have it overwritten by an ***XmText*FontList** in an **app-defaults** file. Although **app-defaults** is of lower priority than **.Xdefaults**, the resource specification set there is more specific, so it takes precedence.

For environment variables, CDE sets values according to the following priorities:

1. **$HOME/.dtprofile** - User-specific variables have top priority.

2. **/etc/dt/config/C/Xsession** - Custom system-wide variables not read by X server.

3. **/etc/dt/config/C/Xconfig** - Custom system-wide variables read by X server.

4. **/usr/dt/config/C/Xsession** - Default system-wide variables not read by X server.

5. **/usr/dt/config/C/Xconfig** - Default system-wide variables read by X server.

6. **/usr/dt/bin/dtlogin** - Built-in default variables have the lowest priority.

For data type and action definitions, CDE looks for **.dt** files according to the following priority:

1. $HOME/.dt/types

2. /etc/dt/appconfig/types/C

3. /usr/dt/appconfig/types/C

Remember, for data types or actions, the first value that it finds is the one it uses. So if you just can't get a file type or action to work, check for a duplicate entry earlier in the file or for an entry in a file with higher priority. Note also that the environment variable DTDATABASESEARCHPATH can be set either in **/etc/dt/config/Xsession** or **$HOME/.dtprofile**, to add directories where CDE can search for file type and action definition information.

Specifying Appearance and Behavior

You need to know only two tricks to specifying appearance and behavior resources in configuration files. The first is to specify the resource and its value correctly. The second is to specify the resource and value in the correct configuration file.

Two caveats involve colors and fonts. The CDE style manager provides a graphical interface for modifying colors and fonts. However, if you specify an application's color or font directly, this specification will override the ability of the style manager to manage that resource for the application.

Typical ways to specify a color or font directly include the following:

- Type the specification on the command line as a startup option.

- Include the specification in the application's **app-defaults** file.

- Use the **xrdb** utility to add resources for the application to the resource database.

The Sequence of Events When CDE Starts

The following section is a blow-by-blow account of what happens when a user logs into CDE. In this particular account, assume a distributed topology like a diskless cluster. The account begins with the boot of the hub system and nodes in step 1. By step 4, X servers are running on each node and login screens are being displayed. By step 6, the user is logged in. By step 11, the session manager is busy re-creating the user's session.

1. The **dtlogin** executable is started as part of the **init** process that occurs during the system boot sequence on the hub machine and each cluster node.

2. **dtlogin** reads **/usr/dt/config/Xconfig** to get a list of resources with which to configure the login process. This is where **dtlogin** first learns about files like **Xaccess**, **Xservers**, **Xresources**, **Xstartup**, **Xsession**, and **Xreset** and gets the values of a number of appearance and behavior resources.

3. **dtlogin** reads two files in **/usr/dt/config**:

   - **Xservers** or the file identified by the **Dtlogin*servers** resource setting in **Xconfig**.

   - **Xresources** or the file identified by the **Dtlogin*resources** resource setting in **Xconfig**.

4. **dtlogin** starts an X server and a child **dtlogin** for each local display.

5. Each child **dtlogin** invokes **dtgreet**, the login screen.

6. When a login and password are validated, a child **dtlogin** sets certain environment variables to default values.

7. The child **dtlogin** runs **/usr/dt/config/Xstartup**.

8. The child **dtlogin** runs **/usr/dt/config/Xsession**.

9. **Xsession** runs **dthello**, the copyright screen.

10. **Xsession** reads **$HOME/.dtprofile**, setting any additional environment variables or overwriting those set previously by **dtlogin**.

11. The child **dtlogin** invokes the session manager, **dtsession**.

12. **dtsession** restores the appropriate session. For example, to restore the current session, **dtsession** reads **dt.resources** and **dt.session** in **$HOME/.dt/sessions/current**.

At logout, the reverse happens. The session is saved and **dtlogin** runs **/usr/dt/config/Xreset**. After **Xreset** completes, **dtlogin** again displays the login screen as in step 4.

CDE and Performance

CDE isn't a monolithic application; it's a set of components layered on top of the operating system, the X Window System, and Motif. Each underlying layer takes its share of RAM before CDE or any other client even starts. Because of the low-level nature of these layers, the RAM they use is hardly ever regained through swapping to disk.

In some cases, operating-system overhead and user-application requirements restrict the amount of RAM available for a graphical user interface to little more than enough to run a window manager such as Motif. Because the CDE workspace manager and the Motif window manager take roughly the same amount of RAM, users can enjoy an enriched graphical environment with the added value of CDE's multiple workspaces at essentially no extra RAM cost over running the Motif window manager.

Tactics for Better Performance

Unless all your users have RAM-loaded powerhouses for systems, you will need to spend some time developing a performance strategy. If you conceive of performance as a bell-shaped curve, satisfaction lies on the leading edge. Your performance strategy should do everything it can to keep your users on the leading edge.

Probably the most logical approach is to start small and grow. In other words, start out with minimal user environments on all the systems on your network. Gradually add software components until you or your users begin to notice performance degradation. Then back off a little. Such an approach might take several weeks or more to evaluate, as you add components and as your users spend several days actually working in the environment to determine the effect of your changes on system performance and their frustration levels.

The most RAM-expensive pieces of CDE are the workspace manager, the session manager, and the file manager. The workspace manager is expensive because portions of it are always in RAM (assuming that you are moving windows around and switching workspaces). The CDE workspace manager is no more expensive than the Motif window manager; if you want a GUI, it's just a price you have to pay. The session manager is expensive only during logout and login, as it saves and restores sessions. The rest of the time, the session manager is dormant and gets swapped out of RAM. Saving your current work session is nice at the end of the day, but it's something to consider giving up if you want to improve your login and logout performance. The file manager is expensive because it wakes up periodically and jumps into RAM to check the status of the file system and update its file manager windows. When it jumps into RAM, it pushes something else out, for example, maybe the desktop publishing program you're using.

Here are some other ideas that you may find useful:

Terminal Emulators   **xterms** are a little less RAM-expensive than **dtterms**. Unless you need the block mode functionality of a **dtterm**,

	xterm might be a better choice for terminal emulation.
Automatic Saves	Some applications automatically save data at periodic intervals. Although this feature can be beneficial, you need to evaluate its effect in light of performance. If the application is central to your users' work, fine, but if not, you might want to disable the automatic save feature.
Scroll Buffers	Large scroll buffers in terminal emulators can be a real convenience, but they can also take up a lot of RAM. Even modestly sized scroll buffers, when multiplied by three or four terminal emulators, consume a lot of RAM.
Background Bitmaps	Avoid large bitmaps; they increase the X server size. Especially avoid switching large bitmaps frequently within a session. If you are hunting for a new background, be sure to restart the X server after you've found the one you want and have included it in the proper **sessionetc** file. The most efficient bitmaps are small ones that can be repeated to tile the background.
Front Panel	Reconfigure the front panel to minimize the number of buttons. Keep just enough to meet user needs. This tactic decreases the workspace manager size in RAM and speeds login and logout.
Pathnames	Whenever possible, use absolute pathnames for bitmap specifications. Although this approach decreases the

flexibility of the system, it speeds access time.

Conclusion

The default CDE is ready to use, but given its power and flexibility, you will inevitably want to customize the CDE environment for your users' work context and optimum performance. Take the time to develop a good idea of what changes you need to make, the order in which to make them, and exactly where to make them. In so doing, all the power and flexibility of CDE will be open to you.

CHAPTER 5

Introduction to the Bash Shell

Different Shells

Most UNIX variants allow you to select among several shells. The shell is important to you as a user because it is your window into the system. The many shells available on UNIX variants are similar in that you use them to issue commands, control many aspects of your user environment, write command files and shell programs, and so on. Because you'll probably be spending a lot of time in your shell, you should develop an understanding of several different shells and see whether you develop a preference of one over the other. A particular shell, such as Bash, does not vary much going from one UNIX variant to another. The shells themselves, however, have some unique features. In general, I don't find that users strongly prefer one shell over another. All the shells are similar in functionality and enjoyable to use once you get to know them. Most UNIX variants allow your system administrator to select from among several different shells when configuring users, so he or she usually has some flexibility concerning the shell that users run. In general, system administrators prefer users to use the same shell making system administration easier in general. Most system administrators, however, will be happy to grant your request for a particular shell if indeed it is available on your system and you have a good reason to use it. I cover the Bash shell in this chapter and the C and KornShell in the following two chapters.

Introduction to Bash

Most UNIX variants allow you to select among several shells. The Linux-based UNIX operating systems I have used configure Bash as the default shell. Bash possesses many of the fine features of other shells, and in fact derives its name from **Bourne Again SHell**, which is a dead giveaway that it possesses at least some of the features of the Bourne shell. Bash is similar to other shells in that it provides a user interface to UNIX. You can use the Bash shell in the following three ways:

- Interactively type commands on the command line.
- Group commonly executed sets of commands into command files that you can execute by typing the name of the file.
- Create Bash shell programs using the structured programming techniques of the shell.

These three techniques are listed in the order in which you'll probably use them. First, you log in and use interactive commands. Then you group together commonly used commands and execute them with a single command. Finally, you may want to create sophisticated shell scripts.

For this reason, describe these aspects of the Bash shell in the order in which they are listed. The command file and programming aspects of the Bash shell are covered as part of the "Shell Programming" chapter. Bash is very similar to the KornShell, which is the shell used in the shell programming chapter. You can, therefore, use the shell programming chapter as an introduction to programming with Bash as well. Keep in mind, however, that differences always occur when programming with one shell vs. another.

Issuing Commands

The first activity you perform after you log into the system is to issue commands at the prompt. A command you may want to issue immediately is **ls -al**. Here is what I see on my system after executing this command to check my present working directory and producing a long listing of all files when logged in as root:

man page

pwd - 3

man page

ls - 2

```
# pwd
# ls -al
total 46
drwxr-xr-x   5 root      root      1024 Nov 26 19:40 .
drwxr-xr-x  20 root      root      1024 Nov  8 20:10 ..
-rw-r--r--   1 root      root       964 Nov 26 19:40 .bash_history
-rw-r--r--   1 root      root       674 Feb  5  1997 .bashrc
-rw-r--r--   1 root      root       602 Feb  5  1997 .cshrc
-rw-r--r--   1 root      root     14815 Nov  8 20:09 .fvwmrc.menus.prep
-rw-r--r--   1 root      root       116 Feb  5  1997 .login
-rw-r--r--   1 root      root       234 Feb  5  1997 .profile
drwxr-xr-x   2 root      root      1024 Nov  8 14:10 .seyon
-rw-r--r--   1 root      root      4276 Nov  8 20:09 XF86Config
-r--r--r--   1 root      root     13875 Nov  8 20:05 XF86Config.bak
drwxrwxrwx   2 root      root      1024 Nov 26 19:40 book
drwxr-xr-x   5 root      root      1024 Nov 14 18:12 lg
-rw-r--r--   1 root      root         0 Nov 26 19:40 typescript
#
```

Among the files produced in the long listing of all files is a Bash startup file called **.bashrc**. The following shows the contents of the **.bashrc** file:

man page

cat - 3

```
# cat .bashrc
# ~/.bashrc --
#   The individual per-interactive-shell startup file for bash

. /etc/profile

# try solve this tedious 'Backspace vs. Delete' problem...
if [ -z "$TERM" ]; then
  echo ".bashrc: TERM empty: this shouldn't happen!" 1>&2
```

```
    echo "   Please contact 'support@lst.de'" 1>&2
else
  case $TERM in
  linux*)
    stty erase '^?'
    ;;
  *)
    stty erase '^H'
    ;;
  esac
fi

# general environment settings
#export GROFF_TYPESETTER=latin1
#export LC_CTYPE=iso-8859-1
export LESSCHARSET=latin1
#export METAMAIL_PAGER=less

HISTSIZE=100

alias which='type -path'
alias h=history
alias j="jobs -l"
alias l="ls -Fax"
alias ll="ls -Alg"
alias pd=pushd
alias z=suspend

#
```

man page

ls - 2

Some interesting contents are in the **.bashrc** file. Among them is a value for *HISTSIZE,* which we'll get into shortly, and a set of aliases. These aliases are "shortcuts" for long commands. When I issue the **ll** command, for instance, I am really issuing the **ls -Alg** command.

I may execute both the local **.profile** shown in the earlier long listing as well as **/etc/profile**. **/etc/profile** usually performs setup for all users who log into the system. The following is a listing of **/etc/ profile**:

man page

cat - 3

```
# cat /etc/profile
# /etc/profile
# System wide environment and startup programs
# Functions and aliases go in $HOME/.bashrc

PATH="/bin:/usr/bin:/opt/bin:/usr/X11R6/bin:/usr/openwin/bin:/usr/TeX/bin:/usr/
local/bin"

umask 022

if [ `id -gn` = `id -un` ] && [ `id -u` != 0 ]; then
  umask 002
fi

if [ -z "$UID" ]; then
  UID=`id -u`
fi

if [ "$UID" = 0 ]; then
  PATH=/sbin:/usr/sbin:$PATH
else
```

```
    PATH=$PATH:
fi
USER=`id -un`
LOGNAME=$USER

export PATH USER LOGNAME

HOSTNAME=`/bin/hostname`
MAIL="/var/spool/mail/$USER"

export HOSTNAME MAIL

if [ -n "$BASH_VERSION" ]; then
  # (aliases now in $HOME/.bashrc, resp. /etc/skel/.bashrc)
  export PS1="[\u@\h \W]\\$ "
  export HISTSIZE=100
fi

#
```

We'll also cover some of the contents of **/etc/profile**.

Initializing the History List in .bashrc

The Bash shell can keep a history list of the commands you have issued. If you wish to reissue a command or view a command you earlier issued, you can use the history list.

You can specify any number of commands to be included in the history list. The following line in **.bashrc** sets the history list to 100:

set history = 100

One hundred commands will be saved in the history list. When you log, out the last 100 commands you have issued are stored in the history list. The next time you log in you can view these 100 commands; however, as you issue commands, the oldest commands fall off the history list. This fact is shown in the following example:

```
# history
    2   more history
    3    ll
    4   cd ..
    5   pwd
    6   cd ..
    7   ll
    8   cd ..
    9   ll
   10   ll log
   11   cd log
   12   more *
   13   l
   14   ll
   15   cd /
   16   ll
   17   cd
   18   XF86Setup
   19   XF86Setup
   20   startx
   21   ll
   22   pwd
   23   ll
   24   ll /
   25   XF86Setup
   26   ll
   27   startx
   28   find / -name XF86Config*
   29   cp /usr/X11R6/lib/X11/XF86Config.eg .
   30   ll
   31   XF86Setup
   32   XF86Setup
   33   startx
   34   ll
   35   mv XF86Config.eg XF86Config
   36   XF86Setup
   37   startx
   38   shutdown -h now
   39   man ls
   40   man ll
   41   man ls
   42   man file
   43   lsr
   44   man chmod
   45   man chmod
   46   shutdown -h now
   47   pwd
   48   ls -l
   49   pwd
   50   ls -a
   51   ls -al
   52   pwd
```

```
 53  ls -al
 54  more .profile
 55  more .bashrc
 56
 57  alias
 58  ll
 59  pwd
 60  script
 61  script
 62  scrit
 63  script
 64  more .bashrc
 65  more .bashrc
 66   ll
 67  more .profile
 68   ll
 69  more .bashrc | grep P
 70  more .profile | grep P
 71  env
 72  more /.profile
 73  more /etc/profile
 74  more /etc/profile | grep PS
 75  find / -name *profile* -print
 76  more .bashrc
 77   more .bashrc
 78  ll /etc/profi*
 79  cp /etc/profile /etc/profile.orig
 80  vi /etc/profile
 81  exit
 82  cp /etc/profile.orig /etc/profile
 83  history
 84
 85  exit
 86  history
 87  history
 88     ll
 89     ll
 90  history
 91  ll /etc/profi*
 92  ll /etc/profi*
 93   more .bashrc
 94    history
 95  ll
 96  cd /root
 97  ll
 98  history | more
 99   history | more
100    exit
101  history
```

Notice in this example that command number 100 is the **exit**, or command to log out, from the last session. Command number 101 is the **history** command I issued immediately upon establishing the next session.

Recalling from the History List

All these commands (**cp, more, find, ll**) are in the history list with their corresponding numbers. You can repeat the last command with **!!**, the 89th command with **!89**, and the last command that started with "m" with **!m**, all of which are shown in the following example:

```
# !!
history
    3   ll
    4   cd ..
    5   pwd
    6   cd ..
    7   ll
    8   cd ..
    9   ll
   10   ll log
   11   cd log
   12   more *
   13   l
   14   ll
   15   cd /
   16   ll
   17   cd
   18   XF86Setup
   19   XF86Setup
   20   startx
   21   ll
   22   pwd
   23   ll
   24   ll /
   25   XF86Setup
   26   ll
   27   startx
   28   find / -name XF86Config*
   29   cp /usr/X11R6/lib/X11/XF86Config.eg .
   30   ll
   31   XF86Setup
   32   XF86Setup
   33   startx
   34   ll
   35   mv XF86Config.eg XF86Config
   36   XF86Setup
   37   startx
   38   shutdown -h now
   39   man ls
   40   man ll
   41   man ls
   42   man file
   43   lsr
   44   man chmod
   45   man chmod
   46   shutdown -h now
   47   pwd
   48   ls -l
```

```
 49  pwd
 50  ls -a
 51  ls -al
 52  pwd
 53  ls -al
 54  more .profile
 55  more .bashrc
 56
 57  alias
 58  ll
 59  pwd
 60  script
 61  script
 62  scrit
 63  script
 64  more .bashrc
 65  more .bashrc
 66   ll
 67  more .profile
 68   ll
 69  more .bashrc | grep P
 70  more .profile | grep P
 71  env
 72  more /.profile
 73  more /etc/profile
 74  more /etc/profile | grep PS
 75  find / -name *profile* -print
 76  more .bashrc
 77   more .bashrc
 78  ll /etc/profi*
 79  cp /etc/profile /etc/profile.orig
 80  vi /etc/profile
 81  exit
 82  cp /etc/profile.orig /etc/profile
 83  history
 84
 85  exit
 86  history
 87  history
 88    ll
 89    ll
 90  history
 91  ll /etc/profi*
 92  ll /etc/profi*
 93   more .bashrc
 94    history
 95  ll
 96  cd /root
 97  ll
 98  history | more
 99   history | more
100    exit
101  history
102  history
# !89
ll
total 44
-rw-r--r--   1 root      root           956 Nov 26 19:33 .bash_history
-rw-r--r--   1 root      root           674 Feb  5  1997 .bashrc
-rw-r--r--   1 root      root           602 Feb  5  1997 .cshrc
-rw-r--r--   1 root      root         14815 Nov  8 20:09 .fvwmrc.menus.prep
-rw-r--r--   1 root      root           116 Feb  5  1997 .login
-rw-r--r--   1 root      root           234 Feb  5  1997 .profile
drwxr-xr-x   2 root      root          1024 Nov  8 14:10 .seyon
-rw-r--r--   1 root      root          4276 Nov  8 20:09 XF86Config
-r--r--r--   1 root      root         13875 Nov  8 20:05 XF86Config.bak
drwxrwxrwx   2 root      root          1024 Nov 13 21:25 book
drwxr-xr-x   5 root      root          1024 Nov 14 18:12 lg
-rw-r--r--   1 root      root             0 Nov 26 19:36 typescript
# !m
more .bashrc
# ~/.bashrc --
#   The individual per-interactive-shell startup file for bash

. /etc/profile
```

```
# try solve this tedious 'Backspace vs. Delete' problem...
if [ -z "$TERM" ]; then
  echo ".bashrc: TERM empty: this shouldn't happen!" 1>&2
  echo "   Please contact 'support@1st.de'" 1>&2
else
  case $TERM in
  linux*)
    stty erase '^?'
    ;;
  *)
    stty erase '^H'
    ;;
  esac
fi

# general environment settings
#export GROFF_TYPESETTER=latin1
#export LC_CTYPE=iso-8859-1
[7m--More--(70%)[m
export LESSCHARSET=latin1
#export METAMAIL_PAGER=less

HISTSIZE=100

alias which='type -path'
alias h=history
alias j="jobs -l"
alias l="ls -Fax"
alias ll="ls -Alg"
alias pd=pushd
alias z=suspend

[root@nycald1 /root]#
Script done on Thu Nov 26 19:39:51 1998
```

Table 5-1 includes some of the more commonly used history list recall commands.

Table 5-1   Recalling from the History List

Command	Description	Example
!*N*	Issue command **N**	**!2**
!!	Issue last command	**!!**
!-*N*	Issue **Nth** command from last command issued	**!-N**
!*str*	Issue last command starting with **str**	**!c**

Command	Description	Example
!?str?	Issue last command that had **str** anyplace in command line	**!?cat?**
!{str1}str2	Append **str2** to last command with **str1**	**!{cd} /tmp**
*^str1^str2^*	Substitute **str2** for **str1** in last command	**^cat^more^**

Editing on the Command Line

Using the history list is a great way of viewing and reissuing commands. Bash also supports command-line editing. You can use the up arrow key to move back one command in the history list. When you press the up arrow key, the last command from the history list appears on the command line. Every time you press the up arrow key, you move back one more command in the history list. When a command appears on the command line, you can press the "Enter" key to issue the command. You can modify the command by using the left and right arrow keys to move to a point in the command line and type additional information, or use the "backspace" and "delete" keys to remove information from the command line.

Aliases in .bashrc

An alias is a name that you select for a frequently used command or series of commands. You can use the **.bashrc** file as a place where your aliases are stored and read every time you log in. In the earlier **.bashrc** file, seven aliases were already set up. You can add additional aliases in the **.bashrc** file or define aliases at the command-line prompt, but these will be cleared when you log out.

Here is a list of the aliases that are already set up for us in the
.bashrc file and an example of running the aliases **l** and **ll**:

```
# alias
alias h='history'
alias j='jobs -l'
alias l='ls -Fax'
alias ll='ls -Alg'
alias pd='pushd'
alias which='type -path'
alias z='suspend'
#
# l
./                      ../                  .bash_history        .bashrc
.cshrc                  .fvwmrc.menus.prep   .login               .profile
.seyon/                 XF86Config           XF86Config.bak       book/
lg/                     typescript
#
# ll
total 44
-rw-r--r--   1 root     root       970 Nov 26 21:35 .bash_history
-rw-r--r--   1 root     root       674 Feb  5  1997 .bashrc
-rw-r--r--   1 root     root       602 Feb  5  1997 .cshrc
-rw-r--r--   1 root     root     14815 Nov  8 20:09 .fvwmrc.menus.prep
-rw-r--r--   1 root     root       116 Feb  5  1997 .login
-rw-r--r--   1 root     root       234 Feb  5  1997 .profile
drwxr-xr-x   2 root     root      1024 Nov  8 14:10 .seyon
-rw-r--r--   1 root     root      4276 Nov  8 20:09 XF86Config
-r--r--r--   1 root     root     13875 Nov  8 20:05 XF86Config.bak
drwxrwxrwx   2 root     root      1024 Nov 26 19:41 book
drwxr-xr-x   5 root     root      1024 Nov 14 18:12 lg
-rw-r--r--   1 root     root         0 Nov 26 21:35 typescript
#
```

These are all very useful indeed, but let's now set up our own
alias. Suppose that we want to know how many processes are running
on the system. We'll create an alias called "procs" that does this for
us. The **ps** command produces a list of processes. We'll issue **ps** and
pipe (|) this output to **wc** with the "l" option to tell us how many lines
are present. The pipe (|) directs the output of **ps** to be used as the input
to **wc**. The **ps** command produces a list of processes and **wc -l** gives us
a count of the number of lines. Therefore, we'll know the total number
of processes running. The following example first shows the output of
ps, then our **alias** command, and finally the output produced by the
alias command:

```
# ps
  PID TTY STAT   TIME COMMAND
  188   2 S      0:00 /sbin/getty tty2 VC linux
  189   3 S      0:00 /sbin/getty tty3 VC linux
  190   4 S      0:00 /sbin/getty tty4 VC linux
```

```
  191   5 S    0:00  /sbin/getty tty5 VC linux
  192   6 S    0:00  /sbin/getty tty6 VC linux
  619   1 S    0:00  login root
  620   1 S    0:00  -bash
  642   1 S    0:00  script
  643   1 S    0:00  script
  644  p0 S    0:00  bash -i
  656  p0 R    0:00  ps
#
# alias procs='echo "Number of processes are: ";ps | wc -l'
#
# procs
Number of processes are: 11
#
```

This alias works great. All we have to type is "procs" to see the number of processes running on our system.

A lot of quoting takes place in this command line. To understand what is taking place on this line, seek the help of Table 5-2.

Table 5-2   Shell Quoting

Character(s)	Description
'cmd'	Single quote means to take the string character literally
"str"	Double quote means allow command and variable substitution
\c	Escape character prevents everything following it from printing, including new line
`str`	Grave means to execute command and substitute output

Applying Table 5-2 to the earlier **procs** alias, we can see what comprises this alias. The alias begins with a single quote, which means execute the command(s) within the single quotes. The first command is the **echo** command, which uses double quotes to specify the characters to **echo**. We could have added the escape character **\c**, which would have prevented a new line from being printed. The semicolons separate commands. **ps** is then run to produce a list of processes, and the output is piped (|) to word count (**wc**), which produces a count of the number of lines, as shown in Figure 5-1.

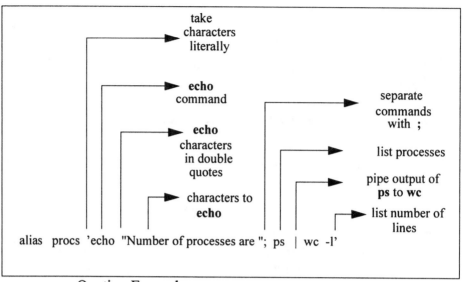

Figure 5-1 Quoting Example

As you can see in Figure 5-1, some of the quoting becomes tricky. An understanding of quoting is important if you wish to modify and reuse existing shell scripts or craft your own.

Command and Path Completion

Bash sometimes knows what you're thinking. You can type part of a command or pathname, and Bash can complete the remainder for you. You can type part of a command or pathname and use the "tab" key to complete the command. If, for instance, you wish to issue the **run-level** command to view the current system run level but can't remember the full command, you can type "run" and the tab key and the command is completed for you as shown in the following example:

```
# run<tab key>level
N 3
```

Bash determined that the only command that starts with "run" is **runlevel** and completed the command.

As long as you issue the command or pathname to the extent that it is unique, then Bash completes it for you. If the command or pathname is not unique, then Bash shows you the options for completing the command. The following example shows typing "ru" and two tabs to get a list of commands that start with "ru":

```
# ru<tab key><tab key>
runlevel   rusers
```

You can see from this example that typing "ru" produced two possible commands - **runlevel** and **rusers**.

This great completion also works for path names. If you change directory to "/b," you get the following result:

man page

cd - 3

```
# cd /b<tab key><tab key>
bin   boot
```

Because two directories at the root level begin with "b," Bash could not determine which of the two you wanted and listed both.

File Name Expansion

Before we can cover the upcoming topics as well as the matieral in the shell programming chapter, you want to take a look at file name expansion. As a user manipulating files, you will surely be preparing shell scripts that deal with file names. An overview of file name expansion is useful to ensure that you're comfortable with this topic before you start writing shell scripts.

Table 5-3 lists some common file name expansion and pattern matching.

Table 5-3   File Name Expansion and Pattern Matching

Character(s)	Example	Description
*	1) ls *.c	Match zero or more characters
?	2) ls conf.?	Match any single character
[list]	3) ls conf.[co]	Match any character in list
[lower-upper]	4) ls libdd.9873[5-6].sl	Match any character in range
str{str1,str2,str3,...}	5) ls ux*.{700,300}	Expand str with contents of {}
~	6) ls -a ~	Home directory
~username	7) ls -a ~gene	Home directory of username

The following descriptions of the examples shown in Table 5-3 are more detailed:

1. To list all files in a directory that end in ".c," you could do the following:

man page

ls - 3

```
$ ls *.c
    conf. SAM.c conf.c
```

2. To find all the files in a directory named "conf" with an extension of one character, you could do the following:

```
$ ls conf.?
    conf.c conf.o conf.1
```

3. To list all the files in a directory named "conf" with only the extension "c" or "o," you could do the following:

```
$ ls conf.{co}
    conf.c conf.o
```

4. To list files with similar names but a field that covers a range, you could do the following:

```
$  ls  libdd9873[5-6].sl
      libdd98735.sl  libdd98736.sl
```

5. To list files that start with "ux," and have the extension "300" or "700," you could do the following:

```
$  ls ux*.{700,300}
      uxbootlf.700  uxinstfs.300
```

6. To list the files in your home directory, you could use ~:

```
$  ls -a ~
   .        .cshrc.org  .login      .shrc.org
   ..       .exrc       .login.org  .cshrc
   .history
```

7. To list the files in the home directory of a user, you can do the following:

```
$   ls -a ~gene
    .              .history      splinedat   under.des
    ..             .login        trail.txt   xtra.part
    .chsrc         .login.org    ESP-File
    .cshrc.org     .profile      Mail
    .exrc          .shrc.org     opt
```

Many of these techniques are useful when writing shell scripts, so become familiar with file name expansion.

Redirection (I/O Redirection)

UNIX is set up such that commands usually take their input from the keyboard, often called standard input, and usually send output to the screen, often called standard output. Commands also send error information to the screen. You do not always want input to come from standard input and output and errors to go to standard output. You are given a lot of control to override these defaults. This is called redirection. Table 5-4 shows many common forms of redirection.

As shown in the table, to redirect the output of a command from standard output to a file, you would use ">". This works almost all the time. If you have an environment variable called **noclobber** set, then redirecting to an existing file does not work (we'll cover environment variables shortly). The **noclobber** does not permit redirection to write over an existing file. If you try to write over an existing file, such as / **tmp/processes** below, you receive a message that the file exists:

man page

ps - 12

```
#  ps  -ef  > /tmp/processes
/tmp/processes:  File exists
```

You can, however, use a "!" with redirection to force a file to be overwritten. Using ">!" forces a file to be overwritten, and ">>!" forces the output to be appended to the end of an existing file. Examples of these are shown in the Table 5-4.

Table 5-4   Commonly Used Redirection Forms

Command or Assignment	Example	Description
<	wc -l < .login	Standard input redirection: execute **wc** (word count) and list number of lines (**-l**) in **.login**
>	ps -ef > /tmp/processes	Standard output redirection: execute **ps** and send output to file **/tmp/processes**
>>	ps -ef >> /tmp/processes	Append standard output: execute **ps** and append output to the end of the file **/tmp/processes**
>!	ps -ef >! /tmp/processes	Append output redirection and override **noclobber**: write over **/tmp/processes** even if it exists
>>!	ps -ef >>! /tmp/processes	Append standard output and override **noclobber**: append to the end of **/tmp/processes**
| (pipe)	ps | wc -l	Run **ps** and use the result as input to **wc**
0 - standard input		
1 - standard output		
2 - standard error	cat program 2> errors	**cat** the file **program** to standard output and redirect errors to the file **errors**
	cat program 2>> errors	**cat** the file **program** to standard output and append errors to the file **errors**
	find / -name '*.c' -print > cprograms 2>errors	**find** all files on the system ending in **.c**, place the list of files in **cprograms** in the current working directory, and send all errors (file descriptor 2) to the file **errors** in current working directory
	find / -name '*.c' -print > cprograms 2>&1	**find** all files on the system ending in **.c**, place the list of files in **cprograms** in the current working directory, and send all errors (file descriptor 2) to the same place as file descriptor 1 (**cprograms**)

Environment Variables

An environment variable is a name associated with a string. The name is the variable and the string is its value. When you issue a command on the system, you usually enter a relative path name, not an absolute pathname. The command you issue is found because the *PATH* variable points to the location of directories where commands are located. Without this *PATH* variable, you would have to type the absolute path name of every command you issue. When you issue a command the shell searches the directories listed in the *PATH* variable in the order in which they are listed. A good way to see many of the environment variables you have set is with the **env** command, as shown below on my Linux system:

```
# env
HISTSIZE=100
HOSTNAME=nycald1.hp.com
LOGNAME=root
MAIL=/var/spool/mail/root
TERM=linux
HOSTTYPE=i386
PATH=/sbin:/usr/sbin:/bin:/usr/bin:/opt/bin:/usr/X11R6/bin:
/usr/openwin/bin:/usr/TeX/bin:/usr/local/bin
HOME=/root
SHELL=/bin/bash
PS1=[\u@\h \W]\$
USER=root
LESSCHARSET=latin1
OSTYPE=Linux
SHLVL=2
_=/usr/bin/env
#
```

As you can see, other environment variables in addition to *PATH* that make working on your UNIX system easier. If you want to know the value of a specific environment variable, you could use the **echo** command to see its value, as shown below for the environment variable *HOME*:

```
$ echo $HOME
/root
```

The "$" preceding the environment variable name specifies that the value of the variable be sent to standard output. In this case, the value of the environment variable *HOME* is **/root**, which means that the current user has a home directory of **/root**.

You can define your own environment variables in Bash with the following syntax:

```
export NAME=value
```

You could set your prompt, defined by the *PS1* environment variable, with the following command:

man page

ps - 12

```
PS1=[\u@\h \W]\$
```

PS1 has now been set to open bracket, user name, at sign, host name, space, home directory, close bracket, dollar sign. As you can see from the previous listing of environment variables, *PS1* has by far the most difficult format.

You can also append to the end of an existing variable with the following format:

```
export NAME="$NAME:appended_information"
```

To add **/root/programs** to the existing *PATH* environment variable, for instance, you would issue the following command:

```
export PATH="$PATH:/root/programs"
```

This appends the path **/root/programs** to the environment variable *PATH*.

I recommend issuing **env** to see the environment variables set for your environment and their values.

Background Jobs and Job Control

When you run a command, as we have done so far in many examples, you don't get back the prompt until the command has completed. Some commands can take a long time to complete, in which case you'll be waiting a long time for the prompt to return. As an alternative to waiting for the prompt to return, you can run the command in the background, meaning that it is running behind the scenes while you perform other work. Because UNIX is multi-tasking, it is happy to run many commands in the background and still provide you with a prompt to issue yet more commands.

In order to run a command in the background, you simply add an ampersand (&) to the end of the command line. When you follow your command with an ampersand, the command is run in the background and the prompt is immediately returned. If you were to issue a recursive listing of all files on your system and redirect this listing to a file, it would take a long time. Probably tens of thousands of files and directories on your system would need to be written. You might be waiting some time for your list of files to be written. Let's now run a command just to see how many files and directories are on the system. What I would like to ultimately produce is a list of these files, but we'll start with a command that tells us how many files and directories are present on the system. The following example shows running the **ls** command with the "a," "-l," and "-R" options to produce a long and recursive listing of all files on the system and piping this output to **wc** with the "-l" option to get a count of the number of lines.

man page

ls - 2

man page

wc - 12

```
#  ls -alR | wc -l
ls: proc/18/exe: No such file or directory
ls: proc/19/exe: No such file or directory
ls: proc/2/exe: No such file or directory
   29982
```

This output shows three errors and a total of 29982 lines. If I want to write all 29982 entries to a file when I issue the **ls -alR** command, I have to sit and wait for the prompt to return. What I would rather do is issue the command to write all these entries to a file followed by an ampersand, in which case the job runs in the background and the prompt returns immediately, as shown in the following example:

```
#  ls -alR > /tmp/files &
[1] 817
ls: proc/18/exe: No such file or directory
ls: proc/19/exe: No such file or directory
ls: proc/2/exe: No such file or directory
```

The result of running this command in the background produces a job number in brackets and the process id, or PID, as the second number. The errors associated with this command, however, are printed to the screen. You can go back to our earlier redirection discussion and redirect both the list of files as well as errors to **/tmp/files** and run the job in the background with the following command:

```
#  ls -alR >& /tmp/files &
[1] 817
```

Now you don't see the errors, because they have been redirected to the file **/tmp/files** along with the listing of files, and you still get the command prompt back immediately. When I search **/tmp/files** for the three errors earlier produced, I can see that they are embedded in the file when they were encountered.

You have control over both foreground jobs, those which have not run in the background, and background jobs. To stop a foreground job, you type the "control" and "z" keys simultaneously, as shown in the following example:

man page

ls - 2

```
#  ls -alR
              .
              ..
              .lgb
              amd
              auto
              bin


ctrl-z
[4]+      Stopped      ls -alR
```

After *ctrl-z* is pressed, the **ls** command is interrupted at the point at which you type *ctrl-z*. The command is suspended at this point and you are shown the job number, in this case "4," and its status is listed as "Stopped," This command has been only suspended; it is not gone forever. You can start this process in the foreground with **fg** or run it in the background with **bg**. Using **bg** runs the command as if you had followed it with an "&." It is started from the point at which you interrupted it. You do not have to supply a job number when you issue the **fg** or **bg** command, because the default is to perform the specified operation on the last job, which in this case is job number 4.

Notice that in this example we have stopped job number 4. This means that other jobs are running with a lower job number. You can use the **jobs** command to get a list of all jobs and their status. You can then control the jobs by issuing commands such as **fg** followed by a "%" and the job number to run the command in the foreground, or a **bg** followed by a "%" and the job number to run the command in the background. If you wish to terminate a job altogether, you can issue the **kill** command followed by a "%" and the job number. In the process of creating the examples in this section, I have started and suspended many jobs. The following example shows listing all jobs with

man page

kill - 6

the **jobs** command, killing jobs 1 and 2 with **kill**, and running job 3 in the background:

man page

kill - 6

```
#  jobs
[1]       Stopped      ls -alR
[2]-      Stopped      run_audit
[3]+      Stopped      run_check
# kill %1
[1]       Stopped
# kill %2
[2]-      Stopped
# bg %3
#
```

Killing jobs 1 and 2 and running job 3 in the background return the prompt so that you can perform additional work.

umask and Permissions

man page

umask - 6

An additional topic to cover before shell programming techniques is file permissions and the way they relate to **umask**. This is important because you will write some shell programs anyone can use and others that you will want only a limited number of users, possibly just the system administrator, to use. **umask** is used to specify permission settings for new files and directories.

man page

ls - 2

Let's start with an example of a long listing of a file. We'll use the alias **ll**, which is **ls -l**, in the following examples:

```
sys1 1: ll script1
-rwxr-xr-x  1  marty  users  120 Jul 26 10:20 script1
```

The access rights for this file are defined by the position of read (r), write (w), and execute (x) when the **ll** command is issued. Figure 5-2 shows the three groups of three access rights for this file.

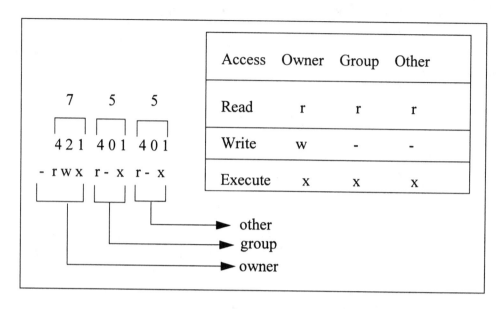

Figure 5-2 Example of File Permissions

The owner of this file has read, write, and execute permissions on the file. The group to which the user belongs has read and execute permissions, and others also have read and execute permissions. The permissions on this file can be specified by the octal sum of each field, which is 755.

What happens if you craft a new shell script or any new file? What permission settings will exist? You will want to execute the shell script, so you will need execute permission for the file. You can use **umask** to define the defaults for all your new files and directories.

You can view your umask with the following command:

```
sys1 2: umask
```

You can set the **umask** in **.cshrc** to define permission settings for new files and directories. The **umask** is used to *disable* access. You start with a **umask** and use the fields to disable some level of access. The **umask** command uses three octal fields. The fields are the sum of the access codes for user, group, and other, as shown in Figure 5-3.

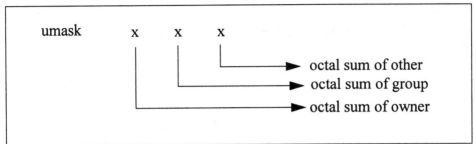

Figure 5-3 **umask** Fields

The *complement* of the umask field is "*anded*" with the default setting to change the **umask**. If you wanted to remove write permissions of files in Figure 5-4 for "group" and "other," you assign a **umask** of 022, as shown.

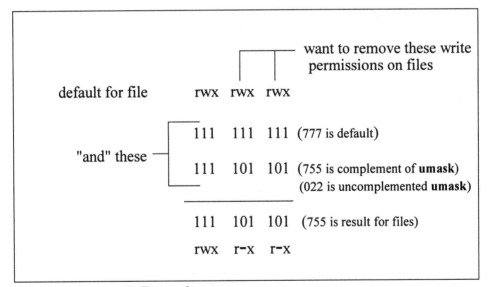

Figure 5-4 **umask** Example

umask 022 changes the file permissions to 755 in this example.

man page

chmod - 3

If you create a new file (**script2**) for your shell script, you may need to make it executable with the **chmod** command. If a file has permissions of 666 (rw-rw-rw-) and you wish to give the owner execute permission, you would issue the following command:

sys1 3: **chmod 766 script2**

CHAPTER 6

Introduction to the KornShell

Different Shells

Most UNIX variants allow you to select among several shells. The shell is important to you as a user, because it is your window into the system. The many shells available on UNIX variants are similar, in that you use them to issue commands, control many aspects of your user environment, write command files and shell programs, and so on. Because you'll probably be spending a lot of time in your shell you should develop an understanding of several different shells and see whether you develop a preference for one over the other. A particular shell, such as Bash, does not vary much from one UNIX variant to another. The shells themselves, however, have some unique features. In general, I don't find that users strongly prefer one shell over another. All the shells are similar in functionality and enjoyable to use once you get to know them. Most UNIX variants allow your system administrator to select from among several different shells when configuring users, so her or she usually has some flexibility concerning the shell that users run. In general, system administrators prefer users to use the same shell, making system administration easier in general. Most system administrators, however, are happy to grant a user request for a particular shell if indeed it is available on your system and you have a good reason to use it. I cover the KornShell in this chapter. Bash is covered in the previous chapter and the C shell in the following chapter.

Introduction to KornShell

man page

ksh - 6

Most UNIX variants allow you to select among several shells. Because of its versatility and ease of use, many system administrators configure the KornShell for new users. The KornShell was derived from the Bourne Shell and has much of the same functionality of the Bourne Shell. The **ksh** is the program you run on your UNIX system that supplies KornShell functionality. It is also often referred to as the K shell. I use **ksh** throughout this chapter. You can use the **ksh** in the following three ways:

- Interactively type commands on the command line.

- Group commonly executed sets of commands into command files that you can execute by typing the name of the file.

- Create KornShell programs using the structured programming techniques of the shell.

These three techniques are listed in the order in which you'll probably use them. First, you log in and use interactive commands. Then you group together commonly used commands and execute them with a single command. Finally, you may want to create sophisticated shell scripts.

For this reason, I describe these aspects of the KornShell in the order in which they are listed. The command file and programming aspects of the KornShell are covered as part of "Shell Programming Chapter."

Most of the examples in this chapter are from a Solaris system. You would probably find both your user setup and the operation of the KornShell on other systems similar to what is covered in this chapter. Much of the setup of any shell is performed by the system administrator, so you will surely find differences in your KornShell setup compared with what is shown in this chapter. In general, however, the operation of the KornShell is similar from one system to another.

Startup Files

The first activity you perform after you log into the system is to issue commands at the prompt. A command you may want to issue immediately is **ls -al**. Here is what I see on my system after executing this command, producing a long listing of all files:

```
martyp $ ls -al
total 22
drwxr-xr-x   2 martyp    staff          512 Mar 15 11:37 .
drwxrwxr-x   4 root      sys            512 Mar  4 09:24 ..
-rw-r--r--   1 martyp    staff          124 Mar 15 11:36 .cshrc
-rw-r--r--   1 martyp    staff          562 Mar  4 09:24 .profile
-rw-------   1 martyp    staff         7056 Apr  6 07:24 .sh_history
martyp $
```

This produces a short list of files. Some of these files, such as **.profile** and **.cshrc**, are startup files for **ksh** and the C shell, respectively. Upon logging in to a system, you normally execute system startup files for your shell and then execute any local startup files that you have in your home directory. In this case, I have a minimal **ksh** startup file in my home directory - only a **.profile** that has very little in it. Virtually all the startup activity for this user comes from the system profile, usually **/etc/profile.** You can usually read **/etc/profile**, so you can see what your system administrator has set up for you and other users. You can then modify your local **.profile** to include a variety of functionality. Your local **.profile** is usually run at login immediately after the system **/etc/profile**.

After running all the startup scripts associated with your **ksh** login, your environment is set up for you. Although our local **.profile** didn't do much, other than set up our prompt, a lot of setup took place with the system files that were run.

Another file you have is called the *Environment* file. This file name is defined by the environment variable **ENV**. This file is usually **.kshrc** in your home directory. Using the environment file, you can define which options, aliases, and other information will be passed to subprocesses. By default, your existing environment variables are passed to subprocesses. You can use the environment file to pass other information along as well.

You should take a look at your **ksh** startup files, including **/etc/profile**, **.profile**, and **.kshrc**.

We'll discuss much of the specific **ksh** functionality provided for you as part of your startup programs in the upcoming sections.

The History File, .sh_history

ksh keeps a history list of the commands you have issued. If you wish to reissue a command or view a command you earlier issued, you can use the history list. By default, **.sh_history** in your home directory is used as a history file. When your system administrator creates your **ksh** home directory, this file is probably present and used as your default history file.

By default, most systems save the 128 most recently executed commands. You can specify any number of commands to be included in the history list. The following line sets the history list to 200:

    HISTSIZE=200

Most users make this entry in their home **.profile**. AFter you have added this line to your **.profile** the history list is set to 200.

Recalling from the History List

You can view the most recent commands issued, along with their corresponding line numbers, with the **history** command, as shown in the following example:

```
martyp $ history
116      history 128
117      history 128 | more
118      history 200
119      alias
120      history 1
121      inv
122      env
123      env | more
124      history 1
125      more .profile
126      env | grep HIS
127      exit
128      env
129      env | grep HIS
130      more .profile
131      history
martyp $
```

Notice in this example that command number 127 is the **exit**, or command to log out, from the last session. Command number 128 is the **env** command I issued immediately upon establishing the next session.

We can also print the history list without line numbers using the **-n** option, as shown in the following example:

```
martyp $ history -n
        history 128 | more
        history 200
```

```
            alias
            history 1
            inv
            env
            env | more
            history 1
            more .profile
            env | grep HIS
            exit
            env
            env | grep HIS
            more .profile
            history
            history -n
martyp $
```

To produce a complete list of commands in the history list, we
issue the following command:

```
martyp $ history 0
5         env
6         more .profile
7         set
8         env | grep CDP
9         env | grep cdp
10        echo $SHELLL
11        echo $SHELL
12        more .profile
13        ll
14        ls -al /etc/profile
15        more /etc/profile
16        more /etc/profile | grep PS
17        exhoecE
18        ECHO
19        echo $ENV
20        env | more
21        echo $ENV
22        env | more
23        env | grep ENV
24        env | grep env
25        more /usr/bin/env
26        ls -al
27        more /etc/.kshrc
28        find / -name .kshrc
29        more /etc/passwd
30        more /etc/passwd | grep /home
31        ll /home/oracle
32        ls -al /home/oracle
33        ll /home
34        ls -al /home
```

```
35    ls -al /home/ptc-nfs
36    ls -al /home/ptc-nfs | more
37    ls -al /root
38    cd /root/users
39    ls -al
40    ls -al verasu
41    ls -al rodtsu
42     cd rodtsu
43    more .kshrc
44    more .env
45    ls
46    ls -l
47    ls -a
48    more .kshrc
49    cd ..
50    ls -al
51    ls -al | more
52    exit
53    ls -al
54    more .sh*
55    history
56    env | grep his
57    env | grep HIS
58    env | grep IS
59    env | more
60     env | grep FC
61    env | grep EDI
62    history
63    echo $HISTIZE
64    echo $HISTSIZE
65    env | more
66    ls -al
67    history 128
68    history
69    history 1 104
70    exit
71    alias
72    more /etc/profile | grep alias
73    ll
74    la -al
75    ls -al
76    more .profile
77    ls -al
78    more .cshrc
79    alias ll="ls -al"
80    aliase
81    alias
82    ll
83    exit
84    alias
85    alias
86    history
```

```
87      fc -l
88      man fc
89      man fc
90      man fc
91      alias
92      ps
93      ps -ef
94      ps -efl
95      ps
96      ls -alF
97      ls -al
98      alias ls="ls -al"
99      alias
100     ls
101     alias
102     unalias ls
103     ls
104     ls -al
105     alias
106     history
107     alias
108     unalias history
109     history
110     fc -l
111     history
112     alias hisotry="fc -l"
113     history
114     alias history="fc -l"
115     history
116     history 128
117     history 128 | more
118     history 200
119     alias
120     history 1
121     inv
122     env
123     env | more
124     history 1
125     more .profile
126     env | grep HIS
127     exit
128     env
129     env | grep HIS
130     more .profile
131     history
132     history 0
martyp $
```

history 0 prints from the very first command, zero, to the present command. Because only 128 commands are saved by default, the first few oldest commands, zero through four, dropped off the history list. This face means that we really started at command number five when we requested to start the list from command number zero.

To produce a list from command 100 to present, we issue the following:

```
martyp $ history 100
100     ls
101     alias
102     unalias ls
103     ls
104     ls -al
105     alias
106     history
107     alias
108     unalias history
109     history
110     fc -l
111     history
112     alias hisotry="fc -l"
113     history
114     alias history="fc -l"
115     history
116     history 128
117     history 128 | more
118     history 200
119     alias
120     history 1
121     inv
122     env
123     env | more
124     history 1
125     more .profile
126     env | grep HIS
127     exit
128     env
129     env | grep HIS
130     more .profile
131     history
132     history 0
133     history
134     history -n
135     history 100
martyp $
```

To list the current command and the 20 commands preceding it, we issue the following:

```
martyp $ history -20
116     history 128
117     history 128 | more
118     history 200
119     alias
120     history 1
121     inv
122     env
123     env | more
124     history 1
125     more .profile
126     env | grep HIS
127     exit
128     env
129     env | grep HIS
130     more .profile
131     history
132     history 0
133     history
134     history -n
135     history 100
136     history -20
martyp $
```

The *-20* goes back from the current command a full 20 commands. In this case, **history** is using the current command as the default place to begin producing the list. You can list the last 20 commands *preceding* the current command by specifying the range *-1 -20*, as shown in the following example:

```
martyp $ history -1 -20
136     history -20
135     history 100
134     history -n
133     history
132     history 0
131     history
130     more .profile
129     env | grep HIS
128     env
127     exit
126     env | grep HIS
125     more .profile
124     history 1
123     env | more
```

```
122       env
121       inv
120       history 1
119       alias
118       history 200
117       history 128 | more
martyp $
```

Notice in this example that the current command, **history -1 -20**, is not shown in the list because the *-1* starts the list with the preceding command. This is effectively producing a range of commands to list.

You can also reverse the order of the last 20 commands by specifying *-20* first and then the *-1,* as shown in the following example:

```
martyp $ history -20 -1
118       history 200
119       alias
120       history 1
121       inv
122       env
123       env | more
124       history 1
125       more .profile
126       env | grep HIS
127       exit
128       env
129       env | grep HIS
130       more .profile
131       history
132       history 0
133       history
134       history -n
135       history 100
136       history -20
137       history -1 -20
martyp $
```

You can also produce a list from the last time a command was issued to the current command. The following example shows producing a list from the last **fc** command to the current command:

```
martyp $ history fc
```

```
110      fc -l
111      history
112      alias hisotry="fc -l"
113      history
114      alias history="fc -l"
115      history
116      history 128
117      history 128 | more
118      history 200
119      alias
120      history 1
121      inv
122      env
123      env | more
124      history 1
125      more .profile
126      env | grep HIS
127      exit
128      env
129      env | grep HIS
130      more .profile
131      history
132      history 0
133      history
134      history -n
135      history 100
136      history -20
137      history -1 -20
138      history -20 -1
139      history
140      history grep
141      history env
142      history
143      history fc
martyp $
```

You can also reverse this list using the *-r* option, as shown in the following example:

```
martyp $ history -r fc
144      history -r fc
143      history fc
142      history
141      history env
140      history grep
139      history
138      history -20 -1
137      history -1 -20
136      history -20
135      history 100
```

```
134     history -n
133     history
132     history 0
131     history
130     more .profile
129     env | grep HIS
128     env
127     exit
126     env | grep HIS
125     more .profile
124     history 1
123     env | more
122     env
121     inv
120     history 1
119     alias
118     history 200
117     history 128 | more
116     history 128
115     history
114     alias history="fc -l"
113     history
112     alias hisotry="fc -l"
111     history
110     fc -l
martyp $
```

Having access to this history list is a great feature of the Korn-Shell. You can view all the commands you have issued, including your typing errors, in any format you wish. In the next section, we start using the commands in the history list by recalling them.

Re-executing Commands with r

You can reissue a command with the **r** commmand. To reissue the last command, you simply type **r**. In the following example, I issue the command **history 5** to view the last five commands from the history list. I then type **r** to reissue the last command, and again the last five commands are listed:

```
martyp $ history -5
301      whoami
302      pwd
303      more /etc/passwd
304       ps -efl
305      cat .profile
306      history -5
martyp $ r
history -5
302      pwd
303      more /etc/passwd
304       ps -efl
305      cat .profile
306      history -5
307      history -5
martyp $
```

You can reissue a specific command number by typing **r**, a space, and the number of the command you wish to reissue. In the following example, I issue the **history** command number 302:

```
martyp $ history
294      history -5
295      whoami
296      pwd
297      more /etc/passwd
298      ps -efl
299      cat /etc/profile
300      history 5
301      whoami
302      pwd
303      more /etc/passwd
304       ps -efl
305      cat .profile
306      history -5
307      history -5
308      history -5
309      history
martyp $ r 302
pwd
/home/martyp
martyp $
```

You can also give the name of the command you wish to reissue. Let's say that you want to reissue the last **fc** command. You would simply give the letter "f" along with the **r** command, and the last command that started with **f** would be reissued, as shown in the following example:

```
martyp $ history
308     history -5
309     history
310     pwd
311     whoami
312     pwd
313     cat /etc/profile
314     ls
315     fc -l
316     env
317     who
318     cat /etc/passwd
319     ls -al
320     history
321     more .profile
322     set
323     history
martyp $ r f
fc -l
309     history
310     pwd
311     whoami
312     pwd
313     cat /etc/profile
314     ls
315     fc -l
316     env
317     who
318     cat /etc/passwd
319     ls -al
320     history
321     more .profile
322     set
323     history
324     fc -l
martyp $
```

man page

vi - 8

You can also perform some substitution with the **r** command. If you issued the **vi** command earlier and want to rerun **vi** but specify a different file name to edit, you can substitute a new file name. The fol-

man page

vi - 8

lowing example shows reissuing an earlier **vi** command, except now we'll replace the original filename we edited, **.profile**, with the new filename we want to edit, **.kshrc**. In this example we'll first run the **history** command, then reissue the **vi** command to edit **.kshrc**, and then run the history command again to see our revised **vi** command:

```
martyp $ history
316     env
317     who
318     cat /etc/passwd
319     ls -al
320     history
321     more .profile
322     set
323     history
324     fc -l
325     vi .profile
326     set
327     ls -al
328     env
329     who
330     more /etc/passwd | grep marty
331     history
martyp $ r vi .profile=.kshrc
martyp $ history
318     cat /etc/passwd
319     ls -al
320     history
321     more .profile
322     set
323     history
324     fc -l
325     vi .profile
326     set
327     ls -al
328     env
329     who
330     more /etc/passwd | grep marty
331     history
332     vi .kshrc
333     history
martyp $
```

This command sustitutes **.kshrc** for **.profile** on the command line.

This leads us to more advanced command line editing. You may want to recall a command earlier issued and edit the command line using **vi** editor commands. The next section covers command line editing.

man page

vi - 8

Fetching Commands Using vi Directives

You can edit entries in your history list with either the **vi** or emacs editor. I will cover the **vi** editor in this chapter, because it is the most widely used on UNIX systems. You can, however, perform all the same functions shown in this chapter with the emacs editor.

You edit the history list using **vi** the same way you edit a file using **vi**. You press the *escape* key and use standard **vi** keys for moving up and down, left and right, inserting deleting, and changing text. In this section, I cover fetching a command from the history list using **vi** commands and then I cover editing the command after you have restored it to the command line. After the command has been edited to your liking, you press *enter* to execute the command and place it at the very bottom of the command list.

Your editor is normally be set in either your local **.profile** or **/etc/profile**. You can view these files to see what editor has been set for you by your system administrator. When I issue the **env** and **set** commands on my system, both report *EDITOR=vi*. This corresponds with my **/etc/profile** that has the editor set to **vi**.

Let's first take a look at fetching some previously issued commands using **vi**. The examples in this section use **vi** functionality that is described in both the **vi** chapter and on the **vi** quick reference card. The **k, j, G,** and search commands in this section operate in the same manner at the command line as they would if you were using **vi** to edit a file.

Pressing the *escape* key and a command allows you to perform various functions in the **ksh**. The following example shows producing the history list and issuing *escape* **k** to recall the previous command:

man page

ksh - 6

```
martyp $ history
125     man fc
126     set | more
127      exit
128     history
129     k
130     env | more
131     set | more
132     more .profile
133     more .profile | grep rof
134     more .profile | grep vi
135     more /etc/profile | grep vi
136     set |grep edit
137     set | grep vi
138     env | grep vi
139     history
140     who
martyp $ history
```

Issuing *escape* **k** recalled the last command issued, in this case the **who** command at line 140. Each time you press **k**, the preceding **ksh** command is fetched. This is the same as pressing *escape* and the - (minus) key. You can specify the number of commands you wish to go back in the history list with *escape* *n***k**, where *n* is the number of commands you want to go back in the history list. The following example shows issuing *escape* **5k** to fetch the fifth command back in the history list:

```
martyp $ history
125     man fc
126     set | more
127      exit
128     history
129     k
130     env | more
131     set | more
132     more .profile
133     more .profile | grep rof
134     more .profile | grep vi
135     more /etc/profile | grep vi
136     set |grep edit
137     set | grep vi
138     env | grep vi
139     history
140     who
martyp $ set |grep edit
```

Issuing *escape* **5k** fetched the fifth command back in the history list at line 136. This is the same as having issued *escape* **5-**.

You can also move forward in the history list, using **j** in the same way we used **k** to move back in the history list. Let's issue *escape* **5k** to move back five commands in the history list to line 136, and then we can use *escape* **3j** to move forward three commands to line 139, as shown in the following example:

```
martyp $ history
125     man fc
126     set | more
127      exit
128     history
129     k
130     env | more
131     set | more
132     more .profile
133     more .profile | grep rof
134     more .profile | grep vi
135     more /etc/profile | grep vi
136     set |grep edit
137     set | grep vi
138     env | grep vi
139     history
140     history
martyp $ who
```

Issuing *escape* **3j** moved us forward to line 139, which is the same as having issued *escape* **3-**.

We can also go back to the oldest command in the history list with *escape* **G**. You can go back to a specific command number from the history list with *escape* **nG**, where *n* is a specific command number from the history file. The following example shows issuing *escape* **126G** to go back to line 126 from the history list:

```
martyp $ history
125     man fc
126     set | more
127      exit
128     history
129     k
130     env | more
131     set | more
```

```
132      more .profile
133      more .profile | grep rof
134      more .profile | grep vi
135      more /etc/profile | grep vi
136      set |grep edit
137      set | grep vi
138      env | grep vi
139      history
140      who
martyp $ set | more
```

man page

more - 3

You can also recall lines from the history list based on searches. If, for instance, you want to recall the most recently issued command from the history list that has in it **profile**, you would issue **/profile**, which is the slash character followed by **profile**, to get the result shown in the following example:

```
martyp $ history
125      man fc
126      set | more
127       exit
128      history
129      k
130      env | more
131      set | more
132      more .profile
133      more .profile | grep rof
134      more .profile | grep vi
135      more /etc/profile | grep vi
136      set |grep edit
137      set | grep vi
138      env | grep vi
139      history
140      who
martyp $ more /etc/profile | grep vi
```

man page

vi - 8

Searching for the most recent occurrence of **profile** produces line 135. Many of the other searches in **vi** work at the command line. The **vi** chapter and **vi** quick reference card have more searching information in them that you may want to try at the command line.

Editing on the Command Line Using vi Directives

After you have "fetched" the command you wish to edit or entered a command that needs editing, you can use your **vi** directives to make modifications on the command line.

The **ksh** puts you in input mode immediately upon fetching a command from the history list. This approach is the converse of the **vi** program that you use to edit files, which puts you in control mode by default. After you have fetched a command from the history list, you must press *escape* in order to move into control mode when using **vi** in **ksh**.

Let's now perform some simple modifications to commands we have fetched from the history list. We recall line number 286 from the history list with the sequence *escape* **286G**. After recalling this command, we insert *cat* at the beginning of the command with **i cat**. **i** is for insert text to the left of the current cursor position. The following example shows the result of both the fetch of line 286 and inserting **cat**:

```
martyp $ history
285      history
286      more /etc/profile | grep vi
287      who
288      whoami
289      who
290      ls -al
291      alias
292      pwd
293      ls -al /home
294      cat .profile
295      history
296      vi .profile
297      cat /etc/passwd
298      cat /etc/passwd | grep donna
299      pwd
300      history
martyp $ cat more /etc/profile | grep vi
```

You can see that **i cat** inserted *cat* at the very beginning of the line.

We can again recall line 286 and use **A** to append text to the very end of the line, as shown in the following example:

```
martyp $ history
285     history
286     more /etc/profile | grep vi
287     who
288     whoami
289     who
290     ls -al
291     alias
292     pwd
293     ls -al /home
294     cat .profile
295     history
296     vi .profile
297     cat /etc/passwd
298     cat /etc/passwd | grep donna
299     pwd
300     history
martyp $ more /etc/profile | grep vieditor
```

man page

more - 3

man page

grep - 10

In this example, we used the squence **A editor** to insert the word *editor* at the very end of the command line we had recalled.

We can recall this line and change *more* at the beginning of the line to *cat* by issuing the sequence **cw cat**, as shown in the following example:

```
martyp $ history
285     history
286     more /etc/profile | grep vi
287     who
288     whoami
289     who
290     ls -al
291     alias
292     pwd
293     ls -al /home
294     cat .profile
295     history
296     vi .profile
```

```
297      cat /etc/passwd
298      cat /etc/passwd | grep donna
299      pwd
300      history
martyp $ cat /etc/profile | grep vi
```

man page

cat - 3

man page

grep - 10

This changes *more* to *cat* on the command line.

To delete the word *more* without replacing it, we fetch line 286 and issue **dw**, as shown in the following example:

```
martyp $ history
285      history
286      more /etc/profile | grep vi
287      who
288      whoami
289      who
290      ls -al
291      alias
292      pwd
293      ls -al /home
294      cat .profile
295      history
296      vi .profile
297      cat /etc/passwd
298      cat /etc/passwd | grep donna
299      pwd
300      history
martyp $  /etc/profile | grep vi
```

If we are unhappy with the most recent command issued we can undo the command by issuing **u**, which undoes the **dw** we used to remove *more* on the command line, as shown in the following example:

```
martyp $ history
285      history
286      more /etc/profile | grep vi
287      who
288      whoami
289      who
290      ls -al
291      alias
```

```
292      pwd
293      ls -al /home
294      cat .profile
295      history
296      vi .profile
297      cat /etc/passwd
298      cat /etc/passwd | grep donna
299      pwd
300      history
martyp $ more /etc/profile | grep vi
```

man page

more - 3

man page

grep - 10

man page

vi - 8

Issuing **u** puts back the *more* that we had removed with **dw**.

You may want to try using both the **vi** commands I have covered here, as well as other commands to add, delete, change, search and replace, copy, and undo at the command line.

Aliases in KornShell

An alias is a name that you select for a frequently used command or series of commands. Many aliases are predefined for you.

The **alias** command, without any arguments, lists all aliases. This list includes both preset aliases as well as those you have set. The following command shows the preset aliases on the system on which I am working:

```
martyp $ alias
autoload='typeset -fu'
command='command '
functions='typeset -f'
history='fc -l'
hyper1=HHLIC='/opt/local/bristol/hyperhelp/licenses/hpptc1;export HHLIC'
hyper36=HHLIC='/opt/local/bristol/hyperhelp/licenses/hpptc36;export HHLIC'
hyper83=HHLIC='/opt/local/bristol/hyperhelp/licenses/hpptc83;export HHLIC'
hyper95=HHLIC='/opt/local/bristol/hyperhelp/licenses/hpptc95;export HHLIC'
integer='typeset -i'
local=typeset
nohup='nohup '
r='fc -e -'
stop='kill -STOP'
suspend='kill -STOP $$'
martyp $
```

Many preset aliases are shown as a result of typing the **alias** command without any options.

Many of these aliases are related to somewhat advanced use of the KornShell, such as job control. Others are useful to you right away. The *history* alias, for instance, lists the commands in the **.sh_history** file and precedes each entry by a line number. The *r* alias allows you to re-run the the last command that appears in the history list.

You are not limited to using only preset aliases. You can set your own aliases. The following example shows setting an alias, producing a list of aliases to see whether indeed our new alias has been set, and then running our alias:

```
martyp $ alias ls="ls -al"
martyp $ alias
autoload='typeset -fu'
command='command '
functions='typeset -f'
history='fc -l'
hyper1=HHLIC='/opt/local/bristol/hyperhelp/licenses/hpptc1;export HHLIC'
hyper36=HHLIC='/opt/local/bristol/hyperhelp/licenses/hpptc36;export HHLIC'
hyper83=HHLIC='/opt/local/bristol/hyperhelp/licenses/hpptc83;export HHLIC'
hyper95=HHLIC='/opt/local/bristol/hyperhelp/licenses/hpptc95;export HHLIC'
integer='typeset -i'
local=typeset
ls='ls -al'
nohup='nohup '
r='fc -e -'
stop='kill -STOP'
suspend='kill -STOP $$'
martyp $ ls
total 26
drwxr-xr-x   2 martyp    staff          512 Mar 15 11:37 .
drwxrwxr-x   4 root      sys            512 Mar  4 09:24 ..
-rw-r--r--   1 martyp    staff          124 Mar 15 11:36 .cshrc
-rw-r--r--   1 martyp    staff          562 Mar  4 09:24 .profile
-rw-------   1 martyp    staff         9058 Apr 10 06:58 .sh_history
martyp $
```

man page

ls - 2

The first command set an alias that executes **ls -al** whenever we type **ls**. I issued the **alias** command to see whether indeed the new alias would appear in the list of aliases. It appears right after *local* and right before *nohup* in the alphabetical list of aliases. The final command shows running **ls**, which produces a listing that you would receive from having run the **ls -al** command.

You don't have to keep an alias for the duration of your session after having set it. If you don't like an alias, you can use the **unalias** command to remove an alias.

To see **unalias** work, let's again produce a list of aliases, use **unalias** to unset the *history* alias, run the *history* command to see whether indeed it has been removed, and then run the **fc -l** command to which the *history* alias was mapped:

```
martyp $ alias
autoload='typeset -fu'
command='command '
functions='typeset -f'
history='fc -l'
hyper1=HHLIC='/opt/local/bristol/hyperhelp/licenses/hpptc1;export HHLIC'
hyper36=HHLIC='/opt/local/bristol/hyperhelp/licenses/hpptc36;export HHLIC'
hyper83=HHLIC='/opt/local/bristol/hyperhelp/licenses/hpptc83;export HHLIC'
hyper95=HHLIC='/opt/local/bristol/hyperhelp/licenses/hpptc95;export HHLIC'
integer='typeset -i'
local=typeset
nohup='nohup '
r='fc -e -'
stop='kill -STOP'
suspend='kill -STOP $$'
martyp $ unalias history
martyp $ history
ksh: history:  not found
martyp $ fc -l
131     ps
132     ls -alF
133     ls -al
134     alias ls="ls -al"
135     alias
136     ls
137     alias
138     unalias ls
139     ls
140     ls -al
141     alias
142     history
143     alias
144     unalias history
145     history
146     fc -l
martyp $
```

When we **unalias** *history* and then run *history,* **ksh** is unable to find it and produces the message *history: not found.* When we run **fc -l** a list of the most recently issued commands with their corresponding numbers is produced. This makes clear that when you run the *history* alias, you are actually running the **fc -l** command.

Command and Path Completion

man page

ksh - 6

ksh sometimes knows what you're thinking. You can type part of a command or pathname and **ksh** can complete the remainder for you. You can type part of a command or pathname and press *escape* key to complete the command. If, for instance, you wish to issue the **uname** command to view the current system run level but can't remember the full command, you can type "un" and *escape* followed by the "=" key and the command is completed for you. In the following example, we'll change to the **/sbin** directory, list its contents, and then type **un***escape*=:

man page

cd - 3

```
martyp $ cd /sbin
martyp $ ls -al
total 11704
drwxrwxr-x   2 root     sys          512 Nov 27 14:55 .
drwxr-xr-x  31 root     root        1024 Apr 19 03:24 ..
-r-xr-xr-x   1 bin      bin       200356 Sep  1  1998 autopush
lrwxrwxrwx   1 root     root          21 Nov 27 14:55 bpgetfile -> ../usr/sbin/e
-r-xr-xr-x   1 bin      bin       470436 Sep  1  1998 dhcpagent
-r-xr-xr-x   1 bin      bin       433064 Sep  1  1998 dhcpinfo
-r-xr-xr-x   1 bin      bin       253664 Sep  1  1998 fdisk
-r-xr-xr-x   1 bin      bin       762816 Sep  1  1998 hostconfig
-r-xr-xr-x   1 bin      bin       535900 Sep  1  1998 ifconfig
-r-xr-xr-x   1 root     sys       516484 Sep  1  1998 init
-r-xr-xr-x   2 bin      root      257444 Sep  1  1998 jsh
-r-xr-xr-x   1 bin      bin       224596 Sep  1  1998 mount
-r-xr-xr-x   1 root     sys         6935 Jan  1  1970 mountall
-rwxr--r--   3 root     sys         2689 Jan  1  1970 rc0
-rwxr--r--   1 root     sys         2905 Jan  1  1970 rc1
-rwxr--r--   1 root     sys         2491 Jan  1  1970 rc2
-rwxr--r--   1 root     sys         1948 Jan  1  1970 rc3
-rwxr--r--   3 root     sys         2689 Jan  1  1970 rc5
-rwxr--r--   3 root     sys         2689 Jan  1  1970 rc6
-rwxr--r--   1 root     sys         9412 Jan  1  1970 rcS
-r-xr-xr-x   2 bin      root      257444 Sep  1  1998 sh
-r-xr-xr-x   1 bin      bin       195300 Sep  1  1998 soconfig
lrwxrwxrwx   1 root     root          13 Nov 27 14:40 su -> ../usr/bin/su
-r-xr-xr-x   1 root     sys       473808 Sep  1  1998 su.static
-r-xr-xr-x   1 root     bin       288544 Sep  1  1998 sulogin
-rwxr--r--   1 root     sys         3138 Jan  1  1970 swapadd
-r-xr-xr-x   1 bin      bin        29736 Sep  1  1998 sync
-r-xr-xr-x   1 root     sys       435004 Sep  1  1998 uadmin
-r-xr-xr-x   1 bin      bin       213408 Sep  1  1998 umount
-r-xr-xr-x   1 root     sys         3292 Jan  1  1970 umountall
-r-xr-xr-x   1 bin      bin       193152 Sep  1  1998 uname
martyp $ un                              ;typed unescape=
1) uname
martyp $ un
```

   ksh determined that the only command that starts with "un" is **uname**. The **uname** command was listed and *un* was again put at the command prompt for me. You can't see the *escape*= I typed after the first "un," so I made a comment to the side showing the full command.

Rather than list all files starting with "un," you can replace the current word with all files that match by typing **un***escape******, as shown in the following example:

man page

cd - 3

man page

ls - 2

```
martyp $ cd /sbin
martyp $ ls -al
total 11704
drwxrwxr-x   2 root     sys          512 Nov 27 14:55 .
drwxr-xr-x  31 root     root        1024 Apr 19 03:24 ..
-r-xr-xr-x   1 bin      bin       200356 Sep  1  1998 autopush
lrwxrwxrwx   1 root     root          21 Nov 27 14:55 bpgetfile -> ../usr/sbin/e
-r-xr-xr-x   1 bin      bin       470436 Sep  1  1998 dhcpagent
-r-xr-xr-x   1 bin      bin       433064 Sep  1  1998 dhcpinfo
-r-xr-xr-x   1 bin      bin       253664 Sep  1  1998 fdisk
-r-xr-xr-x   1 bin      bin       762816 Sep  1  1998 hostconfig
-r-xr-xr-x   1 bin      bin       535900 Sep  1  1998 ifconfig
-r-xr-xr-x   1 root     sys       516484 Sep  1  1998 init
-r-xr-xr-x   2 bin      root      257444 Sep  1  1998 jsh
-r-xr-xr-x   1 bin      bin       224596 Sep  1  1998 mount
-r-xr-xr-x   1 root     sys         6935 Jan  1  1970 mountall
-rwxr--r--   3 root     sys         2689 Jan  1  1970 rc0
-rwxr--r--   1 root     sys         2905 Jan  1  1970 rc1
-rwxr--r--   1 root     sys         2491 Jan  1  1970 rc2
-rwxr--r--   1 root     sys         1948 Jan  1  1970 rc3
-rwxr--r--   3 root     sys         2689 Jan  1  1970 rc5
-rwxr--r--   3 root     sys         2689 Jan  1  1970 rc6
-rwxr--r--   1 root     sys         9412 Jan  1  1970 rcS
-r-xr-xr-x   2 bin      root      257444 Sep  1  1998 sh
-r-xr-xr-x   1 bin      bin       195300 Sep  1  1998 soconfig
lrwxrwxrwx   1 root     root          13 Nov 27 14:40 su -> ../usr/bin/su
-r-xr-xr-x   1 root     sys       473808 Sep  1  1998 su.static
-r-xr-xr-x   1 root     bin       288544 Sep  1  1998 sulogin
-rwxr--r--   1 root     sys         3138 Jan  1  1970 swapadd
-r-xr-xr-x   1 bin      bin        29736 Sep  1  1998 sync
-r-xr-xr-x   1 root     sys       435004 Sep  1  1998 uadmin
-r-xr-xr-x   1 bin      bin       213408 Sep  1  1998 umount
-r-xr-xr-x   1 root     sys         3292 Jan  1  1970 umountall
-r-xr-xr-x   1 bin      bin       193152 Sep  1  1998 uname
martyp $ uname                                   ;typed un escape*
```

You can see in this example that **uname** is replaced right at the prompt with the only command that matched **un***escape******.

The next example shows using **um***escape***=** to get a list of all files that start with "um," then using **um***escape****** to get all files matched to "um," and finally using **um***escape***** to replace the current word with the first file name that starts with "um":

```
martyp $ ls -al
total 11704
drwxrwxr-x   2 root     sys          512 Nov 27 14:55 .
drwxr-xr-x  31 root     root        1024 Apr 19 03:24 ..
-r-xr-xr-x   1 bin      bin       200356 Sep  1  1998 autopush
lrwxrwxrwx   1 root     root          21 Nov 27 14:55 bpgetfile -> ../usr/sbin/e
-r-xr-xr-x   1 bin      bin       470436 Sep  1  1998 dhcpagent
-r-xr-xr-x   1 bin      bin       433064 Sep  1  1998 dhcpinfo
-r-xr-xr-x   1 bin      bin       253664 Sep  1  1998 fdisk
-r-xr-xr-x   1 bin      bin       762816 Sep  1  1998 hostconfig
```

```
-r-xr-xr-x    1 bin      bin        535900 Sep  1  1998 ifconfig
-r-xr-xr-x    1 root     sys        516484 Sep  1  1998 init
-r-xr-xr-x    2 bin      root       257444 Sep  1  1998 jsh
-r-xr-xr-x    1 bin      bin        224596 Sep  1  1998 mount
-r-xr-xr-x    1 root     sys          6935 Jan  1  1970 mountall
-rwxr--r--    3 root     sys          2689 Jan  1  1970 rc0
-rwxr--r--    1 root     sys          2905 Jan  1  1970 rc1
-rwxr--r--    1 root     sys          2491 Jan  1  1970 rc2
-rwxr--r--    1 root     sys          1948 Jan  1  1970 rc3
-rwxr--r--    3 root     sys          2689 Jan  1  1970 rc5
-rwxr--r--    3 root     sys          2689 Jan  1  1970 rc6
-rwxr--r--    1 root     sys          9412 Jan  1  1970 rcS
-r-xr-xr-x    2 bin      root       257444 Sep  1  1998 sh
-r-xr-xr-x    1 bin      bin        195300 Sep  1  1998 soconfig
lrwxrwxrwx    1 root     root           13 Nov 27 14:40 su -> ../usr/bin/su
-r-xr-xr-x    1 root     sys        473808 Sep  1  1998 su.static
-r-xr-xr-x    1 root     bin        288544 Sep  1  1998 sulogin
-rwxr--r--    1 root     sys          3138 Jan  1  1970 swapadd
-r-xr-xr-x    1 bin      bin         29736 Sep  1  1998 sync
-r-xr-xr-x    1 root     sys        435004 Sep  1  1998 uadmin
-r-xr-xr-x    1 bin      bin        213408 Sep  1  1998 umount
-r-xr-xr-x    1 root     sys          3292 Jan  1  1970 umountall
-r-xr-xr-x    1 bin      bin        193152 Sep  1  1998 uname
martyp $ um                                              ;typed umescape=
1) umount
2) umountall
martyp $ umount umountall                               ;typed umescape*
martyp $ umount                                         ;typed umescape\
```

Let's now work with a command and arguments that will be file names. What if the characters you type are not unique, as they were with "un" in the /sbin directory? If the command or pathname is not unique, then ksh shows you the options for completing the command. The following example shows typing ls r*escape*= to get a list of commands that start with "r":

man page

ksh - 6

man page

ls - 2

```
martyp $ ls -al
total 11704
drwxrwxr-x    2 root     sys           512 Nov 27 14:55 .
drwxr-xr-x   31 root     root         1024 Apr 19 03:24 ..
-r-xr-xr-x    1 bin      bin        200356 Sep  1  1998 autopush
lrwxrwxrwx    1 root     root           21 Nov 27 14:55 bpgetfile -> ../usr/sbin/e
-r-xr-xr-x    1 bin      bin        470436 Sep  1  1998 dhcpagent
-r-xr-xr-x    1 bin      bin        433064 Sep  1  1998 dhcpinfo
-r-xr-xr-x    1 bin      bin        253664 Sep  1  1998 fdisk
-r-xr-xr-x    1 bin      bin        762816 Sep  1  1998 hostconfig
-r-xr-xr-x    1 bin      bin        535900 Sep  1  1998 ifconfig
-r-xr-xr-x    1 root     sys        516484 Sep  1  1998 init
-r-xr-xr-x    2 bin      root       257444 Sep  1  1998 jsh
-r-xr-xr-x    1 bin      bin        224596 Sep  1  1998 mount
-r-xr-xr-x    1 root     sys          6935 Jan  1  1970 mountall
-rwxr--r--    3 root     sys          2689 Jan  1  1970 rc0
-rwxr--r--    1 root     sys          2905 Jan  1  1970 rc1
-rwxr--r--    1 root     sys          2491 Jan  1  1970 rc2
-rwxr--r--    1 root     sys          1948 Jan  1  1970 rc3
-rwxr--r--    3 root     sys          2689 Jan  1  1970 rc5
-rwxr--r--    3 root     sys          2689 Jan  1  1970 rc6
-rwxr--r--    1 root     sys          9412 Jan  1  1970 rcS
-r-xr-xr-x    2 bin      root       257444 Sep  1  1998 sh
-r-xr-xr-x    1 bin      bin        195300 Sep  1  1998 soconfig
lrwxrwxrwx    1 root     root           13 Nov 27 14:40 su -> ../usr/bin/su
-r-xr-xr-x    1 root     sys        473808 Sep  1  1998 su.static
-r-xr-xr-x    1 root     bin        288544 Sep  1  1998 sulogin
-rwxr--r--    1 root     sys          3138 Jan  1  1970 swapadd
```

man page

ls - 6

```
-r-xr-xr-x   1 bin     bin        29736 Sep  1  1998 sync
-r-xr-xr-x   1 root    sys       435004 Sep  1  1998 uadmin
-r-xr-xr-x   1 bin     bin       213408 Sep  1  1998 umount
-r-xr-xr-x   1 root    sys         3292 Jan  1  1970 umountall
-r-xr-xr-x   1 bin     bin       193152 Sep  1  1998 uname
martyp $ ls r                               ;typed ls rescape=
1) rc0
2) rc1
3) rc2
4) rc3
5) rc5
6) rc6
7) rcS
martyp $ ls r
```

man page

ksh - 6

You can see from this example that typing **ls -r***escape*= produced a list of seven files. Again, the **ls r** was placed for me at the next prompt. You can use the information left for you at the next prompt to perform additional **ksh** file name expansion. Let's again perform our **ls** *rescape=,* which produces the list of seven files beginning with *r*. Our next prompt will have **ls r** waiting for us, and this time we'll type *escape*,* which will produce a list of all seven files for us on the line:

```
martyp $ ls -al
total 11704
drwxrwxr-x   2 root    sys          512 Nov 27 14:55 .
drwxr-xr-x  31 root    root        1024 Apr 19 03:24 ..
-r-xr-xr-x   1 bin     bin       200356 Sep  1  1998 autopush
lrwxrwxrwx   1 root    root          21 Nov 27 14:55 bpgetfile -> ../usr/sbin/e
-r-xr-xr-x   1 bin     bin       470436 Sep  1  1998 dhcpagent
-r-xr-xr-x   1 bin     bin       433064 Sep  1  1998 dhcpinfo
-r-xr-xr-x   1 bin     bin       253664 Sep  1  1998 fdisk
-r-xr-xr-x   1 bin     bin       762816 Sep  1  1998 hostconfig
-r-xr-xr-x   1 bin     bin       535900 Sep  1  1998 ifconfig
-r-xr-xr-x   1 root    sys       516484 Sep  1  1998 init
-r-xr-xr-x   2 bin     root      257444 Sep  1  1998 jsh
-r-xr-xr-x   1 bin     bin       224596 Sep  1  1998 mount
-r-xr-xr-x   1 root    sys         6935 Jan  1  1970 mountall
-rwxr--r--   3 root    sys         2689 Jan  1  1970 rc0
-rwxr--r--   1 root    sys         2905 Jan  1  1970 rc1
-rwxr--r--   1 root    sys         2491 Jan  1  1970 rc2
-rwxr--r--   1 root    sys         1948 Jan  1  1970 rc3
-rwxr--r--   3 root    sys         2689 Jan  1  1970 rc5
-rwxr--r--   3 root    sys         2689 Jan  1  1970 rc6
-rwxr--r--   1 root    sys         9412 Jan  1  1970 rcS
-r-xr-xr-x   2 bin     root      257444 Sep  1  1998 sh
-r-xr-xr-x   1 bin     bin       195300 Sep  1  1998 soconfig
lrwxrwxrwx   1 root    root          13 Nov 27 14:40 su -> ../usr/bin/su
-r-xr-xr-x   1 root    sys       473808 Sep  1  1998 su.static
-r-xr-xr-x   1 root    bin       288544 Sep  1  1998 sulogin
-rwxr--r--   1 root    sys         3138 Jan  1  1970 swapadd
-r-xr-xr-x   1 bin     bin        29736 Sep  1  1998 sync
-r-xr-xr-x   1 root    sys       435004 Sep  1  1998 uadmin
-r-xr-xr-x   1 bin     bin       213408 Sep  1  1998 umount
-r-xr-xr-x   1 root    sys         3292 Jan  1  1970 umountall
-r-xr-xr-x   1 bin     bin       193152 Sep  1  1998 uname
martyp $ ls r                               ;typed ls rescape=
1) rc0
2) rc1
3) rc2
4) rc3
5) rc5
```

```
6) rc6
7) rcS
martyp $ ls rc0 rc1 rc2 rc3 rc5 rc6 rcS        ;typed escape* to get
seven files
```

escape* listed all seven files beginning with *r* and placed them on the command line.

In the next example we'll issue both the *escape=* and *escape**. We'll then type **ls** *escape_* (underscore), which puts the last word of the last command in the line, which is *rcS*:

man page

ls - 2

```
martyp $ ls -al
total 11704
drwxrwxr-x   2 root    sys         512 Nov 27 14:55 .
drwxr-xr-x  31 root    root       1024 Apr 19 03:24 ..
-r-xr-xr-x   1 bin     bin      200356 Sep  1 1998 autopush
lrwxrwxrwx   1 root    root         21 Nov 27 14:55 bpgetfile -> ../usr/sbin/e
-r-xr-xr-x   1 bin     bin      470436 Sep  1 1998 dhcpagent
-r-xr-xr-x   1 bin     bin      433064 Sep  1 1998 dhcpinfo
-r-xr-xr-x   1 bin     bin      253664 Sep  1 1998 fdisk
-r-xr-xr-x   1 bin     bin      762816 Sep  1 1998 hostconfig
-r-xr-xr-x   1 bin     bin      535900 Sep  1 1998 ifconfig
-r-xr-xr-x   1 root    sys      516484 Sep  1 1998 init
-r-xr-xr-x   2 bin     root     257444 Sep  1 1998 jsh
-r-xr-xr-x   1 bin     bin      224596 Sep  1 1998 mount
-r-xr-xr-x   1 root    sys        6935 Jan  1 1970 mountall
-rwxr--r--   3 root    sys        2689 Jan  1 1970 rc0
-rwxr--r--   1 root    sys        2905 Jan  1 1970 rc1
-rwxr--r--   1 root    sys        2491 Jan  1 1970 rc2
-rwxr--r--   1 root    sys        1948 Jan  1 1970 rc3
-rwxr--r--   3 root    sys        2689 Jan  1 1970 rc5
-rwxr--r--   3 root    sys        2689 Jan  1 1970 rc6
-rwxr--r--   1 root    sys        9412 Jan  1 1970 rcS
-r-xr-xr-x   2 bin     root     257444 Sep  1 1998 sh
-r-xr-xr-x   1 bin     bin      195300 Sep  1 1998 soconfig
lrwxrwxrwx   1 root    root         13 Nov 27 14:40 su -> ../usr/bin/su
-r-xr-xr-x   1 root    sys      473808 Sep  1 1998 su.static
-r-xr-xr-x   1 root    bin      288544 Sep  1 1998 sulogin
-rwxr--r--   1 root    sys        3138 Jan  1 1970 swapadd
-r-xr-xr-x   1 bin     bin       29736 Sep  1 1998 sync
-r-xr-xr-x   1 root    sys      435004 Sep  1 1998 uadmin
-r-xr-xr-x   1 bin     bin      213408 Sep  1 1998 umount
-r-xr-xr-x   1 root    sys        3292 Jan  1 1970 umountall
-r-xr-xr-x   1 bin     bin      193152 Sep  1 1998 uname
martyp $ ls r                                  ;typed ls rescape=
1) rc0
2) rc1
3) rc2
4) rc3
5) rc5
6) rc6
7) rcS
martyp $ ls rc0 rc1 rc2 rc3 rc5 rc6 rcS        ;typed escape* to get
seven files
rc0  rc1  rc2  rc3  rc5  rc6  rcS
martyp $ ls  rcS                               ;typed lsescape_ to get
last word
rcS
martyp $
```

Now that we've seen how to get the last of the words to appear on the command line with *escape_,* how about the third word of the last command? You can specify the third word by typing *escape3_* or substitute for the "3" for any of the words on the last command line. The following example shows listing the third word of the last command:

man page

ls - 2

```
martyp $ ls -al
total 11704
drwxrwxr-x    2 root     sys          512 Nov 27 14:55 .
drwxr-xr-x   31 root     root        1024 Apr 19 03:24 ..
-r-xr-xr-x    1 bin      bin       200356 Sep  1  1998 autopush
lrwxrwxrwx    1 root     root          21 Nov 27 14:55 bpgetfile -> ../usr/sbin/e
-r-xr-xr-x    1 bin      bin       470436 Sep  1  1998 dhcpagent
-r-xr-xr-x    1 bin      bin       433064 Sep  1  1998 dhcpinfo
-r-xr-xr-x    1 bin      bin       253664 Sep  1  1998 fdisk
-r-xr-xr-x    1 bin      bin       762816 Sep  1  1998 hostconfig
-r-xr-xr-x    1 bin      bin       535900 Sep  1  1998 ifconfig
-r-xr-xr-x    1 root     sys       516484 Sep  1  1998 init
-r-xr-xr-x    2 bin      root      257444 Sep  1  1998 jsh
-r-xr-xr-x    1 bin      bin       224596 Sep  1  1998 mount
-r-xr-xr-x    1 root     sys         6935 Jan  1  1970 mountall
-rwxr--r--    3 root     sys         2689 Jan  1  1970 rc0
-rwxr--r--    1 root     sys         2905 Jan  1  1970 rc1
-rwxr--r--    1 root     sys         2491 Jan  1  1970 rc2
-rwxr--r--    1 root     sys         1948 Jan  1  1970 rc3
-rwxr--r--    3 root     sys         2689 Jan  1  1970 rc5
-rwxr--r--    3 root     sys         2689 Jan  1  1970 rc6
-rwxr--r--    1 root     sys         9412 Jan  1  1970 rcS
-r-xr-xr-x    2 bin      root      257444 Sep  1  1998 sh
-r-xr-xr-x    1 bin      bin       195300 Sep  1  1998 soconfig
lrwxrwxrwx    1 root     root          13 Nov 27 14:40 su -> ../usr/bin/su
-r-xr-xr-x    1 root     sys       473808 Sep  1  1998 su.static
-r-xr-xr-x    1 root     bin       288544 Sep  1  1998 sulogin
-rwxr--r--    1 root     sys         3138 Jan  1  1970 swapadd
-r-xr-xr-x    1 bin      bin        29736 Sep  1  1998 sync
-r-xr-xr-x    1 root     sys       435004 Sep  1  1998 uadmin
-r-xr-xr-x    1 bin      bin       213408 Sep  1  1998 umount
-r-xr-xr-x    1 root     sys         3292 Jan  1  1970 umountall
-r-xr-xr-x    1 bin      bin       193152 Sep  1  1998 uname
martyp $ ls r                                ;typed ls rescape=
1) rc0
2) rc1
3) rc2
4) rc3
5) rc5
6) rc6
7) rcS
martyp $ ls rc0 rc1 rc2 rc3 rc5 rc6 rcS      ;typed escape* to get seven
files
rc0  rc1  rc2  rc3  rc5  rc6  rcS
martyp $ ls  rc1                             ;typed lsescape3_ to get
third word
```

Because the previous command included the **ls** command, the third word is not **rc2** but **rc1**, because **ls** was the first entry in the previous command.

The Table 6-1 summarizes the command and path completion used in the previous examples.

Table 6-1   Command and Path Completion in **ksh**

Word or Command (type *escape* before each)	Result
word*escape***=**	Displays a numbered list of file names beginning with **word**.
word*escape******	Replaces **word** with all files matched.
word*escape*****	Replaces **word** with the first file name that starts with **word**.
command word*escape***=**	Displays a numbered list of file names beginning with **word**.
command word*escape******	Replaces **word** with all files matched.
command word*escape***_**	Inserts the last word of the last command at the cursor position.
command word*escape***_3**	Inserts the third word of the last command at the cursor position.

File Name Expansion

man page

ksh - 6

In your general activities working with **ksh**, you have to perform a lot of file-name-related work, including crafting shell scripts that deal with file names. An overview of file name expansion is useful to ensure that you're comfortable with this topic before you start writing shell scripts.

Table 6-2 lists some common filename expansion and pattern matching.

Table 6-2   File Name Expansion and Pattern Matching

Character(s)	Example	Description
*	1) **ls *.c**	Match zero or more characters
?	2) **ls conf.?**	Match any single character
[list]	3) **ls conf.[co]**	Match any character in list
[lower-upper]	4) **ls libdd.9873[5-6].sl**	Match any character in range
str{str1,str2,str3,...}	5) **ls ux*.{700,300}**	Expand str with contents of { }
~	6) **ls -a ~**	Home directory
~username	7) **ls -a ~gene**	Home directory of username

The following are more detailed descriptions of the examples shown in Table 6-2:

1. To list all files in a directory that end in ".c," you could do the following:

```
$ ls *.c
      conf. SAM.c  conf.c
```

2. To find all the files in a directory named "conf" with an extension of one character, you could do the following:

```
$ ls conf.?
      conf.c  conf.o  conf.1
```

3. To list all the files in a directory named "conf" with only the extension "c" or "o," you could do the following:

```
$ ls conf.{co}
      conf.c  conf.o
```

4. To list files with similar names but with a specific field that covers a range, you could do the following:

```
$ ls libdd9873[5-6].sl
      libdd98735.sl  libdd98736.sl
```

man page

ls - 2

5. To list files that start with "ux" and have the extension "300" or "700," you could do the following:

```
$ ls ux*.{700,300}
      uxbootlf.700  uxinstfs.300
```

6. To list the files in your home directory, you could use ~:

```
$ ls -a ~
      .        .cshrc.org .login    .shrc.org
      ..       .exrc      .login.org    .cshrc
      .history
```

7. To list the files in the home directory of a user, you can do the following:

```
$    ls -a ~gene
             .            .history      splinedat    under.des
             ..           .login        trail.txt    xtra.part
      .chsrc              .login.org    ESP-File
      .cshrc.org          .profile      Mail
      .exrc               .shrc.org     opt
```

man page

ksh - 6

Many of these techniques are useful when working with **ksh** and writing shell scripts, so you want to become familiar with file name expansion.

Redirection (I/O Redirection)

UNIX is set up such that commands usually take their input from the keyboard, often called standard input, and usually send output to the screen, often called standard output. Commands also send error information to the screen. You do not always want input to come from standard input and output and errors to go to standard output. You are given a lot of control to override these defaults. This is called redirection. Table 6-3 shows many common forms of redirection.

As shown in Table 6-3, to redirect the output of a command from standard output to a file, you use ">". This works almost all of the time. If you have an environment variable called **noclobber** set, then redirecting to an existing file does not work (we'll cover environment variables shortly). The **noclobber** does not permit redirection to write over an existing file. If you try to write over an existing file, such as /**tmp/processes** below, you receive a message that the file exists:

man page

ps - 12

```
#  ps  -ef  >  /tmp/processes
/tmp/processes:   File exists
```

You can, however, use a "!" with redirection to force a file to be overwritten. Using ">!" forces a file to be overwritten, and ">>!" forces the output to be appended to the end of an existing file. Examples of these are shown in the Table 6-3.

Table 6-3   Commonly Used Redirection Forms

Command or Assignment	Example	Description
<	wc -l < .login	Standard input redirection: execute **wc** (word count) and list number of lines (**-l**) in **.login**
>	ps -ef > /tmp/processes	Standard output redirection: execute **ps** and send output to file **/tmp/processes**

Command or Assignment	Example	Description
>>	ps -ef >> /tmp/processes	Append standard output: execute **ps** and append output to the end of file **/tmp/processes**
>!	ps -ef >! /tmp/processes	Standard output redirection and override **noclobber**: write over **/tmp/processes** even if it exists
>>!	ps -ef >>! /tmp/processes	Append standard output and override **noclobber**: append to the end of **/tmp/processes**
| (pipe)	ps | wc -l	Run **ps** and use the result as input to **wc**
0 - standard input		
1 - standard output		
2 - standard error	cat program 2> errors	**cat** the file **program** to standard output and redirect errors to the file **errors**
	cat program 2>> errors	**cat** the file **program** to standard output and append errors to the file **errors**
	find / -name '*.c' -print > cprograms 2>errors	**find** all files on the system ending in **.c**, place the list of files in **cprograms** in the current working directory, and send all errors (file descriptor 2) to the file **errors** in current working directory
	find / -name '*.c' -print > cprograms 2>&1	**find** all files on the system ending in **.c**, place the list of files in **cprograms** in the current working directory, and send all errors (file descriptor 2) to same place as file descriptor 1 (**cprograms**)

Environment Variables

An environment variable is a name associated with a string. The name is the variable and the string is its value. Environment variables are also available to subshells or processes spawned by the shell. In most cases, you see environment variables capitalized, the convention on most systems.

When you issue a command on the system, you usually enter a relative pathname not an absolute pathname. The command you issue is found because the *PATH* variable points to the location of directories where commands are located. Without this *PATH* variable, you would have to type the absolute pathname of every command you issue. When you issue a command, the shell searches the directories listed in the *PATH* variable in the order in which they are listed. A good way to see many of the environment variables you have set is with the **env** command, as shown below:

```
martyp $ env
_=/usr/bin/env
MANPATH=:/opt/local/ptc/sysadmin/scripts:/opt/local/ptc/man:/
opt/local/altrasofn
_INIT_UTS_RELEASE=5.7
HZ=100
_INIT_UTS_MACHINE=sun4m
EPC=true
PATH=/usr/bin:/usr/ucb:/etc:.
WEB_SERVER=sioux.rose.hp.com
_INIT_UTS_VERSION=Generic
MODEL=SPARCstation-10
OS_REV=5.7
EDITOR=vi
_INIT_RUN_NPREV=0
CLASSPATH=.:/usr/java/lib:
LOGNAME=martyp
_INIT_UTS_NODENAME=sunsys
_INIT_UTS_ISA=sparc
MAIL=/var/mail/martyp
ERASE=^H
OS=solaris
PS1=$PWD
$LOGNAME $TOKEN
_INIT_PREV_LEVEL=S
HOST=sunsys
TESTEXPERT_HOME=/opt/local/svn/te33
TA_HOME=/opt/local/platinum/solaris2/testadvise
MA_HOME=/opt/local/platinum/solaris2/memadvise
CL_LICENSE_FILE=/opt/local/CenterLine/configs/license.dat
SHELL=/bin/ksh
PROFILE_DIR=/opt/local/ptc/sysadmin/profile.d
OSTYPE=solaris2
HOME=/home/martyp
_INIT_UTS_SYSNAME=SunOS
TERM=vt100
LD_LIBRARY_PATH=:/opt/local/parasoft/lib.solaris
MWHOME=/opt/local/mainsoft/mainwin/mw
FMHOME=/opt/local/adobe/frame
PWD=/home/martyp
TZ=US/Pacific
_INIT_RUN_LEVEL=3
```

```
CLEARCASE_BLD_UMASK=02
_INIT_UTS_PLATFORM=SUNW,SPARCstation-10
martyp $
```

As you can see, other environment variables in addition to *PATH* make working on your UNIX system easier. You may want to issue other commmands related to **ksh** variables. Table 6-4 summarizes some **ksh**-related variable commands you may want to issue on your system.

man page

ksh - 6

Table 6-4   **ksh**-Related Variable Commands

Command	Description
env	Lists all environment variables (exported). These variables are normally uppercase and passed to child processes.
set	Prints all local and exported set variables.
set -o	Lists all built-in variables that are set to *on* or *off*.
typeset	Displays all variables and associated attributes, functions, and integers.
typeset +	Displays only the names of variables.

You may want to try all these commands on your system to see what variables have been set for you.

If you want to know the value of a specific environment variable, you could use the **echo** command to see its value, as shown below for the environment variable *HOME*:

```
martyp $ echo $HOME
/home/martyp
```

Similarly, to view the operating system-type on this specific computer, you could issue the following command:

```
martyp $ echo $OSTYPE
solaris2
```

The "$" preceding the environment variable name specifies that the value of the variable be sent to standard output. In this case, the value of the environment variable *HOME* is **/home/martyp**, which means that the current user has a home directory of **/home/martyp**.

You can define your own environment variables in **ksh** with the following syntax:

```
export NAME=value
```

Many users like to customize the **ksh** prompts. Most systems provide four **ksh** prompts by default. You can normally modify the first two prompts. The first, called **PS1**, is the primary prompt. The second, called **PS2**, appears after you have partially typed a command and pressed *enter*. **PS1** is normally set to *$* and **PS2** to *>,* by default.

The following example sets **PS1** to our home directory, a space, the current history number, a space, and dollar sign:

```
PS1="`pwd` ! $ "
```

We'll leave the default for **PS2** as >. The following sequence shows issuing a command at our new **PS1** prompt and the default **PS2** prompt:

```
/home/martyp 187 $ print "This is new PS1
> but default PS2"
This is new PS1
but default PS2
/home/martyp 188 $
```

This example shows the new **PS1**, including the history entry incrementing from 187 to 188, and the default **PS2** when the incomplete **print** command was issued.

You can also append to the end of an existing variable with the following format:

```
export NAME="$NAME:appended_information"
```

To add **/home/martyp/programs** to the existing *PATH* environment variable, for instance, you issue the following command:

```
export PATH="$PATH:/home/martyp/programs"
```

This appends the path **/home/martyp/programs** to the environment variable *PATH*.

man page

ksh - 6

A great deal of flexibility is available in working with **ksh**. You should view all your variables and update those that make your job easier. Some customization, such as updating **PS1** and your **PATH**, can also make your job easier.

Background Jobs and Job Control

When you run a command, as we have done so far in many examples, you don't get back the prompt until the command has completed. These commands have been run in the foreground. Some commands can take a long time to complete, in which case you'll be waiting a long time for the prompt to return. As an alternative to waiting for the prompt to return, you can run the command in the background, meaning that it is running behind the scenes while you perform other work. Because UNIX is multi-tasking it is happy to run many commands in the background and still provide you with a prompt to issue yet more commands.

In order to run a command in the background, you simply add an ampersand (&) to the end of the command line. When you follow your command with an ampersand, the command is run in the background and the prompt is immediately returned.

Let's now run some commands on our Solaris system. We'll first run a command to find all of the files in **/usr** that end in ".c," which takes some time to complete. We'll preface the **find** string with the **time** command, so that we know how long the command takes to complete:

man page

find - 10

```
martyp $ time find /usr -name *.c
                        .
                        .
                        .
/usr/demo/link_audit/src/dumpbind.c
/usr/demo/link_audit/src/env.c
/usr/demo/link_audit/src/hash.c
/usr/demo/link_audit/src/perfcnt.c
/usr/demo/link_audit/src/symbindrep.c
/usr/demo/link_audit/src/truss.c
/usr/demo/link_audit/src/who.c
find: cannot read dir /usr/aset: Permission denied

real    1m21.04s
user    0m1.51s
sys     0m12.67s
```

This commad took roughly one minute and 21 seconds to complete. Because it was run in the foreground we were unable to issue any other commands while it was running, because we had to wait for the prompt to return.

An alternative to running the command in the foreground is to issue the command followed by an ampersand, in which case the job runs in the background and the prompt returns immediately, as shown in the following example:

```
martyp $ time find /usr -name *.c > cprogs 2>&1 &
[3]     16279
martyp $
real    2m10.20s
user    0m1.31s
sys     0m8.62s
```

The result of running this command in the background produces a job number in brackets and the process id, or PID, as the second number. All the outputs of this command, inlcuding errors, are written to the file **cprogs**. The prompt was immediately returned after we issued the command, and after it completed, the output of **time** was sent to the screen. We could have begun issuing additional commands immediately after issuing the command in the background.

You have control over both foreground jobs and background jobs. To suspend a foreground job, you type the "control" and "z" keys simultaneously, as shown in the following example:

man page

find - 10

```
martyp $ find /usr -name *.c
/usr/openwin/share/include/X11/Xaw/Template.c
/usr/openwin/share/src/dig_samples/DnD/main.c
/usr/openwin/share/src/dig_samples/DnD/owner.c
/usr/openwin/share/src/dig_samples/DnD/requestor.c
/usr/openwin/share/src/dig_samples/Tooltalk/olit_tt.c
/usr/openwin/share/src/dig_samples/Tooltalk/
tt_callbacks.c
/usr/openwin/share/src/dig_samples/Tooltalk/tt_code.c
/usr/openwin/share/src/dig_samples/ce1/ce_map1.c
/usr/openwin/share/src/dig_samples/ce2/ce_simple.c
/usr/openwin/share/src/dig_samples/dnd_olit/olitdnd.c
/usr/openwin/share/src/dig_samples/dnd_xview1/
xview_dnd.c
/usr/openwin/share/src/dig_samples/dnd_xview2/
xview_dnd2.c
/usr/openwin/share/src/dig_samples/selection_olit/
olit_sel.c
/usr/openwin/share/src/dig_samples/tooltalk_simple/tt-
send.c
/usr/openwin/share/src/olit/oldials/oldials.c
/usr/openwin/share/src/olit/olitbook/ch10/draw.c
^Z[3] + Stopped (SIGTSTP)        find /usr -name *.c
```

After *ctrl-z* is pressed, the **find** command is interrupted at the point at which you type *ctrl-z*. The command is suspended at this point, and you are shown the job number, in this case "3," and its status is listed as "Stopped". This command has only been suspended; it is not gone forever. You can start this process in the foreground with **fg** or run it in the background with **bg**. Using **bg** runs the command as if you had followed it with an "&". It is started from the point at which you interrupted it. You do not have to supply a job number when you issue the **fg** or **bg** command, because the default is to perform the specified operation on the last job which in this case is job number 3.

Notice that in this example we have stopped job number 3. This means that there are other jobs running with a lower job number. You can use the **jobs** command to get a list of all jobs and their status. You can then control the jobs by issuing commands such as **fg** followed by a "%" and the job number to run the command in the foreground, or a **bg** followed by a "%" and the job number to run the command in the background. If you wish to terminate a job altogether, you can issue the **kill** command followed by a "%" and the job number.

man page

kill - 6

In the process of creating the examples in this section, I have started and suspended many jobs. The following example shows listing all jobs with the **jobs** command, killing jobs 1 and 2 with **kill**, and running job 3 in the background:

```
martyp $ jobs
[3] + Stopped (SIGTSTP) find /usr -name *.c
[2] - Running          time find / -name gnu* > gnu 2>&1 &
[1]   Running          time find / -name *.c > cprogs
2>&1 &
martyp $ kill %1
[1]   Terminated       time find / -name *.c > cprogs
2>&1 &
martyp $ kill %2
[2] - Terminated       time find / -name gnu* > gnu 2>&1 &
martyp $ bg %3
[3]      find /usr -name *.c&
martyp $
```

man page

ksh - 6

Notice that an ampersand was added to job 3 when we requested that it be run in the background. Killing jobs 1 and 2 and running job 3 in the background return the prompt so that you can perform additional work.

umask and Permissions

man page

umask - 6

An additional topic to cover related to **ksh** is file permissions and the way they relate to **umask**. This is important because you may write shell programs, and the permissions control the access that others will have to these programs. **umask** is used to specify permission settings for new files and directories.

Let's start with an example of a long listing of a file. We'll use **ls -l** in the following examples:

```
sys1 1: ls -l script1
-rwxr-xr-x  1  marty  users  120 Jul 26 10:20 script1
```

The access rights for this file are defined by the position of read (r), write (w), and execute (x) when the **ll** command is issued. Figure 6-5 shows the three groups of three access rights for this file.

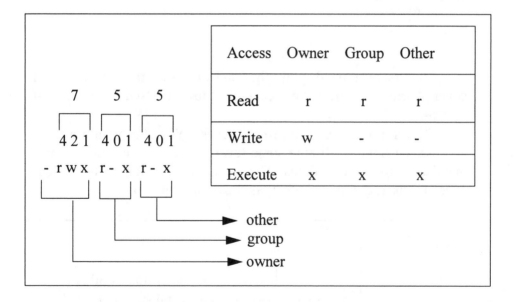

Figure 6-5 Example of File Permissions

The owner of this file has read, write, and execute permissions on the file. The group to which the user belongs has read and execute permissions, and others also have read and execute permissions. The permissions on this file can be specified by the octal sum of each field, which is 755.

What happens if you craft a new shell script or any new file? What permission settings exist? You want to execute the shell script, so you need execute permission for the file. You can use **umask** to define the defaults for all your new files and directories.

By default, most systems start with a permission of 777 for directories and 666 for files. These mean that everyone has complete access to all directories you create and everyone has read and write access to all files you create. These defaults are modified with the value of **umask**.

You can view your **umask** in the following two ways:

```
martyp $ umask
002
martyp $ umask -S
u=rwx,g=rwx,o=rx
martyp $
```

The first example displays the octal value of **umask**, which we'll cover shortly, and the second example shows the symbolic value of **umask**.

The **umask** is used to *disable* access. You start with a **umask** and use the fields to disable some level of access. The **umask** command uses three octal fields. The fields are the sum of the access codes for user, group, and other, as shown in Figure 6-6.

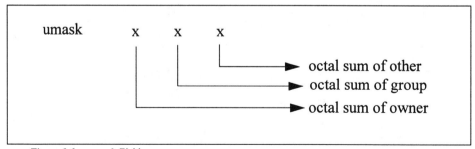

Figure 6-6   umask Fields

The *complement* of the umask field is "*anded*" with the default setting to change the **umask**. You can set **umask** by specifying its value. In our earlier example we viewed **umask** two different ways. To set the **umask**, you simply issue **umask** and the desired value. Setting **umask** to *022*, for example, removes write permissions of directories for "group" and "other," as shown in Figure 6-7:

man page

umask - 6

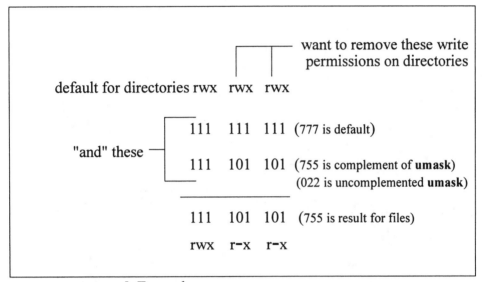

Figure 6-7 **umask** Example

    umask 022 changes the directory permissions to 755 in this example.

    Similarly, a **umask** of 022 changes the default permission of 666 for files to 644, which would be read-only for group and other.

Change File Permissions with chmod

man page

chmod - 3

The **chmod** command is used to change the permissions on a file. Irrespective of what takes place with **umask** as just described you can change a file's permissions at any time with **chmod**. You need to be the owner of the file or superuser to change a file's permissions with **chmod** in most cases. Let's start our discussion of **chmod** with the listing of the file **sort**:

```
$ ls -l sort
-rwxr-x--x   1 marty     users      120 Jul 26 10:20 sort
```

Figure 6-8 shows a breakdown of the permissions on **sort**.

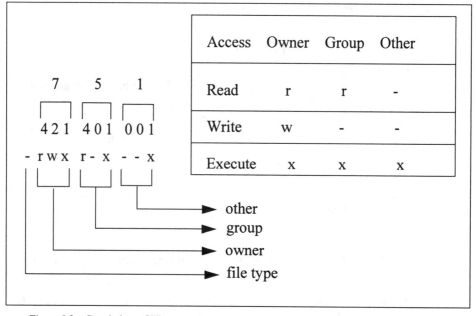

Figure 6-8   Permissions of File **sort**

You have very little control over the type of file defined. You do, however, have a great deal of control over the permissions of this file if it belongs to you. The **chmod** command is used to change the permissions on a file or directory. If you are the owner of the file, you can have a field day changing the permissions on the file.

Two means by which you can change the permissions: symbolic or numeric. I focus first on the numeric mode, because the numbers involved are easy to manage, and I sometimes find new UNIX users get hung up on the meaning of some of the symbols. I'll then cover the symbols and include the symbol meanings in the **chmod** summary.

man page

chmod - 3

First of all, what do I mean by numbers? Looking at the numbers for **sort**, we see permissions of 751: 7 for *owner* (hundreds position), 5 for *group* (tens position), and 1 for *other* (ones position). Figure 6-9 helps with the meanings of the positions.

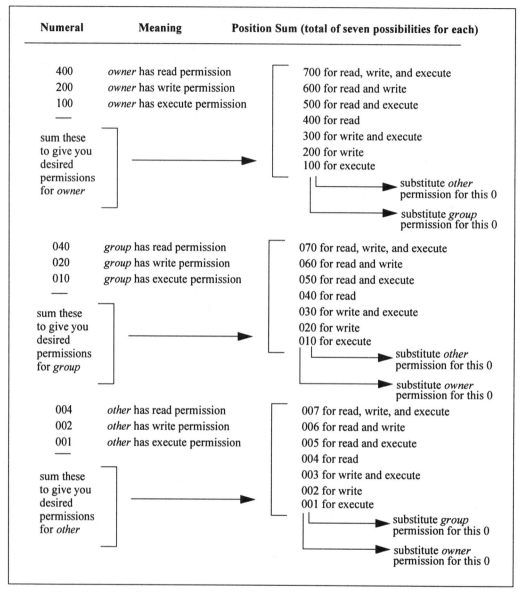

Figure 6-9   Numerical Permissions Summary

Selecting the desired permissions for *owner*, *group*, and *other*, you use the **chmod** command to assign those permissions to a file or

directory. Some of these permission possibilities are infrequently used, such as execute only, because you usually need to have read access to a file in order to execute it; however, I included all possibilities in figure 6-9 for completeness. In addition to the permission mode bits shown in Figure 6-9, there are also miscellaneous mode bits which you don't need to be concerned with at this time.

If you decide that you would like to add write permission of the file **sort** for *group*, and remove all permissions for *other*, you would simply execute the **chmod** command with the appropriate numeric value. The following set of commands first list the existing permissions for **sort**, next change the permissions on **sort**, and finally list the new permissions on **sort**:

man page

chmod - 3

```
$ ls -l sort
-rwxr-x--x   1 marty      users      120 Jul 26 10:20 sort

$ chmod 770 sort

$ ls -l sort
-rwxrwx---   1 marty      users      120 Jul 26 10:20 sort
```

man page

ls - 2

The same set of commands to change the permissions using the symbolic mode would be:

```
$ ls -l sort
-rwxr-x--x   1 marty      users      120 Jul 26 10:20 sort

$ chmod g+w,o-x sort

$ ls -l sort
-rwxrwx---   1 marty      users      120 Jul 26 10:20 sort
```

In symbolic mode, you issue the **chmod** command and specify who will be affected by the change [user (u), group (g), other (o), or all (a)], the operation you wish to perform [add (+), delete (-), or replace (=)], and the permission you wish to specify [read (r), write (w), or execute (x)]. In the previous example using symbolic mode, write (w) permission is being added (+) for *group* (g), and execute (x) permission is being removed (-) for *other* (o).

man page

chmod- 3

The following is a summary of some of the more commonly used symbols of **chmod**:

chmod - Change permissions of specified files using the following symbolic mode list.

Symbol of who is affected:

u	User is affected.
g	Group is affected.
o	Other is affected.
a	All users are affected.

Operation to perform:

+	Add permission.
-	Remove permission.
=	Replace permission.

Permission specified:

r	Read permission.
w	Write permission.
x	Execute permission.
u	Copy user permissions.
g	Copy group permissions.
o	Copy other permissions.

Manual Pages of Some Commands Used in Chapter 6

The following are the HP-UX manual pages for many of the commands used in the chapter. Commands often differ among UNIX variants, so you may find differences in the options or other areas for some commands; however, the following manual pages serve as an excellent reference.

kill

kill - Send signal to a process.

```
kill(1)                                                                kill(1)

NAME
      kill - send a signal to a process; terminate a process

SYNOPSIS

      kill [-s signame] pid ...

      kill [-s signum] pid ...

      kill -l

   Obsolescent Versions:
      kill -signame pid ...

      kill -signum pid ...

DESCRIPTION
      The kill command sends a signal to each process specified by a pid
      process identifier.  The default signal is SIGTERM, which normally
      terminates processes that do not trap or ignore the signal.

      pid is a process identifier, an unsigned or negative integer that can
      be one of the following:


            > 0  The number of a process.

            = 0  All processes, except special system processes, whose
                 process group ID is equal to the process group ID of the
                 sender.

            =-1  All processes, except special system processes, if the user
                 has appropriate privileges.  Otherwise, all processes,
                 except special system processes, whose real or effective
                 user ID is the same as the user ID of the sending process.


            <-1  All processes, except special system processes, whose
                 process group ID is equal to the absolute value of pid and
                 whose real or effective user ID is the same as the user of
                 the sending process.

      Process numbers can be found with the ps command (see ps(1)) and with
      the built-in jobs command available in some shells.

   Options
      kill recognizes the following options:

            -l    (ell)        List all values of signame supported by the
                               implementation.  No signals are sent with this
                               option.  The symbolic names of the signals
```

(without the SIG prefix) are written to
standard output, separated by spaces and
newlines.

-s signame   Send the specified signal name. The default is
                    SIGTERM, number 15. signame can be specified
                    in upper- and/or lowercase, with or without the
                    SIG prefix. These values can be obtained by
                    using the -l option. The symbolic name SIGNULL
                    represents signal value zero. See "Signal
                    Names and Numbers" below.

-s signum   Send the specified decimal signal number. The
                    default is 15, SIGTERM. See "Signal Names and
                    Numbers" below.

-signame   (Obsolescent.) Equivalent to -s signame.

-signum   (Obsolescent.) Equivalent to -s signum.

Signal Names and Numbers
    The following table describes a few of the more common signals that
    can be useful from a terminal. For a complete list and a full
    description, see the header file <signal.h> and the manual entry
    signal(5).

signum	signame	Name	Description
0	SIGNULL	Null	Check access to pid
1	SIGHUP	Hangup	Terminate; can be trapped
2	SIGINT	Interrupt	Terminate; can be trapped
3	SIGQUIT	Quit	Terminate with core dump; can be trapped
9	SIGKILL	Kill	Forced termination; cannot be trapped
15	SIGTERM	Terminate	Terminate; can be trapped
24	SIGSTOP	Stop	Pause the process; cannot be trapped
25	SIGTSTP	Terminal stop	Pause the process; can be trapped
26	SIGCONT	Continue	Run a stopped process

SIGNULL (0), the null signal, invokes error checking but no signal is
actually sent. This can be used to test the validity or existence of
pid.

SIGTERM (15), the (default) terminate signal, can be trapped by the
receiving process, allowing the receiver to execute an orderly
shutdown or to ignore the signal entirely. For orderly operations,
this is the perferred choice.

SIGKILL (9), the kill signal, forces a process to terminate
immediately. Since SIGKILL cannot be trapped or ignored, it is useful
for terminating a process that does not respond to SIGTERM.

The receiving process must belong to the user of the sending process,
unless the user has appropriate privileges.

As a single special case, the continue signal SIGCONT can be sent to
any process that is a member of the same session as the sending
process.

RETURN VALUE
    Upon completion, kill returns with one of the following values:

        0   At least one matching process was found for each pid
             operand, and the specified signal was successfully processed
             for at least one matching process.

```
>0    An error occurred.
```

EXAMPLES

The command:

```
kill 6135
```

signals process number 6135 to terminate. This gives the process an
opportunity to exit gracefully (removing temporary files, etc.).

The following equivalent commands:

```
kill -s SIGKILL 6135
kill -s KILL 6135
kill -s 9 6135
kill -SIGKILL 6135
kill -KILL 6135
kill -9 6135
```

terminate process number 6135 abruptly by sending a SIGKILL signal to
the process. This tells the kernel to remove the process immediately.

WARNINGS

If a process hangs during some operation (such as I/O) so that it is
never scheduled, it cannot die until it is allowed to run. Thus, such
a process may never go away after the kill. Similarly, defunct
processes (see ps(1)) may have already finished executing, but remain
on the system until their parent reaps them (see wait(2)). Using kill
to send signals to them has no effect.

Some non-HP-UX implementations provide kill only as a shell built-in
command.

DEPENDENCIES

This manual entry describes the external command /usr/bin/kill and the
built-in kill command of the POSIX shell (see sh-posix(1)). Other
shells, such as C and Korn (see csh(1) and ksh(1) respectively), also
provide kill as a built-in command. The syntax for and output from
these built-ins may be different.

SEE ALSO

csh(1), ksh(1), ps(1), sh(1), sh-bourne(1), sh-posix(1), kill(2),
wait(2), signal(5).

STANDARDS CONFORMANCE

kill: SVID2, SVID3, XPG2, XPG3, XPG4, POSIX.2

ksh

ksh - Command programming language.

man page

ksh - 6

NAME
     ksh, rksh - shell, the standard/restricted command programming
     language

SYNOPSIS

     ksh [+aefhikmnoprstuvx] [+o option] ... [-c string] [arg ...]
     rksh [+aefhikmnoprstuvx] [+o option] ... [-c string] [arg ...]

DESCRIPTION
     ksh is a command programming language that executes commands read from
     a terminal or a file. rksh is a restricted version of the command
     interpreter ksh, used to set up login names and execution environments
     whose capabilities are more controlled than those of the standard
     shell. See Invoking ksh and Special Commands sections later in this
     entry for details about command line options and arguments,
     particularly the set command.

     Definitions
     metacharacter One of the following characters:

                       ;   &   (   ) | <   >   new-line   space   tab

     blank   A tab or space character.

     identifier   A sequence of letters, digits, or underscores starting
                    with a letter or underscore. Identifiers are used as
                    names for functions and named parameters.

     word   A sequence of characters separated by one or more non-
                    quoted metacharacters .

     command   A sequence of characters in the syntax of the shell
                    language. The shell reads each command and carries out
                    the desired action, either directly or by invoking
                    separate utilities.

     special command
                    A command that is carried out by the shell without
                    creating a separate process. Often called ``built-in
                    commands''. Except for documented side effects, most
                    special commands can be implemented as separate
                    utilities.

     #   The # character is interpreted as the beginning of a
                    comment. See Quoting below.

     Commands
     A simple-command is a sequence of blank-separated words that can be
     preceded by a parameter assignment list. (See Environment below).
     The first word specifies the name of the command to be executed.

Except as specified below, the remaining words are passed as arguments to the invoked command. The command name is passed as argument 0 (see exec(2)). The value of a simple-command is its exit status if it terminates normally, or (octal) 200+status if it terminates abnormally (see signal(5) for a list of status values).

A pipeline is a sequence of one or more commands separated by |. The standard output of each command except the last is connected by a pipe (see pipe(2)) to the standard input of the next command. Each command is run as a separate process; the shell waits for the last command to terminate. The exit status of a pipeline is the exit status of the last command in the pipeline.

A list is a sequence of one or more pipelines separated by ;, &, &&, or ||, and optionally terminated by ;, &, or |&. Of these five symbols, ;, &, and |& have equal precedence. && and || have a higher but also equal precedence. A semicolon (;) causes sequential execution of the preceding pipeline; an ampersand (&) causes asynchronous execution of the preceding pipeline (that is, the shell does not wait for that pipeline to finish). The symbol |& causes asynchronous execution of the preceding command or pipeline with a two-way pipe established to the parent shell (known as a co-process). The standard input and output of the spawned command can be written to and read from by the parent shell using the -p option of the special commands read and print described later. The symbol && (||) causes the list following it to be executed only if the preceding pipeline returns a zero (non-zero) value. An arbitrary number of new-lines can appear in a list, instead of semicolons, to delimit commands.

A command is either a simple-command or one of the following. Unless otherwise stated, the value returned by a command is that of the last simple-command executed in the command.

for identifier [in word ...] do list done
> Each time for is executed, identifier is set to the next word taken from the in word list. If in word ... is omitted, for executes the do list once for each positional parameter set (see Parameter Substitution below). Execution ends when there are no more words in the list.

select identifier [in word...] do list done
> A select command prints on standard error (file descriptor 2), the set of words, each preceded by a number. If in word ... is omitted, the positional parameters are used instead (see Parameter Substitution below). The PS3 prompt is printed and a line is read from the standard input. If this line consists of the number of one of the listed words, the value of the parameter identifier is set to the word corresponding to this number. If this line is empty, the selection list is printed again. Otherwise the value of the parameter identifier is set to null. The contents of the line read from standard input is saved in the parameter REPLY. The list is executed for each selection until a break or end-of-file (eof) is encountered.

case word in [[(] pattern [|pattern] ...) list ;;] ... esac
> A case command executes the list associated with the first pattern that matches word. The form of the patterns is identical to that used for file name generation (see File Name Generation below).

if list then list [elif list then list] ... [else list]fi
> The list following if is executed and, if it returns a

zero exit status, the list following the first then is
executed. Otherwise, the list following elif is
executed and, if its value is zero, the list following
the next then is executed. Failing that, the else list
is executed. If no else list or then list is executed,
if returns a zero exit status.

while list do list done

until list do list done
A while command repeatedly executes the while list, and
if the exit status of the last command in the list is
zero, executes the do list; otherwise the loop
terminates. If no commands in the do list are
executed, while returns a zero exit status; until can
be used in place of while to negate the loop
termination test.

(list)   Execute list in a separate environment. If two
adjacent open parentheses are needed for nesting, a
space must be inserted to avoid arithmetic evaluation
as described below.

{ list;}   Execute list, but not in a separate environment. Note
that { is a keyword and requires a trailing blank to be
recognized.

[[expression]]
Evaluates expression and returns a zero exit status
when expression is true. See Conditional Expressions
below, for a description of expression. Note that [[
and]] are keywords and require blanks between them and
expression.

function identifier {list;}

identifier () {list;}
Define a function referred to by identifier. The body
of the function is the list of commands between { and }
(see Functions below).

time pipeline   pipeline is executed and the elapsed time, user time,
and system time are printed on standard error.

The following keywords are recognized only as the first word of a
command and when not quoted:

if then else elif fi case esac for while until do done { }
function select time [[ ]]

Comments
A word beginning with # causes that word and all subsequent characters
up to a new-line to be ignored.

Aliasing
The first word of each command is replaced by the text of an alias, if
an alias for this word has been defined. An alias name consists of
any number of characters excluding metacharacters, quoting characters,
file expansion characters, parameter and command substitution
characters, and =. The replacement string can contain any valid shell
script, including the metacharacters listed above. The first word of
each command in the replaced text, other than any that are in the
process of being replaced, is tested for additional aliases. If the
last character of the alias value is a blank, the word following the
alias is also checked for alias substitution. Aliases can be used to
redefine special built-in commands, but cannot be used to redefine the

keywords listed above. Aliases can be created, listed, and exported
with the alias command and can be removed with the unalias command.
Exported aliases remain in effect for subshells but must be
reinitialized for separate invocations of the shell (see Invoking ksh
below).

Aliasing is performed when scripts are read, not while they are
executed. Therefore, for it to take effect, alias must be executed
before the command referring to the alias is read.

Aliases are frequently used as a shorthand for full path names. An
option to the aliasing facility allows the value of the alias to be
automatically set to the full path name of the corresponding command.
These aliases are called tracked aliases. The value of a tracked
alias is defined the first time the identifier is read and becomes
undefined each time the PATH variable is reset. These aliases remain
tracked so that the next reference redefines the value. Several
tracked aliases are compiled into the shell. The -h option of the set
command converts each command name that is an identifier into a
tracked alias.

The following exported aliases are compiled into the shell but can be
unset or redefined:

```
autoload='typeset -fu'
false='let 0'
functions='typeset -f'
hash='alias -t -'
history='fc -l'
integer='typeset -i'
nohup='nohup '
r='fc -e -'
stop='kill -STOP'
suspend='kill -STOP $$'
true=':'
type='whence -v'
```

Tilde Substitution
    After alias substitution is performed, each word is checked to see if
    it begins with an unquoted ~. If it does, the word up to a / is
    checked to see if it matches a user name in the /etc/passwd file. If
    a match is found, the ~ and the matched login name are replaced by the
    login directory of the matched user. This is called a tilde
    substitution. If no match is found, the original text is left
    unchanged. A ~, alone or before a /, is replaced by the value of the
    HOME parameter. A ~ followed by a + or - is replaced by the value of
    the parameter PWD and OLDPWD, respectively. In addition, tilde
    substitution is attempted when the value of a parameter assignment
    begins with a ~.

Command Substitution
    The standard output from a command enclosed in parenthesis preceded by
    a dollar sign ($(command)) or a pair of back single quotes (accent
    grave) (`command`) can be used as part or all of a word; trailing
    new-lines are removed. In the second (archaic) form, the string
    between the quotes is processed for special quoting characters before
    the command is executed (see Quoting below). The command substitution
    $(cat file) can be replaced by the equivalent but faster $(<file).
    Command substitution of most special commands (built-ins) that do not
    perform I/O redirection are carried out without creating a separate
    process. However, command substitution of a function creates a
    separate process to execute the function and all commands (built-in or
    otherwise) in that function.

    An arithmetic expression enclosed in double parenthesis preceded by a
    dollar sign ($((expression))) is replaced by the value of the

arithmetic expression within the double parenthesis (see Arithmetic
Evaluation below for a description of arithmetic expressions).

Parameter Substitution
    A parameter is an identifier, one or more digits, or any of the
    characters *, @, #, ?, -, $, and !. A named parameter (a parameter
    denoted by an identifier) has a value and zero or more attributes.
    Named parameters can be assigned values and attributes by using the
    typeset special command. Attributes supported by ksh are described
    later with the typeset special command. Exported parameters pass
    values and attributes to the environment.

    The shell supports a limited one-dimensional array facility. An
    element of an array parameter is referenced by a subscript. A
    subscript is denoted by a [followed by an arithmetic expression (see
    Arithmetic Evaluation below) followed by a]. To assign values to an
    array, use set -A name value .... The value of all subscripts must be
    in the range of 0 through 1023. Arrays need not be declared. Any
    reference to a named parameter with a valid subscript is legal and an
    array is created if necessary. Referencing an array without a
    subscript is equivalent to referencing the first element.

    The value of a named parameter can also be assigned by writing:

        name=value [name=value] ...

    If the -i integer attribute is set for name, the value is subject to
    arithmetic evaluation as described below.

    Positional parameters, parameters denoted by a number, can be assigned
    values with the set special command. Parameter $0 is set from
    argument zero when the shell is invoked.

    The character $ is used to introduce substitutable parameters.

${parameter}	Substitute the value of the parameter, if any. Braces are required when parameter is followed by a letter, digit, or underscore that should not be interpreted as part of its name or when a named parameter is subscripted. If parameter is one or more digits, it is a positional parameter. A positional parameter of more than one digit must be enclosed in braces. If parameter is * or @ all the positional parameters, starting with $1, are substituted (separated by a field separator character). If an array identifier with subscript * or @ is used, the value for each element is substituted (separated by a field separator character). The shell reads all the characters from ${ to the matching } as part of the same word even if it contains braces or metacharacters.
${#parameter}	If parameter is * or @, the number of positional parameters is substituted. Otherwise, the length of the value of the parameter is substituted.
${#identifier[*]}	Substitute the number of elements in the array identifier.
${parameter:-word}	If parameter is set and is non-null, substitute its value; otherwise substitute word.

${parameter:=word}   If parameter is not set or is null, set it to word; then substitute the value of the parameter. Positional parameters cannot be assigned in this way.

${parameter:?word}   If parameter is set and is non-null, substitute its value; otherwise, print word and exit from the shell. If word is omitted, a standard message is printed.

${parameter:+word}   If parameter is set and is non-null, substitute word; otherwise substitute nothing.

${parameter#pattern}

${parameter##pattern}

        If the shell pattern matches the beginning of the value of parameter, the value of this substitution is the value of the parameter with the matched portion deleted; otherwise the value of this parameter is substituted. In the former case, the smallest matching pattern is deleted; in the latter case, the largest matching pattern is deleted.

${parameter%pattern}

${parameter%%pattern}

        If the shell pattern matches the end of the value of parameter, the value of parameter with the matched part is deleted; otherwise substitute the value of parameter. In the former, the smallest matching pattern is deleted; in the latter, the largest matching pattern is deleted.

In the above, word is not evaluated unless it is used as the substituted string. Thus, in the following example, pwd is executed only if d is not set or is null:

echo ${d:-$(pwd)}

If the colon (:) is omitted from the above expressions, the shell only checks to determine whether or not parameter is set.

The following parameters are set automatically by the shell:

#	The number of positional parameters in decimal.
-	Options supplied to the shell on invocation or by the set command.
?	The decimal value returned by the last executed command.
$	The process number of this shell.
_	Initially, the value of _ is an absolute pathname of the shell or script being executed as passed in the environment. Subsequently it is assigned the last argument of the previous command. This parameter is not set for commands which are asynchronous. This parameter is also used to hold the name of the matching MAIL file when checking for mail.
!	The process number of the last background command invoked.
COLUMNS	If this variable is set, its value is used to define the width of the edit window for the shell

edit modes and for printing select lists. In a
windowed environment, if the shell detects that
the window size has changed, the shell updates the
value of COLUMNS.

ERRNO   The value of errno as set by the most recently
failed system call. This value is system
dependent and is intended for debugging purposes.

LINENO   The line number of the current line within the
script or function being executed.

LINES   If this variable is set, the value is used to
determine the column length for printing select
lists. select lists print vertically until about
two-thirds of LINES lines are filled. In a
windowed environment, if the shell detects that
the window size has changed, the shell updates the
value of LINES.

OLDPWD   The previous working directory set by the cd
command.

OPTARG   The value of the last option argument processed by
the getopts special command.

OPTIND   The index of the last option argument processed by
the getopts special command.

PPID   The process number of the parent of the shell.

PWD   The present working directory set by the cd
command.

RANDOM   Each time this parameter is evaluated, a random
integer, uniformly distributed between 0 and
32767, is generated. The sequence of random
numbers can be initialized by assigning a numeric
value to RANDOM.

REPLY   This parameter is set by the select statement and
by the read special command when no arguments are
supplied.

SECONDS   Each time this parameter is referenced, the number
of seconds since shell invocation is returned. If
this parameter is assigned a value, the value
returned upon reference is the value that was
assigned plus the number of seconds since the
assignment.

The following parameters are used by the shell:

CDPATH   The search path for the cd command.

EDITOR   If the value of this variable ends in emacs,
gmacs, or vi and the VISUAL variable is not set,
the corresponding option is turned on (see set in
Special Commands below).

ENV   If this parameter is set, parameter substitution
is performed on the value to generate the path
name of the script to be executed when the shell
is invoked (see Invoking ksh below). This file is
typically used for alias and function definitions.

FCEDIT   The default editor name for the fc command.

FPATH   The search path for function definitions. This
path is searched when a function with the -u
attribute is referenced and when a command is not
found. If an executable file is found, then it is
read and executed in the current environment.

IFS   Internal field separators, normally space, tab,
and new-line that are used to separate command
words resulting from command or parameter
substitution, and for separating words with the
special command read. The first character of the
IFS parameter is used to separate arguments for

	the "$*" substitution (see Quoting below).
HISTFILE	If this parameter is set when the shell is invoked, its value is the path name of the file that is used to store the command history. The default value is $HOME/.sh_history. If the user has appropriate privileges and no HISTFILE is given, then no history file is used (see Command Re-entry below).
HISTSIZE	If this parameter is set when the shell is invoked, the number of previously entered commands accessible to this shell will be greater than or equal to this number. The default is 128.
HOME	The default argument (home directory) for the cd command.
MAIL	If this parameter is set to the name of a mail file and the MAILPATH parameter is not set, the shell informs the user of arrival of mail in the specified file.
MAILCHECK	This variable specifies how often (in seconds) the shell checks for changes in the modification time of any of the files specified by the MAILPATH or MAIL parameters. The default value is 600 seconds. When the time has elapsed the shell checks before issuing the next prompt.
MAILPATH	A list of file names separated by colons (:). If this parameter is set, the shell informs the user of any modifications to the specified files that have occurred within the last MAILCHECK seconds. Each file name can be followed by a ? and a message to be printed, in which case the message undergoes parameter and command substitution with the parameter $_ defined as the name of the changed file. The default message is you have mail in $_.
PATH	The search path for commands (see Execution below). The user cannot change PATH if executing rksh (except in the .profile file).
PS1	The value of this parameter is expanded for parameter substitution, to define the primary prompt string which, by default, is $ followed by a space character. The character ! in the primary prompt string is replaced by the command number (see Command Re-entry below). To include a ! in the prompt, use !!.
PS2	Secondary prompt string, by default > followed by a space character.
PS3	Selection prompt string used within a select loop, by default #? followed by a space character.
PS4	The value of this variable is expanded for parameter substitution and precedes each line of an execution trace. If PS4 is unset, the execution trace prompt is + followed by a space character.
SHELL	The path name of the shell is kept in the environment. When invoked, the shell is restricted if the value of this variable contains an r in the basename.
TMOUT	If set to a value greater than zero, the shell terminates if a command is not entered within the prescribed number of seconds after issuing the PS1 prompt.
VISUAL	Invokes the corresponding option when the value of this variable ends in emacs, gmacs, or vi (see set in Special Commands below).

The shell gives default values to PATH, PS1, PS2, MAILCHECK, TMOUT,

and IFS. HOME, SHELL, ENV, and MAIL are never set automatically by
the shell (although HOME, SHELL, and MAIL are set by login(1)).

Blank Interpretation

After parameter and command substitution, the results of substitution
are scanned for field separator characters (found in IFS), and split
into distinct arguments where such characters are found. ksh retains
explicit null arguments (or '') but removes implicit null arguments
(those resulting from parameters that have no values).

File Name Generation

Following substitution, each command word is processed as a pattern
for file name expansion unless the -f option has been set. The form
of the patterns is the Pattern Matching Notation defined by regexp(5).
The word is replaced with sorted file names matching the pattern. If
no file name is found that matches the pattern, the word is left
unchanged.

In addition to the notation described in regexp(5), ksh recognizes
composite patterns made up of one or more pattern lists separated from
each other with a |. Composite patterns can be formed with one or
more of the following:

?(pattern-list)	Optionally matches any one of the given patterns.
*(pattern-list)	Matches zero or more occurrences of the given patterns.
+(pattern-list)	Matches one or more occurrences of the given patterns.
@(pattern-list)	Matches exactly one of the given patterns.
!(pattern-list)	Matches anything, except one of the given patterns.

Quoting

Each of the metacharacters listed above (See Definitions above) has a
special meaning to the shell and causes termination of a word unless
quoted. A character can be quoted (i.e., made to stand for itself) by
preceding it with a \. The pair \new-line is ignored. All characters
enclosed between a pair of single quote marks (''), are quoted. A
single quote cannot appear within single quotes. Inside double quote
marks (""), parameter and command substitution occurs and \ quotes the
characters \, `, ", and $. $* and $@ have identical meanings when not
quoted or when used as a parameter assignment value or as a file name.
However, when used as a command argument, "$*" is equivalent to
"$1d$2d...", where d is the first character of the IFS parameter,
whereas "$@" is equivalent to "$1" "$2" .... Inside back single quote
(accent grave) marks (``) \ quotes the characters \, `, and $. If the
back single quotes occur within double quotes, \ also quotes the
character ".

The special meaning of keywords or aliases can be removed by quoting
any character of the keyword. The recognition of function names or
special command names listed below cannot be altered by quoting them.

Arithmetic Evaluation

The ability to perform integer arithmetic is provided with the special
command let. Evaluations are performed using long arithmetic.
Constants take the form [base#]n, where base is a decimal number
between two and thirty-six representing the arithmetic base and n is a
number in that base. If base is omitted, base 10 is used.

An arithmetic expression uses the same syntax, precedence, and

associativity of expression of the C language. All the integral
operators, other than ++, --, ?:, and , are supported. Variables can
be referenced by name within an arithmetic expression without using
the parameter substitution syntax. When a variable is referenced, its
value is evaluated as an arithmetic expression.

An internal integer representation of a variable can be specified with
the -i option of the typeset special command. Arithmetic evaluation
is performed on the value of each assignment to a variable with the -i
attribute. If you do not specify an arithmetic base, the first
assignment to the variable determines the arithmetic base. This base
is used when parameter substitution occurs.

Since many of the arithmetic operators require quoting, an alternative
form of the let command is provided. For any command beginning with
((, all characters until the matching)) are treated as a quoted
expression. More precisely, ((...)) is equivalent to let "...".

Prompting
   When used interactively, the shell prompts with the value of PS1
before reading a command. If at any time a new-line is typed and
further input is needed to complete a command, the secondary prompt
(the value of PS2) is issued.

Conditional Expressions.
   A conditional expression is used with the [[compound command to test
attributes of files and to compare strings. Word splitting and file
name generation are not performed on the words between [[and]].
Each expression can be constructed from one or more of the following
unary or binary expressions:

-a file	True if file exists.
-b file	True if file exists and is a block special file.
-c file	True if file exists and is a character special file.
-d file	True if file exists and is a directory.
-f file	True if file exists and is an ordinary file.
-g file	True if file exists and is has its setgid bit set.
-h file	True if file exists and is a a symbolic link.
-k file	True if file exists and is has its sticky bit set.
-n string	True if length of string is non-zero.
-o option	True if option named option is on.
-p file	True if file exists and is a fifo special file or a pipe.
-r file	True if file exists and is readable by current process.
-s file	True if file exists and has size greater than zero.
-t fildes	True if file descriptor number fildes is open and associated with a terminal device.
-u file	True if file exists and is has its setuid bit set.
-w file	True if file exists and is writable by current process.
-x file	True if file exists and is executable by current process. If file exists and is a directory, the current process has permission to search in the directory.
-z string	True if length of string is zero.
-H file	True if file exists and is a hidden directory (see cdf(4)).

```
        -L file              True if file exists and is a symbolic link.

        -O file              True if file exists and is owned by the
                             effective user ID of this process.
        -G file              True if file exists and its group matches the
                             effective group ID of this process.
        -S file              True if file exists and is a socket.
        file1 -nt file2      True if file1 exists and is newer than file2.

        file1 -ot file2      True if file1 exists and is older than file2.

        file1 -ef file2      True if file1 and file2 exist and refer to
                             the same file.
        string = pattern     True if string matches pattern.
        string != pattern    True if string does not match pattern.
        string1 < string2    True if string1 comes before string2 based on
                             ASCII value of their characters.
        string1 > string2    True if string1 comes after string2 based on
                             ASCII value of their characters.
        exp1 -eq exp2        True if exp1 is equal to exp2.
        exp1 -ne exp2        True if exp1 is not equal to exp2.
        exp1 -lt exp2        True if exp1 is less than exp2.
        exp1 -gt exp2        True if exp1 is greater than exp2.
        exp1 -le exp2        True if exp1 is less than or equal to exp2.

        exp1 -ge exp2        True if exp1 is greater than or equal to
                             exp2.
```

A compound expression can be constructed from these primitives by using any of the following, listed in decreasing order of precedence.

```
        (expression)                  True, if expression is true.
                                      Used to group expressions.
        ! expression                  True if expression is false.

        expression1 && expression2    True, if expression1 and
                                      expression2 are both true.
        expression1 || expression2    True, if either expression1 or
                                      expression2 is true.
```

Input/Output

Before a command is executed, its input and output can be redirected using a special notation interpreted by the shell. The following can appear anywhere in a simple-command or can precede or follow a command and are not passed on to the invoked command. Command and parameter substitution occurs before word or digit is used, except as noted below. File name generation occurs only if the pattern matches a single file and blank interpretation is not performed.

```
        <word       Use file word as standard input (file descriptor
                    0).

        >word       Use file word as standard output (file descriptor
                    1). If the file does not exist, it is created.
                    If the file exists, and the noclobber option is
                    on, an error occurs; otherwise, the file is
                    truncated to zero length.

        >|word      Sames as >, except that it overrides the noclobber
                    option.

        >>word      Use file word as standard output. If the file
                    exists, output is appended to it (by first
                    searching for the end-of-file); otherwise, the
                    file is created.
```

`<>word`	Open file word for reading and writing as standard input. If the file does not exist it is created.
`<<[-]word`	The shell input is read up to a line that matches word, or to an end-of-file. No parameter substitution, command substitution, or file name generation is performed on word. The resulting document, called a here-document, becomes the standard input. If any character of word is quoted, no interpretation is placed upon the characters of the document. Otherwise, parameter and command substitution occurs, \new-line is ignored, and \ must be used to quote the characters \, $, `, and the first character of word. If - is appended to <<, all leading tabs are stripped from word and from the document.
`<&digit`	The standard input is duplicated from file descriptor digit (see dup(2)).
`>&digit`	The standard output is duplicated to file descriptor digit (see dup(2)).
`<&-`	The standard input is closed.
`>&-`	The standard output is closed.
`<&p`	The input from the co-process is moved to standard input.
`>&p`	The output to the co-process is moved to standard output.

If one of the above is preceded by a digit, the file descriptor number cited is that specified by the digit (instead of the default 0 or 1). For example:

        ... 2>&1

means file descriptor 2 is to be opened for writing as a duplicate of file descriptor 1.

Redirection order is significant because the shell evaluates redirections referencing file descriptors in terms of the currently open file associated with the specified file descriptor at the time of evaluation. For example:

        ... 1>fname 2>&1

first assigns file descriptor 1 (standard output) to file fname, then assigns file descriptor 2 (standard error) to the file assigned to file descriptor 1; i.e., fname. On the other hand, if the order of redirection is reversed as follows:

        ... 2>&1 1>fname

file descriptor 2 is assigned to the current standard output (user terminal unless a different assignment is inherited). File descriptor 1 is then reassigned to file fname without changing the assignment of file descriptor 2.

The input and output of a co-process can be moved to a numbered file descriptor allowing other commands to write to them and read from them using the above redirection operators. If the input of the current co-process is moved to a numbered file descriptor, another co-process can be started.

If a command is followed by & and job control is inactive, the default
standard input for the command is the empty file /dev/null.
Otherwise, the environment for the execution of a command contains the
file descriptors of the invoking shell as modified by input/output
specifications.

Environment

The environment (see environ(5)) is a list of name-value pairs passed
to an executed program much like a normal argument list. The names
must be identifiers and the values are character strings. The shell
interacts with the environment in several ways. When invoked, the
shell scans the environment and creates a parameter for each name
found, gives it the corresponding value, and marks it export.
Executed commands inherit the environment. If the user modifies the
values of these parameters or creates new ones by using the export or
typeset -x commands, the values become part of the environment. The
environment seen by any executed command is thus composed of any
name-value pairs originally inherited by the shell whose values can be
modified by the current shell, plus any additions which must be noted
in export or typeset -x commands.

The environment for any simple-command or function can be augmented by
prefixing it with one or more parameter assignments. A parameter
assignment argument takes the form identifier=value. For example,

        TERM=450 cmd args

and

        (export TERM; TERM=450; cmd args)

are equivalent (as far as the above execution of cmd is concerned
except for special commands listed below that are preceded by a
dagger).

If the -k option is set, all parameter assignment arguments are placed
in the environment, even if they occur after the command name. The
following echo statement prints a=b c. After the -k option is set,
the second echo statement prints only c:

        echo a=b c
        set -k
        echo a=b c

This feature is intended for use with scripts written for early
versions of the shell, and its use in new scripts is strongly
discouraged. It is likely to disappear someday.

Functions

The function keyword (described in the Commands section above) is used
to define shell functions. Shell functions are read and stored
internally. Alias names are resolved when the function is read.
Functions are executed like commands, with the arguments passed as
positional parameters (see Execution below).

Functions execute in the same process as the caller except that
command substitution of a function creates a new process. Functions
share all files and present working directory with the caller. Traps
caught by the caller are reset to their default action inside the
function. If a function does not catch or specifically ignore a trap
condition, the function terminates and the condition is passed on to
the caller. A trap on EXIT set inside a function is executed after
the function completes in the environment of the caller. Ordinarily,
variables are shared between the calling program and the function.

However, the typeset special command used within a function defines
local variables whose scope includes the current function and all
functions it calls.

The special command return is used to return from function calls.
Errors within functions return control to the caller.

Function identifiers can be listed with the +f option of the typeset
special command. Function identifiers and the associated text of the
functions can be listed with the -f option. Functions can be
undefined with the -f option of the unset special command.

Ordinarily, functions are unset when the shell executes a shell
script. The -xf option of the typeset command allows a function to be
exported to scripts that are executed without reinvoking the shell.
Functions that must be defined across separate invocations of the
shell should be placed in the ENV file.

Jobs

If the monitor option of the set command is turned on, an interactive
shell associates a job with each pipeline. It keeps a table of
current jobs, printed by the jobs command, and assigns them small
integer numbers. When a job is started asynchronously with &, the
shell prints a line resembling:

    [1] 1234

indicating that job number 1 was started asynchronously and had one
(top-level) process whose process ID was 1234.

If you are running a job and want to do something else, type the
suspend character (usually ^Z (Ctrl-Z)) to send a STOP signal to the
current job. The shell then indicates that the job has been
`Stopped', and prints another prompt. The state of this job can be
manipulated by using the bg command to put it in the background,
running other commands (while it is stopped or running in the
background), and eventually restarting or returning the job to the
foreground by using the fg command. A ^Z takes effect immediately and
resembles an interrupt, since pending output and unread input are
discarded when ^Z is typed.

A job run in the background stops if it tries to read from the
terminal. Background jobs normally are allowed to produce output, but
can be disabled by giving the stty tostop command. If the user sets
this tty option, background jobs stop when trying to produce output.

There are several ways to refer to jobs in the shell. A job can be
referred to by the process ID of any process in the job or by one of
the following:

        %number   The job with the given number.
        %string   Any job whose command line begins with
                         string.
        %?string   Any job whose command line contains string.

        %%   Current job.
        %+   Equivalent to %%.
        %-   Previous job.

The shell learns immediately when a process changes state. It informs
the user when a job is blocked and prevented from further progress,
but only just before it prints a prompt.

When the monitor mode is on, each background job that completes
triggers any trap set for CHLD.

Attempting to leave the shell while jobs are running or stopped produces the warning, You have stopped (running) jobs. Use the jobs command to identify them. An immediate attempt to exit again terminates the stopped jobs; the shell does not produce a warning the second time.

Signals
The INT and QUIT signals for an invoked command are ignored if the command is followed by & and the monitor option is off. Otherwise, signals have the values inherited by the shell from its parent, with the exception of signal 11 (but see also the trap command below).

Execution
Substitutions are made each time a command is executed. If the command name matches one of the Special Commands listed below, it is executed within the current shell process. Next, ksh checks the command name to determine whether it matches one of the user-defined functions. If it does, ksh saves the positional parameters and then sets them to the arguments of the function call. The positional parameter 0 is set to the function name. When the function completes or issues a return, ksh restores the positional parameter list and executes any trap set on EXIT within the function. The value of a function is the value of the last command executed. A function is executed in the current shell process. If a command name is not a special command or a user-defined function, ksh creates a process and attempts to execute the command using exec (see exec(2)).

The shell parameter PATH defines the search path for the directory containing the command. Alternative directory names are separated by a colon (:). The default path is /usr/bin: (specifying /usr/bin and the current directory in that order). Note that the current directory is specified by a null path name which can appear immediately after the equals sign, between colon delimiters, or at the end of the path list. The search path is not used if the command name contains a /. Otherwise, each directory in the path is searched for an executable file. If the file has execute permissions but is not a directory or an executable object code file, it is assumed to be a script file, which is a file of data for an interpreter. If the first two characters of the script file are #!, exec (see exec(2)) expects an interpreter path name to follow. exec then attempts to execute the specified interpreter as a separate process to read the entire script file. If a call to exec fails, /usr/bin/ksh is spawned to interpret the script file. All non-exported aliases, functions, and named parameters are removed in this case. If the shell command file does not have read permission, or if the setuid and/or setgid bits are set on the file, the shell executes an agent to set up the permissions and execute the shell with the shell command file passed down as an open file. A parenthesized command is also executed in a sub-shell without removing non-exported quantities.

Command Re-entry
The text of the last HISTSIZE (default 128) commands entered from a terminal device is saved in a history file. The file $HOME/.sh_history is used if the HISTFILE variable is not set or writable. A shell can access the commands of all interactive shells that use the same named HISTFILE. The special command fc is used to list or edit a portion of this file. The portion of the file to be edited or listed can be selected by number or by giving the first character or characters of the command. A single command or range of commands can be specified. If no editor program is specified as an argument to fc, the value of the FCEDIT parameter is used. If FCEDIT is not defined, /usr/bin/ed is used. The edited command is printed and re-executed upon leaving the editor. The editor name - is used to skip the editing phase and to re-execute the command. In this case a substitution parameter of the form old=new can be used to modify the command before execution. For example, if r is aliased to fc -e -,

typing r bad=good c re-executes the most recent command that starts
with the letter c and replaces the first occurrence of the string bad
with the string good.

umask

umask - Display or set creation mask.

```
umask(1)                                                              umask(1)

NAME
     umask - set or display the file mode creation mask

SYNOPSIS

  Set Mask:
  umask mask

  Display Mask:
  umask [-S]

DESCRIPTION
     The umask command sets the value of the file mode creation mask or
     displays the current one.  The mask affects the initial value of the
     file mode (permission) bits for subsequently created files.

  Setting the File Mode Creation Mask
     The umask mask command sets a new file mode creation mask for the
     current shell execution environment.  mask can be a symbolic or
     numeric (obsolescent) value.

     A symbolic mask provides a flexible way of modifying the mask
     permission bits individually or as a group.  A numeric mask specifies
     all the permission bits at one time.

     When a mask is specified, no output is written to standard output.

  Symbolic Mask Value

     A symbolic mask replaces or modifies the current file mode creation
     mask.  It is specified as specified as a comma-separated list of
     operations in the following format.  Whitespace is not permitted.

          [who][operator][permissions][,...]

     The fields can have the following values:

          who           One or more of the following letters:


                        u    Modify permissions for user (owner).
                        g    Modify permissions for group.
                        o    Modify permissions for others.

                     Or:


                        a    Modify permissions for all (a = ugo).


          operator      One of the following symbols:
```

+   Add permissions to the existing mask for who.

-    Delete permissions from the existing mask for who.

=   Replace the existing mask for who with permissions.

permissions   One or more of the following letters:

r   The read permission.
w   The write permission.
x   The execute/search permission.

If one or two of the fields are omitted, the following table applies:

Format Entered	Effect	Input	Equals
who	Delete current permissions for who	g	g=
operator	No action	-	(none)
permissions	Equal to: a+permissions	rw	a+rw
who=	Delete current permissions for who	u=	u=
who+	No action	u+	(none)
who-	No action	u-	(none)
whopermissions	Equal to: who=permissions	ux	u=x
operatorpermissions	Equal to: aoperatorpermissions	-rw	a-rw

Numeric Mask Value (Obsolescent)

A numeric mask replaces the current file mode creation mask. It is specified as an unsigned octal integer, constructed from the logical OR (sum) of the following mode bits (leading zeros can be omitted):

```
0400   ( a=rwx,u-r)  Read by owner
0200   ( a=rwx,u-w)  Write by owner
0100   ( a=rwx,u-x)  Execute (search in directory) by owner
0040   ( a=rwx,g-r)  Read by group
0020   ( a=rwx,g-w)  Write by group
0010   ( a=rwx,g-x)  Execute/search by group
0004   ( a=rwx,o-r)  Read by others
0002   ( a=rwx,o-w)  Write by others
0001   ( a=rwx,o-x)  Execute/search by others
```

Displaying the Current Mask Value
To display the current file mode creation mask value, use one of the commands:

umask -S   Print the current file mode creation mask in a symbolic format:

u=[r][w][x],g=[r][w][x],o=[r][w][x]

The characters r (read), w (write), and x (execute/search) represent the bits that are clear in the mask for u (user/owner), g (group), and o (other). All other bits are set.

umask   Print the current file mode creation mask as an octal value.

The zero bits in the numeric value correspond to the displayed r, w, and x permission characters in the symbolic value. The one bits in the numeric value correspond to the missing permission characters in the symbolic value.

Depending on implementation, the display consists of one to four octal digits; the first digit is always zero (see DEPENDENCIES). The rightmost three digits (leading zeros implied as needed) represent the bits that are set or clear in the mask.

Both forms produce output that can be used as the mask argument to set the mask in a subsequent umask command.

General Operation
When a new file is created (see creat(2)), each bit that is set in the file mode creation mask causes the corresponding permission bit in the the file mode to be cleared (disabled). Conversely, bits that are clear in the mask allow the corresponding file mode bits to be enabled in newly created files.

For example, the mask u=rwx,g=rx,o=rx (022) disables group and other write permissions. As a result, files normally created with a file mode shown by the ls -l command as -rwxrwxrwx (777) become mode -rwxr-xr-x (755); while files created with file mode -rw-rw-rw- (666) become mode -rw-r--r-- (644).

Note that the file creation mode mask does not affect the set-user-id, set-group-id, or "sticky" bits.

The file creation mode mask is also used by the chmod command (see chmod(1)).

Since umask affects the current shell execution environment, it is generally provided as a shell regular built-in (see DEPENDENCIES.

If umask is called in a subshell or separate utility execution environment, such as one of the following:

        (umask 002)
        nohup umask ...
        find . -exec umask ...

it does not affect the file mode creation mask of the calling environment.

The default mask is u=rwx,g=rwx,o=rwx (000).

RETURN VALUE
umask exits with one of the following values:

        0   The file mode creation mask was successfully changed or no
             mask operand was supplied.

        >0   An error occurred.

EXAMPLES
In these examples, each line show an alternate way of accomplishing the same task.

Set the umask value to produce read and write permissions for the file's owner and read permissions for all others (ls -l displays -rw-r--r-- on newly created files):

        umask u=rwx,g=rx,o=rx   symbolic mode

```
umask a=rx,u+w          symbolic mode
umask 022               numeric mode
```

Set the umask value to produce read, and write permissions for the file's owner, read-only for others users in the same group, and no access to others (-rw-r-----):

```
umask a-rwx,u+rw,g+r    symbolic mode
umask 137               numeric mode
```

Set the umask value to deny read, write, and execute permissions to everyone (----------):

```
umask a=                symbolic mode
umask 777               numeric mode
```

Add the write permission to the current mask for everyone (there is no equivalent numeric mode):

```
umask a+w               symbolic mode
```

WARNINGS

If you set a mask that prevents read or write access for the user (owner), many programs, such as editors, that create temporary files will fail because they cannot access the file data.

DEPENDENCIES

The umask command is implemented both as a separate executable file (/usr/bin/umask) and as built-in shell commands.

POSIX Shell and Separate File

All features are supported (see sh-posix(1). The numeric mask display uses a minimum of two digits.

Korn Shell

The -S option is not supported in the Korn shell built-in command (see ksh(1). The numeric mask display uses a minimum of two digits.

C Shell

The -S option and symbolic mask values are not supported in the C shell built-in command (see csh(1). The numeric mask display uses a minimum of one digit.

Bourne Shell

The -S option and symbolic mask values are not supported in the Bourne shell built-in command (see sh-bourne(1). The numeric mask display always consists of four digits.

SEE ALSO

chmod(1), csh(1), ksh(1), sh-posix(1), sh(1), chmod(2), creat(2), umask(2).

STANDARDS CONFORMANCE

umask: SVID2, SVID3, XPG2, XPG3, XPG4, POSIX.2

CHAPTER 7

Introduction to the C Shell

Different Shells

Most UNIX variants allow you to select among several shells. The shell is important to you as a user, because it is your window into the system. The many shells available on UNIX variants are similar in that you use them to issue commands, control many aspects of your user environment, write command files and shell programs, and so on. Because you'll probably be spending a lot of time in your shell you should develop an understanding of several different shells and see if you develop a preference for one over the other. A particular shell, such as Bash, does not vary much from one UNIX variant to another. The shells themselves, however, have some unique features. In general, I don't find that users strongly prefer one shell over another. All the shells are similar in functionality and enjoyable to use once you get to know them. Most UNIX variants allow your system administrator to select from among several different shells when configuring users, so there is usually some flexibility concerning the shell that users run. In general, system administrators prefer users to use the same shell, making system administration easier in general. Most system administrators, however, are happy to grant a user request for a particular shell if indeed it is available on your system and you have a good reason you'd like to use it. I'll cover the C shell in this chapter. Bash and KornShell were covered in the two previous chapters.

Introduction to the C Shell

The C shell is similar to other shells in that it provides a user interface to UNIX. You can use the C shell in the following three ways:

- Interactively type commands on the command line.
- Group commonly executed sets of commands into command files that you can execute by typing the name of the file.
- Create C shell programs using the structured programming techniques of the C shell.

These three techniques are listed in the order in which you'll probably use them. First, you log in and use interactive commands. Then you group together commonly used commands and execute them with a single command. Finally, you may want to create sophisticated shell scripts.

In this chapter I cover login and interactive commands and a lot of useful ways to use the C shell.

Most of the examples in this chapter are from Solaris and HP-UX systems. You probably will find both your user setup and the operation of the C shell on other systems similar to what is covered in this chapter. Much of the setup of any shell is performed by the system administrator, so you will surely find differences in your C shell setup compared with what is shown in this chapter. In general, however, the operation of the C shell is similar from one system to another.

Issuing Commands

The first activity you perform after you log into the system is to issue commands at the prompt. A command you may want to issue immediately is **ls -al**. Here is what I see on my system after executing this:

man page

ls - 2

```
sys1 7: ls -al
total 10
drwxr-x---   2 martyp2     users          96 May   5 09:34 .
drwxr-xr-x  10 root        root         1024 May   5 10:38 ..
-rw-r--r--   1 martyp2     users         814 May   5 09:34 .cshrc
-rw-r--r--   1 martyp2     users         347 May   5 09:34 .exrc
-rw-r--r--   1 martyp2     users         341 May   5 09:34 .login
-rw-r--r--   1 martyp2     users         446 May   5 09:34 .profile
sys1 8:
```

The C shell prompt consists of system name (sys1) followed by the command number and a colon. I cover the prompt shortly.

ls -al shows two files related to the C shell in this user area:

.cshrc and **.login**

Figure 7-1 is the contents of **.cshrc**.

```
# Default user .cshrc file (/usr/bin/csh initialization).

# Usage:  Copy this file to a user's home directory and edit it to
# customize it to taste.  It is run by csh each time it starts up.

# Set up default command search path:
#
# (For security, this default is a minimal set.)

     set path=( $path )

# Set up C shell environment:

     if ( $?prompt ) then        # shell is interactive.
        set history=20           # previous commands to remember.
        set savehist=20          # number to save across sessions.
        set system=`hostname`    # name of this system.
        set prompt = "$system \!: " # command prompt.

     # Sample alias:

     alias      status  '(date; bdf)'

     # More sample aliases:

     alias   d    dirs
     alias   pd   pushd
     alias   pd2  pushd +2
     alias   po   popd
     alias   m    more
     endif
```

Figure 7-1 Sample **.cshrc**

Figure 7-2 shows the contents of **.login**.

```
# @(#) $Revision: 72.3 $


# Default user .login file ( /usr/bin/csh initialization )

# Set up the default search paths:
set path=( $path )

#set up the terminal
eval `tset -s -Q -m ':?hp' `
stty erase "^H" kill "^U" intr "^C" eof "^D" susp "^Z" hupcl ixon ixoff
tostop
tabs

# Set up shell environment:
set noclobber
set history=20
```

Figure 7-2 Sample **.login**

The .cshrc File

The sequence of events after login varies from one UNIX system to another. On many systems, the **.cshrc** is first read and executed by the C shell. You can modify the **.cshrc** file to specify the command-line prompt you wish to use, initialize the history list, and define aliases. The upcoming sections describe the way the **.cshrc** file shown in Figure 7-1 defines these. Let's first take a quick look at the **.login** file in the next section.

The .login File

On many UNIX systems the **.login** file is read after the **.cshrc** file. There are only two issues related to setup present in the example shown. The first is the **tset** command, which sets the **TERM** environment variable. The **eval** preceding **tset** means that the C shell executes **tset** and its arguments without creating a child process. This allows **tset** to set environment variables in the current shell instead of a subshell, which would be useless. The **stty** command is used to set terminal I/O options. The two set commands are used to define shell variables, which I describe shortly. The **noclobber** does not permit redirection to write over an existing file. If you try to write over an existing file, such as **/tmp/processes** below, you receive a message that the file exists:

man page

ps - 12

```
sys1 1:  ps  -ef  >  /tmp/processes
/tmp/processes:  File exists
```

The ">" means to take the output of **ps** and rather than write it to your screen, write it to **/tmp/processes**. The file **/tmp/processes** will not be written over, however, with the output of **ps -ef** because **/tmp/processes** already exists and an environment variable called **noclobber** has been set. If **noclobber** is set, then redirecting output to this file will not take place. This is a useful technique for preventing existing files from being accidently overwritten. There are many forms of redirection that you'll find useful. Redirection is covered later in this chapter.

Initialize History List in .cshrc

The C shell can keep a history list of the commands you have issued. If you wish to reissue a command or view a command you earlier issued, you can use the history list.

The commands issued are referred to by number, so you want to have a number appear at the command prompt. The following line in **.cshrc** provides a number following the system name:

```
set prompt = "$system \!: "

sys1 1:
```

We get into shell and environment variables shortly, but for now it is sufficient to know that **$system** corresponds to system name "sys1."

You can specify the number of previously issued commands you want to save and view when you issue the **history** command. The following line in **.cshrc** sets the history list to 20:

```
set history = 20
```

The last 20 commands issued are displayed when you issue the **history** command.

The *savehist* variable allows you to save a specified number of history commands after logout. By default, when you log out, the history list is cleared. This variable has a value of 20, so that upon the next login there will be 20 commands from the previous session will be saved.

Command-Line History

You can view the history list a variety of different ways. Let's first view the last 20 commands by simply issuing the **history** command:

```
sys1 23: history
     4 whoami
     5 pwd
     6 find / -name login -print &
     7 hostname
     8 who
     9 more /etc/passwd
    10 history
    11 history 5
    12 echo $PATH
    13 more .login
    14 cat .login
    15 exit
    16 exit
    17 history -h
    18 pwd
    19 whoami
    20 cd /tmp
    21 cat database.log
    22 cd
    23 history
sys1 24:
```

We can also print the history list without line number, as shown in the following example:

```
sys1 24: history -h
pwd
find / -name login -print &
hostname
who
more /etc/passwd
history
history 5
echo $PATH
more .login
cat .login
exit
```

```
exit
history -h
pwd
whoami
cd /tmp
cat database.log
cd
history
history -h
sys1 25:
```

Next let's print the history list in reverse order:

```
sys1 25: history -r
    25 history -r
    24 history -h
    23 history
    22 cd
    21 cat database.log
    20 cd /tmp
    19 whoami
    18 pwd
    17 history -h
    16 exit
    15 exit
    14 cat .login
    13 more .login
    12 echo $PATH
    11 history 5
    10 history
     9 more /etc/passwd
     8 who
     7 hostname
     6 find / -name login -print &
sys1 26:
```

We can also select the number of events we want to print from the history list. The following example prints only the last ten commands from the history list:

```
sys1 26: history 10
    17 history -h
    18 pwd
```

```
    19 whoami
    20 cd /tmp
    21 cat database.log
    22 cd
    23 history
    24 history -h
    25 history -r
    26 history 10
sys1 27:
```

You can see that you have a variety of ways to produce a list of commands previously issued. Table 7-1 summarizes the commands issued in this section.

Table 7-1 Command-Line History

Command	Description	Example
history	The history list is produced with each command numbered.	history
history -h	The history list is produced without line numbers.	history -h
history -r	The history list is produced in reverse order with each command numbered.	history -r
history *n*	The last *n* commands from the history list are produced with each command numbered.	history 10

Re-Executing Commands from the History List

You can re-execute commands from the history list using a variety of techniques. We'll re-execute commands from the history using the most common techniques.

You can repeat the last command with **!!**, the second command with **!2**, and the last command that started with "c" with **!c**. Let's issue

the **history** command to get a list of the last 20 commands and then
re-execute some of them:

```
sys1 27: history
       8 who
       9 more /etc/passwd
      10 history
      11 history 5
      12 echo $PATH
      13 more .login
      14 cat .login
      15 exit
      16 exit
      17 history -h
      18 pwd
      19 whoami
      20 cd /tmp
      21 cat database.log
      22 cd
      23 history
      24 history -h
      25 history -r
      26 history 10
      27 history
sys1 28:
```

Let's first reissue the last command with **!!**:

```
sys1 28: !!
history
       9 more /etc/passwd
      10 history
      11 history 5
      12 echo $PATH
      13 more .login
      14 cat .login
      15 exit
      16 exit
      17 history -h
      18 pwd
      19 whoami
      20 cd /tmp
      21 cat database.log
      22 cd
      23 history
      24 history -h
      25 history -r
      26 history 10
```

```
   27 history
   28 history
sys1 29:
```

Let's now reissue the 19th command with **!19**:

```
sys1 29: !19
whoami
martyp2
sys1 30:
```

Let's now reissue the last command beginning with "p" with **!p**:

```
sys1 30: !p
pwd
/home/martyp2
sys1 31:
```

Table 7-2 includes some of the more commonly used history list recall commands.

Table 7-2 Recalling from History List

Command	Description	Example
!N	Issue command N	!2
!!	Issue last command	!!
!-N	Issue **Nth** command from last command issued	!-N
!str	Issue last command starting with **str**	!c
!?str?	Issue last command that had **str** anyplace in command line	!?cat?
!{str}str2	Append **str2** to last command with **str1**	!{cd} /tmp
^str1^str2^	Substitute **str2** for **str1** in last command	^cat^more^

Aliases in .cshrc

An alias is a name that you select for a frequently used command or series of commands. Many aliases are predefined for you.

You can use the **.cshrc** file as a place where your aliases are stored and read every time you log in. You can also define aliases at the command-line prompt, but these are cleared when you log out.

The **alias** command, without any arguments, lists all aliases. This list includes both preset aliases as well as those you have set. The following **alias** command shows all preset aliases on the system on which I am working:

```
sys1 7: alias
d       dirs
m       more
pd      pushd
pd2     (pushd +2)
po      popd
status  (date; bdf)
sys1 8:
```

You are not restricted to using only the preset aliases. To create your own alias, you first issue the **alias** command, the name of the alias, and then the command or commands that are executed when the alias is executed.

Let's now create a few simple aliases. The first creates an alias of "h" for the **history** command:

```
sys1 1: alias h history
sys1 2: h
        history
```

Every time you type **h**, the history command is executed.

The following example creates an alias of a command that contains spaces, so the command is surrounded by single quotes:

```
alias ls='ls -al'
alias
ls
```

man page

ls - 2

The first command creates an alias for "ls" that executes the **ls -al** command. We then issued the **alias** command to see whether indeed the new alias appears in the list of aliases. Then we run **ls** to see whether **ls -al** is run.

You don't have to keep an alias for the duration of your session after having set it. If you don't like an alias you can use the **unalias** command to remove an alias.

To see **unalias** work let's again produce a list of aliases, use **unalias** to unset the **h** alias, and run the **h** command to see if indeed it has been removed.

```
unalias h
h
```

When we issued **unalias** to remove the **h** alias and then try to run *h,* we were told that **h** is not found.

man page

ps - 12

```
sys1 3:alias procs 'echo "Number of processes are: \c";
ps -ef | wc -l'
                        # single quote on outside
                        # double quote on inside
```

When you run **procs**, you see the following:

```
sys1 4: procs
Number of processes are: 44
```

A lot of quoting takes place in this command line. To understand what is taking place on this line turn to Table 7-3 for help.

Table 7-3 Shell Quoting

Character(s)	Description
'cmd'	Single quote means to take the string character literally
"str"	Double quote means to allow command and variable substitution
\c	Escape character that prevents everything following it from printing, including new line
`str`	Grave means to execute command and substitute output

Applying Table 7-3 to the earlier **procs** alias, we can see what comprises this alias. The alias begins with a single quote, which means execute the command(s) within the single quotes. The first command is the **echo** command, which uses double quotes to specify the characters to **echo**. Embedded in the double quotes is the escape character \c, which prevents a new line from being printed. The semicolons separate commands. **ps** is then run to produce a list of processes, and the output is piped (|) to word count (**wc**) which produces a count of the number of lines. There are actually 43 processes running, because an extra line consisting of the **ps** headings is reported by **wc**.

man page

ps - 12

man page

wc - 12

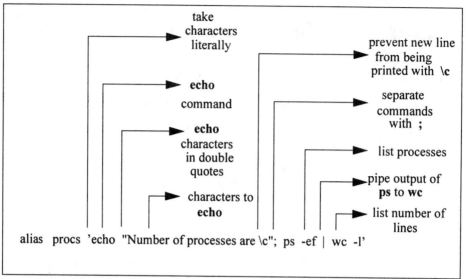

Figure 7-3 Quoting Example

As you can see in Figure 7-3, some of the quoting becomes tricky. An understanding of quoting is important if you wish to modify and reuse existing shell scripts or craft your own.

File-Name Expansion

Another important part of using the C shell is file-name expansion. When we cover shell programming, you will surely be preparing shell scripts that deal with file names. An overview of file-name expansion is useful to ensure that you're comfortable with this topic before you start writing shell scripts.

Table 7-4 lists some common file-name expansion and pattern matching.

Table 7-4   File-Name Expansion and Pattern Matching

Character(s)	Example	Description
*	1) ls *.c	Match zero or more characters
?	2) ls conf.?	Match any single character
[list]	3) ls conf.[co]	Match any character in list
[lower-upper]	4) ls libdd.9873[5-6].sl	Match any character in range
str{str1,str2,str3,...}	5) ls ux*.{700,300}	Expand str with contents of {}
~	6) ls -a ~	Home directory
~username	7) ls -a ~gene	Home directory of username

The following are expanded descriptions of the examples shown in Table 7-4:

1. To list all files in a directory that end in ".c," you could do the following:

man page

ls - 2

    sys1 30: **ls *.c**
        conf. SAM.c conf.c

2. To find all the files in a directory named "conf" with an extension of one character, you could do the following:

    sys1 31: **ls conf.?**
        conf.c conf.o conf.1

3. To list all the files in a directory named "conf" with only the extension "c" or "o," you could do the following:

    sys1 32: **ls conf.{co}**

conf.c conf.o

man page

ls - 2

4. To list files with similar names but with a specific field that covers a range, you could do the following:

sys1 46: **ls libdd9873[5-6].sl**
           libdd98735.sl libdd98736.sl

5. To list files that start with "ux" and have the extension "300" or "700," you could do the following:

sys1 59: **ls ux*.{700,300}**
           uxbootlf.700 uxinstfs.300 unistkern.300
           unistkern.700 unistlf.700

6. To list the files in your home directory, you could use ~:

sys1 62: **ls -a ~**
           .   .cshrc.org .login   .shrc.org
           ..   .exrc   .login.org .vue
           .chsrc .history   .profile   .vueprofile

7. To list the files in the home directory of a user, you can do the following:

sys1 65: **ls -a ~gene**
           .   .history .vue   splinedat
           ..   .login   .vueprofile trail.txt
           .chsrc   .login.org ESP-File under.des
           .cshrc.org .profile Mail   xtra.part
           .exrc   .shrc.org opt

Many of these techniques are useful when writing shell scripts, so you want to become familiar with file-name expansion.

Redirection (I/O Redirection)

UNIX is set up such that commands usually take their input from the keyboard, often called standard input, and usually send output to the screen, often called standard output. Commands also send error information to the screen. You do not always want input to come from standard input and output and errors to go to standard output. You are given a lot of control to override these defaults. This is called redirection. Table 7-5 shows many common forms of redirection.

As shown in the table, to redirect the output of a command from standard output to a file, you would use ">". This works almost all of the time. If you have an environment variable called **noclobber** set, then redirecting to an existing file does not work. The **noclobber** does not permit redirection to write over an existing file. If you try to write over an existing file, such as **/tmp/processes** below, you receive a message that the file exists:

man page

ps - 12

```
#  ps  -ef  > /tmp/processes
/tmp/processes:  File exists
```

You can, however, use a "!" with redirection to force a file to be overwritten. Using ">!" forces a file to be overwritten, and ">>!" will force the output to be appended to the end of an existing file. Examples of these are shown in the Table 7-5.

Table 7-5   Commonly Used Redirection Forms

Command or Assignment	Example	Description
<	wc -l < .login	Standard input redirection: execute **wc** (word count) and list number of lines (**-l**) in **.login**
>	ps -ef > /tmp/processes	Standard output redirection: execute **ps** and send output to file **/tmp/processes**

Command or Assignment	Example	Description
>>	ps -ef >> /tmp/processes	Append standard output: execute **ps** and append output to the end of file **/tmp/processes**
>!	ps -ef >! /tmp/processes	Standard output redirection and override **noclobber**: write over **/tmp/processes** even if it exists
>>!	ps -ef >>! /tmp/processes	Append standard output and override **noclobber**: append to the end of **/tmp/processes**
| (pipe)	ps | wc -l	Run **ps** and use the result as input to **wc**
0 - standard input 1 - standard output 2 - standard error	cat program 2> errors	**cat** the file **program** to standard output and redirect errors to the file **errors**
	cat program 2>> errors	**cat** the file **program** to standard output and append errors to the file **errors**
	cat program >& outfile	**cat** both the file **program** and errors to the file **outfile**
	(cat program > outfile) >& errors	**cat** the file **program** to **outfile** and redirect errors to the file **errors**

Shell and Environment Variables

You are indeed special to your UNIX system. Information about your user environment in the C shell is stored in shell variables and environment variables.

Shell variables are sometimes called "local" variables. Shell variables are known only to the shell in which they were created.

Environment variables are sometimes called "global" variables. Environment variables are defined in the shell where they are created and inherited by all shells spawned from the original shell. Because these variables are passed to shells spawned from the original shell, they are considered global.

You can view shell variables with the **set** command and environment variables with the **env** command, as shown below:

```
sys1 22: set
argv    ()
autologout          600
cwd     /home/martyp2
history 20
home    /home/martyp2
noclobber
path    (/usr/bin /usr/ccs/bin /usr/contrib/bin /opt/net-
tladm/bin /opt/pd/bin /)
prompt  sys1 !:
savehist            20
shell   /usr/bin/csh
status  0
system  sys1
term    vt100
sys1 23: set
argv    ()
autologout          600
cwd     /home/martyp2
history 20
home    /home/martyp2
noclobber
path    (/usr/bin /usr/ccs/bin /usr/contrib/bin /opt/net-
tladm/bin /opt/pd/bin /)
prompt  sys1 !:
savehist            20
shell   /usr/bin/csh
status  0
system  sys1
term    vt100
sys1 24:
```

```
sys1 24: env
HOME=/home/martyp2
PATH=/usr/bin:/usr/ccs/bin:/usr/contrib/bin:/opt/net-
tladm/bin:/opt/pd/bin:/opt/n
LOGNAME=martyp2
TERM=vt100
SHELL=/usr/bin/csh
MAIL=/var/mail/martyp2
COLUMNS=80
LINES=24
```

```
MANPATH=/usr/share/man/%L:/usr/share/man:/usr/contrib/
man/%L:/usr/contrib/man:/n
TZ=PST8PDT
sys1 25:
```

Notice that local variables are in lower case and global variables are in uppercase by convention.

You can see from having issued the **set** command that many local and global variables have been set. You can determine whether a variable has been set by using the special notation *$?*. Placing this special notation in front of a variable name returns a *1* if the variable has been set and a *0* if the variable has not been set. The following example shows using **echo** and this special notation to see whether the variables *history* and *hist* have been set:

```
sys1 25: echo $?history
1
sys1 26: echo $?hist
0
sys1 27:
```

Because a *1* was returned from the *history* variable, we know that this variable was indeed set. We can confirm this from the earlier output of the **set** command, which showed that *history* was set to 20.

Because a *0* was returned from the *hist* variable, we know that this variable is not set.

Using the special metacharacter *$*, we tell the shell to extract the value of a variable. The following example uses **echo** combined with *$* preceding the *history* variable to report its value:

```
sys1 27: echo $history
20
sys1 28: echo $hist
hist: Undefined variable.
sys1 29:
```

Shell variables are defined using **set**. We saw in the **.cshrc** file earlier that the **history** shell variable is set with the following command:

```
set history = 20
```

Environment variables are defined with **setenv**, as in the following command:

```
setenv  EDITOR  vi
```

Background Jobs and Job Control

When you run a command, as we have done so far in many examples, you don't get back the prompt until the command has completed. These commands have been run in the foreground. Some commands can take a long time to complete, in which case you wait a long time for the prompt to return. As an alternative to waiting for the prompt to return, you can run the command in the background, which means it is running behind the scenes while you perform other work. Because UNIX is multi-tasking, it is happy to run many commands in the background and still provide you with a prompt to issue yet more commands.

In order to run a command in the background, you simply add an ampersand (&) to the end of the command line. When you follow your command with an ampersand, the command is run in the background and the prompt is immediately returned.

Let's now run some commands on our Solaris system. We'll first run a command to find all the files in **/usr** that end in ".c," which takes some time to complete. We'll preface the **find** string with the **time** command so that we know how long the command takes to complete:

man page

find - 10

man page

find - 10

```
martyp $ time find /usr -name *.c
                    .
                    .
                    .
/usr/demo/link_audit/src/dumpbind.c
/usr/demo/link_audit/src/env.c
/usr/demo/link_audit/src/hash.c
/usr/demo/link_audit/src/perfcnt.c
/usr/demo/link_audit/src/symbindrep.c
/usr/demo/link_audit/src/truss.c
/usr/demo/link_audit/src/who.c
find: cannot read dir /usr/aset: Permission denied

real    1m21.04s
user    0m1.51s
sys     0m12.67s
```

This command took roughly one minute and 21 seconds to complete. Because it was not run in the foreground, we were unable to issue any other commands while it was running, because we had to wait for the prompt to return.

An alternative to running the command in the foreground is to issue the command followed by an ampersand in which case the job runs in the background and the prompt returns immediately, as shown in the following example:

```
martyp $ time find /usr -name *.c > cprogs 2>&1 &
[3]    16279
martyp $
real    2m10.20s
user    0m1.31s
sys     0m8.62s
```

The result of running this command in the background produces a job number in brackets and the process id, or PID, as the second number. All the output of this command, including errors, are written to the file **cprogs**. The prompt was immediately returned after we issued the command and after it completed, the output of **time** was sent to the screen. We could have begun issuing additional commands immediately after issuing the command in the background.

You have control over both foreground jobs and background jobs. To suspend a foreground job, you type the "control" and "z" keys simultaneously, as shown in the following example:

man page

find - 10

```
martyp $ find /usr -name *.c
/usr/openwin/share/include/X11/Xaw/Template.c
/usr/openwin/share/src/dig_samples/DnD/main.c
/usr/openwin/share/src/dig_samples/DnD/owner.c
/usr/openwin/share/src/dig_samples/DnD/requestor.c
/usr/openwin/share/src/dig_samples/Tooltalk/olit_tt.c
/usr/openwin/share/src/dig_samples/Tooltalk/
tt_callbacks.c
/usr/openwin/share/src/dig_samples/Tooltalk/tt_code.c
/usr/openwin/share/src/dig_samples/ce1/ce_map1.c
/usr/openwin/share/src/dig_samples/ce2/ce_simple.c
/usr/openwin/share/src/dig_samples/dnd_olit/olitdnd.c
/usr/openwin/share/src/dig_samples/dnd_xview1/
xview_dnd.c
/usr/openwin/share/src/dig_samples/dnd_xview2/
xview_dnd2.c
/usr/openwin/share/src/dig_samples/selection_olit/
olit_sel.c
/usr/openwin/share/src/dig_samples/tooltalk_simple/tt-
send.c
/usr/openwin/share/src/olit/oldials/oldials.c
/usr/openwin/share/src/olit/olitbook/ch10/draw.c
^Z[3] + Stopped (SIGTSTP)          find /usr -name *.c
```

After *ctrl-z* is pressed, the **find** command is interrupted at the point at which you type *ctrl-z*. The command is suspended at this point and you are shown the job number, in this case "3," and its status is listed as "Stopped." This command has only been suspended; it is not gone forever. You can restart this process in the foreground with **fg** or run it in the background with **bg**. Using **bg** runs the command as if you had followed it with an "&". It is started from the point at which you interrupted it. You do not have to supply a job number when you issue the **fg** or **bg** command, because the default is to perform the specified operation on the last job, which in this case is job number 3.

Notice that in this example we have stopped job number 3. This means that there are other jobs running with a lower job number. You can use the **jobs** command to get a list of all jobs and their status. You can then control the jobs by issuing commands: such as **fg** followed by a "%" and the job number to run the command in the foreground, or a **bg** followed by a "%" and the job number to run the command in the background. If you wish to terminate a job altogether, you can issue the **kill** command followed by a "%" and the job number.

kill - 6

In the process of creating the examples in this section I have started and suspended many jobs. The following example shows listing all jobs with the **jobs** command, killing jobs 1 and 2 with **kill**, and running job 3 in the background:

```
martyp $ jobs
[3] + Stopped (SIGTSTP) find /usr -name *.c
[2] - Running            time find / -name gnu* > gnu 2>&1 &
[1]   Running              time find / -name *.c > cprogs
2>&1 &
martyp $ kill %1
[1]   Terminated           time find / -name *.c > cprogs
2>&1 &
martyp $ kill %2
[2] - Terminated          time find / -name gnu* > gnu 2>&1 &
martyp $ bg %3
[3]      find /usr -name *.c&
martyp $
```

Notice that an ampersand was added to job 3 when we requested that it be run in the background. Killing jobs 1 and 2 and running job 3 in the background return the prompt so that you can perform additional work.

csh - 7

umask - 6

umask and Permissions

An additional topic to cover related to **csh** is file permissions and the way they relate to **umask**. This is important because you may write shell programs, and the permissions control the access that others have to these programs. **umask** is used to specify permission settings for new files and directories.

man page

umask - 6

Let's start with an example of a long listing of a file. We'll use **ls** -l in the following examples:

man page

ls - 2

```
sys1 1: ls -l script1
-rwxr-xr-x  1  marty  users  120 Jul 26 10:20 script1
```

The access rights for this file are defined by the position of read (r), write (w), and execute (x) when the **ll** command is issued. Figure 7-4 shows the three groups of three access rights for this file.

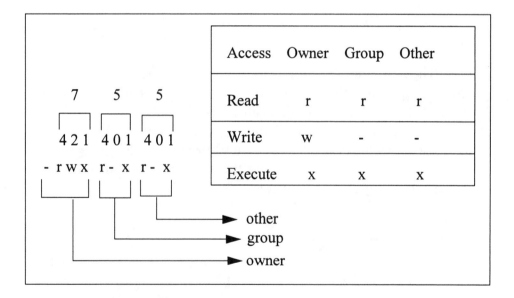

Figure 7-4 Example of File Permissions

The owner of this file has read, write, and execute permissions on the file. The group to which the user belongs has read and execute permissions, and others also have read and execute permissions. The permissions on this file can be specified by the octal sum of each field, which is 755.

man page

umask - 6

What happens if you craft a new shell script or any new file? What permission settings exist? You want to execute the shell script, so you will need execute permission for the file. You can use **umask** to define the defaults for all your new files and directories.

By default, most systems start with a permission of 777 for directories and 666 for files. This means that everyone has complete access to all directories you create and everyone has read and write access to all files you create. These defaults are modified with the value of **umask**.

You can view your **umask** in the following two ways:

```
martyp $ umask
002
martyp $ umask -S
u=rwx,g=rwx,o=rx
martyp $
```

The first example displays the octal value of **umask**, which we'll cover shortly, and the second example shows the symbolic value of **umask**. The **-S** does not work on all UNIX variants.

The **umask** is used to *disable* access. You start with a **umask** and use the fields to disable some level of access. The **umask** command uses three octal fields. The fields are the sum of the access codes for user, group, and other, as shown in Figure 7-5.

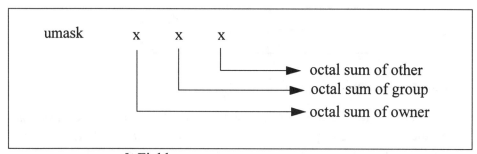

Figure 7-5   **umask** Fields

The *complement* of the umask field is "*anded*" with the default setting to change the **umask**. You can set **umask** by specifying its value. In our earlier example we viewed **umask** two different ways. To set the **umask**, you simply issue **umask** and the desired value. Setting **umask** to *022*, for example, removes write permissions of directories for "group" and "other," as shown in Figure 7-6.

man page

umask - 6

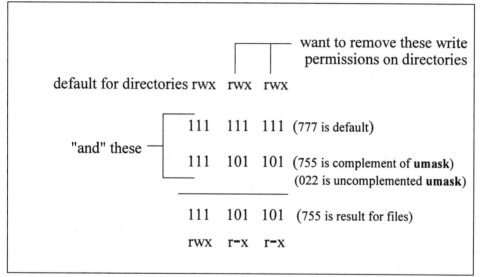

Figure 7-6   **umask** Example

umask   022   changes the directory permissions to 755 in this example.

Similarly, a **umask** of 022 changes the default permission of 666 for files to 644, which is read-only for group and other.

Change File Permissions with chmod

chmod - 3

umask - 6

ls - 2

The **chmod** command is used to change the permissions on a file. Irre-spective of what takes place with **umask**, as just described, you can change a file's permissions at any time with **chmod**. You need to be the owner of the file or superuser to change a file's permissions with **chmod** in most cases. Let's start our discussion of **chmod** with the listing of the file **sort**:

```
$ ls -l sort
-rwxr-x--x   1 marty      users      120 Jul 26 10:20 sort
```

Figure 7-7 shows a breakdown of the permissions on **sort**.

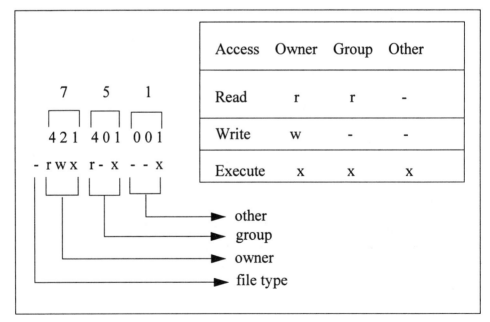

Figure 7-7   Permissions of File **sort**

You have very little control over the type of file defined. You do, however, have a great deal of control over the permissions of this file if it belongs to you. The **chmod** command is used to change the permissions on a file or directory. If you are the owner of the file, you can have a field day changing the permissions on the file.

man page

chmod - 3

There are two means by which you can change the permissions: symbolic or numeric. I'll focus first on the numeric mode, because the numbers involved are easy to manage and I sometimes find that new UNIX users get hung up on the meaning of some of the symbols. I'll then cover the symbols and include the symbol meanings in the **chmod** summary.

First of all, what do I mean by numbers? Looking at the numbers for **sort**, we see permissions of 751: 7 for *owner* (hundreds position), 5 for *group* (tens position), and 1 for *other* (ones position). Figure 7-8 helps with the meanings of the positions.

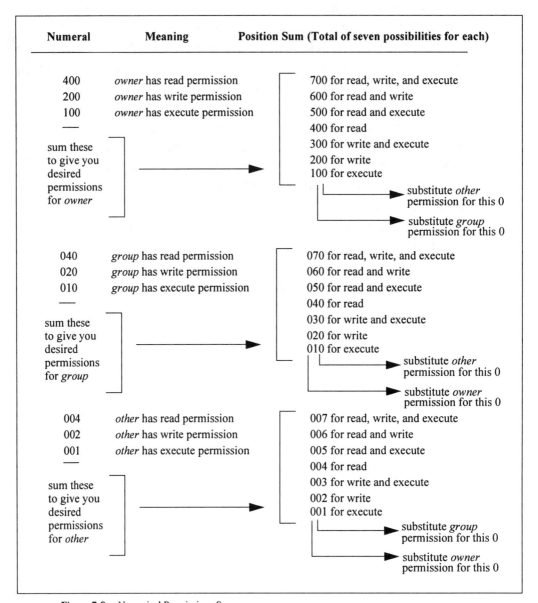

Numeral	Meaning	Position Sum (Total of seven possibilities for each)
400	*owner* has read permission	700 for read, write, and execute
200	*owner* has write permission	600 for read and write
100	*owner* has execute permission	500 for read and execute
—		400 for read
		300 for write and execute
sum these to give you desired permissions for *owner*	→	200 for write
		100 for execute
		substitute *other* permission for this 0
		substitute *group* permission for this 0
040	*group* has read permission	070 for read, write, and execute
020	*group* has write permission	060 for read and write
010	*group* has execute permission	050 for read and execute
—		040 for read
		030 for write and execute
sum these to give you desired permissions for *group*	→	020 for write
		010 for execute
		substitute *other* permission for this 0
		substitute *owner* permission for this 0
004	*other* has read permission	007 for read, write, and execute
002	*other* has write permission	006 for read and write
001	*other* has execute permission	005 for read and execute
—		004 for read
		003 for write and execute
sum these to give you desired permissions for *other*	→	002 for write
		001 for execute
		substitute *group* permission for this 0
		substitute *owner* permission for this 0

Figure 7-8   Numerical Permissions Summary

man page

chmod - 3

Selecting the desired permissions for *owner*, *group*, and *other*, you use the **chmod** command to assign those permissions to a file or

directory. Some of these permission possibilities are infrequently used, such as execute only, because you usually need to have read access to a file in order to execute it; however, I included all possibilities in Figure 7-8 for completeness. In addition to the permission mode bits shown in Figure 7-8, miscellaneous mode bits also exist which you don't need to be concerned with at this time.

If you decided that you would like to add write permission of the file **sort** for *group*, and remove all permissions for *other*, you would simply execute the **chmod** command with the appropriate numeric value. The following set of commands first list the existing permissions for **sort**, next change the permissions on **sort**, and finally list the new permissions on **sort**:

man page

chmod - 3

man page

ls - 2

```
$ ls -l sort
-rwxr-x--x   1 marty      users      120 Jul 26 10:20 sort

$ chmod 770 sort

$ ls -l sort
-rwxrwx---   1 marty      users      120 Jul 26 10:20 sort
```

The same set of commands to change the permissions using the symbolic mode would be:

```
$ ls -l sort
-rwxr-x--x   1 marty      users      120 Jul 26 10:20 sort

$ chmod g+w,o-x sort

$ ls -l sort
-rwxrwx---   1 marty      users      120 Jul 26 10:20 sort
```

In symbolic mode, you issue the **chmod** command and specify who will be affected by the change [user (u), group (g), other (o), or all (a)], the operation you wish to perform [add (+), delete (-), or replace (=)], and the permission you wish to specify [read (r), write (w), or execute (x)]. In the previous example using symbolic mode, write (w) permission is being added (+) for *group* (g), and execute (x) permission is being removed (-) for *other* (o).

man page

chmod - 3

The following is a summary of some of the more commonly used symbols of **chmod**:

chmod - Change permissions of specified files using the following symbolic mode list.

Symbol of who is affected:

u	User is affected.
g	Group is affected.
o	Other is affected.
a	All users are affected.

Operation to perform:

+	Add permission.
-	Remove permission.
=	Replace permission.

Permission specified:

r	Read permission.
w	Write permission.
x	Execute permission.
u	Copy user permissions.
g	Copy group permissions.
o	Copy other permissions.

The C shell functionality covered in this chapter combined with the following manual pages should get you off to a good start with the C shell.

Manual Pages of Some Commands Used in Chapter 7

The following is the HP-UX manual page for **csh**. Commands often differ among UNIX variants, so you may find differences in the options or other areas for this manual page; however, the following manual page serves as an excellent reference.

csh

man page

csh - 7

csh - C shell.

---

csh(1)   csh(1)

NAME
     csh - a shell (command interpreter) with C-like syntax

SYNOPSIS

     csh [-cefinstvxTVX] [command_file] [argument_list ...]

DESCRIPTION
     csh is a command language interpreter that incorporates a command
     history buffer, C-like syntax, and job control facilities.

  Command Options
     Command options are interpreted as follows:

          -c   Read commands from the (single) following argument
                    which must be present. Any remaining arguments are
                    placed in argv.

          -e   C shell exits if any invoked command terminates
                    abnormally or yields a non-zero exit status.

          -f   Suppress execution of the .cshrc file in your home
                    directory, thus speeding up shell start-up time.

          -i   Force csh to respond interactively when called from a
                    device other than a computer terminal (such as another
                    computer). csh normally responds non-interactively.
                    If csh is called from a computer terminal, it always
                    responds interactively, regardless of which options are
                    selected.

          -n   Parse but do not execute commands. This is useful for
                    checking syntax in shell scripts. All substitutions
                    are performed (history, command, alias, etc.).

          -s   Take command input from the standard input.

          -t   Read and execute a single line of input.

          -v   Set the verbose shell variable, causing command input
                    to be echoed to the standard output device after
                    history substitutions are made.

          -x   Set the echo shell variable, causing all commands to be
                    echoed to the standard error immediately before
                    execution.

          -T   Disable the tenex features which use the ESC key for
                    command/file name completion and CTRL-D for listing
                    available files (see the CSH UTILITIES section below)

-V   Set the verbose variable before .cshrc is executed so
            that all .cshrc commands are also echoed to the
            standard output.

-X   Set the echo variable before .cshrc is executed so that
            all .cshrc commands are also echoed to the standard
            output.

After processing the command options, if arguments remain in the
argument list, and the -c, -i, -s, or -t options were not specified,
the first remaining argument is taken as the name of a file of
commands to be executed.

COMMANDS
    A simple command is a sequence of words, the first of which specifies
    the command to be executed. A sequence of simple commands separated
    by vertical bar (|) characters forms a pipeline. The output of each
    command in a pipeline becomes the input for the next command in the
    pipeline. Sequences of pipelines can be separated by semicolons (;)
    which causes them to be executed sequentially. A sequence of
    pipelines can be executed in background mode by adding an ampersand
    character (&) after the last entry.

    Any pipeline can be placed in parentheses to form a simple command
    which, in turn, can be a component of another pipeline. Pipelines can
    also be separated by || or && indicating, as in the C language, that
    the second pipeline is to be executed only if the first fails or
    succeeds, respectively.

Jobs
    csh associates a job with each pipeline and keeps a table of current
    jobs (printed by the jobs command) and assigns them small integer
    numbers. When a job is started asynchronously using &, the shell
    prints a line resembling:

        [1] 1234

    indicating that the job which was started asynchronously was job
    number 1 and had one (top-level) process, whose process id was 1234.

    If you are running a job and want to do something else, you can type
    the currently defined suspend character (see termio(7)) which sends a
    stop signal to the current job. csh then normally indicates that the
    job has been `Stopped', and prints another prompt. You can then
    manipulate the state of this job, putting it in the background with
    the bg command, run some other commands, and then eventually bring the
    job back into the foreground with the foreground command fg. A
    suspend takes effect immediately and is like an interrupt in that
    pending output and unread input are discarded when it is typed. There
    is a delayed suspend character which does not generate a stop signal
    until a program attempts to read(2) it. This can usefully be typed
    ahead when you have prepared some commands for a job which you want to
    stop after it has read them.

    A job being run in the background stops if it tries to read from the
    terminal. Background jobs are normally allowed to produce output, but
    this can be disabled by giving the command stty tostop (see stty(1)).
    If you set this tty option, background jobs stop when they try to
    produce output, just as they do when they try to read input. Keyboard
    signals and line-hangup signals from the terminal interface are not
    sent to background jobs on such systems. This means that background
    jobs are immune to the effects of logging out or typing the interrupt,
    quit, suspend, and delayed suspend characters (see termio(7)).

    There are several ways to refer to jobs in the shell. The character %
    introduces a job name. If you wish to refer to job number 1, you can

name it as %1. Just naming a job brings it to the foreground; thus %1
is a synonym for fg %1 , bringing job 1 back into the foreground.
Similarly, typing %1 & resumes job 1 in the background. Jobs can also
be named by prefixes of the string typed in to start them if these
prefixes are unambiguous; thus %ex normally restarts a suspended ex(1)
job, if there is only one suspended job whose name begins with the
string ex. It is also possible to say %?string which specifies a job
whose text contains string, if there is only one such job.

csh maintains a notion of the current and previous jobs. In output
pertaining to jobs, the current job is marked with a + and the
previous job with a -. The abbreviation %+ refers to the current job
and %- refers to the previous job. For close analogy with the syntax
of the history mechanism (described below), %% is also a synonym for
the current job.

csh learns immediately whenever a process changes state. It normally
informs you whenever a job becomes blocked so that no further progress
is possible, but only just before printing a prompt. This is done so
that it does not otherwise disturb your work. If, however, you set
the shell variable notify, csh notifies you immediately of changes in
status of background jobs. There is also a csh built-in command
called notify which marks a single process so that any status change
is immediately reported. By default, notify marks the current
process. Simply type notify after starting a background job to mark
it.

If you try to leave the shell while jobs are stopped, csh sends the
warning message: You have stopped jobs. Use the jobs command to see
what they are. If you do this or immediately try to exit again, csh
does not warn you a second time, and the suspended jobs are terminated
(see exit(2)).

Built-In Commands
    Built-in commands are executed within the shell without spawning a new
process. If a built-in command occurs as any component of a pipeline
except the last, it is executed in a subshell. The built-in commands
are:

       alias
       alias name

       alias name wordlist
             The first form prints all aliases. The second form
             prints the alias for name. The third form assigns the
             specified wordlist as the alias of name. Command and
             file name substitution are performed on wordlist. name
             cannot be alias or unalias.

       bg [%job ...]
             Put the current (job not specified) or specified jobs
             into the background, continuing them if they were
             stopped.

       break   Causes execution to resume after the end of the nearest
             enclosing foreach or while. The remaining commands on
             the current line are executed. Multi-level breaks are
             thus possible by writing them all on one line.

    breaksw Causes a break from a switch, resuming after the endsw.

       case label:
             A label in a switch statement as discussed below.

       cd

```
cd directory_name

chdir
chdir directory_name
        Change the shell's current working directory to
        directory_name.  If not specified, directory_name
        defaults to your home directory.
        If directory_name is not found as a subdirectory of the
        current working directory (and does not begin with /, ./,
        or ../), each component of the variable cdpath is checked
        to see if it has a subdirectory directory_name.  Finally,
        if all else fails, csh treats directory_name as a shell
        variable.  If its value begins with /, this is tried to
        see if it is a directory.
continue
        Continue execution of the nearest enclosing while or
        foreach.  The rest of the commands on the current line
        are executed.
default:
        Labels the default case in a switch statement.  The
        default should come after all other case labels.
dirs    Prints the directory stack; the top of the stack is at
        the left; the first directory in the stack is the current
        directory.
echo wordlist

echo -n wordlist
        The specified words are written to the shell's standard
        output, separated by spaces, and terminated with a new-
        line unless the -n option is specified.

else
end
endif
endsw   See the descriptions of the foreach, if, switch, and
        while statements below.

eval arguments ...
        (Same behavior as sh(1).) arguments are read as input to
        the shell and the resulting command(s) executed.  This is
        usually used to execute commands generated as the result
        of command or variable substitution, since parsing occurs
        before these substitutions.

exec command
        The specified command is executed in place of the current
        shell.

exit
exit (expression)
        csh exits either with the value of the status variable
        (first form) or with the value of the specified
        expression (second form).

fg [%job ...]
        Brings the current (job not specified) or specified jobs
        into the foreground, continuing them if they were
        stopped.

foreach name (wordlist)

    ...
end     The variable name is successively set to each member of
        wordlist and the sequence of commands between this
        command and the matching end are executed.  (Both foreach
        and end must appear alone on separate lines.)
```

The built-in command continue can be used to continue the
loop prematurely; the built-in command break to terminate
it prematurely. When this command is read from the
terminal, the loop is read once, prompting with ? before
any statements in the loop are executed. If you make a
mistake while typing in a loop at the terminal, use the
erase or line-kill character as appropriate to recover.

glob wordlist
> Like echo but no \ escapes are recognized and words are
> delimited by null characters in the output. Useful in
> programs that use the shell to perform file name
> expansion on a list of words.

goto word
> The specified word is file name and command expanded to
> yield a string of the form label. The shell rewinds its
> input as much as possible and searches for a line of the
> form label: possibly preceded by blanks or tabs.
> Execution continues after the specified line.

hashstat
> Print a statistics line indicating how effective the
> internal hash table has been at locating commands (and
> avoiding execs). An exec is attempted for each component
> of the path where the hash function indicates a possible
> hit, and in each component that does not begin with a /.

history [-h] [-r] [n]
> Displays the history event list. If n is given, only the
> n most recent events are printed. The -r option reverses
> the order of printout to be most recent first rather than
> oldest first. The -h option prints the history list
> without leading numbers for producing files suitable for
> the source command.

if (expression) command
> If expression evaluates true, the single command with
> arguments is executed. Variable substitution on command
> happens early, at the same time it does for the rest of
> the if command. command must be a simple command; not a
> pipeline, a command list, a parenthesized command list,
> or an aliased command. Input/output redirection occurs
> even if expression is false, meaning that command is not
> executed (this is a bug).

if (expression1) then

  ...
else if (expression2) then

  ...
else
  ...
endif   If expression1 is true, all commands down to the first
         else are executed; otherwise if expression2 is true, all
         commands from the first else down to the second else are
         executed, etc. Any number of else-if pairs are possible,
         but only one endif is needed. The else part is likewise
         optional. (The words else and endif must appear at the
         beginning of input lines. The if must appear alone on
         its input line or after an else.)

jobs [-l]
>   Lists active jobs. The -l option lists process IDs in
>   addition to the usual information.

kill % job

kill - sig % job ...

kill pid

kill - sig pid...

kill -l Sends either the TERM (terminate) signal or the specified
>   signal to the specified jobs or processes. Signals are
>   either given by number or by names (as given in
>   /usr/include/signal.h, stripped of the SIG prefix (see
>   signal(2)). The signal names are listed by kill -l.
>   There is no default, so kill used alone does not send a
>   signal to the current job. If the signal being sent is
>   TERM (terminate) or HUP (hangup), the job or process is
>   sent a CONT (continue) signal as well.

limit[-h][resource][maximum_use]
>   Limits the usage by the current process and each process
>   it creates not to (individually) exceed maximum_use on
>   the specified resource. If maximum_use is not specified,
>   then the current limit is displayed; if resource is not
>   specified, then all limitations are given.
>
>   If the -h flag is specified, the hard limits are used
>   instead of the current limits. The hard limits impose a
>   ceiling on the values of the current limits. Only the
>   superuser can raise the hard limits, but a user can lower
>   or raise the current limits within the legal range.
>
>   Controllable resources currently include:
>
>   addresspace Maximum address space in bytes for a process
>
>   coredumpsize Size of the largest core dump that is created
>
>   cputime Maximum number of CPU seconds to be used by each
>   process
>
>   datasize Maximum growth of the data region allowed beyond
>   the end of the program text
>
>   descriptors Maximum number of open files for each process
>
>   filesize Largest single file that can be created
>
>   memoryuse Maximum size to which a process's resident set
>   size can grow
>
>   stacksize Maximum size of the automatically extended stack
>   region
>
>   The maximum_use argument can be specified as a floating-
>   point or integer number followed by a scale factor: k or
>   kilobytes (1024 bytes), m or megabytes, or b or blocks (the
>   units used by the ulimit system call). For both resource
>   names and scale factors, unambiguous prefixes of the names
>   can be used. filesize can be lowered by an instance of csh,
>   but can only be raised by an instance whose effective user
>   ID is root. For more information, refer to the documentation
>   for the ulimit system call.

login
>   Terminates a login shell, replacing it with an instance of
>   /usr/bin/login. This is one way to log off, included for
>   compatibility with sh(1).

logout
>   Terminates a login shell. Especially useful if ignoreeof is
>   set. A similar function, bye, which works for sessions that
>   are not login shells, is provided for historical reasons.
>   Its use is not recommended because it is not part of the
>   standard BSD csh and may not be supported in future
>   releases.

newgrp
>   Changes the group identification of the caller; for details
>   see newgrp(1). A new shell is executed by newgrp so that
>   the current shell environment is lost.

nice
nice +number

nice command

nice +number command
>   The first form sets the nice (run command priority) for this
>   shell to 4 (the default). The second form sets the priority
>   to the given number. The final two forms run command at
>   priority 4 and number respectively. The user with
>   appropriate privileges can raise the priority by specifying
>   negative niceness using nice -number ... command is always
>   executed in a sub-shell, and restrictions placed on commands
>   in simple if statements apply.

nohup [command]
>   Without an argument, nohup can be used in shell scripts to
>   cause hangups to be ignored for the remainder of the script.
>   With an argument, causes the specified command to be run
>   with hangups ignored. All processes executed in the
>   background with & are effectively nohuped as described under
>   Jobs in the COMMANDS section.

notify [job ...]
>   Causes the shell to notify the user asynchronously when the
>   status of the current (job not specified) or specified jobs
>   changes; normally notification is presented before a prompt.
>   This is automatic if the shell variable notify is set.

onintr [-] [label]
>   Controls the action of the shell on interrupts. With no
>   arguments, onintr restores the default action of the shell
>   on interrupts, which action is to terminate shell scripts or
>   return to the terminal command input level. If - is
>   specified, all interrupts are ignored. If a label is given,
>   the shell executes a goto label when an interrupt is
>   received or a child process terminates because it was
>   interrupted.
>
>   If the shell is running in the background and interrupts are
>   being ignored, onintr has no effect; interrupts continue to
>   be ignored by the shell and all invoked commands.

popd [+n]
>   Pops the directory stack, returning to the new top
>   directory. With an argument, discards the nth entry in the
>   stack. The elements of the directory stack are numbered

from 0 starting at the top. A synonym for popd, called rd, is provided for historical reasons. Its use is not recommended because it is not part of the standard BSD csh and may not be supported in future releases.

pushd [name] [+n]
>   With no arguments, pushd exchanges the top two elements of the directory stack. Given a name argument, pushd changes to the new directory (using cd) and pushes the old current working directory (as in csw) onto the directory stack. With a numeric argument, pushd rotates the nth argument of the directory stack around to be the top element and changes to that directory. The members of the directory stack are numbered from the top starting at 0. A synonym for pushd, called gd, is provided for historical reasons. Its use is not recommended since it is not part of the standard BSD csh and may not be supported in future releases.

rehash
>   Causes the internal hash table of the contents of the directories in the path variable to be recomputed. This is needed if new commands are added to directories in the path while you are logged in. This should only be necessary if you add commands to one of your own directories or if a systems programmer changes the contents of one of the system directories.

repeat count command
>   The specified command (which is subject to the same restrictions as the command in the one-line if statement above) is executed count times. I/O redirections occur exactly once, even if count is 0.

set
set name

set name=word

set name[index]=word

set name=(wordlist)
>   The first form of set shows the value of all shell variables. Variables whose value is other than a single word print as a parenthesized word list. The second form sets name to the null string. The third form sets name to the single word. The fourth form sets the indexth component of name to word; this component must already exist. The final form sets name to the list of words in wordlist. In all cases the value is command and file-name expanded.

>   These arguments can be repeated to set multiple values in a single set command. Note, however, that variable expansion happens for all arguments before any setting occurs.

setenv name value
>   Sets the value of environment variable name to be value, a single string. The most commonly used environment variables, USER, TERM, and PATH, are automatically imported to and exported from the csh variables user, term, and path; there is no need to use setenv for these.

shift [variable]
>   If no argument is given, the members of argv are shifted to the left, discarding argv[1]. An error occurs if argv is not set or has less than two strings assigned to it. When variable is specified, shift performs the same function on

the specified variable.

source [-h] name
    csh reads commands from name. source commands can be
    nested, but if nested too deeply the shell may run out of
    file descriptors. An error in a source at any level
    terminates all nested source commands. Normally, input
    during source commands is not placed on the history list.
    The -h option can be used to place commands in the history
    list without being executing them.

stop [%job ...]
    Stops the current (no argument) or specified jobs executing
    in the background.

suspend
    Causes csh to stop as if it had been sent a suspend signal.
    Since csh normally ignores suspend signals, this is the only
    way to suspend the shell. This command gives an error
    message if attempted from a login shell.

switch (string)

case str1:

   ...

breaksw

   ...

default:

   ...

breaksw

endsw
    Each case label (str1) is successively matched against the
    specified string which is first command and file name
    expanded. The form of the case labels is the Pattern
    Matching Notation with the exception that non-matching lists
    in bracket expressions are not supported (see regexp(5)).
    If none of the labels match before a default label is found,
    the execution begins after the default label. Each case
    label and the default label must appear at the beginning of
    a line. The breaksw command causes execution to continue
    after the endsw. Otherwise, control may fall through case
    labels and default labels as in C. If no label matches and
    there is no default, execution continues after the endsw.

time [command]
    When command is not specified, a summary of time used by
    this shell and its children is printed. If specified, the
    simple command is timed and a time summary as described
    under the time variable is printed. If necessary, an extra
    shell is created to print the time statistic when the
    command completes.

umask [value]
    The current file creation mask is displayed (value not
    specified) or set to the specified value. The mask is given
    in octal. Common values for the mask are 002, which gives
    all permissions to the owner and group and read and execute
    permissions to all others, or 022, which gives all
    permissions to the owner, and only read and execute

permission to the group and all others.

unalias pattern
     All aliases whose names match the specified pattern are
     discarded. Thus, all aliases are removed by unalias *. No
     error occurs if pattern does not match an existing alias.

unhash
     Use of the internal hash table to speed location of executed
     programs is disabled.

unset pattern
     All variables whose names match the specified pattern are
     removed. Thus, all variables are removed by unset *; this
     has noticeably undesirable side-effects. No error occurs if
     pattern matches nothing.

unsetenv pattern
     Removes all variables whose names match the specified
     pattern from the environment. See also the setenv command
     above and printenv(1).

wait Waits for all background jobs to terminate. If the shell is
     interactive, an interrupt can disrupt the wait, at which
     time the shell prints names and job numbers of all jobs
     known to be outstanding.

while (expression)

...
end While the specified expression evaluates non-zero, the
     commands between the while and the matching end are
     evaluated. break and continue can be used to terminate or
     continue the loop prematurely. (The while and end must
     appear alone on their input lines.) If the input is a
     terminal (i.e., not a script), prompting occurs the first
     time through the loop as for the foreach statement.

%job Brings the specified job into the foreground.

%job &
     Continues the specified job in the background.

@

@ name=expression

@ name[index]=expression
     The first form prints the values of all the shell variables.
     The second form sets the specified name to the value of
     expression. If the expression contains <, >, &, or |, at
     least this part of the expression must be placed within
     parentheses. The third form assigns the value of expression
     to the indexth argument of name. Both name and its indexth
     component must already exist.

     The operators *=, +=, etc., are available as in C. White
     space can optionally separate the name from the assignment
     operator. However, spaces are mandatory in separating
     components of expression which would otherwise be single
     words.

     Special postfix ++ and -- operators increment and decrement
     name, respectively (e.g., @ i++).

Non-Built-In Command Execution
When a command to be executed is not a built-in command, csh attempts

to execute the command via exec(2). Each word in the variable path
names a directory in which the shell attempts to find the command (if
the command does not begin with /). If neither -c nor -t is given,
the shell hashes the names in these directories into an internal table
so that an exec is attempted only in those directories where the
command might possibly reside. This greatly speeds command location
when a large number of directories are present in the search path. If
this mechanism has been turned off (via unhash), or if -c or -t was
given, or if any directory component of path does not begin with a /,
the shell concatenates the directory name and the given command name
to form a path name of a file which it then attempts to execute.

Commands placed inside parentheses are always executed in a subshell.
Thus

        (cd ; pwd)

prints the home directory then returns to the current directory upon
completion, whereas:

        cd ; pwd

remains in the home directory upon completion.

When commands are placed inside parentheses, it is usually to prevent
chdir from affecting the current shell.

If the file has execute permissions but is not an executable binary
file, it is assumed to be a script file, which is a file of data for
an interpreter that is executed as a separate process.

csh first attempts to load and execute the script file (see exec(2)).
If the first two characters of the script file are #!, exec(2) expects
an interpreter path name to follow and attempts to execute the
specified interpreter as a separate process to read the entire script
file.

If no #! interpreter is named, and there is an alias for the shell,
the words of the alias are inserted at the beginning of the argument
list to form the shell command. The first word of the alias should be
the full path name of the command to be used. Note that this is a
special, late-occurring case of alias substitution, which inserts
words into the argument list without modification.

If no #! interpreter is named and there is no shell alias, but the
first character of the file is #, the interpreter named by the $shell
variable is executed (note that this normally would be /usr/bin/csh,
unless the user has reset $shell). If $shell is not set, /usr/bin/csh
is executed.

If no !# interpreter is named, and there is no shell alias, and the
first character of the file is not #, /usr/bin/sh is executed to
interpret the script file.

History Substitutions
    History substitutions enable you to repeat commands, use words from
    previous commands as portions of new commands, repeat arguments of a
    previous command in the current command, and fix spelling or typing
    mistakes in an earlier command.

    History substitutions begin with an exclamation point (!).
    Substitutions can begin anywhere in the input stream, but cannot be
    nested. The exclamation point can be preceded by a backslash to
    cancel its special meaning. For convenience, an exclamation point is
    passed to the parser unchanged when it is followed by a blank, tab,
    newline, equal sign, or left parenthesis. Any input line that

contains history substitution is echoed on the terminal before it is
executed for verification.

Commands input from the terminal that consist of one or more words are
saved on the history list. The history substitutions reintroduce
sequences of words from these saved commands into the input stream.
The number of previous commands saved is controlled by the history
variable. The previous command is always saved, regardless of its
value. Commands are numbered sequentially from 1.

You can refer to previous events by event number (such as !10 for
event 10), relative event location (such as !-2 for the second
previous event), full or partial command name (such as !d for the last
event using a command with initial character d), and string expression
(such as !?mic? referring to an event containing the characters mic).

These forms, without further modification, simply reintroduce the
words of the specified events, each separated by a single blank. As a
special case, !! is a re-do; it refers to the previous command.

To select words from a command, use a colon (:) and a designator for
the desired words after the event specification. The words of an
input line are numbered from zero. The basic word designators are:

    0   First word (i.e., the command name itself).

    n   nth word.

    ^   First argument. (This is equivalent to 1.)

    $ Last word.

    a-b   Range of words from a through b. Special cases are -y, an
           abbreviation for ``word 0 through word y''; and x-, which
           means ``word x up to, but not including, word $''.

    *   Range from the second word through the last word.

    %   Used with a search sequence to substitute the immediately
           preceding matching word.

The colon separating the command specification from the word
designator can be omitted if the argument selector begins with a ^, $,
*, -, or %.

After word designator can be followed by a sequence of modifiers, each
preceded by a colon. The following modifiers are defined:

    h   Use only the first component of a path name by removing all
           following components.

    r   Use the root file name by removing any trailing suffix
           (.xxx).

    e   Use the file name's trailing suffix (.xxx) by removing the
           root name.

    s /l/r
           substitute the value of r for the value l in the indicated
           command.

    t   Use only the final file name of a path name by removing all
           leading path name components.

    &   Repeat the previous substitution.

p   Print the new command but do not execute it.

q   Quote the substituted words, preventing further
       substitutions.

x   Like q, but break into words at blanks, tabs and newlines.

g   Use a global command as a prefix to another modifier to
       cause the specified change to be made globally. All words
       in the command are changed, one change per word, and each
       string enclosed in single quotes (') or double quotes (") is
       treated as a single word.

Unless preceded by a g, the modification is applied only to the first
modifiable word. An error results if a substitution is attempted and
cannot be completed (i.e., if you ask for a substitution of !11 on a
history buffer containing only 10 commands).

The left hand side of substitutions are strings; not regular
expressions in the sense of HP-UX editors. Any character can be used
as the delimiter in place of a slash (/). Use a backslash to quote a
delimiter character if it is used in the l or r string. The character
& in the right-hand side is replaced by the text from the left. A \
also quotes &. A null l string uses the previous string either from
an l or from a contextual scan string s in !?s?. The trailing
delimiter in the substitution can be omitted if a new-line character
follows immediately, as may the trailing ? in a contextual scan.

A history reference can be given without an event specification (as in
!$). In this case, the reference is to the previous command unless a
previous history reference occurred on the same line, in which case
this form repeats the previous reference. Thus

     !?foo?^ !$

gives the first and last arguments from the command matching ?foo?.

A special abbreviation of a history reference occurs when the first
non-blank character of an input line is a circumflex (^). This is
equivalent to !:s^, providing a convenient shorthand for substitutions
on the text of the previous line. Thus ^lb^lib fixes the spelling of
lib in the previous command.

Finally, a history substitution can be enclosed within curly braces
{ } if necessary to insulate it from the characters which follow.
Thus, after

     ls -ld ~paul

one could execute !{l}a to do

     ls -ld ~paula

while !la would look for a command starting with la.

CHAPTER 8

The vi Editor

The vi Editor

Many UNIX users have a Graphical User Interface (GUI) through which they access their UNIX system. The Common Desktop Environment (CDE) is the most commonly used GUI on UNIX systems. It is based on the X Windows System and Motif, which together provide an advanced windowing environment. A chapter in this book is devoted to CDE. Most UNIX GUIs provide a graphical editor. Despite the fact that these graphical editors are a standard part of most GUIs, the visual editor, **vi**, still remains the most popular UNIX editor. With many fine graphics-based editors as a standard part of most UNIX GUIs and a plethora of editors available as part of personal computer windowing environments, why am I covering **vi**? The answer is twofold. First, not everyone using a UNIX system has access to a graphics display and may therefore need to know and use **vi**. Because **vi** comes with most UNIX-based systems and is a powerful editor, many new UNIX users end up using and liking it. Second,

man page

vi - 8

vi has traditionally been thought of as *the* UNIX editor. Few UNIX users have not used **vi**. This fact does not mean that it is everyone's primary editor; however, virtually all UNIX users have had some experience with **vi**.

Also, a line editor called **ed** comes with many UNIX systems. It is now seldom used because **vi** is a screen editor. Also available is an enhanced version of **ed** called **ex**. **vi** is much more widely used than either of the line editors, so I'll cover only **vi** in this chapter.

I'll cover the *basics* of using **vi** in this chapter. You can experiment with what is covered here, and if you really like it, you can investigate some of the more advanced features of **vi**. A quick reference card summarizing all the **vi** commands covered in this chapter is included with this book.

The following table is a list of tables in this chapter that summarize some of the more commonly used **vi** commands by function:

Table Number	vi Function
Introduction	Modes and Notations in **vi**
1	Starting a **vi** Session
2	Cursor Control Commands in **vi**
3	Adding Text in **vi**
4	Deleting Text in **vi**
5	Changing Text in **vi**
6	Search and Replace in **vi**
7	Copying in **vi**
8	Undo in **vi**
9	Saving Text and Exiting **vi**
10	Options in **vi**
11	Status in **vi**
12	Positioning and Marking in **vi**

Table Number	vi Function
13	Joining Lines in **vi**
14	Cursor Placement and Adjusting Screen in **vi**
15	Shell Escape Commands in **vi**
16	Macros and Abbreviations in **vi**
17	Indenting Text in **vi**
18	Shell Filters in **vi**
19	Pattern Matching in **vi**

Modes and Notations

man page

vi - 8

We're first going to cover some of the fundamentals of the operation of **vi** called modes, and then go over some of the notations used in the tables in this chapter.

A feature of **vi** that often confuses new users is that it has modes. When you are in *command mode*, everything you type is interpreted as a command. In *command mode,* you can specify such actions as the location to which you want the cursor to move. When you are in *input mode,* everything you type is information to be added to the file. *Command mode* is the default when you start **vi**. You can move into *command mode* from *input mode* at any time by pressing the *escape* key. You move into *insert mode* from *command mode* by typing one of the *input mode* commands covered shortly.

vi commands don't really have a standard form. For this reason, I cover common notations. Table 8 - Introduction summarizes modes and commands in **vi**.

Table 8- Introduction Modes and Notations in **vi**

Mode or Notation	Description
Command Mode	You are issuing commands such as moving the cursor or deleting text, rather than inserting or changing text when in command mode. You can switch to insert mode by issuing an insert mode command such as **i** for insert or **a** for add text.
Insert Mode	You are in insert mode when changing or inserting more than one character of text. You can switch to command mode by pressing the *escape* key.
: (colon commands)	Commands that start with a **:** are completed by pressing the *return* key.
control (^) commands	When a command uses the *control* (^) key, you press and hold down the *control* key and then press the next key that is part of the command. For instance, ^**g** means press and hold *control* and then **g** to get the status on the file you are editing.
file for the name of a file	Many commands require you to specify the name of a file. For instance, in the command **vi** *file*, you would substitute the name of the file you wish to edit for *file*.
char for the name of a character	Many commands require you to specify a single character. For instance, in the command **f***char*, you would substitute the character you wish to search for in place of *char*.
cursor_command for a cursor movement command	Many commands require you to specify a cursor command to execute. For instance, in the command **d***cursor_command*, you would substitute for *cursor_command* the command you wish to execute.

Mode or Notation	Description
string for a character string	Many commands require you to specify a character string. For instance, in the command */string*, you would substitute for *string* the character string for which you wish to search.

Starting a vi Session

Let's jump right in and edit a file. For most of the examples in this chapter, I perform various **vi** commands and capture the results in an X Window. The best way to learn any topic is by example. I not only provide many examples, but I also capture each example in an X Window so that you can see the results of each command. From the command line, we type **vi** and the name of the file we wish to edit, in this case **wisdom**.

man page

vi - 8

```
$ vi wisdom
```

We are then editing the file **wisdom** as shown in Figure 8-1. **wisdom** contains a passage from <u>Tao Te Ching</u> or "Book of the Way." We use this file throughout this chapter.

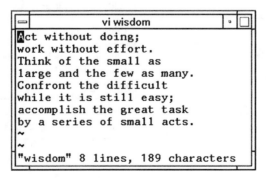

Figure 8-1 Editing the File **wisdom**

The bottom line in Figure 8-1 is the message line in **vi**. After invoking **vi,** the message line indicates the name of the file, the number of lines, and the number of characters in the file. Different messages appear on the message line, depending on the command you issue, as we see in upcoming examples. If a tilde appears on any lines in the file, as it does in the two lines above the message line in **wisdom**, it means that not enough lines exist to fill up the screen. The cursor is the dark box that appears at line 1 in Figure 8-1.

We can specify several file names and after saving the first file move on to the second file by entering **:n**, and continue going through the list of files in this way. Or we can specify a file and position the cursor on the last line in the file. The default is for the cursor to appear over the first character in the file, as shown in Figure 8-1.

Table 8-1 shows some of the ways we can start a **vi** session.

Table 8-1 Starting a **vi** Session

Command	Description
vi *file*	Edit *file.*
vi -r *file*	Edit last saved version of *file* after a crash.
vi -R *file*	Edit *file* in read-only mode.
vi + *n file*	Edit *file* and place cursor at line *n*.
vi + *file*	Edit *file* and place cursor on last line.
vi *file1 file2 file3 ...*	Edit *file1* through *file3*, and after saving changes in *file1*, you can move to *file2* by entering **:n**.
vi +/*string file*	Edit *file* and place cursor at the beginning of the line containing *string*.

Figure 8-2 shows editing wisdom and placing the cursor at line 5 with the command **vi +5 wisdom**.

man page

vi - 8

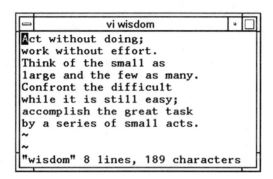

Figure 8-2 Editing the File **wisdom** and Placing Cursor at Line 5 with **vi +5 wisdom**

Figure 8-3 shows editing wisdom and placing the cursor at the last line of the file with the command **vi + wisdom**.

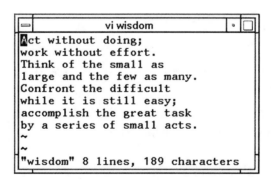

Figure 8-3 Editing the File **wisdom** and Placing Cursor at Last Line with **vi + wisdom**

man page

vi - 8

Figure 8-4 shows editing wisdom and placing the cursor at the line containing task with **vi +/task wisdom**.

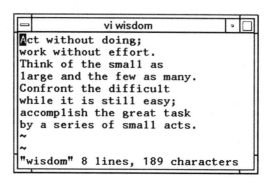

Figure 8-4 Editing the File **wisdom** and Placing Cursor at Line Containing *task* with **vi +/task wisdom**

Cursor Control Commands

A key skill to develop in **vi** is getting the cursor to the desired position. You do this in *command mode*. You have a variety of ways to move the cursor around the screen. Table 8-2 summarizes some of the more commonly used cursor movements.

Table 8-2 Cursor Control Commands In **vi**

Command	Cursor Movement
h or **^h**	Move left one character.
j or **^j** or **^n**	Move down one line.
k or **^p**	Move up one line.
l or **space**	Move right one character.

Table 8-2 Cursor Control Commands In **vi**

Command	Cursor Movement
G	Go to the last line of the file.
nG	Go to line number n.
G$	Go to the last character in the file.
1G	Go to the first line in the file.
w	Go to the beginning of the next word.
W	Go to the beginning of next word, ignore punctuation.
b	Go to the beginning of the previous word.
B	Go to the start of previous word, ignore punctuation.
L	Go to the last line of the screen.
M	Go to the middle line of the screen.
H	Go to the first line of the screen.
e	Move to the end of the next word.
E	Move to the end of the next word, ignore punctuation.
(	Go to the beginning of the sentence.
)	Go to the end of the sentence.
{	Go to the beginning of the paragraph.
}	Go to the beginning of the next paragraph.
0 or |	Go to the first column in the current line.
n|	Go to column n in the current line.
^ (caret)	Go to the first non-blank character in the current line.
$	Go to the last character in the current line.
+ or *return*	Go to the first character in the next line.
-	Go to the first non-blank character in the previous line.

man page

vi - 8

I know that the fact that you have to remember these commands in order to get the cursor to the desired position may seem a little strange at first, but this is the way **vi** works. Let's use **wisdom** to show how some of these cursor movements work. Figures 8-5 and 8-6 show some cursor movements. Like all of the upcoming figures, Figures 8-5 and 8-6 show **wisdom** before a command is entered on the left and the result after the command is entered on the right. The command issued appears in the middle. Some of the commands in upcoming figures use the *enter* and *escape* keys.

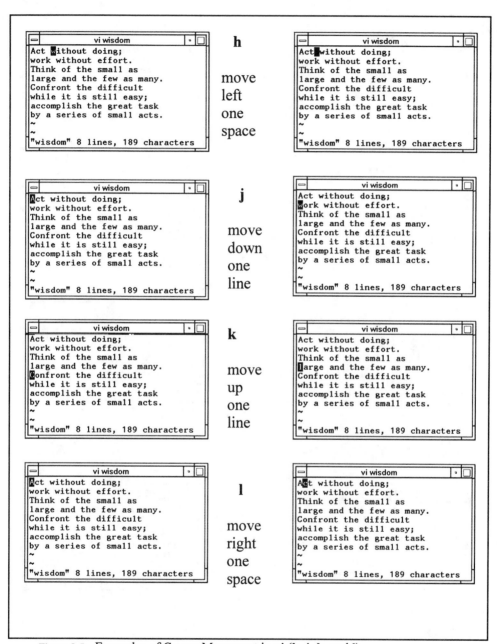

Figure 8-5   Examples of Cursor Movement in vi (h, j, k, and l)

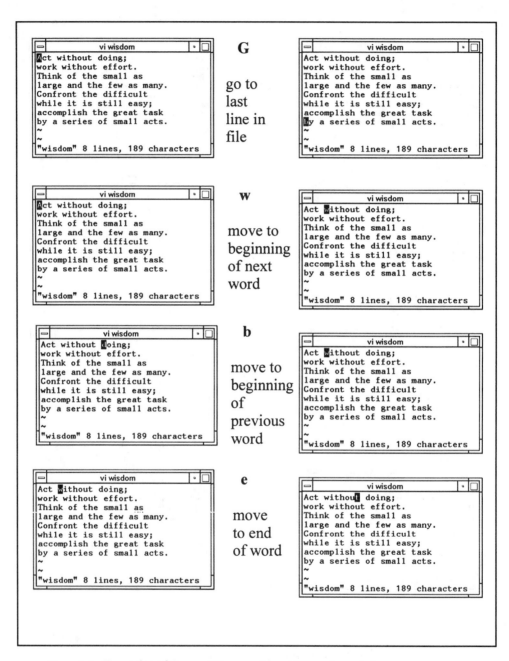

Figure 8-6 Examples of Cursor Movement in **vi** (**G**, **w**, **b**, and **e**)

Adding Text in vi

Now that we know how to move around the cursor, let's do something with it. You need to first learn about cursor movement, because the commands for adding text take place relative to the position of the cursor. Table 8-3 summarizes some commands for adding text.

Table 8-3 Adding Text In **vi**

Command	Insertion Action
a	Append new text after the cursor.
A	Append new text after the end of the current line.
i	Insert new text before the cursor.
I	Insert new text before the beginning of the current line.
o	Open a line below the current line and insert.
O	Open a line above the current line and insert.
:r *file*	Read *file* and insert after the current line.
:*nr file*	Read *file* and insert after line *n*.
escape	Get back to command mode.
^v *char*	Ignore special meaning of *char* when inserting. This is for inserting special characters.

Let's now look at some examples for adding text into **wisdom** in Figure 8-7.

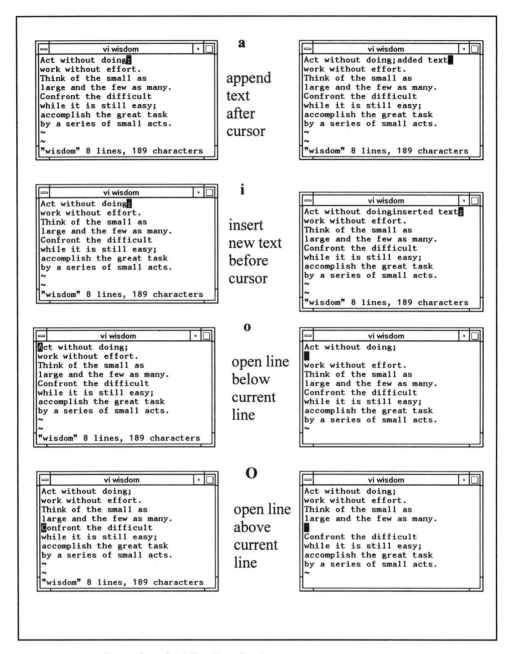

Figure 8-7 Examples of Adding Text in **vi**

Deleting Text in vi

We also need to learn about cursor movement before learning how to delete text, because the commands for deleting text take place relative to the position of the cursor. Table 8-4 summarizes some commands for deleting text.

Table 8-4 Deleting Text In vi

Command	Deletion Action
x	Delete the character at the cursor. You can also put a number in front of x to specify the number of characters to delete.
nx	Delete n characters beginning with the current.
X	Delete the previous character. You can also put a number in front of X to specify the number of previous characters to delete.
nX	Delete previous n characters.
dw	Delete to the beginning of the next word.
$n$dw	Delete the next n words beginning with the current.
dG	Delete lines to the end of the file.
dd	Delete the entire line.
$n$dd	Delete n lines beginning with the current.
db	Delete the previous word.
$n$db	Delete the previous n words beginning with the current.
:n,md	Deletes lines n through m.

Table 8-4 Deleting Text In **vi**

Command	Deletion Action
D or **d$**	Delete from the cursor to the end of the line.
d_cursor_command_	Delete text to the _cursor_command_. **dG** would delete from the current line to the end of the file.
^h or _backspace_	While inserting, delete the previous character.
^w	While inserting, delete the previous word.

Let's now look at some examples for deleting text from **wisdom** in Figures 8-8 and 8-9.

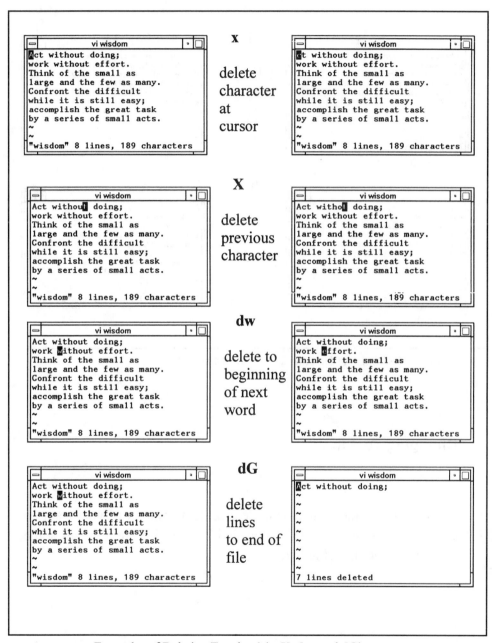

Figure 8-8 Examples of Deleting Text in **vi** (**x**, **X**, **dw**, and **dG**)

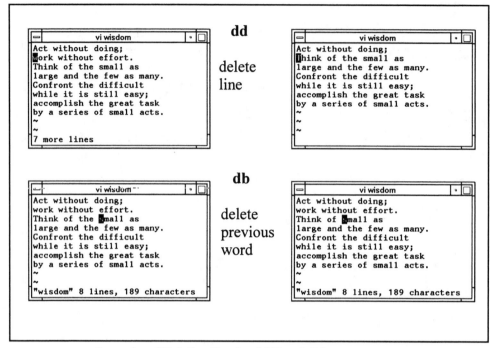

Figure 8-9   Examples of Deleting Text in **vi** (**dd** and **db**)

Changing Text in vi

Okay, you've added text and deleted text, and now you want to change text. **vi** isn't so bad so far, is it? Table 8-5 summarizes some commands for changing text.

Table 8-5 Changing Text In vi

Command (Preceding these commands with a number repeats the commands any number of times.)	**Replacement Action**
r_char_	Replace the current character with _char_.
R_text escape_	Replace the current characters with _text_ until _escape_ is entered.
s_text escape_	Substitute _text_ for the current character.
S or **cc**_text escape_	Substitute _text_ for the entire line.
cw_text escape_	Change the current word to _text_.
C_text escape_	Change the rest of the current line to _text_.
cG _escape_	Change to the end of the file.
c_cursor_cmd_ **text** _escape_	Change to _text_ from the current position to _cursor_cmd_.

Let's now look at some examples of replacing text from **wisdom** in Figures 8-10 and 8-11.

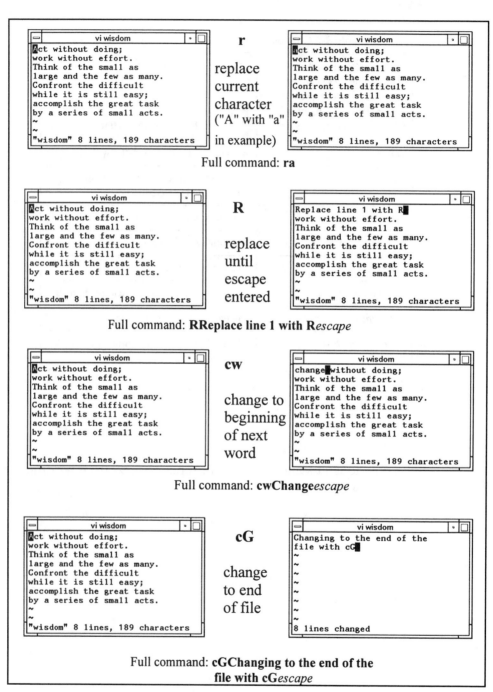

Figure 8-10   Examples of Changing Text in **vi** (**r**, **R**, **cw**, and **cG**)

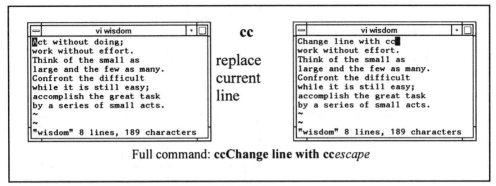

Full command: **ccChange line with cc***escape*

Figure 8-11 Example of Changing Text in **vi** with **cc**

Search and Replace in vi

man page

vi - 8

You have a lot of search and replace functionality in **vi**. Table 8-6 summarizes some of the more common search-and-replace functionality in **vi**.

Table 8-6 Search And Replace In **vi**

Command	Search and Replace Action
/*text*	Search for ***text*** going forward into the file.
?*text*	Search for ***text*** going backward into the file.
n	Repeat the search in the same direction as the original search.
N	Repeat the search in the opposite direction as the original search.
f*text*	Search for *text* going forward in the current line.
F*text*	Search for *text* going backward in the current line.

Table 8-6 Search And Replace In **vi**

Command	Search and Replace Action
t*text*	Search for *text* going forward in the current line and stop at the character before *text*.
T*text*	Search for *text* going backward in the current line to character after *text*.
:set ic	Ignore case when searching.
:set noic	Make searching case-sensitive.
:s/*oldtext*/*newtext*/	Substitute *newtext* for *oldtext*.
:*m,n*s/*oldtext*/*newtext*/	Substitute *newtext* for *oldtext* in lines *m* through *n*.
&	Repeat the last **:s** command.
:g/*text1*/s/*text2*/*text3*	Find line containing *text1*, replace *text2* with *text3*.
:g/*text*/*command*	Run *command* on all lines that contain *text*.
:v/*text*/*command*	Run *command* on all lines that do not contain *text*.

Let's now look at some examples of searching and replacing text in **wisdom** in Figure 8-12.

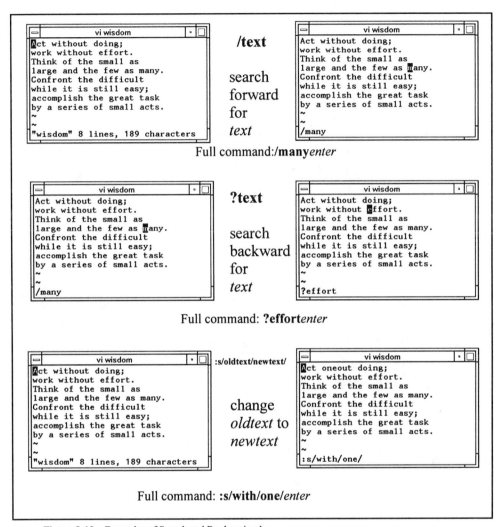

Figure 8-12   Examples of Search and Replace in vi

You can perform advanced searches with **:g** and **:v**. You can find and display all the lines in a file containing **while** with the following command:

```
:g/while/p
```

The /p in this command line is the print command used with the
ex editor. You could find all the lines in the file that contain **while** and
delete those lines with the following command:

```
:g/while/d
```

You can also specify the specific line numbers for which you
want the search to take place. The following command finds all the
lines between 10 and 20 that contain **while** and prints the line number
on which they appear:

```
:10,20g/while/nu
```

:g runs a command on the lines that contain the text for which we
are searching, and **:v** runs a command on the lines that do not contain
the specified text. The following three commands act on the lines that
do not contain **while**, in the same way that the previous three act on
the lines that do contain **while**:

```
:v/while/p
```

```
:v/while/d
```

```
:10,20v/while/nu
```

The first command prints lines that do not contain **while**. The
second command deletes the lines on which **while** does not appear.
The third command prints the line number between 10 and 20 on
which **while** does not appear.

Copying Text in vi

You can copy text in **vi**. Some commands for copying are shown in Table 8-7.

man page

vi - 8

Table 8-7 Copying In **vi**

Command	Copy Action
yy	Yank the current line.
nyy	Yank **n** lines.
p (lower case)	Put the yanked text after the cursor.
p (upper case)	Put the yanked text before the cursor.
*"(a-z)n***yy**	Copy *n* lines into the buffer named in parentheses. Omit *n* for the current line.
*"(a-z)n***dd**	Delete *n* lines into the buffer named in parentheses. Omit *n* for the current line.
*"(a-z)***p**	Put lines named in the buffer in parentheses after current line.
*"(a-z)***P**	Put lines named in the buffer in parentheses before the current line.

Let's now look at some examples of copying text in **wisdom** in Figure 8-13.

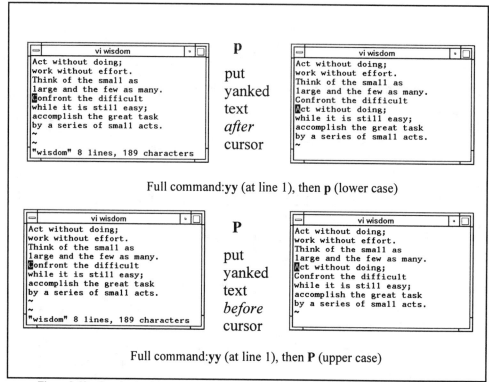

Full command:**yy** (at line 1), then **p** (lower case)

Full command:**yy** (at line 1), then **P** (upper case)

Figure 8-13   Copying in **vi**

Undo and Repeat in vi

You can easily undo changes in **vi** with the commands shown in Table 8-8.

Table 8-8 Unso In **vi**

Command	Undo Action
u	Undo the last change.
U	Undo all changes to the current line.
. (period)	Repeat the last change.
, (comma)	Repeat, in reverse direction, last **f**, **F**, **t**, or **T** search command.
; (semi-colon)	Repeat last **f**, **F**, **t**, or **T** search command.
"_n_**p**	Retrieve the last _n_th delete (a limited number of deletes are in the buffer, usually nine).
n	Repeat last **/** or **?** search command.
N	Repeat, in reverse direction, last **/** or **?** search command.

Save Text and Exit vi

man page

vi - 8

You have a number of different ways to save files and exit **vi**, some of which are summarized in Table 8-9.

Table 8-9 Saving Text and Exiting **vi**

Command	Save and/or Quit Action
:w	Save the file but don't exit **vi**.
:w _file_	Save changes in _file_ but don't quit **vi**.
:wq or **ZZ** or **:x**	Save the file and quit **vi**.

Table 8-9 Saving Text and Exiting **vi**

Command	Save and/or Quit Action
:q!	Quit **vi** without saving the file.
:e!	Re-edit the file, discarding changes since the last write.

Options in vi

man page

vi - 8

There are many options you can set and unset in **vi**. To set an option, you type **:set** *option.* To unset an option, you type **:set no***option.* Table 8-10 summarizes some of the more commonly used options.

Table 8-10 Options In **vi**

Option	Action
:set all	Print all options.
:set no*option*	Turn off *option.*
:set nu	Prefix lines with line number.
:set showmode	Show whether input or replace mode.
:set noic	Ignore case when searching.
:set list	Show tabs (^I) and end of line ($).
:set ts=8	Set tab stops for text input.
:set window=*n*	Set number of lines in a text window to *n*.

Let's now prefix lines with line numbers and show input or
replace mode in Figure 8-14.

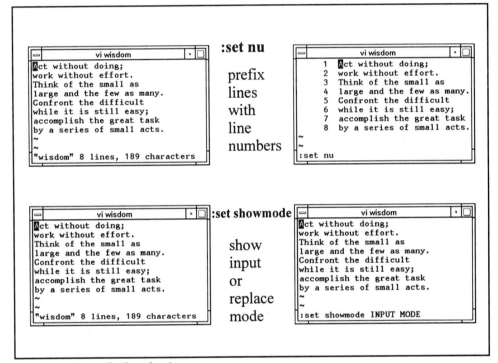

Figure 8-14   Options in vi

Many additional options are available beyond those in Table 8-
10. The following is a list of options produced on a UNIX system
from the **:set all** command. You should issue this command when in
vi to see the options available to you:

```
:set all
noautoindent
autoprint
noautowrite
nobeautify
directory=/var/tmp
nodoubleescape
noedcompatible
noerrorbells
noexrc
flash
hardtabs=8
noignorecase
keyboardedit
nokeyboardedit!
nolisp
nolist
magic
mesg
nomodelines
nonumber
nonovice
nooptimize
paragraphs=IPLPPPQPP LIpplpipnpbp
prompt
noreadonly
redraw
remap
report=5
scroll=11
sections=NHSHH HUuhsh+c
shell=/sbin/sh
shiftwidth=8
noshowmatch
noshowmode
noslowopen
```

```
tabstop=8
taglength=0
tags=tags /usr/lib/tags
tagstack
term=hp
noterse
timeout
timeoutlen=500
ttytype=hp
warn
window=23
wrapscan
wrapmargin=0
nowriteany
noshowmatch
noshowmode
```

Many of the options are preceded by a "no," indicating that the option is not set. You may want to list your options with **:set all** and then experiment with the options of interest to you to see the effect they will have on your **vi** session.

Status in vi

You can obtain a lot of useful status information with some simple commands in **vi**. You can display current line number, number of lines in the file, file name, and other status information with the commands shown in Table 8-11.

Table 8-11 Status In **vi**

Option	Action
:.=	Print the current line number.
:=	Print the number of lines in the file.
^g	Show the file name, current line number, total lines in the file, and percent of file location.
:l	Use the letter "l" to display various special characters such as tab and newline.

Section Positioning and Placing Marks in Text

man page

vi - 8

You can define sections of text to which you can move as well as mark text with characters and move to those marks. Table 8-12 summarizes positioning and marking in **vi**.

Table 8-12 Positioning and Marking In **vi**

Option	Action
{	Insert { in first column to define section.
[[	Go back to beginning of section.
]]	Forward to beginning of next section.
m(a-z)	Mark current position with a letter such as **mz** for mark z.

Table 8-12 Positioning and Marking In **vi**

Option	Action
'(a-z)	Move cursor to specified mark such as 'z for move to z.

Joining Lines in vi

man page

vi - 8

You can join one or more lines in **vi** using the commands shown in Table 8-13.

Table 8-13 Joining Lines In **vi**

Option	Action
J	Join the next line to the end of the current line.
nJ	Join the next n lines.

Cursor Placement and Adjusting the Screen

You can place the cursor anywhere in your file and adjust the screen in a variety of ways using the commands shown in Table 8-14.

Table 8-14 Cursor Placement and Adjusting the Screen In **vi**

Option	Action
H	Move cursor to top line of the screen.
*n***H**	Move cursor to *n* line from the top of the screen.
M	Move cursor to the middle of the screen.
L	Move cursor to the bottom line of the screen.
*n***L**	Move cursor to line *n* from the bottom of the screen.
^e (control-e)	Move screen up one line.
^y	Move screen down one line.
^u	Move screen up one-half page.
^d	Move screen down one-half page.
^b	Move screen up one page.
^f	Move screen down one page.
^l (letter l)	Redraw screen.
z - *return*	Make current line the top of screen.
*n***z** - *return*	Make *n* line the top of screen.
z.	Make current line the middle line.
*n***z.**	Make line *n* the middle line on screen.
z-	Make current line the bottom line.
*n***z-**	Make line *n* the bottom line on screen.

Shell Escape Commands

You can run a UNIX command without exiting **vi** by using shell escape commands. You could do something as simple as start a subshell with the **:sh** command. You could also run a command outside the file you are editing without exiting **vi**. Table 8-15 describes shell escape commands.

man page

vi - 8

Table 8-15 Shell Escape Commands In **vi**

Option	Action
:! *command*	Execute shell command *command* such as **:! ls**.
:!!	Execute last shell command.
:r! *command*	Read and insert output from *command*, such as **:r! ls** to run **ls** and read contents.
:w *!command*	Send currently edited file to *command* as standard input and execute *command*, such as **:w ! grep all**.
:cd *directory*	Change the current working directory to *directory*.
:sh	Start a sub-shell and use **^d** (control-d) to return to **vi**.
:so *file*	Read and execute commands in the shell program *file*.

An example of using **:w** would be to send the file **wisdom** as standard input to **grep** looking for all lines that contain **all**, as in the following example:

```
:w ! grep all
Think of the small as
by a series of small acts.
```

You can issue the **:so** command to read and execute the commands in a file. Issuing the following command when in **vi** would run the commands in the file **file_with_commands**:

```
:so file_with_commands
```

This file contains the following two commands:

```
:set nu
:g/all/p
```

When we issue the earlier **:so** command, line numbers are shown with the **:set nu** command, and the following lines containing *all* are printed:

```
Think of the small as
by a series of small acts.
```

Macros and Abbreviations

man page

vi - 8

You are not limited to issuing individual **vi** commands. You can define strings of **vi** commands and define a key corresponding to this string that you can recall. When defining the keys for your macros, you can't use the following: **K V g q v * =** and function keys. There are also control keys you can't use, so stay away from control keys in general. Table 8-16 shows macros and abbreviations.

Table 8-16 Macros and Abbreviations In **vi**

Option	Action
:map *key command_seq*	Define *key* to run *command_seq*, such as **:map e ea** to append text whenever you use **e** to move to the end of a word.
:map	Display all defined macros on the status line.

Table 8-16 Macros and Abbreviations In vi

Option	Action
:umap *key*	Remove the macro for *key.*
:ab *string1 string2*	Define an abbreviation such that when *string1* is inserted, replace it with *string2.* When inserting text type *string1,* press *escape* key and *string2* will be inserted.
:ab	Display all abbreviations.
:cd *directory*	Change the current working directory to *directory.*
:una *string*	Unabbreviate *string.*
	Avoid control keys, symbols, and don't use characters: **K V g q v * =** and function keys.

An example of using the **map** command would be to automatically add text when you move to the end, as shown with the following **map** command:

```
:map e ea
```

This command maps **e** to **ea**. When you go to the end of the next word with **e**, you are also placed in insert mode with **a** so that you can append new text immediately after the end of the word.

You can also abbreviate long sequences with **ab**. For instance, you could abbreviate *system administration* with *sa* with the following command:

```
:ab sa system administration
```

Now whenever you insert text, type *sa*, and then press the *escape* key to complete the insert, the string *system administration* appears. *sa* is an abbreviation for *system administration.*

Indenting Text

You can indent text a variety of different ways. Table 8-17 shows some of the more commonly used indenting commands.

Table 8-17 Indenting Text In **vi**

Option	Action
^i (control i) or *tab*	While inserting text, insert on shift width. Shift width can be defined.
:set ai	Turn on auto-indentation.
:set sw=*n*	Set shift width to *n* characters.
n<<	Shift *n* lines left by one shift width.
n>>	Shift *n* lines right by one shift width. For example, **3>>** shifts the next three lines right by one shift width.

Before you adjust the shift width, you may want to issue **:set all** in order to see the current number of characters to which the shift width is set. It is usually eight characters by default. To set shift width to 16 characters, issue the following command:

:set sw=16

You can then shift over the next three lines to the right by 16 characters each, with the following command:

3>>

The next three lines are then shifted right by 16 characters.

Shell Filters

You can send information from the file you are editing to a command and then replace the original text with the output of the command. Table 8-18 shows a shell filter.

Table 8-18 Shell Filters In **vi**

Option	Action
!cursor_command command	Send text from the current position to that described by *cursor_command* to the shell *command.* For example, use **!}** **grep admin** to take text from the current position to the end of the paragraph, run this text through **grep** looking for the word *admin*, and replace existing text with the output of **grep**.

Pattern Matching

Pattern matching allows you to find patterns within the file you are editing. You can then perform functions such as changing what you have found in some way. Table 8-19 shows some of the most common pattern matching commands.

Table 8-19 Pattern Matching In vi

Option	Action
^ (caret)	Match the beginning of the line. To search for **Think** at only the beginning of the line, you would use: **/^Think** You can use this in combination with **$**, which matches to the end of the line, to delete all blank lines with: **:g/^$/d.**
$	Match end of line. To match **last.** only when it is followed by a newline character, you would use: **/last.$**
.	Match any single character.
\<	Match beginning of word.
\>	Match end of word.
[string]	Match any single character in *string*. To find **mp, mP, Mp,** or **MP**, use: **/[mM][pP]** Change all occurrences of **input** or **Input** to **INPUT** with: **:%s/[Ii]nput/INPUT/g**
[^string]	Match any character not in *string*.
[a-p]	Match any character between *a* and *p*.

Table 8-19 Pattern Matching In **vi**

Option	Action
*	Match zero or more occurrences of previous character in expression.
\	Escape meaning of next character. To search for [, use the following: \[
\\	Escape the \ character.

You may find pattern matching a little confusing when you first start to use it, so I'll use several simple examples to get you started. Keep in mind that many of the pattern-matching techniques described here also work outside **vi** in your shell.

man page

vi - 8

Matching a Set

We'll begin with the *square bracket operator*. To match any of the single characters **m**, **f**, or **p**, you would use the following:

```
/[mfp]
```

A common pattern to match would be a word with the first letter in the word, either uppercase or lowercase. To match **input** or **Input**, you would use the following:

```
/[Ii]nput
```

After you match either **Input** or **input**, you could then change it to **INPUT** with the following command:

```
:%s/[Ii]nput/INPUT/g
```

You can use sequences of expressions to search for more than one character, as shown in the following example:

```
/[mM][pP]
```

This sequence will match **mp**, **mP**, **Mp**, or **MP**. You are, in effect, searching for any of the four two-character strings.

Matching a Range

You can also use the square bracket operator to match single characters within a range. To find an occurrence of any digit in a file, you could use either of the two following square bracket searches:

```
/[0123456789]
```

or

```
/[0-9]
```

The hyphen denotes a range within the square bracket. To find any character, either uppercase or lowercase, you could use the following:

```
/[a-zA-Z]
```

To search for characters that normally have a special meaning, such as [, you can ignore, or escape, the special meaning by preceding the special character with a \ (backslash). To search for [in **vi**, for instance, you would use the following sequence:

```
/\[
```

This search finds the first occurrence of [.

Beginning and End of Line Search

You can specify that you wish your pattern match to take place at only the beginning or end of a line. To specify a beginning of the line pattern match, use the ^ (caret) preceding your desired pattern, as shown in the following example:

```
/^Think
```

This matches **Think** only when it appears at the beginning of a line.

To specify an end-of-the-line pattern match, use a $ (dollar sign) following your desired pattern, as shown in the following example:

```
/last.$
```

This matches **last.** only when it is followed by a newline.

Manual Pages for Commands Used in Chapter 8

The following section contains copies of the manual pages for **vi**.

vi

vi - Run visual editor.

```
vi(1)                                                                    vi(1)

NAME
     vi, view, vedit - screen-oriented (visual) text editor

SYNOPSIS

     vi [-] [-l] [-r] [-R] [-t tag] [-v] [-V] [-wsize] [-x] [+command] [file
     ...]

  XPG4 Synopsis
     vi [-rR] [-c command] [-t tag] [-w size] [file ...]

  Obsolescent Options
     vi [-rR] [+command] [-t tag] [-w size] [file ...]

     view [-] [-l] [-r] [-R] [-t tag] [-v] [-V] [-wsize] [-x] [+command]
     [file ...]

     vedit [-] [-r] [-R] [-l] [-t tag] [-v] [-V] [-wsize] [-x] [+command]
     [file ...]

  Remarks
     The program names ex, edit, vi, view, and vedit are separate
     personalities of the same program.  This manual entry describes the
     behavior of the vi/view/vedit personality.

DESCRIPTION
     The vi (visual) program is a display-oriented text editor that is
     based on the underlying ex line editor (see ex(1)).  It is possible to
     switch back and forth between the two and to execute ex commands from
     within vi.  The line-editor commands and the editor options are
     described in ex(1).  Only the visual mode commands are described here.

     The view program is identical to vi except that the readonly editor
     option is set (see ex(1)).

     The vedit program is somewhat friendlier for beginners and casual
     users.  The report editor option is set to 1, and the nomagic, novice,
     and showmode editor options are set.

     In vi, the terminal screen acts as a window into a memory copy of the
     file being edited.  Changes made to the file copy are reflected in the
     screen display.  The position of the cursor on the screen indicates
     the position within the file copy.

     The environment variable TERM must specify a terminal type that is
     defined in the terminfo database (see terminfo(4)).  Otherwise, a
     message is displayed and the line-editor is invoked.

     As with ex, editor initialization scripts can be placed in the
     environment variable EXINIT, or in the file .exrc in the current or
     home directory.
```

Options and Arguments
vi recognizes the following command-line options and arguments:

-               Suppress all interactive-user feedback. This is useful
                when editor commands are taken from scripts.

-l   Set the lisp editor option (see ex(1)). Provides
                indents appropriate for lisp code. The (,), {, }, [[,
                and]] commands in vi are modified to function with
                lisp source code.

-r   Recover the specified files after an editor or system
                crash. If no file is specified, a list of all saved
                files is printed. You must be the owner of the saved
                file in order to recover it (superuser cannot recover
                files owned by other users).

-R   Set the readonly editor option to prevent overwriting a
                file inadvertently (see ex(1)).

-t tag   Execute the tag tag command to load and position a
                predefined file. See the tag command and the tags
                editor option in ex(1).

-v   Invoke visual mode (vi). Useful with ex, it has no
                effect on vi.

-V   Set verbose mode. Editor commands are displayed as
                they are executed when input from a .exrc file or a
                source file (see the source command in ex(1)).

-wsize   Set the value of the window editor option to size. If
                size is omitted, it defaults to 3.

-x   Set encryption mode. You are prompted for a key to
                allow for the creation or editing of an encrypted file
                (see the crypt command in ex(1)).

-c command   (XPG4 only.)

+command   (Obsolescent) Begin editing by executing the specified
                ex command-mode commands. As with the normal ex
                command-line entries, the command option-argument can
                consist of multiple ex commands separated by vertical-
                line commands (|). The use of commands that enter input
                mode in this manner produces undefined results.

file   Specify the file or files to be edited. If more than
                one file is specified, they are processed in the order
                given. If the -r option is also specified, the files
                are read from the recovery area.

(XPG4 only.) If both the -t tag and -c command (or the obsolescent
+command) options are given, the -t tag will be processed first, that
is, the file containing the tag is selected by -t and then the command
is executed.

When invoked, vi is in command mode. input mode is initiated by
several commands used to insert or change text.

In input mode, ESC (escape) is used to leave input mode; however, two
consecutive ESC characters are required to leave input mode if the
doubleescape editor option is set (see ex(1)).

In command mode, ESC is used to cancel a partial command; the terminal

bell sounds if the editor is not in input mode and there is no
partially entered command.

WARNING: ESC completes a "bottom line" command (see below).

The last (bottom) line of the screen is used to echo the input for
search commands (/ and ?), ex commands (:), and system commands (!).
It is also used to report errors or print other messages.

The receipt of SIGINT during text input or during the input of a
command on the bottom line terminates the input (or cancels the
command) and returns the editor to command mode. During command mode,
SIGINT causes the bell to be sounded. In general the bell indicates
an error (such as an unrecognized key).

Lines displayed on the screen containing only a ~ indicate that the
last line above them is the last line of the file (the ~ lines are
past the end of the file). Terminals with limited local intelligence
might display lines on the screen marked with an @. These indicate
space on the screen not corresponding to lines in the file. (These
lines can be removed by entering a ^R, forcing the editor to retype
the screen without these holes.)

If the system crashes or vi aborts due to an internal error or
unexpected signal, vi attempts to preserve the buffer if any unwritten
changes were made. Use the -r command line option to retrieve the
saved changes.

The vi text editor supports the SIGWINCH signal, and redraws the
screen in response to window-size changes.

Command Summary
Most commands accept a preceding number as an argument, either to give
a size or position (for display or movement commands), or as a repeat
count (for commands that change text). For simplicity, this optional
argument is referred to as count when its effect is described.

The following operators can be followed by a movement command to
specify an extent of text to be affected: c, d, y, <, >, !, and =.
The region specified begins at the current cursor position and ends
just prior to the cursor position indicated by the move. If the
command operates on lines only, all the lines that fall partly or
wholly within this region are affected. Otherwise the exact marked
region is affected.

In the following description, control characters are indicated in the
form ^X, which represents Ctrl-X. Whitespace is defined to be the
characters space, tab, and alternative space. Alternative space is
the first character of the ALT_PUNCT item described in langinfo(5) for
the language specified by the LANG environment variable (see
environ(5)).

Unless otherwise specified, the commands are interpreted in command
mode and have no special effect in input mode.

      ^B   Scroll backward to display the previous window of
                  text. A preceding count specifies the number of
                  windows to go back. Two lines of overlap are kept if
                  possible.

      ^D   Scroll forward a half-window of text. A preceding
                  count gives the number of (logical) lines to scroll,
                  and is remembered for future ^D and ^U commands.

      ^D   (input mode) Backs up over the indentation provided
                  by autoindent or ^T to the next multiple of

shiftwidth spaces. Whitespace inserted by ^T at
other than the beginning of a line cannot be backed
over using ^D. A preceding ^ removes all indentation
for the current and subsequent input lines of the
current input mode until new indentation is
established by inserting leading whitespace, either
by direct input or by using ^T.

^E   Scroll forward one line, leaving the cursor where it
            is if possible.

^F   Scroll forward to display the window of text
            following the current one. A preceding count
            specifies the number of windows to advance. Two
            lines of overlap are kept if possible.

            (XPG4 only.) The current line is displayed and the
            cursor is moved to the first nonblank character of
            the current line or the first character if the line
            is a blank line.

^G   Print the current file name and other information,
            including the number of lines and the current
            position (equivalent to the ex command f).

^H   Move one space to the left (stops at the left
            margin). A preceding count specifies the number of
            spaces to back up. (Same as h).

^H   (input mode) Move the cursor left to the previous
            input character without erasing it from the screen.
            The character is deleted from the saved text.

^J   Move the cursor down one line in the same column, if
            possible. A preceding count specifies the number of
            lines to move down. (Same as ^N and j).

^L   Clear and redraw the screen. Use when the screen is
            scrambled for any reason.

^M   Move to the first nonwhitespace character in the next
            line. A preceding count specifies the number of
            lines to advance.

^N   Same as ^J and j.

^P   Move the cursor up one line in the same column. A
            preceding count specifies the number of lines to move
            up (same as k).

^R   Redraw the current screen, eliminating the false
            lines marked with @ (which do not correspond to
            actual lines in the file).

^T   Pop the tag stack. See the pop command in ex(1).

^T   (input mode) Insert shiftwidth whitespace. If at the
            beginning of the line, this inserted space can only
            be backed over using ^D.

^U   Scroll up a half-window of text. A preceding count
            gives the number of (logical) lines to scroll, and is
            remembered for future ^D and ^U commands.

^V   In input mode, ^V quotes the next character to permit
            the insertion of special characters (including ESC)

into the file.

^W   In input mode, ^W backs up one word; the deleted characters remain on the display.

^Y   Scroll backward one line, leaving the cursor where it is, if possible.

^[Cancel a partially formed command; ^[sounds the bell if there is no partially formed command.

In input mode, ^[terminates input mode. However, two consecutive ESC characters are required to terminate input mode if the doubleescape editor option is set (see ex(1)).

When entering a command on the bottom line of the screen (ex command line or search pattern with \ or ?), terminate input and execute command.

On many terminals, ^[can be entered by pressing the ESC or ESCAPE key.

^\   Exit vi and enter ex command mode. If in input mode, terminate the input first.

^]   Take the word at or after the cursor as a tag and execute the tagMbobC editor command (see ex(1)).

^^   Return to the previous file (equivalent to :ex #).

space   Move one space to the right (stops at the end of the line). A preceding count specifies the number of spaces to go forward (same as l).

erase   Erase, where erase is the user-designated erase character (see stty(1)). Same as ^H.

kill   Kill, where kill is the user-designated kill character (see stty(1)). In input mode, kill backs up to the beginning of the current input line without erasing the line from the screen display.

susp   Suspend the editor session and return to the calling shell, where susp is the user-designated process-control suspend character (see stty(1)). See ex(1) for more information on the suspend editor command.

!   An operator that passes specified lines from the buffer as standard input to the specified system command, and replaces those lines with the standard output from the command. The ! is followed by a movement command specifying the lines to be passed (lines from the current position to the end of the movement) and then the command (terminated as usual by a return). A preceding count is passed on to the movement command after !.

Doubling ! and preceding it by count causes that many lines, starting with the current line, to be passed.

"   Use to precede a named buffer specification. There are named buffers 1 through 9 in which the editor places deleted text. The named buffers a through z

are available to the user for saving deleted or
yanked text; see also y, below.

$ Move to the end of the current line. A preceding
count specifies the number of lines to advance (for
example, 2$ causes the cursor to advance to the end
of the next line).

% Move to the parenthesis or brace that matches the
parenthesis or brace at the current cursor position.

& Same as the ex command & (that is, & repeats the
previous substitute command).

' When followed by a ', vi returns to the previous
context, placing the cursor at the beginning of the
line. (The previous context is set whenever a
nonrelative move is made.) When followed by a letter
a-z, returns to the line marked with that letter (see
the m command), at the first nonwhitespace character
in the line.

When used with an operator such as d to specify an
extent of text, the operation takes place over
complete lines (see also `).

`  When followed by a `, vi returns to the previous
context, placing the cursor at the character position
marked (the previous context is set whenever a
nonrelative move is made). When followed by a letter
a z, returns to the line marked with that letter (see
the m command), at the character position marked.

When used with an operator such as d to specify an
extent of text, the operation takes place from the
exact marked place to the current position within the
line (see also ').

[[Back up to the previous section boundary. A section
is defined by the value of the sections option.
Lines that start with a form feed (^L) or { also stop
[[.

If the option lisp is set, the cursor stops at each (
at the beginning of a line.

]] Move forward to a section boundary (see [[).

^ Move to the first nonwhitespace position on the
current line.

(Move backward to the beginning of a sentence. A
sentence ends at a ., !, or ? followed by either the
end of a line or by two spaces. Any number of
closing),], ", and ' characters can appear between
the ., !, or ? and the spaces or end of line. If a
count is specified, the cursor moves back the
specified number of sentences.

If the lisp option is set, the cursor moves to the
beginning of a lisp s-expression. Sentences also
begin at paragraph and section boundaries (see { and
[[).

) Move forward to the beginning of a sentence. If a

count is specified, the cursor advances the specified
number of sentences (see ().

{   Move back to the beginning of the preceding
paragraph. A paragraph is defined by the value of
the paragraphs option. A completely empty line and a
section boundary (see [[above) are also interpreted
as the beginning of a paragraph. If a count is
specified, the cursor moves backward the specified
number of paragraphs.

}   Move forward to the beginning of the next paragraph.
If a count is specified, the cursor advances the
specified number of paragraphs (see {).

| Requires a preceding count; the cursor moves to the
specified column of the current line (if possible).

+   Move to the first nonwhitespace character in the next
line. If a count is specified, the cursor advances
the specified number of lines (same as ^M).

,   The comma (,) performs the reverse action of the last
f, F, t, or T command issued, by searching in the
opposite direction on the current line. If a count
is specified, the cursor repeats the search the
specified number of times.

-          The hyphen character (-) moves the cursor to the
first nonwhitespace character in the previous line.
If a count is specified, the cursor moves back the
specified number of times.

_   The underscore character (_) moves the cursor to the
first nonwhitespace character in the current line.
If a count is specified, the cursor advances the
specified number of lines, with the current line
being counted as the first line; no count or a count
of 1 specifies the current line.

.   Repeat the last command that changed the buffer. If
a count is specified, the command is repeated the
specified number of times.

/   Read a string from the last line on the screen,
interpret it as a regular expression, and scan
forward for the next occurrence of a matching string.
The search begins when the user types a carriage
return to terminate the pattern; the search can be
terminated by sending SIGINT (or the user-designated
interrupt character).

When used with an operator to specify an extent of
text, the defined region begins with the current
cursor position and ends at the beginning of the
matched string. Entire lines can be specified by
giving an offset from the matched line (by using a
closing / followed by a +n or -n).

0   Move to the first character on the current line (the
0 is not interpreted as a command when preceded by a
nonzero digit).

:   The colon character (:) begins an ex command. The :
and the entered command are echoed on the bottom

line; the ex command is executed when the user types
a carriage return.

;   Repeat the last single character find using f, F, t,
or T. If a count is specified, the search is
repeated the specified number of times.

<   An operator that shifts lines to the left by one
shiftwidth. The < can be followed by a move to
specify lines. A preceding count is passed through
to the move command.

           When repeated (<<), shifts the current line (or count
lines starting at the current one).

>   An operator that shifts lines right one shiftwidth
(see <).

=   If the lisp option is set, = reindents the specified
lines, as if they were typed in with lisp and
autoindent set. = can be preceded by a count to
indicate how many lines to process, or followed by a
move command for the same purpose.

?   Scan backwards, the reverse of / (see /).

@buffer   Execute the commands stored in the named buffer. Be
careful not to include a <return> character at the
end of the buffer contents unless the <return> is
part of the command stream. Commands to be executed
in ex mode should be preceded by a colon (:).

~   The tilde (~) switches the case of the character
under the cursor (if it is a letter), then moves one
character to the right, stopping at the end of the
line). A preceding count specifies how many
characters in the current line are switched.

A   Append at the end of line (same as $a).

B   Back up one word, where a word is any nonblank
sequence, placing the cursor at the beginning of the
word. If a count is specified, the cursor moves back
the specified number of words.

C   Change the rest of the text on the current line (same
as c$).

D   Delete the rest of the text on the current line (same
as d$).

E   Move forward to the end of a word, where a word is
any nonblank sequence. If a count is specified, the
cursor advances the specified number of words.

F   Must be followed by a single character; scans
backwards in the current line, searching for that
character and moving the cursor to it, if found. If
a count is specified, the search is repeated the
specified number of times.

G   Go to the line number given as preceding argument, or
the end of the file if no preceding count is given.

H   Move the cursor to the top line on the screen. If a

count is given, the cursor moves to count number of
lines from the top of the screen. The cursor is
placed on the first nonwhitespace character on the
line. If used as the target of an operator, entire
lines are affected.

I   Insert at the beginning of a line (same as ^ followed
        by i).

J   Join the current line with the next one, supplying
        appropriate whitespace: one space between words, two
        spaces after a period, and no spaces at all if the
        first character of the next line is a closing
        parenthesis ()). A preceding count causes the
        specified number of lines to be joined, instead of
        just two.

L   Move the cursor to the first nonwhitespace character
        of the last line on the screen. If a count is given,
        the cursor moves to count number of lines from the
        bottom of the screen. When used with an operator,
        entire lines are affected.

M   Move the cursor to the middle line on the screen, at
        the first nonwhitespace position on the line.

N   Scan for the next match of the last pattern given to
        / or ?, but in the opposite direction; this is the
        reverse of n.

O   Open a new line above the current line and enter
        input mode.

P   Put back (replace) the last deleted or yanked text
        before/above the cursor. Entire lines of text are
        returned above the cursor if entire lines were
        deleted or yanked. Otherwise, the text is inserted
        just before the cursor.

        (XPG4 only.) In this case, the cursor is moved to
        last column position of the inserted characters.

        If P is preceded by a named buffer specification (x),
        the contents of that buffer are retrieved instead.

Q   Exit vi and enter ex command mode.

R   Replace characters on the screen with characters
        entered, until the input is terminated with ESC.

S   Change entire lines (same as cc). A preceding count
        changes the specified number of lines.

T   Must be followed by a single character; scan
        backwards in the current line for that character,
        and, if found, place the cursor just after that
        character. A count is equivalent to repeating the
        search the specified number of times.

U   Restore the current line to its state before the
        cursor was last moved to it.

        (XPG4 only.) The cursor position is set to the column
        position 1 or to the position indicated by the
        previous line if the autoindent is set.

W   Move forward to the beginning of a word in the
                  current line, where a word is a sequence of nonblank
                  characters. If the current position is at the
                  beginning of a word, the current position is within a
                  bigword or the character at that position cannot be a
                  part of a bigword, the current position shall move to
                  the first character of the next bigword. If no
                  subsequent bigword exists on the current line, the
                  current position shall move to the first character of
                  the first bigword on the first following line that
                  contains the bigword. For this command, an empty or
                  blank line is considered to contain exactly one
                  bigword. The current line is set to the line
                  containing the bigword selected and the current
                  position is set to the first character of the bigword
                  selected. A preceding count specifies the number of
                  words to advance.

X   Delete the character before the cursor. A preceding
                  count repeats the effect, but only characters on the
                  current line are deleted.

Y   Place (yank) a copy of the current line into the
                  unnamed buffer (same as yy). If a count is
                  specified, count lines are copied to the buffer. If
                  the Y is preceded by a buffer name, the lines are
                  copied to the named buffer.

ZZ   Exit the editor, writing out the buffer if it was
                  changed since the last write (same as the ex command
                  x). Note that if the last write was to a different
                  file and no changes have occurred since, the editor
                  exits without writing out the buffer.

a   Enter input mode, appending the entered text after
                  the current cursor position. A preceding count
                  causes the inserted text to be replicated the
                  specified number of times, but only if the inserted
                  text is all on one line.

b   Back up to the previous beginning of a word in the
                  current line. A word is a sequence of alphanumerics
                  or a sequence of special characters. A preceding
                  count repeats the effect.

c   Must be followed by a movement command. Delete the
                  specified region of text, and enter input mode to
                  replace deleted text with new text. If more than
                  part of a single line is affected, the deleted text
                  is saved in the numeric buffers. If only part of the
                  current line is affected, the last character deleted
                  is marked with a $. A preceding count passes that
                  value through to the move command. If the command is
                  cc, the entire current line is changed.

d   Must be followed by a movement command. Delete the
                  specified region of text. If more than part of a
                  line is affected, the text is saved in the numeric
                  buffers. A preceding count passes that value through
                  to the move command. If the command is dd, the
                  entire current line is deleted.

e   Move forward to the end of the next word, defined as
                  for b. A preceding count repeats the effect.

f   Must be followed by a single character; scan the rest

	of the current line for that character, and moves the cursor to it if found. A preceding count repeats the action that many times.
h	Move the cursor one character to the left (same as ^H). A preceding count repeats the effect.
i	Enter input mode, inserting the entered text before the cursor (see a).
j	Move the cursor one line down in the same column (same as ^J and ^N).
k	Move the cursor one line up (same as ^P).
l	Move the cursor one character to the right (same as <space>).
mx	Mark the current position of the cursor. x is a lowercase letter, a-z, that is used with the ` and ' commands to refer to the marked line or line position.
n	Repeat the last / or ? scanning commands.
o	Open a line below the current line and enter input mode; otherwise like O.
p	Put text after/below the cursor; otherwise like P.
r	Must be followed by a single character; the character under the cursor is replaced by the specified one. (The new character can be a new-line.) If r is preceded by a count, count characters are replaced by the specified character.
s	Delete the single character under the cursor and enter input mode; the entered text replaces the deleted character. A preceding count specifies how many characters on the current line are changed. The last character being changed is marked with a $, as for c.
t	Must be followed by a single character; scan the remainder of the line for that character. The cursor moves to the column prior to the character if the character is found. A preceding count is equivalent to repeating the search count times.
u	Reverse the last change made to the current buffer. If repeated, u alternates between these two states; thus is its own inverse. When used after an insertion of text on more than one line, the lines are saved in the numerically named buffers.
w	Move forward to the beginning of the next word (where word is defined as in b). A preceding count specifies how many words the cursor advances.
x	Delete the single character under the cursor. When x is preceded by a count, x deletes the specified number of characters forward from the cursor position, but only on the current line.
y	Must be followed by a movement command; the specified text is copied (yanked) into the unnamed temporary

buffer. If preceded by a named buffer specification,
"x, the text is placed in that buffer also. If the
command is yy, the entire current line is yanked.

z   Redraw the screen with the current line placed as
             specified by the following options: z<return>
             specifies the top of the screen, z. the center of
             the screen, and z- the bottom of the screen. The
             commands z^ and z+ are similar to ^B and ^F,
             respectively. However, z^ and z+ do not attempt to
             maintain two lines of overlap. A count after the z
             and before the following character to specifies the
             number of lines displayed in the redrawn screen. A
             count before the z gives the number of the line to
             use as the reference line instead of the default
             current line.

Keyboard Editing Keys
   At initialization, the editor automatically maps some terminal
   keyboard editing keys to equivalent visual mode commands. These
   mappings are only established for keys that are listed in the
   following table and defined in the terminfo(4) database as valid for
   the current terminal (as specified by the TERM environment variable).

   Both command and input mode mappings are created (see the map command
   in ex(1)). With the exception of the insertchar keys, which simply
   toggle input mode on and off, the input mode mappings exit input mode,
   perform the same action as the command mode mapping, and then reenter
   input mode.

   On certain terminals, the character sequence sent by a keyboard
   editing key, which is then mapped to a visual mode command, can be the
   same character sequence a user might enter to perform another command
   or set of commands. This is most likely to happen with the input mode
   mappings; therefore, on these terminals, the input mode mappings are
   disabled by default. Users can override the disabling and enabling of
   both the command and input mode keyboard editing key mappings by
   setting the keyboardedit and keyboardedit! editor options as
   appropriate (see ex(1)). The timeout, timeoutlen, and doubleescape
   editor options are alternative methods of addressing this problem.

terminfo entry	command mode map	input mode map	map name	description
key_ic	i	^[	inschar	insert char
key_eic	i	^[	inschar	end insert char
key_up	k	^[ka	up	arrow up
key_down	j	^[ja	down	arrow down
key_left	h	^[ha	left	arrow left
key_right	l	^[la	right	arrow right
key_home	H	^[Ha	home	arrow home
key_il	o^[	^[o^[a	insline	insert line
key_dl	dd	^[dda	delline	delete line
key_clear	^L	^[^La	clear	clear screen
key_eol	d$	^[d$a	clreol	clear line
key_sf	^E	^[^Ea	scrollf	scroll down
key_dc	x	^[xa	delchar	delete char
key_npage	^F	^[^Fa	npage	next page
key_ppage	^B	^[^Ba	ppage	previous page
key_sr	^Y	^[^Ya	sr	scroll up
key_eos	dG	^[dGa	clreos	clear to end of screen

EXTERNAL INFLUENCES
    Support for international codes and environment variables are as
    follows:

Environment Variables
    UNIX95 specifies using the XPG4 behaviour for this command.

    COLUMNS overrides the system-selected horizontal screen size.

    LINES overrides the system-selected vertical screen size, used as the
    number of lines in a screenful and the vertical screen size in visual
    mode.

    SHELL is a variable that shall be interpreted as the preferred
    command-line interpreter for use in !, shell, read, and other commands
    with an operand of the form !string. For the shell command the
    program shall be invoked with the two arguments -c and string. If
    this variable is null or not set, the sh utility shall be used.

    TERM is a variable that shall be interpreted as the name of the
    terminal type. If this variable is unset or null, an unspecified
    default terminal type shall be used.

    PATH determines the search path for the shell command specified in the
    editor commands, shell, read, and write. EXINIT determines a list of
    ex commands that will be executed on editor startup, before reading
    the first file. The list can contain multiple commands by separating
    them using a vertical line (|) character.

    HOME determines a pathname of a directory that will be searched for an
    editor startup file named .exrc.

    LC_ALL This variable shall determine the locale to be used to override
    any values for locale categories specified by the setting of LANG or
    any environment variables beginning with LC_.

    LC_MESSAGES determines the locale that should be used to affect the
    format and contents of diagnostic messages written to standard error
    and informative messages written to standard output.

    LC_COLLATE determines the collating sequence used in evaluating
    regular expressions and in processing the tags file. LC_CTYPE
    determines the interpretation of text as single and/or multi-byte
    characters, the classification of characters as uppercase or lowercase
    letters, the shifting of letters between uppercase and lowercase, and
    the characters matched by character class expressions in regular
    expressions.

    LANG determines the language in which messages are displayed.

    LANGOPTS specifies options determining how text for right-to-left
    languages is stored in input and output files. See environ(5).

    If LC_COLLATE or LC_CTYPE is not specified in the environment or is
    set to the empty string, the value of LANG is used as a default for
    each unspecified or empty variable. If LANG is not specified or is
    set to the empty string, a default of "C" (see lang(5)) is used
    instead of LANG. If any internationalization variable contains an
    invalid setting, the editor behaves as if all internationalization
    variables are set to "C". See environ(5).

International Code Set Support
    Single- and multi-byte character code sets are supported.

WARNINGS
    See also the WARNINGS section in ex(1).

Program Limits
   vi places the following limits on files being edited:

   Maximum Line Length
        LINE_MAX characters (defined in <limits.h>), including 2-3 bytes
        for overhead. Thus, if the value specified for LINE_MAX is 2048,
        a line length up to 2044 characters should cause no problem.

        If you load a file that contain lines longer than the specified
        limit, the lines are truncated to the stated maximum length.
        Saving the file will write the truncated version over the
        original file, thus overwriting the original lines completely.

        Attempting to create lines longer than the allowable maximum for
        the editor produces a line too long error message.

   Maximum File Size
        The maximum file length of 234,239 lines is silently enforced.

   Other limits:

        - 256 characters per global command list.

        - 128 characters in a file name in vi or ex open mode. On
           short-file-name HP-UX systems, the maximum file name length is
           14 characters.

        - 128 characters in a previous insert/delete buffer.

        - 100 characters in a shell-escape command.

        - 63 characters in a string-valued option (:set command).

        - 30 characters in a program tag name.

        - 32 or fewer macros defined by map command.

        - 512 or fewer characters total in combined map macros.

AUTHOR
     vi was developed by the University of California, Berkeley. The 16-
     bit extensions to vi are based in part on software of the Toshiba
     Corporation.

SEE ALSO
     ctags(1), ed(1), ex(1), stty(1), write(1), terminfo(4), environ(5),
     lang(5), regexp(5).

     The Ultimate Guide to the vi and ex Text Editors,
          Benjamin/Cummings Publishing Company, Inc., ISBN 0-8053-4460-8,
          HP part number 97005-90015.

STANDARDS CONFORMANCE
     vi: SVID2, SVID3, XPG2, XPG3, XPG4

CHAPTER 9

Networking

Networking varies greatly from installation to installation. Some installations, such as highly centralized and isolated systems that have only ASCII terminals connected to the system, require the system administrator to pay very little attention to networking. Other installations, such as highly distributed environments in which thousands of systems are connected to a network that may span many geographic sites, may require the system administrator to pay a great deal of attention to networking. In this scenario, the amount of time a system administrator devotes to networking may exceed the amount of time spent on all other system administration functions combined! Rather than ignoring networking altogether, as the first system administrator might, or covering all aspects of network administration, as the second system administrator may require, I cover in this chapter the aspects of networking that apply to most UNIX systems. This content is based on my experience working in a variety of new UNIX installations. In the event that you require more networking background than I cover in this chapter, I recommend the following book as an excellent source of networking information - *UNIX Networks* by Bruce H. Hunter and Karen Bradford Hunter (Prentice Hall, ISBN 0-13-08987-1).

In this chapter, I provide primarily background rather than setup information on many networking topics, because setup is predominately performed by system administrators. Most of what I cover is sometimes called "Internet Services." In general, I am going to cover the basics of networking in this chapter. This includes ARPA and Berkeley Services. Here is a list of topics I cover:

- General UNIX networking background

- Internet Protocol (IP) addressing (classes A, B, and C)

- Subnet mask

- ARPA Services

- Berkeley commands

- Host name mapping

- Network File System (NFS) background

- UNIX networking commands

- Some examples

I provide summaries and examples of many UNIX commands in this chapter. A great deal more detail can be found in the manual pages for these commands. I provide the full manual pages at the end of this chapter for many of the commands covered.

I use a variety of systems in the examples in this chapter, including Solaris, AIX, and HP-UX.

UNIX Networking

Connecting to other machines is an important part of every UNIX network. This means connecting both to other UNIX machines as well as to non-UNIX machines. The machines must be physically connected to one another as well as functionally connected to one another, so that you can perform such tasks as transferring files and logging into other systems. Many commands exist on your UNIX system that provide you with the functionality to log in and transfer files between systems. These are known as the ARPA commands **telnet** and **ftp**.

The **telnet** command allows remote logins in a heterogeneous environment. From your UNIX system, for instance, you can **telnet** to non-UNIX systems and log in. After login on the remote system, you need to have an understanding of the operating system running on that system. If you need to connect to a different computer only for the purpose of transferring files to and from the system, then you can use **ftp**. This command allows you to transfer files between any two systems without having an understanding of the operating system running on the remote system.

These commands are somewhat primitive compared to the commands that can be issued between UNIX systems. To UNIX systems, networking is not an afterthought that needs to be added on to the system. The **ftp** and **telnet** commands come with your UNIX system, as well as more advanced commands and functionality you can use to communicate between your UNIX system and other UNIX systems. These more advanced commands, known as Berkeley commands, allow you to perform many commands remotely, such as copying files and directories and logging in. This functionality continues to increase to a point where you are working with files that can be stored on any system on the network, and your access to these files is transparent to you with the Network File System (NFS).

Let's take a look at some of the basics of UNIX networking.

What Is All This Ethernet, IEEE802.3, TCP/IP Stuff, Anyway?

In order to understand how the networking on your UNIX system works, you first need to understand the components of your network that exist on your UNIX system. Seven layers of network functionality exist on your UNIX system, as shown in Figure 9-1. I cover the bottom four layers at a cursory level so that you can see how each plays a part in the operation of your network and, therefore, be more informed when you configure and troubleshoot networking on your UNIX system. The top layers are the ones that most UNIX system administrators spend time working with because those layers are closest to the functionality to which you can relate. The bottom layers are, however, also important to understand at some level, so that you can perform any configuration necessary to improve the network performance of your system, which has a major impact on the overall performance of your system.

Layer Number	Layer Name	Data Form	Comments
7	Application		User applications here.
6	Presentation		Applications prepared.
5	Session		Applications prepared.
4	Transport	Packet	Port-to-port transportation handled by TCP.
3	Network	Datagram	Internet Protocol (IP) handles routing by going directly to either the destination or default router.
2	Link	Frame	Data encapsulated in Ethernet or IEEE 802.3 with source and destination addresses.
1	Physical		Physical connection between systems. Usually thinnet or twisted pair.

Figure 9-1 ISO/OSI Network Layer Functions

I start reviewing Figure 9-1 at the bottom with layer 1 and then describe each of the four bottom layers. This is the International Standards Organization Open Systems Interconnection (ISO/OSI) model. It is helpful to visualizing the way in which networking layers interact.

Physical Layer

The beginning is the physical interconnect between the systems on your network. Without the **physical layer,** you can't communicate between systems, and all the great functionality you would like to implement is not possible. The physical layer converts the data you would like to transmit to the analog signals that travel along the wire (I'll assume for now that whatever physical layer you have in place uses wires). The information traveling into a network interface is taken off the wire and prepared for use by the next layer.

Link Layer

In order to connect to other systems local to your system, you use the link layer that is able to establish a connection to all the other systems on your local segment. This is the layer where you have either IEEE 802.3 or Ethernet. Your UNIX system supports both of these "encapsulation" methods. This is called encapsulation because your data is put in one of these two forms (either IEEE 802.3 or Ethernet). Data is transferred at the link layer in frames (just another name for data), with the source and destination addresses and some other information attached. You might think that because two different encapsulation methods exist, they must be much different. This assumption, however, is not the case. IEEE 802.3 and Ethernet are nearly identical. For this reason, many UNIX systems can handle both types of encapsulation. So with the bottom two layers, you have a physical connection between your systems and data that is encapsulated into one of two formats with a source and destination address attached. Figure 9-2 lists the components of an **Ethernet** encapsulation and makes comments about IEEE802.3 encapsulation where appropriate.

destination address	6 bytes	address data is sent to
source address	6 bytes	address data is sent from
type	2 bytes	this is the "length count" in 802.3

data	46-1500 bytes	38-1492 bytes for 802.3; the difference in these two data sizes (MTU) can be seen with the **ifconfig** command
crc	4 bytes	checksum to detect errors

Figure 9-2 Ethernet Encapsulation

One interesting item to note is the difference in the maximum data size between IEEE 802.3 and Ethernet of 1492 and 1500 bytes, respectively. This is the Maximum Transfer Unit (MTU). The **ifconfig** command covered shortly displays the MTU for your interface. The data in Ethernet is called a *frame* (the re-encapsulation of data at the next layer up is called a *datagram* in IP, and encapsulation at two levels up is called a *packet* for TCP).

Keep in mind that Ethernet and IEEE 802.3 will run on the same physical connection, but there are indeed differences between the two encapsulation methods. With your UNIX systems, you don't have to spend much, if any, time setting up your network interface for encapsulation.

Network Layer

Next we work up to the third layer, which is the network layer. This layer on UNIX systems is synonymous with Internet Protocol (IP). Data at this layer is called *datagrams*. This is the layer that handles the routing of data around the network. Data that gets routed with IP sometimes encounters an error of some type, which is reported back to the source system with an Internet Control Message Protocol (ICMP) message. We will see some ICMP messages shortly. **ifconfig** and **netstat** are two UNIX commands that are used to configure this routing, which I'll cover shortly.

Unfortunately, the information that IP uses does not conveniently fit inside an Ethernet frame, so you end up with fragmented data. This is really re-encapsulation of the data, so you end up with a lot of inefficiency as you work your way up the layers.

IP handles routing in a simple fashion. If data is sent to a destination connected directly to your system, then the data is sent directly to that system. If, on the other hand, the destination is not connected directly to your system, the data is sent to the default router. The default router then has the responsibility of getting the data to its destination. This routing can be a little tricky to understand, so I'll cover it in detail shortly.

Transport Layer

This layer can be viewed as one level up from the network layer, because it communicates with *ports*. TCP is the most common protocol found at this level, and it forms packets that are sent from port to port. The port used by a program is usually defined in **/etc/services**, along with the protocol (such as TCP). These ports are used by network programs such as **telnet**, **rlogin**, **ftp**, and so on. You can see that these programs, associated with ports, are the highest level we have covered while analyzing the layer diagram.

man page

telnet - 9

man page

rlogin - 9

man page

ftp - 9

Internet Protocol (IP) Addressing

The Internet Protocol address (IP address) is either a class "A," "B," or "C" address (there are also class "D" and "E" addresses I will not cover). A class "A" network supports many more nodes per network than either a class "B" or "C" network. IP addresses consist of four fields. The purpose of breaking down the IP address into four fields is to define a node (or host) address and a network address. Figure 9-3 summarizes the relationships between the classes and addresses.

Address Class	Networks	Nodes per Network	Bits Defining Network	Bits Defining Nodes per Network
A	a few	the most	8 bits	24 bits

Address Class	Networks	Nodes per Network	Bits Defining Network	Bits Defining Nodes per Network
B	many	many	16 bits	16 bits
C	the most	a few	24 bits	8 bits
Reserved	-	-	-	-

Figure 9-3 Comparison of Internet Protocol (IP) Addresses

These bit patterns are significant in that the number of bits defines the ranges of networks and nodes in each class. For instance, a class A address uses 8 bits to define networks, and a class C address uses 24 bits to define networks. A class A address therefore supports fewer networks than a class C address. A class A address, however, supports many more nodes per network than a class C address. Taking these relationships one step further, we can now view the specific parameters associated with these address classes in Figure 9-4.

Figure 9-4 Address Classes

Address Class	Networks Supported	Nodes per Network	Address Range		
A	127	16777215	0.0.0.1	-	127.255.255.254
B	16383	65535	128.0.0.1	-	191.255.255.254
C	2097157	255	192.0.0.1	-	223.255.254.254
Reserved	-	-	224.0.0.0	-	255.255.255.255
Looking at the 32-bit address in binary form, you can see how to determine the class of an address:					

Figure 9-4   Address Classes (Continued)

Class "A"

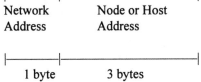

net.host.host.host

A class "A" address has the first bit set to 0. You can see how so many nodes per network can be supported with all the bits devoted to the node or host address. The first bit of a class A address is 0, and the remaining 7 bits of the network portion are used to define the network. Then a total of 3 bytes are devoted to defining the nodes with a network.

Class "B"

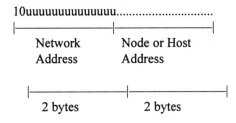

net.net.host.host

A class "B" address has the first bit set to a 1 and the second bit to a 0. More networks are supported here than with a class A address, but fewer nodes per network. With a class B address, 2 bytes are devoted to the network portion of the address and 2 bytes devoted to the node portion of the address.

Figure 9-4   Address Classes (Continued)

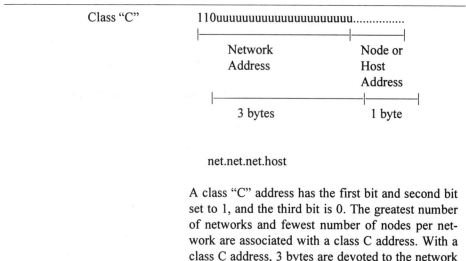

A class "C" address has the first bit and second bit set to 1, and the third bit is 0. The greatest number of networks and fewest number of nodes per network are associated with a class C address. With a class C address, 3 bytes are devoted to the network and 1 byte is devoted to the nodes within a network.

These addresses are used in various setup files that are covered later when the **/etc/hosts** file is described. Every interface on your network must have a unique IP address. Systems that have two network interfaces must have two unique IP addresses.

Subnet Mask

Your UNIX system uses the subnet mask to determine whether an IP datagram is for a host on its own subnet, a host on a different subnet but the same network, or a host on a different network. Using subnets, you can have some hosts on one subnet and other hosts on a different subnet. The subnets can be separated by routers or other networking electronics that connect the subnets.

To perform routing, the only aspects of an address that your router uses are the net and subnet. The subnet mask is used to mask the host part of the address. Because you can set up network addresses in such a way that you are the only one who knows which part of the address is the host, subnet, and network, you use the subnet mask to make your system aware of the bits of your IP address that are for the host and which are for the subnet.

In its simplest form, what you are really doing with subnet masking is specifying which portion of your IP address defines the host, and which part defines the network. One of the most confusing aspects of working with subnet masks is that most books show the subnet masks in Figure 9-5 as the most common.

Address Class	Decimal	Hex
A	255.0.0.0	0xff000000
B	255.255.0.0	0xffff0000
C	255.255.255.0	0xffffff00

Figure 9-5 Subnet Masks

This way of thinking, however, assumes that you are devoting as many bits as possible to the network and as many bits as possible to the host and that no subnets are used. Figure 9-6 shows an example of using subnetting with a class B address.

Address Class	Class B		
host IP address	152.128.	12.	1
breakdown	network	subnet	hostid
number of bits	16 bits	8 bits	8 bits
subnet mask in decimal	255.255.	255.	0
subnet mask in hexadecimal	0xffffff00		
Example of different host on same subnet	152.128.	12.	2

Address Class	Class B
Example of host on different subnet	152.128. 13. 1

Figure 9-6 Class B IP Address and Subnet Mask Example

In Figure 9-6, the first two bytes of the subnet mask (255.255) define the network, the third byte (255) defines the subnet, and the fourth byte (0) is devoted to the host ID. Although this subnet mask for a class B address did not appear in the earlier default subnet mask figure, the subnet mask of 255.255.255.0 is widely used in class B networks to support subnetting.

How does your UNIX system perform the comparison using the subnet mask of 255.255.255.0 to determine that 152.128.12.1 and 152.128.13.1 are on different subnets? Figure 9-7 shows this comparison.

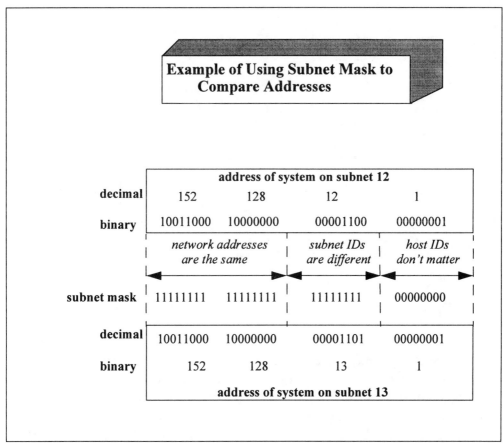

Figure 9-7 Example of Using Subnet Mask to Compare Addresses

Figure 9-8 shows these two systems on the different subnets.

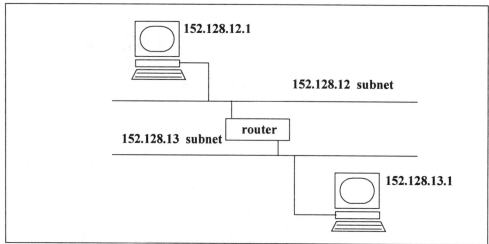

Figure 9-8 Class B Systems on Different Subnets

You don't have to use the 8-bit boundaries to delineate the network, subnet, and host ID fields. If, for instance, you want to use part of the subnet field for the host ID, you can do so. A good reason for this approach would be to accommodate future expandability. You might want subnets 12, 13, 14, and 15 to be part of the same subnet today and make these into separate subnets in the future. Figure 9-9 shows this setup.

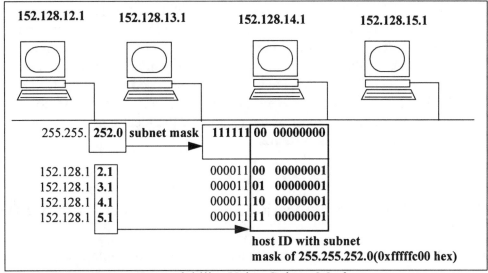

Figure 9-9 Future Expandability Using Subnet Mask

These systems are connected to the same subnet, even though part of the third byte, normally associated with the subnet, is used for the host ID. In the future, the subnet mask could be changed to 255.255.252.0 and have four separate subnets of 12, 13, 14, and 15. This arrangement would require putting routers in place to route to these separate subnets.

Let's now switch to the high level and look at some networking functionality.

Using Networking

The ISO/OSI model is helpful for visualizing the way in which the networking layers interact. The model does not, however, tell you how to use the networking. Two widely used networking services that may be running on your system(s) and are worth taking a look at are ARPA and NFS.

The first networking product to try on your system is what is sometimes called ARPA Services - what I have been calling ARPA.

ARPA is a combination of "ARPA Services" and "Berkeley Services." ARPA Services supports communications among systems running different operating systems, and Berkeley Services supports UNIX systems. The following sections are a list of the most common commands. Although many programs can be run under each of these services, the following are the most commonly used ones in the UNIX world. In some cases, there are examples that show how these commands are used. For most of the examples, the local host is **system1** and the remote host is **system2**.

ARPA Services (Communication among Systems w/ Different OS)

man page

ftp - 9

File Transfer Protocol (ftp) Transfer a file, or multiple files, from one system to another. This is often used when transferring files between a UNIX workstation and a Windows PC, VAX, etc. The following example shows copying the file **/tmp/krsort.c** from system2 (remote host) to the local directory on system1 (local host):

	comments
$ ftp system2	Issue ftp command
Connected to system2.	
system2 FTP server (Version 4.1) ready.	
Name (system2:root): root	Log in to system2
Password required for root.	
Password:	Enter password
User root logged in.	
Remote system type is UNIX.	
Using binary mode to transfer files.	
ftp> **cd /tmp**	**cd** to **/tmp** on system2
CWD command successful	
ftp> **get krsort.c**	Get krsort.c file
PORT command successful	
Opening BINARY mode data connection for **krsort.c**	
Transfer complete.	
2896 bytes received in 0.08 seconds	

	comments
ftp> **bye**	Exit ftp
Goodbye.	
$	

man page

ftp - 9

In this example, both systems are running UNIX; however, the commands you issue through **ftp** are operating-system-independent. The **cd** for change directory and **get** commands used above work for any operating system on which **ftp** is running. If you become familiar with just a few **ftp** commands, you may find that transferring information in a heterogeneous networking environment is not difficult.

Chances are that you are using your UNIX system(s) in a heterogeneous environment and may therefore use **ftp** to copy files and directories from one system to another. Because **ftp** is so widely used, I describe some of the more commonly used **ftp** commands.

ascii   Set the type of file transferred to ASCII. This means that you are transferring an ASCII file from one system to another. This is usually the default, so you don't have to set it.

Example: **ascii**

binary   Set the type of file transferred to binary. This means that you are transferring a binary file from one system to another. If, for instance, you want to have a directory on your UNIX system that holds applications that you copy to non-UNIX systems, then you want to use binary transfer.

Example: **binary**

cd	Change to the specified directory on the remote host.
	Example: **cd /tmp**
dir	List the contents of a directory on the remote system to the screen or to a file on the local system, if you specify a local file name.
get	Copy the specified remote file to the specified local file. If you don't specify a local file name, then the remote file name will be used.
lcd	Change to the specified directory on the local host.
	Example: **lcd /tmp**
ls	List the contents of a directory on the remote system to the screen or to a file on the local system, if you specify a local file name.
mget	Copy multiple files from the remote host to the local host.
	Example: **mget *.c**
put	Copy the specified local file to the specified remote file. If you don't specify a remote file name, then the local file name will be used.
	Example: **put test.c**

mput	Copy multiple files from the local host to the remote host.
	Example: **mput *.c**

bye/quit	Close the connection to the remote host.
	Example: **bye**

Other **ftp** commands are available in addition to those I have covered here. If you need more information on these commands or wish to review additional **ftp** commands, the UNIX manual pages for **ftp** are helpful.

man page

ftp - 9

man page

telnet - 9

man page

rlogin - 9

telnet	Used for communication with another host using the telnet protocol. Telnet is an alternative to using **rlogin**, described later. The following example shows how to establish a telnet connection with the remote host system2:

	comments
$ telnet system2	
Connected to system2.	Telnet to system2
AIX version 4 system2	
login: **root**	Log in as root on system2
password:	Enter password
Welcome to system2. - rs6000 aix 4.3.1.0	
$	AIX prompt on system2

Berkeley Commands (Communication between UNIX Systems)

Remote Copy (rcp)

This program is used to copy files and directories from one UNIX system to another. To copy **/tmp/krsort.c** from system1 to system2, you could do the following:

$ rcp   system2:/tmp/krsort.c /tmp/krsort.c

Your system administrator has to configure some networking files to get this level of functionality. In this example, the user who issues the command is considered "equivalent" on both systems and has permission to copy files from one system to the other with **rcp** (These terms are described shortly).

Remote login (rlogin)

Supports login to a remote UNIX system. To remotely log in to system2 from system1, you would do the following:

$ rlogin system2

password:

Welcome to system2

$

If a password is requested when the user issues the **rlogin** command, the users are not equivalent on the two systems. If no password is requested, then the users are indeed equivalent.

Remote shell (remsh)

man page

remsh - 9

With the **remsh** command, you can sit on one UNIX system and issue a command to be run remotely on a different UNIX system and have the results displayed locally. In this case, a **remsh** is issued to show a long listing of **/tmp/krsort.c**. The command is run on system2, but the result is displayed on system1, where the command was typed:

$ remsh system2 ll /tmp/krsort.c

-rwxrwxrwx 1 root sys 2896 Sept 1 10:54 /tmp/krsort.c

$

In this case, the users on system1 and system2 must be equivalent, or else permission is denied to issue this command.

Remote who (rwho)

man page

rwho - 9

Find out who is logged in on a remote UNIX system. Here is the output of issuing **rwho**:

$ rwho

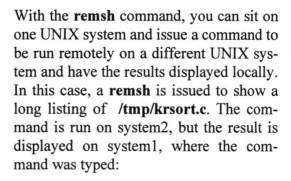

```
root       system1:ttyu0    Sept 1 19:21
root       system2:console  Sept 1 13:17
tomd       system2:ttyp2    Sept 1 13:05
 |          |        |            |      |> time of login
 |          |        |            |> day of login
 |          |        |
 |          |        |> terminal line
 |          |> machine name
 |
 |> user name
```

For **rwho** to work, the **rwho** daemon (**rwhod**) must be running.

Other "r" commands, in addition to those covered are available. Also, variations of these commands occur going from one UNIX variant to another, so you may not run exactly the same "r" command on your UNIX system.

Host Name Mapping

The most important decision related to networking is how your system administrator implements host name mapping in ARPA. Three techniques are available for host name mapping:

- Berkeley Internet Named Domain (BIND)

- Network Information Service (NIS)

- UNIX file **/etc/hosts**

The most common and simplest way to implement host name mapping is with **/etc/hosts**, so I cover this technique in the next section. Keep in mind that there are probably networking manuals for your UNIX variant devoted to many networking topics including NFS, ARPA, and others. These manuals serve as good reference material if you need to know more about networking than is covered here.

Using the **/etc/hosts** file, as you are about to see, becomes very difficult for environments where there are many systems deployed. With this solution there is one **/etc/hosts** file that must be kept up-to-date and propagated to all other systems.

The Domain Name System (DNS) is widely used in large environments. DNS uses Berkeley Internet Name Domain Service (BIND) to resolve names to addresses. There are name servers that fill a request for name data. This is the server side to BIND. There is a client side to BIND called the resolver that accesses the name server(s) to resolve names. Using this client/server model it is much easier to maintain naming information, because it only needs to be kept in a few places as opposed to on each system.

Clients use a file called **/etc/resolv.conf** to configure the resolver. The name server and its corresponding address are the keys to resolving information.

This solution makes it much easier to maintain system names and addresses in large environments. DNS and BIND are primarily a system administration exercise to setup. From a user standpoint, you don't need to know much about them. What I will instead focus on in the upcoming sections are some of the programs in which users are more interested. I will supply some background so that the way in which the programs are used has more meaning. In general, though, I'll concentrate on the user aspect of these networking topics, as opposed to the system administration aspect of them.

/etc/hosts

This file contains information about the other systems to which you are connected. It contains the Internet address of each system, the system name, and any aliases for the system name. If your system administrator modifies your **/etc/hosts** file to contain the names of the systems on your network, they have provided the basis for **rlogin** to another system. Although you can now **rlogin** to other UNIX systems, you cannot yet **rcp** or **remsh** to another system. Although adding **remsh** and **rcp** functionality is easy, it does indeed compromise security, so it is not always set up on all systems. Here is an example **/etc/ hosts** file:

```
127.0.0.1           localhost        loopback
15.32.199.42        a4410827
15.32.199.28        a4410tu8
15.32.199.7         a4410922
15.32.199.21        a4410tu1
15.32.199.22        a4410tu2
```

man page
rlogin - 9

man page
rcp - 9

man page
remsh - 9

15.32.199.62	a4410730	
15.32.199.63	hpxterm1	
15.32.199.64	a4410rd1	
15.32.199.62	a4410750	hp1

This file is in the following format:

<internet_address>   <official_hostname>   <alias>

The Internet Protocol address (IP address) is a class "A," "B," or "C" address. A class "A" network supports many more nodes per network than either a class "B" or "C" network. The purpose of breaking down the IP address into four fields is to define a node (or host) address and a network address. Figures 9-3 through 9-6 described these classes in detail.

Assuming that the above /etc/hosts file contains class "C" addresses, the rightmost field is the host or node address, and the other three fields comprise the network address.

You could use either the official_hostname or alias from the /etc/hosts file when issuing one of the ARPA or Berkeley commands described earlier. For instance, either of the following ARPA commandsl works:

man page

telnet - 9

$ **telnet a4410750**

or

$ **telnet hp1**

Similarly, either of the following Berkeley commands works:

man page

rogin - 9

$ **rlogin a4410750**

or

$ **rlogin hp1**

/etc/hosts.equiv

If your system administrator doesn't want users to have to issue a password when they **rlogin** to a remote system, they can set up equivalent hosts by editing this file. As I mentioned earlier, this is technique sometimes considered a security risk, so it is not always employed. The login names must be the same on both the local and remote systems for **/etc/hosts.equiv** to allow the user to bypass entering a password. You can either list all the equivalent hosts in **/etc/hosts.equiv** or list the host and user name you wish to be equivalent. Users can now use **rcp** and **remsh**, because they are equivalent users on these systems. I usually just enter all the host names on the network. Here is an example of **/etc/hosts.equiv**:

man page

rlogin - 9

man page

rcp - 9

man page

remsh - 9

```
a4410730
a4410tu1
a4410tu2
hpxterm1
a4410827
a4410750
```

Keep in mind the potential security risks of using **/etc/ hosts.equiv**. If a user can log into a remote system without a password, you have reduced the overall level of security on your network. Even though users may find it convenient to not have to enter a password when logging into a remote system, you have given every user in **/etc/hosts.equiv** access to the entire network. If you could ensure that all the permissions on all the files and directories on all systems were properly set up, then you wouldn't care who had access to what system. In the real UNIX world, however, permissions are sometimes not what they are supposed to be. Users have a strong tendency to "browse around," invariably stumbling upon a file they want to copy to which they really shouldn't have access.

/.rhosts

This file is the **/etc/hosts.equiv** for superuser. If you log in as root, you want to have this file configured with exactly the same information as **/etc/hosts.equiv**. If you do, however, you have compounded your network security risk by allowing superuser on any system to log in to a remote system without a root password. If you are the undisputed ruler of your network and you're 100 percent certain that no security holes exist, then you may want to set up **/.rhosts** so that you don't have to issue a password when you log in remotely to a system as superuser. From a security standpoint, however, you should know that this setup is frowned upon.

If your system administrator has made the appropriate entries in **/etc/hosts**, **/etc/hosts.equiv**, and **/.rhosts**, you can use the ARPA Services commands **ftp** and **telnet** as well as the Berkeley commands **rcp**, **rlogin**, **remsh**, and **rwho**.

I have described the process of setting up the appropriate files to get the most commonly used ARPA Services up and running. There is sometimes even more advanced functionality such as BIND is required. Your system administrator may have set up BIND or similar functionality gives you access to some or all the commands covered throughout this section.

Network File System (NFS)

NFS allows you to mount disks on remote systems so that they appear as though they are local to your system. Similarly, NFS allows remote systems to mount your local disk so that it looks as though it is local to the remote system. Configuring NFS to achieve this functionality is simple for your system administrator. Here are the steps your system administrator goes through in order to configure NFS:

1. Start NFS.

2. Specify whether your system will be an NFS Client, NFS Server, or both.

3. Specify which of your local file systems can be mounted by remote systems.

4. Specify the remote disks you want to mount and view as if they were local to your system.

As with ARPA, you could enable other aspects to NFS, but again, I cover what I know to be the NFS functionality that nearly every UNIX installation uses.

Because your system administrator may set up NFS to meet the needs of you and other users, you may want to understand the terminology associated with NFS. The following are commonly used NFS terms:

Node	A computer system that is attached to or is part of a computer network.
Client	A node that requests data or services from other nodes (servers).
Server	A node that provides data or services to other nodes (clients) on the network.
File System	A disk partition or logical volume.
Export	Makes a file system available for mounting on remote nodes using NFS.
Mount	Accesses a remote file system using NFS.

Mount Point   The name of a directory on which the NFS file system is mounted.

Import   Mounts a remote file system.

Some of the specific configuration tasks and related files are different among UNIX variants. This fact is mostly a problem for your system administrator to deal with if they have multiple UNIX variants to manage. The following are some general tasks and examples related to configuring NFS. You system administrator, of course, has to deal with the specifics of configuration on the UNIX variants.

Your system must be an NFS client, NFS server, or both. There are also daemons which must be running to support NFS. Both of these tasks are performed somewhat differently among UNIX variants.

Your system then imports remote file systems to which you have local access and exports local file systems that are accessed by other systems.

A remote file system that you are mounting locally has an entry similar to the one that follows in **/etc/fstab**, **/etc/vfstab**, **/etc/filesystems**, or whatever file is used to mount file systems:

system2:/opt/app3   /opt/app3   nfs   rw,suid   0   0

man page

showmount
- 13

In this case we are mounting **/opt/app3** on *system2* locally as **/opt/app3**. This is an NFS mount with the permissions shown.

You can use the **showmount** command to show all remote systems (clients) that have mounted a local file system. This command is supported on most UNIX variants. **showmount** is useful for determining the file systems that are most often mounted by clients with NFS. The output of **showmount** is particularly easy to read, because it lists the host name and the directory that was mounted by the client. You have the three following options to the **showmount** command:

-a prints output in the format "name:directory"

-d lists all the local directories that have been remotely mounted by clients

-e prints a list of exported file systems

Other Networking Commands and Setup

Setting up networking is an exercise that your system administrator spends a lot of time planning. No two networking environments are alike. There is typically a lot of networking electronics to which your system is connected. There are many useful commands related to testing connectivity to other systems and networking configuration. Should you encounter a problem, you want to have an understanding of some networking commands that can be lifesavers. In addition, you can encounter some tricky aspects to networking setup if you have some networking hardware that your UNIX systems must interface to, such as routers, gateways, bridges, etc. I give an example of one such case: connecting a UNIX system to a router. At the same time, I cover some of the most handy networking commands as part of this description.

Consider Figure 9-10, in which a UNIX system is connected directly to a router.

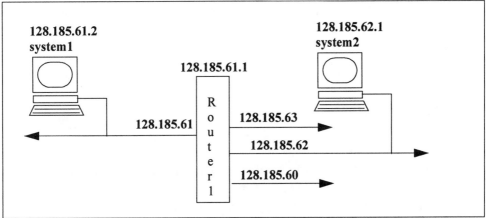

Figure 9-10 UNIX System and Router Example

Here we have a UNIX system connected to segment 128.185.61. This is a class "B" Internet address with subnetting enabled.

The **/etc/hosts** file needs to have in it the UNIX system with node ID 2, the router, and any other systems on this segment or segments on the other side of the router.

If the router is properly configured, we should be able to seamlessly connect from 61 to systems on segments 60, 62, and 63. The router should be configured to allow our system to connect to systems on other segments (60, 62, and 63) by going through the router. Some unforeseen configuration was required to make this simple network operate seamlessly. In this case, a problem occurred getting system1 to connect to systems on the other side of the router on 60, 62, and 63. Before discussing the additional configuration that needed to be done, I first show the **/etc/hosts** file and then use some very useful UNIX commands that show the state of the network. Here is the **/etc/hosts** file showing just the UNIX system and router:

man page

cat - 3

$ cat /etc/hosts

```
127.0.0.1    localhosts loopback
128.185.61.1  router1      # router
128.185.61.2  system1      # UNIX system on 61
128.185.62.1  system2      # UNIX system on 62
```

This host file is simple and allows system1 to connect to router1 and system2. The connection from system1 to system2 takes place by going through the router.

ping

man page

ping - 9

Let's look at one of the most commonly used networking commands - **ping**. This command is used to determine whether or not a connection exists between two networking components. **ping** is a simple command that sends an ICMP echo packet to the host you specify once per second. You may recall that ICMP was covered earlier under the network, or third layer. **ping** stands for Packet InterNet Groper. **ping** differs somewhat among UNIX variants mostly in the reporting that **ping** produces when no options are provided.

man page

ping - 9

Some systems provide performance information when **ping** is issued with no options; others report that the system "is alive". The following is an example of checking the connection between the local system and another system on the network called *austin*:

```
martyp $ ping austin
austin is alive
martyp $
```

Among the additional information you can specify with **ping** are the interval, packetsize, and number of iterations shown in the following example:

```
martyp $ ping -I 5 austin 4096 10
PING austin: 4096 data bytes
4104   bytes   from   austin   (128.185.61.5):   icmp_seq=0.
time=8. ms
4104   bytes   from   austin   (128.185.61.5):   icmp_seq=1.
time=9. ms
4104 bytes from austin (128.15.61.5): icmp_seq=2. time=9.
ms
4104 bytes from austin (128.15.61.5): icmp_seq=3. time=9.
ms
4104 bytes from austin (128.15.61.5): icmp_seq=4. time=8.
ms
4104 bytes from austin (128.15.61.5): icmp_seq=5. time=9.
ms
4104 bytes from austin (128.15.61.5): icmp_seq=6. time=9.
ms
4104 bytes from austin (128.15.61.5): icmp_seq=7. time=9.
ms
4104 bytes from austin (128.15.61.5): icmp_seq=8. time=9.
ms
4104 bytes from austin (128.15.61.5): icmp_seq=9. time=9.
ms

----austin PING Statistics----

10 packets transmitted, 10 packets received, 0% packet
loss
round-trip (ms)  min/avg/max = 9/9/15
martyp $
```

man page
ping - 9

In this example, we **ping** *austin* every five seconds, with a packet size of 4096 bytes at total of ten times.

Let's now get back to our example.

How do I know that I have a connection between system1 and the router and the other systems on the other side of the router? I use the **ping** command. Here is how I know that system1 is connected to router1:

$ ping router1

PING router1: 64 byte packets
64 bytes from 128.185.61.2: icmp_seq=0. time=0. ms
64 bytes from 128.185.61.2: icmp_seq=1. time=0. ms
64 bytes from 128.185.61.2: icmp_seq=2. time=0. ms

Each line of output here represents a response that was returned from the device that was pinged. This means that the device responded. You continue to get this response indefinitely and have to type ^**c** (control c) to terminate the **ping**. If no output is produced, as shown below, then no response occurred and you may have a problem between your system and the device to which you are checking the connection.

$ ping system2

PING router1: 64 byte packets

In this scenario, you would see this message and that is as far as you get. A ^**c** will kill the **ping** and you see that some number of packets were sent and none were received. I did indeed get this response when issuing the **ping** command, so I know that a problem exists with the connection between system1 and router1.

ping should be used only for testing purposes such as manual fault isolation, because it generates a substantial amount of network traffic. You do not want to use **ping** on an ongoing basis such as in a script that is running continuously.

man page

ping - 9

A nice variation of **ping** that I use is to specify a packet size of 4096 bytes, rather than the default of 64 bytes shown in the previous examples, and count the number of times **ping** transmits before terminating, rather than having to type ^c to terminate **ping**. The following example shows this:

$ ping router1 4096 5

PING router1: 64 byte packets
4096 bytes from 128.185.51.2: icmp_seq=0. time=8. ms
4096 bytes from 128.185.51.2: icmp_seq=1. time=8. ms
4096 bytes from 128.185.51.2: icmp_seq=2. time=9. ms
4096 bytes from 128.185.51.2: icmp_seq=3. time=8. ms
4096 bytes from 128.185.51.2: icmp_seq=4. time=8. ms

Notice that the time required to transmit and receive a response, the round-trip time, is substantially longer than with only 64 bytes transmitted. I usually find that the round-trip time for 64 bytes is 0 ms, although this depends on a number of factors, including network topology and network traffic.

netstat

From the earlier description of the subnet mask, you can see that routing from one host to another can be configured in a variety of ways. The path that information takes in getting from one host to another depends on routing.

man page

netstat - 9

You can obtain information related to routing with the **netstat** command. The **-r** option to **netstat** shows the routing tables, which you usually want to know, and the **-n** option can be used to print network addresses as numbers rather than as names. With the **-v** option, you get additional information related to routing, such as subnet mask.

In the following examples, **netstat** is issued with the **-r** option (this is used when describing the **netstat** output), the **-rn** options, and the **-rnv** options, so you can compare the outputs.

```
# netstat -r

Routing tables
Destination     Gateway       Flags   Refs       Use  Interface  Pmtu  PmtuTime
localhost       localhost     UH         0       465  lo0        4608
system1         localhost     UH         2    837711  lo0        4608
default         wellfleet     UG        12   1051826  lan0       1500
169.200.112     system1       U             751821954  lan0      1500
```

```
# netstat -rn

Routing tables
Destination     Gateway         Flags  Refs       Use  Interface  Pmtu  PmtuTime
127.0.0.1       127.0.0.1       UH        0       465  lo0        4608
169.200.112.1   127.0.0.1       UH        2    837735  lo0        4608
default         169.200.112.250 UG       12   1051827  lan0       1500
169.200.112.0   169.200.112.1   U            751821991  lan0      1500
```

```
# netstat -rnv

Routing tables
Dest/Netmask       Gateway       Flags  Refs       Use  Interface  Pmtu  PmtuTime
127.0.0.1/255.255.255.255
                   127.0.0.1     UH        0       465  lo0        4608
169.200.112.1/255.255.255.255
                   127.0.0.1     UH        1    837756  lo0        4608
default/0.0.0.0    169.200.112.250 UG     14   1051834  lan0       1500
169.200.112.0/255.255.255.0
                   169.200.112.1 U            751822050  lan0      1500
```

With **netstat**, some information is provided about the router, which is the middle entry. The **-r** option shows information about routing, but many other useful options to this command are available. Of particular interest in this output is "Flags," which defines the type of routing that takes place. Here are descriptions of the most common flags from the UNIX manual pages:

1=U   Route to a *network* via a gateway that is the local host itself.

3=UG   Route to a *network* via a gateway that is the remote host.

5=UH   Route to a *host* via a gateway that is the local host itself.

7=UGH   Route to a *host* via a remote gateway that is a host.

man page

netstat - 9

The first two lines are for the local host or loopback interface, called **lo0,** at address 127.0.0.1 (you can see this address in the **netstat -rn** example). The UH flags indicate that the destination address is the local host itself. This class A address allows a client and server on the same host to communicate with one another with TCP/IP. A datagram sent to the loopback interface doesn't go out onto the network; it simply goes through the loopback.

The next line is for the default route. This entry says to send packets to router1 if a more specific route can't be found. In this case, the router has a UG under Flags. Some routers are configured with a U; others, such as the one in this example, with a UG. I've found that I usually end up determining through trial and error whether a U or UG is required. If a U is in Flags and I am unable to connect to a system on the other side of a router, a UG usually fixes the problem.

The third line is for the system's network interface **lan0**. Keep in mind that this may be called something other than **lan0** on your system such as **le0**. This means to use this network interface for packets to be sent to 169.200.112.

Also, I use two forms of **netstat** to obtain network statistics, as opposed to routing information. The first is **netstat -i**, which shows the state of interfaces that are autoconfigured. Because I am most often interested in getting a summary of **lan0**, I issue this command. **netstat -i** gives a good rundown of **lan0**, such as the network it is on, its name, and so on.

The following example shows the output of **netstat -i**:

```
# netstat -i
Name  Mtu   Network      Address         Ipkts Ierrs   Opkts Oerrs  Coll
ni0*  0     none         none                0     0       0     0      0
ni1*  0     none         none                0     0       0     0      0
lo0   4608  loopback     127.0.0.1         232     0     232     0      0
lan0  1500  169.200.112  169.200.112.2 3589746     2   45630     0    104
```

man page

netstat - 9

Here is a description of the nine fields in the **netstat** example:

Name	The name of your network interface (Name), in this case, **lan0**.
MTU	The "maximum transmission unit," which is the maximum packet size sent by the interface card.
Network	The network address of the LAN to which the interface card is connected (169.200).
Address	The host name of your system. This is the symbolic name of your system as it appears in the file **/etc/hosts**.

Start of statistical information:

Ipkts	The number of packets received by the interface card, in this case **lan0**.
Ierrs	The number of errors detected on incoming packets by the interface card.
Opkts	The number of packets transmitted by the interface card.
Oerrs	The number of errors detected during the transmission of packets by the interface card.
Collis	The number of collisions that resulted from packet traffic.

netstat provides cumulative data since the node was last powered up; you might have a long elapsed time over which data was accumulated. If you are interested in seeing useful statistical information, you can use **netstat** with different options. You can also specify an interval to report statistics. I usually ignore the first entry, because it shows all data since the system was last powered up. Therefore, the data includes non-prime hours when the system was idle. I prefer to view data at the time the system is working its hardest. This following netstat example provides network interface information every five seconds.

man page

netstat - 9

```
# netstat -I lan0 5
(lan0)-> input         output          (Total)-> input          output
  packets  errs  packets errs colls       packets  errs  packets errs colls
  3590505    2    45714   0   104          3590737    2    45946   0   104
      134    0        5   0     0              134    0        5   0     0
      174    0        0   0     0              174    0        0   0     0
      210    0       13   0     0              210    0       13   0     0
      165    0        0   0     0              165    0        0   0     0
      169    0        0   0     0              169    0        0   0     0
      193    0        0   0     0              193    0        0   0     0
      261    0        7   0     0              261    0        7   0     0
      142    0        8   0     0              142    0        8   0     0
      118    0        0   0     0              118    0        0   0     0
      143    0        0   0     0              143    0        0   0     0
      149    0        0   0     0              149    0        0   0     0
```

With this example, you get multiple outputs of what is taking place on the LAN interface. As I mentioned earlier, you may want to ignore the first output, because it includes information over a long time period. This may include a time when your network was idle, and therefore the data is not important to you.

You can specify the network interface on which you want statistics reported by using **-I interface**; in the case of the example, it was **-I lan0**. An interval of five seconds was also used in this example.

Yet another use of **netstat** is to show the state of network sockets. **netstat -a** produces a list of protocols, queues, local and remote addresses, and protocol states. All this information is useful for showing active communications, as shown in the following example:

```
# netstat -a
Active Internet connections (including servers)
Proto Recv-Q Send-Q Local Address        Foreign Address       (state)
tcp       0      2  system1.telnet       atlm0081.atl.hp..1319 ESTABLISHED
tcp       0      0  *.1095               *.*                   LISTEN
tcp       0      0  *.psmond             *.*                   LISTEN
tcp       0      0  *.mcsemon            *.*                   LISTEN
tcp       0      0  localhost.8886       localhost.1062        ESTABLISHED
tcp       0      0  localhost.1062       localhost.8886        ESTABLISHED
tcp       0      0  *.8886               *.*                   LISTEN
tcp       0      0  *.8887               *.*                   LISTEN
tcp       0      0  *.1006               *.*                   LISTEN
tcp       0      0  *.978                *.*                   LISTEN
tcp       0      0  *.22370              *.*                   LISTEN
tcp       0      0  *.389                *.*                   LISTEN
tcp       0      0  *.8181               *.*                   LISTEN
tcp       0      0  *.1054               *.*                   LISTEN
tcp       0      0  *.1053               *.*                   LISTEN
tcp       0      0  *.diagmond           *.*                   LISTEN
tcp       0      0  *.1045               *.*                   LISTEN
tcp       0      0  *.1038               *.*                   LISTEN
tcp       0      0  *.135                *.*                   LISTEN
tcp       0      0  *.smtp               *.*                   LISTEN
```

```
tcp       0       0   *.1036              *.*            LISTEN
tcp       0       0   *.appconn           *.*            LISTEN
tcp       0       0   *.spc               *.*            LISTEN
tcp       0       0   *.dtspc             *.*            LISTEN
tcp       0       0   *.recserv           *.*            LISTEN
tcp       0       0   *.klogin            *.*            LISTEN
tcp       0       0   *.kshell            *.*            LISTEN
tcp       0       0   *.chargen           *.*            LISTEN
tcp       0       0   *.discard           *.*            LISTEN
tcp       0       0   *.echo              *.*            LISTEN
tcp       0       0   *.time              *.*            LISTEN
tcp       0       0   *.daytime           *.*            LISTEN
tcp       0       0   *.printer           *.*            LISTEN
tcp       0       0   *.auth              *.*            LISTEN
tcp       0       0   *.exec              *.*            LISTEN
tcp       0       0   *.shell             *.*            LISTEN
tcp       0       0   *.login             *.*            LISTEN
tcp       0       0   *.telnet            *.*            LISTEN
tcp       0       0   *.ftp               *.*            LISTEN
tcp       0       0   *.795               *.*            LISTEN
tcp       0       0   *.792               *.*            LISTEN
tcp       0       0   *.*                 *.*            CLOSED
tcp       0       0   *.787               *.*            LISTEN
tcp       0       0   *.783               *.*            LISTEN
tcp       0       0   *.779               *.*            LISTEN
tcp       0       0   *.portmap           *.*            LISTEN
tcp       0       0   *.2121              *.*            LISTEN
udp       0       0   *.1127              *.*
udp       0       0   *.177               *.*
udp       0       0   *.1003              *.*
udp       0       0   *.*                 *.*
udp       0       0   *.*                 *.*
udp       0       0   *.*                 *.*
udp       0       0   *.*                 *.*
udp       0       0   *.nfsd              *.*
udp       0       0   *.976               *.*
udp       0       0   *.22370             *.*
udp       0       0   *.1097              *.*
udp       0       0   *.1095              *.*
udp       0       0   *.1079              *.*
udp       0       0   *.135               *.*
udp       0       0   *.*                 *.*
udp       0       0   *.1045              *.*
udp       0       0   *.snmp              *.*
udp       0       0   *.1040              *.*
udp       0       0   *.tftp              *.*
udp       0       0   *.chargen           *.*
udp       0       0   *.discard           *.*
udp       0       0   *.echo              *.*
udp       0       0   *.time              *.*
udp       0       0   *.daytime           *.*
udp       0       0   *.ntalk             *.*
udp       0       0   *.bootps            *.*
udp       0       0   *.1023              *.*
udp       0       0   *.787               *.*
udp       0       0   *.798               *.*
udp       0       0   *.797               *.*
udp       0       0   *.1037              *.*
udp       0       0   *.*                 *.*
udp       0       0   *.1036              *.*
udp       0       0   *.1035              *.*
udp       0       0   *.777               *.*
udp       0       0   *.portmap           *.*
udp       0       0   *.1034              *.*
udp       0       0   *.syslog            *.*
udp       0       0   *.2121              *.*
Active UNIX domain sockets
Address   Type    Recv-Q Send-Q   Inode    Conn   Refs   Nextref Addr
  bb9c00  stream       0      0    af9000      0      0         0 /tmp/.AgentSoA
  ced700  dgram        0      0    c99400      0      0         0 /opt/dcelocalr
  ce9e00  dgram        0      0    d23000      0      0         0 /opt/dcelocalr
  b0d200  dgram        0      0    b87000      0      0         0 /opt/dcelocalr
  997a00  stream       0      0    b84800      0      0         0 /opt/dcelocal1
  b24e00  dgram        0      0    b84000      0      0         0 /opt/dcelocal1
  d59400  dgram        0      0    b66400      0      0         0 /var/tmp/psb_t
```

```
        d85c00 dgram      0      0  b67000        0        0        0 /var/tmp/psb_t
        c8b200 dgram      0      0  b12000        0        0        0 /opt/dcelocalr
        c8b400 stream     0      0  b78400        0        0        0 /opt/dcelocal5
        c8b300 dgram      0      0  b78000        0        0        0 /opt/dcelocalr
        c90900 dgram      0      0  d22400        0        0        0 /opt/dcelocalr
        c78c00 dgram      0      0  ba1000   c4a180        0        0 /opt/dcelocal0
        b1e900 dgram      0      0  9a4400        0   c32e80        0 /opt/dcelocald
        d64100 stream     0      0  d24c00        0        0        0 /opt/dcelocal5
        9e1600 dgram      0      0  9a4000   d4d940        0        0 /opt/dcelocal2
        d64200 dgram      0      0  cfc800        0   c32c80        0 /opt/dcelocal9
        d12d00 dgram      0      0  cfc000   c32c00        0        0 /opt/dcelocal1
        c5ee00 stream     0      0  b1c000        0        0        0 /opt/dcelocal4
        d19d00 dgram      0      0  ce4800        0        0        0 /opt/dcelocald
        cf0c00 dgram      0      0  a92800        0   af15c0        0 /opt/dcelocal7
        d2d600 dgram      0      0  a93800   c32c00        0   d4db80 /opt/dcelocal0
        c9b900 dgram      0      0  a93c00        0        0        0 /opt/dcelocald
        d6c800 stream     0      0  ba3000        0        0        0 /var/opt/OV/sT
#
```

A lot of information is in this output. You can refer to the manual page at the end of this chapter if you want a detailed explanation of any of the fields.

The first line shows the *Proto tcp* to the *Local Address system1.telnet* as having a *(state)* of *ESTABLISHED*. This is the connection we have initiated to this system. We are sitting on *system1* with a telnet session open to the system on which we ran **netstat**.

man page

netstat - 9

Most of the remaining *tcp* protocol entries are listening. This means that they are listening for incoming connections as indicated by the *LISTEN*. They have a wildcard in the *Foreign Address* field, which will contain the address when a connection has been established. We are one of the few connections that has been made, as indicated by the *ESTABLISHED*.

All the send and receive queues, shown as *Recv-Q* and *Send-Q*, are empty as indicated by the *0*.

The UNIX domain sockets at the end of the output are stream and datagram connections for a variety of services such as NFS.

This output gives you an appreciation of the immense amount of activity taking place from a networking perspective on your UNIX system. Networking and connectivity have been among the most advanced aspects of UNIX since its inception.

man page

netstat - 9

man page

ifconfig - 9

man page

route - 9

route

The information displayed with **netstat** is the routing tables for your system. Some are automatically created with the **ifconfig** command when your system is booted or when the network interface is initialized. Routes to networks and hosts that are not directly connected to your system are entered with the **route** command.

Your system administrator can make routing changes on the fly, as I did to change the Flags from U to UG:

$ /usr/sbin/route add default 128.185.61.1 3

First is the **route** command. Second, we specify that we wish to add a route; the other option is to delete a route. Third, we specify the destination, in this case, the default. This could be a specific host name, a network name, an IP address, or default that signifies the wildcard gateway route that is shown in our example. Fourth is the gateway through which the destination is reached. In the above example, the IP address was used, but this could also be a host name. The 3 corresponds to the count that is used to specify whether the gateway is the local host or a remote gateway. If the gateway is the local host, then a count of 0 is used. If the gateway is a remote host, which is the case in the example, a count of >0 is used. This corresponds to UG for Flags. This manually changed the network routing table by adding a default route with the appropriate Flags. Issuing this command fixed the problem I encountered trying to get system1 to talk to the systems on the other side of the router (remember Figure 9-10?).

Before issuing **/usr/sbin/route** with the **add** option, you can first use the **delete** option to remove the existing default route, which is not working.

route commands usually appear in one of the system's startup files so that every time the system boots, **route** commands are issued. This ensures that the right connectivity information is in place every time the system starts.

ifconfig

man page

ifconfig - 9

The **ifconfig** command provides additional information on a LAN interface. The following example provides the configuration of a network interface:

$ /etc/ifconfig lan0
lan0:   flags=863<UP,BROADCAST,NOTRAILERS,RUNNING>
        inet 128.185.61.2 netmask ffff0000 broadcast 128.185.61.255

From this example, we can quickly see that the interface is up, it has an address of 128.185.61.2, and it has a netmask of ffff0000. Again, keep in mind that your network interface may have a different name, such as **le0**.

You can use **ifconfig** to get the status of a network interface as I have done here to assign an address to a network interface, or to configure network interface parameters. The network address you have falls into classes such as "A," "B," or "C," as mentioned earlier. You want to be sure that you know the class of your network before you start configuring your LAN interface. This example is a class "B" network, so the netmask is defined as ffff0000 (typical for a class "B" address), as opposed to ffffff00, which is typical for a class "C" network. The netmask is used to determine how much of the address to reserve for subdividing the network into smaller networks. The netmask can be represented in hex, as shown above, or in decimal format, as in the **/etc/hosts** file. Here is the **ifconfig** command I issued to configure the interface:

$ /etc/ifconfig lan0 inet 128.185.61.2 netmask 255.255.0.0

- The 255.255.0.0 corresponds to the hex ffff000 shown earlier for the class "B" subnet mask.

- **lan0** is the interface being configured.

- **inet** is the address family, which is currently the only one supported for this system.

- **128.185.61.2** is the address of the LAN interface for system1.

- **netmask** shows how to subdivide the network.

- **255.255.0.0** is the same as ffff0000, which is the netmask for a class "B" address.

man page

netstat - 9

man page

ping - 9

man page

ifconfig - 9

man page

route - 9

I have made good use of **netstat, ping**, and **ifconfig** to help get the status of the network. **ifconfig, route**, and **/etc/hosts** are used to configure the network, should you identify changes you need to make. The subnet examples show how flexible you can be when configuring your network for both your current and future needs. In simple networks, you may not need to use many of these commands or complex subnetting. In complex networks, or at times when you encounter configuration difficulties, you may have to make extensive use of these commands. In either case, network planning is an important part of setting up UNIX systems.

Most of the commands used throughout this chapter are more a part of your system administrator's toolbox than they are of your toolbox. Networking is so vital to the use of UNIX systems, however, that having background in this area can help with your overall understanding of the system and how to use it more effectively.

rpcinfo

man page

rpcinfo - 9

man page

rcp - 9

As a user, you may have a need to NFS mount a directory on another system or perform some other function that you haven't before used on your system. You can determine whether indeed your system administrator has enabled some functionality that you need by evaluating the daemons running on your system. **rpcinfo** allows you to generate a Remote Procedure Call (RPC) on a system, including your local system, by issuing the command **rpc -p** *system_name*.

The following example shows issuing **rpcinfo -p** on our local system:

```
# rpcinfo -p
   program vers proto    port
    100000   2   tcp     111  portmapper
    100000   2   udp     111  portmapper
    100024   1   udp     777  status
    100024   1   tcp     779  status
    100021   1   tcp     783  nlockmgr
    100021   1   udp    1035  nlockmgr
    100021   3   tcp     787  nlockmgr
    100021   3   udp    1036  nlockmgr
    100020   1   udp    1037  llockmgr
    100020   1   tcp     792  llockmgr
    100021   2   tcp     795  nlockmgr
    100068   2   udp    1040  cmsd
    100068   3   udp    1040  cmsd
    100068   4   udp    1040  cmsd
    100068   5   udp    1040  cmsd
    100083   1   tcp    1036  ttdbserver
    100005   1   udp     976  mountd
    100005   1   tcp     978  mountd
    100003   2   udp    2049  nfs
    150001   1   udp    1003  pcnfsd
    150001   2   udp    1003  pcnfsd
    150001   1   tcp    1006  pcnfsd
    150001   2   tcp    1006  pcnfsd
#
```

Many daemons are running on the system that are important to the functionality I like to use. **mountd** is running, which indicates that a server could NFS mount file systems on this computer. There is other setup required for the mount to take place, but at least the daemon is running to support this functionality. In addition, **pcnfsd** is running, meaning that we have support for Windows-based NFS access.

Manual Pages of Some Commands Used in Chapter 9

The following are the HP-UX manual pages for many of the commands used in the chapter. Commands often differ among UNIX variants, so you may find differences in the options or other areas for some commands, however; the following manual pages serve as an excellent reference.

ftp

ftp - Interface for file transfer program.

man page

ftp - 9

```
ftp(1)                                                              ftp(1)

NAME
     ftp - file transfer program

SYNOPSIS

     ftp [-g] [-i] [-n] [-v] [-B size] [server-host]

DESCRIPTION
     ftp is a user interface to the File Transfer Protocol.  ftp copies
     files over a network connection between the local ``client'' host and
     a remote ``server'' host.  ftp runs on the client host.

  Options
     The ftp command supports the following options:

          -g   Disable file name ``globbing''; see the glob command, below.
               By default, when this option is not specified, globbing is
               enabled.

          -i   Disable interactive prompting by multiple-file commands; see
               the prompt command, below.  By default, when this option is
               not specified, prompting is enabled.

          -n   Disable ``auto-login''; see the open command, below.  By
               default, when this option is not specified, auto-login is
               enabled.

          -v   Enable verbose output; see the verbose command, below.  If
               this option is not specified, ftp displays verbose output
               only if the standard input is associated with a terminal.

          -B   Set the buffer size of the data socket to size blocks of
               1024 bytes. The valid range for size is an integer from 1 to
               64 (default is 56).
               Note: A large buffer size will improve the performance of
               ftp on fast links (e.g., FDDI), but may cause long
               connection times on slow links (e.g., X.25).

     The name of the server host that ftp communicates with can be
     specified on the command line.  If the server host is specified, ftp
     immediately opens a connection to the server host; see the open
     command, below.  Otherwise, ftp waits for commands from the user.

     File Transfer Protocol specifies file transfer parameters for type,
     mode, form, and struct.  ftp supports the ASCII, binary, and tenex
     File Transfer Protocol types.  ASCII is the default FTP type.  (It
     should be noted though that, whenever ftp establishes a connection
     between two similar systems, it switches automatically to the more
     efficient binary type.) ftp supports only the default values for the
     file transfer parameters mode which defaults to stream, form which
     defaults to non-print, and struct which defaults to file.
```

COMMANDS

ftp supports the following commands. Command arguments with embedded spaces must be enclosed in quotes (for example, "argument with embedded spaces").

![command [args]]
Invoke a shell on the local host. The SHELL environment variable specifies which shell program to invoke. ftp invokes /usr/bin/sh if SHELL is undefined. If command is specified, the shell executes it and returns to ftp. Otherwise, an interactive shell is invoked. When the shell terminates, it returns to ftp.

$ macro-name [args]
Execute the macro macro-name that was defined with the macdef command. Arguments are passed to the macro unglobbed.

account [passwd]
Supply a supplemental password required by a remote system for access to resources once a login has been successfully completed. If no argument is included, the user is prompted for an account password in a non-echoing input mode.

append local-file [remote-file]
Copy local-file to the end of remote-file. If remote-file is left unspecified, the local file name is used in naming the remote file after being altered by any ntrans or nmap setting.

ascii
Set the file transfer type to network ASCII. This is the default type.

bell Sound a bell after each file transfer completes.

binary
Set the file transfer type to binary.

bye Close the connection to the server host if a connection was open, and exit. Typing an end-of-file (EOF) character also terminates and exits the session.

case Toggle remote computer file name case mapping during mget commands. When case is on (the default is off), remote computer file names with all letters in uppercase are written in the local directory with the letters mapped to lowercase.

cd remote-directory
Set the working directory on the server host to remote-directory.

cdup Set the working directory on the server host to the parent of the current remote working directory.

chmod mode file-name
Change the permission modes of the file file-name on the remote system to mode.

close
Terminate the connection to the server host. The close command does not exit ftp. Any defined macros are erased.

cr   Toggle carriage return stripping during ascii type file retrieval. Records are denoted by a carriage-return/line-feed sequence during ascii type file transfer. When cr is on (the default), carriage returns are stripped from this sequence to conform with the UNIX single line-feed record delimiter. Records on non-UNIX remote systems may contain single line-feeds; when an

ascii type transfer is made, these line-feeds can be
distinguished from a record delimiter only when cr is off.

delete remote-file
Delete remote-file. The remote-file can be an empty directory.
No globbing is done.

dir [remote-directory] [local-file]
Write a remote-directory listing to standard output or optionally
to local-file. If neither remote-directory nor local-file is
specified, list the remote working directory to standard output.
If interactive prompting is on, ftp prompts the user to verify
that the last argument is indeed the target file for dir output.
Globbing characters are always expanded.

disconnect
A synonym for close.

form format
Set the file transfer form to format. The only supported format
is non-print

get remote-file [local-file]
Copy remote-file to local-file. If local-file is unspecified,
ftp uses the specified remote-file name as the local-file name,
subject to alteration by the current case, ntrans, and nmap
settings.

glob Toggle file name globbing. When file name globbing is enabled,
ftp expands csh(1) metacharacters in file and directory names.
These characters are *, ?, [,], ~, {, and }. The server host
expands remote file and directory names. Globbing metacharacters
are always expanded for the ls and dir commands. If globbing is
enabled, metacharacters are also expanded for the multiple-file
commands mdelete, mdir, mget, mls, and mput.

hash Toggle printing of a hash-sign (#) for each 1024 bytes
transferred.

help [command]
Print an informative message about the ftp command called ftp-
command. If ftp-command is unspecified, print a list of all ftp
commands.

idle [seconds]
Set the inactivity timer on the remote server to seconds seconds.
If seconds is omitted, ftp prints the current inactivity timer.

lcd [local-directory]
Set the local working directory to local-directory. If local-
directory is unspecified, set the local working directory to the
user's local home directory.

ls [remote-directory] [local-file]
Write a listing of remote-directory to local-file. The listing
includes any system-dependent information that the server chooses
to include; for example, most UNIX systems produce output from
the command ls -l (see also nlist). If neither remote-directory
nor local-file is specified, list the remote working directory.
If globbing is enabled, globbing metacharacters are expanded.

macdef macro-name
Define a macro. Subsequent lines are stored as the macro macro-
name; an empty input line terminates macro input mode. There is
a limit of 16 macros and 4096 total characters in all defined

macros. Macros remain defined until a close command is executed.
The macro processor interprets $ and \ as special characters. A
$ followed by a number (or numbers) is replaced by the
corresponding argument on the macro invocation command line. A $
followed by an i signals to the macro processor that the
executing macro is to be looped. On the first pass $i is
replaced by the first argument on the macro invocation command
line, on the second pass it is replaced by the second argument,
and so on. A \ followed by any character is replaced by that
character. Use the \ to prevent special treatment of the $.

mdelete [remote-files]
        Delete remote-files. If globbing is enabled, globbing
        metacharacters are expanded.

mdir remote-files local-file
        Write a listing of remote-files to local-file. If globbing is
        enabled, globbing metacharacters are expanded. If interactive
        prompting is on, ftp prompts the user to verify that the last
        argument is indeed the target local file for mdir output.

mget remote-files
        Copy remote-files to the local system. If globbing is enabled,
        globbing metacharacters are expanded. The resulting local file
        names are processed according to case, ntrans, and nmap settings.

mkdir directory-name
        Create remote directory-name.

mls remote-files local-file
        Write an abbreviated listing of remote-files to local-file. If
        globbing is enabled, globbing metacharacters are expanded. If
        interactive prompting is on, ftp prompts the user to verify that
        the last argument is indeed the target local file for mls output.

mode [mode-name]
        Set the FTP file transfer mode to mode-name. The only supported
        mode is stream.

modtime remote-file
        Show the last modification time of remote-file.

mput local-files
        Copy local-files from the local system to the remote system. The
        remote files have the same name as the local files processed
        according to ntrans and nmap settings. If globbing is enabled,
        globbing characters are expanded.

newer file-name
        Get the file only if the modification time of the remote file is
        more recent that the file on the current system. If the file
        does not exist on the current system, the remote file is
        considered newer. Otherwise, this command is identical to get.

nlist [remote-directory] [local-file]
        Write an abbreviated listing of remote-directory to local-file.
        If remote-directory is left unspecified, the current working
        directory is used. If interactive prompting is on, ftp prompts
        the user to verify that the last argument is indeed the target
        local file for nlist output.

nmap [inpattern outpattern]
        Set or unset the filename mapping mechanism. If no arguments are

specified, the filename mapping mechanism is unset. If arguments
are specified, remote filenames are mapped during mput commands
and put commands issued without a specified remote target
filename. If arguments are specified, local filenames are mapped
during mget commands and get commands issued without a specified
local target filename. This command is useful when connecting to
a non-UNIX remote computer with different file naming conventions
or practices. The mapping follows the pattern set by inpattern
and outpattern. inpattern is a template for incoming filenames
(which may have already been processed according to the ntrans
and case settings). Variable templating is accomplished by
including the sequences $1, $2, ..., $9 in inpattern. Use \ to
prevent this special treatment of the $ character. All other
characters are treated literally, and are used to determine the
nmap inpattern variable values. For example, given inpattern
$1.$2 and the remote file name mydata.data, $1 would have the
value mydata, and $2 would have the value data. The outpattern
determines the resulting mapped filename. The sequences $1,
$2, ..., $9 are replaced by any value resulting from the
inpattern template. The sequence $0 is replaced by the original
filename. Additionally, the sequence [seq1,seq2] is replaced by
seq1 if seq1 is not a null string; otherwise it is replaced by
seq2. For example, the command nmap $1.$2.$3 [$1,$2].[$2,file]
would yield the output filename myfile.data for input filenames
myfile.data and myfile.data.old, myfile.file for the input
filename myfile, and myfile.myfile for the input filename
.myfile. Spaces can be included in outpattern, as in the
example: nmap $1 | sed "s/ *$//" > $1 . Use the \ character to
prevent special treatment of the $, [,], and , characters.

ntrans [inchars [outchars]]
    Set or unset the filename character translation mechanism. If no
    arguments are specified, the filename character translation
    mechanism is unset. If arguments are specified, characters in
    remote filenames are translated during mput commands and put
    commands issued without a specified remote target filename. If
    arguments are specified, characters in local filenames are
    translated during mget commands and get commands issued without a
    specified local target filename. This command is useful when
    connecting to a non-UNIX remote computer with different file
    naming conventions or practices. Characters in a filename
    matching a character in inchars are replaced with the
    corresponding character in outchars. If the character's position
    in inchars is longer than the length of outchars, the character
    is deleted from the file name.

open server-host [port-number]
    Establish a connection to server-host, using port-number (if
    specified). If auto-login is enabled, ftp attempts to log into
    the server host.

prompt
    Toggle interactive prompting. By default, ftp prompts the user
    for a yes or no response for each output file during multiple-
    file commands. If interactive prompting is disabled, ftp
    performs the command for all specified files.

proxy ftp-command
    Execute an ftp command on a secondary control connection. This
    command allows simultaneous connection to two remote FTP servers
    for transferring files between the two servers. The first proxy
    command should be an open, to establish the secondary control
    connection. Enter the command proxy ? to see other FTP commands
    executable on the secondary connection. The following commands
    behave differently when prefaced by proxy: open does not define
    new macros during the auto-login process, close does not erase

existing macro definitions, get and mget transfer files from the
host on the primary control connection to the host on the
secondary control connection, and put, mput, and append transfer
files from the host on the secondary control connection to the
host on the primary control connection. Third party file
transfers depend upon support of the FTP protocol PASV command by
the server on the secondary control connection.

put local-file [remote-file]
    Copy local-file to remote-file. If remote-file is unspecified,
    ftp assigns the local-file name, processed according to any
    ntrans or nmap settings, to the remote-file name.

pwd Write the name of the remote working directory to stdout.

quit A synonym for bye.

quote arguments
    Send arguments, verbatim, to the server host. See ftpd(1M).

recv remote-file [local-file]
    A synonym for get.

reget remote-file [local-file]
    reget acts like get, except that if local-file exists and is
    smaller than remote-file, local-file is presumed to be a
    partially transferred copy of remote-file and the transfer is
    continued from the apparent point of failure. This command is
    useful when transferring very large files over networks that tend
    to drop connections.

rhelp [command-name]
    Request help from the server host. If command-name is specified,
    supply it to the server. See ftpd(1M).

rstatus [file-name]
    With no arguments, show status of remote machine. If file-name
    is specified, show status of file-name on remote machine.

rename remote-from remote-to
    Rename remote-from, which can be either a file or a directory, to
    remote-to.

reset
    Clear reply queue. This command re-synchronizes command/reply
    sequencing with the remote FTP server. Resynchronization may be
    necessary following a violation of the FTP protocol by the remote
    server.

restart marker
    Restart the immediately following get or put at the indicated
    marker. On UNIX systems, marker is usually a byte offset into
    the file.

rmdir remote-directory
    Delete remote-directory. remote-directory must be an empty
    directory.

runique
    Toggle storing of files on the local system with unique
    filenames. If a file already exists with a name equal to the
    target local filename for a get or mget command, a .1 is appended
    to the name. If the resulting name matches another existing
    file, a .2 is appended to the original name. If this process
    continues up to .99, an error message is printed, and the
    transfer does not take place. ftp reports the unique filename.

Note that runique does not affect local files generated from a
shell command (see below). The default value is off.

send local-file [remote-file]
     A synonym for put.

sendport
     Toggle the use of PORT commands. By default, ftp attempts to use
     a PORT command when establishing a connection for each data
     transfer. If the PORT command fails, ftp uses the default data
     port. When the use of PORT commands is disabled, ftp makes no
     attempt to use PORT commands for each data transfer. This is
     useful for certain FTP implementations that ignore PORT commands
     but (incorrectly) indicate that they've been accepted. See
     ftpd(1M). Turning sendport off may cause delays in the execution
     of commands.

site arguments
     Send arguments, verbatim, to the server host as a SITE command.
     See ftpd(1M).

size remote-file
     Show the size of remote-file.

status
     Show the current status of ftp.

struct [struct-name]
     Set the FTP file transfer struct to struct-name. The only
     supported struct is file.

sunique
     Toggle storing of files on remote machine under unique file
     names. The remote server reports the unique name. By default,
     sunique is off.

system
     Show the type of operating system running on the remote machine.

tenex
     Set the FTP file transfer type to tenex.

type [type-name]
     Set the FTP file transfer type to type-name. If type-name is
     unspecified, write the current type to stdout. Ascii, binary,
     and tenex are the types currently supported.

umask [newmask]
     Set the default umask on the remote server to newmask. If
     newmask is omitted, the current umask is printed.

user user-name [password] [account]
     Log into the server host on the current connection, which must
     already be open. A .netrc file in the user's local home
     directory can provide the user-name, password, and optionally the
     account; see netrc(4). Otherwise ftp prompts the user for this
     information. The HP-UX FTP server does not require an account.
     For security reasons, ftp always requires a password. It does
     not log into remote accounts that do not have a password.

verbose
     Toggle verbose output. If verbose output is enabled, ftp
     displays responses from the server host, and when a file transfer
     completes it reports statistics regarding the efficiency of the
     transfer.

? [command]
>   A synonym for the help command. Prints the help information for
>   the specified command.

Aborting A File Transfer
>   To abort a file transfer, use the terminal interrupt key (usually
>   Ctrl-C). Sending transfers are halted immediately. ftp halts
>   incoming (receive) transfers by first sending a FTP protocol ABOR
>   command to the remote server, then discarding any further received
>   data. The speed at which this is accomplished depends upon the remote
>   server's support for ABOR processing. If the remote server does not
>   support the ABOR command, an ftp> prompt does not appear until the
>   remote server completes sending the requested file.
>
>   The terminal interrupt key sequence is ignored while ftp awaits a
>   reply from the remote server. A long delay in this mode may result
>   from the ABOR processing described above, or from unexpected behavior
>   by the remote server, including violations of the FTP protocol. If
>   the delay results from unexpected remote server behavior, the local
>   ftp program must be killed manually.

File Naming Conventions
>   Files specified as arguments to ftp commands are processed according
>   to the following rules.

- If the file name - is specified, ftp uses the standard input (for
  reading) or standard output (for writing).

- If the first character of the file name is |, ftp interprets the
  remainder of the argument as a shell command. ftp forks a shell,
  using popen() (see popen(3S)) with the supplied argument, and reads
  (writes) from standard output (standard input). If the shell
  command includes spaces, the argument must be quoted, as in:

      "| ls -lt".

  A particularly useful example of this mechanism is:

      "| dir . | more".

- Otherwise, if globbing is enabled, ftp expands local file names
  according to the rules used by the C shell (see csh(1)); see the
  glob command, below. If the ftp command expects a single local
  file (e.g. put), only the first filename generated by the globbing
  operation is used.

- For mget commands and get commands with unspecified local file
  names, the local filename is named the same as the remote filename,
  which may be altered by a case, ntrans, or nmap setting. The
  resulting filename may then be altered if runique is on.

- For mput commands and put commands with unspecified remote file
  names, the remote filename is named the same as the local filename,
  which may be altered by a ntrans or nmap setting. The resulting
  filename may then be altered by the remote server if sunique is on.

WARNINGS
>   Correct execution of many commands depends upon proper behavior by the
>   remote server.

AUTHOR
     ftp was developed by the University of California, Berkeley.

SEE ALSO
     csh(1), rcp(1), ftpd(1M), netrc(4), ftpusers(4), hosts(4).

ifconfig

man page

ifconfig - 9

ifconfig - Display or configure network interface parameters.

```
ifconfig(1M)                                              ifconfig(1M)

NAME
     ifconfig - configure network interface parameters

SYNOPSIS

     ifconfig interface address_family [address [dest_address]] [parameters]

     ifconfig interface [address_family]

DESCRIPTION
     The first form of the ifconfig command assigns an address to a network
     interface and/or configures network interface parameters.  ifconfig
     must be used at boot time to define the network address of each
     interface present on a machine.  It can also be used at other times to
     redefine an interface's address or other operating parameters.

     The second form of the command, without address_family, displays the
     current configuration for interface.  If address_family is also
     specified, ifconfig reports only the details specific to that address
     family.

     Only a user with appropriate privileges can modify the configuration
     of a network interface.  All users can run the second form of the
     command.

  Arguments
     ifconfig recognizes the following arguments:

          address          Either a host name present in the host name
                           database (see hosts(4)), or a DARPA Internet
                           address expressed in Internet standard dot
                           notation (see inet(3N)).  The host number can be
                           omitted on 10MB/second Ethernet interfaces (which
                           use the hardware physical address), and on
                           interfaces other than the first.

          address_family   Name of protocol on which naming scheme is based.
                           An interface can receive transmissions in
                           differing protocols, each of which may require
                           separate naming schemes.  Therefore, it is
                           necessary to specify the address_family, which
                           may affect interpretation of the remaining
                           parameters on the command line.  The only address
                           family currently supported is inet (DARPA-
                           Internet family).

          dest_address     Address of destination system.  Consists of
                           either a host name present in the host name
                           database (see hosts(4)), or a DARPA Internet
                           address expressed in Internet standard dot
                           notation (see inet(3N)).

          interface        A string of the form nameunit, such as lan0.
```

(See the LAN Card Numbering subsection.)

parameters   One or more of the following operating
                parameters:

        up   Mark an interface "up". Enables
                        interface after an ifconfig down.
                        Occurs automatically when setting
                        the address on an interface.
                        Setting this flag has no effect if
                        the hardware is "down".

        down   Mark an interface "down". When an
                        interface is marked "down", the
                        system will not attempt to
                        transmit messages through that
                        interface. If possible, the
                        interface will be reset to disable
                        reception as well. This action
                        does not automatically disable
                        routes using the interface.

        broadcast   (Inet only) Specify the address
                        that represents broadcasts to the
                        network. The default broadcast
                        address is the address with a host
                        part of all 1's.

        debug   Enable driver-dependent debugging
                        code. This usually turns on extra
                        console error logging.

        -debug   Disable driver-dependent debugging
                        code.

        ipdst   (NS only) This is used to specify
                        an Internet host that is willing
                        to receive IP packets
                        encapsulating NS packets bound for
                        a remote network. In this case,
                        an apparent point-to-point link is
                        constructed, and the address
                        specified is taken as the NS
                        address and network of the
                        destination.

        metric n   Set the routing metric of the
                        interface to n. The default is 0.
                        The routing metric is used by the
                        routing protocol (see gated(1m)).
                        Higher metrics have the effect of
                        making a route less favorable;
                        metrics are counted as additional
                        hops to the destination network or
                        host.

        netmask mask   (Inet only) Specify how much of
                        the address to reserve for
                        subdividing networks into sub-
                        networks or aggregating networks
                        into supernets. mask can be
                        specified as a single hexadecimal
                        number with a leading 0x, with a
                        dot-notation Internet address, or
                        with a pseudo-network name listed
                        in the network table (see

networks(4)). For subdividing
networks into sub-networks, mask
must include the network part of
the local address, and the subnet
part which is taken from the host
field of the address. mask must
contain 1's in the bit positions
in the 32-bit address that are to
be used for the network and subnet
parts, and 0's in the host part.
The 1's in the mask must be
contiguous starting from the
leftmost bit position in the 32-
bit field. mask must contain at
least the standard network
portion, and the subnet field must
be contiguous with the network
portion. The subnet field must
contain at least 2 bits. The
subnet part after performing a
bit-wise AND operation between the
address and the mask must not
contain all 0's or all 1's. For
aggregating networks into
supernets, mask must only include
a portion of the network part.
mask must contain contiguous 1's
in the bit positions starting from
the leftmost bit of the 32-bit
field.

trailers   Request the use of a "trailer"
                      link-level encapsulation when
                      sending. If a network interface
                      supports trailers, the system
                      will, when possible, encapsulate
                      outgoing messages in a manner that
                      minimizes the number of memory-
                      to-memory copy operations
                      performed by the receiver. On
                      networks that support the Address
                      Resolution Protocol, this flag
                      indicates that the system should
                      request that other systems use
                      trailers when sending to this
                      host. Similarly, trailer
                      encapsulations will be sent to
                      other hosts that have made such
                      requests. Currently used by
                      Internet protocols only. See
                      WARNINGS section.

-trailers   Disable the use of a "trailer"
                      link-level encapsulation
                      (default).

LAN Card Numbering
    The name of an interface associated with a LAN card is lan, and its
    unitnumber is determined as follows. The LAN card installed first in
    the system is given interface unit number 0; the next LAN card
    installed is given interface unit number 1; and so on. When there are
    two or more LAN cards installed at the same time, interface unit
    numbers are assigned according to card positions in the backplane:
    the LAN card that appears "first" in the backplane is given the
    interface unit number N; the next LAN card in the backplane is given
    the number N+1.

The lanscan command can be used to display the name and unit number of
each interface that is associated with a LAN card (see lanscan(1M)).

Supernets
 A supernet is a collection of smaller networks. Supernetting is a
 technique of using the netmask to aggregate a collection of smaller
 networks into a supernet. This technique is particularly useful for
 class C networks. A Class C network can only have 254 hosts. This
 can be too restrictive for some companies. For these companies, a
 netmask that only contains a portion of the network part can be
 applied to the hosts in these class C networks to form a supernet.
 This supernet netmask should be applied to those interfaces that
 connect to the supernet using the ifconfig command. For example, a
 host can configure its interface to connect to a class C supernet,
 192.6, by configuring an IP address of 192.6.1.1 and a netmask of
 255.255.0.0 to its interface.

DIAGNOSTICS
 Messages indicate if the specified interface does not exist, the
 requested address is unknown, or the user is not privileged and tried
 to alter an interface's configuration.

WARNINGS
 Currently, all HP 9000 systems can receive trailer packets but do not
 send them. Setting the trailers flag has no effect.

SEE ALSO
 netstat(1), lanconfig(1m), lanscan(1m) hosts(4), routing(7).

netstat

netstat - Display statistics related to networking.

```
netstat(1)                                                              netstat(1)

NAME
     netstat - show network status

SYNOPSIS
     netstat [-aAn] [-f address-family] [system [core]]
     netstat [-mMnrsv] [-f address-family] [-p protocol] [system [core]]
     netstat [-gin] [-I interface] [interval] [system [core]]

DESCRIPTION
     netstat displays statistics for network interfaces and protocols, as
     well as the contents of various network-related data structures.  The
     output format varies according to the options selected.  Some options
     are ignored when used in combination with other options.

     Generally, the netstat command takes one of the three forms shown
     above:

          -  The first form of the command displays a list of active
             sockets for each protocol.

          -  The second form displays the contents of one of the other
             network data structures according to the option selected.

          -  The third form displays configuration information for each
             network interface.  It also displays network traffic data on
             configured network interfaces, optionally updated at each
             interval, measured in seconds.

     Options are interpreted as follows:

          -a                      Show the state of all sockets, including
                                  passive sockets used by server processes.  When
                                  netstat is used without any options (except -A
                                  and -n), only active sockets are shown.  This
                                  option does not show the state of X.25
                                  programmatic access sockets.  The option is
                                  ignored if the -g, -i, -I, -m, -M, -p, -r, -s
                                  or interval option is specified.

          -A                      Show the address of the protocol control block
                                  associated with sockets.  This option is used
                                  for debugging.  It does not show the X.25
                                  programmatic access control blocks.  This
                                  option is ignored if the -g, -i, -I, -m, -M,
                                  -p, -r, -s or interval option is specified.

          -f address-family Show statistics or address control block for
                                  only the specified address-family.  The
                                  following address families are recognized: inet
                                  for AF_INET, and unix for AF_UNIX.  This option
```

applies to the -a, -A and -s options.

-g   Show multicast information for network
              interfaces. Only the address family AF_INET is
              recognized by this option. This option may be
              combined with the -i option to display both
              kinds of information. The option is ignored if
              the -m, -M or -p option is specified.

-i   Show the state of network interfaces.
              Interfaces that are statically configured into
              a system, but not located at boot time, are not
              shown. This option is ignored if the -m, -M or
              -p option is specified.

-I interface Show information about the specified interface
              only. This option applies to the -g and -i
              options.

-m   Show statistics recorded by network memory
              management routines. If this option is
              specified, all other options are ignored.

-M   Show the multicast routing tables. When -s is
              used with the -M option, netstat displays
              multicast routing statistics instead. This
              option is ignored if the -m or -p option is
              specified.

-n   Show network addresses as numbers. Normally,
              netstat interprets addresses and attempts to
              display them symbolically. This option applies
              to the -a, -A, -i, -r and -v options.

-p protocol   Show statistics for the specified protocol.
              The following protocols are recognized: tcp,
              udp, ip, icmp, igmp, arp, and probe. This
              option is ignored if the -m option is
              specified.

-r   Show the routing tables. When -v is used with
              the -r option, netstat also displays the
              network masks in the route entries. When -s is
              used with the -r option, netstat displays
              routing statistics instead. This option is
              ignored if the -g, -m, -M, -i, -I, -p or
              interval option is specified.

-s   Show statistics for all protocols. When this
              option is used with the -r option, netstat
              displays routing statistics instead. When this
              option is used with the -M option, netstat
              displays multicast routing statistics instead.
              This option is ignored if the -g, -i, -I, -m,
              -p or interval option is specified.

-v   Show additional routing information. When -v
              is used with the -r option, netstat also
              displays the network masks in the route
              entries. This option only applies to the -r
              option.

The arguments system and core allow substitutes for the defaults,
/stand/vmunix and /dev/kmem.

If no options or only the -A or -n option is specified, netstat

displays the status of only active sockets. The display of active and
passive sockets status shows the local and remote addresses, send and
receive queue sizes (in bytes), protocol, and the internal state of
the protocol. Address formats are of the form host.port, or
network.port if the host portion of a socket address is zero. When
known, the host and network addresses are displayed symbolically by
using gethostbyname() and getnetbyname(), respectively (see
gethostbyname(3N) and getnetbyname(3N)). If a symbolic name for an
address is unknown, or if the -n option is specified, the address is
displayed numerically according to the address family. For more
information regarding the Internet ``dot format'', refer to inet(3N).
Unspecified or ``wildcard'' addresses and ports appear as an asterisk
(*).

The interface display provides a table of cumulative statistics
regarding packets transferred, errors, and collisions. The network
addresses of the interface and the maximum transmission unit (MTU) are
also displayed. When the interval argument is specified, netstat
displays a running count of statistics related to network interfaces.
This display consists of a column for the primary interface (the first
interface found during auto-configuration) and a column summarizing
information for all interfaces. To replace the primary interface with
another interface, use the -I option. The first line of each screen
of information contains a summary since the system was last rebooted.
Subsequent lines of output show values accumulated over the preceding
interval.

The routing table display indicates the available routes and their
status. Each route consists of a destination host or network, a
netmask and a gateway to use in forwarding packets. The Flags field
shows whether the route is up (U), whether the route is to a gateway
(G), whether the route is a host or network route (with or without H),
whether the route was created dynamically (D) by a redirect or by Path
MTU Discovery, and whether a gateway route has been modified (M), or
it has been marked doubtful (?) due to the lack of a timely ARP
response.

The Netmask field shows the mask to be applied to the destination IP
address of an IP packet to be forwarded. The result will be compared
with the destination address in the route entry. If they are the same,
then the route is one of the candidates for routing this IP packet.
If there are several candidate routes, then the route with the longest
Netmask field (contiguous 1's starting from the leftmost bit position)
will be chosen. (see routing (7).)

The Gateway field shows the address of the immediate gateway for
reaching the destination. It can be the address of the outgoing
interface if the destination is on a directly connected network.

The Refs field shows the current number of active uses of the route.
Connection-oriented protocols normally hold on to a single route for
the duration of a connection, while connectionless protocols normally
obtain a route just while sending a particular message. The Use field
shows a count of the number of packets sent using the route. The
Interface field identifies which network interface is used for the
route.

The Pmtu and PmtuTime fields apply only to host routes. The Pmtu
field for network and default routes is the same as the MTU of the
network interface used for the route. If the route is created with a
static PMTU value (see route(1M)), the corresponding PmtuTime field
contains the word perm, and the PMTU value permanently overrides the
interface MTU. If the route is created dynamically (D in the Flags
field), the value in the corresponding PmtuTime field is the number of
minutes remaining before the PMTU expires. When the PMTU expires, the
system rediscovers the current PMTU for the route, in case it has

changed. The PmtuTime field is left blank when the PMTU is identical
to the MTU of the interface. An asterisk (*) in the Pmtu field
indicates that user has disabled the PMTU Discovery for the route.

DEPENDENCIES
    X.25:
      -A and -a options do not list X.25 programmatic access information.

AUTHOR
    netstat was developed by the University of California, Berkeley.

SEE ALSO
    hosts(4), networks(4), gethostbyname(3N), getnetbyname(3N),
    protocols(4), route(1M), services(4).

ping

man page

ping - 9

ping - Send information over network and get response.

---

ping(1M)   ping(1M)

NAME
     ping - send ICMP Echo Request packets to network host

SYNOPSIS

     ping [-oprv] [-i address] [-t ttl] host [-n count]
     ping [-oprv] [-i address] [-t ttl] host packet-size [[-n] count]

DESCRIPTION
     The ping command sends ICMP Echo Request (ECHO_REQUEST) packets to
     host once per second. Each packet that is echoed back via an ICMP
     Echo Response packet is written to the standard output, including
     round-trip time.

     ICMP Echo Request datagrams ("pings") have an IP and ICMP header,
     followed by a struct timeval (see gettimeofday(2)) and an arbitrary
     number of "pad" bytes used to fill out the packet. The default
     datagram length is 64 bytes, but this can be changed by using the
     packet-size option.

   Options
     The following options and parameters are recognizaed by ping:

          -i address If host is a multicast address, send multicast
                      datagrams from the interface with the local IP
                      address specified by address in ``dot'' notation (see
                      inet_addr(3N)). If the -i option is not specified,
                      multicast datagrams are sent from the default
                      interface, which is determined by the route
                      configuration.

          -o   Insert an IP Record Route option in outgoing packets,
                      summarizing routes taken when the command terminates.

                      It may not be possible to get the round-trip path if
                      some hosts on the route taken do not implement the IP
                      Record Route option. A maximum of 9 Internet
                      addresses can be recorded due to the maximum length
                      of the IP option area.

          -p   The new Path MTU information is displayed when a ICMP
                      "Datagram Too Big" message is received from a
                      gateway. The -p option must be used in conjunction
                      with a large packetsize and with the -v option.

          -r   Bypass the normal routing tables and send directly to
                      a host on an attached network. If the host is not on
                      a directly-connected network, an error is returned.
                      This option can be used to ping the local system
                      through an interface that has no route through it,
                      such as after the interface was dropped by gated (see

gated(1M)).

-t ttl   If host is a multicast address, set the time-to-live field in the multicast datagram to ttl. This controls the scope of the multicast datagrams by specifying the maximum number of external systems through which the datagram can be forwarded.

     If ttl is zero, the datagram is restricted to the local system. If ttl is one, the datagram is restricted to systems that have an interface on the network directly connected to the interface specified by the -i option. If ttl is two, the datagram can forwarded through at most one multicast router; and so forth. Range: zero to 255. The default value is 1.

-v   Verbose output. Show ICMP packets other than Echo Responses that are received.

host   Destination to which the ICMP Echo Requests are sent. host can be a hostname or an Internet address. All symbolic names specified for host are looked up by using gethostbyname() (see gethostbyname(3N)). If host is an Internet address, it must be in "dot" notation (see inet_addr(3N)).

     If a system does not respond as expected, the route might be configured incorrectly on the local or remote system or on an intermediate gateway, or there might be some other network failure. Normally, host is the address assigned to a local or remote network interface.

     If host is a broadcast address, all systems that receive the broadcast should respond. Normally, these are only systems that have a network interface on the same network as the local interface sending the ICMP Echo Request.

     If host is a multicast address, only systems that have joined the multicast group should respond. These may be distant systems if the -t option is specified, and there is a multicast router on the network directly connected to the interface specified by the -i option.

packet-size   The size of the transmitted packet, in bytes. By default (when packet-size is not specified), the size of transmitted packets is 64 bytes. The minimum value allowed for packet-size is 8 bytes, and the maximum is 4095 bytes. If packet-size is smaller than 16 bytes, there is not enough room for timing information. In that case, the round-trip times are not displayed.

count   The number of packets ping will transmit before terminating. Range: zero to 2147483647. The default is zero, in which case ping sends packets until interrupted.

When using ping for fault isolation, first specify a local address for host to verify that the local network interface is working correctly. Then specify host and gateway addresses further and further away to determine the point of failure. ping sends one datagram per second, and it normally writes one line of output for every ICMP Echo Response

that is received. No output is produced if there are no responses.
If an optional count is given, only the specified number of requests
is sent. Round-trip times and packet loss statistics are computed.
When all responses have been received or the command times out (if the
count option is specified), or if the command is terminated with a
SIGINT, a brief summary is displayed.

This command is intended for use in testing, managing and measuring
network performance. It should be used primarily to isolate network
failures. Because of the load it could impose on the network, it is
considered discourteous to use ping unnecessarily during normal
operations or from automated scripts.

AUTHOR
      ping was developed in the Public Domain.

FILES
      /etc/hosts

SEE ALSO
      gethostbyname(3N), inet(3N).

rcp

rcp - Copy files and directories from one system to another.

man page

rcp - 9

rcp(1)   rcp(1)

NAME
     rcp - remote file copy

SYNOPSIS

  Copy Single File
    rcp [-p] source_file1 dest_file

  Copy Multiple Files
    rcp [-p] source_file1 [source_file2]... dest_dir

  Copy One or More Directory Subtrees
    rcp [-p] -r source_dir1 [source_dir2]... dest_dir

  Copy Files and Directory Subtrees
    rcp [-p] -r file_or_dir1 [file_or_dir2]... dest_dir

DESCRIPTION
     The rcp command copies files, directory subtrees, or a combination of
     files and directory subtrees from one or more systems to another. In
     many respects, it is similar to the cp command (see cp(1)).

     To use rcp, you must have read access to files being copied, and read
     and search (execute) permission on all directories in the directory
     path.

  Options and Arguments
    rcp recognizes the following options and arguments:

        source_file   The name of an existing file or directory on a
        source_dir   local or remote machine that you want copied to
                       the specified destination. Source file and
                       directory names are constructed as follows:

                            user_name@hostname:pathname/filename

                       or

                            user_name@hostname:pathname/dirname

                       Component parts of file and directory names are
                       described below. If multiple existing files
                       and/or directory subtrees are specified
                       (source_file1, source_file2, ..., etc.), the
                       destination must be a directory. Shell file name
                       expansion is allowed on both local and remote
                       systems. Multiple files and directory subtrees
                       can be copied from one or more systems to a single
                       destination directory with a single command.

        dest_file   The name of the destination file. If host name
                       and path name are not specified, the existing file

is copied into a file named dest_file in the current directory on the local system. If dest_file already exists and is writable, the existing file is overwritten. Destination file names are constructed the same way as source files except that file name expansion characters cannot be used.

dest_dir   The name of the destination directory. If host name and path name are not specified, the existing file is copied into a directory named dest_dir in the current directory on the local system. If dest_dir already exists in the specified directory path (or current directory if not specified), a new directory named dest_dir is created underneath the existing directory named dest_dir. Destination directory names are constructed the same way as source directory tree names except that file name expansion characters cannot be used.

file_or_dir   If a combination of files and directories are specified for copying (either explicitly or by file name expansion), only files are copied unless the -r option is specified. If the -r option is present, all files and directory subtrees whose names match the specified file_or_dir name are copied.

-p   Preserve (duplicate) modification times and modes (permissions) of source files, ignoring the current setting of the umask file creation mode mask. If this option is specified, rcp preserves the sticky bit only if the target user is superuser.

If the -p option is not specified, rcp preserves the mode and owner of dest_file if it already exists; otherwise rcp uses the mode of the source file modified by the umask on the destination host. Modification and access times of the destination file are set to the time when the copy was made.

-r   Recursively copy directory subtrees rooted at the source directory name. If any directory subtrees are to be copied, rcp recursively copies each subtree rooted at the specified source directory name to directory dest_dir. If source_dir is being copied to an existing directory of the same name, rcp creates a new directory source_dir within dest_dir and copies the subtree rooted at source_dir to dest_dir/source_dir. If dest_dir does not exist, rcp creates it and copies the subtree rooted at source_dir to dest_dir.

Constructing File and Directory Names

As indicated above, file and directory names contain one, two, or four component parts:

user_name   Login name to be used for accessing directories and files on remote system.

hostname   Hostname of remote system where directories and files are located.

pathname   Absolute directory path name or directory path name relative to the login directory of user user_name.

filename   Actual name of source or destination file. File name expansion is allowed on source file names.

dirname   Actual name of source or destination directory subtree. File name expansion is allowed on source directory names.

Each file or directory argument is either a remote file name of the form hostname:path, or a local file name (with a slash (/) before any colon (:)). hostname can be either an official host name or an alias (see hosts(4)). If hostname is of the form ruser@rhost, ruser is used on the remote host instead of the current user name. An unspecified path (that is, hostname:) refers to the remote user's login directory. If path does not begin with /, it is interpreted relative to the remote user's login directory on hostname. Shell metacharacters in remote paths can be quoted with backslash (\), single quotes (''), or double quotes (""), so that they will be interpreted remotely.

The rcp routine does not prompt for passwords. The current local user name or any user name specified via ruser must exist on rhost and allow remote command execution via remsh(1) and rcmd(3). remshd(1M) must be executable on the remote host.

Third-party transfers in the form:

        rcp ruser1@rhost1:path1 ruser2@rhost2:path2

are performed as:

        remsh rhost1 -l ruser1 rcp path1 ruser2@rhost2:path2

Therefore, for a such a transfer to succeed, ruser2 on rhost2 must allow access by ruser1 from rhost1 (see hosts.equiv(4)).

WARNINGS
        The rcp routine is confused by any output generated by commands in a .cshrc file on the remote host (see csh(1)).

        Copying a file onto itself, for example:

                rcp path `hostname`:path

        may produce inconsistent results. The current HP-UX version of rcp simply copies the file over itself. However, some implementations of rcp, including some earlier HP-UX implementations, corrupt the file. In addition, the same file may be referred to in multiple ways, for example, via hard links, symbolic links, or NFS. It is not guaranteed that rcp will correctly copy a file over itself in all cases.

        Implementations of rcp based on the 4.2BSD version (including the implementations of rcp prior to HP-UX 7.0) require that remote users be specified as rhost.ruser. If the first remote host specified in a third party transfer (rhost1 in the example below) uses this older syntax, the command must have the form:

                rcp ruser1@rhost1:path1 rhost2.ruser2:path2

        since the target is interpreted by rhost1. A common problem that is encountered is when two remote files are to be copied to a remote target that specifies a remote user. If the two remote source systems, rhost1 and rhost2, each expect a different form for the remote target, the command:

```
rcp rhost1:path1 rhost2:path2 rhost3.ruser3:path3
```

will certainly fail on one of the source systems. Perform such a
transfer using two separate commands.

AUTHOR
     rcp was developed by the University of California, Berkeley.

SEE ALSO
     cp(1), ftp(1), remsh(1), remshd(1M), rcmd(3), hosts(4),
     hosts.equiv(4).

     ftp chapter in Using Internet Services.

rcp(1)   Secure Internet Services with Kerberos Authentication   rcp(1)

NAME
     rcp - remote file copy

SYNOPSIS

   Copy Single File
     rcp [-k realm] [-P] [-p] source_file1 dest_file

   Copy Multiple Files
     rcp [-k realm] [-P] [-p] source_file1 [source_file2]... dest_dir

   Copy One or More Directory Subtrees
     rcp [-k realm] [-P] [-p] -r source_dir1 [source_dir2]... dest_dir

   Copy Files and Directory Subtrees
     rcp [-k realm] [-P] [-p] -r file_or_dir1 [file_or_dir2]... dest_dir

DESCRIPTION
     The rcp command copies files, directory subtrees, or a combination of
     files and directory subtrees from one or more systems to another. In
     many respects, it is similar to the cp command (see cp(1)).

     To use rcp, you must have read access to files being copied, and read
     and search (execute) permission on all directories in the directory
     path.

     In a Kerberos V5 Network Authentication environment, rcp uses the
     Kerberos V5 protocol while initiating the connection to a remote host.
     The authorization mechanism is dependent on the command line options
     used to invoke remshd on the remote host (i.e., -K, -R, -r, or -k).
     Kerberos authentication and authorization rules are described in the
     Secure Internet Services man page, sis(5).

     Although Kerberos authentication and authorization may apply, the
     Kerberos mechanism is not applied when copying files. The files are
     still transferred in cleartext over the network.

   Options and Arguments
     rcp recognizes the following options and arguments:

          source_file   The name of an existing file or directory on a
          source_dir   local or remote machine that you want copied to
                        the specified destination. Source file and
                        directory names are constructed as follows:

                             user_name@hostname:pathname/filename

                        or

user_name@hostname:pathname/dirname

Component parts of file and directory names are
described below. If multiple existing files
and/or directory subtrees are specified
(source_file1, source_file2, ..., etc.), the
destination must be a directory. Shell file name
expansion is allowed on both local and remote
systems. Multiple files and directory subtrees
can be copied from one or more systems to a single
destination directory with a single command.

dest_file   The name of the destination file. If host name
                 and path name are not specified, the existing file
                 is copied into a file named dest_file in the
                 current directory on the local system. If
                 dest_file already exists and is writable, the
                 existing file is overwritten. Destination file
                 names are constructed the same way as source files
                 except that file name expansion characters cannot
                 be used.

dest_dir   The name of the destination directory. If host
                 name and path name are not specified, the existing
                 file is copied into a directory named dest_dir in
                 the current directory on the local system. If
                 dest_dir already exists in the specified directory
                 path (or current directory if not specified), a
                 new directory named dest_dir is created underneath
                 the existing directory named dest_dir.
                 Destination directory names are constructed the
                 same way as source directory tree names except
                 that file name expansion characters cannot be
                 used.

file_or_dir   If a combination of files and directories are
                 specified for copying (either explicitly or by
                 file name expansion), only files are copied unless
                 the -r option is specified. If the -r option is
                 present, all files and directory subtrees whose
                 names match the specified file_or_dir name are
                 copied.

-k realm   Obtain tickets from the remote host in the
                 specified realm instead of the remote host's
                 default realm as specified in the configuration
                 file krb.realms.

-P   Disable Kerberos authentication. Only applicable
                 in a secure environment based on Kerberos V5. If
                 the remote host has been configured to prevent
                 non-secure access, using this option would result
                 in the generic error,

                     rcmd: connect: <hostname>: Connection refused

                 See DIAGNOSTICS in remshd(1M) for more details.

-p   Preserve (duplicate) modification times and modes
                 (permissions) of source files, ignoring the
                 current setting of the umask file creation mode
                 mask. If this option is specified, rcp preserves
                 the sticky bit only if the target user is
                 superuser.

                 If the -p option is not specified, rcp preserves

the mode and owner of dest_file if it already
exists; otherwise rcp uses the mode of the source
file modified by the umask on the destination
host. Modification and access times of the
destination file are set to the time when the copy
was made.

-r   Recursively copy directory subtrees rooted at the
                      source directory name. If any directory subtrees
                      are to be copied, rcp recursively copies each
                      subtree rooted at the specified source directory
                      name to directory dest_dir. If source_dir is
                      being copied to an existing directory of the same
                      name, rcp creates a new directory source_dir
                      within dest_dir and copies the subtree rooted at
                      source_dir to dest_dir/source_dir. If dest_dir
                      does not exist, rcp creates it and copies the
                      subtree rooted at source_dir to dest_dir.

Constructing File and Directory Names
   As indicated above, file and directory names contain one, two, or four
   component parts:

        user_name   Login name to be used for accessing directories and
                      files on remote system.

        hostname   Hostname of remote system where directories and
                      files are located.

        pathname   Absolute directory path name or directory path name
                      relative to the login directory of user user_name.

        filename   Actual name of source or destination file. File
                      name expansion is allowed on source file names.

        dirname   Actual name of source or destination directory
                      subtree. File name expansion is allowed on source
                      directory names.

Each file or directory argument is either a remote file name of the
form hostname:path, or a local file name (with a slash (/) before any
colon (:)). hostname can be either an official host name or an alias
(see hosts(4)). If hostname is of the form ruser@rhost, ruser is used
on the remote host instead of the current user name. An unspecified
path (that is, hostname:) refers to the remote user's login directory.
If path does not begin with /, it is interpreted relative to the
remote user's login directory on hostname. Shell metacharacters in
remote paths can be quoted with backslash (\), single quotes (''), or
double quotes (""), so that they will be interpreted remotely.

rcp does not prompt for passwords. In a non-secure or traditional
environment, user authorization is checked by determining if the
current local user name or any user name specified via ruser exists on
rhost. In a Kerberos V5 Network Authentication or secure environment,
the authorization method is dependent upon the command line options
for remshd (see remshd(1M) for details). In either case, remote
command execution via remsh(1) and rcmd(3) must be allowed and
remshd(1M) must be executable on the remote host.

Third-party transfers in the form:

      rcp ruser1@rhost1:path1 ruser2@rhost2:path2

are performed as:

```
remsh rhost1 -l ruser1 rcp path1 ruser2@rhost2:path2
```

Therefore, for a such a transfer to succeed, ruser2 on rhost2 must allow access by ruser1 from rhost1 (see hosts.equiv(4)).

WARNINGS

The rcp routine is confused by any output generated by commands in a .cshrc file on the remote host (see csh(1)).

Copying a file onto itself, for example:

```
rcp path `hostname :path
```

may produce inconsistent results. The current HP-UX version of rcp simply copies the file over itself. However, some implementations of rcp, including some earlier HP-UX implementations, corrupt the file. In addition, the same file may be referred to in multiple ways, for example, via hard links, symbolic links, or NFS. It is not guaranteed that rcp will correctly copy a file over itself in all cases.

Implementations of rcp based on the 4.2BSD version (including the implementations of rcp prior to HP-UX 7.0) require that remote users be specified as rhost.ruser. If the first remote host specified in a third party transfer (rhost1 in the example below) uses this older syntax, the command must have the form:

```
rcp ruser1@rhost1:path1 rhost2.ruser2:path2
```

since the target is interpreted by rhost1. A common problem that is encountered is when two remote files are to be copied to a remote target that specifies a remote user. If the two remote source systems, rhost1 and rhost2, each expect a different form for the remote target, the command:

```
rcp rhost1:path1 rhost2:path2 rhost3.ruser3:path3
```

will certainly fail on one of the source systems. Perform such a transfer using two separate commands.

AUTHOR

rcp was developed by the University of California, Berkeley.

SEE ALSO

cp(1), ftp(1), remsh(1), remshd(1M), rcmd(3), hosts(4), hosts.equiv(4), sis(5).

ftp chapter in Using Internet Services.

remsh

remsh - Connect to a remote host and execute a command.

remsh(1)   remsh(1)

NAME
     remsh - execute from a remote shell

SYNOPSIS

     remsh host [-l username] [-n] command
     host [-l username] [-n] command

     rexec host [-l username] [-n] command

DESCRIPTION
     remsh connects to the specified host and executes the specified
     command. The host name can be either the official name or an alias as
     understood by gethostbyname() (see gethostent(3N) and hosts(4)).
     remsh copies its standard input (stdin) to the remote command, and the
     standard output of the remote command to its standard output (stdout),
     and the standard error of the remote command to its standard error
     (stderr). Hangup, interrupt, quit, terminate, and broken pipe signals
     are propagated to the remote command. remsh exits when the sockets
     associated with stdout and stderr of the remote command are closed.
     This means that remsh normally terminates when the remote command does
     (see remshd(1M)).

     By default, remsh uses the following path when executing the specified
     command:

          /usr/bin:/usr/ccs/bin:/usr/bin/X11:

     remsh uses the default remote login shell with the -c option to
     execute the remote command. If the default remote shell is csh, csh
     sources the remote .cshrc file before the command. remsh cannot be
     used to run commands that require a terminal interface (such as vi) or
     commands that read their standard error (such as more). In such
     cases, use rlogin or telnet instead (see rlogin(1) and telnet(1)).

     The remote account name used is the same as your local account name,
     unless you specify a different remote name with the -l option. This
     remote account name must be equivalent to the originating account; no
     provision is made for specifying a password with a command. For more
     details about equivalent hosts and how to specify them, see
     hosts.equiv(4). The files inspected by remshd on the remote host are
     /etc/hosts.equiv and $HOME/.rhosts (see remshd(1M)).

     If command, is not specified, instead of executing a single command,
     you will be logged in on the remote host using rlogin (see rlogin(1)).
     Any rlogin options typed in on the command line are transmitted to
     rlogin. If command is specified, options specific to rlogin are
     ignored by remsh.

     By default, remsh reads its standard input and sends it to the remote
     command because remsh has no way to determine whether the remote
     command requires input. The -n option redirects standard input to

remsh from /dev/null. This is useful when running a shell script
containing a remsh command, since otherwise remsh may use input not
intended for it. The -n option is also useful when running remsh in
the background from a job control shell, /usr/bin/csh or /usr/bin/ksh.
Otherwise, remsh stops and waits for input from the terminal keyboard
for the remote command. /usr/bin/sh automatically redirects its input
from /dev/null when jobs are run in the background.

Host names for remote hosts can also be commands (linked to remsh) in
the directory /usr/hosts. If this directory is specified in the $PATH
environment variable, you can omit remsh. For example, if remotehost
is the name of a remote host, /usr/hosts/remotehost is linked to
remsh, and if /usr/hosts is in your search path, the command

        remotehost command

executes command on remotehost, and the command

        remotehost

is equivalent to

        rlogin remotehost

The rexec command, a link to remsh, works the same as remsh except
that it uses the rexec() library routine and rexecd for command
execution (see rexec(3N) and rexecd(1M)). rexec prompts for a
password before executing the command instead of using hosts.equiv for
authentication. It should be used in instances where a password to a
remote account is known but there are insufficient permissions for
remsh.

EXAMPLES
        Shell metacharacters that are not quoted are interpreted on the local
        host; quoted metacharacters are interpreted on the remote host. Thus
        the command line:

                remsh otherhost cat remotefile >> localfile

        appends the remote file remotefile to the local file localfile, while
        the command line

                remsh otherhost cat remotefile ">>" otherremotefile

        appends remotefile to the remote file otherremotefile.

        If the remote shell is /usr/bin/sh, the following command line sets up
        the environment for the remote command before executing the remote
        command:

                remsh otherhost . .profile 2>&- \; command

        The 2>&- throws away error messages generated by executing .profile
        when stdin and stdout are not a terminal.

        The following command line runs remsh in the background on the local
        system, and the output of the remote command comes to your terminal
        asynchronously:

                remsh otherhost -n command &

        The background remsh completes when the remote command does.

        The following command line causes remsh to return immediately without
        waiting for the remote command to complete:

```
remsh otherhost -n "command 1>&- 2>&- &"
```

(See remshd(1M) and sh(1)). If your login shell on the remote system
is csh, use the following form instead:

```
remsh otherhost -n "sh -c \"command 1>&- 2>&- &\""
```

RETURN VALUE
   If remsh fails to set up the secondary socket connection, it returns
   2. If it fails in some other way, it returns 1. If it fully succeeds
   in setting up a connection with remshd, it returns 0 once the remote
   command has completed. Note that the return value of remsh bears no
   relation to the return value of the remote command.

DIAGNOSTICS
   Besides the errors listed below, errors can also be generated by the
   library functions rcmd() and rresvport() which are used by remsh (see
   rcmd(3N)). Those errors are preceded by the name of the library
   function that generated them. remsh can produce the following
   diagnostic messages:

      rlogin: ...
            Error in executing rlogin (rlogin is executed when the user
            does not specify any commands to be executed). This is
            followed by the error message specifying why the execution
            failed.

      shell/tcp: Unknown service
            The ``shell'' service specification is not present in the
            /etc/services file.

      Can't establish stderr
            remsh cannot establish secondary socket connection for
            stderr.

      <system call>: ...
            Error in executing system call. Appended to this error is a
            message specifying the cause of the failure.

      There is no entry for you (user ID uid) in /etc/passwd
            Check with the system administrator to see if your entry in
            the password file has been deleted by mistake.

WARNINGS
   For security reasons, the /etc/hosts.equiv and .rhosts files should
   exist, even if empty, and should be readable and writable only by the
   owner. Note also that all information, including any passwords asked
   for, is passed unencrypted between the two hosts.

   If remsh is run with an interactive command it hangs.

DEPENDENCIES
   remsh is the same service as rsh on BSD systems. The name was changed
   due to a conflict with the existing System V command rsh (restricted
   shell).

AUTHOR
   remsh was developed by the University of California, Berkeley.

FILES
   /usr/hosts/*   for version of the command invoked only with
                         hostname

SEE ALSO
   rlogin(1), remshd(1M), rexecd(1M), gethostent(3N), rcmd(3N),
```
```

rexec(3N), hosts.equiv(4), hosts(4).

remsh(1)   Secure Internet Services with Kerberos Authentication   remsh(1)

NAME
     remsh - execute from a remote shell

SYNOPSIS

     remsh host [-l username] [-f/F] [-k realm] [-P] [-n] command
     host [-l username] [-f/F] [-k realm] [-P] [-n] command

     rexec host [-l username] [-n] command

DESCRIPTION
     remsh connects to the specified host and executes the specified
     command. The host name can be either the official name or an alias as
     understood by gethostbyname() (see gethostent(3N) and hosts(4)).
     remsh copies its standard input (stdin) to the remote command, and the
     standard output of the remote command to its standard output (stdout),
     and the standard error of the remote command to its standard error
     (stderr). Hangup, interrupt, quit, terminate, and broken pipe signals
     are propagated to the remote command. remsh exits when the sockets
     associated with stdout and stderr of the remote command are closed.
     This means that remsh normally terminates when the remote command does
     (see remshd(1M)).

     By default, remsh uses the following path when executing the specified
     command:

          /usr/bin:/usr/ccs/bin:/usr/bin/X11:

     remsh uses the default remote login shell with the -c option to
     execute the remote command. If the default remote shell is csh, csh
     sources the remote .cshrc file before the command. remsh cannot be
     used to run commands that require a terminal interface (such as vi) or
     commands that read their standard error (such as more). In such
     cases, use rlogin or telnet instead (see rlogin(1) and telnet(1)).

     The remote account name used is the same as your local account name,
     unless you specify a different remote name with the -l option. In
     addition, the remote host account name must also conform to other
     rules which differ depending upon whether the remote host is operating
     in a Kerberos V5 Network Authentication, i.e., secure environment or
     not. In a non-secure, or traditional environment, the remote account
     name must be equivalent to the originating account; no provision is
     made for specifying a password with a command. For more details about
     equivalent hosts and how to specify them, see hosts.equiv(4). The
     files inspected by remshd on the remote host are /etc/hosts.equiv and
     $HOME/.rhosts (see remshd(1M)).

     In a Kerberos V5 Network Authentication environment, the local host
     must be successfully authenticated before the remote account name is
     checked for proper authorization. The authorization mechanism is
     dependent on the command line options used to invoke remshd on the
     remote host (i.e., -K, -R, -r, or -k). For further information on
     Kerberos authentication and authorization see the Secure Internet
     Services man page, sis(5) and remshd(1M).

     Although Kerberos authentication and authorization may apply, the
     Kerberos mechanism is not applied to the command or to its response.
     All information transferred between the local and remote host is still
     sent in cleartext over the network.

     In a secure or Kerberos V5-based environment, the following command
     line options are available:

-f   Forward the ticket granting ticket (TGT) to the remote
            system. The TGT is not forwardable from there.

-F   Forward the TGT to the remote system and have it
            forwardable from there to another remote system. -f and
            -F are mutually exclusive.

-k realm   Obtain tickets from the remote host in the specified
            realm instead of the remote host's default realm as
            specified in the configuration file krb.realms.

-P   Disable Kerberos authentication.

If a command is not specified, instead of executing a single command,
you will be logged in on the remote host using rlogin (see rlogin(1)).
Any rlogin options typed in on the command line are transmitted to
rlogin. If no command and the option -P is specified, rlogin will be
invoked with -P to indicate that Kerberos authentication (or secure
access) is not required. This will mean that if a password is
requested, the password will be sent in cleartext. If a command is
specified, options specific to rlogin are ignored by remsh.

If a command and the option -n are specified, then standard input is
redirected to remsh by /dev/null. If -n is not specified (the default
case), remsh reads its standard input and sends the input to the
remote command. This is because remsh has no way to determine whether
the remote command requires input. This option is useful when running
a shell script containing a remsh command, since otherwise remsh may
use input not intended for it. The -n option is also useful when
running remsh in the background from a job control shell, /usr/bin/csh
or /usr/bin/ksh. Otherwise, remsh stops and waits for input from the
terminal keyboard for the remote command. /usr/bin/sh automatically
redirects its input from /dev/null when jobs are run in the
background.

Host names for remote hosts can also be commands (linked to remsh) in
the directory /usr/hosts. If this directory is specified in the $PATH
environment variable, you can omit remsh. For example, if remotehost
is the name of a remote host, /usr/hosts/remotehost is linked to
remsh, and if /usr/hosts is in your search path, the command

     remotehost command

executes command on remotehost, and the command

     remotehost

is equivalent to

     rlogin remotehost

The rexec command, a link to remsh, works the same as remsh except
that it uses the rexec() library routine and rexecd for command
execution (see rexec(3N) and rexecd(1M)) and does not support Kerberos
authentication. rexec prompts for a password before executing the
command instead of using hosts.equiv for authentication. It should be
used in instances where a password to a remote account is known but
there are insufficient permissions for remsh.

EXAMPLES
     Shell metacharacters that are not quoted are interpreted on the local
     host; quoted metacharacters are interpreted on the remote host. Thus
     the command line:

          remsh otherhost cat remotefile >> localfile

appends the remote file remotefile to the local file localfile, while
the command line

    remsh otherhost cat remotefile ">>" otherremotefile

appends remotefile to the remote file otherremotefile.

If the remote shell is /usr/bin/sh, the following command line sets up
the environment for the remote command before executing the remote
command:

    remsh otherhost . .profile 2>&- \; command

The 2>&- throws away error messages generated by executing .profile
when stdin and stdout are not a terminal.

The following command line runs remsh in the background on the local
system, and the output of the remote command comes to your terminal
asynchronously:

    remsh otherhost -n command &

The background remsh completes when the remote command does.

The following command line causes remsh to return immediately without
waiting for the remote command to complete:

    remsh otherhost -n "command 1>&- 2>&- &"

(See remshd(1M) and sh(1)). If your login shell on the remote system
is csh, use the following form instead:

    remsh otherhost -n "sh -c \"command 1>&- 2>&- &\""

RETURN VALUE
    If remsh fails to set up the secondary socket connection, it returns
    2. If it fails in some other way, it returns 1. If it fully succeeds
    in setting up a connection with remshd, it returns 0 once the remote
    command has completed. Note that the return value of remsh bears no
    relation to the return value of the remote command.

DIAGNOSTICS
    Besides the errors listed below, errors can also be generated by the
    library functions rcmd() and rresvport() which are used by remsh (see
    rcmd(3N)). Those errors are preceded by the name of the library
    function that generated them. remsh can produce the following
    diagnostic messages:

        rlogin: ...
            Error in executing rlogin (rlogin is executed when the user
            does not specify any commands to be executed). This is
            followed by the error message specifying why the execution
            failed.

        shell/tcp: Unknown service
            The ``shell'' service specification is not present in the
            /etc/services file.

        Can't establish stderr
            remsh cannot establish secondary socket connection for
            stderr.

        <system call>: ...
            Error in executing system call. Appended to this error is a

message specifying the cause of the failure.

There is no entry for you (user ID uid) in /etc/passwd
    Check with the system administrator to see if your entry in
    the password file has been deleted by mistake.

rcmd: connect: <hostname>: Connection refused
    One cause for display of this generic error message could be
    due to the absence of an entry for shell in /etc/inetd.conf
    on the remote system. This entry may have been removed or
    commented out to prevent non-secure access.

Kerberos-specific errors are listed in sis(5).

WARNINGS
For security reasons, the /etc/hosts.equiv and .rhosts files should
exist, even if empty, and should be readable and writable only by the
owner.

If remsh is run with an interactive command it hangs.

DEPENDENCIES
remsh is the same service as rsh on BSD systems. The name was changed
due to a conflict with the existing System V command rsh (restricted
shell).

AUTHOR
remsh was developed by the University of California, Berkeley.

FILES
/usr/hosts/*   for version of the command invoked only with
                           hostname

SEE ALSO
rlogin(1), remshd(1M), rexecd(1M), gethostent(3N), rcmd(3N),
rexec(3N), hosts.equiv(4), hosts(4), sis(5).

rlogin

rlogin - Log in to a remote host.

NAME
     rlogin - remote login

SYNOPSIS

     rlogin rhost [-7] [-8] [-ee] [-l username]

     rhost [-7] [-8] [-ee] [-l username]

DESCRIPTION
     The rlogin command connects your terminal on the local host to the
     remote host (rhost). rlogin acts as a virtual terminal to the remote
     system. The host name rhost can be either the official name or an
     alias as listed in the file /etc/hosts (see hosts(4)).

     In a manner similar to the remsh command (see remsh(1)), rlogin allows
     a user to log in on an equivalent remote host, rhost, bypassing the
     normal login/password sequence. For more information about equivalent
     hosts and how to specify them in the files /etc/hosts.equiv and
     .rhosts, see hosts.equiv(4). The searching of the files
     /etc/hosts.equiv and .rhosts occurs on the remote host, and the
     .rhosts file must be owned by the remote user account or by a remote
     superuser.

     If the originating user account is not equivalent to the remote user
     account, the originating user is prompted for the password of the
     remote account. If this fails, a login name and password are prompted
     for, as when login is used (see login(1)).

     The terminal type specified by the current TERM environment variable
     is propagated across the network and used to set the initial value of
     your TERM environment variable on the remote host. Your terminal baud
     rate is also propagated to the remote host, and is required by some
     systems to set up the pseudo-terminal used by rlogind (see
     rlogind(1M)).

     All echoing takes place at the remote site, so that (except for
     delays) the remote login is transparent.

     If at any time rlogin is unable to read from or write to the socket
     connection on the remote host, the message Connection closed is
     printed on standard error and rlogin exits.

  Options
     rlogin recognizes the following options. Note that the options follow
     the rhost argument.

               -7   Set the character size to seven bits. The eighth
                             bit of each byte sent is set to zero (space
                             parity).

               -8   Use an eight-bit data path. This is the default
                             HP-UX behavior.

To use eight-bit characters, the terminal must be
configured to generate either eight-bit characters
with no parity, or seven bit characters with space
parity. The HP-UX implementation of rlogind (see
rlogind(1M)) interprets seven bit characters with
even, odd, or mark parity as eight-bit non-USASCII
characters. You may also need to reconfigure the
remote host appropriately (see stty(1) and
tty(7)). Some remote hosts may not provide the
necessary support for eight-bit characters. In
this case, or if it is not possible to disable
parity generation by the local terminal, use the
-7 option.

-ee   Set the escape character to e. There is no space
            separating the option letter and the argument
            character. To start a line with the escape
            character, two of the escape characters must be
            entered. The default escape character is tilde
            (~). Some characters may conflict with your
            terminal configuration, such as ^S, ^Q, or
            backspace. Using one of these as the escape
            character may not be possible or may cause
            problems communicating with the remote host (see
            stty(1) and tty(7)).

-l username Set the user login name on the remote host to
            username. The default name is the current account
            name of the user invoking rlogin.

Escape Sequences
    rlogin can be controlled with two-character escape sequences, in the
    form ex, where e is the escape character and x is a code character
    described below. Escape sequences are recognized only at the
    beginning of a line of input. The default escape character is tilde
    (~). It can be changed with the -e option.

The following escape sequences are recognized:

    ey If y is NOT a code character described below, pass the
        escape character and y as characters to the remote host.

    ee Pass the escape character as a character to the remote host.

    e. Disconnect from the remote host.

    e! Escape to a subshell on the local host. Use exit to return
        to the remote host.

    If rlogin is run from a shell that supports job control (see
    csh(1), ksh(1), and sh-posix(1)), escape sequences can be used to
    suspend rlogin. The following escape sequences assume that ^Z
    and ^Y are set as the user's susp and dsusp characters,
    respectively (see stty(1) and termio(7)).

    e^Z Suspend the rlogin session and return the user to the shell
        that invoked rlogin. The rlogin job can be resumed with the
        fg command (see csh(1), ksh(1), and sh-posix(1)). e^Z
        suspends both rlogin processes: the one transmitting user
        input to the remote login, and the one displaying output
        from the remote login.

    e^Y Suspend the rlogin session and return the user to the shell

that invoked rlogin. The rlogin job can be resumed with the
fg command (see csh(1), ksh(1), and sh-posix(1)). e^Y
suspends only the input process; output from the remote
login continues to be displayed.

If you "daisy-chain" remote logins (for example, you rlogin from host
A to host B and then rlogin from host B to host C) without setting
unique escape characters, you can repeat the escape character until it
reaches your chosen destination. For example, the first escape
character, e, is seen as an escape character on host A; the second e
is passed as a normal character by host A and seen as an escape
character on host B; a third e is passed as a normal character by
hosts A and B and accepted as a normal character by host C.

Remote Host Name As Command

The system administrator can arrange for more convenient access to a
remote host (rhost) by linking remsh to /usr/hosts/rhost, allowing use
of the remote host name (rhost) as a command (see remsh(1)). For
example, if remotehost is the name of a remote host and
/usr/hosts/remotehost is linked to remsh, and if /usr/hosts is in your
search path, the command:

        remotehost

is equivalent to:

        rlogin remotehost

RETURN VALUES

rlogin sends an error message to standard error and returns a nonzero
value if an error occurs before the connection to the remote host is
completed. Otherwise, it returns a zero.

DIAGNOSTICS

Diagnostics can occur from both the local and remote hosts. Those
that occur on the local host before the connection is completely
established are written to standard error. Once the connection is
established, any error messages from the remote host are written to
standard output, like any other data.

login/tcp: Unknown service

        rlogin was unable to find the login service listed in the
        /etc/services database file.

There is no entry for you (user ID username) in /etc/passwd

        rlogin was unable to find your user ID in the password file.

        Next Step: Contact your system administrator.

system call:...
        An error occurred when rlogin attempted the indicated system
        call. See the appropriate manual entry for information about the
        error.

EXAMPLES

Log in as the same user on the remote host remote:

        rlogin remote

Set the escape character to a !, use a seven-bit data connection, and
attempt a login as user guest on host remhost:

        rlogin remhost -e! -7 -l guest

Assuming that your system administrator has set up the links in
/usr/hosts, the following is equivalent to the previous command:

    remhost -e! -7 -l guest

WARNINGS
    For security purposes, the /etc/hosts.equiv and .rhosts files should
    exist, even if they are empty. These files should be readable and
    writable only by the owner. See host.equiv(4) for more information.

    Note also that all information, including any passwords asked for, is
    passed unencrypted between the two hosts.

    rlogin is unable to transmit the Break key as an interrupt signal to
    the remote system, regardless of whether the user has set stty brkint
    on the local system. The key assigned to SIGINT with the command stty
    intr c should be used instead (see stty(1)).

AUTHOR
    rlogin was developed by the University of California, Berkeley.

FILES
    $HOME/.rhosts   User's private equivalence list
    /etc/hosts.equiv   List of equivalent hosts
    /usr/hosts/*   For rhost version of the command

SEE ALSO
    csh(1), ksh(1), login(1), remsh(1), sh(1), sh-bourne(1), sh-posix(1),
    stty(1), telnet(1), rlogind(1M), hosts(4), hosts.equiv(4),
    inetd.conf(4), services(4), termio(7), tty(7).

rlogin(1)   Secure Internet Services with Kerberos Authentication   rlogin(1)

NAME
    rlogin - remote login

SYNOPSIS

    rlogin rhost [-7] [-8] [-ee] [-f/F] [-k realm] [-l username] [-P]

    rhost [-7] [-8] [-ee] [-f/F] [-k realm] [-l username] [-P]

DESCRIPTION
    The rlogin command connects your terminal on the local host to the
    remote host (rhost). rlogin acts as a virtual terminal to the remote
    system. The host name rhost can be either the official name or an
    alias as listed in the file /etc/hosts (see hosts(4)).

    The terminal type specified by the current TERM environment variable
    is propagated across the network and used to set the initial value of
    your TERM environment variable on the remote host. Your terminal baud
    rate is also propagated to the remote host, and is required by some
    systems to set up the pseudo-terminal used by rlogind (see
    rlogind(1M)).

    All echoing takes place at the remote site, so that (except for
    delays) the remote login is transparent.

    If at any time rlogin is unable to read from or write to the socket
    connection on the remote host, the message Connection closed is
    printed on standard error and rlogin exits.

    In a Kerberos V5 Network Authentication environment, rlogin uses the
    Kerberos V5 protocol to authenticate the connection to a remote host.
    If the authentication is successful, user authorization will be
    performed according to the command line options selected for rlogind

(i.e., -K, -R, -r, or -k). A password will not be required, so a
password prompt will not be seen and a password will not be sent over
the network where it can be observed. For further information on
Kerberos authentication and authorization see the Secure Internet
Services man page, sis(5) and rlogind(1M).

Although Kerberos authentication and authorization may apply, the
Kerberos mechanism is not applied to the login session. All
information transferred between your host and the remote host is sent
in cleartext over the network.

Options
    rlogin recognizes the following options. Note that the options follow
    the rhost argument.

          -7   Set the character size to seven bits. The eighth
                        bit of each byte sent is set to zero (space
                        parity).

          -8   Use an eight-bit data path. This is the default
                        HP-UX behavior.

                        To use eight-bit characters, the terminal must be
                        configured to generate either eight-bit characters
                        with no parity, or seven bit characters with space
                        parity. The HP-UX implementation of rlogind (see
                        rlogind(1M)) interprets seven bit characters with
                        even, odd, or mark parity as eight-bit non-USASCII
                        characters. You may also need to reconfigure the
                        remote host appropriately (see stty(1) and
                        tty(7)). Some remote hosts may not provide the
                        necessary support for eight-bit characters. In
                        this case, or if it is not possible to disable
                        parity generation by the local terminal, use the
                        -7 option.

          -ee   Set the escape character to e. There is no space
                        separating the option letter and the argument
                        character. To start a line with the escape
                        character, two of the escape characters must be
                        entered. The default escape character is tilde
                        (~). Some characters may conflict with your
                        terminal configuration, such as ^S, ^Q, or
                        backspace. Using one of these as the escape
                        character may not be possible or may cause
                        problems communicating with the remote host (see
                        stty(1) and tty(7)).

          -f   Forward the ticket granting ticket (TGT) to the
                        remote system. The TGT is not forwardable from
                        there.

          -F   Forward the TGT to the remote system and have it
                        forwardable from there to another remote system.
                        -f and -F are mutually exclusive.

          -k realm   Obtain tickets from the remote host in the
                        specified realm instead of the remote host's
                        default realm as specified in the configuration
                        file krb.realms.

          -l username   Set the user login name on the remote host to
                        username. The default name is the current account
                        name of the user invoking rlogin.

          -P   Disable Kerberos authentication. Only applicable in a secure environment based on Kerberos V5. When this option is specified, a password is required and the password is sent across the network in cleartext. To bypass the normal login/password sequence, you can login to a remote host using an equivalent account in a manner similar to remsh. See hosts.equiv(4) for details.

rlogin can be controlled with two-character escape sequences, in the form ex, where e is the escape character and x is a code character described below. Escape sequences are recognized only at the beginning of a line of input. The default escape character is tilde (~). It can be changed with the -e option.

The following escape sequences are recognized:

ey   If y is NOT a code character described below, pass the escape character and y as characters to the remote host.

ee   Pass the escape character as a character to the remote host.

e.   Disconnect from the remote host.

e!   Escape to a subshell on the local host. Use exit to return to the remote host.

If rlogin is run from a shell that supports job control (see csh(1), ksh(1), and sh-posix(1)), escape sequences can be used to suspend rlogin. The following escape sequences assume that ^Z and ^Y are set as the user's susp and dsusp characters, respectively (see stty(1) and termio(7)).

e^Z   Suspend the rlogin session and return the user to the shell that invoked rlogin. The rlogin job can be resumed with the fg command (see csh(1), ksh(1), and sh-posix(1)). e^Z suspends both rlogin processes: the one transmitting user input to the remote login, and the one displaying output from the remote login.

e^Y   Suspend the rlogin session and return the user to the shell that invoked rlogin. The rlogin job can be resumed with the fg command (see csh(1), ksh(1), and sh-posix(1)). e^Y suspends only the input process; output from the remote login continues to be displayed.

If you "daisy-chain" remote logins (for example, you rlogin from host A to host B and then rlogin from host B to host C) without setting unique escape characters, you can repeat the escape character until it reaches your chosen destination. For example, the first escape character, e, is seen as an escape character on host A; the second e is passed as a normal character by host A and seen as an escape character on host B; a third e is passed as a normal character by hosts A and B and accepted as a normal character by host C.

Remote Host Name As Command
The system administrator can arrange for more convenient access to a remote host (rhost) by linking remsh to /usr/hosts/rhost, allowing use of the remote host name (rhost) as a command (see remsh(1)). For example, if remotehost is the name of a remote host and /usr/hosts/remotehost is linked to remsh, and if /usr/hosts is in your search path, the command:

    remotehost

is equivalent to:

rlogin remotehost

RETURN VALUES
rlogin sends an error message to standard error and returns a nonzero
value if an error occurs before the connection to the remote host is
completed. Otherwise, it returns a zero.

DIAGNOSTICS
Diagnostics can occur from both the local and remote hosts. Those
that occur on the local host before the connection is completely
established are written to standard error. Once the connection is
established, any error messages from the remote host are written to
standard output, like any other data.

login/tcp: Unknown service

rlogin was unable to find the login service listed in the
/etc/services database file.

There is no entry for you (user ID username) in /etc/passwd

rlogin was unable to find your user ID in the password file.

Next Step: Contact your system administrator.

system call:...
An error occurred when rlogin attempted the indicated system
call. See the appropriate manual entry for information about the
error.

rcmd: connect <hostname>: Connection refused.
One cause for display of this generic error message could be due
to the absence of an entry for login in /etc/inetd.conf on the
remote system. This entry may have been removed or commented out
to prevent non-secure access.

Kerberos-specific errors are listed in sis(5).

EXAMPLES
Log in as the same user on the remote host remote:

rlogin remote

Set the escape character to a !, use a seven-bit data connection, and
attempt a login as user guest on host remhost:

rlogin remhost -e! -7 -l guest

Assuming that your system administrator has set up the links in
/usr/hosts, the following is equivalent to the previous command:

remhost -e! -7 -l guest

WARNINGS
For security purposes, the /etc/hosts.equiv and .rhosts files should
exist, even if they are empty. These files should be readable and
writable only by the owner. See host.equiv(4) for more information.

Note also that all information, including passwords, is passed
unencrypted between the two hosts. In a Kerberos V5 Network
Authentication environment, a password is not transmitted across the
network, so it will be protected.

rlogin is unable to transmit the Break key as an interrupt signal to
the remote system, regardless of whether the user has set stty brkint
on the local system. The key assigned to SIGINT with the command stty
intr c should be used instead (see stty(1)).

AUTHOR
      rlogin was developed by the University of California, Berkeley.

FILES
      $HOME/.rhosts   User's private equivalence list
      /etc/hosts.equiv   List of equivalent hosts
      /usr/hosts/*   For rhost version of the command

SEE ALSO
      csh(1), ksh(1), login(1), remsh(1), sh(1), sh-bourne(1), sh-posix(1),
      stty(1), telnet(1), rlogind(1M), hosts(4), hosts.equiv(4),
      inetd.conf(4), services(4), termio(7), tty(7), sis(5).

route

route - Manipulate network routing tables.

route(1M)   route(1M)

NAME
     route - manually manipulate the routing tables

SYNOPSIS

     /usr/sbin/route [-f] [-n] [-p pmtu] add [net|host] destination
          [netmask mask] gateway [count]

     /usr/sbin/route [-f] [-n] delete [net|host] destination
          [netmask mask] gateway [count]

     /usr/sbin/route -f [-n]

DESCRIPTION
     The route command manipulates the network routing tables manually.
     You must have appropriate privileges.

   Subcommands
     The following subcommands are supported.

          add   Add the specified host or network route to the
                         network routing table. If the route already
                         exists, a message is printed and nothing changes.

          delete   Delete the specified host or network route from
                         the network routing table.

   Options and Arguments
     route recognizes the following options and arguments.

          -f   Delete all route table entries that specify a
                         remote host for a gateway. If this is used with
                         one of the subcommands, the entries are deleted
                         before the subcommand is processed.

          -n   Print any host and network addresses in Internet
                         dot notation, except for the default network
                         address, which is printed as default.

          -p pmtu   Specifies a path maximum transmission unit (MTU)
                         value for a static host route. The minimum value
                         allowed is 68 bytes; the maximum is the MTU of the
                         outgoing interface for this route. This option
                         only applies to adding a host route. In all other
                         cases, this option is ignored and has no effect on
                         a system.

                         You can also disable the Path MTU Discovery for a
                         host route by specifying pmtu as zero.

net   The type of destination address. If this argument
or   is omitted, routes to a particular host are
host   distinguished from those to a network by
                interpreting the Internet address associated with
                destination. If the destination has a local
                address part of INADDR_ANY(0), the route is
                assumed to be to a network; otherwise, it is
                treated as a route to a host.

destination   The destination host system where the packets will
                be routed. destination can be one of the
                following:

                  - A host name (the official name or an alias,
                     see gethostbyname(3N)).
                  - A network name (the official name or an
                     alias, see getnetbyname(3N)).
                  - An Internet address in dot notation (see
                     inet(3N)).
                  - The keyword default, which signifies the
                     wildcard gateway route (see routing(7)).

netmask
mask   The mask that will be bit-wise ANDed with
                destination to yield a net address where the
                packets will be routed. mask can be specified as
                a single hexadecimal number with a leading 0x,
                with a dot-notation Internet address, or with a
                pseudo-network name listed in the network table
                (see networks(4)). The length of the mask, which
                is the number of contiguous 1's starting from the
                leftmost bit position of the 32-bit field, can be
                shorter than the default network mask for the
                destination address. (see routing (7)). If the
                netmask option is not given, mask for the route
                will be derived from the netmasks associated with
                the local interfaces. (see ifconfig (1)). mask
                will be defaulted to the longest netmask of those
                local interfaces that have the same network
                address. If there is not any local interface that
                has the same network address, then mask will be
                defaulted to the default network mask of
                destination.

gateway   The gateway through which the destination is
                reached. gateway can be one of the following:

                  - A host name (the official name or an alias,
                     see gethostbyname(3N)).
                  - An Internet address in dot notation (see
                     inet(3N)).

count   An integer that indicates whether the gateway is a
                remote host or the local host. If the route leads
                to a destination through a remote gateway, count
                should be a number greater than 0. If the route
                leads to destination and the gateway is the local
                host, count should be 0. The default for count is
                zero. The result is not defined if count is
                negative.

Operation
  All symbolic names specified for a destination or gateway are looked
  up first as a host name using gethostbyname(); if the host name is not

found, the destination is searched for as a network name using getnetbyname(). destination and gateway can be in dot notation (see inet(3N)).

If the -n option is not specified, any host and network addresses are displayed symbolically according to the name returned by gethostbyaddr() and getnetbyaddr(), respectively, except for the default network address (printed as default) and addresses that have unknown names. Addresses with unknown names are printed in Internet dot notation (see inet(3N)).

If the -n option is specified, any host and network addresses are printed in Internet dot notation except for the default network address which is printed as default.

If the -f option is specified, route deletes all route table entries that specify a remote host for a gateway. If it is used with one of the subcommands described above, the entries are deleted before the subcommand is processed.

Path MTU Discovery is a technique for discovering the maximum size of an IP datagram that can be sent on an internet path without causing datagram fragmentation in the intermediate routers. In essence, a source host that utilizes this technique initially sends out datagrams up to the the size of the outgoing interface. The Don't Fragment (DF) bit in the IP datagram header is set. As an intermediate router that supports Path MTU Discovery receives a datagram that is too large to be forwarded in one piece to the next-hop router and the DF bit is set, the router will discard the datagram and send an ICMP Destination Unreachable message with a code meaning "fragmentation needed and DF set". The ICMP message will also contain the MTU of the next-hop router. When the source host receives the ICMP message, it reduces the path MTU of the route to the MTU in the ICMP message. With this technique, the host route in the source host for this path will contain the proper MTU.

By default, Path MTU Discovery is enabled for TCP sockets and disabled for UDP sockets.

If the -p pmtu option is specified for a host route, the pmtu value is considered permanent for the host route. Even if the Path MTU Discovery process discovers a smaller pmtu for this route at a later time, the pmtu field in the host route will not be updated. A warning message will be logged with the new pmtu value.

The -p pmtu option is useful only if you knows the network environment well enough to enter an appropriate pmtu for a host route. IP will fragment a datagram to the pmtu specified for the route on the local host before sending the datagram out to the remote. It will avoid fragmentation by routers along the path, if the pmtu specified in the route command is correct.

ping can be used to find the pmtu information for the route to a remote host. The pmtu information in the routing table can be displayed with the netstat -r command (see netstat(1)).

Output
  add destination: gateway gateway

        The specified route is being added to the tables.

  delete destination: gateway gateway

        The specified route is being deleted from the tables.

Flags

The values of the count and destination type fields in the route command determine the presence of the G and H flags in the netstat -r display and thus the route type, as shown in the following table.

Count	Destination Type	Flags	Route Type
=0	network	U	Route to a network directly from the local host
>0	network	UG	Route to a network through a remote host gateway
=0	host	UH	Route to a remote host directly from the local host
>0	host	UGH	Route to a remote host through a remote host gateway
=0	default	U	Wildcard route directly from the local host
>0	default	UG	Wildcard route through a remote host gateway

DIAGNOSTICS

The following error diagnostics can be displayed.

add a route that already exists

The specified entry is already in the routing table.

add too many routes

The routing table is full.

delete a route that does not exist

The specified route was not in the routing table.

WARNINGS

Reciprocal route commands must be executed on the local host, the destination host, and all intermediate hosts if routing is to succeed in the cases of virtual circuit connections or bidirectional datagram transfers.

The HP-UX implementation of route does not presently support a change subcommand.

AUTHOR

route was developed by the University of California, Berkeley.

FILES

/etc/networks
/etc/hosts

SEE ALSO

netstat(1), ifconfig(1M), ping(1M), getsockopt(2), recv(2), send(2), gethostbyaddr(3N), gethostbyname(3N), getnetbyaddr(3N), getnetbyname(3N), inet(3N), routing(7).

rpcinfo

rpcinfo - Report Remote Procedure Call (RPC) information.

man page

rpcinfo - 9

```
rpcinfo(1M)                                                    rpcinfo(1M)

NAME
     rpcinfo - report RPC information

SYNOPSIS
     /usr/sbin/rpcinfo -p [host]
     /usr/sbin/rpcinfo [-n portnum] -u host program [version]
     /usr/sbin/rpcinfo [-n portnum] -t host program [version]
     /usr/sbin/rpcinfo -b program version
     /usr/sbin/rpcinfo -d program version

DESCRIPTION
     rpcinfo makes an RPC call to an RPC server and reports what it finds.

   Options
     rpcinfo recognizes the following command-line options and arguments:

         -p host       Probe the portmapper on host and print a list of
                       all registered RPC programs.  If host is not
                       specified, it defaults to the value returned by
                       hostname (see hostname(1)).

         -n portnum    Use portnum as the port number for the -t and -u
                       options instead of the port number given by the
                       portmapper.

         -u            Make an RPC call to procedure 0 of program on the
                       specified host using UDP and report whether a
                       response was received.

         -t            Make an RPC call to procedure 0 of program on the
                       specified host using TCP and report whether a
                       response was received.

         -b            Make an RPC broadcast to procedure 0 of the
                       specified program and version using UDP and report
                       all hosts that respond.

         -d            Delete registration for the RPC service of the
                       specified program and version.  Only users with
                       appropriate privileges can use this option.

         program       Can be either a name or a number.

         version       If specified, rpcinfo attempts to call that
                       version of the specified program.  Otherwise,
                       rpcinfo attempts to find all the registered
                       version numbers for the specified program by
                       calling version 0, then attempts to call each
                       registered version.  (Version 0 is presumed to not
                       exist, but if version 0 does exist, rpcinfo
```

attempts to obtain the version number information
by calling an extremely high version number
instead.) Note that version must be specified when
the -b and -d options are used.

EXAMPLES

Show all of the RPC services registered on the local machine:

```
rpcinfo -p
```

Show all of the RPC services registered on the machine named klaxon:

```
rpcinfo -p klaxon
```

Show all machines on the local net that are running the Network
Information Service (NIS):

```
rpcinfo -b ypserv 1 | sort | uniq
```

where 1 is the current NIS version obtained from the results of the -p
option in the previous example.

Delete the registration for version 1 of the walld service:

```
rpcinfo -d walld 1
```

[Note that walld is the RPC program name for rwalld (see rwalld(1m))].

WARNINGS

In releases prior to Sun UNIX 3.0, the Network File System (NFS) did
not register itself with the portmapper; rpcinfo cannot be used to
make RPC calls to the NFS server on hosts running such releases. Note
that this does not apply to any HP releases of NFS.

AUTHOR

rpcinfo was developed by Sun Microsystems, Inc.

FILES

/etc/rpc   names for RPC program numbers

SEE ALSO

rpc(4), portmap(1M),
Programming and Protocols for NFS Services.

rwho

rwho - Produce a list of users on a remote system.

```
rwho(1)                                                              rwho(1)

NAME
     rwho - show who is logged in on local machines

SYNOPSIS

     rwho [-a]

DESCRIPTION
     rwho produces output similar to the output of the HP-UX who command
     for all machines on the local network that are running the rwho daemon
     (see who(1) and rwhod(1M)).  If rwhod has not received a report from a
     machine for 11 minutes, rwho assumes the machine is down and rwho does
     not report users last known to be logged into that machine.

     rwho's output line has fields for the name of the user, the name of
     the machine, the user's terminal line, the time the user logged in,
     and the amount of time the user has been idle.  Idle time is shown as:

         hours:minutes

     If a user has not typed to the system for a minute or more, rwho
     reports this as idle time.  If a user has not typed to the system for
     an hour or more, the user is omitted from rwho's output unless the -a
     flag is given.

     An example output line from rwho would look similar to:

         joe_user   machine1:tty0p1  Sep 12  13:28    :11

     This output line could be interpreted as joe_user is logged into
     machine1 and his terminal line is tty0p1.  joe_user has been logged on
     since September 12  at 13:28 (1:28 p.m.).  joe_user has not typed
     anything into machine1 for 11 minutes.

WARNINGS
     rwho's output becomes unwieldy when the number of users for each
     machine on the local network running rwhod becomes large.  One line of
     output occurs for each user on each machine on the local network that
     is running rwhod.

AUTHOR
     rwho was developed by the University of California, Berkeley.

FILES
     /var/spool/rwho/whod.*           Information about other machines.

SEE ALSO
     ruptime(1), rusers(1), rwhod(1M).
```

telnet

man page

telnet - 9

telnet - User interface for TELNET.

```
telnet(1)                                                        telnet(1)

NAME
      telnet - user interface to the TELNET protocol

SYNOPSIS

      telnet [[options]host [port]]

DESCRIPTION
      telnet is used to communicate with another host using the TELNET
      protocol.  If telnet is invoked without arguments, it enters command
      mode, indicated by its prompt (telnet>).  In this mode, it accepts and
      executes the commands listed below.  If telnet is invoked with
      arguments, it performs an open command (see below) with those
      arguments.

      Once a connection has been opened, telnet enters an input mode.  The
      input mode will be either ``character at a time'' or ``line by line'',
      depending on what the remote system supports.

      In ``character at a time'' mode, most text typed is immediately sent
      to the remote host for processing.

      In ``line by line'' mode, all text is echoed locally, and (normally)
      only completed lines are sent to the remote host.  The ``local echo
      character'' (initially ^E) can be used to turn off and on the local
      echo (this would mostly be used to enter passwords without the
      password being echoed).

      In either mode, if the localchars toggle is TRUE (the default in line
      mode; see below), the user's quit and intr characters are trapped
      locally, and sent as TELNET protocol sequences to the remote side.
      There are options (see toggle autoflush and toggle autosynch below)
      which cause this action to flush subsequent output to the terminal
      (until the remote host acknowledges the TELNET sequence) and flush
      previous terminal input (in the case of quit and intr).

      While connected to a remote host, telnet command mode can be entered
      by typing the telnet ``escape character'' (initially ^]).  When in
      command mode, the normal terminal editing conventions are available.

      telnet supports eight-bit characters when communicating with the
      server on the remote host.  To use eight-bit characters you may need
      to reconfigure your terminal or the remote host appropriately (see
      stty(1)).  Furthermore, you may have to use the binary toggle to
      enable an 8-bit data stream between telnet and the remote host.  Note
      that some remote hosts may not provide the necessary support for
      eight-bit characters.

      If, at any time, telnet is unable to read from or write to the server
      over the connection, the message Connection closed by foreign host. is
      printed on standard error.  telnet then exits with a value of 1.
```

telnet supports the TAC User ID (also known as the TAC Access Control System, or TACACS User ID) option. Enabling the option on a host server allows the user to telnet into that host without being prompted for a second login sequence. The TAC User ID option uses the same security mechanism as rlogin for authorizing acces by remote hosts and users. The system administrator must enable the (telnetd) option only on systems which are designated as participating hosts. The system administrator must also assign to each user of TAC User ID the very same UID on every system for which he is allowed to use the feature. (See telnetd(1M) and the System Administration Tasks manual, PN 2355-90051.)

The following telnet options are available:

-8   Enable cs8 (8 bit transfer) on local tty.

-ec   Set the telnet command mode escape character to be ^c instead of its default value of ^].

-l   Disable the TAC User ID option if enabled on the client, to cause the user to be prompted for login username and password. Omitting the -l option executes the default setting.

Commands
   The following commands are available in command mode. You need only type enough of each command to uniquely identify it (this is also true for arguments to the mode, set, toggle, and display commands).

open host [port]
                   Open a connection to the named host at the indicated port. If no port is specified, telnet attempts to contact a TELNET server at the standard TELNET port. The hostname can be either the official name or an alias as understood by gethostbyname() (see gethostent(3N)), or an Internet address specified in the dot notation as described in hosts(4). If no hostname is given, telnet prompts for one.

close   Close a TELNET session. If the session was started from command mode, telnet returns to command mode; otherwise telnet exits.

quit   Close any open TELNET session and exit telnet. An end of file (in command mode) will also close a session and exit.

z   Suspend telnet. If telnet is run from a shell that supports job control, (such as csh(1) or ksh(1)), the z command suspends the TELNET session and returns the user to the shell that invoked telnet. The job can then be resumed with the fg command (see csh(1) or ksh(1)).

mode mode   Change telnet's user input mode to mode, which can be character (for ``character at a time'' mode) or line (for ``line by line'' mode). The remote host is asked for permission to go into the requested mode. If the remote host is capable of entering that mode, the requested mode is entered. In character mode, telnet sends each character to the remote host as it is typed. In line mode, telnet gathers user input into lines and transmits each line to the remote host when the user types carriage return, linefeed, or EOF (normally ^D; see stty(1)). Note that setting line-mode also sets

local echo. Applications that expect to interpret user
input character by character (such as more, csh, ksh,
and vi) do not work correctly in line mode.

status   Show current status of telnet. telnet reports the
              current escape character. If telnet is connected, it
              reports the host to which it is connected and the
              current mode. If telnet is not connected to a remote
              host, it reports No connection. Once telnet has been
              connected, it reports the local flow control toggle
              value.

display [argument ...]
              Displays all or some of the set and toggle values (see
              below).

? [command]   Get help. With no arguments, telnet prints a help
              summary. If a command is specified, telnet prints the
              help information available about that command only.
              Help information is limited to a one-line description
              of the command.

! [shell_command]
              Shell escape. The SHELL environment variable is
              checked for the name of a shell to use to execute the
              command. If no shell_command is specified, a shell is
              started and connected to the user's terminal. If SHELL
              is undefined, /usr/bin/sh is used.

send arguments Sends one or more special character sequences to the
              remote host. Each argument can have any of the
              following values (multiple arguments can be specified
              with each send command):

                    escape   Sends the current telnet escape
                              character (initially ^]).

                    synch   Sends the TELNET SYNCH sequence. This
                              sequence causes the remote system to
                              discard all previously typed (but not
                              yet read) input. This sequence is sent
                              as TCP urgent data (and may not work to
                              some systems -- if it doesn't work, a
                              lower case ``r'' may be echoed on the
                              terminal).

                    brk   Sends the TELNET BRK (Break) sequence,
                              which may have significance to the
                              remote system.

                    ip   Sends the TELNET IP (Interrupt Process)
                              sequence, which should cause the remote
                              system to abort the currently running
                              process.

                    ao   Sends the TELNET AO (Abort Output)
                              sequence, which should cause the remote
                              system to flush all output from the
                              remote system to the user's terminal.

                    ayt   Sends the TELNET AYT (Are You There)
                              sequence, to which the remote system may
                              or may not choose to respond.

                    ec   Sends the TELNET EC (Erase Character)
                              sequence, which should cause the remote

system to erase the last character entered.

el   Sends the TELNET EL (Erase Line) sequence, which should cause the remote system to erase the line currently being entered.

ga   Sends the TELNET GA (Go Ahead) sequence, which likely has no significance to the remote system.

nop   Sends the TELNET NOP (No OPeration) sequence.

?   Prints out help information for the send command.

set variable_name value

Set any one of a number of telnet variables to a specific value. The special value off turns off the function associated with the variable. The values of variables can be shown by using the display command. The following variable_names can be specified:

echo This is the value (initially ^E) which, when in line-by-line mode, toggles between doing local echoing of entered characters (for normal processing), and suppressing echoing of entered characters (for entering, for example, a password).

escape
This is the telnet escape character (initially ^]) which causes entry into telnet command mode (when connected to a remote system).

interrupt
If telnet is in localchars mode (see toggle localchars below) and the interrupt character is typed, a TELNET IP sequence (see send ip above) is sent to the remote host. The initial value for the interrupt character is taken to be the terminal's intr character.

quit If telnet is in localchars mode (see toggle localchars below) and the quit character is typed, a TELNET BRK sequence (see send brk above) is sent to the remote host. The initial value for the quit character is taken to be the terminal's quit character.

flushoutput
If telnet is in localchars mode (see toggle localchars below) and the flushoutput character is typed, a TELNET AO sequence (see send ao above) is sent to the remote host. The initial value for the flush character is ^O.

erase
If telnet is in localchars mode (see toggle localchars below), and if telnet is operating in character-at-a-time mode, then when this character is typed, a TELNET EC sequence (see send ec above)

is sent to the remote system. The initial value
for the erase character is taken to be the
terminal's erase character.

kill If telnet is in localchars mode (see toggle
localchars below), and if telnet is operating in
character-at-a-time mode, then when this character
is typed, a TELNET EL sequence (see send el above)
is sent to the remote system. The initial value
for the kill character is taken to be the
terminal's kill character.

eof If telnet is operating in line-by-line mode,
entering this character as the first character on
a line causes this character to be sent to the
remote system. The initial value of the eof
character is taken to be the terminal's eof
character.

toggle arguments ...

Toggle (between TRUE and FALSE) various flags that
control how telnet responds to events. More than one
argument can be specified. The state of these flags
can be shown by using the display command. Valid
arguments are:

localchars
        If TRUE, the flush, interrupt, quit, erase,
        and kill characters (see set above) are
        recognized locally, and transformed into
        appropriate TELNET control sequences
        (respectively ao, ip, brk, ec, and el; see
        send above). The initial value for this
        toggle is TRUE in line-by-line mode, and
        FALSE in character-at-a-time mode.

autoflush
        If autoflush and localchars are both TRUE,
        whenever the ao, intr, or quit characters are
        recognized (and transformed into TELNET
        sequences - see set above for details),
        telnet refuses to display any data on the
        user's terminal until the remote system
        acknowledges (via a TELNET Timing Mark
        option) that it has processed those TELNET
        sequences. The initial value for this toggle
        is TRUE.

autosynch
        If autosynch and localchars are both TRUE,
        when either the intr or quit character is
        typed (see set above for descriptions of the
        intr and quit characters), the resulting
        TELNET sequence sent is followed by the
        TELNET SYNCH sequence. This procedure should
        cause the remote system to begin discarding
        all previously typed input until both of the
        TELNET sequences have been read and acted
        upon. The initial value of this toggle is
        FALSE.

binary
        Enable or disable the TELNET BINARY option on
        both input and output. This option should be

enabled in order to send and receive 8-bit
characters to and from the TELNET server.

crlf If TRUE, end-of-line sequences are sent as an
ASCII carriage-return and line-feed pair. If
FALSE, end-of-line sequences are sent as an
ASCII carriage-return and NUL character pair.
The initial value for this toggle is FALSE.

crmod
Toggle carriage return mode. When this mode
is enabled, any carriage return characters
received from the remote host are mapped into
a carriage return and a line feed. This mode
does not affect those characters typed by the
user; only those received. This mode is only
required for some hosts that require the
client to do local echoing, but output
``naked'' carriage returns. The initial
value for this toggle is FALSE.

echo Toggle local echo mode or remote echo mode.
In local echo mode, user input is echoed to
the terminal by the local telnet before being
transmitted to the remote host. In remote
echo, any echoing of user input is done by
the remote host. Applications that handle
echoing of user input themselves, such as C
shell, Korn shell, and vi (see csh(1),
ksh(1), and vi(1)), do not work correctly
with local echo.

options
Toggle viewing of TELNET options processing.
When options viewing is enabled, all TELNET
option negotiations are displayed. Options
sent by telnet are displayed as ``SENT'',
while options received from the TELNET server
are displayed as ``RCVD''. The initial value
for this toggle is FALSE.

netdata
Toggles the display of all network data (in
hexadecimal format). The initial value for
this toggle is FALSE.

?   Displays the legal toggle commands.

RETURN VALUE
In the event of an error, or if the TELNET connection is closed by the
remote host, telnet returns a value of 1. Otherwise it returns zero
(0).

DIAGNOSTICS
The following diagnostic messages are displayed by telnet:

telnet/tcp: Unknown service
telnet was unable to find the TELNET service entry in the
services(4) database.

hostname: Unknown host
telnet was unable to map the host name to an Internet
address. Your next step should be to contact the system
administrator to check whether there is an entry for the

remote host in the hosts database (see hosts(4)).

?Invalid command
An invalid command was typed in telnet command mode.

system call>: ...
An error occurred in the specified system call. See the
appropriate manual entry for a description of the error.

AUTHOR
telnet was developed by the University of California, Berkeley.

SEE ALSO
csh(1), ksh(1), login(1), rlogin(1), stty(1), telnetd(1M), hosts(4),
services(4), termio(7).

telnet(1) Secure Internet Services with Kerberos Authentication telnet(1)

NAME
telnet - user interface to the TELNET protocol

SYNOPSIS

telnet [[options]host [port]]

DESCRIPTION
telnet is used to communicate with another host using the TELNET
protocol. If telnet is invoked without arguments, it enters command
mode, indicated by its prompt (telnet>). In this mode, it accepts and
executes the commands listed below. If telnet is invoked with
arguments, it performs an open command (see below) with those
arguments.

Once a connection has been opened, telnet enters an input mode. The
input mode will be either ``character at a time'' or ``line by line'',
depending on what the remote system supports.

In ``character at a time'' mode, most text typed is immediately sent
to the remote host for processing.

In ``line by line'' mode, all text is echoed locally, and (normally)
only completed lines are sent to the remote host. The ``local echo
character'' (initially ^E) can be used to turn off and on the local
echo (this would mostly be used to enter passwords without the
password being echoed).

In either mode, if the localchars toggle is TRUE (the default in line
mode; see below), the user's quit and intr characters are trapped
locally, and sent as TELNET protocol sequences to the remote side.
There are options (see toggle autoflush and toggle autosynch below)
which cause this action to flush subsequent output to the terminal
(until the remote host acknowledges the TELNET sequence) and flush
previous terminal input (in the case of quit and intr).

While connected to a remote host, telnet command mode can be entered
by typing the telnet ``escape character'' (initially ^]). When in
command mode, the normal terminal editing conventions are available.

telnet supports eight-bit characters when communicating with the
server on the remote host. To use eight-bit characters you may need
to reconfigure your terminal or the remote host appropriately (see
stty(1)). Furthermore, you may have to use the binary toggle to
enable an 8-bit data stream between telnet and the remote host. Note
that some remote hosts may not provide the necessary support for
eight-bit characters.

If, at any time, telnet is unable to read from or write to the server over the connection, the message Connection closed by foreign host. is printed on standard error. telnet then exits with a value of 1.

By default (or by use of the -a option or the -l option), this Kerberos version of telnet behaves as a client which supports authentication based on Kerberos V5. As a Kerberos client, telnet will authenticate and authorize the user to access the remote system. (See sis(5) for details on Kerberos authentication and authorization.) However, it will not support integrity-checked or encrypted sessions. telnet supports the TAC User ID (also known as the TAC Access Control System, or TACACS User ID) option. Enabling the option on a host server allows the user to telnet into that host without being prompted for a second login sequence. The TAC User ID option uses the same security mechanism as rlogin for authorizing access by remote hosts and users. The system administrator must enable the (telnetd) option only on systems which are designated as participating hosts. The system administrator must also assign to each user of TAC User ID the very same UID on every system for which he is allowed to use the feature. (See telnetd(1M) and the System Administration Tasks manual)

The following telnet options are available:

-8   Enable cs8 (8 bit transfer) on local tty.

-a   Attempt automatic login into the Kerberos realm and disable
            the TAC User ID option. (Note: this is the default login
            mode.)

            Sends the user name via the NAME subnegotiation of the
            Authentication option. The name used is that of the current
            user as returned by the USER environment variable. If this
            variable is not defined, the name used is that returned by
            getpwnam(3) if it agrees with the current user ID.
            Otherwise, it is the name associated with the user ID.

-e c   Set the telnet command mode escape character to be ^c
            instead of its default value of ^].

-l user   Attempt automatic login into the Kerberos realm as the
            specified user and disable the TAC User ID option. The user
            name specified is sent via the NAME subnegotiation of the
            Authentication option. Omitting the -l option executes the
            default setting. Only one -l option is allowed.

-P   Disable use of Kerberos authentication and authorization.
            When this option is specified, a password is required which
            is sent across the network in a readable form. (See sis(5).)

-f   Allows local credentials to be forwarded to the remote
            system. Only one of -f or -F is allowed.

-F   Allows local credentials to be forwarded to the remote
            system including any credentials that have already been
            forwarded into the local environment. Only one of -f or -F
            is allowed.

Commands
    The following commands are available in command mode. You need only
    type enough of each command to uniquely identify it (this is also true
    for arguments to the mode, set, toggle, and display commands).

    open [-l user] host [port]
                        Open a connection to the named host at the indicated
                        port. If no port is specified, telnet attempts to

contact a TELNET server at the standard TELNET port.
The hostname can be either the official name or an
alias as understood by gethostbyname() (see
gethostent(3N)), or an Internet address specified in
the dot notation as described in hosts(4). If no
hostname is given, telnet prompts for one. The -l
option can be used to specify the user name to use when
automatically logging in to the remote system. Using
this option disables the TAC User ID option.

close   Close a TELNET session. If the session was started
                 from command mode, telnet returns to command mode;
                 otherwise telnet exits.

quit   Close any open TELNET session and exit telnet. An end
                 of file (in command mode) will also close a session and
                 exit.

z   Suspend telnet. If telnet is run from a shell that
                 supports job control, (such as csh(1) or ksh(1)), the z
                 command suspends the TELNET session and returns the
                 user to the shell that invoked telnet. The job can
                 then be resumed with the fg command (see csh(1) or
                 ksh(1)).

mode mode   Change telnet's user input mode to mode, which can be
                 character (for ``character at a time'' mode) or line
                 (for ``line by line'' mode). The remote host is asked
                 for permission to go into the requested mode. If the
                 remote host is capable of entering that mode, the
                 requested mode is entered. In character mode, telnet
                 sends each character to the remote host as it is typed.
                 In line mode, telnet gathers user input into lines and
                 transmits each line to the remote host when the user
                 types carriage return, linefeed, or EOF (normally ^D;
                 see stty(1)). Note that setting line-mode also sets
                 local echo. Applications that expect to interpret user
                 input character by character (such as more, csh, ksh,
                 and vi) do not work correctly in line mode.

status   Show current status of telnet. telnet reports the
                 current escape character. If telnet is connected, it
                 reports the host to which it is connected and the
                 current mode. If telnet is not connected to a remote
                 host, it reports No connection. Once telnet has been
                 connected, it reports the local flow control toggle
                 value.

display [argument ...]
                 Displays all or some of the set and toggle values (see
                 below).

? [command]   Get help. With no arguments, telnet prints a help
                 summary. If a command is specified, telnet prints the
                 help information available about that command only.
                 Help information is limited to a one-line description
                 of the command.

! [shell_command]
                 Shell escape. The SHELL environment variable is
                 checked for the name of a shell to use to execute the
                 command. If no shell_command is specified, a shell is
                 started and connected to the user's terminal. If SHELL
                 is undefined, /usr/bin/sh is used.

send arguments   Sends one or more special character sequences to the

remote host. Each argument can have any of the
following values (multiple arguments can be specified
with each send command):

escape   Sends the current telnet escape
            character (initially ^]).

synch   Sends the TELNET SYNCH sequence. This
            sequence causes the remote system to
            discard all previously typed (but not
            yet read) input. This sequence is sent
            as TCP urgent data (and may not work to
            some systems -- if it doesn't work, a
            lower case ``r'' may be echoed on the
            terminal).

brk   Sends the TELNET BRK (Break) sequence,
            which may have significance to the
            remote system.

ip   Sends the TELNET IP (Interrupt Process)
            sequence, which should cause the remote
            system to abort the currently running
            process.

ao   Sends the TELNET AO (Abort Output)
            sequence, which should cause the remote
            system to flush all output from the
            remote system to the user's terminal.

ayt   Sends the TELNET AYT (Are You There)
            sequence, to which the remote system may
            or may not choose to respond.

ec   Sends the TELNET EC (Erase Character)
            sequence, which should cause the remote
            system to erase the last character
            entered.

el   Sends the TELNET EL (Erase Line)
            sequence, which should cause the remote
            system to erase the line currently being
            entered.

ga   Sends the TELNET GA (Go Ahead) sequence,
            which likely has no significance to the
            remote system.

nop   Sends the TELNET NOP (No OPeration)
            sequence.

?   Prints out help information for the send
            command.

set variable_name value
            Set any one of a number of telnet variables to a
            specific value. The special value off turns off the
            function associated with the variable. The values of
            variables can be shown by using the display command.
            The following variable_names can be specified:

            echo This is the value (initially ^E) which, when in
                 line-by-line mode, toggles between doing local
                 echoing of entered characters (for normal

processing), and suppressing echoing of entered
characters (for entering, for example, a
password).

escape
    This is the telnet escape character (initially ^])
    which causes entry into telnet command mode (when
    connected to a remote system).

interrupt
    If telnet is in localchars mode (see toggle
    localchars below) and the interrupt character is
    typed, a TELNET IP sequence (see send ip above) is
    sent to the remote host. The initial value for
    the interrupt character is taken to be the
    terminal's intr character.

quit If telnet is in localchars mode (see toggle
    localchars below) and the quit character is typed,
    a TELNET BRK sequence (see send brk above) is sent
    to the remote host. The initial value for the
    quit character is taken to be the terminal's quit
    character.

flushoutput
    If telnet is in localchars mode (see toggle
    localchars below) and the flushoutput character is
    typed, a TELNET AO sequence (see send ao above) is
    sent to the remote host. The initial value for
    the flush character is ^O.

erase
    If telnet is in localchars mode (see toggle
    localchars below), and if telnet is operating in
    character-at-a-time mode, then when this character
    is typed, a TELNET EC sequence (see send ec above)
    is sent to the remote system. The initial value
    for the erase character is taken to be the
    terminal's erase character.

kill If telnet is in localchars mode (see toggle
    localchars below), and if telnet is operating in
    character-at-a-time mode, then when this character
    is typed, a TELNET EL sequence (see send el above)
    is sent to the remote system. The initial value
    for the kill character is taken to be the
    terminal's kill character.

eof If telnet is operating in line-by-line mode,
    entering this character as the first character on
    a line causes this character to be sent to the
    remote system. The initial value of the eof
    character is taken to be the terminal's eof
    character.

toggle arguments ...
    Toggle (between TRUE and FALSE) various flags that
    control how telnet responds to events. More than one
    argument can be specified. The state of these flags
    can be shown by using the display command. Valid
    arguments are:

        localchars
            If TRUE, the flush, interrupt, quit, erase,

and kill characters (see set above) are
recognized locally, and transformed into
appropriate TELNET control sequences
(respectively ao, ip, brk, ec, and el; see
send above). The initial value for this
toggle is TRUE in line-by-line mode, and
FALSE in character-at-a-time mode.

autoflush
> If autoflush and localchars are both TRUE,
> whenever the ao, intr, or quit characters are
> recognized (and transformed into TELNET
> sequences - see set above for details),
> telnet refuses to display any data on the
> user's terminal until the remote system
> acknowledges (via a TELNET Timing Mark
> option) that it has processed those TELNET
> sequences. The initial value for this toggle
> is TRUE.

autologin
> Enable or disable automatic login into the
> Kerberos realm. Using this option yields the
> same results as using the -a option. The
> initial value for this toggle is TRUE.

autosynch
> If autosynch and localchars are both TRUE,
> when either the intr or quit character is
> typed (see set above for descriptions of the
> intr and quit characters), the resulting
> TELNET sequence sent is followed by the
> TELNET SYNCH sequence. This procedure should
> cause the remote system to begin discarding
> all previously typed input until both of the
> TELNET sequences have been read and acted
> upon. The initial value of this toggle is
> FALSE.

binary
> Enable or disable the TELNET BINARY option on
> both input and output. This option should be
> enabled in order to send and receive 8-bit
> characters to and from the TELNET server.

crlf If TRUE, end-of-line sequences are sent as an
> ASCII carriage-return and line-feed pair. If
> FALSE, end-of-line sequences are sent as an
> ASCII carriage-return and NUL character pair.
> The initial value for this toggle is FALSE.

crmod
> Toggle carriage return mode. When this mode
> is enabled, any carriage return characters
> received from the remote host are mapped into
> a carriage return and a line feed. This mode
> does not affect those characters typed by the
> user; only those received. This mode is only
> required for some hosts that require the
> client to do local echoing, but output
> ``naked'' carriage returns. The initial
> value for this toggle is FALSE.

echo Toggle local echo mode or remote echo mode.
> In local echo mode, user input is echoed to

the terminal by the local telnet before being
transmitted to the remote host. In remote
echo, any echoing of user input is done by
the remote host. Applications that handle
echoing of user input themselves, such as C
shell, Korn shell, and vi (see csh(1),
ksh(1), and vi(1)), do not work correctly
with local echo.

options
> Toggle viewing of TELNET options processing.
> When options viewing is enabled, all TELNET
> option negotiations are displayed. Options
> sent by telnet are displayed as ``SENT'',
> while options received from the TELNET server
> are displayed as ``RCVD''. The initial value
> for this toggle is FALSE.

netdata
> Toggles the display of all network data (in
> hexadecimal format). The initial value for
> this toggle is FALSE.

?   Displays the legal toggle commands.

RETURN VALUE
> In the event of an error, or if the TELNET connection is closed by the
> remote host, telnet returns a value of 1. Otherwise it returns zero
> (0).

DIAGNOSTICS
> Diagnostic messages displayed by telnet are displayed below. Kerberos
> specific errors are listed in sis(5).

> telnet/tcp: Unknown service
> > telnet was unable to find the TELNET service entry in the
> > services(4) database.

> hostname: Unknown host
> > telnet was unable to map the host name to an Internet
> > address. Your next step should be to contact the system
> > administrator to check whether there is an entry for the
> > remote host in the hosts database (see hosts(4)).

> ?Invalid command
> > An invalid command was typed in telnet command mode.

> system call>: ...
> > An error occurred in the specified system call. See the
> > appropriate manual entry for a description of the error.

AUTHOR
> telnet was developed by the University of California, Berkeley.

SEE ALSO
> csh(1), ksh(1), login(1), rlogin(1), stty(1), telnetd(1M), hosts(4),
> services(4), termio(7), sis(5).

Keep in mind that you may need to start the telnet daemon, telnetd, in order to run telnet.

See the manual page for telnetd for startup instructions if you do not have telnetd running.

telnetd sends options to the client of a telnet session in order to set up a proper communication exchange during a telnet session.

CHAPTER 10

UNIX Tools - grep, awk, sed, and Others

Not All Commands on All UNIX Variants

I cover many useful and enjoyable commands in this chapter. All the commands, however, are not available on all UNIX variants. If a specific command is not available on your system, then you probably have a similar command or can combine more than one command to achieve the desired result.

I cover redirection and viewing files before I cover the more advanced commands. Redirection is important when using many of the commands so it is helpful to cover this topic before going through the commands.

I also cover viewing files. Both redirection and viewing files appeared earlier in the book; however, you may have jumped right to this chapter, so I save you the trouble of flipping back to see how to view files.

Redirection

Before we cover viewing files, let's talk about redirection for a minute because I use some redirection in the upcoming section. I cover redirection under shell programming, but for now I want to give you just a quick introduction to redirection so that we can more effectively cover some of the commands in this chapter.

UNIX is set up such that commands usually take their input from the keyboard, often called *standard input*, and usually send output to the screen, often called *standard output*. Commands also send error information to the screen. It is not always desirable for input to come from standard input and output and errors to go to standard output. You are given a lot of control to override these defaults. This is called redirection. Table 10-1 shows many common forms of redirection.

As shown in the table, to redirect the output of a command from standard output to a file, you would use ">". This works almost all of the time. If you have an environment variable called **noclobber** set, then redirecting to an existing file does not work (we'll cover environment variables shortly). The **noclobber** does not permit redirection to write over an existing file. If you try to write over an existing file, such as **/tmp/processes** below, you receive a message that the file exists:

man page

ps - 12

```
#  ps  -ef  >  /tmp/processes
/tmp/processes:   File exists
```

You can, however, use a "!" with redirection to force a file to be overwritten. Using ">!" forces a file to be overwritten, and ">>!" will force the output to be appended to the end of an existing file. Examples of these are shown in Table 10-1.

Table 10-1   Commonly Used Redirection Forms

Command or Assignment	Example	Description
<	**wc -l < .login**	Standard input redirection: execute **wc** (word count) and list number of lines (**-l**) in **.login**
>	**ps -ef > /tmp/processes**	Standard output redirection: execute **ps** and send output to file **/tmp/processes**
>>	**ps -ef >> /tmp/processes**	Append standard output: execute **ps** and append output to the end of file **/tmp/processes**
>!	**ps -ef >! /tmp/processes**	Append output redirection and override **noclobber**: write over **/tmp/processes** even if it exists
>>!	**ps -ef >>! /tmp/processes**	Append standard output and override **noclobber**: append to the end of **/tmp/processes**
| (pipe)	**ps | wc -l**	Run **ps** and use the result as input to **wc**
0 - standard input		
1 - standard output		
2 - standard error	**cat program 2> errors**	**cat** the file **program** to standard output and redirect errors to the file **errors**
	cat program 2>> errors	**cat** the file **program** to standard output and append errors to the file **errors**
	find / -name '*.c' -print > cprograms 2>errors	**find** all files on the system ending in **.c** and place the list of files in **cprograms** in the current working directory and send all errors (file descriptor 2) to the file **errors** in current working directory
	find / -name '*.c' -print > cprograms 2>&1	**find** all files on the system ending in **.c**, place the list of files in **cprograms** in the current working directory, and send all errors (file descriptor 2) to same place as file descriptor 1 (**cprograms**)

Using the symbols shown in Table 10-1, you can redirect from *standard input* and *standard output*. For instance, rather than display the output on the screen, you can send the output to file. We will use some of these redirection forms in upcoming examples.

Viewing Files with cat, more, pg, head, and tail

man page

cat - 3

To begin with, let's look at a long file. In fact, let's look at a file so long that it will not fit on your screen if you were to print out the contents of the file to your screen.

The **cat** command (short for concatenate) does just this, prints out the file to your screen. If, however, the file is long, then you will only see the end of the file on your screen. Remember the user **denise** from earlier in the book? She had a lot of files in her directory. Let's list the files in her directory and redirect the output to a file called **listing** with the following command:

```
$ ls -a /home/denise > listing
```

When we **cat listing** to the screen we see only the end of it, as shown in Figure 10-1. We know that this is the end of the file, because I have issued **cat** with the **-n** option that includes line numbers. The line numbers indicate that this is not the beginning of the file.

```
┌─────────────────────────────────────────────────────────────┐
│ ▭ │                     cat −n example                   │ □ │▢│
├─────────────────────────────────────────────────────────────┤
││   106   rclock.exe                                          │
││   107   rkhelp.exe                                          │
││   108   sb.txt                                              │
││   109   shellupd.exe                                        │
││   110   smsup2.exe                                          │
││   111   softinit.remotesoftcm                               │
││   112   srvpr.exe                                           │
││   113   tabnd1.exe                                          │
││   114   target.exe                                          │
││   115   tcp41a.exe                                          │
││   116   tnds2.exe                                           │
││   117   trace.TRC1                                          │
││   118   trace.TRC1.Z.uue                                    │
││   119   upgrade.exe                                         │
││   120   uue.syntax                                          │
││   121   v103.txt                                            │
││   122   whoon                                               │
││   123   win95app.exe                                        │
││   124   wsdrv1.exe                                          │
││   125   wsos21.exe                                          │
││   126   wsos22.exe                                          │
││   127   wsos23.exe                                          │
││   128   xferp110.zip                                        │
││$ ▮                                                          │
└─────────────────────────────────────────────────────────────┘
```

Figure 10-1   cat -n Command

Seeing only the end of this file is not what we had in mind. Using the **pg** (for page), we see one screen at time, as shown in Figure 10-2.

```
┌─┬──────────────────────────────────────────────────────────────┬─┬──┐
│ ▭│                         pg example                          │ ▫│▢ │
├──┴──────────────────────────────────────────────────────────────┴──┤
│ .                                                                   │
│ ..                                                                  │
│ .CbtOptSet                                                          │
│ .Xauthority                                                         │
│ .cshrc                                                              │
│ .cshrc.orig                                                         │
│ .elm                                                                │
│ .exrc                                                               │
│ .fmrc                                                               │
│ .fmrc.orig                                                          │
│ .glancerc                                                           │
│ .gpmhp                                                              │
│ .history                                                            │
│ .login                                                              │
│ .lrom                                                               │
│ .mailrc                                                             │
│ .netscape-bookmarks.html                                            │
│ .netscape-cache                                                     │
│ .netscape-history                                                   │
│ .netscape-newsgroups-news.spry.com                                  │
│ .netscape-newsgroups-newsserv.hp.com                                │
│ .netscape-preferences                                               │
│ .newsrc-news.spry.com                                               │
│ :█                                                                  │
└─────────────────────────────────────────────────────────────────────┘
```

Figure 10-2   pg Command

man page

more - 3

The **more** command produces the same output as **pg,** as shown in Figure 10-3.

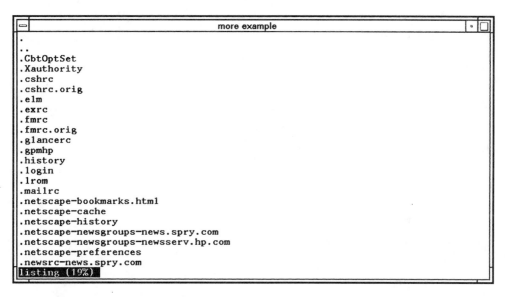

```
⊡                                  more example                          ▫ ▢
.
..
.CbtOptSet
.Xauthority
.cshrc
.cshrc.orig
.elm
.exrc
.fmrc
.fmrc.orig
.glancerc
.gpmhp
.history
.login
.lrom
.mailrc
.netscape-bookmarks.html
.netscape-cache
.netscape-history
.netscape-newsgroups-news.spry.com
.netscape-newsgroups-newsserv.hp.com
.netscape-preferences
.newsrc-news.spry.com
listing (19%)
```

Figure 10-3   more Command

This is more like it; now we can scroll on a screen-by-screen basis with both **pg** and **more**. However, sometimes you want to view only the beginning or end of a file. You can use the **head** command to view the beginning of a file and the **tail** command to view the bottom of a file. The following two examples of **head** and **tail** (see Figures 10-4 and 10-5) show viewing the first 20 lines of **listing** and the last 20 lines of **listing**, respectively.

man page

more - 3

man page

head - 3

man page

tail - 3

```
┌─────────────────────────────── head example ──────────────────────────── □ □ ┐
│ $ head -20 listing                                                             │
│ .                                                                              │
│ ..                                                                             │
│ .CbtOptSet                                                                     │
│ .Xauthority                                                                    │
│ .cshrc                                                                         │
│ .cshrc.orig                                                                    │
│ .elm                                                                           │
│ .exrc                                                                          │
│ .fmrc                                                                          │
│ .fmrc.orig                                                                     │
│ .glancerc                                                                      │
│ .gpmhp                                                                         │
│ .history                                                                       │
│ .login                                                                         │
│ .lrom                                                                          │
│ .mailrc                                                                        │
│ .netscape-bookmarks.html                                                       │
│ .netscape-cache                                                                │
│ .netscape-history                                                              │
│ .netscape-newsgroups-news.spry.com                                             │
│ $ ▆                                                                            │
└────────────────────────────────────────────────────────────────────────────┘
```

Figure 10-4   head Command

```
┌─────────────────────────────── tail example ──────────────────────────── □ □ ┐
│ $ tail -20 listing                                                             │
│ shellupd.exe                                                                   │
│ smsup2.exe                                                                     │
│ softinit.remotesoftcm                                                          │
│ srvpr.exe                                                                      │
│ tabnd1.exe                                                                     │
│ target.exe                                                                     │
│ tcp41a.exe                                                                     │
│ tnds2.exe                                                                      │
│ trace.TRC1                                                                     │
│ trace.TRC1.Z.uue                                                               │
│ upgrade.exe                                                                    │
│ uue.syntax                                                                     │
│ v103.txt                                                                       │
│ whoon                                                                          │
│ win95app.exe                                                                   │
│ wsdrv1.exe                                                                     │
│ wsos21.exe                                                                     │
│ wsos22.exe...                                                                  │
│ wsos23.exe                                                                     │
│ xferp110.zip                                                                   │
│ $ ▆                                                                            │
└────────────────────────────────────────────────────────────────────────────┘
```

Figure 10-5   tail Command

The command you use depends on the information you wish to display. My personal preference, whether viewing the contents of a large file or a long listing of files, is to use **more**. I don't have a good reason for this and all I can say is that we are creatures of habit and I have always used **more**. The following are command summaries for **cat**, **pg**, **more**, **head**, and **tail**. I included some of the most frequently used options associated with these commands. Because none of the commands are difficult to use, I suggest that you try each command and see whether one suits your needs better than the others.

Here are summaries of the **cat, pg, more, head,** and **tail** commands.

cat - Display, combine, append, copy, or create files.

Options

-	Used as a substitute for specifying a file name when you want to use the keyboard for standard input.
-n	Line numbers are displayed along with output lines.
-p	Replace multiple consecutive empty lines with only one empty line.
-s	This is silent mode, which suppresses information about nonexistent files.
-u	Output is unbuffered, which means that it is handled character by character.
-v	Print most nonprinting characters visibly.

pg - Display all or parts of a file.

Options

-number	The number of lines you wish to display.
-p string	Use string to specify a prompt.
-c	Clear the screen before displaying the next page of the file.

-f	Don't split lines being displayed.
-n	A command is issued as soon as a command letter is typed, rather than having to issue a new line character.

man page

more - 3

more - Display all or parts of a file one screen at a time.

Options

-c	Clear the screen before displaying the next page of the file.
-d	Display a prompt at the bottom of the screen with brief instructions.
-f	Wrap text to fit the screen and judge page length accordingly.
-n	The number of lines in the display window is set to n.
-s	Squeeze multiple consecutive empty lines into one empty line.

man page

head - 3

head - Provide only the first few lines of a file.

Options

-c	The output is produced with a specified number of bytes.
-l	The output is produced with a specified number of lines. This is the default.
-n count	The number of bytes or lines is specified by count. You can also use -count to specify the number of bytes or lines, which is shown in the example. The default count is 10.

tail - Provide the last few lines of a file.

man page

tail - 3

Options

-bnumber   Specify the number of blocks from the end of the file you wish to begin displaying.

-cnumber   Specify the number of characters from the end of the file you wish to begin displaying.

-nnumber   Specify the number of lines from the end of the file you wish to begin displaying. You can also specify a number or minus sign and number, as shown in the example, to specify the number of lines from the end of file to begin displaying.

man page

split - 3

split

Some files are just too long. The file **listing** we earlier looked at may be more easily managed if split into multiple files. We can use the **split** command to make **listing** into files 25 lines long, as shown in Figure 10-6.

```
─                              split example                              □ □
$ ll listing
-rw--------    1 denise    users        1430 Dec 19 16:30 listing
$
$ split -1 25 listing
$
$ ll x*
-rw--------    1 denise    users         330 Dec 19 16:40 xaa
-rw--------    1 denise    users         267 Dec 19 16:40 xab
-rw--------    1 denise    users         268 Dec 19 16:40 xac
-rw--------    1 denise    users         256 Dec 19 16:40 xad
-rw--------    1 denise    users         274 Dec 19 16:40 xae
-rw--------    1 denise    users          35 Dec 19 16:40 xaf
$ ■
```

Figure 10-6   **split** Command

Note that the split command produced several files from **listing** called **xaa**, **xab**, and so on. The **-l** option is used to specify the number of lines in files produced by **split**.

Here is a summary of the **split** command:

split - Split a file into multiple files.

Options

    -l line_count   Split the file into files with line_count lines per file.

    -b n   Split the file into files with n bytes per file.

WC

We know that we have split **listing** into separate files of 25 lines each, but how many lines were in **listing** originally? How about the number of words in **listing**? Those of us who get paid by the word for some of the articles we write often want to know. How about the number of characters in a file? The **wc** command can produce a word, line, and character count for you. Figure 10-7 shows issuing the **wc** command with the **-wlc** options, which produce a count of words with the **-w** option, lines with the **-l** option, and characters with the **-c** option.

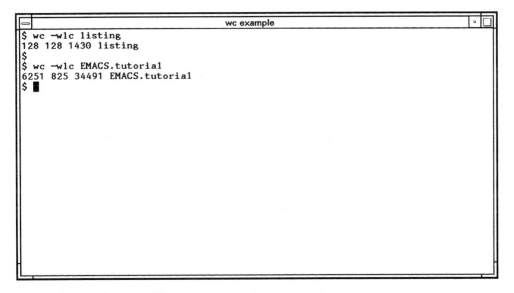

```
wc example
$ wc -wlc listing
128 128 1430 listing
$
$ wc -wlc EMACS.tutorial
6251 825 34491 EMACS.tutorial
$ ▮
```

Figure 10-7   wc Command

man page

wc - 12

Notice that the number of words and lines produced by **wc** is the same for the file **listing**. The reason is that each line contains exactly one word. When we display the words, lines, and characters with the **wc** command for the text file **EMACS.tutorial** we can see that the number of words is 6251, the number of lines is 825, and the number of characters is 34491. In a text file, in this case a tutorial, you would expect many more words than lines.

Here is a summary of the **wc** command:

wc - Produce a count of words, lines, and characters.

Options

-l	Print the number of lines in a file.
-w	Print the number of words in a file.
-c	Print the number of characters in a file.

grep

man page

grep - 10

Here in the information age, we have too much information. We are constantly trying to extract the information we are after from stacks of information. The **grep** command is used to search for text and display it. **grep** stands for General Regular Expression Parser. Let's first look at a few simple searches and display the output with **grep**. Figure 10-8 shows creating a long listing for **/home/denise**, and using **grep**, we search for patterns.

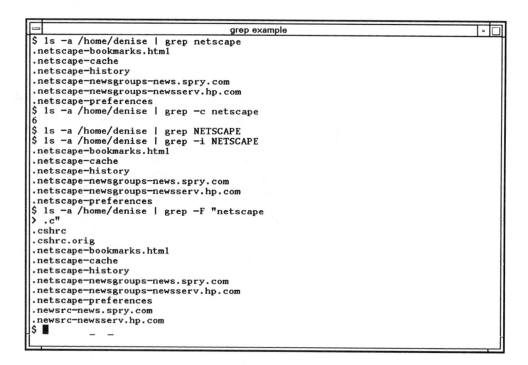

```
                                grep example
$ ls -a /home/denise | grep netscape
.netscape-bookmarks.html
.netscape-cache
.netscape-history
.netscape-newsgroups-news.spry.com
.netscape-newsgroups-newsserv.hp.com
.netscape-preferences
$ ls -a /home/denise | grep -c netscape
6
$ ls -a /home/denise | grep NETSCAPE
$ ls -a /home/denise | grep -i NETSCAPE
.netscape-bookmarks.html
.netscape-cache
.netscape-history
.netscape-newsgroups-news.spry.com
.netscape-newsgroups-newsserv.hp.com
.netscape-preferences
$ ls -a /home/denise | grep -F "netscape
> .c"
.cshrc
.cshrc.orig
.netscape-bookmarks.html
.netscape-cache
.netscape-history
.netscape-newsgroups-news.spry.com
.netscape-newsgroups-newsserv.hp.com
.netscape-preferences
.newsrc-news.spry.com
.newsrc-newsserv.hp.com
$ ▊        _  _
```

Figure 10-8   **grep** Command

First, we search for the pattern **netscape**. This produces a list of files, all of which begin with *.netscape.*

Next we use the **-c** option to create a count for the number of times that *netscape* is found. The result is 6.

man page

grep - 10

Do you think that **grep** is case-sensitive? The next example shows searching for the pattern *NETSCAPE,* and no matching patterns exist.

Using the **-i** option causes **grep** to ignore uppercase and lower case and just search for the pattern, and again all the original matches are found.

Also, more than one pattern can be searched for. Using the **-F** option, both *netscape* and *.c* are searched for and a longer list of matches are found. Notice that two patterns to search for are enclosed in double quotes and are separated by a new line.

Let's now take a look at a couple more advanced searches using **grep**. We'll use the **passwd.test** file as the basis for our searches because each line in it contains a lot of information. To start, the following is the contents of the **passwd.test** file on a Linux system:

man page

cat - 3

```
# cat passwd.test
root:PgYQCkVH65hyQ:0:0:root:/root:/bin/bash
bin:*:1:1:bin:/bin:
daemon:*:2:2:daemon:/sbin:
adm:*:3:4:adm:/var/adm:
lp:*:4:7:lp:/var/spool/lpd:
sync:*:5:0:sync:/sbin:/bin/sync
shutdown:*:6:11:shutdown:/sbin:/sbin/shutdown
halt:*:7:0:halt:/sbin:/sbin/halt
mail:*:8:12:mail:/var/spool/mail:
news:*:9:13:news:/var/spool/news:
uucp:*:10:14:uucp:/var/spool/uucp:
operator:*:11:0:operator:/root:
games:*:12:100:games:/usr/games:
gopher:*:13:30:gopher:/usr/lib/gopher-data:
ftp:*:14:50:FTP User:/home/ftp:
man:*:15:15:Manuals Owner:/:
nobody:*:65534:65534:Nobody:/:/bin/false
col:Wh0yzfAV2qm2Y:100:100:Caldera OpenLinux
    User:/home/col:/bin/bash
```

man page

grep - 10

We can search for a string in the password file just as we did in the earlier **grep** example. The following example searches for *news* in the **passwd.test** file.

```
# grep news passwd.test
news:*:9:13:news:/var/spool/news:
```

Now let's check to see whether there is a user named *bin* in the **passwd.test** file. In order for a user named *bin* to have an entry in the **passwd.test** file, the user name, in this case *bin*, would be the first entry in the line. Here is the result of searching for this user:

```
# grep bin passwd.test
root:PgYQCkVH65hyQ:0:0:root:/root:/bin/bash
bin:*:1:1:bin:/bin:
daemon:*:2:2:daemon:/sbin:
sync:*:5:0:sync:/sbin:/bin/sync
shutdown:*:6:11:shutdown:/sbin:/sbin/shutdown
halt:*:7:0:halt:/sbin:/sbin/halt
nobody:*:65534:65534:Nobody:/:/bin/false
col:Wh0yzfAV2qm2Y:100:100:Caldera OpenLinux
     User:/home/col:/bin/bash
```

Many lines from **passwd.test** are indeed produced that contain the string *bin*; however, we have to search through these lines in order to find the user *bin,* which is the line in which *bin* is the first string that appears. This is more than we wanted when we initiated our search. We wanted to see a user name *bin* that would appear at the beginning of a line. We can further qualify our search, in this case to limit the search to a string at the beginning of a line, by using pattern matching that is much the same as that of **vi**. You can refer to the **vi** chapter or the **vi** Quick Reference Card in this book to view some of the pattern matching options. In this case we want to search only at the beginning of a line for *bin,* so we'll qualify our search with a caret (^)

man page

vi - 8

to restrict the search to only the beginning of the line, as shown in the following example:

man page

grep - 10

```
# grep ^bin passwd.test
bin:*:1:1:bin:/bin:
```

This search results in exactly the information in which we are interested, that is, a line beginning with *bin*. When using special characters, such as the caret(^) in this example, you should enclose the special characters in single quotes ('). Special characters may be interpreted by the shell and cause problems with the arguments we're trying to send to **grep**. Enclosing the search pattern in single quotes will ensures that the search pattern, in this case *^bin*, is passed directly to **grep**. The search pattern in single quotes looks like the following:

```
# grep '^bin' passwd.test
bin:*:1:1:bin:/bin:
```

Because we are going to have to search for this line in the **passwd.test** file after we find it, we may as well print out the line number as well as the line itself by using the -*n* option, as shown in the following example:

```
# grep -n '^bin' passwd.test
2:bin:*:1:1:bin:/bin:
```

The following is a summary of the **grep** command:

grep - Search for text and display results.

Options

-c	Return the number of matches without showing you the text.
-h	Show the text with no reference to file names.
-i	Ignore the case when searching.
-l	Return the names of files containing a match without showing you the text.
-n	Return the line number of the text searched for in a file as well as the text itself.
-v	Return the lines that do not match the text you searched for.
-E	Search for more than one expression (same as **egrep**).
-F	Search for more than one expression (same as **fgrep**).

sed

Most of the editing performed on UNIX systems is done with **vi**. I have devoted a chapter to **vi** in this book, because of its prominence as a UNIX editor. Many times we don't have the luxury of invoking **vi** when we need to edit a file. You may be writing a shell program or piping information between processes and need to edit in a non-interactive manner. **sed** can help here. Its name comes from *stream editor,* and it's a tool for filtering text files.

You can specify the name of the file you wish to edit with **sed** or it takes its input from standard input. **sed** reads one line at a time and performs the editing you specify to each line. You can specify specific line numbers for **sed** to edit as well.

sed uses many of the same commands as **ed**. You can view some of these **ed** commands in the **vi** chapter, and I also supply a summary of these at the end of this **sed** section. Let's view a couple of simple examples of what you can do with **sed**.

Using the **passwd.test** file, lets view this full file, and then view lines 16, 17, and 18 only using *p*.

```
# cat passwd.test
root:PgYQCkVH65hyQ:0:0:root:/root:/bin/bash
bin:*:1:1:bin:/bin:
daemon:*:2:2:daemon:/sbin:
adm:*:3:4:adm:/var/adm:
lp:*:4:7:lp:/var/spool/lpd:
sync:*:5:0:sync:/sbin:/bin/sync
shutdown:*:6:11:shutdown:/sbin:/sbin/shutdown
halt:*:7:0:halt:/sbin:/sbin/halt
mail:*:8:12:mail:/var/spool/mail:
news:*:9:13:news:/var/spool/news:
uucp:*:10:14:uucp:/var/spool/uucp:
operator:*:11:0:operator:/root:
games:*:12:100:games:/usr/games:
gopher:*:13:30:gopher:/usr/lib/gopher-data:
ftp:*:14:50:FTP User:/home/ftp:
man:*:15:15:Manuals Owner:/:
nobody:*:65534:65534:Nobody:/:/bin/false
col:Wh0yzfAV2qm2Y:100:100:Caldera OpenLinux User:/home/col:/bin/bash
#
# sed 16,18p passwd.test
root:PgYQCkVH65hyQ:0:0:root:/root:/bin/bash
bin:*:1:1:bin:/bin:
daemon:*:2:2:daemon:/sbin:
adm:*:3:4:adm:/var/adm:
lp:*:4:7:lp:/var/spool/lpd:
sync:*:5:0:sync:/sbin:/bin/sync
shutdown:*:6:11:shutdown:/sbin:/sbin/shutdown
halt:*:7:0:halt:/sbin:/sbin/halt
mail:*:8:12:mail:/var/spool/mail:
news:*:9:13:news:/var/spool/news:
uucp:*:10:14:uucp:/var/spool/uucp:
operator:*:11:0:operator:/root:
games:*:12:100:games:/usr/games:
gopher:*:13:30:gopher:/usr/lib/gopher-data:
ftp:*:14:50:FTP User:/home/ftp:
man:*:15:15:Manuals Owner:/:
man:*:15:15:Manuals Owner:/:
nobody:*:65534:65534:Nobody:/:/bin/false
nobody:*:65534:65534:Nobody:/:/bin/false
col:Wh0yzfAV2qm2Y:100:100:Caldera OpenLinux User:/home/col:/bin/bash
col:Wh0yzfAV2qm2Y:100:100:Caldera OpenLinux User:/home/col:/bin/bash
#
# sed -n 16,18p passwd.test
man:*:15:15:Manuals Owner:/:
nobody:*:65534:65534:Nobody:/:/bin/false
col:Wh0yzfAV2qm2Y:100:100:Caldera OpenLinux User:/home/col:/bin/bash
```

man page

cat - 3

man page

sed - 10

The first attempt to print only lines 16, 17, and 18 results in all of the lines in the file being printed and lines 16, 17, and 18 being printed twice. The reason is that **sed** reads each line of input and acts on each line. In order to specify the lines on which to act, we used the *-n* switch to suppress all lines from going to standard output. We then specify the lines we want to print and these will indeed go to standard output.

Now that we know how to view lines 16, 17, and 18 of the file, let's again view **passwd.test** and delete those same three lines with *d*:

```
# cat passwd.test
root:PgYQCkVH65hyQ:0:0:root:/root:/bin/bash
bin:*:1:1:bin:/bin:
daemon:*:2:2:daemon:/sbin:
adm:*:3:4:adm:/var/adm:
lp:*:4:7:lp:/var/spool/lpd:
sync:*:5:0:sync:/sbin:/bin/sync
shutdown:*:6:11:shutdown:/sbin:/sbin/shutdown
halt:*:7:0:halt:/sbin:/sbin/halt
mail:*:8:12:mail:/var/spool/mail:
news:*:9:13:news:/var/spool/news:
uucp:*:10:14:uucp:/var/spool/uucp:
operator:*:11:0:operator:/root:
games:*:12:100:games:/usr/games:
gopher:*:13:30:gopher:/usr/lib/gopher-data:
ftp:*:14:50:FTP User:/home/ftp:
man:*:15:15:Manuals Owner:/:
nobody:*:65534:65534:Nobody:/:/bin/false
col:Wh0yzfAV2qm2Y:100:100:Caldera OpenLinux User:/home/col:/bin/bash
#
# sed 16,18d passwd.test
root:PgYQCkVH65hyQ:0:0:root:/root:/bin/bash
bin:*:1:1:bin:/bin:
daemon:*:2:2:daemon:/sbin:
adm:*:3:4:adm:/var/adm:
lp:*:4:7:lp:/var/spool/lpd:
sync:*:5:0:sync:/sbin:/bin/sync
shutdown:*:6:11:shutdown:/sbin:/sbin/shutdown
halt:*:7:0:halt:/sbin:/sbin/halt
mail:*:8:12:mail:/var/spool/mail:
news:*:9:13:news:/var/spool/news:
uucp:*:10:14:uucp:/var/spool/uucp:
operator:*:11:0:operator:/root:
games:*:12:100:games:/usr/games:
gopher:*:13:30:gopher:/usr/lib/gopher-data:
ftp:*:14:50:FTP User:/home/ftp:
```

As with our earlier **grep** example we enclose any special characters in single quotes to make sure that they are not interfered with and are passed directly to **sed** unmodified and uninterpreted by the shell. In this example, we specify the range of lines to delete, 16 through 18, and the *d* for delete. We could specify just one line to delete, such as 16, and not specify an entire range. Because we did not redirect the output as part of the **sed** command line, the result is sent to standard output. The original file remains intact.

We could search for a pattern in a file and delete only those lines containing the pattern. The following example shows searching for *bash* and deleting the lines that contain *bash:*

man page

cat - 3b

```
# cat passwd.test
root:PgYQCkVH65hyQ:0:0:root:/root:/bin/bash
bin:*:1:1:bin:/bin:
daemon:*:2:2:daemon:/sbin:
adm:*:3:4:adm:/var/adm:
lp:*:4:7:lp:/var/spool/lpd:
sync:*:5:0:sync:/sbin:/bin/sync
shutdown:*:6:11:shutdown:/sbin:/sbin/shutdown
halt:*:7:0:halt:/sbin:/sbin/halt
mail:*:8:12:mail:/var/spool/mail:
news:*:9:13:news:/var/spool/news:
uucp:*:10:14:uucp:/var/spool/uucp:
operator:*:11:0:operator:/root:
games:*:12:100:games:/usr/games:
gopher:*:13:30:gopher:/usr/lib/gopher-data:
ftp:*:14:50:FTP User:/home/ftp:
man:*:15:15:Manuals Owner:/:
nobody:*:65534:65534:Nobody:/:/bin/false
col:Wh0yzfAV2qm2Y:100:100:Caldera OpenLinux User:/home/col:/bin/bash
#
# sed '/bash/ d' passwd.test
bin:*:1:1:bin:/bin:
daemon:*:2:2:daemon:/sbin:
adm:*:3:4:adm:/var/adm:
lp:*:4:7:lp:/var/spool/lpd:
sync:*:5:0:sync:/sbin:/bin/sync
shutdown:*:6:11:shutdown:/sbin:/sbin/shutdown
halt:*:7:0:halt:/sbin:/sbin/halt
mail:*:8:12:mail:/var/spool/mail:
news:*:9:13:news:/var/spool/news:
uucp:*:10:14:uucp:/var/spool/uucp:
operator:*:11:0:operator:/root:
games:*:12:100:games:/usr/games:
gopher:*:13:30:gopher:/usr/lib/gopher-data:
ftp:*:14:50:FTP User:/home/ftp:
man:*:15:15:Manuals Owner:/:
nobody:*:65534:65534:Nobody:/:/bin/false
```

man page

sed - 10

Because there may be special characters in a long **sed** command, I used the single quotes.

What if you wanted to delete all lines except those that contain *bash?* You would insert an exclamation mark before the *d* to delete all lines except those that contain *bash,* as shown in the following example:

```
# cat passwd.test
root:PgYQCkVH65hyQ:0:0:root:/root:/bin/bash
bin:*:1:1:bin:/bin:
daemon:*:2:2:daemon:/sbin:
```

```
adm:*:3:4:adm:/var/adm:
lp:*:4:7:lp:/var/spool/lpd:
sync:*:5:0:sync:/sbin:/bin/sync
shutdown:*:6:11:shutdown:/sbin:/sbin/shutdown
halt:*:7:0:halt:/sbin:/sbin/halt
mail:*:8:12:mail:/var/spool/mail:
news:*:9:13:news:/var/spool/news:
uucp:*:10:14:uucp:/var/spool/uucp:
operator:*:11:0:operator:/root:
games:*:12:100:games:/usr/games:
gopher:*:13:30:gopher:/usr/lib/gopher-data:
ftp:*:14:50:FTP User:/home/ftp:
man:*:15:15:Manuals Owner:/:
nobody:*:65534:65534:Nobody:/:/bin/false
col:Wh0yzfAV2qm2Y:100:100:Caldera OpenLinux User:/home/col:/bin/bash
#
# sed '/bash/ !d' passwd.test
root:PgYQCkVH65hyQ:0:0:root:/root:/bin/bash
col:Wh0yzfAV2qm2Y:100:100:Caldera OpenLinux User:/home/col:/bin/bash
```

man page

sed - 10

Now that we have seen how to display and delete specific lines
of the file, let's see how to add three lines to the end of the file:

```
# sed '$a\
> This is a backup of passwd file\
> for viewing purposes only\
> so do not modify' passwd.test
root:PgYQCkVH65hyQ:0:0:root:/root:/bin/bash
bin:*:1:1:bin:/bin:
daemon:*:2:2:daemon:/sbin:
adm:*:3:4:adm:/var/adm:
lp:*:4:7:lp:/var/spool/lpd:
sync:*:5:0:sync:/sbin:/bin/sync
shutdown:*:6:11:shutdown:/sbin:/sbin/shutdown
halt:*:7:0:halt:/sbin:/sbin/halt
mail:*:8:12:mail:/var/spool/mail:
news:*:9:13:news:/var/spool/news:
uucp:*:10:14:uucp:/var/spool/uucp:
operator:*:11:0:operator:/root:
games:*:12:100:games:/usr/games:
gopher:*:13:30:gopher:/usr/lib/gopher-data:
ftp:*:14:50:FTP User:/home/ftp:
man:*:15:15:Manuals Owner:/:
nobody:*:65534:65534:Nobody:/:/bin/false
col:Wh0yzfAV2qm2Y:100:100:Caldera OpenLinux User:/home/col:/bin/bash
This is a backup of passwd file
for viewing purposes only
so do not modify
```

The backslashes (\) are used liberally in this example. Each backslash represents a new line. We go to the end of the file, as designated
by the $, then we add a new line with the backslash, and then add the

text we wish and a new line after the text. These lines are great to add to the end of the file, but we really should add them to the beginning of the file. The following example shows this approach:

man page

sed - 10

```
# sed '1i\
> This is a backup passwd file\
> for viewing purposes only\
> so do not modify\
> ' passwd.test
This is a backup passwd file
for viewing purposes only
so do not modify
root:PgYQCkVH65hyQ:0:0:root:/root:/bin/bash
bin:*:1:1:bin:/bin:
daemon:*:2:2:daemon:/sbin:
adm:*:3:4:adm:/var/adm:
lp:*:4:7:lp:/var/spool/lpd:
sync:*:5:0:sync:/sbin:/bin/sync
shutdown:*:6:11:shutdown:/sbin:/sbin/shutdown
halt:*:7:0:halt:/sbin:/sbin/halt
mail:*:8:12:mail:/var/spool/mail:
news:*:9:13:news:/var/spool/news:
uucp:*:10:14:uucp:/var/spool/uucp:
operator:*:11:0:operator:/root:
games:*:12:100:games:/usr/games:
gopher:*:13:30:gopher:/usr/lib/gopher-data:
ftp:*:14:50:FTP User:/home/ftp:
man:*:15:15:Manuals Owner:/:
nobody:*:65534:65534:Nobody:/:/bin/false
col:Wh0yzfAV2qm2Y:100:100:Caldera OpenLinux User:/home/col:/bin/bash
```

First, we run **sed**, specifying that on line one we are going to begin inserting the text shown. We use the single quote immediately following **sed** and use another single quote on the last line when we are done specifying all the information, except for the input file, which is **passwd.test**.

We have only scratched the surface of commands you can use with **sed**. The following **sed** summary includes the commands we have used (*p* for print; *d* for delete; and *a* for add), as well as others that were not part of the examples.

sed - Stream editor.

Commands

a	Append text.
b	Branch to a label.
c	Replace lines with text.
d	Delete the current text buffer.
D	Delete the first line of the current text buffer.
g	Paste overwriting contents of the hold space.
G	Paste the hold space below the address rather than overwriting it.
h	Copy the pattern space into hold space.
H	Append the contents of pattern space into hold space.
i	Insert text.
l	List the contents of the pattern space.
n	Read the next line of input into the pattern space.
N	Append next line of input to pattern space.
p	Print the pattern space.
P	Print from the start of the pattern space up to and including new line.
r	Read in a file.
s	Substitute patterns.
t	Branch if substitution has been made to the current pattern space.
w	Append the contents of the pattern space to the specified *file*.
x	Interchange the contents of the holding area and pattern space.
y	Translate characters.

awk

awk can pretty much do it all. With **awk**, you can search, modify files, generate reports, and a lot more. **awk** performs these tasks by searching for patterns in lines of input (from standard input or from a file). For each line that matches the specified pattern, it can perform some very complex processing on that line. The code to actually process matching lines of input is a cross between a shell script and a C program.

man page

grep - 10

Data manipulation tasks that would be very complex with combinations of **grep, cut,** and **paste** are very easily done with **awk**. Because **awk** is a programming language, it can also perform mathematical operations or check the input very easily (shells don't do math very well). It can even do floating-point math (shells deal only with integers and strings).

man page

cut - 10

The basic form of an **awk** program looks like this:

man page

paste - 10

```
awk    '/pattern_to_match/    {    program    to    run    }'
input_file_names
```

man page

awk - 10

Notice that the whole program is enclosed in single quotes. If no input file names are specified, **awk** reads from standard input (as from a pipe).

The *pattern_to_match* must appear between the / characters. The pattern is actually called a regular expression. Some common regular expression examples are shown in the examples.

The program to execute is written in **awk** code, which looks something like C. The program is executed whenever a line of input matches the *pattern_to_match*. If */pattern_to_match/* does not precede the program in { }, then the program is executed for every line of input.

awk works with fields of the input lines. Fields are words separated by white space. The fields in **awk** patterns and programs are referenced with *$*, followed by the field number. For example the second field of an input line is *$2*. If you are using an **awk** command in your shell programs, the fields (*$1, $2*, etc.) are not confused with the shell script's positional parameters because the **awk** variables are enclosed in single quotes causing the shell to ignore them.

You really need to see some examples of using **awk** to appreciate its power. The following few examples use a file called **newfiles**, which contains a list of files on a system less than 15 days old. This file is generated as part of a system administration audit program that checks various aspects of a UNIX system. The following shows the contents of **newfiles**:

man page

cat - 3

```
# cat newfiles
PROG>>>> report of files not older than 14 days by find
the file system is /
-rw-r--r--    1 root       root          567 Dec   7 07:16 ./etc/mnttab
-rw-r--r--    1 root       root        20713 Dec   7 07:18 ./etc/rc.log
-rw-r--r--    1 root       root            0 Dec   7 07:17 ./etc/hpC2400/hparray.map
-rw-r--r--    1 root       root            0 Dec   7 07:17 ./etc/hpC2400/hparray.devs
-rw-r--r--    1 root       root            0 Dec   7 07:17 ./etc/hpC2400/hparray.luns
-rw-r--r--    1 root       root            0 Dec   7 07:17 ./etc/hpC2400/hparray.addr
-r-s------    1 root       root            0 Dec   7 07:17 ./etc/hpC2400/pscan.lock
-r-s------    1 root       root            0 Dec   7 07:17 ./etc/hpC2400/monitor.lock
-rw-r--r--    1 root       root        14299 Dec   7 07:17 ./etc/hpC2400/HPARRAY.INFO
-rw-r--r--    1 bin        bin          8553 Dec   7 07:02 ./etc/shutdownlog
-rw-r--r--    1 root       mail        32768 Dec   7 07:16 ./etc/mail/aliases.db
-rw-r--r--    1 root       mail           33 Dec   7 07:16 ./etc/mail/sendmail.pid
-rw-r--r--    1 root       root           13 Dec   7 07:16 ./etc/opt/dce/boot_time
-rw-r--r--    1 root       root          720 Dec   7 13:34 ./etc/utmp
-rw-r--r--    1 root       root            0 Dec   7 07:16 ./etc/xtab
-rw-r--r--    1 root       root            0 Dec   7 07:18 ./etc/rmtab
-rw-r--r--    1 root       root        40814 Dec   7 07:15 ./etc/rc.log.old
-rw-r--r--    1 root       root         4620 Dec   7 13:34 ./etc/utmpx
-rw-r--r--    1 root       root            9 Dec   7 13:17 ./etc/ntp.drift
-rw-r--r--    1 root       root          616 Dec   7 07:15 ./etc/auto_parms.log
-rw-r--r--    1 root       sys           219 Dec   7 07:00 ./etc/auto_parms.log.old
-rw-rw-rw-    1 root       sys           520 Nov 23 12:37 ./.sw/sessions/swlist.last
-r--r--r--    1 root       informix       76 Dec   7 07:17 ./INFORMIXTMP/.inf.shmPSREP
-r--r--r--    1 root       informix       76 Dec   7 07:18 ./INFORMIXTMP/.inf.shmPSDEV
-rw-------    1 autosys    autosys      4052 Nov 25 14:08 ./home/autosys/.sh_history
-rw-------    1 tsaxs      users        2228 Dec   1 13:15 ./home/tsaxs/.sh_history
-rw-------    1 tsfxo      users        2862 Nov 24 10:08 ./home/tsfxo/.sh_history
PROG>>>> report of files not older than 14 days by find
the file system is /usr
-rw-rw-rw-    1 opop6      users          21 Dec   7 13:46 ./local/adm/etc/lmonitor.hst
-rw-r--r--    1 tsgjf      users        1093 Dec   7 13:17
./local/flexlm/licenses/license.log
PROG>>>> report of files not older than 14 days by find
the file system is /opt
-rw-rw-r--    1 bin        bin           200 Dec   7 07:17 ./pred/bin/OPSDBPF
-rw-r--r--    1 root       sys        800028 Dec   7 07:17 ./pred/bin/PSRNLOGD
PROG>>>> report of files not older than 14 days by find
the file system is /var
-rw-r--r--    1 root       sys         45089 Dec   7 07:16 ./adm/sw/swagentd.log
-rw-rw-rw-    1 root       sys           562 Dec   7 07:16 ./adm/sw/sessions/swlist.last
-rw-r--r--    1 root       root        12236 Dec   7 07:16 ./adm/ps_data
-rw-r--r--    1 root       root           65 Dec   7 07:17 ./adm/cron/log
-rw-r--r--    1 root       root          162 Dec   7 07:00 ./adm/cron/OLDlog
-r--r--r--    1 root       root       734143 Dec   7 07:16 ./adm/syslog/mail.log
-rw-r--r--    1 root       root        65743 Dec   7 13:56 ./adm/syslog/syslog.log
-rw-r--r--    1 root       root      4924974 Dec   7 07:02 ./adm/syslog/OLDsyslog.log
-rw-rw-r--    1 adm        adm       2750700 Dec   7 13:52 ./adm/wtmp
-rw-------    1 root       other      145920 Dec   3 14:36 ./adm/btmp
-rw-r--r--    1 lp         lp             33 Dec   7 07:17 ./adm/lp/log
-rw-r--r--    1 lp         lp             67 Dec   7 07:01 ./adm/lp/oldlog
-rw-r--r--    1 root       root         4330 Dec   7 07:18 ./adm/diag/device_table
-rw-r--r--    1 root       root           34 Dec   7 07:18 ./adm/diag/misc_sys_data
-rwxr-xr-x    1 root       root       995368 Nov 22 15:16 ./adm/diag/LOG0190
-rwxr-xr-x    1 root       root       995368 Nov 23 02:05 ./adm/diag/LOG0191
-rwxr-xr-x    1 root       root       453964 Nov 23 07:01 ./adm/diag/LOG0192
-rwxr-xr-x    1 root       root       970448 Nov 23 18:35 ./adm/diag/LOG0193
-rwxr-xr-x    1 root       root       995368 Nov 24 05:24 ./adm/diag/LOG0194
-rwxr-xr-x    1 root       root       995368 Nov 24 16:14 ./adm/diag/LOG0195
-rwxr-xr-x    1 root       root       995368 Nov 25 03:03 ./adm/diag/LOG0196
-rwxr-xr-x    1 root       root       995368 Nov 25 13:52 ./adm/diag/LOG0197
```

```
-rwxr-xr-x   1 root      root       995368 Nov 26 00:41 ./adm/diag/LOG0198
-rwxr-xr-x   1 root      root       995368 Nov 26 11:31 ./adm/diag/LOG0199
-rwxr-xr-x   1 root      root       995368 Nov 26 22:20 ./adm/diag/LOG0200
-rwxr-xr-x   1 root      root       995368 Nov 27 09:09 ./adm/diag/LOG0201
-rwxr-xr-x   1 root      root       995368 Nov 27 19:58 ./adm/diag/LOG0202
-rwxr-xr-x   1 root      root       995368 Nov 28 06:48 ./adm/diag/LOG0203
-rwxr-xr-x   1 root      root       995368 Nov 28 17:37 ./adm/diag/LOG0204
-rwxr-xr-x   1 root      root       995368 Nov 29 04:26 ./adm/diag/LOG0205
-rwxr-xr-x   1 root      root       995368 Nov 29 15:16 ./adm/diag/LOG0206
-rwxr-xr-x   1 root      root       995368 Nov 30 02:05 ./adm/diag/LOG0207
-rwxr-xr-x   1 root      root       452020 Nov 30 06:59 ./adm/diag/LOG0208
-rwxr-xr-x   1 root      root       970448 Nov 30 18:35 ./adm/diag/LOG0209
-rwxr-xr-x   1 root      root       995368 Dec  1 05:24 ./adm/diag/LOG0210
-rwxr-xr-x   1 root      root       995368 Dec  1 16:13 ./adm/diag/LOG0211
-rwxr-xr-x   1 root      root       995368 Dec  2 03:03 ./adm/diag/LOG0212
-rwxr-xr-x   1 root      root       995368 Dec  2 13:52 ./adm/diag/LOG0213
-rwxr-xr-x   1 root      root       995368 Dec  3 00:41 ./adm/diag/LOG0214
-rwxr-xr-x   1 root      root       995368 Dec  3 11:31 ./adm/diag/LOG0215
-rwxr-xr-x   1 root      root       995368 Dec  3 22:20 ./adm/diag/LOG0216
-rwxr-xr-x   1 root      root       995368 Dec  4 09:09 ./adm/diag/LOG0217
-rwxr-xr-x   1 root      root       995368 Dec  4 19:58 ./adm/diag/LOG0218
-rwxr-xr-x   1 root      root       995368 Dec  5 06:48 ./adm/diag/LOG0219
-rwxr-xr-x   1 root      root       995368 Dec  5 17:37 ./adm/diag/LOG0220
-rwxr-xr-x   1 root      root       995368 Dec  6 04:26 ./adm/diag/LOG0221
-rwxr-xr-x   1 root      root       995368 Dec  6 15:15 ./adm/diag/LOG0222
-rwxr-xr-x   1 root      root       995368 Dec  7 02:05 ./adm/diag/LOG0223
-rwxr-xr-x   1 root      root       453964 Dec  7 07:00 ./adm/diag/LOG0224
-rwxr-xr-x   1 root      root       543740 Dec  7 13:57 ./adm/diag/LOG0225
-rw-r--r--   1 root      root        19587 Dec  7 07:16 ./adm/ptydaemonlog
-rw-r--r--   1 root      root           52 Dec  7 07:16 ./adm/conslog.opts
-rw-r--r--   1 root      root            0 Dec  7 07:16 ./adm/rpc.statd.log
-rw-r--r--   1 root      root            0 Dec  7 07:16 ./adm/rpc.lockd.log
-rw-r--r--   1 root      root        24250 Dec  7 07:16 ./adm/vtdaemonlog
-rw-------   1 root      root          214 Dec  7 12:07 ./adm/sulog
-rw-------   1 root      root          381 Dec  3 17:34 ./adm/OLDsulog
-rw-r--r--   1 root      sys          145 Dec  7 07:16 ./adm/rbootd.log
-rw-------   1 sysadm    psoft         60 Dec  1 16:59 ./tmp/EAAa09057
-rw-r--r--   1 tsgjf     users          0 Dec  7 13:17 ./tmp/lockHPCUPLANGS
-rw-r--r--   1 tsgjf     users        175 Dec  7 06:40 ./tmp/.flexlm/lmgrd.1507
-rw-r--r--   1 tsgjf     users        175 Dec  7 13:28 ./tmp/.flexlm/lmgrd.1505
-rw-r--r--   1 lp        lp             0 Dec  7 07:17 ./spool/lp/outputq
-rw-rw-rw-   1 lp        lp             4 Dec  7 07:17 ./spool/lp/SCHEDLOCK
-rw-------   1 root      sys            0 Nov 23 07:00
./spool/cron/tmp/croutAAAa01030
-rw-------   1 root      sys            0 Nov 30 07:00
./spool/cron/tmp/croutAAAa01039
-rw-------   1 root      sys            0 Dec  7 07:00
./spool/cron/tmp/croutAAAb01039
-rw-r--r--   1 root      root            4 Dec  7 07:16 ./run/syslog.pid
-rw-r--r--   1 root      root            4 Dec  7 07:16 ./run/gated.pid
-rw-r--r--   1 root      sys          145 Dec  7 07:16 ./run/gated.version
-rw-r--r--   1 root      sys            3 Dec  7 07:16 ./statmon/state
-rw-r--r--   1 root      root        29771 Dec  7 07:16
./opt/dce/config/dce_config.log
-rw-r--r--   1 root      sys           74 Dec  7 07:16
./opt/dce/rpc/local/00404/srvr_socks
-rw-r--r--   1 root      root           72 Dec  7 07:16
./opt/dce/rpc/local/00927/srvr_socks
-rw-r--r--   1 root      root        32768 Dec  7 07:16 ./opt/dce/dced/Ep.db
-rw-r--r--   1 root      root        32768 Dec  7 07:20 ./opt/dce/dced/Llb.db
-rw-r--r--   1 root      root            0 Nov 30 07:16 ./opt/perf/status.ttd
-rw-r--r--   1 root      root           33 Dec  7 07:17 ./opt/perf/datafiles/RUN
-rwxrwxrwx   1 root      sys      9243180 Dec  7 13:55 ./opt/perf/datafiles/logappl
-rwxrwxrwx   1 root      sys      8697612 Dec  7 13:55 ./opt/perf/datafiles/logdev
-rwxrwxrwx   1 root      sys      9195152 Dec  7 13:55 ./opt/perf/datafiles/logglob
-rwxrwxrwx   1 root      sys        11112 Dec  7 07:17 ./opt/perf/datafiles/logindx
-rwxrwxrwx   1 root      sys     17639080 Dec  7 13:57
./opt/perf/datafiles/logproc
-rwxrwxrwx   1 root      sys         3797 Dec  7 07:17
./opt/perf/datafiles/mikslp.data
-rw-rw-rw-   1 root      sys          105 Nov 30 10:45 ./opt/perf/datafiles/agdb
-rw-r--r--   1 root      root            5 Dec  7 07:17
./opt/perf/datafiles/.perflbd.pid
-rw-rw-rw-   1 root      sys        21176 Dec  7 07:20 ./opt/perf/status.scope
-rw-rw-rw-   1 root      root            5 Nov 30 07:16 ./opt/perf/ttd.pid
```

```
-rw-r--r--    1 root       root              0 Dec   7 07:17 ./opt/perf/status.mi
-rw-rw-rw-    1 root       sys            8254 Dec   7 07:17 ./opt/perf/status.perflbd
-rw-rw-rw-    1 root       sys           21507 Dec   7 07:20 ./opt/perf/status.rep_server
-rw-rw-rw-    1 root       sys           24570 Dec   7 07:20 ./opt/perf/status.alarmgen
-rw-rw-rw-    1 root       sys          160956 Dec   6 21:13 ./opt/omni/log/inet.log
-rw-rw-rw-    1 root       sys          158796 Dec   7 07:17 ./sam/log/samlog
-rw-r--r--    1 root       root          64730 Dec   7 07:17 ./sam/boot.config
-rw-rw-rw-    1 root       sys           11906 Nov  24 14:27 ./sam/poe.iout
-rw-rw-rw-    1 root       sys           11906 Nov  23 09:10 ./sam/poe.iout.old
-rw-rw-rw-    1 root       sys              29 Nov  24 14:27 ./sam/poe.dion
```

man page

awk - 10

You can see that this file contains several fields separated by white space. The next example evaluates the third field to determine whether it equals "adm," and if so, the line is printed:

```
# awk '$3 == "adm" {print}' newfiles
-rw-rw-r--    1 adm        adm         2750700 Dec   7 13:52 ./adm/wtmp
```

There is precisely one line that contains exactly "adm" in the third field.

The next example evaluates the third field to determine whether it approximately equals "adm," meaning that the third field has "adm" embedded in it, and if so, the line is printed:

```
# awk '$3 ~ "adm" {print}' newfiles
-rw-rw-r--    1 adm        adm         2750700 Dec   7 13:52 ./adm/wtmp
-rw-------    1 sysadm     psoft            60 Dec   1 16:59 ./tmp/EAAa09057
```

This result prints the line from the last example, which has "adm" in the third field as well as a line that contains "sysadm."

The next example performs the same search as the previous example; however, this time only fields nine and five are printed:

```
# awk '$3 ~ "adm" {print $9, $5}' newfiles
./adm/wtmp 2750700
./tmp/EAAa09057 60
```

This time only the name of the file, field nine, and the size of the file were printed.

The next example evaluates the third field to determine if it does not equal "root," and if so, prints the entire line:

```
# awk '$3 != "root" {print}' newfiles
PROG>>>>> report of files not older than 14 days by find
the file system is /
-rw-r--r--   1 bin       bin         8553 Dec  7 07:02 ./etc/shutdownlog
-rw-------   1 autosys   autosys     4052 Nov 25 14:08 ./home/autosys/.sh_history
-rw-------   1 tsaxs     users       2228 Dec  1 13:15 ./home/tsaxs/.sh_history
-rw-------   1 tsfxo     users       2862 Nov 24 10:08 ./home/tsfxo/.sh_history
PROG>>>>> report of files not older than 14 days by find
the file system is /usr
-rw-rw-rw-   1 opop6     users         21 Dec  7 13:46 ./local/adm/etc/lmonitor.hst
-rw-r--r--   1 tsgjf     users       1093 Dec  7 13:17
./local/flexlm/licenses/license.log
PROG>>>>> report of files not older than 14 days by find
the file system is /opt
-rw-rw-r--   1 bin       bin          200 Dec  7 07:17 ./pred/bin/OPSDBPF
PROG>>>>> report of files not older than 14 days by find
the file system is /var
-rw-rw-r--   1 adm       adm      2750700 Dec  7 13:52 ./adm/wtmp
-rw-r--r--   1 lp        lp            33 Dec  7 07:17 ./adm/lp/log
-rw-r--r--   1 lp        lp            67 Dec  7 07:01 ./adm/lp/oldlog
-rw-------   1 sysadm    psoft         60 Dec  7 16:59 ./tmp/EAAa09057
-rw-r--r--   1 tsgjf     users          0 Dec  7 13:17 ./tmp/lockHPCUPLANGS
-rw-r--r--   1 tsgjf     users        175 Dec  7 06:40 ./tmp/.flexlm/lmgrd.1507
-rw-r--r--   1 tsgjf     users        175 Dec  7 13:28 ./tmp/.flexlm/lmgrd.1505
-rw-r--r--   1 lp        lp             0 Dec  7 07:17 ./spool/lp/outputq
-rw-rw-rw-   1 lp        lp             4 Dec  7 07:17 ./spool/lp/SCHEDLOCK
```

man page

awk - 10

This command results in many lines printed that do not have "root" in the third field.

newfiles had whitespace to separate the fields. We don't often have this luxury in the UNIX world. The upcoming examples use **passwd.test**, which has a colon(:) as a field separator. **passwd.test** is shown below:

man page

cat - 3

```
# cat passwd.test
root:PgYQCkVH65hyQ:0:0:root:/root:/bin/bash
bin:*:1:1:bin:/bin:
daemon:*:2:2:daemon:/sbin:
adm:*:3:4:adm:/var/adm:
lp:*:4:7:lp:/var/spool/lpd:
sync:*:5:0:sync:/sbin:/bin/sync
shutdown:*:6:11:shutdown:/sbin:/sbin/shutdown
halt:*:7:0:halt:/sbin:/sbin/halt
mail:*:8:12:mail:/var/spool/mail:
news:*:9:13:news:/var/spool/news:
uucp:*:10:14:uucp:/var/spool/uucp:
operator:*:11:0:operator:/root:
games:*:12:100:games:/usr/games:
gopher:*:13:30:gopher:/usr/lib/gopher-data:
ftp:*:14:50:FTP User:/home/ftp:
man:*:15:15:Manuals Owner:/:
nobody:*:65534:65534:Nobody:/:/bin/false
col:WhOyzfAV2qm2Y:100:100:Caldera OpenLinux User:/home/col:/bin/bash
```

You can specify the field separator with the *-F* option followed by a separator, which is a colon(:) in **passwd.test**. The following example specifies the field separator and then evaluates the first field to determine whether it equals "root," and if so, prints out the entire line:

man page

awk - 10

```
# awk -F: '$1 == "root" {print}' passwd.test
root:PgYQCkVH65hyQ:0:0:root:/root:/bin/bash
```

The following example specifies the field separator and then evaluates the fourth field to determine whether it equals "0," which means the user is a member of the same group as root, and if so, prints out the entire line:

```
# awk -F: '$4 == "0" {print}' passwd.test
root:PgYQCkVH65hyQ:0:0:root:/root:/bin/bash
sync:*:5:0:sync:/sbin:/bin/sync
halt:*:7:0:halt:/sbin:/sbin/halt
operator:*:11:0:operator:/root:
```

You can perform many types of comparisons besides == using **awk**. The following examples show the use of several comparison operators on our trusty **passwd.test** file. The first example prints all users who are in a group with a value less than 14:

```
# awk -F: '$4 < 14 {print}' passwd.test
root:PgYQCkVH65hyQ:0:0:root:/root:/bin/bash
bin:*:1:1:bin:/bin:
daemon:*:2:2:daemon:/sbin:
adm:*:3:4:adm:/var/adm:
lp:*:4:7:lp:/var/spool/lpd:
sync:*:5:0:sync:/sbin:/bin/sync
shutdown:*:6:11:shutdown:/sbin:/sbin/shutdown
halt:*:7:0:halt:/sbin:/sbin/halt
mail:*:8:12:mail:/var/spool/mail:
news:*:9:13:news:/var/spool/news:
operator:*:11:0:operator:/root:
```

The next example prints all users who are in a group with a value less than or equal to 14:

```
# awk -F: '$4 <= 14 {print}' passwd.test
root:PgYQCkVH65hyQ:0:0:root:/root:/bin/bash
bin:*:1:1:bin:/bin:
daemon:*:2:2:daemon:/sbin:
adm:*:3:4:adm:/var/adm:
lp:*:4:7:lp:/var/spool/lpd:
sync:*:5:0:sync:/sbin:/bin/sync
shutdown:*:6:11:shutdown:/sbin:/sbin/shutdown
halt:*:7:0:halt:/sbin:/sbin/halt
mail:*:8:12:mail:/var/spool/mail:
news:*:9:13:news:/var/spool/news:
uucp:*:10:14:uucp:/var/spool/uucp:
operator:*:11:0:operator:/root:
```

Let's now print all users who are in a group that does not have a value of 14:

```
# awk -F: '$4 != 14 {print}' passwd.test
root:PgYQCkVH65hyQ:0:0:root:/root:/bin/bash
bin:*:1:1:bin:/bin:
daemon:*:2:2:daemon:/sbin:
adm:*:3:4:adm:/var/adm:
lp:*:4:7:lp:/var/spool/lpd:
sync:*:5:0:sync:/sbin:/bin/sync
shutdown:*:6:11:shutdown:/sbin:/sbin/shutdown
halt:*:7:0:halt:/sbin:/sbin/halt
mail:*:8:12:mail:/var/spool/mail:
news:*:9:13:news:/var/spool/news:
operator:*:11:0:operator:/root:
games:*:12:100:games:/usr/games:
gopher:*:13:30:gopher:/usr/lib/gopher-data:
ftp:*:14:50:FTP User:/home/ftp:
man:*:15:15:Manuals Owner:/:
nobody:*:65534:65534:Nobody:/:/bin/false
col:Wh0yzfAV2qm2Y:100:100:Caldera OpenLinux User:/home/col:/bin/bash
```

Lets now print all users who are in a group with a value greater than or equal to 14:

```
# awk -F: '$4 >= 14 {print}' passwd.test
uucp:*:10:14:uucp:/var/spool/uucp:
games:*:12:100:games:/usr/games:
gopher:*:13:30:gopher:/usr/lib/gopher-data:
ftp:*:14:50:FTP User:/home/ftp:
man:*:15:15:Manuals Owner:/:
nobody:*:65534:65534:Nobody:/:/bin/false
col:Wh0yzfAV2qm2Y:100:100:Caldera OpenLinux User:/home/col:/bin/bash
```

The last example shows all users who are in a group with a value greater than 14:

```
# awk -F: '$4 > 14 {print}' passwd.test
games:*:12:100:games:/usr/games:
gopher:*:13:30:gopher:/usr/lib/gopher-data:
```

```
ftp:*:14:50:FTP User:/home/ftp:
man:*:15:15:Manuals Owner:/:
nobody:*:65534:65534:Nobody:/:/bin/false
col:Wh0yzfAV2qm2Y:100:100:Caldera OpenLinux User:/home/col:/bin/bash
```

There is much more to **awk** than what I have covered in this section. There are additional **awk** examples in the shell programming chapter.

The following table summarizes some of the comparison operators of **awk** covered in this section.

awk - Search a line for a specified pattern and perform operation(s).

Comparison operators:

<	Less than.
<=	Less than or equal to.
==	Equal to.
~	Strings match.
!=	Not equal to.
>=	Greater than or equal to.
>	Greater than.

find

The **find** command is used to locate files by traversing the UNIX tree structure. You can start from any point on the system, even the root level, and traverse through the entire hierarchy. After finding files you can also perform actions.

The most common use of **find** is to produce a list of files. You can produce a list of files in the current working directory, specified by a dot (.), and *print* those files, as shown in the following example:

```
# cd /home
#
# ls -l
total 3
drwxr-xr-x   3 col      users        1024 Nov  8 14:09 col
drwxr-xr-x   6 root     root         1024 Nov  8 14:08 ftp
drwxr-xr-x   6 root     root         1024 Nov  8 14:08 httpd
#
# find . -print
.
./httpd
./httpd/apache
./httpd/apache/doc
./httpd/apache/doc/manual.ps.gz
./httpd/cgi-bin
./httpd/cgi-bin/HelpIndex
./httpd/cgi-bin/HelpScreen
./httpd/html
./httpd/html/dt
./httpd/html/dt/dt.html
./httpd/html/dt/dt.html.idx
./httpd/html/dt/dt.index
./httpd/html/dt/expert.gif
./httpd/html/dt/hint.gif
./httpd/html/dt/index.gif
./httpd/html/dt/info2.gif
./httpd/html/dt/note.gif
./httpd/html/dt/sysadm.gif
./httpd/html/dt/up.gif
./httpd/html/dt/warning.gif
./httpd/icons
./ftp
./ftp/bin
./ftp/bin/gzip
./ftp/bin/ls
./ftp/bin/tar
./ftp/bin/zcat
./ftp/etc
./ftp/etc/group
./ftp/etc/passwd
./ftp/lib
./ftp/pub
./col
./col/.bashrc
./col/.cshrc
./col/.login
./col/.profile
./col/lg
./col/lg/lg_layouts
./col/lg/lg_layouts/User
./col/lg/lg3_prefs
./col/lg/lg3_soundPref
./col/lg/lg3_startup
```

man page

cd - 3

man page

ls - 2

man page

find - 10

This **find** operation was performed from the **/home** directory. Notice that there are only three home directories under **/home**, and the **find** command traverses the hierarchy for each of the three home directories. Keep in mind that you probably don't want to perform this **find** operation at the root level. You will traverse the entire hierarchy and get a list of every file on the system.

When using **find**, you may discover that you receive a message like the following when a file or directory is encountered for which you do not have adequate permission to traverse:

```
find: /var/spool/cron: Permission denied
```

The general form of **find** is the following:

```
find [path] [expression]
```

If you don't specify a *path* or *expression,* you will perform the operation we earlier performed, that is, you will search the current directory and print a list of all files.

A typical find command will specify the path in which to search for a specific file. In this case the *expression* is the *name* of the file for which you wish to search, as shown in the following example:

```
# find /home -name ftp
/home/ftp
```

In this example, we search the *path* **/home** looking for the *name* **ftp**.

You may want to perform a **find** operation to produce a list of files only and not include directories in the operation. The following **find** is similar to that we performed earlier, but this time produces a list of files only:

```
# find /home -type f
/home/httpd/apache/doc/manual.ps.gz
/home/httpd/cgi-bin/HelpIndex
/home/httpd/cgi-bin/HelpScreen
/home/httpd/html/dt/dt.html
/home/httpd/html/dt/dt.html.idx
/home/httpd/html/dt/dt.index
/home/httpd/html/dt/expert.gif
/home/httpd/html/dt/hint.gif
/home/httpd/html/dt/index.gif
/home/httpd/html/dt/info2.gif
/home/httpd/html/dt/note.gif
/home/httpd/html/dt/sysadm.gif
/home/httpd/html/dt/up.gif
```

```
/home/httpd/html/dt/warning.gif
/home/ftp/bin/gzip
/home/ftp/bin/ls
/home/ftp/bin/tar
/home/ftp/etc/group
/home/ftp/etc/passwd
/home/col/.bashrc
/home/col/.cshrc
/home/col/.login
/home/col/.profile
/home/col/lg/lg_layouts/User
/home/col/lg/lg3_prefs
/home/col/lg/lg3_soundPref
/home/col/lg/lg3_startup
```

man page

find - 10

A useful test when performing a **find** operation is for empty files. The following example searches for all empty files and directories on the system:

```
# find / -empty
/lost+found
/var/adm/LST/analyse
/var/spool/lpd
/var/spool/news
/var/spool/uucp
/var/spool/mqueue
/var/spool/atjobs/.SEQ
/var/spool/atspool
/var/spool/cron
/var/spool/fax/outgoing/locks
/var/spool/fax/incoming
/var/spool/voice/incoming
/var/spool/voice/messages
/var/spool/rwho
/var/spool/uucppublic
/var/lib/LST/log
/var/lib/LST/analyse
/var/lib/LST/disks
/var/lib/LST/catalog
/var/lib/LST/conflicts
/var/lib/LST/saved
/var/lib/LST/replaced
/var/lib/LST/deleted
/var/lib/games
/var/local
/var/lock/subsys/inet
/var/lock/subsys/ipx
/var/lock/subsys/syslog
/var/lock/subsys/amd
/var/lock/subsys/cron
/var/lock/subsys/atd
/var/lock/subsys/mta
/var/lock/subsys/rstatd
/var/lock/subsys/httpd
/var/log/httpd/apache/access_log
/var/log/xferlog
/var/log/uucp
/var/log/secure
/var/log/spooler
/var/named
/var/nis
/var/preserve
/var/run/xlaunch
/var/tmp
/var/catman/TeX/cat1
/var/catman/TeX/cat2
/var/catman/TeX/cat3
```

```
/var/catman/TeX/cat4
/var/catman/TeX/cat5
/var/catman/TeX/cat6
/var/catman/TeX/cat7
/var/catman/TeX/cat8
/var/catman/TeX/cat9
/var/catman/TeX/catn
/var/catman/X11/cat1
/var/catman/X11/cat2
/var/catman/X11/cat3
/var/catman/X11/cat4
/var/catman/X11/cat5
/var/catman/X11/cat6
/var/catman/X11/cat7
/var/catman/X11/cat8
/var/catman/X11/cat9
/var/catman/X11/catn
/var/catman/local/cat1
/var/catman/local/cat2
/var/catman/local/cat3
/var/catman/local/cat4
/var/catman/local/cat5
/var/catman/local/cat6
/var/catman/local/cat7
/var/catman/local/cat8
/var/catman/local/cat9
/var/catman/local/catn
/var/catman/openwin/cat1
/var/catman/openwin/cat2
/var/catman/openwin/cat3
/var/catman/openwin/cat4
/var/catman/openwin/cat5
/var/catman/openwin/cat6
/var/catman/openwin/cat7
/var/catman/openwin/cat8
/var/catman/openwin/cat9
/var/catman/openwin/catn
/var/catman/opt/cat1
/var/catman/opt/cat2
/var/catman/opt/cat3
/var/catman/opt/cat4
/var/catman/opt/cat5
/var/catman/opt/cat6
/var/catman/opt/cat7
/var/catman/opt/cat8
/var/catman/opt/cat9
/var/catman/opt/catn
/var/catman/cat1/3725
/var/catman/cat2
/var/catman/cat3
/var/catman/cat4
/var/catman/cat5
/var/catman/cat6
/var/catman/cat7
/var/catman/cat8
/var/catman/cat9
/var/catman/catn
/proc/mounts
/proc/locks
/proc/cmdline
/proc/ioports
/proc/dma
/proc/filesystems
/proc/interrupts
/proc/devices
/proc/stat
/proc/ksyms
/proc/modules
/proc/sys/net/ipv4/arp_confirm_timeout
/proc/sys/net/ipv4/arp_confirm_interval
/proc/sys/net/ipv4/arp_check_interval
/proc/sys/net/ipv4/arp_timeout
/proc/sys/net/ipv4/arp_max_tries
/proc/sys/net/ipv4/arp_dead_res_time
/proc/sys/net/ipv4/arp_res_time
```

```
/proc/sys/net/ethernet
/proc/sys/net/802
/proc/sys/net/unix
/proc/sys/net/core
/proc/sys/vm/bdflush
/proc/sys/vm/freepages
/proc/sys/vm/kswapd
/proc/sys/vm/swapctl
/proc/sys/kernel/real-root-dev
/proc/sys/kernel/panic
/proc/sys/kernel/securelevel
/proc/sys/kernel/file-max
/proc/sys/kernel/file-nr
/proc/sys/kernel/inode-max
/proc/sys/kernel/inode-nr
/proc/sys/kernel/domainname
/proc/sys/kernel/hostname
/proc/sys/kernel/version
/proc/sys/kernel/osrelease
/proc/sys/kernel/ostype
/proc/scsi/scsi
/proc/net/ipx_route
/proc/net/ipx_interface
/proc/net/ipx
/proc/net/dev
/proc/net/rt_cache
/proc/net/route
/proc/net/udp
/proc/net/tcp
/proc/net/sockstat
/proc/net/snmp
/proc/net/raw
/proc/net/igmp
/proc/net/arp
/proc/net/unix
/proc/cpuinfo
/proc/pci
/proc/version
/proc/kmsg
/proc/meminfo
/proc/uptime
/proc/loadavg
/proc/mdstat
/etc/modules/options
/etc/motd
/etc/exports
/etc/ppp/options
/tmp/LST
/tmp/.XF86Setup235/f51cb27-315ae55/ServerOut-2
/tmp/.XF86Setup246/13617839-11c71c71/ServerOut-2
/tmp/.XF86Setup262/1f2cc0a9-aea314d/ServerOut-2
/tmp/.XF86Setup288/17963ff7-21ca966f/ServerOut-2
/tmp/fsslog
/mnt/floppy
/mnt/cdrom
/usr/doc/html/woven/LDP/install-guide-2.2.2.html/images.idx
/usr/lib/games
/usr/lib/groff/tmac/mm/locale
/usr/lib/groff/tmac/mm/se_locale
/usr/lib/kbd/keytables/patch_tables.orig
/usr/lib/perl5/i386-linux/5.003/auto/GDBM_File/GDBM_File.bs
/usr/lib/perl5/i386-linux/5.003/auto/DB_File/DB_File.bs
/usr/lib/perl5/i386-linux/5.003/auto/Fcntl/Fcntl.bs
/usr/lib/perl5/i386-linux/5.003/auto/FileHandle/FileHandle.bs
/usr/lib/perl5/i386-linux/5.003/auto/NDBM_File/NDBM_File.bs
/usr/lib/perl5/i386-linux/5.003/auto/POSIX/POSIX.bs
/usr/lib/perl5/i386-linux/5.003/auto/SDBM_File/SDBM_File.bs
/usr/lib/perl5/i386-linux/5.003/auto/Safe/Safe.bs
/usr/lib/perl5/i386-linux/5.003/auto/Socket/Socket.bs
/usr/lib/perl5/i386-linux/5.003/auto/Text/ParseWords
/usr/lib/perl5/site_perl/i386-linux
/usr/lib/linuxdoc-sgml/null.sty
/usr/etc
/usr/include/g++
/usr/include/netax25
```

```
/usr/include/netipx
/usr/include/readline
/usr/local/bin
/usr/local/doc
/usr/local/etc
/usr/local/games
/usr/local/info
/usr/local/lib
/usr/local/man/man1
/usr/local/man/man2
/usr/local/man/man3
/usr/local/man/man4
/usr/local/man/man5
/usr/local/man/man6
/usr/local/man/man7
/usr/local/man/man8
/usr/local/man/man9
/usr/local/man/mann
/usr/local/sbin
/usr/local/src
/usr/man/man9
/usr/man/mann
/usr/src/linux-2.0.29/include/linux/modules
/usr/src/linux-2.0.29/modules
/usr/src/redhat/BUILD
/usr/src/redhat/RPMS/i386
/usr/src/redhat/SOURCES
/usr/src/redhat/SPECS
/usr/src/redhat/SRPMS
/usr/X11R6/doc
/usr/X11R6/lib/X11/x11perfcomp
/usr/visix/fss/En_US.8859
/usr/visix/vls/En_US.8859
/usr/openwin/share/src/xview
/auto
/initrd
/home/httpd/icons
/home/ftp/lib
/home/ftp/pub
/opt/bin
/opt/man
/root/lg/lg3_hosts
/amd/nycald17auto/.vTRASH
#
# ll /auto
total 0
```

man page

find - 10

All the files and directories listed as a result of this **find** operation are empty. The long listing of **/auto** shown as part of the example
confirms this fact.

There are many useful expressions that can be used with **find**.
The following is a list of some of the more commonly used **find**
expressions.

find - Search for files.

man page find - 10

Commonly used expressions:

-mount   Do not descend directories on other file systems.

-newer *file*

File was modified more recently than *file*.

-name *pattern*

Look for file name of *pattern*.

-type t   File has a type of *t,* such as *d* for directory and *f* for file.

-user *uname*

File is owned by *uname*.

-exec *command ;*

Execute *command.*

-print   Print the current file name.

man page sort - 10

sort

Sometimes the contents of files are not sorted in the way you would like. You can use the **sort** command to sort files with a variety of options.

You may find as you use your UNIX system more and more that your system administrator is riding you about the amount of disk space you are consuming. You can monitor the amount of disk space you are consuming with the **du** command. Figure 10-9 shows creating a file called **disk_space** that lists the amount of disk space consumed by files and directories and shows the first 20 lines of the file.

```
┌──────────────────────────────────────────────────────────────────────────┐
│ ▭                              sort example #1                        • □  │
├──────────────────────────────────────────────────────────────────────────┤
│ $ du -s * > disk_space                                                     │
│ $                                                                          │
│ $ head -20 disk_space                                                      │
│ 1216     27247b.exe                                                        │
│ 240      410pt1.exe                                                        │
│ 288      410pt2.exe                                                        │
│ 74       41mac1.exe                                                        │
│ 368      41ndir.exe                                                        │
│ 736      41nds1.exe                                                        │
│ 1056     41nds4.exe                                                        │
│ 3056     41nwad.exe                                                        │
│ 1696     41rtr2.exe                                                        │
│ 68       EMACS.tutorial                                                    │
│ 2        Mail                                                              │
│ 3520     N3212B6.EXE                                                       │
│ 368      PHNE_6014                                                         │
│ 752      PHNE_6121                                                         │
│ 976      PHNE_6121.depot                                                   │
│ 20       PHNE_6121.text                                                    │
│ 2        Passwd                                                            │
│ 28       SCSI4S.EXE                                                        │
│ 36       aplay.exe                                                         │
│ 4        archives                                                          │
│ $ █                                                                        │
└──────────────────────────────────────────────────────────────────────────┘
```

Figure 10-9   **sort** Command Example #1

man page

sort - 10

Notice that the result is sorted alphabetically. In many cases, this is what you want. If the file were not sorted alphabetically, you could use the **sort** command to do so. In this case, we don't care as much about seeing entries in alphabetical order as we do in numeric order, that is, which files and directories are consuming the most space. Figure 10-10 shows sorting the file **disk_space** numerically with the **-n** option and reversing the order of the sort with the **-r** option so that the biggest numbers appear first. We then specify the output file name with the **-o** option.

```
┌─────────────────────────────────────────────────────────────────────┬───────┐
│ ─ │                            sort example #2                        │ · │ □ │
├───┴─────────────────────────────────────────────────────────────────┴───────┤
│ $ sort −n −r disk_space −o disk_space_numeric                                 │
│ $                                                                             │
│ $ head −20 disk_space_numeric                                                 │
│ 288238    main.directory                                                      │
│ 60336     emacs−19.28.tar                                                     │
│ 8128      c3295n_a.exe                                                        │
│ 5024      trace.TRC1                                                          │
│ 4496      rkhelp.exe                                                          │
│ 3840      tnds2.exe                                                           │
│ 3520      n32e12n.exe                                                         │
│ 3520      N3212B6.EXE                                                         │
│ 3056      41nwad.exe                                                          │
│ 2784      nsh220e2.zip                                                        │
│ 2768      nsh220e3.zip                                                        │
│ 2752      nfs197.exe                                                          │
│ 2688      mbox                                                                │
│ 2160      msie10.exe                                                          │
│ 2032      nsh220e1.zip                                                        │
│ 2000      trace.TRC1.Z.uue                                                    │
│ 1984      plusdemo.exe                                                        │
│ 1840      ja95up.exe                                                          │
│ 1776      hpd10117.exe                                                        │
│ 1712      wsos22.exe                                                          │
│ $ █                                                                           │
└───────────────────────────────────────────────────────────────────────────┘
```

Figure 10-10   **sort** Command Example #2

What if the items being sorted had many more fields than our
two-column disk usage example? Let's go back to the **passwd.test** file
for a more complex sort. Let's **cat passwd.test** so that we can again
see its contents:

man page

cat - 3

```
# cat passwd.test
root:PgYQCkVH65hyQ:0:0:root:/root:/bin/bash
bin:*:1:1:bin:/bin:
daemon:*:2:2:daemon:/sbin:
adm:*:3:4:adm:/var/adm:
lp:*:4:7:lp:/var/spool/lpd:
sync:*:5:0:sync:/sbin:/bin/sync
shutdown:*:6:11:shutdown:/sbin:/sbin/shutdown
halt:*:7:0:halt:/sbin:/sbin/halt
mail:*:8:12:mail:/var/spool/mail:
news:*:9:13:news:/var/spool/news:
uucp:*:10:14:uucp:/var/spool/uucp:
operator:*:11:0:operator:/root:
games:*:12:100:games:/usr/games:
gopher:*:13:30:gopher:/usr/lib/gopher-data:
```

```
ftp:*:14:50:FTP User:/home/ftp:
man:*:15:15:Manuals Owner:/:
nobody:*:65534:65534:Nobody:/:/bin/false
col:Wh0yzfAV2qm2Y:100:100:Caldera   OpenLinux   User:/home/
col:/bin/bash
```

man page

sort - 10

Now let's use **sort** to determine which users are in the same group. Fields are separated in **passwd.test** by a colon (:). The fourth field is the group to which a user belongs. For instance, *bin* is in group 1, *daemon* in group 2, and so on. To sort by group, we would have to specify three options to the **sort** command. The first is to specify the delimiter (or field separator) of colon (:) using the *-t* option. Next we would have to specify the field on which we wish to sort with the *-k* option. Finally, we want a numeric sort, so use the *-n* option. The following example shows a numeric sort of the **passwd.test** file by the fourth field:

```
# sort -t: -k4 -n passwd.test
halt:*:7:0:halt:/sbin:/sbin/halt
operator:*:11:0:operator:/root:
root:PgYQCkVH65hyQ:0:0:root:/root:/bin/bash
sync:*:5:0:sync:/sbin:/bin/sync
bin:*:1:1:bin:/bin:
daemon:*:2:2:daemon:/sbin:
adm:*:3:4:adm:/var/adm:
lp:*:4:7:lp:/var/spool/lpd:
shutdown:*:6:11:shutdown:/sbin:/sbin/shutdown
mail:*:8:12:mail:/var/spool/mail:
news:*:9:13:news:/var/spool/news:
uucp:*:10:14:uucp:/var/spool/uucp:
man:*:15:15:Manuals Owner:/:
gopher:*:13:30:gopher:/usr/lib/gopher-data:
ftp:*:14:50:FTP User:/home/ftp:
col:Wh0yzfAV2qm2Y:100:100:Caldera   OpenLinux   User:/home/
col:/bin/bash
games:*:12:100:games:/usr/games:
nobody:*:65534:65534:Nobody:/:/bin/false
```

man page

sort - 10

The following is a summary of the **sort** command.

sort - Sort lines of files (alphabetically by default).

Options

-b	Ignore leading spaces and tabs.
-c	Check whether files are already sorted, and if so, do nothing.
-d	Ignore punctuation and sort in dictionary order.
-f	Ignore the case of entries when sorting.
-i	Ignore non-ASCII characters when sorting.
-ks	Use field s as the field on which to base the sort.
-m	Merge sorted files.
-n	Sort in numeric order.
-o file	Specify the output file name rather than write to standard output.
-r	Reverse the order of the sort by starting with the last letter of the alphabet or with the largest number, as we did in the example.
+n	Skip n fields or columns before sorting.

man page

cmp - 10

man page

diff - 10

cmp, diff, and comm

A fact of life is that as you go about editing files, you may occasionally lose track of what changes you have made to which files. You may then need to make comparisons of files. Let's take a look at three such commands, **cmp**, **diff** and **comm** and see how they compare files.

man page

comm - 10

Let's assume that we have modified a script called **llsum**. The unmodified version of **llsum** was saved as **llsum.orig**. Using the **head** command we can view the first 20 lines of **llsum** and then the first 20 lines of **llsum.orig**:

man page

head - 3

```
# head -20 llsum
#
#!/bin/sh
# Displays a truncated long listing (ll) and
# displays size statistics
# of the files in the listing.

ll $* | \
awk ' BEGIN { x=i=0; printf "%-25s%-10s%8s%8s\n",\
                       "FILENAME","OWNER","SIZE","TYPE" }
      $1 ~ /^[-dlps]/  {# line format for normal files
            printf "%-25s%-10s%8d",$9,$3,$5
            x = x + $5
              i++
                      }
     $1 ~ /^-/ { printf "%8s\n","file" }  # standard file
types
      $1 ~ /^d/ { printf "%8s\n","dir" }
      $1 ~ /^l/ { printf "%8s\n","link" }
      $1 ~ /^p/ { printf "%8s\n","pipe" }
      $1 ~ /^s/ { printf "%8s\n","socket" }
      $1 ~ /^[bc]/ { # line format for device files
                          printf             "%-25s%-
10s%8s%8s\n",$10,$3,"","dev"
                    }
#
# head -20 llsum.orig
#
#!/bin/sh
# Displays a truncated long listing (ll) and
# displays size statistics
# of the files in the listing.

ll $* | \
awk ' BEGIN { x=i=0; printf "%-16s%-10s%8s%8s\n",\
                       "FILENAME","OWNER","SIZE","TYPE" }
      $1 ~ /^[-dlps]/  {# line format for normal files
            printf "%-16s%-10s%8d",$9,$3,$5
            x = x + $5
              i++
                      }
     $1 ~ /^-/ { printf "%8s\n","file" }  # standard file
types
      $1 ~ /^d/ { printf "%8s\n","dir" }
      $1 ~ /^l/ { printf "%8s\n","link" }
      $1 ~ /^p/ { printf "%8s\n","pipe" }
      $1 ~ /^s/ { printf "%8s\n","socket" }
      $1 ~ /^[bc]/ { # line format for device files
                          printf             "%-16s%-
10s%8s%8s\n",$10,$3,"","dev"
                    }
```

I'm not sure what changes I made to **llsum.orig** to improve it, so
we can first use **cmp** to see whether indeed differences exist between
the files.

man page

cmp - 10

```
$
$ cmp llsum llsum.orig
llsum llsum.orig differ: char 154, line 6
$
```

cmp does not report back much information, only that character
154 in the file at line 6 is different in the two files. There may indeed
be other differences, but this is all we know about so far.

To get information about all of the differences in the two files we
could use the **-l** option to **cmp**:

```
$ cmp -l llsum llsum.orig
    154   62   61
    155   65   66
    306   62   61
    307   65   66
    675   62   61
    676   65   66
```

This is not all that useful an output to me. I want to see not only
the position of the differences, but also he differences themselves.

Now we can use **diff** to describe all the differences in the two
files:

man page

diff - 10

```
$ diff llsum llsum.orig
6c6
< awk ' BEGIN { x=i=0; printf "%-25s%-10s%8s%8s\n",\
---
> awk ' BEGIN { x=i=0; printf "%-16s%-10s%8s%8s\n",\
9c9
<               printf "%-25s%-10s%8d",$9,$3,$5
---
>               printf "%-16s%-10s%8d",$9,$3,$5
19c19
<               printf "%-25s%-10s%8s%8s\n",$10,$3,"","dev"
```

```
---
>         printf "%-16s%-10s%8s%8s\n",$10,$3,"","dev"
$
```

We now know that lines 6, 9, and 25 are different in the two files and these lines are also listed for us. From this listing, we can see that the number 16 in **llsum.orig** was changed to 25 in the newer **llsum** file, and this accounts for all of the differences in the two files. The less than sign (<) precedes lines from the first file, in this case **llsum**. The greater than sign (>) precedes lines from the second file, in this case **llsum.orig**. I made this change, starting the second group of information from character 16 to character 25, because I wanted the second group of information, produced by **llsum,** to start at column 25. The second group of information is the *owner,* as shown in the following example:

```
$ llsum
FILENAME                    OWNER        SIZE    TYPE

README                      denise        810    file
backup_files                denise       3408    file
biography                   denise        427    file
cshtest                     denise       1024     dir
gkill                       denise       1855    file
gkill.out                   denise        191    file
hostck                      denise        924    file
ifstat                      denise       1422    file
ifstat.int                  denise       2147    file
ifstat.out                  denise        723    file
introdos                    denise      54018    file
introux                     denise      52476    file
letter                      denise      23552    file
letter.auto                 denise      69632    file
letter.auto.recover         denise      71680    file
letter.backup               denise      23552    file
letter.lck                  denise         57    file
letter.recover              denise      69632    file
llsum                       denise       1267    file
llsum.orig                  denise       1267    file
llsum.out                   denise       1657    file
llsum.tomd.out              denise       1356    file
psg                         denise        670    file
psg.int                     denise        802    file
psg.out                     denise        122    file
```

```
sam_adduser            denise          1010       file
tdolan                 denise          1024        dir
trash                  denise          4554       file
trash.out              denise           329       file
typescript             denise          2017       file

The files listed occupy 393605 bytes (0.3754 Mbytes)
Average file size is 13120 bytes

$
```

When we run **llsum.orig**, clearly the second group of information, which is the *owner*, starts at column 16 and not column 32:

```
$ llsum.orig
FILENAME         OWNER          SIZE     TYPE

README           denise           810     file
backup_files     denise          3408     file
biography        denise           427     file
cshtest          denise          1024      dir
gkill            denise          1855     file
gkill.out        denise           191     file
hostck           denise           924     file
ifstat           denise          1422     file
ifstat.int       denise          2147     file
ifstat.out       denise           723     file
introdos         denise         54018     file
introux          denise         52476     file
letter           denise         23552     file
letter.auto      denise         69632     file
letter.auto.rec  denise         71680     file
letter.backup    denise         23552     file
letter.lck       denise            57     file
letter.recover   denise         69632     file
llsum            denise          1267     file
llsum.orig       denise          1267     file
llsum.out        denise          1657     file
llsum.tomd.out   denise          1356     file
psg              denise           670     file
psg.int          denise           802     file
psg.out          denise           122     file
sam_adduser      denise          1010     file
tdolan           denise          1024      dir
trash            denise          4554     file
trash.out        denise           329     file
typescript       denise          3894     file
```

```
The files listed occupy 395482 bytes (0.3772 Mbytes)
Average file size is 13182 bytes


script done on Mon Dec 11 12:59:18

$
```

man page

comm - 10

We can compare two sorted files using **comm** and see the lines that are unique to each file, as well as the lines found in both files. When we compare two files with **comm**, the lines that are unique to the first file appear in the first column, the lines unique to the second file appear in the second column and the lines contained in both files appear in the third column. Let's go back to the **/etc/passwd** file to illustrate this comparison. We'll compare two **/etc/passwd** files, the active **/etc/passwd** file in use and an old **/etc/passwd** file from a backup:

```
# comm /etc/passwd /etc/passwd.backup
                    root:PgYQCkVH65hyQ:0:0:root:/root:/bin/bash
                    bin:*:1:1:bin:/bin:
                    daemon:*:2:2:daemon:/sbin:
                    adm:*:3:4:adm:/var/adm:
                    lp:*:4:7:lp:/var/spool/lpd:
                    sync:*:5:0:sync:/sbin:/bin/sync
                    shutdown:*:6:11:shutdown:/sbin:/sbin/shutdown
                    halt:*:7:0:halt:/sbin:/sbin/halt
                    mail:*:8:12:mail:/var/spool/mail:
                    news:*:9:13:news:/var/spool/news:
                    uucp:*:10:14:uucp:/var/spool/uucp:
          operator1:*:12:0:operator:/root:
                    operator:*:11:0:operator:/root:
     games:*:12:100:games:/usr/games:
                    gopher:*:13:30:gopher:/usr/lib/gopher-data:
                    ftp:*:14:50:FTP User:/home/ftp:
                    man:*:15:15:Manuals Owner:/:
                    nobody:*:65534:65534:Nobody:/:/bin/false
                    col:Wh0yzfAV2qm2Y:100:100:Caldera
                    OpenLinux User:/home/col:/bin/bash
```

You can see from this output that the user *games* appears only in the active **/etc/passwd** file, the user *operator1* appears only in the **/etc/passwd.backup** file, and all of the other entries appear in both files.

The following is a summary of the **cmp** and **diff** commands.

man page

cmp - 10

cmp - Compare the contents of two files. The byte position and line number of the first difference between the two files is returned.

man page

diff - 10

Options

-l	Display the byte position and differing characters for all differences within a file.
-s	Work silently, that is only exit codes are returned.

diff - Compares two files and reports differing lines.

Options

-b	Ignore blanks at the end of a line.
-i	Ignore case differences.
-t	Expand tabs in output to spaces.
-w	Ignore spaces and tabs.

man page

dircmp - 10

dircmp

Why stop at comparing files? You will probably have many directories in your user area as well. **dircmp** compares two directories and produces information about the contents of directories.

To begin with let's perform a long listing of two directories:

```
$ ls -l krsort.dir.old
total 168
-rwxr-xr-x   1 denise     users          34592 Oct 31 11:27 krsort
-rwxr-xr-x   1 denise     users           3234 Oct 31 11:27 krsort.c
-rwxr-xr-x   1 denise     users          32756 Oct 31 11:27 krsort.dos
-rw-r--r--   1 denise     users           9922 Oct 31 11:27 krsort.q
-rwxr-xr-x   1 denise     users           3085 Oct 31 11:27 krsortorig.c
$
$ ls -l krsort.dir.new
total 168
-rwxr-xr-x   1 denise     users          34592 Oct 31 15:17 krsort
-rwxr-xr-x   1 denise     users          32756 Oct 31 15:17 krsort.dos
-rw-r--r--   1 denise     users           9922 Oct 31 15:17 krsort.q
-rwxr-xr-x   1 denise     users           3234 Oct 31 15:17 krsort.test.c
-rwxr-xr-x   1 denise     users           3085 Oct 31 15:17 krsortorig.c
$
```

From this listing, you can see clearly that one file unique to each directory. **krsort.c** appears in only the **krsort.dir.old** directory, and **krsort.test.c** appears in only the **krsort.dir.new** directory. Let's now use **dircmp** to inform us of the differences in these two directories:

```
$ dircmp krsort.dir.old krsort.dir.new

krsort.dir.old only and krsort.dir.new only Page 1


./krsort.c              ./krsort.test.c




Comparison of krsort.dir.old krsort.dir.new Page 1


directory        .
same             ./krsort
same             ./krsort.dos
same             ./krsort.q
same             ./krsortorig.c

$
```

This is a useful output. First, the files that appear in only one directory are listed. Then, the files common to both directories are listed.

The following is a summary of the **dircmp** command.

man page

dircmp - 10

dircmp - Compare directories.

Options

-d   Compare the contents of files with the same name in both directories and produce a report of what must be done to make the files identical.

-s   Suppress information about different files.

cut

man page

cut - 10

There are times when you have an output that has too many fields in it. When we issued the **llsum** command earlier, it produced four fields: FILENAME, OWNER, SIZE, and TYPE. What if we want to take this output and look at just the FILENAME and SIZE. We could modify the **llsum** script, or we could use the **cut** command to eliminate the OWNER and TYPE fields with the following commands:

```
$ llsum | cut -c 1-25,37-43
FILENAME                 SIZE
README                    810
backup_files             3408
biography                 427
cshtest                  1024
gkill                    1855
gkill.out                 191
hostck                    924
ifstat                   1422
ifstat.int               2147
ifstat.out                723
```

```
        introdos                       54018
        introux                        52476
        letter                         23552
        letter.auto                    69632
        letter.auto.recover            71680
        letter.backup                  23552
        letter.lck                        57
        letter.recover                 69632
        llsum                           1267
        llsum.orig                      1267
        llsum.out                       1657
        llsum.tomd.out                  1356
        psg                              670
        psg.int                          802
        psg.out                          122
        sam_adduser                     1010
        tdolan                          1024
        trash                           4554
        trash.out                        329
        typescript                        74

        The files listed occupy 3 (0.373
        Average file size is 1305
        $
```

   This has produced a list from **llsum**, which is piped to **cut**. Only characters 1 through 25 and 37 through 43 have been extracted. These characters correspond to the fields we want. At the end of the output are two lines that are only partially printed. We don't want these lines, so we can use **grep -v** to eliminate them and print all other lines. The output of this command is saved to the file **llsum.out** at the end of this output, which we'll use later:

```
$ ./llsum | grep -v "bytes" | cut -c 1-25,37-43
        FILENAME                       SIZE
        README                          810
        backup_files                   3408
        biography                        427
        cshtest                         1024
        gkill                           1855
        gkill.out                        191
        hostck                           924
        ifstat                          1422
        ifstat.int                      2147
        ifstat.out                       723
        introdos                       54018
        introux                        52476
        letter                         23552
        letter.auto                    69632
```

```
letter.auto.recover      71680
letter.backup            23552
letter.lck                  57
letter.recover           69632
llsum                     1267
llsum.orig                1267
llsum.out                 1657
llsum.tomd.out            1356
psg                        670
psg.int                    802
psg.out                    122
sam_adduser               1010
tdolan                    1024
trash                     4554
trash.out                  329
typescript                1242
$ llsum | grep -v "bytes" | cut -c 1-25,37-4_3 > llsum.out
$
```

man page

grep - 10

man page

cut - 10

The following is a summary of the **cut** command, with some of the more commonly used options.

cut - Extract specified fields from each line.

Options

- -c list   Extract based on character position, as shown in the example.
- -f list   Extract based on fields.
- -d char   The character following d is the delimiter when using the -f option. The delimiter is the character that separates fields.

man page

paste - 10

paste

Files can be merged together in a variety of ways. If you want to merge files on a line-by-line basis you can use the **paste** command.

man page

cut - 10

The first line in the second file is pasted to the end of the first line in the first file and so on.

Let's use the **cut** command just covered and extract only the permissions field, or characters 1 through 10, to get only the permissions for files. We'll then save these in the file **ll.out**:

man page

ls - 2

```
$ ls -al | cut -c 1-10

total 798
drwxrwxrwx
drwxrwxrwx
-rwxrwxrwx
-rwxrwxrwx
-rwxrwxrwx
drwxr-xr-x
-rwxrwxrwx
-rw-r--r--
-rwxrwxrwx
-rwxrwxrwx
-rwxr-xr-x
-rw-r--r--
-rw-r--r--
-rwxrwxrwx
-rw-r--r--
-rw-r--r--
-rw-r--r--
-rw-r--r--
-rw-rw-rw-
-rw-r--r--
-rw-r--r--
-rwxrwxrwx
-rwxr-xr-x
-rw-r--r--
-rw-r--r--
-rwxrwxrwx
-rwxr-xr-x
-rw-r--r--
-rwxrwxrwx
drwxr-xr-x
-rwxrwxrwx
-rw-r--r--
-rw-r--r--

$ ls -al | cut -c 1-10 > ll.out
$
```

man page

paste - 10

We can now use the **paste** command to paste the permissions saved in the **ll.out** file to the other file-related information in the **llsum.out** file:

man page

paste - 10

```
$ paste llsum.out ll.out

FILENAME                 SIZE       total 792
README                    810       -rwxrwxrwx
backup_files             3408       -rwxrwxrwx
biography                 427       -rwxrwxrwx
cshtest                  1024       drwxr-xr-x
gkill                    1855       -rwxrwxrwx
gkill.out                 191       -rw-r--r--
hostck                    924       -rwxrwxrwx
ifstat                   1422       -rwxrwxrwx
ifstat.int               2147       -rwxr-xr-x
ifstat.out                723       -rw-r--r--
introdos                54018       -rw-r--r--
introux                 52476       -rwxrwxrwx
letter                  23552       -rw-r--r--
letter.auto             69632       -rw-r--r--
letter.auto.recover     71680       -rw-r--r--
letter.backup           23552       -rw-r--r--
letter.lck                 57       -rw-rw-rw-
letter.recover          69632       -rw-r--r--
ll.out                   1057       -rw-r--r--
llsum                    1267       -rwxrwxrwx
llsum.orig               1267       -rwxr-xr-x
llsum.out                1657       -rw-r--r--
llsum.tomd.out           1356       -rw-r--r--
psg                       670       -rwxrwxrwx
psg.int                   802       -rwxr-xr-x
psg.out                   122       -rw-r--r--
sam_adduser              1010       -rwxrwxrwx
tdolan                   1024       drwxr-xr-x
trash                    4554       -rwxrwxrwx
trash.out                 329       -rw-r--r--
typescript                679       -rw-r--r--

$
```

This has produced a list that includes *FILENAME* and *SIZE* from **llsum.out** and permissions from **ll.out**.

man page

paste - 10

If both the files have the same first field, you can use the **join** command to merge the two files:

The following is a summary of the **paste** and **join** commands, with some of the more commonly used options:

man page

join - 10

paste - Merge lines of files.

Options

        -d list   Use list as the delimiter between columns. You can use special escape sequences for list such as \n for newline and \t for tab.

join - Combine two presorted files that have a common key field.

Options

        -a n   Produce the normal output and also generate a line for each line that can't be joined in 1 or 2.

        -e string Replace empty fields in output with string.

        -t char   Use char as the field separator.

tr

tr translates characters. **tr** is ideal for such tasks as changing case. For instance, what if you want to translate all lowercase characters to upper case? The following example shows listing files that have the suffix "zip" and then translates these files into uppercase:

```
$ ls -al *.zip
file1.zip
file2.zip
file3.zip
file4.zip
file5.zip
file6.zip
file7.zip
$ ls -al *.zip | tr "[:lower:]" "[:upper:]"
```

```
FILE1.ZIP
FILE2.ZIP
FILE3.ZIP
FILE4.ZIP
FILE5.ZIP
FILE6.ZIP
FILE7.ZIP
$
```

We use brackets in this case, because we are translating a class of characters.

The following is a summary of the **tr** command, with some of the more commonly used options.

man page

tr - 10

tr - Translate characters.

Options

-A   Translate on a byte-by-byte basis.

-d   Delete all occurrences of characters specified.

[:class:] Translate from one character class to another such as from lowercase class to uppercase class, as shown in the example.

Manual Pages of Some Commands Used in Chapter 10

The following are the HP-UX manual pages for many of the commands used in the chapter. Commands often differ among UNIX variants, so you may find differences in the options or other areas for some commands; however, the following manual pages serve as an excellent reference.

awk

awk - Pattern-processing language.

man page

awk - 10

NAME
     awk - pattern-directed scanning and processing language

SYNOPSIS
     awk [-Ffs] [-v var=value] [program | -f progfile ...] [file ...]

DESCRIPTION
     awk scans each input file for lines that match any of a set of
     patterns specified literally in program or in one or more files
     specified as -f progfile. With each pattern there can be an
     associated action that is to be performed when a line in a file
     matches the pattern. Each line is matched against the pattern portion
     of every pattern-action statement, and the associated action is
     performed for each matched pattern. The file name - means the
     standard input. Any file of the form var=value is treated as an
     assignment, not a filename. An assignment is evaluated at the time it
     would have been opened if it were a filename, unless the -v option is
     used.

     An input line is made up of fields separated by white space, or by
     regular expression FS. The fields are denoted $1, $2, ...; $0 refers
     to the entire line.

     Options
        awk recognizes the following options and arguments:

            -F fs   Specify regular expression used to separate
                          fields. The default is to recognize space and tab
                          characters, and to discard leading spaces and
                          tabs. If the -F option is used, leading input
                          field separators are no longer discarded.

            -f progfile   Specify an awk program file. Up to 100 program
                          files can be specified. The pattern-action
                          statements in these files are executed in the same
                          order as the files were specified.

            -v var=value Cause var=value assignment to occur before the
                          BEGIN action (if it exists) is executed.

     Statements
        A pattern-action statement has the form:

            pattern { action }

        A missing { action } means print the line; a missing pattern always
        matches. Pattern-action statements are separated by new-lines or
        semicolons.

        An action is a sequence of statements. A statement can be one of the following:

```
if(expression) statement [else statement]
while(expression) statement
for(expression;expression;expression) statement
for(var in array) statement
do statement while(expression)
break
continue
{[statement ...]}
expression                        # commonly var=expression
print[expression-list] [> expression]
printf format [, expression-list] [> expression]
return [expression]
next          # skip remaining patterns on this input line.
delete array [expression]          # delete an array element.
exit [expression]      # exit immediately; status is expression.
```

Statements are terminated by semicolons, newlines or right braces. An
empty expression-list stands for $0. String constants are quoted
(""), with the usual C escapes recognized within. Expressions take on
string or numeric values as appropriate, and are built using the
operators +, -, *, /, %, ^ (exponentiation), and concatenation
(indicated by a blank). The operators ++, --, +=, -=, *=, /=, %=, ^=,
**=, >, >=, <, <=, ==, !=, and ?: are also available in expressions.
Variables can be scalars, array elements (denoted x[i]) or fields.
Variables are initialized to the null string. Array subscripts can be
any string, not necessarily numeric (this allows for a form of
associative memory). Multiple subscripts such as [i,j,k] are
permitted. The constituents are concatenated, separated by the value
of SUBSEP.

The print statement prints its arguments on the standard output (or on
a file if >file or >>file is present or on a pipe if |cmd is present),
separated by the current output field separator, and terminated by the
output record separator. file and cmd can be literal names or
parenthesized expressions. Identical string values in different
statements denote the same open file. The printf statement formats
its expression list according to the format (see printf(3)).

Built-In Functions
  The built-in function close(expr) closes the file or pipe expr opened
  by a print or printf statement or a call to getline with the same
  string-valued expr. This function returns zero if successful,
  otherwise, it returns non-zero.

The customary functions exp, log, sqrt, sin, cos, atan2 are built in.
Other built-in functions are:

blength[([s])]   Length of its associated argument (in bytes)
                    taken as a string, or of $0 if no argument.

length[([s])]   Length of its associated argument (in characters)
                    taken as a string, or of $0 if no argument.

rand()   Returns a random number between zero and one.

srand([expr])   Sets the seed value for rand, and returns the
                    previous seed value. If no argument is given,
                    the time of day is used as the seed value;
                    otherwise, expr is used.

int(x)   Truncates to an integer value

substr(s, m[, n])   Return the at most n-character substring of s
                    that begins at position m, numbering from 1. If
```
```

n is omitted, the substring is limited by the
length of string s.

index(s, t)   Return the position, in characters, numbering
                   from 1, in string s where string t first occurs,
                   or zero if it does not occur at all.

match(s, ere)   Return the position, in characters, numbering
                   from 1, in string s where the extended regular
                   expression ere occurs, or 0 if it does not. The
                   variables RSTART and RLENGTH are set to the
                   position and length of the matched string.

split(s, a[, fs]) Splits the string s into array elements a[1],
                   a[2], ..., a[n], and returns n. The separation
                   is done with the regular expression fs, or with
                   the field separator FS if fs is not given.

sub(ere, repl [, in])
                   Substitutes repl for the first occurrence of the
                   extended regular expression ere in the string in.
                   If in is not given, $0 is used.

gsub   Same as sub except that all occurrences of the
                   regular expression are replaced; sub and gsub
                   return the number of replacements.

sprintf(fmt, expr, ...)
                   String resulting from formatting expr ...
                   according to the printf(3S) format fmt

system(cmd)   Executes cmd and returns its exit status

toupper(s)   Converts the argument string s to uppercase and
                   returns the result.

tolower(s)   Converts the argument string s to lowercase and
                   returns the result.

The built-in function getline sets $0 to the next input record from
the current input file; getline < file sets $0 to the next record from
file. getline x sets variable x instead. Finally, cmd | getline
pipes the output of cmd into getline; each call of getline returns the
next line of output from cmd. In all cases, getline returns 1 for a
successful input, 0 for end of file, and -1 for an error.

Patterns
Patterns are arbitrary Boolean combinations (with ! || &&) of regular
expressions and relational expressions. awk supports Extended Regular
Expressions as described in regexp(5). Isolated regular expressions
in a pattern apply to the entire line. Regular expressions can also
occur in relational expressions, using the operators ~ and !~. /re/
is a constant regular expression; any string (constant or variable)
can be used as a regular expression, except in the position of an
isolated regular expression in a pattern.

A pattern can consist of two patterns separated by a comma; in this
case, the action is performed for all lines from an occurrence of the
first pattern though an occurrence of the second.

A relational expression is one of the following:

    expression matchop regular-expression
    expression relop expression
    expression in array-name
    (expr,expr,...) in array-name

where a relop is any of the six relational operators in C, and a
matchop is either ~ (matches) or !~ (does not match). A conditional
is an arithmetic expression, a relational expression, or a Boolean
combination of the two.

The special patterns BEGIN and END can be used to capture control
before the first input line is read and after the last. BEGIN and END
do not combine with other patterns.

Special Characters
The following special escape sequences are recognized by awk in both
regular expressions and strings:

Escape	Meaning
\a	alert character
\b	backspace character
\f	form-feed character
\n	new-line character
\r	carriage-return character
\t	tab character
\v	vertical-tab character
\nnn	1- to 3-digit octal value nnn
\xhhh	1- to n-digit hexadecimal number

Variable Names
Variable names with special meanings are:

FS	Input field separator regular expression; a space character by default; also settable by option -Ffs.
NF	The number of fields in the current record.
NR	The ordinal number of the current record from the start of input. Inside a BEGIN action the value is zero. Inside an END action the value is the number of the last record processed.
FNR	The ordinal number of the current record in the current file. Inside a BEGIN action the value is zero. Inside an END action the value is the number of the last record processed in the last file processed.
FILENAME	A pathname of the current input file.
RS	The input record separator; a newline character by default.
OFS	The print statement output field separator; a space character by default.
ORS	The print statement output record separator; a newline character by default.
OFMT	Output format for numbers (default %.6g). If the value of OFMT is not a floating-point format specification, the results are unspecified.
CONVFMT	Internal conversion format for numbers (default %.6g). If the value of CONVFMT is not a floating-point format specification, the results are unspecified.

SUBSEP	The subscript separator string for multi-dimensional arrays; the default value is " 34"
ARGC	The number of elements in the ARGV array.
ARGV	An array of command line arguments, excluding options and the program argument numbered from zero to ARGC-1.

The arguments in ARGV can be modified or added to; ARGC can be altered. As each input file ends, awk will treat the next non-null element of ARGV, up to the current value of ARGC-1, inclusive, as the name of the next input file. Thus, setting an element of ARGV to null means that it will not be treated as an input file. The name - indicates the standard input. If an argument matches the format of an assignment operand, this argument will be treated as an assignment rather than a file argument.

ENVIRON	Array of environment variables; subscripts are names. For example, if environment variable V=thing, ENVIRON["V"] produces thing.
RSTART	The starting position of the string matched by the match function, numbering from 1. This is always equivalent to the return value of the match function.
RLENGTH	The length of the string matched by the match function.

Functions can be defined (at the position of a pattern-action statement) as follows:

```
function foo(a, b, c) { ...; return x }
```

Parameters are passed by value if scalar, and by reference if array name. Functions can be called recursively. Parameters are local to the function; all other variables are global.

Note that if pattern-action statements are used in an HP-UX command line as an argument to the awk command, the pattern-action statement must be enclosed in single quotes to protect it from the shell. For example, to print lines longer than 72 characters, the pattern-action statement as used in a script (-f progfile command form) is:

```
length > 72
```

The same pattern action statement used as an argument to the awk command is quoted in this manner:

```
awk 'length > 72'
```

EXTERNAL INFLUENCES
  Environment Variables
    LANG   Provides a default value for the internationalization
                  variables that are unset or null. If LANG is unset or
                  null, the default value of "C" (see lang(5)) is used.
                  If any of the internationalization variables contains
                  an invalid setting, awk will behave as if all
                  internationalization variables are set to "C". See
                  environ(5).

LC_ALL   If set to a non-empty string value, overrides the
                values of all the other internationalization variables.

LC_CTYPE   Determines the interpretation of text as single and/or
                multi-byte characters, the classification of characters
                as printable, and the characters matched by character
                class expressions in regular expressions.

LC_NUMERIC   Determines the radix character used when interpreting
                numeric input, performing conversion between numeric
                and string values and formatting numeric output.
                Regardless of locale, the period character (the
                decimal-point character of the POSIX locale) is the
                decimal-point character recognized in processing awk
                programs (including assignments in command-line
                arguments).

LC_COLLATE   Determines the locale for the behavior of ranges,
                equivalence classes and multi-character collating
                elements within regular expressions.

LC_MESSAGES   Determines the locale that should be used to affect the
                format and contents of diagnostic messages written to
                standard error and informative messages written to
                standard output.

NLSPATH   Determines the location of message catalogues for the
                processing of LC_MESSAGES.

PATH   Determines the search path when looking for commands
                executed by system(cmd), or input and output pipes.

In addition, all environment variables will be visible via the awk
variable ENVIRON.

International Code Set Support
Single- and multi-byte character code sets are supported except that
variable names must contain only ASCII characters and regular
expressions must contain only valid characters.

DIAGNOSTICS
awk supports up to 199 fields ($1, $2, ..., $199) per record.

EXAMPLES
Print lines longer than 72 characters:

Print first two fields in opposite order:

    { print $2, $1 }

Same, with input fields separated by comma and/or blanks and tabs:

    BEGIN { FS = ",[\t]*|[\t]+" }
          { print $2, $1 }

Add up first column, print sum and average:

              { s += $1 }"
    END   { print "sum is", s, " average is", s/NR }

Print all lines between start/stop pairs:

    /start/, /stop/

Simulate echo command (see echo(1)):

```
BEGIN   {                                  # Simulate echo(1)
        for (i = 1; i < ARGC; i++) printf "%s ", ARGV[i]
        printf "\n"
        exit }
```

AUTHOR
awk was developed by AT&T, IBM, OSF, and HP.

SEE ALSO
lex(1), sed(1).
A. V. Aho, B. W. Kernighan, P. J. Weinberger: The AWK Programming
Language, Addison-Wesley, 1988.

STANDARDS CONFORMANCE
awk: SVID2, SVID3, XPG2, XPG3, XPG4, POSIX.2

cmp

man page

cmp - 10

cmp - Compare files.

```
cmp(1)                                                              cmp(1)

NAME
      cmp - compare two files

SYNOPSIS

      cmp [-l] [-s] file1 file2

DESCRIPTION
      cmp compares two files (if file1 or file2 is -, the standard input is
      used).  Under default options, cmp makes no comment if the files are
      the same; if they differ, it announces the byte and line number at
      which the difference occurred.  If one file is an initial subsequence
      of the other, that fact is noted.

      cmp recognizes the following options:

            -l      Print the byte number (decimal) and the differing bytes
                    (octal) for each difference (byte numbering begins at 1
                    rather than 0).

            -s      Print nothing for differing files; return codes only.

EXTERNAL INFLUENCES
   Environment Variables
      LANG determines the language in which messages are displayed.  If LANG
      is not specified or is set to the empty string, a default of "C" (see
      lang(5)) is used instead of LANG.  If any internationalization
      variable contains an invalid setting, cmp behaves as if all
      internationalization variables are set to "C".  See environ(5).

   International Code Set Support
      Single- and multi-byte character code sets are supported.

DIAGNOSTICS
      cmp returns the following exit values:

            0      Files are identical.
            1      Files are not identical.
            2      Inaccessible or missing argument.

      cmp prints the following warning if the comparison succeeds till the
      end of file of file1(file2) is reached.

            cmp: EOF on file1(file2)

SEE ALSO
      comm(1), diff(1).

STANDARDS CONFORMANCE
      cmp: SVID2, SVID3, XPG2, XPG3, XPG4, POSIX.2
```

comm

comm - Produce three-column output of sorted files.

man page

comm - 10

comm(1)   comm(1)

NAME
     comm - select or reject lines common to two sorted files

SYNOPSIS

     comm [-[123]] file1 file2

DESCRIPTION
     comm reads file1 and file2, which should be ordered in increasing
     collating sequence (see sort(1) and Environment Variables below), and
     produces a three-column output:

          Column 1:   Lines that appear only in file1,
          Column 2:   Lines that appear only in file2,
          Column 3:   Lines that appear in both files.

     If - is used for file1 or file2, the standard input is used.

     Options 1, 2, or 3 suppress printing of the corresponding column.
     Thus comm -12 prints only the lines common to the two files; comm -23
     prints only lines in the first file but not in the second; comm -123
     does nothing useful.

EXTERNAL INFLUENCES
   Environment Variables
     LC_COLLATE determines the collating sequence comm expects from the
     input files.

     LC_MESSAGES determines the language in which messages are displayed.

     If LC_MESSAGES is not specified in the environment or is set to the
     empty string, the value of LANG determines the language in which
     messages are displayed. If LC_COLLATE is not specified in the
     environment or is set to the empty string, the value of LANG is used
     as a default. If LANG is not specified or is set to the empty string,
     a default of ``C'' (see lang(5)) is used instead of LANG. If any
     internationalization variable contains an invalid setting, comm
     behaves as if all internationalization variables are set to ``C''.
     See environ(5).

   International Code Set Support
     Single- and multi-byte character code sets are supported.

EXAMPLES
     The following examples assume that file1 and file2 have been ordered
     in the collating sequence defined by the LC_COLLATE or LANG
     environment variable.

     Print all lines common to file1 and file2 (in other words, print
     column 3):

```
comm -12 file1 file2
```

Print all lines that appear in file1 but not in file2 (in other words, print column 1):

```
comm -23 file1 file2
```

Print all lines that appear in file2 but not in file1 (in other words, print column 2):

```
comm -13 file1 file2
```

SEE ALSO
    cmp(1), diff(1), sdiff(1), sort(1), uniq(1).

STANDARDS CONFORMANCE
    comm: SVID2, SVID3, XPG2, XPG3, XPG4, POSIX.2

cut

cut - Cut selected fields from the lines in a file.

```
cut(1)                                                              cut(1)

NAME
     cut - cut out (extract) selected fields of each line of a file

SYNOPSIS
     cut -c list [file ...]
     cut -b list [-n] [file ...]
     cut -f list [-d char] [-s] [file ...]

DESCRIPTION
     cut cuts out (extracts) columns from a table or fields from each line
     in a file; in data base parlance, it implements the projection of a
     relation.  Fields as specified by list can be fixed length (defined in
     terms of character or byte position in a line when using the -c or -b
     option), or the length can vary from line to line and be marked with a
     field delimiter character such as the tab character (when using the -f
     option).  cut can be used as a filter; if no files are given, the
     standard input is used.

     When processing single-byte character sets, the -c and -b options are
     equivalent and produce identical results.  When processing multi-byte
     character sets, when the -b and -n options are used together, their
     combined behavior is very similar, but not identical to the -c option.

  Options
     Options are interpreted as follows:

          list              A comma-separated list of integer byte (-b
                            option), or character (-c option), or field (-f
                            option) numbers, in increasing order, with
                            optional - to indicate ranges.  For example:

                                 1,4,7
                                      Positions 1, 4, and 7.
                                 1-3,8
                                      Positions 1 through 3 and 8.
                                 -5,10
                                      Positions 1 through 5 and 10.
                                 3-  Position 3 through last position.


          -b list           Cut based on a list of bytes.  Each selected byte
                            is output unless the -n option is also specified.


          -c list           Cut based on character positions specified by list
                            (-c 1-72 extracts the first 72 characters of each
                            line).

          -f list           Where list is a list of fields assumed to be
```

separated in the file by a delimiter character
(see -d); for example, -f 1,7 copies the first and
seventh field only. Lines with no field
delimiters will be passed through intact (useful
for table subheadings), unless -s is specified.

-d char   The character following -d is the field delimiter
               (-f option only). Default is tab. Space or other
               characters with special meaning to the shell must
               be quoted. Adjacent field delimiters delimit null
               fields.

-n   Do not split characters. If the high end of a
               range within a list is not the last byte of a
               character, that character is not included in the
               output. However, if the low end of a range within
               a list is not the first byte of a character, the
               entire character is included in the output."

-s   Suppresses lines with no delimiter characters when
               using -f option. Unless -s is specified, lines
               with no delimiters appear in the output without
               alteration.

Hints
  Use grep to extract text from a file based on text pattern recognition
  (using regular expressions). Use paste to merge files line-by-line in
  columnar format. To rearrange columns in a table in a different
  sequence, use cut and paste. See grep(1) and paste(1) for more
  information.

EXTERNAL INFLUENCES
  Environment Variables
    LC_CTYPE determines the interpretation of text as single and/or
    multi-byte characters.

    If LC_CTYPE is not specified in the environment or is set to the empty
    string, the value of LANG is used as a default for each unspecified or
    empty variable. If LANG is not specified or is set to the empty
    string, a default of "C" (see lang(5)) is used instead of LANG. If
    any internationalization variable contains an invalid setting, cut
    behaves as if all internationalization variables are set to "C". See
    environ(5).

  International Code Set Support
    The delimiter specified with the -d argument must be a single-byte
    character. Otherwise, single- and multi-byte character code sets are
    supported.

EXAMPLES
  Password file mapping of user ID to user names:

      cut -d : -f 1,5 /etc/passwd

  Set environment variable name to current login name:

      name=`who am i | cut -f 1 -d " "`

  Convert file source containing lines of arbitrary length into two
  files where file1 contains the first 500 bytes (unless the 500th byte
  is within a multi-byte character), and file2 contains the remainder of
  each line:

      cut -b 1-500 -n source > file1
      cut -b 500- -n source > file2

DIAGNOSTICS

line too long   Line length must not exceed LINE_MAX characters or
                fields, including the new-line character (see
                limits(5).

bad list for b/c/f option
                Missing -b, -c, or -f option or incorrectly specified
                list. No error occurs if a line has fewer fields than
                the list calls for.

no fields   list is empty.

WARNINGS

cut does not expand tabs. Pipe text through expand(1) if tab
expansion is required.

Backspace characters are treated the same as any other character. To
eliminate backspace characters before processing by cut, use the fold
or col command (see fold(1) and col(1)).

AUTHOR

cut was developed by OSF and HP.

SEE ALSO

grep(1), paste(1).

STANDARDS CONFORMANCE

cut: SVID2, SVID3, XPG2, XPG3, XPG4, POSIX.2

diff

diff - File and directory comparison.

```
diff(1)                                                                    diff(1)

NAME
      diff - differential file and directory comparator

SYNOPSIS

      diff [-C n] [-S name] [-lrs] [-bcefhintw] dir1 dir2
      diff [-C n] [-S name] [-bcefhintw] file1 file2
      diff [-D string] [-biw] file1 file2

DESCRIPTION
   Comparing Directories
      If both arguments are directories, diff sorts the contents of the
      directories by name, then runs the regular file diff algorithm
      (described below) on text files that have the same name in each
      directory but are different.  Binary files that differ, common
      subdirectories, and files that appear in only one directory are
      listed.  When comparing directories, the following options are
      recognized:

            -l              Long output format; each text file diff is piped
                            through pr to paginate it (see pr(1)).  Other
                            differences are remembered and summarized after all
                            text file differences are reported.

            -r              Applies diff recursively to common subdirectories
                            encountered.

            -s              diff reports files that are identical but otherwise
                            not mentioned.

            -S name         Starts a directory diff in the middle of the sorted
                            directory, beginning with file name.

   Comparing Files
      When run on regular files, and when comparing text files that differ
      during directory comparison, diff tells what lines must be changed in
      the files to bring them into agreement.  diff usually finds a smallest
      sufficient set of file differences.  However, it can be misled by
      lines containing very few characters or by other situations.  If
      neither file1 nor file2 is a directory, either can be specified as -,
      in which case the standard input is used.  If file1 is a directory, a
      file in that directory whose filename is the same as the filename of
      file2 is used (and vice versa).

      There are several options for output format.  The default output
      format contains lines resembling the following:

            n1 a n3,n4
            n1,n2 d n3
            n1,n2 c n3,n4
```

These lines resemble ed commands to convert file1 into file2. The numbers after the letters pertain to file2. In fact, by exchanging a for d and reading backwards one may ascertain equally how to convert file2 into file1. As in ed, identical pairs where n1=n2 or n3=n4 are abbreviated as a single number.

Following each of these lines come all the lines that are affected in the first file flagged by <, then all the lines that are affected in the second file flagged by >.

Except for -b, -w, -i, or -t which can be given with any of the others, the following options are mutually exclusive:

-e   Produce a script of a, c, and d commands for the ed editor suitable for recreating file2 from file1. Extra commands are added to the output when comparing directories with -e, so that the result is a shell script for converting text files common to the two directories from their state in dir1 to their state in dir2 (see sh-bourne(1)

-f   Produce a script similar to that of the -e option that is not useful with ed but is more readable by humans.

-n   Produce a script similar to that of -e, but in the opposite order, and with a count of changed lines on each insert or delete command. This is the form used by rcsdiff (see rcsdiff(1)).

-c   Produce a difference list with 3 lines of context. -c modifies the output format slightly: the output begins with identification of the files involved, followed by their creation dates, then each change separated by a line containing about twelve asterisks (*)s. Lines removed from file1 are marked with -, and lines added to file2 are marked +. Lines that change from one file to the other are marked in both files with with !. Changes that lie within 3 lines of each other in the file are grouped together on output.

-C n   Output format similar to -c but with n lines of context.

-h   Do a fast, half-hearted job. This option works only when changed stretches are short and well separated, but can be used on files of unlimited length.

-D string
     Create a merged version of file1 and file2 on the standard output, with C preprocessor controls included so that a compilation of the result without defining string is equivalent to compiling file1, while compiling the result with string defined is equivalent to compiling file2.

-b   Ignore trailing blanks (spaces and tabs) and treat other strings of blanks as equal.

-w   Ignore all whitespace (blanks and tabs). For example, if (a == b) and if(a==b) are treated as equal.

-i   Ignores uppercase/lowercase differences. Thus A is treated the same as a.

-t   Expand tabs in output lines. Normal or -c output adds one or more characters to the front of each line. Resulting misalignment of indentation in the original

source lines can make the output listing difficult to
interpret. This option preserves original source file
indentation.

EXTERNAL INFLUENCES
    Environment Variables
        LANG determines the locale to use for the locale categories when both
        LC_ALL and the corresponding environment variable (beginning with LC_)
        do not specify a locale. If LANG is not set or is set to the empty
        string, a default of "C" (see lang(5)) is used.

        LC_CTYPE determines the space characters for the diff command, and the
        interpretation of text within file as single- and/or multi-byte
        characters.

        LC_MESSAGES determines the language in which messages are displayed.

        If any internationalization variable contains an invalid setting, diff
        and diffh behave as if all internationalization variables are set to
        "C". See environ(5).

    International Code Set Support
        Single- and multi-byte character code sets are supported with the
        exception that diff and diffh do not recognize multi-byte alternative
        space characters.

RETURN VALUE
    Upon completion, diff returns with one of the following exit values:

        0   No differences were found.

        1   Differences were found.

        >1   An error occurred.

EXAMPLES
    The following command creates a script file script:

        diff -e x1 x2 >script

    w is added to the end of the script in order to save the file:

        echo w >> script

    The script file can then be used to create the file x2 from the file
    x1 using the editor ed in the following manner:

        ed x1 < script

    The following command produces the difference output with 2 lines of
    context information before and after the line that was different:

        diff -C2 x1 x2

    The following command ignores all blanks and tabs and ignores
    uppercase-lowercase differences.

        diff -wi x1 x2

WARNINGS
    Editing scripts produced by the -e or -f option are naive about
    creating lines consisting of a single dot (.).

    When comparing directories with the -b, -w, or -i options specified,
    diff first compares the files in the same manner as cmp, then runs the
    diff algorithm if they are not equal. This may cause a small amount

of spurious output if the files are identical except for insignificant blank strings or uppercase/lowercase differences.

The default algorithm requires memory allocation of roughly six times the size of the file. If sufficient memory is not available for handling large files, the -h option or bdiff can be used (see bdiff(1)).

When run on directories with the -r option, diff recursively descends sub-trees. When comparing deep multi-level directories, more memory may be required than is currently available on the system. The amount of memory required depends on the depth of recursion and the size of the files.

AUTHOR
diff was developed by AT&T, the University of California, Berkeley, and HP.

FILES
/usr/lbin/diffh   used by -h option

SEE ALSO
bdiff(1), cmp(1), comm(1), diff3(1), diffmk(1), dircmp(1), ed(1), more(1), nroff(1), rcsdiff(1), sccsdiff(1), sdiff(1), terminfo(4).

STANDARDS CONFORMANCE
diff: SVID2, SVID3, XPG2, XPG3, XPG4, POSIX.2

dircmp

man page

dircmp - 10

dircmp - Compare directories and produce results.

```
dircmp(1)                                                              dircmp(1)

NAME
     dircmp - directory comparison

SYNOPSIS

     dircmp [-d] [-s] [-wn] dir1 dir2

DESCRIPTION
     dircmp examines dir1 and dir2 and generates various tabulated
     information about the contents of the directories.  Sorted listings of
     files that are unique to each directory are generated for all the
     options.  If no option is entered, a sorted list is output indicating
     whether the filenames common to both directories have the same
     contents.

          -d        Compare the contents of files with the same name in both
                    directories and output a list telling what must be
                    changed in the two files to bring them into agreement.
                    The list format is described in diff(1).

          -s        Suppress messages about identical files.

          -wn       Change the width of the output line to n characters.  The
                    default width is 72.

EXTERNAL INFLUENCES
   Environment Variables
     LC_COLLATE determines the order in which the output is sorted.

     If LC_COLLATE is not specified in the environment or is set to the
     empty string, the value of LANG is used as a default.  If LANG is not
     specified or is set to the empty string, a default of ``C'' (see
     lang(5)) is used instead of LANG.  If any internationalization
     variable contains an invalid setting, dircmp behaves as if all
     internationalization variables are set to ``C'' (see environ(5)).

   International Code Set Support
     Single- and multi-byte character code sets are supported.

EXAMPLES
     Compare the two directories slate and sleet and produce a list of
     changes that would make the directories identical:

          dircmp -d slate sleet

SEE ALSO
     cmp(1), diff(1).

STANDARDS CONFORMANCE
     dircmp: SVID2, SVID3, XPG2, XPG3
```

find

find - Find files on system by recursively searching through hierarchy.

man page

find - 10

find(1)   find(1)

NAME
     find - find files

SYNOPSIS

     find pathname_list [expression]

DESCRIPTION
     The find command recursively descends the directory hierarchy for each
     path name in pathname_list (that is, one or more path names) seeking
     files that match a Boolean expression written in the primaries given
     below. By default, find does not follow symbolic links.

     The Boolean expression is evaluated using short-circuit evaluation.
     This means that whenever the result of a Boolean operation (AND or OR)
     is known from evaluating the left-hand argument, the right-hand
     argument is not evaluated.

     In the descriptions of the primaries, the argument n represents a
     decimal integer; +n means more than n, -n means less than n, and n
     means exactly n.

     The following primaries are recognized:

     -depth   A position-independent term which causes
                         descent of the directory hierarchy to be done
                         so that all entries in a directory are acted
                         on before the directory itself. This can be
                         useful when find is used with cpio(1) to
                         transfer files that are contained in
                         directories without write permission. It is
                         also useful when using cpio(1) and the
                         modification dates of directories must be
                         preserved. Always true.

     -follow   A position-independent term which causes find
                         to follow symbolic links. Always true.

     -fsonly FStype   A position-independent term which causes find
                         to stop descending any directory whose file
                         system is not of the type specified by
                         FStype, where FStype is one of cdfs, hfs, or
                         nfs, representing the CDFS, HFS, or NFS file
                         system type, respectively.

                         In this context, mount points inherit the
                         FStype of their parent directory. This means
                         that when -fsonly hfs has been specified and
                         find encounters an NFS mount point that is
                         mounted on an HFS file system, the mount
                         point will be visited but entries below that

	mount point will not. It is important to note that when -fsonly nfs has been specified, any HFS file systems that are beneath the mount point of an NFS file system are not traversed. Always true.
-xdev	A position-independent term that causes find to avoid crossing any file system mount points that exist below starting points enumerated in pathname_list. The mount point itself is visited, but entries below the mount point are not. Always true.
-mountstop	Identical to -xdev. This primary is provided for backward compatibility only. -xdev is preferred over -mountstop.
-name file	True if file matches the last component of the current file name. The matching is performed according to Pattern Matching Notation (see regexp(5)).
-path file	Same as -name except the full path (as would be output by -print) is used instead of just the base name. Note that / characters are not treated as a special case. For example, */.profile matches ./home/fred/.profile.
-perm [-]mode	In this primary, the argument mode is used to represent file mode bits. The argument is identical in format to the mode operand as described in chmod(1), with the exception that the first character must not be the - operator. When using the symbolic form of mode, the starting template is assumed to have all file mode bits cleared. If the leading minus is omitted, this primary is true when the file permission bits exactly match the value of mode. Bits associated with the symbolic attributes s (set-user-ID, set-group-ID) and t (sticky bit) are ignored when the minus is omitted. If mode is preceded by a minus, this primary is true if all of the bits that are set in mode are also set in the file permission bits. In this case, the bits associated with the symbolic attributes s and t are significant.
-fstype FStype	True if the file system to which the file belongs is of type FStype, where FStype is one of cdfs, hfs, or nfs, corresponding to the CDFS, HFS, or NFS file system type, respectively.
-type c	True if the type of the file is c, where c is one of:

f	Regular file
d	Directory
b	Block special file
c	Character special file
p	FIFO (named pipe)
l	Symbolic link

s	Socket
n	Network special file
M	Mount point

-links n
True if the file has n links.

-user uname
True if the file belongs to the user uname. If uname is numeric and does not appear as a login name in the /etc/passwd file, it is taken as a user ID. The uname operand can be preceded by a + or - to modify the comparison operation as described previously.

-group gname
True if the file belongs to the group gname. If gname is numeric and does not appear in the /etc/group file, it is taken as a group ID. The gname operand can be preceded by a + or - to modify the comparison operation as described previously.

-nouser
True if the file belongs to a user ID that is not listed in the password database. See passwd(4).

-nogroup
True if the file belongs to a group ID that is not listed in the group database. See group(4).

-size n[c]
True if the file is n blocks long. If n is followed by a c, the size is in bytes.

-atime n
True if the file has been accessed in n days. The access time of directories in pathname_list is changed by find itself.

-mtime n
True if the file has been modified in n days.

-ctime n
True if the file inode has been changed in n days.

-newer file
True if the current file has been modified more recently than the argument file.

-newer[tv1[tv2]] file
True if the indicated time value (tv1) of the current file is newer than the indicated time value (tv2) of file. The time values tv1 and tv2 are each selected from the set of characters:

a	The time the file was last accessed
c	The time the inode of the file was last modified
m	The time the file was last modified

If the tv2 character is omitted, it defaults to m. Note that the -newer option is equivalent to -newermm.

Syntax examples;

    -newera file
    -newermc file

-inum n	True if the file serial number (inode number) is n. Note that file serial numbers are unique only within a given file system. Therefore, matching file serial numbers does not guarantee that the referenced files are the same unless you restrict the search to a single file system.
-linkedto path	True if the file is the same physical file as the file specified by path (i.e., linked to path). This primary is similar to -inum, but correctly detects when a file is hard-linked to path, even when multiple file systems are searched.
-print	Causes the current path name to be printed. Always true.
-exec cmd	True if the executed cmd returns a zero value as exit status. The end of cmd must be punctuated by a semicolon (semicolon is special to the shell and must be escaped). Any command argument {} is replaced by the current path name.
-ok cmd	Same as -exec except that the generated command line is printed with a question mark first, and is executed only if the user responds by typing y.
-cpio device	Write the current file on device in cpio(4) format (5120-byte records). The use of -cpio implies -depth. Always true.
-ncpio	Same as -cpio but adds the -c option to cpio. The use of -ncpio implies -depth. Always true.
-prune	If the current entry is a directory, cause find to skip that directory. This can be useful to avoid walking certain directories, or to avoid recursive loops when using cpio -p. Note, however, that -prune is useless if the -depth option has also been given. See the description of -only and the EXAMPLES section, below, for more information. Always true.
-only	This is a positive-logic version of -prune. A -prune is performed after every directory, unless -only is successfully evaluated for that directory. As an example, the following three commands are equivalent: find . -fsonly hfs -print find . -print -fstype hfs -only find . -print ! -fstype hfs -prune Note, however, that -only is useless if the -depth option has also been given. Always true.
(expression)	True if the parenthesized expression is true. The spaces are required. Parentheses are

special to the shell and must be escaped, as
in \(and \).

Primaries can be combined by using the following operators (in order
of decreasing precedence):

! expression	Logical NOT operator. True if expression is not true.
expression [-a] expression	Logical AND operator. True if both of the expressions are true.
expression -o expression	Logical OR operator. True if either or both of the expressions are true.

If expression is omitted, or if none of -print, -ok, -exec, -cpio, or
-ncpio is specified, -print is assumed.

Access Control Lists
The -acl primary enables the user to search for access control list
entries. It is true if the file's access control list matches an
access control list pattern or contains optional access control list
entries (see acl(5)). It has three forms:

-acl aclpatt	Match all files whose access control list includes all (zero or more) pattern entries specified by the aclpatt pattern.
-acl =aclpatt	Match a file only if its access control list includes all (zero or more) pattern entries specified by the aclpatt pattern, and every entry in its access control list is matched by at least one pattern entry specified in the aclpatt pattern.
-acl opt	Match all files containing optional access control list entries.

The aclpatt string can be given as an operator or short form pattern;
see acl(5).

By default, -acl is true for files whose access control lists include
all the (zero or more) access control list patterns in aclpatt. A
file's access control list can also contain unmatched entries.

If aclpatt begins with =, the remainder of the string must match all
entries in a file's access control list.

The aclpatt string (by default, or the part following =) can be either
an access control list or an access control list pattern. However, if
it is an access control list, aclpatt must include at least the three
base entries ((user.%, mode), (%.group, mode), and (%.%, mode)).

As a special case, if aclpatt is the word opt, the primary is true for
files with access control list entries.

EXTERNAL INFLUENCES
Environment Variables
If an internationalization variable is not specified or is null, it
defaults to the value of LANG.

If LANG is not specified or is null, it defaults to C (see lang(5)).

If LC_ALL is set to a nonempty string value, it overrides the values
of all the other internationalization variables.

If any internationalization variable contains an invalid setting, all
internationalization variables default to C (see environ(5)).

LC_CTYPE determines the interpretation of text as single and/or
multibyte characters, the classification of characters as printable,
and the characters matched by character class expressions in regular
expressions.

LC_MESSAGES determines the locale that should be used to affect the
format and contents of diagnostic messages written to standard error
and informative messages written to standard output.

NLSPATH determines the location of message catalogues for the
processing of LC_MESSAGES.

International Code Set Support
    Single- and multibyte character code sets are supported.

EXAMPLES
    Search the two directories /example and /new/example for files
    containing the string Where are you and print the names of the files:

        find /example /new/example -exec grep -l 'Where are you' {} \;

    Remove all files named a.out or *.o that have not been accessed for a
    week:

        find / \(-name a.out -o -name '*.o' \) -atime +7 -exec rm {} \;

    Note that the spaces delimiting the escaped parentheses are
    required.

    Print the names of all files on this machine. Avoid walking nfs
    directories while still printing the nfs mount points:

        find / -fsonly hfs -print

    Copy the entire file system to a disk mounted on /Disk, avoiding the
    recursive copy problem. Both commands are equivalent (note the use of
    -path instead of -name):

        cd /; find . ! -path ./Disk -only -print | cpio -pdxm /Disk

        cd /; find . -path ./Disk -prune -o -print | cpio -pdxm /Disk

    Copy the root disk to a disk mounted on /Disk, skipping all mounted
    file systems below /. Note that -xdev does not cause / to be skipped,
    even though it is a mount point. This is because / is the starting
    point and -xdev only affects entries below starting points.

        cd /; find . -xdev -print | cpio -pdm /Disk

    Change permissions on all regular files in a directory subtree to mode
    444, and permissions on all directories to 555:

        find <pathname> -type f -print | xargs chmod 444
        find <pathname> -type d -print | xargs chmod 555

    Note that output from find was piped to xargs(1) instead of using
    the -exec primary. This is because when a large number of files
    or directories is to be processed by a single command, the -exec
    primary spawns a separate process for each file or directory,
    whereas xargs collects file names or directory names into
    multiple arguments to a single chmod command, resulting in fewer
    processes and greater system efficiency.

Access Control List Examples
Find all files not owned by user karl that have access control lists
with at least one entry associated with karl, and one entry for no
specific user in group bin with the read bit on and the write bit off:

```
find  /  !  -user karl -acl 'karl.*, %.bin+r-w' -print
```

Find all files that have a read bit set in any access control list
entry:

```
find  /  -acl '*.*+r' -print
```

Find all files that have the write bit unset and execute bit set in
every access control list entry:

```
find  /  -acl '=*.*-w+x' -print
```

Find all files that have optional access control list entries:

```
find  /  -acl opt -print
```

DEPENDENCIES
  NFS
    The -acl primary is always false for NFS files.

WARNINGS
    Because of interoperability goals, cpio does not support archiving
    files larger than 2GB or files that have user/group IDs larger than
    60,000 (60K). Files with user/group IDs greater than 60K are archived
    and restored under the user/group ID of the current process.

AUTHOR
    find was developed by AT&T and HP.

FILES
    /etc/group   Group names
    /etc/mnttab   Mount points
    /etc/passwd   User names

SEE ALSO
    chacl(1), chmod(1), cpio(1), sh(1), test(1), xargs(1), mknod(2),
    stat(2), cpio(4), fs(4), group(4), passwd(4), acl(5), environ(5),
    lang(5), regexp(5).

STANDARDS CONFORMANCE
    find: SVID2, SVID3, XPG2, XPG3, XPG4, POSIX.2

grep

grep - Command to match a specified pattern.

---

grep(1)   grep(1)

NAME
     grep, egrep, fgrep - search a file for a pattern

SYNOPSIS

   Plain call with pattern
     grep [-E|-F] [-c|-l|-q] [-insvx] pattern [file ...]

   Call with (multiple) -e pattern
     grep [-E|-F] [-c|-l|-q] [-binsvx] -e pattern... [-e pattern] ...
          [file ...]

   Call with -f file
     grep [-E|-F] [-c|-l|-q] [-insvx] [-f pattern_file] [file ...]

   Obsolescent:
     egrep [-cefilnsv] [expression] [file ...]

     fgrep [-cefilnsvx] [strings] [file ...]

DESCRIPTION
     The grep command searches the input text files (standard input
     default) for lines matching a pattern. Normally, each line found is
     copied to the standard output. grep supports the Basic Regular
     Expression syntax (see regexp(5)). The -E option (egrep) supports
     Extended Regular Expression (ERE) syntax (see regexp(5)). The -F
     option (fgrep) searches for fixed strings using the fast Boyer-Moore
     string searching algorithm. The -E and -F options treat newlines
     embedded in the pattern as alternation characters. A null expression
     or string matches every line.

     The forms egrep and fgrep are maintained for backward compatibility.
     The use of the -E and -F options is recommended for portability.

   Options
            -E   Extended regular expressions. Each pattern
                                      specified is a sequence of one or more EREs.
                                      The EREs can be separated by newline
                                      characters or given in separate -e expression
                                      options. A pattern matches an input line if
                                      any ERE in the sequence matches the contents
                                      of the input line without its trailing
                                      newline character. The same functionality is
                                      obtained by using egrep.

            -F   Fixed strings. Each pattern specified is a
                                      sequence of one or more strings. Strings can
                                      be separated by newline characters or given
                                      in separate -e expression options. A pattern
                                      matches an input line if the line contains
                                      any of the strings in the sequence. The same

functionality is obtained by using fgrep.

-b   Each line is preceded by the block number on which it was found. This is useful in locating disk block numbers by context. Block numbers are calculated by dividing by 512 the number of bytes that have been read from the file and rounding down the result.

-c   Only a count of matching lines is printed.

-e expression   Same as a simple expression argument, but useful when the expression begins with a hyphen (-). Multiple -e options can be used to specify multiple patterns; an input line is selected if it matches any of the specified patterns.

-f pattern_file   The regular expression (grep and grep -E) or strings list (grep -F) is taken from the pattern_file.

-i   Ignore uppercase/lowercase distinctions during comparisons.

-l   Only the names of files with matching lines are listed (once), separated by newlines. If standard input is searched, a path name of - is listed.

-n   Each line is preceded by its relative line number in the file starting at 1. The line number is reset for each file searched. This option is ignored if -c, -b, -l, or -q is specified.

-q   (Quiet) Do not write anything to the standard output, regardless of matching lines. Exit with zero status upon finding the first matching line. Overrides any options that would produce output.

-s   Error messages produced for nonexistent or unreadable files are suppressed.

-v   All lines but those matching are printed.

-x   (eXact) Matches are recognized only when the entire input line matches the fixed string or regular expression.

In all cases in which output is generated, the file name is output if there is more than one input file. Care should be taken when using the characters $, *, [, ^, |, (,), and \ in expression, because they are also meaningful to the shell. It is safest to enclose the entire expression argument in single quotes ('...').

EXTERNAL INFLUENCES
  Environment Variables
    LANG determines the locale to use for the locale categories when both LC_ALL and the corresponding environment variable (beginning with LC_) do not specify a locale. If LANG is not specified or is set to the empty string, a default of C (see lang(5)) is used.

    LC_ALL determines the locale to use to override any values for locale categories specified by the settings of LANG or any environment variables beginning with LC_.

LC_COLLATE determines the collating sequence used in evaluating regular expressions.

LC_CTYPE determines the interpretation of text as single byte and/or multi-byte characters, the classification of characters as letters, the case information for the -i option, and the characters matched by character class expressions in regular expressions.

LC_MESSAGES determines the language in which messages are displayed.

If any internationalization variable contains an invalid setting, the commands behave as if all internationalization variables are set to C. See environ(5).

International Code Set Support
Single-byte and multi-byte character code sets are supported.

RETURN VALUE
Upon completion, grep returns one of the following values:

0   One or more matches found.
1   No match found.
2   Syntax error or inaccessible file (even if matches were found).

EXAMPLES
In the Bourne shell (sh(1)) the following example searches two files, finding all lines containing occurrences of any of four strings:

```
grep -F 'if
then
else
fi' file1 file2
```

Note that the single quotes are necessary to tell grep -F when the strings have ended and the file names have begun.

For the C shell (see csh(1)) the following command can be used:

```
grep -F 'if\ then\ else\ fi' file1 file2
```

To search a file named address containing the following entries:

```
Ken    112 Warring St.  Apt. A
Judy   387 Bowditch  Apt. 12
Ann    429 Sixth St.
```

the command:

```
grep Judy address
```

prints:

```
Judy  387 Bowditch  Apt. 12
```

To search a file for lines that contain either a Dec or Nov, use either of the following commands:

```
grep -E '[Dd]ec|[Nn]ov' file
```

```
egrep -i 'dec|nov' file
```

Search all files in the current directory for the string xyz:

```
grep xyz *
```

Search all files in the current directory subtree for the string xyz, and ensure that no error occurs due to file name expansion exceeding system argument list limits:

```
find . -type f -print |xargs grep xyz
```

The previous example does not print the name of files where string xyz appears. To force grep to print file names, add a second argument to the grep command portion of the command line:

```
find . -type f -print |xargs grep xyz /dev/null
```

In this form, the first file name is that produced by find, and the second file name is the null file.

WARNINGS
 (XPG4 only.) If the -q option is specified, the exit status will be zero if an input line is selected, even if an error was detected. Otherwise, default actions will be performed.

SEE ALSO
 sed(1), sh(1), regcomp(3C), environ(5), lang(5), regexp(5).

STANDARDS CONFORMANCE
 grep: SVID2, SVID3, XPG2, XPG3, XPG4, POSIX.2

 egrep: SVID2, SVID3, XPG2, XPG3, XPG4, POSIX.2

 fgrep: SVID2, SVID3, XPG2, XPG3, XPG4, POSIX.2

join

man page

join - 10

join - Join two relations based on lines in files.

---

join(1)   join(1)

NAME
     join - relational database operator

SYNOPSIS

     join [options] file1 file2

DESCRIPTION
     join forms, on the standard output, a join of the two relations
     specified by the lines of file1 and file2. If file1 or file2 is -,
     the standard input is used.

     file1 and file2 must be sorted in increasing collating sequence (see
     Environment Variables below) on the fields on which they are to be
     joined; normally the first in each line.

     The output contains one line for each pair of lines in file1 and file2
     that have identical join fields. The output line normally consists of
     the common field followed by the rest of the line from file1, then the
     rest of the line from file2.

     The default input field separators are space, tab, or new-line. In
     this case, multiple separators count as one field separator, and
     leading separators are ignored. The default output field separator is
     a space.

     Some of the below options use the argument n. This argument should be
     a 1 or a 2 referring to either file1 or file2, respectively.

     Options
     -a n   In addition to the normal output, produce a line for each
                    unpairable line in file n, where n is 1 or 2.

     -e s   Replace empty output fields by string s.

     -j m   Join on field m of both files. The argument m must be
                    delimited by space characters. This option and the
                    following two are provided for backward compatibility.
                    Use of the -1 and -2 options (see below) is recommended
                    for portability.

     -j1 m   Join on field m of file1.

     -j2 m   Join on field m of file2.

     -o list   Each output line comprises the fields specified in list,
                    each element of which has the form n.m, where n is a file
                    number and m is a field number. The common field is not
                    printed unless specifically requested.

     -t c   Use character c as a separator (tab character). Every

appearance of c in a line is significant. The character c
is used as the field separator for both input and output.

-v file_number
            Instead of the default output, produce a line only for
            each unpairable line in file_number, where file_number is
            1 or 2.

-1 f   Join on field f of file 1. Fields are numbered starting
            with 1.

-2 f   Join on field f of file 2. Fields are numbered starting
            with 1.

EXTERNAL INFLUENCES
    Environment Variables
        LC_COLLATE determines the collating sequence join expects from input
        files.

        LC_CTYPE determines the alternative blank character as an input field
        separator, and the interpretation of data within files as single
        and/or multi-byte characters. LC_CTYPE also determines whether the
        separator defined through the -t option is a single- or multi-byte
        character.

        If LC_COLLATE or LC_CTYPE is not specified in the environment or is
        set to the empty string, the value of LANG is used as a default for
        each unspecified or empty variable. If LANG is not specified or is
        set to the empty string, a default of ``C'' (see lang(5)) is used
        instead of LANG. If any internationalization variable contains an
        invalid setting, join behaves as if all internationalization variables
        are set to ``C'' (see environ(5)).

    International Code Set Support
        Single- and multi-byte character code sets are supported with the
        exception that multi-byte-character file names are not supported.

EXAMPLES
        The following command line joins the password file and the group file,
        matching on the numeric group ID, and outputting the login name, the
        group name, and the login directory. It is assumed that the files
        have been sorted in the collating sequence defined by the LC_COLLATE
        or LANG environment variable on the group ID fields.

            join -1 4 -2 3 -o 1.1 2.1 1.6 -t: /etc/passwd /etc/group

        The following command produces an output consisting all possible
        combinations of lines that have identical first fields in the two
        sorted files sf1 and sf2, with each line consisting of the first and
        third fields from sorted_file1 and the second and fourth fields from
        sorted_file2:

            join -j1 1 -j2 1 -o 1.1, 2.2, 1.3, 2.4 sorted_file1 sorted_file2

WARNINGS
        With default field separation, the collating sequence is that of sort
        -b; with -t, the sequence is that of a plain sort.

        The conventions of join, sort, comm, uniq, and awk are incongruous.

        Numeric filenames may cause conflict when the -o option is used
        immediately before listing filenames.

AUTHOR
        join was developed by OSF and HP.

SEE ALSO
         awk(1), comm(1), sort(1), uniq(1).

STANDARDS CONFORMANCE
         join: SVID2, SVID3, XPG2, XPG3, XPG4, POSIX.2

paste

paste - Merge lines of files.

NAME
     paste - merge same lines of several files or subsequent lines of one
     file

SYNOPSIS

     paste file1 file2 ...
     paste -d list file1 file2 ...
     paste -s [-d list] file1 file2 ...

DESCRIPTION
     In the first two forms, paste concatenates corresponding lines of the
     given input files file1, file2, etc. It treats each file as a column
     or columns in a table and pastes them together horizontally (parallel
     merging). In other words, it is the horizontal counterpart of cat(1)
     which concatenates vertically; i.e., one file after the other. In the
     -s option form above, paste replaces the function of an older command
     with the same name by combining subsequent lines of the input file
     (serial merging). In all cases, lines are glued together with the tab
     character, or with characters from an optionally specified list.
     Output is to standard output, so paste can be used as the start of a
     pipe, or as a filter if - is used instead of a file name.

     paste recognizes the following options and command-line arguments:

          -d   Without this option, the new-line characters of all but
                    the last file (or last line in case of the -s option)
                    are replaced by a tab character. This option allows
                    replacing the tab character by one or more alternate
                    characters (see below).

          list   One or more characters immediately following -d replace
                    the default tab as the line concatenation character.
                    The list is used circularly; i.e., when exhausted, it
                    is reused. In parallel merging (that is, no -s
                    option), the lines from the last file are always
                    terminated with a new-line character, not from the
                    list. The list can contain the special escape
                    sequences: \n (new-line), \t (tab), \\ (backslash), and
                    \0 (empty string, not a null character). Quoting may
                    be necessary if characters have special meaning to the
                    shell. (For example, to get one backslash, use -
                    d"\\\\").

          -s   Merge subsequent lines rather than one from each input
                    file. Use tab for concatenation, unless a list is
                    specified with the -d option. Regardless of the list,
                    the very last character of the file is forced to be a
                    new-line.

          -         Can be used in place of any file name to read a line from the standard input (there is no prompting).

EXTERNAL INFLUENCES
    Environment Variables
        LC_CTYPE determines the locale for the interpretation of text as
        single- and/or multi-byte characters.

        LC_MESSAGES determines the language in which messages are displayed.

        If LC_CTYPE or LC_MESSAGES is not specified in the environment or is
        set to the empty string, the value of LANG is used as a default for
        each unspecified or empty variable. If LANG is not specified or is
        set to the empty string, a default of "C" (see lang(5)) is used
        instead of LANG.

        If any internationalization variable contains an invalid setting,
        paste behaves as if all internationalization variables are set to "C".
        See environ(5).

    International Code Set Support
        Single- and multi-byte character code sets are supported.

RETURN VALUE
    These commands return the following values upon completion:

        0   Completed successfully.

        >0   An error occurred.

EXAMPLES
    List directory in one column:

        ls | paste -d" " -

    List directory in four columns

        ls | paste - - - -

    Combine pairs of lines into lines

        paste -s -d"\t\n" file

    Notes
        pr -t -m... works similarly, but creates extra blanks, tabs and new-
        lines for a nice page layout.

DIAGNOSTICS
        too many files   Except for the -s option, no more than
                                    OPEN_MAX - 3 input files can be specified
                                    (see limits(5)).

AUTHOR
    paste was developed by OSF and HP.

SEE ALSO
    cut(1), grep(1), pr(1).

STANDARDS CONFORMANCE
    paste: SVID2, SVID3, XPG2, XPG3, XPG4, POSIX.2

sed

sed - Stream text editor.

sed(1)   sed(1)

NAME
     sed - stream text editor

SYNOPSIS

     sed [-n] script [file ...]

     sed [-n] [-e script] ... [-f script_file] ... [file ...]

DESCRIPTION
     sed copies the named text files (standard input default) to the
     standard output, edited according to a script containing up to 100
     commands. Only complete input lines are processed. Any input text at
     the end of a file that is not terminated by a new-line character is
     ignored.

     Options
     sed recognizes the following options:

          -f script_file
                         Take script from file script_file.

          -e script   Edit according to script. If there is just one -e
                         option and no -f options, the flag -e can be omitted.

          -n   Suppress the default output.

     sed interprets all -escript and -fscript_file arguments in the order
     given. Use caution, if mixing -e and -f options, to avoid
     unpredictable or incorrect results.

     Command Scripts
     A script consists of editor commands, one per line, of the following
     form:

          [address [, address]] function [arguments]

     In normal operation, sed cyclically copies a line of input into a
     pattern space (unless there is something left after a D command),
     applies in sequence all commands whose addresses select that pattern
     space, and, at the end of the script, copies the pattern space to the
     standard output (except under -n) and deletes the pattern space.

     Some of the commands use a hold space to save all or part of the
     pattern space for subsequent retrieval.

     Command Addresses
     An address is either a decimal number that counts input lines
     cumulatively across files, a $ which addresses the last line of input,
     or a context address; that is, a /regular expression/ in the style of

ed(1) modified thus:

- In a context address, the construction \?regular expression?, where ? is any character, is identical to /regular expression/. Note that in the context address \xabc\xdefx, the second x stands for itself, so that the regular expression is abcxdef.

- The escape sequence \n matches a new-line character embedded in the pattern space.

- A period (.) matches any character except the terminal new-line of the pattern space.

- A command line with no addresses selects every pattern space.

- A command line with one address selects each pattern space that matches the address.

- A command line with two addresses selects the inclusive range from the first pattern space that matches the first address through the next pattern space that matches the second (if the second address is a number less than or equal to the line number first selected, only one line is selected). Thereafter the process is repeated, looking again for the first address.

sed supports Basic Regular Expression syntax (see regexp(5)).

Editing commands can also be applied to only non-selected pattern spaces by use of the negation function ! (described below).

Command Functions
In the following list of functions, the maximum number of permissible addresses for each function is indicated in parentheses. Other function elements are interpreted as follows:

text   One or more lines, all but the last of which end with \ to hide the new-line. Backslashes in text are treated like backslashes in the replacement string of an s command, and can be used to protect initial blanks and tabs against the stripping that is done on every script line.

rfile   Must terminate the command line, and must be preceded by exactly one blank.

wfile   Must terminate the command line, and must be preceded by exactly one blank. Each wfile is created before processing begins. There can be at most 10 distinct wfile arguments.

sed recognizes the following functions:

(1)a\
text   Append. Place text on the output before reading next input line.

(2)b label   Branch to the : command bearing label. If no label is specified, branch to the end of the script.

(2)c\
text   Change. Delete the pattern space. With 0 or 1 address or at the end of a 2-address range, place text on the output. Start the next cycle.

(2)d   Delete pattern space and start the next cycle.

(2)D   Delete initial segment of pattern space through first
            new-line and start the next cycle.

(2)g   Replace contents of the pattern space with contents of the
            hold space.

(2)G   Append contents of hold space to the pattern space.

(2)h   Replace contents of the hold space with contents of the
            pattern space.

(2)H   Append the contents of the pattern space to the hold
            space.

(1)i\
text   Insert. Place text on the standard output.

(2)l   List the pattern space on the standard output in an
            unambiguous form. Non-printing characters are spelled in
            three-digit octal number format (with a preceding
            backslash), and long lines are folded.

(2)n   Copy the pattern space to the standard output if the
            default output has not been suppressed (by the -n option
            on the command line or the #n command in the script file).
            Replace the pattern space with the next line of input.

(2)N   Append the next line of input to the pattern space with an
            embedded new-line. (The current line number changes.)

(2)p   Print. Copy the pattern space to the standard output.

(2)P   Copy the initial segment of the pattern space through the
            first new-line to the standard output.

(1)q   Quit. Branch to the end of the script. Do not start a
            new cycle.

(1)r rfile Read contents of rfile and place on output before reading
            the next input line.

(2)s/regular expression/replacement/flags
            Substitute replacement string for instances of regular
            expression in the pattern space. Any character can be
            used instead of /. For a fuller description see ed(1).
            flags is zero or more of:

            n   n=1-2048 (LINE_MAX). Substitute for just
                        the nth occurrence of regular expression in
                        the pattern space.

            g   Global. Substitute for all non-overlapping
                        instances of regular expression rather than
                        just the first one.

            p   Print the pattern space if a replacement
                        was made and the default output has been
                        suppressed (by the -n option on the command
                        line or the #n command in the script file).

            w wfile   Write. Append the pattern space to wfile
                        if a replacement was made.

(2)t label   Test. Branch to the : command bearing the label if any
              substitutions have been made since the most recent reading
              of an input line or execution of a t. If label is empty,
              branch to the end of the script.

(2)w wfile   Write. Append the pattern space to wfile.

(2)x   Exchange the contents of the pattern and hold spaces.

(2)y/string1/string2/
              Transform. Replace all occurrences of characters in
              string1 with the corresponding character in string2. The
              lengths of string1 and string2 must be equal.

(2)! function
              Don't. Apply the function (or group, if function is {}
              only to lines not selected by the address or addresses.

(0): label   This command does nothing; it bears a label for b and t
              commands to branch to.

(1)=   Place the current line number on the standard output as a
              line.

(2){   Execute the following commands through a matching } only
              when the pattern space is selected. The syntax is:

              { cmd1
              cmd2
              cmd3
                .
                .
                .
              }

(0)   An empty command is ignored.

(0)#   If a # appears as the first character on the first line of
              a script file, that entire line is treated as a comment
              with one exception: If the character after the # is an n,
              the default output is suppressed. The rest of the line
              after #n is also ignored. A script file must contain at
              least one non-comment line.

EXTERNAL INFLUENCES
   Environment Variables
      LANG provides a default value for the internationalization variables
      that are unset or null. If LANG is unset or null, the default value of
      "C" (see lang(5)) is used. If any of the internationalization
      variables contains an invalid setting, sed will behave as if all
      internationalization variables are set to "C". See environ(5).

      LC_ALL If set to a non-empty string value, overrides the values of all
      the other internationalization variables.

      LC_CTYPE determines the interpretation of text as single and/or
      multi-byte characters, the classification of characters as printable,
      and the characters matched by character class expressions in regular
      expressions.

      LC_MESSAGES determines the locale that should be used to affect the
      format and contents of diagnostic messages written to standard error
      and informative messages written to standard output.

      NLSPATH determines the location of message catalogues for the processing of LC_MESSAGES.

International Code Set Support
Single- and multi-byte character code sets are supported.

EXAMPLES
Make a simple substitution in a file from the command line or from a
shell script, changing abc to xyz:

```
sed 's/abc/xyz/' file1 >file1.out
```

Same as above but use shell or environment variables var1 and var2 in
search and replacement strings:

```
sed "s/$var1/$var2/" file1 >file1.out
```

or

```
sed 's/'$var1'/'$var2'/' file1 >file1.out
```

Multiple substitutions in a single command:

```
sed -e 's/abc/xyz/' -e 's/lmn/rst/' file1
```

or

```
sed -e 's/abc/xyz/' \
-e 's/lmn/rst/' \
file1 >file1.out
```

WARNINGS
sed limits command scripts to a total of not more than 100 commands.

The hold space is limited to 8192 characters.

sed processes only text files. See the glossary for a definition of
text files and their limitations.

AUTHOR
sed was developed by OSF and HP.

SEE ALSO
awk(1), ed(1), grep(1), environ(5), lang(5), regexp(5).

sed: A Non-Interactive Streaming Editor tutorial in the Text
Processing Users Guide.

STANDARDS CONFORMANCE
sed: SVID2, SVID3, XPG2, XPG3, XPG4, POSIX.2

sort

sort - Sort contents of files.

---

sort(1)   sort(1)

NAME
     sort - sort or merge files

SYNOPSIS

     sort [-m] [-o output] [-bdfinruM] [-t char] [-k keydef] [-y [kmem]] [-z
     recsz] [-T dir] [file ...]

     sort [-c] [-AbdfinruM] [-t char] [-k keydef] [-y [kmem]] [-z recsz] [-T
     dir] [file ...]

DESCRIPTION
     sort performs one of the following functions:

          1. Sorts lines of all the named files together and writes the
              result to the specified output.

          2. Merges lines of all the named (presorted) files together and
              writes the result to the specified output.

          3. Checks that a single input file is correctly presorted.

     The standard input is read if - is used as a file name or no input
     files are specified.

     Comparisons are based on one or more sort keys extracted from each
     line of input. By default, there is one sort key, the entire input
     line. Ordering is lexicographic by characters using the collating
     sequence of the current locale. If the locale is not specified or is
     set to the POSIX locale, then ordering is lexicographic by bytes in
     machine-collating sequence. If the locale includes multi-byte
     characters, single-byte characters are machine-collated before multi-
     byte characters.

     Behavior Modification Options
     The following options alter the default behavior:

          -A   Sorts on a byte-by-byte basis using each character's
                      encoded value. On some systems, extended characters
                      will be considered negative values, and so sort
                      before ASCII characters. If you are sorting ASCII
                      characters in a non-C/POSIX locale, this flag
                      performs much faster.

          -c   Check that the single input file is sorted according
                      to the ordering rules. No output is produced; the
                      exit code is set to indicate the result.

          -m   Merge only; the input files are assumed to be already
                      sorted.

-o output   The argument given is the name of an output file to
             use instead of the standard output. This file can be
             the same as one of the input files.

-u   Unique: suppress all but one in each set of lines
             having equal keys. If used with the -c option, check
             to see that there are no lines with duplicate keys,
             in addition to checking that the input file is
             sorted.

-y [kmem]   The amount of main memory used by the sort can have a
             large impact on its performance. If this option is
             omitted, sort begins using a system default memory
             size, and continues to use more space as needed. If
             this option is presented with a value, kmem, sort
             starts using that number of kilobytes of memory,
             unless the administrative minimum or maximum is
             violated, in which case the corresponding extremum
             will be used. Thus, -y 0 is guaranteed to start with
             minimum memory. By convention, -y (with no argument)
             starts with maximum memory.

-z recsz   The size of the longest line read is recorded in the
             sort phase so that buffers can be allocated during
             the merge phase. If the sort phase is omitted via
             the -c or -m options, a popular system default size
             will be used. Lines longer than the buffer size will
             cause sort to terminate abnormally. Supplying the
             actual number of bytes in the longest line to be
             merged (or some larger value) will prevent abnormal
             termination.

-T dir   Use dir as the directory for temporary scratch files
             rather than the default directory, which is is one of
             the following, tried in order: the directory as
             specified in the TMPDIR environment variable;
             /var/tmp, and finally, /tmp.

Ordering Rule Options
  When ordering options appear before restricted sort key
  specifications, the ordering rules are applied globally to all sort
  keys. When attached to a specific sort key (described below), the
  ordering options override all global ordering options for that key.

  The following options override the default ordering rules:

-d   Quasi-dictionary order: only alphanumeric characters
             and blanks (spaces and tabs), as defined by LC_CTYPE
             are significant in comparisons (see environ(5)).

             (XPG4 only.) The behavior is undefined for a sort key
             to which -i or -n also applies.

-f   Fold letters. Prior to being compared, all lowercase
             letters are effectively converted into their
             uppercase equivalents, as defined by LC_CTYPE.

-i   In non-numeric comparisons, ignore all characters
             which are non-printable, as defined by LC_CTYPE. For
             the ASCII character set, octal character codes 001
             through 037 and 0177 are ignored.

-n   The sort key is restricted to an initial numeric
             string consisting of optional blanks, an optional
             minus sign, zero or more digits with optional radix
             character, and optional thousands separators. The

radix and thousands separator characters are defined
by LC_NUMERIC. The field is sorted by arithmetic
value. An empty (missing) numeric field is treated
as arithmetic zero. Leading zeros and plus or minus
signs on zeros do not affect the ordering. The -n
option implies the -b option (see below).

-r   Reverse the sense of comparisons.

-M   Compare as months. The first several non-blank
characters of the field are folded to uppercase and
compared with the langinfo(5) items ABMON_1 < ABMON_2
< ... < ABMON_12. An invalid field is treated as
being less than ABMON_1 string. For example,
American month names are compared such that JAN < FEB
< ... < DEC. An invalid field is treated as being
less than all months. The -M option implies the -b
option (see below).

Field Separator Options
  The treatment of field separators can be altered using the options:

-t char   Use char as the field separator character; char is
not considered to be part of a field (although it can
be included in a sort key). Each occurrence of char
is significant (for example, <char><char> delimits an
empty field). If -t is not specified, <blank>
characters will be used as default field separators;
each maximal sequence of <blank> characters that
follows a non-<blank> character is a field separator.

-b   Ignore leading blanks when determining the starting
and ending positions of a restricted sort key. If
the -b option is specified before the first -k option
(+pos1 argument), it is applied to all -k options
(+pos1 arguments). Otherwise, the -b option can be
attached independently to each -k field_start or
field_end option (+pos1 or (-pos2 argument; see
below). Note that the -b option is only effective
when restricted sort key specifications are given.

Restricted Sort Key
  -k keydef The keydef argument defines a restricted sort key.
The format of this definition is

        field_start[type][,field_end[type]]

which defines a key field beginning at field_start
and ending at field_end. The characters at positions
field_start and field_end are included in the key
field, providing that field_end does not precede
field_start. A missing field_end means the end of the
line. Fields and characters within fields are
numbered starting with 1. Note that this is
different than the obsolete form of restricted sort
keys, where numbering starts at 0. See WARNINGS
below.

Specifying field_start and field_end involves the
notion of a field, a minimal sequence of characters
followed by a field separator or a new-line. By
default, the first blank of a sequence of blanks acts
as the field separator. All blanks in a sequence of
blanks are considered to be part of the next field;
for example, all blanks at the beginning of a line

are considered to be part of the first field.

The arguments field_start and field_end each have the form m.n which are optionally followed by one or more of the type options b, d, f, i, n, r, or M. These modifiers have the functionality for this key only, that their command-line counterparts have for the entire record.

A field_start position specified by m.n is interpreted to mean the nth character in the mth field. A missing n means .1, indicating the first character of the mth field. If the -b option is in effect, n is counted from the first non-blank character in the mth field.

A field_end position specified by m.n is interpreted to mean the nth character in the mth field. If n is missing, the mth field ends at the last character of the field. If the -b option is in effect, n is counted from the first non-<blank> character in the mth field.

Multiple -k options are permitted and are significant in command line order. A maximum of 9 -k options can be given. If no -k option is specified, a default sort key of the entire line is used. When there are multiple sort keys, later keys are compared only after all earlier keys compare equal. Lines that otherwise compare equal are ordered with all bytes significant. If all the specified keys compare equal, the entire record is used as the final key.

The -k option is intended to replace the obsolete [+pos1 [+pos2]] notation, using field_start and field_end respectively. The fully specified [+pos1 [+pos2]] form:

    +w.x-y.z

is equivalent to:

    -k w+1.x+1,y.0 (if z == 0)
    -k w+1.x+1,y+1.z (if z > 0)

Obsolete Restricted Sort Key
   The notation +pos1 -pos2 restricts a sort key to one beginning at pos1 and ending at pos2. The characters at positions pos1 and pos2 are included in the sort key (provided that pos2 does not precede pos1). A missing -pos2 means the end of the line.

   Specifying pos1 and pos2 involves the notion of a field, a minimal sequence of characters followed by a field separator or a new-line. By default, the first blank (space or tab) of a sequence of blanks acts as the field separator. All blanks in a sequence of blanks are considered to be part of the next field; for example, all blanks at the beginning of a line are considered to be part of the first field.

   pos1 and pos2 each have the form m.n optionally followed by one or more of the flags bdfinrM. A starting position specified by +m.n is interpreted to mean character n+1 in field m+1. A missing .n means .0, indicating the first character of field m+1. If the b flag is in effect, n is counted from the first non-blank in field m+1; +m.0b refers to the first non-blank character in field m+1.

   A last position specified by -m.n is interpreted to mean the nth

character (including separators) after the last character of the m th
field. A missing .n means .0, indicating the last character of the
mth field. If the b flag is in effect, n is counted from the last
leading blank in field m+1; -m.1b refers to the first non-blank in
field m+1.

EXTERNAL INFLUENCES
  Environment Variables
    LC_COLLATE determines the default ordering rules applied to the sort.

    LC_CTYPE determines the locale for interpretation of sequences of
    bytes of text data as characters (e.g., single- verses multibyte
    characters in arguments and input files) and the behavior of character
    classification for the -b, -d, -f, -i, and -n options.

    LC_NUMERIC determines the definition of the radix and thousands
    separator characters for the -n option.

    LC_TIME determines the month names for the -M option.

    LC_MESSAGES determines the language in which messages are displayed.

    LC_ALL determines the locale to use to override the values of all the
    other internationalization variables.

    NLSPATH determines the location of message catalogs for the processing
    of LC_MESSAGES.

    LANG provides a default value for the internationalization variables
    that are unset or null. If LANG is unset or null, the default value of
    "C" (see lang(5)) is used.

    If any of the internationalization variables contains an invalid
    setting, sort behaves as if all internationalization variables are set
    to "C". See environ(5).

  International Code Set Support
    Single- and multi-byte character code sets are supported.

EXAMPLES
  Sort the contents of infile with the second field as the sort key:

        sort -k 2,2 infile

  Sort, in reverse order, the contents of infile1 and infile2, placing
  the output in outfile and using the first two characters of the second
  field as the sort key:

        sort -r -o outfile -k 2.1,2.2 infile1 infile2

  Sort, in reverse order, the contents of infile1 and infile2, using the
  first non-blank character of the fourth field as the sort key:

        sort -r -k 4.1b,4.1b infile1 infile2

  Print the password file (/etc/passwd) sorted by numeric user ID (the
  third colon-separated field):

        sort -t: -k 3n,3 /etc/passwd

  Print the lines of the presorted file infile, suppressing all but the
  first occurrence of lines having the same third field:

        sort -mu -k 3,3 infile

DIAGNOSTICS

sort exits with one of the following values:

0   All input files were output successfully, or -c was specified and the input file was correctly presorted.

1   Under the -c option, the file was not ordered as specified, or if the -c and -u options were both specified, two input lines were found with equal keys. This exit status is not returned if the -c option is not used.

>1   An error occurred such as when one or more input lines are too long.

When the last line of an input file is missing a new-line character, sort appends one, prints a warning message, and continues.

If an error occurs when accessing the tables that contain the collation rules for the specified language, sort prints a warning message and defaults to the POSIX locale.

If a -d, -f, or -i option is specified for a language with multi-byte characters, sort prints a warning message and ignores the option.

WARNINGS

Numbering of fields and characters within fields (-k option) has changed to conform to the POSIX standard. Beginning at HP-UX Release 9.0, the -k option numbers fields and characters within fields, starting with 1. Prior to HP-UX Release 9.0, numbering started at 0.

A field separator specified by the -t option is recognized only if it is a single-byte character.

The character type classification categories alpha, digit, space, and print are not defined for multi-byte characters. For languages with multi-byte characters, all characters are significant in comparisons.

FILES

/var/tmp/stm???
/tmp/stm???

AUTHOR

sort was developed by OSF and HP.

SEE ALSO

comm(1), join(1), uniq(1), collate8(4), environ(5), hpnls(5), lang(5).

STANDARDS CONFORMANCE

sort: SVID2, SVID3, XPG2, XPG3, XPG4, POSIX.2

tr

man page

tr - 10

tr - Substitute selected characters.

tr(1)   tr(1)

NAME
     tr - translate characters

SYNOPSIS
     tr [-Acs] string1 string2

     tr -s [-Ac] string1

     tr -d [-Ac] string1

     tr -ds [-Ac] string1 string1

DESCRIPTION
     tr copies the standard input to the standard output with substitution
     or deletion of selected characters. Input characters from string1 are
     replaced with the corresponding characters in string2. If necessary,
     string1 and string2 can be quoted to avoid pattern matching by the
     shell.

     tr recognizes the following command line options:

          -A   Translates on a byte-by-byte basis. When this flag
                          is specified tr does not support extended
                          characters.

          -c   Complements the set of characters in string1,
                          which is the set of all characters in the current
                          character set, as defined by the current setting
                          of LC_CTYPE, except for those actually specified
                          in the string1 argument. These characters are
                          placed in the array in ascending collation
                          sequence, as defined by the current setting of
                          LC_COLLATE.

          -d   Deletes all occurrences of input characters or
                          collating elements found in the array specified in
                          string1.

                          If -c and -d are both specified, all characters
                          except those specified by string1 are deleted. The
                          contents of string2 are ignored, unless -s is also
                          specified. Note, however, that the same string
                          cannot be used for both the -d and the -s flags;
                          when both flags are specified, both string1 (used
                          for deletion) and string2 (used for squeezing) are
                          required.

                          If -d is not specified, each input character or
                          collating element found in the array specified by
                          string1 is replaced by the character or collating

element in the same relative position specified by string2.

-s
: Replaces any character specified in string1 that occurs as a string of two or more repeating characters as a single instance of the character in string2.

If the string2 contains a character class, the argument's array contains all of the characters in that character class. For example:

```
tr -s '[:space:]'
```

In a case conversion, however, the string2 array contains only those characters defined as the second characters in each of the toupper or tolower character pairs, as appropriate. For example:

```
tr -s '[:upper:]' '[:lower:]'
```

The following abbreviation conventions can be used to introduce ranges of characters, repeated characters or single-character collating elements into the strings:

c1-c2 or [c1-c2]
: Stands for the range of collating elements c1 through c2, inclusive, as defined by the current setting of the LC_COLLATE locale category.

[:class:]or [[:class:]]
: Stands for all the characters belonging to the defined character class, as defined by the current setting of LC_CTYPE locale category. The following character class names will be accepted when specified in string1: alnum, alpha, blank, cntrl. digit, graph, lower, print, punct, space, upper, or xdigit, Character classes are expanded in collation order.

When the -d and -s flags are specified together, any of the character class names are accepted in string2; otherwise, only character class names lower or upper are accepted in string2 and then only if the corresponding character class (upper and lower, respectively) is specified in the same relative position in string1. Such a specification is interpreted as a request for case conversion.

When [:lower:] appears in string1 and [:upper:] appears in string2, the arrays contain the characters from the toupper mapping in the LC_CTYPE category of the current locale. When [:upper:] appears in string1 and [:lower:] appears in string2, the arrays contain the characters from the tolower mapping in the LC_CTYPE category of the current locale.

[=c=]or [[=c=]]
: Stands for all the characters or collating elements belonging to the same equivalence class as c, as defined by the current setting of LC_COLLATE locale category. An equivalence class expression is allowed only in string1, or in string2 when it is being used by the combined -d and -s options.

[a*n]   Stands for n repetitions of a. If the first digit
                 of n is 0, n is considered octal; otherwise, n is
                 treated as a decimal value. A zero or missing n
                 is interpreted as large enough to extend string2-
                 based sequence to the length of the string1-based
                 sequence.

The escape character \ can be used as in the shell to remove special
meaning from any character in a string. In addition, \ followed by 1,
2, or 3 octal digits represents the character whose ASCII code is
given by those digits.

An ASCII NUL character in string1 or string2 can be represented only
as an escaped character; i.e. as \000, but is treated like other
characters and translated correctly if so specified. NUL characters
in the input are not stripped out unless the option -d "\000" is
given.

EXTERNAL INFLUENCES
    Environment Variables
        LANG provides a default value for the internationalization variables
        that are unset or null. If LANG is unset or null, the default value of
        "C" (see lang(5)) is used. If any of the internationalization
        variables contains an invalid setting, tr will behave as if all
        internationalization variables are set to "C". See environ(5).

        LC_ALL If set to a non-empty string value, overrides the values of all
        the other internationalization variables.

        LC_CTYPE determines the interpretation of text as single and/or
        multi-byte characters, the classification of characters as printable,
        and the characters matched by character class expressions in regular
        expressions.

        LC_MESSAGES determines the locale that should be used to affect the
        format and contents of diagnostic messages written to standard error
        and informative messages written to standard output.

        NLSPATH determines the location of message catalogues for the
        processing of LC_MESSAGES.

RETURN VALUE
    tr exits with one of the following values:

        0   All input was processed successfully.

        >0 An error occurred.

EXAMPLES
    For the ASCII character set and default collation sequence, create a
    list of all the words in file1, one per line in file2, where a word is
    taken to be a maximal string of alphabetics. Quote the strings to
    protect the special characters from interpretation by the shell (012
    is the ASCII code for a new-line (line feed) character:

        tr -cs "[A-Z][a-z]" "[\012*]" <file1 >file2

    Same as above, but for all character sets and collation sequences:

        tr -cs "[:alpha:]" "[\012*]" <file1 >file2

    Translate all lower case characters in file1 to upper case and write
    the result to standard output.

        tr "[:lower:]" "[:upper:]" <file1

Use an equivalence class to identify accented variants of the base
character e in file1, strip them of diacritical marks and write the
result to file2:

```
tr "[=e=]" "[e*]" <file1 >file2
```

Translate each digit in file1 to a # (number sign), and write the
result to file2.

```
tr "0-9" "[#*]" <file1 >file2
```

The * (asterisk) tells tr to repeat the # (number sign) enough times
to make the second string as long as the first one.

AUTHOR
     tr was developed by OSF and HP.

SEE ALSO
     ed(1), sh(1), ascii(5), environ(5), lang(5), regexp(5).

STANDARDS CONFORMANCE
     tr: SVID2, SVID3, XPG2, XPG3, XPG4, POSIX.2

WC

man page

wc - 10

wc - Count words, bytes, and lines.

---

wc(1)   wc(1)

NAME
    wc - word, line, and byte or character count

SYNOPSIS

    wc [-c|-m] [-lw] [names]

DESCRIPTION
    The wc command counts lines, words, and bytes or characters in the
    named files, or in the standard input if no names are specified. It
    also keeps a total count for all named files.

    A word is a maximal string of characters delimited by spaces, tabs, or
    new-lines.

    wc recognizes the following command-line options:

            -c   Write to the standard output the number of bytes in
                        each input file.

            -m   Write to the standard output the number of characters
                        in each input file.

            -w   Write to the standard output the number of words in
                        each input file.

            -l   Write to the standard output the number of newline
                        characters in each input file.

    The c and m options are mutually exclusive. Otherwise, the l, w, and
    c or m options can be used in any combination to specify that a subset
    of lines, words, and bytes or characters are to be reported.

    When any option is specified, wc will report only the information
    requested by the specified options. If no option is specified, The
    default output is -lwc.

    When names are specified on the command line, they are printed along
    with the counts.

EXTERNAL INFLUENCES
    Environment Variables
        LC_CTYPE determines the range of graphics and space characters, and
        the interpretation of text as single- and/or multi-byte characters.

        LC_MESSAGES determines the language in which messages are displayed.

        If LC_CTYPE or LC_MESSAGES is not specified in the environment or is
        set to the empty string, the value of LANG is used as a default for
        each unspecified or empty variable. If LANG is not specified or is
        set to the empty string, a default of "C" (see lang(5)) is used

instead of LANG.

If any internationalization variable contains an invalid setting, wc behaves as if all internationalization variables are set to "C". See environ(5).

International Code Set Support
Single- and multi-byte character code sets are supported.

WARNINGS
The wc command counts the number of newlines to determine the line count. If a text file has a final line that is not terminated with a newline character, the count will be off by one.

Standard Output (XPG4 only)
By default, the standard output contains an entry for each input file of the form:

"%d %d %d %s\n", <newlines>, <words>, <bytes>, <file>

If the -m option is specified, the number of characters replaces the <bytes> field in this format.

If any options are specified and the -l option is not specified, the number of newlines are not written.

If any options are specified and the -w option is not specified, the number of words are not written.

If any options are specified and neither -c nor -m is specified, the number of bytes or characters are not written.

If no input file operands are specified, no flie name is written and no blank characters preceding the pathname is written.

If more than one input file operand is specified, an additional line is written, of the same format as the other lines, except that the word total (in the POSIX Locale) is written instead of a pathname and the total of each column is written as appropriate. Such an additional line, if any, is written at the end of the input.

Exit Status
The wc utility shall exit with one of the following values

    0   Successful completion.

    >0   An error occured.

EXAMPLES
Print the number of words and characters in file1:

    wc -wm file1

The following is printed when the above command is executed:

    n1 n2 file1

where n1 is the number of words and n2 is the number of characters in file1.

STANDARDS CONFORMANCE
wc: SVID2, SVID3, XPG2, XPG3, XPG4, POSIX.2

CHAPTER 11

Introduction to Shell Programming

Shell Programming

There is much more to a shell than meets the eye. The shell is much more than the command line interpreter everyone is used to using. UNIX shells actually provide a powerful interpretive programming language as well.

In this chapter, we'll cover **ksh** shell programming. I chose **ksh** because most **ksh** programming techniques work with the Bourne shell as well. There is a follow-on to **ksh** programming at the end of the chapter for **csh** because the **csh** employs many different programming techniques than the **ksh**.

We'll cover most important **ksh** programming techniques. The climax of this chapter is a fairly sophisticated shell program to remove files and place them in a directory, rather than just permanently removing files from the system with **rm**. This program employs all the shell programming techiques covered in the chapter. This shell program, called **trash**, with some minor modifications, can be run in the Bourne shell as well.

The shell is one of the most powerful features on any UNIX system. If you can't find the right command to accomplish a task, you can probably build it quite easily using a shell script.

The best way to learn shell programming is by example. There are many examples given in this chapter. Some serve no purpose other than to demonstrate the current topic. Most, however, are useful tools or parts of tools that you can easily expand and adapt into your environment. The examples provide easy-to-understand prompts and output messages. Most examples show what is needed to provide the functionality we are after. They do not do a great deal of error checking. From my experience, however, it only takes a few minutes to get a shell program to do what you want; it can take hours to handle every situation and every error condition. Therefore, these programs are not very dressed up (maybe a sport coat versus a tuxedo). I'm giving you what you need to know to build some useful tools for your environment. I hope that you will have enough knowledge and interest by the time we get to the end of this chapter to learn and do more.

Most of the examples in this chapter were performed on a Solaris system; however, shells are nearly identical going from one system to another so you should be able to get the programs in this chapter running on your system quickly.

Steps to Create Shell Programs

When you craft a shell program, there are some initial steps you want to perform so that you have consistency among all of your programs. The following is a list of some important concepts to employ with your shell programs:

1. **Names of shell programs and their output** - You should give your shell programs and their output a meaningful name. If you call your shell programs *script1*, *script2* and so on these will not have any meaning for you and other potential users of the programs. If your shell program finds files of a particular

type, then you can name the program *filefind* or some other descriptive name. Do the same with the output of shell programs. Don't call the output of a shell program *output1* if there is some descriptive name you can give it such as *filefind.out*. Also avoid naming shell programs and their output names that already exist. You may use commands such as **read** and **test**, so you may create confusion and conflicts if you were to give your program and their output the same names. The first shell program in this chapter shows today's date. If we were to name the program **date**, we would actually run the system **date** command as opposed to our shell program **date**. The reason is that in most cases, the system **date** command would be found before our shell program **date** file.

2. **Repository for shell programs** - If you plan to produce numerous shell programs, you may want to place them in a directory. You can have a directory in your home directory called **bin** or **shellprogs**, in which all programs are located. You can then update your path to include the directory name where your shell programs are located.

3. **Specify shell to execute program** - The very first line of the program specifies the shell to be used to execute the program. The path of the shell is preceeded by **#!**, which is a "magic number" that indicates that the path of the shell is about to follow. The shell programs in this chapter use the **ksh** path.

4. **Formatting of shell programs** - Do not underestimate the importance of proper formatting to enhance the readability of shell programs. You should indent areas of the program to indicate that commands are part of a group. Indenting only three or four spaces is fine for groups of commands. You may also want to set autoindent in **vi** so that the next line starts at the same point as the previous line (try **:set ai** in **vi** to see how this technique works). You can break up long lines by placing a \ at the end of one line and continue the command on the next line.

5. **Comments** - Include detailed comments in your shell program. You can write paragraphs of comments to describe what

an upcoming section of your program will accomplish. These will help you understand your program when you look at it months or years after having originally created it as well as help others understand the program. No limit exists on the amout of comments you can include. Start comment lines with a # (pound sign).

6. **Make the shell program executable** - The **chmod** command covered in the chapters introducing various shells is used to make your program executable.

Following the previous list of recommendations will make creating and using shell programs more efficient. Now we need to cover the types of shell programs.

A shell program is simply a file containing a set of commands you wish to execute sequentially. The file needs to be set with execute permissions so that you can execute it just by typing the name of the script.

There are two basic forms of shell programs exist:

1. **Simple command files** - When you have a command line or set of command lines that you use over and over, you can use one simple command to execute them all.

2. **Structured programs** - The shell provides much more than the ability to "batch" together a series of commands. It has many of the features that any higher-level programming language contains:

   • Variables for storing data

   • Decision-making controls (the **if** and **case** commands)

   • Looping abilities (the **for** and **while** loops)

   • Function calls for modularity

Given these two basic forms you can build everything from simple command replacements to much larger and more complex data manipulation and system administration tools.

ksh Programming

I have created a directory in my home directory called **shellprogs** to serve as a repository for my shell programs. In order to execute these programs without having to specify an absolute path, I have updated my path in **.profile** to include the following line:

```
export PATH=${PATH}:~shellprogs
```

This adds **/home/martyp/shellprogs** to my path. After updating **.profile** you can log out and log in to update your path. You can issue the command below to confirm that your path has indeed been updated to include the directory in which you keep your shell programs:

```
martyp $ echo $PATH
/usr/bin:/usr/ucb:/etc:.:/home/martyp/shellprogs
martyp $
```

Let's now go to the **shellprogs** directory and type a simple command file called **today**:

```
#!/bin/ksh
# This is a simple command file to display today's date.
echo "Today's date is"
date +%x
```

Before we look at each line in the program, let's run it to see the output:

```
martyp $ today
ksh: today: cannot execute
martyp $ ls -al
total 6
```

```
drwxrwxr-x    2 martyp    staff     512 May 21 09:53 .
drwxrwx---    4 martyp    staff     512 May 21 09:25 ..
-rw-rw-r--    1 martyp    staff     100 May 21 09:54 today
martyp $ chmod +x today
martyp $ ls -al
total 6
drwxrwxr-x    2 martyp    staff     512 May 21 09:53 .
drwxrwx---    4 martyp    staff     512 May 21 09:25 ..
-rwxrwxr-x    1 martyp    staff     100 May 21 09:54 today
martyp $ today
Today's date is
05/21/99
martyp $
```

We could not execute **today** because the file was created with execute permissions, which we confirm by performing a long listing. We then add execute permission to the file with **chmod +x**, which is confirmed with the next long listing. We are then able to execute **today** and view its results.

The **umask** discussion in each of the earlier shell chapters describes the defaults for new files. Almost invariably, new files are created without execute permission; therefore, you will have to update the permissions on the file to include execute.

Let's now walk through this simple shell program and analyze each line.

```
#!/bin/ksh
```

The first line specifies that the **ksh** will be used. If you are using Bash, C shell, or any other shell, you would specify its location in this manner. Some systems have multiple versions of shells running on them. It may be that a shell has been updated since the last release and some users may want to maintain the old version of the shell. For this reason, you want to be sure that the absolute path you specify is indeed that of the shell you wish to use. Note that the **#!** must be the very first two characters in the file.

Normally, when you run a shell program, the system tries to execute commands using the same shell you are using for your interactive command lines. If we don't include this line, someone running a shell other than the **ksh** might have unexpected results when trying to run one of our programs.

man page

ksh - 6

As a good practice, you should include **#!shellname** as the first line of every shell program you write.

Let's now view the next line of our program:

```
# This is a simple command file to display today's date.
```

These are comments. Everything after a # in a command line is considered a comment (**#!** on the first line is the one very big exception). Keep in mind my early remarks about including comments liberally. It is a great pleasure to share a well commented shell program with a friend, knowing that you have adequately documented the program with comments.

Here is the next command:

```
echo "Today's date is"
```

The **echo** command generates prompts and messages in shell programs. See the **echo** manual entry to see all the options available with **echo** for formatting your output. We commonly enclose the string to be displayed in double quotes. In this case, we did because we needed to let the shell know that the apostrophe was part of the string and not a single quote that needs a match.

Next is the last command in our program:

```
date +%x
```

This executes the **date** command. There are indeed many options to the **date** command, some of which are not intuitive. In this case, we use one of the simplest forms of the command, which simply produces today's date.

Let's cover one more example of a command file that you may
find useful. This program informs you of the present working directory and then produces a long listing of the files in the directory. The
following is a listing of the shell program **myll**:

```
#!/bin/ksh
# This is a simple shell program that displays the current
# directory name before a long file listing (ll) of that
# directory.
# The script name is myll
echo "Long listing of directory:"
pwd
echo
ll -l
```

This program uses **ll**; you may need to use **ls -al**. The following is
what **myll** looks like when it runs:

```
martyp $ myll
Long listing of directory:
/home/martyp/shellprogs

total 4
-rwxrwxr-x   1 martyp    staff      220 May 24 05:28 myll
-rwxrwxr-x   1 martyp    staff      100 May 21 09:54 today
martyp $
```

This name of the present working directory is **/home/martyp/
shellprogs**. A long listing of the contents of this directory shows the
two programs we have covered so far in this chapter.

Before we can produce more complex shell programs, we need to
learn more about some of the programming features built into the
shell. Let's start with shell variables.

Shell Variables

A shell variable is similar to a variable in any programming language. A variable is simply a name you give to a storage location. Unlike most languages, however, you never have to declare or initialize your variables; you just use them.

Shell variables can have just about any name that starts with a letter (uppercase or lowercase). To avoid confusion with special shell characters (like file name generation characters), keep the names simple and use just letters, numbers, and underscore (_).

To assign values to shell variables, you simply type the following:

```
name=value
```

Note that there are no spaces before and after the = character.

Here are some examples of setting shell variables from the command line. These examples work correctly:

```
$ myname=ralph
$ HerName=mary
```

This one does not work because of the space after "his":

```
$ his name=norton
his: not found
```

The shell assumes that "his" is a command and tries to execute it. The rest of the line is ignored.

This example contains an illegal character (+) in the name:

```
$ one+one=two
one+one=two: not found
```

A variable must start with a letter. A common mistake is to give a variable a name that makes perfect sense to you but does not start with a letter. The following example uses a variable that starts with a number:

```
$ 3word=hi
3word=hi: not found
```

The "3" causes a "not found" to be produced when we attempt to assign this variable.

Now that we can store values in our variables, we need to know how to use those values. The dollar sign ($) is used to get the value of a variable. Any time the shell sees a $ in the command line, it assumes that the characters immediately following it are a variable name. It replaces the *$variable* with its value. Here are some simple examples using variables at the command line:

```
$ myname=ralph
$ echo myname
myname

$ echo $myname
ralph
$ echo $abc123
```

In the first **echo** command there is no $, so the shell ignores **myname**, and **echo** gets **myname** as an argument to be echoed. In the second **echo**, however, the shell sees the $, looks up the value of **myname,** and puts it on the command line. Now **echo** sees **ralph** as its argument (not **myname** or **$myname**). The final **echo** statement is similar, except that we have not given a value to **abc123** so the shell assumes that it has no value and replaces **$abc123** with nothing. Therefore echo has no arguments and echos a blank line.

There may be times when you want to concatenate variables and strings. This is very easy to do in the shell:

```
$ myname=ralph
$ echo "My name is $myname"
My name is ralph
```

There may be times when the shell can become confused if the variable name is not easily identified in the command line:

```
$ string=dobeedobee
$ echo "$stringdoo"
```

We wanted to display "dobeedobee," but the shell thought the variable name was stringdoo, which had no value. To accomplish this we can use curly braces around the variable name to separate it from surrounding characters:

```
$ echo "${string}doo"
dobeedobeedoo
```

You can set variables in shell programs in the same way, but you would also like to do things such as save the output of a command in a variable so that we can use it later. You may want to ask users a question and read their response into a variable so that you can examine it.

Command Substitution

Command substitution allows us to save the output from a command (**stdout**) into a shell variable. To demonstrate this, let's take another look at how our "today" example can be done using command substitution.

```
#!/bin/ksh
d=`date +%x`
echo "Today's date is $d"
```

The back quotes (') around the **date** command tell the shell to execute date and place its output on the command line. The output will then be assigned to the variable **d**. We'll name this updated script **today1** and run it:

```
$ today1
Today's date is 05/24/00
```

We could also have done this task without using the variable **d**. We could have just included the **date** command in the echo string, as shown in the **today2** script shown in the following example:

```
#!/bin/ksh
echo "Today's date is `date +%x`"
```

When we run this program, we see exactly the same output as we did with **today1**:

```
$ today2
Today's date is 05/24/00
```

We'll use shell variables and command substitution extensively in some of the upcoming examples. Let's now cover reading user input.

Reading User Input

The most common way to get information from the user is to prompt him or her and then read the response. The **echo** command is most commonly used to display the prompt; then the **read** command is used to read a line of input from the user (standard input). Words from the input line can be assigned to one or several shell variables.

Here is an example with comments to show you how **read** can be used:

```
#!/bin/ksh
# program: readtest
echo "Please enter your name: \c"      # the \c leaves cursor on
                                       # this line.

read name        # I have no $ because we are doing an assignment
                 # of whatever the user enters into name.

echo "Hello, $name"

echo "Please enter your two favorite colors: \c"

read color1 color2       # first word entered goes into color1
                         # remainder of line goes into color2

echo "You entered $color2 and $color1"
```

If we ran this program, it would look something like this:

```
$ readtest
Please enter your name: gerry
Hello, gerry
Please enter your two favorite colors: blue green
You entered green and blue
$
```

Notice how the **read** command assigned the two words entered for colors into the two respective color variables. If the user entered fewer words than the **read** command was expecting, the remaining variables are set to null. If the user enters too many words, all extra words entered are assigned into the last variable. This technique is how you can get a whole line of input into one variable. Here's an example of what happens if you entered more than two colors:

```
$ readtest
Please enter your name: gerry
Hello, gerry
Please enter your two favorite colors: chartreuse orchid
blue You entered orchid blue and chartreuse
$
```

The program took the last two colors entered and assigned them to *color2*. For this reason, you have to be careful of what a user may enter with the read command and how you map that information to variables.

You may have a built-in variable used with **read** called *REPLY*. With *REPLY*, a line of input is assigned to the variable *REPLY*. I tend not to use this often because I don't like to leave anything to chance. I normally explicitly name a variable to which input is assigned. The example shows the listing and running of **readtest1**, which includes a line that contains only the **read** command, the response of which is assigned to *REPLY*:

man page

cat - 3

```
martyp $cat readtest1

#!/bin/ksh
# program: readtest
echo "Please enter your name: \c"       # the \c leaves cursor on
                                        # this line.

read name        # I have no $ because we are doing an assignment
                 # of whatever the user enters into name.

echo "Hello, $name"

echo "Please enter your two favorite colors: \c"

read color1 color2       # first word entered goes into color1
                         # remainder of line goes into color2

echo "You entered $color2 and $color1"
echo "Where are you from?"
read                                    # read response into $REPLY
echo "I'm sure $REPLY is great"


martyp $ readtest1
Please enter your name: MARTY
Hello, MARTY
Please enter your two favorite colors: RED BLUE
You entered BLUE and RED
Where are you from?
MANY DIFFERENT PLACES
I'm sure MANY DIFFERENT PLACES is great
martyp $
```

You can see in this example that the response I typed of "MANY DIFFERENT PLACES" was indeed read into *REPLY*.

Although **echo** is used throughout this chapter, you may also see **print** used display lines on the screen.

Arguments to Shell Programs

Shell programs can have command-line arguments just like any regular command. Command-line arguments that you use when you invoke your shell program are stored in a special set of variables. These are called the positional parameters.

The first ten words on the command line are directly accessible in the shell program using the special variables **$0-$9**. This is how they work:

$0	The command name
$1	The first argument
$2	The second argument
$3	.
	.
	.
$9	The ninth argument

If you are not sure how many command line arguments you may get when your program is run, there are two other variables that can help:

$#	The number of command-line arguments
$*	A space-separated list all of the command-line arguments (which does not include the command name)

The variable **$*** is commonly used with the **for** loop (soon to be explained) to process shell script command lines with any number of arguments.

Let's now take the **myll** we worked with earlier and modify it to produce a long listing of the directory that we specify when we run the program. Figure 11-1 shows the modified **myll**.

```
#!/bin/ksh
# This is a simple shell program that takes one command line
# argument (a directory name) and then displays the full pathname
# of that directory before doing a long file listing (ll) on
# it.
#
# The script name is myll
cd $1
echo "Long listing of the `pwd` directory:"
echo
ls -l
```

Figure 11-1 **myll** Shell Program

If we run **myll** with a directory name, the script changes directory, echoes the message containing the full path name (notice the command substitution), and then executes the **ls -l** command.

Note that the **cd** in the **myll** program will changes only the working directory of the script; it does not affect the working directory of the shell from which we run **myll**.

```
martyp $ myll /tmp
Long listing of the /tmp directory:

total 2384
-rw-------   1 root     sys       265228 Feb 22 15:21 dtdbcache_:0
-rw-r--r--   1 root     sys        70829 Feb 23 10:44 g
-rw-r--r--   1 root     sys        13642 Feb 23 10:48 i
-rw-rw-rw-   1 root     root       14071 May 24 06:10 license_log
-rwxr-xr-x   1 chrisb   users        317 Apr 20 17:38 ls
-rw-rw-r--   1 root     sys         4441 Mar 25 14:37 mwaps7454
-rw-rw-rw-   1 anne     users       4341 May 20 13:56 ps23974
-rw-r--r--   1 rodt     users       4218 Apr 14 11:17 ps3358
-rw-r--r--   1 rodt     users       4763 Feb 24 07:23 ps6465
-rw-rw-r--   1 root     sys         4446 Mar 25 14:31 ps7036
-rw-rw-r--   1 root     sys         4442 Mar 25 14:35 ps7138
-rw-rw-r--   1 root     sys         4446 Mar 25 14:35 ps7215
-rw-rw-r--   1 root     sys         4498 Mar 25 14:36 ps7342
```

```
-rw-rw-r--    1 root      sys            4446 Mar 25 14:38 ps7622
-rw-rw-r--    1 root      sys            4615 Mar 25 15:30 ps7812
-rw-rw-r--    1 root      sys            5728 Feb 18 11:09 ps_data
-rw-r--r--    1 root      sys               0 Apr 26 10:50 sh20890.1
-rw-r--r--    1 root      sys               0 Apr 26 10:50 sh20891.1
-rw-r--r--    1 root      sys               0 Apr 26 10:51 sh20978.1
-rw-r--r--    1 root      sys               0 Apr 26 10:51 sh20979.1
-rw-r--r--    1 chrisb    users          5325 Mar 26 13:42 sman_9664
-rw-rw-r--    1 root      sys          295996 Mar  1 10:15 ups_data
drwx------    2 root      other            69 Mar  9 11:37 whatis.11526
drwx------    2 root      other            69 Mar  9 11:37 whatis.11686
drwx------    2 root      other            69 Mar  9 11:38 whatis.11853
drwx------    2 root      other            69 Mar  9 11:38 whatis.12014
-rw-r--r--    1 root      sys          354221 Feb 23 10:49 x
-rw-r--r--    1 chrisb    users             0 Feb 23 14:39 xx
martyp $
```

In this case, we could give **myll** no argument and it would still work properly. If we don't provide any command line arguments, then **$1** will be null, so nothing goes on the command line after **cd**. This will make **cd** take us to our home directory and perform the **ll** there.

man page

cd - 6

If we provide more than one argument, only the first is used and any others are ignored.

If we use a command-line argument, it *must* be a directory name; otherwise the **cd** command fails and the script terminates with a "bad directory" error message. Later, I will show how to test for valid directory and file names so that you can work around potential errors.

A more complex example can be used to build new versions of the **ps** command. Below are two examples that use command line arguments and command substitution to help you with your process management.

man page

ps - 12

The **psg** shell program in Figure 11-2 is handy for searching through what is typically a long process status listing to find only cer-

man page

grep - 10

tain commands or user processes. These examples use **grep**. **grep** finds all lines that contain the pattern for which you are searching.

```
#!/usr/bin/sh
# Program name: psg
# Usage: psg some_pattern
#
# This program searches through a process status (ps -ef)
# listing for a pattern given as the first command-line
# argument.
procs=`ps -ef`                  # Get the process listing
head=`echo "$procs" | line`     # Take off the first line (the
                                # headings)
echo "$head"                    # Write out the headings
echo "$procs" | grep -i $1 | grep -v $0 # Write out lines
    # containing $1 but not this program's command line

# Note that $procs MUST be quoted or the newlines in the ps
# -ef listing will be turned into spaces when echoed. $head
# must also be quoted to preserve any extra white space.
```

Figure 11-2 **psg** Shell Program

Here's what **psg** looks like when it runs. In this example we want to look at all the Korn shells running on the system.

```
martyp $ psg ksh
    UID    PID  PPID  C    STIME TTY       TIME CMD
   root   2954  2936  0   Feb 22 ?         0:01 /bin/ksh /usr/dt/bin/Xsession
   root   3002  2999  0   Feb 22 pts/2     0:01 -ksh -c      unset DT;     DISPLg
   root   3067     1  0   Feb 22 ?         0:00 /bin/ksh /usr/dt/bin/sdtvolcheckm
  jnola  11516 11514  0   May 11 pts/3     0:01 -ksh
 martyp  29291 29289  0 09:30:04 pts/4     0:02 -ksh
```

man page

ps - 12

This program also works to find terminal, process ID, parent process ID, start date, and any other information from **ps**.

As a user you may start processes that you wish to stop. You may, for instance, start an application that does not come up on your display. You can identify the process with **psg** and then use the next program to stop the process, provided that you have the rights to stop the process.

The **gkill** shell program in Figure 11-3 searches through a **ps -ef** listing for a pattern (just like **psg**); then it kills all listed processes. The examples use the **cut** command, which allows you to specify a range of columns to retain.

man page

cut - 10

```
#!/usr/bin/sh
# Program name: gkill
# Usage: gkill some_pattern
# This program will find all processes that contain the
# pattern specified as the first command line argument then
# kills those processes.
# get the process listing
procs=`ps -ef`
echo "The following processes will be killed:"
# Here we list the processes to kill. We don't kill this
# process
echo "$procs" | grep -i $1 | grep -v $0
# Allow the user a chance to cancel.
echo "\nPress Return to continue Ctrl-C to exit"
# If the user presses Ctrl-C the program will exit.
# Otherwise this read waits for the next return character and
# continue.
read junk
# find the pattern and cut out the pid field
pids=`echo "$procs" | grep -i $1 | grep -v $0 | cut -c9-15`
# kill the processes
kill $pids
```

Figure 11-3 **gkill** Shell Program

If we don't provide any command-line arguments, **grep** issues an error and the program continues. In the next section, we will learn how to check if **$1** is set and how to gracefully clean up if it's not.

Let's now start a process in the background, use the **psg** program to identify the process number, and then use **gkill** to stop the process:

man page

grep - 10

man page

find - 10

```
martyp $ find / -name .c > cprogs 2>&1 &
[1]     29683
martyp $ psg find
    UID    PID  PPID  C    STIME TTY      TIME CMD
  martyp 29683 29579  7 13:54:19 pts/4    0:02 find / -name .c
martyp $ gkill 29683
The following processes will be killed:
  martyp 29683 29579 10 13:54:19 pts/4    0:03 find / -name .c

Press Return to continue Ctrl-C to exit

martyp $
```

find - 10

kill - 6

When we start the **find** command, we are given its process number. To be sure we don't **kill** the wrong process, I checked for all of the **find** programs running with **psg**. When I was sure of the process number to **kill**, I used **psg** to **kill** the process.

Although the shell programs in this section were simple, they employed many important shell programming techniques. Let's now move to testing and branching, which is one of the most powerful aspects of shell programming.

Testing and Branching

Decision-making is one of the shell's most powerful features. You have two ways to check conditions and branch to a piece of code that can handle that condition.

For example, you may want to ask the user a question and then check whether the answer was yes or no. You may also want to check whether a file exists before you operate on it. In either case, you can use the **if** command to accomplish the task. Here are a few shell script segments that explain each part of the **if** command:

```
echo "Continue? \c"
read ans
if [ "$ans" = "n" ]
then
      echo "Goodbye"
      exit
fi
```

The **echo** and **read** provide a prompt and response, as usual. The **if** statement executes the next command, and if it succeeds, it executes any commands between the **then** and the **fi** (if spelled backwards).

Note that the **\c** in the **echo** command suppresses the new line that **echo** normally generates. This action leaves the cursor on the line immediately after the "Continue? " prompt. This is commonly used when prompting for user input.

The **test** command is the most common command to use with the **if** command. The ["$ans" = "n"] is the **test** command. It performs many types of file, string, and numeric logical tests, and if the condition is true, the test succeeds.

The syntax of the **test** command requires spaces around the [ ] or you will get a syntax error when the program runs. Also notice the double quotes around the response variable **$ans**. These are a strange anomaly with the **test** command. If the user presses only [[RETURN]] at the prompt without typing any other character, the value of **$ans** will be null. If we didn't have the quote marks around **$ans** in the **test** command, it would look like this when the value of **$ans** was substituted into the test command:

```
[ = "n" ]
```

This generates a "test: argument expected" error when you run the program. This is a very common mistake and if you ever get this error, you should look for variables in your **test** commands with null values.

There is another form of the **if** command that is very common. It allows you to do one thing if a condition is met or do something else if not:

```
if [    ]            # if some condition is true
then
                     # do something
else
                     # otherwise do this
fi
```

There are many conditions that the **test** command can test. Table 11-1 shows some of the more common conditions for which you can test.

Table 11-1 **test** Command Conditions

String tests:

["$a" = "string"]	True if $a is equal to "string"
["$a" != "string"]	True if $a is NOT equal to "string"
[-z "$a"]	True if $a is null (zero characters)
[-n "$a"]	True if $a is NOT null

Numeric tests:

[$x -eq 1]	True if $x is equal to 1
[$x -ne 1]	True if $x is NOT equal to 1
[$x -lt 1]	True if $x is less than 1
[$x -gt 1]	True if $x is greater than 1
[$x -le 1]	True if $x is less than or equal to 1
[$x -ge 1]	True if $x is greater than or equal to 1

File tests:

[-d $file]	True if $file is a directory
[-f $file]	True if $file is a file
[-s $file]	True if $file is a file with > 0 bytes
[-r $file]	True if $file is readable
[-w $file]	True if $file is writable
[-x $file]	True if $file is executable

Tests can be combined using **-a** to logically "AND" the tests together, **-o** to logically "OR" two tests, and **!** to "negate" a test. For example, this test statement is true only if the **$interactive** variable is set to true or **$file** is a directory:

```
[ "$interactive" = "TRUE" -o -d $file ]
```

This will be used in some upcoming example programs.

Here is a useful extension to the **gkill** program earlier shown. It checks to see that we have exactly one command-line argument before the program will attempt to do the processing. It uses a numeric test and the *$#* variable, which represents the number of command-line arguments. It should be inserted before any other lines of code in the **gkill** example given above:

```
# If we don't have exactly one command-line argument,
write an
# error and exit.
if [ $# -ne 1 ]
then
    echo "Usage: $0 pattern"
    echo "Some pattern matching the processes to kill must
    echo "be specified"
    exit 1 # Exit 1 terminates the program and tells the
           # calling shell that we had an error.
fi
```

Some other possible extensions to the **gkill** program might be to

man page

kill - 6

- Allow the user to specify a signal to use with the **kill** command. For example:
  ```
  gkill -9 ralph
  ```
  would find all of Ralph's processes and then kill them with **kill -9**.

- Make sure that a valid message is printed if we can't find any processes to kill using the specified pattern.

This same type of command-line check is easily applied to the **psg** program to make sure you that have just exactly one argument representing the pattern for which to search.

When you are reading user input, you may want to check if the user entered a value at all. If not, you would provide a reasonable default value. This is easily done with a variable modifier.

This example reads answer ("ans") from the user and then checks its value using an **if** command:

```
echo "Do you really want to remove all of your files? \c"
read ans
if [ ${ans:-n} = y ]
then
    rm -rf *
fi
```

The **${ans:-n}** statement checks the value of **$ans**. If there is a value in **$ans,** use it in the command line. If the user simply pressed [[RETURN]] at the prompt, **$ans** will be null. In this case, **${ans:-n}** will evaluate to *n* when we do the comparison. Basically, in one small statement it says, "if the user did not provide an answer, assume they meant *n*."

There is another modifier that is often used:

```
${var:=default}
```

It returns the value of **var** if it is set; it returns the default if **var** is not set, and it will also assign the default as the value of **var** for future use.

Making Decisions with the case Statement

The **case** statement is another way to make decisions and test conditions in shell programs. It is most commonly used to check for certain patterns in command-line arguments. For example, if you wanted to determine whether the first command-line argument is an option (starts with a -), the **case** statement is the easiest way to do so. The **case** statement is also used to respond to different user input (such as asking the user to select a choice from a menu).

The **case** statement is probably one of the most complicated shell commands because of its syntax:

```
case pattern_to_match in
        pattern1)   cmdA
                    cmdB
                ;;
        pattern2) cmdC
                ;;
                  ...
        *) cmdZ
                ;;
esac
```

pattern_to_match is usually a shell variable that you are testing (like a command-line argument or a user response). If *pattern_to_match* matches *pattern1*, then commands *cmdA* and *cmdB* are executed. The **;;** separates this pattern's command list from the next pattern. In all cases, when **;;** is reached, the program jumps to the **esac** (**case** spelled backwards).

If *pattern_to_match* matches *pattern2*, then *cmdC* is executed and we jump to **esac**, the end of the **case** statement.

The ***** is provided so that if *pattern_to_match* did not match anything else, it will execute *cmdZ*. It's important to have a default action to handle the case where the user types an invalid entry.

For more robust pattern matching, any file name generation characters (*, [ ], ?) can be used to do special pattern matches. There is also a very useful way to check for multiple patterns in one line using the | symbol, which means logical "OR". Here's an example:

```
echo "Do you want to continue? (y/n) \c"
read ans
case $ans in
        y|Y) echo "Continuing"
                 ...
            ;;
        n|N) echo "Done, Goodbye"
             exit
            ;;
        *) echo "Invalid input"
            ;;
esac
```

Here is another example where we are testing to see whether *$1* (the first command-line argument) is a valid option (a character we recognize that begins with a -).

```
case $1 in
        -l | -d) # Perform a listing
                echo "All files in $HOME:\n"
                ll -R $HOME | more
                ;;
        -i) # -i means set to an interactive flag to true
            interactive="TRUE"
                ;;
        *)  # Invalid input
            echo "$0: $1 is an invalid option"
            exit 1
            ;;
esac
```

A **case** statement is used in an example later in this chapter.

Looping

There are many times when you want to perform an action repeatedly. In the shell, there are two ways to do this:

1. The **for** loop takes a list of items and performs the commands in the loop once for each item in the list.

2. The **while** loop executes some commands (usually the **test** command) if that command executes successfully. (If the test condition is true, then the commands in the loop are executed, and the command is again executed to see whether we should loop again.)

The basic format of the **for** loop is:

```
for var in list_of_items
do
        cmdA
        cmdB
        cmdC
done
```

When the loop starts, the variable **var** has its value set to the first word in the **list_of_items** through which to loop. Then the three commands between the **do** and the **done** statements are executed. After the program reaches the **done** statement, it goes back to the top of the loop and assigns **var** to the next item in the list, executes the commands, and so on. The last time through the loop, the program continues with the next executable statement after the **done** statement.

The **list_of_items** can be any list of words separated by white space. You can type the words or use variables or command substitution to build the list. For example, let's say that we want to copy a new **.kshrc** file into the home directory of several users. A **for** loop is the easiest way to do so:

```
for name in ralph norton alice edith archie
do
        echo $name
        cp /tmp/.kshrc.new /users/$name/.kshrc
done
```

This example can be extended to copy certain files to several machines using the **rcp** command and verify that they got there using the **remsh** command:

```
for host in neptune jupiter mars earth sun
do
        echo $host
        rcp /etc/passwd /etc/hosts $host:/etc
        rcp /.profile $host:/.profile
        remsh $host ll /etc/passwd /etc/hosts /.profile
done
```

You can also process lists of files in the current directory using command substitution to generate the **list_of_items**:

```
for file in `ls`
do
     if [ -r $file ]
     then
             echo "$file is readable
     fi
done
```

Note that **for file in *** would have done the same thing.

If you have a large list of things you would like to loop through and you don't want to type them on the command line, you can enter them in a file instead. Then, using the **cat** command and command substitution, you can generate the **list_of_items**:

```
for i in `cat important_files`
do
    # do something with each of the files listed in the
    # important_files file.
done
```

The **for** loop, however, is most commonly used to process the list of command line arguments (**$***):

```
for name in $*
do
    if [ ! -f $name -a ! -d $name ]
    then
      echo "$name is not a valid file or directory name"
    else
      # do something with the file or directory
    fi
done
```

The upcoming **trash** program contains a **for** loop that processes command-line arguments in a similar way.

The while Loop

The **while** loop has the following format:

```
while cmd1
do
      cmdA
      cmdB
      cmdC
done
```

cmd1 is executed first. If it executes successfully, then the commands between the **do** and the **done** statements are executed. **cmd1** is then executed again; if successful, the commands in the loop are executed again, and so on. When **cmd1** fails, the program jumps past the **done** statement and resumes execution with the next executable statement.

Most of the time, the command executed in place of **cmd1** is the **test** command. You can then perform logical tests as described in the **if** section. If the test succeeds (is true), the commands in the loop are executed and the script tests the condition again. The **while** loop is useful if you have a fixed number of times you want the loop to run or if you want something to happen until some condition is met.

Let's now take a look at an example of using **while**. We'll run the **netstat** command once every 30 seconds a total of ten times, looking for the output of our primarlly LAN interface. In the case of the Solaris system on which we are running this will be *le0*. Keep in mind that your primary LAN interface may have a different name, almost surely if you are not using a Solaris system. Let's first take a look at our short program:

man page

netstat - 9

This program displays the primary LAN interface (lan0) statistics using **netstat** ten times, once every 30 seconds:

```
#!/bin/ksh
i=1
while [ $i -le 10 ]
do
        print $i
        netstat -i | grep le0
        sleep 30
        let i=i+1
done
```

We increment *i* in a very simple fashion by adding one to it each time through the loop. We evaluate the value of *i* every time through the loop to determine whether it is less than or equal to (*le*) ten. If so, we run **netstat -i**.

Before we run this program, called **net1**, let's run the **netstat -i** command to view its output and then run **net1**:

```
martyp $ netstat -i
Name  Mtu  Net/Dest     Address      Ipkts  Ierrs Opkts  Oerrs Collis Queue
lo0   8232 loopback     localhost    18927030 0     18927030 0     0      0
le0   1500 sunsys       sunsys       310417964 0     17193381 52064 7573173
sunsys:/home/martyp/shellprogs
martyp $ net1
1
le0   1500 sunsys       sunsys       310418018 0     17193388 52064 7573173
2
le0   1500 sunsys       sunsys       310418738 0     17193395 52064 7573173
3
le0   1500 sunsys       sunsys       310419579 0     17193401 52064 7573173
4
le0   1500 sunsys       sunsys       310420295 0     17193405 52064 7573173
5
le0   1500 sunsys       sunsys       310421099 0     17193446 52064 7573173
6
le0   1500 sunsys       sunsys       310421786 0     17193455 52064 7573173
7
le0   1500 sunsys       sunsys       310422425 0     17193462 52064 7573173
8
le0   1500 sunsys       sunsys       310423089 0     17193467 52064 7573173
9
le0   1500 sunsys       sunsys       310423749 0     17193471 52064 7573173
10
le0   1500 sunsys       sunsys       310424507 0     17193478 52064 7573173
sunsys:/home/martyp/shellprogs
martyp $
```

net1 produces just the output we want for *le0* every 30 seconds on our system, called *sunsys*. We also print out the value of *i* each time through the loop just so that we can see that we are incrementing it properly.

The **while** loop can also be used to process command-line arguments one at a time, using the number of command-line arguments and the **shift** command:

```
while [ $# -ne 0 ]
do
    case $1 in
    -*) # $1 must be an option because it starts with -
        # Add it to the list of options:
        opts="$opts $1"
        ;;
     *) # $1 must be an argument. Add it to the list of
        # command-line arguments:
        args="$args $1"
        ;;
    esac
    shift
done
```

The **shift** command shifts the remaining arguments in $* to the left by one position and decrements $#. What was the first argument ($1) is now gone forever; what was in $2 is now in $1, etc. In the process of shifting command-line arguments, $# is also decremented to accurately reflect the number of arguments left in $*.

You may want some commands to run until the user stops the program or until some stop condition is met. An infinite **while** loop is the best way to do so. For example, let's say that we are prompting users for some input and we will continue to prompt them until they give us valid input:

```
while true
do
    # prompt users and get their response
    echo "Enter yes or no: \c"
    read ans

    # Check whether the response is valid
    if [ "$ans" = "yes" -o "$ans" = "no" ]
    then
    # If it is valid, stop the looping
    break
  else
    # Otherwise print an error message and try it again
    # from the top of the loop
    echo "Invalid input, try again!\n"
    fi
done
# Now that we have valid input, we can process the user's
# request
    .
    .
    .
```

true is a special command that always executes successfully. The loop does not terminate unless the user stops the program by killing it or until a **break** command is executed in the loop. The **break** command will stop the loop.

Shell Functions

As you write shell programs, you will notice that there are certain sets of commands appear in many places within a program. For example, several times in a script, you may check user input and issue an appropriate message if input is invalid. It can be tedious to type the same lines of code in your program numerous times. It can be a nuisance if you later want to change these lines.

Instead, you can you can put these commands into a shell function. Functions look and act like a new command that can be used inside the script. Here's an example of a basic shell function:

```
# This is a function that may be called from anywhere within
# the program. It displays a standard usage error message
# and then exits the program.

print_usage()
{
    echo "Usage:"
    echo "To trash files: $0 [-i] files_to_trash..."
    echo "Display trashed files: $0 -d"
    echo "Remove all trashed files: $0 -rm"
    echo "Print this message: $0 -help"
    exit 1
}
```

print_usage is now a new command in your shell program. You can use it anywhere in this script.

Shell functions also have their own set of positional parameters ($1-$9, $#, and $*), so you can pass them arguments just like any other command. The only nuance is that **$0** represents the name of the shell program, not the name of the function.

Earlier, we talked about arguments. When you type the name of the shell script, you can supply arguments that are saved in the variables **$1** through **$9**. The first ten words on the command line are directly accessible in the shell program using the special variables **$0–$9**. The following shows how they work:

$0	The command name
$1	The first argument
$2	The second argument
$3	.
	.
	.
$9	The ninth argument

If you are not sure how many command-line arguments you may get when your program is run, there are two other variables that can help:

$#	The number of command line arguments
$*	A space-separated list of all of the command line arguments (which does *not* include the command name).

The variable **$*** is commonly used with a **for** loop to process shell script command lines with any number of arguments.

Figure 11-4 is a fairly complex program that exercises all the concepts we have covered so far. It is a **trash** program that removes files from their original locations. Instead of removing them permanently, it places them in a trash can in your home directory. This is a

fairly robust program, but I'm sure that you can think of many extensions as you read through it.

```
#!/bin/ksh
# for Bourne use /bin/sh
# Program name: trash
# Usage:
#  To trash files:    trash [-i] file_names_to_trash ...
#  Display trashed files:    trash -d
#  Remove all trashed files: trash -rm
#  Print a help message:    trash -help
# This program takes any number of directory or file name
# arguments. If the argument is a file it will be removed
# from its current place in the file system and placed in the
# user's trash directory ($HOME/.trash). If the argument is a
# directory name the program will ask if the user really
# wants to trash the whole directory.
#
# This program also takes an -i (interactive) option. Like
# the rm command, if the -i is the first argument on the
# command line, the program stops and asks if each file
# named in the remaining arguments should be trashed.
#
# The -d (display) option shows the contents of the
# user's trashed files.
#
# The -help option displays a usage message for the user.
```

Figure 11-4 **trash** Shell Program

```
# The -rm (remove) option interactively
# asks the user if each file or directory in the trash
# directory should be removed permanently.
#
# The -h, -d and -rm options may not be used with
# any other command line arguments.

# Possible extensions:
# - Enhance the -rm option to remove a list of files
# from the trash directory from the command line.
# - Create a program to be run by cron once nightly to empty
# everyone's trash directory.

# This is a function that may be called from anywhere within
# the program. It displays a standard usage error message
# then exits the program.
print_usage()
{
  echo "Usage:"
  echo "To trash files: $0 [-i] file_names_to_trash ..."
  echo "Display trashed files:    $0 -d"
  echo "Remove all trashed files: $0 -rm"
  echo "Print this message:       $0 -help"
exit 1
}
# Make sure we have at least one command-line argument before
# we start.
if [ $# -lt 1 ]
then
     print_usage
fi

# If this flag is true then we need to do interactive
# processing.
interactive="FALSE"

# This is the name of the trash can.
trash_dir="$HOME/.trash"

# Make sure the trash directory exists before we go any
# further.
if [ ! -d $trash_dir ]
then
     mkdir $trash_dir
fi
# Sort out the command-line arguments.
case $1 in
   -help) # Print a help message.
      print_usage
      ;;
```

Figure 11-4 trash Shell Program (Continued)

```
-d | -rm) # a -d or -rm were given
       # If it was not the only command-line argument
       # then display a usage message and then exit.
       if [ $# -ne 1 ]
       then
            print_usage
       fi

       # Otherwise do the task requested.
       if [ $1 = "-d" ]
       then
            echo "The contents of $trash_dir:\n"
          ls -l -R $trash_dir | more
       else
            # remove all files from the trash directory
            rm -rf $trash_dir/*
            # get any dotfiles too
            rm -rf $trash_dir/.[!.]*
       fi
       # Now we can exit successfully.
       exit 0
       ;;
-i) # If the first argument is -i ask about each file as it
       # is processed.
       interactive="TRUE"
       # Take -i off the command line so we know that the
       # rest of the arguments are file or directory names.
       shift
       ;;

 -*)# Check for an option we don't understand.
       echo "$1 is not a recognized option."
       print_usage
       ;;
       esac
# Just for fun we'll keep a count of the files that were
# trashed.
count=0

for file in $*
do
 # First make sure the file or directory to be renamed exists.
 # If it doesn't, add it to a list of bad files to be written
 # out later. Otherwise process it.
 if [ ! -f $file -a ! -d $file ]
 then
     bad_files="$bad_files $file"
 else
# If we are in interactive mode ask for confirmation
# on each file. Otherwise ask about directories.
```

Figure 11-4 trash Shell Program (Continued)

```
if [ "$interactive" = "TRUE" -o -d $file ]
then
    # Ask the user for confirmation (default answer is no).
    if [ -d $file ]
    then
        echo "Do you want to trash the dir $file ? (y/n) n\b\c"
    else
        echo "Do you really want to trash $file ? (y/n) n\b\c"
    fi
    read doit

    # If the user answered y then do the move.
    # Otherwise print a message that the file was not touched.
    if [ "${doit:-n}" = y ]
    then
        mv -i $file $trash_dir
        echo "$file was trashed to $trash_dir"
        let count=count+1
    # for Bourne use: count=`expr $count + 1`
    else
        echo "$file was not trashed"
    fi
  else # We are not in interactive mode, so just do it.
      mv -i $file $trash_dir
      let count=count+1
    #for Bourne use: count=`expr  $count + 1`
  fi
fi
done
echo "$0: trashed $count item(s)"
if [ -n "$bad_files" ]
then
    echo "The following name(s) do not exist and \c"
    echo "could not be trashed:"
    echo "$bad_files"
fi
exit 0
```

Figure 11-4 **trash** Shell Program (Continued)

Let's now run the **trash** program. The following example shows issuing just the program named **trash**, the next example shows issuing **trash -help**, the next example shows issuing **trash -i junk** to interactively remove the file **junk**, and the last example shows issuing **trash -d** to display files that have been removed with **trash** and are in the **/home/martyp/trash** directory.

```
martyp $ trash
Usage:
To trash files: trash [-i] file_names_to_trash ...
Display trashed files:    trash -d
Remove all trashed files: trash -rm
Print this message:       trash -help
martyp $ trash -help
Usage:
To trash files: trash [-i] file_names_to_trash ...
Display trashed files:    trash -d
Remove all trashed files: trash -rm
Print this message:       trash -help
martyp $ trash -i junk
Do you really want to trash junk ? (y/n) y
mv: overwrite /home/martyp/.trash/junk (yes/no)? yes
junk was trashed to /home/martyp/.trash
trash: trashed 1 item(s)
martyp $ trash -d
The contents of /home/martyp/.trash:

/home/martyp/.trash:
total 1364
-rw-------  1 martyp    staff      684808 May 30 05:31 core
-rwxrwxr-x  1 martyp    staff         631 May 30 06:45 file1
-rwxrwxr-x  1 martyp    staff          45 May 31 06:04 junk
martyp $
```

Notice, when we removed the file **junk** that **trash** asked us whether we wanted to overwrite a file by the same name that had been earlier removed with **trash** and placed in the **/home/martyp/trash** directory.

The program employs every concept we have covered in this shell programming chapter so far. You may want to take a close look at this program so that you can use these techniques in the program you craft. I have also included comments for the lines that need to be changed to make this program work in the Bourne shell. The Korn-Shell and Bourne shell are very similar, so you can use most of the same techniques when writing the programs for these two shells.

awk in Shell Programs

man page

awk - 10

awk is a very powerful symbolic programming language. A *what*?

Simply stated, **awk** searches for patterns in lines of input (from standard input or from a file). For each line that matches the specified pattern, it can perform some very complex processing on that line. The code to actually process matching lines of input is a cross between a shell script and a C program.

man page

grep - 10

Data manipulation tasks that would be very complex with combinations of **grep**, **cut**, and **paste** are very easily done with **awk**. Because **awk** is a programming language, it can also perform mathematical operations or check the input very easily, a task that is normally difficult with shells. It can even perform floating-point math.

man page

cut - 10

The basic form of an **awk** program looks like this:

man page

paste - 10

```
awk '/pattern_to_match/ { program to run }' input_file_names
```

Notice that the whole program is enclosed in single quotes. If no input file names are specified, **awk** reads from standard input (as from a pipe).

The **pattern_to_match** must appear between the / characters. The pattern is actually called a regular expression. Some common regular expression examples are shown shortly.

The program to execute is written in **awk** code, which looks something like C. The program is executed whenever a line of input matches the **pattern_to_match**. If **/pattern_to_match/** does not precede the program in { }, then the program is executed for every line of input.

awk works with fields of the input lines. Fields are words separated by white space. The fields in **awk** patterns and programs are referenced with **$**, followed by the field number. For example, the second field of an input line is **$2**. If you are using an **awk** command in your shell programs, the fields (**$1, $2**, etc.) are not confused with

man page

awk - 10

the shell script's positional parameters, because the **awk** variables are enclosed in single quotes and the shell ignores them.

But I don't want to just talk about it. Let's take a look at some examples.

This simple example lists just the terminals that are active on your system in which the terminal name is the second field of a **who** listing:

```
who | awk '{ print $2 }'
```

Here is an example of running **who** and then running this one-line command:

```
martyp $ who
thomfsu     console      Feb 22 15:21   (:0)
martyp     pts/3          May 31 06:03  (atlm0216.atl.hp.com)
martyp $ who | awk '{print $2}'
console
pts/3
martyp $
```

man page

cut - 10

This output shows only the active terminals on the system.

Note that **cut** could have done this also, but you would have had to know exactly which columns the terminal name occupied in the **who** output, as shown below:

```
martyp $ who
thomfsu     console      Feb 22 15:21     (:0)
martyp             pts/3                    May  31  06:03
(atlm0216.atl.hp.com)
martyp $ who | cut -c12-20
console
pts/3
martyp $
```

If the user or terminal name is longer than normal in any line, this command does not work. The **awk** example will work because it looks at fields, not columns.

Some trivia to wow your friends with at your next cocktail party: **awk** is the first letter of the last names of its authors: Alfred Aho, Peter Weinberger, and Brian Kernighan.

man page

awk - 10

The next section is a short introduction to C shell programming.

C Shell Programming

Although shell programming techniques apply to all shells, generally speaking, there are some differences exist between the C shell and the KornShell. If you are using the C shell, I want you to get off to a quick start, so I'll cover the basics of C shell programming in this section. I'll cover each shell programming technique briefly and use basic examples to help reinforce each technique. In all the following shell programs, any line beginning with a "#" is a comment. This is true except for the very first line of a shell program in which the shell the script is written for is executed. In all the following programs the C shell is executed with **#!/bin/csh**, which is the path of the C shell on the Solaris system used in the examples.

Command Substitution

The shell variables earlier covered can be used to save the output from a command. You can then use these variables when issuing other commands. The following shell program executes the **date** command and saves the results in the variable **d**. The variable **d** is then used within the **echo** command in the program **cdate**:

```
#!/bin/csh
# program "today" that provides the date
set d=`date +%x`
echo "Today's date is $d"
```

When we run **cdate**, the following is produced:

```
martyp $ cdate
Today's date is 06/01/00
martyp $
```

The "+%x" in the above example produces the current date. Command substitution of this type is used in several upcoming shell scripts.

Reading User Input

Two common methods help you read user input to shell programs. The first is to prompt the user for information, and the second is to provide arguments to shell programs.

To begin, I'll cover prompting a user for information. A character, word, or sentence can be read into a variable. The following example first shows prompting the user for a word, and then a sentence:

```
#!/bin/csh
echo "Please enter your name:"
set name = $<
echo "hello, $name"
echo "Please enter your favorite quote:"
set quote = $<
echo "Your favorite quote is:"
echo $quote
```

Here is an example of running this program:

```
martyp $ userinput
Please enter your name:
Marty
hello, Marty
Please enter your favorite quote:
Creating is the essence of life.
Your favorite quote is:
Creating is the essence of life.
martyp $
```

Using this technique, you can prompt a user for information in a shell program. This technique is used in an upcoming program.

You can also enter command line arguments. When you type the name of the shell script, you can supply arguments that are saved in the variables **$1** through **$9**. The first ten words on the command line are directly accessible in the shell program using the special variables **$0-$9**. This is how they work:

$0	The command name
$1	The first argument
$2	The second argument
$3	.
	.
	.
$9	The ninth argument

If you are not sure how many command-line arguments you may get when your program is run, there are two other variables that can help:

$#	The number of command-line arguments
$*	A space-separated list of all the command line arguments (which does *not* include the command name)

The variable **$*** is commonly used with the **for** loop (soon to be explained) to process shell script command lines with any number of arguments.

The following script changes to the specified directory (**$1**) and searches for the specified pattern (**$2**) in the specified file (**$3**):

```
#!/bin/csh
# search
# Usage: search directory pattern file
echo " "
cd $1                    # change to search dir and
grep -n "$2" $3          # search for $2 in $3
echo " "                 # print line
endif
```

man page

grep - 10

man page

awk - 10

grep is used to search a file for a pattern and print the line in which the pattern was found. **awk** (which will be used later) can be used to pick out a specific field within a line.

Here is an example run of the **search** program:

```
martyp $ search /home/martyp/shellprogs awk ifstat

12:# as one command so it can be easily piped to awk.
18:awk 'BEGIN { printf "%10s%10s%10s%10s%10s\n", "ipkts",
38:' # End of the awk program.

martyp $
```

In this example, we run **search** in the directory **/home/martyp/ shellprogs**, looking for the pattern **awk** in the file **ifstat**. The result of this search produces three lines in the file **ifstat**, in which **awk** appears. These are lines number 12, 18, and 38.

In the next section we'll expand this program somewhat to include testing and branching.

Testing and Branching

There are many kinds of decision-making your shell programs can perform. **if** provides the flexibility to make decisions and take the appropriate action. Let's expand the search script to verify that three arguments have been provided:

```
#!/bin/csh
# search
# Usage: search directory pattern files

if ($#argv != 3) then            # if < 3 args provided

        echo "Usage: search directory pattern files"
                                 # then print Usage
else
        echo " "                 # else print line and
        cd $1                    # change to search dir
        grep -n "$2" $3          # search for $2 in $3
        echo " "                 # print line
endif
```

This program is called **search1**. We run this program using the same arguments as we did with the **search** program; however, **search1** is enhanced to provide a *usage* message if we don't provide arguments when we run it. The following example shows running **search1**:

```
martyp $ search1
Usage: search directory pattern files
martyp $ search1 /home/martyp/shellprogs awk llsum

12:# drwxrwxrwx 2  gerry  aec  24  Mar 21 18:25    awk_ex
15:# awk field numbers:
18:awk ' BEGIN { x=i=0; printf "%-16s%-10s%8s%8s\n",\

martyp $
```

On the first attempt to run **search1**, we provided no arguments. The program checked to see whether we provided fewer than three arguments and produced the *usage* message, because it found fewer than three arguments. Upon seeing the *usage* it became clear how to use the program and we provided the required three arguments on the next attempt to run the program. In this example, we run **search1** in the directory **/home/martyp/shellprogs**, looking for the pattern **awk** in the file **llsum**. The result of this search produces three lines in the file **llsum**, in which **awk** appears. These are lines number 12, 15, and 18.

man page

awk - 10

Here are four commonly used forms of **if**:

1)   if (expression) command

2)   if (expression) then
                            command(s)
                endif

3)   if (expression) then
                            command(s)
                      else
                            command(s)
                endif

4)   if (expression) then
                            command(s)
                    [else if expression) then
                            command(s)]

                            .
                            .
                            .

                    [else
                            command(s)]
                endif

There are many operators that can be used in the C shell to compare integer values, such as the < used in the previous example. Here is a list of operators:

>	greater than
<	less than
>=	greater than or equal to
<=	less than or equal to
==	equal to
!=	not equal to

Looping

The C shell supports a number of techniques to support looping, including:

    1) The **foreach** loop, which takes a list of items and performs the commands in the loop once for each item in the list.

    2) The **while** loop, which executes a command (such as the **test** command) if the command executes successfully.

    The format of the **foreach** loop is

```
foreach name (list)
        command(s)
end
```

    The following example uses a **foreach** loop to test whether or not the systems in the **/etc/hosts** file are connected to the local host.

```
#!/bin/csh
#Program name: csh_hostck

#This program will test connectivity to all other hosts in
#your network listed in your /etc/hosts file.

# It uses the awk command to get the names from the hosts file
#and the ping command to check connectivity.

#Note that we use /bin/echo because csh echo doesn't support
#escape chars like \t or \c which are used in the
#foreach loop.

#Any line in /etc/hosts that starts with a number represents
#a host entry. Anything else is a comment or a blank line.

#Find all lines in /etc/hosts that start with a number and
#print the second field (the hostname).

set hosts=`awk '/^[1-9]/ { print $2 }' /etc/hosts`
                # grave on outside, single quote on inside
```

```
                /bin/echo "Remote host connection status:"

foreach sys ($hosts)
     /bin/echo "$sys - \c"
                    # send one 64 byte packet and look for
                    # the"is alive" message in
                    # the output that indicates success.
                    # messages vary between UNIX variants.

     ping $sys 64 1 | grep "is alive" > /dev/null
     if ( $status == 0 ) then
                echo "OK"
     else
                echo "DID NOT RESPOND"
     endif
end
```

man page

awk - 10

The crazy-looking line with **awk** is used to obtain the name of remote hosts from the **/etc/hosts** file. The **foreach** loop takes all of the items in the list, the hosts in this case, and checks the status of each.

The **hosts** file on this system has three entries, the localhost, the LAN interface, and a DNS system. When we run the program in the following example, we expect to see a result for the testing of all three entries:

```
martyp $ csh_hostck
Remote host connection status:
localhost - OK
sunsys - OK
dnssrv1 - OK
martyp $
```

man page

ping - 9

All three entries in the **hosts** file have been evaluated with **ping** and produce a status of *OK*. When hardcoding information into scripts, such as the path of **ping** and the result you get from the **ping** command, please keep in mind that these may vary among different UNIX variants. One of the reasons you want to liberally comment your shell programs is to make them easy to modify under such circumstances.

You could use the **while** loop to execute commands for some number of iterations. The **while** loop is in the following format:

while (expression)
      command(s)
end

man page

netstat - 9

The following program called **netcheck** runs **netstat** at the desired interval, and prints out the heading once and the status of le0 nine times:

```
#!/bin/csh
# program to run netstat at every specified interval
# Usage: netcheck interval

set limit=9                # set limit on number times
                           # to run netstat

echo " "
netstat -i | grep Name     # print netstat line with head-
ings
set count=0
while ($count<$limit)       # if limit hasn't reached
                           # limit run netstat
        netstat -i | grep le0
        sleep $1           # sleep for interval
                           # specified on command line
        @ count++          # increment limit
end
echo "count has reached $limit, run netcheck again to see
le0 status"
```

Here is an example run of the **netcheck** program:

```
martyp $ netcheck 3

Name Mtu  Net/Dest   Address    Ipkts     Ierrs Opkts    Oerrs Collis Queue
le0  1500 sunsys     sunsys     314374989 0     17252200 52135 7580906
le0  1500 sunsys     sunsys     314375038 0     17252203 52135 7580906
le0  1500 sunsys     sunsys     314375114 0     17252206 52135 7580906
le0  1500 sunsys     sunsys     314375185 0     17252209 52135 7580906
```

```
le0   1500 sunsys       sunsys       314375257 0    17252212 52135 7580906
le0   1500 sunsys       sunsys       314375332 0    17252215 52135 7580906
le0   1500 sunsys       sunsys       314375444 0    17252218 52135 7580906
le0   1500 sunsys       sunsys       314375508 0    17252221 52135 7580906
le0   1500 sunsys       sunsys       314375588 0    17252224 52135 7580906
count has reached 9, run netcheck again to see le0 status
martyp $
```

man page

netstat - 9

The output of **netcheck** produces nine **netstat** outputs at the three-second interval we had specified. Keep in mind that you may have to modify such information as the name of the LAN interface when you use this program on your system.

This program increments the expression with the following:

@ count++

If the expression is true, then the command(s) will execute. The @count++ is an assignment operator in the form of

@ variable_name operator expression

In this case, the variable is first assigned with "=" and is later auto incremented (++). There are a number of operations that can be performed on the variable, as described in Table 11-2.

Table 11-2   Assignment Operators

Operation	Symbol	Example with count = 100	Result
store value	=	@count=100	100
auto increment	++	@count++	101
auto decrement	--	@count--	99
add value	+=	@count+=50	150
subtract value	-=	@count-=50	50
multiply by value	*=	@count*=2	200
divide by value	/=	@count/2	50

There are also comparison operators, such as the "<" used in the example, as well as arithmetic, bitwise, and logical operators. As you craft more and more shell scripts, you will want to use all these operators.

There are a set of test conditions related to files that are useful when writing shell scripts that use files. Using the format **- operator filename** you can use the tests in Table 11-3.

TABLE 11-3   Operator File Name Tests

Operator	Meaning
r	read access
w	write access
x	execute access
o	ownership
z	zero length
f	file, not a directory
d	directory, not a file

The following program, called **filetest,** uses these operators to test the file **.profile**. Because **.profile** is not executable, of zero length, or a directory, I would expect **filetest** to find these false.

Here is a long listing of **.profile**:

```
martyp $ ls -al .profile
-rw-r--r--   1 martyp    staff        594 May 21 09:29 ../.profile
martyp $
```

man page

ls - 2

Here is a listing of the shell script **filetest**:

```csh
#!/bin/csh
#  Program to test file $1

if (-e $1) then
            echo "$1 exists"
            else
            echo "$1 does not exist"
endif

if (-z $1) then
            echo "$1 is zero length"
            else
            echo "$1 is not zero length"
endif

if (-f $1) then
            echo "$1 is a file"
            else
            echo "$1 is not a file"
endif

if (-d $1) then
            echo "$1 is a directory"
            else
            echo "$1 is not a directory"
endif

if (-o $1) then
            echo "you own $1 "
            else
            echo "you don't own $1 "
endif

if (-r $1) then
            echo "$1 is readable"
            else
            echo "$1 is not readable"
endif

if (-w $1) then
            echo "$1 is writable"
            else
            echo "$1 is not writable"
endif

if (-x $1) then
            echo "$1 is executable"
            else
            echo "$1 is not executable"
endif
```

This is a somewhat extreme example of testing a file; however, I wanted to include many of the file tests.

Here is the output of **filetest** using **.profile** as input:

```
martyp $ filetest /home/martyp/.profile
/home/martyp/.profile exists
/home/martyp/.profile is not zero length
/home/martyp/.profile is a file
/home/martyp/.profile is not a directory
you own /home/martyp/.profile
/home/martyp/.profile is readable
/home/martyp/.profile is writable
/home/martyp/.profile is not executable
martyp $
```

The result of having run **filetest** on **.profile** produces the file test results that we expect.

The next section covers a way of making decisions with *switch*.

Decision Making with switch

You can use **switch** to make decisions within a shell program. You can use **switch** to test command-line arguments or interactive input to shell programs as shown in the upcoming example. If, for example, you wanted to create a menu in a shell program and you needed to determine which option a user selected when running this shell program, you can use **switch**.

The syntax of **switch** looks like the following:

```
switch (pattern_to_match)

case pattern1
            commands
            breaksw
```

```
             case pattern2
                     commands
                     breaksw

             case pattern 3
                     commands
                     breaksw

         default
                 commands
                 breaksw
     endsw
```

pattern_to_match is the user input that you are testing, and if it is equal to **pattern1,** then the commands under **pattern1** are executed. If **pattern_to_match** and **pattern2** are the same, then the commands under **pattern2** will be executed, and so on. If no match occurs between **pattern_to_match** and one of the case statement patterns, then the default is executed. The following program allows you to pick from among two scripts through its menu. These are two shell programs we crafted earlier in this chapter. You can expand this script to include as many of your programs as you wish. This example uses **switch**:

```
#!/bin/csh
# Program pickscript to run some of
# the C shell scripts we've created
# Usage: pickscript
echo " ---------------------------------------------"
echo "                  Sys Admin Menu             "
echo "---------------------------------------------"
echo " "
echo " 1            netcheck for network interface "
echo " "
echo " 2            hostck to check connection     "
echo "                 to hosts in /etc/hosts      "
echo "                                             "
echo " ---------------------------------------------"
echo " "
echo " Please enter your selection -> \c"

set pick = $<     # read input which is number of script
echo " "
switch ($pick)    # and assign to variable pick

         case 1          # if 1 was selected execute this
         $HOME/cshscripts/netcheck 5
```

```
                   breaksw

                   case 2          # if 2 was selected, execute this
                   $HOME/cshscripts/hostck
                   breaksw

                   default
                   echo "Please select 1 or 2 next time"
                   breaksw

           endsw
```

This program allows us to select from between two scripts to run. Let's take a look at an example of running this program:

```
martyp $ pickscript
--------------------------------------------
                  Sys Admin Menu
--------------------------------------------

1          netcheck for network interface

2          hostck to check connection
               to hosts in /etc/hosts

--------------------------------------------
 Please enter your selection
1

Name  Mtu  Net/Dest    Address        Ipkts   Ierrs Opkts  Oerrs Collis Queue
le0   1500 sunsys      sunsys         314996747 0   17261251 52135 7580952
le0   1500 sunsys      sunsys         314996862 0   17261256 52135 7580952
le0   1500 sunsys      sunsys         314997189 0   17261266 52135 7580952
le0   1500 sunsys      sunsys         314997319 0   17261269 52135 7580952
le0   1500 sunsys      sunsys         314997420 0   17261272 52135 7580952
le0   1500 sunsys      sunsys         314997630 0   17261275 52135 7580952
le0   1500 sunsys      sunsys         314997774 0   17261278 52135 7580952
le0   1500 sunsys      sunsys         314997904 0   17261281 52135 7580952
le0   1500 sunsys      sunsys         314998020 0   17261284 52135 7580952
count has reached 9, run netcheck again to see lan0 status
martyp $
```

We selected option *1* when we ran **pickscript**. You can use this program as the basis for running the many shell programs you may write.

Debugging C Shell Programs

When you begin C shell programming, you'll probably make a lot of simple syntax-related errors. Using the **-n** option to **csh** you can have the C shell check the syntax of your program without executing it. I also use the **-v** option to produce a verbose output. This can sometimes lead to too much information so I start with **-v** and if there is too much feedback results, I eliminate it.

The following example is the earlier **search1** program that includes a check that three arguments have been provided. When checking to see that **$#argv** is equal to 3, I left off the left parentheses. Here is the listing of the program and a syntax check showing the error:

```
martyp $ cat search1
#!/bin/csh
# search
# Usage: search directory pattern files

if ($#argv !3 3 then              # if < 3 args provided
        echo "Usage: search directory pattern files"
                                  # then print Usage
else
        echo " "                  # else print line and
        cd $1                     # change to search dir
        grep -n "$2" $3           # search for $2 in $3
        echo " "                  # print line
endif

martyp $ csh -nv search1
if ( $#argv != 3 then
Too many ('s
martyp $
```

The **csh -nv** has performed a syntax check with verbose output. First, the line in question is printed and then an error message that tells you what is wrong with the line. In this case, it is clear that I have left off the left parentheses.

After fixing the problem, I can run the program with the **-x**, which causes all commands to be echoed immediately before execution. The following example shows a run of the search program:

```
martyp $ csh -xv search1 shellprogs grep csh_hostck

if ( $#argv != 3 ) then
if ( 3 != 3 ) then

echo " "
echo

cd $1
cd /home/martyp/shellprogs
grep -n "$2" $3
grep -n grep csh_hostck
25:     /usr/sbin/ping $sys 64 1 | grep "is alive" > /dev/
null
echo " "
echo

endif
endif
martyp $
```

You can follow what is taking place on a line-by-line basis. The line beginning with 25 is the line in the file **csh_hostck** that has **grep** in it, that is, the output you would have received if the program had been run without the **-xv** options.

man page

grep - 10

I would recommend performing the syntax check (**-n**) with a new shell program, and then echo all commands with the **-x** option only if you get unexpected results when you run the program. The debugging options will surely help you at some point when you run into problems with the shell programs you craft.

How Long Does It Take?

You can use the **time** command to see a report of the amount of **time** your shell program takes to run. The output of **time** is different for many UNIX variants. You may want to view the manual page for **time** to see what output you can expect. A typical output of **time** when in **csh** is shown in Figure 11-5.

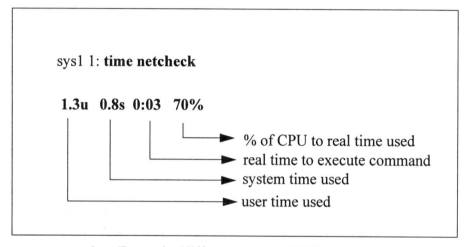

sys1 1: **time netcheck**

1.3u   0.8s   0:03   70%

% of CPU to real time used
real time to execute command
system time used
user time used

Figure 11-5   **time** Example (different among UNIX variants)

Because some of the scripts you write may consume a substantial amount of system resources, you may want to consider investigating some of the job-control capabilities of the C shell. The simplest job control you can use is to run scripts in the background so that the priority of the script is low. By issuing the script name followed by the **&,** you will run the script in the background. If you run several scripts in the background, you can get the status of these by issuing the **jobs** command. This is a more advanced C shell topic, but depending on the level of complexity of scripts you write, you may want to look into job control.

Manual Pages of Some Commands Used in Chapter 11

There are no manual pages included for this chapter. The manual pages for commands used in this chapter appear in many other chapters, including:

csh - Chapter 7
ksh - Chapter 6
grep, **awk**, **sed**, and other tools - Chapter 10

CHAPTER 12

Introduction to System Administration

System Administration

We have been dancing around system adminsitration throughout this book. We have touched on a lot of system adminsitration, such as listing and killing processes in the shell programming chapter, viewing available disk space, and so on. In this chapter, we'll look at many unintrusive system administration commands. By unintrusive, I mean commands that do not alter the setup of your system and commands that a user may typically run.

Your system adminsitrator is responsible for the setup and operation of your system; however, there are many aspects of system setup in which users may be interested. We'll cover many of the most commonly used commands related to system setup and how your system is running. As a user you may be interested in the way in which your system operates and administration-related commands. In addition, there are some commands directly related to the work you are performing, such as listing the processes you are running and how to kill them, that you can run as a user.

At the end of the chapter, I also provide manual pages for many of the commands used in this chapter. Much of what takes place in system administration can only be covered at a cursory level in a user book, and the manual pages provide additional detail but still won't make you a system administration expert.

The examples in this chapter were performed on Solaris, HP-UX, AIX, and Linux systems; however, the commands and files are similar from one system to another, so you should be able to relate the information in this chapter to your UNIX variant.

Most UNIX variants come with a system adminsitration tool. This tool provides a menu-driven way of performing common system administration tasks such as managing the following: users and groups; disks and file systems; networking; printers; and so on. There is no widely used standard for such management tools, so they are different for each UNIX variant. These tools usually require superuser access to run, because the user has control over the most important and critical aspects of the system. Some of these tools allow users other than superuser to perform a subset of tasks as defined by superuser. I do not cover system administration tools, because they are peculiar to the UNIX variant on which they run and are used mostly by the system administrator. I'll cover many of the files used by system administrators and some of the more commonly used unintrusive commands. Some of the following sections also appear in other chapters.

Check Processes with ps

man page

ps - 12

To find the answer to "What is my system doing?," use **ps -ef**. This command provides information about every running process on your system. If, for instance, you want to know whether NFS is running, you simply type **ps -ef** and look for NFS daemons. Although **ps** tells you every process that is running on your system, it doesn't provide a good summary of the level of system resources being consumed. I would guess that **ps** is the most often issued system administration command. There are a number of options you can use with **ps**. I normally use **e** and **f**, which provide information about every ("**e**") running process and lists this information in full ("**f**"). **ps** outputs are almost identical going from system to system. The following three examples are from a Solaris, AIX, and HP-UX system, respectively:

man page

ps - 12

Solaris example:

```
martyp $ ps -ef
       UID    PID  PPID  C    STIME TTY        TIME CMD
      root      0     0  0  Feb 18 ?          0:01 sched
      root      1     0  0  Feb 18 ?          1:30 /etc/init -
      root      2     0  0  Feb 18 ?          0:02 pageout
      root      3     0  1  Feb 18 ?        613:44 fsflush
      root   3065  3059  0  Feb 22 ?          5:10 /usr/dt/bin/sdtperfmeter -f -H -r
      root     88     1  0  Feb 18 ?          0:01 /usr/sbin/in.routed -q
      root    478     1  0  Feb 18 ?          0:00 /usr/lib/saf/sac -t 300
      root     94     1  0  Feb 18 ?          2:50 /usr/sbin/rpcbind
      root    150     1  0  Feb 18 ?          6:03 /usr/sbin/syslogd
      root     96     1  0  Feb 18 ?          0:00 /usr/sbin/keyserv
      root    144     1  0  Feb 18 ?         50:37 /usr/lib/autofs/automountd
      root   1010     1  0  Apr 12 ?          0:00 /opt/perf/bin/midaemon
      root    106     1  0  Feb 18 ?          0:02 /usr/lib/netsvc/yp/ypbind -broadt
      root    156     1  0  Feb 18 ?          0:03 /usr/sbin/cron
      root    176     1  0  Feb 18 ?          0:00 /usr/lib/lpsched
      root    129     1  0  Feb 18 ?          0:00 /usr/lib/nfs/lockd
    daemon    130     1  0  Feb 18 ?          0:01 /usr/lib/nfs/statd
      root  14798     1  0  Mar 09 ?         31:10 /usr/sbin/nscd
      root    133     1  0  Feb 18 ?          0:10 /usr/sbin/inetd -s
      root    197     1  0  Feb 18 ?          0:00 /usr/lib/power/powerd
      root    196     1  0  Feb 18 ?          0:35 /etc/opt/licenses/lmgrd.ste -c /d
      root    213     1  0  Feb 18 ?       4903:09 /usr/sbin/vold
      root    199   196  0  Feb 18 ?          0:03 suntechd -T 4 -c /etc/optd
      root    219     1  0  Feb 18 ?          0:08 /usr/lib/sendmail -bd -q15m
      root    209     1  0  Feb 18 ?          0:05 /usr/lib/utmpd
      root   2935   266  0  Feb 22 ?         48:08 /usr/openwin/bin/Xsun :0 -nobanna
      root  16795 16763  1 07:51:34 pts/4    0:00 ps -ef
      root   2963  2954  0  Feb 22 ?          0:17 /usr/openwin/bin/fbconsole
      root    479     1  0  Feb 18 console   0:00 /usr/lib/saf/ttymon -g -h -p sunc
      root  10976     1  0  Jun 01 ?          0:00 /opt/perf/bin/ttd
      root   7468     1  0  Feb 24 ?          0:13 /opt/perf/bin/pvalarmd
      root    266     1  0  Feb 18 ?          0:01 /usr/dt/bin/dtlogin -daemon
    martyp  16763 16761  0 07:46:46 pts/4    0:01 -ksh
      root  10995     1  0  Jun 01 ?          0:01 /opt/perf/bin/perflbd
      root    484   478  0  Feb 18 ?          0:00 /usr/lib/saf/ttymon
      root    458     1  0  Feb 18 ?         20:06 /usr/lib/snmp/snmpdx -y -c /etc/f
      root  16792  3059  0 07:50:37 ?          0:00 /usr/dt/bin/dtscreen -mode blank
      root    471     1  0  Feb 18 ?          0:07 /usr/lib/dmi/dmispd
      root    474     1  0  Feb 18 ?          0:00 /usr/lib/dmi/snmpXdmid -s
      root    485   458  0  Feb 18 ?        739:44 mibiisa -r -p 32874
      root   2954  2936  0  Feb 22 ?          0:01 /bin/ksh /usr/dt/bin/Xsession
      root   2936   266  0  Feb 22 ?          0:00 /usr/dt/bin/dtlogin -daemon
      root   3061  3059  0  Feb 22 ?          1:32 dtwm
      root   3058     1  0  Feb 22 pts/2     0:01 /usr/dt/bin/ttsession
      root    712   133  0  Feb 18 ?          0:01 rpc.ttdbserverd
      root  11001 11000  0                   0:01 <defunct>
      root   2938     1  0  Feb 22 ?          0:00 /usr/openwin/bin/fbconsole -d :0
      root   2999  2954  0  Feb 22 pts/2     0:16 /usr/dt/bin/sdt_shell -c        unt
      root   3059  3002  0  Feb 22 pts/2   283:35 /usr/dt/bin/dtsession
      root   3063  3059  0  Feb 22 ?          0:03 /usr/dt/bin/dthelpview -helpVolur
      root   3099  3062  0  Feb 22 ?          0:13 /usr/dt/bin/dtfile -geometry +700
      root  11000 10995  0  Jun 01 ?          0:02 /opt/perf/bin/agdbserver -t alar/
      root   3002  2999  0  Feb 22 pts/2     0:01 -ksh -c         unset DT;       DISPLg
      root    730   133  0  Feb 18 ?          1:37 rpc.rstatd
      root   3062  3059  0  Feb 22 ?          2:17 /usr/dt/bin/dtfile -geometry +700
      root   3067     1  0  Feb 22 ?          0:00 /bin/ksh /usr/dt/bin/sdtvolcheckm
```

```
root   3000      1  0   Feb 22 ?      0:00 /usr/dt/bin/dsdm
root   3078   3067  0   Feb 22 ?      0:00 /bin/cat /tmp/.removable/notify0
root  10984      1  0   Jun 01 ?     12:42 /opt/perf/dce/bin/dced -b
root  16761    133  0 07:46:45 ?      0:00 in.telnetd

martyp $
```

man page

ps - 12

AIX example:

```
martyp $ ps -ef
     UID   PID  PPID   C   STIME    TTY   TIME CMD
    root     1     0   0   Feb 24    -    5:07 /etc/init
    root  2208 15520   0   Feb 24    -    8:21 dtwm
    root  2664     1   0   Feb 24    -    0:00 /usr/dt/bin/dtlogin -daemon
    root  2882     1   0   Feb 24    -  158:41 /usr/sbin/syncd 60
    root  3376  2664   5   Feb 24    - 3598:41 /usr/lpp/X11/bin/X -D /usr/lib/
    root  3624  2664   0   Feb 24    -    0:00 dtlogin <:0>            -daemon
    root  3950     1   6   Feb 24    - 5550:30 /usr/lpp/perf/bin/llbd
    root  4144     1   0   Feb 24    -    0:00 /usr/lpp/perf/bin/midaemon
    root  4490     1   0   Feb 24    -    0:48 /usr/lpp/perf/bin/perflbd
    root  4906     1   0   Feb 24    -    0:00 /usr/lib/errdemon
    root  5172     1   0   Feb 24    -    0:00 /usr/sbin/srcmstr
    root  5724  5172   0   Feb 24    -    9:54 /usr/sbin/syslogd
    root  6242  5172   0   Feb 24    -    0:00 /usr/sbin/biod 6
    root  6450  5172   0   Feb 24    -    0:02 sendmail: accepting connections
    root  6710  5172   0   Feb 24    -    7:34 /usr/sbin/portmap
    root  6966  5172   0   Feb 24    -    0:23 /usr/sbin/inetd
    root  7224  5172   0   Feb 24    -    1:09 /usr/sbin/timed -S
    root  7482  5172   0   Feb 24    -   11:55 /usr/sbin/snmpd
    root  8000     1   0   Feb 24    -    9:17 ovspmd
    root  8516  8782   0   Feb 24    -    0:00 netfmt -CF
    root  8782     1   0   Feb 24    -    0:00 /usr/OV/bin/ntl_reader 0 1 1 1
    root  9036  8000   0   Feb 24    -   10:09 ovwdb -O -n5000
    root  9288  8000   0   Feb 24    -    0:44 pmd -Au -At -Mu -Mt -m
    root  9546  8000   0   Feb 24    -   20:05 trapgend -f
    root  9804  8000   0   Feb 24    -    0:28 trapd
    root 10062  8000   0   Feb 24    -    0:47 orsd
    root 10320  8000   0   Feb 24    -    0:33 ovesmd
    root 10578  8000   0   Feb 24    -    0:30 ovelmd
    root 10836  8000   0   Feb 24    -   13:12 ovtopmd -O
    root 11094  8000   0   Feb 24    -   17:50 netmon -P
    root 11352  8000   0   Feb 24    -    0:02 snmpCollect
    root 11954     1   0   Feb 24    -    1:22 /usr/sbin/cron
    root 12140  5172   0   Feb 24    -    0:01 /usr/lib/netsvc/yp/ypbind
    root 12394  5172   0   Feb 24    -    1:39 /usr/sbin/rpc.mountd
    root 12652  5172   0   Feb 24    -    0:29 /usr/sbin/nfsd 8
    root 12908  5172   0   Feb 24    -    0:00 /usr/sbin/rpc.statd
    root 13166  5172   0   Feb 24    -    0:29 /usr/sbin/rpc.lockd
    root 13428     1   0   Feb 24    -    0:00 /usr/sbin/uprintfd
    root 14190  5172   0   Feb 24    -   72:59 /usr/sbin/automountd
    root 14452  5172   0   Feb 24    -    0:17 /usr/sbin/qdaemon
    root 14714  5172   0   Feb 24    -    0:00 /usr/sbin/writesrv
    root 14992     1   0   Feb 24    -  252:26 /usr/lpp/perf/bin/scopeux
    root 15520  3624   1   Feb 24    -   15:29 /usr/dt/bin/dtsession
    root 15742     1   0   Feb 24    -    0:00 /usr/lpp/diagnostics/bin/diagd
    root 15998     1   0   Feb 24  1ft0   0:00 /usr/sbin/getty /dev/console
    root 16304 18892   0   Feb 24  pts/0  0:00 /bin/ksh
    root 16774     1   0   Feb 24    -    0:00 /usr/lpp/perf/bin/ttd
    root 17092  4490   0   Feb 24    -   68:54 /usr/lpp/perf/bin/rep_server -t
    root 17370 19186   3              0:00 <defunct>
    root 17630 15520   0   Mar 25    -    0:00 /usr/dt/bin/dtexec -open 0 -ttp
    root 17898 15520   0   Mar 20    -    0:00 /usr/dt/bin/dtexec -open 0 -ttp
    root 18118 19888   0   Feb 24  pts/1  0:00 /bin/ksh
    root 18366  6966   0   Feb 24    -    0:00 rpc.ttdbserver 100083 1
    root 18446 15520   0   Mar 15    -    0:00 /usr/dt/bin/dtexec -open 0 -ttp
    root 18892 15520   0   Feb 24    -    3:46 /usr/dt/bin/dtterm
    root 19186 16304   0   Feb 24  pts/0  0:01 /usr/lpp/X11/bin/msmit
    root 19450     1   0   Feb 24    -   26:53 /usr/dt/bin/ttsession -s
    root 19684  2208   0   Feb 24    -    0:00 /usr/dt/bin/dtexec -open 0 -ttp
    root 19888 19684   0   Feb 24    -    0:00 /usr/dt/bin/dtterm
```

```
       root 20104 15520   0   Feb 27    -   0:00 /usr/dt/bin/dtexec -open 0 -ttp
       root 20248 20104   0   Feb 27    -   0:03 /usr/dt/bin/dtscreen
       root 20542 29708   0   May 14    -   0:03 /usr/dt/bin/dtscreen
       root 20912 26306   0   Apr 05    -   0:03 /usr/dt/bin/dtscreen
       root 33558     1   0   May 18    -   3:28 /usr/atria/etc/lockmgr -a /var/
       root 33834  6966   3 07:55:49    -   0:00 telnetd
       root 34072     1   0   May 18    -   0:00 /usr/atria/etc/albd_server
     martyp 36296 36608  13 07:56:07 pts/2  0:00 ps -ef
     martyp 36608 33834   1 07:55:50 pts/2  0:00 -ksh
       root 37220 15520   0   May 28    -   0:00 /usr/dt/bin/dtexec -open 0 -ttp
martyp $
```

HP-UX example (partial listing):

man page

ps - 12

```
# ps -ef
    UID   PID  PPID C  STIME   TTY   TIME     COMMAND
    root     0     0 0  Mar  9  ?   107:28 swapper
    root     1     0 0  Mar  9  ?     2:27 init
    root     2     0 0  Mar  9  ?    14:13 vhand
    root     3     0 0  Mar  9  ?   114:55 statdaemon
    root     4     0 0  Mar  9  ?     5:57 unhashdaemon
    root     7     0 0  Mar  9  ?   154:33 ttisr
    root    70     0 0  Mar  9  ?     0:01 lvmkd
    root    71     0 0  Mar  9  ?     0:01 lvmkd
    root    72     0 0  Mar  9  ?     0:01 lvmkd
    root    13     0 0  Mar  9  ?     9:54 vx_sched_thread
    root    14     0 0  Mar  9  ?     1:54 vx_iflush_thread
    root    15     0 0  Mar  9  ?     2:06 vx_ifree_thread
    root    16     0 0  Mar  9  ?     2:27 vx_inactive_cache_thread
    root    17     0 0  Mar  9  ?     0:40 vx_delxwri_thread
    root    18     0 0  Mar  9  ?     0:33 vx_logflush_thread
    root    19     0 0  Mar  9  ?     0:07 vx_attrsync_thread
                            .
                            .
                            .
    root    69     0 0  Mar  9  ?     0:09 vx_inactive_thread
    root    73     0 0  Mar  9  ?     0:01 lvmkd
    root    74     0 19 Mar  9  ?  3605:29 netisr
    root    75     0 0  Mar  9  ?     0:18 netisr
    root    76     0 0  Mar  9  ?     0:17 netisr
    root    77     0 0  Mar  9  ?     0:14 netisr
    root    78     0 0  Mar  9  ?     0:48 nvsisr
    root    79     0 0  Mar  9  ?     0:00 supsched
    root    80     0 0  Mar  9  ?     0:00 smpsched
    root    81     0 0  Mar  9  ?     0:00 smpsched
    root    82     0 0  Mar  9  ?     0:00 sblksched
    root    83     0 0  Mar  9  ?     0:00 sblksched
    root    84     0 0  Mar  9  ?     0:00 strmem
    root    85     0 0  Mar  9  ?     0:00 strweld
    root  3730     1 0 16:39:22 console  0:00 /usr/sbin/getty console console
    root   404     1 0  Mar  9  ?     3:57 /usr/sbin/swagentd
  oracle   919     1 0 15:23:23  ?     0:00 oraclegprd (LOCAL=NO)
    root   289     1 2  Mar  9  ?    78:34 /usr/sbin/syncer
    root   426     1 0  Mar  9  ?     0:10 /usr/sbin/syslogd -D
    root   576     1 0  Mar  9  ?     0:00 /usr/sbin/portmap
    root   429     1 0  Mar  9  ?     0:00 /usr/sbin/ptydaemon
    root   590     1 0  Mar  9  ?     0:00 /usr/sbin/biod 4
    root   442     1 0  Mar  9  ?     0:00 /usr/lbin/nktl_daemon 0 0 0 0 0 1 -2
  oracle  8145     1 0 12:02:48  ?     0:00 oraclegprd (LOCAL=NO)
    root   591     1 0  Mar  9  ?     0:00 /usr/sbin/biod 4
```

```
root     589     1  0  Mar   9  ?     0:00 /usr/sbin/biod 4
root     592     1  0  Mar   9  ?     0:00 /usr/sbin/biod 4
root     604     1  0  Mar   9  ?     0:00 /usr/sbin/rpc.lockd
root     598     1  0  Mar   9  ?     0:00 /usr/sbin/rpc.statd
root     610     1  0  Mar   9  ?     0:16 /usr/sbin/automount -f /etc/auto_master
root     638     1  0  Mar   9  ?     0:06 sendmail: accepting connections
root     618     1  0  Mar   9  ?     0:02 /usr/sbin/inetd
root     645     1  0  Mar   9  ?     5:01 /usr/sbin/snmpdm
root     661     1  0  Mar   9  ?    11:28 /usr/sbin/fddisubagtd
root     711     1  0  Mar   9  ?    30:59 /opt/dce/sbin/rpcd
root     720     1  0  Mar   9  ?     0:00 /usr/sbin/vtdaemon
root     867   777  1  Mar   9  ?     0:00 <defunct>
lp       733     1  0  Mar   9  ?     0:00 /usr/sbin/lpsched
root     777     1  0  Mar   9  ?     8:55 DIAGMON
root     742     1  0  Mar   9  ?     0:15 /usr/sbin/cron
oracle  7880     1  0  11:43:47  ?    0:00 oraclegprd (LOCAL=NO)
root     842     1  0  Mar   9  ?     0:00 /usr/vue/bin/vuelogin
oracle  5625     1  0  07:00:14  ?    0:01 ora_smon_gprd
root     781     1  0  Mar   9  ?     0:00 /usr/sbin/envd
root     833   777  0  Mar   9  ?     0:00 DEMLOG  DEMLOG;DEMLOG;0;0;
root     813     1  0  Mar   9  ?     0:00 /usr/sbin/nfsd 4
root     807     1  0  Mar   9  ?     0:00 /usr/sbin/rpc.mountd
root     815   813  0  Mar   9  ?     0:00 /usr/sbin/nfsd 4
root     817   813  0  Mar   9  ?     0:00 /usr/sbin/nfsd 4
root     835   777  0  Mar   9  ?     0:13 PSMON   PSMON;PSMON;0;0;
```

Here is a brief description of the headings:

UID	The user ID of the process owner.
PID	The process ID (you can use this number to kill the process).
PPID	The process ID of the parent process.
C	Process utilization for scheduling.
STIME	Start time of the process.
TTY	The controlling terminal for the process, if any.
TIME	The cumulative execution time for the process.
COMMAND	The command name and arguments.

man page

ps - 12

ps gives a quick profile of the processes running on your system. To get more detailed information, you can include the "l" option which includes a lot of useful additional information, as shown in the following example:

```
martyp $ ps -efl
 F S       UID   PID  PPID  C PRI NI     ADDR    SZ    WCHAN    STIME TTY        D
19 T      root     0     0  0   0 SY f026f7f0     0            Feb 18 ?          d
 8 S      root     1     0  0  41 20 f5b90808   175 f5b90a30   Feb 18 ?          -
19 S      root     2     0  0   0 SY f5b90108     0 f0283fd0   Feb 18 ?          t
19 S      root     3     0  0   0 SY f5b8fa08     0 f0287a44   Feb 18 ?          6h
 8 S      root  3065  3059  0  40 20 f626d040  1639 f62aab96   Feb 22 ?          c
 8 S      root    88     1  0  40 20 f5b8d708   377 f5b59df6   Feb 18 ?          q
 8 S      root   478     1  0  41 20 f5b8ec08   388 f5b51bb8   Feb 18 ?          0
 8 S      root    94     1  0  41 20 f5b8d008   527 f5b59e46   Feb 18 ?          d
 8 S      root   150     1  0  41 20 f5da1a10   808 f5b59806   Feb 18 ?          d
 8 S      root    96     1  0  67 20 f5da2810   535 f5b59ad6   Feb 18 ?          v
 8 S      root   144     1  0  41 20 f5da0c10  2694 ef69f61c   Feb 18 ?          5d
 8 S      root  1010     1  0   0 RT f61da330   496 f5dbec1c   Apr 12 ?          n
 8 S      root   106     1  0  41 20 f5da1310   485 f5b59e96   Feb 18 ?          s
 8 S      root   156     1  0  51 20 f5b8de08   446 f5b51eb8   Feb 18 ?          n
 8 S      root   176     1  0  53 20 f5da2110   740 f5b59036   Feb 18 ?          d
 8 S      root   129     1  0  56 20 f5d9fe10   447 f5b59cb6   Feb 18 ?          d
 8 S    daemon   130     1  0  41 20 f5d9f710   564 f5b59b76   Feb 18 ?          d
 8 S      root 14798     1  0  45 20 f5b8e508   616 f5b8e730   Mar 09 ?          3d
 8 S      root   133     1  0  51 20 f5e18818   507 f5b59c66   Feb 18 ?          s
 8 S      root   197     1  0  63 20 f5e15e18   284 f5e16040   Feb 18 ?          d
 8 S      root   196     1  0  41 20 f5da0510   429 f5c68f8e   Feb 18 ?          c
 8 S      root   213     1  0  41 20 f5e16518   586 f5c68b2e   Feb 18 ?          4d
 8 S      root   199   196  0  41 20 f5e16c18   451 f5b59f86   Feb 18 ?          i
 8 S      root   219     1  0  41 20 f5e17318   658 f5b59d06   Feb 18 ?          m
 8 S      root   209     1  0  41 20 f5e18118   234 f5c68e4e   Feb 18 ?          d
 8 S      root  2935   266  0  40 20 f61db130  2473 f62aaa56   Feb 22 ?          4
 8 S      root 16800  3059  1  81 30 f626f340  1466 f61b345e 07:59:40 ?          k
 8 S      root  2963  2954  0  40 20 f5f52028   513 f61b313e   Feb 22 ?          e
 8 S      root   479     1  0  55 20 f5ee7120   407 f5fde2c6   Feb 18 console    g
 8 S      root 10976     1  0  65 20 f5f55828   478 f5c6853e   Jun 01 ?          d
 8 S      root  7468     1  0  46 20 f621da38  2851    8306c   Feb 24 ?          d
 8 S      root   266     1  0  41 20 f5ee5520  1601 f5c6858e   Feb 18 ?          n
 8 S    martyp 16763 16761  0  51 20 f6270140   429 f62701ac 07:46:46 pts/4      h
 8 S      root 10995     1  0  41 20 f5b8f308  2350 f5fde5e6   Jun 01 ?          d
 8 S      root   484   478  0  41 20 f5ee4e20   408 f5ee5048   Feb 18 ?          n
 8 S      root   458     1  0  41 20 f5f54a28   504 f5fde906   Feb 18 ?          2m
 8 O      root 16802 16763  1  61 20 f5ee7820   220            08:00:05 pts/4    l
 8 S      root   471     1  0  41 20 f5f53c28   658 f5fde726   Feb 18 ?          d
 8 S      root   474     1  0  51 20 f5f53528   804 f61a58b6   Feb 18 ?          g
 8 S      root   485   458  0  40 20 f5f52e28   734 f607ecde   Feb 18 ?          74
 8 S      root  2954  2936  0  40 20 f626e540   433 f626e5ac   Feb 22 ?          n
 8 S      root  2936   266  0  66 20 f5ee4720  1637 f5ee478c   Feb 22 ?          n
 8 S      root  3061  3059  0  40 20 f5e17a18  2041 f61b359e   Feb 22 ?          m
 8 S      root  3058     1  0  40 20 f61daa30  1067 f62aadc6   Feb 22 pts/2      n
 8 S      root   712   133  0  41 20 f61d8e30   798 f61b390e   Feb 18 ?          d
 8 Z      root 11001 11000  0   0            0                                   >
 8 S      root  2938     1  0  60 20 f5ee6320   513 f601bfb6   Feb 22 ?          0
 8 S      root  2999  2954  0  40 20 f621e138  1450 f61b33be   Feb 22 pts/2      t
 8 S      root  3059  3002  1  51 20 f626de40  4010 f62aafa6   Feb 22 pts/2      2n
 8 S      root  3063  3059  0  50 20 f621e838  1952 f62aa556   Feb 22 ?
 8 S      root  3099  3062  0  40 20 f5f52728  2275 f60a1d18   Feb 22 ?          0
 8 S      root 11000 10995  0  48 20 f626d740  2312    55694   Jun 01 ?          e
 8 S      root  3002  2999  0  43 20 f61d8730   427 f61d879c   Feb 22 pts/2      =
 8 S      root   730   133  0  40 20 f61d9530   422 f62aa9b6   Feb 18 ?          d
 8 S      root  3062  3059  0  61 20 f621b738  2275 f62aa506   Feb 22 ?          0
 8 S      root  3067     1  0  40 20 f5ee5c20   424 f5ee5c8c   Feb 22 ?          d
 8 S      root  3000     1  0  40 20 f61d8030   518 f62aa8c6   Feb 22 ?          m
 8 S      root  3078  3067  0  40 20 f61d9c30   211 f5b512b8   Feb 22 ?          0
 8 S      root 10984     1  0  41 20 f5f54328  2484 eee46e84   Jun 01 ?          1b
 8 S      root 16761   133  0  44 20 f5ee4020   411 f5c6894e 07:46:45 ?          d
martyp $
```

In this example, the first column is *F* for flags. *F* provides octal
information about whether the process is swapped, in core, a system

process, and so on. The octal value sometimes varies from system to system, so check the manual pages for your system to see the octal value of the flags.

S is for state. The state can be sleeping, as indicated by *S* for most of the processes shown in the example, waiting, running, intermediate, terminated, and so on. Again, some of these values may vary from system to system, so check your manual pages.

Some additional useful information in this output is: *NI* for the nice value; *ADDR* for the memory address of the process; *SZ* for the size in physical pages of the process; and *WCHAN,* which is the event for which the process is waiting.

Killing a Process

man page

ps - 12

man page

kill - 6

If you issue the **ps** command and find that one of your processes is hung or if you start a large job that you wish to stop, you can do so with the **kill** command. **kill** is a utility that sends a signal to the process you identify. You can **kill** any process that you own. In addition, superuser can kill almost any process on the system.

To kill a process that you own, simply issue the **kill** command and the Process ID (PID). The following example shows issuing the **ps** command to find all processes owned by *martyp*, killing a process, and checking to see that it has disappeared:

```
martyp $ ps -ef | grep martyp
 martyp 19336 19334   0 05:24:32 pts/4  0:01 -ksh
 martyp 19426 19336   0 06:01:01 pts/4  0:00 grep martyp
 martyp 19424 19336   5 06:00:48 pts/4  0:01 find / -name .login
martyp $ kill 19424
martyp $ ps -ef | grep martyp
  martyp 19336 19334   0 05:24:32 pts/4  0:01 -ksh
  martyp 19428 19336   1 06:01:17 pts/4  0:00 grep martyp
[1] + Terminated         find / -name .login &
martyp $
```

The example shows killing process *19424,* which is owned by *martyp.* We confirm that the process has indeed been killed by reissuing the **ps** command.

man page

ps - 12

You can kill several processes on the command line by issuing **kill** followed by a space-separated list of all of the process numbers you wish to kill.

man page

kill - 6

Take special care when killing processes, if you are logged in as superuser. You may adversely affect the way the system runs and have to manually restart processes or reboot the system.

Signals

When you issue the **kill** command and process number, you are also sending a *signal* associated with the **kill**. We did not specify a *signal* in our **kill** example; however, the default *signal* of 15, or *SIGTERM,* was used. These *signals* are used by the system to communicate with processes. The *signal* of 15 we used to terminate our process is a software termination *signal* that is usually enough to terminate a user process such as the **find** we had started. A process that is difficult to kill may require the *SIGKILL,* or 9 *signal*. This *signal* causes an immediate termination of the process. I use this only as a last resort because processes killed with *SIGKILL* do not always terminate smoothly. To kill such processes as the shell, you sometimes have to use *SIGKILL*.

man page

find - 10

You can use either the *signal* name or number. These signal numbers sometimes vary from system to system, so view the manual page for *signal*, usually in section 5, to see the list of *signals* on your system. A list of some of the most frequently used *signal* numbers and corresponding *signals* follows:

Signal number	Signal
1	SIGHUP
2	SIGINT
3	SIGQUIT
9	SIGKILL

15   SIGTERM
24   SIGSTOP

As I had explained earlier earlier in the book, you can view an on line manual page from a specific section by using the "-s" option with the *section* number. To view the **signal** man page in section five, you would issue the following command:

```
$ man -s 5 signal
```

Your UNIX variant, such as Linux, may require a capital S for the section number option.

To kill a process with id *234* with *SIGKILL,* you would issue the following command:

```
$ kill -9 234
    |    |   |
    |    |   |> process id (PID)
    |    |> signal number
    |> kill command to terminate the process
```

Using **ps** and **kill** as we have covered in these sections works on every UNIX variant. Keep in mind that the signal definitions differ among UNIX variants. There are also two commands that may be supported on your UNIX variant called **pgrep** and **pkill**. **pgrep** finds a process by name or other attributes. We earlier issued **ps** combined with **grep** to find processes owned by user *martyp*. **pgrep** is kind of a combination of these two commands and will find a process based on the name or other attribute you specify. Similarly, **pkill** identifies a process by the attribute you specify and kills it.

System Startup and Shutdown Scripts

Startup and shutdown scripts for newer releases of UNIX variants are based on a mechanism that separates the actual startup and shutdown scripts from configuration information. In order to modify the way your system starts or stops, you don't have to modify scripts, a task that in general is considered somewhat risky; you can instead modify configuration variables. The startup and shutdown sequence is based on an industry standard that is similar on most UNIX variants.

As always, however, there are implementation differences on-going from one UNIX variant to another. What I'll describe here is an implementation that is likely similar to the implementation on your UNIX system.

Startup and shutdown become important if you take on any system administration responsibility. As you load and customize more applications, you will need more startup and shutdown knowledge. What I do in this section is give you an overview of startup and shutdown and the commands you can use to shut down your system.

The following components are in the startup and shutdown model:

Execution Scripts

> Execution scripts read variables from configuration variable scripts and run through the startup or shutdown sequence. These scripts are usually located in **/sbin/init.d**. (These scripts are found in **/etc/init.d** on some systems.)

Configuration Variable Scripts

> These are the files you would modify to set variables that are used to enable or disable a subsystem or perform some other function at the time of system startup or shutdown.

These are located in **/etc/rc.config.d**. (These files do not exist on some systems.)

Link Files   These files are used to control the order in which scripts execute. These are actually links to execution scripts to be executed when moving from one run level to another. These files are located in the directory for the appropriate run level, such as **/sbin/rc0.d** for run level 0, **/sbin/rc1.d** for run level 1, and so on. The files in this directory that begin with an "S" are startup scripts, and those that end in a "K" are shutdown scripts. (These links are found in **/etc** instead of / **sbin** on some systems.)

Sequencer Script

This script invokes execution scripts based on run-level transition. This script is usually **/sbin/rc**.

Figure 12-1 shows a commonly used directory structure for startup and shutdown scripts.

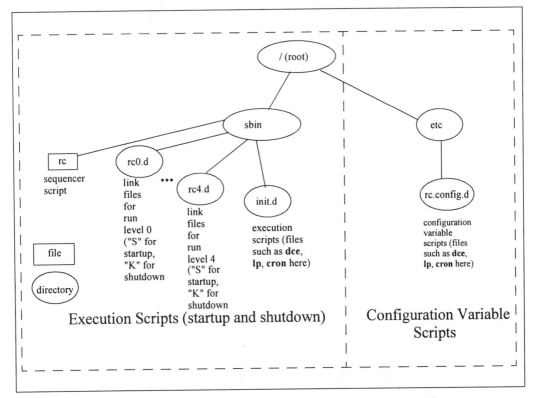

Figure 12-1 Typical Organization of Startup and Shutdown Files

Execution scripts perform startup and shutdown tasks. **/sbin/rc** invokes the execution script, with the appropriate start or stop arguments, and you can view the appropriate start or stop messages on the console. The messages you see will have one of the three following values:

OK   This indicates that the execution script started or shut down properly.

FAIL   A problem occurred at startup or shutdown.

N/A   The script was not configured to start.

In order to start up a subsystem, you would simply edit the appropriate configuration file in **/etc/rc.config.d**. An example showing **/etc/rc.config.d/audio** is shown with the **AUDIO_SERVER** variable set to **1**.

```
#          **********    File:        /etc/rc.config.d/audio
*************
# Audio server configuration.  See audio(5)
#
# AUDIO_SER:       Set to 1 to start audio server daemon
#

AUDIO_SERVER=1
```

This example results in the following message being shown at the time the system boots:

```
Start audio server daemon ........................[ OK ]
```

and this message at the time the system is shut down:

```
Stopping audio server daemon .......................OK
```

I have mentioned run levels several times in this discussion. Both the startup and shutdown scripts described here, as well as the **/etc/inittab** file, depend on run levels. Run levels are different among UNIX variants. I have never seen all the same run-level definitions for different UNIX variants. In general, the lower run levels are used for lower-level functionality, and you initiate more advanced capabilities as the run levels increase. This generalizaion is not always true, so you want to check for the UNIX variant you are using. The following is a list of run levels and how they are used:

0	Halted run level.
s, S	Run level s, also known as single-user mode, is used to ensure that no one else is on the system so that you can proceed with system administration tasks.
0	PROM monitor level on some systems.
1	Run level 1 starts various basic processes for single-user mode.
2	Run level 2 allows users to access the system. This is also known as multi-user mode.
3	Run level 3 is for exporting NFS file systems and sharing other resources on many UNIX variants.
4	Run level 4 starts the graphical manager including Common Desktop Environment (HP CDE), on some UNIX variants and is not used on other UNIX variants.
5	Not used on some UNIX variants and instead used for "HALT" state on other UNIX variants.
6	Not used on some UNIX variants and used to reboot to run level 3 on some UNIX variants.

You can see that run levels differ greatly among UNIX variants so you'll want to check the run levels and their associated function for you UNIX variant.

/etc/inittab is also used to define a variety of processes that will be run, and is used by **/sbin/init**. The **/sbin/init** process ID is 1. It is the first process started on your system and it has no parent. The **init** process looks at **/etc/inittab** to determine the run level of the system.

Entries in the **/etc/inittab** file have the following format:

id:run state:action:process

id:	The name of the entry. The id is up to four characters long and must be unique in the file. If the line in **/etc/inittab** is preceded by a "#," the entry is treated as a comment.
run state:	Specifies the run level at which the command is executed. More than one run level can be specified. The command is executed for every run level specified.
action:	Defines which of 11 actions will be taken with this process. The 11 choices for action are *initdefault, sysinit, boot, bootwait, wait, respawn, once, powerfail, powerwait, ondemand,* and *off.*
process	The shell command to be executed *if* the run level and/or action field so indicates.

Here is an example of an **/etc/inittab** entry:

cons:123456:respawn:/usr/sbin/getty   console console

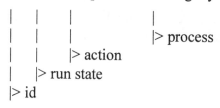

```
 |   |   |          |
 |   |   |          |> process
 |   |   |> action
 |   |> run state
 |> id
```

This is in the **/etc/inittab** file, as opposed to being defined as a startup script, because the console may be killed and have to be restarted whenever it dies, even if no change has occurred in run level.

respawn starts a process if it does not exist and restarts the process after it dies. This entry shows all run states, because you want the console to be activated at all times.

Another example is one of the first lines from **/etc/inittab**:

```
init:3:initdefault:
```

The default run level of the system is defined as 3. On some UNIX variants, this line will look like the following:

```
is:3:initdefault:
```

The only difference between these two examples is the id of the run level. The run level itself and *initdefault* are the same. *initdefault* is an action that is used when **init** is initially invoked.

An Alternative Startup and Shutdown Method

There is another similar startup and shutdown arrangement found on some UNIX variants. I'll first describe the procedure verbally; however, Figure 12-2 depicts it graphically. The **/sbin** directory contains a file for each run level, such as **rcS** through **rc6**. These files contain variables, test conditions, and calls to files that stop and start services. The scripts that are run by **rcS** through **rc6** are under the appropriate run-level directory, such as **/etc/rcS.d** through **/etc/rc6.d**. As in the previous description, files in **/etc/rcS.d** through **/etc/rc6.d** that start with an *S* are used to start processes, and files that start with a *K* are used to stop processes. The directory **/etc/init.d** contains run-control scripts used by the start and kill scripts located in **/etc/rcS.d** through **/etc/rc6.d**. The scripts in **/etc/rcS.d** through **/etc/rc6.d** are links to programs in **/etc/init.d**, meaning that the control scripts in **/etc/init.d** are used in **/etc/rcS.d** through **/etc/rc6.d** by creating links to **/etc/init.d**. You have one version of the script in **/etc/init.d** that is used in many other directories by linking to the script in **/etc/init.d**. You can use the control files in **/etc/init.d** to start and stop programs from this directory. To stop the *lp* service, for instance, you could issue the following command:

```
# /etc/init.d/lp stop
```

The startup files to be run at boot are called from **/etc/inittab** in this startup arrangement. **/etc/inittab** defines the default run level called *initdefault* and the appropriate run files in **/sbin**.

Figure 12-2 shows the organization of the startup and shutdown files discussed in this section.

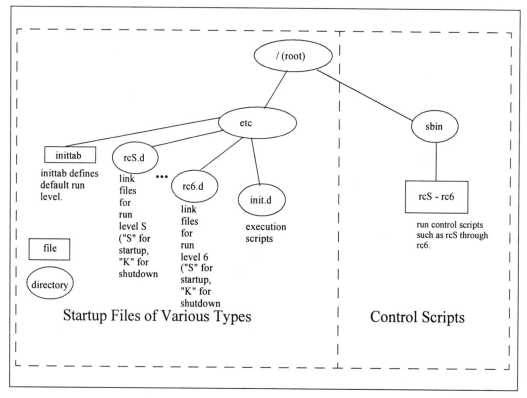

Figure 12-2 Another Organization of Startup and Shutdown Files

The basics of system startup and shutdown described here are important to understand. You may be starting up and shutting down your system and possibly even modifying some of the files described here. Please take a close look at the startup and shutdown files before you begin to modify these. These files and procedures differ enough among UNIX variants to make this process dangerous if you are not careful.

Now let's take a look at the command you can issue to shut down your system.

System Shutdown

What does it mean to shut down the system? Well, in its simplest form, a shutdown of the system simply means issuing the **shutdown** command. The **shutdown** command is used to terminate all processing. It has many options, including the following:

man page

shutdown
- 12

-r	Automatically reboots the system, that is, brings it down and brings it up. This is available on only some UNIX variants.
-h	Halts the system completely. This is available on only some UNIX variants.
-y	Completes the shutdown without asking you any questions it would normally ask.
grace or **-g**	Specifies the number of seconds you wish to wait before the system is shut down, in order to give your users time to save files, quit applications, and log out. This is a **-g** in some UNIX variants.
-i	Specifies the state to which the system will transition.

To shut down and automatically reboot the system, you would type:

man page

shutdown
- 12

```
$ shutdown -r
```

To halt the system, you would type:

```
$ shutdown -h
```

You will be asked whether you want to type a message to users informing them of the impending system shutdown. After you type the message, it is immediately sent to all users. After the specified time elapses (60 seconds is the default), the system begins the shutdown process. After you receive a message that the system is halted, you can power off all your system components.

To shut down the system in two minutes without being asked any questions, type:

```
$ shutdown -h -y 120
```

At times, you will need to go into single-user mode with **shutdown**, to perform some task such as a backup or to expand a logical volume, and then reboot the system to return it to its original state.

To shut down the system into single-user mode, you would type:

```
$ shutdown
```

This command also differs among UNIX variants. Some implementations do not allow you to specify the state; others do not support the *-r* and *-y* options and instead want you to specify the state. Be sure of all the options before you issue this command. This is a high-risk command. You must be sure of such information as who is using the system at the time you wish to shut down. You must exercise great caution in general when using commands that require superuser access.

Users and Groups

Your system administrator considers many options before setting up a user. Once set up, however, user administration is not typically a function that system administrators spend a lot of time managing.

Your system administrator needs to make some basic decisions about every user they setup. Where should users' data be located? Who needs to access data from whom, thereby defining "groups" of users? What kind of particular startup is required by users and applications? Is there a shell that your users will prefer? Then the customization of the graphical user interface used on your system is another consideration.

Among the most important considerations your system administrator has is related to user data. A big system administration headache is rearranging user data, for several reasons. It doesn't fit on a whole disk (and not all UNIX variants have a volume manager that supports volumes spanning multiple disks), users can't freely access one another's data, or even worse, users *can* access one another's data too freely.

We will consider these questions, but first, let's look at the basic steps to adding a user. Here is a list of activities:

- Select a user name to add
- Select a user ID number
- Select a group for the user
- Create an **/etc/passwd** entry
- Assign a user password (including expiration options)
- Select and create a home directory for user
- Select the shell the user will run (there are *bash*, *ksh*, and *csh* chapters in this book)
- Place startup files in the user's home directory
- Test the user account

Most of what you do is entered in the **/etc/passwd** file, where information about all users is stored. You can make these entries to

man page

vipw - 12

the **/etc/passwd** file with the **vipw** command. Figure 12-3 is a sample **/etc/passwd** entry.

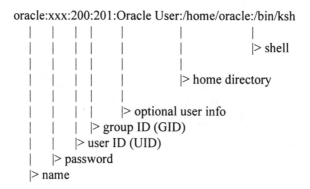

Figure 12-3 Sample **/etc/passwd** Entry

Here is a description of each of these fields:

name.   The user name you assign. This name should be easy for the user and other users on the system to remember. When sending electronic mail or copying files from one user to another, the more easily you can remember the user name, the better. If a user has a user name on another system, you may want to assign the same user name on your UNIX system. Some systems don't permit nice, easy user names, so you may want to break the tie with the old system and start using sensible, easy-to-remember user names on your UNIX system. Remember, no security is tied to the user name; security is handled through the user's password and the file permissions.

password.   This is the user's password in encrypted form. If an asterisk appears in this field, the account can't be used. If it is empty, the user has no password assigned and can log in by typing only his or her user name. I strongly recommend that each user have a password that he or she changes periodically. Every system has different security needs, but at a minimum, every user on every system should have a password. When setting up a new user, you can force the user to create a password at first login by putting a „.. in the password field.

Some features of a good password are:

- A minimum of six characters that should include special characters such as a slash (/), a dot (.), or an asterisk (*).

- No words should be used for a password.

- Don't make the password personal such as name, address, favorite sports team, etc.

- Don't use something easy to type such as *123456* or *qwerty*.

- Some people say that misspelled words are acceptable, but I don't recommend using them. Spell check programs that match misspelled words to correctly spelled words can be used to guess at words that might be misspelled for a password.

- A password generator that produces unintelligible passwords works the best.

user ID (UID).   The identification number of the user. Every user on your system should have a unique UID. Conventions for UIDs are different among UNIX variants. I recommend that you reserve UIDs less than 100 for system-level users. Some UNIX variants recommend that UIDs for general users begin at 1000.

group ID (GID).   The identification number of the group. The members of the group and their GID are in the **/etc/group** file. The system administrator can change the GID assigned if they don't like it, but they may also have to change the GID of many files. As a user creates a file, his or her UID is assigned to the file as well as the GID. This means that if the system administrator changes the GID well after users of the same group have created many files and directories, they may have to change the GID of all these. I usually save GIDs less than 10 for system groups.

optional user info.   In this space, you can make entries, such as the user's phone number or full name. You can leave this blank, but if you manage a system or network with many users, you may want to add the user's full name and extension so that if you need to get in touch with him or her, you'll have the information at your fingertips. (This field is sometimes referred to as the GECOs field.)

home directory. The home directory defines the default location for all the users' files and directories. This is the present working directory at the time of login.

shell. This is the startup program that the user will run at the time of login. The shell is really a command interpreter for the commands the user issues from the command line. The system administrator usually decides what shells are supported based on the setup files they have developed. In general, though, most shells are supported on most systems. See the shell chapters for a description of some of the most commonly used shells.

The location of the user's home directory is another important entry in the **/etc/passwd** file. You have to select a location for the user's "home" directory in the file system where the user's files will be stored. With some of the advanced networking technology that exists, such as NFS, the user's home directory does not even have to be on a disk that is physically connected to the computer he or she is using! The traditional place to locate a user's home directory on a UNIX system is the **/home** directory such as **/home/martyp**.

The **/home** directory is typically the most dynamic in terms of growth. Users create and delete files in their home directory on a regular basis. So, you have to do more planning related to your user area than in more static areas, such as the root file system and application areas. You would typically load UNIX and your applications and then perform relatively few accesses to these in terms of adding and deleting files and directories. The user area is continuously updated, making it more difficult to maintain.

man page

passwd-12

The **passwd** file has a way of getting out-of-date on a regular basis. Users come and go, and in general there are continuous changes made to this file. There is a program on most UNIX variants called **pwck** that checks the integrity of the **passwd** file. Interestingly, this program is often accessible to users as well as the system administrator. The following example shows running **pwck** on the default file used for passwords:

```
martyp $ pwck

webuser:x:80:80::/usr/local/etc/httpd/htdocs:/bin/sh
        Login directory not found

teacher:x:8057:80:Desktop   Classroom   Teacher:/usr/local/etc/
pwserver/www/:/bin/kh
        Login directory not found

oracle:x:200:201:Oracle User:/home/oracle:/bin/ksh
        Login directory not found

opc_op:x:777:77:OpC default operator:/export/home/opc_op:/bin/
sh
        Login directory not found

denise - Login name not found on system
martyp $
```

This example shows that the login directory for several users does not exist. This absence may not be a problem, because some applications require a login name but no home directory is required. On the other hand, there are usually users on the system for which there is no login directory because the directory was removed when the user left the company but their entry in **passwd** was not removed. The last problem, with user *denise*, is a user for which no files or directories exist on the system. **pwck** validates the following information in the password file you specify (this is **passwd** by default):

man page

passwd-12

- Correct number of fields

- Login name

- User ID

- Group ID

- Login directory exists

- User's default shell exists

pwck is a useful program that is underused. I often run audits for system administrators to check the health of their systems and include this program under the many security checks. There is no response if **pwck** finds no errors or warnings to report.

Assigning Users to Groups

After defining all user-related information, the system administrator needs to consider groups. Groups are often overlooked in the UNIX environment until the system administrator finds that all his or her users are in the very same group, even though from an organizational standpoint they are in different groups. Before I cover the groups in general, let's look at a file belonging to a user and the way access is defined for a file:

man page

ls - 2

```
$ ls -l
-rwxr-x--x    1 donna       users      120 Jul 26 10:20 sort
```

For every file on the system, UNIX supports three classes of access:

- User access (u). Access granted to the owner of the file

- Group access (g). Access granted to members of the same group as the owner of the file

- Other access (o). Access granted to everyone else

These access rights are defined by the settings on the permissions of r (read), write (w), and execute (x) when the long listing command is issued. For the long listing (**ls -l**) above, you see the permissions in Table 12-1.

Table 12-1 Long Listing Permissions

Access	User Access	Group Access	Other
Read	r	r	-
Write	w	-	-
Execute	x	x	x

You can see that access rights are arranged in groups of three. Three groups of permissions exist with three access levels each. The owner, in this case, *donna*, is allowed read, write, and execute permissions on the file. Anyone in the group *users* is permitted read and execute access to the file. Others are permitted only execute access of the file.

These permissions are important to consider as you arrange your users into groups. If several users require access to the same files, then the system administrator will want to put those users in the same group. The trade-off here is that you can give all users within a group *rwx* access to files, but then you run the risk of several users editing a file without other users knowing it, thereby causing confusion. On the other hand, you can make several copies of a file so that each user has his or her personal copy, but then you have multiple versions of a file. If possible, assign users to groups based on their work.

The **/etc/group** file contains the group name, an encrypted password (which is rarely used), a group ID, and a list of users in the group. Here is an example of an **/etc/group** file:

```
root::0:root
other::1:root, hpdb
bin::2:root,bin
sys::3:root,uucp
adm::4:root,adm
daemon::5:root,daemon
mail::6:root
lp::7:root,lp
tty::10:
nuucp::11:nuucp
military::25:jhunt,tdolan,vdallesandro
```

```
commercial::30:ccascone,jperwinc,devers
nogroup:*:-2:
```

This **/etc/group** file shows two different groups of users. Although all users run the same application, a desktop publishing tool, some work on documents of "commercial" products while others work on only "military" documents. It made sense for the system administrator to create two groups, one for commercial document preparation and the other for military document preparation. All members of a group know what documents are current and respect one another's work and its importance. System administrators will have few problems among group members who know what each other is doing, and you will find that these members don't delete files that shouldn't be deleted. If you put all users into one group, however, you may find that you spend more time restoring files because users in this broader group don't find files that are owned by other members of their group to be important. Users can change group with the **newgrp** command.

man page

newgrp - 12

The **group** file also has a way of getting out-of-date on a regular basis. As users come and go there are both changes to the **passwd** and **group** files required. There is a program on most UNIX variants called **grpck** that checks the integrity of the **group** file. Interestingly, this program is often accessible to users as well as the system administrator. The following example shows running **grpck** on the default file used for passwords:

```
martyp $ grpck

database:10:
        No users in this group

development1:*:200:nadmin,charles,william
        william - Login name not found in password file

bin::2:root,bin,daemon
```

```
          bin - Duplicate logname entry (gid first occurs
in passwd entry)


sys::3:root,bin,sys,adm
          sys - Duplicate logname entry (gid first occurs
in passwd entry)


adm::4:root,adm,daemon
          adm - Duplicate logname entry (gid first occurs
in passwd entry)


uucp::5:root,uucp
          uucp - Duplicate logname entry (gid first occurs
in passwd entry)


tty::7:root,tty,adm
          tty - Logname not found in password file


lp::8:root,lp,adm
          lp - Duplicate logname entry (gid first occurs in
passwd entry)


nuucp::9:root,nuucp
          nuucp - Duplicate logname entry (gid first occurs
in passwd entry)

martyp $
```

This example shows that there are a variety of potential **group-**related problems on this system. They include: no users in the group *database*; a user in a group for which there is no entry in the **passwd** file; and several duplicate entries. Some of these may not be a problem. However, a typical problem revealed by **grpck** is a user who has been removed from the system but has not been removed from the group of which they were a member. **grpck** validates the following information in the group file you specify (this is **group** by default):

- Correct number of fields

- Group name

• Group ID

• Login name exceeds maximum number of groups

• Login names appear in password file

grpck is a useful program that is underused. I often run audits for system administrators to check the health of their systems and include this program under the many security checks.

Disk-Related Concepts

System administrators typically spend a great deal of time setting up, managing, and monitoring disks and file systems. I'll cover the basics here; however, I don't want to cover any setup procedures, because users typically aren't permitted access to the commands used to set up disks, filesystems, and so on. Some commands associated with initial disk and file system setup are: **newfs**, **dd**, **fsck**, **mknod**, and others. If you see these commands in the user material you use to learn UNIX you can immediately associate this with disk and file system setup and maitenance. It is still very useful, however, to be abe to view they way your system and environment have been set up.

We'll cover a variety of topics in this section including: viewing file systems; viewing swap space; viewing some setup files; and a review of Network File System (NFS) covered in the networking chapter.

Viewing Mounted Filesystems and Swap

One of the first activities you would perform when interested in file systems is to see what file systems are currently mounted on your system and their characteristics. The **df** command produces a listing of mounted file systems and some space-related information on each. The following is an example **df** output from a Solaris system:

df - 12

```
martyp $ df
/proc               (/proc        ):        0 blocks     927 files
/                   (/dev/dsk/c0t3d0s0 ): 2284464 blocks  438864 files
/dev/fd             (fd           ):        0 blocks       0 files
/tmp                (swap         ):   116584 blocks   10390 files
/home/ptc-nfs       (ptc-nfs:/export/users2/home):22467786 blocks      -1 files
/opt/local          (ptc-nfs:/export/opt/local): 1292902 blocks       -1 files
martyp $
```

Issuing the **df** command with no options produces this output. All currently mounted file systems are listed along with capacity information for each. I like to issue **df** with the **-t** option, which produces totals for the file systems and includes the output for swap on most systems. The following is an example or running **df -t**:

```
martyp $ df -t
/proc               (/proc        ):         0 blocks     927 files
                                 total:      0 blocks     988 files
/                   (/dev/dsk/c0t3d0s0 ):  2284464 blocks  438864 files
                                 total:  3806172 blocks  476288 files
/dev/fd             (fd           ):         0 blocks       0 files
                                 total:      0 blocks      66 files
/tmp                (swap         ):    116600 blocks   10390 files
                                 total:   197104 blocks   10455 files
/home/ptc-nfs       (ptc-nfs:/export/users2/home): 22448064 blocks      -1 files
                                 total: 139264000 blocks      -1 files
/opt/local          (ptc-nfs:/export/opt/local):  1292900 blocks      -1 files
                                 total: 31866880 blocks      -1 files
martyp $
```

Included in this output are totals related to swap space, which is a very important aspect of your system. When the entire real memory (RAM) of your system is consumed, some information is moved to the swap area. The information that is moved is different among UNIX variants. Some UNIX variants move idle processes and all their associated information to swap space. Others move only blocks of information that are idle. The important thing to know is that swap is a partition or volume on disk used for this purpose.

One of the most difficult tasks for a system administrator is to determine the amount of swap space required on a system. The rule of thumb most often used is to have swap space equal to twice the amount of RAM on a system.

Most systems also have an area of dump space that is used to hold the contents of RAM should a system crash occur. In the event of a system crash, it can take a long time for all of RAM to be written to disk. Some UNIX variants support writing only the area of RAM that was active to dump space at the time of a crash in order to get the system up and running more quickly.

man page
df - 12

Getting back to our **df** example, the **-t** option allows you to view all of the file systems, including swap.

man page
swap - 13

You can view information specifically related to swap space with the **swap** command. The two following examples show issuing the **swap** command with the **-l** option, to list information about swap areas, and the **-s** option, to produce a summary of swap areas:

```
martyp $  swap -l
swapfile              dev   swaplo blocks    free
/dev/dsk/c0t3d0s1    32,25       8 263080   74200

martyp $  swap -s
total: 99104k bytes allocated + 10200k reserved = 109304k
used, 63252k available
martyp $
```

We'll cover device files later in this chapter. For the purpose of covering this example, however, it is sufficient to know that there is a portion of a disk named **/dev/dsk/c0t3d0s1** that is used for swap. There is a slice of disk **c0t3d0** called **s1** that is reserved for swap, as shown with **swap -l**.

In addition to the list and summary outputs, **swap** can be used to add and delete swap space. Because this is exclusively the domain of the system adminstrator, I won't cover these options.

man page
mount - 12

You can quickly view mounted file systems any time you wish with the **mount** command. This is normally available to users to view mounted file systems; however, as a user, you probably cannot manipulate file systems in any way such as mounting and unmounting them. Most of the commands we have covered in the book produce somewhat different results among UNIX variants. The **mount** command is no exception. The following examples show issuing the **mount** command on Solaris, AIX, and HP-UX, respectively:

man page

mount - 12

```
sun1 $ mount
/proc on /proc read/write/setuid on Thu Feb 18 11:09:14
/ on /dev/dsk/c0t3d0s0 read/write/setuid/largefiles on Thu Feb 18 11:09:14
/dev/fd on fd read/write/setuid on Thu Feb 18 11:09:14
/tmp on swap read/write on Thu Feb 18 11:09:16
/opt/local on ptc-nfs:/export/opt/local read/write/intr/soft/remote on Sun Jul 9
sun1 $
```

```
ibm1 $ mount
  node       mounted         mounted over     vfs       date         options
--------  ---------------  ---------------  ------  ------------  ---------------
           /dev/hd4        /                jfs     Jul 02 19:02  rw,log=/dev/hd8
           /dev/hd2        /usr             jfs     Jul 02 19:02  rw,log=/dev/hd8
           /dev/hd9var     /var             jfs     Jul 02 19:02  rw,log=/dev/hd8
           /dev/hd3        /tmp             jfs     Jul 02 19:02  rw,log=/dev/hd8
           /dev/hd10       /usr/sys/inst.images jfs     Jul 02 19:03  rw,log=/dev/
           /dev/lv00       /opt             jfs     Jul 02 19:03  rw,log=/dev/hd8
           /dev/bakup      /home.bak        jfs     Jul 02 19:03  rw,log=/dev/logl0
           /dev/cd0        /usr/lpp/info/data/techlib cdrfs  Jul 02 19:03  ro
           /dev/lv01       /root/users      jfs     Jul 02 19:03  rw,log=/dev/hd8
           -hosts          /net             autofs Jul 02 19:04  ignore
           auto.users      /users           autofs Jul 02 19:04  ignore
           auto.ptc        /ptc_mnt         autofs Jul 02 19:04  ignore
           auto.indirect   /local_mnt       autofs Jul 02 19:04  ignore
           auto.direct     /home/ptc-nfs    autofs Jul 02 19:04  ignore
           auto.direct     /opt/local       autofs Jul 02 19:04  ignore
ibm1 $
```

```
hp1 22: mount
/ on /dev/vg00/lvol3 log on Wed Jun 16 11:20:07
/stand on /dev/vg00/lvol1 defaults on Wed Jun 16 11:20:10
/var on /dev/vg00/lvol8 delaylog on Wed Jun 16 11:20:21
/usr on /dev/vg00/lvol7 delaylog on Wed Jun 16 11:20:21
/tmp on /dev/vg00/lvol6 delaylog on Wed Jun 16 11:20:22
/opt on /dev/vg00/lvol5 delaylog on Wed Jun 16 11:20:22
/home on /dev/vg00/lvol4 delaylog on Wed Jun 16 11:20:22
hp1 23:
```

Although I haven't been in the habit of showing commands with examples of many different UNIX variants, I decided to include the output of the **mount** command. This is because the three outputs are sufficiently different to illustrate that, although generally the same information is provided, the format of the outputs are different. This fact is especially true of system administration-related commands, which are the area where UNIX variants differ the most. The concepts are the same, but the location of files, their options, and of course the format may differ. As long as you know this information going from one UNIX variant to another you'll be ready to change your thinking just enough to get you through the possible variations in commands.

The file systems that are mounted at the time of boot are in the **/etc/vfstab** or **/etc/fstab** files on most UNIX variants. This file contains information related to the devices to be mounted, mount point, file system type, mount options, and other important mounting information. You can view this file on your system to see what your system administrator has set up as the default file systems.

Determining Disk Usage

man page

du - 12

System administrators like to know the amount of disk space consumed on their system by users, applications, groups, and so on. It's a good idea to know the disk hogs on a system. The **du** command helps with this determination. With **du**, you specify a file for which you want to view disk usage. For the home directory *martyp,* you would issue the following **du** command:

```
martyp $ du
2        ./test
60       ./shellprogs
1366     ./.trash
6024     .
martyp $
```

This output shows that this directory consumes 6024 KBytes or about 6 MBytes. For large directories with many entries in them this can be a lot of output. For a summary only, you could issue the **du** command with the **-s** option and receive the following result for the entire *home* directory:

```
martyp $ du -s /home/nfs/*
0        /home/nfs-home/Mail
0        /home/nfs-home/SomeResults
1        /home/nfs-home/admin
30285    /home/nfs-home/achil
18079    /home/nfs-home/admin1
```

```
12        /home/nfs-home/aguaris
1262210   /home/nfs-home/alfonso
8         /home/nfs-home/amand
395838    /home/nfs-home/andre
28        /home/nfs-home/andrej
94448     /home/nfs-home/annelora
605738    /home/nfs-home/annetest
15        /home/nfs-home/badmin
448544    /home/nfs-home/barryworgo
7         /home/nfs-home/bbnuser
0         /home/nfs-home/bdonalla
0         /home/nfs-home/benilla
2565325   /home/nfs-home/benranos
3         /home/nfs-home/besinerro
                  .
                  .
                  .
273936    /home/nfs-home/thalla
6814      /home/nfs-home/timk
8         /home/nfs-home/tobbaa
298160    /home/nfs-home/tomphon
20        /home/nfs-home/tompsoca
5856      /home/nfs-home/vanhall
657543    /home/nfs-home/verdera
79248     /home/nfs-home/vobollas
24552     /home/nfs-home/waldok
martyp $
```

This is much more managable for large directories. I never would have been able to include the output for *home* in this book without using the summary, because there are roughly 1000 users in this directory.

I encourage users to issue this command on their home directories occasionally so that they'll know the amount of disk space they're consuming. In a development environment it is common for a directory in which you are working to grow very quickly with copies of a code. **du** shows exactly the space your directories are consuming so yhat you know the significant ones from the insignficant ones in terms of space consumed.

man page

du - 12

System Backup

System administrators spend a lot of time worrying about system backup and recovery. I'll talk about some backup and recovery concepts in this section and then cover some backup commands found on most UNIX variants. These commands are widely used because they are available on most systems. In very sophisticated UNIX environments, however, there are very elaborate backup and recovery programs provide advanced functionality. At some point, these programs usually end up calling one of the common programs I'll cover in this section.

To begin, let's consider why you perform backups. A backup is a means of recovering from any system-related problem. System-related problems range from a disk hardware problem that ruins every byte of data on your disk to a user who accidentally deletes a file he or she really needs. The disk hardware problem is a worst-case scenario: You will need an entire (full) backup of your system performed regularly in order to recover from this. The minor problem that your user has created can be recovered from with regular incremental backups. This means you need to perform full system backups regularly and incremental backups as often as possible. Depending on the amount of disk space you have and the backup device you will use, you may be in the comfortable position of performing backups as often as you want. Assuming that you have the backup device, what is the full and incremental backup technique you should employ? I am a strong advocate of performing a full backup, and then performing incremental backups of every file that has changed since the **last full backup**. This means that to recover from a completely "hosed" (a technical term meaning *destroyed*) system, you need your full backup tape and only one incremental tape. If, for instance, you performed a full backup on Sunday and an incremental backup on Monday through Friday, you would need to load only Sunday's full backup tape and Friday's incremental backup tape to completely restore your system.

Here is a brief overview of some commonly used backup programs:

tar   **tar** is the most popular generic backup utility. You will find that many applications are shipped on **tar** tapes. This is the most widely used format for exchanging data with other UNIX systems. **tar** is the oldest UNIX backup method and therefore runs on all UNIX systems. You can append files to the end of a **tar** tape. When sending files to another UNIX user, I would strongly recommend **tar**. **tar** is as slow as molasses, so you won't want to use it for your full or incremental backups. One highly desirable aspect of **tar** is that when you load files onto a tape with **tar** and then restore them onto another system, the original users and groups are retained. For instance, to back up all files belonging to frank and load them onto another system, you would use the following commands:

$ **cd /home/frank**

$ **tar -cvf /dev/rmt/0m** .

The **c** option creates a new **tar** file, the **v** option produces a verbose output, and the **f** option indicates the file or device to be used for the backup, which is the device file **/dev/rmt/0m**. The dot indicates that the backup will start in the present working directory. You could then load frank's files on another system even if the user frank and his group don't yet exist on that system.

cpio   **cpio** is also portable and easy to use, like **tar**. In addition, **cpio** is much faster than **tar**. **cpio** is good for replicating directory trees. **cpio** supports the incremental backup discussed earlier. You simply give **cpio** a list of files and it will perform a backup.

dd   This is a bit-for-bit copy. It is not smart in the sense that it does not copy files and ownerships; it just copies bits. You could not, therefore, select only a file from a **dd** tape as you could with **tar** or **cpio**. **dd** is widely used for copying data from one disk to another to create a mirror image of the first disk.

dump and **ufsdump**

dump and **ufsdump** (depending on your UNIX variant) are programs for producing full or incremental backups. You can specify "levels" of dump which specify the type of incremental backup. You can perform an incremental backup since the last full backup, since the last incrememtal backup, and so on. There are as many as 10 levels of backup you can specify with these commands. Level 0 is the lowest level which is a full backup. You can also specify that a dump record be updated so that you can keep track of when full and incremental backups were performed. You can specify the tape device to which you want to dump information or use a file as the dump destination. Files can later be recoverd with **restore** or **ufsrestore**, again depending on which command is supported by your UNIX variant.

Scheduling Cron Jobs

You can schedule periodic execution of tasks using the **cron** daemon. The **cron** daemon starts when the system boots and remains running.

cron works by reading configuration files and acting on their contents. A typical configuration would have in it the command to be run, the day and time to run the command, and the username under which the command should be run. You can look at this scheduling of jobs as a way of issuing commands at a specific time. The configuration files are called **crontab** files.

The **crontab** file is used to schedule jobs that are automatically executed by **cron**. **crontab** files are usually in the **/var/spool/cron/crontabs** directory. The Red Hat Linux system on which some of the upcoming examples were run are in **/var/spool/cron**.

man page

cron - 12

The format of entries in the **crontab** file are as follows:

minute hour monthday month weekday user name command

minute - the minute of the hour, from 0-59

hour - the hour of the day, from 0-23

monthday - the day of the month, from 1-31

month - the month of the year, from 1-12

weekday - the day of the week, from 0 (Sunday) - 6 (Saturday)

user name - the user who will run the command if necessary (not used in the example)

command - specifies the command line or script file to run

Please be sure to check your UNIX variant to ensure that **crontab** entries are in the same format and that the entries are in the same order.

You have many options in the **crontab** file for specifying the *minute, hour, monthday, month,* and *weekday* to perform a task. You could list one entry in a field and then a space, several entries in any field separated by a comma, two entries separated by a dash indicating a range, or an asterisk, which corresponds to all possible entries for the field.

Let's create the simplest imaginable example to see how **cron** works. We'll create a file called **listing** with the following contents in our home directory (*/root* on a Linux system):

```
* * * * * ls -l / > /root/listing.out
```

This file will produce a long listing of the root directory every minute and send the output to **listing.out** in our home directory.

To "activate" or "install" the **crontab** we simply issue the **crontab** command and the name of the file. We could also specify a username if you wanted to associate the file with a specific user. After installing the **crontab** file, we can issue **crontab -l** to view the installed **crontab** files. The following example shows the process of working with our **crontab** file called **listing**:

man page

cat - 3

man page

ls - 2

```
[root@linux1 /root]# cat listing
* * * * * ls -l / > /root/listing.out
[root@linux1 /root]# crontab listing
[root@linux1 /root]# crontab -l
# DO NOT EDIT THIS FILE - edit the master and reinstall.
# (listing installed on Fri Aug  6 10:40:03 )
# (Cron version -- $Id: crontab.c,v 2.13 03:20:37 vixie Exp $)
* * * * * ls -l / > /root/listing.out
[root@linux1 /root]# ls -l
total 640
-rw-------    1 root     root       647168 Aug  5 23:22 core
-rw-------    1 root     root            7 Aug  6 10:14 dead.letter
-rw-r--r--    1 root     root           39 Aug  6 10:16 listing
-rw-r--r--    1 root     root          909 Aug  6 10:41 listing.out
-rw-------    1 root     root          516 Aug  6 10:15 mbox
-rw-r--r--    1 root     root            0 Aug  6 10:39 typescript
[root@linux1 /root]# cat listing.out
total 1182
drwxr-xr-x    2 root     root         2048 Jun 18 19:38 bin
drwxr-xr-x    2 root     root         1024 Jun 18 19:41 boot
-rw-------    1 root     root      1138688 Aug  5 23:21 core
drwxr-xr-x    5 root     root        34816 Aug  6 09:21 dev
drwxr-xr-x   29 root     root         3072 Aug  6 09:21 etc
drwxr-xr-x    3 root     root         1024 Jun 18 19:36 home
drwxr-xr-x    4 root     root         3072 Jun 18 19:36 lib
drwxr-xr-x    2 root     root        12288 Jun 18 19:26 lost+found
drwxr-xr-x    4 root     root         1024 Jun 18 19:27 mnt
dr-xr-xr-x   56 root     root            0 Aug  6 05:20 proc
drwxr-x---    9 root     root         1024 Aug  6 10:39 root
drwxr-xr-x    3 root     root         2048 Jun 18 19:39 sbin
drwxrwxrwt    6 root     root         1024 Aug  6 10:15 tmp
drwxr-xr-x   20 root     root         1024 Jun 18 19:33 usr
drwxr-xr-x   15 root     root         1024 Jun 18 19:39 var
[root@linux1 /root]# crontab -r
[root@linux1 /root]# crrontab -l
no crontab for root
[root@linux1 /root]#
```

The first command shows the contents of the file **listing** that we created. Next we issue the **crontab** command to install **listing**. Next we issue **crontab -l** to see the file we have installed. Next is a long listing of our home directory, which shows that the file **listing.out** has indeed been produced. Then we **cat** the file to see its contents. Then we remove the installed file with **crontab -r**. Issuing **crontab -l** as the last command shows that there are no **crontab** files installed for the user root.

man page

cat - 3

System administrators get a lot of use out of **cron** by scheduling many time- and resource-consuming jobs during off hours. A typical task that is scheduled at night are backups.

man page

cron - 12

The following hybrid example shows how a system administrator would schedule the full backup on day 6 and the incremental backup on other days. This is a hybrid example whereby you would substitute actual commands for the "full backup command" and "incremental backup commands":

```
$ crontab -l


00 2 * * 6 full backup command
15 12 * * 1-5 incremental backup command
```

The first entry is the full backup, and the second entry is the incremental backup. In the first entry, the *minute* is 00; in the second entry, the *minute* is 15. In the first entry, the *hour* is 2; in the second entry, the *hour* is 12. In both entries, the *monthday* and *month* are all legal values (*), meaning every *monthday* and *month*. In the first entry, the *weekday* is 6 for Saturday (0 is Sunday); in the second entry, the *weekdays* are 1-5, or Monday through Friday. The optional *username* is not specified in either example. And finally, the backup command is provided.

minute	hour	monthday	month	weekday	user name	command
00	2	all	all	6	n/a	full backup
15	12	all	all	1-5	n/a	incremental

man page

cron - 12

man page

find - 12

Another common use of **cron** for system administrators is to find *core* files on a daily or weekly basis. *Core* files are images of memory written to disk when a problem of some kind is encountered on the system. They can be written in a variety of places on the system depending on the problem. These files can sometimes be used to identify the source of the problem, so system administrators like to keep track of them. The following **find** command will be run once a week to find *core* files that have not been accessed in a week and writes the *core* file names to a file in the home directory of root:

```
00 2 * * 6 find / -name core -atime 7 > /root/core.files
```

The system administrator will check this file on Monday to see what core files have been produced over the last week. Like our backup example, this check is run every Saturday at 2:00.

Users sometimes set up **cron** entries to invoke large compilations or large batch jobs during the night when the system is not heavily used. As long as your system administrator has not denied you access to running **cron** jobs, you are free to set up your own jobs. Your system administrator can list users who are permitted to use **cron** in the **cron.allow** file. If you are not listed in this file, the format of which is one user per line, then you cannot run the **crontab** program. If **cron.allow** does not exist, then **cron.deny** is checked to see whether there are any users who have been explicitly denied access to **crontab**.

cron is very easy to use. Simply create your file, such I as had done with **listing** in the earlier example, and run **crontab** against the file. If you have jobs you would like to see run on a regular basis, such as running your **make** at night, **cron** is a useful tool.

If you have a command you wish to schedule to run only one time, you can use the **at** command. You can specify the **at** command, the *time* at which you want a command executed, and then at the "at>"

prompt, the *command* to execute. The following shows an example to remove all core files in **/home/martyp** at 9:00 P.M.:

```
$ at 9:00PM
at> find /home/martyp -name core exec rm {} \;
at>                                        type ^d (control d)
$
```

After issuing **at** and the time the "at>" prompt appears for you to issue the *command*. You then press **^d** (control d) at the next prompt to return to your usual shell prompt.

Networking

Networking is covered extensively in Chapter 11. This is a topic on which system administrators spend a great deal of time both in setup and maintenance, so much so that there are books devoted to networking topics. Chapter 11 covers networking from a user perspective but has more of a system administration tone to it than the other chapters, because many important networking commands are covered, including **ping**, **route**, **ifconfig**, **netstat**, and others. Your system administrator has undoubtedly spent a lot of time planning how your systems fit into the network and configuring them to support this plan. You reap the benefits of this work by having the use of remote file systems mounted as if they were local to your system with NFS, by accessing other systems through remote login with **rlogin**, and many other important network functions. Please see the Networking chapter to view how many important networking commands are used.

man page

ping - 9

man page

route - 9

man page

ifconfig - 9

man page

netstat - 9

syslog and Log Files

When your system administrator encounters a problem of some type on your system they immediately start looking through system log files. Log files are produced from a variety of sources, including utilities and the kernel. There are many log files on a typical UNIX system, but we'll take a look at the most commonly used log file in this section called **syslog**.

Most log files appear in **/var/log**, one of its subdirectories, **/var/adm**, or one of its subdirectories. Unfortunately there is usually a little hunting around required to find log files. Almost all UNIX variants put log files somewhere under **/var**, so at least you have a place to start your search. Some log files require superuser rights to access, so you cannot read all log files on your system.

The most often used log file is **syslog**. It is called the system event logger because it is a comprehensive logging utility. It includes many facilities, so the kernel, mail system, printer spooler, **cron**, and many other programs can use it.

syslog consists of several parts, including a daemon, library routines, and a logger. In all likelihood, your system is running the daemon called **syslogd**. You can check this with **ps**.

The result of using **syslog** is a log file that you can view should you encounter a problem with your system. You'll get messages of varying degrees of importance in **syslog** ranging from nothing more than informational messages to panic situations.

dmesg

Another tool used to report system information is **dmesg**. It looks in the system buffer for recently printed diagnostic messages. It is most often used to print messages produced at the time of system boot. This capability is very helpful in determining what hardware exists on your system. You don't normally have to be superuser to run this command.

The Kernel

The kernel is the heart of the UNIX system. Its configuration and maintenance are the domain of the system administrator. In this section, I'll give a description of the kernel, including the important functionality it provides that is often taken for granted by system users.

In very general terms, the UNIX operating system consists of three levels: hardware, UNIX kernel, and user-level programs.

In this book, we have not discussed hardware, because UNIX is a highly versatile operating system that runs on such a wide variety of hardware that no one could cover it in a book. The vast majority of what we are covering in this book takes place at the user level. Even the commands normally associated with system administration work take place at the user level. The kernel takes care of the interface between all the user-level commands and programs we run and the hardware.

An example of the way in which the kernel handles this interface between hardware and user-level programs is the file system. Every time you make a request to read a file, the kernel handles the interface between the hardware you are accessing to view the file and the user request to read the file.

Another example of functionality provided by the kernel is the illusion that you, as a user, have exclusive use of the system. On most UNIX systems, only a small number of programs can be executing at one time; however, your system may have many programs that need to be run simultaneously. The kernel manages which processes will be using the system CPU(s) at a given time and controls the passing of the CPU(s) from one process to another. This *context switching* takes place many times per second and is one of the most complex functions of the kernel.

System administrators typically update the kernel on a regular basis. There are parameters in the kernel which may need to be *tuned* in order to improve system performance. There are kernel modules, such as those required to support specific hardware, that may need to be included in the kernel.

Many advanced UNIX systems allow modules to be loaded dynamically, while the system is running, without disrupting the users on the system.

To support dynamically loadable kernel modules there is usually an infrastructure providing for a separate system file for each module. Specially created modules can be loaded or unloaded into the kernel without having to reboot the system. This is advanced functionality that is finding its way into more and more UNIX variants.

Your system administrator is solely responsible for the maintaining the kernel; however, all users on the system interact with the kernel with most every command you execute.

Device Files

Device files on UNIX systems allow programs to communicate with system hardware. In the previous section covering the kernel, I talked about the way in which the kernel supports the hardware on your UNIX system. A device driver is loaded into the kernel to ensure that the hardware with which you need to communicate will be handled by the kernel.

Generally speaking, device files on UNIX systems are character or block devices. Character devices expect the driver and other aspects of the UNIX system to manage input and output buffering of data. Block devices expect the filesystem and kernel to perform buffering for them. Most hard disk drives have both a block and character device file. This provides flexibility in the way in which the hardware is used.

A device file provides the UNIX kernel with important information about a specific device. The UNIX kernel needs to know a lot about a device before input/output operations can be performed. Device files are normally found in the **/dev** directory. There may also be a subdirectory under **/dev** used to further categorize the device files. An example of a subdirectory would be **/dev/dsk,** where disk device files are usually located, and **/dev/rmt**, where tape drive device files are located. To give you an idea of what a device file looks like, I have included Figure 12-4, which shows an HP-UX example that is a common device file naming convention.

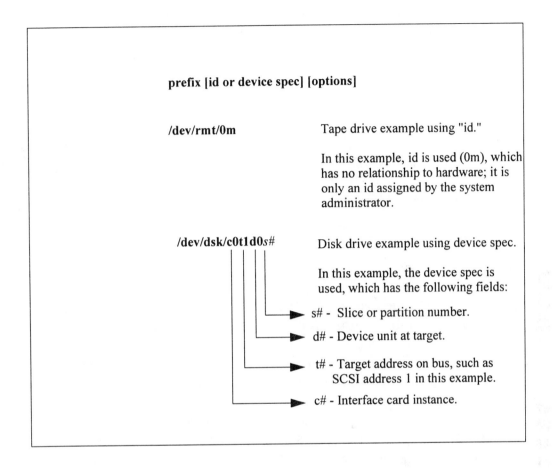

prefix [id or device spec] [options]

/dev/rmt/0m   Tape drive example using "id."

In this example, id is used (0m), which has no relationship to hardware; it is only an id assigned by the system administrator.

/dev/dsk/c0t1d0s#   Disk drive example using device spec.

In this example, the device spec is used, which has the following fields:

s# - Slice or partition number.

d# - Device unit at target.

t# - Target address on bus, such as SCSI address 1 in this example.

c# - Interface card instance.

Figure 12-4 Common Device File Naming Convention

Notice that the disk description for **/dev/dsk/c0t1d0** has slice, or partition, number appearing at the very end of the device file. Some UNIX systems slice up a disk into sections and others use a high-level volume manager to control the way in which disks are used. You may or may not see section numbers on your disks, depending on the way in which disk management takes place.

The following two examples show long listings of the devices from Figure 12-4. The first long listing is that of the tape drive, and the second is the disk:

man page

ls- 2

```
$ ls -l /dev/rmt/0m


crw-rw-rw- 2 bin bin 205 0x003000 Feb 12 03:00 /dev/rmt/0m


$ ls -l /dev/dsk/c0t1d0


brw-r----- 1 bin sys 31 0x001000 Feb 12 03:01 /dev/dsk/
c0t1d0
```

Notice in the device file long listing that there is not a slice, or partition, number in the **/dev/dsk/c0t1d0** listing. The system from which this long listing was obtained employs a volume manager solution that handles the way in which disks are configured and managed. The disks are not sliced in this arrangement; therefore, no disk slices are shown in the example.

There are some important components of which every device file is comprised on UNIX systems. The first is the major number and the second is the minor number. The major number refers to the device driver that the kernel will use for accessing the device. The minor number informs the kernel and device driver what physical unit connected to the system to address. In the disk example above, we have a major number of 31 for the disk driver and a minor number of 0x001000. These numbers may very well look much different on your UNIX variant.

The tape drive device file, **/dev/rmt/0m**, shows a major number of 205 corresponding to that shown for the *character* device driver *stape*. The disk drive device file, **/dev/dsk/c0t6d0**, shows a major number of 31 corresponding to the *block* device driver *sdisk*. Because the tape drive requires only a character device file, this is the only device file that exists for the tape drive. The disk, on the other hand, may be used as either a block device or a character device (also referred to as the *raw device*). Therefore, we should see a character device file, **/dev/rdsk/c0t6d0**, with a major number of 188, as shown in the following example:

```
$ ls /dev/rdsk/c0t0d0
```

```
crw-r-----  1  root  sys  188  0x001000  Feb  12  03:01
/dev/rdsk/c0t1d0
```

The major and minor numbers, as well as the device file naming convention, are different among UNIX variants. In general, though, you will see a major number and minor number associated with device files on all UNIX variants. As a user, you will probably not interact with device files names and numbers; however, this background is good to know.

Software Management

Most UNIX variants have a means of managing software that consists of a series of related commands that allow you to work with software. The basis for software management is software packages. Software packages are typically a group of related files, and the commands are a set of utilities that allow you to work with the packages. Although software packages are conceptually somewhat similar, the names of the utilities and their specific operation is different among UNIX variants.

The utilities allow you to perform a lot of useful tasks related to software packages, such as: getting information about packages; adding and removing packages; checking packages; and so on.

System administrators usually have to become intimately familar with software management, because the operating system, applications, patches, and other software are loaded and maintained from the software utilities running on the UNIX variant.

The names of software management utilities usually give a good indication of the function of the utility. The following examples list some of the software utilities from Solaris and HP-UX.

Solaris *pkg* commands:

man page

ls - 2

```
martyp $ ls -l /usr/sbin/pkg*
-r-xr-xr-x   2 root      sys      102980 Oct   6  1998 /usr/sbin/pkgadd
-r-xr-xr-x   2 root      sys      102980 Oct   6  1998 /usr/sbin/pkgask
-r-xr-xr-x   1 root      sys      157836 Oct   6  1998 /usr/sbin/pkgchk
-r-xr-xr-x   1 root      sys       51084 Oct   6  1998 /usr/sbin/pkgmv
-r-xr-xr-x   1 root      sys       81296 Oct   6  1998 /usr/sbin/pkgrm

martyp $ ls -l /usr/bin/pkg*
-r-xr-xr-x   1 bin       sys       97108 Oct   6  1998 /usr/bin/pkginfo
-r-xr-xr-x   1 bin       bin      118348 Oct   6  1998 /usr/bin/pkgmk
-r-xr-xr-x   1 bin       sys       84356 Oct   6  1998 /usr/bin/pkgparam
-r-xr-xr-x   1 bin       bin       29848 Oct   6  1998 /usr/bin/pkgproto
-r-xr-xr-x   1 bin       bin       68112 Oct   6  1998 /usr/bin/pkgtrans
```

HP-UX *sw* commands:

```
martyp $ ls -l /usr/sbin/sw*
-r-sr-xr-x  11 root      bin     1609728 Dec 15  1998 /usr/sbin/swacl
-r-xr-xr-x   1 bin       bin      446464 Dec 15  1998 /usr/sbin/swagentd
-r-xr--r--   1 bin       bin       16384 Jun 10  1996 /usr/sbin/swapinfo
-r-xr-xr-x   1 bin       bin       24576 Jun 10  1996 /usr/sbin/swapon
-r-xr-xr-x   1 bin       bin       71992 May 30  1996 /usr/sbin/swcluster
-r-sr-xr-x  11 root      bin     1609728 Dec 15  1998 /usr/sbin/swconfig
-r-sr-xr-x  11 root      bin     1609728 Dec 15  1998 /usr/sbin/swcopy
-r-sr-xr-x  11 root      bin     1609728 Dec 15  1998 /usr/sbin/swdepot
-r-sr-xr-x  11 root      bin     1609728 Dec 15  1998 /usr/sbin/swinstall
-r-sr-xr-x  11 root      bin     1609728 Dec 15  1998 /usr/sbin/swjob
-r-sr-xr-x  11 root      bin     1609728 Dec 15  1998 /usr/sbin/swlist
-r-sr-xr-x   2 root      bin      770048 Nov 24  1998 /usr/sbin/swmodify
-r-sr-xr-x   2 root      bin      770048 Nov 24  1998 /usr/sbin/swpackage
-r-sr-xr-x  11 root      bin     1609728 Dec 15  1998 /usr/sbin/swreg
-r-sr-xr-x  11 root      bin     1609728 Dec 15  1998 /usr/sbin/swremove
-r-sr-xr-x  11 root      bin     1609728 Dec 15  1998 /usr/sbin/swverify
```

AIX software management-related commands include **lslpp**, **installp**, and **lppchk**.

Most UNIX variants also supply a graphical interface through which software management can be performed. This interface can usually be invoked from the primary system administration manager running on the system as well. Figure 12-5 shows a screen shot of the graphical utility on Red Hat Linux called **rpm**.

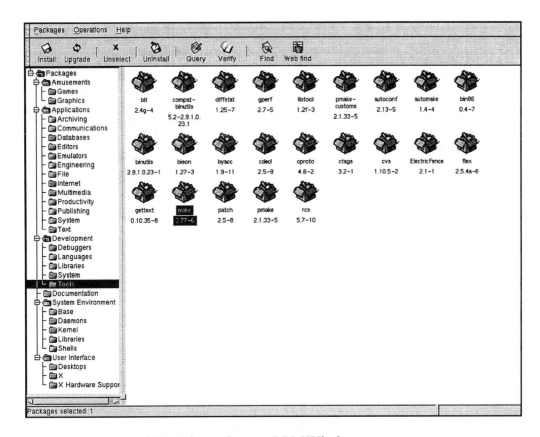

Figure 12-5 Red Hat Linux *Gnome RPM* Window

The left side of the *Gnome RPM* window shows the categories of software packages. The package categories are: *Amusements*, *Applications*, *Development*, *System Environment*, and *User Interface*. I have selected *Tools* under *Development*. The right side of the window shows the tool packages that are loaded with *make* selected. You can see in the top of this window that after selecting a package, we can perform a variety of tasks such as *Insall*, *Upgrade*, *Unselect*, and so on. If we select *Query*, the window shown in Figure 12-6 appears:

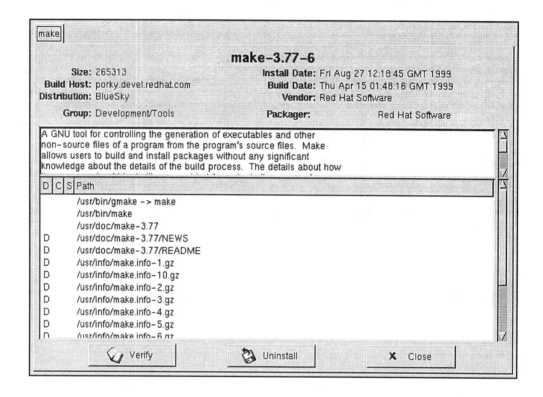

| make |

make-3.77-6

Size: 265313   **Install Date:** Fri Aug 27 12:18:45 GMT 1999
Build Host: porky.devel.redhat.com   **Build Date:** Thu Apr 15 01:48:16 GMT 1999
Distribution: BlueSky   **Vendor:** Red Hat Software

Group: Development/Tools   **Packager:**   Red Hat Software

A GNU tool for controlling the generation of executables and other
non-source files of a program from the program's source files. Make
allows users to build and install packages without any significant
knowledge about the details of the build process. The details about how

D	C	S	Path
			/usr/bin/gmake -> make
			/usr/bin/make
			/usr/doc/make-3.77
D			/usr/doc/make-3.77/NEWS
D			/usr/doc/make-3.77/README
D			/usr/info/make.info-1.gz
D			/usr/info/make.info-10.gz
D			/usr/info/make.info-2.gz
D			/usr/info/make.info-3.gz
D			/usr/info/make.info-4.gz
D			/usr/info/make.info-5.gz
D			/usr/info/make.info-6.gz

Verify   Uninstall   X   Close

Figure 12-6 Red Hat Linux *Package Info* Window

Figure 12-6 contains a lot of useful information about the *make* package we have selected, such as the revision of the software package, its size, and so on.

We could have obtained much of the same information using **rpm** at the command line. The following example shows issuing the **rpm** command with options to produce information about **make**:

```
[root@linux1 /root]# rpm --query -qiv make

Name        : make                     Relocations: /usr
Version     : 3.77                          Vendor: Red Hat Software
Release     : 6                         Build Date: Thu Apr 15 09:48:16 1999
Install date: Fri Aug 27 08:18:45 1999  Build Host: porky.devel.redhat.com
Group       : Development/Tools         Source RPM: make-3.77-6.src.rpm
Size        : 265313                       License: GPL
Packager    : Red Hat Software <http://developer.redhat.com/bugzilla>
Summary     : A GNU tool which simplifies the build process for users.
Description :
A GNU tool for controlling the generation of executables and other
non-source files of a program from the program's source files.  Make
allows users to build and install packages without any significant
knowledge about the details of the build process.  The details about how
the program should be built are provided for make in the program's
makefile.

The GNU make tool should be installed on your system because it .is
commonly used to simplify the process of installing programs.
```

Some system administrators prefer to work with the command line vs. the graphical version of tools such as **rpm**. Most other UNIX variants also include graphical interfaces to software managment tools as well as general management tools, as we had seen earlier in the chapter. In any event, you can usually achieve the same result on UNIX systems a variety of different ways, and when it comes to system administration in particular, the method you use is purely a matter of preference.

Printing

UNIX systems run a variety of programs related to printing called *lp* (for line printing). These programs work together to support printing of text files, formatted documents, graphics files, and so on. We'll cover the basics of printing in this section, including some of the basics of printer administration.

To simply print a file, called **mbox** you would use the **lp** command, as shown in the following example:

```
martyp $ lp mbox
Job number is: 1
martyp $
```

In this example, we have requested that the file **mbox** be printed. You receive a return message from **lp**, indicating the request identification number. You can print multiple files with one **lp** request, as shown in the following example:

man page

ls - 2

```
martyp $ ls -l
total 80
-rw-------   1 martyp    usr    350 Sep 27 07:22 dead.letter
-rw-rw-r--   1 martyp    usr  24576 Sep  6 07:07 inst.out
-rw-rw-r--   1 martyp    usr      0 Aug 21 06:45 lanadmin.list
-rw-------   1 martyp    usr   1485 Sep 27 08:20 mbox
-rw-rw-r--   1 martyp    usr    353 Sep 29 04:57 trip
-rw-rw-r--   1 martyp    perf   635 Mar 21 1999  typescript
martyp $ lp t*
Job number is: 2
martyp $
```

In this example, both files beginning with "t" were printed, and one job number is associated with the printing of both files.

Many UNIX systems have multiple printers connected. You can specify the printer you want to send the file(s) to with the **-d** option followed by the printer name. In the previous examples, we went to the default system printer. We can specify the printer device to which our earlier print of **mbox** will go with the **-d** option, as shown in the following example:

```
martyp $ lp -d ros2228 mbox
Job number is: 3
martyp $
```

This output sends the file *test* to the printer we have specified, and again the job number is specified.

You can specify a default printer, which will be used when you do not specify a printer name, as shown in the following exmaple:

```
martyp $ LPDEST=ros2228
martyp $ export LPDEST
martyp $ lp mbox
Job number is: 4
martyp $
```

The **LPDEST** environment variable is normally associated with a user's default printer. You can also specify the default printer in your startup file.

Print jobs are spooled to a printer so that you can proceed with other work. You don't have to wait until a print job completes without a problem before you move on. You can receive an electronic mail message if there was any problem with your print job using the **-m** option as shown in the following example:

```
martyp $ lp -m t*
Job number is: 5
martyp $
```

In this case, we have again sent the two files beginning with "t" to the default printer we earlier set up. You can assume this print job will complete without any problem unless you receive an electronic mail message informing you otherwise.

You would sometimes like to see the status of printers. The spooling functionality means that several files may be spooled to the printer, which means that you may have to wait for your file to print. There may only be one file ahead of yours in the print queue; however, it may be a very large file such as a report from an ERP system. To obtain the status of printers you use the **lpstat** command. I normally issue this with the **-t** option to obtain a long status listing, as shown in the following example:

```
martyp $ lpstat -t
Queue    Dev   Status      Job    Name        From              To
                           Submitted         Rnk Pri   Blks  Cp          PP %
-------  ----- ---------   ---------         --- ---   ----- ---         ---- --
a464     a464d READY
a464:
         no entries
a438     a438d READY
a438:
         no entries
a570     a570d READY
a570:
         no entries
a654     a654d READY
a654:
         no entries
a662     a662d READY
a662:

a662:

a662:

a662:

a946     a946d READY
a946:
         no entries
a956     a956d READY
a956:
         no entries
a732     a732d READY
a732: ros-ps4: Warning: a732 is down

a732: ros-ps4: Warning: a732 is down

a732: ros-ps4: Warning: a732 is down

a732: ros-ps4: Warning: a732 is down

a732: ros-ps4: Warning: a732 is down

a732: ros-ps4: Warning: a732 is down

a732: ros-ps4: Warning: a732 is down

a732: ros-ps4: Warning: a732 is down

a732: ros-ps4: Warning: a732 is down

a732: ros-ps4: Warning: a732 is down

a732: ros-ps4: Warning: a732 is down

ros2227 ros22 READY
ros2227:
         no entries
ros2228 ros22 READY
ros2228:

ros2228:

ros2228:

ros2228:

ros2228:

ros2228:

ros2228:
```

```
    ros2228:

    ros2228:

    ros2228:

    ros2228:

    ros2228:

    ros2228:

    ros2228:

    ros2228:

martyp $
```

The output shows the status of all printers. You can see in this example that there are many printers connected to this system. I removed several printers from this output, because it was too long to include in the book. Several of the printers report warning messages indicating that they are "down," which of course means that they are unable to print. We won't get into the troubleshooting of such problems here, because this is almost exclusively a problem that would be handled by the system administrator. If you wish to obtain the status of a the default printer, which we just set up, you can do so with the **-d** option, as shown in the following example:

```
martyp $ lpstat -d
Queue   Dev   Status    Job Files             User        PP %  Blks Cp Rnk
------- ----- --------- --- ------------------ ---------- ---- -- ----- --- ---
ros2228 ros22 READY
ros2228:
ros2228:
ros2228:
ros2228:
ros2228:
ros2228:
martyp $
```

I often pull the trigger too quickly on a print job and need to cancel it. After a job is submitted, you can remove it with the **cancel** command, along with the job id. You can use the *job number* shown in earlier examples, along with the cancel command or use the printer name along with **cancel**. Small print jobs will normally be processed and printed too quickly to **cancel**. Large print jobs, however, may be canceled before they are complete.

The **lpstat** command can be used to obtain the job number, in the event that you did not write it down when you submitted the job.

Table 12-2 lists some of the most commonly used lp-related commands. Keep in mind that some of these are associated with system administration work, such as configuring printers and are not normally used by users.

Table 12-2   lp Commands

Command	Description
/usr/sbin/accept	Start accepting jobs to be queued
/usr/bin/cancel	Cancel a print job that is queued
/usr/bin/disable	Disable a device for printing
/usr/bin/enable	Enable a device for printing
/usr/sbin/lpfence	Set minimum priority for spooled file to be printed (not available on all UNIX variants)
/usr/bin/lp	Queue a job or jobs for printing
/usr/sbin/lpadmin	Configure the printing system with the options provided
/usr/sbin/lpmove	Move printing jobs from one device to another
/usr/sbin/lpsched	Start the **lp** scheduling daemon
/usr/sbin/lpshut	Stop the **lp** scheduling daemon
/usr/bin/lpstat	Show the status of printing based on the options provided
/usr/sbin/reject	Stop accepting jobs to be queued

Graphical-Based Management Tools

Most UNIX variants come with a graphical-based system management tool. More precisely, these are menu-driven tools that have both a character and graphical interface, although some come in graphical-only form. Most any system administration function can be performed with a graphical tool including the topics covered in this chapter. There is no standard for such tools, so you'll find that they are different among UNIX variants. Some system administrators perform all their work at the command line, others will perform basic tasks with a graphical tool, and others will perform all but a few system administration tasks with a graphical tool. The method depends on the preference of the system administrator. I have found in 20 years of UNIX use that these tools have gone from non-existent to satisfactory. Many system administrators with whom I work like graphical system administration tools and use them frequently.

The following Figures show the top-level interface that you see when using the graphical system administration tools on Solaris, HP-UX, AIX, and Red Hat Linux, respectively. You really can't gauge much from only a screen shot of the top level other than to see the categories of tasks you can perform. You need to use a tool and find its nuances to determine whether or not it is useful. In general, I think that most UNIX variants have done a good job supplying such tools.

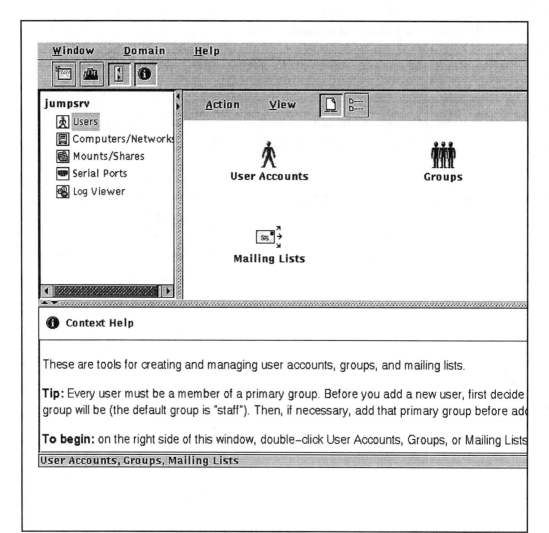

Figure 12-7   Solaris Graphical System Administration Tool - *Users* Top,
Software Bottom. *Browse* Categories Are: *Users, Groups, Hosts,
Printers, Serial Ports,* and *Software.*

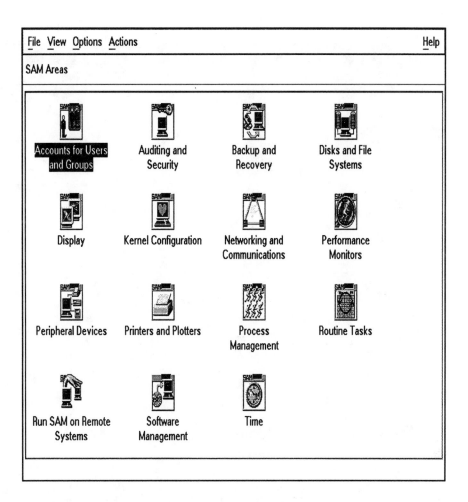

File View Options Actions   Help

SAM Areas

Accounts for Users and Groups Auditing and Security Backup and Recovery Disks and File Systems

Display Kernel Configuration Networking and Communications Performance Monitors

Peripheral Devices Printers and Plotters Process Management Routine Tasks

Run SAM on Remote Systems Software Management Time

Figure 12-8 HP-UX Graphical System Administration Tool

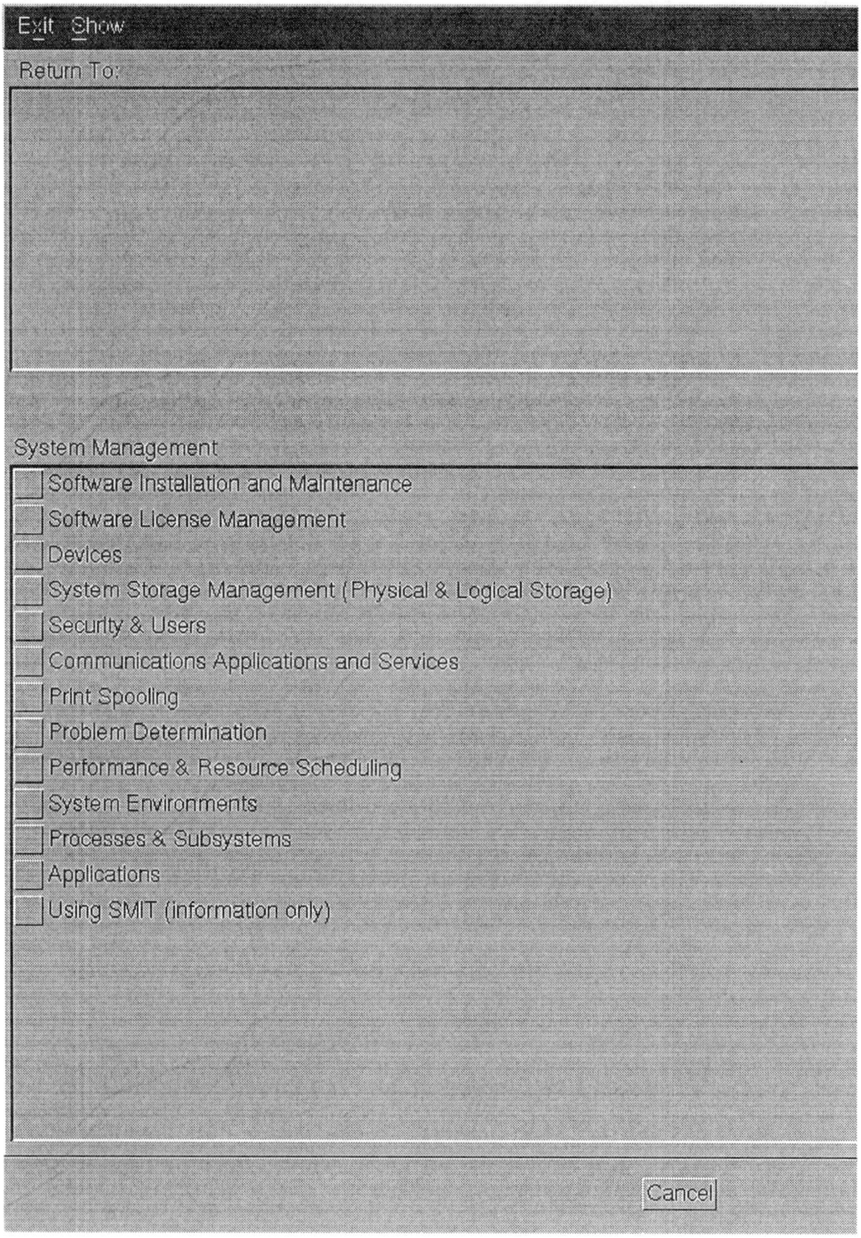

Figure 12-9 AIX Graphical System Administration Tool

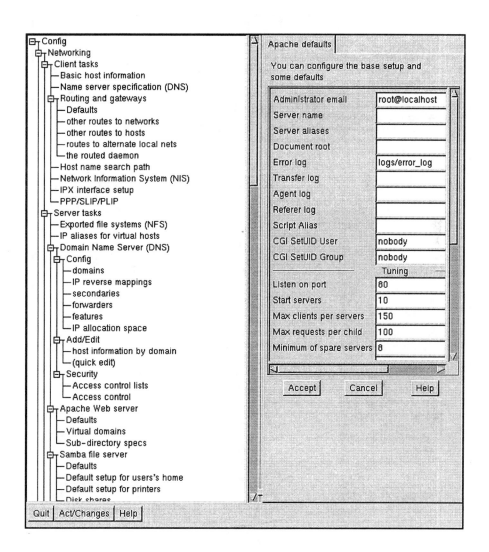

Figure 12-10
Red Hat Linux Graphical System Administration Tool - 1 of 3

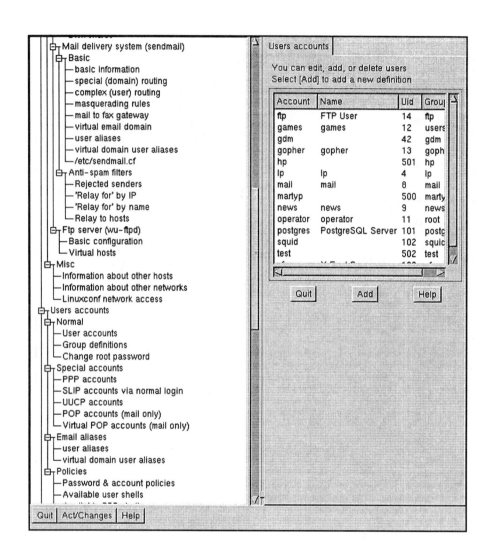

Figure 12-11 Red Hat Linux Graphical System Administration Tool - 2 of 3

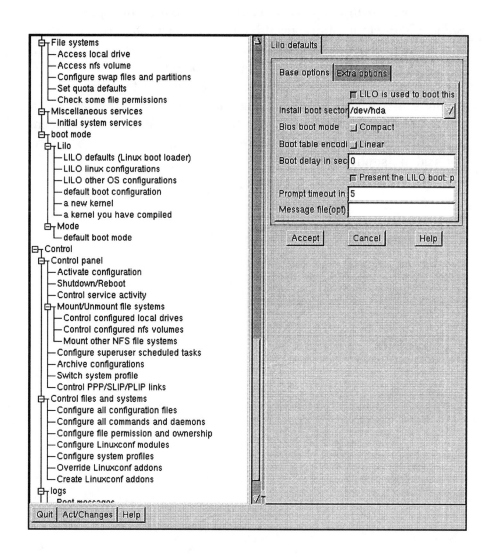

Figure 12-12 Red Hat Linux Graphical System Administration Tool - 3 of 3

As a user, you won't be able to use such a tool. You need special permission, usually superuser, to run a system administration tool. Some of these tools allow specified users to run a subset of the overall functionality, such as initiating backups and adding users, but prevent access to disk configuration and system shutdown.

Some of the tools provide control over many categories, and others are somewhat limited about what system administration tasks they allow you to control. You'll have to manually perform any system administration functions not automated as part of your UNIX variant's administration tool.

Manual Pages of Some Commands Used in Chapter 12

The following are the HP-UX manual pages for many of the commands used in the chapter. Commands often differ among UNIX variants, so you may find differences in the options or other areas for some commands; however, the following manual pages serve as an excellent reference.

cron

cron - Execute commands at specific dates and times.

---

cron(1M)   cron(1M)

NAME
     cron - timed-job execution daemon

SYNOPSIS

     /usr/sbin/cron

DESCRIPTION
     cron executes commands at specified dates and times. Regularly
     scheduled commands can be specified according to instructions placed
     in crontab files. Users can submit their own crontab files with a
     crontab command (see crontab(1)). Users can submit commands that are
     to be executed only once with an at or batch command.

     Since cron never exits, it should be executed only once. This is best
     done by running cron from the initialization process with the startup
     script /sbin/init.d/cron (see init(1M)).

     cron only establishes a schedule for crontab files and at/batch
     command files during process initialization and when it is notified by
     at, batch, or crontab that a file has been added, deleted, or
     modified.

     When cron executes a job, the job's user and group IDs are set to
     those of the user who submitted the job.

   Spring and Autumn Time Transitions
     On the days of daylight savings (summer) time transition (in time
     zones and countries where daylight savings time applies), cron
     schedules commands differently from normal.

     In the following description, an ambiguous time refers to an hour and
     minute that occurs twice in the same day because of a daylight savings
     time transition (usually on a day during the Autumn season). A
     nonexistent time refers to an hour and minute that does not occur
     because of a daylight savings time transition (usually on a day during
     the Spring season). DST-shift refers to the offset that is applied to
     standard time to result in daylight savings time. This is normally
     one hour, but can be any combination of hours and minutes up to 23
     hours and 59 minutes (see tztab(4)).

     When a command is specified to run at an ambiguous time, the command
     is executed only once at the first occurrence of the ambiguous time.

     When a command is specified to run at a nonexistent time, the command
     is executed after the specified time by an amount of time equal to the
     DST-shift. When such an adjustment would conflict with another time
     specified to run the command, the command is run only once rather than
     running the command twice at the same time.

Commands that are scheduled to run during all hours (there is a * is
in the hour field of the crontab entry) are scheduled without any
adjustment.

EXTERNAL INFLUENCES
     Environment Variables
          LANG determines the language in which messages are displayed.

          If LANG is not specified or is set to the empty string, it defaults to
          "C" (see lang(5)). If any internationalization variable contains an
          invalid setting, all internationalization variables default to "C"
          (see environ(5)).

DIAGNOSTICS
          A history of all actions taken by cron is recorded in
          /var/adm/cron/log.

EXAMPLES
          The following examples assume that the time zone is MST7MDT. In this
          time zone, the DST transition occurs one second before 2:00 a.m. and
          the DST-shift is 1 hour.

          Consider the following entries in a crontab file:

# Minute	Hour	Month	Day	Month	Weekday	Command
0	01	*	*	*		Job_1
0	02	*	*	*		Job_2
0	03	*	*	*		Job_3
0	04	*	*	*		Job_4
0	*	*	*	*		Job_hourly
0	2,3,4	*	*	*		Multiple_1
0	2,4	*	*	*		Multiple_2

          For the period of 1:00 a.m. to 4:00 a.m. on the days of DST
          transition, the results will be:

Job	Times Run in Fall	Times Run in Spring
Job_1	01:00 MDT	01:00 MST
Job_2	02:00 MDT	03:00 MDT
Job_3	03:00 MST	03:00 MDT
Job_4	04:00 MST	04:00 MDT
Job_hourly	01:00 MDT	01:00 MST
	02:00 MDT	
	02:00 MST	
	03:00 MST	03:00 MDT
	04:00 MST	04:00 MDT
Multiple_1	02:00 MDT	
	03:00 MST	03:00 MDT
	04:00 MST	04:00 MDT
Multiple_2	02:00 MDT	03:00 MDT
	04:00 MST	04:00 MDT

WARNINGS
     In the Spring, when there is a nonexistent hour because of daylight
     savings time, a command that is scheduled to run multiple times during
     the nonexistent hour will only be run once. For example, a command
     scheduled to run at 2:00 and 2:30 a.m. in the MST7MDT time zone will
     only run at 3:00 a.m. The command that was scheduled at 2:30 a.m.
     will not be run at all, instead of running at 3:30 a.m.

DEPENDENCIES
     HP Process Resource Manager
          If the optional HP Process Resource Management (PRM) software is

installed and configured, jobs are launched in the initial process
resource group of the user that scheduled the job. The user's initial
group is determined at the time the job is started, not when the job
is scheduled. If the user's initial group is not defined, the job
runs in the user default group (PRMID=1). See prmconfig(1) for a
description of how to configure HP PRM, and prmconf(4) for a
description of how the user's initial process resource group is
determined.

AUTHOR
      cron was developed by AT&T and HP.

FILES
      /var/adm/cron   Main cron directory
      /var/spool/cron/atjobs   Directory containing at and batch job
                                       files
      /var/spool/cron/crontabs   Directory containing crontab files
      /var/adm/cron/log   Accounting information

SEE ALSO
      at(1), crontab(1), sh(1), init(1M), cdf(4), queuedefs(4), tztab(4).

      HP Process Resource Manager:
            prmconfig(1), prmconf(4) in HP Process Resource Manager User's
            Guide.

STANDARDS CONFORMANCE
      cron: SVID2, SVID3

df

df - Report the amount of free disk blocks.

man page

df - 12

df(1M)   df(1M)

NAME
     df (generic) - report number of free file system disk blocks

SYNOPSIS
     /usr/bin/df [-F FStype] [-befgiklnv] [-t|-P] [-o specific_options] [-V]
        [special|directory]...

DESCRIPTION
     The df command displays the number of free 512-byte blocks and free
     inodes available for file systems by examining the counts kept in the
     superblock or superblocks. If a special or a directory is not
     specified, the free space on all mounted file systems is displayed.
     If the arguments to df are path names, df reports on the file systems
     containing the named files. If the argument to df is a special of an
     unmounted file system, the free space in the unmounted file system is
     displayed.

   Options
     df recognizes the following options:

          -b   Report only the number of kilobytes (KB) free.

          -e   Report the number of files free.

          -f   Report only the actual count of the blocks in the
                          free list (free inodes are not reported).

          -F FStype   Report only on the FStype file system type (see
                          fstyp(1M)).

          -g   Report the entire structure described in
                          statvfs(2).

          -i   Report the total number of inodes, the number of
                          free inodes, number of used inodes, and the
                          percentage of inodes in use.

          -k   Report the allocation in kilobytes (KB).

          -l   Report on local file systems only.

          -n   Report the file system name. If used with no
                          other options, display a list of mounted file
                          system types.

          -o specific_options
                          Specify options specific to each file system type.
                          specific_options is a comma-separated list of
                          suboptions intended for a specific FStype module

of the command. See the file-system-specific
manual entries for further details.

-P   Report the name of the file system, the size of
                the file system, the number of blocks used, the
                number of blocks free, the percentage of blocks
                used and the directory below which the file system
                hierarchy appears.

-t   Report the total allocated block figures and the
                number of free blocks.

-v   Report the percentage of blocks used, the number
                of blocks used, and the number of blocks free.
                This option cannot be used with other options.

-V   Echo the completed command line, but perform no
                other action. The command line is generated by
                incorporating the user-specified options and other
                information derived from /etc/fstab. This option
                allows the user to verify the command line.

EXTERNAL INFLUENCES
     Environment Variables
        LC_MESSAGES determines the language in which messages are displayed.

        If LC_MESSAGES is not specified in the environment or is set to the
        empty string, the value of LANG is used as a default for each
        unspecified or empty variable. If LANG is not specified or is set to
        the empty string, a default of "C" (see lang(5)) is used instead of
        LANG.

        If any internationalization variable contains an invalid setting, df
        behaves as if all internationalization variables are set to "C". See
        environ(5).

     International Code Set Support
        Single-byte and multi-byte character code sets are supported.

EXAMPLES
     Report the number of free disk blocks for all mounted file systems:

             df

     Report the number of free disk blocks for all mounted HFS file
     systems:

             df -F hfs

     Report the number of free files for all mounted NFS file systems:

             df -F nfs -e

     Report the total allocated block figures and the number of free
     blocks, for all mounted file systems:

             df -t

     Report the total allocated block figures and the number of free
     blocks, for the file system mounted as /usr:

             df -t /usr

FILES
        /dev/dsk/*   File system devices
        /etc/fstab   Static information about the file systems

/etc/mnttab   Mounted file system table

SEE ALSO
     du(1), df_FStype(1M), fsck(1M), fstab(4), fstyp(1M), statvfs(2),
     mnttab(4).

STANDARDS CONFORMANCE
     df: SVID2, SVID3, XPG2, XPG3, XPG4

du

man page

du - 12

du - Report the amount of free disk blocks.

---

du(1)   du(1)

NAME
       du - summarize disk usage

SYNOPSIS

       du [-a|-s] [-brx] [-t type] [name ...]

DESCRIPTION
       The du command gives the number of 512-byte blocks allocated for all
       files and (recursively) directories within each directory and file
       specified by the name operands. The block count includes the indirect
       blocks of the file. A file with two or more links is counted only
       once. If name is missing, the current working directory is used.

       By default, du generates an entry only for the name operands and each
       directory contained within those hierarchies.

   Options
       The du command recognizes the following options:

               -a   Print entries for each file encountered in the
                               directory hierarchies in addition to the normal
                               output.

               -b   For each name operand that is a directory for
                               which file system swap has been enabled, print the
                               number of blocks the swap system is currently
                               using.

               -r   Print messages about directories that cannot be
                               read, files that cannot be accessed, etc. du is
                               normally silent about such conditions.

               -s   Print only the grand total of disk usage for each
                               of the specified name operands.

               -x   Restrict reporting to only those files that have
                               the same device as the file specified by the name
                               operand. Disk usage is normally reported for the
                               entire directory hierarchy below each of the given
                               name operands.

               -t type   Restrict reporting to file systems of the
                               specified type. (Example values for type are hfs,
                               cdfs, nfs, etc.) Multiple -t type options can be
                               specified. Disk usage is normally reported for
                               the entire directory hierarchy below each of the
                               given name operands.

EXAMPLES

Display disk usage for the current working directory and all
directories below it, generating error messages for unreadable
directories:

      du -r

Display disk usage for the entire file system except for any cdfs or
nfs mounted file systems:

      du -t hfs /

Display disk usage for files on the root volume (/) only. No usage
statistics are collected for any other mounted file systems:

      du -x /

WARNINGS
      Block counts are incorrect for files that contain holes.

SEE ALSO
      df(1M), bdf(1M), quot(1M).

STANDARDS CONFORMANCE
      du: SVID2, SVID3, XPG2, XPG3, XPG4

group

group - File that contains information about groups.

```
group(4)                                                              group(4)

NAME
     group, logingroup - group file, grp.h

DESCRIPTION

     group contains for each group the following information:

         - group name

         - encrypted password

         - numerical group ID

         - comma-separated list of all users allowed in the group

     This is an ASCII file.  Fields are separated by colons, and each group
     is separated from the next by a new-line.  No spaces should separate
     the fields or parts of fields on any line.  If the password field is
     null, no password is associated with the group.

     There are two files of this form in the system, /etc/group and
     /etc/logingroup.  The file /etc/group exists to supply names for each
     group, and to support changing groups by means of the newgrp utility
     (see newgrp(1)).  /etc/logingroup provides a default group access list
     for each user via login and initgroups() (see login(1) and
     initgroups(3C)).

     The real and effective group ID set up by login for each user is
     defined in /etc/passwd (see passwd(4)).  If /etc/logingroup is empty
     or non-existent, the default group access list is empty.  If
     /etc/logingroup and /etc/group are links to the same file, the default
     access list includes the entire set of groups associated with the
     user.  The group name and password fields in /etc/logingroup are never
     used; they are included only to give the two files a uniform format,
     allowing them to be linked together.

     All group IDs used in /etc/logingroup or /etc/passwd should be defined
     in /etc/group.  No user should be associated with more than NGROUPS
     (see setgroups(2)) groups in /etc/logingroup.

     These files reside in directory /etc.  Because of the encrypted
     passwords, these files can and do have general read permission and can
     be used, for example, to map numerical group IDs to names.

     The group structure is defined in <grp.h> and includes the following
     members:

         char *gr_name;   /* the name of the group */
         char *gr_passwd; /* the encrypted group password */
         gid_t    gr_gid;    /* the numerical group ID */
```

```
char **gr_mem;    /* null-terminated array of pointers
                      to member names */
```

NETWORKING FEATURES
    NIS
        The /etc/group file can contain a line beginning with a plus (+),
        which means to incorporate entries from Network Information Services
        (NIS). There are two styles of + entries: + means to insert the
        entire contents of NIS group file at that point, and +name means to
        insert the entry (if any) for name from NIS at that point. If a +
        entry has a non-null password or group member field, the contents of
        that field override what is contained in NIS. The numerical group ID
        field cannot be overridden.

        A group file can also have a line beginning with a minus (-), these
        entries are used to disallow group entries. There is only one style
        of - entry; an entry that consists of -name means to disallow any
        subsequent entry (if any) for name. These entries are disallowed
        regardless of whether the subsequent entry comes from the NIS or the
        local group file.

WARNINGS
        Group files must not contain any blank lines. Blank lines can cause
        unpredictable behavior in system administration software that uses
        these files.

        Group ID (gid) 9 is reserved for the Pascal Language operating system
        and the BASIC Language operating system. These are operating systems
        for Series 300/400 computers that can co-exist with HP-UX on the same
        disk. Using this gid for other purposes can inhibit file transfer and
        sharing.

        The length of each line in /etc/group is limited to LINE_MAX, as
        defined in <limits.h>. The maximum number of users per group is
        (LINE_MAX - 50)/9.

        If /etc/group is linked to /etc/logingroup, group membership for a
        user is managed by NIS, and no NIS server is able to respond, that
        user cannot log in until a server does respond.

DEPENDENCIES
    NIS
        EXAMPLES
            Here is a sample /etc/group file:

                    other:*:1:root,daemon,uucp,who,date,sync
                    -oldproj
                    bin:*:2:root,bin,daemon,lp
                    +myproject:::bill,steve
                    +:

            Group other has a gid of 1 and members root, daemon, uucp,
            who, date, and sync. The group oldproj is ignored since it
            appears after the entry -oldproj. Also, the group myproject
            has members bill and steve, and the password and group ID of
            the NIS entry for the group myproject. All groups listed in
            the NIS are pulled in and placed after the entry for
            myproject.

        WARNINGS
            The plus (+) and minus (-) features are part of NIS.
            Therefore if NIS is not installed, these features cannot
            work.

FILES
    /etc/group
```
```

```
/etc/logingroup
```

SEE ALSO
```
groups(1), newgrp(1), passwd(1), setgroups(2), crypt(3C),
getgrent(3C), initgroups(3C), passwd(4).
```

WARNINGS
```
There is no single tool available to completely ensure that
/etc/passwd, /etc/group, and /etc/logingroup are compatible.  However,
pwck and grpck can be used to simplify the task (see pwck(1M) and
grpck(1M)).
```

```
There is no tool for setting group passwords in /etc/group.
```

STANDARDS CONFORMANCE
```
group: SVID2, SVID3, XPG2
```

inittab

inittab - File used by init daemon.

inittab(4)   inittab(4)

NAME
     inittab - script for the boot init process

DESCRIPTION
     The /etc/inittab file supplies the script to the boot init daemon in
     its role as a general process dispatcher (see init(1M)). The process
     that constitutes the majority of boot init's process dispatching
     activities is the line process /usr/sbin/getty that initiates
     individual terminal lines. Other processes typically dispatched by
     boot init are daemons and shells.

     The inittab file is composed of entries that are position-dependent
     and have the following format:

          id:rstate:action:process

     Each entry is delimited by a newline; however, a backslash (\)
     preceding a newline indicates a continuation of the entry. Up to 1024
     characters per entry are permitted. Comments can be inserted in the
     process field by starting a "word" with a # (see sh(1)). Comments for
     lines that spawn gettys are displayed by the who command (see who(1)).
     It is expected that they will contain some information about the line
     such as the location. There are no limits (other than maximum entry
     size) imposed on the number of entries within the inittab file.

     The entry fields are:

          id   A one- to four-character value used to uniquely
                    identify an entry. Duplicate entries cause an error
                    message to be issued, but are otherwise ignored. The
                    use of a four-character value to identify an entry is
                    strongly recommended (see WARNINGS below).

          rstate   Defines the run level in which this entry is to be
                    processed. Run levels correspond to a configuration of
                    processes in the system where each process spawned by
                    boot init is assigned one or more run levels in which
                    it is allowed to exist. Run levels are represented by
                    a number in the range 0 through 6. For example, if the
                    system is in run level 1, only those entries having a 1
                    in their rstate field are processed.

                    When boot init is requested to change run levels, all
                    processes that do not have an entry in the rstate field
                    for the target run level are sent the warning signal
                    (SIGTERM) and allowed a 20-second grace period before
                    being forcibly terminated by a kill signal (SIGKILL).
                    You can specify multiple run levels for a process by
                    entering more than one run level value in any
                    combination. If no run level is specified, the process

is assumed to be valid for all run levels, 0 through 6.

Three other values, a, b and c, can also appear in the rstate field, even though they are not true run levels. Entries having these characters in the rstate field are processed only when a user init process requests them to be run (regardless of the current system run level). They differ from run levels in that boot init can never enter "run level" a, b, or c. Also, a request for the execution of any of these processes does not change the current numeric run level.

Furthermore, a process started by an a, b, or c option is not killed when boot init changes levels. A process is killed only if its line in inittab is marked off in the action field, its line is deleted entirely from inittab, or boot init goes into the single-user state.

action   A keyword in this field tells boot init how to treat the process specified in the process field. The following actions can be specified:

boot   Process the entry only at boot init's boot-time read of the inittab file. Boot init starts the process, does not wait for its termination, and when it dies, does not restart the process. In order for this instruction to be meaningful, the rstate should be the default or it must match boot init's run level at boot time. This action is useful for an initialization function following a hardware boot of the system.

bootwait   Process the entry only at boot init's boot-time read of the inittab file. Boot init starts the process, waits for its termination, and, when it dies, does not restart the process.

initdefault   An entry with this action is only scanned when boot init is initially invoked. Boot init uses this entry, if it exists, to determine which run level to enter initially. It does this by taking the highest run level specified in the rstate field and using that as its initial state. If the rstate field is empty, boot init enters run level 6.

                        The initdefault entry cannot specify that boot init start in the single-user state. Additionally, if boot init does not find an initdefault entry in inittab, it requests an initial run level from the user at boot time.

off   If the process associated with this entry is currently running, send the warning signal (SIGTERM) and wait 20 seconds before forcibly terminating the process via the kill signal (SIGKILL). If the process is nonexistent, ignore the entry.

once   When boot init enters a run level that matches the entry's rstate, start the process and do not wait for its termination. When it dies, do not restart the process. If boot init enters a new run level but the process is still running from a previous run level change, the process is not restarted.

ondemand   This instruction is really a synonym for the respawn action. It is functionally identical to respawn but is given a different keyword in order to divorce its association with run levels. This is used only with the a, b, or c values described in the rstate field.

powerfail   Execute the process associated with this entry only when boot init receives a power-fail signal (SIGPWR see signal(5)).

powerwait   Execute the process associated with this entry only when boot init receives a power-fail signal (SIGPWR) and wait until it terminates before continuing any processing of inittab.

respawn   If the process does not exist, start the process; do not wait for its termination (continue scanning the inittab file). When it dies, restart the process. If the process currently exists, do nothing and continue scanning the inittab file.

sysinit   Entries of this type are executed before boot init tries to access the console. It is expected that this entry will be only used to initialize devices on which boot init might attempt to obtain run level information. These entries are executed and waited for before continuing.

wait   When boot init enters the run level that matches the entry's rstate, start the process and wait for its termination. Any subsequent reads of the inittab file while boot init is in the same run level cause boot init to ignore this entry.

process   This is a sh command to be executed. The entire process field is prefixed with exec and passed to a forked sh as "sh -c 'exec command'". For this reason,

any sh syntax that can legally follow exec can appear
in the process field. Comments can be inserted by
using the ; #comment syntax.

WARNINGS
The use of a four-character id is strongly recommended. Many pty
servers use the last two characters of the pty name as an id. If an
id chosen by a pty server collides with one used in the inittab file,
the /etc/utmp file can become corrupted. A corrupt /etc/utmp file can
cause commands such as who to report inaccurate information.

FILES
/etc/inittab   File of processes dispatched by boot init.

SEE ALSO
sh(1), getty(1M), exec(2), open(2), signal(5).

mount

mount - List mounted file systems or mount file systems.

man page

mount - 12

---

mount(1M)   mount(1M)

NAME
     mount (generic), umount (generic) - mount and unmount file systems

SYNOPSIS
     /usr/sbin/mount [-l] [-p|-v]

     /usr/sbin/mount -a [-F FStype] [-eQ]

     /usr/sbin/mount [-F FStype] [-eQrV] [-o specific_options]
          {special|directory}

     /usr/sbin/mount [-F FStype] [-eQrV] [-o specific_options]
          special directory

     /usr/sbin/umount [-v] [-V] {special|directory}

     /usr/sbin/umount -a [-F FStype] [-v]

DESCRIPTION
     The mount command mounts file systems. Only a superuser can mount
     file systems. Other users can use mount to list mounted file systems.

     The mount command attaches special, a removable file system, to
     directory, a directory on the file tree. directory, which must
     already exist, will become the name of the root of the newly mounted
     file system. special and directory must be given as absolute path
     names. If either special or directory is omitted, mount attempts to
     determine the missing value from an entry in the /etc/fstab file.
     mount can be invoked on any removable file system, except /.

     If mount is invoked without any arguments, it lists all of the mounted
     file systems from the file system mount table, /etc/mnttab.

     The umount command unmounts mounted file systems. Only a superuser
     can unmount file systems.

     Options (mount)
     The mount command recognizes the following options:

          -a   Attempt to mount all file systems described in
                               /etc/fstab. All optional fields in /etc/fstab
                               must be included and supported. If the -F option
                               is specified, all file systems in /etc/fstab with
                               that FStype are mounted. File systems are not
                               necessarily mounted in the order listed in
                               /etc/fstab.

          -e   Verbose mode. Write a message to the standard output indicating which file system is being mounted.

-F FStype   Specify FStype, the file system type on which to operate. See fstyp(1M). If this option is not included on the command line, then it is determined from either /etc/fstab, by matching special with an entry in that file, or from file system statistics of special, obtained by statfsdev() (see statfsdev(3C)).

-l   Limit actions to local file systems only.

-o specific_options

Specify options specific to each file system type. specific_options is a list of comma separated suboptions and/or keyword/attribute pairs intended for a FStype-specific version of the command. See the FStype-specific manual entries for a description of the specific_options supported, if any.

-p   Report the list of mounted file systems in the /etc/fstab format.

-Q   Prevent the display of error messages that result from an attempt to mount already mounted file systems.

-r   Mount the specified file system as read-only. Physically write-protected file systems must be mounted in this way or errors occur when access times are updated, whether or not any explicit write is attempted.

-v   Report the regular output with file system type and flags; however, the directory and special fields are reversed.

-V   Echo the completed command line, but perform no other action. The command line is generated by incorporating the user-specified options and other information derived from /etc/fstab. This option allows the user to verify the command line.

Options (umount)
The umount command recognizes the following options:

-a   Attempt to unmount all file systems described in /etc/mnttab. All optional fields in /etc/mnttab must be included and supported. If FStype is specified, all file systems in /etc/mnttab with that FStype are unmounted. File systems are not necessarily unmounted in the order listed in /etc/mnttab.

-F FStype   Specify FStype, the file system type on which to operate. If this option is not included on the command line, then it is determined from /etc/mnttab by matching special with an entry in that file. If no match is found, the command fails.

-v   Verbose mode. Write a message to standard output indicating which file system is being unmounted.

    -V   Echo the completed command line, but perform no
other action. The command line is generated by
incorporating the user-specified options and other
information derived from /etc/fstab. This option
allows the user to verify the command line.

EXAMPLES

List the file systems currently mounted:

```
mount
```

Mount the HFS file system /dev/dsk/c1d2s0 at directory /home:

```
mount -F hfs /dev/dsk/c1d2s0 /home
```

Unmount the same file system:

```
umount /dev/dsk/c1d2s0
```

AUTHOR

mount was developed by HP, AT&T, the University of California,
Berkeley, and Sun Microsystems.

FILES

/etc/fstab   Static information about the systems
/etc/mnttab   Mounted file system table

SEE ALSO

mount_FStype(1M), mount(2), fstab(4), mnttab(4), fs_wrapper(5),
quota(5).

STANDARDS COMPLIANCE

mount: SVID3

umount: SVID3

newgrp

newgrp - Change the group in which you are a member.

```
newgrp(1)                                                          newgrp(1)

NAME
     newgrp - switch to a new group

SYNOPSIS

     newgrp [-] [group]

DESCRIPTION
     The newgrp command changes your group ID without changing your user ID
     and replaces your current shell with a new one.

     If you specify group, the change is successful if group exists and
     either your user ID is a member of the new group, or group has a
     password and you can supply it from the terminal.

     If you omit group, newgroup changes to the group specified in your
     entry in the password file, /etc/passwd.

     Whether the group is changed successfully or not, or the new group is
     the same as the old one or not, newgrp proceeds to replace your
     current shell with the one specified in the shell field of your
     password file entry.  If that field is empty, newgrp uses the POSIX
     shell, /usr/bin/sh (see sh-posix(1)).

     If you specify - (hyphen) as the first argument, the new shell starts
     up as if you had just logged in.  If you omit -, the new shell starts
     up as if you had invoked it as a subshell.

     You remain logged in and the current directory is unchanged, but
     calculations of access permissions to files are performed with respect
     to the new real and effective group IDs.

     Exported variables retain their values and are passed to the new
     shell.  All unexported variables are deleted, but the new shell may
     reset them to default values.

     Since the current process is replaced when the new shell is started,
     exiting from the new shell has the same effect as exiting from the
     shell in which newgrp was executed.

EXTERNAL INFLUENCES
   International Code Set Support
     Characters from the 7-bit USASCII code set are supported in group
     names (see ascii(5)).

DIAGNOSTICS
     The newgrp command issues the following error messages:

     Sorry                         Your user ID does not qualify as a group
```

                                                member.

          Unknown group   The group name does not exist in
                                         /etc/group.

          Permission denied   If a password is required, it must come
                                         from a terminal.

          You have no shell   Standard input is not a terminal file,
                                         causing the new shell to fail.

     EXAMPLES
          To change from your current group to group users without executing the
          login routines:

               newgrp users

          To change from your current group to group users and execute the login
          routines:

               newgrp - users

     WARNINGS
          There is no convenient way to enter a password into /etc/group.

          The use of group passwords is not recommended because, by their very
          nature, they encourage poor security practices. Group passwords may
          be eliminated in future HP-UX releases.

     FILES
          /etc/group   System group file
          /etc/passwd   System password file

     SEE ALSO
          csh(1), ksh(1), login(1), sh-bourne(1), sh-posix(1), group(4),
          passwd(4), environ(5).

     STANDARDS CONFORMANCE
          newgrp: SVID2, SVID3, XPG2, XPG3, XPG4

passwd

man page

passwd -12

passwd - File that contains information about users (this is different from **passwd** command that is used to change a user's password).

```
passwd(4)                                                              passwd(4)

NAME
      passwd - password file, pwd.h

DESCRIPTION

      passwd contains the following information for each user:

            -  login name
            -  encrypted password
            -  numerical user ID
            -  numerical group ID
            -  reserved field, which can be used for identification
            -  initial working directory
            -  program to use as shell

      This is an ASCII file.  Each field within each user's entry is
      separated from the next by a colon.  Each user is separated from the
      next by a newline.  This file resides in the /etc directory.  It can
      and does have general read permission and can be used, for example, to
      map numerical user IDs to names.  If the password field is null and
      the system has not been converted to a trusted system, no password is
      demanded.

      If the shell field is null, /usr/bin/sh is used.

      The encrypted password consists of 13 characters chosen from a 64-
      character set of "digits" described below, except when the password is
      null, in which case the encrypted password is also null.  Login can be
      prevented by entering in the password field a character that is not
      part of the set of digits (such as *).

      The characters used to represent "digits" are . for 0, / for 1, 0
      through 9 for 2 through 11, A through Z for 12 through 37, and a
      through z for 38 through 63.

      Password aging is put in effect for a particular user if his encrypted
      password in the password file is followed by a comma and a nonnull
      string of characters from the above alphabet.  (Such a string must be
      introduced in the first instance by a superuser.) This string defines
      the "age" needed to implement password aging.

      The first character of the age, M, denotes the maximum number of weeks
      for which a password is valid.  A user who attempts to login after his
      password has expired is forced to supply a new one.  The next
      character, m, denotes the minimum period in weeks that must expire
      before the password can be changed.  The remaining characters define
      the week (counted from the beginning of 1970) when the password was
      last changed (a null string is equivalent to zero).  M and m have
      numerical values in the range 0 through 63 that correspond to the 64-
```

character set of "digits" shown above. If m = M = 0 (derived from the
string . or ..), the user is forced to change his password next time
he logs in (and the "age" disappears from his entry in the password
file). If m > M (signified, for example, by the string ./), then only
a superuser (not the user) can change the password. Not allowing the
user to ever change the password is discouraged, especially on a
trusted system.

Trusted systems support password aging and password generation. For
more information on converting to trusted system and on password, see
the HP-UX System Administration Tasks Manual and sam(1M).

getpwent(3C) designates values to the fields in the following
structure declared in <pwd.h>:

```
struct passwd {
    char    *pw_name;
    char    *pw_passwd;
    uid_t   pw_uid;
    gid_t   pw_gid;
    char    *pw_age;
    char    *pw_comment;
    char    *pw_gecos;
    char    *pw_dir;
    char    *pw_shell;
    aid_t   pw_audid;
    int     pw_audflg;
};
```

It is suggested that the range 0-99 not be used for user and group IDs
(pw_uid and pw_gid in the above structure) so that IDs that might be
assigned for system software do not conflict.

The user's full name, office location, extension, and home phone
stored in the pw_gecos field of the passwd structure can be set by use
of the chfn command (see chfn(1)) and is used by the finger(1)
command. These two commands assume the information in this field is
in the order listed above. A portion of the user's real name can be
represented in the pw_gecos field by an & character, which some
utilities (including finger) expand by substituting the login name for
it and shifting the first letter of the login name to uppercase.

SECURITY FEATURES
    On trusted systems, the encrypted password for each user is stored in
    the file /tcb/files/auth/c/user_name (where c is the first letter in
    user_name). Password information files are not accessible to the
    public. The encrypted password can be longer than 13 characters
    For example, the password file for user david is stored in
    /tcb/files/auth/d/david. In addition to the password, the user
    profile in /tcb/files/auth/c/user_name also contains:

        - numerical audit ID

        - numerical audit flag

    Like /etc/passwd, this file is an ASCII file. Fields within each
    user's entry are separated by colons. Refer to authcap(4) and
    prpwd(4) for details. The passwords contained in /tcb/files/auth/c/*
    take precedence over those contained in the encrypted password field
    of /etc/passwd. User authentication is done using the encrypted
    passwords in this file . The password aging mechanism described in
    passwd(1), under the section called SECURITY FEATURES, applies to this
    password .

NETWORKING FEATURES
    NFS

The passwd file can have entries that begin with a plus (+) or minus
(-) sign in the first column. Such lines are used to access the
Network Information System network database. A line beginning with a
plus (+) is used to incorporate entries from the Network Information
System. There are three styles of + entries:

+   Insert the entire contents of the Network Information
                     System password file at that point;

+name   Insert the entry (if any) for name from the Network
                     Information System at that point

+@name   Insert the entries for all members of the network
                     group name at that point.

If a + entry has a nonnull password, directory, gecos, or shell field,
they override what is contained in the Network Information System.
The numerical user ID and group ID fields cannot be overridden.

The passwd file can also have lines beginning with a minus (-), which
disallow entries from the Network Information System. There are two
styles of - entries:

-name   Disallow any subsequent entries (if any) for name.

-@name   Disallow any subsequent entries for all members of
                     the network group name.

WARNINGS
    User ID (uid) 17 is reserved for the Pascal Language operating system.
    User ID (uid) 18 is reserved for the BASIC Language operating system.
    These are operating systems for Series 300 and 400 computers that can
    coexist with HP-UX on the same disk. Using these uids for other
    purposes may inhibit file transfer and sharing.

    The login shell for the root user (uid 0) must be /sbin/sh. Other
    shells such as sh, ksh, and csh are all located under the /usr
    directory which may not be mounted during earlier stages of the bootup
    process. Changing the login shell of the root user to a value other
    than /sbin/sh may result in a non-functional system.

    The information kept in the pw_gecos field may conflict with
    unsupported or future uses of this field. Use of the pw_gecos field
    for keeping user identification information has not been formalized
    within any of the industry standards. The current use of this field
    is derived from its use within the Berkeley Software Distribution.
    Future standards may define this field for other purposes.

    The following fields have character limitations as noted:

        - Login name field can be no longer than 8 characters;

        - Initial working directory field can be no longer than 63
          characters;

        - Program field can be no longer than 44 characters.

        - Results are unpredictable if these fields are longer than the
          limits specified above.

    The following fields have numerical limitations as noted:

        - The user ID is an integer value between -2 and UID_MAX
          inclusive.

        - The group ID is an integer value between 0 and UID_MAX

inclusive.

- If either of these values are out of range, the getpwent(3C) functions reset the ID value to (UID_MAX).

EXAMPLES
  NFS Example
    Here is a sample /etc/passwd file:

        root:3Km/o4Cyq84Xc:0:10:System Administrator:/:/sbin/sh
        joe:r4hRJr4GJ4CqE:100:50:Joe User,Post 4A,12345:/home/joe:/usr/bin/ksh
        +john:
        -bob:
        +@documentation:no-login:
        -@marketing:
        +:::Guest

    In this example, there are specific entries for users root and joe, in case the Network Information System are out of order.

    - User john's password entry in the Network Information System is incorporated without change.

    - Any subsequent entries for user bob are ignored.

    - The password field for anyone in the netgroup documentation is disabled.

    - Users in netgroup marketing are not returned by getpwent(3C) and thus are not allowed to log in.

    - Anyone else can log in with their usual password, shell, and home directory, but with a pw_gecos field of Guest.

  NFS Warnings
    The plus (+) and minus (-) features are NFS functionality; therefore, if NFS is not installed, they do not work. Also, these features work only with /etc/passwd, but not with a system that has been converted to a trusted system. When the system has been converted to a trusted system, the encrypted passwords can be accessed only from the protected password database, /tcb/files/auth/*/*. Any user entry in the Network Information System database also must have an entry in the protected password database.

    The uid of -2 is reserved for remote root access by means of NFS. The pw_name usually given to this uid is nobody. Since uids are stored as signed values, the following define is included in <pwd.h> to match the user nobody.

        UID_NOBODY   (-2)

FILES
    /tcb/files/auth/*/*   Protected password database used when
                                 system is converted to trusted system.

    /etc/passwd   Standard password file used by HP-UX.

SEE ALSO
    chfn(1), finger(1), login(1), passwd(1), a641(3C), crypt(3C),
    getprpwent(3), getpwent(3C), authcap(4), limits(5).

STANDARDS CONFORMANCE
    passwd: SVID2, SVID3, XPG2

ps

ps - Report status of processes.

---

ps(1)   ps(1)

NAME
     ps - report process status

SYNOPSIS

     ps [-adeflP] [-g grplist] [-p proclist] [-R prmgrplist] [-t termlist]
     [-u uidlist]

XPG4 SYNOPSIS
     ps [-aAcdefHjlP] [-C cmdlist] [-g grplist] [-G gidlist] [-n namelist]
     [-o format] [-p proclist] [-R prmgrplist] [-s sidlist] [-t termlist]
     [-u uidlist] [-U uidlist]

DESCRIPTION
     ps prints information about selected processes. Use options to
     specify which processes to select and what information to print about
     them.

   Process Selection Options
     Use the following options to choose which processes should be
     selected.

     NOTE: If an option is used in both the default (standard HP-UX) and
     XPG4 environments, the description provided here documents the default
     behavior. Refer to the UNIX95 variable under EXTERNAL INFLUENCES for
     additional information on XPG4 behavior.

          (none)   Select those processes associated with the current
                        terminal.

          -A   (XPG4 Only.) Select all processes. (Synonym for
                        -e.)

          -a   Select all processes except process group leaders
                        and processes not associated with a terminal.

          -C cmdlist   (XPG4 Only.) Select processes executing a command
                        with a basename given in cmdlist.

          -d   Select all processes except process group leaders.

          -e   Select all processes.

          -g grplist   Select processes whose process group leaders are
                        given in grplist.

          -G gidlist   (XPG4 Only.) Select processes whose real group ID
                        numbers or group names are given in gidlist.

          -n namelist   (XPG4 Only.) This option is ignored; its presence is allowed for standards compliance.

    -p proclist   Select processes whose process ID numbers are
                            given in proclist.

    -R prmgrplist   Select processes belonging to PRM process resource
                            groups whose names or ID numbers are given in
                            prmgrplist. See DEPENDENCIES.

    -s sidlist   (XPG4 Only.) Select processes whose session
                            leaders are given in sidlist. (Synonym for -g).

    -t termlist   Select processes associated with the terminals
                            given in termlist. Terminal identifiers can be
                            specified in one of two forms: the device's file
                            name (such as tty04) or if the device's file name
                            starts with tty, just the rest of it (such as 04).
                            If the device's file is in a directory other than
                            /dev or /dev/pty, the terminal identifier must
                            include the name of the directory under /dev that
                            contains the device file (such as pts/5).

    -u uidlist   Select processes whose effective user ID numbers
                            or login names are given in uidlist.

    -U uidlist   (XPG4 Only.) Select processes whose real user ID
                            numbers or login names are given in uidlist.

If any of the -a, -A, -d, or -e options is specified, the -C, -g, -G,
-p, -R, -t, -u, and -U options are ignored.

If more than one of -a, -A, -d, and -e are specified, the least
restrictive option takes effect.

If more than one of the -C, -g, -G, -p, -R, -t, -u, and -U options are
specified, processes will be selected if they match any of the options
specified.

The lists used as arguments to the -C, -g, -G, -p, -R, -t, -u, and -U
options can be specified in one of two forms:

    - A list of identifiers separated from one another by a comma.

    - A list of identifiers enclosed in quotation marks (") and
      separated from one another by a comma and/or one or more
      spaces.

Output Format Options
  Use the following options to control which columns of data are
  included in the output listing. The options are cumulative.

    (none)   The default columns are: pid, tty, time, and comm,
                      in that order.

    -f   Show columns user, pid, ppid, cpu, stime, tty,
                      time, and args, in that order.

    -l   Show columns flags, state, uid, pid, ppid, cpu,
                      intpri, nice, addr, sz, wchan, tty, time, and
                      comm, in that order.

    -fl   Show columns flags, state, user, pid, ppid, cpu,
                      intpri, nice, addr, sz, wchan, stime, tty, time,
                      and args, in that order.

-c	(XPG4 Only.) Remove columns cpu and nice; replace column intpri with columns cls and pri.
-j	(XPG4 Only.) Add columns pgid and sid after column ppid (or pid, if ppid is not being displayed).
-P	Add column prmid (for -l) or prmgrp (for -f or -fl) immediately before column pid. See DEPENDENCIES.
-o format	(XPG4 Only.) format is a comma- or space-separated list of the columns to display, in the order they should be displayed. (Valid column names are listed below.) A column name can optionally be followed by an equals sign (=) and a string to use as the heading for that column. (Any commas or spaces after the equals sign will be taken as a part of the column heading; if more columns are desired, they must be specified with additional -o options.) The width of the column will be the greater of the width of the data to be displayed and the width of the column heading. If an empty column heading is specified for every heading, no heading line will be printed. This option overrides options -c, -f, -j, -l, and -P; if they are specified, they are ignored.
-H	(XPG4 Only.) Shows the process hierarchy. Each process is displayed under its parent, and the contents of the args or comm column for that process is indented from that of its parent. Note that this option is expensive in both memory and speed.

The column names and their meanings are given below. Except where noted, the default heading for each column is the uppercase form of the column name.

addr	The memory address of the process, if resident; otherwise, the disk address.
args	The command line given when the process was created. This column should be the last one specified, if it is desired. Only a subset of the command line is saved by the kernel; as much of the command line will be displayed as is available. The output in this column may contain spaces. The default heading for this column is COMMAND if -o is specified and CMD otherwise.
cls	Process scheduling class, see rtsched(1).
comm	The command name. The output in this column may contain spaces. The default heading for this column is COMMAND if -o is specified and CMD otherwise.
cpu	Processor utilization for scheduling. The default heading for this column is C.
etime	Elapsed time of the process. The default heading for this column is ELAPSED.
flags	Flags (octal and additive) associated with the

process:

```
       0    Swapped
       1    In core
       2    System process
       4    Locked in core (e.g., for physical I/O)

       10   Being traced by another process
       20   Another tracing flag
```

The default heading for this column is F.

intpri   The priority of the process as it is stored
            internally by the kernel. This column is provided
            for backward compatibility and its use is not
            encouraged.

gid   The group ID number of the effective process
            owner.

group   The group name of the effective process owner.

nice   Nice value; used in priority computation (see
            nice(1)). The default heading for this column is
            NI.

pcpu   The percentage of CPU time used by this process
            during the last scheduling interval. The default
            heading for this column is %CPU.

pgid   The process group ID number of the process group
            to which this process belongs.

pid   The process ID number of the process.

ppid   The process ID number of the parent process.

pri   The priority of the process. The meaning of the
            value depends on the process scheduling class; see
            cls, above, and rtsched(1).

prmid   The PRM process resource group ID number.

prmgrp   The PRM process resource group name.

rgid   The group ID number of the real process owner.

rgroup   The group name of the real process owner.

ruid   The user ID number of the real process owner.

ruser   The login name of the real process owner.

sid   The session ID number of the session to which this
            process belongs.

state   The state of the process:

```
       0    Nonexistent
       S    Sleeping
       W    Waiting
       R    Running
       I    Intermediate
       Z    Terminated
```

T	Stopped
X	Growing

The default heading for this column is S.

stime	Starting time of the process. If the elapsed time is greater than 24 hours, the starting date is displayed instead.
sz	The size in physical pages of the core image of the process, including text, data, and stack space. Physical page size is defined by _SC_PAGE_SIZE in the header file <unistd.h> (see sysconf(2) and unistd(5)).
time	The cumulative execution time for the process.
tty	The controlling terminal for the process. The default heading for this column is TT if -o is specified and TTY otherwise.
uid	The user ID number of the effective process owner.
user	The login name of the effective process owner.
vsz	The size in kilobytes (1024 byte units) of the core image of the process. See column sz, above.
wchan	The event for which the process is waiting or sleeping; if there is none, a hyphen (-) is displayed.

Notes

ps prints the command name and arguments given at the time of the process was created. If the process changes its arguments while running (by writing to its argv array), these changes are not displayed by ps.

A process that has exited and has a parent, but has not yet been waited for by the parent, is marked <defunct> (see zombie process in exit(2)).

The time printed in the stime column, and used in computing the value for the etime column, is the time when the process was forked, not the time when it was modified by exec*().

To make the ps output safer to display and easier to read, all control characters in the comm and args columns are displayed as "visible" equivalents in the customary control character format, ^x.

EXTERNAL INFLUENCES

Environment Variables

UNIX95 specifies to use the XPG4 behavior for this command. The changes for XPG4 include support for the entire option set specified above and include the following behavioral changes:

  - The TIME column format changes from mmmm:ss to [dd-]hh:mm:ss.

  - When the comm, args, user, and prmgrp fields are included by default or the -f or -l flags are used, the column headings of those fields change to CMD, CMD, USER, and PRMGRP, respectively.

- -a, -d, and -g will select processes based on session rather than on process group.

- The uid or user column displayed by -f or -1 will display effective user rather than real user.

- The -u option will select users based on effective UID rather than real UID.

- The -C and -H options, while they are not part of the XPG4 standard, are enabled.

LC_TIME determines the format and contents of date and time strings. If it is not specified or is null, it defaults to the value of LANG.

If LANG is not specified or is null, it defaults to C (see lang(5)).

If any internationalization variable contains an invalid setting, all internationalization variables default to C (see environ(5)).

International Code Set Support
    Single-byte character code sets are supported.

EXAMPLES
    Generate a full listing of all processes currently running on your machine:

        ps -ef

    To see if a certain process exists on the machine, such as the cron clock daemon, check the far right column for the command name, cron, or try

        ps -f -C cron

WARNINGS
    Things can change while ps is running; the picture it gives is only a snapshot in time. Some data printed for defunct processes is irrelevant.

    If two special files for terminals are located at the same select code, that terminal may be reported with either name. The user can select processes with that terminal using either name.

    Users of ps must not rely on the exact field widths and spacing of its output, as these will vary depending on the system, the release of HP-UX, and the data to be displayed.

DEPENDENCIES
    HP Process Resource Manager
        The -P and -R options require the optional HP Process Resource Manager (PRM) software to be installed and configured. See prmconfig(1) for a description of how to configure HP PRM, and prmconf(4) for the definition of "process resource group."

        If HP PRM is not installed and configured and -P or -R is specified, a warning message is displayed and (for -P) hyphens (-) are displayed in the prmid and prmgrp columns.

FILES
    /dev   Directory of terminal device files

    /etc/passwd   User ID information
    /var/adm/ps_data   Internal data structure

SEE ALSO

kill(1), nice(1), acctcom(1M), exec(2), exit(2), fork(2), sysconf(2), unistd(5).

HP Process Resource Manager: prmconfig(1), prmconf(4) in HP Process Resource Manager User's Guide.

STANDARDS COMPLIANCE
    ps: SVID2, XPG2, XPG3, XPG4

shutdown

shutdown - Terminate all running processes in an orderly fashion.

man page

shutdown
- 12

shutdown(1M)   shutdown(1M)

NAME
     shutdown - terminate all processing

SYNOPSIS

     /sbin/shutdown [-h|-r] [-y] [-o] [grace]

DESCRIPTION
     The shutdown command is part of the HP-UX system operation procedures.
     Its primary function is to terminate all currently running processes
     in an orderly and cautious manner. shutdown can be used to put the
     system in single-user mode for administrative purposes such as backup
     or file system consistency checks (see fsck(1M)), and to halt or
     reboot the system. By default, shutdown is an interactive program.

   Options and Arguments
     shutdown recognizes the following options and arguments.

          -h   Shut down the system and halt.

          -r   Shut down the system and reboot automatically.

          -y   Do not require any interactive responses from the user.
                    (Respond yes or no as appropriate to all questions,
                    such that the user does not interact with the shutdown
                    process.)

          -o   When executed on the cluster server in a diskless
                    cluster environment, shutdown the server only and do
                    not reboot clients. If this argument is not entered the
                    default behavior is to reboot all clients when the
                    server is shutdown.

          grace   Either a decimal integer that specifies the duration in
                    seconds of a grace period for users to log off before
                    the system shuts down, or the word now. The default is
                    60. If grace is either 0 or now, shutdown runs more
                    quickly, giving users very little time to log out.

          If neither -r (reboot) nor -h (halt) is specified, standalone and
          server systems are placed in single-user state. Either -r
          (reboot) or -h (halt) must be specified for a client; shutdown to
          single-user state is not allowed for a client. See dcnodes(1M),
          init(1M).

   Shutdown Procedure
     shutdown goes through the following steps:

          - The PATH environment variable is reset to
             /usr/bin:/usr/sbin:/sbin.

          - The IFS environment variable is reset to space, tab, newline.

- The user is checked for authorization to execute the shutdown command. Only authorized users can execute the shutdown command. See FILES for more information on the /etc/shutdown.allow authorization file.

- The current working directory is changed to the root directory (/).

- All file systems' super blocks are updated; see sync(1M). This must be done before rebooting the system to ensure file system integrity.

- The real user ID is set to that of the superuser.

- A broadcast message is sent to all users currently logged in on the system telling them to log out. The administrator can specify a message at this time; otherwise, a standard warning message is displayed.

- The next step depends on whether a system is standalone, a server, or a client.

    - If the system is standalone, /sbin/rc is executed to shut down subsystems, unmount file systems, and perform other tasks to bring the system to run level 0.

    - If the system is a server, the optional -o argument is used to determine if all clients in the cluster should also be rebooted. The default behavior (command line parameter -o is not entered) is to reboot all clients using /sbin/reboot; entering -o results in the server only being rebooted and the clients being left alone. Then /sbin/rc is executed to shut down subsystems, unmount file systems, and perform other tasks to bring the system to run level 0.

    - If the system is a client, /sbin/rc is executed to bring the system down to run-level 2, and then /sbin/reboot is executed. Shutdown to the single-user state is not an allowed option for clients.

- The system is rebooted or halted by executing /sbin/reboot if the -h or -r option was chosen. If the system was not a cluster client and the system was being brought down to single-user state, a signal is sent to the init process to change states (see init(1M)).

DIAGNOSTICS

device busy

This is the most commonly encountered error diagnostic, and happens when a particular file system could not be unmounted; see mount(1M).

user not allowed to shut down this system

User is not authorized to shut down the system. User and system must both be included in the authorization file /etc/shutdown.allow.

EXAMPLES

Immediately reboot the system and run HP-UX again:

```
        shutdown -r 0
```

Halt the system in 5 minutes (300 seconds) with no interactive
questions and answers:

```
        shutdown -h -y 300
```

Go to run-level s in 10 minutes:

```
        shutdown 600
```

FILES
    /etc/shutdown.allow

        Authorization file.

        The file contains lines that consist of a system host name
        and the login name of a user who is authorized to reboot or
        halt the system. A superuser's login name must be included
        in this file in order to execute shutdown. However, if the
        file is missing or of zero length, the root user can run the
        shutdown program to bring the system down.

        This file does not affect authorization to bring the system
        down to single-user state for maintenance purposes; that
        operation is permitted only when invoked by a superuser.

        A comment character, #, at the beginning of a line causes
        the rest of the line to be ignored (comments cannot span
        multiple lines without additional comment characters).
        Blank lines are also ignored.

        The wildcard character + can be used in place of a host name
        or a user name to specify all hosts or all users,
        respectively (see hosts.equiv(4)).

        For example:

            # user1 can shut down systemA and systemB
            systemA user1
            systemB user1
            # root can shut down any system
            + root
            # Any user can shut down systemC
            systemC +

WARNINGS
    The user name compared with the entry in the shutdown.allow file is
    obtained using getlogin() or, if that fails, using getpwuid() (see
    getlogin(3) and getpwuid(3)).

    The hostname in /etc/shutdown.allow is compared with the hostname
    obtained using gethostbyname() (see gethostbyname(3)).

    shutdown must be executed from a directory on the root volume, such as
    the / directory.

    The maximum broadcast message that can be sent is approximately 970
    characters.

    When executing shutdown on an NFS diskless cluster server and the -o
    option is not entered, clients of the server will be rebooted. No
    clients should be individually rebooted or shutdown while the cluster
    is being shutdown.
```
```

SEE ALSO
    dcnodes(1M), fsck(1M), init(1M), killall(1M), mount(1M), reboot(1M),
    sync(1M), dcnodes(3), gethostbyname(3), getpwuid(3), hosts.equiv(4).

vipw

vipw - Edit the passwd file with locking.

```
vipw(1M)                                                        vipw(1M)

NAME
     vipw - edit the password file

SYNOPSIS

     vipw

DESCRIPTION
     vipw edits the password file while setting the appropriate locks, and
     does any necessary processing after the password file is unlocked.  If
     the password file is already being edited, you will be told to try
     again later.  The vi editor is used unless the environment variable
     EDITOR indicates an alternate editor.  vipw performs a number of
     consistency checks on the password entry for root, and does not allow
     a password file with an incorrectly formatted root entry to be
     installed.

WARNINGS
     An /etc/passwd.tmp file not removed when a system crashes prevents
     further editing of the /etc/passwd file using vipw after the system is
     rebooted.

AUTHOR
     vipw was developed by the University of California, Berkeley.

FILES
     /etc/passwd.tmp

SEE ALSO
     passwd(1), passwd(4).
```

CHAPTER 13

Introduction to UNIX Performance Tools

Introduction

You can take a variety of approaches to performance analysis on your system. These choices range from quick snapshots that take but a few seconds to create, to long-range capacity planning programs that you may want to run for weeks or months before you even begin to analyze the data they produce.

In this chapter, we'll focus on some commonly used UNIX commands and a couple of advanced tools that run on several UNIX variants. These are by no means an exhaustive list of UNIX commands and tools related to performance management; however, I provide enough good information to give you an overview. Your UNIX system may support additional commands and have advanced performance analysis tools. This chapter will give a good overview of performance analysis, including examples of the most commonly used UNIX performance-related commands.

Standard UNIX Commands

To begin, let's look at some commands you can issue from the UNIX-prompt to give you some information about your system. The commands I'll cover are:

- **iostat**
- **vmstat**
- **netstat**
- **ps**
- **kill**
- **showmount**
- **swapinfo and swap**
- **sar**

We'll first look at each of these commands so that you get an understanding of the output produced by each and how this output may be used. There are manual pages for many of the commands covered at the end of this chapter.

Please keep in mind that, like all topics we have covered, the output of these commands may differ somewhat among UNIX variants. The basic information produced on most UNIX variants is the same; however, the format of the outputs may differ somewhat. This usually is not significant if you're viewing the outputs, however, if you're writing programs that accept these outputs and manipulate them in some way, then the format of the outputs is important.

I/O and CPU Statistics with iostat

man page

iostat - 13

The **iostat** command gives you an indication of the level of effort the CPU is putting into I/O and the amount of I/O taking place among your disks and terminals. **iostat** provides a lot of useful information; however, it acts somewhat differently among UNIX variants. The following examples show issuing **iostat** on a Solaris system, an HP-UX system, and an AIX system. **iostat** was not supported on the Linux system I was using for this chapter. Note that on some systems, using the **-t** option for terminal information produces just terminal information, and on some systems it produces a full output. You will, of course, have to determine the best options for your needs on your UNIX variant. The following examples show the **iostat** command:

man page

iostat - 13

Solaris example executed ten times at five-second intervals:

```
# iostat 5 10
        tty          fd0          sd1          sd3          sd6          cpu
 tin tout kps tps serv kps tps serv kps tps serv kps tps serv us sy wt id
   0    0   0   0    0   0   0    0   3   0   57   0  79    0   0  7 49 43
   0   47   0   0    0   0   0    0  14   2   75   0   0    0   0  2  0 98
   0   16   0   0    0   0   0    0   0   0    0   0   0    0   0  1  0 98
   0   16   0   0    0   0   0    0   0   0    0   0   0    0   0  2  0 98
   0   16   0   0    0   0   0    0   0   0    0   0   0    0   0  0  0 100
   0   16   0   0    0   0   0    0   0   0    0   0   0    0   0  0  0 100
   0   16   0   0    0   0   0    0   0   0    0   0   0    0   0  1  0 99
   0   16   0   0    0   0   0    0   0   0    0   0   0    0   0  0  0 100
   0   16   0   0    0   0   0    0   6   1   35   0   0    0   0  4  0 96
   0   16   0   0    0   0   0    0   0   0    0   0   0    0   0  0  0 100
```

HP-UX example includes the **-t** option executed five times at five-second intervals:

```
# iostat -t 5 5

                            tty     cpu
                   tin tout us  ni  sy   id
                     0    3 17   0   3   80

    device    bps    sps    msps

    c0t6d0      0    0.0    1.0
    c5t4d0      0    0.0    1.0
    c4t5d0      0    0.0    1.0
    c4t5d1      0    0.0    1.0
    c5t4d1      0    0.0    1.0
    c5t4d2      0    0.0    1.0
    c5t4d3      0    0.0    1.0

                            tty     cpu
                   tin tout us  ni  sy   id
                     0    0 30   0  12   58

    device    bps    sps    msps

    c0t6d0      0    0.0    1.0
    c5t4d0     20    2.4    1.0
```

```
            c4t5d0        0      0.0      1.0
            c4t5d1       26      2.4      1.0
            c5t4d1        0      0.0      1.0
            c5t4d3        0      0.0      1.0


                                           tty        cpu
                                  tin tout us  ni  sy  id
                                    0    0  36   0  14  51

            device      bps      sps      msps

            c0t6d0        2      0.2      1.0
            c5t4d0       33      3.9      1.0
            c4t5d0        0      0.0      1.0
            c4t5d1       48      4.9      1.0
            c5t4d1        0      0.0      1.0
            c5t4d2        1      0.2      1.0
            c5t4d3        0      0.0      1.0


                                           tty        cpu
                                  tin tout us  ni  sy  id
                                    0    0  25   0  12  64

            device      bps      sps      msps

            c5t4d0        6      1.0      1.0
            c4t5d0        0      0.0      1.0
            c4t5d1       17      2.2      1.0
            c5t4d1        0      0.0      1.0
            c5t4d3        0      0.0      1.0


                                           tty        cpu
                                  tin tout us  ni  sy  id
                                    0    0  31   0  13  56

            device      bps      sps      msps

            c5t4d0       11      1.4      1.0
            c4t5d0        0      0.0      1.0
            c4t5d1       14      1.6      1.0
            c5t4d1        0      0.0      1.0
            c5t4d2        3      0.4      1.0
            c5t4d3        0      0.0      1.0
```

AIX example executed ten times at five-second intervals:

man page

iostat - 13

```
# iostat 5 10
tty:      tin          tout     avg-cpu:  % user    % sys    % idle   % iowait
          0.0          0.0                 0.3       1.0      98.4     0.3

Disks:        % tm_act    Kbps      tps     Kb_read    Kb_wrtn
hdisk0        0.4         2.7       0.4     2366635    959304
hdisk1        0.0         0.0       0.0       18843     37928
hdisk2        0.1         0.6       0.1      269803    423284
hdisk3        0.0         0.0       0.0       20875       172
cd0           0.0         0.0       0.0          14         0

tty:      tin          tout     avg-cpu:  % user    % sys    % idle   % iowait
          0.0          108.2               0.0       0.2      99.8     0.0
```

Disks:	% tm_act	Kbps	tps	Kb_read	Kb_wrtn
hdisk0	0.0	0.0	0.0	0	0
hdisk1	0.0	0.0	0.0	0	0
hdisk2	0.0	0.0	0.0	0	0
hdisk3	0.0	0.0	0.0	0	0
cd0	0.0	0.0	0.0	0	0

tty:	tin	tout	avg-cpu:	% user	% sys	% idle	% iowait
	0.0	108.4		0.2	0.8	99.0	0.0

Disks:	% tm_act	Kbps	tps	Kb_read	Kb_wrtn
hdisk0	0.0	0.0	0.0	0	0
hdisk1	0.0	0.0	0.0	0	0
hdisk2	0.0	0.0	0.0	0	0
hdisk3	0.0	0.0	0.0	0	0
cd0	0.0	0.0	0.0	0	0

tty:	tin	tout	avg-cpu:	% user	% sys	% idle	% iowait
	0.0	108.4		0.4	0.2	99.4	0.0

Disks:	% tm_act	Kbps	tps	Kb_read	Kb_wrtn
hdisk0	0.0	0.0	0.0	0	0
hdisk1	0.0	0.0	0.0	0	0
hdisk2	0.0	0.0	0.0	0	0
hdisk3	0.0	0.0	0.0	0	0
cd0	0.0	0.0	0.0	0	0

tty:	tin	tout	avg-cpu:	% user	% sys	% idle	% iowait
	0.0	108.2		0.4	0.6	99.0	0.0

Disks:	% tm_act	Kbps	tps	Kb_read	Kb_wrtn
hdisk0	0.0	0.0	0.0	0	0
hdisk1	0.0	0.0	0.0	0	0
hdisk2	0.0	0.0	0.0	0	0
hdisk3	0.0	0.0	0.0	0	0
cd0	0.0	0.0	0.0	0	0

tty:	tin	tout	avg-cpu:	% user	% sys	% idle	% iowait
	0.0	108.4		0.0	0.4	99.6	0.0

Disks:	% tm_act	Kbps	tps	Kb_read	Kb_wrtn
hdisk0	0.0	0.0	0.0	0	0
hdisk1	0.0	0.0	0.0	0	0
hdisk2	0.0	0.0	0.0	0	0
hdisk3	0.0	0.0	0.0	0	0
cd0	0.0	0.0	0.0	0	0

tty:	tin	tout	avg-cpu:	% user	% sys	% idle	% iowait
	0.0	108.4		0.6	0.0	99.4	0.0

Disks:	% tm_act	Kbps	tps	Kb_read	Kb_wrtn
hdisk0	0.0	0.0	0.0	0	0
hdisk1	0.0	0.0	0.0	0	0
hdisk2	0.0	0.0	0.0	0	0
hdisk3	0.0	0.0	0.0	0	0
cd0	0.0	0.0	0.0	0	0

tty:	tin	tout	avg-cpu:	% user	% sys	% idle	% iowait
	0.0	108.2		0.2	0.8	99.0	0.0

Disks:	% tm_act	Kbps	tps	Kb_read	Kb_wrtn
hdisk0	0.0	0.0	0.0	0	0
hdisk1	0.0	0.0	0.0	0	0
hdisk2	0.0	0.0	0.0	0	0
hdisk3	0.0	0.0	0.0	0	0
cd0	0.0	0.0	0.0	0	0

tty:	tin	tout	avg-cpu:	% user	% sys	% idle	% iowait
	0.0	108.4		0.4	0.0	99.6	0.0

Disks:	% tm_act	Kbps	tps	Kb_read	Kb_wrtn
hdisk0	0.0	0.0	0.0	0	0
hdisk1	0.0	0.0	0.0	0	0
hdisk2	0.0	0.0	0.0	0	0
hdisk3	0.0	0.0	0.0	0	0

| cd0 | 0.0 | 0.0 | 0.0 | 0 | 0 |

tty:	tin	tout	avg-cpu:	% user	% sys	% idle	% iowait
	0.0	108.4		0.4	0.4	99.2	0.0

Disks:	% tm_act	Kbps	tps	Kb_read	Kb_wrtn
hdisk0	0.0	0.0	0.0	0	0
hdisk1	0.0	0.0	0.0	0	0
hdisk2	0.0	0.0	0.0	0	0
hdisk3	0.0	0.0	0.0	0	0
cd0	0.0	0.0	0.0	0	0

man page

iostat - 13

Here are descriptions of the reports you receive with **iostat** for terminals, the CPU, and mounted file systems. Because the reports are somewhat different, I have included detailed information from the HP-UX output. A more detailed description of these fields is included in the **iostat** manaul page at the end of this chapter. Most of the fields appear in the outputs; however, the outputs of the commands differ somewhat among UNIX variants.

For every terminal you have connected (tty), you see a "tin" and "tout," which represent the number of characters read from your terminal and the number of characters written to your terminal, respectively.

For your CPU, you see the percentage of time spent in user mode ("us"), the percentage of time spent running user processes at a low priority called nice ("ni"), the percentage of time spent in system mode ("sy"), and the percentage of time the CPU is idle ("id").

For every locally mounted file system, you receive information on the kilobytes transferred per second ("bps"), number of seeks per second ("sps"), and number of milliseconds per average seek ("msps"). For disks that are NFS-mounted or disks on client nodes of your server, you will not receive a report; **iostat** reports only on locally mounted file systems.

When viewing the output of **iostat**, there are some parameters to take note of.

First, note that the time that your CPU is spending in the four categories shown. The CPU report is produced with the **-t** option. I have worked on systems with poor performance that the administrator assumed to be a result of a slow CPU when the "id" number was very high, indicating that the CPU was actually idle most of the time. If the CPU is mostly idle, the chances are that the bottleneck is not the CPU but may be I/O, memory, or networking. If the CPU is indeed busy most of the time ("id" is very low), see whether any processes are running "nice" (check the "ni" number). It may be that there are some background processes consuming a lot of CPU time that can be changed to run "nice."

Second, compare the milliseconds per average seek ("msps") for all the disks you have mounted. If you have three identical disks mounted, yet the "msps" for one of the disks is substantially higher than the others, then you may be overworking it while the others remain mostly idle. If so, distribute the workload evenly among your disks so that you get as close to the same number of accesses per disk as possible. Note that a slower disk will always have a higher "msps" than a faster disk, so put your most often accessed information on your faster disks. The "msps" for a disk is usually around 20 milliseconds, and a DVD would have a much higher msps of approximately 200 milliseconds.

Virtual Memory Statistics with vmstat

man page

vmstat - 13

vmstat provides virtual memory statistics. It provides information on the status of processes, virtual memory, paging activity, faults, and the breakdown of the percentage of CPU time. **vmstat** acts somewhat differently among UNIX variants. The following examples show issuing **vmstat** on a Solaris system, an HP-UX system, an AIX system and a Linux system. You will, of course, have to determine the best options for your needs on your UNIX variant. In the following examples, the output was produced nine times at five-second intervals. The first argument to the **vmstat** command is the interval; the second is the number of times you would like output produced.

Solaris example:

```
# vmstat 5 9
 procs     memory            page            disk          faults      cpu
 r b w   swap  free  re  mf pi po fr de sr f0 s1 s3 s6   in   sy   cs us sy id
 0 0 0   4480  4696   0   0  1  0  0  0  0  0  0  0 79  864  130  297  0  7 92
 0 0 0 133020 5916   0   3  0  0  0  0  0  0  3  0  102   42   24  0  2 98
 0 0 0 133020 5916   0   0  0  0  0  0  0  0  0  0   70   48   24  0  0 100
 0 0 0 133020 5916   0   0  0  0  0  0  0  0  0  0   74   42   24  0  0 100
 0 0 0 133020 5916   0   0  0  0  0  0  0  0  0  0   35   45   23  0  0 99
```

```
0 0 0 133020  5916   0   0  0  0  0  0  0  0  0  0  0    65    66   26  0  0 100
0 0 0 133020  5916   0   0  0  0  0  0  0  0  0  0  0    52    44   23  0  1  99
0 0 0 133020  5916   0   0  0  0  0  0  0  0  0  0  0    53    54   24  0  1  99
0 0 0 133020  5916   0   0  0  0  0  0  0  0  0  1  0    60    53   25  0  2  98
```

man page

vmstat - 13

HP-UX example:

```
# vmstat 5 9

procs         memory                        page                          faults           cpu
r  b  w    avm   free  re  at  pi  po  fr  de  sr    in    sy   cs  us sy id
5 240 0  17646  3979   2   0   0   0   0   0   0     0   778  193  17  3 80
4 242 0  16722  4106   0   0   0   0   0   0   0   814 20649  258  89 10  2
4 240 0  16649  4106   0   0   0   0   0   0   0    83 18384  218  91  9  0
4 240 0  16468  4106   0   0   0   0   0   0   0   792 19552  273  89 11  1
5 239 0  15630  4012   9   0   0   0   0   0   0   804 18295  270  93  8 -1
5 241 0  16087  3934   6   0   0   0   0   0   0   920 21044  392  89 10  0
5 241 0  15313  3952  11   0   0   0   0   0   0   968 20239  431  90 10  0
4 242 0  16577  4043   3   0   0   0   0   0   0   926 19230  409  89 10  0
6 238 0  17453  4122   0   0   0   0   0   0   0   837 19269  299  89  9  2
```

AIX example:

```
martyp $ vmstat 5 9
kthr     memory              page                   faults          cpu
----- -----------   ------------------------   ------------   -----------
 r  b    avm  fre   re  pi  po  fr   sr cy   in   sy  cs  us sy id wa
 0  0  16604  246    0   0   0   0    2  0  149   79  36   0  1 98  0
 0  0  16604  246    0   0   0   0    0  0  153  125  41   0  0 99  0
 0  0  16604  246    0   0   0   0    0  0  143   83  33   0  0 99  0
 0  0  16604  246    0   0   0   0    0  0  140   94  35   0  1 99  0
 0  0  16604  246    0   0   0   0    0  0  166   62  32   0  0 99  0
 0  0  16604  246    0   0   0   0    0  0  150  102  38   1  0 99  0
 0  0  16604  246    0   0   0   0    0  0  183   78  34   0  0 99  0
 0  0  16604  246    0   0   0   0    0  0  132   87  33   0  1 99  0
 0  0  16604  246    0   0   0   0    0  0  147   84  38   0  0 99  0
```

Linux example:

```
# vmstat 5 5
   procs                       memory     swap        io     system        cpu
 r  b  w   swpd  free  buff  cache  si  so   bi  bo   in    cs  us sy id
 1  0  0   9432  1160   656  12024   1   2   14   1  138   274   3  1 96
 1  0  0   9684   828   652  12148   0  50    0  14  205  8499  82 18  0
 1  0  0   9684   784   652  11508   0   0    0   1  103  8682  81 19  0
 1  0  0   9684   800   652  10996   0   0    0   0  101  8683  80 20  0
 0  0  0   9772   796   652   9824  12  18    3   4  160  6577  66 17 18
```

You certainly get a lot for your money out of the **vmstat** command. Here is a brief description of the categories of information produced by **vmstat**. I have included a description of the fields in the HP-UX example because the manual page that appears at the end of this chapter for HP-UX. You can see, however, that the outputs are very similar.

Processes are classified into one of three categories: runnable ("r"), blocked on I/O or short-term resources ("b"), or swapped ("w").

Next you will see information about memory. "avm" is the number of virtual memory pages owned by processes that have run within the last 20 seconds. If this number is roughly the size of physical memory minus your kernel, then you are near paging. The "free" column indicates the number of pages on the system's free list. It doesn't mean that the process is finished running and these pages won't be accessed again; it just means that they have not been accessed recently. I suggest that you ignore this column.

Next is paging activity. The first field ("re") is particularly useful. It shows the pages that were reclaimed. These pages made it to the free list but were later referenced and had to be salvaged. Check to see that "re" is a low number. If you are reclaiming pages that were thought to be free by the system, then you are wasting valuable time salvaging these. Reclaiming pages is also a symptom that you are short on memory.

Next you see the number of faults in three categories: interrupts per second, which usually come from hardware ("in"), system calls per second ("sy"), and context switches per second ("cs").

The final output is CPU usage percentage for user ("us"), system ("sy"), and idle ("id"). This is not as complete as the **iostat** output, which also shows **nice** entries.

man page

iostat - 13

You want to verify that the runnable processes ("r") value is higher than the blocked ("b") value and the runnable but swapped ("w") processes value. If too many processes are blocked and swapped, your users will get a slower response time.

Whenever you see entries in the blocked ("b") or runnable-but-swapped ("w") columns, you see evidence that processes are standing still. You want to identify the source of the blocked and runnable-but-swapped processes. The reason will usually be insufficient RAM in your system. Swapped processes are those that have been moved from RAM to disk in an effort to free up RAM for other processes.

The following output shows a system in which there are many swapped processes occur:

#vmstat 5 15:

procs			memory				page					faults			cpu		
r	b	w	avm	free	re	at	pi	po	fr	de	sr	in	sy	cs	us	sy	id
0	0	19	9484	91	0	0	0	0	0	0	0	65	84	20	7	0	93
0	0	22	10253	68	0	0	0	0	0	0	0	214	939	127	72	7	21
0	0	25	10288	90	0	0	0	0	0	0	9	289	988	152	73	5	22
0	0	25	10300	89	0	0	0	0	0	0	9	325	820	151	76	3	21
0	0	24	10298	90	0	0	0	0	0	0	2	139	629	94	94	4	2
0	0	21	9889	86	0	0	0	0	0	0	1	189	782	111	72	5	23
0	0	20	9886	77	0	0	0	0	0	0	0	220	998	135	73	5	22
0	0	21	10274	77	0	0	0	0	0	0	0	220	723	124	69	3	28
0	0	22	10285	73	0	0	0	0	0	0	0	265	606	94	90	3	7
0	0	22	10291	69	0	0	0	0	0	0	0	156	872	122	71	5	24
0	0	20	10292	60	0	0	0	0	0	0	0	192	989	139	72	5	23
0	0	21	9913	257	0	0	0	0	0	0	1	282	736	118	81	2	17
0	0	22	9915	257	0	0	0	0	0	0	9	209	596	84	89	5	6
0	0	22	10699	237	0	0	0	0	0	3	7	165	945	117	70	7	23
0	0	21	10211	229	0	0	0	0	0	3	1	331	677	127	71	5	24

From this example, you can see that runnable ("r") and blocked ("b") processes are zero, but swapped ("w") processes are roughly 20 for each five-second interval. This result is indicative of a system that has a severe memory shortage. Note also that the active virtual memory ("avm") is around 10,000 blocks, which is roughly 40 MBytes on this system.

Network Statistics with netstat

man page

netstat - 9

netstat provides information related to network statistics. Because network bandwidth has as much to do with performance as the CPU and memory in some networks, you want to get an idea of the level of network traffic you have.

I use two forms of **netstat** to obtain network statistics. The first is **netstat -i**, which shows the state of interfaces that are autoconfigured. Although **netstat -i** gives a good rundown of the primary LAN interface, such as the network it is on, its name, and so on, it does not show useful statistical information.

The following diagram shows the output of **netstat -i**:

```
# netstat -i
```

Name	Mtu	Network	Address	Ipkts	Ierrs	Opkts	Oerrs	Col
lan0	1497	151.150	a4410.e.h.c	242194	120	107665	23	19884

netstat provides a concise output. Put another way, most of what you get from **netstat** is useful. Here is a description of the nine fields in the **netstat** example:

Name	The name of your network interface (Name), in this case, "lan0."
Mtu	The "maximum transmission unit," which is the maximum packet size sent by the interface card.
Network	The network address of the LAN to which the interface card is connected (151.150).
Address	The host name of your system. This is the symbolic name of your system as it appears in the **/etc/hosts** file if your networking is configured to use **/etc/hosts**.

Below is the statistical information. Depending on the system you are using, you may not see some of these commands:

Ipkts	The number of packets received by the interface card, in this case, "lan0."
Ierrs	The number of errors detected on incoming packets by the interface card.
Opkts	The number of packets transmitted by the interface card.
Oerrs	The number of errors detected during the transmission of packets by the interface card.
Col	The number of collisions that resulted from packet traffic.

man page

netstat - 9

netstat provides cumulative data since the node was last powered up; you might have a long elapsed time over which data was accumulated. If you are interested in seeing useful statistical information, you can use **netstat** with different options. You can also specify an interval to report statistics. I usually ignore the first entry, because it shows all data since the system was last powered up. This means that the data includes non-prime hours when the system was idle. I prefer to view data at the time the system is working its hardest. The following examples show running **netstat -I** and specifying the lan interface for Solaris, HP-UX, and AIX. These outputs are nearly identical, although the name of the network interface does vary among UNIX variants. The **netstat** command is run at an interval of five seconds. The Linux version of this command, which is not shown, does not allow me to specify an interval.

Solaris example:

```
# netstat -I le0 5
     input   le0       output              input   (Total)   output
packets errs  packets errs  colls  packets errs  packets errs  colls
116817990 0     3299582 11899 1653100 116993185 0    3474777 11899 1653100
185       0     3       0     0      185     0     3       0     0
273       0     8       0     0      273     0     8       0     0
153       0     3       0     0      153     0     3       0     0
154       0     3       0     0      154     0     3       0     0
126       0     3       0     0      126     0     3       0     0
378       0     2       0     0      378     0     2       0     0
399       0     4       0     0      399     0     4       0     0
286       0     2       0     0      286     0     2       0     0
```

HP-UX example:

man page

netstat - 9

```
# netstat -I lan0 5
```

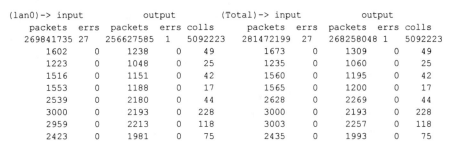

```
(lan0)-> input            output        (Total)-> input            output
    packets  errs  packets errs colls        packets errs  packets errs colls
 269841735  27   256627585  1  5092223     281472199  27  268258048 1  5092223
      1602   0       1238   0    49            1673   0      1309   0    49
      1223   0       1048   0    25            1235   0      1060   0    25
      1516   0       1151   0    42            1560   0      1195   0    42
      1553   0       1188   0    17            1565   0      1200   0    17
      2539   0       2180   0    44            2628   0      2269   0    44
      3000   0       2193   0   228            3000   0      2193   0   228
      2959   0       2213   0   118            3003   0      2257   0   118
      2423   0       1981   0    75            2435   0      1993   0    75
```

AIX example:

```
# netstat -I en0 5
   input   (en0)     output            input  (Total)   output
 packets errs  packets errs colls  packets errs  packets errs colls
46333531   0  1785025   0    0  47426087   0  2913405   0    0
     203   0        1   0    0       204   0        2   0    0
     298   0        1   0    0       298   0        1   0    0
     293   0        1   0    0       304   0       12   0    0
     191   0        1   0    0       191   0        1   0    0
     150   0        2   0    0       151   0        3   0    0
     207   0        3   0    0       218   0       15   0    0
     162   0        3   0    0       162   0        4   0    0
     120   0        2   0    0       120   0        2   0    0
```

With this example, you get multiple outputs of what is taking place on the LAN interface, including the totals on the right side of the output. As I mentioned earlier, you may want to ignore the first output, because it includes information over a long time period. This may include a time when your network was idle, and therefore the data may not be important to you.

You can specify the network interface on which you want statistics reported by using **-I interface**; in the case of the example, it was **-I** and either *le0*, *lan0*, or *en0*. An interval of five seconds was also used in this example.

Analyzing **netstat** statistical information is intuitive. You want to verify that the collisions (Colls) are much lower than the packets transmitted (Opkts). Collisions occur on output from your LAN interface. Every collision your LAN interface encounters slows down the network. You will get varying opinions about what is too many collisions. If your collisions are less than 5 percent of "Opkts," you're probably in good shape and better off spending your time analyzing some other system resource. If this number is high, you may want to consider segmenting your network in some way such as installing networking equipment between portions of the network that don't share a lot of data.

As a rule of thumb, if you reduce the number of packets you are receiving and transmitting ("Ipkts" and "Opkts"), then you will have less overall network traffic and fewer collisions. Keep this in mind as you plan your network or upgrades to your systems. You may want to have two LAN cards in systems that are in constant communication. That way, these systems have a "private" LAN over which to communicate and do not adversely affect the performance of other systems on the network. One LAN interface on each system is devoted to intrasystem communication. This provides a "tight" communication path among systems that usually act as servers. The second LAN interface is used to communicate with any systems that are usually clients on a larger network.

man page

netstat - 9

You can also obtain information related to routing with **netstat** (see "Networking" chapter). The **-r** option to **netstat** shows the routing tables, which you usually want to know, and the **-n** option can be used to print network addresses as numbers rather than as names. In the following examples, **netstat** is issued with the **-r** option (this will be used when describing the **netstat** output) and the **-rn** options, so that you can compare the two outputs:

$ netstat -r

Routing tables

Destination	Gateway	Flags	Refs	Use	Interface	Pmtu
hp700	localhost	UH	0	28	lo0	4608
default	router1	UG	0	0	lan0	4608
128.185.61	system1	U	347	28668	lan0	1500

$ netstat -rn

Routing tables

Destination	Gateway	Flags	Refs	Use	Interface	Pmtu
127.0.0.1	127.0.0.1	UH	0	28	lo0	4608
default	128.185.61.1	UG	0	0	lan0	4608
128.185.61	128.185.61.2	U	347	28668	lan0	1500

man page

netstat - 9

With **netstat**, some information is provided about the router, which is the middle entry. The **-r** option shows information about routing, but there are many other useful options to this command are available. Of particular interest in this output is "Flags," which defines the type of routing that takes place. Here are descriptions of the most common flags, which may be different among UNIX variants, from the manual page at the end of this chapter.

1=U   Route to a *network* via a gateway that is the local host itself.

3=UG   Route to a *network* via a gateway that is the remote host.

5=UH   Route to a *host* via a gateway that is the local host itself.

7=UGH   Route to a *host* via a remote gateway that is a host.

The first line is for the local host or loopback interface called **lo0** at address 127.0.0.1 (you can see this address in the **netstat -rn** example). The UH flags indicate that the destination address is the local host itself. This class A address allows a client and server on the same host to communicate with one another with TCP/IP. A datagram sent to the loopback interface won't go out onto the network; it will simply go through the loopback.

The second line is for the default route. This entry says to send packets to router1 if a more specific route can't be found. In this case, the router has a UG under Flags. Some routers are configured with a

U; others, such as the one in this example, with a UG. I've found that I usually end up determining through trial and error whether a U or UG is required. If there is a U in Flags and I am unable to ping a system on the other side of a router, a UG usually fixes the problem.

The third line is for the system's network interface **lan0**. This means to use this network interface for packets to be sent to 128.185.61.

Check Processes with ps

kill - 6

ps - 12

Knowing about the processes running on your system, and knowing how to stop them, are important to both system administration and performance. Therefore, this process section, the **kill** command, and signals appear in both this chapter and the system administration chapter.

To find the answer to "What is my system doing?," use **ps -ef**. This command provides information about every running process on your system. If, for instance, you want to know whether NFS is running, you simply type **ps -ef** and look for NFS daemons. Although **ps** tells you every process that is running on your system, it doesn't provide a good summary of the level of system resources being consumed. I would guess that **ps** is the most often issued system administration command. There are a number of options you can use with **ps**. I normally use **e** and **f**, which provide information about every ("**e**") running process and lists this information in full ("**f**"). **ps** outputs are almost identical from system to system. The following three examples are from a Solaris, AIX, and HP-UX system, respectively:

Solaris example:

```
martyp $ ps -ef
    UID   PID  PPID  C    STIME TTY      TIME CMD
   root     0     0  0  Feb 18 ?        0:01 sched
   root     1     0  0  Feb 18 ?        1:30 /etc/init -
   root     2     0  0  Feb 18 ?        0:02 pageout
   root     3     0  1  Feb 18 ?      613:44 fsflush
   root  3065  3059  0  Feb 22 ?        5:10 /usr/dt/bin/sdtperfmeter -f -H -r
```

```
     root    88     1   0   Feb 18 ?       0:01 /usr/sbin/in.routed -q
     root   478     1   0   Feb 18 ?       0:00 /usr/lib/saf/sac -t 300
     root    94     1   0   Feb 18 ?       2:50 /usr/sbin/rpcbind
     root   150     1   0   Feb 18 ?       6:03 /usr/sbin/syslogd
     root    96     1   0   Feb 18 ?       0:00 /usr/sbin/keyserv
     root   144     1   0   Feb 18 ?      50:37 /usr/lib/autofs/automountd
     root  1010     1   0   Apr 12 ?       0:00 /opt/perf/bin/midaemon
     root   106     1   0   Feb 18 ?       0:02 /usr/lib/netsvc/yp/ypbind -broadt
     root   156     1   0   Feb 18 ?       0:03 /usr/sbin/cron
     root   176     1   0   Feb 18 ?       0:00 /usr/lib/lpsched
     root   129     1   0   Feb 18 ?       0:00 /usr/lib/nfs/lockd
   daemon   130     1   0   Feb 18 ?       0:01 /usr/lib/nfs/statd
     root 14798     1   0   Mar 09 ?      31:10 /usr/sbin/nscd
     root   133     1   0   Feb 18 ?       0:10 /usr/sbin/inetd -s
     root   197     1   0   Feb 18 ?       0:00 /usr/lib/power/powerd
     root   196     1   0   Feb 18 ?       0:35 /etc/opt/licenses/lmgrd.ste -c /d
     root   213     1   0   Feb 18 ?    4903:09 /usr/sbin/vold
     root   199   196   0   Feb 18 ?       0:03 suntechd -T  4 -c /etc/optd
     root   219     1   0   Feb 18 ?       0:08 /usr/lib/sendmail -bd -q15m
     root   209     1   0   Feb 18 ?       0:05 /usr/lib/utmpd
     root  2935   266   0   Feb 22 ?      48:08 /usr/openwin/bin/Xsun :0 -nobanna
     root 16795 16763   1   07:51:34 pts/4 0:00 ps -ef
     root  2963  2954   0   Feb 22 ?       0:17 /usr/openwin/bin/fbconsole
     root   479     1   0   Feb 18 console 0:00 /usr/lib/saf/ttymon -g -h -p sunc
     root 10976     1   0   Jun 01 ?       0:00 /opt/perf/bin/ttd
     root  7468     1   0   Feb 24 ?       0:13 /opt/perf/bin/pvalarmd
     root   266     1   0   Feb 18 ?       0:01 /usr/dt/bin/dtlogin -daemon
   martyp 16763 16761   0   07:46:46 pts/4 0:01 -ksh
     root 10995     1   0   Jun 01 ?       0:01 /opt/perf/bin/perflbd
     root   484   478   0   Feb 18 ?       0:00 /usr/lib/saf/ttymon
     root   458     1   0   Feb 18 ?      20:06 /usr/lib/snmp/snmpdx -y -c /etc/f
     root 16792  3059   0   07:50:37 ?     0:00 /usr/dt/bin/dtscreen -mode blank
     root   471     1   0   Feb 18 ?       0:07 /usr/lib/dmi/dmispd
     root   474     1   0   Feb 18 ?       0:00 /usr/lib/dmi/snmpXdmid -s
     root   485   458   0   Feb 18 ?     739:44 mibiisa -r -p 32874
     root  2954  2936   0   Feb 22 ?       0:01 /bin/ksh /usr/dt/bin/Xsession
     root  2936   266   0   Feb 22 ?       0:00 /usr/dt/bin/dtlogin -daemon
     root  3061  3059   0   Feb 22 ?       1:32 dtwm
     root  3058     1   0   Feb 22 pts/2   0:01 /usr/dt/bin/ttsession
     root   712   133   0   Feb 18 ?       0:01 rpc.ttdbserverd
     root 11001 11000   0                  0:01 <defunct>
     root  2938     1   0   Feb 22 ?       0:00 /usr/openwin/bin/fbconsole -d :0
     root  2999  2954   0   Feb 22 pts/2   0:16 /usr/dt/bin/sdt_shell -c      unt
     root  3059  3002   0   Feb 22 pts/2 283:35 /usr/dt/bin/dtsession
     root  3063  3059   0   Feb 22 ?       0:03 /usr/dt/bin/dthelpview -helpVolur
     root  3099  3062   0   Feb 22 ?       0:13 /usr/dt/bin/dtfile -geometry +700
     root 11000 10995   0   Jun 01 ?       0:02 /opt/perf/bin/agdbserver -t alar/
     root  3002  2999   0   Feb 22 pts/2   0:01 -ksh -c      unset DT;     DISPLg
     root   730   133   0   Feb 18 ?       1:37 rpc.rstatd
     root  3062  3059   0   Feb 22 ?       2:17 /usr/dt/bin/dtfile -geometry +700
     root  3067     1   0   Feb 22 ?       0:00 /bin/ksh /usr/dt/bin/sdtvolcheckm
     root  3000     1   0   Feb 22 ?       0:00 /usr/dt/bin/dsdm
     root  3078  3067   0   Feb 22 ?       0:00 /bin/cat /tmp/.removable/notify0
     root 10984     1   0   Jun 01 ?      12:42 /opt/perf/dce/bin/dced -b
     root 16761   133   0   07:46:45 ?     0:00 in.telnetd
   martyp $
```

AIX example:

man page

ps - 12

```
martyp $ ps -ef
     UID   PID  PPID  C   STIME   TTY  TIME CMD
    root     1     0  0   Feb 24    -  5:07 /etc/init
    root  2208 15520  0   Feb 24    -  8:21 dtwm
    root  2664     1  0   Feb 24    -  0:00 /usr/dt/bin/dtlogin -daemon
    root  2882     1  0   Feb 24    - 158:41 /usr/sbin/syncd 60
    root  3376  2664  5   Feb 24    - 3598:41 /usr/lpp/X11/bin/X -D /usr/lib/
    root  3624  2664  0   Feb 24    -  0:00 dtlogin <:0>           -daemon
    root  3950     1  6   Feb 24    - 5550:30 /usr/lpp/perf/bin/llbd
    root  4144     1  0   Feb 24    -  0:00 /usr/lpp/perf/bin/midaemon
    root  4490     1  0   Feb 24    -  0:48 /usr/lpp/perf/bin/perflbd
    root  4906     1  0   Feb 24    -  0:00 /usr/lib/errdemon
```

```
root  5172     1  0  Feb 24    -   0:00 /usr/sbin/srcmstr
root  5724  5172  0  Feb 24    -   9:54 /usr/sbin/syslogd
root  6242  5172  0  Feb 24    -   0:00 /usr/sbin/biod 6
root  6450  5172  0  Feb 24    -   0:02 sendmail: accepting connections
root  6710  5172  0  Feb 24    -   7:34 /usr/sbin/portmap
root  6966  5172  0  Feb 24    -   0:23 /usr/sbin/inetd
root  7224  5172  0  Feb 24    -   1:09 /usr/sbin/timed -S
root  7482  5172  0  Feb 24    -  11:55 /usr/sbin/snmpd
root  8000     1  0  Feb 24    -   9:17 ovspmd
root  8516  8782  0  Feb 24    -   0:00 netfmt -CF
root  8782     1  0  Feb 24    -   0:00 /usr/OV/bin/ntl_reader 0 1 1 1
root  9036  8000  0  Feb 24    -  10:09 ovwdb -O -n5000
root  9288  8000  0  Feb 24    -   0:44 pmd -Au -At -Mu -Mt -m
root  9546  8000  0  Feb 24    -  20:05 trapgend -f
root  9804  8000  0  Feb 24    -   0:28 trapd
root 10062  8000  0  Feb 24    -   0:47 orsd
root 10320  8000  0  Feb 24    -   0:33 ovesmd
root 10578  8000  0  Feb 24    -   0:30 ovelmd
root 10836  8000  0  Feb 24    -  13:12 ovtopmd -O
root 11094  8000  0  Feb 24    -  17:50 netmon -P
root 11352  8000  0  Feb 24    -   0:02 snmpCollect
root 11954     1  0  Feb 24    -   1:22 /usr/sbin/cron
root 12140  5172  0  Feb 24    -   0:01 /usr/lib/netsvc/yp/ypbind
root 12394  5172  0  Feb 24    -   1:39 /usr/sbin/rpc.mountd
root 12652  5172  0  Feb 24    -   0:29 /usr/sbin/nfsd 8
root 12908  5172  0  Feb 24    -   0:00 /usr/sbin/rpc.statd
root 13166  5172  0  Feb 24    -   0:29 /usr/sbin/rpc.lockd
root 13428     1  0  Feb 24    -   0:00 /usr/sbin/uprintfd
root 14190  5172  0  Feb 24    -  72:59 /usr/sbin/automountd
root 14452  5172  0  Feb 24    -   0:17 /usr/sbin/qdaemon
root 14714  5172  0  Feb 24    -   0:00 /usr/sbin/writesrv
root 14992     1  0  Feb 24    - 252:26 /usr/lpp/perf/bin/scopeux
root 15520  3624  1  Feb 24    -  15:29 /usr/dt/bin/dtsession
root 15742     1  0  Feb 24    -   0:00 /usr/lpp/diagnostics/bin/diagd
root 15998     1  0  Feb 24  lft0  0:00 /usr/sbin/getty /dev/console
root 16304 18892  0  Feb 24  pts/0 0:00 /bin/ksh
root 16774     1  0  Feb 24    -   0:00 /usr/lpp/perf/bin/ttd
root 17092  4490  0  Feb 24    -  68:54 /usr/lpp/perf/bin/rep_server -t
root 17370 19186  3             0:00 <defunct>
root 17630 15520  0  Mar 25    -   0:00 /usr/dt/bin/dtexec -open 0 -ttp
root 17898 15520  0  Mar 20    -   0:00 /usr/dt/bin/dtexec -open 0 -ttp
root 18118 19888  0  Feb 24  pts/1 0:00 /bin/ksh
root 18366  6966  0  Feb 24    -   0:00 rpc.ttdbserver 100083 1
root 18446 15520  0  Mar 15    -   0:00 /usr/dt/bin/dtexec -open 0 -ttp
root 18892 15520  0  Feb 24    -   3:46 /usr/dt/bin/dtterm
root 19186 16304  0  Feb 24  pts/0 0:01 /usr/lpp/X11/bin/msmit
root 19450     1  0  Feb 24    -  26:53 /usr/dt/bin/ttsession -s
root 19684  2208  0  Feb 24    -   0:00 /usr/dt/bin/dtexec -open 0 -ttp
root 19888 19684  0  Feb 24    -   0:00 /usr/dt/bin/dtterm
root 20104 15520  0  Feb 27    -   0:00 /usr/dt/bin/dtexec -open 0 -ttp
root 20248 20104  0  Feb 27    -   0:03 /usr/dt/bin/dtscreen
root 20542 29708  0  May 14    -   0:03 /usr/dt/bin/dtscreen
root 20912 26306  0  Apr 05    -   0:03 /usr/dt/bin/dtscreen
root 33558     1  0  May 18    -   3:28 /usr/atria/etc/lockmgr -a /var/
root 33834  6966  3 07:55:49   -   0:00 telnetd
root 34072     1  0  May 18    -   0:00 /usr/atria/etc/albd_server
martyp 36296 36608 13 07:56:07 pts/2 0:00 ps -ef
martyp 36608 33834  1 07:55:50 pts/2 0:00 -ksh
root 37220 15520  0  May 28    -   0:00 /usr/dt/bin/dtexec -open 0 -ttp
martyp $
```

HP-UX example (partial listing):

man page

ps - 12

```
martyp $ ps -ef
    UID    PID   PPID C  STIME   TTY    TIME   COMMAND
    root     0      0 0  Mar  9    ?  107:28 swapper
    root     1      0 0  Mar  9    ?    2:27 init
```

```
   root      2     0  0  Mar  9  ?      14:13 vhand
   root      3     0  0  Mar  9  ?     114:55 statdaemon
   root      4     0  0  Mar  9  ?       5:57 unhashdaemon
   root      7     0  0  Mar  9  ?     154:33 ttisr
   root     70     0  0  Mar  9  ?       0:01 lvmkd
   root     71     0  0  Mar  9  ?       0:01 lvmkd
   root     72     0  0  Mar  9  ?       0:01 lvmkd
   root     13     0  0  Mar  9  ?       9:54 vx_sched_thread
   root     14     0  0  Mar  9  ?       1:54 vx_iflush_thread
   root     15     0  0  Mar  9  ?       2:06 vx_ifree_thread
   root     16     0  0  Mar  9  ?       2:27 vx_inactive_cache_thread
   root     17     0  0  Mar  9  ?       0:40 vx_delxwri_thread
   root     18     0  0  Mar  9  ?       0:33 vx_logflush_thread
   root     19     0  0  Mar  9  ?       0:07 vx_attrsync_thread
                            .
                            .
                            .
   root     69     0  0  Mar  9  ?       0:09 vx_inactive_thread
   root     73     0  0  Mar  9  ?       0:01 lvmkd
   root     74     0 19  Mar  9  ?    3605:29 netisr
   root     75     0  0  Mar  9  ?       0:18 netisr
   root     76     0  0  Mar  9  ?       0:17 netisr
   root     77     0  0  Mar  9  ?       0:14 netisr
   root     78     0  0  Mar  9  ?       0:48 nvsisr
   root     79     0  0  Mar  9  ?       0:00 supsched
   root     80     0  0  Mar  9  ?       0:00 smpsched
   root     81     0  0  Mar  9  ?       0:00 smpsched
   root     82     0  0  Mar  9  ?       0:00 sblksched
   root     83     0  0  Mar  9  ?       0:00 sblksched
   root     84     0  0  Mar  9  ?       0:00 strmem
   root     85     0  0  Mar  9  ?       0:00 strweld
   root   3730     1  0  16:39:22 console   0:00 /usr/sbin/getty console console
   root    404     1  0  Mar  9  ?       3:57 /usr/sbin/swagentd
 oracle    919     1  0  15:23:23 ?       0:00 oraclegprd (LOCAL=NO)
   root    289     1  2  Mar  9  ?      78:34 /usr/sbin/syncer
   root    426     1  0  Mar  9  ?       0:10 /usr/sbin/syslogd -D
   root    576     1  0  Mar  9  ?       0:00 /usr/sbin/portmap
   root    429     1  0  Mar  9  ?       0:00 /usr/sbin/ptydaemon
   root    590     1  0  Mar  9  ?       0:00 /usr/sbin/biod 4
   root    442     1  0  Mar  9  ?       0:00 /usr/lbin/nktl_daemon 0 0 0 0 0 1 -2
 oracle   8145     1  0  12:02:48 ?       0:00 oraclegprd (LOCAL=NO)
   root    591     1  0  Mar  9  ?       0:00 /usr/sbin/biod 4
   root    589     1  0  Mar  9  ?       0:00 /usr/sbin/biod 4
   root    592     1  0  Mar  9  ?       0:00 /usr/sbin/biod 4
   root    604     1  0  Mar  9  ?       0:00 /usr/sbin/rpc.lockd
   root    598     1  0  Mar  9  ?       0:00 /usr/sbin/rpc.statd
   root    610     1  0  Mar  9  ?       0:16 /usr/sbin/automount -f /etc/auto_master
   root    638     1  0  Mar  9  ?       0:06 sendmail: accepting connections
   root    618     1  0  Mar  9  ?       0:02 /usr/sbin/inetd
   root    645     1  0  Mar  9  ?       5:01 /usr/sbin/snmpdm
   root    661     1  0  Mar  9  ?      11:28 /usr/sbin/fddisubagtd
   root    711     1  0  Mar  9  ?      30:59 /opt/dce/sbin/rpcd
   root    720     1  0  Mar  9  ?       0:00 /usr/sbin/vtdaemon
   root    867   777  1  Mar  9  ?       0:00 <defunct>
     lp    733     1  0  Mar  9  ?       0:00 /usr/sbin/lpsched
   root    777     1  0  Mar  9  ?       8:55 DIAGMON
   root    742     1  0  Mar  9  ?       0:15 /usr/sbin/cron
 oracle   7880     1  0  11:43:47 ?       0:00 oraclegprd (LOCAL=NO)
   root    842     1  0  Mar  9  ?       0:00 /usr/vue/bin/vuelogin
 oracle   5625     1  0  07:00:14 ?       0:01 ora_smon_gprd
   root    781     1  0  Mar  9  ?       0:00 /usr/sbin/envd
   root    833   777  0  Mar  9  ?       0:00 DEMLOG   DEMLOG;DEMLOG;0;0;
   root    813     1  0  Mar  9  ?       0:00 /usr/sbin/nfsd 4
   root    807     1  0  Mar  9  ?       0:00 /usr/sbin/rpc.mountd
   root    815   813  0  Mar  9  ?       0:00 /usr/sbin/nfsd 4
```

```
root   817   813   0  Mar  9  ?    0:00 /usr/sbin/nfsd 4
root   835   777   0  Mar  9  ?    0:13 PSMON   PSMON;PSMON;0;0;
```

Here is a brief description of the headings:

UID	The user ID of the process owner.
PID	The process ID (you can use this number to kill the process).
PPID	The process ID of the parent process.
C	Process utilization for scheduling.
STIME	Start time of the process.
TTY	The controlling terminal for the process.
TIME	The cumulative execution time for the process.
COMMAND	The command name and arguments.

man page

ps - 12

ps gives a quick profile of the processes running on your system. To get more detailed information, you can include the "l" option, which includes a lot of useful additional information as shown in the following example:

```
martyp $ ps -efl
 F S     UID   PID  PPID  C PRI NI    ADDR     SZ    WCHAN    STIME TTY       D
19 T    root     0     0  0   0 SY f026f7f0      0            Feb 18  ?        d
 8 S    root     1     0  0  41 20 f5b90808    175 f5b90a30   Feb 18  ?        -
19 S    root     2     0  0   0 SY f5b90108      0 f0283fd0   Feb 18  ?        t
19 S    root     3     0  0   0 SY f5b8fa08      0 f0287a44   Feb 18  ?       6h
 8 S    root  3065  3059  0  40 20 f626d040   1639 f62aab96   Feb 22  ?        c
 8 S    root    88     1  0  40 20 f5b8d708    377 f5b59df6   Feb 18  ?        q
 8 S    root   478     1  0  41 20 f5b8ec08    388 f5b51bb8   Feb 18  ?        o
 8 S    root    94     1  0  41 20 f5b8d008    527 f5b59e46   Feb 18  ?        d
 8 S    root   150     1  0  41 20 f5da1a10    808 f5b59806   Feb 18  ?        d
 8 S    root    96     1  0  67 20 f5da2810    535 f5b59ad6   Feb 18  ?        v
 8 S    root   144     1  0  41 20 f5da0c10   2694 ef69f61c   Feb 18  ?       5d
 8 S    root  1010     1  0   0 RT f61da330    496 f5dbec1c   Apr 12  ?        n
 8 S    root   106     1  0  41 20 f5da1310    485 f5b59e96   Feb 18  ?        s
 8 S    root   156     1  0  51 20 f5b8de08    446 f5b51eb8   Feb 18  ?        n
 8 S    root   176     1  0  53 20 f5da2110    740 f5b59036   Feb 18  ?        d
 8 S    root   129     1  0  56 20 f5d9fe10    447 f5b59cb6   Feb 18  ?        d
 8 S  daemon   130     1  0  41 20 f5d9f710    564 f5b59b76   Feb 18  ?        d
 8 S    root 14798     1  0  45 20 f5b8e508    616 f5b8e730   Mar 09  ?       3d
 8 S    root   133     1  0  51 20 f5e18818    507 f5b59c66   Feb 18  ?        s
 8 S    root   197     1  0  63 20 f5e15e18    284 f5e16040   Feb 18  ?        d
 8 S    root   196     1  0  41 20 f5da0510    429 f5c68f8e   Feb 18  ?        c
 8 S    root   213     1  0  41 20 f5e16518    586 f5c68b2e   Feb 18  ?       4d
 8 S    root   199   196  0  41 20 f5e16c18    451 f5b59f86   Feb 18  ?        i
 8 S    root   219     1  0  41 20 f5e17318    658 f5b59d06   Feb 18  ?        m
 8 S    root   209     1  0  41 20 f5e18118    234 f5c68e4e   Feb 18  ?        d
 8 S    root  2935   266  0  40 20 f61db130   2473 f62aaa56   Feb 22  ?        4
 8 S    root 16800  3059  1  81 30 f626f340   1466 f61b345e 07:59:40  ?        k
```

```
8 S     root    2963   2954   0   40 20  f5f52028    513 f61b313e  Feb 22 ?        e
8 S     root     479      1   0   55 20  f5ee7120    407 f5fde2c6  Feb 18 console  g
8 S     root   10976      1   0   65 20  f5f55828    478 f5c6853e  Jun 01 ?        d
8 S     root    7468      1   0   46 20  f621da38   2851     8306c  Feb 24 ?        d
8 S     root     266      1   0   41 20  f5ee5520   1601 f5c6858e  Feb 18 ?        n
8 S   martyp  16763  16761   0   51 20  f6270140    429 f62701ac 07:46:46 pts/4    h
8 S     root   10995      1   0   41 20  f5b8f308   2350 f5fde5e6  Jun 01 ?        d
8 S     root     484    478   0   41 20  f5ee4e20    408 f5ee5048  Feb 18 ?        n
8 S     root     458      1   0   41 20  f5f54a28    504 f5fde906  Feb 18 ?       2m
8 O     root   16802  16763   1   61 20  f5ee7820    220            08:00:05 pts/4  1
8 S     root     471      1   0   41 20  f5f53c28    658 f5fde726  Feb 18 ?        d
8 S     root     474      1   0   51 20  f5f53528    804 f61a58b6  Feb 18 ?        g
8 S     root     485    458   0   41 20  f5f52e28    734 f607ecde  Feb 18 ?       74
8 S     root    2954   2936   0   40 20  f626e540    433 f626e5ac  Feb 22 ?        n
8 S     root    2936    266   0   66 20  f5ee4720   1637 f5ee478c  Feb 22 ?        n
8 S     root    3061   3059   0   40 20  f5e17a18   2041 f61b359e  Feb 22 ?        m
8 S     root    3058      1   0   40 20  f61daa30   1067 f62aadc6  Feb 22 pts/2    n
8 S     root     712    133   0   41 20  f61d8e30    798 f61b390e  Feb 18 ?        d
8 Z     root   11001  11000   0    0                                              >
8 S     root    2938      1   0   60 20  f5ee6320    513 f601bfb6  Feb 22 ?        0
8 S     root    2999   2954   0   40 20  f621e138   1450 f61b33be  Feb 22 pts/2    t
8 S     root    3059   3002   1   51 20  f626de40   4010 f62aafa6  Feb 22 pts/2   2n
8 S     root    3063   3059   0   50 20  f621e838   1952 f62aa556  Feb 22 ?        0
8 S     root    3099   3062   0   40 20  f5f52728   2275 f60a1d18  Feb 22 ?        0
8 S     root   11000  10995   0   48 20  f626d740   2312    55694  Jun 01 ?        e
8 S     root    3002   2999   0   43 20  f61d8730    427 f61d879c  Feb 22 pts/2    =
8 S     root     730    133   0   40 20  f61d9530    422 f62aa9b6  Feb 18 ?        d
8 S     root    3062   3059   0   61 20  f621b738   2275 f62aa506  Feb 22 ?        0
8 S     root    3067      1   0   40 20  f5ee5c20    424 f5ee5c8c  Feb 22 ?        d
8 S     root    3000      1   0   40 20  f61d8030    518 f62aa8c6  Feb 22 ?        m
8 S     root    3078   3067   0   40 20  f61d9c30    211 f5b512b8  Feb 22 ?        0
8 S     root   10984      1   0   41 20  f5f54328   2484 eee46e84  Jun 01 ?       1b
8 S     root   16761    133   0   44 20  f5ee4020    411 f5c6894e 07:46:45 ?       d
martyp $
```

In this example, the first column is *F* for flags. *F* provides octal information about whether the process is swapped, in core, a system process, and so on. The octal value sometimes varies from system to system, so check the manual pages for your system to see the octal value of the flags.

S is for state. The state can be sleeping, as indicated by *S* for most of the processes shown in the example, waiting, running, intermediate, terminated, and so on. Again, some of these values may vary from system to system, so check your manual pages.

Some additional useful information in this output are: *NI* for the nice value; *ADDR* for the memory address of the process; *SZ* for the size in physical pages of the process; and *WCHAN*, which is the event for which the process is waiting.

Killing a Process

man page

ps - 12

man page

kill - 6

If you issue the **ps** command and find that one of your processes is hung, or if you started a large job that you wish to stop, you can do so with the **kill** command. **kill** is a utility that sends a signal to the process you identify. You can **kill** any process that you own. In addition, superuser can kill almost any process on the system.

To kill a process that you own, simply issue the **kill** command and the Process ID (PID). The following example shows issuing the **ps** command to find all processes owned by *martyp*, killing a process, and checking to see that it has disappeared:

man page

grep - 10

```
martyp $ ps -ef | grep martyp
   martyp 19336 19334 0 05:24:32 pts/4  0:01 -ksh
   martyp 19426 19336 0 06:01:01 pts/4  0:00 grep martyp
   martyp 19424 19336 5 06:00:48 pts/4  0:01 find / -name .login
martyp $ kill 19424
martyp $ ps -ef | grep martyp
   martyp 19336 19334 0 05:24:32 pts/4  0:01 -ksh
   martyp 19428 19336 1 06:01:17 pts/4  0:00 grep martyp
[1] + Terminated                  find / -name .login &
martyp $
```

The example shows killing process *19424,* which is owned by *martyp*. We confirm that the process has indeed been killed by reissuing the **ps** command.

You can kill several processes on the command line by issuing **kill** followed by a space-separated list of all the process numbers you wish to kill.

Take special care when killing processes if you are logged in as superuser. You may adversely affect the way the system runs and have to manually restart processes or reboot the system.

Signals

When you issue the **kill** command and process number, you are also sending a *signal* associated with the **kill**. We did not specify a *signal* in our **kill** example; however, the default *signal* of 15, or *SIGTERM*, was used. These *signals* are used by the system to communicate with processes. The *signal* of 15 we used to terminate our process is a software termination *signal* that is usually enough to terminate a user process such as the **find** we had started. A process that is difficult to kill may require the *SIGKILL*, or 9 *signal*. This *signal* causes an immediate termination of the process. I use this only as a last resort because processes killed with *SIGKILL* do not always terminate smoothly. To kill such processes as the shell, you sometimes have to use *SIGKILL*.

man page
kill - 6

man page
find - 10

You can use either the *signal* name or number. These signal numbers sometimes vary from system to system, so view the manual page for *signal*, usually in section 5, to see the list of *signals* on your system. A list of some of the most frequently used *signal* numbers and corresponding *signals* follows:

Signal number	Signal
1	SIGHUP
2	SIGINT
3	SIGQUIT
9	SIGKILL
15	SIGTERM
24	SIGSTOP

To kill a process with id *234* with *SIGKILL*, you would issue the following command:

```
$ kill -9 234
     |    |   |
     |    |   |> process id (PID)
     |    |> signal number
     |> kill command to terminate the process
```

Show Remote Mounts with showmount

man page

showmount
- 13

showmount is used to show all remote systems (clients) that have mounted a local file system. **showmount** is useful for determining the file systems that are most often mounted by clients with NFS. The output of **showmount** is particularly easy to read because it lists the host name and the directory that was mounted by the client.

NFS servers often end up serving many NFS clients that were not originally intended to be served. This situation ends up consuming additional UNIX system resources on the NFS server, as well as additional network bandwidth. Keep in mind that any data transferred from an NFS server to an NFS client consumes network bandwidth, and in some cases may be a substantial amount of bandwith if large files or applications are being transferred from the NFS server to the client. The following example is a partial output of **showmount** taken from a system. **showmount** runs on the HP-UX, AIX, and Linux systems I have been using throughout this chapter, but not the Solaris system:

```
# showmount -a

sys100.ct.mp.com:/applic

sys101.ct.mp.com:/applic

sys102.cal.mp.com:/applic

sys103.cal.mp.com:/applic

sys104.cal.mp.com:/applic

sys105.cal.mp.com:/applic

sys106.cal.mp.com:/applic

sys107.cal.mp.com:/applic

sys108.cal.mp.com:/applic

sys109.cal.mp.com:/applic
```

```
# showmount -a
```

sys200.cal.mp.com:/usr/users

sys201.cal.mp.com:/usr/users

sys202.cal.mp.com:/usr/users

sys203.cal.mp.com:/usr/users

sys204.cal.mp.com:/usr/users

sys205.cal.mp.com:/usr/users

sys206.cal.mp.com:/usr/users

sys207.cal.mp.com:/usr/users

sys208.cal.mp.com:/usr/users

sys209.cal.mp.com:/usr/users

man page

showmount
- 13

The three following options are available to the **showmount** command:

-**a** prints output in the format "name:directory," as shown above.

-**d** lists all the local directories that have been remotely
mounted by clients.

-**e** prints a list of exported file systems.

The following are examples of **showmount -d** and **-e**:

```
# showmount -d
```

/applic

/usr/users

/usr/oracle

/usr/users/emp.data

/network/database

/network/users

showmount -d

/tmp/working

showmount -e

export list for server101.cal.mp.com

/applic

/usr/users

/cdrom

Show System Swap

If your system has insufficient main memory for all the information it needs to work with, it will move pages of information to your swap area or swap entire processes to your swap area. Pages that were most recently used are kept in main memory, and those not recently used will be the first moved out of main memory.

System administrators spend a lot of time determining the right amount of swap space for their systems. Insufficient swap may prevent a system from starting additional processes, hang applications, or not permit additional users to get access to the system. Having sufficient swap prevents these problems from taking place. System administrators usually go about determining the right amount of swap by considering many important factors, including the following three:

1. How much swap is recommended by the application(s) you run? Use the swap size recommended by your applications. Application vendors tend to be realistic when recommending swap space. There is sometimes competition among application vendors to claim the lowest memory and CPU requirements in order to keep the overall cost of solutions as low as possible, but swap space recommendations are usually realistic.

2. How many applications will you run simultaneously? If you are running several applications, sum the swap space recommended for each application you plan to run simultaneously. If

you have a database application that recommends 200 MBytes of swap and a development tool that recommends 100 MBytes of swap, then configure your system with 300 MBytes of swap minimum.

3. Will you be using substantial system resources on periphery functionality such as NFS? The nature of NFS is to provide access to file systems, some of which may be very large, so this use may have an impact on your swap space requirements.

Swap is listed and manipulated on different UNIX variants with different commands. The following example shows listing the swap area on a Solaris system with **swap -l**:

man page

swap - 13

```
# swap -l
swapfile              dev  swaplo blocks    free
/dev/dsk/c0t3d0s1    32,25      8 263080 209504
```

These values are all in 512 KByte blocks. In this case, the free blocks are 209504, which is a significant amount of the overall swap allocated on the system.

You can view the amount of swap being consumed on your HP-UX system with **swapinfo**. The following is an example output of **swapinfo**:

man page

swapinfo - 13

```
# swapinfo
```

TYPE	Kb AVAIL	Kb USED	Kb FREE	PCT USED	START/ LIMIT	Kb RESERVE	PRI	NAME
dev	49152	10532	38620	21%	0	-	1	/dev/vg00/lvol2
dev	868352	10888	759160	1%	0	-	1	/dev/vg00/lvol8
reserve	-	532360	-532360					
memory	816360	469784	346576	58%				

Following is a brief overview of what **swapinfo** gives you.

In the previous example, the "TYPE" field indicated whether the swap was "dev" for device, "reserve" for paging space on reserve, or "memory," which is RAM that can be used to hold pages if all the paging areas are in use.

"Kb AVAIL" is the total swap space available in 1024-byte blocks. This includes both used and unused swap.

"Kb USED" is the current number of 1024-byte blocks in use.

"Kb FREE" is the difference between "Kb AVAIL" and "Kb USED."

"PCT USED" is "Kb USED" divided by "Kb AVAIL."

"START/LIMIT" is the block address of the start of the swap area.

"Kb RESERVE" is "-" for device swap or the number of 1024-byte blocks for file system swap.

"PRI" is the priority given to this swap area.

"NAME" is the device name for the swap device.

man page

swapinfo
- 13

You can also issue the **swapinfo** command with a series of options. Here are some of the options you can include:

-m to display output of **swapinfo** in MBytes rather than in 1024-byte blocks.

-d prints information related to device swap areas only.

-f prints information about file system swap areas only.

man page

sar - 13

sar: The System Activity Reporter

sar is another UNIX command for gathering information about activities on your system. You can gather data over an extended time period with **sar** and later produce reports based on the data. **sar** is similar among UNIX variants in that the options and outputs are similar. The Linux system I was using for the examples did not support **sar,** but the Solaris, HP-UX, and AIX systems had the same options and nearly identical outputs. The following are some useful options to **sar,** along with examples of reports produced with these options where applicable:

sar -o	Save data in a file specified by "o." After the file name, you would usually also enter the time interval for samples and the number of samples. The following example shows saving the binary data in file **/tmp/sar.data** at an interval of 60 seconds 300 times:

man page
sar - 13

```
# sar -o /tmp/sar.data 60 300
```

The data in **/tmp/sar.data** can later be extracted from the file.

sar -f	Specify a file from which you will extract data.

sar -u	Report CPU utilization with headings %usr, %sys, %wio, %idle with some processes waiting for block I/O, %idle. This report is similar to the **iostat** and **vmstat** CPU reports. You extract the binary data saved in a file to get CPU information, as shown in the following example. The following is a **sar -u** example:

man page
iostat - 13

man page
vmstat - 13

man page
sar - 13

```
# sar -u -f /tmp/sar.data

Header Information for your system

12:52:04     %usr     %sys     %wio     %idle
12:53:04       62        4        5        29
12:54:04       88        5        3         4
12:55:04       94        5        1         0
12:56:04       67        4        4        25
12:57:04       59        4        4        32
```

12:58:04	61	4	3	32
12:59:04	65	4	3	28
13:00:04	62	5	16	17
13:01:04	59	5	9	27
13:02:04	71	4	3	22
13:03:04	60	4	4	32
13:04:04	71	5	4	20
13:05:04	80	6	8	7
13:06:04	56	3	3	37
13:07:04	57	4	4	36
13:08:04	66	4	4	26
13:09:04	80	10	2	8
13:10:04	73	10	2	15
13:11:04	64	6	3	28
13:12:04	56	4	3	38
13:13:04	55	3	3	38
13:14:04	57	4	3	36
13:15:04	70	4	5	21
13:16:04	65	5	9	21
13:17:04	62	6	2	30
13:18:04	60	5	3	33
13:19:04	77	3	4	16
13:20:04	76	5	3	15

.
.
.

14:30:04	50	6	6	38
14:31:04	57	12	19	12
14:32:04	51	8	20	21
14:33:04	41	4	9	46
14:34:04	43	4	9	45
14:35:04	38	4	6	53
14:36:04	38	9	7	46
14:37:04	46	3	11	40
14:38:04	43	4	7	46
14:39:04	37	4	5	54
14:40:04	33	4	5	58
14:41:04	40	3	3	53
14:42:04	44	3	3	50
14:43:04	27	3	7	64
Average	57	5	8	30

sar -b
Report buffer cache activity. A database application such as Oracle would recommend that you use this option to see the effectiveness of buffer cache use. You extract the binary data saved in a file to get CPU information, as shown in the following example:

man page

sar - 13

```
# sar -b -f /tmp/sar.data
```

Header information for your system

	bread/s	lread/s	%rcache	bwrit/s	lwrit/s	%wcache	pread/s	pwrit/s
12:52:04								
12:53:04	5	608	99	1	11	95	0	0
12:54:04	7	759	99	0	14	99	0	0
12:55:04	2	1733	100	4	24	83	0	0
12:56:04	1	836	100	1	18	96	0	0
12:57:04	0	623	100	2	21	92	0	0
12:58:04	0	779	100	1	16	96	0	0
12:59:04	0	1125	100	0	14	98	0	0
13:00:04	2	1144	100	9	89	89	0	0
13:01:04	10	898	99	11	76	86	0	0
13:02:04	0	1156	100	0	14	99	0	0
13:03:04	1	578	100	2	22	88	0	0
13:04:04	5	1251	100	0	12	99	0	0
13:05:04	3	1250	100	0	12	97	0	0
13:06:04	1	588	100	0	12	98	0	0
13:07:04	1	649	100	2	15	86	0	0
13:08:04	1	704	100	2	15	86	0	0
13:09:04	1	1068	100	0	18	100	0	0
13:10:04	0	737	100	1	44	99	0	0
13:11:04	0	735	100	1	13	95	0	0
13:12:04	0	589	100	1	15	93	0	0
13:13:04	0	573	100	0	16	99	0	0
13:14:04	1	756	100	1	16	91	0	0
13:15:04	1	1092	100	9	49	81	0	0
13:16:04	2	808	100	6	82	93	0	0
13:17:04	0	712	100	1	9	93	0	0
13:18:04	1	609	100	0	13	97	0	0
13:19:04	1	603	100	0	10	99	0	0
13:20:04	0	1127	100	0	14	98	0	0
		.						
		.						
		.						
14:30:04	2	542	100	1	22	94	0	0
14:31:04	10	852	99	12	137	92	0	0
14:32:04	2	730	100	10	190	95	0	0
14:33:04	4	568	99	2	26	91	0	0
14:34:04	4	603	99	1	13	91	0	0
14:35:04	1	458	100	1	13	89	0	0
14:36:04	13	640	98	1	24	98	0	0
14:37:04	21	882	98	1	18	95	0	0
14:38:04	7	954	99	0	19	98	0	0
14:39:04	3	620	100	1	11	94	0	0
14:40:04	3	480	99	2	15	85	0	0
14:41:04	1	507	100	0	9	98	0	0
14:42:04	1	1010	100	1	10	91	0	0

14:43:04	5	547	99	1	9	93	0	0
Average	3	782	100	3	37	91	0	0

man page

sar - 13

sar -d

Report disk activity. You get the device name, percent that the device was busy, average number of requests outstanding for the device, number of data transfers per second for the device, and other information. You extract the binary data saved in a file to get CPU information, as shown in the following example:

```
# sar -d -f /tmp/sar.data
```

Header information for your system

12:52:04	device	%busy	avque	r+w/s	blks/s	avwait	avserv
12:53:04	c0t6d0	0.95	1.41	1	10	16.76	17.28
	c5t4d0	100.00	1.03	20	320	8.36	18.90
	c4t5d1	10.77	0.50	13	214	5.02	18.44
	c5t4d2	0.38	0.50	0	3	4.61	18.81
12:54:04	c0t6d0	0.97	1.08	1	11	10.75	14.82
	c5t4d0	100.00	1.28	54	862	9.31	20.06
	c4t5d1	12.43	0.50	15	241	5.21	16.97
	c5t4d2	0.37	0.50	0	3	3.91	18.20
12:55:04	c0t6d0	1.77	1.42	1	22	13.32	14.16
	c5t4d0	100.00	0.79	26	421	8.33	16.00
	c4t5d1	14.47	0.51	17	270	5.30	13.48
	c5t4d2	0.72	0.50	0	7	4.82	15.69
12:56:04	c0t6d0	1.07	21.57	1	22	72.94	19.58
	c5t4d0	100.00	0.60	16	251	6.80	13.45
	c4t5d1	8.75	0.50	11	177	5.05	10.61
	c5t4d2	0.62	0.50	0	6	4.79	15.43
12:57:04	c0t6d0	0.78	1.16	1	9	13.53	14.91
	c5t4d0	100.00	0.66	15	237	7.60	13.69
	c4t5d1	9.48	0.54	13	210	5.39	13.33
	c5t4d2	0.87	0.50	1	10	4.86	14.09
12:58:04	c0t6d0	1.12	8.29	1	17	54.96	14.35
	c5t4d0	100.00	0.60	11	176	7.91	14.65
	c4t5d1	5.35	0.50	7	111	5.23	10.35
	c5t4d2	0.92	0.50	1	10	4.63	16.08
12:59:04	c0t6d0	0.67	1.53	1	8	18.03	16.05

	c5t4d0	99.98	0.54	11	174	7.69	14.09
	c4t5d1	3.97	0.50	5	83	4.82	9.54
	c5t4d2	1.05	0.50	1	11	4.69	16.29
13:00:04	c0t6d0	3.22	0.67	3	39	8.49	16.53
	c5t4d0	100.00	0.60	65	1032	8.46	14.83
	c4t5d1	21.62	0.50	31	504	5.30	8.94
	c5t4d2	6.77	0.50	5	78	4.86	14.09
13:01:04	c0t6d0	4.45	3.08	5	59	25.83	11.49
	c5t4d0	100.00	0.65	42	676	7.85	14.52
	c4t5d1	21.34	0.55	30	476	5.87	18.49
	c5t4d2	4.37	0.50	3	51	5.32	13.50

.

.

.

14:42:04	c0t6d0	0.53	0.83	0	7	12.21	16.33
	c5t4d0	100.00	0.56	7	107	6.99	14.65
	c4t5d1	6.38	0.50	7	113	4.97	15.18
	c5t4d2	0.15	0.50	0	2	4.53	16.50
14:43:04	c0t6d0	0.52	0.92	0	7	11.50	15.86
	c5t4d0	99.98	0.92	17	270	8.28	18.64
	c4t5d1	10.26	0.50	9	150	5.35	16.41
	c5t4d2	0.12	0.50	0	1	5.25	14.45
Average	c0t6d0	1.43	108.80	2	26	0.00	14.71
Average	c5t4d0	100.00	0.74	25	398	7.83	-10.31
Average	c4t5d1	19.11	0.51	25	399	5.26	-13.75
Average	c5t4d2	1.71	0.53	1	21	5.29	13.46

man page

sar - 13

sar -q   Report average queue length. You may have a problem any time the run queue length is greater than the number of processors on the system:

```
# sar -q -f /tmp/sar.data

Header information for your system

12:52:04 runq-sz %runocc swpq-sz %swpocc
12:53:04    1.1      20     0.0        0
12:54:04    1.4      51     0.0        0
12:55:04    1.3      71     0.0        0
12:56:04    1.1      22     0.0        0
```

12:57:04	1.3	16	0.0	0
12:58:04	1.1	14	0.0	0
12:59:04	1.2	12	0.0	0
13:00:04	1.2	21	0.0	0
13:01:04	1.1	18	0.0	0
13:02:04	1.3	20	0.0	0
13:03:04	1.2	15	0.0	0
13:04:04	1.2	20	0.0	0
13:05:04	1.2	43	0.0	0
13:06:04	1.1	14	0.0	0
13:07:04	1.2	15	0.0	0
13:08:04	1.2	26	0.0	0
13:09:04	1.5	38	0.0	0
13:10:04	1.5	30	0.0	0
13:11:04	1.2	23	0.0	0
13:12:04	1.3	11	0.0	0
13:13:04	1.3	12	0.0	0
13:14:04	1.4	16	0.0	0
13:15:04	1.4	27	0.0	0
13:16:04	1.5	20	0.0	0
13:17:04	1.3	21	0.0	0
13:18:04	1.1	15	0.0	0
13:19:04	1.2	19	0.0	0
13:20:04	1.4	22	0.0	0

.
.
.

14:30:04	1.5	5	0.0	0
14:31:04	1.6	12	0.0	0
14:32:04	1.4	9	0.0	0
14:33:04	1.1	6	0.0	0
14:34:04	1.3	3	0.0	0
14:35:04	1.1	4	0.0	0
14:36:04	1.2	6	0.0	0
14:37:04	1.4	5	0.0	0
14:38:04	1.2	10	0.0	0
14:39:04	1.3	4	0.0	0
14:40:04	1.1	3	0.0	0
14:41:04	1.6	3	0.0	0
14:42:04	1.1	4	0.0	0
14:43:04	1.3	1	0.0	0
Average	1.3	17	1.2	0

sar -w   Report system swapping activity.

```
# sar -w -f /tmp/sar.data
```

Header information for your system

12:52:04	swpin/s	bswin/s	swpot/s	bswot/s	pswch/s
12:53:04	1.00	0.0	1.00	0.0	231
12:54:04	1.00	0.0	1.00	0.0	354
12:55:04	1.00	0.0	1.00	0.0	348
12:56:04	1.00	0.0	1.00	0.0	200
12:57:04	1.00	0.0	1.00	0.0	277
12:58:04	1.00	0.0	1.00	0.0	235
12:59:04	1.02	0.0	1.02	0.0	199
13:00:04	0.78	0.0	0.78	0.0	456
13:01:04	1.00	0.0	1.00	0.0	435
13:02:04	1.02	0.0	1.02	0.0	216
13:03:04	0.98	0.0	0.98	0.0	204
13:04:04	1.02	0.0	1.02	0.0	239
13:05:04	1.00	0.0	1.00	0.0	248
13:06:04	0.97	0.0	0.97	0.0	170
13:07:04	1.00	0.0	1.00	0.0	166
13:08:04	1.02	0.0	1.02	0.0	209
13:09:04	0.98	0.0	0.98	0.0	377
13:10:04	1.00	0.0	1.00	0.0	200
13:11:04	1.00	0.0	1.00	0.0	192
13:12:04	0.87	0.0	0.87	0.0	187
13:13:04	0.93	0.0	0.93	0.0	172
13:14:04	1.00	0.0	1.00	0.0	170
13:15:04	1.00	0.0	1.00	0.0	382
13:16:04	1.00	0.0	1.00	0.0	513
13:17:04	1.00	0.0	1.00	0.0	332
13:18:04	1.00	0.0	1.00	0.0	265
13:19:04	1.02	0.0	1.02	0.0	184
13:20:04	0.98	0.0	0.98	0.0	212
.					
.					
.					
14:30:04	0.00	0.0	0.00	0.0	301
14:31:04	0.00	0.0	0.00	0.0	566
14:32:04	0.00	0.0	0.00	0.0	539
14:33:04	0.00	0.0	0.00	0.0	400
14:34:04	0.00	0.0	0.00	0.0	242

```
14:35:04     0.00     0.0     0.00     0.0     286
14:36:04     0.00     0.0     0.00     0.0     295
14:37:04     0.00     0.0     0.00     0.0     249
14:38:04     0.00     0.0     0.00     0.0     300
14:39:04     0.00     0.0     0.00     0.0     296
14:40:04     0.00     0.0     0.00     0.0     419
14:41:04     0.00     0.0     0.00     0.0     234
14:42:04     0.00     0.0     0.00     0.0     237
14:43:04     0.00     0.0     0.00     0.0     208

Average      0.70     0.0     0.70     0.0     346
```

timex to Analyze a Command

man page

timex - 13

If you have a specific command you want to find out more about, you can use **timex**, which reports the elapsed time, user time, and system time spent in the execution of a command you specify.

timex is a good command for users because it gives you an idea of the system resources you are consuming when issuing a command. The following two examples show issuing **timex** with no options to get a short output of the amount of cpu consumed, and the second example shows issuing **timex -s** to report "total" system activity on a Solaris system:

```
martyp $ timex listing

real        0.02
user        0.00
sys         0.02


martyp $ timex -s listing

real        0.02
user        0.00
sys         0.01


SunOS 5.7 Generic sun4m    08/21

07:48:30    %usr    %sys    %wio    %idle
07:48:31      32      68       0        0

07:48:30 bread/s lread/s %rcache bwrit/s lwrit/s %wcache pread/s pwrit/s
07:48:31       0       0     100       0       0     100       0       0

Average        0       0     100       0       0     100       0       0

07:48:30    device          %busy   avque   r+w/s  blks/s  avwait  avserv
```

```
07:48:31   fd0                      0    0.0      0      0    0.0    0.0
           nfs1                     0    0.0      0      0    0.0    0.0
           nfs219                   0    0.0      0      0    0.0    0.0
           sd1                      0    0.0      0      0    0.0    0.0
           sd1,a                    0    0.0      0      0    0.0    0.0
           sd1,b                    0    0.0      0      0    0.0    0.0
           sd1,c                    0    0.0      0      0    0.0    0.0
           sd1,g                    0    0.0      0      0    0.0    0.0
           sd3                      0    0.0      0      0    0.0    0.0
           sd3,a                    0    0.0      0      0    0.0    0.0
           sd3,b                    0    0.0      0      0    0.0    0.0
           sd3,c                    0    0.0      0      0    0.0    0.0
           sd6                      0    0.0      0      0    0.0    0.0

Average    fd0                      0    0.0      0      0    0.0    0.0
           nfs1                     0    0.0      0      0    0.0    0.0
           nfs219                   0    0.0      0      0    0.0    0.0
           sd1                      0    0.0      0      0    0.0    0.0
           sd1,a                    0    0.0      0      0    0.0    0.0
           sd1,b                    0    0.0      0      0    0.0    0.0
           sd1,c                    0    0.0      0      0    0.0    0.0
           sd1,g                    0    0.0      0      0    0.0    0.0
           sd3                      0    0.0      0      0    0.0    0.0
           sd3,a                    0    0.0      0      0    0.0    0.0
           sd3,b                    0    0.0      0      0    0.0    0.0
           sd3,c                    0    0.0      0      0    0.0    0.0
           sd6                      0    0.0      0      0    0.0    0.0

07:48:30 rawch/s canch/s outch/s rcvin/s xmtin/s mdmin/s
07:48:31       0       0     147       0       0       0

Average        0       0     147       0       0       0

07:48:30 scall/s sread/s swrit/s  fork/s  exec/s rchar/s wchar/s
07:48:31    2637       0      95   15.79   15.79       0   19216

Average     2637       0      95   15.79   15.79       0   19216

07:48:30 swpin/s bswin/s swpot/s bswot/s pswch/s
07:48:31    0.00     0.0    0.00     0.0     116

Average     0.00     0.0    0.00     0.0     116

07:48:30  iget/s namei/s dirbk/s
07:48:31       0     195     121

Average        0     195     121

07:48:30 runq-sz %runocc swpq-sz %swpocc
07:48:31     2.0     526

Average      2.0     526

07:48:30  proc-sz  ov  inod-sz   ov  file-sz   ov   lock-sz
07:48:31   45/986   0  973/4508   0  357/357    0    0/0

07:48:30   msg/s  sema/s
07:48:31    0.00    0.00

Average     0.00    0.00

07:48:30  atch/s  pgin/s ppgin/s  pflt/s  vflt/s slock/s
07:48:31    0.00    0.00    0.00  505.26 1036.84    0.00

Average     0.00    0.00    0.00  505.26 1036.84    0.00

07:48:30 pgout/s ppgout/s pgfree/s pgscan/s %ufs_ipf
07:48:31    0.00     0.00     0.00     0.00     0.00

Average     0.00     0.00     0.00     0.00     0.00

07:48:30 freemem freeswap
07:48:31   15084  1224421
```

```
Average      15084   1224421

07:48:30 sml_mem    alloc   fail  lg_mem    alloc   fail  ovsz_alloc  fail
07:48:31 2617344  1874368        0 17190912 10945416       0    3067904      0

Average    186953    133883        0 1227922  781815       0     219136      0
```

More Advanced and Graphical Performance Tools

The command line is a way of life when working with UNIX. UNIX grew out of the command line and is still primarily command-line-based. Although you need to know a lot when issuing commands, especially when it comes to system performance, you can dig deeply very quickly with many of the commands I just covered.

You have the option with most UNIX variants to buy graphical performance tools. Some systems come with basic graphical performance tools as well. You usually end up buying an advaced performance analysis tool if you want to perform advanced performance analysis. We'll take a quick look at a few performance tools in upcoming sections.

Figure 13-1 shows three performance tools that came with the Red Hat Linux system I used for many of the examples in this chapter.

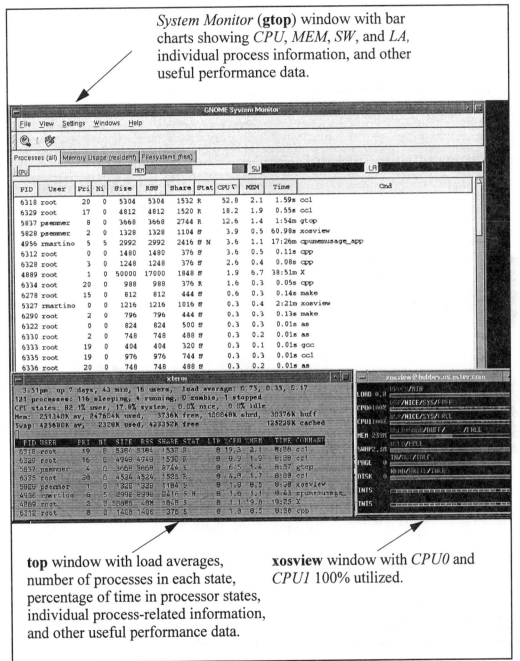

System Monitor (**gtop**) window with bar charts showing *CPU, MEM, SW,* and *LA,* individual process information, and other useful performance data.

top window with load averages, number of processes in each state, percentage of time in processor states, individual process-related information, and other useful performance data.

xosview window with *CPU0* and *CPU1* 100% utilized.

Figure 13-1 Red Hat Linux Performance Tools Screen Shot

man page

top - 13

The three performance tools shown in this diagram are **xosview** in the lower right, the *System Monitor* across the top of the screen, and **top** shown in the lower left. The *System Monitor* provides bar charts across the top of the screen that indicate the amount of CPU, Memory, Swap, and LAN utilization taking place. There is then tabular data supplied for every process on the system. The *System Monitor* is a graphical version of **top** that I invoked with the command **gtop** for graphical **top**. **xosview** is a small load meter that you can keep running that provides bar charts of system activity shown in the bottom right window. This is the **X** Windows **operating system view** program, hence the name **xosview**. You can't see the bar charts clearly in this diagram, because this is a color-based application and the book is printed in only black and white. The bar charts are, however, clear on the computer screen. The final, and most often used, tool on UNIX systems is the character version of **top** that is running in the bottom left **xterm**. **top** is found on many UNIX variants and supplies a lot of useful system information.

Among the useful **top** system data displayed is the following:

- Load averages in the last one, five, and fifteen minutes.

- Number of existing processes and the number of processes in each state.

- Percentage of time spent in each of the processor states per processor on the system.

This same information is included in the bottom of the *System Monitor* window that is covered by the **top** and **xosview** windows.

Next in the *top* window is memory data, including used, free, and shared.

man page

ps - 12

Data is also provided for individual process in a format similar to **ps**, including the following:

PID - Process ID number.

USER - Name of the owner of the process.

PRI - Current priority of the process.

NI - Nice value ranging from -20 to +20.

SIZE - Total size of the process in kilobytes.

RSS - Resident size of the process in kilobytes.

STATE - Current state of the process.

TIME - Number of system and CPU seconds the process has consumed.

%CPU - CPU percentage.

%MEM - Memory percentage.

COMMAND - Name of the command the process is currently running.

man page

top - 13

As with all commands we have been covering, **top** is different among UNIX variants. You may see some different fields on the different UNIX variants. I am usually confident when I sit down at any UNIX system that I can run **top** and quickly see how the system is running. Most versions of **top** I have run are character-based applications, so you don't even need a graphics terminal to run them. I have run **top** in this example in character mode within an X terminal.

The system used in this example has two CPUs. If you look carefully in the **xosview** window, you'll see that both *CPU0* and *CPU1* are 100 percent used. At the time this screen shot was obtained, I was compiling the Linux kernel on this system, which consumed all the

man page

top - 13

CPU resources on the system for a short period of time. You can see from both the **top** and *System Monitor* windows that the program **cc1**, used to compile the kernel, was consuming a substantial amount of the CPU resources on the system.

Figure 13-1 helps illustrate how different tools help with viewing how system resources are consumed. **xosview** provides a quick-reference graphical overview of how much system resources are being consumed. **top** and *System Monitor* can then be used to determine the specific process consuming the most system resources.

HP GlancePlus/UX

Using UNIX commands to get a better understanding of what your system is doing requires you to do a lot of work. In the first case, issuing UNIX commands gives you the advantage of obtaining data about what is taking place on your system that very second. Unfortunately, you can't always issue additional commands to probe more deeply into an area, such as a process, about which you want to know more.

Now I'll describe another technique - a tool that can help get useful data in real time, allow you to investigate a specific process, and not bury you in reports. This tool is HP GlancePlus/UX (GlancePlus). This tool runs on several UNIX variants, including Solaris, HP-UX, and AIX.

GlancePlus can be run in character mode or in graphic mode. I chose to use the character-based version of GlancePlus, because this will run on any display, either graphics- or character-based, and the many colors used by the Motif version of GlancePlus do not show up well in a book. My examples are displayed much more clearly in the book when using the character mode. I recommend that you try both versions of GlancePlus to see which you prefer.

The system used in the examples has eight processors, 4 GBytes of RAM, and a substantial amount of EMC Symmetrix disk connected to it.

Figure 13-2 shows one of several interactive screens of Glance-Plus. This one is the *Process List* screen, also referred to as the *Global* screen. This is the default screen when bringing up GlancePlus.

Two features of the screen shown in Figure 13-2 are worth noticing immediately:

1. Four histograms at the top of the screen give you a graphical representation of your CPU, Disk, Memory, and Swap Utilization in a format much easier to assimilate than a column of numbers.

man page

ps - 12

2. The "Process Summary" has columns similar to **ps -ef**, with which many system administrators are familiar and comfortable. GlancePlus, however, gives you the additional capability of filtering out processes that are using very few resources by specifying thresholds.

Using GlancePlus, you can take a close look at your system in many areas, including the following:

- Process List
- CPU Report
- Memory Report
- Swap Space
- Disk Report
- LAN Detail
- NFS by System
- PRM Summary (Process Resource Manager)
- I/O by File System
- I/O by Disk
- I/O by Logical Volume

- System Tables

Figure 13-2 is a GlancePlus screen shot.

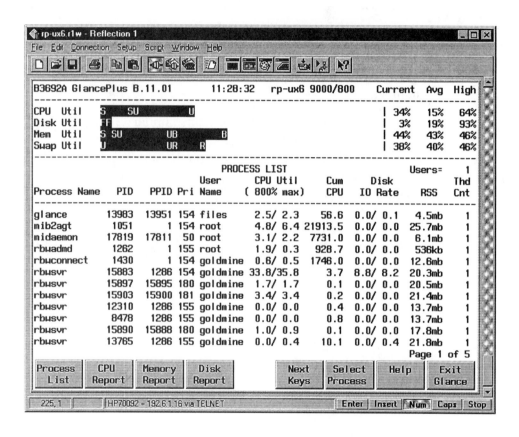

Figure 13-2   HP GlancePlus/UX *Process List* Screen Shot

Because the *Process List* shown in the example tells you where
your system resources are going at the highest level, I'll start my
description here. I am using a terminal emulator on my portable computer to display GlancePlus. I find that many system administrators
use a PC and a terminal emulator to perform UNIX management functions. Keep in mind that the information shown on this screen can be

updated at any interval you choose. If your system is running in a steady-state mode, you may want to have a long interval because you don't expect things to much change. On the other hand, you may have a dynamic environment and want to see the histograms and other information updated every few seconds. In either case, you can change the update interval to suit your needs. You can use the function keys at the bottom of the screen to go into other functional areas.

Process List Description

The *Process List* screen provides an overview of the state of system resources and active processes.

The top section of the screen (the histogram section) is common to the many screens of GlancePlus. The bottom section of the screen displays a summary of active processes.

Line 1 provides the product and version number of GlancePlus, the time, name of your system, and system type. In this case, we are running version 11.01 of GlancePlus.

Line 3 provides information about the overall state of the CPU. This tends to be the single most important piece of information that administrators want to know about their system - Is my CPU over-worked?

The CPU Utilization bar is divided into the following parts:

1. "S" indicates the amount of time spent on "system" activities such as context switching and system calls.

2. "N" indicates the amount of time spent running "nice" user processes (those run at a low priority).

3. "U" indicates the amount of time spent running user processes.

4. "R" indicates real-time processes.

5. "A" indicates the amount of time spent running processes at a negative "nice" priority.

The far right of line 3 shows the percentage of CPU utilization. If your system is "CPU-Bound," you will consistently see this number near 100 percent. You get statistics for Current, Average (since analysis was begun), and High.

Line 4 shows Disk Utilization for the busiest mounted disk. This bar indicates the percentage of File System and Virtual Memory disk I/O over the update interval. This bar is divided into two parts:

1. "F" indicates the amount of file system activity of user reads and writes and other non-paging activities.

2. "V" indicates the percentage of disk I/O devoted to paging virtual memory.

The Current, Avg, and High statistics have the same meaning as in the CPU Utilization description.

Line 5 shows the system memory utilization. This bar is divided into three parts:

1. "S" indicates the amount of memory devoted to system use.

2. "U" indicates the amount of memory devoted to user programs and data.

3. "B" indicates the amount of memory devoted to buffer cache.

The Current, Avg, and High statistics have the same meaning as in the CPU Utilization description.

Line 6 shows swap space information, which is divided into two parts:

1. "R" indicates reserved but not in use.

2. "U" indicates swap space in use.

All three of these areas (CPU, Memory, and Disk) may be further analyzed by using the F2, F3, and F4 function keys, respectively. Again, you may see different function keys, depending on the version of GlancePlus you are running. When you select one of these keys, you move from the *Process List* screen to a screen that provides more in-depth functions in the selected area. In addition, more detailed screens are available for many other system areas. Because most investigation beyond the *Process List* screen takes place on the CPU, Memory, and Disk screens, I'll describe these in more detail shortly.

The bottom of the *Process List* screen shows the active processes running on your system. Because there are typically many processes running on a UNIX system, you may want to consider using the **o** command to set a threshold for CPU utilization. If you set a threshold of five percent, for instance, then only processes that exceed the average CPU utilization of 5 percent over the interval will be displayed. There are other types of thresholds that can be specified such as the amount of RAM used (Resident Size). If you specify thresholds, you see only the processes you're most interested in, that is, those consuming the greatest system resources.

There is a line for each active process that meets the threshold requirements you defined. There may be more than one page of processes to display. The message in the bottom-right corner of the screen indicates which page you are on. You can scroll forward to view the next page with **f** and backwards with **b**. Usually only a few processes consume most of your system resources, so I recommend setting the thresholds so that only one page of processes is displayed. There are a whole series of commands you can issue in GlancePlus. The final figure in this section shows the commands recognized by GlancePlus.

Here is a brief summary of the process headings:

Process Name   The name or abbreviation used to load the executable program.

PID   The process identification number.

PPID   The PID of the parent process.

Pri   The priority of the process. The lower the number, the higher the priority. System-level processes usually run between 0 and 127. Other processes usually run between 128 and 255. "Nice" processes are those with the lowest priority and they have the largest number.

User Name   Name of the user who started the process.

CPU Util   The first number is the percentage of CPU utilization that this process consumed over the update interval. Note that this is 800% maximum for our eight-processor system. The second number is the percentage of CPU utilization that this process consumed since GlancePlus was invoked. I'm skeptical of using GlancePlus, or any other UNIX command, to get data over an extended period. I rarely use the second number under this heading. If you have been using GlancePlus for some time but only recently started a process that consumes a great deal of CPU, you may find that the second number is very low. The reason is that the process you are analyzing has indeed consumed very little of the CPU since GlancePlus was invoked, despite being a highly CPU-intensive process.

Cum CPU   The total CPU time used by the process. Glance-Plus uses the "midaemon" to gather information. If the **midaemon** started before the process, you will get an accurate measure of cumulative CPU time used by the process.

Disk IO Rate   The first number is the average disk I/O rate per second over the last update interval. The second number is the average disk I/O rate since Glance-Plus was started or since the process was started. Disk I/O can mean a lot of different things. Disk I/O could mean taking blocks of data off the disk for the first time and putting them in RAM, or it could be entirely paging and swapping. Some processes will simply require a lot more Disk I/O than others. When this number is very high, however, take a close look at whether or not you have enough RAM.

RSS Size   The amount of RAM in KBytes that is consumed by the process. This is called the Resident Size. Everything related to the process that is in RAM is included in this column, such as the process's data, stack, text, and shared memory segments.

This is a good column to inspect. Because slow systems are often erroneously assumed to be CPU-bound, I always make a point of looking at this column to identify the amount of RAM that the primary applications are using. This is often revealing. Some applications use a small amount of RAM but use large data sets, a point often overlooked when RAM calculations are made. This column shows all the RAM your process is currently using.

Block On   The reason the process was blocked (unable to run). If the process is currently blocked, you will see why. If the process is running, you will see why it was last blocked. There are many reasons a process could be blocked. After *Thd Cnt* is a list of the most common reasons for the process being blocked.

Thd Cnt   The total number of threads for this current process.

Abbreviation	Reason for the Blocked Process
CACHE	Waiting for a cache buffer to become available
DISK	Waiting for a disk operation to complete
DUX	Waiting for a diskless transfer to complete
INODE	Waiting for an inode operation to complete
IO	Waiting for a non-disk I/O to complete
IPC	Waiting for a shared memory operation to complete
LAN	Waiting for a LAN operation to complete
MBUF	Waiting for a memory buffer

MESG	Waiting for a message queue operation to complete
NFS	Waiting for an NFS request to complete
PIPE	Waiting for data from a pipe
PRI	Waiting because a higher-priority process is running
RFA	Waiting for a Remote File Access to complete
SEM	Waiting for a semaphore to become available
SLEEP	Waiting because the process called **sleep** or **wait**
SOCKT	Waiting for a socket operation to complete
SYS	Waiting for system resources
TERM	Waiting for a terminal transfer
VM	Waiting for a virtual memory operation to complete
OTHER	Waiting for a reason GlancePlus can't determine

CPU Report Screen Description

If the *Process List* screen indicates that the CPU is overworked, you'll want to refer to the *CPU Report* screen shown in Figure 13-3. It can provide useful information about the seven types of states that GlancePlus reports.

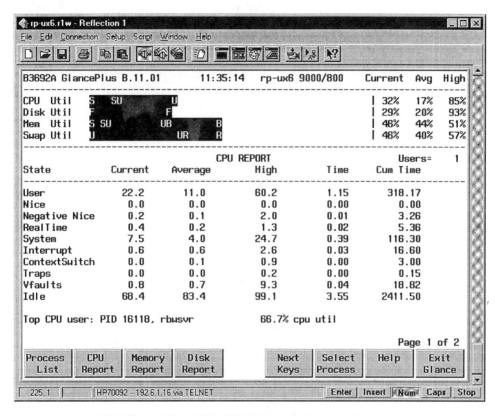

Figure 13-3 HP GlancePlus/UX *CPU Report* Screen Shot

For each of the seven types of states there are columns that provide additional information. Following is a description of the columns:

Current   Displays the percentage of CPU time devoted to this state over the last time interval.

Average   Displays the average percentage of CPU time spent in this state since GlancePlus was started.

High	Displays the highest percentage of CPU time devoted to this state since GlancePlus was started.
Time	Displays the CPU time spent in this state over the last interval.
Cum Time	Displays the total amount of CPU time spent in this state since GlancePlus was started.

A description of the seven states follows:

User	CPU time spent executing user activities under normal priority.
Nice	CPU time spent running user code in nice mode.
Negative Nice	CPU time spent running code at a high priority.
Realtime	CPU time spent executing real-time processes that run at a high priority.
System	CPU time spent executing system calls and programs.
Interrupt	CPU time spent executing system interrupts. A high value here may indicate of a lot of I/O, such as paging and swapping.
ContSwitch	CPU time spent context switching between processes.
Traps	CPU time spent handling traps.
Vfaults	CPU time spent handling page faults.
Idle	CPU time spent idle.

The *CPU Report* screen also shows your system's run queue length or load average. This would be displayed on the second page of the *CPU Report* screen. The current, average, and high values for the number of runnable processes waiting for the CPU are shown. You may want to get a gauge of your system's run queue length when the system is mostly idle and compare these numbers with those you see when your system is in normal use.

The final area reported on the *CPU Report* screen is load average, system calls, interrupts, and context switches. I don't inspect these too closely, because if one of these is high, it is normally the symptom of a problem and not the cause of a problem. If you correct a problem, you will see these numbers reduced.

You can use GlancePlus to view all the CPUs in your system, as shown in Figure 13-4. This is an eight-processor system.

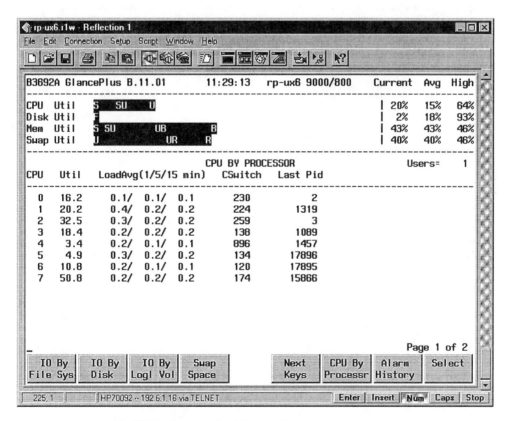

Figure 13-4 *All CPUs* Screen in GlancePlus

Memory Report Screen Description

The *Memory Report* Screen shown in Figure 13-5 provides information on several types of memory management events. The statistics shown are in the form of counts, not percentages. You may want to look at these counts for a mostly idle system and then observe what takes place as the load on the system is incrementally increased. My experience has been that many more memory bottlenecks occur than CPU bottlenecks, so you may find this screen revealing.

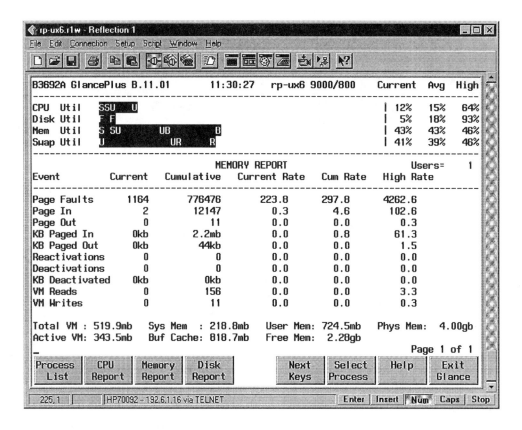

Figure 13-5 HP GlancePlus/UX *Memory Report* Screen Shot

The following five statistics are shown for each memory management event:

Current   The number of times an event occurred in the last interval. The count changes if you update the interval, so you may want to select an interval you are comfortable with and stick with it.

Cumulative   The sum of all counts for this event since GlancePlus started.

Current Rate   The number of events per second.

Cum Rate   The sum of events.

High Rate   The highest rate recorded.

Following are brief descriptions of the memory management events for which the statistics are provided:

Page Faults   A fault takes place when a process tries to access a page that is not in RAM. The virtual memory of the system will handle the "page in." Keep in mind that the speed of the disk is much slower than RAM, so there is a large performance penalty for the page in.

Page In/Page Out Pages of data moved from virtual memory (disk) to physical memory (page in) or vice versa.

KB Paged In   The amount of data paged in because of page faults.

KB Paged Out   The amount of data paged out to disk.

Reactivations and Deactivations

                 The number of processes swapped in and swapped out of memory. A system low on RAM will spend a lot of time swapping processes in and out of RAM. If a lot of this type of swapping is taking place, you may see high CPU utilization and see some other statistics go up as well. These may only be symptoms that a lot of swapping is taking place. You may see Reactivations and Deactivations.

KB Reactivated	The amount of information swapped into RAM as a result of processes having been swapped out earlier due to insufficient RAM. You may see KB Reactivated.
KB Deactivated	The amount of information swapped out when processes are moved to disk. You may see KB Deactivated.
VM Reads	The total count of the number of physical reads to disk. The higher this number, the more often your system is going to disk.
VM Writes	The total count of the number of physical writes to disk.

The following values are also on the Memory screen:

Total VM	The amount of total virtual memory used by all processes.
Active VM	The amount of virtual memory used by all active processes.
Sys Mem	The amount of memory devoted to system use.
Buf Cache Size	The current size of buffer cache.
User Mem	The amount of memory devoted to user use.
Free Memory	The amount of RAM not currently allocated for use.
Phys Memory	The total RAM in your system.

This screen gives you a lot of information about how your memory subsystem is being used. You may want to view some statistics when your system is mostly idle and when it is heavily used and compare the two. Some good numbers to record are "Avail Memory" (to see whether you have any free RAM under either condition) and "Total VM" (to see how much virtual memory has been allocated for all your processes). A system that is RAM-rich will have available memory; a system that is RAM-poor will allocate a lot of virtual memory.

Disk Report Screen Description

The *Disk Report* screen appears in Figure 13-6. You may see groupings of "local" and "remote" information.

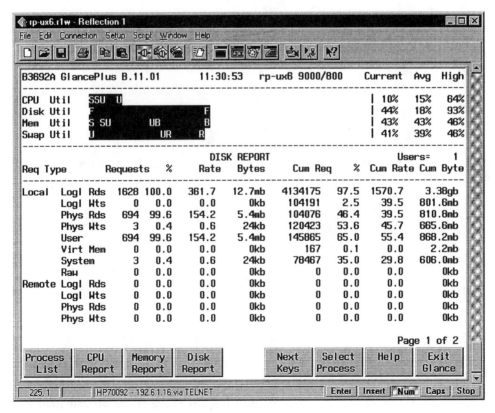

Figure 13-6 HP GlancePlus/UX *Disk Report* Screen Shot

There are eight disk statistics provided for eight events related to logical and physical accesses to all the disks mounted on the local system. These events represent all the disk activity taking place on the system.

Here are descriptions of the eight disk statistics provided:

Requests	The total number of requests of that type over the last interval.
%	The percentage of this type of disk event relative to other types.
Rate	The average number of requests of this type per second.
Bytes	The total number of bytes transferred for this event over the last interval.
Cum Req	The cumulative number of requests since GlancePlus started.
%	The relative percentage of this type of disk event since GlancePlus started.
Cum Rate	The sum of requests.
Cum Bytes	The total number of bytes transferred for this type of event since GlancePlus started.

Next are descriptions of the disk events for which these statistics are provided, which may be listed under "Local" on your system:

Logl Rds and Logl Wts

> The number of logical reads and writes to a disk. Because disks normally use memory buffer cache, a logical read may not require physical access to the disk.

Phys Rds

> The number of physical reads to the disk. These physical reads may be due to either file system logical reads or to virtual memory management.

Phys Wts	The number of physical writes to the disk. This may be due to file system activity or virtual memory management.
User	The amount of physical disk I/O as a result of user file I/O operations.
Virtual Mem	The amount of physical disk I/O as a result of virtual memory management activity.
System	The amount of physical disk I/O as a result of system calls.
Raw	The amount of raw mode disk I/O.

A lot of disk activity may also take place as a result of NFS mounted disks. Statistics are provided for "Remote" disks as well.

Disk access is required on all systems. The question to ask is: What disk activity is unnecessary and slowing down my system? A good place to start is to compare the amount of "User" disk I/O with "Virtual Mem" disk I/O. If your system is performing much more virtual memory I/O than user I/O, you may want to investigate your memory needs.

GlancePlus Summary

In addition to the Process List, or Global, screen and the CPU, Memory, and Disk screens described earlier, there are many other useful screens including the following:

Swap Space	Shows details on all swap areas. May be called by another name in other releases.
Netwk By Intrface	Gives details about each LAN card configured on your system. This screen may have another name in other releases.

NFS Global   Provides details on inbound and outbound
                           NFS mounted file systems. May be called
                           by another name in other releases.

Select Process   Allows you to select a single process to
                           investigate. May be called by another
                           name in other releases.

I/O By File Sys   Shows details of I/O for each mounted
                           disk partition.

I/O By Disk   Shows details of I/O for each mounted
                           disk.

I/O By Logl Vol   Shows details of I/O for each mounted
                           logical volume.

System Tables   Shows details on internal system tables.

Process Threshold   Defines which processes will be displayed
                           on the Process List screen. May be called
                           by another name, such as Global screen, in
                           other releases.

As you can see, although I described the four most commonly
used screens in detail, you can use many others to investigate your
system further.

There are also many commands you can issue within GlancePlus.
Figures 13-7 and 13-8 show the *Command List* screens in GlancePlus.

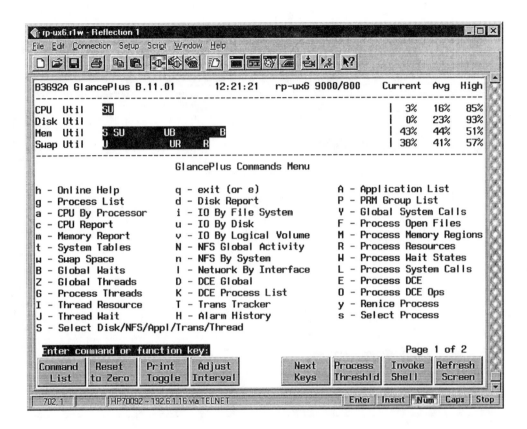

Figure 13-7 HP GlancePlus/UX *Command List* Screen 1

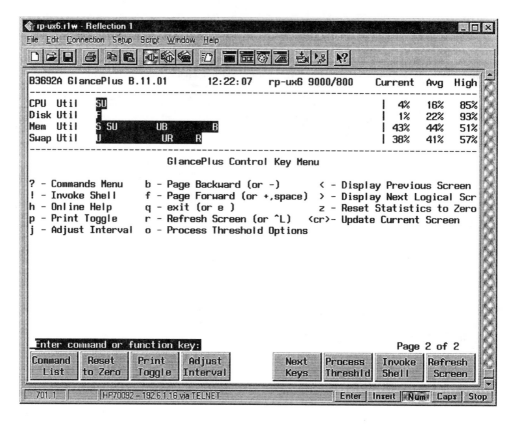

Figure 13-8 HP GlancePlus/UX *Command List* Screen 2

What Should I Look for When Using GlancePlus?

Because GlancePlus provides a graphical representation of the way in which your system resources are being used, the answer is simple: See which bars have a high "Avg" utilization. You can then probe further into the process(es) causing this high utilization. If, for instance, you find that your memory is consistently 99 percent utilized, press the F3 function key and have GlancePlus walk you through an investigation of which of your applications and users are memory hogs.

Similarly, you may be surprised to find that GlancePlus shows low utilization of your CPU or other system resources. Many slow systems are assumed to be CPU-bound. I have seen GlancePlus used to determine that a system is in fact memory-bound, resulting in a memory upgrade instead of a CPU upgrade.

The difference between using GlancePlus to determine the level of CPU resources being used and the first two approaches given in this chapter is that GlancePlus takes out a lot of the guesswork involved. If you are going to justify a system upgrade of some type to management, it is easier to do this with the hard and fast data Glance-Plus provides, than the detective work you may need to do with UNIX commands.

Use the GlancePlus screens I showed you to look for the following bottlenecks:

1. CPU Bottleneck
   Use the "Global Screen" and "CPU Detail Screen" to identify these common CPU bottleneck symptoms:

   - Low CPU idle time. Greater than 85% CPU utilization for an extended period of time is high.

   - High CPU utilization in system mode. Greater than 10% utilization in system mode means that a substantial amount of time is spent handling system tasks.

   - High interrupt time. Greater than 10% interrupt time is high.

   - High context switching. Greater than 5% spent context switching is high.

2. Memory Bottleneck
   Use the "Global Screen," "Memory Screen," and "Tables Screen" to identify these common Memory bottleneck symptoms:

   - High swapping activity.

   - High paging activity. Greater than five page outs per second is high.

- Little or no free memory available. Greater than 80% memory utilization for an extended period is high.

- High CPU usage in System mode.

3. Disk Bottleneck
Use "Global Screen," "Disk I/O Screen," and others to identify these common Disk Bottleneck symptoms:

  - High disk activity.

  - High idle CPU time waiting for I/O requests to complete.

  - Long disk queues.

The best approach to take for understanding where your system resources are going is to become familiar with all three techniques described in this chapter. You can then determine which information is most useful to you.

The most important aspect of this process is to regularly issue commands and review accounting data so that small system utilization problems don't turn into catastrophes and adversely affect all your users.

You may need to go a step further with more sophisticated performance tools. HP can help you identify more sophisticated tools based on your needs.

HP MeasureWare and HP PerfView

There are performance tools that track data over a long period of time and chart this data. System Administrators often call this exercise "capacity planning." The goal of capacity planning is to view what system resources have been consumed over a long period of time and determine what adjustments or additions can be made to the system to improve performance and plan for the future. We'll use HP MeasureWare Agent and HP PerfView together to take a look at the performance of a system. These tools run on HP-UX and are similar to many advanced tools that run on other UNIX variants.

The MeasureWare agent is installed on individual systems throughout a distributed environment. It collects resource and performance measurement data on the individual systems. The PerfView management console, which you would typically install on a management system, is then used to display the historical MeasureWare data. You could also set alarms that are set off by exception conditions using the MeasureWare agent. For instance, if the MeasureWare agent detects an exception condition, such as CPU utilization greater than 90%, it produces an alarm message. The alarm messages are then displayed with PerfView. We're going to use the PerfView Analyzer in our upcoming examples; however, PerfView consists of the following three components:

Monitor   Provides alarm monitoring capability by accepting alarms from MeasureWare and displays alarms. This is not part of the base PerfView product.

Planner   Provides forecasting capability by extrapolating MeasureWare data for forecasts. This is not part of the base PerfView product.

Analyzer   Analyzes MeasureWare data from multiple systems and displays data. You can view the data from multiple systems simultaneously. This is the base product.

In our example, we will be working with a single system. We'll take the MeasureWare data, collected over roughly a one-week period, and display some of it. In this example, we won't take data from several distributed systems and we'll use only one server in the example.

HP MeasureWare Agent produces log files that contain information about the system resource consumption. The longer HP MeasureWare Agent runs, the longer it records data in the log files. I am often called to review systems that are running poorly to propose system upgrades. I usually run HP MeasureWare Agent for a minimum of a week so that I obtain log information over a long enough period of time to obtain useful data. For some systems, this time period is months. For other systems with a regular load, a week may be enough time.

After having run MeasureWare for a week, I invoked PerfView to see the level of system resource utilization that took place over the week. The graphs we'll review are CPU, Memory, and Disk. Figure 13-9 shows *Global CPU Summary* for the week.

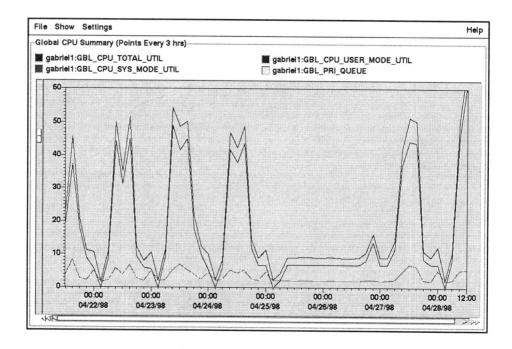

Figure 13-9   HP PerfView *Global CPU Summary*

You can adjust every imaginable feature of this graph with PerfView. Unfortunately, the color in this graph is lost in the book. The colors used allow you to discern the parameters when viewing the graph on the computer screen. Total CPU utilization is always the top point in the graph and it is the sum of system and user mode utilization.

Figure 13-9 shows classic CPU utilization with prime hours reflecting high CPU utilization and non-prime hours reflecting low CPU utilization. In some respects, however, this graph can be deceiving. Because there is a data point occurs every three hours, hence the eight ticks per 24-hour period, you don't get a view of the actual CPU utilization during a much smaller window of time. We can't, for instance, see precisely what time in the morning the CPU becomes heavily used. We can see that it is between the second and third tick, but this is a long time period - between 6:00 and 9:00 am. The same lack of granularity is true at the end of the day. We see a clear fall-off in CPU utilization between the fifth and seventh ticks, but this does not give us a well defined view. Figure 13-10 shows CPU utilization during a much shorter time window.

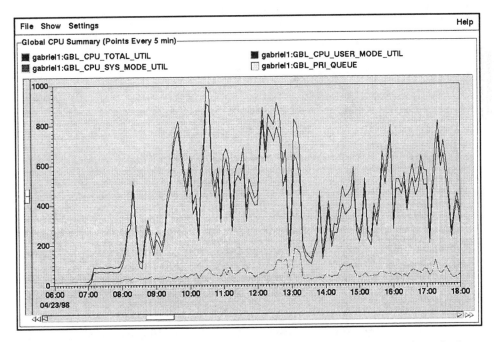

Figure 13-10 HP PerfView *Global CPU Summary* - Short Time Period

Figure 13-10 shows a finer granularity of CPU utilization during the shorter time window. The much finer granularity of this window makes clear the activity spikes that occur throughout the day. For instance, a clear login spike occurs at 8:30 am.

Memory utilization can also be graphed over the course of the week, as shown in Figure 13-11.

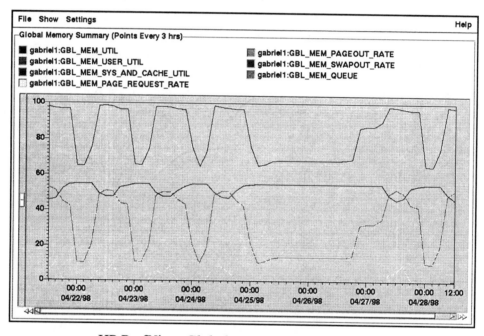

Figure 13-11   HP PerfView *Global Memory Summary*

The user memory utilization is the bottom line of the graph, which roughly corresponds to the CPU utilization shown earlier. User memory utilization is low during non-prime hours and high during prime hours.

System memory utilization is the middle line of the graph, which remains fairly steady throughout the week.

Total memory utilization is always the top line of the graph, and it is the sum of system and user utilization. It rises and drops with user utilization, because system memory utilization remains roughly the same.

The three-hour interval between data points on this graph may not give us the granularity we require. Figure 13-12 shows memory utilization during a much shorter time window.

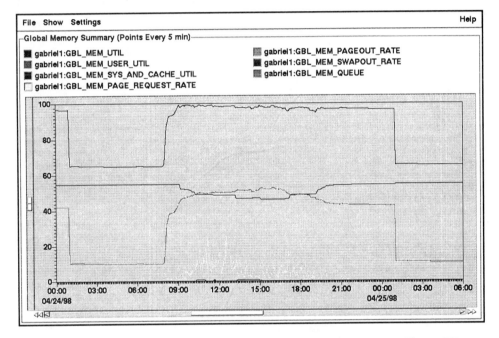

Figure 13-12 HP PerfView *Global Memory Summary* - Short Time Period

Figure 13-12 shows a finer granularity of memory utilization during the shorter time window. You can now see precisely how memory utilization is changing over roughly one day.

Disk utilization can also be graphed over the course of the week, as shown in Figure 13-13.

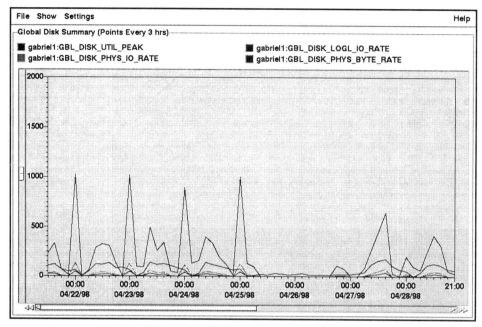

Figure 13-13 HP PerfView *Global Disk Summary*

Like the CPU and memory graph, this is an entire week of disk usage. Because many spikes occur on this graph, we would surely want to view and analyze much shorter time windows.

Figure 13-14 shows disk utilization during a much shorter time window.

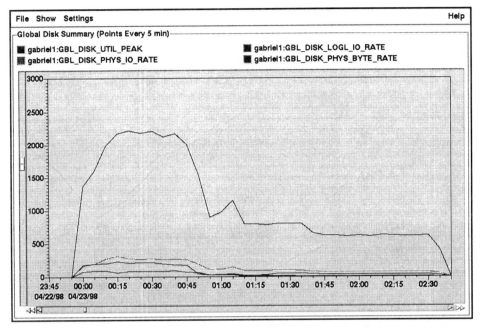

Figure 13-14 HP PerfView *Global Disk Summary* - Short Time Period

This much shorter time window, of roughly three hours, shows a lot more detail. There are tremendous spikes in disk activity occurring in the middle of the night. These could take place for a variety of reasons, including batch job processing or system backup.

You are not limited to viewing parameters related to only one system resource at a time. You can also view the way many system resources are used simultaneously, as shown in Figure 13-15.

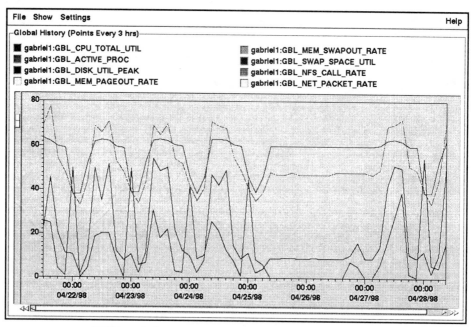

Figure 13-15 HP PerfView *Global Summary*

Many system resources are present on this graph, including CPU, disk, and memory. You would surely want to view a much shorter time period when displaying so many system resources simultaneously.

Figure 13-16 shows the same parameters during a much shorter time window.

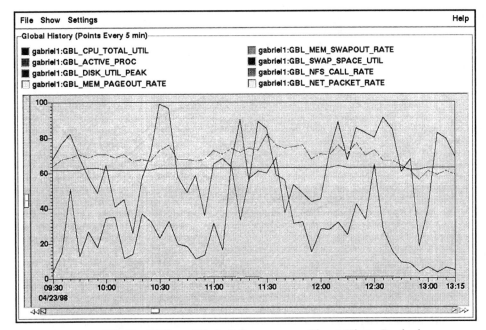

Figure 13-16 HP PerfView *Global Summary* - Short Time Period

Figure 13-16 shows a finer granularity of the utilization of many system resources during the shorter time window. You can now view the ways in which various system resources are related to other system resources.

You can find the status of PerfView running on your system with a useful command called **perfstat**. The following example shows issuing the **perfstat** command with the **-?** option to see all perfstat options:

```
# perfstat -?

usage: perfstat [options]

  Unix option   Function
  -----------   --------
       -?       List all perfstat options.
       -c       Show system configuration information.
       -e       Search for warnings and errors from
                  performance tool status files.
```

```
          -f          List size of performance tool status files.
          -p          List active performance tool processes.
          -t          Display last few lines of performance tool
                      status files.
          -v          List version strings for performance tool files.
          -z          Dump perfstat info to a file and tar tape.
```

Using the **-c** option, you get information about your system configuration, as shown in the following listing:

```
# perfstat -c

*****************************************************************
** perfstat for rp-ux6 on Fri May 15 12:20:06 EDT
*****************************************************************

system configuration information:

uname -a: HP-UX ux6 B.11.00 E 9000/800 71763 8-user license

mounted file systems with disk space shown:
Filesystem              kbytes      used   avail %used Mounted on
/dev/vg00/lvol3          86016     27675   54736  34% /
/dev/vg00/lvol1          67733     44928   16031  74% /stand
/dev/vg00/lvol8         163840     66995   90927  42% /var
/dev/vg00/lvol7         499712    358775  132155  73% /usr
/dev/rp06vgtmp/tmp     4319777   1099297 3134084  26% /tmp
/dev/vg00/lvol6         270336    188902   76405  71% /opt
/dev/vgroot1/var        640691     15636  605834   3% /newvar
/dev/vgroot1/usr        486677    356866  115210  76% /newusr
/dev/vgroot1/stand       67733     45109   15850  74% /newstand
/dev/vgroot1/root        83733     21181   54178  28% /newroot
/dev/vgroot1/opt        263253    188109   67246  74% /newopt
/dev/vg00/lvol5          20480      1109   18168   6% /home

LAN interfaces:
Name     Mtu      Network        Address      Ipkts      Opkts
lo0      4136     127.0.0.0      localhost    7442       7442
lan0     1500     192.60.11.0    rp-ux6       7847831    12939169

************* (end of perfstat -c output) ***************
```

Using the **-f** option shows the size of the performance tools status files, as shown in the following listing:

```
# perfstat -f

*************************************************************
** perfstat for ux6 on Fri May 15 12:20:08 EDT
*************************************************************

ls -l list of performance tool status files in /var/opt/perf:

-rw-rw-rw-  1 root  root   7812 May 10 19:35 status.alarmgen
-rw-r--r--  1 root  root      0 May 10 02:40 status.mi
-rw-rw-rw-  1 root  root   3100 May 10 02:40 status.perflbd
-rw-rw-rw-  1 root  root   3978 May 10 02:40 status.rep_server
-rw-r--r--  1 root  root   6079 May 11 23:30 status.scope
-rw-r--r--  1 root  root      0 Mar 31 07:26 status.ttd

************* (end of perfstat -f output) ****************
```

Using the **-v** option shows the version strings for the performance tools running, as shown in the following listing:

```
# perfstat -v

*************************************************************
** perfstat for ux6 on Fri May 15 12:20:08 EDT
*************************************************************

listing version strings for performance tool files:

NOTE:   The following software version information can be com-
pared
with the version information shown in the /opt/perf/ReleaseNotes
file(s).

MeasureWare executables in the directory /opt/perf/bin
        scopeux   C.01.00      12/17/97 HP-UX 11.0+
            ttd   A.11.00.15   12/15/97 HP-UX 11.00
        perflbd   C.01.00      12/17/97 HP-UX 11.0+
       alarmgen   C.01.00      12/17/97 HP-UX 11.0+
      agdbserver   C.01.00      12/17/97 HP-UX 11.0+
        agsysdb   C.01.00      12/17/97 HP-UX 11.0+
     rep_server   C.01.00      12/17/97 HP-UX 11.0+
        extract   C.01.00      12/17/97 HP-UX 11.0+
        utility   C.01.00      12/17/97 HP-UX 11.0+
            mwa   A.10.52      12/05/97
       perfstat   A.11.01      11/19/97
         dsilog   C.01.00      12/17/97 HP-UX 11.0+
        sdlcomp   C.01.00      12/17/97 HP-UX 11.0+
```

```
                 sdlexpt    C.01.00        12/17/97 HP-UX 11.0+
              sdlgendata    C.01.00        12/17/97 HP-UX 11.0+
                 sdlutil    C.01.00        12/17/97 HP-UX 11.0+

Measureware libraries in the directory /opt/perf/lib
              libmwa.sl    C.01.00        12/17/97 HP-UX 11.0+
              libarm.a     A.11.00.15     12/15/97 HP-UX 11.00
              libarm.sl    A.11.00.15     12/15/97 HP-UX 11.00

Measureware metric description file in the directory /var/opt/
perf
              metdesc    C.01.00       12/17/97

All critical MeasureWare files are accessible

            libnums.sl    B.11.00.15     12/15/97 HP-UX 11.00
            midaemon      B.11.00.15     12/15/97 HP-UX 11.00
             glance    B.11.01          12/16/97 HP-UX 11.00
               gpm    B.11.01          12/16/97 HP-UX 11.00

************* (end of perfstat -v output) ****************
```

Manual Pages of Some Commands Used in Chapter 13

Many useful commands are in this chapter. I provided a brief description of many of the commands along with some of the examples. The following are the HP-UX manual pages for many of the commands used in the chapter. The manual pages are thorough and provide much more detailed descriptions of each of the commands.

iostat

iostat - Interactively report I/O and CPU statistics.

---

iostat(1)   iostat(1)

NAME
     iostat - report I/O statistics

SYNOPSIS

     iostat [-t] [interval [count]]

DESCRIPTION
     iostat iteratively reports I/O statistics for each active disk on the
     system. Disk data is arranged in a four-column format:

          Column Heading   Interpretation
               device   Device name
               bps   Kilobytes transferred per second
               sps   Number of seeks per second
               msps   Milliseconds per average seek

     If two or more disks are present, data is presented on successive
     lines for each disk.

     To compute this information, seeks, data transfer completions, and the
     number of words transferred are counted for each disk. Also, the
     state of each disk is examined HZ times per second (as defined in
     <sys/param.h>) and a tally is made if the disk is active. These
     numbers can be combined with the transfer rates of each device to
     determine average seek times for each device.

     With the advent of new disk technologies, such as data striping, where
     a single data transfer is spread across several disks, the number of
     milliseconds per average seek becomes impossible to compute
     accurately. At best it is only an approximation, varying greatly,
     based on several dynamic system conditions. For this reason and to
     maintain backward compatibility, the milliseconds per average seek (
     msps) field is set to the value 1.0.

     Options
          iostat recognizes the following options and command-line arguments:

               -t   Report terminal statistics as well as disk
                           statistics. Terminal statistics include:

                           tin   Number of characters read from terminals.

                           tout   Number of characters written to
                                  terminals.
                           us   Percentage of time system has spent in
                                  user mode.
                           ni   Percentage of time system has spent in
                                  user mode running low-priority (nice)
                                  processes.
                           sy   Percentage of time system has spent in

> system mode.
>
> id   Percentage of time system has spent idling.

interval   Display successive lines which are summaries of the last interval seconds. The first line reported is for the time since a reboot and each subsequent line is for the last interval only.

count   Repeat the statistics count times.

EXAMPLES

Show current I/O statistics for all disks:

```
iostat
```

Display I/O statistics for all disks every 10 seconds until INTERRUPT or QUIT is pressed:

```
iostat 10
```

Display I/O statistics for all disks every 10 seconds and terminate after 5 successive readings:

```
iostat 10 5
```

Display I/O statistics for all disks every 10 seconds, also show terminal and processor statistics, and terminate after 5 successive readings:

```
iostat -t 10 5
```

WARNINGS

Users of iostat must not rely on the exact field widths and spacing of its output, as these will vary depending on the system, the release of HP-UX, and the data to be displayed.

AUTHOR

iostat was developed by the University of California, Berkeley, and HP.

FILES

/usr/include/sys/param.h

SEE ALSO

vmstat(1).

sar

man page

sar - 13

sar - System activity reporter.

---

sar(1M)   sar(1M)

NAME
     sar - system activity reporter

SYNOPSIS

     sar [-ubdycwaqvmAMS] [-o file] t [n]

     sar [-ubdycwaqvmAMS] [-s time] [-e time] [-i sec] [-f file]

DESCRIPTION
     In the first form above, sar samples cumulative activity counters in
     the operating system at n intervals of t seconds. If the -o option is
     specified, it saves the samples in file in binary format. The default
     value of n is 1. In the second form, with no sampling interval
     specified, sar extracts data from a previously recorded file, either
     the one specified by -f option or, by default, the standard system
     activity daily data file /var/adm/sa/sadd for the current day dd. The
     starting and ending times of the report can be bounded via the -s and
     -e time arguments of the form hh[:mm[:ss]]. The -i option selects
     records at sec-second intervals. Otherwise, all intervals found in
     the data file are reported.

     In either case, subsets of data to be printed are specified by option:

          -u   Report CPU utilization (the default); portion of time
               running in one of several modes. On a multi-processor
               system, if the -M option is used together with the -u
               option, per-CPU utilization as well as the average CPU
               utilization of all the processors are reported. If the -M
               option is not used, only the average CPU utilization of all
               the processors is reported:

                    cpu   cpu number (only on a multi-processor
                                 system with the -M option);

                    %usr   user mode;

                    %sys   system mode;

                    %wio   idle with some process waiting for I/O
                                 (only block I/O, raw I/O, or VM
                                 pageins/swapins indicated);

                    %idle   otherwise idle.

          -b   Report buffer activity:

                    bread/s   Number of physical reads per second
                                 from the disk (or other block devices)
                                 to the buffer cache;

bwrit/s   Number of physical writes per second from the buffer cache to the disk (or other block device);

lread/s   Number of reads per second from buffer cache;

lwrit/s   Number of writes per second to buffer cache;

%rcache   Buffer cache hit ratio for read requests e.g., 1 - bread/lread;

%wcache   Buffer cache hit ratio for write requests e.g., 1 - bwrit/lwrit;

pread/s   Number of reads per second from character device using the physio() (raw I/O) mechanism;

pwrit/s   Number of writes per second to character device using the physio() (i.e., raw I/O) mechanism; mechanism.

-d   Report activity for each block device, e.g., disk or tape drive. One line is printed for each device that had activity during the last interval. If no devices were active, a blank line is printed. Each line contains the following data:

     device   Logical name of the device and its corresponding instance. Devices are categorized into the following four device types:

         disk1 - HP-IB disks (CS/80)
         disk2 - CIO HP-FL disks (CS/80)
         disk3 - SCSI and NIO FL disks
         sdisk - SCSI disks;

     %busy   Portion of time device was busy servicing a request;

     avque   Average number of requests outstanding for the device;

     r+w/s   Number of data transfers per second (read and writes) from and to the device;

     blks/s   Number of bytes transferred (in 512-byte units) from and to the device;

     avwait   Average time (in milliseconds) that transfer requests waited idly on queue for the device;

     avserv   Average time (in milliseconds) to service each transfer request (includes seek, rotational latency, and data transfer times) for the device.

-y   Report tty device activity:

rawch/s	Raw input characters per second;
canch/s	Input characters per second processed by canon();
outch/s	Output characters per second;
rcvin/s	Receive incoming character interrupts per second;
xmtin/s	Transmit outgoing character interrupts per second;
mdmin/s	Modem interrupt rate (not supported; always 0).

-c   Report system calls:

scall/s	Number of system calls of all types per second;
sread/s	Number of read() and/or readv() system calls per second;
swrit/s	Number of write() and/or writev() system calls per second;
fork/s	Number of fork() and/or vfork() system calls per second;
exec/s	Number of exec() system calls per second;
rchar/s	Number of characters transferred by read system calls block devices only) per second;
wchar/s	Number of characters transferred by write system calls (block devices only) per second.

-w   Report system swapping and switching activity:

swpin/s	Number of process swapins per second;
swpot/s	Number of process swapouts per second;
bswin/s	Number of 512-byte units transferred for swapins per second;
bswot/s	Number of 512-byte units transferred for swapouts per second;
pswch/s	Number of process context switches per second.

-a   Report use of file access system routines:

iget/s	Number of file system iget() calls per second;

namei/s	Number of file system lookuppn() (pathname translation) calls per second;
dirblk/s	Number of file system blocks read per second doing directory lookup.

-q   Report average queue length while occupied, and percent of
     time occupied. On a multi-processor machine, if the -M
     option is used together with the -q option, the per-CPU run
     queue as well as the average run queue of all the
     processors are reported. If the -M option is not used,
     only the average run queue information of all the
     processors is reported:

cpu	cpu number (only on a multi-processor system and used with the -M option)
runq-sz	Average length of the run queue(s) of processes (in memory and runnable);
%runocc	The percentage of time the run queue(s) were occupied by processes (in memory and runnable);
swpq-sz	Average length of the swap queue of runnable processes (processes swapped out but ready to run);
%swpocc	The percentage of time the swap queue of runnable processes (processes swapped out but ready to run) was occupied.

-v   Report status of text, process, inode and file tables:

text-sz	(Not Applicable);
proc-sz	The current-size and maximum-size of the process table;
inod-sz	The current-size and maximum-size of the inode table (inode cache);
file-sz	The current-size and maximum-size of the system file table;
text-ov	(Not Applicable);
proc-ov	The number of times the process table overflowed (number of times the kernel could not find any available process table entries) between sample points;
inod-ov	The number of times the inode table (inode cache) overflowed (number of times the kernel could not find any available inode table entries) between sample points;
file-ov	The number of times the system file table overflowed (number of times the kernel could not find any available file table entries) between sample

points.

-m   Report message and semaphore activities:

     msg/s   Number of System V msgrcv() calls per
                          second;

     sema/s   Number of System V semop() calls per
                          second;

     select/s   Number of System V select() calls per
                          second. This value will only be
                          reported if the "-S" option is also
                          explicitly specified.

-A   Report all data. Equivalent to -udqbwcayvm.

-M   Report the per-processor data on a multi-processor system
       when used with -q and/or -u options. If the -M option is
       not used on a multi-processor system, the output format of
       the -u and -q options is the same as the uni-processor
       output format and the data reported is the average value of
       all the processors.

EXAMPLES
    Watch CPU activity evolve for 5 seconds:

        sar 1 5

    Watch CPU activity evolve for 10 minutes and save data:

        sar -o temp 60 10

    Review disk and tape activity from that period later:

        sar -d -f temp

    Review cpu utilization on a multi-processor system later:

        sar -u -M -f temp

WARNINGS
    Users of sar must not rely on the exact field widths and spacing of
    its output, as these will vary depending on the system, the release of
    HP-UX, and the data to be displayed.

FILES
    /var/adm/sa/sadd   daily data file, where dd is two digits
                                   representing the day of the month.

SEE ALSO
    sa1(1M).

STANDARDS CONFORMANCE
    sar: SVID2, SVID3

showmount

showmount- Show all remote mounts.

```
showmount(1M)                                                      showmount(1M)
```

NAME
     showmount - show all remote mounts

SYNOPSIS

     /usr/sbin/showmount [-a] [-d] [-e] [host]

DESCRIPTION
     showmount lists all clients that have remotely mounted a filesystem
     from host. This information is maintained by the mountd server on
     host (see mountd(1M)). The default value for host is the value
     returned by hostname (see hostname(1)).

     Options
     -a   Print all remote mounts in the format

              name:directory

          where hostname is the name of the client, and directory is the
          directory or root of the file system that was mounted.

     -d   List directories that have been remotely mounted by clients.

     -e   Print the list of exported file systems.

WARNINGS
     If a client crashes, executing showmount on the server will show that
     the client still has a file system mounted. In other words, the
     client's entry is not removed from /etc/rmtab until the client reboots
     and executes:

          umount -a

     Also, if a client mounts the same remote directory twice, only one
     entry appears in /etc/rmtab. Doing a umount of one of these
     directories removes the single entry and showmount no longer indicates
     that the remote directory is mounted.

AUTHOR
     showmount was developed by Sun Microsystems, Inc.

SEE ALSO
     hostname(1), exportfs(1M), mountd(1M), exports(4), rmtab(4).

swapinfo

swapinfo - Report system paging information.

swapinfo(1M)   swapinfo(1M)

NAME
        swapinfo - system paging space information

SYNOPSIS

        /usr/sbin/swapinfo [-mtadfnrMqw]

DESCRIPTION
        swapinfo prints information about device and file system paging space.
        (Note: the term `swap' refers to an obsolete implementation of
        virtual memory; HP-UX actually implements virtual memory by way of
        paging rather than swapping. This command and others retain names
        derived from `swap' for historical reasons.)

        By default, swapinfo prints to standard output a two line header as
        shown here, followed by one line per paging area:

                     Kb   Kb   Kb   PCT   START/ Kb
              TYPE   AVAIL   USED   FREE   USED   LIMIT   RESERVE PRI   NAME

        The fields are:

        TYPE   One of:

                    dev   Paging space residing on a mass storage device,
                                either taking up the entire device or, if the
                                device contains a file system, taking up the
                                space between the end of the file system and
                                the end of the device. This space is
                                exclusively reserved for paging, and even if it
                                is not being used for paging, it cannot be used
                                for any other purpose. Device paging areas
                                typically provide the fastest paging.

                    fs   Dynamic paging space available from a file
                                system. When this space is needed, the system
                                creates files in the file system and uses them
                                as paging space. File system paging is
                                typically slower than device paging, but allows
                                the space to be used for other things (user
                                files) when not needed for paging.

                    localfs   File system paging space (see fs above) on a
                                file system residing on a local disk.

                    network   File system paging space (see fs above) on a
                                file system residing on another machine. This
                                file system would have been mounted on the
                                local machine via NFS.

                    reserve   Paging space on reserve. This is the amount of
                                paging space that could be needed by processes

that are currently running, but that has not yet been allocated from one of the above paging areas. See "Paging Allocation" below.

memory   Memory paging area (also known as pseudo-swap). This is the amount of system memory that can be used to hold pages in the event that all of the above paging areas are used up. See "Paging Allocation" below. This line appears only if memory paging is enabled.

Kb AVAIL   The total available space from the paging area, in blocks of 1024 bytes (rounded to nearest whole block if necessary), including any paging space already in use.

For file system paging areas the value is not necessarily constant. It is the current space allocated for paging (even if not currently used), plus the free blocks available on the file system to ordinary users, minus RESERVE (but never less than zero). AVAIL is never more than LIMIT if LIMIT is non-zero. Since paging space is allocated in large chunks, AVAIL is rounded down to the nearest full allocation chunk.

For the memory paging area this value is also not necessarily constant, because it reflects allocation of memory by the kernel as well as by processes that might need to be paged.

Kb USED   The current number of 1-Kbyte blocks used for paging in the paging area. For the memory paging area, this count also includes memory used for other purposes and thus unavailable for paging.

Kb FREE   The amount of space that can be used for future paging. Usually this is the difference between Kb AVAIL and Kb USED. There could be a difference if some portion of a device paging area is unusable, perhaps because the size of the paging area is not a multiple of the allocation chunk size, or because the tunable parameter maxswapchunks is not set high enough.

PCT USED   The percentage of capacity in use, based on Kb USED divided by Kb AVAIL; 100% if Kb AVAIL is zero.

START/LIMIT For device paging areas, START is the block address on the mass storage device of the start of the paging area. The value is normally 0 for devices dedicated to paging, or the end of the file system for devices containing both a file system and paging space.

For file system paging areas, LIMIT is the maximum number of 1-Kbyte blocks that will be used for paging, the same as the limit value given to swapon. A file system LIMIT value of none means there is no fixed limit; all space is available except that used for files, less the blocks represented by minfree (see fs(4)) plus RESERVE.

RESERVE   For device paging areas, this value is always ``-''. For file system paging areas, this value is the number of 1-Kbyte blocks reserved for file system use by ordinary users, the same as the reserve value given to swapon.

PRI   The same as the priority value given to swapon. This value indicates the order in which space is taken from the

	devices and file systems used for paging. Space is taken from areas with lower priority values first. priority can have a value between 0 and 10. See "Paging Allocation" below.

NAME   For device paging areas, the block special file name whose
                major and minor numbers match the device's ID. The
                swapinfo command searches the /dev tree to find device
                names. If no matching block special file is found,
                swapinfo prints the device ID (major and minor values),
                for example, 28,0x15000.

                For file system swap areas, NAME is the name of a
                directory on the file system in which the paging files are
                stored.

Paging Allocation
  Paging areas are enabled at boot time (for device paging areas
  configured into the kernel) or by the swapon command (see swapon(1M)),
  often invoked by /sbin/init.d/swap_start during system initialization
  based on the contents of /etc/fstab. When a paging area is enabled,
  some portion of that area is allocated for paging space. For device
  paging areas, the entire device is allocated, less any leftover
  fraction of an allocation chunk. (The size of an allocation chunk is
  controlled by the tunable parameter swchunk, and is typically 2 MB.)
  For file system paging areas, the minimum value given to swapon
  (rounded up to the nearest allocation chunk) is allocated.

When a process is created, or requests additional space, space is
reserved for it by increasing the space shown on the reserve line
above. When paging activity actually occurs, space is used in one of
the paging areas (the one with the lowest priority number that has
free space available, already allocated), and that space will be shown
as used in that area.

The sum of the space used in all of the paging areas, plus the amount
of space reserved, can never exceed the total amount allocated in all
of the paging areas. If a request for more memory occurs which would
cause this to happen, the system tries several options:

1.   The system tries to increase the total space available by
      allocating more space in file system paging areas.

2.   If all file system paging areas are completely allocated and the
      request is still not satisfied, the system will try to use memory
      paging as described on the memory line above. (Memory paging is
      controlled by the tunable parameter swapmem_on, which defaults to
      1 (on). If this parameter is turned off, the memory line will
      not appear.)

3.   If memory paging also cannot satisfy the request, because it is
      full or turned off, the request is denied.

Several implications of this procedure are noteworthy for
understanding the output of swapinfo:

-     Paging space will not be allocated in a file system paging area
      (except for the minimum specified when the area is first enabled)
      until all device paging space has been reserved, even if the file
      system paging area has a lower priority value.

-     When paging space is allocated to a file system paging area, that
      space becomes unavailable for user files, even if there is no
      paging activity to it.

-     Requests for more paging space will fail when they cannot be

satisfied by reserving device, file system, or memory paging,
even if some of the reserved paging space is not yet in use.
Thus it is possible for requests for more paging space to be
denied when some, or even all, of the paging areas show zero
usage - space in those areas is completely reserved.

- System available memory is shared between the paging subsystem
  and kernel memory allocators. Thus, the system may show memory
  paging usage before all available disk paging space is completely
  reserved or fully allocated.

Options
   swapinfo recognizes the following options:

   -m   Display the AVAIL, USED, FREE, LIMIT, and RESERVE values in
        Mbytes instead of Kbytes, rounding off to the nearest whole
        Mbyte (multiples of 1024^2). The output header format
        changes from Kb to Mb accordingly.

   -t   Add a totals line with a TYPE of total. This line totals
        only the paging information displayed above it, not all
        paging areas; this line might be misleading if a subset of
        -dfrM is specified.

   -a   Show all device paging areas, including those configured
        into the kernel but currently disabled. (These are normally
        omitted.) The word disabled appears after the NAME, and the
        Kb AVAIL, Kb USED, and Kb FREE values are 0. The -a option
        is ignored unless the -d option is present or is true by
        default.

   -d   Print information about device paging areas only. This
        modifies the output header appropriately.

   -f   Print information about file system paging areas only. This
        modifies the output header appropriately.

   -n   Categorize file system paging area information into localfs
        areas and network areas, instead of calling them both fs
        areas.

   -r   Print information about reserved paging space only.

   -M   Print information about memory paging space only.

        The -d, -f, -n, -r and -M options can be combined. The
        default is -dfnrM.

   -q   Quiet mode. Print only a total "Kb AVAIL" value (with the
        -m option, Mb AVAIL); that is, the total paging space
        available on the system (device, file system, reserve, or
        memory paging space only if -d, -f, -r, or -M is specified),
        for possible use by programs that want a quick total. If -q
        is specified, the -t and -a options are ignored.

   -w   Print a warning about each device paging area that contains
        wasted space; that is, any device paging area whose
        allocated size is less than its total size. This option is
        effective only if -d is also specified or true by default.

RETURN VALUE
    swapinfo returns 0 if it completes successfully (including if any
    warnings are issued), or 1 if it reports any errors.

DIAGNOSTICS

swapinfo prints messages to standard error if it has any problems.

EXAMPLES
List all file system paging areas with a totals line:

        swapinfo -ft

WARNINGS
swapinfo needs kernel access for some information. If the user does
not have appropriate privileges for kernel access, swapinfo will print
a warning and assume that the defaults for that information have not
been changed.

Users of swapinfo must not rely on the exact field widths and spacing
of its output, as these will vary depending on the system, the release
of HP-UX, and the data to be displayed.

The information in this manual page about paging allocation and other
implementation details may change without warning; users should not
rely on the accuracy of this information.

AUTHOR
swapinfo was developed by HP.

SEE ALSO
swapon(1M), swapon(2), fstab(4), fs(4).

timex

timex - Time a command and produce a system activity report.

```
timex(1)                                                            timex(1)

NAME
     timex - time a command; report process data and system activity

SYNOPSIS

     timex [-o] [-p[fhkmrt]] [-s] command

DESCRIPTION
     timex reports in seconds the elapsed time, user time, and system time
     spent in execution of the given command.  Optionally, process
     accounting data for command and all its children can be listed or
     summarized, and total system activity during the execution interval
     can be reported.

     The output of timex is written on the standard error.

     Options
            -o          Report the total number of blocks read or written
                        and total characters transferred by command and
                        all its children.

            -p[fhkmrt]  List process accounting records for command and
                        all its children.  The suboptions f, h, k, m, r,
                        and t modify the data items reported.  They behave
                        as defined in acctcom(1M).  The number of blocks
                        read or written and the number of characters
                        transferred are always reported.

            -s          Report total system activity (not just that due to
                        command) that occurred during the execution
                        interval of command.  All the data items listed in
                        sar(1) are reported.

EXAMPLES
     A simple example:

          timex -ops sleep 60

     A terminal session of arbitrary complexity can be measured by timing a
     sub-shell:

          timex -opskmt sh

             session commands

          EOT

WARNINGS
     Process records associated with command are selected from the
     accounting file /var/adm/pacct by inference, since process genealogy
     is not available.  Background processes having the same user-ID,
     terminal-ID, and execution time window are spuriously included.
```

```
SEE ALSO
      sar(1), acctcom(1M).

STANDARDS CONFORMANCE
      timex: SVID2, SVID3
```

top

top - Provide information about top processes on the system.

```
top(1)                                                                    top(1)

NAME
     top - display and update information about the top processes on the
     system

SYNOPSIS

     top [-s time] [-d count] [-q] [-u] [-n number]

DESCRIPTION
     top displays the top processes on the system and periodically updates
     the information.  Raw CPU percentage is used to rank the processes.

  Options
     top recognizes the following command-line options:

          -s time      Set the delay between screen updates to time seconds.
                       The default delay between updates is 5 seconds.

          -d count     Show only count displays, then exit.  A display is
                       considered to be one update of the screen.  This
                       option is used to select the number of displays to be
                       shown before the program exits.

          -q           This option runs the top program at the same priority
                       as if it is executed via a nice -20 command so that
                       it will execute faster (see nice(1)).  This can be
                       very useful in discovering any system problem when
                       the system is very sluggish.  This option is
                       accessibly only to users who have appropriate
                       privileges.

          -u           User ID (uid) numbers are displayed instead of
                       usernames.  This improves execution speed by
                       eliminating the additional time required to map uid
                       numbers to user names.

          -n number    Show only number processes per screen.  Note that
                       this option is ignored if number is greater than the
                       maximum number of processes that can be displayed per
                       screen.

  Screen-Control Commands
     When displaying multiple-screen data, top recognizes the following
     keyboard screen-control commands:

          j            Display next screen if the current screen is not the
                       last screen.

          k            Display previous screen if the current screen is not
                       the first screen.

          t            Display the first (top) screen.
```

Program Termination
   To exit the program and resume normal user activities, type q at any
   time.

Display Description
   Three general classes of information are displayed by top:

   System Data:
      The first few lines at the top of the display show general
      information about the state of the system, including:

      - System name and current time.

      - Load averages in the last one, five, and fifteen
        minutes.

      - Number of existing processes and the number of
        processes in each state (sleeping, waiting, running,
        starting, zombie, and stopped).

      - Percentage of time spent in each of the processor
        states (user, nice, system, idle, interrupt and
        swapper) per processor on the system.

      - Average value for each of the processor states (only
        on multi-processor systems).

   Memory Data
      Includes virtual and real memory in use (with the amount of
      memory considered "active" in parentheses) and the amount of
      free memory.

   Process Data
      Information about individual processes on the system. When
      process data cannot fit on a single screen, top divides the
      data into two or more screens. To view multiple-screen
      data, use the j, k, and t commands described previously.
      Note that the system- and memory-data displays are present
      in each screen of multiple-screen process data.

      Process data is displayed in a format similar to that used
      by ps(1):

      CPU   Processor number on which the process is
                  executing (only on multi-processor
                  systems).

      TTY   Terminal interface used by the process.

      PID   Process ID number.

      USERNAME   Name of the owner of the process. When the
                  -u option is specified, the user ID (uid)
                  is displayed instead of USERNAME.

      PRI   Current priority of the process.

      NI   Nice value ranging from -20 to +20.

      SIZE   Total size of the process in kilobytes.
                  This includes text, data, and stack.

      RES   Resident size of the process in kilobytes.
                  The resident size information is, at best,

	an approximate value.
STATE	Current state of the process. The various states are sleep, wait, run, idl, zomb, or stop.
TIME	Number of system and CPU seconds the process has consumed.
%WCPU	Weighted CPU (central processing unit) percentage.
%CPU	Raw CPU percentage. This field is used to sort the top processes.
COMMAND	Name of the command the process is currently running.

EXAMPLES

top can be executed with or without command-line options. To display five screens of data at two-second intervals then automatically exit, use:

```
top -s2 -d5
```

AUTHOR

top was developed by HP and William LeFebvre of Rice University.

vmstat

vmstat - Report process, virtual memory, trap, and CPU activity.

```
vmstat(1)                                                        vmstat(1)

NAME
     vmstat - report virtual memory statistics

SYNOPSIS

     vmstat [-dnS] [interval [count]]

     vmstat -f | -s | -z

DESCRIPTION
     The vmstat command reports certain statistics kept about process,
     virtual memory, trap, and CPU activity.  It also can clear the
     accumulators in the kernel sum structure.

  Options
     vmstat recognizes the following options:

             -d        Report disk transfer information as a separate section,
                       in the form of transfers per second.

             -n        Provide an output format that is more easily viewed on
                       an 80-column display device.  This format separates the
                       default output into two groups: virtual memory
                       information and CPU data.  Each group is displayed as a
                       separate line of output.  On multiprocessor systems,
                       this display format also provides CPU utilization on a
                       per CPU basis.

             -S        Report the number of processes swapped in and out (si
                       and so) instead of page reclaims and address
                       translation faults (re and at).

             interval  Display successive lines which are summaries over the
                       last interval seconds.  If interval is zero, the output
                       is displayed once only.  If the -d option is specified,
                       the column headers are repeated.  If -d is omitted, the
                       column headers are not repeated.

                       The command vmstat 5 prints what the system is doing
                       every five seconds.  This is a good choice of printing
                       interval since this is how often some of the statistics
                       are sampled in the system; others vary every second.

             count     Repeat the summary statistics count times.  If count is
                       omitted or zero, the output is repeated until an
                       interrupt or quit signal is received.  From the
                       terminal, these are commonly ^C and ^\, respectively
                       (see stty(1)).

             -f        Report on the number of forks and the number of pages
                       of virtual memory involved since boot-up.
```

-s   Print the total number of several kinds of paging-
            related events from the kernel sum structure that have
            occurred since boot-up or since vmstat was last
            executed with the -z option.

-z   Clear all accumulators in the kernel sum structure.
            This requires write file access permission on
            /dev/kmem. This is normally restricted to users with
            appropriate privileges.

If none of these options is given, vmstat displays a one-line summary
of the virtual memory activity since boot-up or since the -z option
was last executed.

Column Descriptions
The column headings and the meaning of each column are:

procs   Information about numbers of processes in various
            states.

            r   In run queue

            b   Blocked for resources (I/O, paging, etc.)

            w   Runnable or short sleeper (< 20 secs) but
                    swapped

memory   Information about the usage of virtual and real
            memory. Virtual pages are considered active if they
            belong to processes that are running or have run in
            the last 20 seconds.

            avm   Active virtual pages

            free   Size of the free list

page   Information about page faults and paging activity.
            These are averaged each five seconds, and given in
            units per second.

            re   Page reclaims (without -S)

            at   Address translation faults (without -S)

            si   Processes swapped in (with -S)

            so   Processes swapped out (with -S)

            pi   Pages paged in

            po   Pages paged out

            fr   Pages freed per second

            de   Anticipated short term memory shortfall

            sr   Pages scanned by clock algorithm, per
                    second

faults   Trap/interrupt rate averages per second over last 5
                seconds.

                in   Device interrupts per second (nonclock)

                sy   System calls per second

                cs   CPU context switch rate (switches/sec)

cpu   Breakdown of percentage usage of CPU time

                us   User time for normal and low priority
                        processes

                sy   System time

                id   CPU idle

EXAMPLES
     The following examples show the output for various command options.
     For formatting purposes, some leading blanks have been deleted.

     1.   Display the default output.

     vmstat

```
        procs              memory                      page
                  faults          cpu
        r    b     w       avm     free    re   at    pi    po    fr    de    sr
            in    sy      cs  us sy id
        0    0     0      1158      511     0    0     0     0     0     0     0
           111    18       7   0  0 100
```

     2.   Add the disk tranfer information to the default output.

     vmstat -d

```
        procs              memory                      page
                  faults          cpu
        r    b     w       avm     free    re   at    pi    po    fr    de    sr
            in    sy      cs  us sy id
        0    0     0      1158      511     0    0     0     0     0     0     0
           111    18       7   0  0 100
```

```
Disk Transfers
   device    xfer/sec
   c0t6d0        0
   c0t1d0        0
   c0t3d0        0
   c0t5d0        0
```

     3.   Display the default output in 80-column format.

     vmstat -n

```
VM
    memory                        page                          faults
    avm     free   re   at    pi   po    fr   de    sr     in     sy   cs
   1158      430    0    0     0    0     0    0     0    111     18    7
CPU
        cpu           procs
    us sy id     r     b     w
```

```
    0  0 100    0     0     0
```

4. Replace the page reclaims and address translation faults with
    process swapping in the default output.

```
vmstat -S

    procs              memory                    page
            faults         cpu
    r    b    w    avm    free   si   so   pi   po   fr   de   sr
         in   sy   cs us sy id
    0    0    0   1158    430    0    0    0    0    0    0    0
         111  18    7  0  0 100
```

5. Display the default output twice at five-second intervals. Note
    that the headers are not repeated.

```
vmstat 5 2

    procs              memory                    page
            faults         cpu
    r    b    w    avm    free   re   at   pi   po   fr   de   sr
         in   sy   cs us sy id
    0    0    0   1158    456    0    0    0    0    0    0    0
         111  18    7  0  0 100
    0    0    0   1221    436    5    0    5    0    0    0    0
         108  65   18  0  1 99
```

6. Display the default output twice in 80-column format at five-
    second intervals. Note that the headers are not repeated.

```
vmstat -n 5 2

VM
    memory                      page                      faults
    avm    free   re   at   pi   po   fr   de   sr   in   sy   cs
   1221    436    0    0    0    0    0    0    0   111   18    7
CPU
       cpu          procs
    us sy id   r    b    w
     0  0 100   0    0    0
   1221    435    2    0    2    0    0    0    0   109   35   17
     0  1 99    0    0    0
```

7. Display the default output and disk transfers twice in 80-column
    format at five-second intervals. Note that the headers are
    repeated.

```
vmstat -dn 5 2

VM
    memory                      page                      faults
    avm    free   re   at   pi   po   fr   de   sr   in   sy   cs
   1221    435    0    0    0    0    0    0    0   111   18    7
CPU
       cpu          procs
    us sy id   r    b    w
     0  0 100   0    0    0

Disk Transfers
    device    xfer/sec
    c0t6d0         0
```

```
      c0t1d0        0
      c0t3d0        0
      c0t5d0        0

VM
   memory                          page                              faults
   avm    free   re   at    pi   po    fr   de    sr     in    sy    cs
   1219   425    0    0     0    0     0    0     0      111   54    15
CPU
       cpu           procs
   us sy id    r     b      w
   1   8 92    0     0      0

Disk Transfers
   device    xfer/sec
   c0t6d0        0
   c0t1d0        0
   c0t3d0        0
   c0t5d0        0
```

8. Display the number of forks and pages of virtual memory since
    boot-up.

```
vmstat -f

24558 forks, 1471595 pages, average=  59.92
```

9. Display the counts of paging-related events.

```
vmstat -s

0 swap ins
0 swap outs
0 pages swapped in
0 pages swapped out
1344563 total address trans. faults taken
542093 page ins
2185 page outs
602573 pages paged in
4346 pages paged out
482343 reclaims from free list
504621 total page reclaims
124 intransit blocking page faults
1460755 zero fill pages created
404137 zero fill page faults
366022 executable fill pages created
71578 executable fill page faults
0 swap text pages found in free list
162043 inode text pages found in free list
196 revolutions of the clock hand
45732 pages scanned for page out
4859 pages freed by the clock daemon
36680636 cpu context switches
1497746186 device interrupts
1835626 traps
87434493 system calls
```

WARNINGS
    Users of vmstat must not rely on the exact field widths and spacing of
    its output, as these will vary depending on the system, the release of
    HP-UX, and the data to be displayed.

AUTHOR
    vmstat was developed by the University of California, Berkeley and HP.

FILES
        /dev/kmem

SEE ALSO
        iostat(1).

CHAPTER 14

Introduction to Software Development

1- Introduction

UNIX is a mature and robust operating environment, designed for performance, reliability, and scalability. Initially developed by researchers, UNIX has become the development platform of choice for many applications, including business critical applications.

As seen in previous chapters of this book, the UNIX system includes hundreds of utilities also referred to as commands. When these commands are combined in the form of scripts, they create programs to solve problems.

Script languages, however, do have several shortcomings. They are flexible and easy to use, but ill-suited to manipulate the computer's memory and I/O devices directly. Script languages are also interpreted languages. The commands typed into the scripts are read and evaluated only when the script is executed. This fact makes them inefficient because the commands must be reinterpreted each time the script is executed.

Command scripts for shell programs are sufficient in some cases, but for more complex problem solving and functionality, a programming language is necessary.

This chapter will introduce you to programming basics and three popular languages: C, C++ and Java. The content and structure is targeted at beginner programmers, working through basic concepts. The upcoming programming sections are only an introduction. They don't provide enough of information to be used as a reference for a specific programming language. You want to supplement each of these sections with a book dedicated to the language(s) you'll be using.

I don't normally number the sections in a chapter; however, because there is so much material covered in this chapter, I have numbered the major sections. The major section numbers will help you find a topic if you wish to turn directly to one of the following sections:

1- Introduction

2 - Understanding Computer Programs

3 -. Compiled vs. Interpreted Languages

4 - Programming Constructs

5 - Programming Design

6 - The Next Step: Object-Oriented Method and Design

7 - Development Life Cycle

8 - SCCS - Source Code Control System

9 - C and C++ - The History

10 - C and C++ - Compilers

11 - C and C++ - Make Utility

12 - C and C++ - Debugging

13 -. C Language

14 - C++ Language

15 - Internet Programming Basics

16 - Java

2 - Understanding Computer Programs

Computer programs are instructions that we give the computer to perform a task or solve a problem. Human-readable instructions are called *source code*.

Unfortunately, computers only understand *machine language*. Machine language, a collection of binary numbers, is unintelligible to us. A developer has to program in terms of binary numbers that corresponded directly to specific machine instructions and locations in the computer's memory. A machine language fragment such as:

```
000000010101111001010
000000010111111001000
000000011001110101000
```

is not as clear as source code found in modern programming languages, which may look similar to:

```
k = i + j.
```

Languages originally needed to evolve further for ease of use and readability.

Next came *assembly languages*. Instead of using sequences of binary numbers, an assembly language allows the programmer to use symbolic names to perform various operations and to refer to specific memory locations. A sequence of binary numbers within a machine language program may tell the computer to store a number. The symbolic equivalent may be **store x**.

Machine and assembly languages are referred to as *low-level languages*. Low-level languages are time-consuming and difficult to use. Simple programming operations, such as adding two numbers together, require multiple low-level operations. Using the example above, **k = i + j**, assembly language requires the following operations:

load i, **add j**, and **store k**. Each step requires an explicit statement for the programmer to write.

There is still a one-to-one correspondence between each assembly language statement and a specific machine instruction. The machine instruction sets vary for different computer systems. Therefore, a programmer must learn the machine instruction set for each type of computer system used.

Low-level languages create programs that are not portable. This means the program will not run on a different computer system without being rewritten, due to differences in the machine instruction sets. Because assembly language programs are written in terms of these instruction sets, they are machine-dependent.

In contrast, *programming languages* are considered *higher-level languages*. C, C++, and Java are examples of programming languages. These languages are more human-readable. Multiple steps in lower-level languages are implied in single statements of higher-level languages. Programming time, effort, and difficulty are reduced. Even UNIX, originally written in assembly language, was rewritten in C language.

The syntax of the higher-level languages became standardized across varying computer systems. There was no longer a need to be concerned with developing a program for a particular computer system's instruction set. Programmers could now write source code, allowing machine-independent programs to be written. Thus, programming in higher-level languages allowed for portability.

But the computer system could not understand the source code. It needed to be translated into machine language. To solve this problem, a special computer program was developed, called a compiler.

3 - Compiled vs. Interpreted Languages

Source code must be translated into machine language for a computer to understand. A compiled language requires a compiler to convert source code into a machine language. An interpreted language requires an interpreter to convert source code into a machine language.

A major difference between compiled and interpreted languages is *when* this translation occurs.

An interpreted language, such as Java or UNIX script programs, translates into machine language at runtime. Whenever the program is executed, the translation is performed. Interpreted languages tend to be slower and less efficient than compiled languages. There is very little time for an interpreted language to attempt to optimize the resulting machine language for execution. This is shown in Figure 14-1.

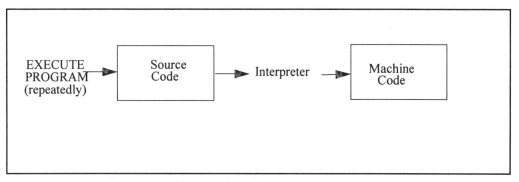

Figure 14-1 Interpreted Execution Flow

On the other hand, a compiled language, such as C or C++, allows the translation into machine language to occur before execution time.

The programmer creates the source code, runs the compiler, and executes the program, using the resulting executable. Not only is the compiler given more time to find optimizations, but also the translation into machine language happens only once, at compile time. Compiling does not occur again unless changes are made to the source code, as shown in Figure 14-2.

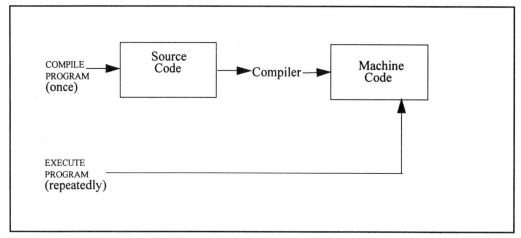

Figure 14-2 Compiled Execution Flow

Another distinction between compiled and interpreted languages is the potential for portable "executable" code or *executables*.

An *executable* is the file that runs the program. If the file name is entered into the computer, the program will run. For example, in C and C++, the executable is the machine code generated by the compiler.

A compiler translates source code into a *target language*. The target language is machine language for C and C++. The target language for Java is *bytecode*.

Important Note: Java is both a compiled and interpreted language. Source code is compiled into bytecode, and the bytecode is then interpreted when the program is executed. This discussion is referring to the interpreted aspect of Java programs.

A compiled language needs compiler software on the computer system performing the compile. The compiler is written specifically for that type of computer system. The executable generated by the compiler can only be moved to other computer systems using the same machine instruction set.

For example, all HP 9000 computer systems running HP-UX can run the same C or C++ executable without forcing a recompile on the individual computers. The same executable will not run on IBM, Sun, or DEC computer systems.

If a C or C++ program is to execute on a different computer system, a compiler for that computer system must be obtained and the source code must be recompiled.

Executables for C and C++ are not portable.

In contrast, the target language for Java, bytecode, is portable to different computer systems. Any computer system compiling with a Java compiler will generate a standard bytecode. The bytecode is usable on any computer system, and thus is portable.

The difference is that a Java-compliant *virtual machine* must be on the computer system executing the Java bytecode. A Java virtual machine, or JVM, accepts bytecode at execution time and interprets it into machine language. The JVM is performing the translation into machine language; therefore, virtual machines are written for specific computer systems.

For example, bytecode generated on a HP 9000 HP-UX computer system can be executed on a Sun Solaris computer system without performing a recompile. The Sun computer system must have a JVM. The JVM used on the HP computer system cannot be used on the Sun computer system.

Thus, the bytecode for Java is portable; the JVM is not.

4 - Programming Constructs

To program, you need to understand a few of the logical tools available. Specific syntax for these logical constructs will be provided in the individual programming sections.

Programming constructs are logical tools that can be used in creating an algorithm, or logical steps, for your program. This section will give you an idea of how to solve problems.

A generic format, or *pseudocode*, is used to help gain an understanding of what these constructs do.

Pseudocode is the expression of a program or statements in a program with simple English that parallels the form of a computer language.

Assignment

Values can be assigned to variables. Variables are locations in computer memory and have a name given by the programmer. Each variable contains a value assigned to it by the programmer.

Variables can be thought of as mailboxes. The mailbox is assigned a name by the programmer. The computer address can be thought of as the postal address to your mailbox. The computer knows where to find the mailbox in memory by its address. The mail placed inside your mailbox equates to the value assigned to it.

```
BankAccount = 100
```

In the example above, the name *BankAccount* is assigned to the variable by the programmer. *BankAccount* is in the computer memory, and can be found by the computer via a computer address. A programmer will reference the name *BankAccount* and the computer will translate that name into a computer address. After the variable is found in memory by the computer, the information inside can be looked at, changed, or deleted by the programmer. In this case, the programmer is putting the value 100 inside the variable named *BankAccount*.

Mathematical Operators

Addition, subtraction, multiplication, division, integer remainder, and exponentiation are standard operators.

```
BankAccount = BankAccount + 500
```

This statement is adding 500 to the value already in the *BankAccount* variable. The result is then put back into the *BankAccount* variable.

Assuming that *BankAccount* already has the value 100 in it, after this statement is complete, *BankAccount* will contain 600.

Comparison Expressions

The simplest expression is a comparison. A comparison evaluates to a TRUE or FALSE value. *Less than, greater than, equal to, less than or equal to, greater than or equal to, or,* as well as *and* are available.

```
BankAccount < 1000
```

The example above is stating, "The value in *BankAccount* less than 1000." Either the statement is TRUE or FALSE.

If the value in *BankAccount* is 600, this expression evaluates to TRUE; "600 is less than 1000" is a true statement.

If *BankAcount* contains 2000, the expression evaluates to FALSE; "2000 is less than 1000" is a false statement.

Loops

Loops can be divided roughly into two groups, depending on whether or not we can predict the number of times the loop will be executed. A *definite* iteration is executed a predetermined number of times. By contrast, the number of executions of an *indefinite* iteration is not known; the number is determined during the execution of the program.

An example of a definite iteration loop is a program that prints all the numbers between one and ten. A single statement can be inserted in a loop and run ten times instead of writing ten separate statements, one for each number printed:

```
LOOP ten times
    Print number
    Add one to number
```

If we start with 1, the result of the definite loop would be:

```
1 2 3 4 5 6 7 8 9 10
```

An indefinite iteration loop decides when to stop the looping while the program is running. A while loop is one example, loop while the number printed is 10 or less. Once the number is 11 or higher, the loop stops and the next statement outside the loop is executed:

```
WHILE number is less than or equal to 10
    Print number
    Add one to number
```

If we started with 1 again, the result of the indefinite loop would be:

```
1 2 3 4 5 6 7 8 9 10
```

Although the results are the same, the way we got there is different. In the first loop, a definite loop, we told it to loop ten times, and then stop. The second loop, an indefinite loop, does not know how many times it will loop until it reaches the number 10.

Let's start with 5 and see what the results would be.

The result from the definite loop:

```
5 6 7 8 9 10 11 12 13 14
```

The result from the indefinite loop:

```
5 6 7 8 9 10
```

The difference is that the definite loop was told to loop ten times, whereas the indefinite loop was told to loop *until the number was 10*. The indefinite loop had to loop five times to reach the number 10. The definite loop didn't care whether it reached the number 10; it is instructed to loop ten times regardless.

Loops can also be nested, one loop inside the other. One common area of use for nested loops is when dealing with tables. One loop can handle the columns; another loop can handle the rows.

Using the example in Figure 14-3, nested loops can help calculate the number of total hours worked.

```
LOOP through three rows of employees
            LOOP through seven columns of days of the week
                    Add number of hours worked
```

	Sunday	Monday	Tuesday	Wednesday	Thursday	Friday	Saturday
Liz	8	8	5	8	8	3	0
Carly	0	3	8	8	3	0	0
Kit	5	0	0	0	3	8	8

Figure 14-3 Hours Worked Table

The outer loop will start with the first row, row one, labeled Liz. The inner loop will then loop through all the columns for row one, Sunday through Saturday, adding the hours worked. After the inner loop is completed, control will then be passed back to the outer loop, which will move to row two, labeled Carly. Again, the inner loop will be activated and loop through all the columns for row two, adding the hours. Once the inner loop is completed, it will again pass control to the outer loop and move to the row labeled Kit. The inner loop will once again loop through the days of the week, accumulating the hours. The end result is the total number of hours worked by all employees for that week, 86.

Choice

An *if...then...else* statement allows a choice to be made. An evaluation is made on an expression. This expression is either TRUE or FALSE. If the expression is TRUE, any statements found in the *then* section are executed. If the expression is FALSE, any statements found in the *else* section are executed.

```
IF bank account balance is equal to or greater than $10
THEN
              Withdraw $10
ELSE
              Print Insufficient Funds
```

An *else* is not always necessary. If there is not an *else*, then *if* the expression is *FALSE*, do nothing.

The *if...then...else* statement can be nested, one inside the other. This possibility allows for sequential choice, as shown in Figure 14-4.

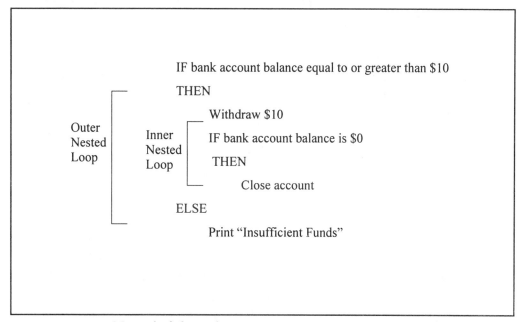

Figure 14-4 Nested *if-then-else*

Notice that the *ELSE* is associated with the first *IF* statement. The nested *IF* statement does not have a corresponding *ELSE*, because action only needs to be taken if the balance of the account is $0.

A *case* statement uses the value of an expression to select one of several choices for execution:

```
CASE part number for UNIX software

            101:   Print Linux
            102:   Print RedHat Linux
            103:   Print HP-UX
            104:   Print Solaris

ELSE
            Print bad part number
END
```

The *case* statement attempts to match the part number it was given with the numbers in the list. If there is a match occurs, then the name of the part is printed. If no match occurs, the *ELSE* statement is executed and a bad part number message is printed.

For example, if the part number requested is 102, "RedHat Linux" is printed. If the part number is 200, the bad part number message is printed.

Data Structures

So what happens to the data in a program? Data or information in a program can get confusing. We need a way to organize it. Programming languages allow a programmer to logically group data into something called *structures*. When a programmer wants to refer to the data, the name of the structure can be used.

For example, a program may know about an employee's name and pay rate, as well as the pay rate for the employee's manager. We would not want to confuse the two if our program generates paychecks. All the information regarding an employee can be put into a structure called *Employee_Record* and all the manager's information into a structure called *Manager_Record*. Both the *Employee_Record* and *Manager_Record* would have two entries, employee name and their respective pay rates.

```
STRUCTURE Employee_Record
          Employee_Name
          Hourly_Pay_Rate
END

STRUCTURE Manager_Record
          Employee Name
          Salary_Pay_Rate
END
```

By organizing the information into logical structures, the readability and understandability of a program is enhanced. It is also important to make the names of the structures as descriptive as possible. Now a programmer can see what information regarding an employee and a manager the program knows about. Because this makes the program logic clearer, it is less likely that the employee pay rate would be confused with the manager pay rate.

5 - Programming Design

Programs need to be planned before the programming begins. A little planning up front will save time and frustration later.

For beginners, the hardest part is learning to think like a computer. There are a few basic concepts that will help. A computer performs instructions one step at a time. The computer does not have previous knowledge about the problem to be solved. The computer needs to be told everything step by step, and it only knows what you tell it.

All computer programs do the same thing. They instruct a computer to accept data (input), to manipulate the data (process), and to produce reports or information back to a user (output).

So where do you start? Start by answering a few questions.

- What is the problem to be solved by the computer?

- How does the output from the program look?

- What are the logical steps (algorithm) to achieve this output?

- What inputs are needed?

After you have defined the input, output, and logical steps, take a moment to step through them one by one as if you were the computer. Does it solve the problem? Does it achieve the expected output?

Next, consider how the program will be organized.The importance of organizing a program is not readily apparent for small programs. When it comes to larger programs, it is easy to get lost when trying to understand the logic, find errors or enhance the code.

Programming logic can be broken into *modules*, smaller pieces of logic performing one or two functions required by the program, otherwise known as *decomposability*. Modules are small subprograms, each accepts input, processes data, and produces output. Modules can be arranged in a logical and easy-to-understand order to form a complete program. This capability is referred to as *modular programming*.

Let's look at an example of designing for modular programming. To design a simple employee weekly pay program, we would have to consider the following:

Statement of problem: To compute an employee's weekly gross and net pay, deducting before tax medical benefit costs.

Input: Employee Name
                Hourly Pay Rate

Output: Report with Employee's gross and net pay

Algorithm:
      1. Calculate Gross Pay
      2. Calculate Net Pay
      3. Generate report with Employee Name, gross pay and net pay.

Look at the logical steps in the algorithm. Can one or a combination of them become a subprogram, accepting input, processing data and producing an output?   Let's name them and see whether they qualify as modules:

```
1. MODULE:         Calc_Gross_Pay

Description:       Calculate one week gross pay

Input:             Hourly Pay Rate

Output:            Gross Pay

Algorithm:         Hourly Pay Rate * 40


2. MODULE:         Calc_Net_Pay

Description:       Calculate net pay, deduct medical benefit costs and taxes

Input:             Gross Pay

Output:            Net Pay

Algorithm:         Calculate medical benefit costs
                   Deduct medical benefits cost from Gross Pay
                   Calculate tax
                   Calculate Net Pay


3. MODULE:         Generate_Report

Description:       Generate report with Employee Name, Gross Pay, and Net Pay

Input:             Employee Name, gross pay, and net pay

Output:            Employee weekly earnings statement

Algorithm:         Format report and print it
```

Each algorithm step fulfills the requirements for a module. Next, connect the modules so that they logically flow together. This characteristic is known as composability. The arrows show that the output of one module becomes the input to another in Figure 14-5.

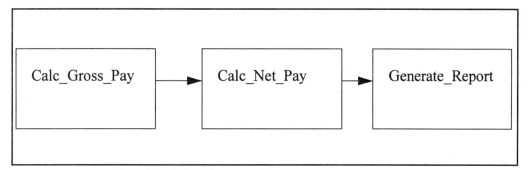

Figure 14-5 One Module after Another

Take a look at the module *Calc_Net_Pay*. This module has the responsibility for calculating medical benefit costs and income tax. The source code to compute this can become long, detailed, and confusing.

One possibility is to break this module into two, one to calculate the cost of medical benefits and the other for income tax.

The names for the new modules will be *Calc_Medical* and *Calc_Tax*. The *Calc_Medical* module needs the output from *Calc_Gross_Pay,* because some benefit costs may be a percentage of gross pay. The output from *Calc_Medical* will now be gross pay minus medical benefits, because medical benefit costs are pre-tax. This total can now be sent to the *Calc_Tax* module, allowing for the correct income tax to be computed, as shown in Figure 14-6.

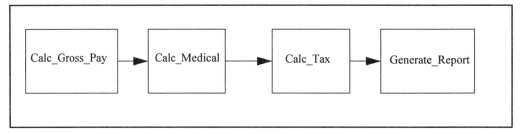

Figure 14-6 Break Module into Two Modules

Remember, design is an iterative process. As you progress from one level of detail into the next, it may become apparent that breaking the logic into more modules will help the clarity and readability of the program.

For example, precise algorithms need to be developed for the medical benefits. We would need to know the type of benefits offered by the employer and how to price them. More detail is needed; therefore, additional design focus should be given to this module. And there is a possibility of breaking up this module into even more modules.

How does this process equate to programming? Each module has a function to perform, and is, in a sense, a mini-program. These mini-programs can be pieced together to create a complete program.

In C language, modules are referred to as functions. Java and C++ have the concept of functions as well, but these languages are object-oriented languages. Therefore, a module may be a class. Classes contain functions, but they also do a lot more, as discussed in the next section.

6 - The Next Step: Object-Oriented Method and Design

If you never plan to program in C++, Java, or any other object-oriented language, then you can skip this section. With that said, let me say that if you plan to take programming seriously at all, explore object-oriented programming. Most feel it is either a revolution in or an evolution of software development. Either way, you are bound to feel its impact.

Our previous definition of modules needs to be stronger when dealing with object-oriented modules. Extendibility, reusability, and reliability are our principal goals.

Extendibility

Because modules are to be designed with reusability in mind, the programmer cannot foresee all the data and operations a module will need in its lifetime. Therefore, the programmer will design the module for possible future changes and extensions. This approach is referred to as Extendibility.

Two principals are key to improving extendibility:

- Simplicity in Design: A simple architecture can be adapted for changes easier than a complex one.

- Decentralization: The more autonomous the modules, the better the chances that a change will affect just one or a small number of modules. Modules that have interdependencies throughout an architecture may trigger a chain reaction of change over the whole program.

Reusability

Software elements or modules that can be used for the construction of many different software applications (programs) are referred to as having high *reusability*.

The need for reusability comes from the observation that software applications frequently follow similar patterns. Many will require the same or similar functionality as found in previously developed software. This should be taken advantage of to reduce the time, effort, and cost associated with software development.

Reliability

Without reliability, our software application would be essentially useless. A few design concepts will help with reliability:

- Designing for compatibility is designing for ease of combining software elements with others. Frequently there are conflicting assumptions made about the rest of the world.

The key to compatibility lies in design homogeneity and agreeing on standardizing conventions. This may be done within a work group, a corporation, or even a software development community of interest.

For example, a workgroup may agree to extract information only from text files, which contains a sequence of characters, rather than binary files, which are machine-dependent. If part of the work-group develops software on a Windows NT system and another on a UNIX system, there is a greater opportunity for software reuse.

- Designing with efficiency in mind will minimize the demands on the hardware resources, such as processor time, space occupied in memory, and bandwidth used for communication. If software is designed without consideration for efficiency, it may take too long to run, or use too many resources when executing on a smaller system.

- If portability is not considered, software may only be useful on one type of computer system. There may be some justified portability issues, but other portability issues may be reconcilable.

- Ease of use will help to ensure that anyone using the software can learn to use it and apply it properly in solving problems.

- Verifiability means that the software is designed to detect failures, and trace them to errors.

- Integrity designed into a software system will allow it to protect itself against unauthorized access and modification.

As you learn more about individual languages, you will begin to see how these issues are handled. Each language has its own set of tools; how to apply them will become apparent.

Next let's look at different programming paradigms.

Procedural Paradigm

The original programming paradigm is procedural programming. Procedural programming focuses on what steps are taken to solve a problem. Functions or subprograms are used to create some order in the program. A program consists of a series of functions, and these functions manipulate data.

To understand the procedural approach, let's try an example to see how it might work.

A program is created that maintains an employee's salary and generates a paycheck. First, a structure called *EMPLOYEE* is created. The structure contains the employee's *NAME* and *SALARY*. At some point, we may want to give a raise to the employee. A function is written called *IncreasePay()*. The *EMPLOYEE* structure would be passed as input to the function *IncreasePay()*. The function would increase the salary of the employee and store it in *SALARY* within the *EMPLOYEE* structure.

This simple program may cause problems later for the procedural programmer. This program may need enhancements in the future. More information may be included in the *EMPLOYEE* structure, such as job title, phone number, location, social security number, and so on. Changes or additions made to the *EMPLOYEE* structure would, in most cases, cause the programmer to make changes in the functions using it.

As programs grow in complexity, so does the ability to maintain and enhance them. In the procedural paradigm, there is no inherent connection exists between data and the functions manipulating the data. In addition, if the behavior of the function needs modification, there is no easy way to do so without rewriting it. For example, if you want to use a more complex method of giving a pay increase, the only way to reuse the existing code is to cut and paste it into a new function.

Problems have become more sophisticated and complex. In today's world, procedural programming is no longer sufficient. A new paradigm called *object-oriented* becomes necessary.

Object-Oriented Paradigm

Object-oriented languages allow programmers to more closely model the real world by building a strong link between the data structures and methods (functions) that manipulate the data. More importantly, programmers no longer think about data structures and functions to manipulate the data; they think instead of *objects*.

Object-oriented languages use the concepts of "class" and "object" as the basic building blocks. Because object-oriented programming models how we perceive our world, it can best be explained using a real-world example. Most people know how to drive a car, but do they need to know how to build one to use it? Of course not. There are many things in the world that we are capable of using without knowing anything about how they are built, or implemented. The reason that things are easy to use without knowledge of their implementation is that they are designed for use via a well defined public interface. The interface is dependent upon the implementation, but it hides the complexity of it from the users. The implementation may change, but if the public interface doesn't; users typically don't need to know or care.

If a person purchases a new model of a car he currently owns, he may not care whether the engine has been redesigned. If the new model has more power than the previous model, the user will only notice it when driving the car. The user still knows how to use the car because the public interface has remained the same. If the auto manufacturer decided to implement a braking feature with a knob on the dashboard instead of a pedal on the floor, the purchaser of the car may become quite upset. This is because the public interface changed and the user is no longer familiar with it.

One of the fundamental concepts in object-oriented languages is just this philosophy. All implementation issues should be hidden from their users behind a well defined, consistent public interface. Users need to know about the interface, but are never allowed to see its implementation.

Most understand what is meant by the term "car," even though one may not be visible. The reason for this is, most of us own or use cars. Cars are a part of our life. We know that all cars are used for travel, and they share certain attributes such as an engine, seats, steering wheel and so on. We have also seen cars that allow us to turn them on and off with a key, accelerate, brake, and turn left and right. Essentially we have the concept, called a car, which captures the notion of data and behavior of all cars. This concept is known as a *"class."* The physical car in your driveway is an *"object"* (or *instance*) of the car class. The relationship between the notion of class and object is called the *"instantiation relationship."* A car object is said to be *instantiated* from the car class, while the car class is said to be the *generalization* of all car objects.

If I said that my coffee table accelerated from 0 to 60 in five seconds, you would think that I was crazy. If I told you that my car did the same thing, you would consider that to be reasonable, if not impressive, behavior. The reason is that the name of a class not only implies a set of attributes, it also gives an indication of the behavior. This relationship between data and behavior is key to the object-oriented paradigm.

Encapsulation

In a procedural language, it is easy to see the data dependencies on a function. To find data dependencies, look for all the data input to, used by, and returned from a function. Variables may be used inside functions. If they are created, used, and destroyed inside the function each time the function is executed, they are referred to as local variables. This relationshiop is shown in Figure 14-7.

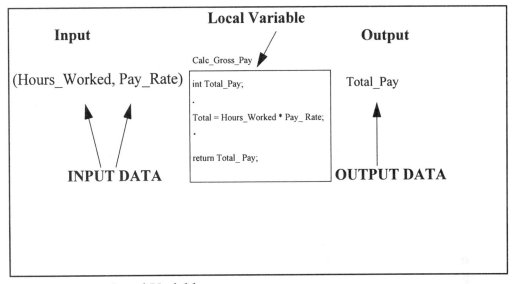

Figure 14-7 Local Variables

One problem with a procedural language is the ability to find the functional dependencies on a piece of data. Looking for functional dependencies on data means that we must look for every function that uses the data or otherwise depends upon the data. To do this, we must examine all the code, looking for these functions. If we need to change how our data looks or how it is used, this can become a very large and error-prone process. The larger the program, the bigger our problem becomes.

An object-oriented language solves these issues. Both types of dependencies, data dependencies on a function and functional dependencies on data, are readily available. Objects are tightly bound entities. Everything they know about (data) and everything they can do (all their methods) are tied together into a neat bundle. This arrangement is referred to as *encapsulation*.

Again, working with a program that deals with payroll, a user of an *EMPLOYEE* class does not need to know or care how the employee pay is stored within the class. All the user cares about is that the *Total_Pay* can be retrieved for a particular object of type *EMPLOYEE*. This task could be done with a method called *Get-*

Pay(). A user could even give a raise to the employee by calling the *EMPLOYEE* member function *GiveARaise()*.

Both methods, *GetPay()* and *GiveARaise()*, are contained in the class *EMPLOYEE* and are part of *EMPLOYEE*'s public interface. The interface is a contract that *EMPLOYEE* makes with its users: it tells the users what the class can do. This is shown in Figure 14-8.

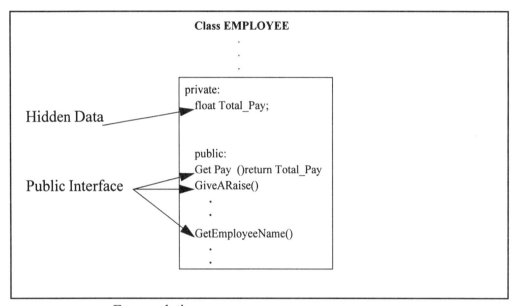

Figure 14-8 Encapsulation

In the example above, the user can ask for or do the following via the public interface of *EMPLOYEE*:

- Retrieve the employee name (*GetEmployeeName()*)
- Give a raise to the employee (*GiveARaise()*)
- Retrieve the total amount of pay due the employee (*GetPay()*)

A user cannot directly alter or even see the variable *Total_Pay* in the *EMPLOYEE* class. It is only accessible via methods in the *EMPLOYEE* class. Any actions performed on *Total_Pay* can only be done through the *EMPLOYEE* class's methods *GetPay()* and *GiveARaise()*.

Total_Pay is a member variable. A member variable is a variable that is part of a class. If, at a later date, *Total_Pay* is to be extracted from a database, this can be done without impact to the user. The user does not know from where *Total_Pay* comes. The internal representation of *Total_Pay* is invisible to users. This is called information or data hiding, and is a natural outcome of encapsulation. As long as users use the public interface, they are guaranteed access to the private data (via methods), regardless of how it is stored.

Inheritance

Inheritance is one of the more important relationships within object-oriented languages. It is best captured as "a-kind-of" relationship between classes. An example is that a FordTaurus is a-kind-of car. Or the relationship can be hierarchical in nature, as in A Dog is a-kind-of Animal, a Dalmatian is a-kind-of Dog. Its primary purpose is twofold: it allows expression of commonality between two classes (generalization), and it is used to indicate that one class is a special type of another class (specialization).

Usually in the first version of software, designers will attempt to generalize. Designers will decide that two or more classes have something in common, such as data, behavior, or a common interface. Typically, this information is collected and put in a more general class from which these classes can inherit.

For example, if I have a Dalmatian class and a Dachshund class, there are some obvious common traits and there are some obvious differences, as shown in Figure 14-9.

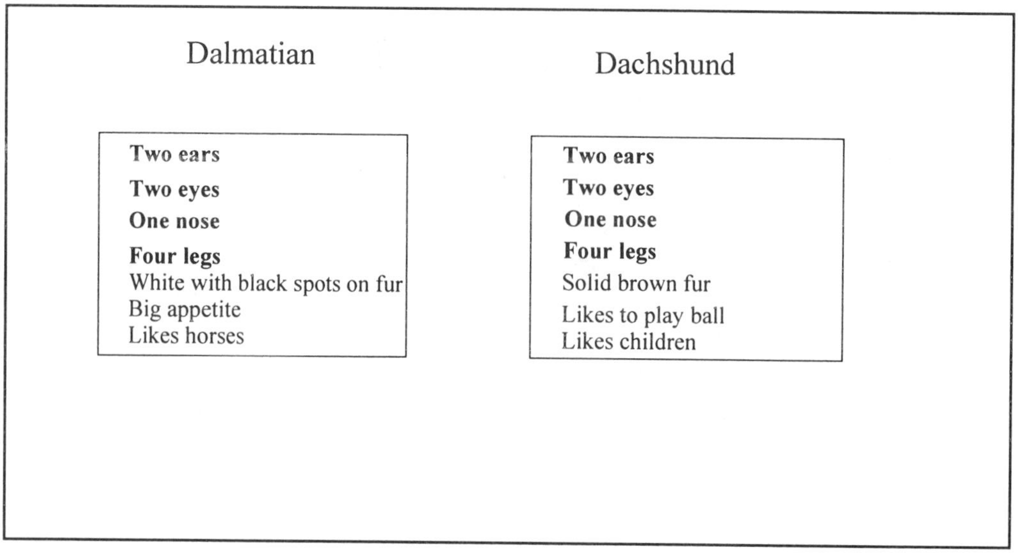

Dalmatian   Dachshund

Two ears
Two eyes
One nose
Four legs
White with black spots on fur
Big appetite
Likes horses

Two ears
Two eyes
One nose
Four legs
Solid brown fur
Likes to play ball
Likes children

Figure 14-9 Common Traits and Differences

These are two very different breeds of dog, but they have the attributes of a dog in common, such as two ears, two eyes, one nose, and four legs. We can take these attributes and put them in a separate class called Dog, allowing the Dalmatian and Dachshund classes to inherent these common attributes.

Specialization, on the other hand, is more prevalent after generalized classes have been decided upon or a mature program requires modification. As the design evolves, the programmer realizes that some classes will require special treatment. Inheritance is ideal for implementing these cases.

A class called Dog may be too general for a user's needs. What may be needed is a special kind of dog, perhaps a search and rescue dog, a hunting dog, a show dog, or a dog of a certain breed. Specialization allows us to start with a generic class and use it as part of a new class through inheritance. The new class can be customized to meet specific needs.

Inheritance is referred to as the reusability mechanism because it helps adapt standard components into specific areas of the software.

To understand inheritance, we need to understand some terms. If a class inherits from another class, it is referred to as a subclass or derived class. If a class is inherited by another class, it is referred to as a superclass or base class.

Figure 14-10 is a graphical view of the inheritance of data.

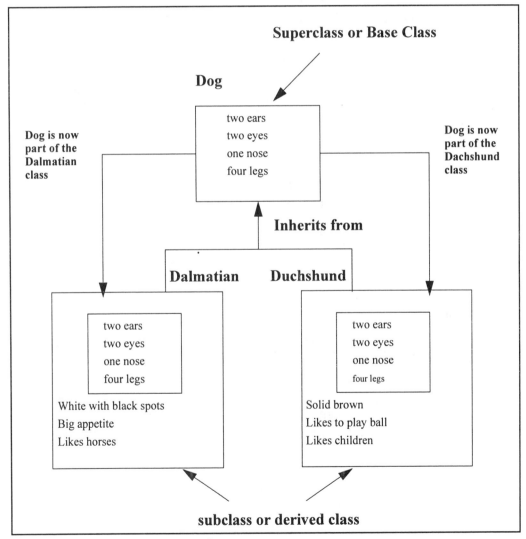

Figure 14-10   Inheritance of Data

The class Dog is the base class. Both the Dalmatian and Dachshund classes inherit from the class Dog. There exists a set of common attributes to describe a dog, and it is expressed once in class Dog. Any class that is intended to be of type dog, but is more than just a generic dog, can inherit from the base class Dog and add attributes to create a special kind of dog.

Inheritance is a better way to reuse code. You reuse code by creating a new class, but instead of rebuilding all the logic, you integrate classes that have already been built and debugged. It is certainly better than cutting and pasting source code.

Polymorphism

Polymorphism is an essential feature in object-oriented languages. With polymorphism, a developer can allow a class to be extensable or grown not only during its initial creation, but also when new features are necessary.

If a class is built to deal with dogs, the developer will more than likely miss specifying some types of dogs required by future users of the class.

Classes can be designed in a way that the actual type of dog is dealt with at the time of execution (loose coupling) instead of at compile time. This means that the base class of Dog is not written with any specific type of dog in mind. The base class deals with the generic aspect of all Dogs. The original writer of the base class does not know what type of dogs are needed by the user, nor does he care. Loose coupling allows us to deal with a "virtual" dog, a dog of no specific type until the type of dog is determined at a later date by a user of the base class.

For example, let's say that each type of dog has its own special bark. As the developer of the base class called Dog, I want the class to handle any type of dog and its bark. So when someone using my class tells the dog to *bark()*, they don't have to worry about telling my base class of Dog what type of dog is going to *bark()*. They just ask the Dog to *bark()*, which is like saying "Hey dog, bark." They don't have to say "Hey Dalmatian, bark."

But if the user of my base class just tells the Dog to *bark()*, I still want the right *bark()* for that type of Dog. If I have a virtual *bark()* method in my base class of Dog, I am not giving the details of any specific *bark()*s. After the base class has been developed and debugged, I can make it available to anyone for use. A user of my base class can inherit it to create a new, derived class. The derived class may be for a specific type of Dog, say a Jack Russell Terrier Show Dog. The derived class developer knows what type of dog it is designed to be and how that Dog's *bark()* sounds. Because the derived class is familiar with the *bark()* specifics, it will provide the details.

Each derived class will know what type of dog they are dealing with and what the *bark()* sounds like. When they ask the class Dog for a *bark()*, the "virtual" *bark()* in the base class is replaced with the specific *bark()* from the derived class and the correct one is used. Such a program is extensable because you can add new functionality through inheritance without modifying the base class.

If the example was implemented without polymorphism, the base class developer would have to consider every type of dog needed, both now and in the future. Let's say that I built the base class Dog to handle a Dalmatian, Jack Russell Terrier, and a Labrador Retriever. If I ask for a *bark()*, I have to think about what type of dog I'm asking to *bark()*. I can't just ask the Dog class to *bark()*; it may give the wrong *bark()*. If I want a Poodle to *bark()* and Poodle is not part of the class, the class would have to be edited to include Poodle information, recompiled and retested. This class is not extensable. It is not reusable when the type dog requested isn't already part of the class.

This may be confusing, but the concept of polymorphism is usually described with C++ examples and terminology. It becomes clearer once you learn more about the C++ programming language.

How to Design for Object-Oriented Languages

You need to remain focused on what you want the system to do. To collect this type of information, try use cases. Ask the question "What does the system do if...". For example, what would a payroll system do if today was the last day of the month? Use-cases describe what actions the system (program) will take when a specific event occurs.

Use-cases will identify some key aspects of your program that will identify some of the fundamental classes to be created.

Describe what the classes will look like and how they will interact. Write down for each class:

1. The name of the class. Make it descriptive, so that when referring to it later, you will have an idea of what the class does.

2. The responsibilities or what a class should do. Write down the names of member functions, such as *GetPay()* or *GiveARaise()*.

3. The collaboration or with what other classes it interacts.

You may not find all the classes or determine all the interactions and responsibilities. More will be discovered as the design process progresses.

The design phase of an object is not limited to the time when the program is being written. Instead, the design happens over a series of stages. You don't need to strive for perfection immediately, instead understanding what an object does and what it should looks like happens over a period of time. The key stages where your understanding may evolve are listed below. These stages are summarized from Bruce Eckel's book *Thinking in C++* .

- During the initial analysis of a program, objects may be discovered by examination of external factors and boundaries. Looking for duplications of elements within the program, and smaller logical units or modules may reveal more objects.

- While building an object, the need for new objects may become apparent. Internal functionality of the object may require new classes.

- When pulling together classes and constructing the program, you may discover more requirements for objects may be discovered. Communication and interconnection of objects in the program may require new classes or changes in existing classes.

- Adding new features to a completed program may reveal inadequacies in the previous design. Extending the existing program may very possibly require the addition of new classes.

- Object reuse is a true indication of completeness in class design. If the class is reused in an entirely new situation, there may be some shortcomings may occur.

Design is not an exact science; it is more of an evolution. Expect and be open to improvements in design. It becomes apparent, given the list above, that object design continues and evolves throughout the lifecycle of the class.

7 - Development Life Cycle

Whether you will be programming for yourself or for a large project, being familiar with the development process will be helpful. Understanding the development life cycle becomes a necessity when programming for a larger project with multiple developers.

Software projects are broken into three basic phases: Analysis phase, Development phase, and Test phase. These three phases are described in the upcoming three sections.

Analysis Phase

A program or application has a community of users. Changes in business needs or interests require either the creation of new programs or enhancements to existing ones. These requests are given to the development community. Writers and architects work to interpret the requests into a comprehensive statement of work, outlining changes needed to the application.

Designers model these changes, creating or enhancing design documents.

Development Phase

Programmers make changes to or create new source code to meet the requirements outlined in the design documents.

A programmer will create or edit a source file with an editor. The source file contains source code, which is readable text instructions or commands written in a programming language.

After the source code is complete, the developer compiles the program. A compiler will check for syntax errors. Syntax errors occur if the programmer has not followed the programming language's rules (syntax) for entering text instructions. If any syntax errors occur, they must be corrected in the source code and recompiled. This process continues until a compile completes successfully and an executable is created.

Test Phase

Next, a programmer begins the Test phase. *Unit test* occurs first, allowing the programmer to test the new or enhanced programming logic. The program is executed and the output is checked to ensure that it meets the requirements outlined in the design phase.

After the programmer is satisfied, the source code is sent to *integration test*. This allows the programmer to integrate and test her source code with other programmers source code. This is a particularly important phase when more than one programmer is working on the same program.

If the integration test phase is completed successfully, the source code is moved into *system test*. Most programming projects have either staff testers or a testing organization with the responsibility for test the whole application against the user and design requirements. If at any stage logical errors are found, they are brought to the attention of the programmer. If the errors are due to a design flaw, the process reverts to the design phase. After the fix has occurred, the cycle begins again, moving forward from that point.

The final test phase is called *acceptance test*. The program is tested either in the production environment or on a separate computer system emulating the production environment.

After acceptance test, the program is moved into the production environment and is available to its user community.

Different programming organizations may have a variation of this process, using different terminology, inserting more steps, or consolidating others. Regardless, organizations will feel the impact of errors in logic or design. Because an error causes a role back to a previous process or phase, and every step after it must be performed again, there is a cost associated with it.

Errors found during the Development phase are much more expensive in both time and cost than errors found during the Analysis phase. And likewise, errors discovered late in the Test phase are very expensive. Errors found in production are the most expensive to repair.

It is important that the analysis and design of a problem is performed with due diligence. Assuming that ambiguities or design adjustments will be ironed out later in the process is not good practice. Every issue dealt with early in the development cycle will save an enormous amount of effort, cost, and time in the end.

8 - SCCS - Source Code Control System

Most programs consist of more than one file, frequently many files. Source code for a single program can be in multiple source files. The source code in these files evolve over the life of the program. It is very hard to keep track of the different versions of each file. Source and documentation files change frequently as errors are fixed, programs are enhanced, and new versions of the software are released to production. Frequently, customers are using one version while programmers are working on a new version. It is easy to loose track of the versions and accidentally lose changes that were already made.

Source files usually reside in a directory and are accessible to developers. Consider the following scenario:

Developer A needs to make a change to a source file. Developer A makes a copy of the source file from the public directory where the source files are stored. The source file is copied to Developer A's home directory. Developer A begins to make changes to the source code in the file.

Meantime, Developer B also needs to make a change to the same source file. Developer B also makes a copy from the public directory and puts the source file in his home directory. Developer B has no idea that Developer A has a copy of this file and is currently making her own changes. Developer B begins to make changes.

Developer A has now completed changes made to the source code in the source file. Developer A compiles the source code successfully and performs a unit test of the code. Developer A returns the source file to the public directory where the source files are stored. Developer A performs an integration test, which is successful.

Developer B has now completed his changes. Developer B compiles and unit tests his changes. Developer B copies the source file back to the public directory and overwrites Developer A's changes. Both Developer B and Developer A have no idea this has happened. Developer B performs integration test.

The software is moved to system test. An external organization begins testing, and notices that Developer A's changes are not there. Developer A is notified and now must redo her work.

How was this scenario avoidable? To help with these problems, UNIX provides utilities for managing and tracking changes to files called SCCS.

man page

sccs - 14

SCCS enables organizations and individuals to have some control over their files. SCCS can control who is allowed to update the files thus preventing overwrites. For each update to a file, it records who made the changes and saves notes or comments regarding the reason for the changes. Because SCCS stores the original version of the file as well as any changes made to it, it is possible to regenerate previous versions of a file. SCCS will save only the changes, not a whole copy of the new version. This approach helps keep the size of an SCCS file under control. A history of changes made to files can also be requested. The history output of a file SCCS will list the version, date, time, author, and comments.

SCCS allows developers to generate a read-only copy of a version of a file. SCCS also allows a file to be "taken out for edit." This phrase means that the copy given is intended for edit, and any subsequent requests for an editable copy will be denied until the original is "returned." In other words, SCCS locks a file that is out for edit, to prevent overwrites.

SCCS Revision Versioning

man page

sccs - 14

When an SCCS file is taken out for edit and returned, a change is recorded. The change is referred to as a *delta*. Changes to the software are referred to as *revisions to the software*.

Each delta has an associated version number consisting of either two or four components. The first two, which are always used, are the release and level numbers. When an SCCS file is initially created, the default release number and level number are 1, which corresponds to Version 1.1 or Delta 1.1. When subsequent revisions occur, SCCS automatically assigns subsequent numbers - 1.2, 1.3, and so on. The user does have control over the version numbers and can skip level numbers or change the release number. Normally, release numbers only change when there is a major revision to the software occurs, i.e., Version 1 to Version 2.

File versions follow a sequential pattern, where each delta or revision includes all previous deltas or revisions. The last box in Figure 14-11 illustrates a change to the release number to reflect a major software revision.

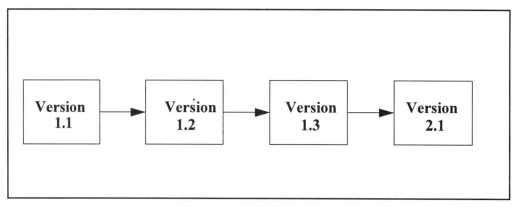

Figure 14-11   Sequential Pattern of SCCS Software Revisions

However, there are cases when an intermediate version is necessary. For example, version 2.1 of the software is under development.
The previous version, 1.3, is currently in production. A feature in the
production version 1.3 has an error in it and an emergency fix is
needed. The development version 2.1 is not ready for production;
therefore, an intermediate version of the production file becomes necessary. A branch delta is created, as shown in Figure 14-12.

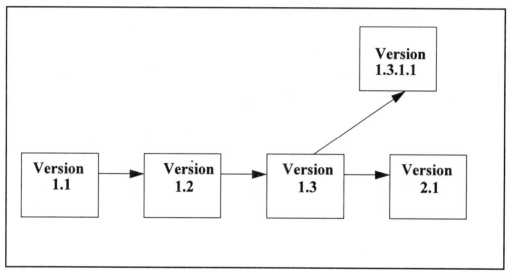

Figure 14-12 Branch Delta Created

Any revisions made in the branch starting with version 1.3.1.1
will not be included in version 2.1 and beyond. All revisions made to
the branched versions of the file will not impact the primary version
flow. If the error is part of version 2.1, the fix will need to be manually
entered into a new version, 2.2.

SCCS Commands

man page

sccs - 14

SCCS provides a number of commands to allow a user to manage software versions. All SCCS files begin with "s." followed by the name of the file to be tracked in SCCS. When an SCCS file is initially created, the "s." file is created. This file will contain all the software changes, comments, dates, times, IDs of the developers making the change, and revision information.

Admin Command

The **admin** command is one of the most important SCCS utilities. It is used to create SCCS files, control the availability of revisions to the software, and change the requirements for submitting a revision.

All SCCS files must be initialized using the admin command before any other action can be performed. These files can be initialized as empty files or with the contents of a file.

To create an SCCS file with an empty initial revision, the following command is used:

```
$ admin -n s.payroll.txt
```

where "s." is the SCCS file prefix and payroll.txt is the file to be tracked with SCCS.

To create an SCCS file with initial contents from another file, use:

```
$ admin -i payroll.txt s.payroll.txt
```

where the SCCS file, **s.payroll.txt**, will be initialized with the contents of payroll.txt.

A simpler method of creating SCCS files is:

```
$ sccs create payroll.txt
```

The file **s.payroll.txt** will automatically be created in the directory where this command is run.

get Command

man page

sccs - 14

The **get** command will allow a copy to be generated from an existing SCCS file. Any version can be retrieved either by version number or by date.

Without any options, SCCS will generate a copy of the latest version of the file with read-only permissions, because it assumes that you will not be making any changes and creating a new revision.

```
$ get s.payroll.txt
  1.1
  4 lines
  No id keywords
```

This command prompted the generation of three lines. The first line, 1.1 is the current revision number of the software, the second line is the number of lines in the file, and the third states how many keywords were expanded. The read-only file can be found in the directory where this command was executed.

If a user wishes to make changes to the file and create a new revision of the software, the following command can be used:

```
$ get -e s.payroll.txt
  1.1
  new delta 1.2
  4 lines
```

The first line is the current revision number, the second is the new revision number, and the third line is the number of lines in the file. The **-e** option indicates that the most recent revision of the file payroll.txt is out for editing. The get command generates a writable copy and creates a lock file called p.payroll.txt. This lock prevents other users from retrieving the same version of the file for editing until this file is checked back in using the delta or unget commands. Read-only copies can still be generated.

The **-e** option allows for different versions of the same file to be out for edit at the same time. Both of these versions cannot be on the same revision path. For example, if a revision is out for edit from the primary revision path, any other revisions taken out for edit at the same time can only be from branches.

The default revision of the file generated by the get command is the most recent revision. Using the **-p** and **-c** options allow other revisions of the files to be generated. Both options can be combined with the **-e** option.

SCCS also allows the retrieval of the highest revision within a version of the software with the **-r** option:

```
$ get -r2 s.payroll.txt
  2.3
  4 lines
  No id keywords
```

In this example, revision 2.3 was the highest revision number within version 2 of the software.

To retrieve a revision by date, use the **-c** option:

```
$ get -c991129 s.payroll.txt
  1.1
  4 lines
  No id keywords
```

The date is specified in the following format; time is optional:

```
YY[MM[DD[HH[MM[SS]]]]]
```

The **sccs** command simplifies the functionality of the **get** command.

To retrieve a read-only copy of the latest revision:

```
$ sccs get payroll.txt
```

To retrieve a read-only copy of revision 1.4:

```
$ sccs get -r1.4 payroll.txt
```

To retrieve the most recent revision of **payroll.txt** for edit:

man page

sccs - 14

```
$ sccs edit payroll.txt
```

The **sccs** command accepts all the **get** flags. It also accepts the file name, the user does not have to specify the SCCS file with the "s." prefix. The **sccs** command performs the translation.

unget Command

This command cancels the **get -e** or edit command, preventing a new delta from being created and deleting any lock associated with the file.

delta Command

The **delta** command is used to submit files that have been edited and need to return to SCCS as a new revision. This is also called *creating a delta* or *submitting a file*.

To submit a file, use the following command:

```
$ delta s.payroll.txt
  comments? Add fifth line
  No id keywords (cm7)
  1.5
  1 inserted
  0 deleted
  3 unchanged
```

The **delta** command prompts the user for comments. Once entered, the **delta** command lists the new revision number, how many lines were inserted, how many were deleted, and how many lines experienced no change at all.

Delta removes the writable version of the file by default. If the -**n** flag is used, the writable version remains. If more than one revision is out for edit, use the -**r** flag to specify with which revision path the file should be associated.

man page

sccs - 14

The **sccs** command can be used with **delta** much the same as it is used with **edit**.

prs command

The **prs** command allows a user to print reports from SCCS information found in the "s." files. The following command will produce a history file:

```
$ prs s.payroll.txt
```

The UNIX manual page will give information about how to customize output from the **prs** command.

sact Command

The **sact** command provides a report on the revisions that are checked out for editing and what the revisions will become after they are checked back in.

9 - C and C++ - The History

The C and C++ history starts with the C language. C language was pioneered by Dennis Ritchie at AT&T Bell Laboratories in the early 1970s. The primary reason for creating this language was so Bell Labs programmers could write their UNIX operating system for a new DEC (Digital Equipment Corporation) computer. By the late 1970s, C compilers were ready for commercial applications and C language began to grow in popularity.

As its popularity increased, more and more vendors began marketing their own compilers. Unfortunately, due to some ambiguity in the definition of C, vendors were left to interpret some aspects of the language on their own. This resulted in the fragmentation of the language. This meant that programmers creating C programs were not guaranteed that their source files would compile with someone else's version of the C compiler.

In the early 1980s The American National Standards Institute (ANSI) standardized the definition of the C language. As a result, any programmer that has compiled a C program with an ANSI C compiler is ensured that it will compile without modification on any system that has an ANSI C compiler.

C++ language was developed by Bjarne Stroustrup in AT&T Bell Laboratories. The name C++ was given to the language in 1983 by Rick Mascitti. C++ language is a superset of C language. Because of this, compilers for C++ will correctly compile C programs. This implies it is still possible to program procedurally in C++.

C was chosen as a base language for C++ instead of designing the whole language from scratch. The reason was that designing a new language had problems and so did C language, but C language problems were at least known.

Earlier versions of C++ were known as "C with Classes." Over time it evolved to become the language it is today. The implementation of classes is not the only feature differentiating C++ from C. C++ also has other features such as operator overloading, references, and virtual functions.

In 1989, ANSI became involved with C++ standardization at the initiative of Hewlett-Packard. Today an ANSI C++ standard is widely used.

10 - C and C++ - Compilers

Compilers are nothing more than complex programs designed to convert a language's source code text into computer-readable machine language. A compiler is written for a specific computer language on a specific computer platform. A compiler written for an IBM system is a different program from a compiler written for a Sun system. Check with your computer vendors for compatible compiler software.

A program that is to be compiled is first entered into a file on the computer system. Most programmers use the editors **vi, ed**, or **emacs**. A file containing source code is referred to as a source file. A source file for C must end with ".c" and a source file for C++ ends with ".cc" or ".cpp," depending upon the compiler. An example of a valid C source file name is **payroll.c**, and a valid C++ source file name is **payroll.cc** or **payroll.cpp**.

The program entered into the source file is usually referred to as source code or the source program. After the source code has been entered into the source file, it can be compiled. For simplicity, the file extension ".c" will be used but is interchangeable with ".cc" or ".cpp".

Compiling Programs

The compiling is initiated by using a special command. When the command is used, it will include the name of the source file to be compiled.

ANSI C compilers may initiate a compile with an "a" in front of the compile commands, while others will use "CC" to denote a C++ compiler. For simplicity, the **cc** command will be used in this book. Check with your compiler software for the exact command.

When a programmer invokes the compile command, the system traverses four major components: preprocessor, compiler, assembler, and link editor.

The overall compiler process can be described as consisting of two major processes:

1) The compile process, consisting of the preprocessor, compiler, and assembler

2) For more complex programs, the link process, where object files are linked together to form a single executable program

These are shown in Figure 4-13.

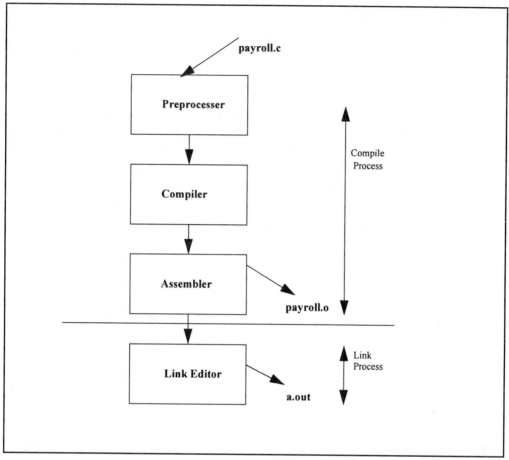

Figure 14-13 Single Executable

When compiling, the source program must go through a preprocessor before it can be compiled. This occurs automatically. The preprocessor will prepare the source code for the compiler. For example,
there are *preprocessor directives* that cause information to be
included for the compiler. This aspect is explored further when discussing C and C++ programming.

The compiler creates assembly language that corresponds to the
programming instructions found in the source file.

The assembler generates machine-readable object code. One object file is created for each source file. Each object file has the same name as the source file, with the exception of the prefix, it is replaced with ".o."

The programmer does not necessarily write every function in a program. Some functions are pre-written and reside in libraries. The compiler vendor supplies some of these libraries for basic functionality, such as reading and writing to a file, math functions, and so on. There are also software companies who provide even more libraries, and a programmer can also create his or her own libraries.

During the final phase, the link editor searches specified libraries for the functions used by the program and combines their object files with the programmer object files to create an executable.

When the C compiler successfully completes all phases of the process for a program, an *executable* file (executable) is created and the object file is automatically removed. The default name of the executable is a.out.

Type the name of the executable to run the program, in this case the executable file name is a.out.

To compile a program, type:

```
$ cc payroll.c
```

Compiler Options

Compilers can compile one source file, as previously seen. But in some cases, various pieces of a program may be in multiple source files. This arrangement is usually the case for larger programs and programming projects.

To compile multiple source files:

```
$ cc payroll_1.c payroll_2.c employee.c
```

The **a.out** default name for the executable is not very descriptive. The **-o** option allows the programmer to specify the name of the executable to be generated. For example, if three source code files contain all the code for a payroll system and I want the executable to be called myPayroll, the following command is used:

```
$ cc -o myPayroll payroll_1.c payroll_2.c employee.c
```

The executable generated by the compile is called **myPayroll**. To run the **payroll** program, type:

```
$ myPayroll
```

If the programmer wants to compile but wants to stop before the link process, the **-c** option can be used. The **-c** option will not generate an executable, but the user will see the object files. In this case, **payroll_1** and **payroll_2** source files will have corresponding object files, but no executable will be generated.

```
$ cc -c payroll_1.c payroll_2.c
```

After all the object files for the source code have been generated, the programmer is ready to generate the executable and can do so using the object files instead of the source files in the compile command.

```
$ cc -o myPayroll payroll_1.o payroll_2.o employee.o
```

The compiler recognizes the file extension of .o, and recognizes that the files only need to be linked. You can also include both **.c** and **.o** files on a single command line. The compiler will compile and link the **.c** files whereas the **.o** files will only be linked. The compiler also accepts assembly language files ending in **.s** and handles them appropriately, assembling and linking them.

When working with large programs that have many different source files, the ability to compile separately and link them together later can save time. If only one source file is impacted out of many, the compiler will only compile the one, and link the others.

man page

make - 14

Figuring out which files to compile can also be automated with the **make** utility.

11 - C and C++ - Make Utility

We saw in the previous section that compiling must go through two primary processes, compile and link. The **make** utility allows management of this process throughout the development life cycle. This section is an introduction to **make**; however, the utility varies to a degree among UNIX variants. Consult the UNIX man pages for specifics on your system.

A program consisting of multiple source files will greatly benefit from the **make** utility. It is a powerful, nonprocedural, template-based method to maintain sets of file interdependencies. For example, **make** can be used to manage changes to C, C++, or even HTML source code. The relationship between object and executable files are described via the **make** utility, and it will update the latter when the former changes. Although **make** can be invoked directly from a shell or run from the command line, complex build processes are usually captured in a file called a **makefile**.

Makefiles

A **makefile** is a text file containing any of four types of lines: target lines, shell command lines, macro lines, and make directive lines. Comments can be included in a **makefile** and start with a pound sign (#).

To invoke a **makefile**, the programmer types **make**. The **make** command will look for a file named **makefile** in the current working directory. If **makefile** does not exist, then **make** searches for a file named **Makefile**. The **make** utility can also look for names other than the defaults, via command options discussed in "Running make from the Command Line" section later in this chapter. If **makefile** or **Makefile** is not used as a file name for a file containing **make** commands, the extension ".mk" is added as a convention.

man page

make - 14

Targets and Dependencies

Target lines indicate what can be built. They consist of a list of target files, followed by a colon (:), followed by a list of dependencies or prerequisite files.

A target file is a file that depends upon one or more *prerequisite files*. The prerequisite files are also referred to as dependencies. If a dependency is updated more recently than the target file, **make** updates the target file based on *construction commands* that follow the target line. The **make** utility will stop if an error is encountered during the construction process. A simple **makefile** will have the following format:

```
target:dependencies_list
    construction_commands
```

The *construction_commands* are regular commands to the shell that construct the target file, usually by compiling and/or linking. The following code shows the target line with construction commands for a file called **payroll_form**. Its dependencies are **form.o** and **pay_info.o**. A **cc** command constructs the target:

```
payroll_form:form.o payinfo.o
    cc -o payroll_form form.o payinfo.o
```

A target list can contain multiple targets, but typically only one target is listed per target line. The target list cannot be empty; however the list of dependencies can be empty. Target line examples are listed below:

```
target_1:    dependency_1 dependency_2 # target with two de-
pendencies
```

```
target_2:     # target with no dependencies
```

Dependencies are used to ensure that the components are built before the overall executable file. The target must be newer than its dependencies. If any of the dependency is newer than the current target or if the dependency does not exist, the dependencies and then the current target must be made. If the list of dependencies is empty, the target is always made.

It may help to construct a dependency graph. A dependency graph will also show dependencies upon header files.

When several symbolic constant and macro definitions are used in different source files of a program, they can be collected together into a single file called a header file or an include file. By convention, these files end in **.h**.

Symbolic constants are names that can be used in a source program in place of a constant value. For example, if a payroll program needs to calculate employee reimbursements for automobile mileage, you may want to associate the cost per mile with a symbolic constant, *AUTO_MILEAGE*.

```
#define     AUTO_MILEAGE     .33
```

Anywhere this cost is needed, the programmer can use *AUTO_MILEAGE* instead of the actual value of $.33. When the federal government changes the reimbursement per mile charge, the symbolic constant value is changed in one place, most likely in a header file. Anyone including that header file in the source file and in the **makefile** as a dependency, and using *AUTO_MILEAGE* within the program, will see the change.

Macros are similar to short functions and can also be included in header files. For example, if I need a short function throughout my program to ensure that the salary total for an employee does not fall below zero after deductions, I may want to include it as a macro and put it in a header file for multiple source files to use:

```
# define     isWageValid(n) ( n >= 0 )
```

In the graph in Figure 14-14, the executable **payroll_form** depends upon two object files and the object files each depend on their respective source files and a header **form.h**. In turn **form.h** depends on two other header files.

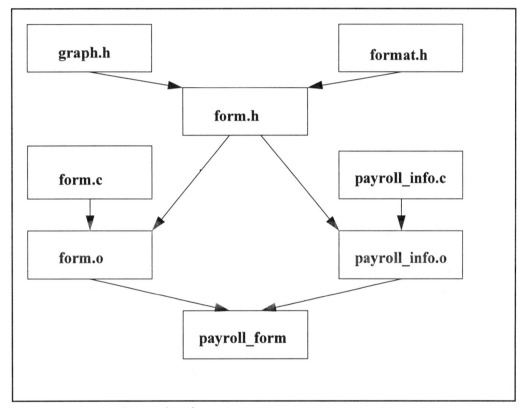

Figure 14-14   Dependencies

Each of the dependencies can be a target on another dependency. For example, both **form.o** and **payroll_info.o** are targets on one line and dependencies for other targets on another line. Nesting dependencies can create a complex hierarchy that specifies relationships among may files.

The following **makefile** corresponds to the complete dependency graph shown above.

```
payroll_form:form.o payroll_info.o
cc -o payroll_form form.o payroll_info.o

form.o:      size.c form.h
cc -c size.c

payroll_info.o:payroll_info.c form.h
cc -c payroll_info.c

form.h:       graph.h format.h
cat graph.h format.h > form.h
```

The last line illustrates how shell commands can be put on a construction line, although concatenation of two files to create a third is not common practice.

Library Targets

Libraries consist of multiple functions or classes. Functions or classes are usually logically grouped together and placed in a library with a descriptive name for reuse by multiple programs. If a target or dependency includes parentheses (()), then it is concidered to be a library.

An example of a target line with library targets is as follows:

```
payroll_lib.a(payroll_tools.o):payroll_tools.c  payroll.h
```

Do not use spaces between parentheses, because they result in an error.

Rule Targets

man page

make - 14

A powerful feature of **make** is the ability to specify generic targets known as suffix rules, inference rules, or simply rules. Rules are a shorthand method used to tell **make** only once how to build certain type of targets. Consider the following excerpt from a **makefile** (the -I compile option tells the compiler where to look for header files):

```
payroll.o:    payroll.c
cc -c payroll.c -I. -I/user/local/include

screens.o:    screens.c
cc -c screens.c -I. -I/user/local/include

main.o:       main.c
cc -c main.c -I. -I/user/local/include

main:         payroll.o screens.o main.o
cc  payroll.o screens.o main.o
```

This has a great deal of redundancy. All the shell command lines are identical, except the file being compiled into an executable. The following rule tells **make** how to transform a file ending in **.c** to a file ending in **.o**:

```
.c.o:
    cc -c $< -I. -I/user/local/include
```

This rule has a special macro, $<, which will substitute the current source file in the body of a rule. Using this rule, **.c.o**, simplifies the previous **makefile** excerpt to:

```
.c.o:
    cc -c $< -I. -I/user/local/include

main:         payroll.o screens.o main.o
    cc payroll.o screens.o main.o
```

Macros

Macros can be used to simplify references to commonly used text, increase maintainability by providing a single place where information is defined, and improve readability.

The basic syntax for defining macros with a **makefile** is:

```
name = valuelist
```

man page

make - 14

The name may consist of any combination of upper- and lower-case letters, digits (0-9), and underlines or underbars (_). Macro names appear in all uppercase by convention.The **make** utility allows name to be replaced with an identifying name.

The valuelist may contain zero, one, or more entries. The value-name can be replaced with a list of file names. The valuelist can be quite long, and the backslash (\) newline escape can be used to continue a definition on another line and the backslash is seen as a space.

A macro definition can be used to represent a group of header files frequently used within the **makefile**.

```
HEADERS = payroll.h companies.h benefits.h
```

The **makefile** can make use of HEADERS by using:

```
process.o: $(HEADERS)
```

Running make from the Command Line

The **make** utility has methods of configuration from within a **makefile,** but it also has command-line options. These options are used when executing the **makefile.**

A typical sequence of **make** command-line arguments can appear in any order:

man page

make - 14

Make [-f makefile] [options] [macro definitions] [targets]

Option items are enclosed in [].

Command-line options are preceded with a (-) followed by the option, for example **make -d**. The following is a list of some of the more common options used:

COMMAND LINE OPTIONS FOR make

-d   Enables debug mode. Debug mode will produce a large amount of messages and should only be turned on as a last resort when debugging a **makefile**.

-f   FilenameDenotes the name of the file to be used as a **makefile**. A space must appear between the option and the file name.

-p   Prints all macro definitions and rules.

-i   **Make** will ignore nonzero error codes returned by commands. Instead of terminating the build of all targets, it will continue.

-k   Will kill work on the current target if a nonzero error code is returned by a command. Work on other targets will continue. This is the opposite of **-s** mode.

-s   Puts **make** into silent mode. Normally commands are executed to standard out.

-t   The files are touched; commands associated with a rule are not issued.   See the UNIX **touch** command.

12 - C and C++ - Debugging

After programs have been successfully debugged from syntactic errors, allowing the compiler to generate an executable, the program must be tested for runtime and logical errors. Debuggers help a programmer find where these errors have occurred.

The C and C++ compilers are liberal about the kinds of constructs they allow in programs. The compiler assumes that you mean what you've entered.   This assumption allows for various errors to occur while running the program. A serious error, called a segmentation violation will stop the program from executing. A message such as *Segmentation violation - Core dumped* is displayed and creates a core file. A core file contains information about the state of the program and the system when the failure occurred. A stack trace is part of the information put into the core file. The trace indicates the source line where the core dump occurred and the functions that were called to reach that line.

Debuggers like **sdb** (symbolic debugger) or **dbx** use the core file to help programmers find and fix the problem. The debuggers sdb and dbx each have their own look and feel, but they provide similar capabilities. Both allow the programmer to monitor and control the execution of a program. The program can be stepped through line by line, allowing an examination of the state of the execution environment. They also allow the core file to be examined. The debugger can also be told on which line or lines to pause execution via breakpoints. After the execution has been paused, the programmer can check the system and values found in variables and structures. The programmer may choose to watch the execution step by step and the execution can be resumed at any point.

Lint is another useful tool. The **lint** command examines the source code for possible problems. The code may compile completely and cleanly, but it may execute incorrectly. Lint is stricter than the compiler. It detects and reports on a wide variety of problems and potential problems, including variables that are used before a value has been assigned to it, arguments to functions that are never used, and functions using return values that were never returned.

You are free to ignore Lint's warnings and complete the compile, but a warning typically means that the program has a bug or a non-portable construct, or that you have violated a standard of good programming. Paying attention to Lint's warnings is a good way not only to debug your programs but also to hone your programming skill.

13 - C Language

There are many programming basics that span both C and C++. These basics will be introduced using C language. The upcoming programming sections are only an introduction. They don't provide enough of information to be used as a reference for the C language. You want to supplement this section with a book dedicated to the C language.

C programs are written in terms of functions. A program will go into functions, execute the logic and leave. Frequently, functions are made up of other functions and statements. Statements are lines of code that carry out a task.

A C program must have a function called main(). Within the main() function is the body of the program as shown in Figure 14-15. The body consists of statements and functions. Preprocessor directives are listed outside and above the main() function.

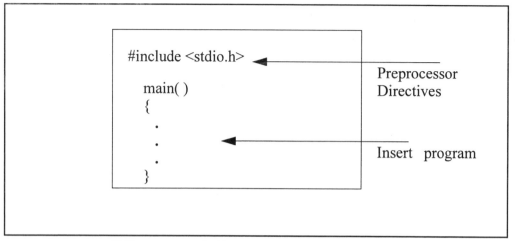

Figure 14-15   C Program main( )

Many find it helpful to look at a simple but complete C program to see all of it's parts.

The C program **TestAverage.c** in Figure 14-16 will perform arithmetic operations and print the results. Any comments in the program are between the /* and */ symbols. Comments are ignored by the compiler and are for readability. It is considered good programming practice to include comments.

```
/* file name TestAverage.c
This program will compute the average of three test scores and print the
results using a print function supplied in a C library */        ◄──────  comment

#include <stdio.h>                                                ◄──────  preprocessor directive

main()                                                            ◄──────  main function
{                                                                 ◄──────  block begins
    int grade1, grade2, grade3, total_score;                      ◄──────  variable declarations
    float average;

    grade1=96;                          /*assign grades*/
    grade2=89;
    grade3=99;

    total_score = grade1 + grade2 + grade3;  /*add grades*/

    average = total_score/3;                 /*find average grade*/

    printf("For test scores %d, %d and %d the final grade is %f",
            grade1, grade2, grade3, average);                     ◄──────  print statement from
                                                                           a c library prints to
    /* programs and functions should end with a return statement*/         screen

    return;
}                                                                 ◄──────  block ends
```

Figure 14-16   C Program **TestAverage.c**

Preprocessor directives are listed first, followed by the main()
function. The left curly brace ({) indicates the beginning of the block
of code known as the body of the function. Variables representing the
grades are assigned data types and are populated with values. Additional variables are declared to hold the sum and the average of the
grades. The grades are added together, and the average is computed.
The printf() function is part of the standard C libraries and will print to
the screen. The last line of the source code in the body of the function
is the return statement. A return statement allows a function to send
back a value to the function from which it was invoked. If the main()
function is returning a value, it is sent to the UNIX shell. All functions

should end with a return statement. The right curly brace (}) denotes the end of the block of code.

For now, review the program to become familiar with its overall format. The output of the program is minimal. The test scores are printed along with the final grade, which is the average of the three test scores.

Format of a C Program

C is known as a *free-form* language. That is, the programming statements can start at any column of any line. Blank lines are allowed and are recommended for readability. Interestingly enough, C language does not require each statement to be on a separate line. All statements can be one continuous line with semicolons (;) denoting the end of a statement. This style is not recommended, however. A C program can look confusing enough. Programmers need to be concerned with maintainability. If the program is not easy to read, it will not be easy to maintain.

Good Programming Practices

There are a few things that can be done to keep a C program readable.

First, use comments to explain the functionality. It is a good idea to put a comment in the very beginning of the source file, explaining what the functions in the file do. If the source file contains the main() function, describe the program. Some suggested information to include is the source file name, the author, the date it was created, and what the program does.

Use variable names that are descriptive of the data they hold. Function names should also be descriptive, giving some idea of their purpose and/or behavior.

Put C statements on individual lines.

Make good use of white space; separating lines and statements with spaces or tabs helps clarity. Surround functions with white space.

This helps the function stand out as a block of code so that the reader's eye will drop to it.

Indent the source code inside the braces:

```
function_1()

{

        (body of function is indended)

}
```

Use comments throughout the program.

Comments

Comments help readability and therefore, maintainability. Comments start with /* and end with */. Everything between is considered a comment and will be ignored by the compiler.

A comment can be on one line of code or can span multiple lines. Comments can be inserted before a statement on a line or appended to the end.

You want to comment as you program while the thought is fresh in your mind. Some programmers may decide to fill in comments after the source code is complete but it is frequently neglected due to lack of time. Also, comments inserted after the fact may not be as clear or as helpful.

Uppercase and Lowercase

Upper- and lowercase letters are more significant in C language than most other programming languages. You may have noticed that most of the program in TestAverage.c is in lowercase. No commands in C language have uppercase letters. Preprocessor directives are the one exception. They will be covered later in this chapter.

C Language Nuts and Bolts

Now that you've had the chance to look at a C program and become familiar with some good programming practices, it is time to discuss the C language itself. We will start with the basics and begin to develop an understanding of some key concepts, using C programs or fragments of programs to illustrate various topics.

Standard Library

The standard library comes with the compiler and contains a substantial number of functions. These functions are pre-written and tested and provide standard functionality for reading data from a keyboard, reading information from files, displaying information to a screen, and mathematical routines, to name only a few.

It would take a chapter of significant size to address all the functionality supplied by the standard library. Books dedicated to teaching C programming address a majority of the most popular functions. Also, they usually supply a comprehensive list of header files with a brief description of the functions contained within.

To use the standard library facilities, standard header files need to be included in the source file using the preprocessor directive *#include*.

Constants

We've previously discussed the concept of a variable, a place in the computer memory that has a name and contents that can be changed. A constant is also a value stored in computer memory, but the value cannot be changed.

A constant can be assigned to a variable, but you can not assign new values to a constant. Below is an example of how a constant can be assigned to variables:

```
pens = 10;
```

This shows how the constant 10 can be assigned to the variable pens. Essentially, the value of 10 has been placed in the pens variable.

There are a few types of constants. An integer constant can be formed using the digits 0 through 9. The character constants are enclosed within single quotes ('Z'). Floating-point constants use the digits 0 through 9 and a decimal point.

Symbolic Constants

Symbolic constants are names or identifiers that can be used in a program instead of the actual value of a constant. When the program is compiled, the preprocessor searches the source code for every occurrence of the symbolic constant identifier and substitutes it with the actual constant value.

The *define directive* is used to create a symbolic constant. The define directive is a preprocessor directive that assigns a name or identifier to the constant. *Preprocessor directives* are statements beginning with a pound sign (#). The define directive consists of #define followed by an identifier and then a constant. The following directive defines a symbolic constant for the value of pi:

```
#define PI   3.14
```

Symbolic constants are useful in situations where a constant is used throughout a program and may change. A good example is a program that includes calculations for mileage reimbursements. The per-mile reimbursement value may change occasionally. If the reimbursement value changes from .32 to .33, a programmer would have to search the program for every occurrence of .32 and change it to .33.

A better method is to assign the constant to an identifier using the define directive. The directive

```
#define PER_MILE    .32
```

appears once, either at the top of the source file or in a header file. The programmer uses the identifier PER_MILE instead of the actual constant value of .32 through out the program. When the reimbursement value changes, the programmer only updates the define directive.

Escape Sequences

Using certain character constants can be problematic. Expressing 'newline' or 'tab' as character constants cannot be done directly, when entered, they will go to a new line or a tab within the source file.

These control characters can be entered as constants by means of an escape sequence. An escape sequence is an indirect way of specifying these control characters. Escape sequences always begin with a backslash (\).

The escape sequences are shown in Table 14-1.

Table 14-1   Escape Sequences

Control Character	Escape Sequence
new line	\n
horizontal tab	\t
vertical tab	\v
backspace	\b
carraige return	\r
form feed	\f
alert - bell	\a
backslash	\\
single quote	\'
double quote	\"
question mark	\?

Data Types

There are four basic data types in C: integer, floating point, double precision floating point, and character data. Another data type discussed will be the void data type. C language needs to know what type of data it is manipulating. Data types are used to define the type of data a variable will be used for and the type of data returned from a function. Data types and functions require a more comprehensive discussion and will be addressed in the "Functions" section.

For example, a program is created to give directions to the Statue of Liberty from anywhere in the country. The program has a variable called *road_exit* to indicate which numbered exit should be used when entering or leaving a particular highway. This variable contains whole numbers, because exit numbers can be 12, but not 12.5. The program defines the variable *road_exit* to contain only data of type integer.

The definitions of variables are found before the programming statements in the body of a function.

```
void directions_home()

{
      int road_exit;    /* Variable is defined with data type and goes here */

      /* Programming statements inserted below */
}
```

When the program knows what type of data it is dealing with, it will know how to treat the data, and what operations are legal and which are illegal. Data types are assigned to variables before they are used in the body of the function. The format for declaring a variable is data type, variable name followed by a semicolon:

```
            data_type    variable_name;
```

To declare multiple variables of the same data type on a single line, separate the variable names with a comma:

```
            data_type    variable_name1, variable_name2;
```

A constant can be assigned to a variable at the time the data type is declared. This action is referred to as initializing the variable, or giving it a starting value:

```
            data_type   variable_name1 = constant;
```

Variables can also be initialized after they are declared, in the body of the function, by assigning it a value.

```
            variable_name1 = constant;
```

Each basic data type is described in the upcoming sections.

Integer

An integer is any positive or negative number that does not have a decimal point. Integers are also known as whole numbers. C refers to these numbers as integer constants. A variable of type integer is denoted by int within a C program:

```
int grade1;
```

Integers may be preceded with a "+" or "-" sign. Integers cannot contain commas, decimal points, or special symbols such as a "$". Examples of valid integers are:

```
10   -15   +999   256   -26112
```

Each computer system has its own internal limit on the size of a number that can be used in a variable of type integer. This is dependent upon the storage allocated by the computer for each type of data. A computer will allocate storage by bytes. Each byte consists of bits. A bit is the smallest piece of information a computer can handle, and will contain the value of either 0 or 1. A byte consists of eight bits, and can represent a single character, digit, or symbol.

To determine the storage allocation for your computer system, refer to the computer's reference manual. Some common storage allocations are listed in Table 14-2.

Table 14-2 Common Storage Allocations

Storage Allocated	Max Integer Value	Min Integer Value
1 byte	127	-128
2 bytes	32767	-32768
4 bytes	2147483647	-2147483648

If the integer maximum for your machine is too small, the qualifier unsigned can be used:

```
unsigned int my_bank_acct;
```

Unsigned means that all numbers in the variable will be a positive number, negatives are not allowed. Unsigned int would change the storage table to look like that of Table 14-3.

Table 14-3   Unsigned Storage Allocations

Storage Allocated	Max Integer Value	Min Integer Value
1 byte	255	0
2 bytes	65535	0
4 bytes	4294967295	0

Floating Point

Floating-point numbers are any numbers containing decimal points. Variables containing floating-point numbers are denoted as type *float* in C language:

```
float acct_total;
```

Valid floating point numbers are:

```
+16.776   5.   -6.2   3244.25 0.0   0.222   11.0
```

As with integers, commas and special symbols are not allowed. The number of digits stored in a variable of type float is dependent upon your computer system.

Floating-point variables can represent extremely large and extremely small numbers, but there are limits exist, just as there are with integer numbers. The minimum positive value that a variable of type float can have is 1.0e-37, or a 1 preceded by a decimal point and 36 zeros. The maximum value is 1.0e38, or a 1 followed by 38 zeros.

Double Precision

Double-precision numbers are similar to type float. Double precision is denoted with double:

```
double acct_total;
```

It is used whenever the accuracy provided by a *float* is not sufficient. Variables declared to be of type double might store roughly twice as many significant digits as can a variable of type *float*. The precise number of digits stored depends upon the computer system. Like variables of type *float*, variables of type *double* do not allow commas and special symbols.

The minimum and maximum values for a double-precision number are dependent upon the computer system. They can greatly extend the maximum and minimum found in floating-point number variables.

Exponential Notation

Floating-point and double-precision numbers can be written in *exponential notation. Exponential notation* is commonly used to express either very large or very small numbers using a compact notation.

In exponential notation, the letter e is used to indicate the *exponent*. The number following the *e* represents a power of 10, which indicates the number of places the decimal point should be moved to obtain the standard format for a decimal number. If the number after the e is a positive number, the decimal point should be moved that many places to the right. If the number is negative, the decimal point is moved to the left.

For example, *e5* tells us to move the decimal point five places to the right, and the number 5.897e5 becomes 589700. The *e-3* in number 1.664e-3 tells use to move the decimal point three places to the left, and the number becomes .001664.

Character

The fourth basic data type recognized by the C language is the *character type*. Characters can be letters of the alphabet, one of the ten digits 0 through 9, and special symbols such as ! * $, + @. A single character consists of any one letter, digit, or special symbol enclosed by single quotes. For example:

```
'A'      '9'      'r'      '!'      '+'      'c'
```

A variable of type character is declared as follows:

```
char   letter_grade;
```

Do not confuse single characters with a string of characters.

For example, the single characters 'B', 'e', 'a', 'c', 'h' are different from the string "Beach." Each of the letters represented as 'B', 'e', 'a', 'c', 'h' is viewed by the computer as a separate letter, in spite of the fact that we may automatically read the word Beach. The 'B' may be stored in one place in memory, the 'e' may be somewhere else, and so on. The computer sees each letter as its own logical unit.

Because humans read the word Beach, C language gave us a way to logically lump the characters together into a "word" or string. A string consists of a series of characters, digits between 0 and 9, and special characters, surrounded by double quotes (" "). The characters in the "Beach" string are actually stored contiguously inside the computer, or one next to the other. C language makes our job a little easier by supplying a standard set of string functions for use since it would be difficult to deal with each character individually. We will learn more about strings a little later.

Void

The data type of void is a generic data type that has no specific size or range of values associated with it. A void value is nonexistent, values cannot be stored in a variable of the data type void. If you attempt to assign a value to it, the compiler will issue an error message.

This data type seems a little ridiculous, but there are uses for it. Void can signal to the compiler that a function will not be returning a return value.

```
main()
{
    void function_1();
}
```

This topic will be discussed in greater depth in the "Functions" section.

Arithmetic Expressions

Integers, floating-point, and double-precision numbers can be added (+), subtracted (-), multiplied (*) and divided (/). I recommend that math operations be performed on like data types, although math operations between different data types are allowable. Arithmetic operations are also allowed on character data types.

Each arithmetic operator (+, -, *, /) is a binary operation, requiring two operands. This means that there must be something on each side of the arithmetic operator to perform the arithmetic operation on. They associate from left to right. This means the operator (+ - * /) uses the left operand first, and then applies the right. Examples of arithmetic expressions are shown in Figure 14-17.

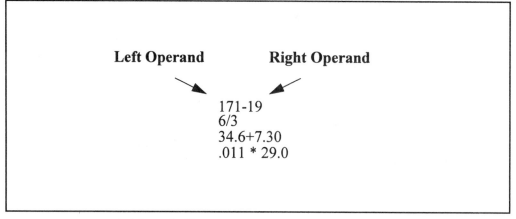

Spaces around the operators are not required but may be included for clarity.

There are two basic rules governing the type of data used and the resulting data type for these arithmetic expressions. They are as follows:

1. If all operands are integers (int), the resulting value is an integer.

2. If any operand is a floating-point (float) or a double precision (double) data type, the result is a double-precision number.

The fifth arithmetic operator, the modulus (%) operator, is also a binary operation. This operator results in the remainder of the first operand after it is divided by the second. As an example, the result of 7%4 is 3 because seven divided by four yields a dividend of 1 with a remainder of 3. The dividend is ignored, and the remainder is the resulting value.

The modulus operator only works with integer numbers. If a variable of any other data type is used, the compiler will generate an error.

Figure 14-8 is a program using the modulus operator to calculate a leap year. The program will print "Enter the year: " on the screen of the computer. This is called prompting for input. The user then enters a year. The *scanf()* function allows a value for the year to be accepted from the keyboard while the program is running. Notice the *if..else* statement is used. This helps us print the correct message, determining whether the year evaluated is a leap year. We check the result of the modulus operator, which resides in the *leap_year* variable, to determine which message to print. The *if...else* statement will be further addressed in the "Choice" section. The \n in the *printf()* function will generate a new line after the message is printed. The *printf()* function also uses %d to print integer variables, %f for floating-point variables, and %c for character variables.

/* The program leapyear.c will except a year from the user and determine whether the year is a leap year. The appropriate message will be displayed to the user.*/

```c
#include <stdio.h>
main()
{
    int year;
    int leap_year;

    printf("Enter the year: ");       /* Prompt the user */

    scanf("%d", &year);               /* Accept year from user */

    leap_year = year % 4;             /* Use modulus operator */

    if (leap_year == 0)                    /* Leap year */
            printf("%d is a leap year.\n", year)

    else                                   /* Not a leap year */
            printf("%d is not a leap year.\n", year)

    return;
}
```

Figure 14-18   C Program **leapyear.c**

Unary arithmetic operators have only one operand. The result of applying a unary minus(-) operator is the negative of the operand value. For example, the unary minus turns a positive number into a negative and a negative number into a positive. The applying the plus (+) operator has no effect on the operand value.

Below is a fragment of C code illustrating this:

```
count = 10;

a_difference = -count; /* a _difference now contains -10 because the value
                          of count was changed by the unary minus operator */

no_difference = +a _difference;
                    /* no_difference contains -10 because the unary plus
                       operator had no effect on the value of a_difference */

no_difference = -a_difference;
                    /* no_difference now contains a 10 because the unary
                       minus operator changed the value of a_difference  */
```

Increment and Decrement Operators

The increment (++) operator adds one to the value of an operand, and the decrement (--) operator will subtract one. These are unary operators because they require one operand. You can think of these operators as shorthand notation for adding or subtracting 1 from a value.

For example, to add one to a number using the addition operator, you would do the following:

```
counter = counter + 1;
```

This same calculation can be expressed more easily using the increment operator:

```
counter++;
```

Both statements do the same thing, add 1 to a value in the counter variable. You can use the increment and decrement operators with any numeric operand, such as integer, floating point and double precision numbers.

There are two variations on the increment and decrement operators: When the operator is used in front of the operand, known as a prefix increment (++counter) or decrement (--counter), and when the operator follows the operand, known as a *postfix* increment (counter++) or decrement (counter--). A prefix operator changes the operand before it is used, and the postfix operator changes the operand after it is used.

To illustrate this situation, below is a fragment of C code:

```
int bottles = 3;        /* declare variable and initialize */
int cans = 2;

bottles++;              /* bottles is now 4 */

cans = bottles++;       /* after cans is assigned 4 from bottles,
                           bottles is incremented to 5.
                           cans now has 4
                           bottles now has 5 */

bottles++;              /* bottles now has 6 */

cans = --bottles;       /* bottles is decremented first to 5,
                           and then 5 is assigned to cans
                           bottles now has 5
                           cans now has 5 */
```

Assignment Operators

Assignment operators allow a value to be given to a variable. The most basic assignment operator is the equal sign (=). To assign a value, place the variable on the left and the value to be assigned on the right.

```
dalmatians = 101;
```

The variable dalmatians contains 101.

In addition to =, C language has other assignment operators that combine assignment with another operation for a shorthand notation.

A statement normally written:

```
biscuits  = biscuits * 2;
```

can be written with an assignment operator combined with the multiplication operator as:

```
biscuits *= 2;
```

A slightly more involved expression is:

```
biscuits /= kibbles + treats;
```

which would be identical to:

```
biscuits = biscuits / ( kibbles + treats );
```

The valid combinations involving assignment operators are:

```
+=    -=    *=    /=    %=
```

Type Conversion

C allows *type conversion*, which is a temporary change in the data type of a variable, constant, or expression after it has been declared, usually to help match up different data types between operands. Conversion of data types either occurs automatically in the compiler according to compiler rules, or when a programmer explicitly requests it with a cast operator.

Whenever an expression consists of variables, constants, or expressions of different data types, the compiler must decide what to do. For example, a floating point of 3.0 divided by an integer of 2 will result in 1.5. This number will not fit into an integer, but it will fit into a floating point number. The best solution for the compiler is to put the result into a floating point number and continue evaluating the expression.

The general rule is that a compiler will convert the expression to a common data type before the calculation is done. The compiler will promote or convert the number to the largest data type present. For example, if an expression consists of integers and floating point numbers, all numbers will be promoted to floating-point numbers. If an expression contains integer, floating-point and double-precision numbers, all numbers will be promoted to double-precision numbers. If a demotion were to occur, part of the larger number would be discarded to fit into a smaller data type.

A demotion can occur when the left operand of the assignment operator is a smaller data type than the right operand. For example, if an expression consists floating-point numbers, the resulting value will also be a floating-point number. If this number is stored in an integer variable, a demotion occurs. The accuracy or precision of the floating point number is lost.

```
float data1=3.0, data2=2.0;

int results;

results = data1/data2;
```

The right operand of the assignment operator, the expression data1/data2, evaluates to the floating-point number 1.5. This number is assigned to the left operand, the integer variable results. The number actually stored in the integer variable results is 1, because the floating-point number 1.5 is truncated and precision is lost.

C provides the cast operator, allowing programmers to convert a variable, constant, or expression to another data type after the original declaration has occurred. Casting does not permanently affect the original variable or its contents; it temporarily casts the variable to the data type requested.

The cast operator has the form of (data type), a data type enclosed by parentheses. The cast operator will convert the constant, variable, or expression immediately following it into the data type of the cast operator.

The format for casting is as follows:

```
( data type ) variable
```
or
```
( data type ) constant
```
or
```
( data type ) (expression)
```

The example below shows the casting of a single variable in an expression to a floating-point number.

```
float results, data_3 = 5.5;

int data_1 = 3, data_2 = 2;

results = ((float)data_1/data_2) * data_3;
```

By casting the *data_1* variable to float in the expression *data_1/ data_2*, the compiler is forced to promote the integer variable *data_2* to a floating-point number. This promotion ensures that the precision is not lost when dividing the integer numbers. The resulting floating-point number is not truncated; it is used in evaluating the rest of the expression.

Precedence

It is very important to understand the concept of precedence when evaluating complex expressions. C language has rules of precedence and associativity. These rules determine the order of evaluation of expressions. The rules are fairly simple. Apply operators with the highest precedence first; if two or more operators are of equal precedence, then the associativity determines the order.

Table 14-4 lists operators in their order of precedence, starting with the highest precedence.

Table 14-4   C Operators in Order of Precedence

Operator	Associativity
( )	Left to right
unary +, unary -, sizeof(), ++, --, (type)	Right to left
*, /, %	Left to right
binary +, binary -	Left to right
=, +=, -=, *=, /=, %=	Right to left

The compiler evaluates operators with a higher precedence first. If two operators of the same precedence are to be evaluated, the associativity tells the compiler how to "break the tie" and which one to process first. Depending upon the associativity, the compiler may start with the right-most operator and evaluate moving left, or vice versa.

Pay particular attention to the parentheses operator on the top line of the table. This operator forces evaluation of an enclosed expression first, because it has the highest priority.

```
total = 2 + 8 * 8 / 2        /* The result evaluates to 34 */
```

In the above example, the * and / operators are of equal precedence. Associativity tells us to evaluate left to right. The * operator is evaluated first, 8 * 8, resulting in 64. Next the / operator is evaluated, 64 / 2, resulting in 32. The binary + is evaluated next, because it is of lower precedence, 2 + 32, resulting in 34.

When the parentheses operator is used, the answer is different.

```
total = (2 + 8) * 8 / 2   /* The result evaluates to 40 */
```

The parentheses are of highest precedence; therefore, anything inside is evaluated first. The expression 2 + 8 results in 10. Next, because the * and / operators are of equal precedence, they are evaluated left to right; 10 * 8 is 80 and 80 / 2 is 40. The final result of this equation is different from the previous example, due to the higher precedence of the parentheses operator.

Parentheses can also be nested, and the compiler always evaluates the parentheses within the innermost parentheses first, and then proceeds to the next innermost parentheses and so on until the last expression is evaluated. Below is a logical breakdown of how an expression with nested parentheses is evaluated:

```
int a = 3, b = 2, c = 6, d = 2;
int e = 3, f = 4, g = 5;

total =  ( a - ( b + ( ( c * d ) / e ) * f ) + g ) - 1;
                           ^
                           |
                  Evaluates to 12

total =  ( a - ( b + ( 12 / e ) * f ) + g ) - 1;
                          ^
                          |
                  Evaluates to 4

total =  ( a - ( b + 4 * f ) + g ) - 1;
                      ^
                      |
              Evaluates to 18

total =  ( a - 18 + g ) - 1;
               ^
               |
      Evaluates to -10

total =  -10 - 1;

total = -11
```

Looping

Now that you've been exposed to some of the foundation needed for C language programming, it is time to investigate some of the control statements needed to build more complex programs. C language has a small but powerful set of control statements.

In this section, you will learn how to perform repetitive actions by executing some statements more than once. This is referred to as *looping*.

There are two principal types of loops: *while* and *for*, with a variation of the while loop called do while. The basic constructs of loops and their behaviors were previously discussed in general terms in the "Programming Constructs" section. This section will discuss C looping syntax.

When working with or describing loops, I make references to return values from expressions. These values are either TRUE or

FALSE, where TRUE is a nonzero number and FALSE is a zero. For simplicity, the words TRUE and FALSE will be used. A programmer can use define directives for these values in a program.

For Loops

For loops are used to control definite looping, when we know how many times we want to loop. The syntax for this statement is:

```
for ( initialize expression; loop condition; update expression)
            statement;
```

The three expressions, initialize expression, loop condition, and update expression, set up and control the environment for the loop. The statement that immediately follows is the body of the loop consisting of any valid C statement.

If the body of the loop consists of more than one statement, curly braces ({ }) are used to define the body.

```
for ( initialize expression; loop conditon; update expression)

{
            statement;
            statement;
}
```

The first component of the *for* loop is labeled *initialize expression*. This is used to set the initial value of the control variable before the loop begins. An example of a valid expression is x = 0;. The variable x is assigned the value of zero before the loop begins. The initialize expression is performed once, at the start of the loop.

The second component, *loop condition*, specifies the condition or set of conditions that are necessary for the loop to continue. After the loop condition is satisfied, the looping stops. The loop condition is specified with a relational expression. A *relational expression* compares variables using relational operators.

Relational operators provide a means to compare variables, constants and expressions. There are six operators in C that can test the relationships between two values, as shown in Table 14-5:

Table 14-5 Relational Operators

Relational Operator	Meaning	Example
<	Less than	j < 19
>	Greater than	counter > 10
==	Equal to	flag == DONE
!=	Not equal to	dog != cat
<=	Less than or equal to	temp <= freezing
>=	Greater than or equal to	air_miles >= premier

Expressions using these operators will evaluate to either TRUE or FALSE. Relational operators have a lower precedence than arithmetic operators.

One word of caution: do not confuse the relational operator "is equal to" (==) with the assignment operator (=). The expression

```
count == 2;
```

tests whether the value of count is equal to 2 and evaluates to either TRUE or FALSE. The expression

```
count = 2;
```

assigns the value 2 to the variable *count*.

The choice of relational operator for a loop will depend upon the particular test to be made. Do I want to stop when a variable equals a value? Or do I want to stop only when it is greater than? By asking these types of questions, you can figure out which operator makes the most sense.

The looping condition is tested immediately after the initialize expression. If the looping condition evaluates to FALSE, the loop will perform the statements in the body of the loop. If the looping condition evaluates to TRUE, the loop will stop, leave the loop, and go to the next statement in the program after the body of the loop.

The third component, update expression, is performed after the statements in the body of the loop are executed.   It allows the controlling variables to be updated. After the update expression is performed, the looping condition is re-tested to determine whether the loop should continue.

The following example illustrates the for loop:

```
int x;         /* control variable used in the for loop */

for ( x = 0; x < 3; x++ )/* loop exactly 3 times */
{
        printf("%d ", x);/* print the control variable, x */
}

printf("\nThe loop is complete.\n");
```

In the example above, x is declared as an integer and used in the for loop. The following is a step-by-step list, demonstrating how the loop is executed:

1. The first time the loop is reached, the initialize expression assigns 0 to x.

2. Next, the looping condition asks whether x is less than 3. Since this is a TRUE statement,

3. The printf() function prints 0 to the screen.

4. The update expression is evaluated and x is incremented by one. The value of x is now 1.

5. The looping condition asks whether x is less than 3. Because this is a TRUE statement,

6. The printf() function prints 1 to the screen.

7. The update expression is evaluated and x is incremented by one. The value of x is now 2.

8. The looping condition asks whether x is less than 3. Since this is a TRUE statement,

9. The printf() function prints 2 to the screen.

10. The update expression is evaluated and x is incremented by one. The value of x is now 3.

11. The looping condition asks whether x is less than 3. Since this is a FALSE statement, all looping is discontinued and

12. The printf() function immediately below the body of the loop prints "The loop is complete." to the screen.

While Loops

The while loop allows you to repeat execution of the body of the while loop until some predetermined condition occurs. This condition is known as indefinite looping. The while loop is not looping a predetermined number of times, but instead will continue looping until a predetermined condition occurs.

The syntax of a while loop is:

```
while ( loop condition )

       statement;
```

If the loop has more than one statement to execute, the body of the loop is surrounded by curly braces ({ }):

```
while ( loop condition )
{
          statement_1;
          statement_2;
}
```

The loop condition or expression in the parentheses is evaluated first. If the results of the expression are TRUE, then the body of the while loop is executed. After the execution of the body of the loop, the expression is evaluated again. If the expression is still TRUE, the body of the loop will be executed again. If the expression is FALSE, the looping will stop.

As an example of a while loop's use, the following fragment of source code will count up to the number 5:

```
int count = 1;

while ( count <= 5 )      /* loop while count is <= to 5 */

{
          printf ("%d ", count );      /* print count */
          count++;                      /* increment count */
}
```

The output is:

```
1 2 3 4 5
```

The while loop stops when the expression evaluates to FALSE. We are not telling it how many times to loop; we are only saying "loop until count is greater than 5, and then stop." To illustrate this point, let's use the same while loop, but initialize count to equal 3:

```
int count = 3;

while ( count <= 5 )      /* loop while count is <= to 5 */
{
          printf ("%d ", count );      /* print count */
          count++;                      /* increment count */
}
```

The output is:

```
3 4 5
```

This is the same while loop, with different results because we started with another number.

Do While Loops

Both loops discussed previously test the loop condition before executing the loop. A *do while* loop will execute the loop first and then test the loop condition. The syntax for a *do while* loop is as follows:

```
do
{
        statement_1;
        statement_2;
}
while ( loop condition );
```

The execution is in the following order: The body of the loop is executed first, and then the loop condition is tested. If the loop condition is TRUE, the body of the loop is executed again; if it is FALSE, the loop will stop.

Break Statement

At times you may want to leave a loop if a certain condition occurs in the body of the loop. A break statement is used for this purpose. Execution of a break statement will cause the loop to immediately stop execution and leave the loop body. The break statement is as follows:

```
break;
```

Continue Statement

A continue statement is similar to the break statement, except that it doesn't cause the loop to terminate. Any statements after the continue statement in the body of the loop will not be executed; they are actually skipped. The execution of the loop otherwise continues as normal. The *continue* statement is as follows:

```
continue;
```

Logical Operators

Logical operators can be used to create compound relational tests for complex looping conditions. There are three logical operators in C, as shown in Table 14-6.

Table 14-6   Logical Operators

Operator	Meaning
!	NOT
&&	AND
||	OR

The logical operators will return TRUE or FALSE. NOT is a unary operator that returns FALSE if its operand is TRUE and TRUE if its operand is FALSE. For instance, if an integer variable z has a value of zero (representative of FALSE), then !z is TRUE. If z has any other value (representative of TRUE), then !z is FALSE.

AND and OR logical operators are binary operators, using two operands. AND returns TRUE if both operands are TRUE, and returns FALSE otherwise. OR returns TRUE if either operand is TRUE; otherwise, FALSE is returned.

For example, the following compound relational expression is using logical AND. The expression returns TRUE because both operands are TRUE.

Since checking = 100 and savings = 100, the following statement is true:

```
checking > 50 && savings < 200
```

Because both sides of the equation are TRUE, the AND evaluates to TRUE. If one or both operands were FALSE, the AND operator would evaluate to FALSE.

For an OR operator, only one operand needs to be TRUE. For example, the following expression will evaluate to TRUE:

Because checking = 100 and savings = 100, the following statement is false:

```
checking > 500 || savings < 200
```

Only one operand needs to be TRUE for the whole expression to be TRUE. An expression using the OR operator will also evaluate to TRUE if both operands are TRUE. If both operands are FALSE, the OR operator will return FALSE.

Expressions with logical operators can be used in a loop for the looping condition.

Nested Loops

Loops can be nested, with one loop in the body of another. A while loop can be inside a for loop and vice versa. The outer loop is executed once, the inner loop is executed until completion, control is passed back to the outer loop, and the process is continued until the outer looping condition is FALSE. Below is a fragment of C source code and its output, illustrating nested loop behaviors:

```
int outer, inner;

for ( outer = 0; outer <= 4; outer++ )
/*outer loop prints the letter 'A' and a new line */

{

            printf( "%c\n", 'A' );
            for ( inner = 0; inner < 4; inner++ )
                    /* inner loop prints the letter 'b' */
            {

            printf( "    %c ", 'b' );
            }
            printf("\n"); /* new line for end of b's line */

}
```

The output for this code fragment is:

```
A
b    b    b
A
b    b    b
A
b    b    b
A
b    b    b
```

Notice that the outer loop is executed for a single loop, and then the inner loop is executed to completion. The outer loop is executed once again for a single loop, and the inner loop is restarted and executed to completion. The nested loops are complete after the looping condition for the outermost loop is FALSE.

Choice

The capability to make decisions is another fundamental property needed to program. The control statements introduced in this section allow the flow of a program to be modified via decisions.

The if Statement

One of the programming constructs that provides general decision-making capability is the if statement. The format of an if statement is as follows:

```
if ( expression )
          statement;
```

If there are more than one statement to perform, curly braces ({ }) can be used to denote the body of the if statement.

```
if ( expression )
{
                statement_1;
                statement_2;
}
```

An if statement can be translated into a statement such as "If the car is $100, then I will buy it." This could be written as:

```
if (car == 100 )
                printf( "I'll buy it!\n" );
```

The printf() function is executed only if the expression evaluates to be TRUE. If it evaluates to FALSE then there is no action taken.

The if...else Statement

An *if...else* statement allows an action to be taken if the expression evaluates to TRUE, and allows another action to be taken if the expression evaluates to FALSE. The syntax for this construct is:

```
if ( expression )
                statement;
else
                statement;
```

If multiple statements need to be executed, the curly braces ({ }) can be used:

```
if ( expression )
{
                statement_1;
                statement_2;
}
else
{
                statement_1;
                statement_2;
}
```

An example of an if...else statement is as follows:

I want to buy a car if it is $100 or less. If the car is more than $100, I want to negotiate with the seller. This can be expressed as:

```
if ( car <= 100 )
            printf( "I'll take it!\n");
else
            printf( "Let's talk about the price.\n");
```

Nested if and if...else and else if Statements

Nested *if* and *if...else* statements can be constructed by placing one *if* or *if...else* statement inside another. Be sure to manage the indenting of statements correctly. If the indenting of an *if* does not match appropriately with its corresponding *else*, it can become very confusing. The following is a properly constructed example:

```
if ( expression_1 )
{
            if (expression_2 )
                statement_1;
}
else
{           if ( expression_3 )
                statement_2;
}
```

Statement_1 is only reached if expression_1 in the outer if...else statement and its imbedded if statement's expression_2 evaluates to TRUE.

Statement_2 is reached if the outer if statement's expression_1 evaluates to FALSE and the outer else's imbedded if statement's expression_3 evaluates to TRUE.

The else if statement can help simplify the nested structure above:

```
if ( expression_1 )
{
            if (expression_2 )
```

```
                    statement_1; }
else if (expression_3 )
            statement_2;
```

The else and its nested if statement are combined on one line.

Logical Operators

If statements used thus far set up simple relational tests between two values. Logical operators can be used to create compound relational tests, as described under "Logical Operators" in the "Loops" section earlier in this chapter. An example of this is:

```
if ( car <= 100 && car_year  > 1992)
            printf ("I'll take it!\n");
```

The car is purchased when both of the expressions are TRUE: the car is $100 or less and the car was made after 1992.

The switch Statement

The switch statement is an alternative to the *if...else* statements for creating multiple branches. Its general format is:

```
switch ( expression )
{
            case value_1:
                statement;
                statement;
                .  .  .
                break;

            case value_2:
                statement;
                statement;
                .  .  .
                break;

            case value_n:
                statement;
                statement;
                .  .  .
```

```
        break;

    default:
        statement;
        statement;
        . . .
        break;
}
```

The expression enclosed within parentheses is compared against *value_1*, *value_2*, through *value_n*, which must be constants or constant expressions. If a value is found to match the value of the expression, the statements associated with it are executed. If no matches are found, control flows to *default* and its statements are executed.

If I am willing to pay for a car based upon the year it was made, the following switch statement can be used:

```
switch ( car_year )
{
        case 1999:
            printf("I'll offer you $8,000 for the car.\n");
            break;
        case 1998:
            printf("I'll offer you $6,000 for the car.\n");
            break;
        case 1997:
            printf("I'll offer you $3,500 for the car.\n");
            break;
        case 1996:
            printf("I'll offer you $2,100 for the car.\n");
            break;
        case 1995:
            printf("I'll offer you $1,000 for the car.\n");
            break;
        case 1994:
            printf("I'll offer you $800 for the car.\n");
            break;
        case 1993:
            printf("I'll offer you $400 for the car.\n");
            break;
        default:
            printf("No thank you, the car is too old.\n");
            break;
}
```

When a match is found, the statements associated with the match are executed. If the year of the car is earlier than 1993, no match is found and the switch statement executes the default case.

Functions

Functions are the basic building blocks of C programs. We have already encountered some functions, such as the *printf()* for printing to a screen and *scanf()* to read data into the program from the keyboard. And we have seen that every C program must begin with a function called *main()*.

When do you use a function? If the operation has already been created as a function and tested, use it. There is no sense in recreating it.

When do you create a function? In a few cases. First, if an operation is used in two or more places within a program, it is a candidate for becoming a function. Second, a function should be created if an operation is used between two or more programs. Third, when an operation yields a single result, it can become a function. Fourth, an operation should be a function if it is a separate or unique task, even if it is used only once. Fifth, if a program is too long, it should be broken up into functions for readability.

When functions are used in a program, they are first defined and then called. A function is defined by writing it as a separate piece of source code, and it is called by referencing the name within other functions.

Many useful functions are already part of a standard library that comes with the C compiler. You want to become familiar with them. They will make programming easier.

Function Call

The syntax to call a function is:

```
function_name ( arg_1, arg_2, ...)
```

A function (called function) is called from within another function (calling function) when the operation contained in the called function is needed as part of the operation of the calling function.

To call a function, the function's name is used as part of the format of the call. The function name uses the same rules as for naming a variable. A function name begins with a letter and contains only letters, digits, or underscores. The parentheses following the function name contain arguments. Arguments are references to values, and these values are passed into the function for use. Arguments are separated by commas, and can be constants, variables, or expressions. If a function does not need any values passed into it, the arguments can be omitted.

A function calls another function by referring to the function's name and including the necessary arguments between the parentheses. There are two things accomplished by a function call. First, the function is executed. Second, a value is returned to the calling function.

Defining a Function

The syntax for defining a function is:

```
return_type function_name( parameter list)
{
            statement(s);
}
```

A function has four elements:

1. Return type: Because a function can return a value, the data type for that value must be specified. If no value is to be returned by the function, the data type void is used. The data type precedes the function name with a type declaration. For example:

```
int price_service (int service_type, float cost_per_service )
{
       /* Statements to calculate the price of a service */
}
```

2. Function name: The maximum length of a function name in C is 31 characters. The function name can be longer, but most compilers will only recognize the first 31 characters.

```
int price_service(int service_type, float cost_per_service )
{
        /* Statements to calculate the price of a service */
}
```

3. Parameter list: The parameter is optional, but the parentheses are required. The term parameter and argument refer to the same value in different places. An argument is a value in the function call statement that equates to a parameter in the function definition. Parameters are variables that are separated by commas inside the parentheses of the function definition. A parameter is a combination of a data type and the name of a variable. Any arguments sent to the function via a function call statement must match in number, data type, and order with the parameters in the function definition.

```
int price_service(int service_type, float cost_per_service )
{
        /* Statements to calculate the price of a service */
}
```

4. Function body: The body of a function is enclosed with curly braces ({ }). Statements to perform the operation required of the function are contained here.

```
int price_service(int service_type, float cost_per_service )
{
        /* Statements to calculate the price of a service */
}
```

The relationship between a function call and a function definition is fairly straightforward.

When defining a function, you decide what to call the function (function name), the operations it will perform (body), the value to be returned from the function (return value), and what type of information needs to be sent into the function (parameter list) to perform the operation.

The body of a function definition contains the source code for that function. The parameters in the parameter list describe what data type the arguments must be, in what order, and how many. By making a call to a function, you are passing the arguments that correspond to the function definition's parameters and executing the code found in the body of the function definition. These concepts are shown in Figure 14-19.

```
main()
{
        int flag;              /* returned from function, 0 indicates successful completion, non-zero
                                  indicates that an error occured within the function*/

        float service_cost;
        ...
        flag = price_service(1, service_cost);          function call and arguments for
        ...                                              price_service()
        return;
}
int price_service(int service_type, float cost)         function definition and parameters for
{                                                        price_service()
        /*statements to price service */
        ...
        return (0)
}
```

Figure 14-19 Anatomy of a Function

Prototypes

When calling a function, the compiler associates parameters in the function definition with arguments when calling a function. The compiler will assign the first argument to the first parameter, the second argument to the second parameter, and so on. The number of arguments must match the number of parameters. If the arguments are not matched appropriately with the parameters, errors can occur.

Prototypes are used to allow compilers to check argument types against parameters. A function prototype is basically a restatement of the first line of the function definition, ended with a semicolon (;). The prototype for the function price_service() in the above example would be:

```
int price_service ( int service_type, float cost);
```

The variable names are not necessary in the prototype and can be excluded:

```
int price_service ( int, float );
```

A prototype provides information about a function to the compiler so that the compiler can verify the correctness of data types in function calls.

Arrays

Arrays allow programmers to define a large amount of memory at one time. If a program is dealing with a calendar or calculating bowling scores, there is a fair amount of similar data needed. By declaring an array, a programmer is setting up a series of like data types.

When individual pieces of data are declared in a program, the computer assigns memory to it. Where the data is stored does not follow a pattern; the information could be anywhere, as shown in Figure 14-20.

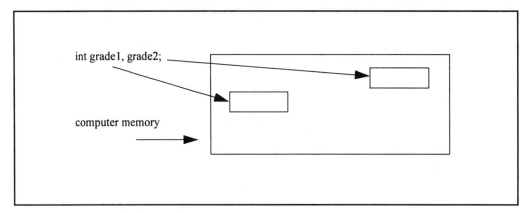

Figure 14-20 Information Anywhere

When an array is used, the information is stored contiguously, or one next to the other, as shown in Figure 14-21.

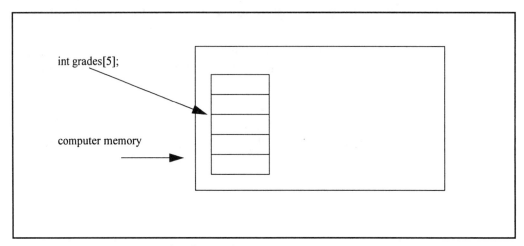

Figure 14-21 Array of Information

In the example above, there are five elements in the *grades* array, all of type integer.

Arrays allow the declaration of large amounts of data with the same data type in one statement. This arrangement is much easier than typing in a separate statement for each data type and variable. Accessing and using the information is simplified and less confusing. Arrays also help enhance readability of source code.

The syntax for declaring arrays is as follows:

```
data_type array_name[array_size];
```

Only integers are used to specify the size of the array. Constants, symbolic constants, or constant expressions can all be used when specifying the size, but they must all result in an integer value.

Each member of an array is called an *element*. Each element is a variable of the same data type as the array.

Elements within an array can be referenced using an integer *index*. Arrays in C always start with an index of zero. This arrangement is referred to as *zero-based indexing*. Figure 14-22 shows an array with index numbers.

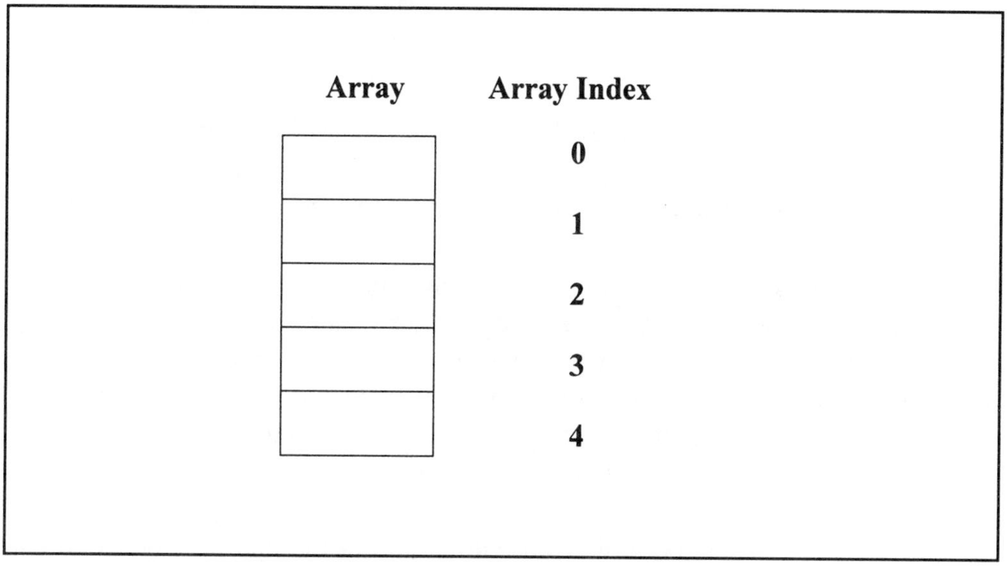

Array	Array Index
	0
	1
	2
	3
	4

Figure 14-22 Arrays

To reference an element in the array, the index number is used. To refer to a specific element, use the array name followed by the index number between square brackets ([ ]). The index number is referred to as a subscript when accessing information in an array. The code fragment below is declaring an array called grades and placing a value into the first and third elements of the array:

```
int grades[ 5 ];

    . . .

grades[ 0 ] = 100;

grades[ 2 ] = 87;
```

Loops are very useful when dealing with arrays. If a program has populated the array called grades with five student test scores, the sum of the grades in the array can be found with the following for loop:

```
for ( x = 0; x < 5; x ++ )          /* loop five times */
            sum += grades[x];       /* short hand for sum =
                                       sum + grades[x] */
```

The for loop traverses the array, starting with the first element, grades[0]. The loop occurs five times, once for each element in the array. The x variable is used as a subscript to reference the elements in the array.

One of the more common errors in C is when the index is out of range. If x <= 5 were used in the conditional expression of the loop, it would have looped a 6th time and tried to access grades[5], which does not exist. This error would not show up at compile time; it would be seen only during the execution of the program. You may get unpredictable results, or it could result in a segmentation violation and core dump.

An array can be initialized with values at the time it is declared by using:

```
int grades[5] = {100, 98, 97, 87, 99};
```

The compiler will map the values into the array. You can initial-ize using less values than the number of elements in the array, but never more.

Multidimensional Arrays

The arrays discussed thus far have been linear arrays, dealing with a single dimension. Arrays can be multidimensional. One of the more common uses for multidimensional arrays is as a two-dimen-sional array for matrixes or tables as shown in Figure 14-23.

A 3 by 5 matrix can be declared as

```
int array_m[3][5];
```

If you think of this in terms of rows and columns, the first square bracket represents the number of rows, and the second represents the number of columns.

To access elements, both indexes must be used.

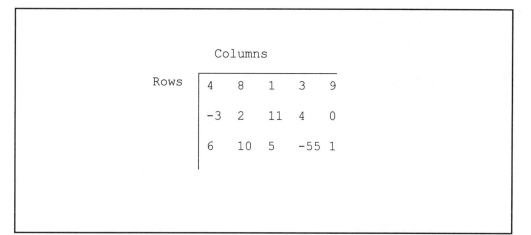

Figure 14-23 Multidimensional Array

The reference array_m[0][4] is referencing the first row, last column, or the element in the upper right corner, 9.

Passing Arrays to Functions

It is possible to pass the value of an element or an entire array as an argument to a function.

To pass in a single element, a function call and function definition would look as follows:

```c
#include <stdio.h>

void print_grade(int);                    /* function prototype */

main()
{
          int grades[5] = {100, 98, 97, 87, 99};
                                          /* declare array */
          . . .

          print_grade( grades[0] );

          /* send the first element of the array grades into
                              the function as an argument */

          . . .

          return;
}
. . .
void print_grade( int a_grade)
{
          printf("The grade is %d.\n", a_grade);
}
```

The output of the program would be:

```
The grade is 100.
```

To access a whole array inside a function, it is only necessary to list the array name without any square brackets ([ ]) or subscripts. To find the lowest grade, the whole array is passed into the function minimum_grade():

```
lowest = minimum_grade(grades);
```

The function definition looks like:

```
int minimum_grade(int all_grades[5])
{
        /* statements */
        . . .
        return ( minimum );
}
```

The function definition does not need the array size included. The array in the function definition can also be declared as int all_grades[].

Arrays are useful structures; this section covered a beginner's view.

Strings

As previously discussed in the "Data Types" section of this chapter, *strings* allow us to "string" together characters into words or sentences. A string is not one of the basic data types, but is a rather special type of character array.

A string and a character array are not the same. A string is a character array containing a sequence of character values that end with a null value ('\0'). A character array does not have to contain a string; it can be an array of character values, none of which are null. The following is an array of characters:

```
char array_of_chars[5] = { 'h', 'e', 'l', 'l', 'o' };
```

The following is an array containing a string:

```
char string_array[6] = "hello";
```

Strings can be *string constants* and *string arrays*. A string constant is a sequence of characters enclosed by double quotes (" "). The null character at the end is implied in a string constant. A string array is a character array that contains a string.

A character array containing four letters can be declared as *char letters[3];*. A string containing a four-letter word can be declared as *char words[4];*. The character array and the string both contain four letters, but the string needs one more spot in the character array for the null value.

A string can be declared and initialized in one statement with a string constant as follows:

```
char student_name[10] = "Carly";
```

The string does not have to take up the whole character array, but it must be long enough for each character in the string plus the null.

The initializing a string with a string constant using the equals assignment operator is allowable only when declaring the character array:

```
char student_name = "Carly"
```

Initializing a string or changing its value in the body of a program using this method is not allowable:

NOT ALLOWED

```
student_name = "Carly";
```

To do this, C provides a library function called strcpy(). A standard set of string functions is provided with the compiler. To correctly copy a string, use the following:

ALLOWED

```
strcpy( student_name, "Carly");
```

The prototype for this function can be found in the string.h header file. When using any string library function, be sure to include the following processor directive at the top of your source file:

```
#include  <string.h>
```

There are many more string functions not addressed in this section.

Structures

Arrays allow information of the same data type to be grouped together and the contents referenced using subscripts.

C also provides a tool called for grouping information together called structures. *Structures* provide a way to group information of different data types together so that they can be handled as a single entity.

What are the reasons for using a structure? They are several. Structures allow a programmer to organize logically related data items under a common name in a common memory structure. For example, grouping together personal information regarding an employee makes sense. An employee has a name, address, salary, benefits, job title, and so on. Each piece of data is logically related to an employee, but is made up of different data types.

Structures also minimize the number of arguments passed into a function. If a function wanted to print all the information it has on an employee, each piece of data would require an argument; name, address, salary, and so on. When all this information is grouped under a structure, only the structure is passed into a function.

Structures are great tools for enhancing readability. If a program grouped all its employee information into one data structure, it would be easy to find.

A structure is declared using the following syntax:

```
struct tag
        {
```

```
        member_list;
        } name_list;
```

The keyword *struct* tells the compiler that this is a structure declaration, with its member list enclosed in curly braces ({ }).

The *member_list* contains information of other data types that are part of the structure, and can also include other structures.

The *tag* is an identifier or name for the structure's template. A structure's template describes the layout or design of the structure; the tag is used to identify that template.

The *name_list* is a list of identifiers or names for the structure's variables. In other words, the variable names used to reference this type of structure are listed in the name_list. The variable name of a structure represents the computer memory allocated according to the template design.

Structures are declared in two steps. First the layout or template of the structure is declared; second the variable is declared and memory is allocated. These steps can be accomplished in two steps or in the same statement. The example shows declaration of a structure in two steps:

```
struct employee_jobs
{
        char job_title[30];
        float monthly_salary;
        int job_level;
};
```

This contains all the elements we want to have associated with the structure. This declaration does not include the variable name; this is done by using the tag *employee_jobs* in the following format:

```
        struct employee_jobs manager;
```

The variable manager is of type struct employee_jobs.

Other types of employee_jobs can be declared:

```
struct employee_jobs analyst;
struct employee_jobs ceo;
```

Referencing an element in a structure is slightly different. Using the variable name of the structure followed by a period, and then the member name accesses a member of a structure. To set the CEO's salary, use the following statement:

```
ceo.monthly_salary = 60000.00;
```

A structure can also be passed in its entirety to a function with one argument. Consider the example in Figure 14-24.

```
struct time
{
        int hour;  ◄────────────────────────────  structure template declaration
        int minute;
};

int time_in_minutes ( struct time t );  ◄───────────────  function prototype

main()
{
        struct time_now;  ◄────────────────────  structure variable declaration
        int minutes;

        time.hour = 10;
                                    ◄──────────────  assigning values to
        time.minute = 15;                                member functions

        minutes = time_in_minute ( time_now );  ◄───  function call with variable
                                                       structure
     printf("%d hours and %d minutes comes to a total of %d minutes\n",
                 time_now.hour, time_now.minutes, minutes);

        return;

}


/* function to calculate the total number of minutes */

int time_in_minutes ( structure time t )  ◄───────────  function declaration has a
{                                                        structure as a parameter
        int total_minutes;


        total_minutes = t.hour*60;   /* add minutes */

        return ( total_minutes );

}
```

Figure 14-24   Passing a Structure into a Function

Notice that the time_now structure passed into the function *time_in_minutes* is declared as variable *t* in the function declaration and used as t within the function body. Also, notice that the information was only read from the time structure; the contents of the time structure was not altered. If the function *time_in_minutes()* did attempt to alter the time structure's contents, it would not be seen in the *main()* function. This is because a copy of the structure was passed to the function. If any changes were made to the structure in the *time_in_minutes()* function, they would only be to the copy, and the copy is destroyed after we return to the *main()* function.

To pass the actual structure so the contents can be altered within a function, a pointer must be used. Pointers are discussed in the next section.

Structures can be a detailed topic; this section has provided a brief overview. For more examples and information regarding structures, refer to the books recommended at the end of this chapter.

Pointers

The last topic covered in this section is pointers. Pointers are a fairly sophisticated topic and one of the most powerful in C. Pointers can be used instead of indexes to access array elements or allow arguments to be altered within a function. Pointers also allow C to work with *dynamically allocated memory*. This means that the size of the variable is not included in the declaration. It is dealt with in the body of the function.

A pointer is a spot in memory containing an address to something else, or pointing to another spot in memory. Pointer contents are similar to integer data previously used, except that the data can be used to access other data.

Pointers can take the form of a constant or a variable in computer memory. Pointer variables can be defined and initialized. The values in pointer variables can be changed. The values in pointer constants, like other constants we've seen, cannot be changed.

A pointer variable can be defined using the following syntax:

```
data_type *pointer_name;
```

The data_type is the same as the data types seen previously. The data type indicates what type of information to which the pointer will be pointing. If a pointer is to point to a float, the pointer should be declared as *float *salary_ptr;*. Figure 14-25 depicts this concept.

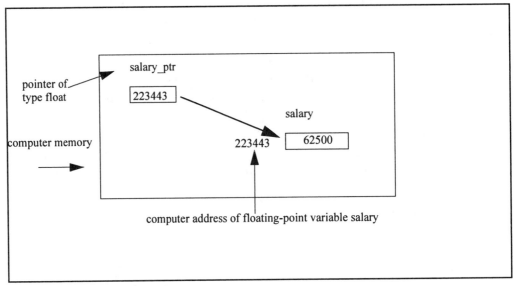

Figure 14-25 Pointer

A variable declared as a pointer contains the address of the variable to which it is "pointing." The pointer salary_ptr must be declared as type float since it is pointing to the variable salary of type float.

Pointer Operators

There are two operators often used with pointers. The *address* operator (&) allows the addresses to be obtained. The *indirection* operator (*) allows you to access values at address locations. These operators perform opposite operations. If placed next to each other, they cancel each other out. When assigning an address to a pointer, use the address operator (&). When accessing the data using a pointer, use the indirection operator (*).

Figure 14-26 illustrates the use of pointers.

```
main()
{
        int a_number = 10, num_from_ptr;
        int *num_ptr;

        num_ptr = &a_number;          ◄──────  take the address from variable a_number and put
                                               it into the pointer variable num_ptr

        num_from_ptr = *num_ptr;      ◄──────  access the value at the address found in
                                               num_ptr and put the value in num_from_ptr
            print f("a_number = %d, num_from_ptr = %d\n",
                        a_number, num_from_prt);

}
```

Figure 14-26   Pointer Operations in Program

The printf() statement produces the following output:

```
a_number = 10, num_from_ptr = 10
```

If we were to print the value in *num_ptr*, the output would be the address of the *a_number* variable. Figure 14-27 is a graphical representation of the program.

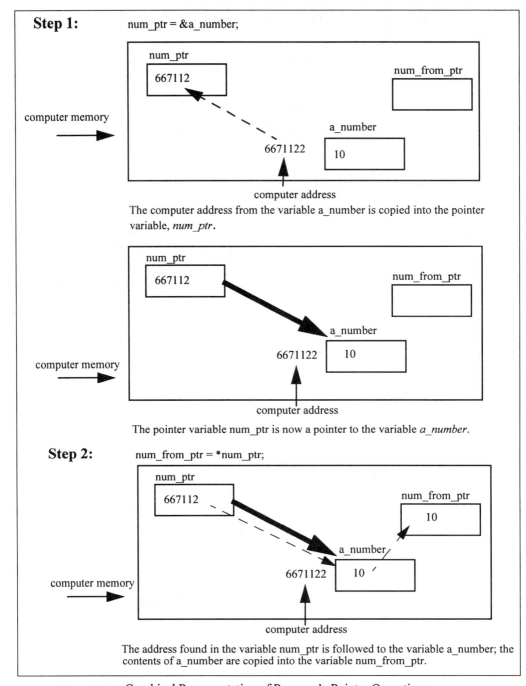

Step 1:   num_ptr = &a_number;

The computer address from the variable a_number is copied into the pointer variable, *num_ptr*.

The pointer variable num_ptr is now a pointer to the variable *a_number*.

Step 2:   num_from_ptr = *num_ptr;

The address found in the variable num_ptr is followed to the variable a_number; the contents of a_number are copied into the variable num_from_ptr.

Figure 14-27   Graphical Representation of Program's Pointer Operations

Pointers and Structures

Pointers can point to structures as well. Consider the following structure declaration:

```
struct time
{
        int hour;
        int minute;
};
```

Previously, we defined variables as type struct time:

```
struct time time_now;
```

We can also define a variable to be a pointer to a *struct time* variable:

```
struct time *time_pointer;
```

Using the following statement, we can assign the address of the structure variable *time_now* to the pointer variable *time_pointer*:

```
time_pointer = &time_now;
```

After the assignment is made, we can indirectly access the members of the *time* structure via the *time_pointer*:

```
(*time_pointer).hour = 16;
```

Structures can also contain pointers, as in the example:

```
struct time
{
        int hour;
        int minute;
        int *seconds_ptr;
}
```

The structure *time* can have a pointer, called *seconds_ptr*, point to an integer containing a number of seconds.

Pointers and Functions

Pointers can also be passed as arguments to a function. When this occurs, we are not passing a copy of the variable, as previously shown, but we are passing a pointer to the actual variable. If any changes are made to the variable contents within the function, this time they will be retained.

Arguments in function calls and parameters in function definitions and prototypes need to be defined to accept pointers.

A prototype defined to accept two integer pointers is as follows:

```
int time_in_minutes( int *hour_ptr, int *minute_ptr );
```

The function definition would look like:

```
int time_in_minutes( int *hour_ptr, int *minute_ptr )
{
            /* statements */
}
```

The fragment of code below illustrates a call to a function that requires integer pointers. In this example, the variables are defined as integers. To use the function, the variable addresses need to be sent into the function using the address operator (&):

```
int hour, minute, total_min;

hour = 10;
minute = 33;

total_min = time_in_minutes( &hour, &minute );
```

In the example below, additional variables are declared as integer pointers. The integer variables are populated with values, and their addresses are assigned to the integer pointer variables. Because the integer pointer variables already contain addresses, they can be used without any of the pointer operators:

```
int hour, minute, total_min;
int *hour_ptr, *minute_ptr;

hour = 10;
minute = 33;

hour_ptr = &hour;
minute_ptr = &minute;

total_min = time_in_minutes( hour_ptr, minute_ptr );
```

Pointer variables can also be declared as pointers to structures. Either the address to the structure can be sent into a function using the address operator (&), or a structure pointer variable can be used.

Referencing the member variables of a pointer to a structure is different from referencing member values directly from a structure.

Referencing member variables directly from a structure is done with a period (.) between the variable name of the structure and the member variable name. We have already seen examples of this, similar to the code fragment below:

```
struct time
{
        int hour;
        int minute;
};

main()
{
        . . .
        struct time mytime;
        . . .
        mytime.hour = 9;
        mytime.minute = 45;
        . . .
}
```

When referencing member values from a pointer to a structure, instead of a period, use the pointer symbol (->) between the variable name of the pointer to the structure and the member variable name.

This symbol is a combination of two characters, the dash (-) and the greater-than sign (>).

Figure 14-28 contains examples of referencing member variables from both a structure and a pointer to a structure. The function *time_in_minutes()* has been modified to accept a pointer to the structure time.

```
      struct time
      {
              int hour;
              int minute;
      };

      int time_in_minutes ( struct time * );        /* function prototype */

      main()
      {
              struct time mytime;                /* declare variable as type struct time */
              struct time *time_ptr;             /*  declare pointer as type struct time */
              int total_min;


              mytime. hour = 9;                  /*  assign data to member variables */
              mytime.minute = 45;


              time_ptr = &mytime;                /* assign adress of structure mytime
                                                    to pointer time_ptr */

              total_min = time_in_minutes( &mytime)    /* send in address of mytime structure

              printf("Hours = %d", mytime.hour);        sending in the address of the variable
              printf("Minutes = %d", mytime.minute);
              printf("Total minutes = %d", total_min);

              total_min = time_in_minutes( time_ptr ); /* Send in structure to mytime pointer */

              printf("Hours = %d", time_prt->hour);
              printf("Minutes = %d", time_prt->minute);
              printf("Total minutes = %d", time_prt->tot_min);
      }
      /* function to calculate total number of minutues */

      int time_in_minutes( struct time *t )           function declaration has a pointer to the
      {                                                structure as a parameter
       int total_minutes;
       total_minutes = t->hour*60;             /*convert hours to minutes*/
       total_minutes +=t->minute;             /*add minutes*/
       return ( total_minutes);
      }
```

Figure 14-28 Referencing Member Variables

In the main() function, the pointer to the time structure, time_ptr is declared. Notice that when referencing the member variables of *time_ptr*, the period (.) is no longer used, but the -> symbol is.

Because the function *time_to_minutes()* has been modified to accept a structure pointer, the pointer symbol (->) is now used within the function to access the member variables. Also, the function call has changed when using the variable of a structure. Because the function now accepts a pointer to the structure, the structure variable must send its address using the address operator (&). When sending the pointer to the structure, no pointer operator is needed. It is also worth noting that any changes to the contents of the member variables within a function defined in this manner will be retained after leaving the function.

For more information regarding pointers, please refer to the recommended books at the end of this chapter.

More Data Types

Each variable that is declared in a C program has a data type and a storage class. The data type determines how much storage a variable will use, what kind of data it can hold, where the variable can be used, when it exists, and how it is initialized.

C language allows a programmer to assign a name to a data type with the typedef data type.

Storage Classes

There are three properties determined by the storage class of a variable. The compiler may or may not initialize a variable with a starting value when it allocates space for it; this action is referred to as initialization. The lifetime of a variable is when a program creates and destroys a variable during execution. A variable may be created within a function and destroyed after the function is complete. The third property, scope, determines through which programming area a variable is accessible. A variable may be globally accessible, which means that it was declared outside a function and is accessible by all the functions, or a variable may be local, accessible from within a function only.

Automatic Storage Class

Variables in the automatic storage class are local to the function in which they are defined. This means the lifetime and scope of the variable are limited to the function. In other words, a variable in the automatic storage class comes into existence when the function is executed; it is only used within the function, and is automatically destroyed when leaving a function. The format is:

```
auto data_type variable_name;
```

Static Storage Class

Variables of the static storage class are sometimes referred to as global, because their scope and lifetime are not restricted to a function. The existence of a static variable is the lifetime of the program. The scope of the variable depends upon how it is defined. The format is:

```
static data_type variable_name;
```

There are three ways to declare a static variable, starting with a narrow scope and moving to wider scopes:

1. A static variable declared inside a function restricts the static variable to that function. A non-static variable declared in a function is destroyed after the function execution is complete. A static variable will not be destroyed after the function execution is complete. If a value is assigned to the variable, the value will still be there the next time the function is executed.

2. A static variable declared outside all functions in a file has a scope that includes all functions in that source file. Using static vari-

ables prohibits functions in other source files from accessing the variable.

3. A variable can be accessible from other source files if it is declared outside all functions, static is not used, and it is accessed from functions in other source files using the qualifier extern. The variable needs a declaration in each of the source files. One will have the variable declaration, and all others will have the declaration with the extern qualifier.

Typedef

Typedef allows a programmer to assign their names to data types. The convention is uppercase letters are used for names so that they are easily distinguishable. For example, some programs may use bytes in their logic. A programmer may want to declare every variable used as a byte as an unsigned char. It would be easier to use the typedef keyword and assign the word BYTE to the data type unsigned char with the following statement:

```
typedef unsigned char BYTE;
```

Variables can be declared as:

```
BYTE intial_byte;
BYTE new_byte;
```

Essentially, any variable declared as type BYTE is really declared as unsigned char. This will help with organization and program readability.

Enumerations

Enumerations provide the ability to create a variable that has a limited set of possible values that can be referred to by name. When defining an enumeration, the result will be a list of named integer constants. These constants can be used anywhere an integer is used. The format for declaring an enumeration is as follows:

```
enum enum_type_name { enumeration list } variable_list;
```

For example, a variable can be created that will only accept the days of the week. This is defined as follows:

```
enum Week { Sunday, Monday, Tuesday, Wednesday, Thursday, Fri-
day, Saturday };
```

The enumerated data type called Week and variables of this type can only have the values listed between the curly braces ({ }). If the variable Week is set to any other value, an error is generated.

Each day of the week is automatically defined as representing a fixed integer value. For example, Sunday will have a value of 0, Monday has a value of 1, and so on.

The variable yesterday can be declared as an instance of the enumeration type Week with an initial value of Thursday, using the following statement:

```
enum Week yesterday = Thursday;
```

Dynamic Memory Allocation

There are times when a programmer does not know how much memory a program will need for its data. For example, a program accepts input from a keyboard, perhaps a sentence. A program can allocate a large piece of memory to put the sentence in, but the programmer really doesn't know how long it will be. If the programmer allocates a large amount of memory and the sentence is short, memory is wasted. If the programmer makes an assumption that the sentence will only be 100 words, there is always the possibility of a 101-word sentence being entered. A solution is to allocate memory while a program is executing.

A standard library function, malloc(), allows a programmer to allocate only the amount of memory needed and only when it is needed. When the memory is no longer needed, it can be released or freed with a call to another standard library function called free(). Dynamic memory allocation allows a programmer to control the life-time of the memory usage.

Pointers play an essential role in dynamic memory allocation. Pointers contain the address of the memory allocated. The pointer is defined in advance, but the memory that the pointer will point to is made available while the program is running.

When memory is needed, a programmer can use malloc(), speci-fying the size of memory needed, and the computer will populate the pointer with the address of the assigned memory. A call can be made to malloc() as follows:

```
char * ptr;

ptr = ( char * )malloc( size );
```

Malloc() locates a block of contiguous memory of the requested size and returns a void pointer to the first byte in the block. The results of malloc() should be cast to match the type of pointer on the left side of the assignment operator. For example, a call to create a block to be used for integers would be:

```
int * ptr;

ptr = (int * )malloc(size );
```

The malloc() function will return a NULL pointer if there was a failure. NULL is a pointer with a value of zero that points to type void. The return value of malloc() needs to be tested for a NULL value to determine whether it was successful.

```
if ( ptr == NULL)
{
printf("Memory allocation error.\n");
return;
}
```

After the memory block is no longer needed, release it back to the operating system by calling the free() function as follows:

```
free( ptr );
```

The memory will now be available for reuse. After the program ends, all memory is automatically freed. It is good programming practice to free memory within the program.

The C programming section was intended to give you a quick overview of the language and a basis for understanding C++. The C language section should be supplemented with a C programming book to provide more detail and comprehensive coverage of the topics we've just touched upon.

14 - C++ Language

Programming languages have evolved in response to a primary issue; increasing complexity of programs. As a project increases in size, so does the ability to manage its complexity. At some point, the complexity exceeds the ability of a programmer to manage it. This situation has driven the need for better ways to manage complexity. Out of this need emerged object-oriented programming. C, already a popular language among programmers, did not support object-oriented programming. This prompted enhancements to C, and C++ was born.

C++ was built using C as a foundation, creating a smooth migration path to object-oriented programming for programmers already familiar with C. Because C++ is a superset of C, both C and C++ programs can be compiled with a C++ compiler. This capability implies that programmers need to make an effort to create object-oriented programs; the language does not force it.

The concepts and syntax already explored in the "C Language" section can be directly applied here. However, there are some differences where the C++ language has made syntax simplifications, enhancements, or introduced new concepts for object-oriented programming. These differences will be addressed in this section, first with enhancements to functionality already found in C, followed by new concepts and syntax added to the C++ standard.

For readers interested in programming with C++, this section should be supplemented with a book dedicated to C++ programming. Book recommendations will be listed at the end of this chapter.

C++ Basics

A C++ program uses the same format as a C program. A C++ program may also have definitions of classes in header files or included in the source file. This will be addressed later in this section.

A C++ source file extension is .cpp.

Enhancements

As previously discussed, C++ has simplified some syntax and enhanced functionality already found in C. This section will discuss these differences.

Comments

C++ has simplified a single-line comment. A single-line comment is proceeded with a double forward slash (//):

```
// a single-line comment
```

Comments can still start with /* and end with */, but these notations are typically reserved for multiple-line comments.

I/O System

I/O stands for input and output. I/O operations are how we get information read into or sent out of a program. In the "C Language" section, we used two of the C I/O functions, scanf() (input) and printf() (output).

C++ has defined its own I/O system, because it needs to handle more than just the base data types. C++ I/O is object-oriented and can be made aware of objects that a programmer creates. For more information on the C++ I/O system, refer to one of the recommended C++ books listed at the end of this chapter.

Output Statement

In C, the function printf() caused a message to be displayed on the screen. C++ allows us to use cout, which stands for console out:

```
cout << "Let's go to the beach\n";
```

The statement above outputs the string "Let's go to the beach" to the screen using the insertion operator (<<).

Variables can also be printed to the screen just as easily:

```
int num_rooms = 4;

cout << "My new house has " << num_rooms << " bedrooms.";
```

When using cout in a program, be sure to include the following processor directive:

```
#include <iostream>
using namespace std;
```

For more information regarding the use of namespaces, refer to the "Namespace" section later in this chapter.

If your compiler is older, it may not support the new style headers. Both statements must be replaced with the following for an older compiler:

```
#include <iostream.h>
```

Input Statement

In C, we used the scanf() function to read user-entered information from the keyboard. C++ provides cin, which stands for console in, although input is usually accepted from the keyboard:

```
int length;
cout << "Enter the length of the vehicle:   ";
cin >> length;
```

The code fragment above prompts the user for input, and then accepts input from the keyboard, using cin and the extraction operator (>>).

When using cin, be sure to include the following processor directive:

```
#include <iostream> using namespace std;
```

For more information regarding the use of namespaces, refer to the "Namespace" section.

If your compiler is older, it may not support the new style headers. Both statements must be replaced with the following for an older compiler:

```
#include <iostream.h>
```

Headers

Older versions of the C++ compiler force the use of the .h file extension for header files in #include statements. An example of an old style #include statement for the iostream header is as follows:

```
#include <iostream.h>
```

This causes the preprocessor to include the iostream.h file in the program. The old style specification uses a file name. This is not the case for the newer C++ standard.

The newer C++ standard does not specify file names for header files, they specify standard identifiers. The headers are an abstraction that ensures the appropriate information required by the program is included. The identifiers may or may not map to a file name. An example is as follows:

```
#include <iostream>
```

When including the newer style C++ headers, the contents of the headers are contained in the std namespace. For more information regarding namespaces, see the "Namespace" section later in this chapter.

Enumerations

In C++, when declaring a variable of type enumeration Week, the following statement:

```
enum Week yesterday;
```

can be written as:

```
Week yesterday;
```

Precedence

The precedence of a few new operators needs to be included. Scope resolution (::) has the highest order of precedence; see the "Namespace" section later in this chapter for more information. C++ has included four new casting operators; see the "Casting Operators" section later in this chapter for more information.

Table 14-7 lists operators in their order of precedence, starting with the highest precedence.

Table 14-7   C++ Operators in Order of Precedence

Operator	Associativity
::	Left to right
( )	Left to right
unary +, unary -, sizeof(), ++, --, (type)	Right to left
static_cast, dynamic_cast, const_cast	
reintrept_cast	
*, /, %	Left to right
binary +, binary -	Left to right
=, +=, -=, *=, /=, %=	Right to left

New Features of C++

The following features are part of the C++ standard and do not have their foundations in C. Many of these features provide enhanced capabilities and enable object-oriented programming.

Namespace

Namespaces are a recent addition to the C++ standard. For this reason, namespaces may not be supported in older C++ compilers.

Namespaces are designed to avoid name collisions. Prior to namespaces, all these names competed for slots in the global namespace. Global namespace or global scope can be thought of as an area outside all functions and classes. In both C and C++, any variable declared at the top of a source file, outside a function, will be global. This makes them accessible by all functions. Contention for names in the global namespace has become an issue, especially in the C++ programming environment, where there are a larger number of variable, function, and class names.

For example, the standard library contains a function called abs(), which returns the absolute value of an integer. If a program defined its own function called abs(), it would collide in the global namespace with the standard library function abs(). Even if the programmer was careful to use a function name not found in the standard library, there still could be a collision with third-party libraries. It becomes impossible to guarantee the uniqueness of a function, variable or class name.

A namespace is a region within a program that is assigned its own name, and all names declared within that region are local to that namespace. Any names declared within a namespace will have the name of the namespace associated with them. Figure 14-29 illustrates two namespaces.

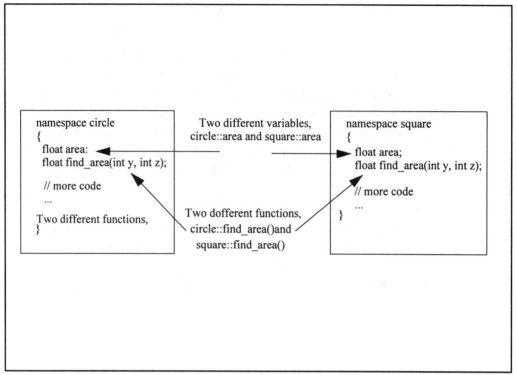

Figure 14-29 Two Namespaces

In each namespace there is a variable called area. Each variable is associated with separate namespaces. They may look the same, but the actual variable names are *circle::area* and *square::area*. The same holds true for the functions *circle::find_area()* and *square::find_area()*. This naming prevents any potential clashes between them.

The standard library namespace is **std**. Any names defined in the standard library have the **std** name associated with them. For example, the complete name of the console out statement, *cout*, is *std::cout*. A statement to display the contents of a variable can be written as:

```
std::cout << value1;
```

The operator *::* is the *scope resolution operator*. This operator tells the compiler where to look for the definition of a name. In the example above, the compiler will look for the definition of *cout* in the standard library.

The using directive allows all the names in the namespace to be used without qualification. The format of the *using directive* is:

```
using namespace namespace_name;
```

The namespace can be declared at the top of a function. When the namespace is declared this way, it is no longer necessary to use the namespace, scope resolution operator, and the name. Just the name can be used. This fact is illustrated with a code fragment that has the same operation as the example above:

```
. . .
using namespace std;
. . .
cout << value1;
. . .
```

This simplifies the code, but needs to be used with caution. Ambiguities can result.

For code simplification, a better solution would be using the using declaration instead of the using directive. The format of a using declaration is:

```
using namespace_name::identifier;
```

If a program is using cout frequently, the using declaration can be used as follows:

```
using std::cout;
```

More Data Types and Operators

C++ supports several other data types and operators. Also discussed will be dynamic memory allocation for C++.

Access Modifiers

There are two access modifiers that are used to control the way variables can be accessed and modified. The first, *const*, is also part of C language. The second, volatile, is found only in C++.

When variables are declared with the *const* modifier, their values cannot be modified during the execution of the program. For example,

```
const int hours_in_day = 24;
```

creates an integer variable called *hours_in_day,* which contains the value 24. This value cannot be modified during the execution of the program.

The volatile modifier tells the compiler that the variable's value may be modified asynchronously by an external process. The intent of this modifier is to prohibit the compiler from performing optimization on that variable. The compiler may optimize by referencing a previously loaded value for the variable to reduce overhead. The volatile modifier forces the value of the variable to be retrieved each time it is used.

For example, if a variable called time needs to be updated every second by the computer's clock mechanism, the compiler should not reuse the previously retrieved value. A new value must be obtained from the computer's clock mechanism. The variable time needs to be declared as:

```
volatile int time;
```

This will ensure that the variable time will be populated with a new value each time it is referenced.

Dynamic Memory Allocation

C++ has two new operators for dynamic memory allocation: new and delete. New allocates memory, and delete de-allocates or frees memory allocated by new. The formats are as follows:

```
pointer_variable = new data_type;
delete pointer_variable;
```

The *pointer_variable* is a pointer of type *data_type*. The new operator allocates sufficient memory to hold a value of type *data_type* and returns a pointer to it.

The delete operator frees the memory pointed to by *pointer_variable*.

Memory can be initialized when using the new operator by specifying a value inside the parentheses after the data_type. For example:

```
#include <iostream>
using namespace std;

int main()
{
        int *num_ptr;

        num_ptr = new int  (346); // initialize with 346
        if (!num_ptr)
        {
             cout << "Memory allocation failure.\n");
             return 1;
        }

        cout << "Memory was successfully
                 allocated for num_ptr contajning " << *p;

        delete p;// clean up memory

        return 0;
}
```

Arrays can also be allocated using *new*. To allocate a single dimension array:

```
pointer_variable = new variable_type[size];
```

Size refers to the number of elements in the array.
To free a dynamically allocated array, use:

delete [ ] pointer_variable;

Function Overloading

Function overloading is a feature in C++ where two or more
functions can share the same name, as long as their parameter declarations are different. When functions are sharing the same name, they
are said to be *overloaded*. Function overloading is one way that C++
achieves polymorphism.

Consider the following program:

```
// overload the function three times

#include <iostream>
using namespace std;
void print_values( int x );// function prototypes - integer param
void print_values( int x, int y);// two integer parameters
void print_values(double z );// double parameter

int main()
{
            print_values(346);
            print_values(3, 346);
            print_values(10.25);
            return 0;
}

void print_values(int x )
{
            cout << "The value is " << x;
}

void print_values(int x, int y)
{
            cout << "The value is " << x << " and " << y;
}

void print_values(double z)
{
        cout << "The value is " << z;
}
```

The *print_values()* function is overloaded three times, allowing
the function to accept three different parameter lists.

Overloading of a function is intended for closely related operations. For example, overloading a function called *square()*, once for the square of an integer and the other for the square root of a floating point number, would not be good programming practice. The variations of the overload function are not closely related. If the square() function accepted an integer and squared it, and overloaded the function to accept a floating-point number and squared it, this would be a case where operations were closely related and overloading makes sense.

Default Function Arguments

C++ allows a parameter to have a default value if the function is called with no corresponding value. For example, if a function is called with an integer and a character in the parameter list, each of these values can be given a default value:

```
void price_widgets(int num_widgets = 1, char widget_type = 'A')
{
              // code for pricing widgets
              . . .
}
```

The function is then called in the following ways:

```
price_widgets( 3, 'D' );// passes values to all parameters
price_widgets( 7);         // passes in the number of widgets,
              // but uses the default value for the widget type
price_widgets();           // uses default values for both parameters
```

The first function call passes values to all the parameters. Because the second function call does not have a value for *widget_type*, the default of 'A' is used. In the third function call, both parameters are not passed; the default values of 1 for the number of widgets and 'A' for the widget type are used.

Classes

The class is the foundation of C++'s support for object-oriented programming. It allows programs to be written in terms of objects.

The keyword class is used to define a new data type, a data type that can be used to create objects. A class defines and contains both the data and the code that operates upon the data. The packaging together of data members and functions that operate on the data within an object is referred to as *encapsulation*.

When a class is declared, an object is created. The object is the physical existence that occupies space in memory and is an instance of the class. Each object of a class has its own copy of the data defined within the class. The format of a class declaration is as follows:

```
class class_name {
                    private data and functions
   public:
                    public data and functions
} object_list;
```

Private data and functions are only usable by the functions within the class. Any private data and functions are inaccessible and are protected from outside interference. This protection is known as data hiding.

If a program managed bank accounts, the data within the accounts needs to be protected from other parts of the program that may attempt to directly access or change the account balance. A class would provide that protection by declaring account balances as private. An example of a class may be:

```
// This creates a class for a bank account

class bank_acct {
                double acct_balance;
            public:
                void init();
                double retrieve_balance();
                void update_balance();
                    . . .
};
```

By default, all items in a class are private. In this class, acct_balance is private and can only be accessed by other members of the bank_acct class. All items defined after the public specifier are accessible by all other functions in the program. Typically, the program will access the private items within a class through its public functions. The functions *init()*, *retrieve_balance()*, and *update_balance()* are called *member functions* and make up the *public interface*. Because the prototypes for the member functions are within the class definition, they do not need to be prototyped elsewhere.

After the class has been defined, an object can be created of that type by using the class name. The class name becomes a new data type specifier. To create two objects, checking and savings, the following statement is used:

```
bank_acct checking, savings;
```

To implement a member function such as *retrieve_balance()*, the compiler must be told which class the function belongs to by qualifying the function name with the class name. The source code for *retrieve_balance()* function is:

```
double bank_acct::retrieve_balance()
{
            return( acct_balance );
}
```

The :: symbol is the scope *resolution operator*. This tells the compiler that this version of the function, *retrieve_balance()*, belongs to the class *bank_acct*.

To call a member function from part of the program that is not part of the class, the object's name and the dot operator must be used. The following is a call to the *retrieve_balance()* function for object checking:

```
bank_acct checking, savings;
double checking_balance;

checking_balance = checking.retrieve_balance();
```

This will retrieve the account balance for the checking object only.

Constructor

It is common for some part of an object to require initialization at the time it is created. In the bank_acct class, the acct_balance should be set to 0.0. This is done with a *constructor function*. If a constructor function is not provided, the compiler will supply a default constructor. The object for the class is created in a constructor, which is all the default constructor will do.

A constructor function is a special function that is a member of a class and has the same name as a class. When the object is created, the object's constructor is called. An example of a constructor function for the class *bank_acct* is:

```
// Constructor function
bank_acct::bank_acct()
{
            acct_balance = 0.0;
}
```

For global objects, the constructor is called before the main() function. For local objects, the constructor is called each time an object declaration is encountered.

A constructor can also accept parameters. It would look as follows:

```
// This creates a class for a bank account

class bank_acct {
```

```
            double acct_balance;

public:
            bank_acct(double starting_balance);
                    // constructor accepting a parameter
            ~bank_acct();               // destructor
            void init();
            double retrieve_balance();
            void update_balance();
                . . .
};

// constructor function

bank_acct::bank_acct( double balance )
{
            acct_balance = balance;
}
```

The argument to the constructor function is passed in when the object is declared using either method below:

```
            bank_acct checking = bank_acct( 120.05 );
```

or

```
            bank_acct checking( 120.05 );
```

Destructor

When objects are destroyed, the *destructor function* is called. This function is called when the object is destroyed.

A destructor function is a member of a class and has the same name of the class, but the destructor's name is preceded with ~. An example of a destructor function for the class *bank_acct* is:

```
// Destructor Function
bank_acct::~bank_acct()
{
            // write account information to a log file
                . . .
}
```

If the source code for a function, constructor, or destructor resides within the class, the class name and scope resolution operator are not needed.

Friend Functions

Members of a class can be private or public. Private ensures that only other members of the class can use anything private. Public members are accessible by other classes and functions outside the scope of the class in which they are declared.

A function that is not a member of a class but can access all its members is called a *friend function*. This allows non-member functions to access the private members of a class. To make a function a friend of a class, use the *friend* keyword in the public section of the class, and include the function's prototype. For example:

```
// This creates a class for a bank account

class bank_acct {
            double acct_balance;
public:
            bank_acct(double starting_balance);
                            // constructor accepting a parameter
            ~bank_acct();       // destructor
            void init();
            double retrieve_balance();
            void update_balance();
            friend void irs_audit(bank_acct x);
                    // irs_audit function is not part of the class
                . . .     // but can access private members
};


// irs_audit function - NOTE it is not a member function of any class

void irs_audit( bank_acct x )

{
            // code for audit
                . . .
}
```

The *irs_audit()* function can access all members of the class bank_acct directly. For example, the *irs_audit()* function can access the account balance in the bank_acct class using:

```
x.acct_balance;
```

String Objects

C++ provides a *string type*, which is defined by a *class*. Essentially, a class simply introduces a new type in the language. In practice, using a class-defined type is no different from using one of the basic data types.

Null-terminating strings, like those used in C, cannot be manipulated by any of the standard C++ operators. The standard string class was introduced to solve this issue as well as for convenience and to prevent the overrun of array boundaries.

Declaring a String Object

An object of type string contains a string of characters of type *char*. To declare an object of type string as an empty string, use the following statement:

```
string student_name;
```

To declare and initialize a string, use:

```
string student_name = "Glenn";
```

or, by using a function notation, as in:

```
string student_name ( "Glenn" );
```

The stored string does not need a null-terminating character. The string object keeps track of the length of the string.

String Assignment

A string can be assigned a value of a string literal or another string, simply by using the assignment operator.

```
string valedictorian = "Carly";// declares and initializes a string
string student_1 = "Liz";      // declares and initializes a string

valedictorian = student_1;     // modifies contents of valedictorian
```

Concatenation

Strings can be joined together using the addition operator; this is known as *concatenation*. The following example demonstrates concatenation.

```
string valedictorian = "Carly";// declares and initializes a string
string student_1 = "Liz";// declares and initializes a string

string announcement = valedictorian + " and " + student_1 +  " have
won awards."
```

Comparison

When entire strings need to be compared, string objects can be used with any of the comparison operators. The comparison operators are:

>   >=   <   <=   ==   !=

An example of string comparisons is:

```
string animal_1 = "dog";
string animal_2 = "cat";

if (animal_1 == animal_2 )
            cout << "Both animals are the same.\n");
else
            cout << "These animals are different.\n");
```

Inheritance

Inheritance allows new classes to be created by reusing and expanding existing classes. C++ supports inheritance by allowing one class to incorporate another class into its declaration.

A *base class* is used to create a new, specialized class or *derived class*, as shown in Figure 14-30.

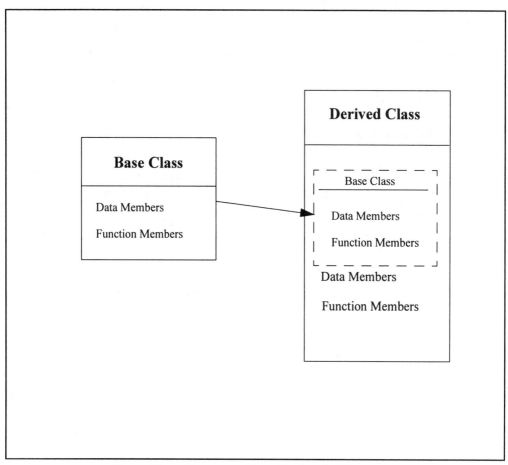

Figure 14-30   Base Class Creates a New Derived Class

The format for inheritance is as follows:

```
Class derived_class : access base_class
{
          body of new class
}
```

Access is optional, but if it is present, it must be public, private, or protected.

The following class, *automobile*, is a generic and broad description of a car. It has the number of doors, number of wheels, and number of cylinders in the engine:

```
class automobile
{
            int doors;
            int wheels;
            int cylinders;
public:
            void set_doors(int num_d) {door = num_d; }
            int get_doors() { return doors; }
            void set_wheels(int num_w) {wheels = num_w; }
            int get_wheels() { return wheels; }
            void set_cylinders(int num_c) {cylinders = num_c; }
            int get_cylinders() { return cylinders; }
};
```

This base definition of an *automobile* can be used to help define a specific object. For example, this base class, automobile, can be used to define a class called *station_wagon*:

```
class station_wagon : public automobile
{
            int hatch_space;
public:
            void set_hatch(int size)   {hatch_space = size; }
            int get_hatch() { return hatch_space; }
            void display_features();
};
```

Because *station_wagon* inherits automobile, the class *station_wagon* includes all members of the class automobile and adds information and member functions about the hatch space in the back of the vehicle for cargo.

Access Control

When one class inherits from another, the members of the base class become members of the derived class. The ability to access the base class members inside the derived class is determined by the access specifier used in the inheritance declaration.

The base class can have access specifiers of *public, private,* or *protected.* If the access specifier is not included in the inheritance declaration, the default of private is used. But this is only true if the derived class is a class. A derived class may also be a structure, and in that case, the default access is public.

What are the implications of all this specification? The access specifier affects the ability of the derived class to access members of the base class.

First of all, individual members of a class can be declared as public, private, or protected. A public member of a class is accessible by the class and anything external to the class. A private member of the class is only accessible by member functions of the class. A protected class member allows access to a derived class when inherited; otherwise, it behaves like a private member of the class.

Inheritance affects the access of base class member functions, and the base class also has an access specifier associated with it. When a class is derived or inherits from a base class, a base class access specifier of public, private, or protected is chosen. The impact to the base class members can be described in a total of nine cómbinations of base class access and member function access.

When the inheritance of the base class is public, the access status of the inherited members is unchanged. (1.) Inherited public members are public, (2.) inherited protected members are protected, and (3.) inherited private members are private.

When the inheritance of the base class is protected, (4.) inherited public members of the base class become protected members in the derived class. (5.) The inherited protected members of the base class remain protected. (6.) The inherited private members of the base class remain private.

When the inheritance of the base class is private, (7.) inherited public and (8.) protected members of the base class become private to the derived class. They are accessible by member functions of the derived class but not accessible outside the derived class, even when the derived class is inherited by another derived class. (9.) Private members of the base class remain private in the derived class.

Polymorphism

Polymorphism is an advanced topic in C++. An overview will be addressed here. C++ polymorphism is the process by which different implementations of a function can be accessed via the same name and is sometimes referred to as "one interface, multiple methods." Polymorphism only operates within a class hierarchy, making the ability to derive one class from another a fundamental capability.

C++ polymorphism is supported at both compile time and runtime. Function overloading is an example of compile-time polymorphism. C++ also allows runtime polymorphism via derived classes and *virtual functions*.

Base Class Pointers

The foundation of runtime polymorphism is the base class pointer. Pointers to base classes and derived classes have a special relationship that differs from other pointers. We've previously seen that a pointer of one type cannot point to an object of another type. Base class pointers and derived objects are the exception to the rule. A base class pointer can be used to point to an object of any class derived from that base. For example, given the base class of automobile and the derived class of station_wagon, any pointer declared as a pointer to automobile can also be a pointer to station_wagon:

```
class automobile
{
            int doors;
            int wheels;
            int cylinders;
public:
            void set_doors(int num_d) {door = num_d; }
            int get_doors() { return doors; }
            void set_wheels(int num_w) {wheels = num_w; }
```

```
                    int get_wheels() { return wheels; }
                    void set_cylinders(int num_c) {cylinders = num_c; }
                    int get_cylinders() { return cylinders; }
};
class station_wagon : public automobile
{
                    int hatch_space;
public:
                    void set_hatch(int size)    {hatch_space = size; } int
get_hatch() {  return hatch_space; }
                    void display_features();
};
```

Given the following:

```
automobile p*;              // pointer to object of type automobile
automobile auto_object; // object of type automobile station_wagon
stwgn_object;               // object of type station_wagon
```

both statements below are valid:

```
p = &auto_object;   // pointer points to object of type automobile
p = &station_wagon;// pointer points to object of type station_wagon
```

The pointer *p* can access all elements of *station_wagon* inherited from *automobile*. However, elements specific to type *station_wagon* cannot be referenced with p unless a type cast is used.

Virtual Functions

Polymorphism is accomplished through a combination of inheritance and virtual functions.

A *virtual function* is declared as virtual in the base class and is redefined in one or more derived classes. This definition allows each derived class to have its own version of the virtual function. A virtual function is called through a base class pointer. C++ determines which version of the virtual function to call based upon the type of the object pointed to by the pointer at runtime. The compiler dynamically binds the function in any class that is derived from the base class. The type of object pointed to determines the version of the virtual function to execute.

The following program demonstrates the use of virtual functions:

```cpp
#include <iostreadm>
using namespace std;

class base_print
{
public:
        virtual void print_me()
        {
        cout << "Print statement from the base class.\n";
        }
};

class first_print : public base_print
{
public:
        void print_me() { cout << "Print statement from
                                 first_print class.\n"; }
};

class second_print : public base_print
{
public:
        void print_me() { cout << "Print statement from
                                 second_print class.\n" }
};

int main()
{
        base_print base_object;
        base_print ptr;
        first_print first_object;
        second_print second_object;

        p = & base_object;
        p->print_me();// prints from base_print class

        p = &first_object;
        p->print_me();// prints from first_object class

        p = &second_object;
        p->print_me();// prints from second_object class

        return 0;
}
```

The program prints:

```
Print statement from the base class.
Print statement from the first_print class.
Print statement from the second_print class.
```

Casting Operators

In addition to the traditional method of casting seen in the "C Language" section, C++ has defined four casting operators: *dynamic_cast, const_cast, reinterpret_cast,* and *static_cast.* These operators were added to enable additional control over how casting is performed.

dynamic_cast

The dynamic_cast verifies the validity of a cast at runtime. The purpose of a dynamic_cast is to perform casts on polymorphic types. Basically, a dynamic_cast will succeed if the pointer or reference being cast is a pointer or reference to either an object of the target type or an object derived from the target type.

The format of a dynamic_cast is:

```
dynamic_cast<target_type> (expression)
```

const_cast

The const_cast is used to override a const or volatile in a cast. The format of a const_cast is:

```
const_cast<target_type> (expression)
```

static_cast

A static_cast performs a non-polymorphic cast. This is a substitute for the original cast operator, discussed in the "C Language" section. The format of a static_cast is:

```
static_cast<data type>(expression)
```

reinterpret_cast

A reinterpret_cast operator converts a type into a fundamentally different type. For example, it can change a pointer into an integer and vice versa. It can also be used to cast incompatible pointer types. The format of a reinterpret_cast is:

```
reinterpret_cast<data_type>(expression)
```

Exception Handling

An exception is an error that occurs at runtime. C++ allows programmers to handle runtime exceptions in a controlled manner. Errors or exceptions can be caught and handled easily with an error handling routine.

There are three keywords for exception handling: *try, catch,* and *throw*. Programming statements to be monitored are contained in a try block. If an exception occurs within the try block, it is thrown using throw. The exception is caught using catch and is processed by an error-handling routine.

The throw generates an exception based upon the error encountered. The throw is executed from within a try block or from a function within the try block. The format for a throw statement is:

```
throw exception;
```

The general form of a try and catch is:

```
try
{
        // statements to check for errors - try block
```

```
                    // contains a throw statement or a function
                    // that contains a throw statement
     }
     catch (type1 arg)
     {
                    // catch block
     }
     catch (type2 arg)
     {
                    //catch block
     }
                        . . .
     catch (typeN arg)
     {
                    // catch block
     }
```

The C++ programming section was intended to give you a quick overview and should be supplemented with a C++ programming book to provide more detail and comprehensive coverage of the topics we've just touched upon.

15 - Internet Programming Basics

Internet programming is defined many ways. This section will discuss the Internet, what it is, its history, and some methods of programming used.

Internet Basics

What is the Internet? Most people have accessed web pages, but the Internet is more. The Internet is the world's largest computer network, providing access to people and information around the globe. It isn't a single network; it is a vast network of networks. We can send and receive mail, listen to music, watch videos. We can create our own web pages and access others' web pages. The Internet can even work for us by performing services.

The Internet is evolving. The number of people around the world gaining access to the Internet is growing. Businesses now see the Internet as a place of business, a potential for new revenue. It has motivated new ideas and technology. And it is still young. It is an information revolution, and we can all be a part of it.

History

The Internet can trace its history to as early as the 1960s, when researchers began experimenting with creating links between computers via telephone hook-ups using funds provided by the U.S. Defense Department's Advanced Research Projects Agency (DARPA).

DARPA was interested in determining whether computers in different locations could communicate with a new technology called packet switching. This technology allowed several computers to share one communications line, when previously the computers had to have a line between each of them.

Packet switching sends information that has been broken into pieces or packets. The packets are sent to the proper destination, and then reassembled in the appropriate order for use by the receiving computer can use them, as seen in Figure 14-31. Each packet contains information about its destination. Because information travels the network in packets many computers can share a single line, with packets, filling it like vehicles on a data highway. This enables packet-switched networks.

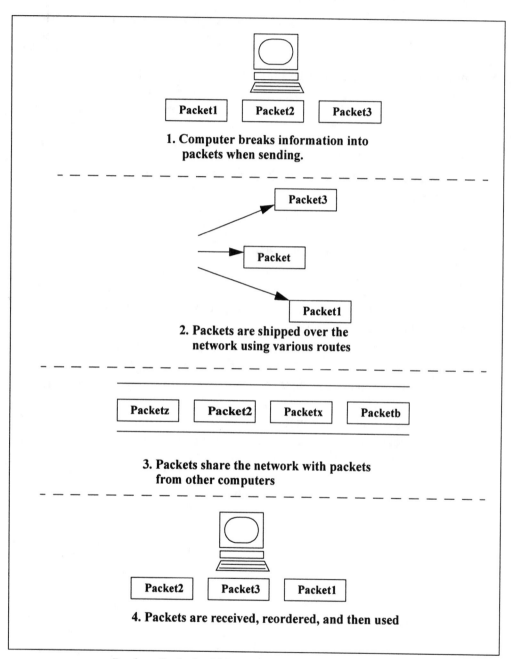

Figure 14-31   Packet-Switched Network

Unlike circuit-switched networks that make up our telephone system, packet-switched networks do not require a single, unbroken connection between packet sender and packet recipient. The packets can take many routes to a destination. For example, if a piece of information is broken into five packets, each packet can take a different route through the network, and then all five packets are assembled at the destination and used. In contrast, the telephone system is a circuit-switched network, requiring a part of the network to be dedicated to a single connection. This connection is open whether someone is speaking or not. A circuit-switched network and a packet-switched network can be seen in Figure 14-32.

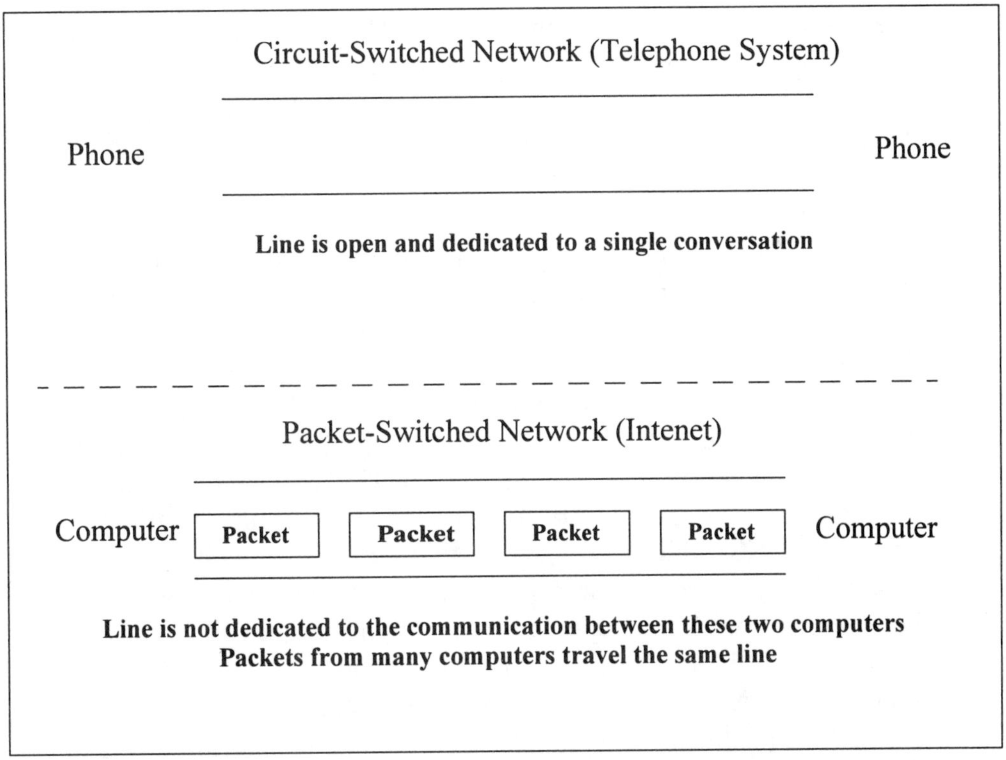

Figure 14-32 Circuit-Switched Network vs. Packet-Switched Network

The packet-switching technology was a success and became known as ARPANet. A few enterprising students developed a way to conduct online conferences, and eventually people recognized the power of online communication.

In the 1970s, ARPA supported the development of protocols, or rules, for transferring data between different computer networks. These internetworking or internet protocols enabled the development of the Internet. The end of the 1970s saw the establishment of links between ARPANet and similar networks in other countries. The networking "web" began encompassing the globe.

Expansion of the Internet began at a phenomenal rate in the 1980s. Universities and colleges, government agencies, and research companies began to connect to this worldwide network.

The 1990s saw the invention of the Internet browser, which facilitated explosive growth. Now the data could be displayed in more creative formats, and the Internet began drawing the interest of more than hobbyists and researchers. Data transfer speeds increased, and commercial internetworking services emerged with speeds comparable to the government system. By mid-1994, the U.S. government removed itself from the day-to-day operations over the Internet.

The Internet is more than information displayed on a browser. It is a network that carries a variety of data. The World Wide Web, or Web, is the fastest growing part of the Internet. It is an Internet facility that links documents locally and remotely and was developed at the European Center for Nuclear Research (CERN) in Geneva for sharing nuclear physics research information. Its origins lie in a proposal by Tim Berners-Lee in 1989. Soon after, in 1991, the first command-line browser was introduced, followed by the Voila X Window browser in 1993, which provided the first graphical capability for the Web. In the same year, CERN introduced its Macintosh browser and the National Center for Supercomputing Applications (NCSA) introduced the X Window version of Mosaic. Soon afterwards, Netscape brought its browser to market, followed by Microsoft.

Browsers allowed the graphical representation and formatting of data that, for the first time, gave the Internet mass appeal.

Today most new users interact with the Internet via web browsers, but prior to that, command-line UNIX utilities were and can still be used. Programs and files were listed using the Archie utility, and information was downloaded via FTP (File Transfer Protocol). Telnet was used to log on to a computer over the Internet to run programs. Gopher provided hierarchical menus describing Internet files, and Veronica allowed more sophisticated searches on Gopher sites. In 1994, when web browsers were in their infancy, there were approximately 500 web sites. Today, there are millions of web sites with more coming online every day.

Client-Server Model of the Internet

Architectures for programming have evolved over the years. The front-end, or client, is a machine that interfaces with the user and sends information to and receives information from the back-end. A back-end, or server, is a machine or a set of machines that sends information to and receives information from the client. This client-server architecture is illustrated in Figure 14-33.

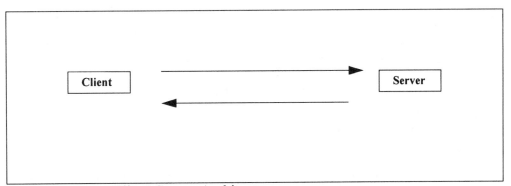

Figure 14-33 Client-Server Architecture

Early architectures consisted of "dumb" terminals as the client, with super computers as the server. Dumb terminals only knew how to display text information. Later, X-terminals were introduced allowing some graphical representations. The server handled most everything, from number crunching and algorithms to field validation. This setup presented a problem when a field had to be validated against business logic; the contents were sent over the network to the server, validated, and sent back. If there was an error in the field, the process was repeated. This architecture increased the network traffic, and the users frequently experienced delays in response.

As technology evolved and PCs became more prevalent, the development community realized that logic, such as field validations, could reside on the client and that pre-validated information could be sent to the server, minimizing network traffic and enhancing user response time. Because clients were more sophisticated, customized and flashy graphical interfaces could be implemented. But they had a price. Complex client software had to be developed, along with server software. All software residing on the client had to be shipped to each user and installed by each user. This meant that any revisions to the client software had to be communicated to the user community, and the user was responsible to perform the update. Eventually the Internet could be used to distribute the software, allowing the users to download new versions of client software. But there was still the problem of ensuring the user community had the correct version of the client software. And because each user had to do his or her own software updates, this opened up the possibility of errors occurring on individual systems, which meant more user support. Each user spent time performing the update, so the cost of a single client software update became expensive. If each user had to spend ten to twenty minutes on an update, multiplied by hundreds or thousands of users, the time spent for a single client update becomes enormous.

When the World Wide Web and browsers became popular, development communities began to see a possible solution to their dilemma. Browsers could be sent a standard set of commands over the Internet and instructed to display information per these commands. Therefore, developers no longer created client software; and users no longer had to update client software, they used a browser instead. But this has limitations. A developer could only create an interface using the methods provided by the browser. This solution wasn't perfect either. The browser's capabilities were inferior to the interfaces that developers were now accustom to building. At first, browsers only provided static pages. Many client-server applications needed dynamic attributes from their client, such as buttons and field validation. Eventually Java, Javascript, and other new technologies were created, which enabled dynamic web pages. Now developers could begin using the browser as the client software and by combining various techniques, create a fully functioning application on the web without the hassle of client software updates. The technology is still young and there are limitations. Developers created simple client-server applications at first, but as the technology matures, so does the ability to implement more complex applications.

When using the Internet, connection between the client and server is maintained only during the actual exchange of information. After the information is transferred from the server to the client, the connection between the two is broken, but the connection to the Internet remains.

Protocols

A protocol is a standard or set of rules for hardware and software governing transmission and receipt of data. This facilitates data exchanges via a "conversation." The following is a conceptual exchange managed by a communications protocol:

Computer 1 wishes to send data to Computer 2.

Computer 1: Are you there?
Computer 2: Yes.

Computer 1: Are you ready to receive data?
Computer 2: Yes.

Computer 1: The message is ...(data is sent). Did you receive it?
Computer2: Yes.

Computer 1: Here is more...(data is sent). Did you receive it?
Computer 2: No.

Computer 1: Here it is again...(data is re-sent). Did you receive it?
Computer 2: Yes.

Computer 1: I have no more data. Goodbye.
Computer 2: Goodbye.

This seemingly simple idea makes it possible for computers and networks all over the world to share information and messages on the Internet.

When using the Internet, a connection between the client and server is maintained only during the actual exchange of information. After the information is transferred between the client and server the connection is broken, but the Internet connection remains.

As mentioned in the previous section, data is broken into packets, sent, reassembled at the destination, and used. This process is the job of two of the most important communications protocols on the Internet, TCP (Transmission Control Protocol) and IP (Internet Protocol).

TCP/IP

TCP/IP is a communications protocol that was designed as an open protocol to enable all types of computers to transmit data to each other. The Internet uses TCP/IP because it's a packet-switched network.

TCP is a connection-oriented protocol and sets up a connection between two computers. It will guarantee reliable delivery of the data, tests for errors, and will request a retransmission of data if necessary.

TCP/IP is a routable protocol, which means that all messages contain the address of the destination. IP provides the routing mechanism. The routing mechanism uses an IP address.

An IP address consists of four numbers separated by dots, such as 15.199.45.11. The first part of the address is the network address or netid; the second part is the host or hostid. Every client and server must have an IP address so that it can be found on the Internet.

Basically, TCP is responsible for breaking down and reassembling packets and IP is responsible for ensuring that the packets are sent to the correct destination.

HTTP

HTTP (HyperText Transfer Protocol) is the communications protocol used to connect to servers on the World Wide Web. It establishes a connection with a Web server and facilitates the transmission of HTML pages to the client's browser.

Web addresses begin with the HTTP protocol of **http://**. Web browsers will typically default an address to the HTTP protocol if the protocol is not entered. For example, the complete address of the Netscape site is

http://netscape.com

If netscape.com is typed without the HTTP protocol, the browser will default to it and put the **http://** prefix on the address.

The HTTP connection between the client and server is maintained only while the data is transferred to the client's browser. After it is complete, the HTTP connection between the client and server is broken. When the HTTP connection closes, the TCP/IP connection to the Internet remains. Therefore, the client is still connected to the Internet but is no longer connected to the server.

HTTPS

HTTPS (HyperText Transfer Protocol Secure) is a protocol for accessing a secure web server. Most web servers use the default port number of 80. The web address using **https://** directs the message to a secure port number rather than the default port number. The session is then managed by a security protocol.

This protocol is used when entering a secure web page. The **https://** prefix will appear in the web address instead of **http://**.

Web Browsers

As previously mentioned, the Web uses a client /server model. A web browser is client software that serves as an interface to the World Wide Web on the Internet. Published information or documents on the Web can be found and viewed using a web browser.

Documents may contain graphics, text, executable programs such as a Java applet, or a link to another document. A browser will read the document and render it in a human-understandable format.

Browsers are available for many different computer systems. When selecting a browser, be sure that it is compatible with your computer system. Many computer systems have pre-installed browsers. PCs with Microsoft Windows typically have the Internet Explorer browser, while UNIX systems will more than likely have the Netscape browser. Some Internet Service Providers may provide their own browser software.

Most information on the Web is found via linked pages located on different computers that are connected to the Internet. These network computers, called servers, store and deliver information.

Information is requested via a Uniform Resource Locator or URL. The network uses the URL to find the server that has the document and request a copy. The URL contains the protocol prefix and a domain name. It may also contain a port number, subdirectory names and a document name. If no document name is given, index.html is assumed. The components of a fictional URL are labeled and described below:

URL: http://www.lizards.com:80/neon/products.html

Protocol Prefix:http://
Domain Name:www.lizards.com
Port Number::80/
Subdirectory:neon/
Document Name:products.html

Browsers accept URLs as a means of requesting a document on the Web. URLs can be either typed into a browser or can be displayed as part of a document, known as a link. A user can click on a link and jump to that document.

When a URL is entered or a link clicked, the domain name is mapped to an IP address. An IP address can be used in place of the domain name in a URL, but this is less popular since it is easier to remember a name than a series of numbers. The IP address is used to find the appropriate server, and makes a request for a copy of the document. The server sends a copy over the Web and back to your computer. When the data arrives, the browser interprets the data into a document, displaying any images, and running any Java applets.

16 - Java

Introduction

Java, the programming language, has gained tremendous popularity since its introduction in late 1995 by Sun Microsystems. Java was initially created to build applications for heterogeneous consumer electronic devices. The World Wide Web was experiencing explosive growth and developers craved more than static web pages. Java developers soon realized that an architecture independent language like Java filled this technology gap. Since the Internet ran on a variety of machines, the ability to write a program once and having the potential to execute the program on all of those machines was extremely advantageous. This fueled the opportunity for widespread adoption of Java.

Java's creators wanted a programming language that would be easy to learn and familiar to most programmers. C and C++ languages were already widely accepted and used. When designing Java, many

C and C++ constructs were retained and a number of features found in C and C++ were removed. Most of the features removed either led to poor programming practices or were rarely used. One example is Java does not use pointers. Many programming errors are as a result of poor pointer implementation, therefore they were removed.

Architecture Independence

Executables generated from C or C++ programs run only on the computer platform it was compiled on. These executables are not portable. In the highly heterogeneous world of the Internet, this presents a problem. In many cases, even the source code for a C or C++ program will not compile on a given computer platform.

Java allows for architecture independence. It is a language that is both compiled and interpreted. The Java compiler generates architecture neutral bytecodes rather than native machine code. The bytecode is the same regardless of the platform on which it was compiled. This allows for the easy transport of Java programs to multiple platforms.

Java programs can only be run on a computer platform that has the Java Virtual Machine (JVM). This allows for Java programs to execute without a re-compile or a change to source code. Once Java bytecodes arrive on a computer system, the Java interpreter within the JVM interprets them into native machine code.

Figure 14-34 illustrates the compiled and interpreted nature of Java. The Java source code resides on computer A, and is compiled into bytecode. When a request is made for the bytecode via the Internet, a copy is sent over the network. Computer B has made the request and receives a copy of the bytecode. The bytecode is interpreted into the native machine code understood by Computer B, executing the Java program.

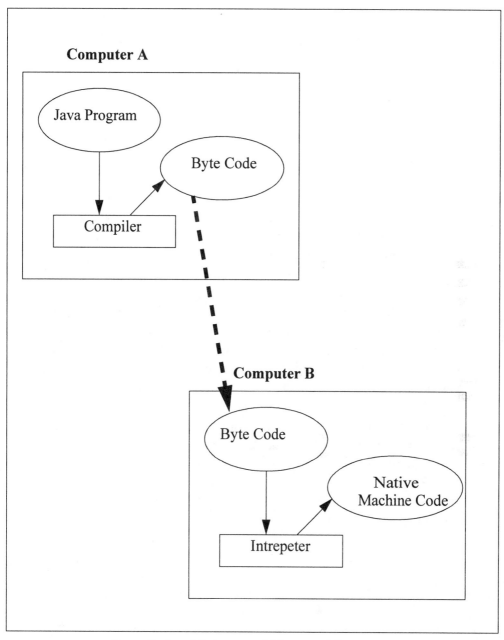

Figure 14-34 Compiled and Interpreted Nature of Java

Not all Java programs are written to traverse the network. Many programmers use Java to create portable software. This is useful to prevent recompiles and, in some cases, rewrites, that may be necessary for other languages to run on different computer platforms.

The Java Platform

A platform is typically the hardware and software environment in which a program runs. In contrast, the Java platform is a software-only platform that runs on top of other hardware platforms.

Java consists of two components, the JVM and the Java Application Programming Interface (Java API).

The JVM, which has been previously discussed, is part of what makes a Java program portable. JVM's are not portable, they must be written for a specific computer platform. JVM's interpret the Java bytecode into machine dependent code for execution. A Java program can not be run on a computer system unless it has a JVM.

The Java API is a large collection of frequently used software components. The Java API's are grouped into libraries or packages of related components. The Java API's enable quick development by providing pre-written components for use by a developer.

Figure 14-35 shows a Java program running on a Java platform. It illustrates how the Java API's and JVM insulate the program from computer platform dependencies.

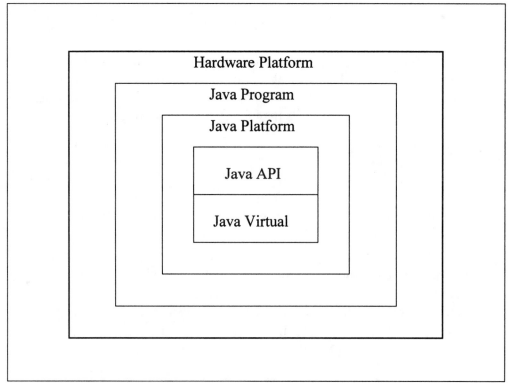

Figure 14-35 Java Program on a Java Platform

Java is a platform independent environment, but there is a cost associated with this. Since Java portability is enabled through a JVM which must interpret bytecode into machine code, Java can be slower than native code.

Just-in-time compilers, well-tuned interpreters, smarter compilers, and technologies like HotSpot are brining Java's performance closer to that of native code without threatening portability.

Dynamic

A separate linking phase, such as can be found in a C or C++ compile process, is basically absent from the Java environment. Linking in Java is actually the process of loading new classes by the Class Loader. This is a more incremental and lightweight process.

The portable and interpreted nature of the Java language produces a highly dynamic and dynamically-extensible system. The Java language was designed to adapt to evolving environments. Java classes are linked when needed and can be downloaded from the network.

The interpreted environment enables fast prototyping or updates to continuously running executables without waiting for the traditional compile and link cycle. An exception is the applet, which is executed by a web browser. Most web browsers cache information and changes will only be seen once the browser is restarted.

Java v.s. C and C++

Java and C/C++ have many similarities, but there are a number of important differences as well. One of the primary differences between Java and C language is Java is object oriented.

Those familiar with C++ will find much of the syntax the same, those familiar with C will notice the analogies are not as strong. The familiar Java syntax and keywords deceive many C++ programmers. Differences are significant enough to warrant a closer examination of the language.

Java Environment

To begin development in Java, the Java development tools, such as those provided in the Java Developers Kit (JDK) is needed. A JDK can be downloaded from most hardware vendor sites. A JDK will provide the Java compiler, Java API's, the JVM, and an applet viewer along with other useful components.

Many think of Java as a language enabling a program to run over the Web, in web browsers. While this is true, Java is also an application language that can reside on servers with a main() method, similar to C and C++.

When a Java applet is executed within a web browser, the applet class is used instead of a main() method. It should be noted that a Java applet is not an application but a Java class that is loaded and run by an already running Java application such as a web browser or applet viewer.

If the Java program is to run on a server as an application, the main() method is used. This chapter will discuss the applet class in more depth since the intent is to discuss internet programming. Discussions regarding the server applications will be limited to a few paragraphs.

Java source code resides in a file with the .java extension. It contains an optional package statement, followed by any number of import statements, followed by one or more class or interface definitions. The package statement specifies which package the code in the file is part of. The import statement makes Java classes available to the current class. If more than one class or interface is defined in a Java source file, only one of the classes can be declared as public (made available outside of the package). The source file name must have the same name as the public class or interface plus the .java extension. For example, a Java source file called games.java will contain only one public class or interface called games.

The Java compiler generates the equivalent of object files containing bytecode in <file>.class files. Each class or interface definition in a Java source file is compiled into a separate file with the **.class** extension and must have the same name as the class or interface they define. For example, the class Solitare would be stored in the file Solitare.class.

The command line argument **javac** is used when compiling followed by the Java source file.

javac [*options*] *files*

Check with the vendor of your JDK for the exact argument.

To execute a Java application on a server by invoking the interpreter, the java command line argument is used followed by the class name and any arguments.

java [*interpreter options*] *classname* [*program arguments*]

To execute a debugging version of the interpreter, use java_g.

java_g [*interpreter options*] *classname* [*program arguments*]

The main() method is used by the Java interpreter to start a Java program. It must have the following prototype:

public static void main(String args[])

The Java interpreter will continue to run until the main() method reaches the end or the method returns.

The argument to the main() method is an array of strings called *args* or *argv*. The length of the array, passed as argc in C is available as argv.length, like all Java arrays. When dealing with command line arguments within the application, note that the first element of the array of arguments is not the name of the class as a C programmer might expect.

The main() method must be declared to return *void*. A return value from a Java program cannot use a return statement in the main() method. If a return value is needed, the System.exit() with an integer value is used.

Java cannot read operating system environment variables since they are platform-dependent. Instead, Java has a system properties list, which allows textual values to be associated with names. Properties can be added to this listed to allow for easy customization of application behavior.

Name Space

Java is designed to support dynamic loading of modules over the entire Internet and must take special care to avoid name space conflicts. Java does not have any global variables, functions or procedures.

The directory structure under which the class files are stored contain the same components as the package name. For example, if the fully qualified name of a class is

gameworld.games.multi_player.doom.landscapes,

the full path of the class file must be

gameworld/games/multi_player/doom/landscapes.class.

The file name is interpreted relative to the Java class path.

The Java class path is an environmental variable set by the developer to tell the Java interpreter where to look for the user-defined classes. The interpreter knows where the standard system classes are installed and will append that location to the end of the path specified in this environmental variable. To set the class path for the example above:

```
setenv CLASSPATH .:/home/gameworld/games/multi_player/doom
```

Comments

Java supports three comment types, the standard C-style beginning with /* and ending with */, a C++ style starting with // and continuing to the end of the line, and a special doc comment. The doc comment begins with /** and continues to the next */ and may not be nested. The doc comments are specially processed by a javadoc program to produce simple on-line documentation from the Java source code.

No Preprocessor

Java does not have any preprocessors, and does not support #define, #include, and #ifdef.

Constants

A variable declared as final in Java is a constant and the value may never be changed. The Java equivalent of a C #define constant is a static final variable declared within a class definition.

No Macros

Java does not have an equivalent for the C macro, which saves the overhead of a function call. Many Java compilers and virtual machines "inline" short Java methods where appropriate. This method of inlining does not leave the developer with control of which methods are inlined and which are not.

No Include Files

Java does not have a #include directive since class names are fully qualified and the Java compiler knows where to find it without the use of a special directive.

Data Types

The primitive types of byte and boolean were added by Java to the standard set of C types.

Java also strictly defines the size and signedness of its types. In C, an float may be 16, 32 or 64 bits, and a char may behave as signed or unsigned depending on the platform. In Java, the size and signedness remains consistant across platforms.

In C, an uninitialized variable usually contains garbage as its value. Java assigns default values for all variables. Table 14-8 below shows the data type, the default value, and the size.

Table 14-8   Data Types and Sizes

Relational Operator	Meaning	Example
boolean	false	1 bit
char	\u0000	16 bits
byte	0	8 bits
short	0	16 bits
int	0	32 bits
long	0	64 bits
float	0.0	32 bits
double	0.0	64 bira

Integral Types

Java integral types are byte, short char, int, and long. All integral types, other than char, are signed. The keywords unsigned, long and short are no longer valid syntax. A long constant will have the character l or L appended to it.

Reference Data Types

Non-primitive data types in Java are objects and arrays and are often called "reference types". These types are handled by reference, meaning the address of the object or array is stored in a variable and passed to methods.

In C, value by reference can be manipulated using the & operator and dereferenced using the * and -> operators. These operators do not exist in Java.

Modifiers

Modifiers may be applied to variable and/or method declarations to provide additional information or to place restrictions. Java defines a number of modifier keywords.

The final keyword can be applied to classes, methods and variables. A final class may never be a subclass. A final method may never be overwritten. A final variable may never have its value set.

The native keyword is a modifier that may applied to method declarations, indicating that the method is implemented elsewhere in C or another platform dependent implementation.

The synchronized keyword prevents concurrent modification of the class does not occur, indicating that the class is not thread-safe.

The transient keyword can be applied to instance fields within a class, indicating that the field is not part of an object's persistent state and does not need to be serialized with the object.

The volatile keyword indicates that synchronized threads are using a field, and the compiler should not attempt to perform optimizations with it. For example, it may indicate that the value of the variable should be read from memory every time and should not have a copy saved on the stack.

No Pointers

Java automatically handles the referencing and dereferencing of objects. Java does not allow the developer to manipulate pointers or memory addresses of any kind. It will not allow casting of objects or array references into integers and vise versa. It will not allow pointer arithmetic. There is no sizeof operator.

Null

Variables of all reference types have the default value of null, which means "no object" or absence of a reference. NULL in C is a constant defined to be 0. Java has made null a reserved keyword.

No Structure or Unions

Struct and union types ae not supported. It is important to note two things, first a class is essentially the same as a struct with more features, and two, a union can be simulated by using subclassing.

No Enumerated Types

Java does not support the C enum keyword. Enumerated types can be partially simulated with the use of static final constant values.

No Typedef

The typedef keyword, which defines aliases for type names, is not supported in Java. This is due to Java's simpler type naming scheme.

Object Creation

To create a new object, the new keyword is used, followed by the object's class or type, and an optional argument list. These arguments are passed to a constructor method for the class, which initializes internal variables in the new object.

The following is an example of creating a class.

```
TempBuffer s = new TempBuffer(name);
```

Because strings are created so frequently, Java provides the following short cut for creating a string object:

```
String s = "346 Ocean Blvd";
```

The memory needed for the newly created object is dynamically allocated. Creating an object with new in Java is the equivalent of calling malloc() in C. It is even more similar to using the new operator in C++.

Accessing Objects

To access fields of an object is with a dot. The following is an example of assigning a value to a field in an object using a dot.

```
Circle c = new Circle();
c.radius = 2.0;
```

Garbage Collection

Java allows objects to be created and space allocated using new, but there is no corresponding method to free the space. Java uses a technique called garbage collection to automatically detect when objects are no longer in use. Java determines that an object is no longer used when there are no references to it.

Arrays

Just like objects, arrays are manipulated by reference, dynamically created with new, and when they are no longer referred to, they are automatically garbage collected.

There are two ways to create an array. The first method uses new with a specification for the size of the array:

```
int lottery_numbers[]= new int[6];
```

The elements in an array created with this method automatically has its elements set to the data type default.

The second method creates an array with initializing values, and looks like it does in C:

```
int lottery_numbers[]= {1, 7, 11, 17, 26, 29};
```

This method initializes the elements of the array to specific values.

Accessing elements in an array is the same as C and C++, an integer-valued expression is placed between square brackets after the name of the array.

Strings

Java strings are not null-terminated arrays of characters as in C, but are instances of the String class. String literals are widely used, therefore, Java allows them to appear between quotes just as they do in C.

The String class does not contain a method that allows the contents to be changed. If the contents need to be modified, a String-Buffer object is used.

The for Loop

Most control statements found in C and C++ are identical to those found in Java. The only statement with enough of a difference to warrant a mention is the for loop. There are only two differences between the Java for loop and the C for loop. Java does not support the comma operator, which allows multiple expressions to be joined into a single expression. Java allows multiple comma-separated expression in the initialization and increment sections of the loop syntax, but not in the test section.

The second difference is regarding the C++ capability to declare local loop variables in the initialization section of the loop.

```
for (int x = 0; x < max_shells; x++)
System.out.println("current number of shells = " + x);
```

Although the variable declared has the for loop as its scope, the Java compiler will not allow the declaration of a loop variable that has the same name as an already existing variable or parameter.

Exception and Exception Handling

Exception handling is a new feature in Java although it is similar to C++ exception handling. An exception is a signal indicating that some exceptional condition such as an error has occurred. To throw an exception is to signal an exceptional condition. An exception is caught when the exception is handled along with actions necessary to recover from it.

If the block of code that throws the exception does not catch the exception, it will move up to the next higher block of code. If an exception is never caught, it eventually moves to the main() method and causes the Java interpreter to print an error message and a stack trace, and exit.

An exception in Java is an object that has two standard sub-classes representing Error and Exception. Any exceptions that are of subclasses Error generally indicate unrecoverable errors and should not be caught. Exceptions that are of subclasses Exception indicate conditions that may be caught and recovered from, such as end of file, or array out of bounds.

The *try/catch/finally* statement is Java's exception handling mechanism. try establishes a block of code that will have exceptions and abnormal exits handled. The try block is followed by zero or more catch clauses. The catch clause is optionally followed by a finally block that contains "clean-up" code.

The try/catch/finally statement looks as follows:

```
try {
    // Block of code that will normally run without any
    // problems, but may run into exceptions.
}

catch (AnException e) {
    // Handles the exception object, catching it
}

finally {
    // This code will always execute after leaving the try
    // clause regardless of how we leave it.
```

```
        // This section will be executed whether the run was
        // normal, an exception was caught, an exception was not
        // caught or the code was broken out of with a break,
        // continue or return statement.
}
```

Various pieces of code can anticipate exceptions being thrown at some point. For example, if a program requires a user to enter an integer, there is a strong possibility that something other than an integer may be entered. The following fragment of code requires that an integer is passed into the main() method via arguments on the command line.

```
try { i = Integer.parseInt(argv[0]); }
catch (NumberFormatException e) {
    System.out.println("Argument must be an integer.");
    return;
}
```

Applets

Applets are a kind of small application designed to be run by a web browser, or an applet viewer. They differ from regular applications in two ways. First, there are a number of security restrictions regarding applets and what they can do. An applet may consist of untrusted code, so it must not be allowed to access the local file system, for example.

Programmers will notice another difference between applets and applications, applets do not have a main() method. An applet is a subclass that is loaded into a piece of software already running Java, such as a web browser or applet viewer.

How does it work? First, a java class is created using the applet class. An html file is created and an HTML tag is used to reference the applet and request it from the local machine or a machine on the Internet. It is then loaded into the browser or applet viewer and executed. It will be come clearer after creating your first applet.

Creating a First Applet

The first step is creating a Java source file. Create a file named HelloWorld.java with the Java code below:

```
import java.applet.Applet;
import java.awt.Graphics;

public class HelloWorld extends Applet {
    public void paint (Graphics g) {
        g.drawString("Hello World!!", 50, 25);
    }
}
```

Next, compile the source file using the Java compiler. If the compile is successful, a file called HelloWorld.class is created in the same directory.

An HTML file needs to be created to invoke the applet. Create a file called **HelloWorld.html** in the same directory as the HelloWorld.class file. Insert the following text:

```
<HTML>
<BODY>
<APPLET code="HelloWorld.class" WIDTH= 150 HEIGHT=50>
</APPLET>
</BODY>
</HTML>
```

To run the applet, the HTML file needs to be loaded into a program that can run Java applets. Examples are a Java-enabled browser or the applet viewer provided with the JDK. To load the file the URL of the HTML file needs to be entered. An example is listed below:

```
file:/home/kit/applet/HTML/HelloWorld.html
```

The command when using an applet viewer may look as follows:

```
appletviewer file:/home/kit/applet/HTML/HelloWorld.html
```

Importing Classes and Packages

The first two lines of the applet import java.applet.Applet and java.awt.Graphics. If these lines where not included, the following changes would need to be made to the applet source code:

```
Public class HelloWorld extends java.applet.Applet {
    Public void paint(java.awt.Graphics g) {
        g.drawString("Hello World!!", 50, 25);
    }
}
```

Importing the classes allows the program to refer to them without any prefixes.

Defining Applet Subclass

In the applet source code, the keyword extends indicates that HelloWorld is a subclass of the class following it, in this case Applet. Applets inherit functionality from the Applet class, one of the more important is the ability to respond to browser requests.

An applet isn't restricted to defining one class, it can define custom classes.

Applets as Graphical User Interfaces

The very nature of applets encourages the use of User Interface (UI) components. The AWT and Swing libraries contain pre-made graphical components. AWT libraries were some of the first graphical components. The Swing libraries followed, providing the capability of customizing the graphical look and feel of a component. For example, Swing libraries enable a Windows look and feel for the graphical components regardless of the platform.

Some of the basic components are buttons, check boxes, single-line text fields, editing areas, field labels, lists, pop-up lists, sliders and scrollbars, and menus.

A layout manager will help the developer arrange the components and produce a well-designed applet.

Java has many API's and libraries with pre-written components. Anyone interested in learning more should also investigate these libraries. They can be found and described in most books with a sizable Java section.

Manual Pages of Some Commands Used in Chapter 14

The following are the HP-UX manual pages for many of the commands used in the chapter. Commands often differ among UNIX variants, so you may find differences in the options or other areas for some commands, however; the following manual pages serve as an excellent reference.

make

make - Maintain, update, and regenerate groups of files.

make(1)   make(1)

NAME
       make - maintain, update, and regenerate groups of programs

SYNOPSIS

       make [-f makefile] [-bBdeiknpqrsSt] [macro_name=value] [names]

DESCRIPTION
    Makefile Structure
       A makefile can contain four different kinds of lines: target lines,
       shell command lines, macro definitions, and include lines.

       TARGET LINES:
       Target lines consist of a blank-separated, non-null list of targets,
       followed by a colon (:) or double colon (::), followed by a (possibly
       null) list of prerequisite files called dependents. Pattern Matching
       Notation (see regexp(5)) is supported for the generation of file names
       as dependents.

       SHELL COMMAND LINES:
       Text following a semicolon (;) on a target line, and all following
       lines that begin with a tab are shell commands to be executed to
       update the target (see the Environment section below about SHELL).
       The first line that does not begin with a tab or # begins a new target
       definition, macro definition, or include line. Shell commands can be
       continued across lines by using a <backslash><new-line> sequence.

       Target lines with their associated command lines are called rules.

       MACROS:
       Lines of the form string1 = string2 are macro definitions. Macros can
       be defined anywhere in the makefile, but are usually grouped together
       at the beginning. string1 is the macro name; string2 is the macro
       value. string2 is defined as all characters up to a comment character
       or an unescaped new-line. Spaces and tabs immediately to the left and
       right of the = are ignored. Subsequent appearances of $(string1)
       anywhere in the makefile (except in comments) are replaced by string2.
       The parentheses are optional if a single character macro name is used
       and there is no substitute sequence. An optional substitute sequence,
       $(string1 [:subst1=[subst2]]) can be specified, which causes all
       nonoverlapping occurrences of subst1 at the end of substrings in the
       value of string1 to be replaced by subst2. Substrings in a macro
       value are delimited by blanks, tabs, new-line characters, and
       beginnings of lines. For example, if

             OBJS = file1.o file2.o file3.o

       then

             $(OBJS:.o=.c)

evaluates to

    file1.c file2.c file3.c

Macro values can contain references to other macros (see WARNINGS):

    ONE =1

    TWELVE = $(ONE)2

The value of $(TWELVE) is set to $(ONE)2 but when it is used in a
target, command, or include line, it is expanded to 12. If the value
of ONE is subsequently changed by another definition further down in
the makefile or on the command line, any references to $(TWELVE)
reflect this change.

Macro definitions can also be specified on the command line and
override any definitions in the makefile.

(XPG4 only. Macros on the command line are added to the MAKEFLAGS
environment variable. Macros defined in the MAKEFLAGS environment
variable, but without any command line macro, adds the macro to the
environment overwriting any existing environment variable of the same
name.)

Certain macros are automatically defined for make (see Built-in
Macros). See the Environment section for a discussion of the order in
which macro definitions are treated.

The value assigned to a macro can be overridden by a conditional macro
definition. A conditional macro definition takes on the form target
:= string1 = string2. When the target line associated with target is
being processed, the macro value specified in the conditional macro
definition is in effect. If string1 is previously defined, the new
value of string1 will override the previous definition. The new value
of string1 takes effect when target or any dependents of target are
being processed.

INCLUDE LINES:
If the string include appears as the first seven letters of a line in
a makefile, and is followed by one or more space or tab characters,
the rest of the line is assumed to be a file name and is read and
processed by the current invocation of make as another makefile after
any macros in the filename have been expanded.

General Description
    make executes commands previously placed in a makefile to update one
    or more target names. Target names are typically names of programs.
    If no -f option is specified, the filenames makefile, Makefile,
    s.makefile, SCCS/s.makefile, s.Makefile and SCCS/s.Makefile are tried
    in that order. If -f - is specified, the standard input is used.
    More than one -f option can be specified. The makefile arguments are
    processed in the order specified. A space between the -f and the
    filename must be present, and multiple makefile names must each have
    their own -f option preceding them. The contents of a makefile
    override the built-in rules and macros if they are present.

    If no target names are specified on the command line, make updates the
    first target in the (first) makefile that is not an inference rule. A
    target is updated only if it depends on files that are newer than the
    target. Missing files are deemed to be out-of-date. All dependents
    of a target are recursively updated, if necessary, before the target
    is updated. This effects a depth-first update of the dependency tree
    for the target.

    If a target does not have any dependents specified after the separator on the target line (explicit dependents), any shell commands associated with that target are executed if the target is out-of-date.

A target line can have either a single or double colon between the target name or names and any explicit dependent names. A target name can appear on more than one target line, but all of those lines must be of the same (single- or double-colon) type. For the usual single-colon case, at most one of these target lines can have explicit commands associated with it. If the target is out-of-date with any of its dependents on any of the lines, the explicit commands are executed, if they are specified, or else a default rule can be executed. For the double-colon case, explicit commands can be associated with more than one of the target lines containing the target name; if the target is out-of-date with any of the dependents on a particular line, the commands for that line are executed. A built-in rule may also be executed.

Target lines and their associated shell command lines are also referred to as rules. Hash marks (#) and new-line characters surround comments anywhere in the makefile except in rules. Comments in the rules depend on the setting of the SHELL macro.

The following makefile says that pgm depends on two files: a.o and b.o, and that they in turn depend on their corresponding source files (a.c and b.c) and a common file incl.h:

```
OBJS = a.o b.o

pgm: $(OBJS)
    cc $(OBJS) -o pgm

a.o: incl.h a.c
    cc -c a.c

b.o: incl.h b.c
    cc -c b.c
```

Command lines are executed one at a time, each by its own shell. Each command line can have one or more of the following prefixes: -, @, or +. These prefixes are explained below.

Commands returning non-zero status normally terminate make. The -i option or the presence of the special target .IGNORE in the makefile cause make to continue executing the makefile regardless of how many command lines cause errors, although the error messages are still printed on standard output. If - is present at the beginning of a command line, any error returned by that line is printed to standard output but make does not terminate. The prefix - can be used to selectively ignore errors in a makefile. If the -k option is specified and a command line returns an error status, work is abandoned on the current target, but continues on other branches that do not depend on that target. If the -k option is present in the MAKEFLAGS environment variable, processing can be returned to the default by specifying the -S option.

The -n option specifies printing of a command line without execution. However, if the command line has the string $(MAKE) or ${MAKE} in it or + as a prefix, the line is always executed (see discussion of the MAKEFLAGS macro under Environment). The -t (touch) option updates the modified date of a file without executing any commands.

A command line is normally printed before it is executed, but if the line has a @ at the beginning, printing is suppressed. The -s option or the presence of the special target .SILENT: in the makefile suppresses printing of all command lines. The @ can be used to selectively turn off printing. Everything printed by make (except the initial tab) is passed directly to the shell without alteration. Thus,

```
echo a\
b
```

produces

```
ab
```

just as the shell would.

The -b option allows old makefiles (those written for the old version of make) to run without errors. The old version of make assumed that if a target did not have any explicit commands associated with it, the user intended the command to be null, and would not execute any .DEFAULT rule that might have been defined. The current version of make operates in this mode by default. However, the current version of make provides a -B option which turns this mode off so that if a target does not have explicit commands associated with it and a .DEFAULT rule is defined, the .DEFAULT rule is executed. Note that the -b and -B options have no effect on the search and possible location and execution of an appropriate inference rule for the target. The search for a built-in inference rule other than .DEFAULT is always performed.

The signals SIGINT, SIGQUIT, SIGHUP, and SIGTERM (see signal(5)) cause the target to be deleted unless the target depends on the special name .PRECIOUS.

Options

The following is a brief description of all options and some special names. Options can occur in any order. They can be specified separately, or together with one -, except for the -f option.

-b   Compatibility mode for old (Version 7) makefiles. This option is turned on by default.

-B   Turn off compatibility mode for old (Version 7) makefiles.

-d   Debug mode. Print out detailed information on files and times examined. (This is very verbose and is intended for debugging the make command itself.)

-e   Environment variables override assignments within makefiles .

-f makefile   Description file name, referred to as the makefile. A file name of - denotes the standard input. The contents of the makefile override the built-in rules and macros if they are present. Note that the space between -f and makefile must be present. Multiple instances of this option are allowable (except for -f -), and are processed in the order specified.

-p   Write to standard output the complete set of macro definitions and target descriptions.

-i   Ignore error codes returned by invoked commands. This mode is also entered if the special target name .IGNORE appears in the makefile.

-k   When a command returns nonzero status, abandon work on the current entry, but continue on other branches that do not depend on that target. This is the opposite of

-S. If both -k and -S are specified, the last one
specified is used.

-n   No execute mode. Print commands, but do not execute
            them. Even lines beginning with an @ are printed.
            However, lines that contain the string $(MAKE) or
            ${MAKE} or that have + as a prefix to the command are
            executed.

-q   Question. The make command returns a zero or non-zero
            status code, depending on whether the target file is or
            is not up-to-date. Targets are not updated with this
            option.

-r   Clear suffix list and do not use the built-in rules.

-s   Silent mode. Command lines are not printed to standard
            output before their execution. This mode is also
            entered if the special target name .SILENT appears in
            the makefile.

-S   Terminate if an error occurs while executing the
            commands to bring a target up-to-date. This is the
            default and the opposite of -k. If both -k and -S are
            specified, the last one given is used. This enables
            overriding the presence of the k flag in the MAKEFLAGS
            environment variable.

-t   Touch the target files (causing them to be up-to-date)
            rather than issue the usual commands.

[macro_name=value]
            Zero or more command line macro definitions can be
            specified. See the Macros section.

[names]   Zero or more target names that appear in the makefile.
            Each target so specified is updated by make. If no
            names are specified, make updates the first target in
            the makefile that is not an inference rule.

Environment
    All variables defined in the environment (see environ(5)) are read by
    make and are treated and processed as macro definitions, with the
    exception of the SHELL environment variable which is always ignored.
    make automatically sets SHELL to /usr/bin/sh. Variables with no
    definition or empty string definitions are included by make.

    There are four possible sources of macro definitions which are read in
    the following order: internal (default), current environment, the
    makefile(s), and command line. Because of this order of processing,
    macro assignments in a makefile override environment variables. The
    -e option allows the environment to override the macro assignments in
    a makefile. Command-line macro definitions always override any other
    definitions.

    The MAKEFLAGS environment variable is processed by make on the
    assumption that it contains any legal input option (except -f, -p, and
    -d) defined for the command line. The MAKEFLAGS variable can also be
    specified in the makefile.

    (XPG4 only. MAKEFLAGS in the makefile replaces the MAKEFLAGS
    environment variable. Command line options have precedence over
    MAKEFLAGS environment variable.)

    If MAKEFLAGS is not defined in either of these places, make constructs
    the variable for itself, puts the options specified on the command

line and any default options into it, and passes it on to invocations
of commands. Thus, MAKEFLAGS always contains the current input
options. This proves very useful for recursive makes. Even when the
-n option is specified, command lines containing the string $(MAKE) or
${MAKE} are executed; hence, one can perform a make -n recursively on
an entire software system to see what would have been executed. This
is possible because the -n is put into MAKEFLAGS and passed to the
recursive invocations of $(MAKE) or ${MAKE}. This is one way of
debugging all of the makefiles for a software project without actually
executing any of the commands.

Each of the commands in the rules is given to a shell to be executed.
The shell used is the shell command interpreter (see sh(1)), or the
one specified in the makefile by the SHELL macro. To ensure the same
shell is used each time a makefile is executed, the line:

>   SHELL=/usr/bin/sh

or a suitable equivalent should be put in the macro definition section
of the makefile.

Suffixes
>   Target and/or dependent names often have suffixes. Knowledge about
>   certain suffixes is built into make and used to identify appropriate
>   inference rules to be applied to update a target (see the section on
>   Inference Rules). The current default list of suffixes is:

>   .o .c .c~ .C .C~ .cxx .cxx~ .cpp .cpp~ .cc .cc~
>   .y .y~ .l .l~ .s .s~ .sh .sh~
>   .h .h~ .H .H~ .p .p~ .f .f~ .r .r~

>   These suffixes are defined as the dependents of the special built-in
>   target .SUFFIXES. This is done automatically by make.

>   Additional suffixes can be specified in a makefile as the dependents
>   list for .SUFFIXES. These additional values are added to the default
>   values. Multiple suffix lists accumulate. The order of the suffix
>   list is significant (see the Inference Rules section). If the user
>   wishes to change the order of the suffixes, he must first define
>   .SUFFIXES with a null dependent list, which clears the current value
>   for .SUFFIXES, and then define .SUFFIXES with the suffixes in the
>   desired order. The list of suffixes built into make on any machine
>   can be displayed by:

>   make -fp - 2>/dev/null </dev/null

>   The list of built-in suffixes incorporated with the definitions in a
>   given makefile called mymakefile can be displayed by:

>   make -fp mymakefile 2>/dev/null </dev/null

Inference Rules
>   Certain target or dependent names (such as those ending with .o) have
>   inferable dependents such as .c and .s, etc. If no update commands
>   for such a name appear in the makefile, and if an inferable dependent
>   file exists, that dependent file is compiled to update the target. In
>   this case, make has inference rules that allow building files from
>   other files by examining the suffixes and determining an appropriate
>   inference rule to use. There are currently default inference rules
>   defined for:

Single Suffix Rules
>   .c .c~
>   .C .C~ .cxx .cxx~ .cpp .cpp~ .cc .cc~
>   .sh .sh~
>   .p .p~

```
        .f .f~
        .r .r~
```

Double Suffix Rules
```
        .c.o  .c~.o  .c~.c  .c.a  .c~.a
        .C.o  .C~.o  .C~.C  .C.a  .C~.a
        .cxx.o  .cxx~.o  .cxx~.cxx  .cxx.a  .cxx~.a
        .cpp.o  .cpp~.o  .cpp~.cpp  .cpp.a  .cpp~.a
        .cc.o  .cc~.o  .cc~.cc  .cc.a  .cc~.a
        .s.o  .s~.o  .s~.a
        .p.o  .p~.o  .p~.p  .p.a  .p~.a
        .f.o  .f~.o  .f~.f  .f.a  .f~.a
        .r.o  .r~.o  .r~.r  .r.a  .r~.a
        .y.o  .y~.o  .y.c  .y~.c
        .l.o  .l~.o  .l.c
        .h~.h  .H~.H  .hxx~.hxx  .hpp~.hpp
        .C.o  .C~.o  .C.a  .C~.a
```

Double suffix inference rules (.c.o) define how to build x.o from x.c.
Single suffix inference rules (.c) define how to build x from x.c. In
effect, the first suffix is null. Single suffix rules are useful for
building targets from only one source file; e.g., shell procedures and
simple C programs.

A tilde in the above rules refers to an SCCS file (see sccsfile(4)).
Thus, the rule .c~.o would transform an SCCS C source file into an
object file (.o). Since the s. of the SCCS files is a prefix, it is
incompatible with make's suffix point-of-view. Hence, the tilde is a
way of changing any file reference into an SCCS file reference.

A rule to create a file with suffix .o from a file with suffix .c is
specified as an entry with .c.o as the target and no dependents.
Shell commands associated with the target define the rule for making a
.o file from a .c file. Any target name that has no slashes in it and
starts with a dot is identified as an inference (implicit) rule
instead of a target (explicit) rule. Targets with one dot are single
suffix inference rules; targets with two dots are double suffix
inference rules. Users can, in a makefile, define additional
inference rules and either redefine or cancel default inference rules.

The default inference rule for changing a .c file into a .o file might
look like this:

```
    .c.o:
        $(CC) $(CFLAGS) -c $<
```

and the default inference rule for changing a yacc file to a C object
file might look like this:

```
    .y.o:
        $(YACC) $(YFLAGS) $<
        $(CC) $(CFLAGS) -c y.tab.c
        rm y.tab.c
    mv y.tab.o $@
```

Certain macros are used in the default inference rules to permit the
inclusion of optional matter in any resulting commands. For example,
CFLAGS, LDFLAGS, and YFLAGS are used for compiler options to cc(1),
lex(1), and yacc(1), respectively. LDFLAGS is commonly used to
designate linker/loader options. These macros are automatically
defined by make but can be redefined by the user in the makefile.

The macro LIBS is, by convention, used to specify the order of
inclusion of any special libraries during the linking phase of
compilation. To specify a particular order of inclusion for a

particular set of libraries, the existing single suffix rule for a .c
file,

```
$(CC) $(CFLAGS) $< $(LDFLAGS) -o $ @
```

can be redefined as

```
$(CC) $(CFLAGS) $< $(LDFLAGS) -o $ @ $(LIBS)
```

as well as defining LIBS in the makefile.

There are also some special built-in macros used in the inference
rules (@, <). See the Built-in Macros section.

If a target does not have explicit dependents, or if a dependent does
not also have a target that matches it with associated explicit rules,
make looks for the first inference rule that matches both the target's
(dependent's) suffix (which may be null) and a file which matches the
other suffix of the rule. Since it conducts this search by going
through the list of .SUFFIXES values front to back, the order in which
.SUFFIXES is defined is significant.

To print out the rules compiled into the make on any machine, type:

```
make -fp - 2>/dev/null </dev/null
```

Since make defines an inference rule .c.o, the example in the General
Description section can be rewritten more simply:

```
OBJS = a.o b.o
    pgm: $(OBJS)
          cc $(OBJS) -o pgm
    $(OBJS): incl.h
```

Libraries
   If a target or dependent name contains parentheses, it is assumed to
   be an archive library, the string within parentheses referring to a
   member within the library. Thus lib(file.o) and $(LIB)(file.o) both
   refer to an archive library that contains file.o (this assumes the LIB
   macro has been previously defined). The expression $(LIB)(file1.o
   file2.o) is not valid. Rules pertaining to archive libraries have the
   form .xx.a where xx is the suffix from which the archive member is to
   be made. An unfortunate byproduct of the current implementation
   requires the xx to be different from the suffix of the archive member.
   Thus, one cannot have lib(file.o) depend upon file.o explicitly. The
   most common use of the archive interface follows. Here, we assume the
   source files are all C type source:

```
lib: lib(file1.o) lib(file2.o) lib(file3.o)
    @echo lib is now up-to-date
.c.a:
    $(CC) -c $(CFLAGS) $<
    ar rv $@ $*.o
    rm -f $*.o
```

(See the section on Built-in Macros for an explanation of the <, @,
and * symbols.) In fact, the .c.a rule listed above is built into make
and is unnecessary in this example. This rule is applied to each
dependent of lib in turn. The following example accomplishes this
more efficiently:

```
lib: lib(file1.o) lib(file2.o) lib(file3.o)
    $(CC) -c $(CFLAGS) $(?:.o=.c)
    ar rv lib $?
    rm $?
```

```
            @echo lib is now up-to-date
      .c.a:;
```

Here substitution in the macros is used. The $? list is defined to
be the set of object file names (inside lib) whose C source files are
out-of-date. The substitution sequence translates the .o to .c.
(Unfortunately, one cannot as yet transform to .c~; however, this may
become possible in the future.) Note also, the disabling of the .c.a
rule, which would have created and archived each object file, one by
one. This particular construct speeds up archive library maintenance
considerably, but becomes very cumbersome if the archive library
contains a mix of assembly programs and C programs.

Kernel entry points are designated by double parentheses around the
entry point name, lib((entry_name)), but are otherwise handled as
described above.

Built-In Targets

make has knowledge about some special targets. These must be
specified in the makefile to take effect (with the exception of
.SUFFIXES, which is automatically set by make but can be changed by
the user).

.DEFAULT	If a file must be made but there are no explicit commands or relevant built-in rules for it, the commands associated with the target name .DEFAULT are used if .DEFAULT has been defined in the makefile. .DEFAULT does not have any explicit dependents.
.PRECIOUS	Dependents of this target are not removed when QUIT, INTERRUPT, TERMINATE, or HANGUP are received.
.SILENT	Same effect as the -s option. No dependents or explicit commands need to be specified.
.IGNORE	Same effect as the -i option. No dependents or explicit commands need to be specified.
.SUFFIXES	The explicit dependents of .SUFFIXES are added to the built-in list of known suffixes and are used in conjunction with the inference rules. If .SUFFIXES does not have any dependents, the list of known suffixes is cleared. There are no commands associated with .SUFFIXES.

Built-in Macros

There are five internally maintained macros that are useful for
writing rules for building targets. In order to clearly define the
meaning of these macros, some clarification of the terms target and
dependent is necessary. When make updates a target, it may actually
generate a series of targets to update. Before any rule (either
explicit or implicit) is applied to the target to update it, recursion
takes place on each dependent of the target. The dependent, upon
recursion, becomes a target itself, and may have or generate its own
dependents, which in turn are recursed upon until a target is found
that has no dependents, at which point the recursion stops. Not all
targets processed by make appear as explicit targets in the makefile;
some of them are explicit dependents from the makefile while others
are implicit dependents generated as make recursively updates the
target. For instance, when the following makefile is executed:

```
pgm: a.o b.o
     cc a.o b.o -o pgm
```

the following series of targets to be made is generated:

--- pgm   with two dependents and an explicit rule to follow

--- a.o   (recursively) with an implicit dependent of a.c which matches the implicit rule .c.o

--- a.c   (recursively) with no implicit dependents and no implicit rules. This stops the recursion and simply returns the last modification time of the file a.c.

--- b.o   (recursively) with an implicit dependent of b.c which matches the implicit rule .c.o

--- b.c   (recursively) with no implicit dependents and no implicit rules. This stops the recursion and merely returns the last modification time of the file b.c.

In the definitions below, the word target refers to a target specified in the makefile, an explicit dependent specified in the makefile which becomes the target when make recurses on it, or an implicit dependent (generated as a result of locating an inference rule and file that match the suffix of the target) which becomes the target when make recurses on it. The word dependent refers to an explicit dependent specified in the makefile for a particular target, or an implicit dependent generated as a result of locating an appropriate inference rule and corresponding file that matches the suffix of the target.

It may be helpful to think of target rules as user specified rules for a particular target name, and inference rules as user or make specified rules for a particular class of target names. It may also be helpful to remember that the value of the target name and its corresponding dependent names change as make recurses on both explicit and implicit dependents, and that inference rules are only applied to implicit dependents or to explicit dependents which do not have target rules defined for them in the makefile.

$@   The $@ macro is the full target name of the current target, or the archive filename part of a library archive target. It is evaluated for both target and inference rules.

$%   The $% macro is only evaluated when the current target is an archive library member of the form libname(member.o) or libname((entry.o)). In these cases, $@ evaluates to libname and $% evaluates to member.o or entry.o. $% is evaluated for both target and inference rules.

$?   The $? macro is the list of dependents that are out-of-date with respect to the current target; essentially, those modules that have been rebuilt. It is evaluated for both target and inference rules, but is usually only used in target rules. $? evaluates to one name only in an inference rule, but may evaluate to more than one name in a target rule.

$<   In an inference rule, $< evaluates to the source file name that corresponds to the implicit rule which matches the suffix of the target being made. In other words, it is the file that is out-of-date with respect to the target. In the .DEFAULT rule, the $< macro evaluates to the current target name. $< is evaluated only for inference rules. Thus, in the .c.o rule, the $< macro would evaluate to the .c file. An example for making optimized .o files from .c files is:

```
            .c.o:
                cc -c -O $*.c

    or:

            .c.o:
                cc -c -O $<
```

$* The macro $* is the current target name with the suffix deleted. It is evaluated only for inference rules.

These five macros can have alternative forms. When an uppercase D or F is appended to any of the five macros, the meaning is changed to ``directory part'' for D and ``file part'' for F. Thus, $(@D) refers to the directory part of the string $@. If there is no directory part, ./ is generated. When the $? macro contains more than one dependent name, the $(?D) expands to a list of directory name parts and the $(?F) expands to a list of the filename parts.

In addition to the built-in macros listed above, other commonly used macros are defined by make. These macros are used in the default inference rules, and can be displayed with the -p option. These macros can be used in target rules in the makefile. They can also be redefined in the makefile.

$$@ The $$@ macro has meaning only on dependency lines. Macros of this form are called dynamic dependencies because they are evaluated at the time the dependency is actually processed. $$@ evaluates to exactly the same thing as $@ does on a command line; i.e., the current target name. This macro is useful for building large numbers of executable files, each of which has only one source file. For instance, the following HP-UX commands could all be built using the same rule:

```
                CMDS = cat echo cmp chown
                $(CMDS) : $$@.c
                    $(CC) -O $? -o $@
```

If this makefile is invoked with make cat echo cmp chown, make builds each target in turn using the generic rule, with $$@ evaluating to cat while cat is the target, to echo when the target is echo, and so forth.

The dynamic dependency macro can also take the F form, $$(@F) which represents the filename part of $$@. This is useful if the targets contain pathnames. For example:

```
                INCDIR = /usr/include
                INCLUDES = $(INCDIR)/stdio.h \
                            $(INCDIR)/pwd.h   \
                            $(INCDIR)/dir.h   \
                            $(INCDIR)/a.out.h
                $(INCLUDES) : $$(@F)
                    cp $? $@
                    chmod 0444 $@
```

Special Macros
The VPATH macro allows make to search a colon separated list of directories for dependents. Lines of the form VPATH= path1:path2 ... causes make to first search the current directory for a dependent and

if the dependent is not found, make searches path1 and continues until
the directories specified in the VPATH macro are exhausted.

EXTERNAL INFLUENCES
   Environment Variables
      LANG provides a default value for the internationalization variables
      that are unset or null. If LANG is unset or null, the default value of
      "C" (see lang(5)) is used. If any of the internationalization
      variables contains an invalid setting, make will behave as if all
      internationalization variables are set to "C". See environ(5).

      LC_ALL If set to a non-empty string value, overrides the values of all
      the other internationalization variables.

      LC_CTYPE determines the interpretation of text as single and/or
      multi-byte characters, the classification of characters as printable,
      and the characters matched by character class expressions in regular
      expressions.

      LC_MESSAGES determines the locale that should be used to affect the
      format and contents of diagnostic messages written to standard error
      and informative messages written to standard output.

      NLSPATH determines the location of message catalogues for the
      processing of LC_MESSAGES.

      PROJECTDIR provides a directory to be used to search for SCCS files
      not found in the current directory. In all of the following cases, the
      search for SCCS files will be made in the directory SCCS in the
      identified directory. If the value of PROJECTDIR begins with a slash,
      it is considered an absolute pathname; otherwise, the home directory
      of a user of that name is examined for a subdirectory src or source.
      If such a directory is found, it is used. Otherwise, the value is used
      as a relative pathname.

      If PROJECTDIR is not set or has a null value, the search for SCCS
      files will be made in the directory SCCS in the current directory.

      The setting of PROJECTDIR affects all files listed in the remainder of
      this utility description for files with a component named SCCS.

   International Code Set Support
      Single and multi-byte character code sets are supported.

RETURN VALUES
      make returns a 0 upon successful completion or a value greater than 0
      if an error occurred. If the -q option is specified, make returns 0
      if the target was up-to-date and a value greater than 0 if the target
      was not up-to-date.

EXAMPLES
      The following example creates an executable file from a C source code
      file without a makefile, if program.c exists in the current directory:

         make program

      The following example shows more than one makefile specified and some
      command line macros defined, and updates the first target in module1:

         make -f module1 -f module2 RELEASE=1.0 CFLAGS=-g

      The following example updates two targets in a default makefile
      currently residing in the current directory:

         make clobber prog

The following example updates the prog target in a specified makefile, allows environment variables to override any common variables in the makefile, clears the built-in suffix list and ignore the built-in rules, and outputs exhaustive debugging information:

    make -erd -f module1 prog

WARNINGS
Be wary of any file (such as an include file) whose access, modification, and last change times cannot be altered by the make-ing process. For example, if a program depends on an include file that in turn depends on another include file, and if one or both of these files are out-of-date, make tries to update these files each time it is run, thus unnecessarily re-makeing up-to-date files that are dependent on the include file. The solution is to manually update these files with the touch command before running make (see touch(1)). (Note that it is generally a bad idea to include the touch(1) command in your makefile, because it can cause make to update a program that otherwise did not need to be updated.)

Some commands return non-zero status inappropriately; use -i to overcome the difficulty.

File names with the characters = : @ $ do not work.

Built-in commands that are directly executed by the shell such as cd (see cd(1)), are ineffectual across new-lines in make.

The syntax (lib(file1.o file2.o file3.o) is illegal.

You cannot build lib(file.o) from file.o.

The macro $(a:.o=.c~) does not work.

Expanded target lines cannot contain more than 16384 characters, including the terminating new-line.

If no makefile exists in the current directory, typing

        make filename

results in make attempting to build filename from filename.c

If make is invoked in a shell script with a quoted argument that evaluates to NULL (such as $@), make fails.

DEPENDENCIES
  NFS Warning:
  When comparing modification times of files located on different NFS servers, make behaves unpredictably if the clocks on the servers are not synchronized.

FILES
    [Mm]akefile
    s.[Mm]akefile
    SCCS/s.[Mm]akefile

SEE ALSO
    cc(1), cd(1), lex(1), mkmf(1), sh(1), yacc(1), environ(5), lang(5), regexp(5).

    A Nutshell Handbook, Managing Projects With Make by Steve Talbot, Second Edition, O'Reilly & Associates, Inc., 1986.

STANDARDS CONFORMANCE
    make: SVID2, SVID3, XPG2, XPG3, XPG4, POSIX.2

sccs

man page

sccs - 14

sccs - Source code control system.

---

sccs(1)   sccs(1)

NAME
     sccs - front-end utility program for SCCS commands

SYNOPSIS

     sccs [-r] [-d rootpath] [-p dirpath] command [options] [file ...]

DESCRIPTION
     The sccs command is a straightforward front end to the various
     programs comprising the Source Code Control System. It includes the
     capability of running set-user-id to another user to allow shared
     access to the SCCS files. sccs reduces the need to explicitly
     reference the SCCS filenames. The SCCS filenames are generated by
     prepending the string SCCS/s. to the working files specified. The
     default SCCS subdirectory name can be overridden with the -p dirpath
     option.

     The command supplied to the sccs command can either be an SCCS program
     or a pseudo command. The SCCS programs that sscs handles include
     admin, cdc, comb, delta, get, help, prs, rmdel, sact, unget, val, what
     and sccsdiff. The pseudo commands are:

          check   Prints a list of all files being edited. Returns a
                     non-zero exit status if a file is being edited. The
                     intent is to allow an 'install' entry in a makefile
                     to verify that everything is included in the SCCS
                     file before a version is installed. See the info
                     pseudo command for a description of the -b, -u user
                     and -U options.

          clean   Removes all files from the current directory or the
                     named directory that can be recreated from the SCCS
                     files. Does not remove files that are in the process
                     of being edited. If -b is given, branches (i.e.
                     SID's with three or more components) are ignored in
                     determining which files are being edited. Therefore,
                     any edits on branches can be lost.

          create   Creates the initial SCCS file, taking the contents
                     from file. Any options to admin are accepted. If the
                     files are created successfully, the original files
                     are renamed with a , (comma) on the front. Read-only
                     copies are retrieved with get. The renamed files
                     should be removed after you have verified that the
                     SCCS files have been created successfully.

          delget   Runs delta on the named files and then get the new
                     versions. The new versions of the files have
                     expanded identification keywords, and cannot be
                     edited. The [-mprsy] options are passed to delta,
                     and the [-bceiklsx] options are passed to get.

deledit	Equivalent to delget, except that the get phase includes the -e option.
diffs	Gives a diff listing between the current version of the files being edited and the versions in SCCS format. The [-rcixt] options are passed to get. The [-lsefhb] options are passed to diff. The -C option is passed to diff as -c.
edit	Equivalent to get -e.
enter	Equivalent to create, except get is omitted. This pseudo command is useful when you want to run the edit command immediately after creating the SCCS file.
fix	Removes a named delta, but leaves a copy of the delta in the current directory. The -r SID option is required and must point to a leaf in the source tree. Since a record of the changes is not preserved, fix should be used carefully.
info	Lists all the files being edited. The -b option ignores branches in determining which files are being edited. The -u user option lists only the files being edited by user. The -U option is equivalent to -u current_user.
print	Prints information about named files. Equivalent to prs -a followed by get -p -m -s.
tell	Lists all the files being edited, with a newline after each entry. See the info section for a description of the -b, -u user and -U options.
unedit	Equivalent to unget. Any changes made since the last get are lost. Use with caution.

Certain commands, admin, cdc, check, clean, diffs, info, rmdel, sccsdiff, and tell cannot use the set-user-id feature, as this would allow anyone to change the authorizations. These commands are always run as the real user.

Options

The options supplied to the SCCS commands are documented in the corresponding SCCS man pages. The options supplied to the pseudo commands are documented in the above section. All other options preceding command are documented as follows:

-r	Runs sccs as the real user rather than the effective user sccs is set-user-id to.
-d rootpath	Gives the pathname to be used as the root directory for the SCCS files. rootpath defaults to the current directory. This flag takes precedence over the PROJECTDIR environment variable.
-p dirpath	Specifies the pathname for the SCCS files. The default is the SCCS directory. dirpath is appended to rootpath and is inserted before the final component of the pathname.

The command sccs -d /usr -p cmd get src/b converts to get /usr/src/cmd/s.b. This can be used to create aliases. For example, the command alias syssccs="sccs -p /usr/src/cmd" makes syssccs an alias that can be used in commands like syssccs get b.

EXTERNAL INFLUENCES
   Environment Variables
      If the PROJECTDIR environment variable is set, its value is used to determine the -d rootpath option value for rootpath. If PROJECTDIR begins with a / (slash), the value is used directly; otherwise, the value is assume to be a login name and the home directory corresponding to login name is examined for a subdirectory named src or source. If found, this directory path is used. Otherwise, the value is used as a relative path name.

      LC_CTYPE determines the interpretation of text within file as single- and/or multi-byte characters.

      LC_MESSAGES determines the language in which messages are displayed.

      If LC_CTYPE or LC_MESSAGES is not specified in the environment or is set to the empty string, the value of LANG is used as a default for each unspecified or empty variable. If LANG is not specified or is set to the empty string, a default of "C" (see lang(5)) is used instead of LANG.

      If any internationalization variable contains an invalid setting, sccs behaves as if all internationalization variables are set to "C". See environ(5).

   International Code Set Support
      Single-byte and multi-byte character code sets are supported.

EXAMPLES
   To create a new SCCS file:
       sccs create file

   To get a file for editing, edit it, create a new delta and get file for editing:
       sccs edit file.c
       ex file.c
       sccs deledit file.c

   To get a file from another directory (/usr/src/cmd/SCCS/s.cc.c):
       sccs -d /usr/src get cmd/cc.c

   To make a delta of a large number of files in the current directory, enter:
       sccs delta *.c

   To get a list of files being edited that are not on branches, enter:
       sccs info -b

   To get a list of files being edited by you, enter:
       sccs tell -u

   In a makefile, to get source files from an SCCS file if it does not already exist, enter:
       SRCS = <list of source files>
       $ (SRCS) :
           sccs get $(REL) $@

RETURN VALUE
   A successful completion returns 0. On error, sccs exists with a value from <sysexits.h> or the exit value from the command that was invoked. The only exception is the check pseudo command which returns a non-zero exit status if a file is being edited.

SEE ALSO

admin(1), cdc(1), comb(1), delta(1), get(1), prs(1), rmdel(1),
sact(1), sccsdiff(1), sccshelp(1), unget(1), val(1), vc(1), what(1),
sccsfile(4).

SCCS: Source Code Control System chapter in Programming on HP-UX.

STANDARDS CONFORMANCE
        sccs: XPG4

CHAPTER 15

The X Window System

Interoperability Topics

I could spend another 1000 pages covering just Windows and UNIX interoperability. There are hundreds of technologies and products that enhance Windows and UNIX interoperability. Because covering even a small fraction of these technologies and products in this book would not be feasible, I decided to devote a few chapters to technologies that bridge the gap between some fundamental Windows and UNIX differences in operation. The following is a list of what I consider to be the top interoperability topics, which are covered in the interoperability chapters of this book Chapters 15-20:

- **UNIX Application Server That Displays on Windows Using the X Window System (covered in this chapter)** - X Windows is a networked windowing environment that is the standard on UNIX systems. If you install X Windows on your Windows system, you can run applications on your UNIX system and use X Windows on your Windows system to manage those applications. The UNIX system is acting as the application server, but the applications are controlled from X Windows running on the Windows system.

- **Network File System (NFS) Used to Share Data (Covered in Chapter 16)** - The next chapter covers using NFS to share data between Windows and UNIX systems. NFS comes with UNIX, and by loading NFS on a Windows system, you can freely access the UNIX file systems on the Windows systems and vice versa. I focus only on accessing UNIX file systems on the Windows systems because, as I earlier mentioned, I think it is more likely that the UNIX system will act as a data and application server and the Windows system will act as a client. There is, however, no reason that NFS could not be used to access Windows file systems while on a UNIX system.

- **Windows Functionality on UNIX (Covered in Chapter 17)** - Putting the X Window System and NFS on Windows brings important UNIX functionality to the Windows operating system. It is equally useful to bring WindowsWindows functionality to UNIX. Advanced Server 9000 is a software product that runs on HP-UX and brings important Windows functionality such as file and print services to HP-UX. Chapter 17 is devoted to Advanced Server 9000.

- **Services For UNIX (Covered in Chapter 18)** - Microsoft Services For UNIX (SFU) provides interoperability between UNIX and Windows in many essential areas. Microsoft has packaged several widely used third-party interoperability products in SFU. Such important UNIX and Windows interoperability functions as NFS, Telnet, and UNIX utilities are part of SFU.

- **Common Set of Commands (Covered in Chapter 19)** - The Windows Resource Kit provides countless useful utilities, including a set of POSIX commands that are familiar to UNIX system administrators. Commands such as **chmod**, **ls**, and **mv** run on Windows. Chapter 14 is devoted to these utilities.

- **Samba (Covered in Chapter 20)** - Samba is an application that allows a UNIX host to act as a file server for Windows systems. The Windows systems can access UNIX filesystems and printers using their native Windows networking.

Although the system administration topics are pretty much the same going from operating system to operating system, the peculiarities of each operating system define how you perform a given function. For this reason, system administration is seldom covered as a general topic; rather, it is covered for a particular operating system. In this book, however, the assumption is that you have both Windows and UNIX in your environment. You need to manage both and manage them separately for the most part; however, advantages exist to implementing technology that can enhance interoperability between the two operating systems.

What I cover in the interoperability chapters of this book (Chapters 15-20) are some of the most basic, and at the same time some of the most useful, technologies you can put in place to help with interoperability between Windows and UNIX.

You could certainly go beyond the interoperability topics I cover to much more advanced functionality; however, what I cover in the interoperability chapters is a big interoperability gain for very little cost and effort.

This chapter and the next work together and build on one another. In this chapter, I cover Windows and UNIX interoperability by running an X server program on a Windows system, which provides graphical access to an UNIX system. Then in Chapter 16, I use a networking product on the Windows system that provides transparent access to the data on the UNIX system using Network File System (NFS). Using the X Window System (X Windows), you have a graphical means of connecting a Windows system to a UNIX system, and using NFS, you have a way of easily sharing data between these two systems. These two technologies, X Windows and NFS, provide the foundation for a variety of other useful interoperability between the two operating systems.

Why the X Window System?

The Windows user environment and the UNIX user environment, which is based on X Windows, are much different. There is no bundled support whatever for accessing Windows from UNIX and UNIX from Windows.

To go beyond logging into a Windows system to perform Windows system administration and logging into an UNIX system to perform UNIX system administration, you need some way of getting access to one of these systems from the other. The X Window System is an ideal way to get remote access to a UNIX system while sitting at your Windows system.

X Window System Background

X Windows is a *network*-based windowing environment, not a system-based windowing environment. For this reason, it is ideal for giving you a window into your UNIX system from your Windows system.

X Windows is an industry standard for supporting windowed user interfaces across a computer network. Because it is an industry standard, many companies offer X server products for operating systems, such as Windows (we'll get into the "server" and "client" terminology of X Windows shortly). X Windows is not just a windowing system on your computer but a windowing system across the network.

X Windows is independent of the hardware or operating system on which it runs. All it needs is a server and a client. The server and client may be two different systems or the same system; that detail doesn't matter. The server is a program that provides input/output devices such as your display, keyboard, and mouse. The client is the program that takes commands from the server such as an application.

The client and server roles are much different from those we normally associate with these terms. The X Windows server is on your local system (in this chapter, it is your Windows system), and the X Windows client is the application that communicates with the server (in this chapter, it will be the UNIX system running a program such as a System Administration Tool). We normally think of the small desktop system as the client and the larger, more powerful system as the server. With X Windows, however, it is the system that controls X Windows that is the server, and the system that responds to the commands is the client. I often refer to a powerful client as the "host," in order to minimize confusion over this distinction.

In X Windows, the software that manages a single screen, keyboard, and mouse is known as an X server. A client is an application that displays on the X server. The X client sends requests to the X server, such as a request for information. The X server accepts requests from multiple X clients and returns information and errors to the X client.

Sitting on one of the Windows systems on a network, you could open an X Window into several UNIX hosts. You could therefore have one window open to UNIX_System1, another window open to UNIX_System2, and so on.

The X server performs the following functions:

• Displays drawing requests on the screen.

• Replies to information requests.

• Reports an error associated with a request.

• Manages the keyboard, mouse, and display.

• Creates, maps, and removes windows.

The X client performs the following functions:

• Sends requests to the server.

• Receives events and errors from the server.

X Server Software

There are many fine X Server products on the market. I loaded Exceed 6 from Hummingbird Communications Ltd. on my system for demonstrating how X Windows can be used in a Windows and UNIX environment. I will use Exceed 6 in the examples in this chapter. Figure 15-1 shows the full menu structure from having loaded Hummingbird's X Windows product Exceed.

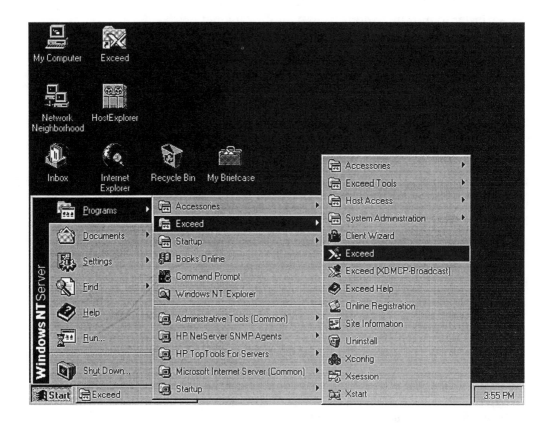

Figure 15-1 The *Programs-Exceed* Menu

Selecting the Exceed icon from the very top of Figure 15-1 produces a group of Exceed icons that is an alternative to accessing items
from the menu of Figure 15-1. Figure 15-2 shows the icon group.

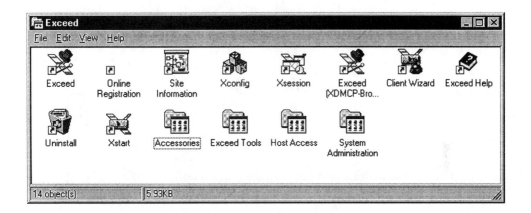

Figure 15-2 The *Exceed* Group

The *Exceed* menu pick from Figure 15-1 allows you to establish
an X Windows connection between your Windows system and UNIX
system. You can specify the host to which you want to connect, the
UNIX system in this case, the user you want to be connected as on the
host, and the command to run on the UNIX system. Figure 15-3
shows the *Xstart* window.

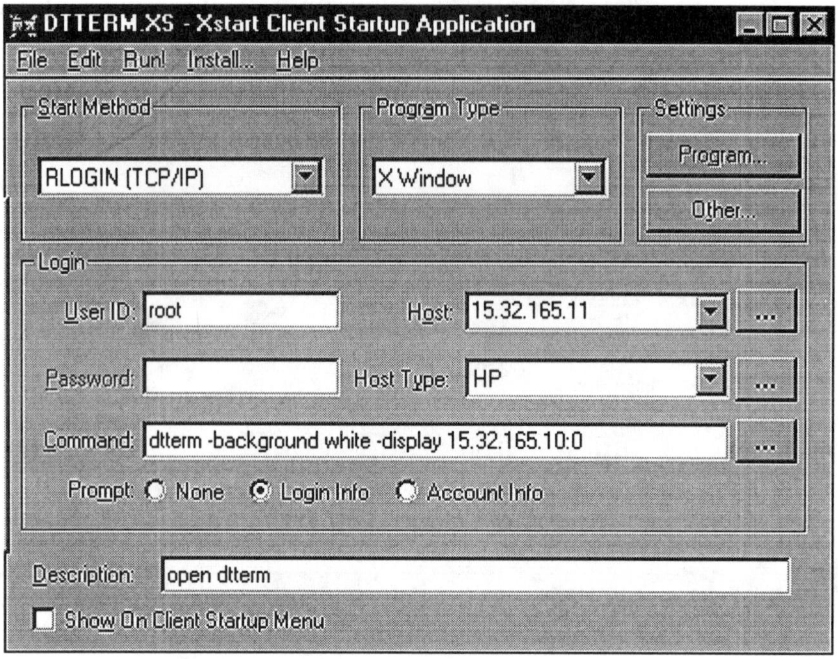

Figure 15-3 Establishing an X Windows Connection

The window in Figure 15-3 is labeled "DTTERM.XS." After you set up the *Xstart* window with the information you want, you can save the configuration. In this case, I am issuing the **dtterm** command, so I saved the window under this name. The system type can be most any system running X Windows. I used an HP-UX system in the upcoming examples, so the *Host Type* is *HP*. The complete **dtterm** command used will run on most UNIX systems running the Common Desktop Environment and is shown below:

dtterm -background white -display 15.32.165.10:0

Selecting *Run!* from the window in Figure 15-3 brings up the window in Figure 15-4, in which you can issue the *Password* and make other changes.

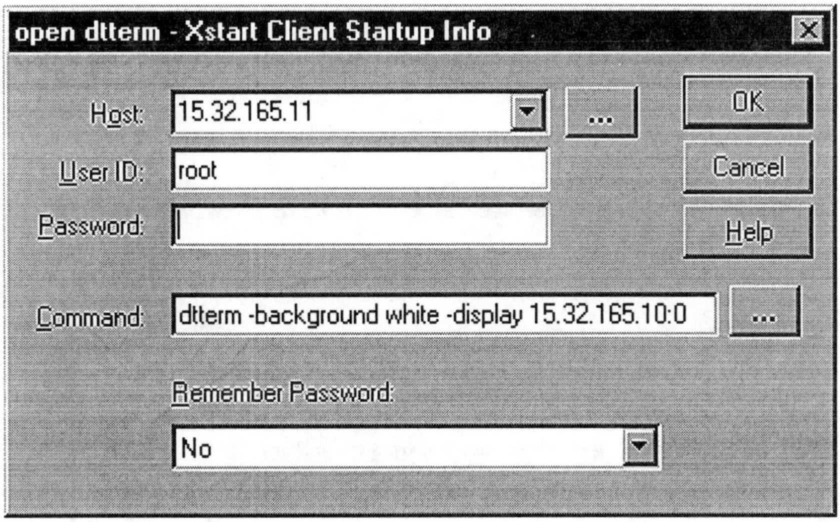

Figure 15-4 Establishing an X Windows Connection

This command starts a **dtterm** window, which is a standard window program on UNIX with a white background, and displays the window on the system at the IP address 15.32.165.11. The IP address in this case is the Windows system on which you are issuing the command, which is the X Windows server. The ":0" indicates that the first display on the Windows system will be used for **dtterm**, because in the X Windows world, you can have several displays on a system. The system on which the command runs is 15.32.165.10. This is the UNIX system that acts as the X Windows client.

Although you are typing this information on your Windows system, this command is being transferred to the UNIX system you specified in the *Xstart* box. This transfer will have the same result as typing the **dtterm** command shown on the UNIX system directly.

When you type your password and click *OK,* a **dtterm** window appears on your Windows system that is a window into your UNIX

system. Figure 15-5 shows the **dtterm** window open on the Windows
system.

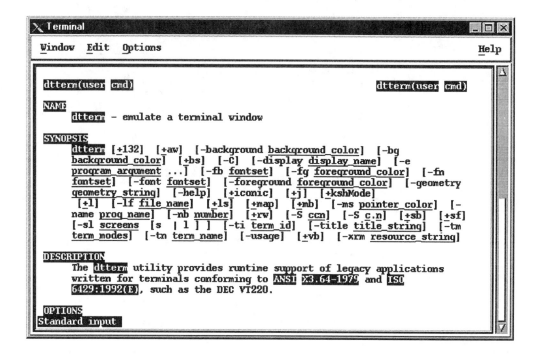

Figure 15-5 **dtterm** Running on UNIX and Displayed on Windows

Figure 15-5 is a **dtterm** window displayed on the Windows system but running on the UNIX system. The window currently has open
the HP-UX manual page for **dtterm**. You can issue any commands in
this **dtterm** window that you could issue if you were sitting on the
UNIX system directly. Keep in mind, though, that your access to the
UNIX system is based on the rights of the user you specified in the
Xstart window.

You can use *Xstart* to run any program for which you have
appropriate permissions on the UNIX system. Figure 15-6 shows an

xterm window that is displayed on the Windows system but is running on the UNIX system.

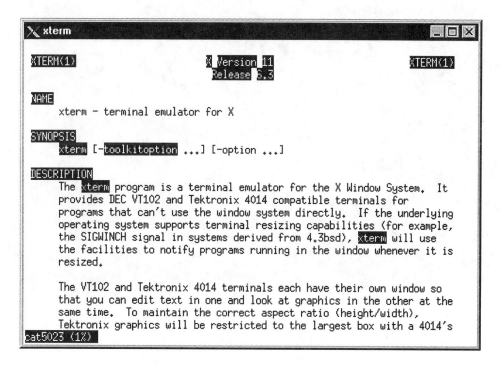

```
┌─────────────────────────────────────────────────────────────────────┐
│  ✕ xterm                                                  [─][□][✕]   │
│ ┌───────────────────────────────────────────────────────────────┐    │
│ │ XTERM(1)                    X Version 11              XTERM(1)  │    │
│ │                             Release 5.3                         │    │
│ │                                                                 │    │
│ │ NAME                                                            │    │
│ │       xterm - terminal emulator for X                           │    │
│ │                                                                 │    │
│ │ SYNOPSIS                                                        │    │
│ │       xterm [-toolkitoption ...] [-option ...]                  │    │
│ │                                                                 │    │
│ │ DESCRIPTION                                                     │    │
│ │       The xterm program is a terminal emulator for the X Window System.  It │
│ │       provides DEC VT102 and Tektronix 4014 compatible terminals for    │
│ │       programs that can't use the window system directly.  If the underlying │
│ │       operating system supports terminal resizing capabilities (for example, │
│ │       the SIGWINCH signal in systems derived from 4.3bsd), xterm will use │
│ │       the facilities to notify programs running in the window whenever it is │
│ │       resized.                                                  │    │
│ │                                                                 │    │
│ │       The VT102 and Tektronix 4014 terminals each have their own window so │
│ │       that you can edit text in one and look at graphics in the other at the │
│ │       same time.  To maintain the correct aspect ratio (height/width), │
│ │       Tektronix graphics will be restricted to the largest box with a 4014's │
│ │ cat5023 (1%)                                                    │    │
│ └───────────────────────────────────────────────────────────────┘    │
└─────────────────────────────────────────────────────────────────────┘
```

Figure 15-6 **xterm** Running on UNIX and Displayed on Windows

You are by no means limited to running only terminal windows such as **dtterm** and **xterm** under X Windows in this environment. You can invoke your commonly used applications or perform system management functions as well. Figure 15-7 shows the System Administration Manager (SAM), which is the primary system administration tool on HP-UX, running on the UNIX system and displayed on the Windows system with *Kernel Configuration* selected.

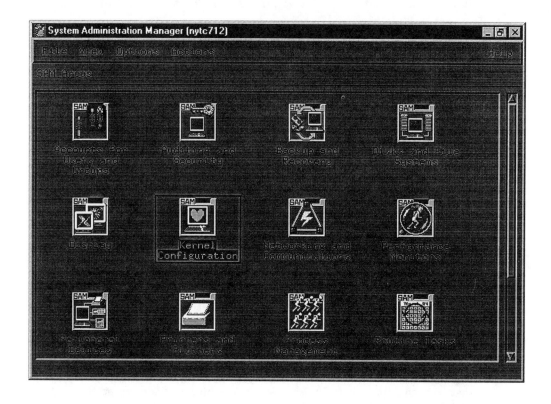

Figure 15-7 SAM Running on HP-UX and Displayed on Windows

You have no reason, however, to limit your use of Exceed to opening single windows or single applications. Exceed can also be used to run the Common Desktop Environment (CDE) used on most UNIX operating systems. CDE is a windowing environment that allows you to open several "desktops," which results in many windows.

By modifying a few parameters in Exceed, you can specify that the entire CDE environment run on your Windows system. CDE allows you to have multiple workspaces in with which you can organize the functional tasks you are performing. Figure 15-8 shows CDE running on our Windows system with the first of the workspaces selected called *program.*

Figure 15-8 CDE *program* Workspace

program is the first of the four workspaces shown on the bottom middle of Figure 15-8. There are three other workspaces for this user that we will view labeled *sam, files,* and *icon.*

Figure 15-9 shows the *sam* workspace in which we have invoked the System Administration Manager.

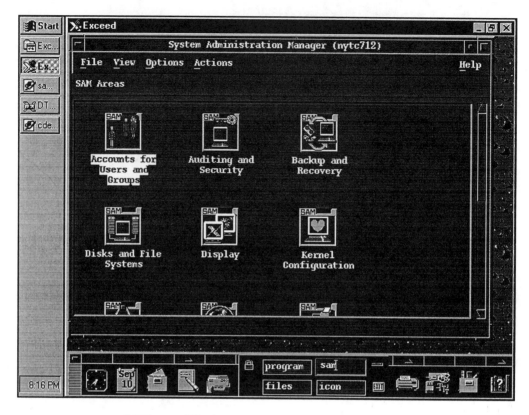

Figure 15-9 CDE *sam* Workspace

Figure 15-10 shows the *files* workspace in which we have invoked the File Manager from CDE.

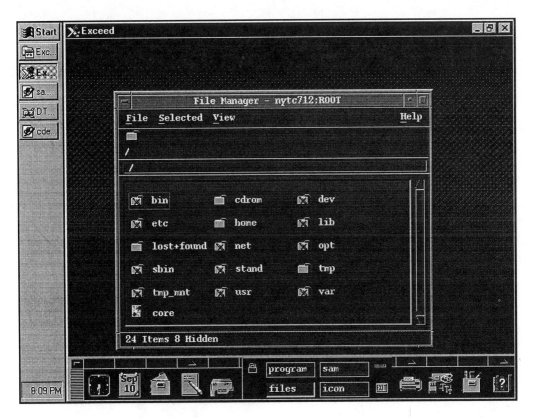

Figure 15-10 CDE *files* Workspace

Figure 15-11 shows the *icon* workspace in which we have invoked the icon editor.

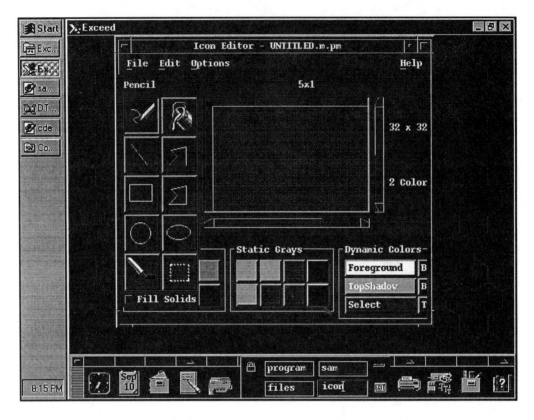

Figure 15-11 CDE *icon* Workspace

This technique, using X Windows on the Windows system to display applications running on the UNIX system, is powerful in this heterogeneous environment. It is also inexpensive and simple to install. You have a choice using Exceed to either open individual UNIX windows while working on your Windows system or run the entire Common Desktop Environment from your Windows system. I find that users who spend a majority of their time working on the UNIX system, such as UNIX developers, like to run the entire Common Desktop Environment on their Windows system. Users who spend a majority of time on their Windows systems and need only occasional access to UNIX usually open a **dtterm** or **xterm** window from the Windows system. Exceed gives you the flexibility to access UNIX from Windows using either technique.

We can also take this interoperability one step further by introducing data sharing into this mixed environment. Just as X Windows on UNIX and the Windows user interface are not compatible, the ways in which data is shared in UNIX and Windows environments are different. Chapter 16 covers a way in which data sharing between UNIX and Windows takes place.

CHAPTER 16

Networking

Why Cover Interoperability?

Although system administration topics are pretty much the same going from operating system to operating system, the peculiarities of each operating system define how you perform a given function. For this reason, system administration is seldom covered as a general topic; rather, it is covered for a particular operating system. In this book, however, the assumption is that you have both Windows and UNIX in your environment. You need to manage both and manage them separately for the most part; however, advantages to implementing technology exist that can enhance interoperability between the two operating systems.

What I cover in the interoperability chapters of this book (Chapters 15 through 20) are some of the most basic, and at the same time some of the most useful, technologies you can put in place to help with interoperability between Windows and UNIX.

You could certainly go beyond the interoperability topics I cover to much more advanced functionality; however, what I cover in the interoperability chapters is a big interoperability gain for very little cost and effort.

This chapter and Chapter 15 combine to provide background of some useful interoperability. In this chapter, I use a networking product on the Windows system that provides transparent access to the data on the UNIX system using Network File System (NFS). In Chapter 15, I covered Windows and UNIX interoperability by running an X server program on a Windows system, providing graphical access to a UNIX system. Using the X Window System (X Windows), you have a graphical means of connecting a Windows system to a UNIX system, and using NFS, you have a way of easily sharing data between these two systems. These two technologies, X Windows and NFS, provide the foundation for a variety of other useful interoperability between the two operating systems.

Although I provide TCP/IP background earlier in the book, I am going to include it again here so that you don't have to flip back and forth if you have to review TCP/IP.

TCP/IP Networking Background

You can see the seven layers of network functionality in the ISO/OSI model shown in Figure 16-1. I'll cover these layers at a cursory level, so that you have some background into this networking model. The top layers are the ones that you spend time working with, because they are closest to the functionality to which you can relate. The bottom layers are, however, also important to understand at some level, so that you can perform any configuration necessary to improve the network performance of your system and have a major impact on the overall performance of your system.

Layer Number	Layer Name	Data Form	Comments
7	Application		User applications here.
6	Presentation		Applications prepared.
5	Session		Applications prepared.

Layer Number	Layer Name	Data Form	Comments
4	Transport	Packet	Port-to-port transportation handled by TCP.
3	Network	Datagram	Internet Protocol (IP) handles routing by going directly to the destination or default router.
2	Link	Frame	Data encapsulated in Ethernet or IEEE 802.3 with source and destination addresses.
1	Physical		Physical connection between systems. Usually thinnet or twisted pair.

Figure 16-1 ISO/OSI Network Layer Functions

I'll start reviewing Figure 16-1 at the bottom, with layer 1, and describe each of the four bottom layers. This model is the International Standards Organization Open Systems Interconnection (ISO/ OSI) model. It is helpful to visualize the way in which networking layers interact.

Physical Layer

The beginning is the physical interconnect between the systems on your network. Without the **physical layer**, you can't communicate between systems, and all the great functionality you would like to implement will not be possible. The physical layer converts the data you would like to transmit to the analog signals that travel along the wire (I'll assume for now that whatever physical layer you have in place uses wires). The information traveling into a network interface is taken off the wire and prepared for use by the next layer.

Link Layer

In order to connect to other systems local to your system, you use the link layer that is able to establish a connection to all the other systems on your local segment. This is the layer where you have either IEEE 802.3 or Ethernet. These are "encapsulation" methods, named so because your data is put in one of these two forms (either IEEE 802.3 or Ethernet). Data is transferred at the link layer in frames (just another name for data), with the source and destination addresses and some other information attached. You might think that because there are two different encapsulation methods they must be much different. This conclusion, however, is not the case. IEEE 802.3 and Ethernet are nearly identical. So with the bottom two layers, you have a physical connection between your systems and data that is encapsulated into one of two formats with a source and destination address attached. Figure 16-2 lists the components of an *Ethernet* encapsulation and includes comments about IEEE802.3 encapsulation where appropriate.

destination address	6 bytes	address to which data is sent
source address	6 bytes	address from which data is sent
type	2 bytes	the "length count" in 802.3
data	46-1500 bytes	38-1492 bytes for 802.3
crc	4 bytes	checksum to detect errors

Figure 16-2 Ethernet Encapsulation

One interesting item to note is the difference in the maximum data size between IEEE 802.3 and Ethernet of 1492 and 1500 bytes, respectively. This is the Maximum Transfer Unit (MTU). The data in

Ethernet is called a *frame* (the re-encapsulation of data at the next layer up is called a *datagram* in IP, and encapsulation at two levels up is called a *packet* for TCP.)

Keep in mind that Ethernet and IEEE 802.3 can run on the same physical connection, but there are indeed differences between the two encapsulation methods.

Network Layer

Next we work up to the third layer, which is the network layer. This layer is synonymous with Internet Protocol (IP). Data at this layer is called a *datagram*. This is the layer that handles the routing of data around the network. Data that gets routed with IP sometimes encounters an error of some type, which is reported back to the source system with an Internet Control Message Protocol (ICMP) message.

Unfortunately, the information that IP uses does not conveniently fit inside an Ethernet frame, so you end up with fragmented data. This is really re-encapsulation of the data, so you end up with a lot of inefficiency as you work your way up the layers.

IP handles routing in a simple fashion. If data is sent to a destination connected directly to your system, then the data is sent directly to that system. If, on the other hand, the destination is not connected directly to your system, the data is sent to the default router. The default router, sometimes called a gateway, then has the responsibility to handle getting the data to its destination.

Transport Layer

This layer can be viewed as one level up from the network layer, because it communicates with *ports*. TCP is the most common protocol found at this level, and it forms packets that are sent from port to port. These ports are used by network programs such as **telnet, rlogin, ftp,** and so on. You can see that these programs, associated with ports, are the highest level I have covered while analyzing the layer diagram.

Internet Protocol (IP) Addressing

The Internet Protocol address (IP address) is a class "A," "B," or "C" address (class "D" and "E" addresses exist that I will not cover). A class "A" network supports many more nodes per network than a class "B" or "C" network. IP addresses consist of four fields. The purpose of breaking down the IP address into four fields is to define a node (or host) address and a network address. Figure 16-3 summarizes the relationships between the classes and addresses.

Address Class	Networks	Nodes per Network	Bits Defining Network	Bits Defining Nodes per Network
A	a few	the most	8 bits	24 bits
B	many	many	16 bits	16 bits
C	the most	a few	24 bits	8 bits
Reserved	-	-	-	-

Figure 16-3 Comparison of Internet Protocol (IP) Addresses

These bit patterns are significant in that the number of bits defines the ranges of networks and nodes in each class. For instance, a class A address uses 8 bits to define networks, and a class C address uses 24 bits to define networks. A class A address therefore supports fewer networks than a class C address. A class A address, however, supports many more nodes per network than a class C address. Taking these relationships one step further, we can now view the specific parameters associated with these address classes in Figure 16-4.

Figure 16-4 Address Classes

Address Class	Networks Supported	Nodes per Network	Address Range		
A	127	16777215	0.0.0.1	-	127.255.255.254
B	16383	65535	128.0.0.1	-	191.255.255.254
C	2097157	255	192.0.0.1	-	223.255.254.254
Reserved	-	-	224.0.0.0	-	255.255.255.255

Looking at the 32-bit address in binary form, you can see how to determine the class of an address:

Class "A"

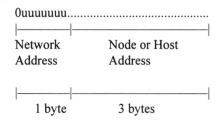

net.host.host.host

A class "A" address has the first bit set to 0. You can see how so many nodes per network can be supported with all the bits devoted to the node or host address. The first bit of a class A address is 0, and the remaining 7 bits of the network portion are used to define the network. There are then a total of 3 bytes devoted to defining the nodes within a network.

Figure 16-4 Address Classes (Continued)

Class "B"

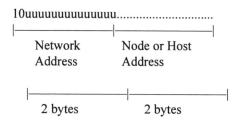

net.net.host.host

A class "B" address has the first bit set to a 1 and the second bit to a 0. There are more networks supported here than with a class A address, but fewer nodes per network. With a class B address, there are 2 bytes devoted to the network portion of the address and 2 bytes are devoted to the node portion of the address.

Class "C"

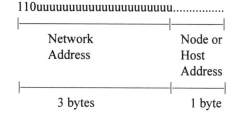

net.net.net.host

A class "C" address has the first bit and second bit set to 1, and the third bit is 0. The greatest number of networks and fewest number of nodes per network are associated with a class C address. With a class C address, there are 3 bytes devoted to the network and 1 byte is devoted to the nodes within a network.

Every interface on your network must have a unique IP address. Systems that have two network interfaces must have two unique IP addresses. I will cover some networking commands in Windows in an upcoming chapter.

NFS Background

I am not going to limit the discussion and examples in this chapter to NFS. There are other services used to share files that are also useful, such as File Transfer Protocol (FTP) which I'll show examples of as well. Because NFS is so widely used in the UNIX user community, it is one of my goals to expose you to how NFS can be used in a Windows and UNIX environment.

NFS allows you to mount disks on remote systems so that they appear as though they are local to your system. Similarly, NFS allows remote systems to mount your local disk so that it looks as though it is local to the remote system.

NFS, like X Windows, has a unique set of terminology. Here are definitions of some of the more important NFS terms:

Node   A computer system that is attached to or is part of a computer network.

Client   A node that requests data or services from other nodes (servers).

Server   A node that provides data or services to other nodes (clients) on the network.

File System	A disk partition or logical volume, or in the case of a workstation, this might be the entire disk.
Export	To make a file system available for mounting on remote nodes using NFS.
Mount	To access a remote file system using NFS.
Mount Point	The name of a directory on which the NFS file system is mounted.
Import	To mount a remote file system.

Before any data can be shared using NFS, the UNIX system must be set up with exported file systems. The **/etc/exports** file is often used on UNIX to define what file systems are exported.

This file has in it the directories exported and options such as "ro" for read only and "anon," which handles requests from anonymous users. If "anon" is equal to 65535, then anonymous users are denied access.

The following is an example **/etc/exports** file in which **/opt/app1** is exported to everyone but anonymous users, and **/opt/app1** is exported only to the system named system2:

```
/opt/app1    -anon=65534
/opt/app2    -access=system2
```

You may need to run a program such as **exportfs** **-a** on your UNIX system if you add a file system to export.

Although we are going to focus on exporting UNIX file systems to be mounted by Windows systems in this chapter, I can think of no reason that we could not do the converse as well. Windows file systems can be mounted on a UNIX system just as UNIX file systems are mounted in Windows. Remote file systems to be mounted locally on a UNIX system are often put in **/etc/fstab**. Here is an example of an entry in **/etc/fstab** of a remote file system that is mounted locally. The remote directory **/opt/app3** on system2 is mounted locally under **/opt/ opt3**:

system2:/opt/app3   /opt/app3   nfs   rw,suid   0   0

You can use the **showmount** command available on many UNIX systems to show all remote systems (clients) that have mounted a local file system. **showmount** is useful for determining the file systems that are most often mounted by clients with NFS. The output of **showmount** is particularly easy to read because it lists the host name and the directory that was mounted by the client. You have the three following options to the **showmount** command:

-a prints output in the format "name:directory," as shown above.

-d lists all the local directories that have been remotely mounted by clients.

-e prints a list of exported file systems.

Using Windows and UNIX Networking

I use the NFS Maestro product from Hummingbird Communications Ltd. on Windows to demonstrate the networking interoperability in this chapter.

You would typically run your NFS client, such as NFS Maestro, on your Windows system in order to mount file systems on a UNIX system. This setup means that all your Windows clients would run NFS Maestro. Depending on the number of Windows systems you have, you may find loading an NFS client on each and every system to be a daunting task. Hummingbird Communications has an alternative. Rather than loading the NFS client on each system, you can use a Windows system to act as a gateway between your Windows systems and your UNIX systems. NFS Maestro Gateway bridges your Windows network to your UNIX network. All Windows clients go through the NFS Maestro Gateway system in order to perform NFS access to the UNIX systems, thereby simplifying the installation and administration of NFS on Windows.

NFS Maestro Gateway bridges your Microsoft Server Message Block (SMB) network to your UNIX network by acting as a proxy. It forwards SMB requests from a Windows client to a UNIX NFS server and vice-versa.

The performance of using a dedicated NFS Maestro client is superior to that of using NFS Maestro Gateway. Like many system administration topics, there is a trade-off takes place between simplicity and performance. In this chapter I'll cover using a dedicated NFS Maestro client to access file systems on a UNIX server.

Figure 16-5 shows the menu for the Maestro product after I installed it.

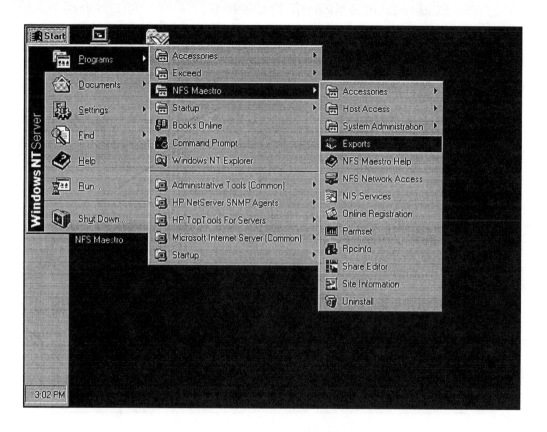

Figure 16-5 Hummingbird Maestro Menu in Windows

As you can see in Figure 16-5, there is much more than NFS functionality is part of NFS Maestro. I will cover some additional functionality later in this chapter; however, my specific objectives are to cover the most important Windows and UNIX interoperability topics related to networking.

The NFS icons can also be accessed as part of a group from the *NFS Maestro* icon, as shown in Figure 16-6.

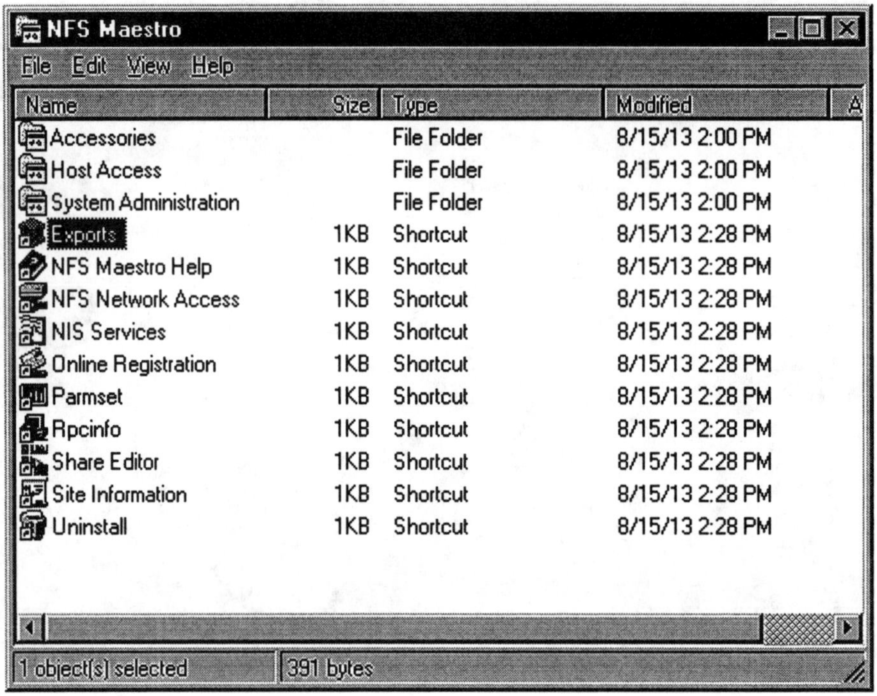

Name	Size	Type	Modified	A
Accessories		File Folder	8/15/13 2:00 PM	
Host Access		File Folder	8/15/13 2:00 PM	
System Administration		File Folder	8/15/13 2:00 PM	
Exports	1KB	Shortcut	8/15/13 2:28 PM	
NFS Maestro Help	1KB	Shortcut	8/15/13 2:28 PM	
NFS Network Access	1KB	Shortcut	8/15/13 2:28 PM	
NIS Services	1KB	Shortcut	8/15/13 2:28 PM	
Online Registration	1KB	Shortcut	8/15/13 2:28 PM	
Parmset	1KB	Shortcut	8/15/13 2:28 PM	
Rpcinfo	1KB	Shortcut	8/15/13 2:28 PM	
Share Editor	1KB	Shortcut	8/15/13 2:28 PM	
Site Information	1KB	Shortcut	8/15/13 2:28 PM	
Uninstall	1KB	Shortcut	8/15/13 2:28 PM	

Figure 16-6 *NFS* Group

Before we use NFS with our Windows and UNIX systems, let's first see what file systems we have available to us.

Using the Common Desktop Environment (CDE) on our Windows system from Chapter 15, we can sit at the Windows system and work on the UNIX system. Figure 16-7 shows the Common Desktop Environment with a *Terminal* window open.

Figure 16-7 Common Desktop Environment on UNIX with **/etc/ exports** Shown

There are several file systems exported on this UNIX system. Some, such as **/home** and **/tmp,** have no restrictions on them; others do have restrictions. We don't, however, have to open a *Terminal* in order to see this file. We can use the NFS Maestro menu pick *Exports* to bring up the window shown in Figure 16-8.

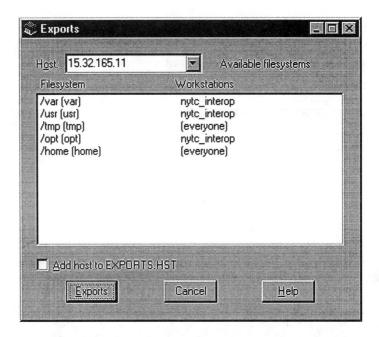

Figure 16-8 *Exports* Window Showing Exported File Systems

You can use the IP address, as shown in Figure 16-8, or the host name to specify the host on which you wish to view the exported file systems. You can see that this window takes the **/etc/exports** file and clarifies some of the entries. The entries that have no restrictions now have an "(everyone)" associated with them, and only system *nytc_interop* may mount the other file systems.

Now we can specify one or more of these exported file systems on the UNIX system that we wish to mount on the Windows system. Using the *NFS Network Access* from the NFS Maestro menu, we can specify one of these file systems to mount. Figure 16-9 shows mounting **/home/hp** on the UNIX system on the **F:** drive of the Windows system. Note that we are UNIX user *hp* when we mount this file system.

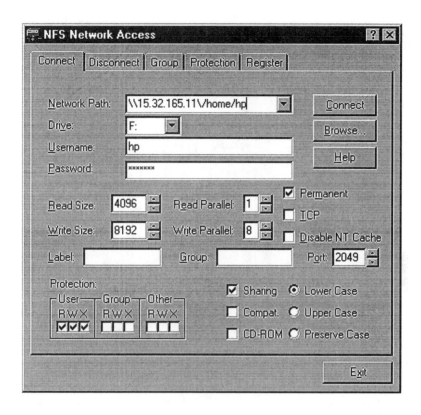

Figure 16-9 *NFS Network Access* Window Mounting **/home/hp** as **F:**

After you click the *Connect* button in the window, you have
/home/hp mounted as **F:**. The means by which you specify the system
and file system you wish to mount with NFS Maestro is two slashes
preceding the IP address or system name, another slash following the
IP address or system name, and then the name of the file system you
wish to mount. Note that the forward slash is part of the file system
name. I used the IP address of the system. To view all the mounted
file systems on the Windows system, you can invoke Windows
Explorer. Figure 16-10 shows several file systems mounted in an
Explorer window, including **/home/hp** on **F:**.

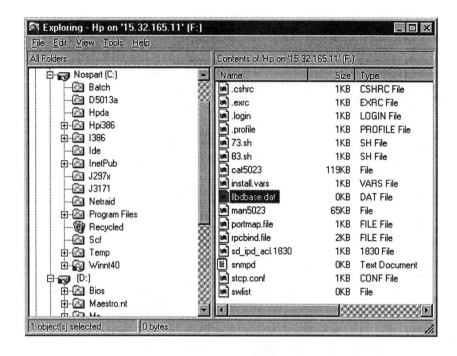

Figure 16-10 Windows *Explorer* Showing **/home/hp** as **F:**

This window shows **/home/hp** on drive **F:**. On the right side of
the window is a listing of files in **/home/hp** on the UNIX system.
These files are now fully accessible on the Windows system (provided
that the appropriate access rights have been provided). You may need
to adjust the *Explorer* to *Show all files* in order to see the hidden
UNIX files. You can now manipulate these UNIX files in *Explorer* on
the Windows system just as if they were local to the system. This is a
powerful concept - to go beyond the barrier of only the Windows file
system to freely manipulate UNIX files.

The permissions of these NFS mounted files are not shown in the
Explorer window. We can select specific files and view their properties. Figure 16-11 shows viewing the **.cshrc** file.

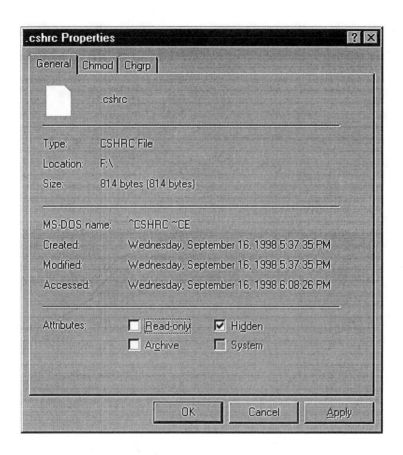

Figure 16-11 Viewing the Properties of **.cshrc**

The **.cshrc** file is *Hidden* and is not *Read-only*, meaning that we can manipulate this file.

Next let's view the properties of **install.vars**, as shown in Figure 16-12.

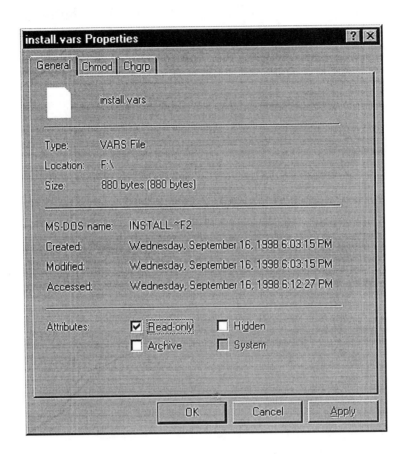

Figure 16-12 Viewing the Properties of **install.vars**

install.vars is *Read-only* because this file is owned by *root* on the UNIX system and not by user *hp*, which is the UNIX user under which we mounted **/home/hp**.

We are unable to *Chmod*, or modify the permissions on this file, because it is owned by root and we have mounted **/home/hp** as the user *hp*, as shown in Figure 16-13.

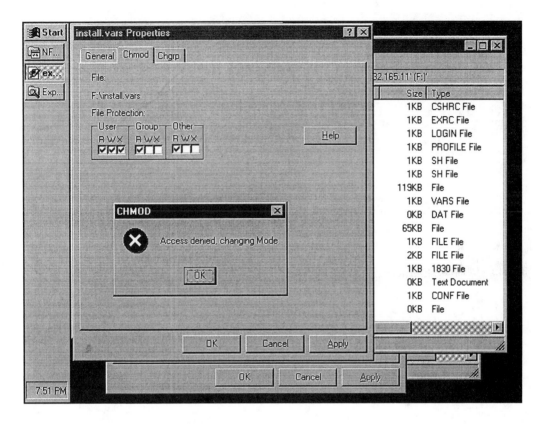

Figure 16-13   Failed Attempt to Change Permissions of **install.vars**

This error indicates that we are prevented from changing the permissions on **install.vars**.

An example of how you might go about using *Explorer* is to copy a Windows NT directory to UNIX. Figure 16-14 shows two *Explorer* windows. The top window has an **nfs** directory on the Windows system, which is being copied to a directory of the same name on the UNIX system in the bottom window. As the copy from the Windows system to the UNIX system takes place, a status window

appears, which shows the name of the file within the **nfs** directory
(**exp2.bmp**) being copied.

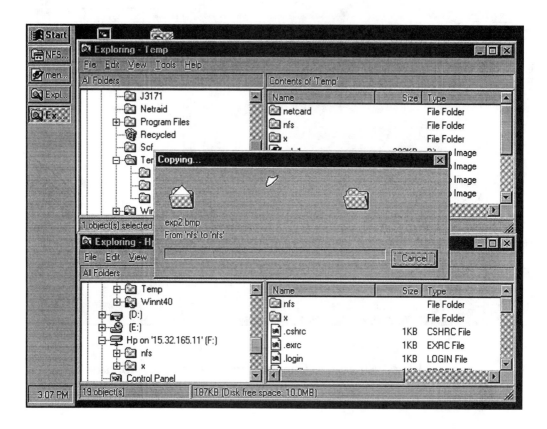

Figure 16-14 Copying a Windows NT Directory to UNIX Using
Explorer

This copy from Windows to UNIX using *Explorer* demonstrates
the ease with which files can be shared between these two operating
systems.

File Transfer Protocol (FTP)

I started this chapter covering NFS on Windows and UNIX for interoperability, because NFS is the predominant means of sharing files in the UNIX world. NFS is used almost universally to share data among networked UNIX systems. NFS allows you to share data in real time, meaning that you can work on a UNIX file while sitting at your Windows system. This approach is file sharing. You can also copy data between your Windows and UNIX systems using FTP. This approach is not file sharing; however, the FTP functionality of NFS Maestro makes it easy to transfer files between Windows and UNIX.

Figure 16-15 shows the dialog box that you would use to establish a connection to a UNIX system from Windows.

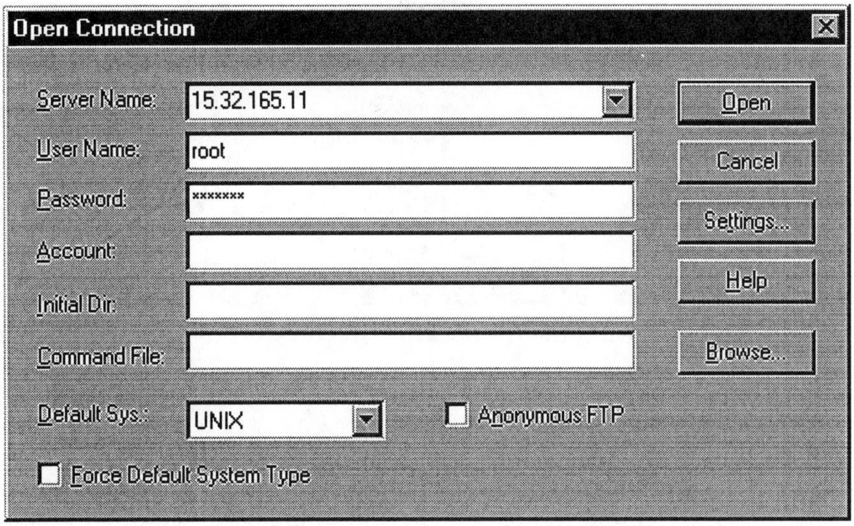

Figure 16-15 Establishing a Connection to UNIX from Windows

After having established the connection, a window appears in which you can traverse the UNIX file systems while working at your Windows system. Figure 16-16 shows viewing the **/home/hp** directory on a UNIX system through the *FTP* window.

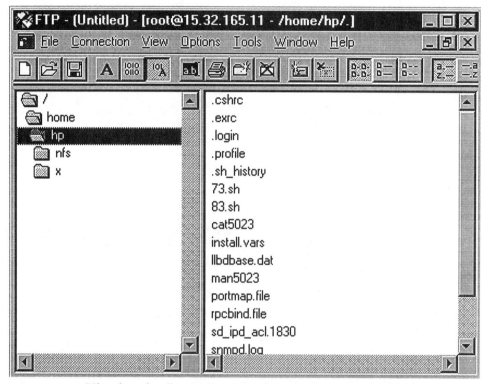

Figure 16-16 Viewing the **/home/hp** Directory Using the *FTP* Window

You can also copy files graphically using FTP. You can open two *FTP* windows and copy files and directories from one system to the other. Figure 16-17 shows copying the directory **c:\temp\x** on the Windows system to **/home/hp/x** on the UNIX system. This was performed using the icons in the two windows. The **x** directory did not exist on the UNIX system and was created as part of the copy. As the copy from the Windows system to the UNIX system takes place, a status window appears, which shows the name of the file within the **x** directory (**xmenu2.bmp**) being copied.

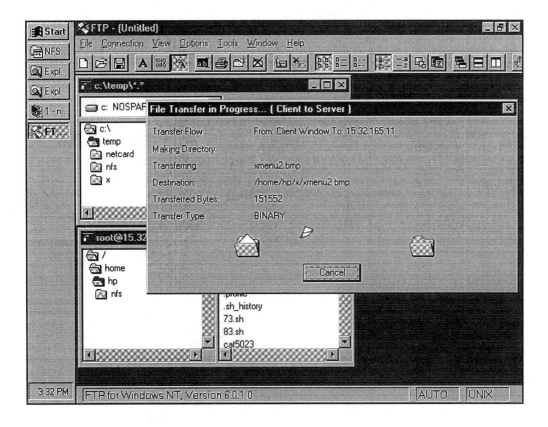

Figure 16-17 Using FTP to Copy a Directory from Windows to UNIX

There are a variety of options you can select when running FTP. Notice in Figure 16-17 that the "Transfer Type:" is binary. This is one of the options I selected prior to initiating the transfer.

Although this functionality is not as extensive as the file sharing of NFS, it is widely used to copy files from system to system and therefore can play a role in Windows and UNIX interoperability.

I used icons to specify the information to be copied in this example. You could also have used the FTP command. The following is an overview of FTP, including an example of running it from the command line and a command summary.

File Transfer Protocol (FTP)   Transfer a file, or multiple files, from one system to another, such as Windows to UNIX. The following example shows copying the file **/tmp/krsort.c** from system2 (remote host) to the local directory on system1 (local host).

	comments
$ ftp system2	Issue ftp command
Connected to system2.	
system2 FTP server (Version 16.2) ready.	
Name (system2:root): root	Log in to system2
Password required for root.	
Password:	Enter password
User root logged in.	
Remote system type is UNIX.	
Using binary mode to transfer files.	
ftp> **cd /tmp**	**cd** to **/tmp** on system2
CWD command successful	
ftp> **get krsort.c**	Get **krsort.c** file
PORT command successful	
Opening BINARY mode data connection for **krsort.c**	
Transfer complete.	
2896 bytes received in 0.08 seconds	

	comments
ftp> **bye**	Exit ftp
Goodbye.	
$	

In this example, both systems are running UNIX; however, the commands you issue through **FTP** are operating-system-independent. The **cd** for change directory and **get** commands used above work for any operating system on which **FTP** is running. If you become familiar with just a few **FTP** commands, you may find that transferring information in a heterogeneous networking environment is not difficult.

Because **FTP** is so widely used, I describe some of the more commonly used **FTP** commands.

ftp - File Transfer Protocol for copying files across a network.

The following list includes some commonly used **ftp** commands. This list is not complete.

ascii   Set the type of file transferred to ASCII. This means that you will be transferring an ASCII file from one system to another. This is the default, so you don't have to set it.

Example: **ascii**

binary   Set the type of file transferred to binary. This means that you'll be transferring a binary file from one system to another. If, for instance, you want to have a directory on your UNIX system that will hold applications that you will copy to non-UNIX systems, then you will want to use binary transfer.

Example: **binary**

cd   Change to the specified directory on the remote host.

Example: **cd /tmp**

dir   List the contents of a directory on the remote system to the screen or to a file on the local system if you specify a local file name.

get   Copy the specified remote file to the specified local file. If you don't specify a local file name, then the remote file name is used.

lcd   Change to the specified directory on the local host.

Example: **lcd /tmp**

ls   List the contents of a directory on the remote system to the screen or to a file on the local system if you specify a local file name.

mget   Copy multiple files from the remote host to the local host.

Example: **mget *.c**

       put   Copy the specified local file to the specified remote file. If you don't specify a remote file name, then the local file name is used.

Example: **put test.c**

      mput   Copy multiple files from the local host to the remote host.

Example: **mput *.c**

    system   Show the type of operating system running on the remote host.

Example: **system**

  bye/quit   Close the connection to the remote host.

Example: **bye**

FTP commands exist in addition to those I have covered here.

Other Connection Topics

There are other means by which you can connect to the UNIX system. Two popular techniques for connecting to other systems are FTP, which was just covered, and TELNET. NFS Maestro supplies the capability for both of these. I could sit at the Windows system using TELNET with a window open on the UNIX system and issue commands.

Figure 16-18 shows the *HostExplorer* window used to specify the characteristics of your TELNET session.

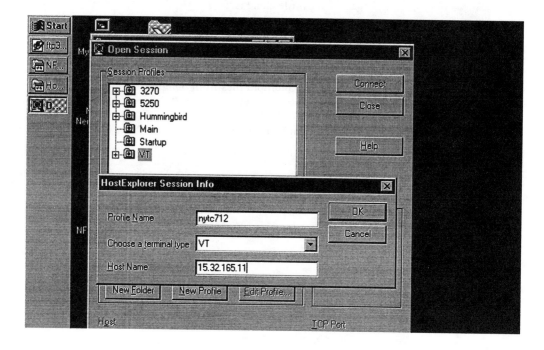

Figure 16-18 Specifying Characteristics of a *HostExplorer* Session

I selected *VT* in the *HostExplorer* window and was able to log in to the UNIX system, as shown in Figure 16-19.

```
1 - hp (15.32.165.11)
File  Edit  Transfer  Fonts  Options  Macro  View  Window  Help

$ ll -a
total 398
drwxr-xr-x   3 hp      users        1024 Sep 16 18:25 .
drwxr-xr-x   4 root    root           96 Sep 16 17:37 ..
-rw-r--r--   1 hp      users         814 Sep 16 17:37 .cshrc
-rw-r--r--   1 hp      users         347 Sep 16 17:37 .exrc
-rw-r--r--   1 hp      users         341 Sep 16 17:37 .login
-rw-r--r--   1 hp      users         446 Sep 16 17:37 .profile
-rw-------   1 hp      users          14 Sep 16 18:25 .sh_history
-rw-r--r--   1 root    sys            23 Sep 16 18:03 73.sh
-rw-r--r--   1 root    sys            23 Sep 16 18:03 83.sh
-rw-rw-rw-   1 root    sys        120922 Sep 16 18:03 cat5023
-rw-r--r--   1 root    sys           880 Sep 16 18:03 install.vars
-r--r--r--   1 root    sys             0 Sep 16 18:03 llbdbase.dat
-rw-rw-rw-   1 root    sys         66113 Sep 16 18:03 man5023
drwx------   2 hp      users        1024 Sep 16 18:17 nfs
-rw-------   1 root    sys           484 Sep 16 18:03 portmap.file
-rw-------   1 root    sys          1692 Sep 16 18:03 rpcbind.file
-rw-r--r--   1 root    sys            74 Sep 16 18:03 sd_ipd_acl.183
-rwxrwxrwx   1 root    sys             0 Sep 16 18:03 snmpd.log
-rw-r--r--   1 root    sys            60 Sep 16 18:03 stcp.conf
-rw-r--r--   1 root    sys             0 Sep 16 18:03 swlist
$
```

Figure 16-19 telnet Window

In this window, we can issue UNIX commands just as if we were sitting at a terminal connected directly to the UNIX system. This window shows **/home/hp**, including the **nfs** directory copied earlier, and permissions, owner, and group of all files and directories.

telnet is widely used in heterogenous environments. With X Windows, you get graphical functionality that is not part of telnet.

The protocols running on the UNIX system are assigned to ports. We can view these ports, protocols, and associated information, using the **rpcinfo** command on the UNIX system, as shown in Figure 16-20.

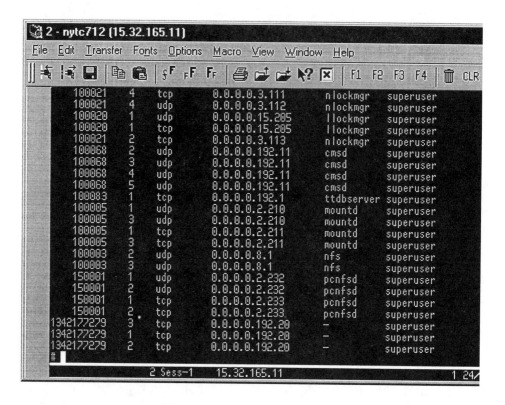

Figure 16-20   **rpcinfo** Command on UNIX

There is a lot of information in this window in which we are interested related to NFS. We do not, however, have to establish a telnet sessionwith the UNIX system and issue **rpcinfo** to see this information. The *Rpcinfo* menu pick under Maestro will query the UNIX host and list the services it is running. Figure 16-21 shows this window.

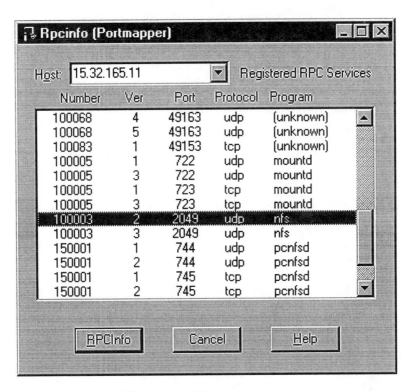

Figure 16-21 *Rpcinfo* Window on Windows

RPC stands for Remote Procedure Call. There are a variety of programs for which there is RPC-related information. Several programs are required to achieve the Windows and UNIX interoperability.

The first number shown is the program number. There are widely accepted RPC numbers for various programs. For NFS, the program number is 100003. The next number is the version of the protocol. In this case, NFS is version 2. The next number is the port. The port number is used by both the client, which is the Windows system in our case, and the server, which is the UNIX system in our case, to communicate using NFS. The next field is the protocol used, which is usually UDP or TCP. The final field is the program name.

In the case of NFS, I had to ensure that NFS, portmapper, mountd, and pcnfsd were running on my UNIX system before I could use the NFS Maestro NFS product.

Rpcinfo is a useful tool for viewing all the information on the host to which your Windows system will connect.

CHAPTER 17

Advanced Server for UNIX

Windows Functionality on UNIX

To this point, we have been discussing moving UNIX functionality such as X Windows and NFS onto Windows in order to achieve interoperability. Why not do the converse? Having some Windows functionality on UNIX would certainly be helpful in some cases. UNIX resources such as printers and disks could then be shared with several Windows systems on the network.

Advanced Server for UNIX® is an AT&T product that serves as the basis for many products that bring Windows functionality to UNIX. Advanced Server for UNIX Systems is the result of a joint development agreement between AT&T and Microsoft Corporation. It provides Windows functionality that facilitates Windows and UNIX interoperability. With Advanced Server for UNIX, a UNIX system can act as a Primary or Backup Domain Controller, a file server, a print server, or other Windows functional component. Most major UNIX vendors have a product that is based on Advanced Server for UNIX. This chapter will use the HP-UX implementation of Advanced Server for UNIX called Advanced Server/9000. Other implementations of Advanced Server for UNIX are similar, so you can use the examples in this chapter as a basis of understanding for other such implementations.

This chapter makes use of some of the **net** commands of Windows, especially the **net share** command. When I am working on the UNIX system (*dloaner*) in this chapter, I use the command line including some **net** commands. When I am working on the Windows system (*hpsystem1*) in this chapter, I will use graphical Windows functionality, which is preferable to issuing commands on the command line. I use both the command line and graphical methods so that you can see the difference in the two approaches. You may want to explore some of these **net** commands described in the "Command Line" chapter (Chapter 19) and using the online help of your Windows system as you progress through this chapter. Here is a list of some widely used **net** commands and a brief explanation of each:

net accounts   Used to maintain the user accounts database.

net computer   Used to add or delete computers from the domain database.

net config server

                       Displays or changes settings for a server service on which the command is executed.

net config workstation

                       Displays or changes settings for the workstation service on which the command is executed.

net continue   Reactivates a Windows service that has been suspended with the **net pause** command.

net file	Used for network file manipulation, such as listing ID numbers, closing a shared file, removing file locks, and so on.
net group	Used to add, display, or modify global groups on servers.
net help	Displays a listing of help options for any net commands.
net helpmsg	Displays explanations of Windows network messages such as errors, warnings, and alerts.
net localgroup	Used to modify local groups on computers.
net name	Used to add or delete a "messaging name" at a computer, which is the name to which messages are sent.
net print	Used to list print jobs and shared queues.
net send	Sends messages to other users, computers, and "messaging names" on the network.
net session	Used to list or disconnect sessions between the computer and other computers on the network.

net share   Shares a server's resources with other com-
                       puters on the network.

net start   Used to start services such as *server*.

net statistics   Displays the statistics log for the local Work-
                       station or Server service.

net stop   Used to stop services such as *server*.

net time   Synchronizes the computer's clock with
                       another computer on the domain.

net use   Displays, connects, or disconnects a com-
                       puter with shared resources.

net user   Creates or modifies user accounts.

net view   Lists resources being shared on a computer.

Installing Advanced Server/9000 on UNIX

You can easily install and configure Advanced Server/9000 on your
UNIX system. Advanced Server/9000 is installed using Software Dis-
tributor on your HP-UX system, just as you would load any other software. After installing Advanced Server/9000, you run the

configuration script called **asu_inst**. The following text shows running **asu_inst** to configure the UNIX system *dloaner* to be a Backup Domain Controller (BDC) for the Windows system *hpsystem1*:

```
# /opt/asu/lanman/bin/asu_inst
```

This request script will prompt you for information which is necessary
to install and configure your Advanced Server for UNIX Systems.

There are two installation modes:

Express Setup - the installation scripts use default settings so
installation is quick and easy. You may change these settings
after installation completes. The server is installed as a
primary domain controller in its own domain.

Custom Setup - this mode allows you to specify the settings at the
beginning of installation. If you select this mode, you must
specify the server's name, the domain it will participate in,
and the role in that domain.

NOTE: The installation requires a password for the administrative account.
A default password of 'password' will be used, although you may elect to
be prompted for a different password at the end of the installation.

If you are installing many servers it is strongly recommended that you use
the default password for all installations. Be sure to change these
passwords after determining that your network is operating correctly.

Do you want Express Setup [y/n]? y

Advanced Server for UNIX provides a NETLOGON service which simplifies the
administration of multiple servers. A single user accounts database can be
shared by multiple servers grouped together into an administrative
collection called a domain. Within a domain, each server has a designated
role. A single server, called the primary domain controller, manages all
changes to the user accounts database and automatically distributes those
changes to other servers, called backup domain controllers, within the same
domain. You may now supply a server name (the name which this server
will be known on the network), the role that this server will perform
in that domain (primary or backup), and a domain name.

Enter the name of the server
or press Enter to select 'dloaner':

Each server must be given a role in a domain. The possible roles are:

primary domain controller:
     Administration server. Distributes user accounts information
             to backup domain controllers. Validates network logon requests.
     There can be only one primary domain controller per domain.

backup domain controller:
             Receives user account information from the primary domain
             controller. Validates network logon requests and can be promoted
     to primary if the primary domain controller is not accessible.

Enter role (primary or backup): backup

```
This installation will configure the server as a backup domain controller.
You will be prompted to enter the name of the primary domain controller,
and an administrative account name on the primary along with its password.
In order for this installation to complete successfully, the primary domain
controller must be running and connected to the network.

Enter the name of the primary domain controller (eg, abc_asu): hpsystem1

Confirm choices for server dloaner:
                           role   : backup
                           primary: hpsystem1
Is this correct [y/n]? y
_&a0y0C_J
Enter the name of an administrative account on the primary
domain controller 'hpsystem1' or press Enter to select 'administrator':

This procedure requires the password for the administrative account on
'hpsystem1'. If the password is the default ('password') created
during installation, you will not need to be prompted for a password.
If you have changed the password, you should allow this program  to prompt
for a password after the files have been installed.

Do you want to use the default password [y/n]? y

Advanced Server/9000
Copyright (c) 1988, 1991-1996 AT&T and Microsoft
Copyright (c) 1992-1996 Hewlett-Packard
All rights reserved

Adding Advanced Server for UNIX Systems administrative users and groups
Add
Comment <Advanced Server account>
Home Dir </opt/asu/lanman>
UID <100>
GID <99>
Shell </sbin/false>
Name <lanman>
pw_name: lanman
pw_passwd: *
pw_uid: 100
pw_gid: 99
pw_age: ?
pw_comment:
pw_gecos: Advanced Server account
pw_dir: /opt/asu/lanman
pw_shell: /sbin/false
enter addusr
pw_name = lanman
pw_passwd = *
pw_uid = 100
pw_gid = 99
pw_gecos = Advanced Server account
pw_dir = /opt/asu/lanman
pw_shell = /sbin/false
enter_quiet_zone()
exit_quiet_zone()
exiting addusr, error = 0
Add
Comment <Advanced Server Administrator>
Home Dir </var/opt/asu/lanman/lmxadmin>
GID <99>
Name <lmxadmin>
pw_name: lmxadmin
pw_passwd: *
pw_uid: 0
```

```
pw_gid: 99
pw_age: ?
pw_comment:
pw_gecos: Advanced Server Administrator
pw_dir: /var/opt/asu/lanman/lmxadmin
pw_shell:
enter addusr
pw_name = lmxadmin
pw_passwd = *
pw_uid = 0
pw_gid = 99
pw_gecos = Advanced Server Administrator
pw_dir = /var/opt/asu/lanman/lmxadmin
pw_shell =
enter_quiet_zone()
exit_quiet_zone()
exiting addusr, error = 0
Add
Comment <Advanced Server GUEST Login>
Shell </sbin/false>
GID <99>
Name <lmxguest>
pw_name: lmxguest
pw_passwd: *
pw_uid: 0
pw_gid: 99
pw_age: ?
pw_comment:
pw_gecos: Advanced Server GUEST Login
pw_dir:
pw_shell: /sbin/false
enter addusr
pw_name = lmxguest
pw_passwd = *
pw_uid = 0
pw_gid = 99
pw_gecos = Advanced Server GUEST Login
pw_dir = /usr/lmxguest
pw_shell = /sbin/false
enter_quiet_zone()
exit_quiet_zone()
exiting addusr, error = 0
Add
Comment <Advanced Server World Login>
Shell </sbin/false>
GID <99>
Name <lmworld>
pw_name: lmworld
pw_passwd: *
pw_uid: 0
pw_gid: 99
pw_age: ?
pw_comment:
pw_gecos: Advanced Server World Login
pw_dir:
pw_shell: /sbin/false
enter addusr
pw_name = lmworld
pw_passwd = *
pw_uid = 0
pw_gid = 99
pw_gecos = Advanced Server World Login
pw_dir = /usr/lmworld
pw_shell = /sbin/false
enter_quiet_zone()
exit_quiet_zone()
```

```
exiting addusr, error = 0

Creating Directory: /home/lanman
Setting owner, group, and permissions for installed files....

Enter the password for administrator on hpsystem1:
Re-enter password:

Contacting the server 'hpsystem1' ... Success

Creating Advanced Server for UNIX Systems accounts database.

Starting the Advanced Server for UNIX Systems...

The Advanced Server for UNIX Systems is now operational.
#
```

After the installation and configuration are complete, you have **netdemon** running, which is an essential component of Advanced Server/9000, as shown in the following **ps** command:

man page

ps - 12

```
# ps -ef | grep netdemon
    root  1100     1  0 10:18:38 ?          0:00 /opt/lmu/netbios/bin/netde-
mon
    #
```

In addition to **netdemon**, NetBIOS must also be running.

Advanced Server/9000 starts several processes on your UNIX system in addition to **netdemon**. You can also verify that the Advanced Server/9000 server is running by viewing its processes with the **ps** command:

```
# ps -ef | grep lm
    root  3285     1  0 10:37:19 ?      0:00 lmx.dmn
    root  3200     1  0 10:36:57 ?      0:00 lmx.ctrl
    root  3262  3200  0 10:37:07 ?      0:00 lmx.srv -s 1
    root  3295     1  0 10:37:20 ?      0:00 lmx.sched
    root  3289     1  0 10:37:19 ?      0:00 lmx.browser
    root  1100     1  0 10:18:38 ?      0:00 /opt/lmu/netbios/bin/netdemon
    #
```

Many process are shown here, such as *lmx.dmn,* which is the daemon; *lmx.ctrl,* which is the control process; *lmx.sched,* which is the scheduler; *lmx.browser* which is the browser; and *lmx.srv,* which is a client session. If Advanced Server/9000 is not running, you would use the **net start server** command to start the server. Similarly, you stop the server with **net stop server**.

In addition, you have several users and groups that have been created on your UNIX system to facilitate using Advanced Server/9000 with your Windows systems. The new users are shown in the upcoming **/etc/passwd** file, and the new groups are shown in the upcoming **/etc/group** file:

man page

cat - 3

```
# cat /etc/passwd
root:jThTuY9OhNxGY:0:3::/:/sbin/sh
daemon:*:1:5::/:/sbin/sh
bin:*:2:2::/usr/bin:/sbin/sh
sys:*:3:3::/:
adm:*:4:4::/var/adm:/sbin/sh
uucp:*:5:3::/var/spool/uucppublic:/usr/lbin/uucp/uucico
lp:*:9:7::/var/spool/lp:/sbin/sh
nuucp:*:11:11::/var/spool/uucppublic:/usr/lbin/uucp/uucico
hpdb:*:27:1:ALLBASE:/:/sbin/sh
nobody:*:-2:-2147483648::/:
lanman:*:100:99:Advanced Server account:/opt/asu/lanman:/sbin/false
lmxadmin:*:202:99:Advanced Server Administrator:/var/opt/asu/lanman/lmxadmin:
lmxguest:*:203:99:Advanced Server GUEST Login:/usr/lmxguest:/sbin/false
lmworld:*:204:99:Advanced Server World Login:/usr/lmworld:/sbin/false
# cat /etc/group
root::0:root
other::1:root,hpdb
bin::2:root,bin
sys::3:root,uucp
adm::4:root,adm
daemon::5:root,daemon
mail::6:root
lp::7:root,lp
tty::10:
nuucp::11:nuucp
users::20:root
nogroup:*:-2:
DOS----::99:lanman
DOS-a--::98:lanman
DOS--s-::97:lanman
DOS---h::96:lanman
DOS-as-::95:lanman
DOS-a-h::94:lanman
DOS--sh::93:lanman
DOS-ash::92:lanman
#
```

In addition to the UNIX system modifications that have automatically taken place, the Windows Primary Domain Controller (PDC) now recognizes the UNIX system as the backup domain controller. Figure 17-1 shows a screen shot from the Windows system *hpsystem1*, which is the primary domain controller. The screen shot shows *dloaner* acting as the backup domain controller and the default

shared directories on the UNIX system *dloaner*. The share properties
for one of the shares, **C:\opt\asu\lanman**, are also shown.

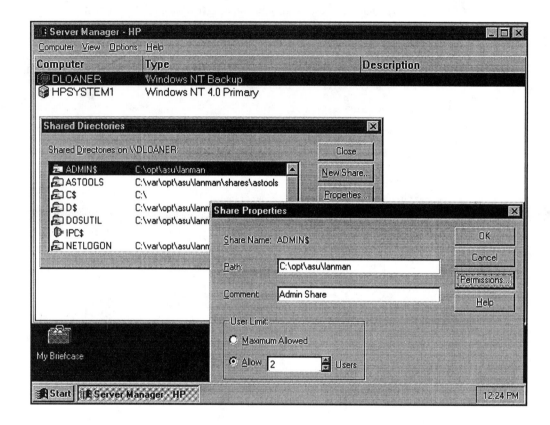

Figure 17-1 Default Shares after Loading and Configuring Advanced
Server/9000

These shares can also be viewed on the command line of the
UNIX system using the net command, as shown in the following output:

```
# /opt/asu/lanman/bin/net share

Sharename    Resource                           Remark
-------------------------------------------------------------------------
ADMIN$       C:\OPT\ASU\LANMAN                   Admin Share
IPC$                                            IPC Share
C$           C:\                                 Root Share
D$           C:\VAR\OPT\ASU\LANMAN\SHARES        SystemRoot Share
ASTOOLS      C:\VAR\OPT\ASU\LANMAN\SHARES...     Advanced Server Tools
DOSUTIL      C:\VAR\OPT\ASU\LANMAN\SHARES...     DOS Utilities
NETLOGON     C:\VAR\OPT\ASU\LANMAN\SHARES...     Logon Scripts Directory
PATCHES      C:\VAR\OPT\ASU\LANMAN\SHARES...     Client Patches
PRINTLOG     C:\VAR\OPT\ASU\LANMAN\SHARES...     LP printer messages
USERS        C:\HOME\LANMAN                      Users Directory
The command completed successfully.
#
```

These are the default shares that have been set up by Advanced Server/9000. Those followed by a $ are hidden shares used only for administrative purposes. When you run *Windows Explorer,* you don't see these hidden directories.

You can set up additional shares, such as the printer and disk we will set up in the upcoming sections *"Sharing a Printer"* and *"Sharing a File System"* respectively.

Sharing a Printer

In addition to the default sharing that takes place with Advanced Server/9000, there may be additional resources you may want to share between Windows and UNIX systems.

For example, you may have a printer used in your UNIX environment, to which you want Windows systems to have access. The following commands show adding a shared printer and viewing it in UNIX.

The first command is **lpstat** on UNIX, which shows the status of the existing printer *laser*:

```
# lpstat -t
scheduler is running
system default destination: laser
device for laser: /dev/c2t0d0_lp
laser accepting requests since Feb 11 17:23
printer laser is idle.  enabled since Feb 11 17:23
fence priority : 0
no entries
#
```

Next we run the **net** command and specify the printer *laser* as a shared printer device.

```
# /opt/asu/lanman/bin/net net share laser=laser /print
laser was successfully shared
```

To see the configuration of the printer, we can issue the **net print** command, as shown below:

```
# net print laser /options
Printing options for LASER

Status              Queue Active
Remark
Print Devices       laser
Driver              HP-UX LM/X Print Manager
Separator file
Priority            5
Print after         12:00 AM
Print until         12:00 AM
Print processor
Parameters          COPIES=1 EJECT=AUTO BANNER=YES
The command completed successfully.
#
```

After printing a text file from the Windows system onto the device *laser* connected to the UNIX system running Advanced Server/9000, I received a bunch of unintelligible information on the printed sheet. The Advanced Server/9000 printer was not configured raw. I issued the following command to make the printer raw:

```
# net print laser /parms:types=-oraw
The command completed successfully.
```

The new configuration, with the *TYPES=-oraw*, is shown in the following output. This device successfully printed from the Windows system to the UNIX system running Advanced Server/9000 to which *laser* is connected:

```
# net print laser /options
Printing options for LASER

Status              Queue Active
Remark
Print Devices       laser
Driver              HP-UX LM/X Print Manager
Separator file
Priority            5
Print after         12:00 AM
Print until         12:00 AM
Print processor
Parameters          COPIES=1 TYPES=-oraw EJECT=AUTO BANNER=YES
The command completed successfully.
#
```

We can now view all the shared devices with the **net** command:

```
# /opt/asu/lanman/bin/net share

Sharename   Resource                      Remark
---------------------------------------------------------------------------
ADMIN$      C:\OPT\ASU\LANMAN             Admin Share
IPC$                                      IPC Share
C$          C:\                           Root Share
D$          C:\VAR\OPT\ASU\LANMAN\SHARES  SystemRoot Share
ASTOOLS     C:\VAR\OPT\ASU\LANMAN\SHARES... Advanced Server Tools
DOSUTIL     C:\VAR\OPT\ASU\LANMAN\SHARES... DOS Utilities
NETLOGON    C:\VAR\OPT\ASU\LANMAN\SHARES... Logon Scripts Directory
PATCHES     C:\VAR\OPT\ASU\LANMAN\SHARES... Client Patches
PRINTLOG    C:\VAR\OPT\ASU\LANMAN\SHARES... LP printer messages
USERS       C:\HOME\LANMAN                Users Directory
LASER       laser                         Spooled
The command completed successfully.
#
```

The last item in this listing is the printer *laser* that was added with the **net** command. All the previous commands were issued on the UNIX system running Advanced Server/9000. We can now view the shared devices of *dloaner* on the Windows system using *Explorer* to confirm that the printer *laser* is a shared device, as shown in Figure 17-2.

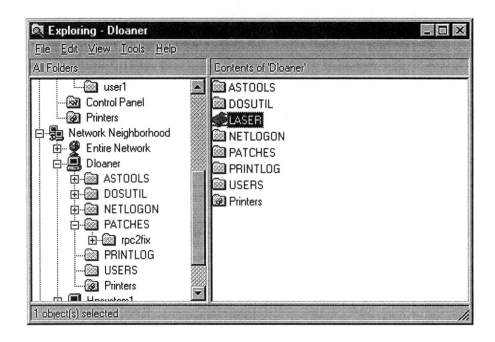

Figure 17-2 Windows Explorer Showing Printer *Laser*

The details of this shared printer can be viewed in *Printers* under *Control Panel*.

Sharing a File System

With the printer having been added, the shares that are now set up on the UNIX system running Advanced Server/9000 look like the following:

```
# /opt/asu/lanman/bin/net share

Sharename      Resource                          Remark
-----------------------------------------------------------------------
ADMIN$         C:\OPT\ASU\LANMAN                  Admin Share
IPC$                                             IPC Share
C$             C:\                               Root Share
D$             C:\VAR\OPT\ASU\LANMAN\SHARES       SystemRoot Share
ASTOOLS        C:\VAR\OPT\ASU\LANMAN\SHARES...    Advanced Server Tools
DOSUTIL        C:\VAR\OPT\ASU\LANMAN\SHARES...    DOS Utilities
NETLOGON       C:\VAR\OPT\ASU\LANMAN\SHARES...    Logon Scripts Directory
PATCHES        C:\VAR\OPT\ASU\LANMAN\SHARES...    Client Patches
PRINTLOG       C:\VAR\OPT\ASU\LANMAN\SHARES...    LP printer messages
USERS          C:\HOME\LANMAN                     Users Directory
LASER          laser                             Spooled
The command completed successfully.
#
```

The shares shown include the printer that was added. We could now issue the **net share** command and add a UNIX file system to be shared. To share the **/home** directory on the UNIX system *dloaner*, we would issue the following command:

```
# /opt/asu/lanman/bin/net share home=c:/home
home was shared successfully
```

Note that the UNIX notation for the directory was issued with the slash (/) rather than the backslash (\), as you would on a Windows system. We can now view the shares on *dloaner*, including the new *HOME* share, with the **net** command:

```
# /opt/asu/lanman/bin/net share

Sharename      Resource                          Remark
-----------------------------------------------------------------------
ADMIN$         C:\OPT\ASU\LANMAN                  Admin Share
IPC$                                             IPC Share
C$             C:\                               Root Share
D$             C:\VAR\OPT\ASU\LANMAN\SHARES       SystemRoot Share
ASTOOLS        C:\VAR\OPT\ASU\LANMAN\SHARES...    Advanced Server Tools
DOSUTIL        C:\VAR\OPT\ASU\LANMAN\SHARES...    DOS Utilities
HOME           C:\HOME
NETLOGON       C:\VAR\OPT\ASU\LANMAN\SHARES...    Logon Scripts Directory
PATCHES        C:\VAR\OPT\ASU\LANMAN\SHARES...    Client Patches
PRINTLOG       C:\VAR\OPT\ASU\LANMAN\SHARES...    LP printer messages
USERS          C:\HOME\LANMAN                     Users Directory
LASER          laser                             Spooled
The command completed successfully.
#
```

You could now view this share on the Windows system and map
it to a drive, as shown in Figure 17-3.

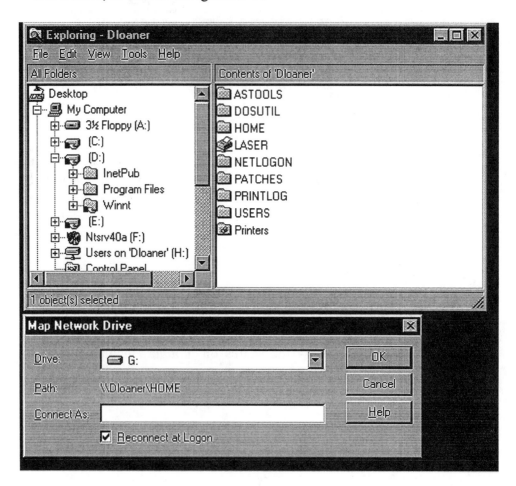

Figure 17-3 Windows *Explorer* Showing New Share *HOME*

I covered only a small subset of Advanced Server/9000 functionality in this chapter. I covered using a UNIX system running Advanced Server/9000 as a backup domain controller, sharing a UNIX connected printer with a Windows network, and sharing a UNIX connected disk with a Windows network. These are some of the more common uses for Advanced Server/9000. Nearly everything you can do with a Windows system can be done with Advanced Server/9000, so don't limit yourself to only the functionality covered in this chapter.

CHAPTER 18

Services for UNIX (SFU)

Introduction to SFU

Microsoft Services for UNIX (SFU) provides interoperability between UNIX and Windows in many essential areas. Microsoft has packaged several widely used third-party interoperability products in SFU. Such important UNIX and Windows interoperability functions as NFS, Telnet, and UNIX utilities are part of SFU. Figure 18-1 shows these functions as menu picks that are produced when SFU is loaded on a Windows system. We'll go through the most important functional areas of SFU in the upcoming sections, starting with NFS.

Using the Network File System (NFS) Functionality of SFU

With the NFS functionality of SFU, you would typically run your NFS client, such as the one included with SFU, on your Windows system in order to mount file systems on a UNIX system.

The NFS client of SFU bridges your Microsoft Server Message Block (SMB) network to your UNIX network by acting as a proxy. It forwards SMB requests from a Windows client to a UNIX NFS server and vice versa. I always concentrate on the *client* aspect of NFS running on Windows, because the UNIX systems are usually bigger, more centralized systems to which Windows users want to get access. Therefore, Windows users usually mount UNIX directories on their Windows systems and not vice versa.

This situation is not necessarily the case. With SFU, you can also set up your Windows system as an NFS Server. Figure 18-1 shows the menu structure of SFU after it has been installed. The *Server for NFS* menu pick is selected.

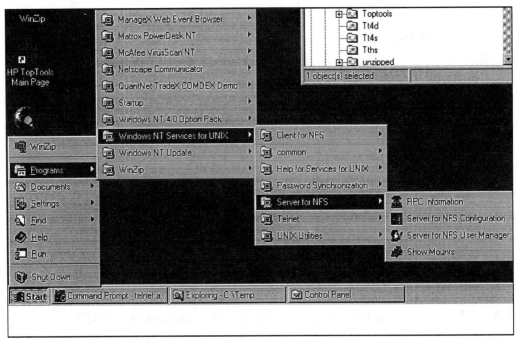

Figure 18-1   SFU Menu Structure

To begin, we'll focus on the *Client for NFS*, because this is very commonly used in mixed Windows and UNIX environments, and we'll then come back to the *Server for NFS* later in the chapter.

Under *Client for NFS Configuration* are the following six categories of information to enter related to NFS:

Authentication
Mount Options
File Access
Filenames
Configured NFS LANs
Symbolic Links

Let's walk through each of these, beginning with *Authentication,* shown in Figure 18-2.

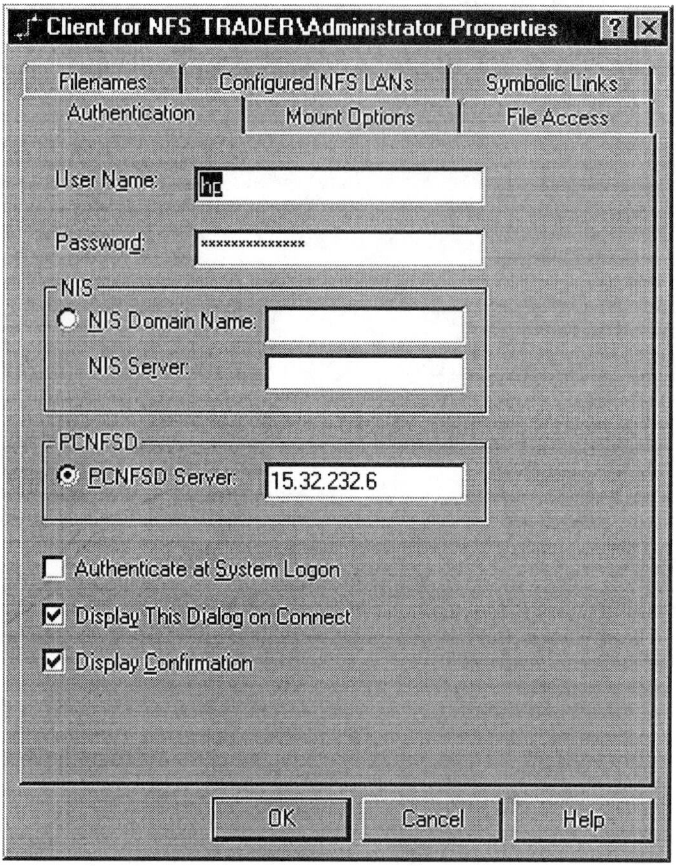

Figure 18-2 SFU *Authentication*

Authentication requires us to add some basic information about our connection to the NFS server. The *User Name* and *Password* are those we use to connect to the NFS Server. These should be set up on the server in advance of attempting to make a connection to the server. You also have the option to use NIS, which won't be part of this example. The server to which you are making an NFS connection must be running the PC NFS daemon. You can check to see whether your server is running this daemon. Figure 18-3 shows checking for **pcnfsd** on the NFS server:

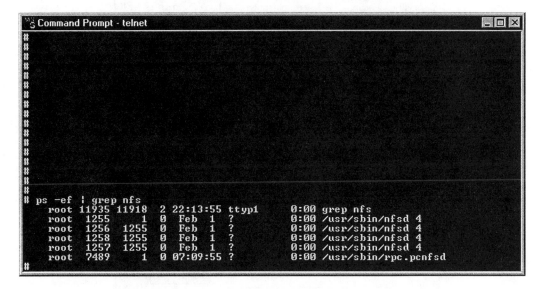

```
# ps -ef | grep nfs
  root 11935 11918  2 22:13:55 ttyp1   0:00 grep nfs
  root  1255     1  0  Feb  1  ?       0:00 /usr/sbin/nfsd 4
  root  1256  1255  0  Feb  1  ?       0:00 /usr/sbin/nfsd 4
  root  1258  1255  0  Feb  1  ?       0:00 /usr/sbin/nfsd 4
  root  1257  1255  0  Feb  1  ?       0:00 /usr/sbin/nfsd 4
  root  7489     1  0 07:09:55  ?      0:00 /usr/sbin/rpc.pcnfsd
#
```

Figure 18-3   Checking for **pcnfsd** on a UNIX System

man page

ps - 12

The last entry, using **ps**, shows that **pcnfsd** is indeed running on our NFS server.

With the *User Name, Password,* and *PCNFSD Server* specified, we can move on to *Configured NFS LANs*. Figure 18-4 shows that I have configured two LANs on which I want to use NFS.

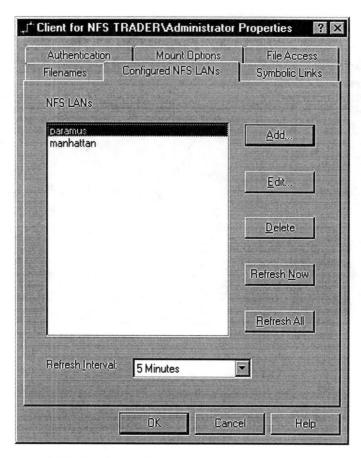

Figure 18-4 SFU *Configured NFS LANs*

You can *Edit...* these LANs to include such information as the *Broadcast Address,* as shown in Figure 18-5.

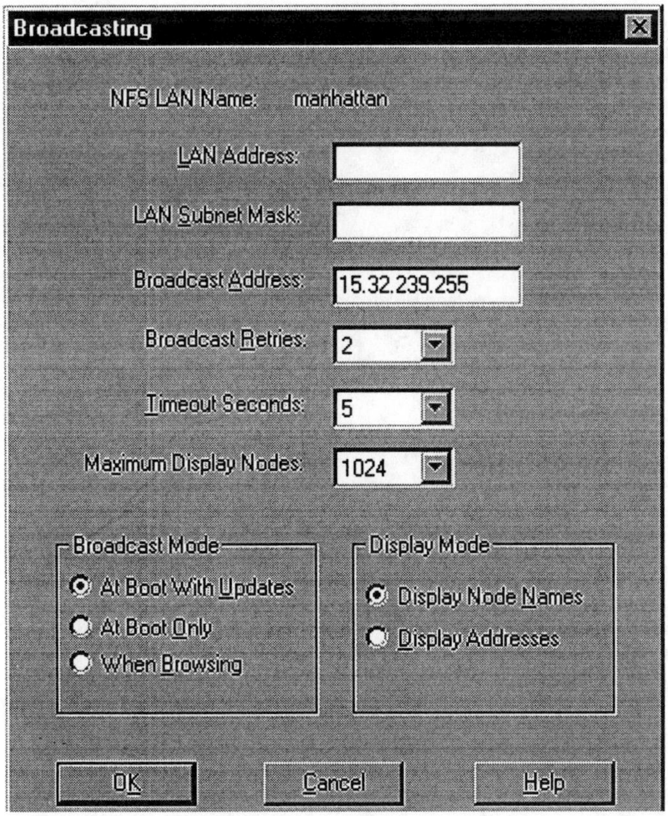

Figure 18-5 Edit a Specific LAN

Next you have options for the way symbolic links will be handled when you establish a client NFS connection. Symbolic links are a
way of mapping a file or directory to an existing file or directory. If
you select *Resolve Symbolic Links,* then you will be shown the actual
path name to which the link is set. The options available for *Symbolic
Links* are shown in Figure 18-6.

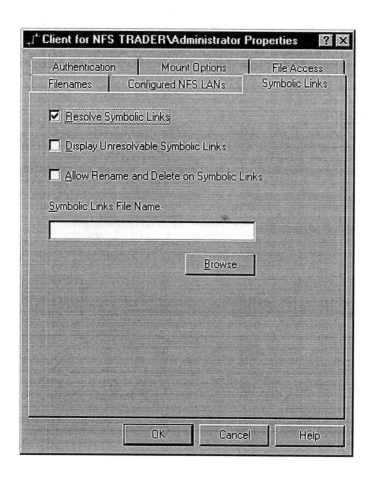

Figure 18-6 SFU *Client for NFS*

I typically like to resolve symbolic links but don't care to manipulate existing links or display those that cannot be resolved.

There are somewhat different conventions used in file naming
on Windows and UNIX. SFU gives you several options related to
Filenames, as shown in Figure 18-7.

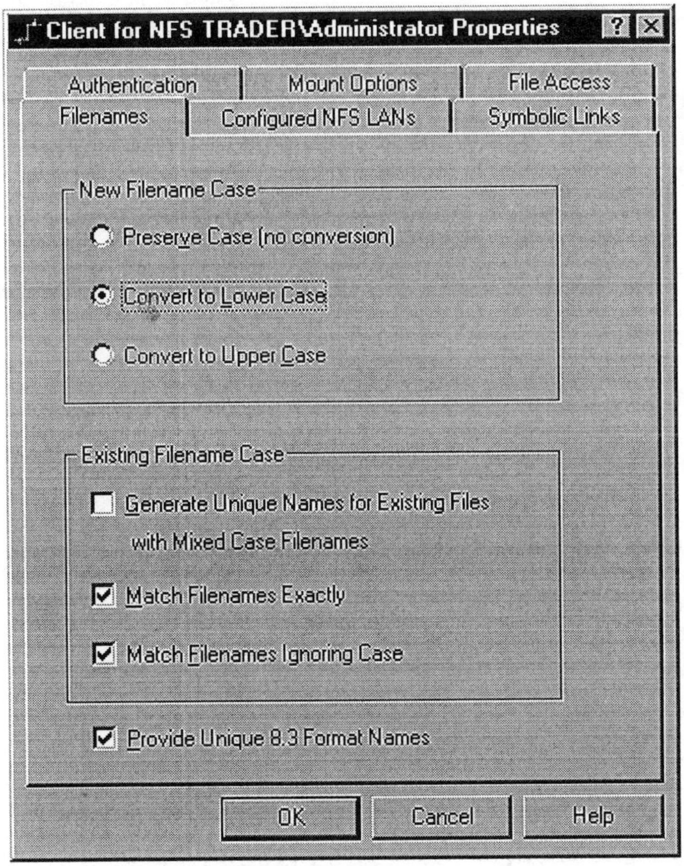

Figure 18-7 SFU *Client for NFS*

I like all new file names to be lowercase. This seems to result in the minimum amount of confusion when working with multiple operating systems. I also like to work with existing file names exactly as they exist, as indicated by the options I have chosen in Figure 18-7.

There are many mount options that you have when working with NFS. Figure 18-8 shows the *Mount Options* window.

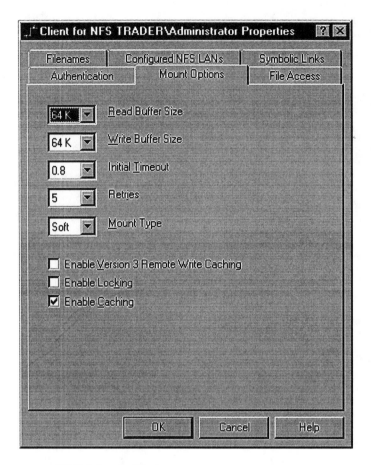

Figure 18-8   SFU *Mount Options*

We are using the default *Read Buffer Size* of 64,000 bytes. I like
to keep this number large, because it is the data part of the packet used
during NFS reads. In general, bigger is better. The same is true of the
Write Buffer Size. The *Initial_Timeout* specifies the amount of time to
wait for a response from the server before a retry. *Retries* specifies the
number of times you'll attempt to access the server before dropping
the operation altogether. I also use a *Mount Type* of *Soft,* as opposed
to *Hard* and *Enable Caching*.

File Access allows you to specify privileges for users establishing NFS mounts. These are the privileges you're accustomed to seeing when working with files, as shown in Figure 18-9.

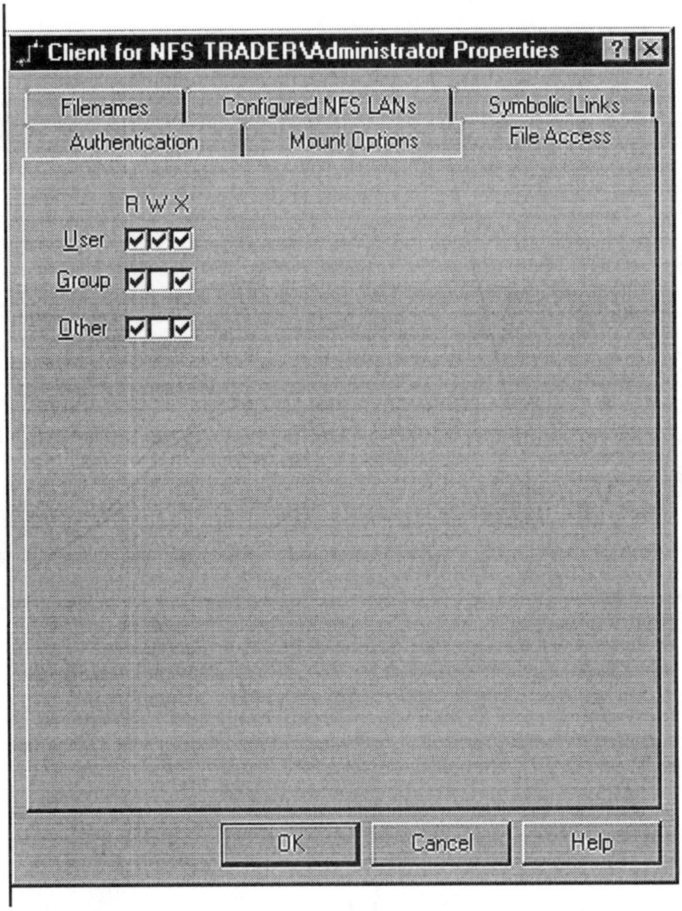

Figure 18-9 SFU *File Access*

By default, *User* will have unlimited access to files, and those in the *Group* and *Other* will have read (R) and execute (X) access only. These are common privilege assignments.

We can easily establish our NFS connection by selecting *OK* from the *Authentication* window shown in Figure 18-2. A box appears asking you to confirm the user name and other information, such as that shown in Figure 18-10.

Figure 18-10 NFS *Login Successful*

The *Username, UID,* and *Primary GID* correspond to those on the UNIX NFS server. If we view the **passwd** file on the UNIX NFS server system and look for our user, *hp*, we'll see the following entry:

```
hp:EkyXw/N.EwFNw:104:20::/home/hp:/sbin/sh
```

The information in this **passwd** entry corresponds to that shown in our NFS Login window.

After login takes place, we can view the file systems exported on the UNIX NFS server using Explorer on our Windows system. Figure 18-11 shows the *Manhattan* LAN, with a specific system selected.

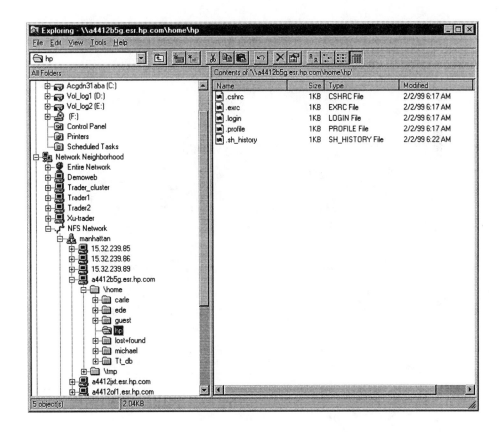

Figure 18-11 Viewing the NFS Mounted File System

\home\hp is selected, and the right Explorer window shows the files in the **\home\hp** directory. We have permission to manipulate the files in the **hp** directory. We can check this by selecting a file, such as

.cshrc, and viewing its properties. Figure 18-12 shows the *Properties* window.

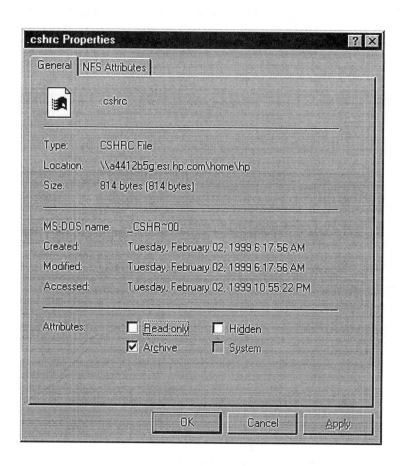

Figure 18-12 SFU *Properties*

The *Read-only* box in this window is not checked; therefore, we have full access to this file.

Telnet Client

There is also a Telnet client loaded as part of SFU. Selecting *Telnet - Telnet Client* from the SFU menu produces the Telnet window shown in Figure 18-13.

```
Telnet Client                                                    _ □ ×
# ls -al   /home/hp
total 12
drwxr-xr-x   2 hp        users         96 Feb  2 07:17 .
drwxr-xr-x   9 root      root        1024 Feb  2 07:17 ..
-rw-r--r--   1 hp        sys          814 Feb  2 07:17 .cshrc
-rw-r--r--   1 hp        sys          347 Feb  2 07:17 .exrc
-rw-r--r--   1 hp        sys          341 Feb  2 07:17 .login
-rw-r--r--   1 hp        users        446 Feb  2 07:17 .profile
-rw-------   1 hp        sys          144 Feb  2 07:22 .sh_history
#
#
#
#
#
#
#
#
#
#
#
#
#
#
```

Figure 18-13 SFU *Telnet Client*

man page

ls - 2

I have created a long listing of the contents of **/home/hp** in this Telnet window.

Telnet Server

There is also a Telnet server loaded as part of SFU. This means you can connect from a UNIX system, or any other system with a Telnet client, to a Windows NT system with the SFU Telnet server. Figure 18-14 shows accessing the Windows Telnet server from a UNIX system.

```
Command Prompt - telnet a4412b5g                                    _ □ ✕
*==============================================================================
Welcome to Microsoft Telnet Server.
*==============================================================================
C:\>dir sfu
 Volume in drive C is ACGDN31ABA
 Volume Serial Number is 3E28-1006

 Directory of C:\sfu

02/02/99  05:12p       <DIR>          .
02/02/99  05:12p       <DIR>          ..
02/02/99  05:12p       <DIR>          common
02/02/99  05:12p       <DIR>          Telnet
02/02/99  05:12p       <DIR>          Shell
02/02/99  05:12p       <DIR>          DiskAccess
02/02/99  05:12p       <DIR>          help
02/09/99  06:08p       <DIR>          DiskShare
02/09/99  06:08p       <DIR>          PswdSync
               9 File(s)              0 bytes
                           586,285,056 bytes free

C:\>
```

Figure 18-14 SFU *Telnet Server*

In Figure 18-14, I have initiated a Telnet session from my UNIX system to my Windows system. After receiving the welcome information from the Microsoft Telnet server, I can issue commands, such as the **dir** shown, exactly as I would from the prompt if I were working directly on the Windows system.

The Telnet server functionality of SFU gives some direct access from UNIX to Windows, which is a big help in mixed environments.

This functionality is further enhanced by many UNIX utilities that you can run on the Windows system through this Telnet connection or on the Windows system directly. The next section "UNIX Utilities" covers these utilities.

UNIX Utilities

One highly desirable capability of SFU is a UNIX Command Shell invoked with *Unix Utilities - Unix Command Shell*. Figure 18-15 shows a window open with the UNIX utilities listed.

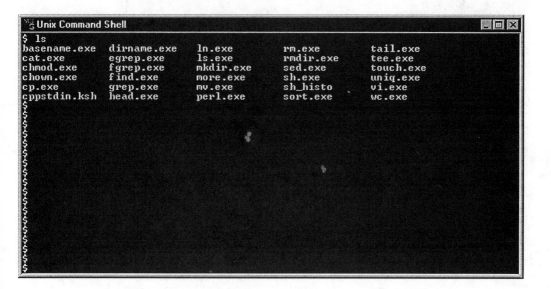

Figure 18-15 SFU UNIX Utilities Listed

The utilities listed in Figure 18-15 work in SFU just the way they work in UNIX. You also have access to these UNIX utilities through the Telnet session that you can establish from another system. To give you an idea how these utilities work, let's issue a few commands, as shown in Figure 18-16.

```
Unix Command Shell
$ pwd
C:/SFU/Shell
$ cd /
$ pwd
C:/
$ ls
AUTOEXEC.ADT              Multimedia Files
AUTOEXEC.BAT              NT4SP3
Acrobat3                  NTOPTION
BOOT.BAK                  Program Files
COMMAND.COM               SETUP
CONFIG.SYS                SFU
DMI                       TT4D
FIRSTBOO.TXT              TT4S
HP_INFO                   TTHS
I386                      Temp
IE401SP1                  Toptools
Inetpub                   WINNT
Internet Explorer 4.01 SP1 Setup  boot.ini
LAN                       pagefile.sys
MOUSE                     webhelp
MktData
$
$
$
$
```

Figure 18-16 SFU Example of Using Some UNIX Utilities

This window shows that when we invoke *Unix Utilities,* we are in the **C:/SFU/Shell** directory on our Windows system. We change directory to **C:** by issuing **cd /**, as we would on a UNIX system. **pwd** confirms that we are at the **C:** level. We then issue an **ls** to see the files in **C:**.

Let's issue two more of the *Unix Utilities* to get a better feel for how these utilities perform in Windows, as shown in Figure 18-17.

```
 ▚ Unix Command Shell                                                    ▭ ▯ ☒
$ ls | grep -i s
CONFIG.SYS
FIRSTBOO.TXT
IE401SP1
Internet Explorer 4.01 SP1 Setup
MOUSE
Multimedia Files
NT4SP3
Program Files
SETUP
SFU
TT4S
TTHS
Toptools
pagefile.sys
$ ls | grep -i s | wc
     14      20      166
$
$
$
$
$
$
$
$_
```

Figure 18-17 SFU Example of Using Some UNIX Utilities

In this window, we issued an **ls** and a **grep** command that ignored case (-i) and searched for *s*. Files that contained both upper- and lowercase *s* were listed. We then piped this same output to **wc** to get a word count.

NFS Server

Not only can the Windows system act as an NFS client, but it can also act as an NFS server with SFU. A system running NFS can mount a file system exported on the Windows system.

Under *Server for NFS Configuration,* you can configure all aspects of your NFS server setup. The defaults for most categories of configuration are fine for initial testing, which we'll perform here. You may want to later perform additional configuration to tune your NFS server.

For our example, I've created one *Share Name,* as shown in Figure 18-18.

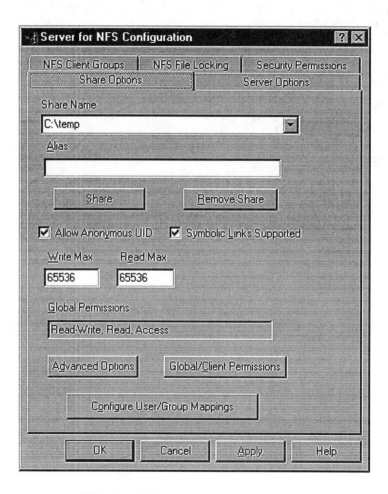

Figure 18-18   SFU *Share Name*

By selecting **Server for NFS Configuration** from the menu and then *Share Options,* I entered the *Share Name* **C:\tem**p shown in Figure 18-18.

We can view *Mount Information* to see what file systems we have exported, as shown in Figure 18-19.

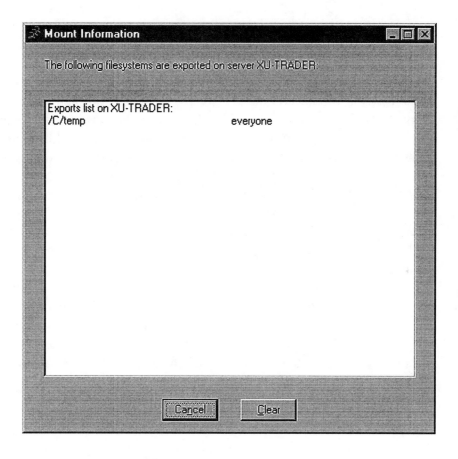

Figure 18-19 SFU *Mount Information*

Our file system of **C:\temp** is indeed in the exported list with no restrictions on who may access it.

With this *Share Name* having been established, we can use the defaults for all other categories of NFS server configuration and mount **C:\temp** on a UNIX system. To mount **C:\temp**, you would issue the following command on your UNIX system:

man page

mount - 12

```
# mount 19.32.23.112:C:\temp /ntmount
```

This command will work on most UNIX systems. We have first specified the mount command, which you would normally issue as root. Next is the name of the Windows system that has the file system we wish to mount on it; in this case, I have used the IP address rather than the system name. The system name, or IP address, is followed by a colon (:). Next is the name of the file system we wish to mount, as it appears on the Windows system, in this case **C:\temp**. Last is the name of the directory on the UNIX system under which we'll mount **C:\temp**, in this case **/ntmount**. You can also add a variety of different options with the **mount** command, but we'll use all defaults in our example.

Let's now check to see whether indeed the NFS mount we specified has been established on the UNIX system. The following example shows issuing the **bdf** command, which is somewhat similar to the **df** command covered earlier in the book, on the UNIX system to see whether the mount has been established, then a **cd** to the **ntmount** directory, and finally an **ls** of the files in this directory:

man page

df - 12

```
# bdf
Filesystem            kbytes      used    avail %used Mounted on
/dev/vg00/lvol3       151552     53165    92162   37% /
/dev/vg00/lvol1        47829     14324    28722   33% /stand
/dev/vg00/lvol8       163840     87595    71039   55% /var
/dev/vg00/lvol7       339968    314984    23189   93% /usr
/dev/vg00/lvol6       102400     62284    37607   62% /tmp
/dev/vg00/lvol5      1048576    656649   367439   64% /opt
```

```
/dev/vg00/lvol4        69632     32448     34850   48%  /home
/dev/vgCE/lvpatch    1024000      1357    958732    0%  /ce/patches
/dev/vgCE/lvfw        512000      1294    478856    0%  /ce/firmware
/dev/vgCE/cetmp       512000    419166     87028   83%  /ce/ce-tmp
19.32.23.112:temp    2096160   1523360    572800   73%  /ntmount
# cd /ntmount
# ls
_istmp0.dir         test.html       ~df8ec8.tmp        ~dfd65e.tmp
_istmp1.dir         tt2.exe         ~df8ee7.tmp        ~dfd65f.tmp
_istmp2.dir         tt3.exe         ~dfa393.tmp        ~dfd660.tmp
ie401sp1.exe        ttdemo.zip      ~dfa394.tmp        ~dfd66b.tmp
ie4setup.exe        ttwiz(1).exe    ~dfa3a3.tmp        ~dfd66c.tmp
jack.log            wbemcore.exe    ~dfa3a4.tmp        ~dfe649.tmp
jack1.log           winzip70.exe    ~dfb2a.tmp         ~dfe64a.tmp
jack2.log           ~df7e2f.tmp     ~dfb39.tmp         ~dfe64b.tmp
mmc14.tmp           ~df7e40.tmp     ~dfb3a.tmp         ~dfe64c.tmp
mmcaaa7.tmp         ~df7e41.tmp     ~dfd63c.tmp        ~dfe659.tmp
mmcaaad.tmp         ~df7e42.tmp     ~dfd63d.tmp        ~dfe65a.tmp
mmcaab1.tmp         ~df7e4f.tmp     ~dfd64c.tmp        ~dfe65b.tmp
nph-ntfinal.exe     ~df7e50.tmp     ~dfd64d.tmp        ~dfe65c.tmp
ntagt33e.exe        ~df7e51.tmp     ~dfd64e.tmp        ~dfe65d.tmp
ntoption.exe        ~df7e52.tmp     ~dfd64f.tmp        ~dfe669.tmp
sfu                 ~df7e53.tmp     ~dfd65b.tmp
sfu1                ~df8e99.tmp     ~dfd65c.tmp
temp.log            ~df8ea9.tmp     ~dfd65d.tmp
```

man page

cd - 3

man page

ls - 2

After issuing this command, we see **/ntmount** as one of the file systems mounted on the UNIX system. At this point, I changed to a user other than root, because it is inadvisable in general for root to be manipulating files on an NFS mounted file system. I changed to user *hp*. We can change directory to **/ntmount** and view its contents that correspond to those under **C:\temp** on the Windows system. Issuing a long listing, we see the files with ownership of *hp*:

```
$ ll
total 5710
drwxrwxrwx    2 hp        users           64 Feb  9 17:58 _istmp0.dir
drwxrwxrwx    3 hp        users           96 Feb  2 10:18 _istmp1.dir
drwxrwxrwx    2 hp        users           64 Feb  2 10:19 _istmp2.dir
-rwxrwxrwx    1 hp        users     24227193 Feb  1 19:50 ie401sp1.exe
-rwxrwxrwx    1 hp        users       443160 Jan 10 10:21 ie4setup.exe
-rwxrwxrwx    1 hp        users          218 Feb 10  1999 jack.log
-rwxrwxrwx    1 hp        users          218 Feb 10  1999 jack1.log
-rwxrwxrwx    1 hp        users          218 Feb 10  1999 jack2.log
-rwxrwxrwx    1 hp        users        60416 Feb  2 15:26 mmc14.tmp
-rwxrwxrwx    1 hp        users       102400 Feb  9 09:24 mmcaaa7.tmp
-rwxrwxrwx    1 hp        users       102400 Feb  9 12:40 mmcaaad.tmp
-rwxrwxrwx    1 hp        users       102400 Feb  9 12:40 mmcaab1.tmp
-rwxrwxrwx    1 hp        users       464200 Feb  1 19:33 nph-ntfinal.exe
-rwxrwxrwx    1 hp        users      5514240 Feb  1 17:43 ntagt33e.exe
-rwxrwxrwx    1 hp        users     38940572 Feb  1 20:07 ntoption.exe
drwxrwxrwx   20 hp        users          640 Feb  3 09:58 sfu
drwxrwxrwx    5 hp        users          160 Feb 10  1999 sfu1
-rwxrwxrwx    1 hp        users          218 Feb  2 11:34 temp.log
```

```
-rwxrwxrwx    1 hp        users           35 Feb  1 19:48 test.html
-rwxrwxrwx    1 hp        users      7046429 Feb  1 20:19 tt2.exe
-rwxrwxrwx    1 hp        users      5758110 Feb  1 20:21 tt3.exe
-rwxrwxrwx    1 hp        users      3232301 Feb  3 15:18 ttdemo.zip
-rwxrwxrwx    1 hp        users      1086772 Feb  1 16:53 ttwiz(1).exe
-rwxrwxrwx    1 hp        users      3456925 Feb  1 19:55 wbemcore.exe
-rwxrwxrwx    1 hp        users       943949 Feb  3 15:51 winzip70.exe
-rwxrwxrwx    1 hp        users         4096 Feb  2 15:26 ~df7e2f.tmp
-rwxrwxrwx    1 hp        users         3584 Feb  2 15:26 ~df7e40.tmp
-rwxrwxrwx    1 hp        users         3584 Feb  2 15:26 ~df7e41.tmp
-rwxrwxrwx    1 hp        users         3584 Feb  2 15:26 ~df7e42.tmp
-rwxrwxrwx    1 hp        users         3072 Feb  2 15:26 ~df7e4f.tmp
-rwxrwxrwx    1 hp        users         3072 Feb  2 15:26 ~df7e50.tmp
-rwxrwxrwx    1 hp        users         3584 Feb  2 15:26 ~df7e51.tmp
-rwxrwxrwx    1 hp        users         3584 Feb  2 15:26 ~df7e52.tmp
-rwxrwxrwx    1 hp        users         3584 Feb  2 15:26 ~df7e53.tmp
-rwxrwxrwx    1 hp        users         9728 Feb  9 09:24 ~df8e99.tmp
-rwxrwxrwx    1 hp        users         3072 Feb  9 09:24 ~df8ea9.tmp
-rwxrwxrwx    1 hp        users         5120 Feb  9 09:24 ~df8ec8.tmp
-rwxrwxrwx    1 hp        users         3584 Feb  9 09:24 ~df8ee7.tmp
-rwxrwxrwx    1 hp        users         6144 Feb  2 15:26 ~dfa393.tmp
-rwxrwxrwx    1 hp        users         9728 Feb  2 15:26 ~dfa394.tmp
-rwxrwxrwx    1 hp        users         3072 Feb  2 15:26 ~dfa3a3.tmp
-rwxrwxrwx    1 hp        users         5120 Feb  2 15:26 ~dfa3a4.tmp
-rwxrwxrwx    1 hp        users         3072 Feb  9 09:24 ~dfb2a.tmp
-rwxrwxrwx    1 hp        users         3072 Feb  9 09:24 ~dfb39.tmp
-rwxrwxrwx    1 hp        users         3072 Feb  9 09:24 ~dfb3a.tmp
-rwxrwxrwx    1 hp        users         4608 Feb  9 09:24 ~dfd63c.tmp
-rwxrwxrwx    1 hp        users        16384 Feb  9 09:24 ~dfd63d.tmp
-rwxrwxrwx    1 hp        users         4608 Feb  9 09:24 ~dfd64c.tmp
-rwxrwxrwx    1 hp        users         3072 Feb  9 09:24 ~dfd64d.tmp
-rwxrwxrwx    1 hp        users         3072 Feb  9 09:24 ~dfd64e.tmp
-rwxrwxrwx    1 hp        users         3072 Feb  9 09:24 ~dfd64f.tmp
-rwxrwxrwx    1 hp        users         3072 Feb  9 09:24 ~dfd65b.tmp
-rwxrwxrwx    1 hp        users         3072 Feb  9 09:24 ~dfd65c.tmp
-rwxrwxrwx    1 hp        users         3072 Feb  9 09:24 ~dfd65d.tmp
-rwxrwxrwx    1 hp        users         3072 Feb  9 09:24 ~dfd65e.tmp
-rwxrwxrwx    1 hp        users         3072 Feb  9 09:24 ~dfd65f.tmp
-rwxrwxrwx    1 hp        users         8192 Feb  9 09:24 ~dfd660.tmp
-rwxrwxrwx    1 hp        users         4608 Feb  9 09:24 ~dfd66b.tmp
-rwxrwxrwx    1 hp        users         3072 Feb  9 09:24 ~dfd66c.tmp
-rwxrwxrwx    1 hp        users         4096 Feb  9 09:24 ~dfe649.tmp
-rwxrwxrwx    1 hp        users         3584 Feb  9 09:24 ~dfe64a.tmp
-rwxrwxrwx    1 hp        users         3584 Feb  9 09:24 ~dfe64b.tmp
-rwxrwxrwx    1 hp        users         3584 Feb  9 09:24 ~dfe64c.tmp
-rwxrwxrwx    1 hp        users         3584 Feb  9 09:24 ~dfe659.tmp
-rwxrwxrwx    1 hp        users         3072 Feb  9 09:24 ~dfe65a.tmp
-rwxrwxrwx    1 hp        users         3072 Feb  9 09:24 ~dfe65b.tmp
-rwxrwxrwx    1 hp        users         3584 Feb  9 09:24 ~dfe65c.tmp
-rwxrwxrwx    1 hp        users         3584 Feb  9 09:24 ~dfe65d.tmp
-rwxrwxrwx    1 hp        users         3584 Feb  9 09:24 ~dfe669.tmp
$
```

We do indeed see that the user *hp* and the corresponding group of *users* are part of this long listing.

The NFS Server setup we have performed in this section can be combined with the NFS Client setup performed earlier to allow the Windows file system to be exported, as part of NFS Server, and imported, as part of NFS Client. The extent to which you use NFS as part of your file-sharing strategy depends on the makeup of your environment. Because NFS is available on most all UNIX variants, you may find that using NFS on Windows makes sense for your environment. If you expect heavy NFS use in a mixed Windows and UNIX environment, you may want to start small, with a few key directories shared using NFS, and test its performance to make sure that it is adequate for your users. As you can see from the previous examples, NFS on Windows can greatly enhance the overall file sharing in your mixed Windows and UNIX environment.

Password Synchronization

SFU synchronizes Windows passwords to UNIX. I didn't include an example of this synchronization. There is an encrypted file sent from Windows to UNIX containing password information. The file should be set to read-only for root. There is also a daemon that is required to implement the password synchronization. After the setup is complete, user passwords on UNIX will be synchronized with those on Windows.

CHAPTER 19

The Windows Command Line: NET Commands, POSIX Utilities, and Others

Introduction for UNIX System Administrators

UNIX system administration is performed mostly from the command line. There are very good system administration interfaces through which many routine system administration tasks can be performed; however, the command line is still used before any graphical tool for most UNIX system administrators. The converse is true for Windows. With Windows, most system administration functions are performed with "point and click." There are, however, many functions you can perform from the command line in Windows. In this UNIX and Windows interoperability chapter I will cover the Windows command line in general, and a group of POSIX utilities that give you UNIX functionality in Windows in particular.

man page

grep - 10

I'll begin with Windows "NET" commands, which are system administration commands for Windows. I'll then cover the POSIX commands you can run at the Windows command line that give you UNIX functionality in Windows, such as **grep**, **ls**, and so on. I'll then cover some additional Windows commands you can issue to perform such tasks as backup and running a command at a specific time.

man page

ls - 2

The POSIX commands are what really constitute the UNIX and Windows portion of this chapter. I think, however, that covering the other Windows commands gives UNIX system administrators an idea of the type of Windows system administration commands available.

The Windows Command Line

The whole Windows operating system is based on performing system administration tasks through the graphical user interface. Why, then, would I include a chapter on the command line? Well, many of us have used operating systems for which the lion's share of system administration work takes place at the command line - and old habits die hard.

The purpose of this chapter is to demonstrate some useful commands that are issued at the command line. You can then decide whether using such commands is helpful to the administration of your Windows server or whether you wish to use only the graphical user interface of Windows.

NET Commands

This section describes some of the **net** commands of Windows. Here is a list of some widely used **net** commands and a brief explanation of each:

net accounts   Used to maintain the user accounts database.

net computer   Used to add or delete computers from the domain database.

net config server

> Displays or changes settings for a server service on which the command is executed.

net config workstation

> Displays or changes settings for the workstation service on which the command is executed.

net continue Reactivates a Windows service that has been suspended with the **net pause** command.

net file Used for network file manipulation, such as listing ID numbers, closing a shared file, removing file locks, and so on.

net group Used to add, display, or modify global groups on servers.

net help Displays a listing of help options for any net commands.

net helpmsg Displays explanations of Windows network messages, such as errors, warnings, and alerts.

net localgroup Used to modify local groups on computers.

net name	Used to add or delete a "messaging name" at a computer, which is the name to which messages are sent.
net print	Used to list print jobs and shared queues.
net send	Sends messages to other users, computers, and "messaging names" on the network.
net session	Used to list or disconnect sessions between the computer and other computers on the network.
net share	Shares a server's resources with other computers on the network.
net start	Used to start services such as *server*.
net statistics	Displays the statistics log for the local Workstation or Server service.
net stop	Used to stop services such as *server*.
net time	Synchronizes the computer's clock with another computer on the domain.
net use	Displays, connects, or disconnects a computer with shared resources.

        net user   Creates or modifies user accounts.

        net view   Lists resources being shared on a computer.

    The following are brief descriptions of some of the NET commands and examples of using them.

    Many of the descriptions include command summaries that were obtained by typing the command name followed by a /?. For instance, to get a command summary for the **NET ACCOUNTS** command, you would type the following:

```
C:\ NET ACCOUNTS /?
```

    You can also get detailed help information by typing **HELP** and the command name, as shown in the following example:

```
C:\ HELP NET ACCOUNTS
```

NET ACCOUNTS

NET ACCOUNTS - Maintains user account database.

The following is a summary of the **NET ACCOUNTS** command.

```
C:\ NET ACCOUNTS /?
NET ACCOUNTS [/FORCELOGOFF:{minutes | NO}] [/MINPWLEN:length]
             [/MAXPWAGE:{days | UNLIMITED}] [/MINPWAGE:days]
             [/UNIQUEPW:number] [/DOMAIN]
NET ACCOUNTS [/SYNC]
```

Some commonly used options follow:

/DOMAIN	Perform the specified action on the domain controller rather than the current computer.
/FORCELOGOFF	Line numbers are displayed, along with output lines.
/MINPWLEN:length	Specify the minimum number of characters for a password with *length*.
/MAXPWAGE:days	Specify the maximum number of *days* a password is valid, or use the *unlimited* option to specify no limit on password validity.
/MINPWAGE:days	Specify the minimum number of *days* that must pass before a user

is permitted to change their password.

/UNIQUEPW:number

A user password must be unique for the number of changes specified by *number*.

/SYNCH

Synchronize the account database.

The following example shows **NET ACCOUNTS** with no options specified:

```
C:\ NET ACCOUNTS

Force user logoff how long after time expires?:      Never
Minimum password age (days):                         0
Maximum password age (days):                         42
Minimum password length:                             0
Length of password history maintained:               None
Lockout threshold:                                   Never
Lockout duration (minutes):                          30
Lockout observation window (minutes):                30
Computer role:                                       BACKUP
Primary Domain controller for workstation domain:    \\NISDEV
The command completed successfully.
```

We'll now issue **NET ACCOUNTS** with the *MINPWLEN* option to change the minimum password length to five characters:

```
C:\ NET ACCOUNTS /MINPWLEN:5

The request will be processed at the primary domain controller for domain
NSDNIS

The command completed successfully.
```

Reissuing **NET ACCOUNTS** with no options reflects the new minimum password length:

```
C:\ NET ACCOUNTS

Force user logoff how long after time expires?:      Never
Minimum password age (days):                         0
Maximum password age (days):                         42
Minimum password length:                             5
Length of password history maintained:              None
Lockout threshold:                                   Never
Lockout duration (minutes):                          30
Lockout observation window (minutes):                30
Computer role:                                       BACKUP
Primary Domain controller for workstation domain:   \\NISDEV
The command completed successfully.
```

NET COMPUTER

NET COMPUTER - Adds or deletes computers from the domain database.

The following is a summary of the **NET COMPUTER** command:

```
C:\ NET COMPUTER /?

NET COMPUTER  \\computername {/ADD | /DEL}
```

Some commonly used options follow:

\\computername	Name of the computer to be added or deleted.
/ADD	Add the computer.
/DEL	Delete the computer.

The following example shows adding a computer using the / *ADD* option:

```
C:\ NET COMPUTER \\SYSTEM2 /ADD

The request will be processed at the primary domain controller for domain
NSDNIS.

The command completed successfully.
```

NET CONFIG SERVER

NET CONFIG SERVER - As a member of Administrator's group, you can change the settings for a service.

The following is a summary of the **NET CONFIG SERVER** command.

```
C:\ NET CONFIG SERVER /?

NET CONFIG SERVER   [/AUTODISCONNECT:time]
                    [/SRVCOMMENT:"text"]
                    [/HIDDEN:{YES | NO}]
```

Some commonly used options follow:

/AUTODISCONNECT:time   Use *time* to specify the number of minutes that pass before an inactive account is disconnected.

/SRVCOMMENT:"text"

/HIDDEN:{YES|NO}

NET CONTINUE

NET CONTINUE - Reactivates a Windows service that had been suspended with **NET PAUSE**.

The following is a summary of the **NET CONTINUE** command.

```
C:\ NET CONTINUE /?
NET CONTINUE service
```

You can pause and continue many Windows services with the **NET PAUSE** and **NET CONTINUE** commands, respectively. The following example shows using the **NET PAUSE** command to pause the **NET LOGON** service and then restart it with the **NET CONTINUE** command.

Figure 19-1 is the *Services* dialog box from a system, showing some of the services running on a system.

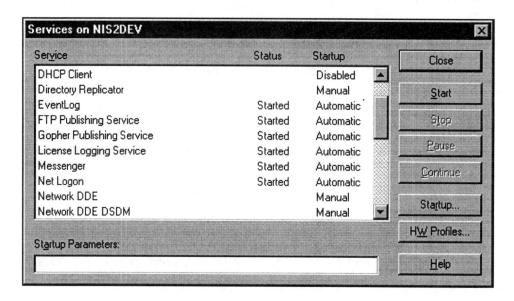

Figure 19-1 *Service* Dialog Box with Net Logon Started

We'll now use the **NET PAUSE** command to pause the *Net Logon* service:

```
C:\NET PAUSE NTLOGON
The Net Logon service was paused successfully.
```

Figure 19-2 shows the *Services* dialog box showing that the *Net Logon* service has indeed been paused.

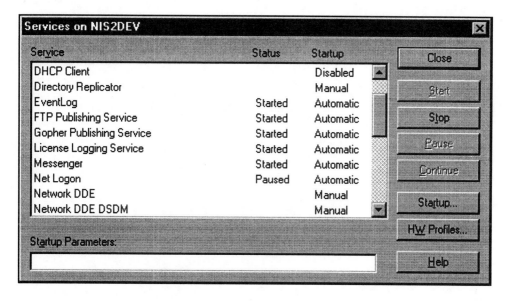

Figure 19-2 *Service* Dialog Box with Net Logon Paused

We can now resume the *Net Logon* service with the following **NET CONTINUE** command:

```
C:\NET CONTINUE NTLOGON

The Net Logon service was continued successfully.
```

NET FILE

NET FILE - This command lists and closes open files.

The following is a summary of the **NET FILE** command.

```
C:\ NET FILE /?

NET FILE   [id [/CLOSE]]
```

Some commonly used options follow:

<table>
<tr>
<td>id</td>
<td>Specify the identification number of the file you wish to view.</td>
</tr>
<tr>
<td>id /CLOSE</td>
<td>Close the file specified by the id number.</td>
</tr>
</table>

The following example shows issuing the **NET FILE** command with no options:

```
C:\ NET FILE

ID         Path                                    User name          # Locks

--------------------------------------------------------------------------------
97         C:\tif_map_proj\sql                     leung_k            0
147        \PIPE\samr                              administrator      0
148        \PIPE\lsarpc                            administrator      0
The command completed successfully.
```

This output shows the open files on the server. You can close one of these shared files or remove locks from the file.

NET GROUP

NET GROUP - This command displays and allows you to manipulate groups
on a server. Without specifying any option, this command lists groups.

The following is a summary of the **NET GROUP** command.

```
C:\ NET GROUP /?
NET GROUP [groupname [/COMMENT:"text"]] [DOMAIN]
          groupname {/ADD [/COMMENT:"text"] | /DELETE} [/DOMAIN]
          groupname username [...] {/ADD | /DELETE} [/DOMAIN]
```

Some commonly used options follow:

/ADD	Add a group to a domain or a *username* to a group.
/DELETE	Delete a group from a domain or a *username* from a group.
groupname	Specify the *groupname* for the operation. With no options, the users who are part of the group are displayed. You can also use the *ADD* or *DELETE* options with the *groupname* to specify a *username* to add to the group.
/COMMENT:"text"	Add this comment to the *groupname*.
/DOMAIN	The operation will be performed on the primary domain control-

ler. This option is the default for Windows server systems.

username   This user will be added or removed from the group. Any number of users can be specified.

The following example shows issuing the **NET GROUP** command to add the group *hp consultants*:

```
C:/ NET GROUP "hp consultants" /ADD
The request will be processed at the primary domain controller for domain
NSDNIS.

The command completed successfully.
```

Next we add the user *marty* to the group *hp consultants* on the local system:

```
C:\ NET GROUP "hp consultants" marty /ADD
The request will be processed at the primary domain controller for domain
NSDNIS.

The command completed successfully.
```

Next we add a comment to *hp consultants*:

```
C:\ NET GROUP "hp consultants" /COMMENT:"Group For HP Consultants"
The request will be processed at the primary domain controller for domain
NSDNIS.

The command completed successfully.
```

We can now view our handiwork by looking at the information we have added associated with the group *hp consultants*:

```
C:\ NET GROUP "hp consultants"

Group name       hp consultants
Comment          Group For HP Consultants

Members

-------------------------------------------------------------------------
marty
The command completed successfully.
```

This output confirms that we have created the group *hp consultants*, that *marty* is a member of this group, and that our comment has indeed been associated with the group.

NET HELP

NET HELP - Use this command to get help on any of the NET commands.

A commonly used option follows:

NET HELP command | more   This provides information about
                                         the *command* you specify.

The following example shows issuing the **NET HELP** command to get a list of commands for which help is available:

```
C:\ NET HELP

The syntax of this command is:

NET HELP command
      -or-
NET command /HELP

    Commands available are:

        NET ACCOUNTS            NET HELP            NET SHARE
        NET COMPUTER            NET HELPMSG         NET START
        NET CONFIG             NET LOCALGROUP      NET STATISTICS
        NET CONFIG SERVER      NET NAME            NET STOP
        NET CONFIG WORKSTATION NET PAUSE           NET TIME
        NET CONTINUE           NET PRINT           NET USE
        NET FILE               NET SEND            NET USER
        NET GROUP              NET SESSION         NET VIEW

    NET HELP SERVICES lists the network services you can start.
    NET HELP SYNTAX explains how to read NET HELP syntax lines.
    NET HELP command | MORE displays Help one screen at a time.
```

The following example shows issuing the **NET HELP** command to get information about the **NET GROUP** command:

```
C:\ NET HELP NET GROUP

The syntax of this command is:

NET GROUP [groupname [/COMMENT:"text"]] [/DOMAIN]
          groupname {/ADD [/COMMENT:"text"] | /DELETE}   [/DOMAIN]
          groupname username [...] {/ADD | /DELETE} [/DOMAIN]

NET GROUP adds, displays, or modifies global groups on servers. Used
without parameters, it displays the groupnames on the server.
```

groupname	Is the name of the group to add, expand, or delete. Supply only a groupname to view a list of users in a group.
/COMMENT:"text"	Adds a comment for a new or existing group. The comment can have as many as 48 characters. Enclose the text in quotation marks.
/DOMAIN	Performs the operation on the primary domain controller of the current domain. Otherwise, the operation is performed on the local computer. This parameter applies only to Windows Workstation computers that are members of a Windows Server domain. By default, Windows Server computers perform operations on the primary domain controller.
username[...]	Lists one or more usernames to add to or remove from a group. Separate multiple username entries with a space.
/ADD	Adds a group, or adds a username to a group.
/DELETE	Removes a group, or removes a username from a group.

NET HELP command | MORE displays Help one screen at a time.

NET HELPMSG

NET HELPMSG - Gets information on four-digit network message codes. Use only the four digits to get information on the code.

The following is the format of the **NET HELPMSG** command:

NET HELPMSG message#	Provides information about the four-digit *messagenumber* you specify.

The following command shows issuing the **NET GROUP** command to add a group to a system. After issuing this command, an error number is provided:

```
C:\ NET GROUP "hp consultants" /ADD

The group already exists.

More help is available by typing NET HELPMSG 2233.
```

We can now use the **NET HELPMSG** command to get information about the specific four-digit code:

```
C:\ NET HELPMSG 2223

The group already exists.

EXPLANATION

You tried to create a group with a group name that already exists.

ACTION

Use a different group name for the new group. To display
a list of group names established on the server, type:
                NET GROUP
```

NET LOCALGROUP

NET LOCALGROUP - This command displays and allows you to manipulate groups on a computer. Without specifying any option, this command lists groups.

The following is a summary of the **NET LOCALGROUP** command.

```
C:\ NET LOCALGROUP /?

NET LOCALGROUP [groupname [/COMMENT:"text"]] [DOMAIN]
               groupname {/ADD [/COMMENT:"text"] | /DELETE} [/DOMAIN]
               groupname name [...] {/ADD | /DELETE} [/DOMAIN]
```

Some commonly used options follow:

/ADD	Add a group to a domain or a *username* to a group.
/DELETE	Delete a group from a domain or a *username* from a group.
groupname	Specify the *groupname* for the operation. With no options, the users who are part of the local group are displayed. You can also use the *ADD* or *DELETE* options with the *groupname* to specify a *username* to add to the group.
/COMMENT:"text"	Add this comment to the *groupname.*

/DOMAIN

The operation will be performed on the primary domain controller. If this option is not used, the operation will take place on the local computer. This is the default for Windows server systems.

name

This is the user name(s) or group name(s) to be added or removed from the group. Any number can be specified.

NET NAME

NET NAME - This command adds or deletes a messaging name from a computer. This command is not to be confused with **NET USER,** which adds or deletes user accounts on a system.

The following is a summary of the **NET NAME** command.

```
C:\ NET NAME /?

NET NAME [name [/ADD | DELETE]]
```

Some commonly used options follow:

name   Name to add or delete.

/ADD   Adds a name to the computer.

/DELETE   Deletes a name from the com-
                                        puter.

NET PAUSE

NET PAUSE - Suspends a Windows service.

The following is a summary of the **NET PAUSE** command:

```
C:\ NET PAUSE /?
NET PAUSE service
```

You can pause and continue many Windows services with the **NET PAUSE** and **NET CONTINUE** commands, respectively. The following example shows using the **NET PAUSE** command to pause the **NET LOGON** service and then to restart it with the **NET CONTINUE** command.

Figure 19-3 shows the *Services* dialog box from a system, showing some of the services running on a system.

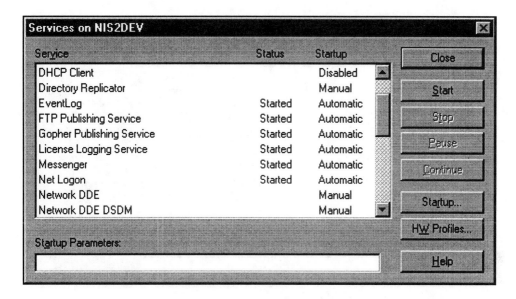

Figure 19-3 *Service* Dialog Box with Net Logon Started

We now use the **NET PAUSE** command to pause the *Net Logon* service:

```
C:\NET PAUSE NTLOGON

The Net Logon service was paused successfully.
```

Figure 19-4 shows the *Services* dialog box showing that the *Net Logon* service has indeed been paused.

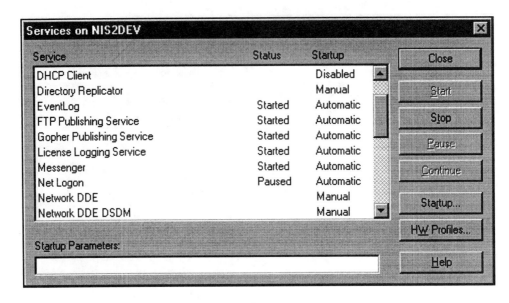

Figure 19-4 *Service* Dialog Box with Net Logon Paused

We can now continue the *Net Logon* service with the following
NET CONTINUE command:

```
C:\NET CONTINUE NTLOGON
The Net Logon service was continued successfully.
```

NET PRINT

NET PRINT - This command lists print jobs and shared queues.

The following is a command summary of the **NET PRINT** command.

```
C:\ NET PRINT /?

NET PRINT \\computername\sharename
          [\\computername] job# [/HOLD | /RELEASE | /DELETE]
```

Some commonly used options follow:

\\computername	The *computername* sharing the print queues.
sharename	The print queue *sharename*.
job#	The unique number assigned to a print job.
/HOLD	The job is assigned a status of *HOLD,* which means that it will not be printed until it is released or deleted.
/RELEASE	Releases a print job so that it can be printed.
/DELETE	Deletes a print job from the print queue.

NET SEND

NET SEND - Sends messages to other users, computers, or messaging names on the network.

The following is a summary of the **NET SEND** command.

```
C:\ NET SEND /?
NET SEND {name | * | /DOMAIN[:name] | /USERS} message
```

Some commonly used options follow:

<table>
<tr>
<td>name</td>
<td>The user name, computer name, or messaging name to which the message is to be sent. Use quotation marks if there are blank characters in the name.</td>
</tr>
<tr>
<td>*</td>
<td>Use * to send a message to all users within your group rather than an individual name.</td>
</tr>
<tr>
<td>/DOMAIN[:domainname]</td>
<td>Use /DOMAIN to send a message to all users in the /DOMAIN. You can also specify a domainname to which you want the message sent.</td>
</tr>
<tr>
<td>message</td>
<td>This is the text message you want sent.</td>
</tr>
</table>

The following example shows issuing the **NET SEND** command to send a message to a specific user:

```
NET SEND marty Our NetServer LXr has arrived for installation.
```

Figure 19-5 shows the alert box that appears on the screen of the computer on which *marty* is working.

Figure 19-5 Alert Box Produced from the **NET SEND** Command

NET SESSION

NET SESSION - Views or disconnects sessions between computers.

The following is a summary of the **NET SESSION** command.

```
C:\ NET SESSION /?
NET SESSION [\\computername] [/DELETE]
```

Some commonly used options follow:

\\computername	Lists session-related information for *computername*.
/DELETE	Terminates a session between the local computer and *computername*, closing open files. Without a *computername*, all sessions are ended.

NET SHARE

NET SHARE - This command is used to list information about existing shares or to share a server's resources with other network users. The command lists information about existing shares if you don't specify any options.

The following is a summary of the **NET SHARE** command.

```
C:\ NET SHARE /?

NET SHARE sharename
        sharename=drive:path [USERS:number | /UNLIMITED]
                             [REMARK:"text"]
        sharename [/USERS:number | /UNLIMITED]
                  [/REMARK:"text"]
        {sharename | devicename | drive:path} /DELETE
```

Some commonly used options follow:

sharename	Network name of the shared resource. Using the *sharename* only displays information about the share.
devicename	Used to specify printers to be shared with *sharename*. Use LP1-LPT9 as a *devicename*.
drive:path	Use this option to specify that a specific drive and path for a directory are to be shared.
/USERS:number	Use this option to specify the maximum number of users that can simultaneously access a shared resource.

/UNLIMITED	An unlimited number of users may simultaneously access a shared resource.
/REMARK:"text"	Associates a remark with the specified shared resource.
/DELETE	Sharing is deleted for the specified resource.

Let's now use **NET SHARE** to set up a new share on a system. To begin, let's look at the existing shares using the **NET SHARE** command with no options:

```
D:\ NET SHARE


Share name    Resource                         Remark

----------------------------------------------------------------------------
ADMIN$        D:\WINNT                         Remote Admin
IPC$                                           Remote IPC
C$            C:\                              Default share
print$        D:\WINNT\system32\spool\drivers  Printer Drivers
D$            D:\                              Default share
E$            E:\                              Default share
net_share     C:\net_share
NETLOGON      D:\WINNT\system32\Repl\Import\S  Logon server share
HPLaserJ5     LPT1:                   Spooled  HP LaserJet 5MP
The command completed successfully.
```

Now we can set up a share of the **c:\measureware** directory with a sharename of *measure* and a maximum number of five users:

```
C:\ NET SHARE measure=c:\measureware /users:5

measure was shared successfully
```

Issuing the NET SHARE command shows that the share named "measureware" has been established.

```
C:\ NET SHARE

Share name    Resource                       Remark

------------------------------------------------------------------------
D$            D:\                            Default share
ADMIN$        D:\WINNT                       Remote Admin
IPC$                                         Remote IPC
C$            C:\                            Default share
print$        D:\WINNT\system32\spool\drivers Printer Drivers
E$            E:\                            Default share
measure       c:\measureware
net_share     C:\net_share
NETLOGON      D:\WINNT\system32\Repl\Import\S Logon server share
HPLaserJ5     LPT1:             Spooled  HP LaserJet 5MP
The command completed successfully.
```

NET START

NET START - This command starts services that have been stopped using the **NET STOP** command or that have not been started. Issue **NET START** without options to see a list of currently running services.

The following is a summary of the **NET START** command.

```
C:\ NET START /?

NET START [service]
```

The following example shows issuing the **NET START** command without any options to list currently running services:

```
C:/ NET START

These Windows services are started:

   Alerter
   Computer Browser
   EventLog
   FTP Publishing Service
   Gateway Service for NetWare
   Gopher Publishing Service
   License Logging Service
   MeasureWare Agent
   MeasureWare Transaction Manager
   Messenger
   Net Logon
   NT LM Security Support Provider
   OracleServiceTMI
   OracleStartTMI
   OracleTNSListener
   Plug and Play
   Remote Procedure Call (RPC) Locator
   Remote Procedure Call (RPC) Service
   Schedule
   Server
   Spooler
   STP/A - TCP/IP Page Server (TMI)
   TCP/IP NetBIOS Helper
   UPS
   Workstation
   World Wide Web Publishing Service

The command completed successfully.
```

There are many services listed in the example that are not native to Windows. For instance, MeasureWare (HP performance tools) and Oracle services. These can be started and stopped with the **NET START** and **NET STOP** commands, respectively.

NET STATISTICS

NET STATISTICS - Use this command to display the statistics log for a service. Issue **NET STATISTICS** without options to display statistics for all services.

The following is a summary of the **NET STATISTICS** command:

```
C:\ NET STATISTICS /?
NET STATISTICS [WORKSTATION | SERVER]
```

Some commonly used options follow:

SERVER	Displays server service statistics.
WORKSTATION	Displays workstation service statistics.

The following example shows issuing the **NET STATISTICS** command with no options:

```
C:\ NET STATISTICS
Server Statistics for \\NISDEV

Statistics since 1/21/98 8:49 AM

Sessions accepted                   3
Sessions timed-out                  32
Sessions errored-out                32

Kilobytes sent                      165941
Kilobytes received                  33118

Mean response time (msec)           0

System errors                       0
Permission violations               2
Password violations                 0

Files accessed                      12787
Communication devices accessed      0
```

```
Print jobs spooled              0

Times buffers exhausted

 Big buffers                    0
 Request buffers                0

The command completed successfully.
```

NET STOP

NET STOP - This command stops a service that was started using the **NET START** command.

The following is a summary of the **NET STOP** command.

```
C:\ NET STOP /?
NET STOP service
```

One option to the **NET STOP** command is:

service   The name of a service that can
                                                         be stopped.

NET TIME

NET TIME - This command is used to display the time for a computer or to synchronize the clock of a computer with the clock on another computer.

The following is a summary of the **NET TIME** command.

```
C:\ NET TIME /?

NET TIME [\\computername | /DOMAIN[:domainname]] [/SET]
```

Some commonly used options follow:

\\computername   The computer with which you
                                        want to synchronize the time or
                                        of which you want to display the
                                        time.

/DOMAIN[:domainname]   The domain name with which
                                        you want to synchronize the
                                        time.

/SET   Sets the computer's time with
                                        the time on the specified com-
                                        puter or domain.

NET USE

NET USE - Lists the connections of a computer, or establishes or removes shared resources. Without options, this command lists the connections of a computer.

The following is a summary of the **NET USE** command.

```
C:\ NET USE /?

NET USE [devicename | *] [//computername\sharename[/volume] [password | *]]
        [/USER:[domainname\]username]
        [[/DELETE] | [/PERSISTENT:{YES | NO}]]

NET USE [devicename | *] [password | *]] [/HOME]

NET USE [PERSISTENT:{YES | NO}]
```

Some commonly used options follow:

devicename	Specifies a name to be connected or disconnected. The possibilities include such names as drives and printers.
//computername	This is the name of the computer that controls the shared resource.
/sharename	The network name of the shared device.
password	The password that is required to get access to the shared resource.
*	Produces a password prompt for the user attempting to use the shared resource.

/USER	Specifies a different user name for the connection.
domainname	A different domain from the current domain is used.
username	Specifies a user logon name.
/HOME	Connects a user to their home directory.
/DELETE	Cancels a network connection and removes it from the list of persistent connections.
/PERSISTENT {yes | no}	Specifying *yes* means that the connections are re-established at the next logon. Specifying *no* does not save the connection for future logons.

The following example shows issuing the **NET USE** command with no options:

```
C:\ NET USE

New connections will be remembered.

Status      Local    Remote                     Network
-------------------------------------------------------------------------
OK          P:       \\DEVSYS\Disk_C            Microsoft Windows Network
The command completed successfully.
```

The directory *Disk_C* on remote system *DEVSYS* is viewed under **P:** on the local system.

NET USER

NET USER - This command creates and modifies accounts on computers. This can also be used without options to list accounts.

The following is a summary of the **NET USER** command.

```
C:\ NET USER /?

NET USER [username [password | *] [options]] [/DOMAIN]
         username {password | *} /ADD [options] [/DOMAIN]
         username [/DELETE] [/DOMAIN]
```

Some commonly used options follow:

/ADD	Adds a user account.
/DELETE	Removes a user account.
username	The name of the account to manipulate. You can add, delete, modify, or view the account.
password	Assigns or changes the password of a user account.
*	Displays the password prompt.
/DOMAIN	The action is to be performed on the primary domain controller.

additional options

You have many additional options such as expiration date, of the account, path of the users logon profile, and many others.

The following example shows issuing the **NET USER** command with no options:

```
C:\ NET USER

User accounts for \\NIS2DEV

-------------------------------------------------------------------------
Administrator            arleo_j                 burgos_c
Guest                    IUSR_NIS2DEV            IUSR_NISDEV
johnt                    leung_k                 marty
mckenna_b
The command completed successfully.
```

Using the second form of the command shown earlier, we can add a new user to the system:

```
C:\ NET USER amyp * /ADD

Type a password for the user:

Retype the password to confirm:

The request will be processed at the primary domain controller for domain DEV.

The command completed successfully.
```

The asterisk in the **NET USER** command means that we want to be prompted for the password for the new user *amyp*.

NET VIEW

NET VIEW - This command lists the resources being shared on a computer. You can use this command without options to display a list of computers on the domain.

The following is a summary of the **NET VIEW** command.

```
C:\ NET VIEW /?

NET VIEW [\\computername | /DOMAIN[:domainname]]
NET VIEW /NETWORK:NW [\\computername]
```

Some commonly used options follow:

//computername	Specifies the name of the computer for which you want to view shared resources.
/DOMAIN:domainname	Specifies the name of the domain for which you wish to view shared resources.
/NETWORK:NW	Displays NetWare servers on the network.

The following example shows issuing the **NET VIEW** command with no options, producing a list of computers in the current domain:

```
C:\ NET VIEW

Server Name          Remark

--------------------------------------------------------------------------
\\NIS2DEV
\\NISDEV
The command completed successfully.
```

The following example shows issuing the **NET VIEW** command while specifying the *DOMAIN* to be viewed:

```
C:\ NET VIEW /DOMAIN:nisdomain

Server Name            Remark

-------------------------------------------------------------------------
\\HPSYSTEM1
\\KITTY
\\NIS
The command completed successfully.
```


The following example shows issuing the **NET VIEW** command while specifying a specific *computername* in the current domain to view:

```
C:\ NET VIEW \\nisdev

Shared resources at \\hpsystem1

Share name   Type          Used as   Comment

-------------------------------------------------------------------------
HPLaserJ5    Print                   HP LaserJet 5MP
measure      Disk
net_share    Disk
NETLOGON     Disk                    Logon server share
The command completed successfully.
```

POSIX Utilities

The Microsoft Windows NT Server *Resource Kit* (referred to as *Resource Kit* throughout this chapter) has on it several POSIX utilities that UNIX system administrators find useful when using Windows. The *Resource Kit* in general is a fantastic system administration resource. Although I will focus on only POSIX utilities in this book, the *Resource Kit* has in it a wealth of information. The *Resource Kit* is available from Microsoft Press, Redmond, WA. The POSIX utilities include such useful commands as **cat, chmod, find, ls, mv,** and others. The commands that are available on the *Resource Kit* vary somewhat from architecture to architecture. In this chapter, I focus on only the "I386" utilities and not the utilities for other architectures.

man page

cat - 3

The *Resource Kit* has on it the file **POSIX.WRI**, which describes the POSIX utilities in detail. In this chapter, I'll just provide a brief overview of the utilities and examples of using some of the utilities. Most UNIX system administrators are familiar with these utilities in UNIX but may find differences in the options to these utilities when using the *Resource Kit* version.

man page

chmod - 3

I have made every effort to limit the number of "add-on" products, to Windows and UNIX covered in this book. The *Resource Kit*, however, is so useful to Windows system administrators that not covering at least some part of it, such as the POSIX utilities, would leave a void in the discussion of Windows system administration. You can find out more information about the *Resource Kit* on the Microsoft Web site. You can buy it at many computer, electronic, and book stores. Be sure to buy the *Resource Kit* for the version of Windows you are running. There is also a *Resource Kit* for both the Server and Workstation versions of Windows. I used the Server *Resource Kit* for the POSIX commands covered in this chapter.

man page

find - 10

man page

ls - 2

man page

mv - 3

Both the source code and executables for the POSIX utilities are on the *Resource Kit*. The following is a listing of the POSIX executables for I386 on the *Resource Kit* CD-ROM. I used the POSIX utility **ls -l** to produce this listing:

```
F:\I386\GNU\POSIX> ls -l

-rwxrwxrwx   1 Everyone Everyone   101748 Sep  6 12:39 CAT.EXE
-rwxrwxrwx   1 Everyone Everyone   116188 Sep  6 12:39 CHMOD.EXE
-rwxrwxrwx   1 Everyone Everyone   110920 Sep  6 12:39 CHOWN.EXE
-rwxrwxrwx   1 Everyone Everyone   111208 Sep  6 12:39 CP.EXE
-rwxrwxrwx   1 Everyone Everyone   173580 Sep  6 12:39 FIND.EXE
-rwxrwxrwx   1 Everyone Everyone   144256 Sep  6 12:39 GREP.EXE
-rwxrwxrwx   1 Everyone Everyone    90960 Sep  6 12:39 LN.EXE
-rwxrwxrwx   1 Everyone Everyone   128532 Sep  6 12:39 LS.EXE
-rwxrwxrwx   1 Everyone Everyone    88984 Sep  6 12:39 MKDIR.EXE
-rwxrwxrwx   1 Everyone Everyone    99096 Sep  6 12:39 MV.EXE
-rwxrwxrwx   1 Everyone Everyone   114564 Sep  6 12:39 RM.EXE
-rwxrwxrwx   1 Everyone Everyone    85004 Sep  6 12:39 RMDIR.EXE
-rwxrwxrwx   1 Everyone Everyone   362528 Sep  6 12:39 SH.EXE
-rwxrwxrwx   1 Everyone Everyone    91244 Sep  6 12:39 TOUCH.EXE
-rwxrwxrwx   1 Everyone Everyone   287628 Sep  6 12:39 VI.EXE
```

```
-rwxrwxrwx    1 Everyone Everyone    95392 Sep  6 12:39 WC.EXE
```

The directory in which these utilities are located is the **F:** drive, which is my CD-ROM, in **I386\GNU\POSIX**, which is the I386 version of these utilities. The following list is command summaries of the POSIX utilities. A brief description of some the utilities as well some of the more commonly used options to the utilities is included. In some cases, you also have an example of having run the utility. The **POSIX.WRI** file on the *Resource Kit* provides an exhaustive description of each utility.

cat

man page

cat - 3

cat - Display, combine, append, copy, or create files.

Some commonly used options follow:

-n   Line numbers are displayed, along with output lines.

-u   Output is unbuffered, which means that it is handled character-by-character.

-v   Prints most nonprinting characters visibly.

The following example shows using the **-n** option with **cat**:

```
D:\WINNT\system> cat -n setup.inf

    1  [setup]
    2      help = setup.hlp
    3
    4  ;    Place any programs here that should be run at the end of setup.
    5  ;    These apps will be run in order of their appearance here.
    6  [run]
    7
    8  [dialog]
    9      caption   = "Windows Setup"
   10      exit      = "Exit Windows Setup"
   11      title     = "Installing Windows 3.1"
   12      options   = "In addition to installing Windows 3.1, you can:"
   13      printwait = "Please wait while Setup configures your printer(s)..."

                                    .
                                    .
                                    .

   20  [data]
```

```
21  ; Disk space required
22  ; <type of setup>= <Full install space>, <Min install space>
23
24      upd2x386full = 10000000,6144000 ; 10.0 Mb,  6.144 Mb
25      upd2x286full = 9000000,6144000  ;  9.0 Mb,  6.144 Mb
26      upd3x386full = 5500000,5000000  ;  5.5 Mb,  5.0 Mb
27      upd3x286full = 5500000,5000000  ;  5.5 Mb,  5.0 Mb
28
29      new386full   = 10000000,6144000 ; 10.0 Mb,  6.144 Mb
30      new286full   = 9000000,6144000  ;  9.0 Mb,  6.144 Mb
31
32      netadmin     = 16000000         ; 16.0 Mb
33      netadminupd  = 16000000         ; 16.0 Mb
34      upd2x386net  = 300000           ;   .3 Mb
35      upd3x386net  = 300000           ;   .3 Mb
36      upd2x286net  = 300000           ;   .3 Mb
37      upd3x286net  = 300000           ;   .3 Mb
38      new386net    = 300000,300000    ;   .3 Mb,   .3 Mb
39      new286net    = 300000,300000    ;   .3 Mb,   .3 Mb
40
41
42
43  ; Defaults used in setting up and names of a few files
44      startup   = WIN.COM
```

chmod

man page

chmod - 3

chmod - Changes permissions of specified files using symbolic or absolute (sometimes called numeric) modes. Symbolic mode is described below.

Symbol of who is affected:

u	User is affected.
g	Group is affected.
o	Other is affected.
a	All users are affected.

Operation to perform:

+	Add permission.
-	Remove permission.
=	Replace permission.

Permission specified:

r	Read permission.
w	Write permission.
x	Execute permission.
u	Copy user permissions.
g	Copy group permissions.
o	Copy other permissions.

The following example uses both modes. Using absolute or numeric mode, the permissions on the file **cat1.exe** are changed from 666 to 777. Using symbolic mode, the execute permissions are then removed for all users:

```
D:\> ls -l cat1.exe

-rw-rw-rw-    1 Administ Administ      71323 Feb 20 11:34 cat1.exe

D:\> chmod 777 cat1.exe

D:\> ls -l cat1.exe


-rwxrwxrwx    1 Administ Administ      71323 Feb 20 11:34 cat1.exe

D:\> chmod a-x cat1.exe

D:\> ls -l cat1.exe

-rw-rw-rw-    1 Administ Administ      71323 Feb 20 11:34 cat1.exe
```

man page

ls - 2

man page

chmod - 3

cp

man page

cp - 3

cp - Copies files and directories.

Some commonly used options follow:

          -i   Interactive copy whereby you are prompted to confirm whether or not you wish to overwrite an existing file.

          -f   Forces existing files to be overwritten by files being copied if a conflict occurs in file names.

          -p   Preserves permissions when copying.

          -R   Copies recursively which includes subtrees.

The following example shows using the **cp** command to copy **cat1.exe** to **cat2.exe,** and then a listing of all files beginning with **cat** is produced:

man page

ls - 2

```
D:\> cp cat1.exe cat2.exe

D:\> ls -l cat*

-rw-rw-rw-   1 Administ Administ     71323 Feb 20 11:34 cat1.exe
-rw-rw-rw-   1 Administ Administ     71323 Feb 20 11:47 cat2.exe
```

find

find - Recursively descends a directory structure looking for the file(s) listed.

man page

find - 10

Some commonly used options follow:

-f   Specifies a file hierarchy for **find** to traverse.

-s   When symbolic links are encountered, the file refer-
            enced by the link and not the link itself will be used.

-x   Doesn't descend into directories that have a device
            number different from that of the file from which the
            descent began.

-print   Prints pathname to standard output.

-size n   True if the file's size is n.

grep

man page

grep - 10

grep - Searches for text and displays result.

The following example shows using grep to find the expression "shell" everywhere it appears inside the file **setup.inf**:

```
D:\> grep shell setup.inf

[shell]
00000000="shell versions below 3.01",,unsupported_net
00030100="shell versions below 3.21",,novell301
00032100="shell versions 3.21 and above",,novell321
00032600="shell versions 3.26 and above",,novell326
    #win.shell, 0:
    #win.shell, 0:
[win.shell]
    shell.dll
    system.ini, Boot,     "oldshell"        ,"shell"
```

ls

man page

ls - 2

ls - Lists the contents of a directory.

Some commonly used options:

-a	List all entries.
-c	Use time file was last modified for producing order in which files are listed.
-d	List only the directory name, not its contents.
-g	Include the group in the output.
-i	Print the inode number in the first column of the report.
-q	Nonprinting characters are represented by a "?".
-r	Reverse the order in which files are printed.
-s	Show the size in blocks instead of bytes.
-t	List in order of time saved with most recent first.
-u	Use time of last access instead of last modification for determining order in which files are printed.
-A	Same as -a, except current and parent directories aren't listed.
-C	Multicolumn output produced.
-F	Directory followed by a "/", executable by an "*", symbolic link by an "@".
-L	List file or directory to which link points.
-R	Recursively list subdirectories.

I include several examples on the next few pages.

man page

ls - 2

```
D:\> ls -a

Blue Monday 16.bmp
Blue Monday.bmp
Coffee Bean 16.bmp
Coffee Bean.bmp
Config
Cursors
FORMS
FeatherTexture.bmp
Fiddle Head.bmp
Fonts
Furry Dog 16.bmp
Furry Dog.bmp
Geometrix.bmp
Gone Fishing.bmp
Greenstone.bmp
Hazy Autumn 16.bmp
Help
Hiking Boot.bmp
Leaf Fossils 16.bmp
Leather 16.bmp
Maple Trails.bmp
Media
NETLOGON.CHG
NOTEPAD.EXE
Petroglyph 16.bmp
Prairie Wind.bmp
Profiles
REGEDIT.EXE
Rhododendron.bmp
River Sumida.bmp
Santa Fe Stucco.bmp
Seaside 16.bmp
Seaside.bmp
ShellNew
Snakeskin.bmp
Soap Bubbles.bmp
Solstice.bmp
Swimming Pool.bmp
TASKMAN.EXE
TEMP
Upstream 16.bmp
WIN.INI
WINFILE.INI
WINHELP.EXE
Zapotec 16.bmp
Zapotec.bmp
_DEFAULT.PIF
black16.scr
clock.avi
control.ini
explorer.exe
inetsrv.mif
inf
lanma256.bmp
lanmannt.bmp
network.wri
poledit.exe
printer.wri
repair
setup.old
setuplog.txt
system
system.ini
system32
vmmreg32.dll
welcome.exe
winhlp32.exe
```

```
D:\> ls -l

-rwxrwxrwx   1 Administ NETWORK      8310 Aug  9  1996 Blue Monday 16.bmp
-rwxrwxrwx   1 Administ NETWORK     37940 Aug  9  1996 Blue Monday.bmp
-rwxrwxrwx   1 Administ NETWORK      8312 Aug  9  1996 Coffee Bean 16.bmp
-rwxrwxrwx   1 Administ NETWORK     17062 Aug  9  1996 Coffee Bean.bmp
drwx---rwx   1 Administ Administ        0 Feb 10 10:39 Config
drwx---rwx   1 Administ Administ        0 Feb 10 16:22 Cursors
drwxrwxrwx   1 Administ NETWORK         0 Feb 10 16:23 FORMS
-rwxrwxrwx   1 Administ NETWORK     16730 Aug  9  1996 FeatherTexture.bmp
-rwxrwxrwx   1 Administ NETWORK     65922 Aug  9  1996 Fiddle Head.bmp
drwx---rwx   1 Administ Administ     8192 Feb 10 10:39 Fonts
-rwxrwxrwx   1 Administ NETWORK     18552 Aug  9  1996 Furry Dog 16.bmp
-rwxrwxrwx   1 Administ NETWORK     37940 Aug  9  1996 Furry Dog.bmp
-rwxrwxrwx   1 Administ NETWORK      4328 Aug  9  1996 Geometrix.bmp
-rwxrwxrwx   1 Administ NETWORK     17336 Aug  9  1996 Gone Fishing.bmp
-rwxrwxrwx   1 Administ NETWORK     26582 Aug  9  1996 Greenstone.bmp
-rwxrwxrwx   1 Administ NETWORK     32888 Aug  9  1996 Hazy Autumn 16.bmp
drwx---rwx   1 Administ Administ        0 Feb 19 15:10 Help
-rwxrwxrwx   1 Administ NETWORK     37854 Aug  9  1996 Hiking Boot.bmp
-rwxrwxrwx   1 Administ NETWORK     12920 Aug  9  1996 Leaf Fossils 16.bmp
-rwxrwxrwx   1 Administ NETWORK      6392 Aug  9  1996 Leather 16.bmp
-rwxrwxrwx   1 Administ NETWORK     26566 Aug  9  1996 Maple Trails.bmp
drwx---rwx   1 Administ Administ        0 Feb 10 16:23 Media
-rwxrwxrwx   1 Administ NETWORK     65536 Feb 11 10:35 NETLOGON.CHG
-rwxrwxrwx   1 Administ NETWORK     45328 Aug  8  1996 NOTEPAD.EXE
-rwxrwxrwx   1 Administ NETWORK     16504 Aug  9  1996 Petroglyph 16.bmp
-rwxrwxrwx   1 Administ NETWORK     65954 Aug  9  1996 Prairie Wind.bmp
drwxrwxrwx   1 Administ NETWORK      4096 Feb 10 16:32 Profiles
-rwxrwxr-x   1 Administ NETWORK     71952 Aug  8  1996 REGEDIT.EXE
-rwxrwxrwx   1 Administ NETWORK     17362 Aug  9  1996 Rhododendron.bmp
-rwxrwxrwx   1 Administ NETWORK     26208 Aug  9  1996 River Sumida.bmp
-rwxrwxrwx   1 Administ NETWORK     65832 Aug  9  1996 Santa Fe Stucco.bmp
-rwxrwxrwx   1 Administ NETWORK      8312 Aug  9  1996 Seaside 16.bmp
-rwxrwxr-x   1 Administ NETWORK     17334 Aug  9  1996 Seaside.bmp
drwxrwxrwx   1 Administ NETWORK         0 Feb 10 16:22 ShellNew
-rwxrwxrwx   1 Administ NETWORK     10292 Aug  9  1996 Snakeskin.bmp
-rwxrwxrwx   1 Administ NETWORK     65978 Aug  9  1996 Soap Bubbles.bmp
-rwxrwxr-x   1 Administ NETWORK     17334 Aug  9  1996 Solstice.bmp
-rwxrwxrwx   1 Administ NETWORK     26202 Aug  9  1996 Swimming Pool.bmp
-rwxrwxrwx   1 Administ NETWORK     32016 Aug  8  1996 TASKMAN.EXE
drwxrwxrwx   1 Administ NETWORK         0 Feb 20 09:59 TEMP
-rwxrwxrwx   1 Administ NETWORK     32888 Aug  9  1996 Upstream 16.bmp
-rwxrwxrwx   1 Administ NETWORK       239 Feb 10 16:23 WIN.INI
-rwxrwxr-x   1 Administ NETWORK         3 Aug  8  1996 WINFILE.INI
-rwxrwxr-x   1 Administ NETWORK    256192 Aug  8  1996 WINHELP.EXE
-rwxrwxrwx   1 Administ NETWORK      8312 Aug  9  1996 Zapotec 16.bmp
-rwxrwxrwx   1 Administ NETWORK      9522 Aug  9  1996 Zapotec.bmp
-rwxrwxr-x   1 Administ NETWORK       707 Aug  8  1996 _DEFAULT.PIF
-rwx---r-x   1 Administ Administ     5328 Aug  8  1996 black16.scr
-rwx---r-x   1 Administ Administ    82944 Aug  8  1996 clock.avi
-rwxrwxrwx   1 Administ NETWORK         0 Feb 10 11:18 control.ini
-rwx---r-x   1 Administ Administ   234256 Aug  8  1996 explorer.exe
-rwxrwxrwx   1 Administ NETWORK      1628 Feb 10 11:20 inetsrv.mif
drwx---rwx   1 Administ Administ    47104 Feb 10 10:56 inf
-rwx---r-x   1 Administ Administ   157044 Aug  8  1996 lanma256.bmp
-rwx---r-x   1 Administ Administ   157044 Aug  8  1996 lanmannt.bmp
-rwx---r-x   1 Administ Administ    67328 Aug  8  1996 network.wri
-rwx---r-x   1 Administ Administ   123152 Aug  8  1996 poledit.exe
-rwx---r-x   1 Administ Administ    34816 Aug  8  1996 printer.wri
drwx---rwx   1 Administ Administ        0 Feb 10 16:24 repair
-rwxrwxrwx   1 Administ NETWORK      2499 Feb 10 16:23 setup.old
-rwxrwxrwx   1 Administ NETWORK       138 Feb 10 16:22 setuplog.txt
drwx---rwx   1 Administ Administ     4096 Feb 20 10:07 system
-rwx---r-x   1 Administ Administ       219 Aug  8  1996 system.ini
drwx---rwx   1 Administ Administ   167936 Feb 20 09:50 system32
-rwx---r-x   1 Administ Administ    24336 Aug  8  1996 vmmreg32.dll
-rwx---r-x   1 Administ Administ    22288 Aug  8  1996 welcome.exe
-rwx---r-x   1 Administ Administ   310032 Aug  8  1996 winhlp32.exe
```

```
D:\> ls -C

Blue Monday 16.bmpGreenstone.bmpRhododendron.bmpWINFILE.INI        poledit.exe
Blue Monday.bmp Hazy Autumn 16.bmpRiver Sumida.bmpWINHELP.EXE      printer.wri
Coffee Bean 16.bmpHelp          Santa Fe Stucco.bmpZapotec 16.bmprepair
Coffee Bean.bmp Hiking Boot.bmp Seaside 16.bmp  Zapotec.bmp        setup.old
Config          Leaf Fossils 16.bmpSeaside.bmp  _DEFAULT.PIF       setuplog.txt
Cursors         Leather 16.bmp  ShellNew        black16.scr        system
FORMS           Maple Trails.bmpSnakeskin.bmp   clock.avi          system.ini
FeatherTexture.bmpMedia         Soap Bubbles.bmpcontrol.ini        system32
Fiddle Head.bmp NETLOGON.CHG    Solstice.bmp    explorer.exe       vmmreg32.dll
Fonts           NOTEPAD.EXE     Swimming Pool.bmpinetsrv.mif       welcome.exe
Furry Dog 16.bmpPetroglyph 16.bmpTASKMAN.EXE    inf                winhlp32.exe
Furry Dog.bmp   Prairie Wind.bmpTEMP            lanma256.bmp
Geometrix.bmp   Profiles        Upstream 16.bmp lanmannt.bmp
Gone Fishing.bmpREGEDIT.EXE     WIN.INI         network.wri
```

mkdir

man page

mkdir - 3

mkdir - Creates specified directories.

The following is a commonly used option:

-p   Creates intermediate directories to achieve the full
            path. If you want to create several layers of directories
            down, use **-p**.

mv

man page

mv - 3

mv - Renames files and directories.

Some commonly used options follow:

-i   Interactive move whereby you are prompted to con-
            firm whether or not you wish to overwrite an existing
            file.

-f   Forces existing files to be overwritten by files being
            moved if a conflict occurs in file names.

rm

rm - Removes files and directories.

Some commonly used options follow:

-d   Removes directories as well as other file types.

-i   Interactive remove whereby you are prompted to con-
        firm whether or not you wish to remove an existing
        file.

-f   Forces files to be removed.

-r (-R) Recursively removes the contents of the directory and
        then the directory itself.

touch

touch - Changes the modification and/or last access times of a file, or creates a file.

Some commonly used options:

-c   Does not create a specified file if it does not exist.

-f   Forces a touch of a file regardless of permissions.

The following example creates **file1** with **touch**:

man page

ls - 2

```
D:\> ls -l file1
ls:file1: No such file or directory

D:\> touch file1

D:\> ls -l file1

-rw-rw-rw-    1 Administ Administ      0 Feb 20 11:45 file1
```

WC

wc - Produces a count of words, lines, and characters.

man page

wc - 10

Some commonly used options follow:

-l   Prints the number of lines in a file.

-w   Prints the number of words in a file.

-c   Prints the number of characters in a file.

The first example lists the contents of a directory and pipes the output
to **wc**. The second example provides **wc** information about the file
system.ini.

```
D:\> ls

CAT.EXE
CHMOD.EXE
CHOWN.EXE
CP.EXE
FIND.EXE
GREP.EXE
LN.EXE
LS.EXE
MKDIR.EXE
MV.EXE
RM.EXE
RMDIR.EXE
SH.EXE
TOUCH.EXE
VI.EXE
WC.EXE

D:\> ls | wc -wlc

      16       16      132

D:\> wc -wlc system.ini

      13       17       219 system.ini
```

Additional Commands

There are many additional commands in Windows that can be issued at the command line. I will present some of these commands in an informal manner.

Networking Commands

You have access to many useful networking commands on the command line in Windows. Some of the commands not covered here that you may want to look into include the following:

man page

ftp - 9

man page

telnet - 9

man page

rcp - 9

- **lpr**
- **route**
- **finger**
- **rexec**
- **ftp**
- **telnet** (opens a telnet window in the Windows environment)
- **hostname**
- **lpq**
- **tracert**
- **rcp**
- **rsh**
- **tftp**

You can find out more about these commands by typing the command name and /? at the command prompt, such as **telnet /?**. In the upcoming sections, I cover some additional commands that I often use.

arp

arp is used to display and edit the Address Resolution Protocol (arp) cache, which maps IP addresses to physical hardware addresses. The cache has in it one or more addresses of recently accessed systems. The following example shows issuing the **arp** command on a Windows system at address 113 and the address of the system most recently accessed at 111, with its physical hardware address shown.

```
d: arp -a

Interface: 159.260.112.113 on Interface 2
    Internet Address       Physical Address      Type
    159.260.112.111        08-00-09-f0-bc-40     dynamic
```

There are several options to the **arp** command that you can view by issuing the **arp /?** command.

ipconfig

ipconfig is used to display the current networking interface parameters. The following example shows issuing the **ipconfig** command on a Windows system at address 113 with the **/all** option set, which shows all information related to the networking interface:

```
d: ipconfig /all

Windows IP Configuration

                Host Name . . . . . . . . . : hpsystem1
                DNS Servers . . . . . . . . :
                Node Type . . . . . . . . . : Broadcast
                NetBIOS Scope ID. . . . . . :
                IP Routing Enabled. . . . . : No
                WINS Proxy Enabled. . . . . : No
                NetBIOS Resolution Uses DNS : No

Ethernet adapter Hpddnd31:

                Description . . . . . . . . : HP DeskDirect
                                        10/100 LAN Adapter
                Physical Address. . . . . . : 08-00-09-D9-
      9A-8A
                DHCP Enabled. . . . . . . . : No
                IP Address. . . . . . . . . : 159.260.112.113
                Subnet Mask . . . . . . . . : 255.255.255.0
                Default Gateway . . . . . . : 159.260.112.250
```

There are several options to the **ipconfig** command that you can view by issuing the **ipconfig /?** command.

netstat

man page

netstat - 9

netstat provides network protocol statistics. The following **netstat** example uses the **-e** and **-s** options, which show Ethernet statistics and statistics for various protocols, respectively. The Ethernet statistics associated with the **-e** option are under "Interface Statistics" and end with "IP Statistics":

```
d: netstat -e -s

Interface Statistics
```

	Received	Sent
Bytes	3182007276	2446436
Unicast packets	11046	9604
Non-unicast packets	21827982	7932

```
Discards                              0                    0
Errors                                0                    1
Unknown protocols               4946670
```

IP Statistics

```
Packets Received                           = 20489869
Received Header Errors                     = 133441
Received Address Errors                    = 28222
Datagrams Forwarded                        = 0
Unknown Protocols Received                 = 0
Received Packets Discarded                 = 0
Received Packets Delivered                 = 20328206
Output Requests                            = 12004
Routing Discards                           = 0
Discarded Output Packets                   = 0
Output Packet No Route                     = 0
Reassembly Required                        = 0
Reassembly Successful                      = 0
Reassembly Failures                        = 0
Datagrams Successfully Fragmented          = 0
Datagrams Failing Fragmentation            = 0
Fragments Created                          = 0
```

ICMP Statistics

```
                             Received    Sent
Messages                     3702        23
Errors                       0           0
Destination Unreachable      4           5
Time Exceeded                0           0
Parameter Problems           0           0
Source Quenchs               0           0
Redirects                    3680        0
Echos                        5           13
Echo Replies                 13          5
Timestamps                   0           0
Timestamp Replies            0           0
Address Masks                0           0
Address Mask Replies         0           0
```

TCP Statistics

```
Active Opens                        = 27
Passive Opens                       = 8
Failed Connection Attempts          = 1
Reset Connections                   = 15
Current Connections                 = 2
Segments Received                   = 1888
Segments Sent                       = 1854
Segments Retransmitted              = 3
```

```
UDP Statistics

    Datagrams Received    = 607489
    No Ports              = 19718827
    Receive Errors        = 0
    Datagrams Sent        = 10124
```

man page

netstat - 9

There are several options to the **netstat** command that you can view by issuing the **netstat /?** command. If you wish to see the changes in the value of statistics, you can specify an interval after which the statistics will again be displayed.

ping

man page

ping - 9

ping is used to determine whether or not a host is reachable on the network. **ping** causes an echo request that sends packets that are returned by the destination host you specify. There are several options to the ping command you can specify. The following example uses the **-n** option to specify the number of times you want to send the packets, and **-l** specifies the length of packets for which the maximum of 8192 is used:

```
d: ping -n 9 -l 8192 system2

Pinging system2 [159.260.112.111] with 8192 bytes of da-
ta:

Reply from 159.260.112.111: bytes=8192 time=20ms TTL=255
Reply from 159.260.112.111: bytes=8192 time=20ms TTL=255
Reply from 159.260.112.111: bytes=8192 time=21ms TTL=255
Reply from 159.260.112.111: bytes=8192 time=20ms TTL=255
Reply from 159.260.112.111: bytes=8192 time=10ms TTL=255
Reply from 159.260.112.111: bytes=8192 time=30ms TTL=255
Reply from 159.260.112.111: bytes=8192 time=30ms TTL=255
Reply from 159.260.112.111: bytes=8192 time=20ms TTL=255
Reply from 159.260.112.111: bytes=8192 time=20ms TTL=255
```

There are several additional options to the **ping** command that you can view by issuing the **ping /?** command.

Permissions with cacls

You can view and change permissions of files from the command line with **cacls**. Figure 19-6 shows the help screen for the **cacls** command.

```
 Command Prompt                                                    _ □ ×
D:\>help cacls
Displays or modifies access control lists (ACLs) of files

CACLS filename [/T] [/E] [/C] [/G user:perm] [/R user [...]]
               [/P user:perm [...]] [/D user [...]]
   filename        Displays ACLs.
   /T              Changes ACLs of specified files in
                   the current directory and all subdirectories.
   /E              Edit ACL instead of replacing it.
   /C              Continue on access denied errors.
   /G user:perm    Grant specified user access rights.
                   Perm can be: R  Read
                                C  Change (write)
                                F  Full control
   /R user         Revoke specified user's access rights (only valid with /E).
   /P user:perm    Replace specified user's access rights.
                   Perm can be: N  None
                                R  Read
                                C  Change (write)
                                F  Full control
   /D user         Deny specified user access.
Wildcards can be used to specify more that one file in a command.
You can specify more than one user in a command.

D:\>
◄                                                                     ▓ ►
```

Figure 19-6 **cacls** Help Screen

cacls is used to display and modify the access control lists of files. You can see in Figure 19-6 that you have four different types of access rights for files that were described in detail earlier. The following list shows the abbreviations for access rights that are associated with the **cacls** command:

N	None
R	Read
C	Change
F	Full Control

Figure 19-7 shows using both **cacls** and the *File Permissions* window to view the existing permissions for **D:\WINNT\REGE-DIT.EXE**. This is one of the most important files on the system that was used in an earlier chapter to view and modify registry information on the system. This is a file that you want to carefully manage access rights to, in order to avoid any operating system mishaps.

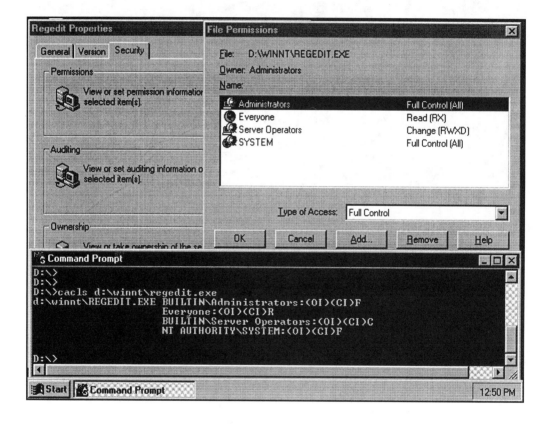

Figure 19-7   D:\WINNT\REGEDIT.EXE Permissions

Notice that *Server Operators* do indeed have *Change* rights to this file. You can, of course, modify the permissions on this or any file on the system. The *File Permissions* window and the output of the

cacls command are in different formats; however, they contain the same information.

Command-Line Backup

An alternative to using the graphical tools to initiate backups is to use the command line. Using the **NTBACKUP** command, you can initiate backups at the command line or build batch files using this command. You can combine the **NTBACKUP** command with the **AT** command to schedule backups. Provided that the *SCHEDULE* service is started, you can specify the time for which a job will be scheduled. Let's take a closer look at these two commands to see how they may be combined to schedule backups.

NTBACKUP

NTBACKUP - This command is used to initiate backups at the command line.

The following is a summary of the **NTBACKUP** command:

```
C:\ NTBACUKP /?
NTBACKUP operation path [/a][/v][/r][/d"text"][/b][/hc:{on | off}]
                        [/t{option}][/l"filename"][/e][/TAPE:{n}]
```

Some commonly used options follow:

operation	The *operation* to perform, such as *backup*.
path	The directories you wish to back up.
/a	Append this backup to those on the tape rather than replacing the contents of the tape with the current job.
/b	Include the local registry in the backup.
/d"text"	Description of the backup set is defined by the text in quotation marks.
/e	The backup log will contain only exceptions rather than the full backup log.

/hc:{on |off}	Specify whether or not to use hardware compression for the backup. You can use this option only if you don't use the /a option.
/L"filename"	The file name to be used for the backup log.
/r	Restricted access to the tape will be used. You can use this option only if you don't use the /A option.
/t option	Specify the type of backup, such as normal, copy, incremental, differential, or daily.
/tape:{n}	Specify the tape drive to be used if indeed the server has more than one tape drive.
/v	Verify the operation.

To back up the **oracle** directory with a *normal* backup, recording exceptions only in the log file, performing tape verification, and including a description of "oracle backup," you would issue the following command.

```
C:\ NTBACKUP backup d:/oracle /e /v /t normal /d "oracle backup"
```

AT

AT - This command is used to schedule jobs.

The following is a summary of the **AT** command:

```
C:\ AT /?

AT [//computername] [id] [/DELETE] | /DELETE [/YES]]

AT [//computername] time [/INTERACTIVE] [/EVERY:date[,...] | [/NEXT:date[,...]]
"command"
```

Some commonly used options follow:

//computername	Computer on which the command will execute.
id	The identification number assigned to a scheduled command.
/DELETE	Cancel a scheduled command. You can use an id to cancel jobs associated with that *id* or cancel all scheduled commands.
/YES	Reply *YES* as confirmation of canceled jobs.
time	The *time* at which the job should be scheduled, in 24-hour format.
/INTERACTIVE	The job will run interactively rather than in the background.

/EVERY:date[,...]	Repeating jobs are scheduled with *dates* (Monday, Tuesday, and so on) or a day of the month (1-31).
/NEXT:date[,...]	Use this option to schedule a job the next time *date* occurs. Specify one or more dates (Monday, Tuesday, and so on) or a day of the month (1-31).
"command"	The *command* to be executed.

We can now combine the previous **NTBACKUP** command with **AT,** to perform a scheduled backup. By placing the previous **NTBACKUP** command in the file **backup,** we can issue the following command:

```
C:\ AT 03:00 /every:Monday,Tuesday,Wednesday,Thursday,Friday "backup"
```

CHAPTER 20

Samba

Samba Overview

Samba is an application that allows a UNIX host to act as a file server for Windows systems. The Windows systems can access UNIX filesystems and printers using their native Windows networking.

Our goal in this chapter is to give an overview of the setup of Samba and demonstrate a subset of its functionality. We'll focus on the file server functionality only. We'll set up shares on the remote UNIX system that will appear as a drive letters and icons on a Windows system. Because Samba comes with the Red Hat Linux software used throughout the book we'll set up and run Samba on a Linux system. Samba is available for most UNIX variants.

Samba provides this file-sharing functionality using Server Message Block (SMB) protocol. SMB runs on top of TCP/IP. In our example in this chapter, both the Windows system and UNIX system are running TCP/IP and SMB. These provide all of the technology that is required to establish file sharing between the two systems.

Chapter 16 covered Network File System (NFS) running on a Windows system and accessing files on a UNIX system. This functionality is similar to that which we'll cover with Samba in this chapter. In addition to the file-sharing capability, Samba also provides printer sharing and addtional user access control capability. We won't focus on these capabilities in this chapter, however, Samba does indeed provide some advanced functionality in these areas.

At the time of this writing Samba contains the functinality just mentioned file-sharing, printer sharing, and advanced user access control of files. There are many advancements taking place with Samba and other software provided under GNU Public License (GPL) as free software. Because the software is free, many individuals have access to it and spend time enhancing the software. For this reason you may find that additional functionality is included in Samba and other such software. There are many enhancements planned for Samba including an administration tool and other advancements that were not available at the time this chapter was written. There is more information about obtaining Samba and other free software at the end of this chapter.

Setup

Because Samba is supplied on the Red Hat Linux CD-ROM, we'll walk through a simple Samba setup using Red Hat Linux. When installing Red Hat Linux, you can select the software packages you wish to load, as you can on most all UNIX variants. If you did not load Samba at the time you originally loaded the operating system, you can use the *Gnome RPM* tool or **rpm** from the command line to load Samba or any other software. These tools were briefly discussed in the System Administration chapter.

Using *linuxconf,* we'll perform some simple tasks to set up Samba. Figure 20-1 shows the *linuxconf* window *Disk Shares* under *Samba file server* with three disk shares we'll be using in this example.

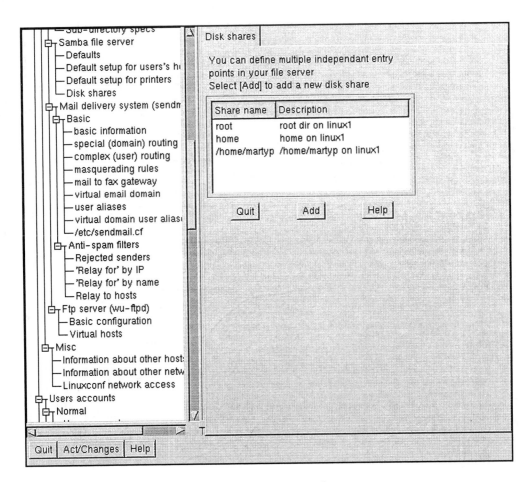

Figure 20-1 Share Information in *Linuxconf*

There are three share names on our Linux system that we will make available to other systems running SMB. Figure 20-2 shows more detailed information about the middle share called *home*.

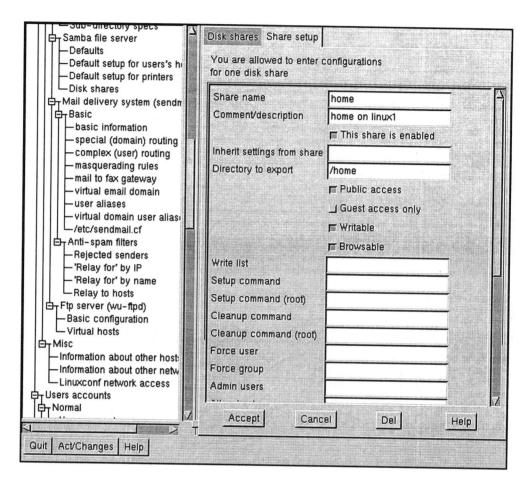

Disk shares | Share setup

Figure 20-2 **/home** Share Information in *Linuxconf*

This share is for the **/home** directory on linux1. Note the four selections related to permissions in the figure. We have granted *Public access*, *Writable*, and *Browsable* rights on this share. We have not restricted it to *Guest only access*. On this share, we have been unrestrictive with respect to the rights granted it. You'll want to consider these rights carefully on your system as you go about assigning these rights. Keep in mind that we're not using any user authentication in our examples, in order to keep them simple. In practice, however, you'll want to make sure that you assign appropriate rights to the shares.

With three shares having been assigned, we'll use *Linuxconf* to start *smb*. We do so by enabling *smb* in *Control service activity,* as shown in Figure 20-3.

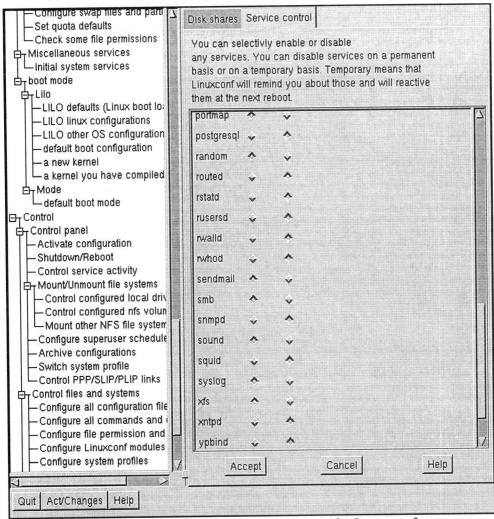

Figure 20-3 Start *smb* in *Control service activity* in *Linuxconf*

smb has been enabled so that the service will start when the system boots.

Before we begin using SMB, let's perform a couple of quick checks on the work we have performed with *Linuxconf*. We could have accomplished manually everything we have done with *Linuxconf*.

The first check is to view the file **/etc/smb.conf**. This is the file that contains all our SMB configuration information. For now, let's go right to the "Share Definitions" section to confirm that the three shares we configured in *Linuxconf* have proper entries in **/etc/smb.conf**:

```
#=============== Share Definitions ==========================
[homes]
     comment = Home Directories
     browseable = no
     writable = yes

# Un-comment the following and create the netlogon directory for
Domain Logons
; [netlogon]
;    comment = Network Logon Service
;    path = /home/netlogon
;    guest ok = yes
;    writable = no
;    share modes = no


# Un-comment the following to provide a specific roving profile
share
# the default is to use the user's home directory
;[Profiles]
;    path = /home/profiles
;    browseable = no
;    guest ok = yes


# NOTE: If you have a BSD-style print system there is no need to
# specifically define each individual printer
[printers]
     comment = All Printers
     path = /var/spool/samba
     browseable = no
# Set public = yes to allow user 'guest account' to print
     guest ok = no
     writable = no
     printable = yes
```

```
[root]
    comment = root dir on linux1
    available = yes
    path = /
    public = yes
    guest only = no
    writable = yes
    browseable = yes
    only user = no
[home]
    comment = home on linux1
    available = yes
    path = /home
    public = yes
    guest only = no
    writable = yes
    browseable = yes
    only user = no
[/home/martyp]
    comment = /home/martyp on linux1
    available = yes
    path = /home/martyp
    public = yes
    guest only = no
    writable = yes
    browseable = yes
    only user = no
```

There are indeed entries in **/etc/smb.conf** for the three shares we configured in *Linuxconf* with the permissions we set up. These are shown near the end of the listing. Next we'll run a Samba utilitiy called **testparm**. This utility will check our **/etc/smb.conf** file for errors. This utility produces a very long output which I won't include here, but you'll want to run this and check for any warnings or errors it produces.

For our **/etc/smb.conf** file **testparm** produced only one warning that appeared at the very beginning of the file, which is shown in the following listing:

```
# testparm smb.conf

Load smb config files from /etc/smb.conf
Processing section "[homes]"
Processing section "[printers]"
Processing section "[root]"
```

```
Processing section "[home]"
Processing section "[/home/martyp]"
Loaded services file OK.
WARNING: You have some share names that are longer than 8 chars
These may give errors while browsing or may not be accessible
to some older clients
Press enter to see a dump of your service definitions
```

•

•

•

testparm produced the warning for a long share name and also included a list of our three shares, which looked to be in order. We won't address the long share name warning because the Windows system used in the example can handle the long name. If, however, we were on a DOS system, there would be a problem with this name. We'll see shortly how these potential name icompatibilities are addressed by Linux.

The next check we want to perform is to see that the daemon for Samba called **smbd** is indeed running, as shown in the following listing:

man page

ps - 12

```
# ps -efl | grep smbd
140 S root      490      1  0  60   0    -   553 do_sel Sep28 ?      00:00:00 [smbd]
140 S root     1493    490  0  60   0    -   896 do_sel Sep29 ?      00:00:00 smbd -D
000 S root     1976   1951  0  70   0    -   288 pipe_r 09:09 pts/1  00:00:00 grep smbd
```

This **ps** output shows that **smbd** is running. Next let's check that the *netbios-ssn* service is running in the "LISTEN" state, as shown in the following example:

man page

netstat - 9

man page

grep - 10

```
# netstat -a | grep netbios
tcp     0     0 linux1:netbios-ssn     f4457mfp2:1047      ESTABLISHED
tcp     0     0 *:netbios-ssn          *:*                 LISTEN
udp     0     0 linux1:netbios-dgm     *:*
udp     0     0 linux1:netbios-ns      *:*
udp     0     0 *:netbios-dgm          *:*
udp     0     0 *:netbios-ns           *:*
```

The output of this listing shows that netbios is running. There is an "ESTABLISHED" connection shown which you won't see until you have created a connection to your Samba server. I had already established this connection as I prepared the examples in this chapter.

We can also use the Samba client to access files on the Windows system from our Linux system. Although we won't cover this capability, mostly because the Linux system will normally act as a file server and not the other way around, there is a utility called **smbclient** that provides a lot of useful information. Let's now get the overall status of the Samba setup with the **smbclient** utility, as shown in the following listing:

```
# smbclient -L linux1

Added interface ip=192.168.1.1 bcast=192.168.1.255 nmask=255.255.255.0

Domain=[MYGROUP] OS=[Unix] Server=[Samba 2.0.3]            .

                Sharename       Type        Comment
                ---------       ----        -------
                root            Disk        root dir on linux1
                home            Disk        home on linux1
                /home/martyp     Disk        /home/martyp on linux1
                IPC$            IPC         IPC Service (Samba Server)
                lp              Printer

                Server                      Comment
                ---------                   -------
                LINUX1                      Samba Server

                Workgroup                   Master
                ---------                   -------
                ATLANTA2                    F4457MFP2
                MYGROUP                     LINUX1
```

This utility produces a useful summary of the Samba setup including the three shares we set up, the Samba server for our example, and other useful information.

We could continue to test Samba on the server, but the listings we viewed give every indication that Samba is running. Let's now move to the Windows client and use *explorer* to access the shares we made available on our Samba server.

Using Shares

Using *explorer,* we'll now map a network drive. We'll map **/root** on the Samba server *linux1* to drive **E:** on the Windows system, as shown in Figure 20-4.

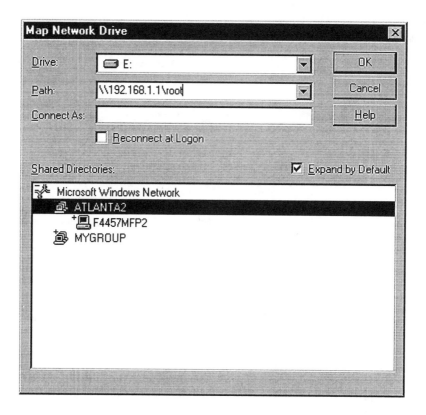

Figure 20-4   Map Drive **E:** to **/root**

We could have mapped this network drive at the command line on the PC using **net use E:\\192.168.1.1\root**. After having success-fully mapped **E:** to / on linux1 using *explorer,* we can access this directory on our Windows system.

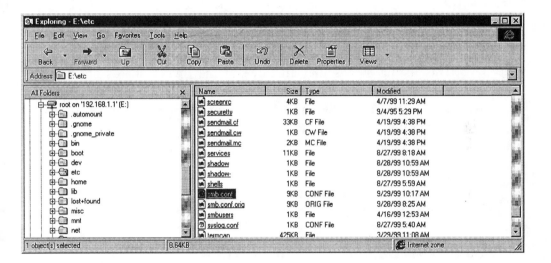

Figure 20-5   View **E:\etc** on Windows System

In Figure 20-5, we have changed to the **/etc** directory on linux1 and have selected the **smb.conf** file. You can see from this example that / on linux1 is fully accessable on the Windows system. We have access to all three shares on linux1, as the following listing shows on the Windows system:

```
c: net view \\192.168.1.1

Shared resources at \\192.168.1.1

Samba Server

Share name    Type           Used as   Comment

-------------------------------------------------------------
/home/martyp   Disk          G:        /home/martyp on linux1
home           Disk          F:          home on linux1
lp             Print
root           Disk           E:         root dir on linux1
The command completed successfully.
```

This listing shows that all three of the linux1 shares are now available on the Windows system. We have not configured any printer sharing, which is also included as part of Samba functionality, so there is no reference to any printers.

Additional Samba Topics

Samba Web Configuration Tool (SWAT)

SWAT is a Web-based administration tool for Samba. It is easy to configure and provides a simple interface for most Samba configuration tasks. On our Red Hat Linux system, the following steps had to be performed to get SWAT running. If you have a different UNIX variant, then your steps will be different.

Confirm that the following line exists in **/etc/services**:

```
swat              901/tcp
```

Next, uncomment the following line in **/etc/inetd.conf**. This line was already in the file as part of the Linux operating system load:

```
swat stream tcp nowait.400 root /usr/sbin/swat swat
```

Kill the **inetd** process by first finding its Process ID (PID) and then issuing the kill command of that PID:

man page

ps - 12

```
# ps -ef | grep inetd
```

```
# kill -1 PID of inetd
```

man page

grep - 10

Now we can run SWAT from a browser interface, in this case Netscape, by specifying the IP address of the Samba server and the port number 901:

man page

```
# netscape http://192.168.1.1:901
```

kill - 6

The browser requests a user name and password when SWAT is invoked to ensure that only users with sufficient rights can make modifications to the Samba configuration in SWAT.

Figure 20-6 shows the SWAT interface. It includes links for *HOME, GLOBALS, SHARES, PRINTERS, STATUS, VIEW,* and *PASSWORD.*

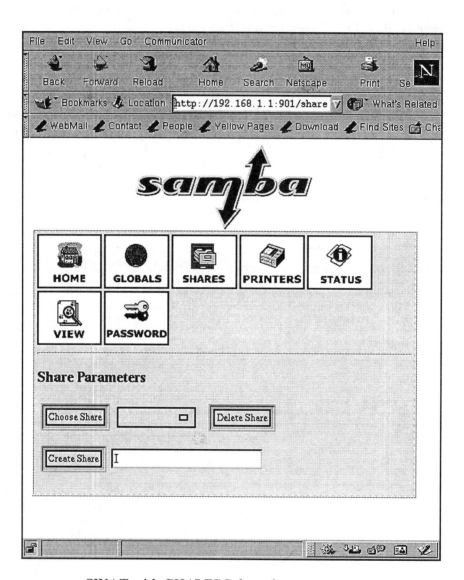

Figure 20-6 SWAT with *SHARES* Selected

The three shares we had earlier conifgured are available in SWAT by selecting *SHARES* from Figure 20-6. SWAT is a good interface for Samba configuration, but there is no substitute for knowing some of the manual processes we experienced earlier in the chapter.

For changes to take effect that are made with SWAT, we had to restart **smbd** with the following command:

```
# /etc/rc.d/init.d/smb restart
```

There is great documentation on our Linux system describing SWAT and all of its capabilities. Figure 20-7 shows the *HOME* page for SWAT with documentation on many of the topics we have covered in this chapter.

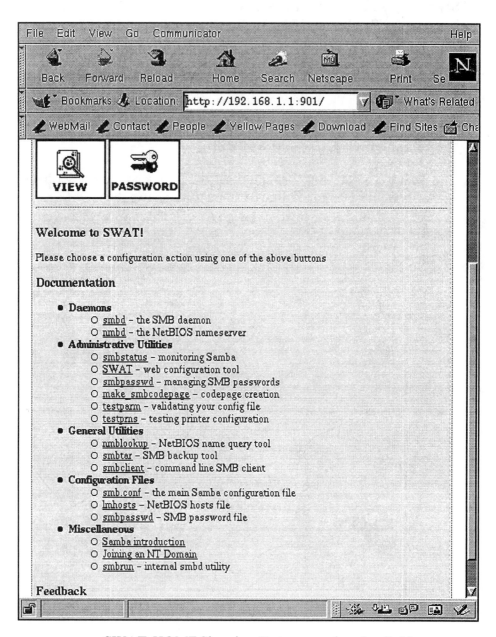

Figure 20-7   SWAT *HOME* Showing Documentation Available

There is also extensive online documentation for all Samba-related software at *www.samba.org*.

Log Files

Like most UNIX applications, Samba provides extensive logging. The **smb.conf** file contains a section that allows you to specify the level of Samba logging you wish to take place. The short section below shows that you can have separate log files for each Windows machine that connects, and you can specify the maximum size of the log file:

```
# this tells Samba to use a separate log file for each machine
# that connects
    log file = /var/log/samba/log.%m

# Put a capping on the size of the log files (in Kb).
    max log size = 50
```

The directory **/var/log/samba** contains a variety of Samba log files, including the log file for the Windows system used in our examples in this chapter called *f4457mfp2,* as shown in the following listing:

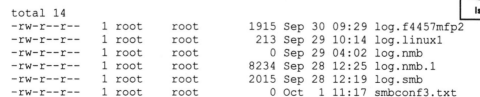

man page

ls - 2

```
# ls -l /var/log/samba

total 14
-rw-r--r--   1 root     root          1915 Sep 30 09:29 log.f4457mfp2
-rw-r--r--   1 root     root           213 Sep 29 10:14 log.linux1
-rw-r--r--   1 root     root             0 Sep 29 04:02 log.nmb
-rw-r--r--   1 root     root          8234 Sep 28 12:25 log.nmb.1
-rw-r--r--   1 root     root          2015 Sep 28 12:19 log.smb
-rw-r--r--   1 root     root             0 Oct  1 11:17 smbconf3.txt
```

File Name Mangling

Among the many Windows and UNIX incompatibilities that exist are file names. Depending on the version of Windows you are using there may be extensive file name incompatibilities with UNIX. Figure 20-6 is an *explorer* window with the file **gnome_private** selected, which is on the Linux server. On our Windows NT system, this file name looks fine. However, also in this figure is a *Properties* window showing that the DOS name for this file would change dramatically if we were on a DOS system.

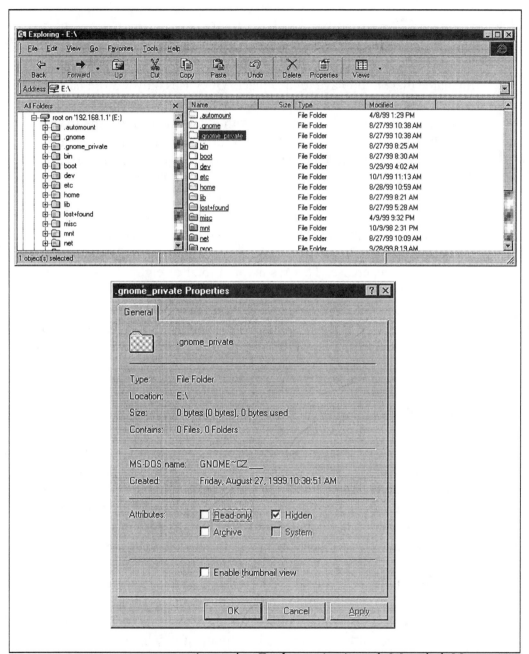

Figure 20-8 **.gnome_private** in *Explorer* (top) and Mangled Name (bottom)

In the case of my Windows system there is no problem handling the file name **.gnome_privagte** as it appears on the Linux system. In the case of a DOS system, there would be extensive "mangling" of the file name that would have to take place. DOS uses only 8.3 file names, or those with eight characters and a three character extension.

Samba mangles files that start with a dot, such as the one in this example, by removing the leading dot, printing the first five characters and then a tilde, and then applying a hash algorithm to the original filename to come up with the last two characters. This results in a total of eight characters for the filename. All the characters are uppercase.

If the file does not begin with a dot, then the file name will be generated in the same way as described in the previous paragraph. The extension consists of the first three characters to the right of the dot converted to uppercase. This results in a total of eight characters for the filename and three for the extension.

In our example, the filename **.gnome_private** would be given a DOS name of **GNOME~CZ**. You have some control over mangling in the **smb.conf** file.

User Issues

I have avoided making a serious user-related configuration in this chapter, in the interest of keeping the examples simple. You will probably not have this luxury unless you are in an environment where you are the only user on both the Windows and UNIX systems.

Users and groups have always been an important part of every UNIX system. Users and groups were not as important in the Windows world until more recently. This change results in some Windows environments in which there is not a complete user and group policy in place which could be used by Samba.

Samba takes into account an environment in which you have set up Windows users and groups and one in which you may not have worked out all the issues related to Windows users and groups. User-level authentication in Samba is set up in such a way that a client can use a given service if they supply the correct user name and password. Share-level authentication takes place by granting access based on the rights of the "guest account" on the UNIX system. This is true unless a client used a user name and password in this or a previous session. Needless to say, there is a lot to consider with user authentication.

The **smb.conf** file has an entry in which you can specify the security as "user" or "share," as shown in the following lines:

```
security = user
security = share
```

Most systems employ user-level security. When this is done users are checked against their names in the **passwd** file and access is granted accordingly.

There are many additional issues related to user authentication that you'll want to investigate if you set up Samba. The documentation supplied with Samba as part of Red Hat Linux is excellent, and the background information on the Web sites listed later in this chapter is informative as well.

Samba Utilities and Programs

We have used several Samba utilities and programs in this chapter. The following list gives a description of the most often used Samba-related commands. There are manual pages for all these that are part of most Samba installations.

- **smbd** - This is the daemon that provides file and print services to SMB clients, such as the Windows system used in our examples throughout this chapter.

- **nmbd** - This is the daemon that provides NetBIOS name server capability and browsing.

- **smbclient** - A program that gives the server access to remotely mounted SMB shares on other servers.

- **testparm** - A test program for **/etc/smb.conf**.

- **smbstatus** - Program that displays status information about current Samba connections.

- **smbpasswd** - Program used to change a user's SMB password on the local machine.

- **smbrun** - Program that runs shell commands for **smbd**.

- **smbtar** - Program to back up SMB shares directly to a UNIX tape drive.

- **smbmount** - Used to mount an SMB file system.

- **smbumount** - Used to unmount an SMB file system.

The online manual pages for these and other Samba-related commands provide more detail. Even in a simple setup such as the one performed in this chapter, you will want to run some of these programs.

Obtaining Samba

In the examples used throughout this chapter, we set up Samba on a Linux system that had Samba installed on it as part of the Red Hat Linux CD-ROM. If Samba does not come on the CD-ROM provided with your UNIX variant or if you wish to be sure that you're loading the very latest Samba, then you can obtain Samba from the Web.

www.samba.org is the place to start. From this Web site you can select a "download site" in your country. You can also select "Web sites" on *www.samba.org* that provide a wealth of information on

Samba, including the GNU General Public License mentioned earlier in the chapter.

There is extensive documentation on Samba-related Web sites, including detailed descriptions of the programs that I listed earlier and used in this chapter.

If you decide to download Samba, you'll probably be given an option of loading a precompiled Samba on your system or building and compiling Samba yourself. The choice you make depends on a lot of factors. If you have a good, reliable Samba distribution, as we did in this chapter when working with Red Hat Linux, then working with a precompiled Samba may be best. If you're interested in learning more about how Samba works and is configured, and want the very latest and greatest version, then download the source and compile yourself.

Even if you have a great prepackaged Samba, as we did in this chapter, it is still worth visiting the Samba-related Web sites to view the extensive documentation available.

INDEX

M

Hewlett-Packard Computer Education and Training

Hewlett-Packard's world-class education and training offers hands on education solutions including:

- Linux
- HP-UX System and Network Administration
- Y2K HP-UX Transition
- Advanced HP-UX System Administration
- IT Service Management using advanced Internet technologies
- Microsoft Windows NT
- Internet/Intranet
- MPE/iX
- Database Administration
- Software Development

HP's new IT Professional Certification program provides rigorous technical qualification for specific IT job roles including HP-UX System Administration, Network Management, Unix/NT Servers and Applications Management, and IT Service Management. For more information, go to http://education.hp.com/hpcert.htm.

In addition, HP's IT Resource Center is the perfect knowledge source for IT professionals. Through a vibrant and rich Web environment, IT professionals working in the areas of UNIX, Microsoft, networking, or MPE/iX gain access to continually updated knowledge pools.

http://education.hp.com

In the U.S. phone 1-800-HPCLASS (472-5277)

LICENSE AGREEMENT AND LIMITED WARRANTY

age by you. EXCEPT FOR THE EXPRESSED WARRANTIES SET FORTH ABOVE, THE COMPANY DISCLAIMS ALL WARRANTIES, EXPRESS OR IMPLIED, INCLUDING WITHOUT LIMITATION, THE IMPLIED WARRANTIES OF MERCHANTABILITY AND FITNESS FOR A PARTICULAR PURPOSE. EXCEPT FOR THE EXPRESS WARRANTY SET FORTH ABOVE, THE COMPANY DOES NOT WARRANT, GUARANTEE, OR MAKE ANY REPRESENTATION REGARDING THE USE OR THE RESULTS OF THE USE OF THE SOFTWARE IN TERMS OF ITS CORRECTNESS, ACCURACY, RELIABILITY, CURRENTNESS, OR OTHERWISE.

IN NO EVENT, SHALL THE COMPANY OR ITS EMPLOYEES, AGENTS, SUPPLIERS, OR CONTRACTORS BE LIABLE FOR ANY INCIDENTAL, INDIRECT, SPECIAL, OR CONSEQUENTIAL DAMAGES ARISING OUT OF OR IN CONNECTION WITH THE LICENSE GRANTED UNDER THIS AGREEMENT, OR FOR LOSS OF USE, LOSS OF DATA, LOSS OF INCOME OR PROFIT, OR OTHER LOSSES, SUSTAINED AS A RESULT OF INJURY TO ANY PERSON, OR LOSS OF OR DAMAGE TO PROPERTY, OR CLAIMS OF THIRD PARTIES, EVEN IF THE COMPANY OR AN AUTHORIZED REPRESENTATIVE OF THE COMPANY HAS BEEN ADVISED OF THE POSSIBILITY OF SUCH DAMAGES. IN NO EVENT SHALL LIABILITY OF THE COMPANY FOR DAMAGES WITH RESPECT TO THE SOFTWARE EXCEED THE AMOUNTS ACTUALLY PAID BY YOU, IF ANY, FOR THE SOFTWARE.

SOME JURISDICTIONS DO NOT ALLOW THE LIMITATION OF IMPLIED WARRANTIES OR LIABILITY FOR INCIDENTAL, INDIRECT, SPECIAL, OR CONSEQUENTIAL DAMAGES, SO THE ABOVE LIMITATIONS MAY NOT ALWAYS APPLY. THE WARRANTIES IN THIS AGREEMENT GIVE YOU SPECIFIC LEGAL RIGHTS AND YOU MAY ALSO HAVE OTHER RIGHTS WHICH VARY IN ACCORDANCE WITH LOCAL LAW.

ACKNOWLEDGMENT

YOU ACKNOWLEDGE THAT YOU HAVE READ THIS AGREEMENT, UNDERSTAND IT, AND AGREE TO BE BOUND BY ITS TERMS AND CONDITIONS. YOU ALSO AGREE THAT THIS AGREEMENT IS THE COMPLETE AND EXCLUSIVE STATEMENT OF THE AGREEMENT BETWEEN YOU AND THE COMPANY AND SUPERSEDES ALL PROPOSALS OR PRIOR AGREEMENTS, ORAL, OR WRITTEN, AND ANY OTHER COMMUNICATIONS BETWEEN YOU AND THE COMPANY OR ANY REPRESENTATIVE OF THE COMPANY RELATING TO THE SUBJECT MATTER OF THIS AGREEMENT.

Should you have any questions concerning this Agreement or if you wish to contact the Company for any reason, please contact in writing at the address below.

Robin Short
Prentice Hall PTR
One Lake Street
Upper Saddle River, New Jersey 07458

About the CD

This CD-ROM contains a great trial software for many UNIX variants. The performance software on the CD-ROM is a 60-day trial of GlancePlus. GlancePlus was covered in the Performance chapter of the book. You need to have root access on most systems in order to install these tools.

There is a README file on the CD-ROM that provides detailed instructions on loading the trial software. The README file contains the following seven sections:

1. INSTALLING TRIAL SOFTWARE AND PRINTING DOCUMENTS FROM THE CD-ROM

    1.1 Interactive installation

    1.2 Batch installation

2. STOPPING AND RESTARTING PERFORMANCE TOOLS FOR INSTALLATIONS

3. REMOVING TRIAL SOFTWARE FROM YOUR SYSTEM

4. PRINTABLE DOCUMENT INFORMATION

5. OVERVIEW OF HP GLANCEPLUS

6. PRODUCT VERSION INFORMATION

7. WHERE TO GET HELP (phone numbers, fax numbers, and email addresses)

No system should be without good multi-vendor performance tools like those on the CD-ROM. I hope you find these tools useful in your installation.

Technical Support

Prentice Hall does not offer technical support for this software. However, if there is a problem with the media, you may obtain a replacement copy by e-mailing us with your problem at:

disc_exchange@prenhall.com